lonely planet

California

Andrea Schulte-Peevers
Sara Benson
Marisa Gierlich-Burgin
Scott McNeely
Kurt Wolff

LONELY PLANET PUBLICATIONS
Melbourne • Oakland • London • Paris

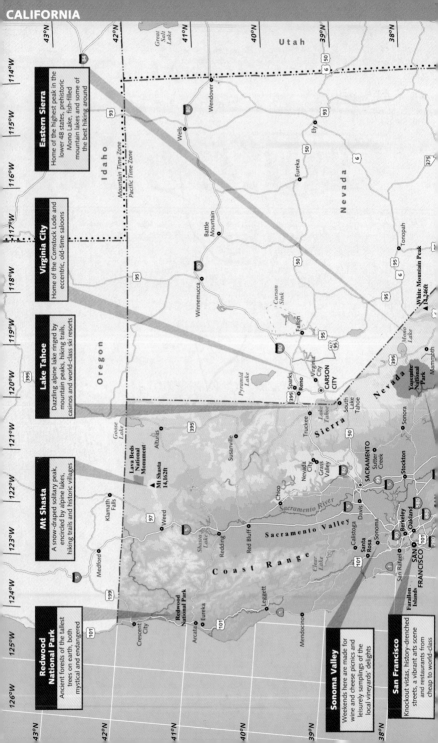

CALIFORNIA

Redwood National Park
Ancient forests of the tallest trees on earth, both mystical and endangered

Mt Shasta
A snow-draped solitary peak, encircled by alpine lakes, hiking trails and historic villages

Lake Tahoe
Dazzling alpine lake ringed by mountain peaks, hiking trails, casinos and world-class ski resorts

Virginia City
Home of the Comstock Lode and eccentric, old-time saloons

Eastern Sierra
Home of the highest peak in the lower 48 states, prehistoric Mono Lake, fish-filled mountain lakes and some of the best hiking around

Sonoma Valley
Weekends here are made for wine and cheese picnics and leisurely samplings of the local vineyards' delights

San Francisco
Knockout vistas, history-drenched streets, a vibrant arts scene and restaurants from cheap to world-class

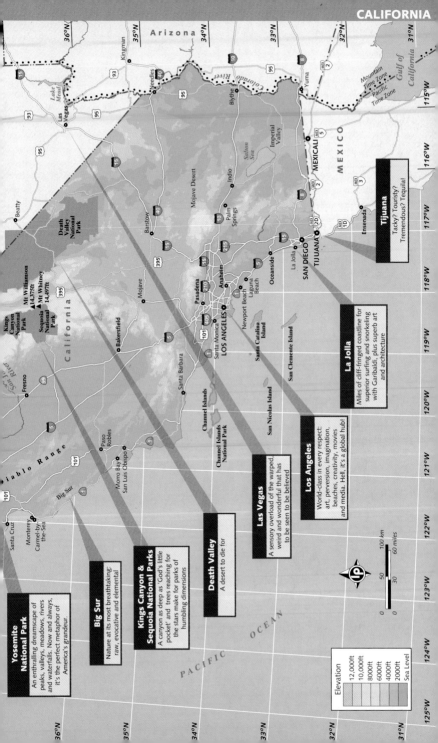

CALIFORNIA

Yosemite National Park
An enthralling dreamscape of peaks, valleys, meadows, rivers and waterfalls. Now and always, it's the perfect metaphor of America's grandeur.

Big Sur
Nature at its most breathtaking; raw, evocative and elemental

Kings Canyon & Sequoia National Parks
A canyon as deep as 'God's little pocket' and trees reaching for the stars make for parks of humbling dimensions

Death Valley
A desert to die for

Las Vegas
A sensory overload of the warped, weird and wonderful that has to be seen to be believed

Los Angeles
World-class in every respect: art, perversion, imagination, beaches, creativity, movies and media. Hell, it's a global hub!

La Jolla
Miles of cliff-fringed coastline for superior surfing and snorkeling with Garibaldi, plus superb art and architecture

Tijuana
Tacky? Touristy? Tremendous? Tequila!

Elevation
12,000ft
10,000ft
8000ft
6000ft
4000ft
2000ft
Sea Level

0   50   100 km
0   30   60 miles

California
3rd edition – March 2003
First published – May 1996

Published by
Lonely Planet Publications Pty Ltd ABN 36 005 607 983
90 Maribyrnong St, Footscray, Victoria 3011, Australia

Lonely Planet Offices
Australia Locked Bag 1, Footscray, Victoria 3011
USA 150 Linden St, Oakland, CA 94607
UK 10a Spring Place, London NW5 3BH
France 1 rue du Dahomey, 75011 Paris

Photographs
Many of the images in this guide are available for licensing from
Lonely Planet Images.
W www.lonelyplanetimages.com

Front cover photograph
Palms on red wall in California (Grant V. Faint/Getty Images)

ISBN 1 86450 331 9

text & maps © Lonely Planet Publications Pty Ltd 2003
photos © photographers as indicated 2003

Printed by The Bookmaker International Ltd
Printed in China

Contents – Text

2 Contents – Text

SAN FRANCISCO BAY AREA   160

WINE COUNTRY   219

NORTH COAST   241

Contents – Maps

6 Contents – Maps

CALIFORNIA MAP INDEX

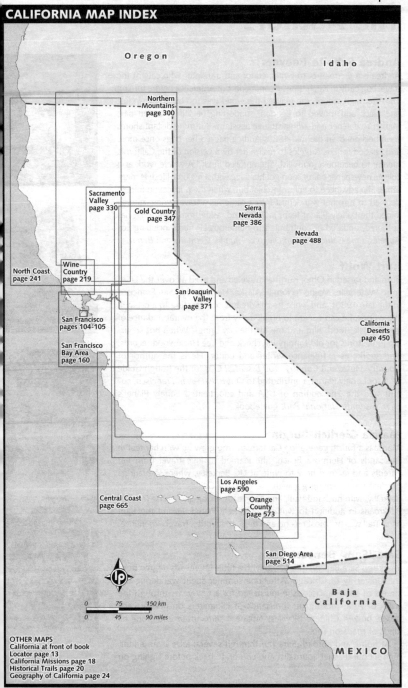

Oregon

Idaho

Northern
Mountains
page 300

Sacramento
Valley
page 330

Gold Country
page 347

Sierra
Nevada
page 386

Nevada
page 488

North Coast
page 241

Wine
Country
page 219

San Joaquin
Valley
page 371

California
Deserts
page 450

San Francisco
pages 104-105

San Francisco
Bay Area
page 160

Los Angeles
page 590

Orange
County
page 573

Central Coast
page 665

San Diego Area
page 514

Baja
California

0   75   150 km
0   45   90 miles

OTHER MAPS
California at front of book
Locator page 13
California Missions page 18
Historical Trails page 20
Geography of California page 24

MEXICO

The Authors

Andrea Schulte-Peevers

Andrea is a German-born writer, editor and translator who caught the travel bug early in life, hitting all continents but Antarctica before turning 18. After high school, she realized the world was too big to live in just one place and moved to London, supporting herself as an au pair, market researcher and administrative assistant. But more distant shores soon beckoned. In the mid-1980s Andrea packed her bags once more and headed for Los Angeles to realize her own version of the California dream: to become a journalist. She enrolled in UCLA where work as a college newspaper editor soon got her a gig with a regional lifestyle magazine. She advanced to editor-in-chief but, when the publication folded, decided to turn her wanderlust into a career as a travel writer. Andrea joined the Lonely Planet team in 1995 and, aside from *California*, has authored, updated or contributed to numerous LP titles, including *Los Angeles, Baja California, San Diego & Tijuana, Germany* and *Berlin*.

Kurt Wolff

Born and raised in Ohio, Kurt has traveled and lived all over the USA, from Waterville, Maine to Kenai, Alaska. He settled in San Francisco in the late 1980s, and while he still dreams of retreating to a cabin in the woods, he can't seem to break away from the overabundance of good music, food, film and friends the city brings. When not scouring junk stores for old Johnny Paycheck and Lee Hazlewood records, Kurt works as a freelance writer and editor. He is the author of *Country Music* and *Country: 100 Essential CDs* for the Rough Guide and, for Lonely Planet, contributed to *Out to Eat – San Francisco*, co-authored the 2nd edition of *USA* and coordinated Lonely Planet's new *Yosemite National Park* guidebook.

Marisa Gierlich-Burgin

Marisa is a fourth generation Californian who grew up with her feet in the sands of Hermosa Beach. She learned to love travel from her parents and learned how to write at UC Berkeley, where she landed her first travel-writing gig with the Berkeley Guides. She still lives in Berkeley, with husband Paul, and now leads hiking and biking trips for Backroads in addition to writing for Lonely Planet. Hiking the John Muir Trail was her most recent, and thus far, favorite, travel experience.

Sara 'Sam' Benson

Years ago Sara Benson graduated with a futile liberal arts degree from the University of Chicago. After one summer spent wandering the streets of San Francisco, she journeyed for a few years through the wilds of Asia, racking up thousands of kilometers on rickety Laos buses, broken Chinese bicycles, Japanese *shinkansen* and along all kinds of roads on foot.

At home and abroad, Sara ran through several jobs as an editor, high school teacher, journalist and corporate hack before signing on

with Lonely Planet many moons ago. She now resides in the Bay Area of Northern California, escaping whenever she can to the hot springs, redwoods forests and brewpubs along the coast. A writer by passion and a traveler by trade, she has worked on over a dozen titles for Lonely Planet.

Scott McNeely

Scott was raised in Los Angeles and is actually fond of the place. After graduating from UC Berkeley, Scott spent a few years living in New York, Istanbul and Dublin. He eventually grew homesick for the Golden State and returned to San Francisco in 1997. Scott has written for numerous guidebooks and magazines, and continues to dabble in travel writing despite a full-time job as Lonely Planet's Digital Publisher. His long-term goal is to found an empire of barber shop–tea house–cocktail bars.

FROM THE AUTHORS

Andrea Schulte-Peevers The biggest bouquet of thanks goes to my husband, David Peevers, who not only joined me in exploring this glorious state but also penned some of the funniest passages in this book. John Mock and Kimberley O'Neil deserve big thanks for their work on LP's *Hiking in the Sierra Nevada*, which formed the basis of the special section 'Hiking in Yosemite'. Kudos also to my co-authors, in particular to Kurt Wolff for lending his expertise to the music section. I'd like to thank my editors – Tom Downs, Suki Gear, Elaine Merrill and Helen Yeates – for their encouragement, patience and understanding, as well as the entire production team for creating another book we can all be proud of. Finally, a big round of applause to the small army of locals, friends, tourism officials and fellow travelers whose insights, tips and contributions were invaluable in the creation of this book.

Kurt Wolff Kurt would like to thank all who gave him information, encouragement, hot tips and even the occasional hot meal during this project, including Amy Ventura, Eric Moore, Jeanne Kearsley, Elgy Gillespie, Suki Gear, Tom Downs, Andrea Schulte-Peevers, Victoria Merkel, Yvette Bozzini, Ben Cooney, Carla Avitabile, Randi Stephens, Gerald Haslam, Margaret Lutz, Roger Taylor and Laura Mitchell.

Marisa Gierlich-Burgin Never-ending are the thanks and credits I give to my parents for encouraging, accompanying and connecting me on my travels. Paul is equally supportive and deserves a medal for his willingness to eat dinner alone for three months out of every year. This edition of *California* brought joyous help from Sarah and Kelly; gifts of time and space from the Burgins; great suggestions from Todd, Jen, Alex, Gidon and other San Diegans I know and love; and research assistance from Paul who sacrificed a few days' surf to wander the streets of his home town.

Sara 'Sam' Benson Thanks to LP hangers-on who shepherd-
ed this guide through the tumult from Down Under, especially
Tom Downs, Suki Gear and Elaine Merrill. Special thanks to
Andrea Schulte-Peevers for being understanding at crunch time.
Heaped spoonfuls of gratitude are for my father, who came along
for the ride – and what's more, survived. To Ipsita Chatterjea, con-
grats on being the first person I've lived with who didn't want to
shoot me when the book came due. And to all the SoHummers,
Jeffersonians, Fort Braggarts, forest rangers and other good folk
who helped me out up north, thank you.

Scott McNeely Scott would like to thank Teal Lewsadder,
Aimee Panyard, Jim Stanley, Maggie Fost, Kelly Green, Noel Mor-
rison, Kurt Hobson, Emily Hobson, John Turco, Tim Mitchell, Ray
Klinke, Lisa Reile, Kip Gebhardt, Ada Vassilovski, Pete Cramer,
David, Michelle and Lela Hepler, Greg and Deborah Mooradian,
Peter Puhvel, Jonathan, Molly and Lucinda Gelber, Virginie
Boone, and the following Lonely Planet staff who generously dis-
closed details of their favorite wineries: Heather Davis, Becky
Ayers, Jenny Weiner, Suzanne Koett, Amy Willis, Andrew
Nystrom, Neda Nazem, Carl Bruce, David Lauterborn, Christine
Lee and Laura Santiago.

This Book

The 1st edition of *California & Nevada* was researched and written by James Lyon, Tony Wheeler, Marisa Gierlich, Nancy Keller and John Gottberg. The 2nd edition was updated by Andrea Schulte-Peevers, David Peevers, Nancy Keller, Marisa Gierlich and Scott McNeely. This 3rd edition of *California* was updated by Andrea Schulte-Peevers (coordinating author), Sara (Sam) Benson, Kurt Wolff, Marisa Gierlich-Burgin and Scott McNeely. Andrea wrote the introductory chapters and the Sierra Nevada, Orange County, Los Angeles and Central Coast chapters. Sara wrote the North Coast and Northern Mountains chapters. Kurt wrote the San Francisco, San Francisco Bay Area, Sacramento Valley, San Joaquin Valley and Nevada chapters. Marisa wrote the Gold Country, California Deserts and San Diego Area chapters. Scott wrote the Wine Country chapter. Special thanks are due to John Mock and Kimberley O'Neil who wrote LP's *Hiking in the Sierra Nevada*, on which the special section 'Hiking in Yosemite' is based.

From the Publisher

This 3rd edition of *California* was produced in Lonely Planet's Melbourne office. Elaine Merrill was the Commissioning Editor. In Melbourne, Project Manager Eoin Dunlevy kept everything on track. Helen Yeates coordinated the editing and most of the proofing; Isabelle Young took over the reins for the rest of proofing and layout. Helen and Isabelle were assisted by Elizabeth Swan, Danielle North, James Lyon, Jenny Mullaly, Lara Morcombe, Linda Suttie and Sally O'Brien. On the cartography side were Csanad Csuturos, Anneka Imkamp, Karen Fry, Laurie Mikkelsen, Herman So, Andrew Smith and, in the US, Fineline Maps. Cameron Duncan was responsible for the design and layout of the book. Sonya Brooke and Nick Stebbing put together the colourwraps. Ruth Askevold designed the cover. Hugh D'Andrade, Haydn Foell, Justin Marler and Rini Keagy drew the illustrations. Thanks to Pepi Bluck for coordinating the illustrations; LPI for coordinating the photographic images; and to Chris Lee Ack and Lachlan Ross for technical support.

THANKS
Many thanks to the travellers who used the last edition and wrote to us with helpful hints, advice and interesting anecdotes. Your names appear in the back of this book.

Foreword

ABOUT LONELY PLANET GUIDEBOOKS

The story begins with a classic travel adventure: Tony and Maureen Wheeler's 1972 journey across Europe and Asia to Australia. There was no useful information about the overland trail then, so Tony and Maureen published the first Lonely Planet guidebook to meet a growing need.

From a kitchen table, Lonely Planet has grown to become the largest independent travel publisher in the world, with offices in Melbourne (Australia), Oakland (USA), London (UK) and Paris (France).

Today Lonely Planet guidebooks cover the globe. There is an ever-growing list of books and information in a variety of media. Some things haven't changed. The main aim is still to make it possible for adventurous travellers to get out there – to explore and better understand the world.

At Lonely Planet we believe travellers can make a positive contribution to the countries they visit – if they respect their host communities and spend their money wisely. Since 1986 a percentage of the income from each book has been donated to aid projects and human rights campaigns, and, more recently, to wildlife conservation.

Although inclusion in a guidebook usually implies a recommendation we cannot list every good place. Exclusion does not necessarily imply criticism. In fact there are a number of reasons why we might exclude a place – sometimes it is simply inappropriate to encourage an influx of travellers.

UPDATES & READER FEEDBACK

Things change – prices go up, schedules change, good places go bad and bad places go bankrupt. Nothing stays the same. So, if you find things better or worse, recently opened or long-since closed, please tell us and help make the next edition even more accurate and useful.

Lonely Planet thoroughly updates each guidebook as often as possible – usually every two years, although for some destinations the gap can be longer. Between editions, up-to-date information is available in our free, monthly email bulletin *Comet* (w www.lonelyplanet.com/newsletters). You can also check out the *Thorn Tree* bulletin board and *Postcards* section of our website, which carry unverified, but fascinating, reports from travellers.

Tell us about it! We genuinely value your feedback. A well-travelled team at Lonely Planet reads and acknowledges every email and letter we receive and ensures that every morsel of information finds its way to the relevant authors, editors and cartographers.

Everyone who writes to us will find their name listed in the next edition of the appropriate guidebook. The very best contributions will be rewarded with a free guidebook.

We may edit, reproduce and incorporate your comments in Lonely Planet products such as guidebooks, websites and digital products, so let us know if you don't want your comments reproduced or your name acknowledged.

How to contact Lonely Planet:
Online: e talk2us@lonelyplanet.com.au, w www.lonelyplanet.com
Australia: Locked Bag 1, Footscray, Victoria 3011
UK: 10a Spring Place, London NW5 3BH
USA: 150 Linden St, Oakland, CA 94607

Introduction

California could not possibly have been more aptly named the 'Golden State.' Of course, it was the 19th-century gold rush that gave it this moniker, but even today there's 'gold' in so many aspects of California. The sunlight, the beaches, the gods and goddesses of cinema: these are the images that play their siren song to the world from screens large and small. But 'golden opportunity' is truly the spine, fuel and spirit of what makes California the singular power that it is. Imagine something on a Monday and by Tuesday it may well be a reality here where the American 'can-do' spirit shines brightest and the boundaries of the possible are without limits.

Hula hoops? Aerobics? The Internet? Personal computers? Cryogenics? In-line skating? Kite surfing? Plunk a creative or wacky idea down on California soil and its tendrils will soon be enveloping cities and farm villages all over the world. Life in California is like living in the future. It's an intellectual playground; a petri dish where ideas, cultures and trends take hold, thrive, multiply, morph and spread at dazzling speed. Dreamers run the show but the 'brick and mortar' aspects of the state are no less dazzling.

California's economy is larger than that of China or France (in fact, its gross domestic product is the fifth largest in the world). Its area exceeds that of either the United Kingdom and Italy. But beyond its economic and creative influence is the California of unparalleled natural beauty. And it's chiefly because of this that the state receives nearly 300 million foreign and domestic visitors each year. They come to experience the 'California Dreamin' found in such national parks as Yosemite and Redwoods. They come to explore 1200mi of coastal roads and to witness the teeming wildlife – whales, dolphins, sea lions etc – of the Pacific. They come to see the tallest point in the lower 48 states (Mt Whitney) and the lowest (Death Valley). They head inland to discover some of the world's most fertile agricultural and wine producing country and to climb or hike among peaks and wilderness areas of striking beauty.

And when visitors head for California's cities they find – in such places as San Francisco and Los Angeles – microcosms of what the state once was, and what it's still becoming. There endures the architectural legacy of the California missions right alongside cutting-edge developments such as the Walt Disney Hall in Downtown LA. There are the Chinatowns and Nob Hills of yesterday rubbing shoulders with altogether new immigrant communities housing people from Cambodia to Ethiopia. And the Latino and African-American cultures that have shaped so much of the state's history are becoming evermore influential in what the future here may bring.

Perhaps in California as with nowhere else does the rule, 'Change is the only constant' apply. Today's matinee idol is tomorrow's has-been. Stellar technology is scrapped overnight with the invention of a single new silicon chip. Buildings and neighborhoods disappear and are reincarnated within months. Here today and…*there* tomorrow. It's sometimes hard to trust your senses while drinking in all that California is. The dreams create the realities which become the myths in an endless cycle of invention and excitement. Perhaps the best advice to travelers in general is 'surrender'. California will provide you with dreams enough for a lifetime. *Real* ones.

Facts about California

HISTORY
The Beginnings
It's generally accepted that the first people in the Americas came from east Asia, over a land bridge to Alaska across what is now the Bering Strait. This land bridge, called Beringia, occurred when sea levels lowered during an ice age between 10,000 and 25,000 years ago. The first immigrants were probably nomadic hunters following large game animals which moved south and east to all corners of the Americas. Among the earliest known inhabitants of North America were the makers of stone tools found near Clovis, New Mexico, which have been dated to around 11,000 years ago.

Californian archaeological sites indicate the state was also inhabited very early on. Stone tools found in the Bakersfield area have been dated to around 8000 to 12,000 years ago. Many other sites across the state have yielded evidence, from large middens of sea shells along the coast to campfire sites in the mountains, of people from around 4000 to 8000 years ago.

The most spectacular artifact left behind by California's early inhabitants is their rock art, dating from 500 to 3000 years ago. It gives some idea of the cultural diversity of the indigenous populations, with five identifiable styles of pictographs (designs painted on rock with one or more colors) and five styles of petroglyphs (designs pecked, chipped or abraded onto the rock). Many of the sites are closed to the public in the interest of preservation, but accessible areas include the Indian Grinding Rock State Historic Park in the Gold Country (see the Gold Country chapter); the Chumash Painted Cave State Historic Park, near Santa Barbara (see the Central Coast chapter); and various sites in the Ridgecrest area (see the California Deserts chapter).

California's Indians
The archaeological evidence, combined with accounts from early European visitors and later ethnographic research, gives quite a clear picture of the Indians at the time of European contact. The native peoples of California belonged to more than 20 language groups with around 100 dialects. Their total population ranged somewhere between 150,000 and 300,000, though some estimates run considerably higher. The Indians lived in small groups and villages, often migrating with the seasons from the valleys and the coast up to the mountains. The largest villages of which there are traces, in the Central Valley, are reckoned to have had 1500 to 2000 residents.

Acorn meal was their dietary staple, supplemented by small game, such as rabbits and deer, and fish and shellfish along the coast. Other plants were used for food and the fiber used in making baskets and clothing. California Indians used earthenware pots, fish nets, bows, arrows and spears with chipped stone points, but their most developed craft was basket making. They wove baskets with local grasses and plant fibers and decorated them with attractive geometric designs. Some baskets were so tightly woven that they would hold water. Examples can be seen in many museums.

There was some trade between the groups, especially between coastal and inland people, but generally they did not interact much, partly because even neighboring villages spoke different languages. Conflict among the groups was almost nonexistent. California Indians did not have a class of warriors or a tradition of warfare, at least not until the Europeans arrived.

Several museums have good exhibits on Native American archaeology and anthropology, such as the Phoebe Hearst Museum of Anthropology at UC Berkeley, the Museum of Man in San Diego and the Southwest Museum in Los Angeles.

European Discovery
Following the conquest of Mexico in the early 16th century, the Spanish turned their attention toward exploring the edges of their new empire. There was much fanciful speculation about a golden island beyond Mexico's western coast, and California was actually named before it was explored, after a mythical island in a Spanish novel. The precise etymology and meaning of the name 'California' have never been convincingly established, though there is now wide consensus that it is a derivation of 'Calafia,' the

novel's heroine queen, who ruled a race of gold-rich black Amazons.

In 1542 the Spanish crown engaged Juan Rodríguez Cabrillo, a Portuguese explorer and retired conquistador, to lead an expedition up the West Coast to find the fabled land. He was also charged with finding the equally mythical Strait of Anian, an imagined sea route between the Pacific and the Atlantic.

When Cabrillo's ships sailed into San Diego Harbor (which Cabrillo named San Miguel), he and his crew became the first Europeans to see mainland California. The ships sat out a storm in the harbor, then sailed on, following the coast north. They made a stop on the Channel Islands where, in 1543, Cabrillo fell ill, died and was buried. The expedition continued north as far as Oregon, but returned with no evidence of a sea route to the Atlantic, no cities of gold and no islands of spice. The Spanish authorities were unimpressed and showed no further interest in California for the next 50 years.

Around 1565, Spanish ships began plying the Pacific, carrying Mexican silver to the Philippines to trade for the exotic goods of Asia. These 'Manila galleons' often took a northerly route back to the Americas to catch the westerly winds, and they sometimes landed along the California coast. The galleons were harassed by English pirates, including Sir Francis Drake, who sailed up the California coast in 1579. He missed the entrance to San Francisco Bay, but pulled in near Point Reyes (at what is now Drakes Bay) to repair his ship, which was literally bursting with the weight of plundered Spanish silver. He claimed the land for Queen Elizabeth, named it Nova Albion (New England), then left for other adventures. (He wrote that he left a brass plate nailed to a post to record his visit. A plate was supposedly found there in 1937 – probably a fake – and is now in the Bancroft Library at UC Berkeley.)

In 1596 the Spanish decided they needed to secure some ports on the Pacific coast, and sent Sebastián Vizcaíno to find them. Vizcaíno's first expedition was a disaster that didn't get past Baja California, but in his second attempt, in 1602, he rediscovered the harbor at San Diego and gave it its present name. Contrary to his orders, he renamed many of the features of the coast

and made glowing reports of the value of his 'discoveries,' in particular Monterey Bay, which he described as a protected harbor. Perhaps no-one believed Vizcaíno's reports, because they were pigeonholed for 160 years, as Spain continued to ignore its remotest territory.

The Mission Period

Around the 1760s, as Russian ships came to California's coast in search of sea otter pelts, and British trappers and explorers were spreading throughout the West, the Spanish king became worried that they might occupy the coast and become a threat to Spain's claim on the land. Also, the Catholic Church was anxious to start missionary work among the native peoples. A combination of Catholic missions and military forts (presidios) was founded in the new territory. The Indian converts would live in the missions, learn trade and agricultural skills and ultimately establish pueblos that would be like little Spanish towns.

The first Spanish colonizing expedition, called the 'Sacred Expedition,' was a major undertaking, with land-based parties and supply ships converging on San Diego in 1769. On July 1 that year, a sorry lot of about 100 missionaries and soldiers, led by the Franciscan priest Junípero Serra and the military commander Gaspar de Portolá, gimped ashore at San Diego Bay. They had just spent several weeks at sea on their journey from Baja California, where Serra had already founded one mission. About half of their cohorts had died en route, and many of the survivors were sick or near death. It was an inauspicious beginning for the Mission San Diego de Alcalá, the 'mother' of the chain of 21 Northern California missions.

While Serra stayed in San Diego, Gaspar de Portolá continued north with instructions to establish a second Spanish outpost at Monterey. Portolá went right past Monterey, as he didn't see anything like the fine protected harbor that Vizcaíno had described. His party continued until they arrived at a large bay, later named San Francisco. Returning disappointed to San Diego, Portolá found Serra's party desperately awaiting an overdue supply ship, and without a single Indian convert after eight months of missionary activity. They were on the point of abandoning the expedition, but after a day of prayer, the supply ship arrived just in time. Portolá returned north to the unpromising site at Monterey with Serra in tow. Although they realized that the lack of a good harbor made the site less than ideal, a second mission, along with a presidio, was established.

Over time, three more presidios were founded, in San Diego (1769), Santa Barbara (1782) and San Francisco (1776). Ostensibly, the purpose of the presidios was to protect the missions and deter foreign intruders. In fact, these garrisons created more threats than they deterred, as the soldiers aroused hostility by raiding the Indian camps to rape and kidnap women. Not only were the presidios militarily weak, but their weakness was well known to Russia and Britain and did nothing to strengthen Spain's claims to California.

With the Indians decimated by disease, the Spanish attempted to build up the pueblos in California with the families of soldiers and with civilians from Mexico. The first group came overland from Sonora, led by Juan Bautista de Anza on a route across the southern desert. They settled on the San Francisco peninsula in 1776 and named the place Yerba Buena (Good Herb), for the *Satureja douglasi* that grew wild in the area. The Spanish established other civilian pueblos at San Jose (1777) and Los Angeles (1781), but they attracted few settlers from Mexico, and those who came were neither farmers who could cultivate the land nor soldiers who could defend it.

The missions were more successful at agriculture, and by 1800 they were growing grapes, fruit trees and wheat, raising cattle and supplying enough food for themselves and the presidios. During the Mexican war for independence from Spain, from 1810 to 1821, supplies from Mexico were cut off completely, and California was, of necessity, self-sufficient.

As a way of colonizing the wilds of California and converting the natives to Christianity, the mission period was an abject failure. The Spanish population remained small; the missions achieved little better than mere survival; foreign intruders were not greatly deterred; and more Indians

The Missions

In all, there are 21 missions in California, mostly along El Camino Real, the 'King's Highway,' which is traced by today's Hwy 101. Except for the one at Sonoma, which dates back to the Mexican period, all the missions were founded by Spanish friars. The first mission was established by Padre Junípero Serra, who spent the rest of his life nurturing the mission chain. His successor, Father Fermin Francisco de Lasuen, continued Serra's work, but the missions were never wholly successful.

All the missions had similar structures, with a church and residences surrounded by fields, vineyards and ranch land. Although military protection was necessary, and became increasingly important as the Indians became less and less happy about the intruders, the missions tried to keep the military, and even more importantly civilian settlers, at arm's length.

To the Spanish, converting the 'heathen' was as important as economic development or military control, but in the end extinction rather than conversion was the result of their efforts. Consolidating the Indians in small communities greatly increased the spread of disease and decimated the population.

The Spanish missionaries had little respect for the Native Americans, who were a gentle people according to the descriptions of early settlers. The converted Indians, known as 'neophytes,' were overworked by the missionaries and maltreated by the military and civilians. If disease didn't kill them, they often drifted away from the alien missions.

A severe earthquake in 1812 damaged many of the mission buildings, and after independent Mexico ended its support in 1834, they gradually crumbled into ruin. Ownership of most of the mission lands, and what remained of the buildings, was returned to the Catholic Church by Abraham Lincoln.

Today the missions are a mixed lot – some of them remarkably preserved, others completely restored, some only vaguely related to the originals. Even during the Spanish period the missions had been a movable feast. The second mission marked the birth of Monterey and then was moved to Carmel a year later. The present Santa Clara mission is actually the sixth church on the fifth site; earlier versions were washed away by floods, tumbled by earthquakes or engulfed by fire.

CALIFORNIA MISSIONS

PACIFIC OCEAN

San Francisco de Solano (1823)

San Rafael Arcángel (1817)

San Francisco de Asís (Mission Dolores) (1776)

San José de Guadalupe (1797)

Santa Clara de Asís (1777)

Santa Cruz (1791)

San Carlos Borromeo de Carmelo (1770)

San Juan Bautista (1797)

Nuestra Señora de la Soledad (1791)

San Antonio de Padua (1771)

San Miguel Arcángel (1797)

El Camino Real

San Luis Obispo de Tolosa (1772)

La Purísima Concepción (1787)

Santa Inés (1804)

Santa Barbara (1786)

San Buenaventura (1782)

San Fernando Rey de España (1797)

San Gabriel Arcángel (1771)

San Juan Capistrano (1776)

El Camino Real

0   40   80 km
0   25   50 miles

San Luis Rey de Francia (1798)

San Diego de Alcalá (1769)

died than were converted. Conflict between the Spanish and Indians persisted, with a major revolt in Santa Barbara as late as 1824.

The Rancho Period

Upon Mexican independence in 1821 many of the new nation's people looked to California to satisfy their thirst for private land. By the mid-1830s the missions had been secularized, with a series of governors doling out hundreds of free land grants. This process gave birth to the rancho system. The new landowners were called rancheros or Californios; they prospered quickly and became the social, cultural and political fulcrums of California. The average rancho was 16,000 acres in size and largely given over to livestock to supply the trade in hide and tallow.

Enterprising rancheros often sold 75,000 or more hides a year, for an average price of $2 each. Although some made fortunes – they paid no taxes and footed the bill for no public works projects – they were largely illiterate and usually lived in nonpermanent dwellings without wooden floors, windows or running water. Schools were nonexistent too. Most of the work was done by mestizos born of European and Indian parents, and the Indians were almost totally marginalized.

When frontiersman Jedediah Smith turned up in San Diego in 1827, the Mexican authorities were alarmed to discover that the route from the east was not impassable. Frontiersman Kit Carson helped forge the Santa Fe Trail to Los Angeles in 1832. Another interloper whose name was linked to California's destiny was Swiss-born John Sutter, who, in 1839, persuaded the California governor to grant him 50,000 acres in the Sacramento Valley. It happened that his ranch was at the western end of another trail, over the Truckee Pass, on which the first American wagon trundled into California in 1841 and which the Donner Party followed in 1846 (see the boxed text 'The Donner Party' in the Sierra Nevada chapter).

American explorers, trappers, traders, whalers, settlers and opportunists increasingly showed interest in California, seizing on many of the prospects for profit that the Californios ignored in favor of ranching. Some of the Americans who started businesses became Catholics, married locals, and assimilated into Californio society. One American, Richard Henry Dana, author of

Two Years Before the Mast (1840), worked on a ship in the hide trade in the 1830s and wrote disparagingly of Californians as 'an idle and thriftless people who can make nothing for themselves.'

The Bear Flag Republic & Statehood

Impressed by California's potential wealth and imbued with Manifest Destiny (the imperialist doctrine to extend the US border from coast to coast), US president Andrew Jackson sent an emissary to offer the financially strapped Mexican government $500,000 for California. Though American settlers were by then showing up by the hundreds, especially in Northern California, Jackson's emissary was tersely rejected. A political storm was brewing.

In 1836, Texas had seceded from Mexico and declared itself an independent republic. When the US annexed Texas in 1845, Mexico broke off diplomatic relations and ordered all foreigners without proper papers to be deported from California. Outraged Northern California settlers revolted, captured the nearest Mexican official and, supported by a company of US soldiers led by Captain John C Frémont, declared California's independence from Mexico in June 1846 by raising their 'Bear Flag' over the town of Sonoma. The Bear Flag Republic existed for all of one month. (The banner lives on, however, as the California state flag.)

Meanwhile, the US had declared war on Mexico after the two countries clashed over the disputed Texas territory. That gave the US all the justification it needed to invade Mexico. By July, US naval units occupied every port on the California coast, including the capital, Monterey. But in the big picture, California was a side show, as the war was really won and lost in mainland Mexico.

When US troops captured Mexico City in September 1847, putting an end to the war, the Mexican government had little choice but to cede much of its northern territory to the US. The Treaty of Guadalupe Hidalgo, signed on February 2, 1848, turned over California, Arizona and New Mexico to the US. Only two years later, California was admitted as the 31st state of the United States. (An interesting feature of this treaty guaranteed the rights of Mexican citizens living in areas taken over by the US. Many Mexicans feel that this provision still entitles them to live and work in those states, regardless of their country of birth.)

The Gold Rush

By an amazing coincidence, gold was discovered in Northern California within days of the signing of the treaty with Mexico, incidentally on land owned by John Sutter (remember him?). The discovery of gold quickly transformed the newest American outpost. The population surged from about 14,000 at the time Mexican rule ended to more than 90,000 by 1849, as people from throughout the US and other countries flocked to California.

The growth and wealth stimulated every aspect of life, from agriculture and banking to construction and journalism. As a result of mining, hills were stripped bare, erosion wiped out vegetation, streams silted up and mercury washed down to San Francisco Bay. San Francisco became a hotbed of gambling, prostitution, drink and chicanery.

Ostensibly under military rule, California had little effective government at all. The currency was a mixture of debased coinage, gold slugs, and foreign cash; the main law was 'miners law,' an arbitrary and often harsh way of dealing with crimes – real or imagined.

Land ownership was uncertain. The rancheros still claimed title to most of California's usable lands, but thousands of new immigrants were squatting as homesteaders in the expectation that they would be able to claim a 160-acre lot for $200. In 1851 Congress sent a land commission west to adjudicate the land claims. Everyone who had received a land grant two decades earlier was now forced to prove its legitimacy with documents and witnesses. By 1857 some 800 cases had been reviewed by tribunal, 500 in favor of the original, pre-rancho landowners. Many other ranchos now passed into the hands of the US government.

California experienced a second boom with the discovery of the Comstock silver lode in 1860, though the lode was actually over the border in what would soon become Nevada. Exploiting it required deep-mining techniques, which meant companies, stocks, trading and speculation. San Francisco made more money out of stocks than Nevada did out of mining: huge mansions sprouted on Nob Hill, and Californian businessmen became renowned for their audacity – *not* their scruples.

The Transcontinental Railroad

The transcontinental railroad was simple in conception, vast in scale and revolutionary in impact. It shortened the trip from New York to San Francisco from two months to four or five days and opened up markets on both coasts. Tracks were built simultaneously from the east and the west, eventually converging in Utah in 1869. The track going east from Sacramento was financed by the Central Pacific Railroad, which hired thousands of Chinese laborers to get the job done. One of its principals, Leland Stanford, became state governor in 1863.

The Civil War (1861–65) slowed down the import of goods from the East Coast to California, thus spurring local industry to pick up the slack. Agriculture diversified, with new crops, especially oranges, being grown for export. As California oranges found their way onto New York grocery shelves, coupled with a hard-sell advertising campaign, more and more Easterners heeded the advice of crusading magazine

and newspaper publisher Horace Greeley to 'Go west, young man.' California's population increased by 47% during the 1860s and by another 54% in the 1870s.

Inevitably the boom was followed by a bust in the late 1870s. Speculation had raised land prices to levels no farmer or immigrant could afford, the railroad brought in products that undersold the goods made in California, and some 15,000 Chinese workers, no longer needed for rail construction, flooded the labor market. A period of labor unrest ensued, which culminated in anti-Chinese laws and a reformed state constitution in 1879.

Industry & Agriculture

Los Angeles was not connected to the transcontinental railroad until 1876, when the Southern Pacific Railroad laid tracks from San Francisco to the fledgling city. The SP monopoly was broken in 1887, when the Atchison, Topeka & Santa Fe Railroad Company laid tracks linking LA across the Arizona desert to the East Coast. The competition greatly reduced the cost of transport and led to more diverse development across the state, particularly in Southern

HISTORIC TRAILS

California and the San Joaquin Valley. The lower fares spurred the so-called 'boom of the '80s' a major real estate boom lasting from 1886 to 1888. More than 120,000 migrants, mostly from the Midwest, came to Southern California in those years. Many settled in the 25 new towns laid out by AT&SF in the eastern part of Los Angeles County.

Much of the land granted to the railroads was sold in big lots to speculators who also acquired, with the help of corrupt politicians and administrators, a lot of the farm land that was released for new settlement. A major share of the state's agricultural land thus became consolidated as large holdings in the hands of a few city-based landlords, establishing the pattern (which continues to this day) of big, industrial-scale 'agribusiness' rather than small family farms. These big businesses were well placed to provide the substantial investment and the political connections required to bring irrigation water to the farmland. They also established a need for cheap farm workers, which was met by poor immigrants.

In the absence of coal, iron ore or abundant water, heavy industry developed slowly, although the 1892 discovery of oil in the Los Angeles area stimulated the development of petroleum processing and chemical industries.

The 20th Century

The population, wealth and importance of California increased dramatically throughout the 20th century. The big San Francisco earthquake and fire of 1906 destroyed most of the city, but it was barely a hiccup in the state's development – the population increased by 60% in the decade to 1910, reaching 2,378,000. The revolutionary years in Mexico, from 1910 to 1921, caused a huge influx of emigrants from south of the border, re-establishing the Latino heritage that had been largely smothered by American dominance. The Panama Canal, completed in 1914, made bulk shipping feasible between the East Coast and West Coast.

During the 1920s, California's population grew by 2.25 million people to 5.677 million: a mammoth 66% increase, the highest growth rate since the gold rush. The Great Depression saw another wave of emigrants, this time from the impoverished prairie states of the Dust Bowl. Outbreaks of social and labor unrest led to a rapid growth of the Democratic party in California. Some of the Depression-era public works projects had lasting benefits, great and small, from San Francisco's Bay Bridge to the restoration of mission buildings.

WWII had a major impact on California, and not just from the influx of military and defense workers and the development of new industries. Women were co-opted into war work and proved themselves in a range of traditionally male jobs. Anti-Asian sentiments resurfaced at this time, many Japanese Americans were interned, and more Mexicans crossed the border to fill labor shortages. Many of the service people who passed through California actually liked the place so much that they returned to settle after the war. In the 1940s the population grew by 53% (reaching 10,643,000 in 1950), and during the 1950s by 49% (15,863,000 in 1960).

Throughout the 20th century, a number of aspects of California life emerged as recurring themes.

Growth, Migration & Minorities California's population has grown exponentially since it was admitted to the union in 1850, and most of the growth has come from immigration. This has resulted in a richly multicultural society, but also one in which race relations have often been strained.

Immigrants are typically welcomed in times of rapid growth, only to be rejected when times get tough. Chinese railroad workers, for instance, were in great demand in the 1860s but ended up victimized in the 1870s. The Webb Alien Land Law of 1913 prevented some Asian minorities from owning land. During WWII, 93,000 people of Japanese heritage – many of them American citizens – were forcibly placed in internment camps. African Americans came in large numbers to take jobs in the postwar boom, but often became unemployed when the economy took a downturn.

Mexican and Latin American workers still do most of the farm labor and domestic work, but in 1994, in the face of increasing unemployment and state government deficits, Californians voted in favor of Proposition 187, which denied illegal immigrants access to state government services, including schools and hospitals. It is estimated that as many as 2.3 million illegal immigrants are currently in California, despite such efforts as Operation Gatekeeper, a costly attempt to police the US-Mexican border through a metal fence, lots more border patrol agents and infrared scopes. Still, for every undocumented worker arrested, at least two manage to slip across into the US.

Today's California has an astonishingly diverse population that is both its strength and its weakness. Racial tensions have become a common occurrence. Occasionally, these receive high-profile exposure as with the 1992 Los Angeles riots following the acquittal of four white police officers charged with beating Rodney King. But at the same time, the arrival of people from every corner of the globe makes California one of the most tolerant, cosmopolitan and open-minded societies anywhere. On an errand run, you might be dropping off shirts with your Japanese dry cleaner, picking up groceries from the Mexican shopkeeper, having your nails done by a Vietnamese cosmetologist and getting a parking ticket from a Greek police officer. The world has definitely come to California.

The Military Although California has never been the scene of a major conflict, it must be one of the most militarized places on earth. During and after WWI, Douglas and the Lockheed brothers in Los Angeles, and Curtiss in San Diego, established aircraft industries. Two decades later, with another world war brewing, the aviation industry helped lift California out of the Great Depression. By the end of WWII, billions of federal dollars had been poured into Southern California military contracts.

Following the Japanese bombing of Pearl Harbor, the headquarters of the US Pacific fleet moved from Hawaii to San Diego, where it has remained ever since. Camp Pendleton, a big Marine Corps base, was established in southern Orange County, and the Colorado Desert, in Southern California, temporarily became one of the biggest military training grounds in history. Shipbuilding started in San Francisco, aircraft plants in Los Angeles turned out planes by the thousands, and the movie industry turned to producing propaganda films.

After WWII the state retained a big slice of the military-industrial complex, with some very high-tech Cold War industries, from avionics and missile manufacturing to helicopter and nuclear submarine maintenance. Military activities include recruit training for the Marine Corps, advanced training for navy fighter pilots, submarine bases, aircraft testing facilities, several air force bases, weapons and gunnery ranges, and home ports for the US Navy. Military spending peaked in the 1980s under President Ronald Reagan, a former California governor, but by 1990 it had become clear that the honeymoon was over. Budget cutbacks resulted in the closure of numerous bases and forced hundreds of defense-related companies to downsize and restructure, a process that is still ongoing.

The Film Industry Few industries have symbolized California, and especially Los Angeles, more than movie making. Independent producers were attracted here beginning in 1908 for numerous reasons. Southern California's sunny climate allowed indoor scenes to be shot outdoors – essential given the unsophisticated photo technology of the day. Any location, from ocean to desert to alpine forest, could be realized nearby. What's more, the proximity of the Mexican border enabled filmmakers to rush their equipment to safety when challenged by the collection agents of patent holders such as Thomas Edison.

The industry has done a lot to promote California's image throughout the country and the world. As film, and later TV, became the predominant entertainment medium of the 20th century, California moved to center stage in the world of popular culture.

Social Change Unconstrained by the burden of traditions, bankrolled by affluence and promoted by film and television, California has always been a leader in new attitudes and social movements. As early as the 1930s, Hollywood was promoting fashions and fads for the middle classes, even as strikes and social unrest rocked San Francisco and author John Steinbeck articulated a new concern for the welfare and worth of working-class people.

With 1950s affluence, the 'Beat' movement in San Francisco reacted against the banality and conformism of suburban life, turning to coffeehouses for jazz, philosophy, poetry and pot. When the postwar baby boomers hit their late teens, many took up where the Beat generation left off, rejecting their parents' values, doing drugs, dropping out and screwing around in a mass display of adolescent rebellion that climaxed, but didn't conclude, with the San Francisco 'Summer of Love' in 1967. Though the hippie 'counter-culture' was an international phenomenon, California was at the leading edge of its music, its psychedelic art and its new liber-tarianism. Sex, drugs and rock and roll were big on the West Coast.

In the late '60s and early '70s, New Left politics, the anti–Vietnam War movement and Black Liberation forced their way into the po-litical limelight, and flower power and give-peace-a-chance politics seemed instantly naive. The 1968 assassination of Robert Kennedy in Los Angeles, the sometimes vio-lent repression of demonstrations, such as those at Berkeley in 1968, and the death of a spectator at a Rolling Stones concert at the hands of their security guards (Hell's Angels they had hired for the occasion) all served to strip the era of its innocence.

California has spawned a number of social movements. Gay Pride exploded in San Francisco in the '70s, and San Francisco is still the most openly, exuberantly gay city in the world.

In the late 1980s and '90s, California cat-apulted right to the forefront of the healthy lifestyle, with more aerobic classes and self-actualization workshops than you could shake your totem at. Leisure activities like in-line skating, snowboarding and mountain biking are industries spawned by California. Be careful what you laugh at. From pet rocks to soy burgers, California's flavor of the month will probably be next year's world trend.

Technology California has always been at the forefront of the technology revolution. In the 1950s, Stanford University in Palo Alto needed to raise some money to finance the university's postwar growth. The university built Stanford Industrial Park, leasing space only to high-tech companies that might be in some way beneficial to the university. Hewlett-Packard, Lockheed and General Electric were among the first to move in. This step is now considered the germ cell of Sili-con Valley (although the term itself didn't ap-pear until 1971 in a series of articles by Don C Hoefler). Major Silicon Valley milestones were the inventions of the microchip by Intel

in 1971 and the first personal computer, the Apple I, in 1976.

In 1969 a UCLA computer science pro-fessor named Len Kleinrock first succeeded at sending data from a computer in Los An-geles to another in Stanford, 360mi away. He typed in 'L' and, sure enough, the letter appeared on the screen in Palo Alto. He typed the letter 'O'. Same thing. Then he typed 'G' – and the system crashed. But the Internet was born.

It would take several more decades be-fore computer-based communication would be as much a part of our daily lives as the telephone, but there can be no doubt that a revolution had been set in motion.

Digital technology did indeed reinvent the world and the way we view and create almost everything. In the fat years of the 1990s, it be-came the lemming-like mantra for leaders in every area of commerce and creativity. Movies increasingly rely on digital enhance-ments, at the very least, to create virtual worlds that would have been unthinkable only a scant decade ago. At the same time, more and more companies jumped on the dot-com bandwagon. Many went through the economic roof, fueled by misplaced opti-mism, and with equal velocity, crashed right through the floor when the stock market bub-ble burst after the turn of the millennium. But history is still being written.

GEOGRAPHY

The third-largest state after Alaska and Texas, California covers about 156,000 sq mi and is larger than Great Britain or Italy. It is bordered by Oregon in the north, Mexico in the south, Nevada and Arizona in the east, and the 1200mi of Pacific coastline to the west. The northern edge of California is at the same latitude as New York or Rome, and the southern edge is at the same latitude as Savannah, Georgia, or Tel Aviv. Moun-tain ranges and water, or lack of it, deter-mine the state's prominent geographic regions. California's five largest cities are Los Angeles (3.7 million), San Diego (2.7 million), San Jose (923,000), San Francisco (801,000) and Long Beach (467,000).

Coast

The Coast Range runs along most of Cali-fornia's coastline, its west side plunging straight into the Pacific and its eastern side

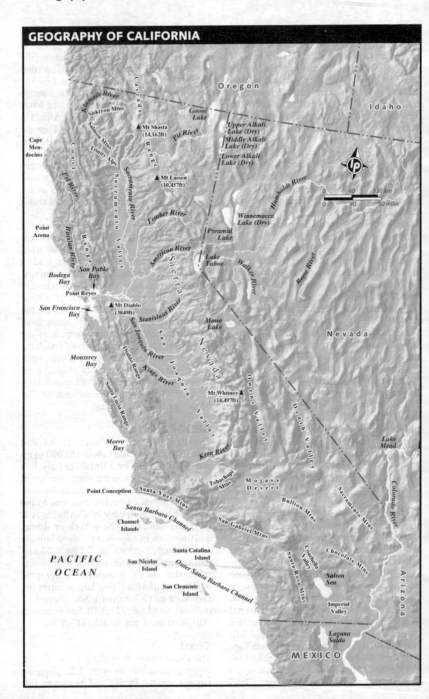

GEOGRAPHY OF CALIFORNIA

rolling gently toward the Central Valley. San Francisco Bay divides the range roughly in half: the North Coast, famous for its coast redwoods, is sparsely populated and very foggy and the Central Coast, from Monterey to Ventura, has a milder climate, more sandy beaches and more people.

Three-quarters of the way down the state, the Coast Range is joined to the Sierra by a series of mountains called the Transverse Ranges. These mountains, mostly around 5000ft high, divide the state into Southern and Northern California. To the south, the Los Angeles Basin directly fronts the ocean, bordered by a series of mountains that extend into Mexico. San Diego, on the edge of this plateau 120mi south of LA, is right on the border with Mexico.

Sierra Nevada & Cascade Range
The prominent Sierra Nevada stretches 400mi along California's eastern border and joins the southern end of the Cascade Range just north of Lake Tahoe. Although the two ranges appear to form an almost continuous line, they contain very different geology: the Sierra Nevada is a westward-tilted fault block with glacier-carved valleys, but the Cascade Range is a chain of distinctly volcanic peaks.

Peaks in the Sierra Nevada are higher at the southern end, culminating with 14,497ft Mt Whitney – the highest mountain in the contiguous US. The Cascade Range, which extends to Oregon and Washington, is dominated by Mt Lassen (10,457ft) and Mt Shasta (14,162ft). East of the Cascades, on the Oregon border, sits the sparsely populated Modoc Plateau. West of the Cascades, the rugged Klamath Mountains have been carved by the unruly Klamath and Trinity Rivers.

Central Valley
Between the Sierra Nevada and the Coast Range lies California's Central Valley, a fertile 430mi-long agricultural region. The Central Valley is composed of two river valley systems – the Sacramento Valley in the north, and the San Joaquin Valley in the south. The two meet at the Sacramento Delta and flow west to the Pacific via San Francisco Bay.

Deserts
The Mojave Desert spreads east and north of Los Angeles, south of the Sierra and east into Nevada. East of the Coast Range, and south of the Mojave, the low desert includes the Imperial and Coachella Valleys, now heavily irrigated farmland, and the Salton Sea. East of the Sierra Nevada, Owens Valley and Death Valley are on the edge of the Great Basin of Nevada and Utah.

GEOLOGY
The gold rush may have started it all, but California is still the nation's single biggest mining state today. In 2001 it accounted for 8.4% of all US mining activity, generating $3.38 billion in revenue. There are about 1000 active mines producing some 32 industrial minerals. California is the single biggest producer of sand and gravel and the only producer of boron and asbestos. Gold is still being mined in 16 active mines, about half of them in the historic Gold Country. In 2000, 553,000oz of gold saw the light of day, worth almost $155 million. Only Nevada and Utah produce more.

California's soil may be full of useful minerals, but it's also pretty unstable. There isn't a day without at least one earthquake, although most of them are too small or too remote to be felt by human beings. California sits on one of the world's major earthquake fault zones on the edge of two plates: the Pacific Plate, which consists of the Pacific ocean floor and the coast line, and the North American Plate, which covers all of North America and part of the Atlantic ocean floor. The primary boundary between the two is the infamous San Andreas Fault, which runs for 650mi and has spawned numerous smaller faults.

The most famous earthquake in California was the 1906 one in San Francisco, which measured 7.8 on the Richter scale and left more than 3000 people dead. San Francisco made headlines again in 1989 with the Loma Prieta earthquake (7.1), which caused a section of the Bay Bridge to collapse and killed 62 people. LA's last 'big one' occurred in 1994 with the 6.7 Northridge quake causing death to 57 people.

CLIMATE
California has a great diversity of climates. San Francisco is famous for its fog. A typical weather forecast for San Francisco, at any time of year, as indeed for most of the North Coast, is 'fog night and morning, burning off by midday.' Fog along the coast

LOS ANGELES

Elevation – 77m/256ft

SAN FRANCISCO

Elevation – 38m/128ft

YOSEMITE VILLAGE

Elevation – 1189m/3963ft

DEATH VALLEY

Elevation – -58m/-194ft

thick that you can't see through it. For more on tule fog, see the boxed text in the San Joaquin Valley chapter.

Not surprisingly, summer temperatures are also unpleasantly high in the deserts; Death Valley often records the highest temperatures in the country. In winter, though, they're warm, dry and extremely pleasant. The Mojave is actually higher than Death Valley and not quite so hot in summer, and cool to cold in winter.

Nights can be chilly in most of the state nearly year-round.

ECOLOGY & ENVIRONMENT

California is a success story in many ways, but development and growth have often come at the expense of the environment. The gold rush and subsequent mining battered hills and valleys, and hydraulic mining clogged up rivers in Northern California with debris. The creation of the Hetch Hetchy Reservoir and the Los Angeles Aqueduct nurtured the evolution of San Francisco and LA, respectively, but also spelled doom to the Hetch Hetchy Valley and the Owens Valley. The pollution and destruction of wetlands in the Central Valley and on the coast eliminated stopovers for birds migrating along the Pacific Flyway. Ever more motor vehicles caused unhealthy levels of air pollution. And then there's overgrazing, logging, overfishing, oil spills, acid rain and so on.

Ironically, despite the grim realities, California has also shown great environmental awareness. As early as 1864 the incomparable beauty of Yosemite was given protection under the Yosemite Grant and it was John Muir who lobbied successfully for the creation of Yosemite National Park, which was established in 1890. Sequoia National Park was formed the same year. Muir, of course, went on to found the Sierra Club, now one of the most influential environmental groups, in 1892.

Air Pollution

The good news: the air quality in California has markedly improved over the past two decades. The bad news: it's still pretty bad. Auto exhaust and industrial emission are the chief culprits in generating such pollutants as carbon monoxide, nitrogen oxides and particulate matter (PM). An even greater health hazard – especially for people with

is especially noticeable in summer, when hot inland temperatures cause a mist to rise from the cooler ocean waters. In the south the coast is warmer year-round, mild in winter, not too hot in summer, but still subject to marine fog in the morning.

The mountainous eastern part of the state, at a much higher elevation, is pleasant in summer and gets snow at higher elevations in winter.

The San Joaquin and Sacramento river valleys are extremely hot in summer but tend to be cool in winter and foggy with 'tule fog,' which hugs the ground and is so respiratory problems – is ozone, which forms when sunshine causes nitrogen oxides and organic gases to react.

In general, air pollution is less of a problem along the coast, where offshore breezes provide some relief, than in the inland areas. Pollution concentration also varies by season, changing as weather conditions shift. While carbon monoxide and PM levels are highest in fall and winter, ozone levels reach their peak during sun-intensive summer days. Summer also brings the greatest number of inversion days, when a warm air layer traps the noxious fumes.

California has stringent motor vehicle emission standards and has introduced several clean fuel programs. As a result, even Los Angeles, the state's (in)famous 'smog capital,' has measurably improved air quality. In 2001, for instance, federal ozone level standards were exceeded on 36 days, compared to 130 days a decade earlier. Still, levels were also exceeded in other urban areas, especially in Riverside–San Bernardino (east of LA), Fresno, Bakersfield and Sacramento. High PM concentrations are more prevalent in rural and agricultural areas such as the San Joaquin Valley, the Coachella Valley (in the California Desert) and the Owens Valley (Eastern Sierra).

Water

At the time of writing, California was once again experiencing a drought, although it had not been as severe as the 'big one' that lasted from 1987 to 1992 when precipitation levels plunged to as low as 60% below normal. In response back then, the state government implemented a number of steps to cut back on water use. A Drought Information Center helped educate the public about water conservation, and water utilities offered consumer rebates on low-flush toilets. Furthermore, the Department of Water Resources set up a water bank to facilitate transfers and sales of water between communities during drought periods. Some cities began to reuse wastewater, and a few coastal towns developed desalination systems to remove salt from seawater.

Water has always been at the heart of conflict between agricultural, urban and environmental interests in California. The US Bureau of Reclamation's Central Valley Project (CVP), set up in the 1930s, dams most of Northern California's major rivers to irrigate 2.6 million acres of farmland in the Central Valley. While this has resulted in one of the most fertile agricultural regions in the world, success has come at the expense of the Sacramento and San Joaquin Rivers and the delta ecosystem from which the water is diverted. Fish populations have declined in number and about 100 species of fish, birds, mammals and other animals are threatened or endangered because of loss of habitat. The 1992 Central Valley Project Improvement Act provided some relief by encouraging conservation and protection of fish and wildlife populations, but its impact has been minor.

The other big water issue is the diversion of water from the Sierra Nevada via the Los Angeles Aqueduct, so poignantly portrayed in the movie *Chinatown*. To this day, Los Angeles gets about 75% of its water in this manner; a further 10% is coaxed from the Colorado River and brought here via a 300mi aqueduct. Only the remaining 15% comes from local underground reservoirs called aquifers.

For details about the issue, see the boxed texts 'Water for a Thirsty Giant' in the Los Angeles chapter and 'Mono Lake' in the Sierra Nevada chapter.

Waste

California produces about 60 million tons of solid waste each year. Its landfills are pushing capacity, causing environmental planners to become increasingly worried about what to do with the mountains of garbage produced each year. Much of the problem lies with the state's burgeoning population, which undermines evermore efficient waste management systems. A state law passed in 1995 required California communities to reduce waste production by at least 25% by 2000. Recycling glass, aluminum, paper products and some plastics is becoming more widespread, but in most cities this target has not been met. Public education about waste reduction is an important step toward waste reduction and schools now integrate the subject within their curricula. A **hotline** (☎ *800-CLEANUP*), operated by the California Integrated Waste Management Board, provides zip code–specific information on reducing, reusing, recycling and composting waste.

Energy

The California energy crisis of 2000–01 made headlines around the world. It came about because of deregulation legislation passed in 1996 under then governor Pete Wilson, ostensibly to lower energy costs to consumers by opening up the state's electricity industry to competition. Under deregulation the utility companies had to sell off their power plants to electricity wholesalers from whom they would later buy back the energy. The rates they could charge were capped until they had sold all their plants, which was expected to happen by 2002.

Meanwhile, demand for electricity surged by about 6% a year, as the state went increasingly high-tech and private Internet use multiplied faster than rabbits on speed. At the same time, California's economy – and that of adjacent states – grew faster than expected, as did the overall population. To make things worse, no new power plants had been built throughout the 1990s; the old ones were less efficient and often closed for maintenance or repairs.

Because of the spike in demand, unregulated wholesale energy prices rose sharply, but the rates the utility companies were able to charge customers remained capped. This deficit eventually brought the state's two largest utilities – PG&E and SoCal Edison – to the brink of bankruptcy. To avert a collapse, the state government intervened in January 2001 and bought electricity for the utilities, thus depleting its own coffers and plunging the state budget into the red. Despite such efforts, Californians experienced a number of outages and rolling blackouts (where electricity is turned off in selected areas for relatively short periods of time to keep the state's power grid from disintegrating).

There have been allegations that the crisis was artificially created by energy companies deliberately limiting the supply to justify higher wholesale prices; several investigations into this matter are under way, while long-term solutions are still being discussed.

FLORA

Deserts, forests, high alpine zones, wetlands: California is home to just about every type of ecosystem and enjoys tremendously varied flora (and fauna), much of which is easily seen and experienced. California is home to three 'superlative' tree species: the world's tallest (coast redwood), largest (sequoia) and oldest (bristlecone pine).

Coast

Coastal ecosystems range from drenched to parched. The northern end of the Coast Range, which parallels much of California's coastline, has stands of coast redwoods *(Sequoia sempervirens)*, giant beauties with spongy red bark, flat needles and olive-size cones. The lush forest floor surrounding these trees supports sword ferns, redwood sorrel and other plants. (See also the boxed text 'Coast Redwoods, the Tallest Trees on Earth' in the North Coast chapter.)

Along the Central Coast, the Monterey cypress and Monterey pine have thick, rough, grayish bark; long, reaching branches clustered at their tops; and long needles.

Southern California, by comparison, is a much more arid region. Species thriving here include live oak, with holly-like evergreen leaves and fuzzy acorns; aromatic California laurel, with long slender leaves that turn purple; and Eastwood and Cuyamaca manzanita, treelike shrubs with intensely red bark and small berries.

The Torrey pine, a species adapted to sparse rainfall and sandy, stony soils, is an extremely rare tree. The last stands are near San Diego and on Santa Rosa Island, which is part of the Channel Islands National Park.

Sierra Nevada

The Sierra Nevada has three distinct ecozones: the dry western foothills covered with oak and chaparral; conifer forests from about 2000ft to 8000ft; and a high-alpine zone above 8000ft. The tree to see in the forests is the giant sequoia, which is unique to California. Its enormous trunks, covered with red shaggy bark, stand like arboreal armies in isolated groves primarily in Yosemite and Sequoia National Parks. The bark, incidentally, is similar to that of the incense cedar, which also grows here, as do lodgepole and ponderosa pines, sugar pine and red and white fir.

Deciduous trees, found mostly near water, include the beautiful Pacific dogwood, whose greenish-white flowers bloom in late May; shimmery quaking aspen, whose large circular leaves turn butter-yellow in fall; black cottonwood, which has small white flowers that shed a fibrous fluff in the wind;

and white alder, which has reddish bark and small cones.

Wildflowers such as bright red Indian paintbrush, purple lupine, yellow-orange monkeyflower and deep purple bowl-tubed iris bloom in alpine meadows between April and June, and later in the higher elevations such as Yosemite's Tuolumne Meadows.

Deserts

Desert plants have adapted to the arid climate with thin, spiny leaves that resist moisture loss (and deter grazing animals), and seed and flowering mechanisms that kick into full gear during the brief rain periods.

The most conspicuous and familiar desert flower is the bright orange California poppy, the state flower, which blooms in March and April.

Desert cacti are perhaps the most intriguing life forms out here. The cholla cactus, for instance, appears so furry that one variety is nicknamed 'teddy-bear cactus.' But do resist giving it a hug: the 'fur' actually consists of extremely sharp, barbed spines that can bury themselves in skin at the slightest touch. It produces a bright yellow flower in spring.

Like something from a Dr Seuss book, Joshua trees are a type of yucca and are related to the lily. Named by immigrant Mormons, who saw them as Joshua welcoming them to the promised land, they grow in the Mojave Desert and, of course, Joshua Tree National Park. Almost as widespread are prickly pears, flat cacti that produce showy flowers ranging in color from pink and magenta to yellow and orange. The smoke tree, a small, fine-leafed tree with a smoky blue color, is said to indicate the presence of underground water.

The cactus-like creosote is actually a small bush with hard leaves and a distinctive smell. There's also the spiky ocotillo shrub, with its canelike branches that sprout leaves after rainfall and produce bright red-orange flowers in spring; and catclaw, which has garnered the moniker 'wait-a-minute bush' for its small, sharp, hooked spikes that scratch you or grab your clothing if you brush past.

Known widely from Western movies, tumbleweed grows quickly to become a ball of tough branches attached to the ground by a single stem, which uproots and tumbles across the desert in the summer wind.

The only palm tree native to California is the Washingtonia palm, which is found naturally in desert oases and produces stalks of rather tasty small black berries.

FAUNA
Coast

The coast offers many chances to see pinnipeds in the wild, including elephant and harbor seals, California sea lions and sea otters. The best places to observe these friendly creatures are along the Central Coast, for instance at the Point Lobos State Reserve near Carmel, Piedras Blancas just north of Hearst Castle and on some of the Channel Islands off Santa Barbara. The Año Nuevo State Reserve on the San Francisco Peninsula is also a major elephant seal breeding ground.

Gray whales can be spotted all along the coast from December to March during their annual migration to warm waters in Mexico (see the boxed text 'Gray Whales' in the San Francisco Bay Area chapter). Bottlenosed dolphins and porpoises swim quite close to shore in groups called 'pods.' They can be seen year-round from Morro Bay to Mexico.

Coastal birds include California brown pelicans, gulls and grebes, terns, cormorants, sandpipers and cute little sanderlings that like to chase waves from the shore. The California condor, a black and white bird with a 9ft to 10ft wingspan, has long been one of the state's most endangered animals but is making a comeback (see the boxed text on the following page).

Monarch butterflies, beautiful orange creatures that follow remarkable migration patterns, spend winter in California, mostly on the Central Coast in such places as Pismo Beach, Pacific Grove and San Simeon.

Sierra Nevada

Environmental factors that vary according to elevation – notably precipitation and food supply – determine where animals live in the Sierra. For example, gray squirrels, common throughout the lower ranges, can't survive winter above 7000ft. Valley pocket gophers and Swainson's thrushes are also found below 7000ft, though their ecological counterparts, mountain pocket gophers and hermit thrushes, can survive at higher elevations.

California Condors: Giants of the Skies

The California condor (*Gymnogyps californianus*) is one of the largest flying birds in the world. It weighs up to 20lb and has a life span of about 20 years. Even more impressive is its wingspan, which averages 9ft and allows it to soar and glide for hours without beating its wings. In the wild, carrion is the main diet of this giant vulture.

Until a few years ago, however, not a single condor remained in the wild; they were a species brought to the brink of extinction by human intrusion. Although killing condors has been illegal for about a century, their numbers declined steadily as a result of contamination and pollution, as well as accidents such as collisions with power lines. In 1967 the depleted condors limped onto the federal endangered species list.

To turn things around, a team of scientists launched extensive conservation efforts, but it was too little too late. In the mid-'80s the world's last surviving 27 condors were captured and taken to breeding programs in the San Diego and LA zoos. It was a risky gamble, but the consensus was that there was nothing to lose.

Fortunately, this tale has a happy ending. The first condor chick was hatched in captivity in 1988, and in 1992 the first captive-bred birds soared back into the wild. By May 2002 their total population had climbed back up to 207, including 74 in the wild. Challenges do remain, however. While a few released condor pairs have started to breed, so far none of the eggs have hatched. Only the future will tell whether the condor is truly back in full swing.

Some creatures survive winter by migrating to the lower elevations. These include mule deer, bighorn sheep, and birds such as Steller's jays, hummingbirds and woodpeckers. High in the Sierra you'll find yellow-bellied marmots and chipmunks.

Black bears are plentiful from 3000ft to about 8000ft. They weigh around 300lb and are omnivorous, feeding on berries, nuts, roots, grasses, insects, eggs, small mammals, fish and carrion.

Deserts

Most desert wildlife is nocturnal and thus rarely visible during the day. Roadrunners, little gray birds with long, straight tails and a poof of feathers on top of their heads, can often be spotted on the side of the road. A rarer sight are desert tortoises, whose slow pace has landed them on the endangered species list because they're often overrun by cars. Other desert inhabitants, all extremely shy, are the reddish kit fox, bobcat (which has no tail), coyote, jackrabbit, kangaroo rat and a variety of snakes, lizards and spiders.

NATIONAL PARKS

National parks protect the most beautiful and cherished parts of the state. Yosemite and Sequoia, created in 1890, were California's first national parks. Today there are seven, plus 16 other areas protected by the National Park Service (NPS), such as national preserves (like the Mojave National Preserve in the California Desert) and national monuments (eg, Devil's Postpile in the Eastern Sierra). The NPS was created in 1916 to 'promote and regulate their use' and to 'conserve the scenery…and the wildlife…for the enjoyment of future generations.' It maintains a useful website at **w** www.nps.gov with detailed information about each park.

In the Sierra Nevada, **Yosemite** is California's – and one of America's – most famous and heavily visited park, known for its solid granite monoliths and numerous waterfalls. South of here, **Kings Canyon & Sequoia**, run as one unit, are home to giant sequoia trees (found nowhere else in the world), the deepest canyon in North America and excellent hiking.

In the California Desert, **Death Valley** has an enigmatically beautiful landscape of salt pillars and sun-cracked flats rimmed by dramatic peaks. South of here, **Joshua Tree** is a mecca for rock climbers and is known for its Joshua trees and Mojave yuccas. Desert parks are best visited from October to April, before the thermostat starts soaring above the 100°F (37°C) mark.

Coastal parks include the **Channel Islands**, a group of five islands off the coast of Santa Barbara that are prized for their underwater life and populations of seals, sea lions and sea otters. On the North Coast, near the border with Oregon, is **Redwood**, home to giant coast redwoods, the tallest trees in the world.

In the Northern Mountains, **Lassen Volcanic National Park** centers on Mt Lassen, which is considered an active volcano although it has been quiet since 1916.

Unfortunately, several of California's national parks – Yosemite especially – have become too popular for their own good. Overcrowding is putting severe strain on the environment and making it increasingly difficult to balance access and wilderness. If you can't stand crowds when communing with nature, don't come in summer, and get away from the roads and parking lots. Lesser-known areas, especially in the northern part of the state, contain mountains, rivers and canyons that go relatively unvisited for much of the year.

GOVERNMENT & POLITICS
The United States is governed according to the provisions of the Constitution, drawn up in 1787 and since amended 27 times. The Constitution provides for separate executive, legislative and judiciary arms of government, with various checks and balances between them. It also provides for a sharing of powers between federal and state government.

US citizens over the age of 18 are eligible to vote, although barely half choose to do so. Nevertheless, elections are hotly contested, and politicians and parties spend many millions of dollars on political campaigns that can become acrimonious.

Two parties dominate US politics. The Republicans, nicknamed the Grand Old Party (GOP) and symbolized by an elephant, are traditionally more conservative, opposed to big government and in favor of states' rights. The Democrats, symbolized by a donkey, tend to be more liberal and support a more active role for the federal government. Smaller parties, such as the Green Party or the Libertarian Party, are insignificant in terms of their elected representation.

It's common for the president to be from one party while one or both houses of Congress have a majority from the other party. In this situation of 'divided government', there is generally a limited output of new legislation and an increase in presidential vetoes.

US Government
The national legislature is made up of the bicameral Congress – the Senate and the House of Representatives. The Senate has two senators from each of the 50 states, and the 435-member House is composed of several members from each state, depending on the state's population. Senators are elected for six years and representatives are elected for two.

The judicial branch is headed by the Supreme Court whose nine justices are appointed for life by the president and approved by the Senate. The court can overrule any federal or state law or executive action that violates the Constitution.

The executive branch consists of the president and the cabinet. Cabinet members are appointed by the president but are subject to Senate approval. The president has the power to veto laws passed by Congress, although a veto can be overridden if two-thirds of the members vote in its favor the second time.

The president is not elected directly by the people, but by an electoral college consisting of a number of individual electors from each state equivalent to its number of senators and representatives combined. These electors vote in accordance with the popular vote within their state. To be elected, the president must obtain a majority of 270 of the total 538 electoral votes. California, as the most populous state, has 54 electors. The president may serve only two four-year terms.

California Government
The US is a federal system, and powers not delegated to the federal government by the Constitution are retained by the states. Among other things, states are responsible for education, criminal justice, prisons, hospitals and maintenance of highways.

Each state has its own constitution and a government that generally mirrors that of the federal government, with the governor as the state's chief executive. In California the legislature consists of a state senate (40 members) and a state assembly (80 members). Term limits restrict the governor and senators to two four-year terms; assembly members can be re-elected three times to two-year terms.

Traditionally, Northern California and most urban areas, especially Los Angeles, vote predominantly Democrat, while the state's rural heartland and affluent Orange and San Diego counties favor Republican candidates.

California is currently helmed by Gray Davis, who became the state's first Democratic governor since the late 1970s when elected in 1998. In November 2002, voters gave Davis a second term with 47.5% of the votes; his Republican challenger, Bill Simon, garnered 42.4%, while the candidate for the Green Party, Peter Miguel Camejo, had a surprisingly strong showing with 5.2%.

ECONOMY

California has an extremely large and diverse economy with a gross domestic product of $1.358 trillion and a labor force of more than 17.5 million people (2001 figures). An interesting statistic comparing California's GDP with that of major nations puts the state's rank at number five, behind the US, Japan, Germany and the UK, but before France and China! The top three nonfarming employment sectors are service industries (6.75 million jobs), retail (3 million) and government/military (2.5 million).

Californians have a per capita income of $32,150, which is about 9% above the US average. The richest counties, all in the Bay Area, are Marin, San Francisco and San Mateo. The poorest, with an average income of less than $19,000 are Kings, Del Norte and Lassen counties, all in the inland areas. In June 2002, California's unemployment rate stood at 6.4%, up 1.2% from June 2001, and 0.5% above the US rate.

Although it accounts for only a small fraction of jobs (about 728,000), California's output is the highest of any state, with around 7.5 million acres of irrigated farmland producing cattle, cotton, dairy products, wine grapes, fruit, vegetables, grain and more. Farming is a highly mechanized corporate industry, aptly described as 'agribusiness,' with huge investment in land and a workforce of poorly paid, mostly Latino, laborers.

Many secondary industries are based on the processing of primary products, including fish packing, fruit and vegetable canning and packaging, wine making, petroleum processing and timber milling. Not well endowed with resources for heavy industry, California has successfully concentrated on the manufacture of aircraft, aero-

space components, electronics, computers and high-tech consumer goods. The construction industry, civil engineering and military hardware are all huge and highly developed industries.

Nevertheless, California is postindustrial in the range of its tertiary industries – banking, finance, education, research and development, computer software, TV, movies, tourism, corporate services and so on.

POPULATION & PEOPLE

In 2002, about 34.5 million people lived in California, making it the most populous state in the US. It is also one of the fastest growing, posting a population increase of more than 5 million between 1990 and 2000. Projections estimate that there will be about 50 million people in the state by 2025. The median age is 33 years.

The state's racial makeup is undergoing changes, as Hispanics, Latino and Asian populations show a steady increase, while whites post a decline. The US census of 2000 found the following racial breakdown:

White (non-Hispanic)	46.7%	15.82 million
Hispanic & Latino	32.4%	10.97 million
African American	7.4%	2.5 million
Asian & Pacific Islander	11.6%	4.36 million
American Indian	1.9%	627,000

California is an amazingly diverse society. In 2002, about one in four residents was foreign-born, an increase of 37% over 1990 figures; about 30% of the US's immigrants live in California. Of these, immigrants from Mexico are the largest group, followed by those from the Philippines, El Salvador, Vietnam, China, Korea, India, UK, Canada and Germany (in that order). California also has large populations of Iranians, Armenians, Indians and other cultures. This makes for a lot of diversity in language, religion and every other element of culture, especially in the urban areas where most immigrants live.

EDUCATION

Education is a state responsibility but the school system is actually run by local school districts at a city or county level and is funded by local property taxes (with some federal and state funding). This means that there is some correlation between the price of real estate and the quality of primary and secondary education. Generally, elementary (or primary) school runs from grades one to six (ages five to 11), junior high (or middle) school is grades seven to nine (ages 12 to 14) and senior high school is grades 10 to 12 (ages 15 to 17).

California has 8575 public schools, which are coeducational, nonreligious and open to all races. Schools often reflect the racial make-up of the local community with a student body of virtually all one race. Some cities have a program of 'busing' students across town to other districts in order to achieve more racially and socially integrated schools. Apart from the public schools, an increasing number of students now attend fee-based private or religious schools, where parents feel they have more control over the curriculum and how funds are spent. There are about 4250 such schools in California.

California's public higher education system is set up in three tiers and is based on the premise that every resident is entitled to continued learning, be it toward a PhD or a certificate in cosmetology.

Community colleges – or two-year colleges – fulfill a variety of functions, including vocational education, academic education for transfer to a four-year university, remedial education and continuing education for life enrichment and skill improvement. California has 108 such colleges, which are low-cost and don't have any entry requirements.

Public universities include the 23 campuses of the California State University system and the 10 campuses of the University of California system. UCLA and UC Berkeley are the top schools of the latter, boasting international teaching and research reputations and numerous Nobel laureates on their faculties.

Private top universities include Stanford University in Palo Alto, California Institute of Technology in Pasadena (Los Angeles) and Arts Center College of Design, also in Pasadena.

ARTS

San Francisco and Los Angeles are California's most dynamic cultural hubs, although many smaller towns, such as Carmel and Laguna Beach, also have lively arts communities. San Francisco's liberalism and humanistic tradition have made it an important center for publishing, and writers have been flocking there for inspiration for years. Jazz, opera, public theater and splendid museums make San Francisco a very livable city. Few, if any, cities in the US can boast the artistic diversity of Los Angeles. And thanks to the movie industry, no other city can claim the cultural influence – both high and low – that LA exerts worldwide.

Music
California is a mecca for musical talent, whether native or imported.

Classical Music Several important early-20th-century composers joined LA's community of exiled European artists – which included at that stage both Bertolt Brecht and Thomas Mann – in the '30s and '40s. Their ranks included Otto Klemperer, who later became music director of the LA Philharmonic, Kurt Weill and Arnold Schoenberg, arriving in 1936, who took a professorship at UCLA and composed his *Fourth Quartet*. Igor Stravinsky settled in Hollywood in 1940 and, as an Angeleno, wrote his *Symphony in C* and the opera *Rake's Progress*.

Jazz Jazz first came to California in the 1920s when horn player Kid Ory became conductor of a recording orchestra in LA, but it didn't hit the big time until the 1940s, especially on Central Ave, the main commercial strip of the African-American community. It was while holding a nightly gig in Hollywood that Charlie Parker was offered a seven-month 'engagement' in Camarillo State Hospital's drug rehab ward. Looking back on that experience, he later recorded 'Relaxing at Camarillo' for LA's Dial label. Many great jazzmen were born or raised in Los Angeles: Dexter Gordon, Charles Mingus and Art Pepper among them.

In the '50s, West Coast jazz was born with artists such as Pepper, Buddy Collette, Gerry Mulligan, Chet Baker and Shelly Manne performing under the Pacific's relaxing influence. At clubs such as Shelly's Manne-Hole in Hollywood and the Lighthouse at Hermosa Beach (in Los Angeles), and Bimbo's 365 Club and the Blackhawk in San Francisco's North Beach, they created a soothing, harmonically sophisticated style of jazz that stole the 'edge' from the East Coast–oriented bop scene.

Jazz fell into a slump in the '60s, as rhythm and blues, soul, and rock and roll became more popular, but the scene picked up again in the 1980s. Jazz continues to appeal to new generations up and down the state, at clubs like Yoshi's in Oakland and the Catalina Bar & Grill and the Jazz Bakery in Los Angeles. The styles and sounds of the swing revival too, continue to draw fans to hear the sassy, bluesy belting of Lavay Smith and Her Red Hot Skillet Lickers and the Western-influenced grooves of Big Sandy and His Fly-Rite Boys, among others.

Rhythm & Blues From the '40s through the '60s, South Central LA was home to a number of outstanding nightclubs presenting blues, R&B, jazz and soul. The Watts area of LA churned out vocal groups in the doo-wop tradition, including the Penguins, who first recorded 'Earth Angel' for LA's Doo-Tone records. A juke-joint crawl in the mid-'50s would likely have included sets played by T-Bone Walker, Amos Milburn or Charles Brown.

At the hub of a thriving Watts musical scene, Johnny Otis brought many forms of music to the public's attention with his popular Johnny Otis Orchestra – featuring Little Esther Phillips – and his record label, DIG. (Johnny Otis still plays in the Bay Area and can be heard on his Saturday morning R&B radio show on KPFA 94.1 FM in Berkeley and KPFK 90.7 FM in LA.) Starting in the early '60s, Sam Cooke performed hit after hit and ran his SAR record label, attracting soul and gospel talent from around the country to Los Angeles.

Rock & Roll Though rock and roll was recorded in California from the beginning, the first homegrown talent to make it big in the '50s was Richie Valens, whose 'La Bamba' was a rockified traditional Mexican folk song. In the early '60s, a new highly popular style of rock and roll called 'surf music' emerged, especially in Southern California's beach towns. It combined lifted Chuck Berry riffs, easy-to-enjoy rock and roll rhythms, innovative use of harmonies, and young California themes – cars, girls and surf. Dick Dale and his Del-tones, the Beach Boys, and Jan and Dean are the best-known performers of this genre.

In the mid-'60s, a group of UCLA students – among them the 'lizard king,' Jim Morrison – formed the Doors, who grooved on the Sunset Strip for half a decade.

Meanwhile, San Francisco had begun a heady ferment that was the beginning of the psychedelic revolution. Apart from big-name acts like the Grateful Dead and the Jefferson Airplane, Bay Area artists like Janis Joplin, Big Brother & the Holding Company, the Charlatans, Sly & the Family Stone and Credence Clearwater Revival were key players in defining the era's sound. Carlos Santana formed the band Santana during the late '60s and succeeded in blending Latin American rhythm with rock and roll. Master-promoter Bill Graham, often referred to as the 'godfather of San Francisco rock,' used these groups to revolutionize the way popular music was presented and by doing so set the stage for a new era of world-class entertainers.

In direct revolt against the love-bead status quo, the singular Frank Zappa, with his band, the Mothers of Invention, began his career with the album *Freak Out* in the mid-'60s. The Mothers' satire took on all comers, from conservative war hawks to mind-numbed hippies.

With a voice rusted over from bottom-shelf bourbon and filterless cigarettes, Tom Waits has brought the world music built on sounds dragged out from a Tin Pan Alley junkyard, influenced by the varied likes of Louis Armstrong, Kurt Weill and Charles Bukowski.

The late '70s and early '80s saw the emergence of California's brand of punk, which grew up around (of all things) skateboard culture. In Los Angeles the band X stood out. Though not strictly punk, X's combination – the vocals of Exene Cervenka and John Doe over the rockabilly guitar licks of Billy Zoom – created an original, decidedly Angeleno sound that simply blew the doors off the local punk scene. For a more pronounced punk sound, Black Flag led the way with the rants of singer Henry Rollins.

In the mid-'80s, Los Lobos emerged from East LA with a Mexican-influenced rock sound and tremendous musicianship that crossed racial boundaries. Also bred locally, the Red Hot Chili Peppers exploded on the national scene in the late '80s with a highly charged, funk-punk sound.

San Francisco (whose now-defunct Winterland Ballroom was the scene of the Sex Pistols' final concert) produced the Avengers and the Dead Kennedys. Jello Biafra, the lead singer of the DKs, ran for mayor of San Francisco in the mid-'80s. One of his better-remembered campaign promises was to require San Francisco's police force to dress in clown suits while patrolling the city streets.

San Diego didn't really play much of a role until generating a couple of alternative rock bands in the 1990s that hit the national stage. The debut album of singer-songwriter Jewel sold 11 million copies, while pop punksters blink-182 have also had great success since releasing *Dude Ranch* in 1997.

Rap The area stretching from South Central LA down to Long Beach is the local rap hotbed. Seminal rappers Eazy E, Ice Cube and Dr Dre all got their start in the group NWA, the band that put Compton and West Coast rap on the map. Dr Dre went on to found Death Row Records with Suge Knight, launching such popular artists as TuPac Shakur and Snoop Doggy Dog. Eazy E, NWA's driving force, founded Ruthless Records, which launched acts including Kid Frost (one of the first well-known Latino rappers) and Grammy award–winning Bone Thugs-n-Harmony. Cypress Hill, a uniquely successful crossover hip-hop outfit, emerged from the LA scene, as have popular rappers such as Coolio and Eminem.

The northern state also produced some noteworthy acts with less edge, including Digital Underground, the ribald Too Short, and the brooding Disposable Heroes of Hiphoprisy.

Ranchero If you flip through radio stations and hear something like a polka, except with lyrics in Spanish, you've hit a ranchero station. German settlers brought polka with them to the Southwest, where it merged with the indigenous Spanish-influenced folk music. It's mostly melodramatic stuff featuring a vocalist and combo music, maybe with a mariachi backing.

Dance

The San Francisco Bay Area is one of the best areas in the US for dance. The internationally renowned San Francisco Ballet is the oldest resident ballet company in the country. It draws dancers and commissions works from all over the world. The city also has many modern dance companies, including ODC/San Francisco, Lines Contemporary Ballet and Joe Goode Performance Group – and independent choreographers.

The Oakland Ballet is more community based than the San Francisco Ballet. It relies heavily on local dancers for talent and is generally more traditional in its repertoire and less expensive than the San Francisco Ballet. Oakland also has a lively ethnic dance scene.

In Los Angeles the trend has always been toward the experimental and the avant-garde. Martha Graham, Alvin Ailey and Bella Lewitzky were among those who got their start here. One of the oldest local companies, the American Repertory Company (1969), is dedicated to keeping alive the legacy of early-20th-century modern dance pioneers, including Graham and Isadora Duncan. Lula Washington Dance Theater is one of the premier African-American dance companies on the West Coast, known for its unique blend of African, modern and jazz techniques.

Fascinating, if slightly bizarre, is the critically acclaimed Diavolo Dance Theatre, which practices a cutting-edge dance form called hyperdance. It involves dancers performing in custom-built spaces by literally slamming their bodies into walls, doors or objects. Another LA jewel is the modern dance company Loretta Livingston & Dancers; Loretta herself used to dance with the now-retired Bella Lewitzky for 10 years.

Painting & Sculpture

The earliest California artists were American Indians who used pigment to make pictographs on rocks and caves, often as part of shamanistic rituals intended to ensure successful hunting. Different tribes had different decorative styles, but the Chumash, who used whimsical designs and bright colors, are considered the most accomplished.

19th-Century Landscape Artists California's first landscape painters were essentially tourists who recorded the state's gentle light and natural landscape in their works. Many such artists were trained cartographers accompanying Spanish explorers to record images of California. An impressive reproduction of a scene painted by the artist who accompanied Sebastián Vizcaíno adorns the walls of the Santa Barbara Courthouse.

The California gold rush in the 1850s also drew artists out west. When the mines ran dry, many fell back on painting to make a living. Thomas Hill and German-born Albert Bierstadt are the two most famous gold rush–era artists, both inspired by the same natural splendor that still draws scores of visitors today. Bierstadt voiced the general sentiment of early painters in writing that California 'holds land and light that can not be found in such quality nor quantity anywhere else.'

As California's popularity grew, lithographers Currier & Ives sent landscape artists such as Thomas A Ayers and Charles Nahl to create lithographs of California scenes, which they sold in mail-order catalogs. While most of this work is in the Library of Congress in Washington, DC, a few pieces are in the Haggin Museum in Stockton and at the Oakland Museum.

The Early 20th Century From the late 19th century until about 1940, California saw an influx of painters migrating to sunnier climes from the East Coast. Many settled around San Francisco, Los Angeles, Carmel and Laguna Beach. Known as the 'Eucalyptus School', they specialized in pleasant impressionist-style landscapes with natural and pastel color palettes. Working outdoors on location – or 'plein air' – they presented an idealized vision of California as a paradise as yet unspoiled by the realities of industrialization that had gripped other parts of the country. Interest in art was stimulated by the Panama-Pacific Expositions held in San Francisco in 1915 and in San Diego in 1916. Guy Rose was one of the most influential painters at the time.

While the plein air artists painted in oil, the California Regionalists or 'Scene Painters' turned to watercolor, which they applied in broad brush strokes and saturated colors. In their subject matter they took a more realistic approach and often focused on documenting daily life.

Good places to see these works are in the galleries of Carmel and Laguna Beach, which still maintain active art colonies. Laguna Beach's annual Festival of the Arts and

Sawdust Arts Festival are two of California's largest arts festivals.

Modern Art California debuted on the national art scene, previously confined to New York and Chicago, in 1940, when Man Ray moved to Los Angeles. Man Ray brought surrealism and dadaism, both well suited to California's off-the-wall, rebellious lifestyle, to the West Coast and spurred artists to venture away from traditionalism. Artists began to explore texture and shadow, intensified by California's light.

In the '40s and '50s, California art reflected the strong abstract expressionist movement in New York. Then in 1951, San Francisco artist David Park submitted a painting of a woman's figure to a competition, signifying the first move away from abstract expressionism. Elmer Bischoff soon followed Park's lead, and together they revitalized the exploration of painting figures that came to be known as the 'Bay Area figurative art movement.' The large following included Richard Diebenkorn, who eventually took his interpretation of space and light to a more abstract level.

The 1950s were also when Asian art began influencing California artists, especially in Los Angeles. Sam Francis, famous for his abstract landscapes, multicolored spatterings and Zen-influenced paintings in which bands of color surround a large blank canvas, played a key part in this Cal-Asian movement. His Japanese wife, an accomplished artist herself, helped connect Japanese art dealers and aspiring California artists.

Pop Art In the Bay Area, as artists rejected the rigid, contrived categories of stylized art, an art form that deviated from previous definitions of 'art' emerged. This 'funk art,' as it came to be known, incorporated everyday objects – lampshades, seashells, cigarettes – into elaborate sculptures and pieces of bricolage. At the same time, Los Angeles saw the development of the 'light and space' movement, which also resisted the overcommercialization of art, in the work of James Turrell and Robert Irwin.

In the 1960s, California artists were caught up in the nation's growing chaos and confusion, and California art turned remarkably disillusioned and dark. Romantic landscapes portraying California as the land of opportunity turned to 'freeway-scapes' showing smog and overcrowding, with much allusion to the lost or tempered American dream. Wayne Thiebaud's pop interpretations of freeways and city streets are strong examples.

San Francisco, with Haight-Ashbury as a focal point, saw a huge output of psychedelic work by poster and album cover artists such as Rick Griffin, Stanley Mouse and Allen Kelley. R Crumb and his art in *Zap Comix* (remember 'Keep on truckin'?) was also very influential in this movement.

Museums The best places to see early California landscapes are the Oakland Museum, the Haggin Museum in Stockton, the Crocker Art Museum in Sacramento and the Long Beach Art Museum.

In Los Angeles the three branches of the Museum of Contemporary Art (MOCA) put on some provocative and often avant-garde shows. The San Francisco Museum of Modern Art (SFMOMA) has a substantial, if more conservative, permanent collection. Across the bay the UC Berkeley Art Museum is a bit hit or miss, but it often has excellent contemporary exhibits. The two branches of San Diego's Museum of Contemporary Art show mostly European works.

The Los Angeles County Museum of Art (LACMA), and the Asian Art Museum and the MH de Young Museum in San Francisco, have large and varied permanent collections and get world-class traveling exhibits. San Francisco's Palace of the Legion of Honor, in Lincoln Park, has an important collection of European work, as does the Getty Center in Los Angeles.

Funk and pop art pieces grace many a poster shop in San Francisco, mostly on Haight St. Public art, especially in the form of street murals, is especially prevalent in Los Angeles.

Architecture

California's architecture is a jumble of styles, uses a hodgepodge of materials and reflects various degrees of quality and care. It is as diverse as the state's population.

Spanish-Mexican Period The first Spanish missions were built around a courtyard where a garden and kitchen could be kept, with buildings for livestock and horses nearby. Building materials reflected what the natives and padres found on hand: adobe, limestone and grass.

Though the missions themselves crumbled into disrepair as the padres' influence waned, the building style was practical for California's climate. The Californios often adopted the original Spanish Mission style, creating the California rancho or rancho adobe. There are outstanding examples of adobes in Old Town in San Diego, in Monterey State Historic Park and in Santa Barbara.

Victorian Also known as Queen Anne or Eastlake style, Victorian architecture became popular in the late 19th century, especially in San Francisco and on the North Coast. California's upper class built grand Victorian mansions (such as the Carson Mansion in Eureka, the Governor's Mansion in Sacramento and the Meux Home in Fresno) to keep up with East Coast fashion that reflected the style popular during the reign of Queen Victoria. Soon smaller, less detailed versions were being produced in great quantities. Their bulging bay windows were good for San Francisco's hills, as they allowed views of more than the neighbors' walls, and prefabricated construction made them cheap. In Southern California the Hotel del Coronado in San Diego is one of the best-known Victorians, and a few examples remain near Downtown Los Angeles as well.

Mission Revival With its simpler, classical lines, Spanish Colonial architecture – as mission revival is also called – was a rejection of the frilly Queen Anne style and a nostalgic hearkening back to the early days of California missions. Hallmarks are arched doors and windows, long covered porches, fountains, courtyards, solid walls and red-tile roofs. The style's heyday lasted from 1890 to 1915. Construction of Leland Stanford Jr University in Palo Alto, and the arrival of William Templeton Johnson and the young Irving Gill on the architectural scene, fortified this trend.

The Amtrak train depots in Stockton, Davis, Los Angeles, San Juan Capistrano and San Diego were built in this style. San Diego's Balboa Park also has some outstanding examples that are a legacy of the 1915–16 Panama-California Expositions.

Craftsman The Craftsman – or Arts and Crafts – movement was started and raised to an art form by Bernard Maybeck, Charles and Henry Greene and Julia Morgan. Simplicity and harmony were key design principles as practitioners blended Asian, European and American influences into single-family homes that were well crafted and both functional and comfortable. The typical house is a bungalow, a one-story wood structure with low-pitched gabled roofs, often with exposed rafters. Overhanging eaves, terraces and sleeping porches function as transitions between, and extensions of, the house and its natural environment.

Some of California's most beautiful buildings are in the Craftsman style, including Bernard Maybeck's First Church of Christ Science (1906) in Berkeley, the Greenes' Gamble House (1908) in Pasadena, and Irving Gill's Marston House (1905) in San Diego. William Wurster, who started with rigid classical buildings and softened under the Arts and Crafts influence, is one of California's most prolific architects; his work is mostly in Stockton and the Bay Area.

Revival & Eclectic In the early 1920s, copying earlier styles was very popular. They were often blended to create an architectural hodgepodge that was surprisingly aesthetic. No style was safe, including neoclassical, baroque, Tudor, pueblo and French Norman; exotic elements were even borrowed from Mayan, Aztec and Egyptian architecture.

Good examples abound throughout the state, especially in the form of public buildings such as courthouses, civic auditoriums, museums and exposition spaces. Examples include San Francisco's Civic Center and Palace of Fine Arts, the Central Library in Downtown LA and the California Quadrangle in San Diego's Balboa Park. Hearst Castle – a mixture of Gothic, Moorish and Spanish Romanesque – is also a perfect example of the eclectic style.

Art Deco & Streamline Moderne Art Deco was a favorite style in the 1920s and 1930s, especially for public and office buildings. It is characterized by vertical lines and symmetry that create a soaring effect, often mitigated by a stepped pattern toward the top. Ornamentation is heavy, especially above doors and windows, and may consist of floral motifs, sunbursts or zigzags. Excellent examples are the Wiltern Theater and the former Bullocks-Wilshire department store in Los Angeles. Downtown Oakland also has many fine examples of Art Deco buildings.

Related to Art Deco, Streamline Moderne sought to incorporate the machine aesthetic and, in particular, the aerodynamic aspects of airplanes and ocean liners. Horizontal bands of smallish, circular windows – like ship portholes – and smooth, curved facades were typical, as were simulated railings and the use of aluminum and stainless steel. The Maritime Museum in San Francisco is a good example of this style.

Modernism Also called the 'International style,' modern architecture was initiated in Europe (mostly Germany) by Bauhaus architects Walter Gropius, Ludwig Mies van der Rohe and Le Corbusier. Characteristics include a boxlike shape, open floor plans, flat roofs, plain and unadorned facades and interior walls and the abundant use of glass.

In LA, Rudolph Schindler and Richard Neutra, both of whom had come to Southern California from their native Austria, were early modernists. Both were influenced by Frank Lloyd Wright, one of America's preeminent architects. Schindler collaborated with Wright on the Hollyhock House in LA, which was built in a style Wright called California Romanza and which incorporated pre-Columbian motifs. Wright also created 'textile block' houses, made from blocks of prefab concrete.

Postmodernism One response to the starkness of the International Style was to re-emphasize the structural form of the building and the spaces between its different parts, as in the heavy-duty concrete blocks of Louis Kahn's Salk Institute in La Jolla (San Diego).

Arguably the best American architect today is Canadian-born Frank Gehry, whose trademark curves and stainless steel finishes are inspired by the shapes and surfaces of fish. Gehry has been greatly influenced by installation art and often uses unconventional materials such as plastic sheering, wire-mesh screens, corrugated aluminum and chain-link fencing in his designs, which often look like deconstructivist collages.

LA has several examples of his work, the most high-profile being the new Walt Disney Hall in Downtown.

Another architect who has managed to perfect and transcend the Modernist vision is Richard Meier, who conceived the Getty Center, also in LA.

Mimetic Architecture California's free and easy style also allowed for zany structures influenced by whim and imagination. Often dubbed 'California roadside vernacular,' these buildings usually have an imitative character: a hot-dog stand shaped like a hot dog, a doughnut shop that *is* a huge doughnut, an advertising firm shaped like a pair of binoculars, an Orange Julius stand in the form of (what else?) a giant navel orange. Southern California, LA in particular, is a global center for these wacky expressions.

Literature

Gold Rush to the 1920s Mark Twain came west to work in Carson City, Nevada, but was almost immediately enticed to Virginia City, where he worked on a newspaper during the frenzied rush to the Comstock Lode. *Roughing It* (1872) covers his stagecoach journey to the West, his mining days and his experience of an earthquake. More of Twain's tales from the gold rush are recounted in *The Celebrated Jumping Frog of Calaveras County, and Other Sketches.*

Another pioneering visitor to the Bay Area, Scottish-born Robert Louis Stevenson, lived briefly in Monterey and San Francisco. His honeymoon near an abandoned silver mine in Calistoga led to *The Silverado Squatters* (1883). Professional hell-raiser Jack London was San Francisco-born and Oakland-bred. London turned out a massive volume of writings, including his own suitably fictionalized biography under the title *Martin Eden* (1909).

The Modern Era Arguably the most influential author to emerge from California was John Steinbeck. Steinbeck turned attention to the farms of the Central Valley and the down and out of Monterey County. His first California novel – *Tortilla Flat* (1935) – dealt with the Mexican-American community of Monterey, while *Grapes of Wrath* (1939) tells of the struggles of migrant farm workers in California's Central Valley. *Cannery Row* (1945) is a humorous description of the work-

ing class in and around Monterey's cannery district. See also the boxed text 'John Steinbeck' in the Central Coast chapter.

Another writer who tried to capture life in rural California was William Saroyan, who wrote extensively of the Armenian immigrant community of Fresno where he grew up.

Eugene O'Neill took his 1936 Nobel prize money and transplanted to the sleepy suburban village of Danville near San Francisco, where he wrote the plays *The Iceman Cometh* (1946) and *Long Day's Journey into Night*.

Aldous Huxley's novel *After Many a Summer Dies the Swan* (1939) is a fine and ironic work based on the life of newspaper magnate William Randolph Hearst (as was Orson Welles' film *Citizen Kane).*

Nathanael West's *Day of the Locust* (1939) is one of the best – and most cynical – novels about Hollywood ever written. Two other novels that make sharply critical observations about the early years of Hollywood are F Scott Fitzgerald's final work, *The Last Tycoon* (1940), and Budd Schulberg's *What Makes Sammy Run?* (1941). Evelyn Waugh's *The Loved One* (1948) takes a viciously humorous look at the funeral trade in Hollywood.

Poet-playwright Kenneth Rexroth began his San Francisco tenure of literary domination with his first collection entitled *In What Hour* (1940). Rexroth, also an influential critic, was instrumental in advancing the careers of several Bay Area artists, notably those of the Beat generation.

The Pulps In the '30s, San Francisco and Los Angeles became the twin capitals of the pulp detective novel. Dashiell Hammett's Sam Spade (*The Maltese Falcon*, 1930) and Nick and Nora Charles (*The Thin Man*, 1932) plied their trade in San Francisco, and Raymond Chandler's Philip Marlowe (*The Big Sleep*, 1939) found trouble in the hills of Los Angeles. Hammett made San Francisco's fog a sinister side character in his books; Chandler played on differences between the haves and the have-nots in sunny LA.

Latter-day practitioners of the art include Elmore Leonard *(Get Shorty*, 1990) and Walter Mosley *(Devil in a Blue Dress,* 1990, and *White Butterfly,* 1992).

The Beats After the chaos of WWII the Beat generation brought about a new style of writing: short, sharp and alive. Based in San Francisco, the scene revolved around Jack Kerouac, Allen Ginsberg and Lawrence Ferlinghetti, the Beats' patron and publisher. (For more on the Beats, see the boxed text 'The Beat Generation' in the San Francisco chapter.)

With the Beats came a sort of glasnost that spread to other art forms, notably standup comedy. This was the first time in the US that comedians began to ruthlessly explore the underbelly of the American experience. Lenny Bruce, Lord Buckley, Mort Sahl, Bob Newhart and Jonathan Winters were in the vanguard of the new comedy.

The 1960s San Francisco dominated the literary scene in California during the '60s. Essayist Joan Didion captures a '60s sense of upheaval in *Slouching Towards Bethlehem* (1968), giving a caustic look at flower power and Haight-Ashbury. Tom Wolfe also puts '60s San Francisco in perspective with *The Electric Kool-Aid Acid Test* (1968), which blends together the Grateful Dead, the Hell's Angels and Ken Kesey's band of Merry Pranksters, who began their acid-laced 'magic bus' journey in Santa Cruz. A precursor to the spirit of the era, Kesey's own *One Flew over the Cuckoo's Nest* (1962) pits a free-thinking individual against stifling authority.

East Bay writer Philip K Dick is chiefly remembered for his science fiction, notably *Do Androids Dream of Electric Sheep?* (1968), which under the title *Blade Runner* became a classic sci-fi film. Frank Herbert of *Dune* fame was also a local during these years, as was Thomas Pynchon, whose *Crying of Lot 49* (1966) takes place in 1960s Berkeley.

The 1970s & Beyond The bloated excess of '70s California became a favorite target for writers. Hunter S Thompson portrayed the collapse of the hippie dream in *Hell's Angels* (1970) and chronicled its death throes in his masterwork *Fear and Loathing in Las Vegas* (1971).

For novels about LA, 1970 was a bumper year. Terry Southern's *Blue Movie* concerns the decadent side of Hollywood; Joan Didion's *Play It As It Lays* looks at Angelenos with a dry and not-too-kind wit; and *Post Office*, by Charles Bukowski, captures the down-and-out side of Downtown LA. Later

works continued to look at the city with a critical eye. *Chicano* (1970), by Richard Vasquez, takes a dramatic look at the Latino barrio of East LA, and LA's cocaine-addled '80s got the treatment in Bret Easton Ellis' *Less than Zero* (1985).

No writer watched San Francisco's gay fraternity emerge from the closet with clearer vision than Armistead Maupin with his *Tales of the City* series. Starting as newspaper serials in 1979, they became a smash hit collection of literary soap operas, light as a feather but great to read and a clear-as-day re-creation of the heady days of pre-AIDS excess. The late Randy Shilts, author of *And the Band Played On* (1987), a moving account of the early years of AIDS awareness, also wrote for the *Examiner* and *Chronicle*.

The West Coast has always attracted artists and writers, and today the California literary community is stronger than ever. Alice Walker, Pulitzer Prize–winning author of *The Color Purple*; Amy Tan, author of *The Joy Luck Club*; Chilean novelist Isabel Allende *(The House of Spirits)*; romance novelist Danielle Steele; Anne Lamott; Dorothy Allison; Maxine Hong Kingston; Elmore Leonard; Walter Mosley; Pico Iyer; and James Ellroy all make their homes there.

Among writers about the American West was the prolific Zane Grey; the list of California writers would not be complete without Wallace Stegner, whose prize-winning novels and nonfiction qualify him as one of the great writers of the American West.

Film
California culture is unique in that the state's primary art form, film, is also a major export. It's a medium with a powerful presence in the lives of people around the world. Images of California are distributed far beyond the state's boundaries. Few people can come here without having some cinematic association with the place, and many who have settled here make every effort to live up to the image.

LA in particular has turned the camera incessantly on itself. Billy Wilder's *Sunset Boulevard* (1950), starring Gloria Swanson and William Holden, is a fascinating study of the way in which Hollywood discards its aged stars.

Perhaps the greatest film about Los Angeles is *Chinatown* (1974). Directed by Roman Polanski and starring Jack Nicholson and

Faye Dunaway, this is the story of LA's early-20th-century water wars.

Blade Runner (1982) is a sci-fi thriller directed by Ridley Scott and starring Harrison Ford, Rutger Hauer and Sean Young. The film projects modern Los Angeles into the future, with newer buildings reaching further into the sky – icy fortresses contrasting starkly with chaotic, poisonous streets.

In *LA Story* (1991), comedian Steve Martin parodies the city that he calls home. Just about every aspect of LA life – from enemas to earthquakes to traffic – gets the irreverent Martin treatment.

John Singleton's *Boyz N the Hood* (1991), starring Cuba Gooding Jr, offers a major reality check on coming of age as a black teen in today's inner city. Meanwhile, Lawrence Kasdan's *Grand Canyon* (1991), starring Danny Glover and Kevin Kline, presents a glimmer of hope as black and white families cope with the sobering realities of racial tensions in modern LA.

Falling Down (1992) offers a much more cynical treatment of racial tensions in modern LA. It stars Michael Douglas as a frustrated white man who goes on an angry rampage through the city's ethnic neighborhoods.

The Player, released in 1992, is Robert Altman's contemporary comment on Hollywood. Starring Tim Robbins and Fred Ward, this is a classic satire on the movie-making machinery, featuring dozens of cameos by the very actors being spoofed.

The films of Quentin Tarantino are self-consciously influenced by noir classics, Westerns and even Hong Kong thrillers. *Pulp Fiction* (1994) is a humorous, horrifying and ironic view of LA from the bottom up. In 1997, *LA Confidential*, starring Kevin Spacey, Russell Crowe, Kim Basinger and Danny DeVito, proved another brilliant entry in the noir department.

Filmed in San Jose and Los Angeles, *American Beauty* (1999) is a black comedy about a middle-aged man who realizes that the trappings of his life are indeed traps and his determined steps to escape them.

Julia Roberts garnered an Oscar for the lead role in *Erin Brokovich* (2000), a movie about a single mother who, while employed as a clerk in an LA law firm, discovers that the residents of a small Southern California town have been poisoned by industrial pollution created by a large utility company.

Surrealist David Lynch's most recent offering, *Mulholland Drive* (2001), is the story of a woman (played by Laura Harring) who tries to put the pieces of her life back together after suffering from amnesia. Her journey takes her through encounters with weird and terrifying people living out their lives on various edges of dark Los Angeles mindscapes.

San Francisco has made a great backdrop for an amazing number of movies. Almost everything in the Hollywood lexicon, from comedies to sci-fi, has used the 'City by the Bay' as a stage. A number of big production companies are based in the Bay Area, including Francis Ford Coppola's Zoetrope and – most famously, in Marin County – George Lucas' Lucasfilm and Industrial Light & Magic, the high-tech company that produces the computer-generated special effects for Hollywood's biggest releases.

The first big San Francisco movie was, of course, Clark Gable's *San Francisco* (1936), which relives the 1906 quake. *The Joy Luck Club* (1993), the film of Amy Tan's bestselling book, explores China old and China new, anchored in the city's Chinatown.

The hit film *The Graduate* (1967), set in status-hungry middle-class California, is notable for Dustin Hoffman's unique ability to get to Berkeley by crossing the Bay Bridge in the San Francisco direction – his red Alfa Romeo simply looks better on the top deck.

We've all hurtled up and down San Francisco's streets with Steve McQueen in *Bullit*, the 1968 thriller that has served as the benchmark for good car chases ever since, and Clint Eastwood's *Dirty Harry* (1971) also found San Francisco familiar territory.

Alfred Hitchcock's movies often made use of San Francisco locales. *Vertigo* (1958) starred Kim Novak and James Stewart and wandered all over San Francisco, with lengthy pauses at the Palace of the Legion of Honor and at Fort Point. Pesky feathered fiends made nuisances of themselves just north of San Francisco in 1963's *The Birds*.

Of course, the classic San Francisco private eye was Dashiell Hammett's Sam Spade. His screen double, Humphrey Bogart, appeared in *The Maltese Falcon* (1941), a classic murder mystery directed by John Huston.

The Wild One (1954) was one of the first movies to exploit the 'rebellious youth' theme: Marlon Brando leads a motorcycle gang that invades a town in rural California.

For a taste of life in a small Central Valley town (Modesto to be exact) on a June night in '62, check George Lucas' tribute to cruising, *American Graffiti* (1973). For a glimpse of the Malibu surf scene at about the same time, *Big Wednesday* (1978) is worth a rental (although it was actually filmed in Santa Barbara). Santa Cruz became the haunt of Generation X vampires in *The Lost Boys* (1987).

Billy Wilder's classic Marilyn Monroe comedy *Some Like It Hot* (1959) elegantly captures in black and white all the splendor of San Diego's Hotel del Coronado. The schmaltzy *Pretty Woman* (1990) stars Julia Roberts as the luckiest hooker in LA – but it's filmed partly in San Diego.

RELIGION

About half of California's 34.5 million people are affiliated with an organized church. Mirroring the rest of the US, the various Christian faiths dominate, with about 45% of Californians professing to being Protestant and 25% to being Roman Catholic. About 5% of the population is Jewish and 7% are of other faiths; 18% express no sectarian preference. Still, only 9% say they are not at all religious; 22% describe themselves as very religious; 47% as fairly religious; and 22% as slightly religious.

Protestants are divided into many different subfaiths with the largest groups being Methodists, Presbyterians, Episcopalians, Lutherans and Baptists. Mormons and Evangelical and Pentecostal Christians are smaller groups but they have the fastest-growing congregations. Thanks to global immigration, California has also sizable numbers of Muslims, Hindus, Sikhs, Baha'is and members of every other faith you can think of. Mosques, temples, synagogues and religious centers of all stripes abound throughout the state, especially in the cities. Forty percent of all Buddhists living in the US reside in the LA area, and there are more Jews here (about half a million) than in Tel Aviv.

Of course, as the 'cereal state' (all fruit, flakes and nuts), California is also home to a number of unusual religious persuasions, from satanic churches to faith healers. From its earliest days, the state has had utopian religious communities tucked away in isolated places.

LANGUAGE

About 43% of Californians over five years old speak a language other than English at home. Of those languages, Spanish is by far the most prevalent, spoken by about 5.5 million people, or 17%. Still, American English predominates on the streets and in places of business. You're most likely to hear foreign languages in the ethnic communities of the big cities. Los Angeles, San Francisco and most San Joaquin Valley towns have neighborhoods where Spanish, Chinese, Japanese, Vietnamese, Korean or Cambodian is the dominant language.

Street signs, billboards and menus in San Francisco's Chinatown are mostly in Chinese characters without English translation. In Southern California, geographical features and towns have Spanish names – Santa Barbara, San Diego, La Mesa, El Cajon – but these reflect early history rather than current demography (though rural areas in Southern California and the Central Valley are increasingly Latino). The many Spanish names of suburban streets reflect the desire of developers to come up with something more exotic than Main St or 5th Ave. Wouldn't you rather live on Via de la Valle than Valley Road?

Visitors to the major national parks will often find introductory brochures printed in Spanish, German, French or Japanese.

Greetings & Civilities

Greetings are fairly uncomplicated, with the standard 'hello,' 'hi,' 'good morning,' 'good afternoon,' 'how are you?' and the more colloquial 'hey,' 'hey there' and 'howdy' among the options. There's more variety with a farewell, including 'bye,' 'goodbye,' 'bye-bye,' 'see ya,' 'take it easy,' 'later,' 'take care,' 'don't work too hard' and the loathsome 'have a nice day.'

While Americans run short on 'please,' they say 'thank you' after almost anything. You'll hear 'excuse me' instead of 'sorry.' In a conversation the listener will interject 'mm-hmmm' or 'uh-huh' frequently to let the speaker know they're paying attention and want them to go on. It's a much more enthusiastic style than the judgment-reserving 'mmm.' For some talkers the enthusiastic 'uh-huhs' aren't enough, and they will pepper their speech with 'y'know' or 'you hear what I'm saying?' – which is not a strictly literal question.

So-Cal Speak

California's most recognized dialect, the style presented in songs and movies, comes from the beaches and shopping malls of Southern California, 'So-Cal'. This casual manner of speaking – which is forever evolving – is usually called 'surfer' or 'valley' talk (as in San Fernando Valley). While it may be difficult to believe that people actually talk this way…it's like totally true. Check it out, dude.

The most common zones (places) to scope out (observe) this lingo (language) are on So-Cal (Southern California) beaches, especially where there is killer (good) wave action (surf) and a mellow scene (ambience). This kind of rap (talk) doesn't necessarily reflect the speaker's intelligence or level of education as much as where he or she has been hangin' (as in hanging around).

Killer, *bitchin'*, *awesome*, *sweet*, *stylin'* and *stellar* basically mean 'really good.'

Bunk, *nappy*, *shitty* and *slack* mean 'really bad,' and *hairy* means 'scary.' *Gnarly* and *insane* can mean anything extreme, just like *totally* or *hella* put before a word makes its meaning more significant (for example, gnarly or insane waves might be totally killer or totally hairy). *Vibes* are feelings or indications you get from a person or place, and can be good, bad or *weird* (strange).

A *dude* can be male or female and is often precluded by *hey*, the common term for 'hi.' To *cruise* means 'to go,' by foot, car, bike or skateboard. *All right* and *right on* are confirmations that you and whoever you're speaking with are *on the same wavelength* (have a similar understanding).

Lots of subcommunities based on common work and leisure interests generate new words and usages at an incredible rate. Californian language is not constrained by tradition. And the catch-all *cool*.

Facts for the Visitor

PLANNING
When to Go

California is a great place to visit year-round, although most visitors arrive between June and September. Naturally, this is also when tourist attractions get the biggest crowds and cheap rooms are harder to find.

You can enjoy hiking, canoeing, rafting and other warm-weather outdoor activities in summer, spring and fall; skiing is good from about late November to early spring. Beaches are scenic all year, but swimming is only comfortable at the height of summer in Northern California and from around May to October in Southern California, though surfers and divers hit the waters year-round in wet suits. Winter is whale-watching season, when gray whales migrate down the coast from Alaska.

Wildflowers bloom everywhere in spring and summer; trees, orchards and vineyards change colors in fall; and winter weather is beautiful and temperate in the desert areas. Many of the most scenic mountain areas, national forests and parks are, however, inaccessible in winter because of heavy snow. Urban attractions – museums, music and cultural performances, cafés and restaurants, zoos and aquariums – are enjoyable any time.

Summer & Winter Prices

Summer is the main holiday season for Americans. For the tourist industry, summer means the period from Memorial Day (the last Monday in May) to Labor Day (the first Monday in September). Some hotels and attractions raise their prices during these months, reverting to regular rates during the rest of the year. This difference is usually denoted with summer and winter in this book.

Maps

The American Automobile Association (AAA) publishes superb city and road maps, which are available at the organization's offices throughout California (check the phone book for local branches). They cost about $4 each but are free to members of AAA or one of its foreign affiliates (bring your membership card and/or letter of introduction). AAA also produces the *Northern California & Nevada* and *Southern California & Las Vegas*) tour books, which list all AAA-certified lodgings ($13.95 each for nonmembers).

Visitor centers and chambers of commerce often have quite good local maps, free or at low cost. At national park entrances, you'll be given an illustrated color map with the price of admission. For detailed trail and topographical maps drop in at the park visitor center or the forest ranger's station. The best are those published by the US Geological Survey (USGS), which are generally available at camping supply stores and travel bookshops.

Many convenience stores and gas stations sell detailed folding maps of local areas that include street name indexes for about $3.50.

What to Bring

Take along as little as possible; if you forget it, you can buy it in California. Dress is generally casual in public places. Men will only need a jacket and tie for the fanciest restaurants or for formal business meetings. Dress in layers, as weather can change drastically from region to region and from day to day; even hot days can be followed by chilly nights.

You'll need warm clothes in winter, especially when traveling in Northern California. Cold, rainy weather can still catch you anywhere, at any time. Be prepared for snow and below-freezing temperatures in the mountains. For very hot weather, you'll need a hat, sunscreen and some light, loose clothing and pants. A water bottle and sunglasses are also essential. In the desert, long-sleeved, light clothing and long pants will aid in the protection from sun- and windburn and help retain moisture.

A sleeping bag is a good idea if you'll be using hostels. You can bring a tent, but rentals may be available near parks and camping areas. Basic utensils like a cup, bowl and spoon allow you to have cereal and a drink for a light breakfast, and they're useful for kids.

RESPONSIBLE TOURISM

Water is a precious resource and too much of it gets wasted every single day. You can help by taking short showers and by being conservative in your use of towels; don't use three when one will suffice. To help conserve energy, turn off lights and the air-conditioner when leaving your hotel room. Littering is loathed and most people just don't do it, and not just out of fear of hefty fines. While hiking in the woods, stay on the trails and don't pick wildflowers. Take out everything you bring in – this includes *any* kind of garbage you create. See the Activities chapter for more on low-impact hiking and backpacking.

TOURIST OFFICES

The **California Division of Tourism** (☎ 800-463-2543) has an excellent website at w www.visitcalifornia.com packed with useful pre-trip planning information. The office will also mail out a free Official State Visitors Guide, but it contains little over and beyond the website.

The state government also maintains several California Welcome Centers in various regions. Staff dispenses maps and brochures and can help with finding accommodation. There are branches in Anderson (Northern Mountains), Arcata (North Coast), Barstow (California Deserts), Los Angeles, Merced (San Joaquin Valley), Oceanside (San Diego), Santa Ana (Orange County), San Francisco and Yucca Valley (California Deserts). See the relevant chapters for contact details.

The US has no government-affiliated tourist offices in other countries.

VISAS & DOCUMENTS
Passports & Visas

Canadian nationals can enter the US with proof of Canadian citizenship, such as a citizenship card with photo identification, or a passport. Visitors from other countries must have a valid passport, and many must also obtain a visa from a US consulate or embassy in their own country.

In most countries this process can be done by mail or through a travel agent. The relevant authority is the US Immigration and Naturalization Service (INS). Note that since the September 11 terrorism attacks, requirements for obtaining visas have been tightened and new changes may still be introduced. For up-to-date information about visas, immigration etc, check the website of the US State Department (w www.travel.state.gov/visa_services.html).

Under the Visa Waiver Program, citizens of certain countries may enter the USA without a visa for stays of 90 days or less. Currently these are Andorra, Austria, Australia, Belgium, Brunei, Denmark, Finland, France, Germany, Iceland, Ireland, Italy, Japan, Liechtenstein, Luxembourg, Monaco, the Netherlands, New Zealand, Norway, Portugal, San Marino, Singapore, Slovenia, Spain, Sweden, Switzerland, the United Kingdom and Uruguay. Under this program you *must* have a round-trip or onward ticket to any foreign destination other than a territory bordering on the US (ie, Mexico and Canada) that is nonrefundable in the US, and you will not be allowed to extend your stay beyond 90 days.

Your passport must be valid for at least six months longer than your intended stay in the US. You'll need to submit a recent photo 1½ inches square (37mm x 37mm) with the visa application (plus a fee of about $65). Documents of financial stability and/or guarantees from a US resident are sometimes required, particularly for those from developing countries. In addition, it may be necessary to 'demonstrate binding obligations' that will ensure their return back home. Because of this requirement, those planning to travel through other countries before arriving in the US are generally better off applying for their US visa while they are still in their home country, rather than while on the road.

The most common tourist visa is a Non-immigrant Visitors Visa, type B1 (for business) and type B2 (for pleasure or medical treatment). The visa's validity period depends on your home country and specifically prohibits you from taking paid employment in the US. The actual length of time you'll be allowed to stay in the US is determined by the INS at the port of entry.

For information on work visas and employment in the US, see the Work section later in this chapter.

Visa Extensions If you want, need or hope to stay in the US longer than the date stamped on your passport, go to the local INS office (call ☎ 800-375-5283 for the nearest branch) *before* the stamped date to apply for an extension. Any time after that will usually lead to an unamusing conversation with an INS official who will assume you want to work illegally. If you find yourself in that situation, it's a good idea to bring a US citizen with you to vouch for your character and to have some verification that you have enough money to support yourself. Note that if you entered the US under the Visa Waiver Program, no extensions of stay can be granted.

Travel Insurance

No matter how you're traveling, make sure you take out travel insurance. Ideally, coverage should not only include medical expenses and luggage theft or loss, but also cover you in case of cancellations or delays in your travel arrangements. The best policies are those that also extend to the worst possible scenario, such as an accident that requires hospitalization and return flight home. Check your medical policy at home, since some may already provide worldwide coverage.

Ask both your insurer and your ticket-issuing agency to explain the finer points, especially what supporting documentation you need to file a claim. Buy travel insurance as early as possible. If you buy it the week before you leave, you may find, for instance, that you're not covered for delays to your flight caused by strikes or other industrial action that may have been in force before you took out the insurance.

Wide varieties of policies are available and your travel agent should have recommendations. Some policies specifically exclude 'dangerous activities' like scuba diving, motorcycling and even trekking. If these activities are on your agenda, search for policies that include them.

While you may find a policy that pays doctors or hospitals directly, be aware that many healthcare professionals still demand payment at the time of service, especially from nonlocals. Except in emergencies, it's wise to call around for a doctor willing to accept your insurance. Be sure to keep all receipts and documentation. Some policies ask you to call back (reverse charges) to a center in your home country for an immediate assessment of your problem.

Driver's License & Permits

Most visitors over 18 can legally drive in California for up to a year using their valid home driver's license as long as that license remains valid. Visitors between 16 and 18 years old may drive in California for only 10 days after their arrival. After 10 days, they must obtain a Nonresident Minor's Certificate from the Department of Motor Vehicles (DMV).

An International Driving Permit (IDP) is a useful, though not mandatory, accessory. Local traffic police are more likely to accept it as valid identification than an unfamiliar document from another country. Permits are usually available for a small fee from your national automobile association and are valid for one year. Make sure to also bring your valid national license. Driver's licenses are also a useful form of identification when seeking access to bars, shows or other age-restricted facilities.

Travel Discounts

Many hostels in California are members of **Hostelling International-American Youth Hostel** *(HI-AYH;* w *www.iyhf.org)*, which is affiliated with the International Youth Hostel Federation (IYHF). You don't need an HI/AYH card in order to stay at these hostels, but having one saves you $3 a night. You can also buy one at the hostel when checking in.

If you're a student, bring along an International Student Identity Card (ISIC), a plastic ID with your photograph. These are available at your university or at student-oriented travel agencies and often entitle you to discounts on transportation and admission to sights and attractions. If you're a US student, carry your school or university's ID card.

People over the age of 65 (sometimes 55, 60 or 62) often qualify for the same discounts as students; any identification showing your birth date should suffice as proof of age. The American Association of Retired Persons (AARP; see Senior Travelers later in this chapter) offers membership cards for even greater discounts and extends its coverage to citizens over 50 and those of other countries.

Members of AAA or one of its foreign affiliates also qualify for lodging and other discounts. Also see Special Deals under Money later in this chapter.

Copies

All important documents (your passport's personal data and visa pages, credit cards, travel insurance policy, air/bus/train tickets, driver's license) should be photocopied before you leave home. Leave one copy with someone at home and keep another with you, separate from the originals. If a document is lost or stolen, having photocopies will make replacing it much easier.

EMBASSIES & CONSULATES
US Embassies & Consulates

Visas and other documents are usually handled by consulates, not by embassies. While embassies are in a country's capital, the US also maintains consulates in many other major cities. To find the US consulate nearest to you, contact the US embassy in your country.

Australia (☎ 02-6214 5600) Moonah Place, Yarralumla, ACT 2600
Canada (☎ 613-238 5335) 4900 Sussex Dr, Ottawa, Ontario K1N 1G8
France (☎ 01 43 12 22 22) 2 Ave Gabriel, 75008 Paris
Germany (☎ 030-830 50) Neustädtische Kirchstrasse 4–5, 10117 Berlin
Ireland (☎ 01-668 8777) 42 Elgin Rd, Dublin 4
Israel (☎ 03-519 7575) 71 Hayarkon St, Tel Aviv
Italy (☎ 06-467 41) Via Veneto 119/A, 00187 Rome
Japan (☎ 03-3224 5000) 1–10–5 Akasaka, Minato-ku, Tokyo
Netherlands (☎ 070-310 9209) Lange Voorhout 102, 2514 EJ The Hague
New Zealand (☎ 04-462 6000) 29 Fitzherbert Terrace, Thorndon, Wellington
UK (☎ 020-7499 9000) 24 Grosvenor Square, London W1A 1AE

Embassies & Consulates in the US

Most foreign embassies are in Washington, DC, but many countries, including the following, have consular offices in Los Angeles and San Francisco.

To get in touch with an embassy in Washington, DC, call that city's directory assistance (☎ 202-555-1212).

Australia (☎ 310-229-4800) 2049 Century Park E, 19th floor, Los Angeles; (☎ 415-362-6160) 1 Bush St, San Francisco
Canada (☎ 213-346-2700) 550 S Hope St, 9th floor, Los Angeles

France (☎ 310-235-3200) 10990 Wilshire Blvd, Suite 300, Los Angeles; (☎ 415-397-4330) 540 Bush St, San Francisco
Germany (☎ 323-930-2703) 6222 Wilshire Blvd, Suite 500, Los Angeles; (☎ 415-775-1061) 1960 Jackson St, San Francisco
Ireland (☎ 415-392-4214) 44 Montgomery St, Suite 3830, San Francisco
Italy (☎ 310-826-5998) 12400 Wilshire Blvd, Suite 300, Los Angeles; (☎ 415-931-4924) 2590 Webster St, San Francisco
Japan (☎ 213-617-6700) 350 S Grand Ave, Suite 1700, Los Angeles; (☎ 415-777-3533) 50 Fremont St, Suite 2300, San Francisco
Netherlands (☎ 310-268-1598) 11766 Wilshire Blvd, Suite 1150, Los Angeles
New Zealand (☎ 310-207-1605) 12400 Wilshire Blvd, 11th floor, Los Angeles
South Africa (☎ 310-651-5902) 6300 Wilshire Blvd, Suite 600, Los Angeles
UK (☎ 310-477-3322) 11766 Wilshire Blvd, Suite 400, Los Angeles; (☎ 415-981-3030) 1 Sansome St, San Francisco

Your Own Embassy

It's important to realize what the embassy of the country of which you are a citizen can and can't do. Generally speaking, it won't be much help in emergencies if the trouble you're in is remotely your own fault. You're bound by the laws of the country you're visiting and embassy officials won't be sympathetic if you've committed a crime locally, even if such actions are legal in your own country.

You might get some assistance in genuine emergencies, but only if other channels have been exhausted. For example, if you need to get home urgently, a free ticket home is exceedingly unlikely – the embassy would expect you to have insurance. If you have all your money and documents stolen, it will assist you in getting a new passport, but forget about a loan for onward travel.

CUSTOMS

US customs allows each person over the age of 21 to bring 1 liter of liquor, 100 cigars and 200 cigarettes duty free into the country. US citizens and permanent residents are allowed to import, duty free, $400 worth of gifts from abroad, while non-US citizens are allowed to bring in $100 worth. US law permits you to bring in, or take out, up to $10,000 in cash, traveler's checks, money orders and the like without formality. There's no maximum limit, but any larger amount must be declared to customs.

California is an important agricultural state. To prevent the spread of pests, fungi and other diseases, most food products – especially fresh, dried and canned meat, fruit, vegetables and plants – may not be brought into the state. Don't bring any such items with you or, if you arrive by air, leave them on the plane or discard them before going through customs. Bakery items or cured cheeses are admissible.

If you drive into California across the border from Mexico or the neighboring states of Oregon, Nevada or Arizona, you may have to stop for a quick inspection and questioning by officials of the California Department of Food and Agriculture.

MONEY
Currency
The US dollar is divided into 100 cents (¢). Coins come in denominations of 1¢ (penny), 5¢ (nickel), 10¢ (dime), 25¢ (quarter) and the seldom seen 50¢ (half dollar). Quarters are the most commonly used coins in vending machines and parking meters, so have a stash of them. Notes, commonly called 'bills,' come in $1, $2, $5, $10, $20, $50 and $100 denominations – $2 bills are rare, but perfectly legal. Also rare is the $1 coin; you may get one as change from ticket and stamp machines.

Exchange Rates
Banks in cities will exchange cash or traveler's checks in major foreign currencies, though banks in outlying areas don't do so very often, and it may take them some time. Thomas Cook, American Express and exchange counters at international airports also offer exchange services, though you'll probably get a better rate at a bank.

At the time of writing, exchange rates were as follows:

country	unit		dollars
Australia	A$1	=	0.56
Canada	C$1	=	0.64
euro zone	€1	=	1.01
Hong Kong	HK$10	=	0.13
Japan	¥100	=	0.83
New Zealand	NZ$1	=	0.50
UK	£1	=	1.59

Exchanging Money
Though carrying cash is more risky, it's still a good idea to travel with some for the convenience, especially when tipping or for making small purchases. Traveler's checks offer greater protection from theft and loss and can be used as cash in many places as long as they're in US currency. American Express and Thomas Cook are widely accepted and have efficient replacement policies. Keeping a record of check numbers and the checks you have used (separate from the check themselves) is vital when replacing lost checks. For refunds for lost or stolen traveler's checks call American Express (☎ 800-221-7220) or Thomas Cook (☎ 800-223-7373).

Automated teller machines (ATMs) operate around the clock and are convenient for obtaining cash from a bank account back home. Nearly all banks have them and they're also common at airports and in supermarkets, shopping malls and convenience stores. ATMs are usually affiliated with several networks, such as Cirrus, Plus, Star and Interlink. Check fees and availability of services with your bank before you leave.

Most ATMs also allow you to withdraw money using a credit card, but this can be quite expensive because, in addition to a withdrawal fee, you'll be charged interest immediately (ie, there's no grace period as with other purchases).

Many ATM cards now double as debit cards and are increasingly accepted at supermarkets, gas stations and other businesses. Debit cards deduct payment directly from the user's bank account for a small transaction fee. Check with your bank to confirm that your debit card will be accepted in California.

Major credit cards are accepted at hotels, restaurants, gas stations, shops and car rental agencies throughout California. In fact, you'll find it hard or impossible to perform certain transactions – such as renting a car, making a room reservation or buying tickets over the phone – without one.

Even if you prefer to rely on ATMs and/or traveler's checks, it's a good idea to carry a credit card for emergencies. Visa and MasterCard are the most widely accepted.

Carry copies of your credit card numbers separately from the cards. If you lose your credit cards or they get stolen, contact the company immediately:

American Express	☎	800-528-4800
Diners Club	☎	800-234-6377
Discover	☎	800-347-2683
MasterCard	☎	800-826-2181
Visa	☎	800-336-8472

Security

Be cautious – but not paranoid – about carrying money. Use the safe at your hotel or hostel for your valuables and excess cash. Don't display large amounts of cash in public. A money belt worn under your clothes is a good place to carry excess cash when you're on the move or otherwise unable to stash it in a safe. The back pocket of your pants is a prime target for pickpockets, as are handbags and the outside pockets of daypacks and fanny packs (bum bags).

Costs

The cost of travel in California depends a great deal on the degree of comfort you require. Generally it's more expensive to travel alone, and moving around a lot costs more than having longer stays in fewer places. The main expenses are transportation, accommodations, food and drink, and sightseeing.

The easiest and most comfortable way to see California is by car, except in a few central city areas, like downtown San Francisco or the Strip in Las Vegas, Nevada. Car rental is available in most towns and rates can be as low as $120 a week, plus insurance.

Intercity buses are inexpensive – Los Angeles to San Francisco can be as little as $30 on a special Greyhound fare. Trains are more expensive than buses, though there may be cheap round-trip deals. The cost of flying varies greatly, but cheap tickets are available, and the prices can be competitive with bus fares. See the Getting There & Away and Getting Around chapters for more details.

Lodging costs are highest between Memorial Day (late May) and Labor Day (early September) and around Thanksgiving and Christmas. At ski resorts, prices naturally skyrocket in winter.

It's free to camp backcountry or sleep in your car in many national forest and Bureau of Land Management (BLM) areas. The cost for campgrounds depends on the degree of comfort offered (flush toilets, hot showers etc) and ranges from $5 for basic sites to $25 for fully developed sites.

Hostels cost from $8 to $24 for a bunk bed in a dorm and from $40 for a private room. Facilities are almost always shared. Basic motels start at around $35 for two people. Comfortable mid-range accommodations cost $80 to $150 in most places and the sky's the limit for luxurious top end hotels and resorts. In the US, B&Bs are not for budget travelers but start at about $100 and can go as high as $250. Any place near a beach, national park or major attraction will be more expensive in the tourist season and as much as double during special events or holidays. Also see the Accommodations section later in this chapter.

If you don't insist on lavish, sit-down meals, you need not spend much money on food. Besides the ubiquitous fast-food chains, you can fill up cheaply at often excellent, if simple, hole-in-the-wall establishments. If you want a more substantial hot meal, lunch is usually cheaper than dinner. Chinese and Thai restaurants are among those offering special set lunches for $7 or less. Dinners don't have to cost much either – even at fancier restaurants – if you stick to one main course and a single nonalcoholic beverage.

Restaurants are notorious for huge markups on beer, wine and even bottled water. If you're concerned about money, stick with tap water; it's perfectly safe to drink. If you want alcohol, order beer or wine by the glass and avoid expensive cocktails.

Remember that your final bill will be swelled by sales tax and a tip (15% to 20%).

Many of the best and most interesting things to see and do cost nothing – like walking across the Golden Gate Bridge, enjoying the coastal views in Big Sur or checking the scene at Venice Beach. Museum admission ranges from free to as much as $15, although most charge between $3 and $8. Theme parks and major attractions – like Disneyland, the San Diego Zoo or Universal Studios – charge considerably more, as much as $45, but offer discounts for seniors and children. Many museums have an admission-free day or evening once a week. Entrance to national parks and historic sites costs $4 to $20 per vehicle and is good for multiple entries over seven days.

Tipping

Gratuities are not really optional in the US, as most people in service industries are paid minimum wages and rely upon making a reasonable living through tips. However, if service is truly appalling, don't tip. Customary tipping amounts are:

Bellhops, skycaps in airports – $1 to $1.50 per bag
Concierges – nothing for simple information (like directions or restaurant recommendations); $5 to $20 for special services like securing hard-to-get concert tickets
Housekeeping staff – $1 to $2 per guest, left on the pillow each day
Parking valets – $1 to $2 unless posted signs call for more when you retrieve your car
Restaurant servers, bartenders – 15% to 20% of the pretax bill
Taxi drivers – 10% to 15%

Special Deals

The US is probably the most promotion-oriented society on the earth. Though bargaining as such is not common, you can sometimes save by asking for a discount. AAA discounts, student discounts or cash discounts may be available. At hotels in the off-season, mentioning a competitor's rate may prompt a manager to lower the quoted price. Or politely ask if they have any rooms under $40, or whatever you'd like to pay.

Discount coupons for local attractions, restaurants and accommodations are widely available. Check circulars in Sunday newspapers, at supermarkets, tourist offices and hotel and motel lobbies. Other good sources are the freebie ad rags available at gas stations, roadside restaurants and tourist offices. There's usually a catch with these coupons. 'Free Pizza,' can mean a free version of their smallest, cheapest pizza, with purchase of another pizza of equal or greater value; offer not valid after 5pm or on weekends; tax and gratuity not included. Or the bargain room rate advertised on the coupon may only apply to a hotel's crummiest rooms for stays from Sunday to Thursday with a two-night minimum stay. Read the small print! On the other hand, $2 off the admission price of an attraction you wanted to see anyway is not to be sneezed at.

For more ideas on how to save money, see the Travel Discounts section under Visas & Documents earlier in this chapter.

Taxes

Almost everything you pay for in the US is taxed. Occasionally, the tax is included in the advertised price (for example, plane tickets, gas, drinks in a bar and tickets for museums or theaters). With restaurant meals and drinks, accommodations and most purchases, the tax is added to the advertised cost.

The basic California sales tax is 7.25%, but many cities add a local sales tax which can be 1% or higher. In addition, other local (city or county) taxes may be added on to lodging, restaurant and car rental bills. Unless otherwise stated, prices in this book do not include taxes.

POST & COMMUNICATIONS
Postal Rates

Postage rates increase every few years. As of July 2002, the rate for 1st-class mail within the US is 37¢ for letters up to 1oz (23¢ for each additional ounce) and 23¢ for postcards.

International airmail rates (except to Canada and Mexico) are 80¢ for a 1oz letter, with each additional ounce costing from 80¢ to 95¢, depending on the country. International postcard rates are 70¢.

Letters to Canada are 60¢ for a 1oz letter and 25¢ for each additional ounce. Letters to Mexico are 60¢ for 1oz, 80¢ for 2oz and 40¢ for each additional ounce. Sending a postcard to either country costs 50¢. Aerograms are 70¢ anywhere.

The cost for parcels sent Priority Mail anywhere within the US is $3.85 up to 1lb, increasing by weight and distance mailed. Books, periodicals and computer disks can be sent by a cheaper (but slower) rate called book rate or media mail.

For specifics and complete updates, call ☎ 800-275-8777 or check w www.usps.com.

Sending & Receiving Mail

If you have the correct postage, you can drop any mail weighing less than 16oz into any blue mailbox. To buy stamps, weigh your mail or send a package 16oz or heavier, go to a post office. There are branch post offices in most towns and post office centers in many supermarkets and drugstores. For the address of the nearest, call ☎ 800-275-8777 and follow the instructions. Post offices in main towns are usually open 8am to 5pm weekdays and 8am to 2pm Saturday, but it all depends on the branch.

General Delivery mail (ie, poste restante) can be sent to you c/o General Delivery at any post office that has its own zip (postal) code.

Mail is usually held for 10 days before it's returned to sender. Ask your correspondents to write 'Hold for Arrival' on their letters. Bring your passport or picture ID to collect mail.

American Express and Thomas Cook offer a free client-mail service. The sender should include the words 'Client Mail' somewhere on the envelope. Branches will hold letters for 30 days but won't accept registered post or parcels.

Telephone

All US phone numbers consist of a three-digit area code followed by a seven-digit local number. For a number within the same area code, just dial the seven-digit number. If you are calling long distance, dial ☎ 1 plus the three-digit area code plus the seven-digit number.

For direct international calls, dial ☎ 011 plus the country code plus the area code and phone number (country codes are listed in phone books or call the international operator at ☎ 00).

If calling from abroad, the international country code for the US is 1.

For local directory assistance, dial ☎ 411. For directory assistance outside your area code, dial ☎ 1 plus the three-digit area code of the place you want to call plus 555-1212 (for example, ☎ 415-555-1212 for a number in San Francisco). Area codes are listed in telephone directories or call the operator (☎ 0).

If you're staying at expensive hotels, resist making calls from your room. Most add a service charge of 50¢ to $1.50 per call, even for local and toll-free calls, and have especially hefty surcharges for direct long-distance calls. Incoming calls, of course, are free. You can save by relaying your hotel and room number to the person you're calling and asking them to call you back. Paradoxically, the cheaper the hotel, the lower the surcharge; in some places local calls are free.

The 800, 866, 877 and 888 area codes are designated for toll-free numbers within the US and sometimes Canada as well. For directory assistance on a toll-free number, dial ☎ 1-800-555-1212 (no charge). Numbers beginning with 900 – phone sex, horoscopes, jokes etc – are charged at premium rates.

Pay Phones Local calls cost a minimum of 35¢. Long-distance rates vary depending on the destination and the telephone company – call the operator (☎ 0) for rate information. Be sure to decline the operator's offer to put your call through, though, because operator-assisted calls are considerably more expensive than direct-dial calls.

Making long-distance or international calls from pay phones using coins is expensive and frustrating, because phones are only equipped to take quarters and dimes. You will be required to deposit sufficient coins to pay for the first three minutes (after you've dialed the number, a robot voice will tell you the minimum amount that must be deposited).

Some pay phones allow the use of credits cards, but be sure to read the small print about rates before punching in your number. The best method is to use a prepaid calling card. You can save if the person you're calling is willing to call you back; but determine if the pay phone is equipped to handle incoming calls (some are blocked from doing so).

Prepaid Calling Cards These allow purchasers to pay in advance, then make calls from any phone by dialing a toll-free 800 number, followed by the card code listed on the card itself. Available in various amounts (eg, $5, $10, $20 or $50), these cards are sold in supermarkets, convenience stores, tourist offices and gas stations. They're definitely more convenient than coins when using pay phones.

Although these cards are usually a good deal, be sure to read the small print. Many charge a per-call 'connection fee' in addition to the per-minute rate. There have also been reports of fraud where the cards promised more minutes of calls than they actually offered.

Lonely Planet's eKno global communication service provides low-cost international calls – for local calls you're usually better off with a local phonecard. It also offers free messaging services, email, travel information and an online travel vault, where you can securely store all your important documents. You can join online at ⓦ www.ekno.lonelyplanet.com, where you will find the local-access numbers for the 24-hour customer-service centre. Once you have joined, always check the eKno website for the latest access numbers for each country and updates on new features.

Fax

Internet cafés and shops that specialize in office services are the best and most reasonably priced locations from which to send and receive faxes. Mail Boxes Etc and the 24-hour Kinko's Copies have franchises throughout California. Hotel business service centers are more costly and may charge as much as $1.50 per page within the US and up to $10 per page overseas. Most hotels don't charge for receiving faxes. Faxes can also be sent from most post offices, but fees are fairly high as well.

Email & Internet Access

Traveling with a portable computer is a great way to stay in touch with life back home, but unfortunately it's fraught with potential problems. Make sure that your AC adaptor is compatible with 110V (most are). To make sure that your PC-card modem will work in the US, have a reputable 'global' modem installed before leaving home. Keep in mind that the US uses a telephone socket different from other countries, so ensure that you have an adapter that works with your modem. You may also need a US plug adapter available at electronics stores, including Radio Shack and Circuit City with branches throughout California.

For more information on traveling with a portable computer, visit w www.teleadapt .com or w www.warrior.com.

If you do intend to rely on Internet cafés, you'll need to know your incoming (POP or IMAP) mail server name, your account name and your password. Your ISP or network supervisor will be able to give you these.

DIGITAL RESOURCES

The World Wide Web is a rich resource for travelers. You can research your trip, hunt down bargain airfares, book hotels, check on weather conditions or chat with locals and other travelers about the best places to visit (or avoid!).

There's no better place to start your Web explorations than the Lonely Planet website (w www.lonelyplanet.com). You'll find succinct summaries on traveling to most places on earth, postcards from other travelers and the Thorn Tree bulletin board, where you can ask questions before you go or dispense advice when you get back. You can also find travel news and updates to many of our most

popular guidebooks, and the subwwway section links you to many of the most useful travel resources elsewhere on the Web.

Here are a few other resources that may be helpful if you're planning a trip to California:

California State Government (w www.ca.gov) Contains general information, history, culture, doing business and environmental protection.

California State Parks (w www.calparks.ca.gov) History, information and reservations for all of California's state parks.

Caltrans (w www.dot.ca.gov) Packed with tourist assistance, route planning, mapping assistance, highway and weather conditions.

Hostels (w www.hostel.com) This has a worldwide hostel database plus lots of travel tips and tales.

National Park Service (w www.nps.gov) Provides information on every national park, historic site, monument etc.

Roadside America (w www.roadsideamerica.com) The 'online guide to offbeat attractions' covers lots of stuff you won't see at the CVB.

BOOKS

Most books are published in different editions by different publishers in different countries. Therefore, a book might be a hardcover rarity in one country while it's readily available in paperback in another. To find any of the titles listed here, ask your bookstore or library clerk to search by title or author or do your own research at online vendors like w www.amazon.com.

Lonely Planet publishes several titles that visitors to California might find useful. The city guides to *San Francisco*, *Los Angeles* and *San Diego & Tijuana* are chock-full of in-the-know sightseeing, entertainment, restaurant and lodging tips.

Hiking in the Sierra Nevada is an excellent guide for anyone planning an in-depth exploration of that part of the state.

Lonely Planet also publishes a series of diving and snorkeling guides, including those to *Monterey Peninsula & Northern California*, *California's Central Coast* and *Southern California & the Channel Islands*. California also features prominently in LP's new cycling guide *USA – West Coast*.

All books are available at good bookstores or may be ordered from w www .lonelyplanet.com.

Most of the main guidebook publishers have guides to California or to Californian cities. The AAA tour books, free to members and affiliates, have good editions on California, including specific parts of the state, like the desert areas or Lake Tahoe, as well as guides to the main cities. Some specialized guidebooks for specific activities, like hiking and skiing, are listed in the Activities chapter. Other guides to local areas may be mentioned in the sections under those places.

A variety of books will help you identify Californian plants and animals, tell you where you can see them and give you insight into their biology.

The Peterson Field Guide series has almost 40 excellent books, including *Mammals* by William H Burt and Richard P Grossenheider; *Western Birds* by Roger Tory Peterson; *Western Reptiles & Amphibians* by Robert C Stebbins; *Western Butterflies* by Paul A Opler, James W Tilden and Amy Bartlett Wright; and *Southwestern & Texas Wildflowers* by Theodore Niehaus.

There are numerous other field guides. The series of Audubon Society field guides covers birds, plants and animals, arranged by color using photos – a departure from the standard field guides, which are arranged by biological type. The Audubon Society Nature Guide *Deserts* by James A MacMahon, gives a fine overview of the southwestern deserts and the most important plants and animals of these regions. The Golden Field Guide series is known for its simple approach and is often preferred by beginners. The National Geographic Society's *Field Guide to the Birds of North America* is well done and one of the most detailed.

For an overall history of California, try *California: an Interpretive History*, by Walton Bean and James Rawls. A history of the US will help you get an understanding of California in context, because the state has a particular place in the national history and the national psyche. For a more social history, read some of the fictional works set in California at various periods (see Literature under Arts in the Facts about California chapter). To get a picture of the first European settlements, read some of the works by early visitors and residents.

One of the first travelers to record his impressions of California was Richard Henry Dana, whose visits to California in 1835, during the Mexican rancho period, are recounted in *Two Years Before the Mast*. It's a good read and is widely available. Dana Point, south of LA, is named for the author.

Several well-known writers have aimed their pens at Las Vegas. The infamous *Fear & Loathing in Las Vegas* is mostly about Hunter S Thompson's reactions to a wide variety of drugs, but you may have similar reactions to the city itself.

Cadillac Desert: The American West and Its Disappearing Water, by Marc Reisner, is a thorough account of how the exploding populations of Western states have exploited and argued over every drop of available water.

The best introduction to Native Americans for the serious student is the 20-volume *Handbook of North American Indians* edited by Robert Heizer. California is covered in volume 8. Heizer also co-wrote, with MA Whipple, *The California Indians: A Source Book*, another authoritative text.

If Hollywood history piques your interest, try *Hollywood Babylon* by Kenneth Anger or *Behind the Scenes* by Rudy Behlmer.

NEWSPAPERS & MAGAZINES

Over 1500 daily newspapers are published in the US. The newspaper with the highest circulation is the *Wall Street Journal*, followed by *USA Today*, the *New York Times* and the *Los Angeles Times*, which are all available in major cities. Apart from the *Los Angeles Times*, California's most widely read newspapers are the *San Francisco Chronicle* and the *San Diego Union-Tribune*. These newspapers' Sunday editions have supplements listing the coming week's events in arts and entertainment.

Most other cities have a local daily newspaper. These papers are worth looking at to get an idea of the local issues in the areas you visit.

Free newspapers such as the *SF Weekly*, the *San Francisco Bay Guardian*, the *LA Weekly* and the *San Diego Reader* have well-written stories concerning local and national news and current entertainment listings including restaurant and theater reviews.

RADIO & TV

All rental cars have car radios. Most stations have a range of less than 100mi, so you'll have to keep changing stations as you drive. In Southern California, Mexican stations can easily be picked up, but they're hard to distinguish from the US stations broadcasting in Spanish. In and near major cities, there's a wide variety of music and entertainment. In rural areas, be prepared for a predominance of country-and-western music, Christian programming, local news and 'talk radio'.

National Public Radio (NPR) features a more level-headed approach to news, discussion and music. NPR normally broadcasts on the lower end of the FM band.

Even the cheapest motel rooms have a color TV, though sometimes the set won't work very well. TVs receive the local affiliates of the five networks that dominate American broadcast television – ABC, CBS, NBC, FOX and PBS. PBS, the Public Broadcasting System, is not commercial, and has a good news service and some thoughtful current ffairs programming, including the *NewsHour with Jim Lehrer*. Other PBS programs feature educational shows, classical music and theater and quite a few BBC productions.

Better motels and most hotels have TV with access to cable stations, usually ESPN (all sports), CNN (all news), the Weather Channel (you guessed it) and HBO (movies). Pay-per-view events or movies are going to cost you and usually only the large, mid-priced to upscale hotels offer the service.

VIDEO SYSTEMS

The US uses the NTSC color TV standard. Unless converted it is not compatible with other standards such as PAL – used in Africa, Europe, Asia and Australia – or the French SECAM.

PHOTOGRAPHY & VIDEO

Print film is widely available at supermarkets and discount drugstores. In general, buy film for the purpose you intend to use it. For general shooting – either prints or slides – 100 ASA film is just about the most useful and versatile, as it gives you good color and enough speed to capture most situations on film. If you plan to shoot in dark areas or in brightly lit night scenes without a tripod, switch to 400 ASA.

The best and most widely available films are made by Fuji and Kodak. Fuji Velvia and Kodak Elite are easy to process and provide good slide images. Stay away from Kodachrome: it's difficult to process quickly and generates lots of headaches if not handled properly. For print film, you can't

beat Kodak Gold, though Fuji is comparable and Agfa is coming along.

Film can be damaged by excessive heat, so avoid leaving your camera and film in the car or placing them on the dash while you're driving.

Carry a spare battery to avoid disappointment when your camera dies in the middle of nowhere. If you're buying a new camera for your trip, do so several weeks before you leave and practice using it.

Drugstores are good places to get your film processed cheaply. If you drop it off by noon, you can usually pick it up the next day. A roll of 100 ASA 35mm color film with 24 exposures will cost about $6 to get processed. Many places offer double sets of prints for much less than double the cost. One-hour processing services charge up to $11 per 24-exposure roll.

For tips on how to take good pictures while on the road, check out Lonely Planet's *Travel Photography: A Guide to Taking Better Pictures*.

Video cartridges are widely available. You don't have to worry about whether it is compatible with your camera. If it fits, it will work, but you will only be able to play it back on a video player that is compatible with your camera.

Airport Security

In general, airport X-ray technology used to inspect carry-on baggage isn't supposed to jeopardize lower-speed film (under 1600 ASA). However, new high-powered machines designed to inspect *checked* luggage have been installed at major airports around the world. These machines are capable of conducting high-energy scans that will damage unprocessed film.

Make sure that you carry all unprocessed film and loaded cameras in your hand-luggage. If you are told that your carry-on luggage must be stowed with the checked luggage or go through a second scan, remove all unprocessed film. Ask airport security people to inspect your film manually, especially if you'll be passing through five or more check points throughout your trip. Pack all your film into a clear plastic bag that you can quickly whip out of your luggage. This not only saves time at the inspection points but also helps minimize confrontations with security staff. In this age of terrorism, their job is tough but they can also add to your preflight hell if not treated with respect.

TIME

California is in the Pacific Time Zone, which is Greenwich Mean Time minus eight hours. When it's noon in Los Angeles, it's 8pm in London, 3pm in New York, 4am (the next day) in Singapore and 6am (the next day) in Sydney or Auckland. Daylight saving time is in effect from the first Sunday in April to the last Sunday in October. Clocks are set ahead one hour in spring (spring forward), and set back one hour in fall (fall back).

ELECTRICITY

Electric current is 110V and plugs are either two-prong (two flat pins) or three-prong (two flat, one round). If your appliance is made for another electrical system, you will need a transformer or adapter available in drugstores, hardware or electronics stores.

WEIGHTS & MEASURES

Distances are in inches, feet, yards and miles. Three feet equal 1yd (0.914m); 1760yd, or 5280ft, equal 1mi (1.6km). Dry weights are in ounces (oz), pounds (lb) and tons (16oz equal 1lb; 2000lb equal 1 ton). There are 454 grams in 1lb.

Liquid measures differ from dry measures. One pint equals 16 fluid oz; 2 pints is 1 quart, 4 quarts make a US gallon (3.8L). Gasoline is also dispensed by the US gallon.

Temperature is given in degrees Fahrenheit, whereby 32° is the freezing point (0° Celsius).

A conversion chart is at the back of this book.

LAUNDRY

Most towns of any size and better campgrounds have self-service coin-operated laundry facilities. Washing a load costs about $1.25, and drying it about another $1. Coin-operated vending machines sell single-wash packages of detergent, but it's usually cheaper to pick up a small box at the supermarket. Some laundries have attendants who will wash, dry and fold your clothes for you for an additional charge. To find a laundry, look under 'Laundries' or 'Laundries – Self-Service' in the Yellow Pages of the telephone directory. Dry cleaners are also listed under 'Laundries' or 'Cleaners'.

TOILETS

Foreign visitors will soon realize that a certain prudery is common in the US concerning this most basic human need. Toilets are never called 'toilets' but a slew of euphemisms such as 'restroom,' 'bathroom,' 'powder room,' 'men's room,' 'ladies' room,' 'washroom' and 'little boys' room' or 'little girls' room'.

Public toilets are basically nonexistent, so you have to get a little more assertive and creative in finding facilities. Shopping malls and department stores, hotel lobbies, museums and other public places are your best bets. Ducking into a bar is an OK alternative, though keep in mind that you have to be over 21 to even enter. Casual restaurants, like diners or cafés, are usually an option, though fancy ones (where you have to pass a host or hostess) may refuse you.

Though ubiquitous, gas station toilets can be dirty, and you often have to ask the cashier for the key. Many public beaches have decent facilities.

HEALTH

For most foreign visitors, no immunizations are required for entry, though cholera and yellow fever vaccinations may be required of travelers from areas with a history of those diseases.

Generally speaking, the US is a healthy place to visit. No prevalent diseases or risks are associated with traveling here, and the country is well served by hospitals. However, because of the high cost of health care, international travelers should take out comprehensive travel insurance before they leave home. Without it, some hospitals may refuse care in all but life-threatening emergencies or refer you to a public or county hospital where you may be faced with long waits and possibly inferior care. If you have a choice between lower or higher medical expense options, take the higher one for visiting the US. Also see Travel Insurance earlier in this chapter.

In a serious emergency, call ☎ 911 for an ambulance to take you to the nearest hospital emergency room (ER), but note that both the ambulance and the ER will be incredibly expensive. Many city hospitals have less costly 'urgent care clinics' designed to deal with walk-in clients with less than catastrophic injuries and illnesses.

Food & Water

Stomach upsets are the most common health problem for travelers, but the majority of these will be relatively minor. US standards of cleanliness in places serving food and drink are very high. Tap water is always OK to drink, though not always very tasty. Bottled water is widely available.

In hot climates, make sure you drink enough water – don't rely on feeling thirsty to know when you should drink. Not needing to urinate or very dark yellow urine are danger signs. Always carry a water bottle with you on long trips and *never* drink directly from any stream or river, regardless how fresh the water might look. It may contain giardia or 'beaver fever' – a most unpleasant little bugger that makes being seasick seem pleasant by comparison. *Always* thoroughly purify any water taken from rivers and streams.

Heat Exhaustion & Heatstroke

Dehydration or salt deficiency can cause heat exhaustion. Take time to acclimatize to high temperatures and make sure that you get enough liquids. Salt deficiency is characterized by fatigue, lethargy, headaches, giddiness and muscle cramps. Salt tablets may help. Vomiting or diarrhea can also deplete your liquid and salt levels. Always carry a water bottle in hot weather and take frequent drinks.

Insufficient fluids and long, continuous exposure to high temperatures can leave you vulnerable to heatstroke, a serious and sometimes fatal condition. It occurs when the body's heat-regulating mechanism breaks down and body temperature rises to dangerous levels. Avoid excessive alcohol intake or strenuous activity when you first arrive in a hot climate.

Symptoms include feeling unwell, lack of perspiration and a high body temperature of 102°F to 105°F (39°C to 41°C). Hospitalization is essential for extreme cases, but meanwhile get out of the sun, remove clothing, cover with a wet sheet or towel and fan continually.

Hypothermia

Temperatures in the mountains or desert can drop from balmy to below freezing, while a sudden soaking and high winds can lower your body temperature too rapidly.

If possible, avoid traveling alone; partners are more likely to help you avoid hypothermia successfully. If you must travel alone, especially when hiking, be sure someone knows your route and when you expect to return.

Seek shelter when bad weather is unavoidable. Woolen clothing and synthetics, which retain warmth even when wet, are superior to cottons. A quality sleeping bag is a worthwhile investment, although goose down loses much of its insulating qualities when wet. Carry high-energy, easily digestible snacks like chocolate or dried fruit.

Get hypothermia victims out of the wind or rain, remove their clothing if it's wet and replace it with dry, warm clothing. Give them hot liquids – not alcohol – and high-calorie, easily digestible food. In advanced stages, it may be necessary to place victims in warm sleeping bags and get in with them. Do not rub victims, but place them near a fire or, if possible, in a warm (not hot) bath.

Altitude Sickness

Acute mountain sickness (AMS) occurs at high altitude and can be fatal. In the thinner atmosphere of the high mountains, lack of oxygen may cause headaches, nausea, nosebleeds, shortness of breath, physical weakness and other symptoms. These can lead to very serious consequences, especially if combined with heat exhaustion, sunburn or hypothermia. Most people recover within a few hours or days. If the symptoms persist, it's imperative to quickly descend to lower elevations. For mild cases, everyday painkillers such as aspirin will relieve symptoms until the body adapts.

There is no hard and fast rule as to how high is too high: AMS has been fatal at altitudes of 10,000ft, although it is much more common above 11,500ft. It is always wise to sleep at a lower altitude than the greatest height reached during the day. A number of other measures can prevent or minimize AMS:

- Ascend slowly. Take frequent rest days, spending two to three nights at each rise of 3000ft. If you reach a high altitude by trekking, acclimatization takes place gradually and you are less likely to be affected than if you fly directly to a high altitude.
- Drink extra fluids. Mountain air is dry and cold and you lose moisture as you breathe.

- Eat light, high-carbohydrate meals for more energy.
- Avoid alcohol, which may increase the risk of dehydration.
- Avoid sedatives.

Ticks

Ticks are parasitic arachnids that may be present in brush, forest and grasslands. They may carry Lyme disease or borelliosis (relapsing fever), both transmitted by bite. Check your clothes, hair and skin after hiking, and your sleeping bag if it has been out under the trees. Early symptoms of both diseases are similar to the flu: chills, high fever, headache, digestive problems and general aching. Advanced Lyme disease may result in arthritis, meningitis, and neurological or cardiac problems.

Giardiasis

Giardiasis is a water-borne intestinal disease that results in chronic diarrhea, abdominal cramps, bloating, fatigue and weight loss (not a fun way to slim down). Don't drink stream, lake or snow water without boiling it for five minutes or treating it with a giardia-rated water filter or iodine-based purifier.

WOMEN TRAVELERS

California is a relatively safe place to travel, even for women traveling alone. Of course, this doesn't mean you can let your guard down and trust your life to every stranger. Simply use the same common sense as you would at home.

If you are assaulted, call the police on ☎ 911. In some rural areas where ☎ 911 is not active, just dial ☎ 0 for the operator. The cities and larger towns have rape crisis centers and women's shelters that provide help and support; they are listed in the telephone directory, or if not, the police should be able to refer you to them.

GAY & LESBIAN TRAVELERS

By far the most established gay communities are in San Francisco and Los Angeles, where gays and lesbians can live their lives openly. Californians tend to be tolerant, although there have been cases of 'gay bashing' even in metropolitan areas, and away from major cities 'tolerance' is sometimes more of a 'don't ask, don't tell' policy.

Apart from the Castro District in San Francisco, the Hillcrest area of San Diego, West Hollywood and Silver Lake in LA, and Palm Springs/Cathedral City have established gay communities. All these places have gay and alternative newspapers that list what's happening and provide phone numbers of local organizations. Same-sex marriages are increasingly popular, but not yet recognized by the state of California.

The classic gay travel guides are those published by Damron (w www.damron .com), including *Women's Traveller* and the *Men's Travel Guide*, both updated annually. Damron also publishes *Damron Accommodations* listing gay-owned and gay-friendly hotels, B&Bs and guesthouses nationwide. Ferrari Guides' *Women's Travel in Your Pocket* is another established source for women's travel worldwide. A good online resource is the **Gay & Lesbian Yellow Pages** (w www.glyp.com).

Several national and worldwide organizations also have a Web presence. These include the **National Gay/Lesbian Task Force** (NGLTF; w www.ngltf.org) and the **Gay and Lesbian Alliance Against Defamation** (GLAAD; w www.gladd.org) and the **Lambda Legal Defense Fund** (w www .lambdalegal.org).

DISABLED TRAVELERS

Travel within the US is becoming easier for people with disabilities, and California is as good as its gets. The Americans with Disabilities Act (ADA) requires that all public buildings (including hotels, restaurants, theaters and museums) be wheelchair accessible. Buses and trains must have wheelchair lifts and telephone companies are required to provide relay operators (available via TTY numbers) for the hearing impaired. Many banks now provide ATM instructions in Braille, and you'll find dropped curbs at most intersections and occasionally audible crossing signals as well.

Larger private and chain hotels have suites for disabled guests. Major car rental agencies offer hand-controlled vehicles and vans with wheelchair lifts at no extra charge, but you must reserve them well in advance.

All major airlines, Greyhound buses and Amtrak trains allow service animals like guide dogs to accompany passengers.

Airlines must accept wheelchairs as checked baggage and have an onboard chair available, though some advance notice may be required. Airlines will also provide assistance for connecting, boarding and deplaning flights – just ask for assistance when making your reservation.

Most national and state parks and recreation areas have paved or boardwalk-style nature trails. For free admission to national parks, blind or permanently disabled US citizens and permanent residents can get a Golden Access Passport (see the boxed text 'National Parks Passes' later in this chapter). Books worth checking out include *California Parks Access* by Linda and Allen Mitchell, and *Easy Access to National Parks* by Wendy Roth and Michael Tompane.

Organizations & Resources

A number of organizations and tour providers specialize in serving disabled travelers:

Access-Able Travel Source (☎ 303-232-2979, fax 303-239-8486, W www.access-able.com) This is an excellent website with many links.
Mobility International USA (☎ 541-343-1284, fax 541-343-6812, W www.miusa.org) Advises disabled travelers on mobility issues and runs an educational exchange program.
Moss Rehabilitation Hospital's Travel Information Service (☎ 215-456-9600, TTY 456-9602, W www.mossresourcenet.org/travel.htm) This has a concise list of useful contacts.
Twin Peaks Press (☎ 360-694-2462, 800-637-2256, W http://home.pacifier.com/~twinpeak) Publishes a quarterly newsletter, plus directories and access guides.

SENIOR TRAVELERS

Though the age when the benefits begin varies with the attraction, travelers as young as 50 can expect to receive cut rates and benefits. Be sure to inquire about such seniors' rates at hotels, museums and restaurants. Visitors to national parks qualify for the Golden Age Passport (see the boxed text 'National Parks Passes' later in this chapter).

Some national advocacy groups that can help in planning your travels include the following:

American Association of Retired Persons (AARP, ☎ 800-424-3410, W www.aarp.org) An advocacy group for Americans 50 years and older

and a good resource for travel bargains. A one-year membership is $8 for US residents and $10 for foreigners.
Elderhostel (☎ 877-426-8056, W www.elderhostel.org) A nonprofit organization that offers those over 55 the opportunity to attend academic college courses and study tours throughout the US and Canada.

TRAVEL WITH CHILDREN

Successful travel with young children requires planning and effort. Don't try to overdo things; even for adults, packing too much into the time available can cause problems. And make sure the activities include the kids as well – balance that morning at the art museum with a visit to the zoo or the beach. Include the kids in the trip planning; if they've helped to work out where you are going, they will be much more interested when they get there. For more information, advice and anecdotes, look at LP's *Travel with Children* by Cathy Lanigan.

Children's discounts are widely available for everything from museum admissions to bus fares and motel stays. The definition of a child varies – in some places anyone under 18 is eligible, while others only include children under six. Unless specified, prices quoted for children in this book refer to those aged three to 12.

Many hotels and motels allow children to share a room with their parents for free or for a modest fee, though B&Bs rarely do and many don't allow children at all. Larger hotels often have a baby-sitting service, and other hotels may be able to help you make arrangements. Alternatively, look in the Yellow Pages for local agencies. Be sure to ask whether sitters are licensed and bonded, what they charge per hour, whether there's a minimum fee and whether they charge extra for meals and transportation.

Most car rental firms have children's safety seats for hire at a nominal cost, but be sure to book them in advance. The same goes for highchairs and cribs; they're common in many restaurants and hotels, but numbers are limited. The choice of baby food, infant formulas, soy and cow's milk, disposable diapers (nappies) and other necessities is great in supermarkets throughout California. Diaper changing stations can be found in many public toilets in malls, department stores and even in many restaurants.

It's perfectly fine to bring your kids, even toddlers, along to casual restaurants (though not to many upscale ones at dinnertime), cafés and daytime events.

USEFUL ORGANIZATIONS

See also the organizations listed previously for women, seniors, gays and lesbians, and disabled travelers.

American Automobile Association (AAA) Motoring information, maps, tours books, car insurance, towing services, travel planning etc, for members, including those of affiliated foreign clubs (also see the Getting Around chapter).

National Parks Passes

If you're going to be visiting several national parks or are planning on making multiple trips within a one-year period, consider buying the National Parks Pass, an annual pass costing $50. It entitles the holder and anyone else in the vehicle to unlimited admission to any national park for one year from the month of purchase. You can buy it at park entrances or in advance by calling ☎ 888-467-2757 or online at **W** www.nationalparks.org.

For an additional $15, a **Golden Eagle** hologram will be affixed to your National Parks Pass, giving you and your group admission to sites managed by other federal agencies, such as the US Fish and Wildlife Service, the US Forest Service and the Bureau of Land Management, in addition to all national parks. It's valid until your National Parks Pass expires.

If you're a US citizen or permanent resident older than 62, you qualify for the **Golden Age Passport**, which costs $10 and is good for unlimited free admission to all national parks, monuments, historic sites, recreation areas and national wildlife refuges for the rest of your life. You also get 50% discount on camping, parking and other fees. The pass is only available in person at an entrance station to a federal recreation area and you must show proof of age.

Finally, there's the **Golden Access Passport**, available to citizens or permanent residents of the US who are blind or permanently disabled. It works the same way as the Golden Age Passport, except that there is no age restriction and it is free.

Bureau of Land Management (BLM) Manages public use of federal lands other than national parks or forests and offers no-frills camping, often in remote settings.

National Park Service (NPS) Administers national parks, monuments, historic sites and other protected federal areas. Most NPS areas charge entrance fees, valid for multiple entries during a seven-day period, of $4 to $20 per vehicle (usually half price or less for walk-in or biking visitors). Some places are free, and some don't collect entrance fees during periods of low visitation (usually late fall to early spring). Additional fees apply for camping and other activities.

US Forest Service (USFS) Administers national forests which enjoy less protection than parks, usually allowing logging, privately owned recreational facilities and such activities as hunting, fishing, snowmobiling, 4WD use and mountain biking. Entrance to most forests is free, although in some areas you will need to purchase a National Forest Adventure Pass (see the boxed text in the Activities chapter).

DANGERS & ANNOYANCES

By and large, California is not a dangerous place. The most publicized problem is violent crime, but this is mostly confined to areas few visitors would go. Travel in deserts and mountain areas can be hazardous and wildlife presents some potential dangers. And then there is the dramatic but unlikely possibility of a natural disaster, such as an earthquake. See the California Deserts chapter for advice on minimizing the risks of desert travel.

Crime

The good news is that tourists will rarely get tricked, cheated or conned simply because they're tourists. The bad news is that violent crime is a problem for tourists as well as locals, especially in the cities. Gang violence is a serious issue, notably in parts of Oakland, South San Francisco, Bakersfield, Modesto and Stockton, and LA suburbs such as Compton, East LA and Watts. Avoid these neighborhoods, especially after dark.

If you find yourself in a neighborhood where you'd rather not be, do your best to look confident; don't stop every few minutes to look at your map. Hail a taxi and get out of there if you can. If you're accosted by a mugger, there's no 100% recommended policy, but handing over whatever the mugger wants is better than getting knifed, shot or beaten up. Don't carry too much cash or valuables and don't have it all in the same pocket or wallet. Keep some money, say $50, separate, and hand it over fast. Muggers are not too happy to find their victims penniless.

While traveling, stash your money in several places, including a money belt worn underneath your clothing. At hotels, use their safe deposit boxes or at least place valuables in a locked bag. Always lock cars and put valuables out of sight. If your car is bumped from behind by another vehicle in a remote area, try to keep going to a well-lit area, gas station or even a police station.

Panhandlers & Homeless People

You're likely to bump into beggars on the streets of California. Many are homeless people suffering from medical or psychiatric problems, or the effects of alcohol and drug abuse. Although a nuisance, most of them are harmless. Often they have witty signs like: 'residentially challenged,' 'nonaggressive panhandler' and 'Let's be honest, I need a beer'.

It's an individual judgment call whether to offer them money or anything else – you might just offer food if you have it. If you want to contribute toward a long-term solution, consider a donation to a charity that cares for the homeless.

Wildlife

Drivers should watch for stock or deer on highways. Hitting a large animal at 55 mph will total your car, kill the animal and might kill you as well. Snakes, spiders, scorpions and other venomous creatures are found throughout California, and not just in wilderness areas. Attacks or fatalities, however, are exceedingly rare and the following descriptions are largely for general interest.

Bears are attracted to campgrounds where they may find accessible food in bags, tents, cars or picnic baskets. The boxed text 'Bears, Your Food & You' in the Activities chapter has details.

Mountain lions – also called 'cougars' or 'pumas' – are most common in the lower western Sierra, and the mountains and forests east of Los Angeles and San Diego, especially in areas with lots of deer. Attacks on humans are rare. Rangers recommend you stay calm if you encounter one, hold your ground and try to appear large by raising your arms or grabbing a stick. If the lion gets aggressive or attacks, fight back, shout and throw objects at it.

Watch your step when hiking, especially on hot summer afternoons and evenings when rattlesnakes like to bask in the middle of the trail. They are often active at night. There are many species of rattler, most easily identified by the 'rattle' of dried segments of skin at the tip of the tail, which emit a rapid rattling sound when the snake is disturbed. Most rattlesnakes have roughly diamond-shaped patterns along their backs and vary in length from 2ft to 6ft. If you are bitten, you will experience rapid swelling, very severe pain and possible temporary paralysis, but victims rarely die. Antivenin is available in most hospitals. If the snake is dead, bring it in for identification, but don't attempt to catch it if there is even a remote possibility of being bitten again.

Scorpions spend their days under rocks or woodpiles, so use caution when around these. The long stinger curving up and around the back is characteristic of these animals. The stings can be very painful but are almost never fatal; small children are at highest risk.

The most dangerous spider in the area is the black widow, a species that has gained notoriety because the venomous female eats her mate after sex. The female has a small, round body marked with a red hourglass shape under its abdomen. She makes very messy webs, so avoid these, as the widow will bite if harassed. Bites are very painful but rarely fatal, except in young children. Antivenin is available.

The large (up to 6 inches in diameter) and hairy tarantula looks much worse than it is – it bites very rarely and then usually when it is roughly handled. The bite is not very serious, although it is temporarily quite painful.

Earthquakes

Earthquakes happen frequently but most are so tiny they can only be detected by sensitive seismological instruments. If you're caught in a serious earthquake, stay indoors and take cover under a desk, table or doorway. Stay clear of windows, mirrors or anything with a danger of falling. Don't use the elevators. If you're in a shopping mall or large public building, expect the alarm and/or sprinkler systems to come on.

If outdoors, get away from buildings, trees and power lines. If you are driving, pull over to the side of the road away from bridges, overpasses and power lines. Stay inside the car until the shaking stops. If you are on a sidewalk near buildings, duck into a doorway to protect yourself from falling bricks, glass and debris. Prepare for aftershocks. Use the telephone only if absolutely necessary. Turn on the radio and listen for bulletins.

EMERGENCIES

Throughout most of the US, dial ☎ 911 for emergency service of any sort. This is a free call from any phone. A few rural phones might not have this service, in which case dial ☎ 0 for the operator and ask for emergency assistance – it's still free.

International visitors in need of emergency or travel assistance can contact ☎ 888-US-1-INFO (☎ 888-871-4636) for help in 140 languages.

LEGAL MATTERS

If you are stopped by the police for any reason, bear in mind that there is no system of paying fines on the spot. For traffic offenses, the police officer will explain the options to you. Attempting to pay the fine to the officer is frowned upon at best and may even result in a charge of bribery. There is usually a 30-day period to pay a fine.

If you are arrested for more serious offenses, you are allowed to remain silent and are presumed innocent until proven guilty. There is no legal reason to speak to a police officer if you don't wish. All persons who are arrested are legally allowed the right to make one phone call. If you don't have a lawyer, friend or family member to help you, call your embassy. The police will give you the number upon request.

The legal drinking age is 21, and you can be asked for a photo ID to prove your age. Stiff fines, jail time and other penalties can be incurred for driving under the influence of alcohol or drugs. A blood alcohol content of 0.08% or higher is illegal, even if you're still able to drive.

Penalties are severe for DUI or driving under the influence of alcohol or drugs. Police can give roadside sobriety checks ('touch your nose, walk along this line' etc) to assess if you've been drinking or using drugs. If you fail, they'll require you to take a breath test, urine test or blood test to determine the level of alcohol in your body. Refusing to be tested is treated the same as taking and failing the test. Penalties for DUI range from license suspension and fines to jail time. If you're in a group, you can avoid a DUI by assigning one of you as the 'designated driver' who agrees not to consume alcohol or drugs.

It is also illegal to carry open containers of alcohol inside a vehicle, even in the passenger section, even if they are empty. Containers that are full and sealed may be carried, but if they have ever been opened, they must be stored in the trunk.

During festive holidays and special events, roadblocks are sometimes set up to deter drunk drivers.

In California, possession of under 1oz of marijuana is a misdemeanor, and though it is punishable by up to one year in jail, a fine is more likely. Possession of any other drug, including cocaine, ecstasy, LSD, heroin, hashish or more than an ounce of weed is a felony, punishable by lengthy jail sentences, depending on the circumstances. Conviction of any drug offense is grounds for deportation of a foreigner.

BUSINESS HOURS

In any large city, a few supermarkets, restaurants and the main post office are open 24 hours. Shops are usually open from 9am or 10am to 5pm or 6pm (often until 9pm in shopping malls), except Sunday when hours are noon to 5pm (often later in malls). Post offices are open weekdays 8am to 4pm or 5:30pm, and some are open 8am to 2pm on Saturday. Banks are usually open from 9am or 10am to 5pm or 6pm weekdays; a few banks are also open until 1pm or 2pm on Saturday. Check with an individual branch for precise hours.

PUBLIC HOLIDAYS

National public holidays are celebrated throughout the US. Banks, schools and government offices (including post offices) are closed and transportation, museums and other services operate on a Sunday schedule. Holidays falling on a weekend are usually observed the following Monday.

New Year's Day	January 1
Martin Luther King Jr Day	3rd Monday in January
Presidents' Day	3rd Monday in February
Memorial Day	last Monday in May
Independence Day	July 4 (also called 'Fourth of July')
Labor Day	1st Monday in September
Columbus Day	2nd Monday in October
Veterans' Day	November 11
Thanksgiving Day	4th Thursday in November
Christmas Day	December 25

CULTURAL EVENTS

Besides the holidays mentioned previously, the US celebrates a number of other events, reflecting the rich mixture of cultures in this country. The following are the most widely observed.

January/February

Chinese New Year Held in late January/early February, Chinese New Year has free festivities, firecrackers, parades and lots of food, with the biggest celebrations held in San Francisco and Los Angeles.

Valentine's Day Celebrated on February 14, this is a day of roses, sappy greeting cards and packed restaurants. Some people wear red and give out 'Be My Valentine' candies.

March

St Patrick's Day Ireland's patron saint is honored on March 17 by all those who feel the Irish in their blood. Everyone wears green (or you can get pinched), stores sell green bread, bars serve green beer, and towns and cities put on frolicking parades.

April

Easter Travel during this weekend is usually expensive and crowded. Good Friday is usually not observed as a holiday.

May

Cinco de Mayo This celebrates the day (May 5) the Mexicans wiped out the French army in 1862, with big festivities in San Diego, San Jose, Los Angeles, Oceanside, Calexico, San Francisco and other towns with large Mexican populations.

June

Juneteenth On June 17 the emancipation of African-American slaves is remembered with large celebrations in Oakland, Berkeley and other communities with large African-American populations.

July

Independence Day Held on July 4, this is a big national holiday with parades, barbecues, fireworks and American flags everywhere.

October

Halloween Kids and adults dress in costumes, children go 'trick-or-treating' for candy, adults go to parties to act out their alter egos. It's held on October 31 and there are big parades and balls in San Francisco and LA.

November

Day of the Dead On November 2, Mexican families honor dead relatives and make breads and sweets resembling skeletons, skulls and such.

Thanksgiving Held on the last Thursday in November, this commemorates the 1621 celebration of the first successful harvest reaped by the Pilgrims with the help of the native Americans. This important family gathering is celebrated with a bounty of food, football games on TV and a big parade in New York City (seen throughout the country). Christmas shopping season officially kicks off the following day.

December

Kwanzaa This African-American holiday celebrates family, heritage and community. It's held from December 26 to 31.

Hanukkah An eight-day Jewish holiday celebrating the rededication of the Temple of Jerusalem.

SPECIAL EVENTS

Apart from national holidays and cultural events, many local celebrations, sporting events, art festivals, county fairs, car shows, Native-American powwows and so on, are quite common in California. Most of these are annual, usually scheduled for a weekend at about the same time every year.

Country events include all the amusements of small town life. Each county has an annual fair, where competitions are held for everything from prize pigs to apple pie, and they also put forth music, arts and crafts, rodeos and carnival rides.

We can only list a small selection of events. For the complete, up-to-date lowdown, with exact dates, contact the California Division of Tourism (see Tourist Offices earlier in this chapter) or check its website.

January & February

Tournament of Roses (☎ 626-449-4400, **W** www.tournamentofroses.com) The famous New Year's Day parade of flower-coated floats, marching bands and equestrians held in the Los Angeles suburb of Pasadena.

Whalefest (☎ 831-784-6464) Held in Monterey each year, is a celebration of the gray whales' annual migration, with music, exhibits and art.

Riverside County Fair & National Date Festival (☎ 760-863-8247, 800-811-3247, W www .datefest.org) Combines a county fair with a celebration of the date industry, plus pig, camel and ostrich races.

Vietnamese New Year, or Tet A big celebration in San Jose.

March & April

San Diego Latino Film Festival (☎ 619-230-1938, W www.sdlatinofilm.com) Screens films from throughout Latin America and the US.

Sacramento Valley Scottish Games & Gathering (☎ 916-557-0764) A celebration of Scottish culture, with bagpipes, dancing, Scottish athletics and more; Woodland.

Toyota Grand Prix of Long Beach (☎ 888-827-7333, W www.longbeachgp.com) A week-long auto racing spectacle drawing world-class drivers through city streets.

Red Bluff Round-Up (☎ 530-527-1000) The largest three-day rodeo in the country.

San Francisco International Film Festival (☎ 995-275-9490, W www.sfss.org) The country's oldest film festival, in late April to early May.

May

Stanford Powwow (☎ 650-723-4078, W http:// powwowstanford.edu) A big intertribal gathering in Palo Alto.

Calaveras County Fair & Jumping Frog Jubilee (☎ 209-736-2561, W www.frogtown.org) A classic county fair, with a famous frog jumping contest, held in Frogtown, 2mi south of Angels Camp.

Bay to Breakers (☎ 415-359-2800, W www. baytobreakers.com) The largest and craziest footrace in the world, is a mob of costumed runners, world-class athletes and weekend warriors; San Francisco.

June

West Coast Antique Fly-In (☎ 800-446-5353) An air show with old and home-built aircraft; Merced.

San Francisco Pride (☎ 415-864-3733, W www .sfpride.org) Lesbian, Gay, Bisexual and Transgender Pride Parade, in late June, attracts thousands of people to San Francisco.

July

Festival of the Arts & Pageant of the Masters (☎ 800-487-3378, W www.foapom.com) Features exhibits by hundreds of artists and a pageant of art masterpieces 're-created' using real people; in Laguna Beach.

Valhalla Arts & Music Festival (☎ 888-632-5859, W www.Valhalla-tallac.com) An extravaganza of jazz and classical music, fine arts exhibits and theater at the Tallac Historic Site on the lake; South Lake Tahoe.

Gilroy Garlic Festival (☎ 408-842-1625, W www .gilroygarlicfestival.com) The focus here is on the 'stinking rose' with lots of garlic food and jokes.

Jazz Jubilee (☎ 760-934-2478, W www.mam mothjazz.org) Top-notch bands perform Dixieland, big band, zydeco and swing jazz; Mammoth Lakes.

Annual US Open Sandcastle Competition (☎ 619-424-6663) Amazing sandcastle competition; Imperial Beach, San Diego.

August

Steinbeck Festival (☎ 831-796-3833, W www .steinbeck.org) Celebrates California's Nobel laureate with films, theater and lectures on John Steinbeck in Salinas.

Old Spanish Days Fiesta (☎ 805-962-8101, W www.oldspanishdays-fiesta.org) Celebrates early rancho culture with parades, rodeo, crafts exhibits and shows; in Santa Barbara.

California State Fair (☎ 916-263-3247) The largest of the state's county fairs with a firework display, a livestock nursery, giant midway, horse-racing and good food, beer and wine; in Sacramento.

Concours D'Elegance (☎ 831-659-0663, W www .pebblebeachconcours.net) presents vintage vehicles to modern concept cars in a world-class car parade; Pebble Beach.

African Marketplace and Cultural Faire (☎ 323-734-1164, W www.africanmarketplace.org) Celebrates African-American culture with traditional food, art and entertainment on three weekends in late August and early September; in Los Angeles.

September

Fringe Festival (☎ 415-931-1094, W www.sff ringe.org) This theater marathon brings a variety of performers from around the world to SanFrancisco.

Monterey Jazz Festival (☎ 831-373-3366, W www.montereyjazzfestival.org) This is a long-running, big-name festival of traditional and modern styles of jazz, with workshops and exhibitions.

Simon Rodia Watts Towers Jazz Festival (☎ 213-847-4646) Features jazz, gospel, R&B, and other sounds, in the shadow of the Watts Towers; Los Angeles.

Oktoberfest Throughout September and October, this is a celebration of German heritage in many of the state's cities with music, dancing, costumes and rivers of beer. The one in Mammoth Lakes is a good one.

Kern County Fair (☎ 661-833-4900, W www .kerncountyfair.com) Music and entertainment, livestock shows, carnival rides, rodeo and more; in Bakersfield.

October

San Francisco Jazz Festival (☎ 415-788-7353, 800-850-7353, W www.sfjazz.com) Features live music from top and new artists throughout the city.

World Championship Pumpkin Weigh-Off (☎ 650-726-4485, W www.miramarevents .com) In Half Moon Bay, this is a competition of West Coast pumpkin growers.

November

Christmas Tree Lighting In late November many communities kick off the Christmas season by lighting up a large tree in a public place.

Hollywood Christmas Parade (☎ 323-469-2337) Features celebrities waving at fans lining Hollywood Boulevard, classic cars, floats, marching bands.

Doo Dah Parade (☎ 626-440-7379) This irreverent spoof of the parade tradition features thousands participants in outrageous costumes; in Pasadena.

December

Truckers Christmas Convoy (☎ 707-442-5744) This memorable parade features 100 big rigs decked out with lively Christmas decorations; Eureka.

Christmas Boat Parade (☎ 949-729-4400) A parade of 150 or so brightly illuminated boats floating in Newport Beach harbor.

First Night Santa Cruz This is a New Year's Eve street festival with dance, theater and music but no alcohol. Santa Rosa, Stockton and Monterey also have First Night celebrations.

WORK

If you're not a US citizen or legal resident (with a Green Card), there's a lot of red tape involved in getting work in the US, and rather severe penalties (a heavy fine for your employer, deportation for yourself) if you're caught working illegally. For foreigners to work legally, they need to apply for a work visa with the American embassy before leaving their home country.

The type of visa varies depending on how long you're staying and the kind of work you plan to do. A J1 visa, for exchange students, is issued to young people (age limits vary) for student vacation employment, work in summer camps and short-term traineeships with a specific employer. Organizations to contact for help with obtaining such a visa include the **American Institute for Foreign Study** (AIFS; W www.aifs.com) and the **Council on International Education and Exchange** (CIEE; W www.ciee.org).

For nonstudent jobs, either temporary or permanent, you need to be sponsored by a US employer who will have to arrange one of the various H-category visas. These are not easy to obtain, since the employer has to prove that no US citizen or permanent resident is available to do the job. Seasonal work is possible in national parks and other tourist sites, especially ski areas.

ACCOMMODATIONS

California's accommodations cover the full spectrum from primitive campsites to luxurious resorts. Rates are generally higher in summer and around such major holidays as Memorial Day, Independence Day, Labor Day, Thanksgiving and Christmas. Ski resorts charge premium rates in winter.

Prices listed in this book are the official ones supplied by the hotel or motel. They do not – in fact cannot – take into account special promotional rates that may become available at any given time. Some hotels give better rates if you book over the Internet. In general, make it a habit to ask about discounts when booking a room.

Also look out for freebie ad rags packed with hotel and other discount coupons often available at gas stations and tourist offices. Flashing the membership card of the American Automobile Association (AAA) or a foreign affiliate or the American Association of Retired People (AARP) often gets you 10% or more off published rates. You might also cash in on discounts for university students, military personnel and travel-industry workers.

Where available, we have listed a property's toll-free information and reservation number in this book. If you're having trouble finding accommodations, consider using a hotel reservation service such as **Hotel Reservations Network** (☎ 800-964-6835; W www.hoteldiscount.com) or **Central Reservation Service** (☎ 800-873-4683; W www.reservation-services.com). The service itself is free but its rates may not be the best ones.

Budget hotels and motels may not accept reservations, but at least phone from the road to see what's available. Chain hotels will take reservations days or months ahead with a credit-card guarantee. If you don't show up and don't call to cancel, you'll usually be charged the first night's rental. Cancellation policies vary.

Camping

Campgrounds abound in California, but many – especially in the mountains and in Northern California – are not open year-round. Actual opening and closing dates vary slightly each year, depending on the weather and road conditions. Camping in the desert in summer may be uncomfortably hot.

There are campgrounds on public land, including in state and national parks, national forests and BLM lands, as well as on private land. Facilities vary widely. Backcountry campgrounds are likely to be undeveloped or primitive and have little more than pit toilets and fire rings but no potable water. Basic campsites usually have toilets, fire pits, picnic benches and drinking water and are most common in national forests and on BLM land. The state and national park campgrounds tend to be the best equipped, featuring flush toilets, sometimes hot showers and RV (recreational vehicle) hookups.

Private campgrounds are usually close to a town or recreational area and cater more to the RV crowd with small areas set aside for tenters. Hot showers and flush toilets are commonplace and many also have a convenience store, laundry facilities, and sometimes a pool or playground. Kampgrounds of America (KOA) is a network of private campgrounds offering sites from $22 for tents to around $30 with hookups. Get the free annual directory from **KOA** (☎ 406-248-7444, 800-548-7239; W www.koa.com).

Many campgrounds on public land accept advance reservations for all or some of their sites. Reservations are handled by different organizations, all of which maintain searchable websites with maps and detailed descriptions of each campground, driving directions, availability and more. These include:

National Forests – Reserve USA (☎ 877-444-6777, 518-885-3639 from outside the US, W www.reserveusa.com); up to 240 days in advance; $9 per reservation

California State Parks – Reserve America (☎ 800-444-7275, W www.reserveamerica.com); up to 240 days in advance; $9.50 per reservation

National Parks – National Park Reservation Service (NPRS; ☎ 800-365-2267, 301-722-1257 from outside the US or Canada, W reservations.nps .gov); up to five months in advance beginning the 15th of each month; free. For Yosemite National Park call ☎ 800-436-7275.

Free dispersed camping is possible in national forests and on BLM land in any area where you can safely park your vehicle next to a road without blocking traffic. You are not allowed to park off undesignated roads (ie, roads that are not shown on maps and that do not have signs that show the road number). Dispersed camping is not permitted in national parks, except for backpackers holding the appropriate permit. Check with the ranger station if you're unsure about where you can legally camp. Rangers also issue fire permits (usually free). You won't have any facilities like toilets, running water, a fire pit or a picnic table and need to pack out whatever you pack in. Read the section 'Low-Impact Hiking & Backpacking' in the Activities chapter for details.

Backcountry camping is different only in that it implies that you've hiked to your camping area. Depending on who has jurisdiction over the area (National Forest, BLM, National Parks etc), you can either pitch a tent anywhere you like, or must do so in designated areas (usually the case in national parks).

Hostels

HI-AYH Currently 23 hostels in California are affiliated with **Hostelling International-American Youth Hostels** (HI-AYH; W www .hiayh.org). All are covered in detail in their respective geographic chapters throughout this book.

Dorm beds range from $8 to $24 ($3 more for nonmembers). Some hostels also have private rooms, which cost from $25 to $40 for two up to $75 for a family. Dormitories are gender-segregated and alcohol and smoking are prohibited. Facilities vary but generally include an equipped, communal kitchen, a laundry room and a common room with TV, games, magazines and books. Most hostels close during the day; some require guests to do small chores.

Reservations are advised during peak season and are available for dorm beds only with a two-night minimum stay. Most hostels take reservations by phone, fax and email with a credit card. At 17 of the 23 hostels, you can make reservations via the central toll-free ☎ 800-909-4776. If you're using snail mail, you'll need to include a check, US bank draft or money order as well as a self-addressed and stamped envelope. Cancellations or changes must be made at least 24 hours before your arrival to avoid having one night's stay charged to your credit card.

Places in San Francisco and the San Francisco Bay Area with HI-AYH hostels are San Francisco (with three), Sausalito, Los Altos Hills, Montara, Pescadero, Point Reyes National Seashore, Santa Cruz and San Jose. Los Angeles has two hostels, and there is one in Fullerton (near Disneyland) and two in San Diego. Other places in California with HI-AYH hostels include Klamath (Redwood National Park), Sacramento, Merced, Independence (Eastern Sierra), Midpines (near Yosemite), Death Valley/Tecopa, Monterey and San Luis Obispo.

Independent Hostels There are also a growing number of independent hostels with similar prices and facilities to the HI-AYH hostels. Major differences are mixed dorms (although sometimes women-only rooms are available), no curfew and more relaxed alcohol and smoking rules. Often these hostels are convivial places with regular guest parties and other events. Some include a light breakfast or other meals in their rates, arrange local tours and pick up guests at transportation hubs.

Some hostels say they accept only international travelers, basically to keep out destitute locals. In fact, Americans who look like they will fit in with the other guests are usually admitted as well. A passport, HI-AYH card or international plane ticket should help establish your traveler credentials satisfactorily.

B&Bs

These are for people who want a comfortable, atmospheric alternative to impersonal motel rooms. They tend to be for the well-heeled rather than the slim-wallet crowd and are typically in restored old houses with floral wallpaper, antique furnishings and a cute, cozy ambience. Rates include a generous breakfast but rooms with your own TV and phone are the exception rather than the rule. Some rooms may share facilities. Many, if not most, B&Bs require advance reservations, though some owners will be happy to oblige the occasional drop-in. Smoking is almost always prohibited. It's hard to find a B&B under $100 and most charge considerably more.

Many of these places belong to the **California Association of Bed & Breakfast Inns** (**w** *www.cabbi.com*).

Motels & Hotels

Hotels differ from motels in that they do not surround a parking lot and usually have some sort of a lobby. Hotels may offer extra services such as laundry, but these can be very expensive. Many motels and hotels are affiliated with well-publicized national chains, and clusters of these establishments huddle together around freeway exits.

Rooms are often priced by the number and size of beds in a room, rather than the number of occupants. A room with one double or queen-size bed usually costs the same for one or two people, while a room with a king-size bed or two beds costs more. Rooms with two double or queen-size beds sleep up to four people, although there is usually a small surcharge for the third and fourth person. Many places advertise that 'kids stay free,' but sometimes you will have to pay extra for a crib or a 'rollaway' (portable bed).

Room location may also affect the price; recently renovated or larger rooms, or those with a view, are likely to cost a bit more. Hotels facing a noisy street may charge more for quieter rooms.

As a rule, motels offer the best lodging value for money. Although rooms won't win style awards, they're usually comfortably furnished and clean. Amenities vary, of course, but telephone, TV, private bathroom, heating and air-conditioning are fairly standard. Better places also have a small refrigerator, coffeemaker and/or microwave. Many even have a swimming pool and spa, a coin laundry and phones with free local calls.

Reservations at chain hotels or motels can be made by calling a central toll-free number (see the boxed text), although it may be better to call an individual property directly to find out about specific amenities and possible local promotions. You'll find direct numbers listed throughout this book.

Resorts & Lodges

Luxury resorts offer so many amenities that they're often destinations in themselves. Ski resorts usually have a central reservations

Hotel & Motel Chains

National hotel chains are heavily represented throughout California.

Budget

Days Inn	☎ 800-325-2525
Econo Lodge	☎ 800-446-6900
Motel 6	☎ 800-466-8356
Super 8 Motel	☎ 800-800-8000
Vagabond Inns	☎ 800-522-1555

Mid-Range

Best Western	☎ 800-528-1234
Comfort Inns	☎ 800-228-5150
Howard Johnson	☎ 800-654-2000
Quality Inn	☎ 800-228-5151
Ramada Inns	☎ 800-272-6232
Travelodge	☎ 800-255-3050

Top End

Doubletree	☎ 800-222-8733
Hilton	☎ 800-445-8667
Holiday Inns	☎ 800-465-4329
Hyatt	☎ 800-228-9000
Marriott	☎ 800-228-9290
Radisson	☎ 800-333-3333
Sheraton	☎ 800-325-3535

hotline to fill their full range of accommodations, from motel rooms to condos. They might charge $250 or more in midwinter and drop prices to less than half that in summer.

Lodges in attractive scenic areas typically affect a rustic style (with lots of logs and stonework) but are usually very comfortable inside. Restaurants are on the premises, and tour services are often available. In national parks, the only accommodations other than camping are in park lodges. They are usually operated as a concession and are fairly comfortable if usually overpriced for what they offer. In summer, they tend to be fully booked months in advance.

Houseboating

In some parts of California, mostly in the north, an alternative to land-based accommodations is a stay on fully equipped, fully operational houseboats that tour lakes and rivers. You'll have all the necessities, including hot water, linens and cooking facilities.

Renting a boat for a weekend or a week is typically cost-effective for groups of four or more. Most houseboats sleep 10, though eight people would be more comfortable. Peak season is June to September, with rates plunging during low and shoulder seasons. Most companies have a minimum rental of three days/two nights. Week-long rentals are a significantly better deal, and discounts of around 20% for accompanying smaller boats are frequent.

For a 10-person houseboat, low-season/high-season rates average $1000/2000 for three weekend or four midweek nights and $1700/3000 for a weekly rental. The only way to get the best deal is to be thorough when inquiring about amenities (ice chests/refrigerators, air-conditioning, stereo, TV, water slide), exactly how many nights are counted in a 'weekend' and a 'week' (it varies) and what discounts or packages are offered.

For houseboat rentals, go online to W www.houseboats.com or contact the following outfits:

Bidwell Canyon Marina (☎ 530-589-3165; W www.funtime-fulltime.com) rents boats on Lake Oroville in the Sacramento Valley.

Forever Resorts Houseboat Rentals (☎ 800-255-5561; W www.foreverresorts.com) operates on Trinity Lake near Weaverville in Northern California, on Lake Pedro near Sonora in the Southern Gold Country and on the Sacramento River Delta.

Seven Crown Resorts (☎ 800-752-9669; W www.sevencrown.com) rents on Lake Shasta and in the California Delta near Stockton.

FOOD

California's dining scene is as diverse as the state's population. It is possible to eat Mexican *huevos rancheros* for breakfast, a Thai curry for lunch and fish and chips for dinner – without venturing out of one neighborhood. Of course this is primarily true in big cities, but even small towns are likely to have a variety of eating establishments. Standard American fare is served at diners, coffee shops and fast-food chains. Pizza is ubiquitous.

You can save a lot by putting together your own meals. Supermarkets, many of them open 24 hours, have the lowest prices and a wide selection of groceries; some also have salad bars, delis and bakeries. Health food stores and natural foods markets have organic produce, bulk food and a deli section, but prices are higher than at supermarkets. You'll also find '99 cents' stores, where everything costs just that, though their food items are usually limited to nonperishables such as canned goods and candy. Trader Joes is a popular food market offering gourmet fare at discount prices, but it's not as common as the regular supermarkets.

Breakfast

Big breakfasts are an affordable way to fill yourself up, provided you can stomach large quantities of food before noon. A breakfast of pancakes, eggs and sausage or a hearty omelet costs around $5 to $8. Breakfast often includes home fries (diced potatoes fried with onions, bell peppers or spices) or hash browns (shredded or sliced potatoes fried until golden brown), toast and 'bottomless cups' (unlimited refills) of coffee. You get a choice of how your eggs are cooked – scrambled, sunny-side up, over easy (flipped, but with a runny yolk), or over hard (flipped with a hard yolk). Typically, the low-price breakfast special is available from about 6am to 11am.

Lunch

Usually served from 11:30am to 2pm, lunch is another inexpensive meal. Prices may be more than one third less expensive than the dinner menu, though the food and portions are identical. For a bustling, energetic lunch scene, head to the business district of any city – like San Francisco's Financial District – where the number of suit-clad businesspeople is an indication of the best or cheapest places to eat. Many ethnic eateries, such as Indian, Thai, Chinese usually have set three-course lunches for around $7.

Dinner

In large cities, many restaurants offer 'early-bird specials,' which feature a complete meal (usually the menu is limited) for around $7, between 4pm to 6pm. Spending a few dollars on drinks during 'happy hour' (usually between 4pm to 7pm) will often get you free appetizers, which can be anything from a bowl of peanuts to a full hot buffet. Sports bars and bars in large hotel chains have the best deals. People tend to eat early, and many restaurants are closed or deserted by 10pm.

Cuisines

Eating healthy is very much part of the California lifestyle, which gave birth to 'California cuisine' in the mid-1980s. Pioneers like Berkeley-based Alice Waters and Wolfgang Puck in Los Angeles created gourmet concoctions revolving around fresh seasonal ingredients, unusual flavor fusions and artistic presentation.

An offshoot of California cuisine is California Asian (Cal-Asian) – sometimes also called 'Pacific Rim' – food. Its focus is on the pairing of local ingredients with Chinese or Japanese seasonings and cooking methods. Meats and fish are flavored with adventurous combinations of turmeric, cilantro (fresh coriander), ginger, garlic, chili paste and fresh fruit juices (usually citrus), and served with Asian staples like rice, sweet potatoes or buckwheat *udon* noodles.

Also available is California French (Cal-French) food, basically a slimmed down version of Gallic fare, banishing much of the butter and cream and instead relying on the flavors produced by top quality vegetables and other ingredients.

Mexican food is a staple of many a Californian's diet, and until you've eaten *carnitas* (pork) or fish tacos washed down by a Pacifico, you have not experienced California culture. The fast-food chain Taco Bell serves Americanized Mexican food – good for the faint of stomach. Traditional Mexican food is very rich and makes liberal use of lard and cheese, though places specializing in healthier versions have cropped up in recent years, among them Baja Fresh, a popular chain. *Taquerias* are, strictly speaking, little places serving tacos, but they are cheap, good and usually have other dishes as well.

A fairly recent trend is the upscale version of Latin food, commonly referred to as Nuevo Latino cuisine. Long popular on the East Coast, it combines the food culture from numerous Latin American countries, Panama to Patagonia. Dishes are veritable flavor bombs blending exotic produce like jicama, plaintains, yucca root and mango with chilies, epazote and other spices in bold combinations.

Fish and shellfish figure big on Californian menus, especially along the coast. What's served often depends on the day's catch, which has the obvious advantage of complete freshness. In Northern California, Dungeness crab is in season from November to March. South of San Francisco, seafood often takes on a Mexican flair and may be served as fish tacos or Vera Cruz style (cooked with tomatoes, peppers and onions and served over rice).

California being the quintessential ethnic cauldron, you also find food from many countries here, Thai, Chinese, Indian and Italian being the most prevalent.

Fast Food

Predictable, unexciting and certainly not healthy, fast-food chains are cheap, reliable standbys any time of day. For hamburgers, the main choices are McDonald's, Burger King and Carl's Jr. Unique to California is the venerable In-N-Out Burger, which has a no-nonsense menu and a die-hard clientele. Taco Bell and Del Taco serve Mexican fast food. Domino's Pizza and Pizza Hut are dominant pizza delivery companies.

Dining Etiquette

Dining out in California tends toward the casual, although you should still dress appropriately. That definitely means shoes and shirt; a jacket is appropriate for men at some upscale restaurants. If in doubt, call ahead and ask about the dress code. If you're heading for a popular eatery – especially on Friday or Saturday nights – make a reservation. It's customary to wait by the entrance until the host or hostess seats you; only in very casual places and self-service restaurants may you pick a table yourself.

Most restaurants figure on several seatings per night, so the expectation is that you'll leave soon after you've finished your meal. In most cases, your server will bring you the bill automatically; in some top restaurants it may be presented only after you've requested it (though to hustle you along, someone might come by your table every two minutes asking if you'd like to order anything else). Smoking inside restaurants and bars is prohibited by state law and local bylaws increasingly enforce this rule in outdoor patios as well.

DRINKS

Nonalcoholic Drinks

Restaurants provide customers with free ice water; it's tap water and safe to drink. All the usual soft drinks are available, although you may be asked to accept Coke instead of Pepsi and vice versa. Lemonade is a lemon-sugar-ice-water mix: if you want the clear, fizzy stuff that the British call lemonade, ask for Sprite or 7-Up.

Many restaurants offer milk, including low-fat varieties. You can often get fresh-squeezed orange juice at better restaurants, but packaged juices are more common.

Coffee is served much more often than tea, usually with a choice of regular or 'decaf.' Tea is less commonly offered and often served as a cup of hot water with a tea bag next to it. Milk is almost never added, but a slice of lemon often is. Iced tea is available in cans as well.

Alcoholic Drinks

If you're under 21 (ie, a minor), you may not consume alcohol in California. Carry a driver's license or passport as proof of age to enter a bar, to order alcohol at a restaurant or buy alcohol at a supermarket. Servers have the right to ask to see your ID and may refuse service without it. Minors are not allowed in bars and pubs, even to order nonalcoholic beverages, although they're OK in restaurants where alcohol may be served.

The big name brands of domestic beer are available everywhere, though many find them lacking in taste. Check the supermarket or liquor store shelves for imported beers. Many California restaurants are only licensed to serve wine and beer and not 'hard liquor' like cognac and whiskey. Microbreweries, or brewpubs, offer beers brewed on the premises, and you can get up to a dozen types on tap.

Beer sold in the US has a lower alcohol content than that in most other countries, which may be why many visitors find it bland. Imported beers must conform to the same restriction on alcohol content and are often specially made for export to the US. If you're particularly fond of Foster's, Heineken or Moosehead at home, you *will* be disappointed to find that it's been wimped down for the American market. For example, the Foster's Lager sold in the US is actually made in Canada and doesn't taste much like the Foster's sold in Australia at all.

California produces excellent varietal wines and some very affordable generic wines that are great value for the tippler on a tight budget. The first California wine growing dates from the Spanish mission period, when grapes were grown to make sacramental wines. The industry is now very sophisticated, and its best wines are respected the world over. The most prestigious wines hail from the Wine Country north of San Francisco, although there are also up-and-coming wineries throughout the Central Coast, such as those in Santa Barbara, San Luis Obispo and Monterey.

California white wines include sauvignon blanc, fumé blanc, Riesling, gewürztraminer, chenin blanc, zinfandel and – the most popular – chardonnay. The most common reds are merlot, cabernet sauvignon and pinot noir. Zinfandel is a varietal unique to California and is available as a red, blush and white.

All bars have a wide range of 'hard liquor': gin, brandy, rum, vodka and whiskey, invariably served with lots of ice (on the rocks) unless you ask for it 'straight up.' If you ask for whiskey, you'll get American whiskey. If you want Scotch whiskey, ask for Scotch. Tequila, from Mexico, is popular on its own or in such cocktails as margaritas or a tequila sunrise.

ENTERTAINMENT
Cinemas

Nearly every town – and just about every shopping mall – in California has a movie theater, usually in the form of a multiplex with anywhere from three to 20 screens. A few small, independent theaters showing alternative, classic and foreign films survive in some cities. Historic movie palaces abound in Los Angeles but can also be found in other cities.

The average movie ticket now costs $9 or $9.50, although smaller theaters and those in rural areas sometimes charge as little as $7. Shows before 6pm are often discounted, but popcorn, candy and soda concessions are outrageously priced and can easily double the cost of your ticket. For movie listings, check the entertainment sections of local papers or the what's-on freebies published in many towns.

Clubs

Nightclubs have long been popular in California. In the 1950s, many dance styles originated on Hollywood stages, at beach parties, and in Los Angeles nightclubs.

Hollywood and San Francisco have the greatest concentration of dance clubs, with a few good spots in San Diego and Fresno's Tower District. The club scene ranges from polished spots like the House of Blues to grunt-sweat-don't-care-what-you-look-like places such as the Garage in Hollywood and the Stork Club in Oakland. A cover charge

(what you must pay to enter) can range from free to $20, with higher prices on weekends. Some places have free entrance but a two drink minimum, or charge half price before 9pm (most clubs don't start to 'happen' until after 10pm). Each club has its own musical style, but hip-hop, house and techno are still popular. Dancing alone or in groups is quite acceptable.

Concerts

Big-name performers from Madonna to Tom Jones usually make the same California route: the San Diego Sports Arena; the Staples Center in Los Angeles; Shoreline Theater in the Bay Area or Oakland's Coliseum; and Cal Expo in Sacramento. Cities also have many smaller venues where you can hear anything from Ukrainian folk music to punk rock every night of the week. San Francisco also has some good medium-size venues like the Fillmore, the Warfield and the Great American Music Hall. Oakland has great jazz and blues.

Theater

Los Angeles is California's undisputed theater capital, launching many plays and musicals that go on to gain international acclaim. A big reason for this is the abundance of talent hanging around Hollywood, waiting for a big break. Actors and actresses who have already 'made it' also like to perform live theater. The Mark Taper Forum is well-known for its quality productions, but lots of the smaller theaters, many of which line Santa Monica Blvd in West Hollywood, also present good work. Mainstream musicals are generally performed at the Shubert Theater, Ahmanson Theatre or Pantages Theater.

San Diego, partly because it's close enough to LA to be accessible to the Hollywood pool of actors, directors and designers, has an excellent reputation for theater. Top venues around town include the Repertory Theater, La Jolla Playhouse and Old Globe Theater.

While San Francisco doesn't share the same talent pool as Southern California, its theater productions are conceptually strong. The many small theater fringe and avant-garde adaptations are often excellent, though not always for the faint-hearted. The nearby Berkeley Repertory Theatre has a national reputation for its productions and has won numerous awards.

Many theaters offer 'rush' or 'student rush' tickets, available for reduced prices a few hours before the performance. Half-price tickets for the day of the performance are available in all three cities (see the respective chapters).

Classical Music & Opera

San Francisco and Los Angeles both have outstanding symphonies. LA Philharmonic director Esa Peka Salonen is considered one of the finest conductors in the world and enjoys strong public support. Performances take place at the Dorothy Chandler Pavilion during the season and at the Hollywood Bowl in summer (the orchestra will begin its residency at the new Walt Disney Hall in late 2003). San Francisco performances are at Davies Symphony Hall, where even bad seats are pretty good. The Berkeley Symphony, conducted by Kent Nagano – who is also a principal conductor at the LA Opera – is excellent. The San Diego and San Jose symphonies are very good, but in a totally different class.

The LA Opera, which has only been in existence since 1985, came under the stewardship of Placido Domingo as artistic director in 2000. San Francisco Opera's performances range from mediocre to quite good. Unless you spend at least $75 on a ticket (or have good luck getting a last-minute rush seat), you're basically guaranteed a bad seat. The San Diego Opera has a season from January to May, in the Civic Theater, and reasonably good seats are affordable.

SPECTATOR SPORTS

Including preseason, the National Football League (NFL) season runs from August to mid-January, Major League Baseball (MLB) from March to October, National Basketball Association (NBA) from November to April, Women's National Basketball Association (WNBA) from June to August, National Hockey League (NHL) ice hockey from October to April and Major League Soccer (MLS) from March to November.

If you're into sports, California is the perfect place in the US to visit as it has more professional teams than any other state: three NFL teams (the San Diego Chargers, the San Francisco 49ers and the Oakland Raiders); five MLB teams (the LA Dodgers, the Disney-owned Anaheim Angels, San Diego Padres, San Francisco Giants and Oakland A's); four NBA teams (the Sacramento Kings, LA Lakers, LA Clippers and Golden State Warriors, in Oakland); two WNBA teams (the LA Sparks and the Sacramento Monarchs); three NHL teams (the LA Kings, Mighty Ducks, in Anaheim, and San Jose Sharks) and two MLS teams (the San Jose Clash and LA Galaxy). Games can be sold out – especially 49ers, Lakers and Kings games – so buy tickets early.

Beach volleyball is becoming more popular each year. Beach towns in Los Angeles host several professional tournaments each summer, with the Hermosa Open and Manhattan Open being the most important.

Motor sports are a huge obsession, especially in Bakersfield, which has multiple race tracks. The Mazda Raceway Laguna Seca, between Monterey and Salinas, is also popular. Long Beach hosts the Toyota Grand Prix, a Formula 1 race, every April.

SHOPPING

The sheer variety and quantity of consumer goods – in the US, generally, and in California, particularly – is staggering to many visitors. Most of the shopping is done in giant malls these days, which house more or less the same array of chain stores. Most feature clothing stores like the Gap, Banana Republic and Ann Taylor; cosmetics and toiletries at The Body Shop; unusual and trendy gadgets at Brookstone or Sharper Image; and, of course, big department stores such as Macy's, Robinsons-May, Nordstrom and Bloomingdale's.

In rural areas, you're more likely to find sprawling shopping districts filled with vast outlets of the big national retailers, including K-Mart, Target, Home Depot etc. Aside from the malls, the big cities – San Francisco and Los Angeles in particular – have neighborhood shopping streets lined with unique boutiques, art galleries and specialty stores.

If it's antiques you're after, you'll come across plenty of antique malls and flea markets. The larger cities usually have several such markets, which operate on a particular weekend every month. Antique malls offer great browsing, especially for Americana, but bargains are hard to find. The best place to buy movie memorabilia is – no surprise here – Los Angeles.

Outlet malls, where famous and mainstream stores sell off their stock at reduced prices, are still all the rage. While bargains here are possible, it's worth noting that items are often damaged, irregular, left over from the previous season or rejected from regular department stores. That lime-green shirt that was so fashionable last year may get you ticketed by the fashion police this summer. Service in these stores is minimal with small sales staff and fewer dressing rooms and mirrors.

California is a major agricultural producer and as you're driving through the growing areas you'll often see roadside stands selling the local product. These abound especially in Monterey County around Salinas, in the San Joaquin Valley (along I-5, I-80 or small side roads), around Palm Springs and in parts of San Diego County. The Napa and Sonoma valleys produce superb wines, as do growing areas around Santa Barbara, Paso Robles and Monterey. You can enjoy tastings and buy wine directly from the wine estate although, ironically, prices tend to be lower in wine and liquor stores and supermarkets.

California's diverse communities also offer some interesting things to buy. The Chinatowns in San Francisco and LA have Chinese bookstores and apothecaries that carry ginger and ginseng products said to promote long life and vitality. You can also find exotic teas and garments. Los Angeles' Olvera St and Old Town in San Diego have traditional Mexican crafts such as leather, shoes and belts, candles and embroidered fabrics. For an array of imported goods – from Guatemalan jackets to Indian temple incense – head to Berkeley's Telegraph Ave or to Venice Beach in LA.

Second-Hand Shopping

Bargain hunters will have plenty of opportunity to separate treasure from trash. For some of the best prices, browse the thrift shops. These are usually operated by charities, such as Goodwill, Junior League or the Salvation Army, and sell donated used clothing, household items, books, furniture and other items, often at ridiculously low prices. Most of the proceeds benefit the charity.

For those traveling on a tight budget, thrift stores can be a godsend. For a fraction of what you'd pay in department stores, you can replace that only pair of shorts you ruined with red wine or look stylish in a thrift shop dress or blazer when showing up at that sudden dinner party.

A spin-off of the thrift shop is the vintage clothing store where you can stock up on used clothing from earlier periods. If you want a flared '50s skirt or '40s zoot suit, this is where you'd look. Bargains are less common in these stores.

As you're driving through neighborhoods on Friday and Saturday, you'll probably notice signs attached to traffic signals and telephone poles announcing a 'Moving Sale', 'Estate Sale', 'Multi-Family Sale', 'Garage Sale' and so on. For those holding the sale, it's a way to clean out the closets and make a buck on the side. For treasure hunters, garage sales can yield everything from vintage earrings to furniture at rock-bottom prices. Haggling, of course, is just part of the fun.

Activities

California is the only place in the USA where you can surf in the morning and ski in the afternoon, or go from the lowest to the highest point in the lower 48 states in one weekend. This chapter explores some of the many options, ranging from near universals like hiking and backpacking to more esoteric activities like surfing and hot-air ballooning. Though each pursuit has specialized gear shops (usually the best source for local information), Recreational Equipment Incorporated (REI) coop stores are excellent for all-around outdoor needs. The knowledgeable staff sells everything from karabiners to wool socks to stoves and kayak paddles, and rents out tents, skis, stoves, bikes and kayaks. REI stores can be found in Los Angeles, Berkeley and elsewhere. Call ☎ 800-426-4840 to find the branch nearest to you.

HIKING & BACKPACKING

There is perhaps no better way to appreciate the beauty of California – its secluded beaches, rugged coast, lofty glacial peaks and peaceful dense forests – than on foot along the trail. Even if you take just a few days (or

even hours) for a break from the highway to explore the great outdoors, you'll feel refreshed and develop a heightened appreciation of the scenery that goes whizzing past day after day. Some travelers experience one good hike and decide to plan the rest of their trip around wilderness or hiking areas.

With California's diverse landscapes, it's possible to explore coastal, desert, mountain and foothill scenery in a fairly pristine state. About half of California's land is public and managed and – to varying degrees – protected by the National Park Service (NPS), the United States Forest Service (USFS) and the Bureau of Land Management (BLM).

While all these are federal agencies, the state park system is administered by the California Department of Parks and Recreation. California has about 270 state parks with more than 2000mi of trails. Parks near urban centers often function as year-round recreational getaways for locals and tend to get crowded on weekends. Mt Tamalpais in San Francisco and Will Rogers in Los Angeles fall into this category.

All national and state parks have easy, well-marked short trails, many under 2mi.

Pacific Crest Trail

A truly amazing thing about the West Coast of the USA is that you can walk from Mexico to Canada, across the entire expanse of California, Oregon and Washington, almost without leaving national park or national forest lands. Simply follow the Pacific Crest Trail (PCT).

This 2638mi trail passes through 24 national forests, seven national parks, 33 designated wilderness areas, and five state parks, following the crest of the Sierra Nevada in California and the Cascade Range in Oregon and Washington, at an average elevation of 5000ft.

To hike the trail in its entirety, at a good clip of 15mi a day, would take nearly six months, the California portion about four months. But you don't have to undertake such a dramatic, cross-state trek to take advantage of the PCT. Day or weekend hikers can plan short trips on many accessible segments of the trail.

Some of California's most spectacular wilderness areas are traversed by the PCT, from the Anza-Borrego Desert State Park in the very south, through Kings Canyon and Sequoia National Parks, Yosemite National Park, Lake Tahoe and Lassen Volcanic Park.

Another long-distance trail, the 212mi **John Muir Trail**, which links Yosemite Valley and Mt Whitney, parallels the PCT for long stretches, veering from it only in the Devils Postpile area and at the Mt Whitney summit.

The **Pacific Crest Trail Association** (☎ 916-349-2109; ⓦ www.pcta.org) headquartered in Sacramento, can provide detailed information on the trail, as well as addresses for regional USFS and wilderness area offices, tips on long and short backpacking trips, weather conditions and which areas require wilderness permits.

They're primarily aimed at people with little hiking experience, low fitness levels or limited time. Many have interpretive displays and are marked on maps as nature trails or self-guided interpretive trails. These trails are the forest equivalent of freeways: fast, easy to navigate and efficient, but not terribly thrilling. Wilderness areas and forests rarely have these types of trails. Most designated wilderness areas are on USFS land; the BLM wilderness areas can be among the best for sheer solitude.

For longer day-hikes, trails are almost always well marked, so you won't need a topographic map or compass as long as you stick to the main routes. Ask at a ranger station or visitor center for suggestions about trails to suit your interest and ability. For any walk longer than one hour, take water, snack food and, if inclement weather is on the horizon, a sweater and raincoat.

Overnight hiking, or backpacking, may not guarantee solitude but it should enable you to get away from the masses, except on weekends and holidays in the most popular parks. Hikers seeking true wilderness may find a more rewarding experience in lesser known national forests and wilderness areas rather than the national parks. Yosemite National Park has a route of High Sierra Camps for people who enjoy backpacking without carrying a heavy load.

Hiking aficionados should look into Lonely Planet's *Hiking in the Sierra Nevada*, which contains detailed descriptions of several dozen hikes in California's largest and most spectacular mountain range.

Wilderness Permits

Most national parks and some forests and wilderness areas require overnight hikers (and occasionally day-hikers) to carry backcountry permits, also called wilderness permits, available from visitor centers or ranger stations. Some trails – including the Main Mt Whitney Trail and trails in the Inyo National Forest and Desolation Wilderness near Lake Tahoe – are subject to a quota system limiting the number of hikers and/or backpackers who start out daily from each trailhead. This system prevents overcrowding and reduces the impact on wilderness areas. Quota periods are only in effect during peak periods, usually from late spring to early fall.

A varying percentage of the available permits may be allocated by advance reservations, with the remaining permits issued on a first-come, first-served basis. Permits are usually free, though reservations are not and camping fees are also extra. Some less impacted trails have self-issuing permits available at the trailhead or outside range stations.

Details about how to obtain wilderness permits are provided throughout this book.

Fees

Most state parks levy a small fee ranging from $2 to $7 per vehicle per entry. Wilderness areas and most national forests are free (for exceptions, see the boxed text 'National Forest Adventure Pass' on the facing page). The entrance fee to national parks varies from $4 to $20 per vehicle and is good for unlimited entries for seven days. If you're going to visit many national parks, in California or elsewhere, consider getting a National Parks Pass. For details, see the boxed text 'National Parks Passes' in the Facts for the Visitor chapter.

Low-Impact Hiking & Backpacking

The popularity of hiking and backpacking is placing great pressure on the environment. Ask yourself what you can do to lessen the negative impact your hike might have. Perhaps the most important single action you can take is to keep the size of your hiking party small. Smaller groups are quieter and do less damage. Avoid overvisited hiking areas and travel during the off-peak season when possible.

Garbage Carry out all your trash, including those easily forgotten items, such as foil, orange peel, cigarette butts and plastic wrappers. Empty packaging weighs very little anyway and should be stored in a dedicated trash bag.

Never bury your trash: digging disturbs soil and ground cover and encourages erosion. Buried trash will probably be dug up by animals, who may be injured or poisoned by it. It may also take years to decompose, especially at high altitudes.

Minimize the waste you must carry out by taking minimal packaging and taking no more food than you will need. If you

National Forest Adventure Pass

Day-use fees at state and national parks have been commonplace in California and Nevada for several years now. In 1996, however, Congress authorized a controversial pilot project requiring anyone visiting certain national forests by car to purchase a National Forest Adventure Pass (NFAP). The list includes four forests in Southern California: San Bernardino, Cleveland, Angeles and Los Padres. Passes cost $5 per day or $30 per year (seniors and disabled $15) and must be displayed on the windshield. If you buy a Golden Eagle Passport (see the boxed text 'National Parks Passes' in the Facts for the Visitor chapter) at a forest service office, the Adventure Pass is included.

Adventures Passes are good for one year from the month of purchase and are transferable. Any USFS ranger station in Southern California sells them or you can order one over the telephone (☎ 909-884-6634 ext 3127) using a credit card, or by writing a check to San Bernardino National Forest, Fee Project Headquarters, 1824 S Commercenter Circle, San Bernardino, CA 92408. Checks (US banks only) must be made out to USDA Forest Service.

About 80% of the revenue is supposed to flow right back into the budgets of these national forests toward such improvements as more and cleaner restrooms, graffiti and trash removal and trail repair.

Passes are not needed if you're just driving through the forest without stopping, if you're stopping at a ranger station or visitor center, or if you are already paying another forest-use fee (eg, camping or cabin fees). There's a penalty of $100 if you're caught without the NFAP.

For more information, or to find a list of vendors, go to W www.fsadventurepass.org.

---

can't buy in bulk, repackage your food into re-usable containers like plastic bags.

Rather than bringing bottled water, use water from a natural source and purify it with iodine or by boiling it vigorously for at least one minute. Don't bring beverages in aluminum cans and glass. Sanitary napkins, tampons and condoms should also be carried out, despite the inconvenience. They burn and decompose poorly. Pick up any trash you find on the trail.

Human Waste Disposal Contamination of water sources by human feces can lead to the transmission of hepatitis, typhoid and intestinal parasites such as giardia, amoebas and roundworms, causing severe health risks not only to members of your party, but also to local residents and wildlife.

Use toilets where available or bury your waste by digging a small hole 6in to 8in (15cm to 20cm) deep and at least 100yd from any water source, campsite or trail. Consider carrying a lightweight trowel for this purpose. Use leaves in lieu of toilet paper (just make sure it's not poison oak!). If using toilet paper, burn it or carry it out to avoid animals digging it up. Cover your waste with soil and a rock. For more on the subject, read *How to Shit in the Woods* by Kathleen Meyer.

Washing Don't use detergents, shampoo or toothpaste, even if they are biodegradable, in or near bodies of water. Use biodegradable soap and a water container (or even a lightweight, portable basin) at least 50yd away from open water sources. Wash cooking utensils 50yd from bodies of water, using a scouring brush, sand or snow instead of detergent.

Erosion Hillsides and mountain slopes, especially at high altitudes, are prone to erosion. Stick to existing trails and avoid shortcuts that bypass switchbacks. If you blaze a new trail straight down a slope, it will turn into a watercourse with the next heavy rainfall and eventually cause soil loss and deep scarring.

If a well-used track passes through a mud patch, walk through the mud; walking around the edge will increase the size of the patch. Avoid removing the plant life that keeps topsoil in place.

Fires & Low-Impact Cooking Developed campgrounds usually have fire pits but cooking on a gas stove is the environmentally preferred way in the backcountry. If you light a fire, use an existing fireplace rather than creating a new one. Use only dead, fallen wood and only as much as needed for cooking.

Ensure that you fully extinguish a fire after use. Spread the embers and douse them with water. Then stir them and douse again. A fire is only truly safe to leave when you can comfortably place your hand in it.

Safety

Hiking and backpacking carry inherent risks, especially in mountain areas. To help make your hike a safe one, plan to be self-sufficient. Obtain the best available maps.

Bears, Your Food & You

California's forests are home to an estimated 16,000 to 24,000 black bears, which actually range in color from black to cinnamon and grow about 3½ft tall (standing on all four feet). Stories about bears fraying nerves and causing big damage by breaking into cars (even RVs) or tents in search of food have been big news in recent years. While these incidents always make good headlines, they are a real concern to visitors and administrators of national parks, especially in Yosemite, but also Kings Canyon and Sequoia and forests in the Sierra Nevada and elsewhere.

With humans increasingly encroaching upon the bears' natural habitat, many have ditched their traditional diet of berries, nuts, roots, grasses and other vegetation in favor of all that they consider 'people food'; this includes everything from toothpaste and suntan lotion to cough syrup and yesterday's sandwich leftovers. Bears have an extraordinary ability to recognize food and food containers by sight and smell, and they've developed uncanny proficiency in getting at what they want. Locked cars, zipped tents or garbage cans are easily and quickly accessed with cleverly honed techniques. Mother bears have even been observed passing along these thieving skills to their cubs.

This is bad news for you, but also for the bears. As they get more habituated to human food, bears also become more aggressive in getting at it and eventually may have to be killed. Everyone must take precautions at all times to protect their food and other scented personal belongings, for their own and the bears' sake. Here are a few basic rules:

- When camping, store all food products, toiletries and other smelly things in bear-resistant metal food lockers now in place at all developed campsites in bear country.
- When camping in the backcountry, use bear-resistant food canisters, which may be rented for a few dollars at ranger stations, visitor centers, grocery stores and other places. Canisters weigh 2½lb and fit inside your backpack or may be strapped to its outside. Put all your food and toiletries inside the canister and place it 50ft from your camp. Hanging your food in a tree no longer works, because most bears have figured out how to get at it anyway.
- Even if staying overnight in a cabin or motel in some areas, especially in Yosemite, remove everything that even remotely looks like food from your car. This includes lipstick and empty candy wrappers. Some parking lots near trailheads also have bear boxes; use them.
- While bears usually won't bother you when you're cooking or eating, be sure to clean the camp of food and trash before leaving or going to sleep. Be paranoid about this. If you have sex while camping, clean up very well after yourself, as bears associate the attendant smells with food. Seriously, folks.
- Never, ever feed bears or pick up a cub (yes, people actually do this).
- If you encounter a bear at a campsite or on the trail, yell, clap your hands, throw stones, bang pots and try to look big. The goal is to show the bear that you may be a danger to it. In campgrounds, you may need to do this more than once until Mr Bear gets the message, but the more racket you make the first time, the less likely it is to make a repeat visit.
- If a bear huffs at you and shows its profile, it may be about to bluff-charge you. Stand your ground, or step back very slowly. Again, make yourself look big and make big noise. Don't stare, but keep eye contact. As the bear backs away, you should too.
- Never run from a bear, as this only triggers its instinct to chase, and you cannot outrun a bear.
- Never get between a mother bear and her cubs, which may be up a nearby tree.
- Bears are not known to make unprovoked attacks, but if attacked, fight back using any means available like throwing rocks, hitting it with your gear or a big stick.

Be prepared for changeable weather by carrying adequate clothing and equipment. In some higher elevations, you may go to bed under a clear sky and wake up in 2ft of snow, even in mid-August. Afternoon thunderstorms are very common in the Sierra Nevada. Backpackers should have a pack liner (heavy-duty garbage bags work well), a full set of rain gear and food that does not require cooking.

Choose a hike that is within your range of physical ability and commitment and seek local advice on trails, equipment and weather before heading out. Be aware of your hike's objective dangers and pay attention on the trail. A minor injury, a twisted ankle or a fall down a hillside can be life-threatening if you're alone. Always let someone know where you are going and how long you plan to be gone. Use sign-in boards at trailheads or ranger stations. Increasingly, hikers and campers are finding that a cellular phone is a useful piece of gear.

Promote mountain safety by following a few basic rules: don't hike alone, don't hike too high too fast and don't hike without the required permits.

When footbridges and natural bridges such as fallen logs or a series of rocks are absent, you may have to ford a river or stream swollen with snowmelt. Look for the widest and most shallow place to ford. Before stepping out from the bank, ease one arm out of the shoulder strap of your pack and unclip the belt buckle (your pack is expendable, you are not). Avoid crossing barefoot. River cobbles will suck body heat right out of your feet, numbing them and making it impossible to navigate. Bring a pair of lightweight canvas sneakers to avoid sloshing around in wet boots for the rest of your hike.

If linking hands with others, grasp at the wrist; this gives a tighter grip than a handhold. If you're fording alone, plant a stick or your hiking poles upstream to give you greater stability and help you to lean against the current. Use these supports to feel the way forward and walk side-on to the direction of the flow so that your body presents less of an obstacle to the rushing water. Even if the cold water makes you want to cross as quickly as possible, don't rush things.

If you get wet, wring your clothes out immediately, wipe off all the excess water on your body and hair and put on any dry clothes you might have. Synthetic fabrics and wool retain heat when they get wet, but cotton does not.

Western poison oak can be found in forests throughout California, especially in elevations below 5000ft. It's a shrub most easily identified by its shiny triple-lobed reddish-green leaves, which turn crimson in autumn. Remember the following trail adage: 'Leaves of three, let it be.'

Touching the plant or even inadvertently brushing up against it along the trail can contaminate you and your clothes with a nearly invisible oily resin, which contains a toxic chemical called urushiol. This produces a miserable progressive skin rash that develops into itchy blisters; swelling may also be present. The rash can appear as soon as 30 minutes after exposure and last as long as two weeks. If you're exposed to poison oak, wash the affected area quickly with soap and water. Remove any contaminated pieces of clothing, being careful not to place them in your tent against your sleeping bag or other clothing. An antihistamine may offer symptomatic relief, but otherwise you'll just have to ride it out.

Books

The best California-specific guides are those available from Wilderness Press in Berkeley, CA, which publishes *The John Muir Trail*, *The Pacific Crest Trail*, *Sierra North*, *Lassen Volcanic National Park* and *Yosemite*; and The Mountaineers in Seattle, WA, whose books include *California's Central Sierra & Coast Range*, *Best Day Hikes of the California Northwest* and *The West Coast Trail*.

Also consider *LA Times* columnist John McKinney's excellent series of hiking guides published by Olympic Press. These include *Day Hiker's Guide to Southern California*, *Day Hiker's Guide to California State Parks*, *Walking the California Coast*, *Walking the East Mojave Desert* and *Walking Los Angeles: Adventures on the Urban Edge*.

Maps

A reliable map is essential for any hiking trip. NPS and USFS ranger stations usually stock topographical maps that cost $2 to $9. In the absence of a ranger station, try the local stationery store, gas station or hardware store.

The **US Geological Survey** (*USGS;* ☎ *888-275-8747;* w *www.usgs.gov*), an agency of the Department of the Interior, publishes very detailed topographic maps of the entire country at different scales. The USGS 1:125,000 maps with 200ft contour intervals and 1:100,000 maps with 150ft contour intervals are useful planning and backpacking maps. For a map index and price list, contact USGS on the phone number provided. The website also has the full product catalog and a data base of retailers near you. The USFS also produces good topographical maps of national forests.

BICYCLING & MOUNTAIN BIKING

Whether you're taking the bike out for an hour's spin along the beach or for multi-day bike tours, traveling by bicycle is healthy, fun and good for the environment. California's cities are becoming increasingly bike-friendly, especially the smaller and mid-size places such as Santa Barbara, Santa Cruz, Davis, Berkeley and parts of San Diego. San Francisco also has many ardent cyclists; though its hills and traffic might be daunting, the city's compact size makes the bicycle an ideal form of transportation.

Mountain biking is hugely popular. Marin County (specifically Mt Tamalpais) lays claim to being the birthplace of mountain biking. Just across the Golden Gate Bridge from San Francisco, the Marin Headlands offer a bonanza of beautiful biking trails (although on weekends things can get more frenzied than a three-legged dog on ice skates).

In summer, some ski areas open trails and chairlifts to mountain bikes, including Mt Shasta and Big Bear Lake, east of Los Angeles. California's current MTB mecca, however, is Mammoth Mountain whose mountain bike park has a slalom course and obstacle area, plus miles of steep dirt just begging for fat tires. Some sections of the Tahoe Rim Trail are open to mountain bikers as well, and the challenging Flume Trail on Lake Tahoe's Nevada shore gives even seasoned bikers an adrenaline kick. Other good places include the Montaña de Oro State Park on the Central Coast and Anza-Borrego Desert State Park, east of San Diego. In the Gold Country, the Downieville Downhill is a top-rated mountain bike course.

Bikes are often banned from designated wilderness areas and national park hiking trails (although the paved roads are OK), but can usually be used on national forest and BLM single-track trails. Be sure to stay on the tracks and not to create new ones.

Rental bikes are widely available and cost about $5 per hour or $10 to $30 per day, depending on the type of bike and the rental location.

Dogwood Mountain Bike Adventures (☎ 916-966-6777; w *www.river-rat.com/dogwood.htm*) runs guided tours through the Sierra Nevada. **Backroads** (☎ 510-527-1555, 800-245-3874; w *www.backroads.com*) offers a Wine Country bicycle tour through the Napa Valley.

Also see the Bicycle section in the Getting Around chapter for other useful information.

Information

If you're serious about bicycling around California, get your hands on a copy of Lonely Planet's *Cycling USA West Coast*. It contains detailed descriptions of 42 rides through spectacular countryside, from quick and easy daylong hops in the saddle to long-distance adventures likely to blister the butts of all but the most seasoned bikers.

The local tourist offices are useful sources of information about bike rentals and usually have area maps for free or purchase. To get the inside scoop on the local scene, you'll probably get better information by talking with the folks in rental shops.

The California Department of Transportation (Caltrans) publishes free bicycle touring maps of the California North Coast and the Central Coast, available by calling Caltrans offices at ☎ 916-653-0036, ☎ 614-688-2597 or ☎ 510-286-5598. There's also an Eastern Sierra map, but for now it's only available online; for a download, go to w www.cabobike.org/publications.htm.

This website, maintained by the **California Association of Bicycle Organizations** (☎ 510-828-5299), also features online maps of several California counties, including Ventura, Los Angeles, Orange, San Luis Obispo, San Francisco and Sacramento, plus links to organizations that publish their own maps. While these are not free, they may be easier to read and contain more information than the free Caltrans maps.

One such organization is the **Adventure Cycling Association** (☎ 416-721-1776, 800-775-2453; **w** www.adv-cycling.org), whose website also contains trip-planning resources, an online store and lots of links. It publishes the *Adventure Cyclist* and *The Cyclist's Yellow Pages*, the latter being accessible through its website. For bike maps of the San Diego area, contact the **San Diego County Bicycle Coalition** (☎ 619-685-7742; **w** www.sdcbc.org).

SKIING

The sweeping mountains of the Sierra Nevada provide excellent territory for skiing, snowboarding and other snow-related activities. High mountains and reliable snow conditions have attracted investors and multimillion-dollar ski resorts equipped with the very latest in chairlift technology, snow-grooming systems and facilities. Skiing season generally lasts from about December to early April, although in some years it has snowed as early as October and as late as June.

With no fewer than 17 downhill and seven cross-country resorts, Lake Tahoe offers the greatest concentration and variety and is easily the most popular skiing destination in California. Along with famous places like Squaw Valley USA, site of the 1960 Winter Olympic Games, and Heavenly, you'll find smaller operations with fewer lifts and cheaper ticket prices good for beginners and families. Since the lake is partly in Nevada, which permits gambling, you can schuss all day on the slopes and spend the evening watching casino shows, drinking free cocktails and trying to win back the price of that expensive lift ticket.

About two hours south of Tahoe, in the Eastern Sierra, Mammoth Mountain is another high-caliber resort, which draws largely from the Southern California market. It has a rollicking après-ski scene where people party as hard as they ski. If you want something quieter, consider neighboring June Mountain. Yosemite's Badger Pass is another low-key place ideal for beginners and families. In the Gold Country's Ebbetts Pass area, there's downhill and cross-country skiing in Bear Valley.

In Northern California Mt Shasta Board & Ski Park is probably the most popular ski area, although there's also skiing in the Plumas-Eureka State Park and at Cedar Pass Snow Park in the Modoc National Forest.

There's a smaller pocket of ski slopes in the San Bernardino Mountains east of Los Angeles, including Big Bear Lake and Lake Arrowhead. While these don't compare in size and variety to the Sierra resorts, they're very popular with day-trippers and people on a short getaway. Traffic to and from the slopes can be horrendous, especially on Friday and Sunday evenings.

No matter where you ski, there's usually no shortage of lodgings, restaurants, shops, entertainment venues and childcare facilities both on and off the mountain. Most ski resorts have at least one comfortable base lodge with a rental office, ski shop and lockers. If you don't ski there are cafeterias and lounges or bars, where you can relax in warmth in front of a bay window looking out over the scene. You do not have to buy a lift ticket or trail pass or pay to enjoy the base lodge. If money saving is your goal, buy food at a grocery store and pack your own lunch. Use lockers and you won't have to tote your food around and worry about falling on your blueberry muffin.

Many resorts offer free or low-cost shuttle buses to area hotels.

Downhill Skiing

Ski areas sell half-day, full-day and multi-day lift tickets. Prices vary tremendously and can be as low as $25 or as high as $56 per day. As a rule, children pay considerably less, although the definition of 'children' varies from resort to resort. Students and seniors may also qualify for discounted rates. Sometimes the best value is in vacation packages, which include lift tickets, accommodation and transport. Look for offers on the Internet, in newspaper travel sections or consult with a travel agent.

Equipment rentals are available at or near even the smallest ski areas, though renting equipment in a nearby town can be cheaper if you can transport it to the slopes.

If you're planning on taking lessons, there's no need to pay separately for rentals since the price of a lesson usually includes all necessary gear with no discount for having your own. Children's ski schools are popular places to stash the kids for a day, offering lessons, day-care facilities and providing lunch.

Cross-Country Skiing

Cross-country or Nordic skiing offers the combined benefit of exercising while experiencing natural beauty at close quarters. Royal Gorge, near Truckee west of Lake Tahoe, is North America's largest cross-country ski resort and a mecca for enthusiasts. Yosemite and Kings Canyon–Sequoia National Parks close many of their roads in winter and maintain cross-country trails into the parks' backcountry. In Lassen Volcanic National Park, you can ski around bubbling fumaroles and mud pots.

One of the most delightful cross-country experiences is skiing into a remote lodge where you wake up to a hearty breakfast, ski all day and return to a homemade dinner, hot tub and roaring fire. Ostrander Ski Hut in Yosemite is a favorite destination for hardcore backcountry skiers, while the Montecito-Sequoia Lodge (just outside Kings Canyon–Sequoia National Park) is easily accessed and popular with families.

The USFS sometimes maintains summer hiking trails as cross-country ski trails during winter. Some resorts specialize in cross-country skiing and offer weekend or week-long packages that include lodging, meals and equipment rentals. Occasionally, downhill resorts (eg, Northstar-at-Tahoe) also have cross-country areas, and some city parks and golf courses are given over to ski trails in winter offering terrain especially suited to beginners.

Snowboarding

This sport has swept the nation's ski culture and taken on a huge following of its own. Many ski resorts now have dedicated snowboard parks with half pipes, jumps and obstacle courses. Snowboard lessons and rental equipment are widely available. Once you get past all the annoying pop-up ads, w www.snowboards.com has some valuable general information and product evaluations.

Other Winter Activities

Cross-country skiers often compete for space with snowmobiles, which have surged in popularity. While fun and exhilarating, snowmobiles are certainly not low-impact. Besides damaging the forest, they also cause considerable noise and air pollution. Nevertheless, equipment rentals are widely available. Snowshoeing is another increasingly popular activity and a great way to get into the backcountry without cross-country skis. When lakes freeze hard, ice-skating is a possibility, although the sport is more commonly practiced in year-round rinks.

Books & Magazines

In the annually updated *Skiing America & Canada*, Charles Leocha has compiled facts and figures about all of North America's big ski resorts. *Ski* (w www.skimag.com) and *Skiing* (w www.skiingmag.com) are both year-round, widely available magazines, featuring travel articles, how-to advice, and equipment tests.

Useful books on snowboarding include *Let It Rip: The Ultimate Guide to Snowboarding* by Greg Daniels, *The Complete Snowboarder* by Jeff Bennett & Scott Downey and *Snowboarding* by Greg Goldman. Also try *50 Classic Backcountry Ski and Snowboard Summits in California: Mount Shasta to Mount Whitney* by Paul Richins Jr and Jane Crosen.

Popular magazines, many with informative websites, include *Powder Magazine* (w www.powdermag.com), *Boarder Line* (w www.theboarderline.com), *Mountain Zone* (w www.mountainzone.com), *Snowboarder Magazine* (w www.snowboarder mag.com) and *Heckler Magazine* (w www .heckler.com).

ROCK CLIMBING & MOUNTAINEERING

The granite monoliths and glacial peaks of the Sierra Nevada and singular volcanic domes of the Cascades entice the world's best climbers and mountaineers. El Capitan and Half Dome in Yosemite National Park are both legendary climbs up the face of sheer granite walls. Joshua Tree National Monument is also popular with rock climbers, especially for those who value technique and finesse more than magnitude. The peaks of Mt Shasta, Lassen Peak and Mt Ritter (all above 13,000ft) are impressive mountaineering destinations, and Mt Whitney, the highest peak in the lower 48 states at 14,497ft, has a mountaineers' route that is a 'perfect balance of fun and challenge' according to the owner of the Whitney Portal store, who has made the ascent over 50 times.

Recently, rock climbers have subordinated the idea of reaching summits to testing their skills on varied routes on difficult terrain. Getting to the summit is no longer the primarily goal; the climbing technique is more important.

Climbing and mountaineering are demanding activities requiring top physical condition, an understanding of the composition of various rock types and their hazards, other hazards of the high country and familiarity with a variety of equipment, including ropes, chocks, bolts, karabiners and harnesses. Many climbers prefer granite, like that found in the Sierra, because of its strength and frequent handholds, but some climbers like limestone for a challenge. Some sedimentary rock is suitable for climbing, but crumbling volcanic rock, common at Pinnacles National Monument, can be very difficult, though it's popular too.

Hikers, climbers and mountaineers categorize routes into five classes: Class I is hiking with possible scrambling, while Class II involves off-trail scrambling on unstable materials like talus and may require use of the hands for keeping balance, especially with a heavy pack. Class III is simple climbing or scrambling, with moderate exposure possible; ropes may be needed. Class IV is intermediate climbing and involves steep rock, smaller holds and great exposure, with obligatory use of ropes and knowledge of knots and techniques like belaying and rappelling; a fall could be serious. Class V divides into a dozen or more subcategories based on degree of difficulty and requires advanced techniques, including proficiency with rope.

Minimum Impact

Many climbers are now following guidelines similar to those established for hikers to preserve the resource on which their sport relies, concentrating impact in high-use areas by using established roads, trails and routes for access; dispersing use in pristine areas and avoiding the creation of new trails; refraining from creating or enhancing handholds; and eschewing the placement of bolts wherever possible. Climbers should also take special caution to respect archaeological and cultural resources, such as rock art, and refrain from climbing in such areas.

Climbing Schools

Budding rock hounds will find a couple of good schools in the Sierra Nevada. **Alpine**

Skills International (☎ 530-426-9108, fax 530-426-3063; ⓦ www.alpineskills.com), based at Donner Pass west of Lake Tahoe, conducts seminars in rock climbing, mountaineering, ski mountaineering, backcountry skiing and avalanche survival. Its courses and trips are a great way to break into the mountaineering scene.

The **Yosemite Mountaineering School** (☎ 209-372-8344 Sept-May, ☎ 209-372-8435 June-Aug), headquartered in Yosemite National Park, has daily beginner and intermediate classes and world-class guides who lead instructional trips up some of the park's star routes. See the Yosemite section in the Sierra Nevada chapter for more details on the Yosemite Mountaineering School.

In Joshua Tree National Park, **Uprising Adventure Guides** (☎ 760-320-6630, 888-254-6266; ⓦ www.uprising.com) offers instruction and guides.

Books

For Yosemite, Don Reid is the most respected rock-climbing writer with multiple books in publication, including *Yosemite Free Climbs*, *Rock Climbing Yosemite's Select* and *Rock Climbs of Tuolumne Meadows*. For the Tahoe area, the best source is *Rock Climbing Lake Tahoe* by Mike Carville and Mike Clelland. *The High Sierra: Peaks, Passes and Trails* by RJ Secor has details about climbs around Mt Whitney. For Joshua Tree, a recommended guide is *Rock Climbing: Joshua Tree* by Randy Vogel.

HORSEBACK RIDING

You may rent a horse for a short ride in many areas in California – in parks, on beaches, and in most rural areas. Casual riders will find rides expensive, as visitors during the short summer tourist season end up paying for the cost of feeding these hay burners over winter. Rates for guided tours start around $20 per hour or $35 for two hours, with full day trips costing around $80. Experienced riders may want to let the horse's owners know of their ability or else they may be saddled with an excessively docile stable nag.

Pack Trips

A 100-year tradition of transporting hikers into the backcountry remains popular. These are high-impact outings where hikers ride horses and have their gear and food put onto pack animals (typically mules), and the whole show, called a pack string, is led along the trail by real-life cowboys. Outfitters are licensed to run pack trips from specific trailheads following specific trails. Most of these are in the Eastern Sierra Nevada, where the steeper and higher elevation approaches to the backcountry make pack trips attractive.

The Sierra Nevada chapter provides full contact details for numerous outfitters; Bishop is the main hub for this kind of thing.

RAFTING

California offers numerous places for practicing one of the most exhilarating outdoor activities: white-water rafting. Commercial outfitters provide white-water experiences ranging from short, inexpensive morning or afternoon trips to overnight and multi-day expeditions. Outfitters on NPS, USFS and BLM lands operate under permits from the appropriate agency, but individuals and groups with their own equipment sometimes also need a permit. People not ready for white-water excitement can try more sedate float or tube trips.

Runoff from typical early-season snowmelt creates massive flows and lots of big rapids. Later in the season, lower flows and river levels often create more technical rapids.

Nearest to Sacramento are the American and Stanislaus Rivers. The South Fork American River (Class II-III, April to October) is ideal for beginners and families. The neighboring North Fork American River (Class IV, April to June) and Middle Fork American River (Class IV, May to September) are more challenging. The North Fork Stanislaus River (Class IV, May to September) offers the most continuous white water of any river in California.

Two rivers descend from Yosemite National Park. The Merced River (Class III-IV, April to July) is the Sierra's best one-day intermediate trip. The Tuolumne River (Class IV, March to October) is considered the best all-around white-water trip. From the highest reaches of the Kings-Kern Divide flows the Kern River, which cuts a steep canyon through Sequoia National Park. Trips on the Lower Kern River (Class III, April to September) and Upper Kern River (Class III, April to July), both staged from near Bakersfield, have the best white water in the southern Sierra. There's also rafting

on the Truckee River (Class II to III, June to September).

White-water trips take place in either large rafts seating a dozen or more people, or smaller rafts seating half a dozen; the latter are more interesting and exciting because the ride over the rapids can be rougher and everyone participates in paddling. Most outfitters also rent white-water kayaks and canoes, which require more skill and maneuvering; instruction is usually provided.

While white-water trips are not without danger, and it's not unusual for participants to fall out of the raft in rough water, serious injuries are rare and the majority of trips are without incident. All participants must wear US Coast Guard-approved life jackets, and even nonswimmers are welcome. All trips have at least one river guide trained in lifesaving techniques.

Rivers and rapids are ranked on the international six-point scale:

Class I (easy) – flat water to occasional series of mild rapids

Class II (medium) – frequent stretches of rapids with waves up to 3ft high and easy chutes, ledges and falls. The best route is easy to identify, the entire river can be run in open canoes and no great skill or maneuvering is required.

Class III (difficult) – numerous rapids with high, irregular waves and difficult chutes and falls that often require scouting. These rivers are for experienced paddlers who either use kayaks or rafts or have spray covers for their canoes.

Class IV (very difficult) – long stretches of high, irregular waves, powerful back eddies and even constricted canyons. Scouting is mandatory, and rescues can be difficult in many places. Rafts or white-water kayaks in which paddlers are equipped with helmets are suitable for these rivers.

Class V (extremely difficult) – continuous violent rapids, large drops, powerful rollers and high, extreme hydraulics and holes, unavoidable waves and haystacks. These rivers are only for professional rafters and white-water kayakers who are proficient in the Eskimo roll.

Class VI (highest level of difficulty) – rarely run except by highly experienced kayakers under ideal conditions. The likelihood of serious injury or worse is high.

Organized Trips

The most popular destination for river running is the South Fork of the American River. Operators, concentrated in the small town of Coloma (see the Gold Country chapter), run half-day trips and multi-day adventures that include meals and camp accommodations. Half-day options are usually more action-packed and economical than full-day trips, though overnighters are the most fun.

OARS (☎ 209-736-4677, 800-346-627; [w] www.oars.com; PO Box 67, Angels Camp, CA 95222) runs white-water rafting and kayak trips on the American, Kern and Tuolumne Rivers.

Another excellent outfitter is **Whitewater Voyages** (☎ 800-488-7238; [w] www.white watervoyages.com; 5225 San Pablo Dam Rd, El Sobrante, CA 94803), which offers rafting trips on such rivers as the Klamath, California Salmon, American and Kern.

Through the University of California recreation department, **Cal Adventures** (☎ 510-642-4000) offers economical raft and kayak classes on the South Fork of the American River.

Tributary Whitewater Tours (☎ 530-346-6812, 800-6723-8464; [w] http://whitewater tours.com) runs rafting trips on just about all major California rivers.

KAYAKING

This quiet, unobtrusive sport allows you to visit unexplored islands and stretches of coast and view marine life at close range. Sea kayaks, which hold one or two people, are larger and more stable than white-water boats, making them safer and easier to navigate. They also have storage capacity, so you can take them on overnight or even weeklong trips. Imagine paddling to a secluded beach on one of the Channel Islands and setting up camp for a week.

The most popular destinations for sea kayaking are the Channel Islands, off the Central Coast, and Catalina Island further south. These places are ideal overnight destinations for experienced kayakers. Day trips are also rewarding, especially in areas where you are likely to see seals and sea lions, such as Morro Bay, Monterey Bay and Richardson Bay in Sausalito.

There's also kayaking on the lower Sacramento River near Woodson Bridge State Recreation Area; on the Russian River and on Mono Lake and Lake Tahoe.

Outfitters renting kayak equipment and offering tours are mentioned wherever it's possible to practice this sport.

SURFING & WINDSURFING

Surfing is California's signature sport. Invented by Pacific Islanders, surfing was made popular by Duke Kahanamoku in Hawaii in the 1920s but actually arrived in California in 1914. It has imbued a look, language and way of life that is 'typically' Californian: laid-back, easy-going and totally dedicated to sun and sea.

California's 'big three' surf spots are Rincon, Malibu and Trestles, all point breaks (where swells peak up into steep waves as they encounter a shelf-like point) known for consistently clean, glassy, big waves. Beginner and intermediate surfers should be content to watch the action at these places (which also get very crowded).

The best places to learn surfing are at beach breaks or long, shallow bays where waves are small and rolling. San Onofre and San Diego's Tourmaline are good beginner spots. Huntington Beach is Orange County's surf mecca, with a surfing museum, a surfing walk of fame and a pro/am surf series championship contested each September. There's also a surfing competition in Oceanside, San Diego county, held every June.

Long boards are heavy and unwieldy compared to the short boards most commonly used, but they're actually easier to balance on and less likely to 'pearl' (when the tip of the board takes a dive). Morey Doyle boards, made of spongy foam, are the ultimate beginner's tool.

You'll find surfboard rental stands on every beach where surfing is possible. Rentals cost around $10 per hour, and lessons (inquire at surf shops) start at about $20.

Northern California has its own surf scene, with colder water, bigger waves and an abundance of sharks. The Santa Cruz coast is good, and Mavericks (near Half Moon Bay), made famous when professional surfer Mark Foo died there in 1994, has waves that rival Hawaii's. Humboldt County grows its own crop of big-wave surfers, right along with its marijuana plants.

Crowds are a problem, especially on fine weekends. Any surf spot with a parking lot facing the ocean is likely to be crowded, but breaks that require a long walk or paddle are usually better. There's a territorial local scene at many places, notably in Oxnard and at San Diego's Windansea. Try hooking up with a local surfer for an introduction.

Surfers – real and armchair ones – may enjoy Daniel Duane's *Caught Inside: A Surfer's Year on the California Coast*, published as part of Lonely Planet Journeys series. Orange County-based *Surfer* magazine has travel reports that cover just about every inch of the US coastline. Order copies from ☎ 949-661-5147 or on the Net at [w] www .surfermag.com/travel.

Windsurfing is also popular in California. Though you can put in with your windsurfing board at any beach or public boat launch, few places rent windsurfing equipment, making it necessary for serious boarders to have their own. Beginners and casual boarders will find rental facilities and relatively calm conditions at San Diego's Mission Bay, Marina Del Rey in Los Angeles and the Berkeley Marina. California's premiere windsurfing locales include the San Francisco Bay, Rio Vista in the Sacramento River Delta, and Lopez Lake, just east of San Luis Obispo.

DIVING & SNORKELING
The waters off the coast of California are wonderful playgrounds for divers and snorkelers. Rock reefs, shipwrecks and kelp beds all invite exploration and attract a variety of fish. There are sites suited for all levels of skills and experience; wet suits are advisable year-round. For detailed information about diving in California, check out Lonely Planet's diving and snorkeling guides to the *Monterey Peninsula & Northern California*; *California's Central Coast* and *Southern California & the Channel Islands*.

If you want to try diving for the first time, some dive operations offer a short beginner's course that includes a brief instruction, followed by a shallow beach or boat dive. The cost ranges from $60 to $100. Great places, especially for first-time divers, are in La Jolla, Monterey Bay and Catalina Island, where kelp beds house a rich marine environment close to the surface. Local dive shops are the best resources for equipment, guides and instructors. Otherwise, to get into the depth of California's waters, you must be certified. To dive with an operator, or to have tanks filled, the minimum qualification required is an open-water certificate from PADI, NAUI or another recognized organization like BSAC. An open-water certificate course costs from $300 to $400. For a list of instructors and dive schools, contact the **National Association for Underwater Instruction** *(NAUI;* ☎ *813-628-6284, 800-553-6284;* [w] *www.naui.org).*

If you don't have the time, money or desire to dive deep, rent a snorkel, mask and fins, which are widely available from concessionaires close to the respective snorkeling sites.

Rodale's Scuba Diving ([w] www.scuba diving.com) and *Sport Diver* ([w] www.sport diver.com) published by PADI, are widely available magazines dedicated entirely to underwater pursuits.

FISHING
Thousands of lakes and hundreds of rivers make trout fishing a popular pastime in California. Native rainbow, cutthroat and golden trout still live in a few places, but introduced brown and brook trout are more abundant. Many lakes and rivers on USFS land are stocked annually.

The Klamath, Eel, Trinity and Pit Rivers are excellent for trout, as are Lake Shasta and the Whiskeytown Reservoir. The lakes and rivers of the Eastern Sierra – including Virginia Lakes, Twin Lakes, Crowley Lake, Convict Lake, June, Grant and Silver – are also prime fishing territory.

Deep-sea fishing for salmon, halibut and yellowfin tuna is popular off the Central Coast (for example Monterey and Morro Bay). Boats also leave from Long Beach, Newport Beach and San Diego.

A California state sport fishing license is required for people over 16, except if fishing from a public ocean pier. Licenses cost $30.45 for California residents and $81.65 for nonresidents and are valid for one calendar year. One-, two- and 10-day licenses are $7.10, $11.05 and $30.45 respectively. They're available from 2350 licensed agents throughout the state, including sporting goods stores, boat companies and bait and tackle shops. For more details, contact the **California Department of Fish and Game** *(*☎ *916-653-7664;* [w] *www .dfg.ca.gov)* in Sacramento.

RUNNING
Running is a great way to stay fit without any equipment except perhaps a pair of comfortable running shoes. Jogging is big in California, especially in the early morning and evening hours. Favorite running places are along the beaches, in parks and forests and

even in the streets. Running competitions, including marathons, take place year-round throughout the state. The popular magazine *California Track & Running News* is among those listing upcoming races in print as well as online at w www.caltrack.com.

CAVING

Experienced spelunkers can explore caves in several areas of limestone bedrock, especially in the Sierra Nevada foothills. Several caves are open to casual visitors for guided tours, without need of equipment or experience. These include Black Chasm Cavern, Moaning Cavern, California Caverns and Mercer Caverns in the Gold Country; Boyden Cavern and Crystal Cave in Kings Canyon and Sequoia National Parks; Subway Cave in the Lassen National Forest; Lava Bed National Monument near Tulelake and the Lake Shasta Caverns near Redding. For fairly easy, self-guided explorations, Balconies Caves in the Pinnacles National Monument is an ideal candidate. Anyone with some mobility can see La Jolla Caves in San Diego.

Because of the delicate and tightly circumscribed subterranean environments, cavers must make special efforts to respect the ecosystem and its inhabitants by leaving no trace of human presence, avoiding contact with sensitive formations and refraining from disturbing bats and other animals.

GOLF

Golf, once the domain of aging, well-off males, has blossomed into a veritable obsession with everyone from kids to grandmas enjoying the sport. As a result, golf courses have proliferated faster than rabbits on Viagra and even small towns now have their own greens.

Most regions of California have various courses open to the public with reasonable fees, although there are still such exclusive enclaves as Pebble Beach and Spyglass Hill. In Southern California, San Diego and Palm Springs are the undisputed golfing meccas, each supporting more than 90 courses. Other areas, including San Luis Obispo County and Monterey/Salinas on the Central Coast, have also jumped on the bandwagon.

HOT-AIR BALLOONING

Floating above California in a wicker gondola has its attractions, given the scenery, but it's not cheap at the relatively few locations that offer it commercially. Most flights leave at dawn and go 1000ft to 2000ft above ground. The most popular spot is the Napa Valley, where most operators offer fancy gondola treats like champagne, local wine and cheese. Other popular ballooning spots include Del Mar in San Diego's North County and Palm Springs area.

SKYDIVING

If jumping out of a plane and falling at 150mi an hour before opening your chute 3000ft above the ground sounds like fun, then you should head to Perris Valley in Southern California. At the **Perris Valley Skydiving School** (☎ *213-759-3483, 714-759-3483, 800-832-8818; 2091 Goetz Rd, Perris, CA 92570*) you can go from the classroom to the sky in half an hour with an instructor, or in six hours if you want to go solo. You must be over 18 years of age and weigh no more than 230lbs. The school is in Riverside County, about two hours east of Los Angeles or north of San Diego.

Getting There & Away

AIR

US domestic airfares vary tremendously depending on the season you travel, the day of the week you fly, the length of your stay and the flexibility the ticket allows for flight changes and refunds. Still, nothing determines fares more than demand, and when business is slow, regardless of the season, airlines will lower their fares to fill empty seats. Airlines are very competitive, and at any given time any one of them could have the cheapest fare. Expect less fluctuation with international fares.

Airports & Airlines

Los Angeles International Airport (LAX; 310-646-5252; W www.lawa.org) has eight terminals. Some of the larger US airlines, like United and American, have their own terminals from which they operate both domestic and international flights. Most international carriers land at the Tom Bradley International Terminal. Midsize LA area airports, mostly for domestic travel, are in **Burbank-Glendale-Pasadena** (☎ 818-840-8847; W www.burbankairport.com), **Ontario/San Bernardino County** (☎ 909-937-2700; W www.lawa.org/ont), **Long Beach** (☎ 562-570-2600; W www.lgb.org) and **John Wayne-Orange County** (☎ 949-252-5200; W www.ocair.com).

San Diego International Airport (☎ 619-686-6200; W www.portofsandiego.org) gets mostly domestic travel as well as one flight daily from London Gatwick by British Airways.

Most international flights to the Bay Area land at **San Francisco International Airport** (SFO; ☎ 650-821-8211; W www.flysfo.com) on the west side of the bay. Most international airlines, as well as the international services of several US carriers, are based at the International Terminal.

The airports in **Oakland** (☎ 510-577-4000; W www.flyoakland.com) and **San Jose** (☎ 408-501-7600; W www.sjc.org) are important domestic gateways.

McCarran International Airport (☎ 702-261-5211; W www.mccarran.com) in Las Vegas, Nevada, has direct flights to and from most US cities and a few from Canada and Europe.

Reno-Tahoe International Airport (☎ 775-328-6400; W www.renoairport.com) in Reno, Nevada, is also served by numerous US airlines.

Major domestic airlines serving California include:

Alaska (☎ 800-426-0333, W www.alaskaair.com)
American Airlines (☎ 800-433-7300, W www.aa.com)
America West (☎ 800-235-9292, W www.america west.com)
Continental (☎ 800-525-0280, W www.continental.com)
Delta (☎ 800-221-1212, 800-241-4141, W www.delta.com)
Jet Blue (☎ 800-538-2583, W www.jetblue.com)
Northwest (☎ 800-225-2525, W www.nwa.com)
Southwest (☎ 800-435-9792, W www.southwest.com)
United Airlines (☎ 800-241-6522, 800-538-2929, W www.united.com)
US Airways (☎ 800-428-4322, W www.usairways.com)

Major international airlines include:

Aeromexico (☎ 800-237-6639, W www.aeromexico.com)
Air Canada (☎ 888-247-2262, W www.aircanada.com)
Air France (☎ 800-237-2747, W www.airfrance.com)
Air New Zealand (☎ 800-262-1234, W www.airnewzealand.com)

Warning

The information in this chapter is particularly vulnerable to change. Prices for international travel are volatile, routes are introduced and cancelled, schedules change, special deals come and go, and rules and visa requirements are amended. You should check directly with the airline or a travel agent to make sure you understand how a fare (and ticket you may buy) works and be aware of the security requirements for international travel.

The upshot of this is that you should get opinions, quotes and advice from as many airlines and travel agents as possible before you part with your hard-earned cash. The details given in this chapter should be regarded as pointers and are not a substitute for your own careful, up-to-date research.

Alitalia (☎ 800-223-5730, W www.alitalia usa.com)
British Airways (☎ 800-247-9297, W www .britishairways.com)
Cathay Pacific (☎ 800-228-4297, W www .cathaypacific.com)
Japan Airlines (☎ 800-525-3663, W www .japanair.com)
KLM (☎ 800-374-7747, W www.klm.com)
Lufthansa (☎ 800-645-3880, W www.luft hansa.com)
Mexicana (☎ 800-531-7921, W www.mexicana .com)
Qantas (☎ 800-227-4500, W www.qantas.com)
Singapore Airlines (☎ 800-742-3333, W www .singaporeair.com)
Virgin Atlantic (☎ 800-862-8621, W www.virgin .com/atlantic)

Buying Tickets

All major international airlines fly to the USA, and a variety of one-way, round-trip and round-the-world fares is available. Fares are highest during peak season from June to early September (ie, the northern summer). May and October are 'shoulder' periods and the low season runs from November to April, except for the weeks around the Thanksgiving and Christmas holidays.

If you're flying to California from outside the US, your plane ticket is likely to be the biggest expense in your budget. Fortunately, world aviation has never been so competitive, making air travel better value than ever. The Internet is a useful resource and most travel agencies and airlines have their own websites. Research the options carefully to make sure you get the best deal.

As a general rule, start shopping for your ticket as early as possible, because some of the cheapest fares must be bought weeks or months in advance, and popular flights sell out early. Full-time students and people under 26 usually qualify for better deals than other travelers.

When you're looking for bargain airfares, there is almost never an advantage to buying a ticket directly from the airline, although attractive online deals may occasionally be available. Discounted tickets are released to selected travel agents and specialist discount agencies, and these are usually the cheapest deals going. Online travel agencies also list some of the cheapest fares around. If you're looking for last-minute airfares and are very flexible about travel dates and times, you could also try websites like W www.price line.com and W www.hotwire.com. These can offer excellent bargains, although there are usually some strings attached. Be sure to read the rules and regulations before committing to these tickets.

The days when some travel agents fleeced travelers by running off with their money are, happily, almost over. Paying by credit card generally offers protection, as most card issuers provide refunds if you can prove you didn't get what you paid for.

Firms with a good reputation include STA Travel with offices worldwide, Travel CUTS in Canada, and Flight Centre in Australia; all offer competitive prices to most destinations, especially to students and those under 26.

Always make a photocopy of your ticket and keep it somewhere separate. This will simplify obtaining a replacement in case of loss or theft.

Remember to buy travel insurance as early as possible (see Visas & Documents in the Facts for the Visitor chapter for details).

Air Passes Most US airlines offer some sort of an air pass to overseas visitors. Passes are sold only in conjunction with an international plane ticket and in order to get the best deal, you have to buy the pass and the international flight from the same airline or a from a 'partner' airline.

The passes are actually a book of coupons. Typically, the minimum number of coupons is three or four and the maximum is eight or 10, with each coupon equaling one flight. One catch is that if a connection is not a direct flight (ie, if it involves a change of flight number), that counts as two coupons. It's therefore worth getting your pass with an airline that offers direct flights between the cities you want to visit.

Most airlines require you to plan your itinerary in advance and to complete your flights within 60 days of arrival in the US, but rules may vary between airlines. A few airlines may allow you to use coupons on standby, in which case you should call the airline a day or two before the flight and make a 'standby reservation.' Such a reservation gives you priority over all other standby travelers. The conditions and cost structures are quite complicated, so check your options carefully with your travel agent.

Round-the-World Tickets Round-the-World (RTW) tickets may be the most economical option if you intend to visit other parts of the world in addition to California. They're usually more expensive than a regular round-trip to the USA, but the extra stops come pretty cheap. They're of most value for trips that combine the USA with two other continents.

Official airline RTW tickets are usually put together by a combination of airlines or a whole alliance. They permit you to fly to a specified number of stops and/or a maximum mileage on their routes, so long as you don't backtrack. You may have to book the first sector in advance and cancellation penalties apply. The tickets are valid for a fixed period, normally one year. An alternative type of RTW ticket is one put together by a travel agent using a combination of discounted tickets.

Most RTW fares restrict the number of stops within the USA and Canada. The cheapest fares permit only one stop, and some airlines black out a few heavily traveled routes (like Honolulu to Tokyo). In most cases a 14-day advance purchase is required. After the ticket is purchased, dates can sometimes be changed without penalty and tickets can be rewritten to add or delete stops for an extra charge.

Getting Bumped

Airlines routinely overbook and count on some passengers canceling or not showing up. Occasionally, almost everybody does show up for a flight, and then some passengers must be 'bumped' onto another flight. Getting bumped can be a nuisance because you have to wait around for the next flight. But if you have a day's leeway, you can turn this to your advantage.

When you check in at the airline counter, ask if the flight is full and if there may be a need for volunteer 'bumpees'; if yes, get your name on the list. Depending on how oversold the flight is, compensation may range from a discount voucher toward your next flight to a fully paid round-trip ticket or even cash. Be sure to try to confirm a later flight so you don't get stuck in the airport on standby. If you have to spend the night, airlines frequently foot the hotel bill for their bumpees. You don't have to accept the airline's first offer and can haggle for a better deal.

However, be aware that being just a little late for boarding could get you bumped with none of these benefits.

Baggage & Other Restrictions

On most domestic and international flights, the checked bag limit is two. A charge may be levied if you have more bags or if the size of a bag exceeds the airline's limits. On international flights the luggage allowance is based on weight, with a maximum allowance of 32kg (70.4lb) per bag. A ski bag, snowboard, golf clubs or packed bicycle are usually OK, but a surfboard or windsurfer may cost extra. Check details with the airlines, preferably before buying your ticket.

If your luggage is delayed upon arrival, some airlines will provide you with cash to purchase necessities. If sporting equipment is misplaced, the airline may pay for rentals. Should the luggage be lost, it is important to submit a claim. The airline doesn't have to pay the full amount of the claim. Rather, they can estimate the value of your lost items. It may take anywhere from six weeks to three months to process the claim.

Items that are illegal to take on a plane, either as check or carry-on baggage, include aerosols, tear gas and pepper spray, camp stoves with fuel and full divers' tanks. Under stepped-up security measures imposed since the September 11, 2001 terrorist attacks, now anything on board that could potentially be used as a weapon (including scissors, razors, knitting needles, metal nail files etc) is prohibited.

Smoking is forbidden on all domestic flights and on most international flights to and from the USA.

Arriving in the USA

Even if you are continuing immediately to another city, the first US airport you land at is where you must carry out immigration and customs formalities.

If you don't have a US passport or Green Card, you must complete an Arrival/Departure Record (form I-94) before you appear at the immigration desk. This form is handed out on the plane, along with the customs declaration which must be filled out by all arriving passengers. After immigration, you collect your baggage and then pass through customs. If you have nothing to declare, you'll probably clear customs quickly and without a baggage search, but random searches have increased in these heightened security times.

Although the vast majority of visitors to the US ultimately have no problem entering the country, immigration and customs officials are entitled to question anyone trying to do so and may even prevent you from being admitted to the US. Aside from trying to detect potential members of terrorist organizations, they are also interested in ferreting out those likely to work illegally or overstay.

You may be subjected to a barrage of questions concerning your length of stay and itinerary, whether you have relatives in the US, whether you have sufficient funds etc. Be prepared to show your return flight ticket and that you have $300 or $400 for every week of your intended stay. These days, a couple of major credit cards will go a long way toward establishing 'sufficient funds.' Don't make too much of having friends, relatives or business contacts in the USA – the INS official may decide that this will make you more likely to overstay. Try to remain as calm as possible and answer all questions politely. Be aware that until you have passed through the last formality, you have few rights.

Departure Tax

Taxes for US airports and an arrivals tax are included in the cost of tickets. They may not be included in an advertised fare but will always be added on at some stage.

Other Parts of the USA

STA Travel (*☎ 800-777-0112; w www.statravel.com*) is a reputable discount travel agent, especially for students and those under 26, with offices around the world. Special fares are also available through other discount agents. Check the ads in the Sunday travel sections of the larger newspapers such as the *New York Times*, *Los Angeles Times*, *Chicago Tribune* and *San Francisco Chronicle*. To scour the Web for cheap fares try w www.orbitz.com, w www.expedia.com or w www.travelocity.com.

Fares are usually lower on the major 'air highways,' especially between San Francisco or LA and major East Coast cities like New York and Washington, DC. Flights to Chicago and Miami are also fairly competitive, but fares go up for flights to smaller cities in the South or Midwest, which may also involve plane changes.

Nonstop flights between the coasts take about 4½ hours eastbound and 5½ hours westbound, because of prevailing winds. Round-trip tickets between, say LA and Boston, New York or Washington can be as low as $300. Expect to pay about $200 for a ticket to LA from Chicago, Houston and Miami; and $100 or less if coming from San Francisco, Las Vegas and Phoenix.

Canada

Travel CUTS/Voyages Campus (*☎ 866-246-9672; w www.travelcuts.com*) is Canada's nationwide student and discount travel agency with offices in Toronto (☎ 416-979-2406; 187 College St), Vancouver (☎ 604-659-2845; 1114 Burnaby St) and other major cities. Also check the travel sections of the *Globe & Mail*, the *Montreal Gazette*, the *Toronto Star* or the *Vancouver Sun* for travel agents' ads. There are daily flights to San Francisco and Los Angeles from Vancouver and Toronto, and other Canadian cities have connections as well.

The UK

One of the busiest, most competitive air sectors in the world is the UK to the USA, with several direct flights from London to San Francisco and Los Angeles daily. Discount air travel is big business in London. For the latest fares, check out the travel page ads of the Sunday newspapers, *Time Out* and the freebie *TNT*. Fares from London to California range roughly from £300 to £500.

Most British travel agents are registered with the ABTA (Association of British Travel Agents). If you have paid an ABTA-registered agent for your flight, and the agent then goes out of business, ABTA will guarantee a refund or an alternative. Using an unregistered agent is not recommended.

STA Travel (*☎ 0870-160-0599; w www.statravel.co.uk*) has 50 branches throughout the UK. Other recommended travel agencies include **Trailfinders** (*w www.trailfinders.co.uk*), with 10 branches throughout the UK and Ireland; **Bridge the World** (*☎ 0870-444-7474; w www.bridgetheworld.com*) with two branches in London and **Flightbookers** (*☎ 0870-010-7000; w www.ebookers.com*), also in London. Call or check the websites for the nearest branch.

For online bookings, you could also try W www.travelocity.co.uk or W www.expedia.co.uk.

Continental Europe

Many airlines, including KLM, Air France, Lufthansa, Alitalia and Iberia, have direct flights to Los Angeles or San Francisco. Many other international and US airlines arrive via a stop in a gateway city (usually Chicago or Miami) and continue on domestic flights. Recommended travel agents include:

Belgium Airstop (☎ 07 023 31 88, W www .airstop.be) 28 Wolvengracht, Brussels; Connections (☎ 02 550 01 00, W www.connec tions.be); 19-21 Rue du Midi, Brussels. Both have branches in other Belgian cities.
France OTU Voyages (☎ 01 44 41 38 50, W www .otu.fr) 39 Ave Georges Bernanos, Paris, with 32 branches around the country; Nouvelles Frontières (☎ 08 03 33 33 33, W www .nouvelles-frontieres.fr) 5 Ave de l'Opéra, Paris; Voyageurs du Monde (☎ 01 42 86 16 00, W www.vdm.com) 55 rue Ste-Anne, Paris
Germany STA Travel (W www.statravel.de) has offices in all major cities; Travel Overland (☎ 030-217 38 90, W www.travel-overland.de) Goltzstrasse 14, Berlin, (☎ 089-27 27 61 00) Barer Strasse 73, Munich.
Italy CTS (W www.cts.it) has 170 branches throughout the country.
Switzerland SSR (☎ 01 261 2955, W www.ssr.ch) Leonhardstrasse 10, Zurich; owned by STA Travel and has branches in all major Swiss cities.

Australia & New Zealand

Some flights go from Sydney and Melbourne direct to Los Angeles and San Francisco and quite a few more go via Auckland. Prices are higher if you stop over in Hawaii or plan to stay abroad for more than two months.

The weekend travel sections of newspapers such as *The Age* in Melbourne, the *Sydney Morning Herald* and the *New Zealand Herald* are useful sources for discounted airfares.

In Australia, the main discount travel agencies, **STA Travel** (☎ 1300 360 960; W www.statravel.com.au) and **Flight Centre** (☎ 133 133; W www.flightcentre.com.au) have offices in all main cities. British discount agency **Trailfinders** (☎ 03-9600 3022; W www.trailfinders.com.au) now has branches in major cities. Fares are likely to hover around A$1450 in low season and A$1800 in high season.

In New Zealand, the two main agencies are also **STA Travel** (☎ 09-309 0458; W www.sta travel.co.nz; 10 High St, Auckland) and **Flight Centre** (☎ 09-309 6171; W www.flight centre.co.nz; 205-225 Queens St, Auckland), plus additional offices in other cities. Air New Zealand has regular flights from Auckland direct to Los Angeles, while flights from Christchurch and Wellington require a change in Auckland or one of the Pacific islands. Fares are roughly the same as from Australia.

Asia

Bangkok, Singapore, Kuala Lumpur, Hong Kong, Seoul and Tokyo all have good connections to the US West Coast on national airlines. Many flights go via Honolulu and allow a stopover. Bangkok is the discount fare capital of the region, though its cheapest agents can be unreliable. STA Travel has branches in Hong Kong, Tokyo, Singapore, Bangkok and Kuala Lumpur.

Mexico

There are regular flights from San Francisco and Los Angeles to the major cities and tourist destinations in Mexico. Travelers headed for Southern California may find it cheaper at times to fly to Tijuana instead of Los Angeles or even San Diego. Tijuana is the northernmost Mexican city, just across the border from San Diego and only three hours by car or bus from Los Angeles.

Central & South America

The main gateway from Central and South America is Miami, but there are also many direct flights to Houston and Los Angeles. Most countries' international flag carriers (like Aerolineas Argentinas and LanChile), as well as US airlines like United and American, serve these destinations, with onward connections.

BUS

Greyhound (☎ 800-231-2222; W www .greyhound.com) is the main national bus carrier, with service throughout California and the rest of the USA. See the Getting Around chapter for contact information and details about fares and reservations.

If California is part of a wider US itinerary, you may be able to save money by purchasing one of Greyhound's unlimited travel passes, available for periods of seven, 10, 15, 21, 30, 45 or 60 consecutive days.

In 2002, the **Domestic Ameripass**, available to citizens and permanent residents of the US and Canada, cost $197 for seven days, $235 for 10 days, $305 for 15 days, $350 for 21 days, $404 for 30 days, $449 for 45 days and $566 for 60 days. Passes may be bought at any Greyhound terminal as late as the day of travel or online at least two weeks prior to your departure.

Overseas travelers qualify for the slightly cheaper **International Ameripass** ($183/228/282/327/381/417/516 for seven/ 10/15/21/30/45/60 days), which is available from select ticket agents around the world and online at least 21 days before the first Greyhound trip. The company's website allows you to search for the nearest agent in your home country.

Students and seniors over 62 qualify for a 10% discount, children get 50% off. Check the website for current fares, details and other passes.

TRAIN

Amtrak operates an extensive rail system throughout the US. The trains are comfortable and equipped with dining and lounge cars on long-distance routes. See the Getting Around chapter for contact information and details about intra-California routes, tickets and reservations.

Four interstate trains pass through California:

California Zephyr Daily between Chicago and Emeryville, near San Francisco, via Omaha, Denver and Salt Lake City.

Coast Starlight Goes up the West Coast daily between Los Angeles and Seattle, with stops in Oakland, Sacramento and Portland.

Southwest Chief Daily departures between Chicago and Los Angeles via Kansas City, Albuquerque and Flagstaff.

Sunset Limited Thrice weekly service between Los Angeles and Orlando via Tucson, El Paso and New Orleans.

Amtrak also offers a variety of passes that may come in handy if you're planning on exploring other parts of the US.

The **USA Rail Pass** is available to non-US or Canadian citizens only and is sold by travel agents outside North America and Amtrak offices in the US (show your passport).

The pass offers unlimited coach-class travel within a specific US region for either 15 or 30 consecutive days, with the price depending on the region, number of days and season traveled. In summer of 2002 the **West Rail Pass**, for instance, which is good for travel anywhere west of Chicago and New Orleans, cost $325/405 for 15/30 day periods between June and early September and $200/270 the rest of the year.

Amtrak's **North America Rail Pass**, available to anyone, offers unlimited travel on US and Canadian railways for 30 consecutive days. Prices are around $674 for travel between June and mid-October and $475 at other times of the year.

CAR & MOTORCYCLE

Much of the information and advice on driving contained within the Getting Around chapter also applies to driving longer distances to and from other parts of the USA; see that chapter for further details.

Drive-Away Cars

Drive-away cars belong to owners who can't drive them to a specific destination but are willing to allow someone else to drive for them. To be a driver, you must be over 21 and present a valid driver's license, personal references and a $200 to $400 cash deposit that is refunded upon safe delivery of the car. Some drive-away agencies also require a printout of your driving record, a major credit card or three forms of identification. You pay nothing for the use of the car, but you do pay for the fuel you use and any incidental expenses such as lodging and food. The agency pays *you* nothing to drive the car, but they do cover the insurance. Inspect the car carefully for damage when it's handed over.

You must deliver the car to its destination at a specified time; the time allotted for a trip usually works out to about six hours of driving per day. Maximum mileage is also stipulated, so you have to follow the shortest route. Be clear about the conditions for the deposit refund.

There may or may not be cars available when and to where you want to travel, so it helps to be flexible and to contact several companies. Availability depends on demand, with coast-to-coast routes the most easily available.

To find a drive-away agency, check the Yellow Pages under 'Automotive Transport & Drive-Away Companies'. The website **w** www.movecars.com is another excellent source.

ORGANIZED TOURS

Group travel can be an enjoyable and often economical way to go, especially for single travelers of the sociable type. Try to pick a tour that will suit you in terms of age, gender and interests. Tours usually include a mix of nationalities but few Americans. This can be a drawback, since you'll only be stopping briefly at most destinations, making an immersion in local culture less likely. The best source for organized travel is a travel agent back in your home country. The companies listed here have all been around for a while and enjoy a good reputation. Check their websites for details.

Green Tortoise (☎ *415-956-7500, 800-867-8647;* **w** *www.greentortoise.com; 494 Broadway, San Francisco, CA 94133)* offers alternative bus tours with stops at places like hot springs and national parks. Green Tortoise operates like a mobile commune. You travel in converted sleeper coaches outfitted with mattresses on raised platforms and bunk beds, couches, tables, kitchen appliances and stereos, but no restrooms (the bus will make stops 'as necessary'). Smoking and alcohol are not allowed on the bus. The National Parks Loop from San Francisco takes 16 days and, in 2002, cost $629 plus $191 toward the food fund. They also have three-day trips to Death Valley ($180) and two-day ($130) and three-day ($170) trips to Yosemite, including food fund money. Tours generally depart from San Francisco.

Adventure Planet (☎ *208-726-8410, 888-737-5263;* **w** *www.adventurebus.com)* operates on a similar scheme as Green Tortoise, running its trips in converted Greyhound buses. Tours start in LA (or Las Vegas) but immediately take you beyond California to the scenic wonders and national parks of the West and Southwest.

Trek America (☎ *973-983-1144, 800-221-0596* ● ☎ *01295-256 777 in the UK;* **w** *www.trekamerica.com)* offers activity-oriented tours in 14-seat vans. Most nights are spent camping in tents, and everyone helps with the camping chores. Stops are often for two or three nights to permit hiking and more individual sightseeing. The standard Trek America trips are for the 18- to 38-year-old age group, but the 'Footloose' trips are designed for older travelers. The seven-day 'Western Wonder' tour (from $529), for instance, starts in San Francisco and takes in Yosemite National Park, Las Vegas and the Grand Canyon before ending up in LA. The same tour in reverse is offered starting in LA.

AmeriCan Adventures (☎ *310-324-3562, 800-873-5872;* **w** *www.americanadventures .com)* is based in LA and also offers small-size group tours for the budget-conscious throughout the US, with half a dozen around the West. Tours start in LA and include the seven-day 'California Cooler' (from $499) which goes to Yosemite, San Francisco, the Pacific Coast Highway, Los Angeles and Disneyland, plus such non-California highlights as Las Vegas and the Grand Canyon. Group size is limited to 13; nights are spent camping or in hostels or budget hotels. Tours are open to anyone over 18. Bookings and inquiries from outside the US or Canada should be directed to the UK office (☎ *01295-756200, fax 01295-756240;* **e** *info@ameri canadventures.co.uk)*. If dialing from outside the UK, you must first dial your country's international access code, plus 44 for the UK, then drop the first zero.

Similar deals are available from **Suntrek** (☎ *707-523-1800, 800-786-8735, fax 707-523-1911;* **w** *www.suntrek.com)*. One-week trips include the 'Western Sun' from LA via the Grand Canyon, Las Vegas, Death Valley, Mono Lake and Yosemite to San Francisco (from $549), and the 'Surf & Sun' tour from San Francisco to Tijuana, Mexico via the Pacific Coast Highway (from $499).

Bicycling, hiking and multisport tours are offered by Berkeley-based **Backroads** (☎ *510-527-1555, 800-462-2848;* **w** *www .backroads.com)*, although they tend to be somewhat more expensive.

Getting Around

AIR

Flying within California is convenient if your time is limited and you want to cover great distances quickly. Depending on such factors as your departure airport, your destination, the time of year and how far in advance you buy your ticket, air travel can sometimes be less expensive than going by bus, train or rental car.

Besides the big airports in San Francisco and Los Angeles, flights also depart from smaller regional airports, including Sacramento, Oakland, San Jose, San Luis Obispo, Monterey, Burbank, Ontario, Long Beach, Orange County and San Diego.

Major routes with service hourly or better include San Francisco (SF)–Los Angeles (LA), SF–Burbank, SF–Orange County, SF–San Diego, SF–Reno, Oakland–LA and LA–Las Vegas. It's possible to just show up at the airport, buy your ticket and hop on, though the best fares usually require advance purchase. See the Getting There & Away chapter for more about buying tickets – much of the same advice applies.

Airlines offering flights within California include America West, American Airlines, Continental, Delta, Southwest, United Airlines and US Airways (see Airports & Airlines under Air in the Getting There & Away chapter for contact information for these airlines).

BUS

Greyhound is the major long-distance bus company with routes throughout California and to the rest of the USA.

Missing Link Tours (☎ 702-453-7193, 800-209-8586; [w] www.tmltours.com), based in Las Vegas, operates a shuttle to/from Los Angeles up to three times weekly in either direction. Tickets include free pick-up from some area hostels and hotels.

Greyhound

Greyhound (☎ 800-231-2222; [w] www.greyhound.com) runs buses several times daily on major highways between cities, stopping at smaller towns along the way. The actual frequency of service varies but even remote destinations get at least one bus coming through daily. The most popular routes have buses every hour or so, sometimes around the clock.

Greyhound buses are often the cheapest way to cover long distances and are favored by impecunious students, low-budget travelers and those from the less affluent strata of US society. Many middle-class Americans wouldn't dream of 'riding the dog,' but by the standards of most countries services are really quite good.

Generally, buses are clean, comfortable and reliable. Amenities include onboard lavatories, air-conditioning and reclining seats. Smoking is not permitted. Buses break for meals every three to four hours, usually at fast-food restaurants or cafeteria-style truck stops.

Bus stations can be pretty depressing places and are often in unsafe areas of big cities. In small towns, buses stop at a given location, such as a McDonald's, a post office or the Amtrak train station. To board at these stops, know exactly where and when the bus arrives, be emphatic when you flag it down and be prepared to pay the driver with exact change.

Tickets may be bought in person at the terminal, through a ticket agent, over the phone (☎ 800-229-9424) or online with a major credit card. They can be mailed to a US address if purchased at least 10 days in advance or be picked up at the ticket counter with proper identification.

The table over the page lists some sample fares; contact Greyhound for other routes.

Prices listed in the table reflect the unrestricted walk-up fares for adults. Children under 12 pay half price; seniors who join Greyhound's 'Seniors Club' ($5) qualify for 10% off; and students can buy the 'Student Advantage Card' for $22.50 (☎ 877-256-4672; [w] www.studentadvantage.com) to get 15% off regular fares. International student travelers get 10% off by presenting their ISIC card.

Lower fares also apply if you buy your tickets at least seven days in advance. Also check the website for special promotions which become available all the time. For information about Greyhound's Domestic and International Ameripasses, see the Getting There & Away chapter.

Greyhound Bus Routes & Fares

route	fare ($)	duration (hr)	frequency
San Francisco–Los Angeles	42	7½-13½	up to 16 direct buses per day
San Francisco–Truckee	41	5½	up to three buses
San Francisco–Merced (for Yosemite)	29	4-5	four direct buses
San Francisco–Mt Shasta (transfer in Sacramento)	56	8½ & 12	two buses
San Francisco–Red Bluff (for Lassen Volcanic National Park, transfer in Sacramento)	37	6-9½	up to five buses
Los Angeles–San Diego	14	2¼-4¼	hourly buses
Los Angeles–Merced	34	6¼-7½	up to 11 direct buses
Los Angeles–Las Vegas	34	5¼-9	buses hourly between 6am and 11pm

TRAIN

Amtrak (☎ 800-872-7245; ⓦ www.amtrak
.com) operates train services throughout
California, with buses providing connections
to and from rural towns.

A pleasant way to travel between San
Diego and San Luis Obispo (SLO) is aboard
the sleek new double-deck *Pacific Surfliner*
with seating in coach and business class.
All seats have laptop computer outlets, and
there's a café car as well. Up to 11 trains
daily ply the LA–San Diego route (via Anaheim), with four trains continuing north to
Santa Barbara and two of these plunging on
SLO. The trip itself, which hugs the coastline
for much of the way, is a treat because of the
beautiful scenery.

The *Coast Starlight* travels daily between
LA and Seattle. Stops within California
include SLO, Paso Robles, Oakland, Sacramento, Chico, Redding and Dunsmuir.

The *Capitol Corridor* connects San Jose
and Oakland with Sacramento and Auburn
in the Northern Gold Country and has up to
18 departures daily.

The *San Joaquins* heads inland from
Emeryville (near San Francisco) to Bakers-
field via Merced (where buses connect to
Yosemite National Park). From Bakersfield,
there's coach service to Santa Barbara, Las
Vegas, Los Angeles and Anaheim.

California is also served by four interstate trains, which are described in the Getting There & Away chapter. Tickets are
available in person, by phone and online.
Fares depend on the day of travel, the route,
the type of seating and other factors. The

standard fare for travel from LA to Oakland
aboard the *Coast Starlight*, for example,
is $67 (11½ hours). San Diego to Santa
Barbara on the *Pacific Surfliner* costs $31
(5½ hours), and San Francisco (Emeryville)
to Merced on the *San Joaquins* is $29
(three hours). Amtrak's website lets you
check fares and schedules and alerts you to
special offers.

Generally, seniors aged 62 and up qualify
for a 15% discount, while children aged two
to 15 get 50% off standard fares. Students
can also receive a 15% discount, if they first
obtain a **Student Advantage Card** (☎ 877-
256-4672, ⓦ www.studentadvantage.com;
cost $22.50). Fares are generally lower from
January through May and from September
to mid-December.

Reservations can be made any time from
11 months in advance to the day of departure;
reserve as early as possible, because space is
limited and this gives you the best chance at
getting a discount fare.

If you're planning on doing a lot of traveling, look into a rail pass. At the time of
writing, the California Pass entitles you to
unlimited travel for seven days within a 21-
day period throughout the entire state for
$159. The Southern California Pass and
Northern California Pass are good for five
days of travel within a seven-day period in
the respective regions and cost $99.

CAR

Most Californian roads are excellent, and as a
result, motoring can be a pleasant way to tour
the state. It certainly is the most convenient

way to travel and pretty much the only way for close-up explorations of the countryside. A car makes it easy to visit small, rural towns, cross sprawling suburbs and explore wide-open spaces, many of which are hard or impossible to reach by public transport.

For road conditions anywhere in California, call the **California Department of Transportation** (Caltrans; ☎ 800-427-7623).

Three major north-south routes run along the length of California. Hwy 1, known as the Pacific Coast Hwy (PCH), is the most scenic but also the slowest and curviest route, passing by sandy beaches and clinging to rugged cliffs that drop steeply into the ocean.

The inland route Hwy 101 also traverses some nice countryside but is not as spectacular as PCH. Finally, there's I-5, the fastest but most boring route, which cuts through the flat San Joaquin Valley and heads up the center of the state into Oregon.

The two main roads flanking the Sierra Nevada are Hwy 99 on the western side, which runs from south of Sacramento to south of Bakersfield via Merced and Fresno; and Hwy 395, which starts in the Mojave Desert, about two hours northeast of Los Angeles, and runs along the Eastern Sierra to Reno and points farther north.

Major east-west highways include I-80, heading northeast from San Francisco through Reno and on to Salt Lake City; I-15, traveling northeast out of Los Angeles through Las Vegas and on to Salt Lake City; I-40, heading east from Barstow to Flagstaff and the Grand Canyon; I-10, heading east from Los Angeles to Phoenix; and I-8, heading east from San Diego to Tucson.

Road Rules

The *California Driver Handbook* explains everything you need to know about driving in California. It's available free at any office of the Department of Motor Vehicles (DMV) or you can access it (as well as the motorcycle handbook) on the Internet at **w** www.dmv.ca.gov.

Seatbelts must be worn at all times. Children under four years old, or those weighing less than 40lbs, must ride in approved child safety seats.

During winter months, especially at the higher elevations, tire chains may be required on snowy or icy roads. Keep a set of chains in the trunk, since icy or snowy roads are sometimes closed to cars without chains or four-wheel drive. (Note that most rental car companies specifically prohibit the use of chains on their vehicles. You are responsible for any damage due to chains.) Roadside services might be available to attach chains to your tires for a fee (around $20). Other cold-weather precautions include keeping a wool blanket, a windshield ice scraper, a spade or snow shovel, flares and an extra set of gloves and boots in the trunk for emergencies.

A few hints for first-time drivers in California: unless a sign indicates otherwise, you can turn right at a red light, as long as you don't impede intersecting traffic, which has the right of way. At intersections with four-way stop signs, cars proceed in the order in which they arrived. If two cars arrive simultaneously, the one on the right has the right of way. This can be an iffy situation, as opinions may differ over who arrived first, so don't insist on going first, even if it's your right.

On freeways, you may pass slower cars on either the left or the right lane; if two cars are trying to get into the same central lane, the one further to the right has priority. Some freeways and highways have lanes marked with a diamond symbol and the words 'car pool.' These lanes are reserved for cars with two or more passengers. Fines for driving in this lane without the minimum number of people are prohibitively stiff.

If you encounter ambulances with their sirens wailing going in your direction, do everything you safely can to steer over to the right curb and halt until they've passed.

For details about penalties for drinking and driving, see the Legal Matters section in the Facts for the Visitor chapter.

Speed Limits Speed limits, unless posted otherwise, are 35mph (56km/h) on city streets and 65mph (104km/h), sometimes 70mph (112km/h) or even 75mph (120km/h) on interstates, freeways and some highways. Most drivers exceed these limits by a few miles per hour, however. California has a 'Basic Speed Law' that says you may never drive faster than is safe for the present conditions, regardless of the posted speed limit, and tickets can be given for driving too slow as well as for speeding, based on the police officer's assessment of the safe speed.

In cities and residential areas, watch for school zones, where limits can be as low as 15mph when children are present. These speeds are strictly enforced. *Never* pass a school bus when its rear red lights are flashing: it means that children are getting off the bus.

Littering California has an aggressive campaign against littering. If you are seen throwing anything from a vehicle onto the roadway, such as bottles, cans, trash, a lighted cigarette, or anything else, you can be fined as much as $1000. Littering convictions are shown on your driving record the same as other driving violations. Keep any trash with you inside the vehicle until you get to a place to discard it.

Parking Beware colored curbs (red is no parking or stopping, yellow is loading zone, white is five-minute parking for adjacent businesses, green is 10-minute limit from 9am to 6pm, blue is disabled parking), since parking patrols issue tickets relentlessly. If you're parked at a meter, be sure to feed it enough coins: fines may be as much as $30 for simply being 30 seconds late in returning to your vehicle. Always study signposts for restrictions. Parking on residential streets, especially those near nightlife areas, is often reserved for residents. Be sure to keep your vehicle off the road during street cleaning hours – usually early on a weekday morning – which are posted as well. And of course, don't block driveways or park too close to fire hydrants or bus stops.

American Automobile Association

If you'll be doing much driving, whether in your own vehicle, someone else's or in a rental car, membership in the American Automobile Association (AAA, called 'triple A'; ☎ 800-874-7532; W www.aaa.com) is an excellent thing to have. Having a AAA card entitles you to free 24-hour roadside emergency service anywhere in the US (☎ 800-222-4357) in the event of an accident, breakdown or locking your keys in the car. AAA also dispenses free maps, tour books and other travel literature, gives advice on how to buy a used car, sells reasonably priced car insurance, and runs a travel agency and other services.

The AAA membership card may entitle you to discounts for lodging, car rental and admission charges. AAA offices are found throughout California and the rest of the country. Call or check the website for addresses. The cost of AAA membership varies slightly by city but should be around $65 for the first year, $45 per year thereafter; additional family members are $20 each.

Members of foreign AAA affiliates, like the Automobile Association in the UK or the ADAC in Germany, are entitled to the same services as AAA members if they bring along their membership cards.

Rental

Renting a car is good value if you want to get around quickly and easily, especially with two or more people to share the costs. Most of the big international rental companies have desks at the airports, in all major cites and most smaller towns. To check rates or make reservations, you can also contact the companies on their toll-free number or online:

Alamo (☎ 800-327-9633, W www.alamo.com)
Avis (☎ 800-831-2847, W www.avis.com)
Budget (☎ 800-527-0700, W www.budget.com)
Dollar (☎ 800-800-4000, W www.dollar.com
Enterprise (☎ 800-325-8007, W www.enterprise .com)
Hertz (☎ 800-654-3131, W www.hertz.com
National (☎ 800-328-4567, W www.nationalcar .com)
Rent-A-Wreck (☎ 800-535-1391, W www.rent-a-wreck.com)
Thrifty (☎ 800-367-2277, W www.thrifty.com)

You must have a drivers' license in order to rent a car and many companies also require you to have a credit card. Prices vary widely, depending on such factors as the type of car, the rental location (big cities are cheaper), the drop-off location, the number of drivers etc. Costs are highest in summer and around major holiday periods, when demand is high. In general, expect to pay from $30 to $50 per day, $150 to $250 per week for a mid-size car, more in peak season and for larger cars. Most rental agencies require that drivers be at least 21; drivers under 25 must normally pay a surcharge of $5 to $15 per day. Rates usually include unlimited mileage but not the sales tax or insurance other than basic liability.

You may be able to get better rates when pre-booking from your home country. If you get a fly-drive package, local taxes may be an extra charge when you collect the car. Several online travel reservation networks have up-to-the-minute information on car rental rates at all the main airports. Compare their rates with any fly-drive package you're considering.

Liability insurance is required by law, but is usually not automatically included in California rental contracts because many Americans are covered for rental cars under their own car liability insurance. Check your policy carefully and don't pay extra if you're already covered. If you're not, expect to pay about $11 per day. Foreign visitors should check their travel insurance policy to see if it covers any rental car risks.

Insurance against damage to the car itself, called Collision Damage Waiver (CDW) or Loss Damage Waiver (LDW) is usually optional ($12 to $15 per day), but may still require you to pay for the first $100 to $500 of any repairs (called the 'deductible').

Some credit cards, such as American Express or the gold and platinum versions of MasterCard and Visa, cover your CDW for rentals up to 15 days, provided you charge the entire cost of the rental to the card. Check with your credit card company to determine if this service is offered and the extent of coverage.

Purchase

If you'll be in the US for three months or longer, purchasing a car is worth considering, but for shorter periods car rentals are probably cheaper and certainly less hassle.

Cars bought from a dealer cost more but may come with warranties and/or financing options. Dealers are often concentrated in certain areas, so you can look at lots of vehicles in a short time and compare prices.

Buying from an individual is usually cheaper; look in the newspaper classified ads or special ad publications for used vehicles. Private sellers will be spread all over the town or city, so you'll need a car to look for a car. Bargaining when buying a used car is standard practice.

Check the *Kelley Blue Book* (available at public libraries, bookstores or online at w www.kbb.com) for the official value of the model and year of the vehicle you're considering and have it checked out by a mechanic or diagnostic service before you buy. Inspect the title carefully; the owner's name that appears on the title must match the identification of the person selling you the car. Also be sure that the car's emissions have been tested and ask the seller for the 'smog certificate' that verifies that the vehicle meets California standards.

If you buy from an individual, you must register the vehicle with any DMV office within 10 days of purchase. Take the smog certificate, proof of insurance, along with the ownership title (the 'pink slip') and bill of sale. If you buy from a dealer, you can usually skip the DMV: the paperwork is done for you and the registration follows in the mail.

As your departure from the USA approaches, set aside time to sell the car. Rather than sell it to a used-car dealer for a pittance, take out an ad in a local newspaper or advertise it in hostels, at universities, supermarkets and other such places. Be sure to officially notify the DMV that you've sold the vehicle, or you may be held liable for someone else's parking tickets.

Every owner or driver of a motor vehicle must 'maintain financial responsibility' to protect the health and property of others in case of an accident by having auto liability insurance.

If you buy a car, you must take out liability insurance, and this can be difficult if you don't have a local license. A car dealer or the AAA (see earlier in this chapter) may be able to suggest an insurer. Even with a local license, insurance can be expensive and difficult to obtain if you don't have evidence of a safe driving record. Bring copies of your home auto insurance policies if they can help to establish that you are a good risk.

Recreational Vehicles

A recreational vehicle, or RV, is fitted out for sleeping and eating. RVs are very popular for travel in California and campgrounds with hookups for electricity and water are ubiquitous, although not in big cities. RVs are more expensive than cars to rent or buy, and they're bulky and not as economical to drive, but they solve all your transport, accommodation and cooking needs. Companies renting RVs and campervans include **Cruise America**

(☎ 800-327-7799; W *www.cruiseamerica*
.com) and LA-based **Happy Travel Camper
Rental & Sales** *(☎ 310-675-1335, 800-370-
1262;* W *www.camperusa.com).*

Ride-Sharing
If you're looking for someone to ride with
to share the cost of fuel, ask around, post
a notice in hostels, check the ride boards
at universities or the newspaper classified
ads. Hostels can be especially good places
to find riders, not only for long trips but
also for sharing car rental costs for local
day trips.

MOTORCYCLE
Riding a bike in America is an almost
mythic experience, with a heritage going
back beyond *Easy Rider* and *The Wild One.*
You'll need a valid motorcycle license,
and an International Driving Permit en-
dorsed for motorcycles will simplify the
rental process.

The free *California Motorcycle Handbook,* which details the rules of the road for
motorcyclists, may be picked up free from
any DMV office or online at W www.dmv
.ca.gov. Helmets are mandatory for all riders.
Motorcycles of less than 150cc engine size
may not be driven on freeways.

Motorcycle rentals and insurance are not
cheap, especially if you've got your eye on a
Harley-Davidson. **EagleRider** *(☎ 310-536-
6777, 888-900-9901;* W *www.eaglerider
.com)* has rental outlets in San Francisco, Los
Angeles, San Diego, Santa Barbara, San Jose,
Palm Springs and Las Vegas. It charges $75
to $135 per day for a Harley, depending on
the rental location, the size of the bike and the
length of the rental. Rates include a helmet or
two, unlimited miles and liability insurance,
but collision insurance (CDW) is extra.

BICYCLE
Bicycling is a great way to travel around
California. It's nonpolluting and inexpensive, you'll be well exercised and also have
your own transport at your destination. The
downside is that the distances involved
make it hard to cover a lot of territory
quickly and some of the more mountainous
regions require a very high level of fitness.

Bicycles may be rented by the hour, day
week or month. They can be bought new at
sporting goods stores, discount warehouse

stores and bicycle shops, or used at flea
markets and from notice boards at hostels;
you could also check the newspaper classified ads. Prices, of course, vary drastically
depending on what you get.

Books and other publications on cycling
and route planning are available at bookstores, bicycle shops and tourist offices. See
the Activities chapter for some suggestions.

Bicycling is allowed on all roads and
highways and even on freeways if there's
no suitable alternative, such as a smaller
parallel road. All mandatory exits are
marked. It is, for instance, possible to bicycle on the I-5 all the way from the Oregon border to just north of Los Angeles.
With few exceptions, there's no mountain
biking in wilderness areas and in national
parks, although cycling on the main roads is
fine. Bicycles, including mountain bikes,
are allowed on national forest and BLM
single-track trails. Trail etiquette requires
that cyclists yield to other users.

The California Department of Transportation (Caltrans) publishes bicycle maps of the
northern and central (but not southern) parts
of the state and will mail them to you free of
charge. Contact ☎ 916-653-0036, ☎ 614-
688-2597 or ☎ 510-286-5598. Another excellent source for maps, bike routes, gadgets
and more is the **Adventure Cycling Association** *(☎ 416-721-1776, 800-775-2453).* Also
check its website at W www.adv-cycling.org.

If you plan a long bicycling trip and get
tired of pedaling, or if you want to avoid
the hilliest spots or bad weather, you can
always take your bike along on public transport. Some local bus services have buses
equipped with bike racks; for more details
call the companies' telephone numbers provided throughout this book.

Greyhound carries bicycles as luggage
provided the bicycle is disassembled and
placed in a special bike box sold at stations
for $15.

Amtrak will also transport bicycles a
checked baggage, but again they must be
broken down to fit into their boxes available
for $10 at the stations. Some trains on the
*San Joaquins, Pacific Surfliner, Coast Star
light* and *Capitol Corridor* routes have car
with bicycle storage areas. Check specific
when making a reservation.

Most airlines will carry boxed bicycles a
sporting equipment for no additional cost

Some carriers, however, impose an over-size-baggage charge for bikes that aren't disassembled first – check details with the airline before buying your ticket.

Helmets may not be chic or may do funny things to your hair but, let's face it, wearing one simply makes good sense. For those under 18, helmets are not optional. If you're pedaling around at night, you'll need a headlight and reflectors; wearing reflective or bright clothing is a good idea, too. Carry water with you, and a repair kit in case of a flat tire or other problem.

Bicycle theft is big business, so use a heavy-duty bicycle lock, some of which even come with theft insurance. Etch your driver's license number or other ID onto the frame of your bike. It takes only a few minutes to do, and most police stations have etching equipment available. Then register your bicycle with the police.

HITCHHIKING

Hitching is never entirely safe anywhere in the world and is not recommended. Travelers undeterred by the potential risk should be aware that on the whole, hitchhiking is uncommon in modern-day America and hitchers are generally viewed with suspicion. Few motorists are willing to stop for a thumb. Use extreme caution, both when hitchhiking and picking up hitchhikers.

At the risk of sounding sexist, women should never hitchhike alone or even with another woman. Drivers are often reluctant to pick up lone men, so a man and a woman together have the best chance of getting a ride and of being safe. You can hitchhike on roads and highways; on freeways you must stand at the on-ramp. The best method for hitching a ride might be to ask someone pulling into a gas station; this also allows you to check out the person (and vice versa). Be prepared for more refusals than offers.

BOAT

Boating is not an option for getting around California, although there are a few local services, notably to Santa Catalina Island off the coast of Los Angeles. On San Francisco Bay, ferry routes operate between San Francisco and Sausalito, Tiburon, Larkspur, Oakland, Alameda and Vallejo. Some small ferries and water taxis operate in San Diego Bay. Details are given in the appropriate chapters.

PUBLIC TRANSPORT

Cities and larger towns have local bus systems, but many are designed for commuter service and provide limited service in the evening, sometimes none at all on weekends. These services are discussed in the geographical chapters.

Bay Area Rapid Transit (BART) is an underground (and underwater) train network around the San Francisco Bay Area. Metro Rail is Los Angeles' budding subway system, while Metro Link is a system of commuter trains linking LA with the surrounding counties. *Coaster* commuter trains operate along the coast of San Diego county from Oceanside to downtown.

Other local trains, some of them historic, operate primarily as tourist attractions. Notable among these are the *Skunk Train* between Willits and Fort Bragg; the *Blue Goose* from Yreka to Montague; the *Napa Valley Wine Train* between Napa and St Helena; the *Santa Cruz, Big Trees & Pacific Railway* from Felton to Santa Cruz; the *Mother Lode Cannon Ball* operating from Jamestown in the Gold Country and the *Sacramento Southern Railroad* from Sacramento to Hood.

Taxis are metered, with charges from $1.50 to $2.50 at flag fall, plus $1.20 to $1.80 per mile. There may be an extra charge for handling baggage and drivers expect a 10% to 15% tip. If you don't spot a taxi cruising, you can phone for one; look under 'Taxi' in the Yellow Pages.

ORGANIZED TOURS

Tours run the gamut from white-water rafting through remote wilderness areas to sightseeing tours of major attractions in the urban centers. Whether you go on a long-distance tour lasting several days, a local sightseeing tour of a few hours or a theme tour (such as wine tasting or horseback riding), tours are often an easy and efficient way to get around, especially if time is limited. Travel agents and tourist offices have bundles of information and brochures about tours; specific tours are also mentioned throughout this book. Longer tours are mentioned in the Getting There & Away chapter.

San Francisco

Head up to San Francisco's Twin Peaks on a clear summer evening and you'll see a postcard-perfect view: rows of Victorian houses stretching over more than 40 hills, a curvaceous bay speckled with sailboats, two of the world's best-loved bridges, and perhaps a few harmless shreds of the city's famous fog colored in shades of red and pink by the setting sun. It's easy to see why San Francisco consistently tops the polls as America's favorite city. No other city in the US can offer such a seductive sight.

Like all great cities, San Francisco (population 801,400) is an amalgam of distinct neighborhoods – vital urban pockets hidden among the hills, compressed into the 7mi by 7mi thumbnail of a peninsula. Colorful, crowded and frenetic Chinatown jostles up against ritzy Union Square and quickly fades to the bars, cafés and Italian restaurants of North Beach, the Beat center of the 1950s. North Beach blends into Fisherman's Wharf, an unapologetic tourist center and jumping-off point for Alcatraz. A hike up hoity-toity Nob Hill segues down to the troubled Tenderloin, which is itself adjacent to the theater district, the swank department stores of Union Square and the sleek towers of the Financial District. South of Market (SoMa) offers its own contrasts – a busy warehouse district during the day, nightclub central after dark. The Mission District, a Latino enclave interspersed with hip bars and restaurants, also embodies several personalities. The nearby Castro was claimed by gays in the 1970s, and it remains predominantly gay today, though projecting an assured, almost mainstream, air.

San Francisco is not a cheap place to live or visit. Hotel rates can be quite high, and if you're not careful, you could easily drop a week's wages during a splashy night on the town. Residents have felt the crunch too. During the dot-com boom of the 1990s, housing prices reached astronomical heights, driving many longtime residents out of the city. The dot-com boom has abated in recent years, yet housing rates are still among the nation's highest. You can't just drop in here expecting to live on the cheap the way many folks did back in the hippie and Beat days – or even just a decade or two ago.

Highlights

- A perfect Sunday – art at San Francisco Museum of Modern Art, live music and a picnic at Yerba Buena Gardens
- The zany Bay to Breakers race at the end of May – over 100,000 costumed (and un-costumed) runners
- The (colorful) streets of San Francisco – Haight St, Mission St, Castro St, Grant Ave and Columbus Ave
- Folsom St Fair – leather, whips and naked strutting
- World-class movie houses – the Castro Theatre, the Roxie and the Balboa

San Francisco
pages 104-115

Nonetheless, despite the roller-coaster economy, the city still abounds with creative energy, much of this fed by the richness of its diverse cultures and lifestyles. You can see it in the various museums, galleries and performances around town, or by just walking down the streets of neighborhoods such as Chinatown, the Mission, North Beach and the Haight. Perhaps the aspect of San Francisco life that best reflects this cultural exchange is the vast diversity of its cuisine. The city is one of the world's great dining centers, with everything from Mexican and Asian cheap eats to stylish restaurants that liberally mix traditions from every continent on the planet. Sit down, dig in and enjoy the feast.

HISTORY

San Francisco is a new city. Though the Miwok and Ohlone Indians settled the area around 1100 BC, it was less than 250 years ago that San Francisco Bay was 'discovered' by Gaspar de Portolá. In 1769 Portolá and his party had been sent north from San Diego to establish a Spanish mission at Monterey Bay, which Sebastián Vizcaíno, an earlier Spanish explorer, had described as a 'fine, enclosed harbor.' Portolá actually found Monterey Bay, but because the bay did not match Vizcaíno's description, Portolá's party continued north. In early November 1769 a detachment of the expedition, led by Sergeant José Ortega, first set eyes on San Francisco Bay. Realizing they had gone too far, Portolá turned back.

In 1772 a second party led by Don Pedro Fages and Father Juan Crespi set off from the recently built mission in Monterey to have a better look at the bay Ortega had discovered. They were understandably impressed by what they saw; as Crespi noted, 'It is a harbor such that not only the navy of our most Catholic Majesty but those of all Europe could take shelter in it.' The Spanish returned in 1775, when Juan Manuel de Ayala sailed into the bay and became the first European to enter what was later nicknamed the 'Golden Gate.' The following year the presidio was built just above the Golden Gate, and the Misión San Francisco de Asís (Mission Dolores) was established 3mi south, at a site that today is in the heart of the Mission District.

The mission settlement never really prospered: the soil was sandy and difficult to farm, the presidio rarely exceeded 20 soldiers and the harbor saw little trade. Not until Mexico gained its independence from Spain did the local economy, based on the hide and tallow trade, begin to show some life. Trading posts, houses, grocery stores and grog shops appeared on the slopes that rose from the bay.

In 1846 war broke out between the US and Mexico. With the American victory in the Mexican War, Mexico ceded the land to the US – excellent timing, because gold was discovered in 1848 in the nearby Sierra Nevada foothills. Almost overnight the sleepy village of Yerba Buena, newly renamed San Francisco, grew into a full-fledged city. By 1850, the year California was admitted as the 31st state in the union, San Francisco's population had exploded from 800 to 25,000 people. The newcomers, called '49ers, were mostly men under the age of 40. To keep them entertained, some 500 saloons and 20 theaters opened in the space of five years, not to mention casinos and bordellos, opium dens and distilleries. Certain sin-loving streets in the vicinity of the port (now the northeastern edge of the Financial District) were well on their way to earning the sobriquet 'Barbary Coast,' a reference to the pirate-plagued coast of North Africa, home to the Berbers.

San Francisco remained a world-class hotbed of murder and mayhem until April 18, 1906, when the 'Big One' – an earthquake estimated at 8.3 on the yet-to-be-invented Richter scale – and dozens of ensuing fires leveled more than half the city and killed over 3000 people. The earthquake destroyed much of the red-light district, giving the city an opportunity to rebuild itself. San Francisco rapidly developed into a bustling modern city. In 1915 San Francisco hosted the Panama-Pacific Exposition, allowing it to flaunt its stylish new image.

San Francisco still suffered through the Great Depression and, like other cities, gigantic public-works projects were undertaken in an attempt to yank the economy out of the doldrums. The Bay Area certainly got its money's worth from these 1930s projects; the Bay Bridge, built in 1936, and the Golden Gate Bridge, built the following year, are still magnificent symbols of the city.

During WWII, the Bay Area became a major launching pad for military operations in the Pacific and huge shipyards soon sprang up around the bay.

The decades that followed were marked by the prominence of colorful subcultures: the Beats spearheaded the '50s counterculture, and the hippies followed in the '60s. Marijuana and LSD were the drugs of choice, accompanied by guitar-driven rock music, long hair and 'flower power.' In January 1967 an estimated 20,000 'hippies' – the term was originally a put-down coined by the now-older beatniks who didn't dig these younger hipsters – congregated in Golden Gate Park for a free concert, kicking off the 'Summer of Love.'

Across the bay, however, peace and love were not the order of the day. While hippies in the Haight were tripping, grooving and wearing flowers in their hair, Berkeley revolutionaries were leading the worldwide student upheavals of the late '60s, slugging it out with the cops and the university administration over civil rights. In Oakland, Bobby Seale and Huey Newton founded the Black Panther Party for Self-Defense, the most militant of the groups involved in the black-power movement of that era.

After the realignments and upheavals of the '60s, the '70s were comparatively relaxed. The hippies had led a sexual revolution but it was a predominantly heterosexual one; a homosexual revolution followed in the '70s, as San Francisco's gays stepped decisively out of the closet. Gay Pride became a rallying call, and the previously underground homosexual community 'came out' in all its glory.

The 1980s were not especially kind to San Francisco. The first cases of AIDS – at the time known as GRID or Gay-Related Immune Deficiency – were reported in 1981. By the end of the 1980s, AIDS had claimed thousands of lives. The late 1980s witnessed yet another startling catastrophe – the Loma Prieta earthquake, which struck on 17 October 1989. It measured 7.1 on the Richter scale, and its damage was far-reaching. A section of the Bay Bridge was damaged, parts of the Marina District crumpled and burned and, in the quake's worst disaster, a double-decker section of I-880 in Oakland collapsed, killing 42 people.

The 1990s ushered in one of the city's great periods of growth, the economy driven sky-high by a plethora of start-up Web businesses and other dot-com delights. The get-rich-quick delirium helped boost the city's restaurant and nightclub industry too, and older neighborhoods – the Mission being a prime example – were soon inundated with new businesses and an increasingly yuppie clientele. This remarkable growth trend didn't last; by the late 1990s, dot-coms were going bust, unemployment levels were rising and the economy was shaking all over. Things have thankfully leveled off, and today everyone – employers and employees, restaurateurs and habitual clubgoers – seems a bit wiser from the experience.

ORIENTATION

San Francisco is one of the most compact cities in the US, an area of approximately 46 sq mi covering the tip of a 30mi-long

Scenic 49-Mile Drive

Make some stops along the way, and the 49-Mile Scenic Drive could take you all day. Devised for the 1939–40 Treasure Island Exposition, the drive covers almost all the city's highlights, from Coit Tower to the Golden Gate Bridge. Although the route is well signposted with instantly recognizable seagull signs, a map and an alert navigator are still helpful. Pick up a map at the San Francisco Visitors Information Center.

peninsula, with the Pacific Ocean on one side and San Francisco Bay on the other. The city can be neatly divided into three sections. The central part resembles a slice of pie, with Van Ness Ave and Market St marking the two sides and the Embarcadero marking the rounded edge of the pie. Squeezed into this compact slice are the Union Square area, the Financial District, the Civic Center area, Chinatown, North Beach, Nob Hill, Russian Hill and Fisherman's Wharf.

To the south of Market St lies the South of Market (SoMa) area, an upwardly mobile warehouse zone. SoMa fades into the Mission, the city's Latino quarter, and then the Castro, the city's gay quarter.

The third and final part of the city is physically the largest – the long sweep from Van Ness Ave all the way to the Pacific Ocean. It's a varied area encompassing upscale neighborhoods such as the Marina and Pacific Heights, suburban zones such as the Richmond and Sunset districts and areas with flavors all of their own, such as Japantown, the Fillmore and the Haight. The city's three great parks – the Presidio, Lincoln Park and Golden Gate Park – are also here.

Maps

Quality maps of San Francisco are available from bookstores, but giveaway maps available from a variety of sources are generally adequate for most visitors. The best of the free maps is the *San Francisco Street Map & Visitor Guide*, available at many of the city's hotels. If you're going to explore the city by public transportation, the MUNI (San Francisco Municipal Railway) *Street & Transit Map* is a smart $2 investment.

Get a copy at the Visitors Information Center or any large bookstore. The **Rand McNally Map Store** *(Map 2; ☎ 415-777-3131; cnr Market & 2nd Sts)* is a good place to pick up maps.

For convenience and durability, Lonely Planet publishes a laminated San Francisco street map ($6). Bay Area street atlases with greater detail are published by **Thomas Bros Maps** *(☎ 415-981-7520; cnr Jackson St & Columbus Ave)*.

INFORMATION
Tourist Offices
In the heart of the city, a stone's throw from Union Square and by the most popular cable car turnaround, is the **San Francisco Visitors Information Center** *(Map 2; ☎ 415-391-2000, fax 415-227-2602; w www.sfvisitor .org; lower level, Hallidie Plaza, cnr Market & Powell Sts; open 8:30am-5pm Mon-Fri, 9am-3pm Sat & Sun)*. Here you can get maps, guidebooks, brochures and phonecards.

The center has a 24-hour phone service offering recorded information on major entertainment, sports and special events in English *(☎ 415-391-2001)*, French *(☎ 415-391-2003)*, German *(☎ 415-391-2004)*, Italian *(☎ 415-391-2002)*, Japanese *(☎ 415-391-2101)* and Spanish *(☎ 415-391-2122)*.

The local AAA (American Automobile Association) office, here called the **California State Automobile Association** *(☎ 415-565-2141; 150 Van Ness Ave)*, can help members with maps and hotel reservations.

Money
Banks are ubiquitous in San Francisco and usually offer the best rates for currency exchange. At San Francisco International Airport, there are currency exchange offices on the third level of the International Terminal run by **Travelex** *(☎ 650-821-0900; open 6:30am-10pm daily)*.

Post & Telephone
Mail can be sent to you at the **Civic Center post office** *(Map 2; ☎ 415-563-7284, 800-725-2161; 101 Hyde St)*. It should be marked c/o General Delivery, Civic Center Post Office, 101 Hyde St, San Francisco, CA 94142, USA. There's also a post office on Union Square in the basement of Macy's department store *(open 10am-5:30pm Mon-Sat, 11am-5pm Sun)*.

Public phones usually cost between 35¢ and 50¢ for local calls, more if you're calling to Marin County, the East Bay or the Peninsula. The cheapest and most convenient method is to use a phonecard, available from most grocery and drug stores.

San Francisco and Marin County are within the ☎ 415 area code. The area code for the East Bay (including Berkeley and Oakland) is ☎ 510; for the Peninsula and Palo Alto it's ☎ 650; and for San Jose it's ☎ 408.

Email & Internet Access
The city's public libraries are equipped to allow Internet and email access, though for most you need a California library card. An exception is the **Main Library** *(Map 2; ☎ 415-557-4400; cnr Larkin & Grove Sts)*, near the Civic Center BART (Bay Area Rapid Transit)/MUNI station, which has six 'express' terminals on the 1st floor available for 15 minutes on a first-come, first-served basis. Library staff also can provide information on Internet access throughout the city, as can the folks at the Visitors Information Center.

Free Web access is available at **CompUSA** *(Map 2; ☎ 415-391-9778; 750 Market St)*. Far nicer, however, are the various Internet cafés scattered around town. Downtown try **Cafe.com** *(Map 2; ☎ 415-922-5322; 970 Market St)*, which charges $7 per hour. In the Haight, **Quetzal** *(Map 2; ☎ 415-673-4181; 1234 Polk St)* charges $10 per hour. The Castro District's **CHAT Cafe** *(Map 5; cnr 18th & Sanchez Sts)* offers free high-speed Internet access to its customers.

Travel Agencies
Good travel agencies include **STA Travel** *(☎ 415- 391-8407, 800-781-4040; w http:// statravel.com; 36 Geary Blvd • ☎ 415-421-3473; 530 Bush St)*, which specializes in cheap tickets for students and nonstudents.

Bookstores
Many city bookstores are open late, and several hold excellent readings. The city's most famous bookstore, **City Lights Bookstore** *(Map 3; ☎ 415-362-8193; 261 Columbus Ave, North Beach)*, was the first paperbacks-only store in the US. It was also the center of the Beat scene in the '50s and is still owned by its founder, Lawrence Ferlinghetti.

[Continued on page 116]

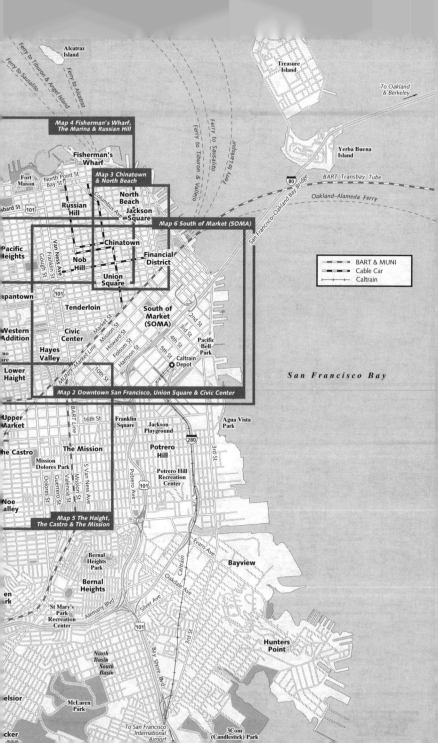

MAP 2 DOWNTOWN SAN FRANCISCO, UNION SQUARE & CIVIC CENTER

see MAP 3
CHINATOWN &
NORTH BEACH

North
Beach

Chinatown

Powell-Hyde St Cable Car Line

Powell-Mason Cable Car Line

Powell-Mason & Powell-Hyde St Cable Car Lines

Powell-Hyde St Cable Car Line

Mini
Park

Vallejo St
Broadway
Pacific Ave
Broadway
Pacific Ave
Jackson St
Clay St
Sacramento St
Clay St
California St
Pine St
Bush St
Sutter St
Post St
Geary St
O'Farrell St
Ellis St

Vallejo St
Broadway
Pacific Ave

Van Ness Ave
Polk St
Larkin St
Hyde St
Leavenworth St
Jones St
Taylor St
Mason St
Powell St
Stockton St
Grant Ave
Column

Stockton St
Clay St
Joice St

Chinese
Playground

Ports
P.

Chinese
Playground

California St Cable Car Lines

Grace
Cathedral

Huntington
Park

Nob Hill

Lafayette Park

Sacramento St
California St

California St
Cable Car
Turnaround

Pine St

Bush St

Sutter St

Post St

Geary St

Union
Square

Stockton Tunnel

Maiden

Tenderloin

Geary Blvd
Post St
Geary St
O'Farrell St
Ellis St
Eddy St
Turk St

Olive St
Willow St

Powell St
Cable Car
Turnaround

Hallidie
Plaza

Bloomin
Powell St BA
& MUNI Stat
San Francisco
Shopping
Centre

Jefferson
Square
Turk Blvd
Hayward
Playground
Golden Gate Ave

Eddy St
Larch St
Turk St
Elm St
Redwood St

Opera
Plaza

Federal
Building

Golden Gate Ave

Civic
Center

Market St

Mary St

Minna St
Natoma St
Russ St
Moss St
Sherman St
Columbi

Howard St
Tehama St
6th St

Mission St
Stevenson St

Langton St
Ringold St
9th St

State
Building

State
Building
Court
House

Veterans
Building
War
Memorial
Opera
House

City
Hall

Health
Department

Davies
Symphony
Hall

AAA

Ballet
Association

Ballet
Association

McAllister St
Ash St
Fulton St
Birch St
Grove St
Ivy St
Hayes St
Linden St
Fell St
Hickory St
Hayes St

McAllister St

Civic Center
Plaza

Main
Library

Bill Graham
Civic Auditorium

State
Building

Federal
Building

United
Nations
Plaza

Civic Center
BART & MUNI Station

McAllister St
Grove St
Hayes St
Ivy St

South of
Market
(SOMA)

Van Ness
MUNI
Station

Hayes
Valley

11th St
Mission St
Grace St
Dore Alley
10th St
Washburn St

12th St
Otis St
S Van Ness Ave
Folsom St
Ringold St
Kissling St
11th St

MUNI Metro

Lily St
Page St
Rose St
Haight St

Central Fwy
BART
Market St

Laguna St
Gough St
Valencia St
McCoppin St
Lafayette St
Guerrero St

see MAP 5 THE HAIGHT,
THE CASTRO &
THE MISSION

0   150   300m
0   150   300yd

Walton Park
Jackson St
Pier 1
Bostonship Plaza
Pier 1/2
Ferry To Oakland/Alameda
Embarcadero Center
Justin Herman Plaza
Ferry Building
Ferry Terminal Plaza
Clay St
Drumm St
Davis St
Redwood Park
Sacramento St
Transamerica Pyramid
Financial District
California St Cable Car Turnaround
Pier 2
California St
San Francisco Bay
Bank of California Building
Halleck St
Front St
To Oakland & Berkeley
Pine St
Bank of America Building
Embarcadero BART & MUNI Station
Rincon Center
Rincon Tower
Bush St
Market St
Battery St
Sansome St
Belden Al
Claude Ln
Crocker Galleria
Montgomery BART & MUNI Station
New Montgomery St
1st St
2nd St
Ecker St
Jessie St
Stevenson St
Annie St
Mission St
Beale St
Main St
Spear St
Steuart St
Folsom St MUNI Station
Howard St
Fremont St
Pier 22½
Pier 24
San Francisco-Oakland Bay Bridge
80
Minna St
Natoma St
Trenton St
Clementina St
Pier 26
Pier 28
South of Market (SOMA)
Harrison St
Folsom St
Pier 30
Pier 32
Yerba Buena Gardens
Hawthorne St
Howard St
3rd St
Pier 34
Brannan St MUNI Station
George R Moscone Convention Center
Folsom St
Shipley St
Clara St
Harrison St
80
e MAP 6 SOUTH MARKET (SOMA)
4th St
5th St
6th St
Harriet St
Bluxome St
Townsend St
Brannan St
7th St
Caltrain

PLACES TO STAY	PLACES TO EAT	OTHER
4 Pacific Tradewinds Guest House	1 Hyde Street Bistro	2 Cable Car Barn & Museum
10 Hyatt Regency; Equinox	3 Redwood Park	7 Wells Fargo History Museum
13 Nob Hill Inn	5 Palio Paninoteca	8 Museum of Money of the American West
14 Huntington Hotel	6 Rubicon	26 Russ Building
15 Fairmont Hotel; Tonga Room	9 Aqua	27 Pacific Stock Exchange
16 Mark Hopkins Inter-Continental; Top of the Mark	11 Swan Oyster Depot	29 101 California St Building
17 Renaissance Stanford Court Hotel	12 Cordon Bleu	49 Children's Fountain
19 Hotel Triton; Café de la Presse	18 Masa's	50 Folk Art International Building
28 Mandarin Oriental San Francisco	20 Café Claude	51 Lotta's Fountain
30 Petite Auberge	21 Tomato & Basil	53 Hobart Building
31 White Swan Inn	23 Plouf	54 Rand McNally Map Store
32 Sheehan Hotel	24 Café Bastille	69 Macy's
33 Golden Gate Hotel	25 Sam's Grill and Seafood Restaurant	70 Neiman-Marcus
34 Grant Hotel	40 Borobudur	72 CompUSA
37 York Hotel	41 Fleur de Lys	74 Glide Memorial United Methodist Church
39 Commodore Hotel; Red Room	44 Farallon	77 San Francisco Visitors Information Center
42 Dakota Hotel	46 Sears Fine Foods	81 Civic Center Post Office
43 Hotel Beresford	59 Dottie's True Blue Cafe	86 Asian Art Museum
45 Inn at Union Square	61 Grand Café	
47 Sir Francis Drake Hotel; Scala's Bistro; Harry Denton's Starlight Room	63 Postrio	
48 Grand Hyatt San Francisco	84 Stars	
52 Palace Hotel; Pied Piper Bar	88 Jardinière	
56 Days Inn	89 Vicolo	
57 Hotel Beresford Arms	90 Caffè delle Stelle	
60 Adelaide Hostel	93 Zuni Cafe	
62 Clift Hotel; Redwood Room		
63 Diva Hotel	CAFÉS	
66 Maxwell Hotel	36 Quetzal	
67 Westin St Francis Hotel; Compass Rose	38 Cup-A-Joe	
68 HI San Francisco Downtown	83 Cafe.com	
73 HI San Francisco City Center	BARS & CLUBS	
75 Globetrotters Inn	22 Carnelian Room	
76 Hotel Bijou	35 Hemlock Tavern	
79 Embassy Hotel	55 Edinburgh Castle	
80 Phoenix Motel; Backflip	58 Blue Lamp	
82 Central YMCA Hotel	65 Biscuits & Blues	
85 Abigail Hotel; Millennium	72 Great American Music Hall	
87 Aida Hotel	78 John's Grill	
92 New Central Hostel	91 Hayes & Vine	

Pier 23
Pier 19
Pier 21
Pier 17
Pier 15
Pier 9
Whaleship Plaza

Pier 27

MUNI Metro
Davis St
Front St

Bostonship Plaza
Walton Park

The Embarcadero (Herb Caen Way...)

Lewis Plaza

●6

Front St

Green St
John Maher St
Battery St
Vallejo St
Broadway
Pacific Ave

Jackson Square

Custom House Place

Battery St

Ice House Alley

Sansome St

Cold St

Hotaling

Lombard St

Sansome St

Osgood Pl

37 ▼

Greenwich Steps
Filbert Steps
Alta St
Calhoun Terrace

Bartol St

Montgomery St

Darrell Steps

Montgomery St

Vallejo Steps

29 ▼ Broadway

Pioneer Park

Castle St

Dunnes Al

28 ■

William Saroyan Place

35 ☐

36 ☐

Sentinel Building ▲ 40

Colt Tower
Telegraph Hill

Kearny St

Fresno St

27 ▼

38 ▼

39 ▼

41 ▼

Telegraph Hill Blvd

Genoa Pl

Sonoma St

11 ▼

Romolo St

26 ●

Columbus Ave

33 ●

34 ☐

Beckett St

Kearny St

Varennes St

Union St

Green St

21 ☐

Jack Kerouac Alley

Grant Ave

Child St

Grant Ave

Bannam Pl

Church of Saint Francis of Assisi

19 ▼

20 ☐ ☐ 23

22 ▼

25 ▼

Broadway

32 ■

Filbert St

Jasper Pl

▼15

■16

17 ☐

18 ☐

Vallejo St

Stockton St

Cordelia St

31 ▼

North Beach

14 🏛

2 ▼

3 ■

▼ 4

☐ 5

Saints Peter & Paul Church

Washington Square

▼ 7

▼ 9

Turk Murphy La

30 ☐

Stockton St

▼ 8

10 ▼

12 ▼

13 ☐

24 ☐

Powell St

John St

Chestnut St
Fielding St
Lombard St

Powell St

Via Buffano

North Beach Playground

Columbus Ave

Mason St

Venard Al

● 1 Scotland St

Powell-Mason Cable Car

Russian Hill

Broadway Robert Levy Tunnel

Mason St

Jansen St

Filbert St

Valparaiso St

Union St

Green St

Ina Coolbrith Park

Vallejo St Steps

Taylor St

Bernard St

see MAP 4 FISHERMAN'S WHARF, THE MARINA & RUSSIAN HILL

MAP 4 FISHERMAN'S WHARF, THE MARINA & RUSSIAN HILL

PLACES TO STAY
- 6 Dockside Boat & Bed
- 12 Radisson Fisherman's Wharf
- 19 HI Fisherman's Wharf
- 26 San Remo Hotel
- 29 Best Inn
- 30 Travelodge
- 31 Comfort Inn
- 36 Marina Motel

PLACES TO EAT
- 8 Alioto's
- 9 Tarantino's
- 14 Greens
- 21 Ana Mandara
- 22 Buena Vista Café
- 24 Gary Danko
- 32 Zarzuela
- 33 I Fratelli
- 37 Home Plate
- 38 Bistro Aix
- 39 Mel's Drive-In
- 41 Betelnut

BARS & CLUBS
- 10 Lou's Pier 47
- 11 Steelhead Brewing Company
- 27 Bimbo's 365 Club
- 34 Liverpool Lil's
- 35 Final Final
- 40 Comet Club
- 42 Perry's
- 43 Bus Stop

OTHER
- 1 SS Jeremiah O'Brien
- 2 USS Pampanito
- 3 Venetian Carousel
- 4 Blue & Gold Fleet Ticket Office (for Alcatraz)
- 5 Blue & Gold Fleet Ticket Office
- 7 Aquarium of the Bay
- 13 Wave Organ
- 15 Museo Italo-American
- 16 Museum of Craft & Folk Art
- 17 Magic Theatre
- 18 African-American Historical & Cultural Society
- 20 Maritime Museum
- 23 Cobb's Comedy Club
- 25 Blazing Saddles
- 28 San Francisco Art Institute

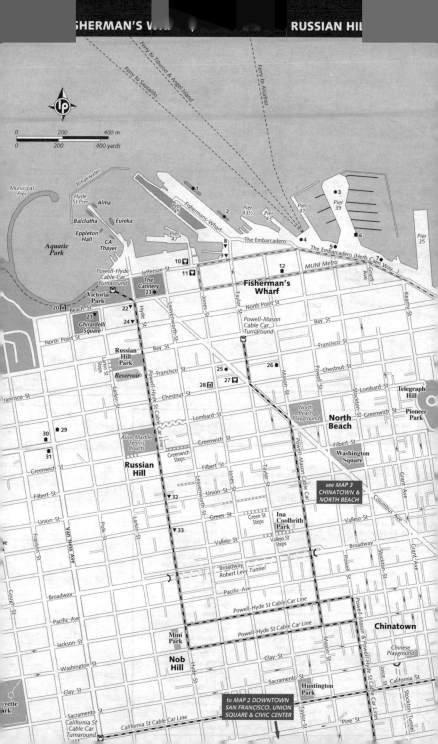

Ferry to Tiburon & Angel Island
Ferry to Sausalito
Ferry to Alcatraz

Municipal Pier

Breakwater

Hyde St Pier
Alma
Balclutha
Eureka
Eppleton Hall
CA Thayer

Aquatic Park

● 1

Fishermans Wharf

Pier 45

2 ●

Pier 47

Pier 43½

Pier 43

● 3

Pier 41

Pier 39

● 4

5 ●

● 6

Pier 35

The Embarcadero

The Embarcadero (Herb Caen Way...)

7 ●

8 ▼
9 ▼

10 ▢
11 ▢

MUNI Metro

12 ■

Jefferson St

Powell-Hyde Cable Car Turnaround

The Cannery 23 ●

Victoria Park

20 ■

22 ▼
24 ▼

Beach St

21 ■
Ghirardelli Square

North Point St

Russian Hill Park

Reservoir

Bay St

Francisco St

Chestnut St

Fisherman's Wharf

North Point St

Powell-Mason Cable Car Turnaround

Bay St

Francisco St

25 ●

26 ■

28 ■ 27 ■

Chestnut St

North Beach Playground

North Beach

Telegraph Hill

Pioneer Park

Lombard St

Greenwich St

Greenwich Steps

Alice Marble Tennis Courts

30 ■ ■ 29

31 ■

Greenwich St

Russian Hill

Lombard St

Greenwich St

Filbert St

Filbert St

Washington Square

Filbert St

see MAP 3 CHINATOWN & NORTH BEACH

Union St

▼ 32

Green St

Green Steps

Leavenworth St

Vallejo St

▼ 33

Green St

Ina Coolbrith Park

Vallejo St Steps

Vallejo St

Broadway

Broadway, Robert Levy Tunnel

Pacific Ave

Powell-Hyde St Cable Car Line

Broadway

Pacific Ave

Jackson St

Washington St

Clay St

Nob Hill

Mini Park

Powell-Hyde St Cable Car Line

Clay St

Sacramento St

Huntington Park

Chinatown

Chinese Playground

California St

to MAP 2 DOWNTOWN SAN FRANCISCO, UNION SQUARE & CIVIC CENTER

Sacramento St

California St Cable Car Turnaround

California St Cable Car Line

Pine St

Tunnel

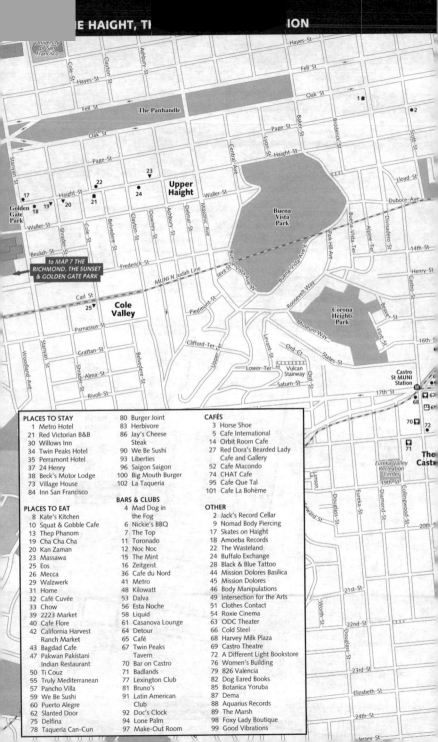

University of San Francisco

The Panhandle

Upper Haight

Golden Gate Park

Buena Vista Park

to MAP 7 THE RICHMOND, THE SUNSET & GOLDEN GATE PARK

MUNI N Judah Line

Cole Valley

Corona Heights Park

Vulcan Stairway

Castro St MUNI Station

Eureka Valley Recreation Center

The Castr

PLACES TO STAY
1 Metro Hotel
21 Red Victorian B&B
30 Willows Inn
34 Twin Peaks Hotel
35 Perramont Hotel
37 24 Henry
38 Beck's Motor Lodge
73 Village House
84 Inn San Francisco

PLACES TO EAT
8 Kate's Kitchen
10 Squat & Gobble Cafe
13 Thep Phanom
19 Cha Cha Cha
20 Kan Zaman
23 Massawa
25 Eos
26 Mecca
29 Walzwerk
31 Home
32 Café Cuvée
33 Chow
39 2223 Market
40 Cafe Flore
42 California Harvest Ranch Market
43 Bagdad Cafe
47 Pakwan Pakistani Indian Restaurant
50 Ti Couz
55 Truly Mediterranean
57 Pancho Villa
59 We Be Sushi
60 Puerto Alegre
62 Slanted Door
75 Delfina
78 Taqueria Can-Cun

80 Burger Joint
83 Herbivore
86 Jay's Cheese Steak
90 We Be Sushi
93 Liberties
96 Saigon Saigon
100 Big Mouth Burger
102 La Taqueria

BARS & CLUBS
4 Mad Dog in the Fog
6 Nickie's BBQ
7 The Top
11 Toronado
12 Noc Noc
15 The Mint
16 Zeitgeist
36 Cafe du Nord
41 Metro
48 Kilowatt
53 Dalva
56 Esta Noche
58 Liquid
61 Casanova Lounge
64 Detour
65 Café
67 Twin Peaks Tavern
70 Bar on Castro
71 Badlands
77 Lexington Club
81 Bruno's
91 Latin American Club
92 Doc's Clock
94 Lone Palm
97 Make-Out Room

CAFÉS
3 Horse Shoe
5 Cafe International
14 Orbit Room Cafe
27 Red Dora's Bearded Lady Cafe and Gallery
52 Cafe Macondo
74 CHAT Cafe
95 Cafe Que Tal
101 Cafe La Bohème

OTHER
2 Jack's Record Cellar
9 Nomad Body Piercing
17 Skates on Haight
18 Amoeba Records
22 The Wasteland
24 Buffalo Exchange
28 Black & Blue Tattoo
44 Mission Dolores Basilica
45 Mission Dolores
46 Body Manipulations
49 Intersection for the Arts
51 Clothes Contact
54 Roxie Cinema
63 ODC Theater
66 Cold Steel
68 Harvey Milk Plaza
69 Castro Theatre
72 A Different Light Bookstore
76 Women's Building
79 826 Valencia
82 Dog Eared Books
85 Botanica Yoruba
87 Dema
88 Aquarius Records
89 The Marsh
98 Foxy Lady Boutique
99 Good Vibrations

MAP 6 SOUTH OF M

San Francisco Bay

To Oakland & Berkeley

To Oakland/Alameda

Ferry to Oakland/Alameda

Pier 2
Pier 24
Pier 26
Pier 28
Pier 30
Pier 32
Pier 34
Pier 36
Pier 38
Pier 40
Pier 48
Pier 50
Pier 52
Pier 54

San Francisco-Oakland Bay Bridge

Ferry Terminal Plaza

Justin Herman Plaza

Breakwater

South Beach Harbor Park

Pacific Bell Park

Terry Francois St

Illinois St

Lefty O'Doul Bridge

Mission Creek Channel

Embarcadero South St

Folsom St/MUNI Station
Brannan St/MUNI Station
2nd & King St MUNI Station
4th & King St MUNI Station

Caltrain Depot

Caltrain

Financial District

Rincon Center

Embarcadero BART & MUNI Station

Montgomery BART & MUNI Station

Chinatown
Chinese Playground
Portsmouth

Union Square

Crocker Galleria
Maiden Lane
Bloomingdale's
San Francisco Shopping Centre
Powell St BART & MUNI Station
Hallidie Plaza
Powell St Cable Car Turnaround

South Park

George R Moscone Convention Center

Yerba Buena Gardens

South Of Market (SOMA)

Tenderloin

Civic Center
United Nations Plaza
Civic Center Plaza
City Hall
Civic Center BART & MUNI Station
Van Ness MUNI Station

The Mission

see MAP 3 CHINATOWN & NORTH BEACH

see MAP 2 DOWNTOWN SAN FRANCISCO, UNION SQUARE & CIVIC CENTER

see MAP 5 THE HAIGHT, THE CASTRO & THE MISSION

500 m
500 yards
0 250
0 250

PLACES TO STAY
3 Hotel Griffon
4 Harbor Court Hotel
15 Mosser's Victorian Hotel
24 Hotel Britton
25 Carriage Inn
26 Americania
34 San Francisco International Student Center
36 Globe Hostel

OTHER
2 Magnes Museum
8 Adolf Gasser
10 Cartoon Art Museum
11 Yerba Buena Center for the Arts
12 San Francisco Museum of Modern Art (SFMOMA)
16 Sony Metreon
18 Zeum; Yerba Buena Ice Skating & Bowling Center
20 Photographer's Supply
21 Jeremy's
33 Brain Wash

PLACES TO EAT
1 Boulevard
5 Yank Sing
6 Yank Sing
13 Hawthorne Lane
14 Fifth Floor
17 Tu Lan
19 LuLu
22 Caffe Centro
23 South Park Cafe
29 Bacar
30 Fringale
35 Julie's Supper Club

BARS & CLUBS
7 111 Minna
9 Kate O'Brien's
27 Covered Wagon Saloon
28 Hotel Utah Saloon
31 1015 Folsom
32 Endup
37 TheStud
38 Slim's
39 El Bobo
40 DNA Lounge
41 The Eagle

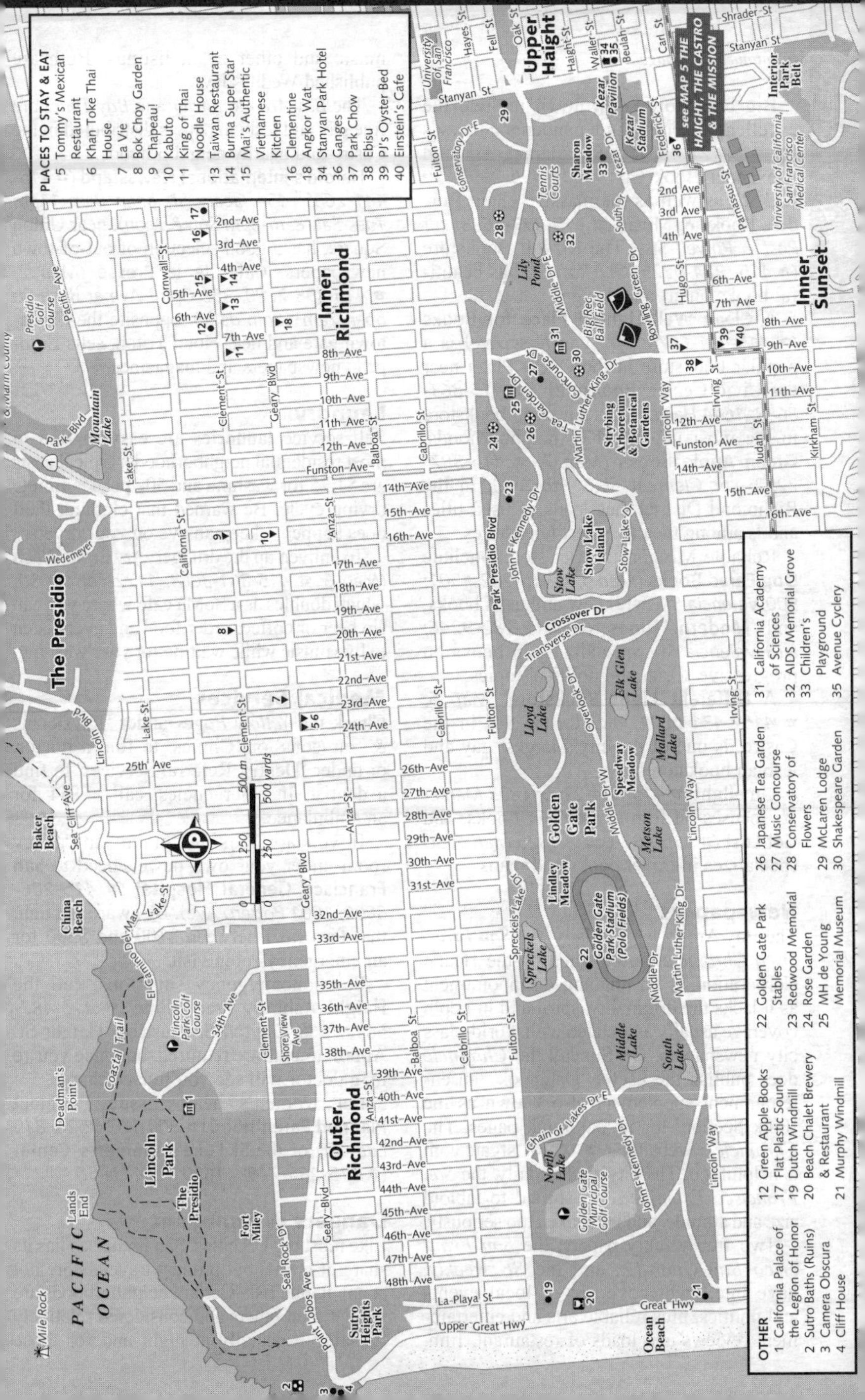

MAP 7 THE RICHMOND, THE SUNSET & GOLDEN GATE PARK

PLACES TO STAY & EAT

5 Tommy's Mexican Restaurant
6 Khan Toke Thai House
7 La Vie
8 Bok Choy Garden
9 Chapeau!
10 Kabuto
11 King of Thai
13 Taiwan Restaurant
14 Burma Super Star Noodle House
15 Mai's Authentic Vietnamese Kitchen
16 Clementine
18 Angkor Wat
34 Stanyan Park Hotel
36 Ganges
37 Park Chow
38 Ebisu
39 PJ's Oyster Bed
40 Einstein's Cafe

OTHER

1 California Palace of the Legion of Honor
2 Sutro Baths (Ruins)
3 Camera Obscura
4 Cliff House
12 Green Apple Books
17 Flat Plastic Sound
19 Dutch Windmill
20 Beach Chalet Brewery & Restaurant
21 Murphy Windmill
22 Golden Gate Park Stables
23 Redwood Memorial
24 Rose Garden
25 MH de Young Memorial Museum
26 Japanese Tea Garden
27 Music Concourse
28 Conservatory of Flowers
29 McLaren Lodge
30 Shakespeare Garden
31 California Academy of Sciences
32 AIDS Memorial Grove
33 Children's Playground
35 Avenue Cyclery

see MAP 5 THE HAIGHT, THE CASTRO & THE MISSION

[Continued from page 103]

Big bookstores downtown include the excellent, friendly independents Stacey's (☎ 415-421-4687; 581 Market St) and Alexander Book Co (☎ 415-495-2992; 50 2nd St), as well as the massive chain Borders Books & Music (☎ 415-399-1633; cnr Post & Powell Sts). The Rizzoli Bookstore (☎ 415- 984-0225; 117 Post St) has beautiful books on art and design.

A Clean Well-Lighted Place for Books (☎ 415-441-6670; 601 Van Ness Ave) is a popular bookstore in the Opera Plaza near the Civic Center. **Booksmith** (☎ 415-863-8688; 1644 Haight St) is a general bookstore in the most ungeneral of neighborhoods. **Green Apple Books** (Map 7; ☎ 415-387-2272; cnr Clement St & 6th Ave), in the Richmond District, has loads of used titles and is among the city's best bookstores.

Reliable Mission District stores include **Dog Eared Books** (Map 5; ☎ 415-282-1901; 900 Valencia St), with new and used books, and **Modern Times** (☎ 415-282-9246; 818 Valencia St), specializing in books on progressive social and political topics.

A Different Light Bookstore (Map 5; ☎ 415- 431-0891; 489 Castro St), in the Castro, is one of the city's largest gay and lesbian bookstores.

Limelight (☎ 415-864-2265; 1803 Market St) focuses on film and theater books, and **Get Lost** (☎ 415-437-0529; 1825 Market St) specializes in travel books and maps.

Newspapers

The Bay Area's largest daily, the *San Francisco Chronicle*, now owned by the Hearst Corporation, is an ongoing disappointment as it lacks the originality, spirit and in-depth coverage usually associated with world-class city newspapers. On Sunday the *Chronicle* does publish the useful 'Datebook,' an entertainment supplement also known as the 'Pink Section' for its pale pink pages. The *Chronicle*'s website at **w** www .sfgate.com is helpful too. The city's other daily, the *San Francisco Examiner*, has shifted to tabloid size and attitude, and isn't taken too seriously.

Two free weekly papers, the *San Francisco Bay Guardian* and the *SF Weekly*, have intelligent coverage of local events and politics, plus reliable arts and entertainment reviews and loads of restaurant, film,

music and other event listings. Both are published Wednesday.

The *Bay Area Reporter* and *Bay Times* are free gay and lesbian papers distributed in the Castro and nearby neighborhoods.

Harold's International Newsstand (☎ 415-441-2665; 454 Geary St; open 8am-11pm Tues-Sat, 8am-8pm Sun & Mon), near Union Square, has a good selection of out-of-town newspapers. **Café de la Presse** (Map 2; ☎ 415-398-2680; 352 Grant Ave at Bush St; open 7am-10pm daily), opposite the Chinatown gate and near Hotel Triton, sells European newspapers and magazines.

Laundry

Self-service laundries are easy to find in most residential neighborhoods; typical costs are $1.75 for washing and 50¢ per 15-minute drying cycle. Be warned that clothing theft does happen – keep an eye on your dryers.

To enliven up the drudgery, try **Brain Wash** (Map 6; ☎ 415-861-3663; 1122 Folsom St), which doubles as a SoMa café where you can sip beer or coffee, order food and even listen to live music while waiting for your washing.

Medical Services

Check the *Yellow Pages* under 'Physicians & Surgeons' or 'Clinics' to find a doctor, or under 'Dentist Referral Services' to find a dentist. In emergencies, call ☎ 911 for an ambulance.

If you are looking for an emergency room under your own power, head to **San Francisco General Hospital** (☎ 415-206-8000; 1001 Potrero Ave). Be aware, though, that fees *start* between $100 and $500 for an emergency-room visit.

For nonemergency situations, call the **Haight Ashbury Free Clinic** (☎ 415-487-5632; 558 Clayton St), just off Haight St. Appointments are required, but once you're in, a doctor will see you free of charge.

For women's health issues, contact **Planned Parenthood** (☎ 800-967-7526; 815 Eddy St) or the **St Luke's Women's Center** (☎ 415-285-7788; 1650 Valencia St).

Dangers & Annoyances

Like most big US cities, San Francisco has its share of crime, but prudent travelers are not at any undue risk. Certain neighborhoods are seedier than others and considered relatively 'unsafe,' especially at night and for those walking alone. These include the Tenderloin, parts of the Mission, the Western Addition and 6th and 7th Sts South of Market. However, these areas are not always sharply defined, and travelers should be aware of their surroundings wherever they walk in the city.

After dark, some of the city's parks, including Mission Dolores Park and Buena Vista Park, become havens for drug dealing and sleazy sex. Bayview-Hunters Point, a poor and largely African-American neighborhood north of 3Com (Candlestick) Park, where the 49ers play, is not a place for wandering tourists.

The city's homeless population is unnaturally high (we won't get into who's to blame). Most people asking for spare change are harmless, some even friendly; a smile of acknowledgment, or a few coins if you can, and they'll be on their way. Some are earning money selling the *Street Sheet*, a locally published newspaper on homeless issues ($1). For aggressive panhandlers, the best strategy is to simply say 'I'm sorry' and keep walking.

If you find yourself somewhere you would rather not be, act confident and sure of yourself; then go into a store and call a taxi.

UNION SQUARE (Map 2)

Union Square, which gets its name from the pro-Union rallies that took place there during the Civil War, is San Francisco's downtown tourist center. The square is surrounded on all sides by pricey hotels, airline offices, upscale shops and major department stores such as Macy's and Neiman-Marcus. The center of the square is dominated by the 97ft-high **Dewey Monument**, built in 1903 to commemorate Admiral George Dewey's 1898 defeat of the Spanish fleet at Manila Bay, which paved the way for the Philippines to become a US territory. Among the buildings flanking the square is the 1904 **Westin St Francis Hotel** (335 Powell St), which features in many Dashiell Hammett novels, most notably *The Maltese Falcon*. Hammett lived in San Francisco during the 1920s and '30s.

In the Grand Hyatt plaza, on Stockton St just off the square, sculptor Ruth Asawa's bronze **Children's Fountain** portrays San Francisco's history in intricate and playful detail. It's worth stepping into **Neiman-Marcus** (150 Stockton St) just to look up at its stained-glass dome, a hallmark feature of the 1909 City of Paris store that occupied the site before this 1982 structure.

On the east side of the square, **Maiden Lane** is crowded with pricey salons and boutiques. This lane had a previous incarnation very much at odds with its present upscale image. Before the 1906 earthquake, Maiden Lane, then called Morton St, was lined with bordellos and was known as one of the bawdiest dives in a city renowned for racy living. During the rebuilding, the city fathers endowed it with its hopeful new name and cleaned up its image to match. The 1949 **Folk Art International Building** (140 Maiden Lane) is the city's only Frank Lloyd Wright building. Have a look at its interior – the spiral walkway marks it as Wright's practice run for the Guggenheim Museum in New York.

The city's famous **cable cars** groan along Powell St, on the west side of Union Square, to and from the Hallidie Plaza terminus, named after the cable car's inventor. This is the most popular spot to catch a cable car.

San Francisco's dense **theater district** lies immediately southwest of the square, crumbling directly into the dismal Tenderloin.

CIVIC CENTER (Map 2)

The compact Civic Center area is a study in contrasts, where the city's architectural and cultural aspirations collide head-on with its human problems. Separating City Hall and the Opera House from downtown are the grubby blocks of the **Tenderloin**, an area plagued by drunks, prostitutes, dirty needles and sticky-floored strip clubs. As you proceed south down Jones St, each block, from Post to Geary to O'Farrell, is slightly more dicey than the previous one. Ellis St, one block below O'Farrell, is the scene of considerable gang activity. Grittiness aside, though, the area does have good cheap restaurants, cool old bars and a few hipper-than-thou nightclubs.

Despite its proximity to the Tenderloin (and the seemingly inevitable homeless population in its plaza), Civic Center tries its best to maintain a stately aura. The crown jewel is the impressively restored **City Hall** (☎ 415-554-4000; cnr Van Ness Ave & Grove St). The 1906 disaster razed the earlier city hall, which was replaced in 1915 with the present Beaux Arts–style structure modeled after St Peter's Basilica in Vatican City. City Hall was badly damaged in the 1989 earthquake; it reopened in 1999 after a $300 million renovation program, and San Franciscans seem pleased with its new light-filled rotunda and flashy gilt dome.

Currently in City Hall's South Light Court is the **Museum of the City of San Francisco** (☎ 415-255-9400; W www.sfmuseum.org; admission free; open 8am-8pm Mon-Fri, noon-4pm Sat), which has interesting photos and exhibits on the city's history. The museum may, however, soon move to Pier 45 at Fisherman's Wharf.

Facing City Hall across the plaza is the old Main Library, a 1917 building slated to reopen in early 2003 as the new **Asian Art Museum** (☎ 415-379-8800; W www.asianart .org; cnr Larkin & McAllister Sts; adult/child $10/6; 10am-5pm Tues-Sun, until 9pm Thur). The museum is home to superb art from the Middle East, the Indian subcontinent, Southeast Asia, Tibet, China, Korea and Japan. Down the street is the new **Main Library** (☎ 415-557-4400), which opened in 1996 and cost $134 million. Even if you hate books, the library is worth visiting for its architecture – five stories built around a naturally lit, semicircular atrium – and its newspaper and magazine reading room (free and stocked with many international titles).

Across Hyde St beyond the two library buildings is United Nations Plaza, built to commemorate the signing of the UN Charter in San Francisco in 1945. A farmers market is held at the plaza every Wednesday and Sunday.

Across from City Hall, the **War Memorial Opera House** (☎ 415-864-3330; 301 Van Ness Ave), built in 1932, is the venue for performances by the city's acclaimed opera and ballet companies. Adjacent to the Opera House is the Veterans Building, housing the **Herbst Theatre** (☎ 415-392-4400), where the UN Charter was signed in 1945. One block south is the **Louise M Davies Symphony Hall** (☎ 415-864-6000).

The three blocks of Hayes St between Franklin and Laguna Sts, just west of the opera house, constitute a small neighborhood of galleries, coffeehouses and restaurants known as Hayes Valley.

SOUTH OF MARKET (Map 6)

South of Market (or SoMa) is a combination of office buildings spilling out of the Financial District, fancy condominiums along the Embarcadero near the Bay Bridge, a busy and still-expanding museum and convention precinct around **Yerba Buena Gardens**, and a thriving and throbbing late-night entertainment scene. Be warned that parking here is in short supply; public transportation is easily accessed nearby and is highly recommended.

Yerba Buena Gardens is the open-air public center of SoMa, a pleasant urban oasis begging a lunchtime picnic. Here you'll find the **Yerba Buena Center for the Arts** (☎ 415-978-2787; cnr Mission & 3rd Sts; W www.yerbabuenaarts.org; adult/student $6/3; open 11am-6pm Tues-Sun), which features concerts, film events and rotating contemporary art exhibits that are among the city's most exciting. Linked to the gardens by a bridge across Howard St is the **George R Moscone Convention Center** (☎ 415-974-4000), the city's ever-expanding main exhibition hall.

The bright, brash **Sony Metreon** (☎ 415-369-6000; cnr 4th & Mission Sts; open 10am-10pm daily) is basically a shopping center with a high-tech theme; inside are stores, restaurants, a fancy video arcade, 15 movie screens, an IMAX theater and the children's attraction **Where the Wild Things Are** (admission $6), an indoor playground with artificial forests, sound effects and oversized creatures from Maurice Sendak's books.

Across Howard St from the Metreon, on the roof of the Moscone Convention Center, **Zeum** (☎ 415-777-2800; W www.zeum.org; adult/child $7/5; open 11am-5pm Tues-Sun) is a hands-on art and technology museum that encourages young people to create and produce their own works with audio, video, computer animation and more. Zeum also has a restored carousel ($2), originally from Playland at the Beach, an amusement park on San Francisco's Ocean Beach from 1921 to 1972.

Also on the rooftop of the Moscone Center is a more prosaic attraction, the **Yerba Buena Ice Skating and Bowling Center** (☎ 415-777-3727; adult/child $6.50/5, skate rental $2.50; open daily). The bowling center costs $4/2.50 per adult/child per game, or $20 per hour.

The excellent **San Francisco Museum of Modern Art** (SFMOMA; ☎ 415-357-4000; W www.sfmoma.org; 151 3rd St; adult/student $10/6; open 10am-6pm Fri-Tues, until 9pm Thur) is directly across from the Yerba Buena Gardens in a striking but somewhat cold building designed by Swiss architect Mario Botta. The permanent collection is particularly strong in American abstract expressionism, with major works by Clyfford Still, Jackson Pollock and Philip Guston. The SF-MOMA's photography collection is also world renowned. Note that admission is free the first Tuesday of the month, and half price on Thursday evening.

The worthwhile **Cartoon Art Museum** (☎ 415-227-8666; W www.cartoonart.org; 655 Mission St; adult/student $4/3; open 11am-5pm Tues-Sun) features constantly changing exhibits of cartoon art.

The **Magnes Museum** (☎ 415-591-8800; W www.jmsf.org; 121 Steuart St; adult/student $4/3; open noon-5pm Sun-Wed, 2pm-7pm Thur), the new joint venture between the Jewish Museum of San Francisco and Berkeley's Judah L Magnes Museum, has changing exhibits on Jewish life. The museum is planning to move to a splashy new Yerba Buena building in 2005.

The **Mexican Museum** (☎ 415-202-9700; W www.mexicanmuseum.org) is moving from Fort Mason to its new home in Yerba Buena Gardens, and is scheduled to open in 2004.

Close to the waterfront, the historic **Rincon Center** occupies the block bounded by Mission, Howard, Steuart and Spear Sts. Modern shops and offices aside, the main building is itself a treasure, a WPA (Works Progress Administration) project and former post office designed by Gilbert Stanley Underwood, who also designed Yosemite's Ahwahnee Hotel. Look for the dolphin friezes on the facade and the massive murals inside depicting California's history. The latter were completed in 1948 by Anton Refregier.

Situated between Bryant, Brannan, 2nd and 3rd Sts is **South Park**, a picturesque oval of green in the midst of the city's once-burgeoning 'Multimedia Gulch.' Built in 1852 to mimic a London city square, it's surrounded by offices and cafés.

Southeast of South Park is **Pacific Bell Park**, home of the San Francisco Giants (see Spectator Sports later in this chapter).

FINANCIAL DISTRICT (Map 2)

The city's tall buildings are densely concentrated in the blocks from Union Square to the bay. This is the city's banking center, San Francisco's core business since banks started to appear in the 1850s to handle the state's gold rush fortunes. It's a frantically busy area during the day, with taxis, power-dressed business people and suicidal bike messengers all competing for street space. Come dark it's a different animal; apart from a handful of restaurants and bars, the district is nearly deserted.

Visiting the Financial District is essentially an architectural experience. The completion of the **Bank of America Building** (555 California St) in 1969 ushered in a new era for San Francisco's previously low-rise skyline. Not only was the 52-story, 779ft building much higher than any earlier structure, but the use of red South Dakota granite in its construction made it look very different from the city's consistent pale coloring.

Probably the most recognizable single building in San Francisco is the 853ft **Transamerica Pyramid** (600 Montgomery St), the tallest in town. It was completed in 1972 and though initially reviled, today it's accepted as a modern symbol of the city. Adjacent to the Pyramid is a half-acre stand of redwood trees known as **Redwood Park**.

The Gothic 1928 **Russ Building** (253 Montgomery St) was the tallest in the city from its creation until 1964.

Other buildings of note in the district include the **Pacific Stock Exchange** (301 Pine St), which was built in 1915 and remodeled in 1930, the 1916 **Hobart Building** (582 Market St) and the 1908 **Bank of California Building** (400 California St), fronted by Corinthian columns and housing the **Museum of Money of the American West** (☎ 415-765-0400; admission free; open 10am-4pm Mon-Fri) in its basement.

The small but interesting **Wells Fargo History Museum** (☎ 415-396-2619; 420 Montgomery St; admission free; open 9am-5pm Mon-Fri) tells the story of Wells Fargo Bank, the company founded in 1852 to provide banking and stagecoach delivery services to miners and businesses throughout the West Coast.

The odd-looking **Lotta's Fountain** (cnr Geary & Market Sts), recently restored to its shiny glory, was donated to the city in 1875 by vaudeville entertainer Lotta Crabtree. A popular gathering point after the 1906 earthquake, a handful of survivors still gather here at 5am each April 18.

The luxurious **Palace Hotel** (☎ 415-512-1111; cnr Market & New Montgomery Sts) opened in 1875 as the most opulent hotel in the city. Along the way, it contributed to the death of its creator, William Ralston, who was driven to bankruptcy and a heart attack by financial pressures. Take afternoon tea in the leafy Garden Court and contemplate the 1991 renovation, which cost more than $100 million.

The waterfront Embarcadero, once the city's busiest area, was killed first by the two bridges across the bay, which ended the ferry boat era, and then by the death of the old-style wharves, superseded by the containership era. The tearing down of the elevated Embarcadero Freeway in the aftermath of the 1989 earthquake led to redevelopment of the area, including a palm-lined roadway and MUNI streetcars.

The **Ferry Building**, with its distinctive clock tower, has been a beacon at the bottom of California and Market Sts since 1898. Currently it's undergoing a major restoration, which will include a revitalized ferry terminal, expanded public areas and shops.

Four skyscrapers mark the huge **Embarcadero Center**, between Sacramento and Clay Sts, starting on Embarcadero at Justin Herman Plaza, a popular lunch spot for Financial District workers. At the base of the buildings (Embarcadero 1 to 4) are shops, restaurants, a movie theater and a post office.

NOB HILL (Map 2)

Nob Hill is a classy district perched atop one of the city's famous hills. When the cable cars arrived in the 1870s and made the 338ft summit accessible, the elite moved in and promptly built the most opulent mansions in the city. Mark Hopkins and Collis P Huntington were the builders who, with fellow 'robber barons' Charles Crocker and Leland Stanford (collectively known as the 'Big Four'), made fortunes from the Central Pacific Railroad. Several Nob Hill hotels are named after Stanford, Huntington and Hopkins – The Huntington, Mark Hopkins and Stanford Court. Crocker's name is applied to a bank, and Stanford went on to become governor of California and founder of Stanford University.

Besides hotels and their top-floor bars, Nob Hill is home to **Grace Cathedral** (☎ 415-749-6300; 1100 California St). The bronze doors are casts of Ghiberti's Gates of Paradise in the Cathedral Baptistry of St John in Florence, Italy, and the magnificent rose window was made in Chartres, France, in 1964. Also of note is the Keith Haring altarpiece, *The Life of Christ*, dedicated in 1995 by the AIDS Memorial Chapel Project.

The **Cable Car Barn & Museum** (☎ 415-474-1887; 1201 Mason St; admission free; open 10am-5pm daily, to 6pm summer) dates from 1910 and is the site of the power plant that tows all the cable cars, the garage where

Cable Cars

The Transamerica Pyramid and the Golden Gate Bridge make fine city symbols, but San Francisco has another, older icon: the beloved cable car. Cable cars were conceived by English mining engineer Andrew Hallidie as a replacement for the horse-pulled trams, for which the city's steep streets were difficult and dangerous.

From Hallidie's first experimental line on Clay St in 1873, cable cars quickly caught on, and by 1890 the cable car system had eight operators, 500 cable cars and a route network of more than 100mi. By the turn of the century, the system was already past its heyday and shrinking in the face of newfangled electric streetcars. The 1906 earthquake was a disaster for the cable car system, but the death knell sounded in January 1947, when the mayor announced the last lines would be replaced by bus services. But he hadn't reckoned with Friedel Klussmann's Citizens Committee to Save the Cable Cars and a groundswell of public support that brought about the reprieve of the Powell St lines.

San Franciscans may have saved the system from politicians and accountants, but saving it from old age became a new problem as derailments and runaways became increasingly frequent. A six-month shutdown in 1979 for a million dollars' worth of repairs was just a Band-Aid solution, and in 1982 the system was finally closed for a $60 million complete overhaul. The rebuilt system, which reopened in 1984, consists of 40 cars on three lines covering a total of 12mi.

the cable cars park at night, and a museum displaying, among other things, inventor Andrew Hallidie's original Clay St cable car.

CHINATOWN (Map 3)

Chinatown is the most densely packed pocket of the city, and perhaps the most colorful. There are no essential sights, but it's a great place for casual wandering, soaking up the hectic atmosphere and stumbling across interesting little corners and alleys.

Packed with shops and restaurants, **Grant Ave** has had a colorful history from its inception as Calle de la Fundación, the main street of the Mexican village of Yerba Buena. Renamed Dupont St, or Du Pon Gai to the Chinese, the street became known for brothels, gambling dives, opium dens and brawling *tongs* (Chinese gangs). Dupont St was renamed after president and Civil War general Ulysses S Grant when he died in 1885.

Get off touristy Grant Ave for a more authentic Chinatown experience – scruffy apothecary shops, multicolored overhanging balconies and backstreet restaurants with glazed ducks dangling in the windows. The most colorful time to visit is during the Chinese New Year in late January/early February, when there is a parade and fireworks and other festivities, though the day-to-day bustle of Chinatown is reason enough to visit.

Chinatown visits usually begin at the dragon-studded **Chinatown Gate** at the Bush St entrance to Grant Ave. The Taoist **Ching Chung Temple** (☎ 415-433-2623; 532 Grant Ave; open daily) isn't a spectacular sight, but this is as good a look at behind-the-scenes Chinatown as you're likely to get. (Though no-one is likely to tell you so, shorts and T-shirts are not respectful attire here, and photography is frowned upon.) At the intersection with California St is **Old St Mary's Church** (☎ 415-986-4388); its 90ft tower made it the city's tallest building when it was completed in 1854. St Mary's Square, off California St, is one of few large open spaces in Chinatown. When Chinatown was cleaned up in the late 19th century, the brothels, gambling dens and bars from all over the area were concentrated here, only to burn down in the aftermath of the 1906 earthquake.

Visitors are welcome in the **Kong Chow Temple** (☎ 415-434-2513; 55 Stockton St), above the post office, to see what's claimed to be the oldest Chinese altar in the US. The **Chinese Consolidated Benevolent Building** (843 Stockton St) houses its namesake organization, also known as the 'Six Companies,' which during the 19th century fought for Chinese legal rights and served as an arbitrator in disputes between Chinese people.

For a good idea of off-the-main-street Chinatown, duck into colorful **Waverly Place**, between Grant Ave and Stockton St, with its many open balconies and upstairs temples. Just to the right, when you emerge onto Washington St, is **Sam Wo's** (☎ 415-982-0596), a hole-in-the-wall Chinese restaurant where Jack Kerouac supposedly learned how to use chopsticks.

A few steps in the opposite direction along Washington St, take a right turn into narrow **Ross Alley**, another picturesque lane. Known at one time as Gau Leuie Sung Hong or 'Old Spanish Alley,' this small street was wall-to-wall gambling dens and brothels in the late 1870s. A favorite location for filmmakers, it has featured in films such as *Big Trouble in Little China*. Here **Golden Gate Fortune Cookies** (☎ 415-781-3956; 56 Ross Alley) turns out crispy treats, which, incidentally, are a San Francisco invention, dreamed up for the Japanese Tea Garden in Golden Gate Park.

Portsmouth Square (Kearny & Washington Sts) almost always has a crowd of young and old people talking or playing checkers, chess or mah jong. It was originally the plaza for the Mexican settlement of Yerba Buena, and its name comes from John B Montgomery's sloop, the *Portsmouth*. Montgomery arrived in 1846 to claim the city for the US, and a plaque commemorates the spot where the Stars and Stripes was first raised in San Francisco.

A pedestrian bridge crosses from Portsmouth Square to the **Chinese Culture Center** (☎ 415-986-1822; w www.c-c-c.org; Holiday Inn, 750 Kearny St; admission free; open 10am-4pm Tues-Sun) on the 3rd floor of the Holiday Inn building. It has free changing exhibitions on Chinese art and culture.

Turn down Kearny St and left onto Commercial St to the **Pacific Heritage Museum** (☎ 415-362-4100; 608 Commercial St; admission free; open 10am-4pm Tues-Sat), which has exhibits on the city's Asian and Pacific connections.

The **Chinese Historical Society of America Museum** (☎ *415-391-1188;* W *www.chsa .org; 965 Clay St; admission $3; open 11am-4pm Tues-Fri, noon-4pm Sat & Sun*) recounts the story of the city's Chinese community. It is located in a one-time YMCA building designed by Julia Morgan.

NORTH BEACH (Map 3)

North Beach started as the city's Italian quarter, and its Italian heritage lives on in the area's restaurants and bars. The Beats took over in the '50s and added cafés, jazz clubs and the City Lights Bookstore to the mix.

The Beat Generation

From the days of the gold rush, San Francisco has been a freewheeling city. Artists, musicians and writers often sang its praises in their works, but it wasn't until the mid-1950s that national attention was first focused on 'the City' as the birthplace of a scene of its own. When Jack Kerouac and Allen Ginsberg, upstart students at Columbia University, fled the indifference of New York City and joined forces with the San Francisco Renaissance, a poets' movement begun by poet and literary critic Kenneth Rexroth, the Beat Generation was given a voice.

They engaged in a new style of writing – short, sharp and alive. Their bible was Kerouac's *On the Road* (1957); Ginsberg's 'Howl' (1956) was their angry anthem. A writer himself, Lawrence Ferlinghetti became the Beats' patron and publisher, and today their era lives on at his City Lights Bookstore in North Beach, still churning out the hipsters after 40 years.

The Beats spoke of a life unbound by social conventions and motivated by spontaneous creativity rather than greed and ambition. Kerouac is widely credited with creating the term 'Beat Generation' after hearing poet Herbert Huncke say, 'Man, I'm beat.' The phrase echoed Hemingway's 'Lost Generation' and alluded to the supreme happiness preached in the Beatitudes of Jesus. The term 'beatnik' came along later, created, it is claimed, by *San Francisco Chronicle* columnist Herb Caen, fusing the 'far out' Beats with the just-launched Sputnik satellite.

Today, despite gentrification and an onslaught of tourists – not to mention the sex emporiums along Broadway – North Beach is one of the liveliest parts of the city and a great place for a cheap meal, a cold beer and the best cappuccino in town.

At the corner of Kearny St, the 1905 **Columbus Tower**, with its green copper cupola, has been the property of film-maker Francis Ford Coppola since 1970. The offices of Coppola's film company, Zoetrope, are in the building.

The block of Columbus Ave from Pacific Ave to Broadway can lay claim to being the literary heart of the city. A drink at **Vesuvio Cafe**, where Dylan Thomas and Jack Kerouac are known to have pissed away a few evenings, is a fine segue to a visit to **City Lights Bookstore** (☎ *415-362-8193*), just across Jack Kerouac Alley. City Lights was founded in 1953 by poet Lawrence Ferlinghetti, who still owns it. City Lights Publishers, with offices above the bookstore, became famous in 1957 when it published Ginsberg's poem 'Howl,' which was promptly banned for obscenity. A highly publicized court ruling finally allowed distribution of the poem.

At the junction of Broadway and Columbus and Grant Aves, there's another historic San Francisco cultural site. The **Condor Bistro** is a very bland replacement for the old Condor Club where, as a plaque solemnly announces, silicon-enhanced Carol Doda first went topless on June 19, 1964 and bottomless on September 3, 1969.

The **Museum of North Beach** (☎ *415-391-6210; 1435 Stockton St; admission free; open 9am-5pm Mon-Fri*), in the Bay View Bank mezzanine, has photographs and memorabilia tracing the history of this colorful area in the late 19th and early 20th centuries.

The 1924 **Saints Peter & Paul Church** (*666 Filbert St*) overlooks **Washington Square**, North Beach's cultural focal point and its only open public space. The church is the largest Catholic church in San Francisco; each October the Santa Maria del Lume (patron saint of fishermen) procession makes its way down Columbus Ave to Fisherman's Wharf to bless the fishing fleet.

Atop Telegraph Hill, the 210ft **Coit Tower** (☎ *415-362-0808; open 10am-6pm daily*) is one of San Francisco's prime landmarks.

Built in 1934, it was financed by San Francisco eccentric Lillie Hitchcock Coit, who often dressed as a man to gamble in North Beach, wore short skirts to go ice skating and harbored a lifelong passion for a good fire. In 1863 the 15-year-old Lillie was adopted as the mascot of the Knickerbocker Hose Company No 5, and it's said she 'rarely missed a blaze.'

Inside the tower is a superb series of Diego Rivera–style murals of San Franciscans at work, painted by 25 local artists as part of a '30s WPA project. The ride to the top of the tower costs $3. Avoid driving here, as parking is limited. Those who make the hike can then follow the wooden Filbert St Steps, which lead down past the picturesque cottages of Darrell Place and Napier Lane to Levi's Plaza and the Embarcadero.

RUSSIAN HILL (Map 4)

West of North Beach are the roller-coaster streets of Russian Hill, with some of the city's prime real estate and the famous Lombard St switchback. This stretch of Lombard, touted as 'the world's crookedest street,' wiggles down the hillside, notching up 10 turns. Originally, the crooked block was as straight as any other, but its 27% incline was too steep for cars to manage, so in 1922 the curves were added.

The top of Russian Hill is so steep that not all the roads manage to surmount it, making way for pocket-size patches of green – affording some incredible views of the city below – such as Ina Coolbrith Park (Vallejo St), and steep stairways such as Macondray Lane (between Leavenworth & Taylor Sts). The latter was the model for Barbary Lane in Armistead Maupin's Tales of the City. Another lane of literary interest is Russell St where, at No 29, Jack Kerouac drafted On the Road and several other works in 1952 while living with Neal and Carolyn Cassady.

The San Francisco Art Institute (☎ 415-771-7020; 800 Chestnut St), founded during the 1870s, has public exhibitions in its Walter and McBean Gallery (open Mon-Sat 11am-6pm) and the student-directed Diego Rivera Gallery (open 8am-9pm Mon-Sat); the latter features public art receptions every Tuesday at 5:30pm. The institute's cloisters and courtyards date from 1926, with a 1970 addition. The school has a surprisingly good café and excellent views over the bay.

For Russian Hill hangouts and stores, head to Polk St, which slopes down to Ghirardelli Square.

FISHERMAN'S WHARF (Map 4)

Most San Franciscans view Fisherman's Wharf as a necessary evil. On the plus side, it brings in tourist dollars and concentrates all the tackiest tourist traps in a single part of town. On the minus side, the area has been developed almost entirely with tourism in mind, and most 'attractions' are nothing more than thinly disguised shopping malls.

At one time, though, the wharf was alive with the hustle and bustle of honest fishermen, a substantial heritage celebrated at the distinguished San Francisco Maritime National Historic Park (☎ 415-561-7100). The park includes the Maritime Museum (300 Beach St; admission free; open 10am-5pm daily), which overlooks Aquatic Park and recounts the Bay Area's nautical history, and five classic ships moored at Hyde St Pier (2905 Hyde St; adult/child $6/2; open 9:30am-5:30pm daily), including the Balclutha, an iron-hull square-rigger from 1886.

Two more historic watercraft await at Pier 45. The USS Pampanito (☎ 415-775-1943; adult/senior & child $7/4; open 9am-8pm Thur-Tues, 9am-6pm Wed) is a WWII US Navy submarine that made six Pacific patrols during the last years of the war and sank six Japanese ships, including two carrying British and Australian POWs. The SS Jeremiah O'Brien (☎ 415-544-0100; Pier 45; adult/child $7/4; open 9am-5pm daily) is the sole surviving WWII Liberty ship in complete working order. It has an illustrious history, including 11 voyages as part of the D-Day landings at Normandy.

If there's a single focus for the Fisherman's Wharf crush, it's undoubtedly Pier 39, a remodeled working pier with a huge collection of cheesy shops and touristy restaurants. Attractions include a Venetian carousel ($2) and the Aquarium of the Bay (☎ 888-732-3483; adult/child $13/6.50; open 10am-6pm daily, extended hours in summer), an enormous marine aquarium highlighted by two clear underwater tunnels that put you at eye level with the bay's creatures.

Another attraction turned up around 1990, when California sea lions began to haul out on a section of the walkways beside Pier 39. Today, the takeover is complete, and hundreds of sea lions bask in the sun, barking noisily.

The Fisherman's Wharf area includes two shopping centers recycled from factories and industrial zones: **Ghirardelli Square** *(900 North Point St)*, once home to the San Francisco chocolatier Ghirardelli (there are still two shops in the square); and the **Cannery** *(2801 Leavenworth St)*, occupying the old Del Monte fruit canning factory.

Note that Fisherman's Wharf is the jumping-off point for Alcatraz (see The Bay later in this chapter).

THE MARINA & COW HOLLOW (Map 4)

The Marina, with its pick-up bars and high-priced rental units, is where grown-up frat boys and sorority girls live after they've landed high-paying jobs downtown. Chestnut St is the main commercial strip of the Marina; a few blocks south, Union St is the spine of the Cow Hollow neighborhood, named after a local dairy farm that once occupied the area. In between the Marina and Cow Hollow is motel-lined Lombard St, which connects the Golden Gate Bridge with Van Ness Ave.

The Marina was just mud flats before the 1915 Panama-Pacific International Exposition. Waterfront marshland was reclaimed to create the grounds for that exhibition, which commemorated the Panama canal's completion and San Francisco's rebirth-post-earthquake. One of the few surviving structures from the Exposition is the stunning **Palace of Fine Arts** *(Baker St at Bay St)*, bordering the Presidio. Bernard Maybeck's artificial classical ruin was so popular that it was spared from its intended demolition when the exhibition closed. In the early '60s, the decaying stucco building was resurrected in durable concrete.

Behind the ruin is the **Exploratorium** *(☎ 415-561-0360; W www.exploratorium .edu; 3601 Lyon St; adult/child $10/6; open 10am-5pm Tues, Thur-Sun, 10am-9:30pm Wed, extended hours in summer)*, founded in 1969 by physicist Frank Oppenheimer (brother of Manhattan Project director Robert Oppenheimer) as a museum blending art, science and human perception. Take the

time to visit, as it's an excellent experience, popular with both children and adults. A highlight is the Tactile Dome, a pitch-black dome that you can crawl, climb and slide through (advance reservations required).

Cyclists, in-line skaters, joggers and kite fliers all enjoy the waterfront strip of **Marina Green**, a great place for lounging when the weather's decent.

At the tip of the breakwater, past the Golden Gate Yacht Club, is the curious **Wave Organ**, developed by artist Peter Richards and installed (with help from the Exploratorium) in 1986. Incoming and outgoing tides produce sounds in the organ's pipes; it's subtle, so don't expect Beethoven's Ninth. The organ and jetty are constructed out of stone from a demolished cemetery.

Between Aquatic Park and the Marina lies **Fort Mason Center** *(☎ 415-441-3400; W www.fortmason.org)*, first a Spanish and then a US military fort. The buildings and surrounding acreage were handed over to the Golden Gate National Recreation Area in the 1970s. The cultural complex now houses nonprofits, theaters, galleries and museums, including the **Museum of Craft & Folk Art** *(☎ 415-775-0991)*, the **Museo Italo-American** *(☎ 415-673-2200)* and the **African-American Historical & Cultural Society** *(☎ 415-441-0640)*. The popular HI Fisherman's Wharf is just up the hill (see Places to Stay later in this chapter).

PACIFIC HEIGHTS

This wealthy residential area is loosely located on the hilltop south of the Marina, between Van Ness Ave and the Presidio. If you like wandering streets lined with impressive mansions, this is your neighborhood. Many of the city's finest historic residences survive here, because Van Ness Ave was where the fire after the 1906 quake stopped. There's no real itinerary to follow, just wander and look; if you want a guided view, see Walking Tours later in this chapter.

Most houses are not open to the public. The exception is the **Haas-Lilienthal House** *(☎ 415-441-3004; 2007 Franklin St)*, built in Queen Anne style between 1882 and 1886. The exterior is impressive, and the house is full of period furniture, but the hour-long tour can be slow. Tours ($5/3 per adult/child) are offered noon to 3pm Wednesday and Saturday, and 11am to 4pm Sunday.

Another standout is the huge baroque Spreckels Mansion at 2080 Washington St, built in 1912 by George Applegarth (who also created the Palace of the Legion of Honor) for sugar magnate Adolph Spreckels. It was purchased by novelist Danielle Steele in 1990.

Fillmore St, climbing uphill from Union St and sloping down to Japantown, is the main drag. The Pacific Heights section (roughly Jackson to Sutter Sts) is chock full of good but pricey restaurants and upscale clothing boutiques.

JAPANTOWN & FILLMORE DISTRICT

Japanese people have lived in San Francisco since the 1860s, and today only a tiny portion of them live in the compact Japantown area, just to the south of Pacific Heights around Fillmore St. Known as Nihonjinmachi in Japanese, the area was populated by Japanese after the 1906 earthquake. The WWII internment of Japanese and Japanese Americans devastated the community, and many of the former residents were unable to reclaim their homes after the war.

During WWII the area, known also as **The Fillmore**, became populated by African Americans, with a once-thriving jazz community along Fillmore St one of the side benefits. Since then, the Fillmore has been the subject of various redevelopment ideas, and now boasts towering condos alongside its day-to-day salons and shops and the famous Fillmore concert venue (see Bars & Clubs under Entertainment later in this chapter).

As for Japantown, today it's centered on the north side of Geary Blvd and is primarily a small commercial district, its focal point being the sprawling **Japan Center** *(cnr Geary Blvd & Fillmore St)*, opened in 1968. Japan Center's three malls are packed with excellent restaurants, the Kabuki 8 cinema and many interesting shops, including a large Japanese bookstore.

While Japantown isn't really a neighborhood in the sense that Chinatown is, it does come alive during the two-weekend Cherry Blossom Festival every April, and during the two-day Nihonmachi Street Fair on the first weekend in August.

For a communal bath, try **Kabuki Springs & Spa** *(☎ 415-922-6000; 1750 Geary Blvd; spa $15-18; open 10am-10pm daily)*. Nights for women are Sunday, Wednesday and Friday; men's nights are Monday, Thursday and Saturday. Tuesday is co-ed and swimsuits are required. Massage and other treatments are also available by appointment.

THE HAIGHT (Map 5)

Just east of Golden Gate Park, the Haight-Ashbury area, locally known as 'the Haight,' is roughly divided into two sections: the **Upper Haight**, from Golden Gate Park to Masonic Ave; and the **Lower Haight**, a colorful few blocks of grungy clubs and bars from Scott St east to Webster St. South of the Upper Haight, quiet **Cole Valley** is an upscale residential area with cafés and shops centered on Carl and Cole Sts.

Though Haight-Ashbury was the epicenter of the Summer of Love and flower power during the heady years of '65, '66 and '67, the seminal events of San Francisco's hippie scene actually occurred in other parts of town. Ken Kesey's Trips Festival, in which thousands of people grooved to live music and dropped acid, took place in 1965 at the Longshoremen's Hall, near Fisherman's Wharf, while the 1967 Gathering of the Tribes (aka the Human Be-In), which ushered in the Summer of Love, was held in Golden Gate Park. But it was to the somewhat run-down Victorian Haight-Ashbury that the idealistic 'hippies' gravitated. They were drawn by low rents, proximity to the park and a preexisting bohemian community that had grown out of North Beach's Beat scene.

The 'San Francisco sound' – the LSD-inspired psychedelic rock typified by groups such as the Charlatans and the Grateful Dead – gestated in Haight St clubs such as the Straight Theater. The neighborhood was populated with musicians who would become the legends of the '60s: the Dead, Jefferson Airplane, Janis Joplin, Big Brother and the Holding Company, and Country Joe and the Fish were all neighbors as the Haight-Ashbury reached its full flowering.

It proved to be a brief, if glowing, heyday. By late '67 drug overdoses had become commonplace, and incidences of violence were increasing among the hippies, gawkers, media and police. By the early '70s, Haight St was skid row for burnt-out hippies, and as the hippie scene faded the street became a hub of gay nightlife.

Today, despite what the throngs of tie-dyed stragglers and some wide-eyed tourists might like to believe, the Summer of Love is just a dreamlike memory on Haight St. About all that remains unchanged from the era is the street sign at the corner of Haight and Ashbury Sts. Still, if you don't mind dodging grubby panhandlers and other LSD casualties, the Haight is worth a wander. Dive into a few boutiques, stop for a cheap meal, down some strong coffee and check out the used clothing and record stores – that's what it's all about. Deadheads should pass by **710 Ashbury St**, the one-time communal home of the Grateful Dead (now a private residence).

THE CASTRO (Map 5)

The compact Castro is the focal point of gay life in San Francisco. Don't mistake it for a center of radicalism, though: it's mostly a residential neighborhood with an upper-middle-class vibe. Yet it's not entirely sedate, as residents do indulge in wackiness, especially during such celebratory events as Gay Pride Month (June) and Halloween.

The magnificent **Castro Theatre** (see Entertainment later in this chapter) is the highlight of Castro St and the center for the annual Gay and Lesbian Film Festival. **Harvey Milk Plaza** (cnr Market & Castro Sts), at the MUNI station, is dedicated to the unofficial 'mayor of Castro St,' and the first openly gay man elected to public office in San Francisco. He was murdered along with Mayor Moscone in 1978.

The AIDS epidemic has claimed thousands of lives here since the 1980s, but the neighborhood has never lost its spirit; it's marked still by colorful characters and a bustling street life. In fact, the Castro remains one of the city's best neighborhoods for people-watching, indulging in a leisurely lunch, browsing for books and clothes, or grabbing a beer.

Continue south along Castro or Noe Sts, and you'll come to **Noe Valley**, another of San Francisco's colorful small neighborhoods. The mix of Victorian homes, restaurants and eclectic shops gives it a villagey feel; the main drag is the stretch of 24th St

Gay San Francisco

In the early 1950s, a chapter of the Mattachine Society, the first serious homosexual rights organization in the US, sprang up in San Francisco, and in 1955 the Daughters of Bilitis (DOB), the nation's first lesbian organization, was founded in San Francisco.

During the 1959 mayoral campaign, challenger Russell Wolden accused incumbent mayor George Christopher of turning San Francisco into 'the national headquarters of the organized homosexuals in the United States.' Christopher was re-elected, but was not about to be accused of being soft on queers. He responded with a massive police crackdown on gay male cruising areas, raids which resulted in a public blacklist of gay citizens.

Resistance to this persecution did not come out of the homophile movement but out of bars, and one in particular: the Black Cat, dubbed by Allen Ginsberg as 'the greatest gay bar in America.' (José Sarria, a drag performer at the Black Cat, ran for city supervisor in 1961, becoming the first openly gay person to run for public office in the US.)

The age of tolerance had not yet arrived, however. In 1965 a dance sponsored by the Council on Religion and the Homosexual was raided by the police, and everyone in attendance was arrested and photographed. The city was outraged and even the media denounced the police behavior. This event helped to turn the tide in the city's perception of the gay community. The crackdown on gay bars stopped, and a gay person was appointed to sit on the police community relations board.

With the 1977 election of gay activist Harvey Milk to the Board of Supervisors, recognition of the gay rights movement reached a new peak, but the euphoria was to be short-lived. The following year, Milk and Mayor George Moscone were assassinated by Dan White, an avowedly anti-gay former police officer.

Their deaths marked the beginning of the end of the heyday, the opulence of which further faded when the first cases of AIDS – at the time known as GRID (Gay-Related Immune Deficiency) – were reported in San Francisco in 1981.

Heather Harris

between Church and Castro Sts, full of clothing and gift boutiques, book and record stores, and lots of baby strollers.

THE MISSION (Map 5)

The Mission, one of the oldest parts of the city, is a largely Spanish-speaking enclave, a center for bohemian and alternative living and one of the city's best spots for a good, cheap meal. The heart of the district stretches east–west, between Dolores St and South Van Ness Ave, and north–south, between 16th and 25th Sts. Valencia and Mission Sts are the two main streets for shops and restaurants.

Long considered a trendy spot for hip nightlife and edgy art happenings, the Mission became one of the neighborhoods most visibly affected by the dot-com boom. Apartments and commercial spaces were always a little cheaper here than elsewhere in San Francisco, but as citywide prices began skyrocketing, local landlords jumped on the bandwagon, leasing and selling to the highest bidder. Because of all this, many longtime residents and businesses were forced out, making way for high-priced restaurants and expensive lofts and condos. These trends have been tempered somewhat by the recent dot-com (and overall economic) downturn.

It's a pleasure to find that the throngs of yuppies and trend-seeking nightclubbers haven't entirely ruined either the Mission's bohemian vibe or its neighborly Latino charm. Latino residents still number 50%, and the culture is still intact along local streets. Just take a stroll down shaded 24th St, between Mission and Potrero Sts, and you'll find the true heart of the neighborhood.

The Mission District takes its name from **Mission Dolores** (☎ 415-621-8203; *Dolores & 16th Sts; admission $2; open 9am-4pm daily*), the oldest building in San Francisco. Originally Misión San Francisco de Asís, it was the sixth mission founded by Father Junípero Serra for the Spanish. Its site was consecrated on June 29, 1776, but a more sturdy structure was built in 1782 by Franciscan monks, with Native American labor. Today, the humble mission building is overshadowed by the adjoining basilica, built in 1913.

A few blocks south, **Mission Dolores Park** is a popular spot on sunny days with both sunbathers and Latino families holding family barbecues. After dark the park remains a seedy enclave best avoided. The park was once a Jewish cemetery.

One prime Mission attraction is its hundreds of colorful **murals**, depicting everything from San Francisco's labor history to Central American independence struggles, the women's movement and local streetlife. One of the most amazing examples of mural art is on the **Women's Building** (*3543 18th St*), between Valencia and Guerrero Sts. Narrow **Balmy Alley**, between Folsom and Harrison Sts and 24th and 25th Sts, is lined end-to-end with murals.

If you're especially interested in murals stop by the **Precita Eyes Mural Arts and Visitors Center** (☎ 415-285-2287; w *www .precitaeyes.org; 2981 24th St*). The center sells postcards, books, art supplies and a mural walking tour map ($4). It also conducts walking tours (see Walking Tours later in this chapter).

THE PRESIDIO

The northwest corner of the San Francisco peninsula was for many decades occupied by a rather low-key army base. As a result the area has not been developed, and most of it remains green, despite the fact that Hwys 1 and 101 meet in the middle of the Presidio and lead to the Golden Gate Bridge.

The Presidio was established in 1776 by the Spanish as the site of their first fort, or *presidio*. The Presidio's military role ended in 1994, when the 1480-acre plot became part of the Golden Gate National Recreation Area. Since then, debates have raged over how best to use the valuable land, and to make the park financially sustainable. One new tenant is George Lucas, who is building a film production facility on the site of the old Letterman hospital.

The **Presidio Visitors Center** (☎ 415-561-4323; *cnr Montgomery St & Lincoln Blvd*) has exhibits and information on the park's facilities.

Facing the bay is Crissy Field, a recently restored tidal marsh that features beautiful hiking and biking trails and the **Crissy Field Center** (☎ 415-561-7690; *cnr Mason & Halleck Sts; open 9am-5pm Wed-Sun*), which has a café and bookstore.

Under American rule, **Fort Point** was built at the start of the 1861–65 Civil War to guard the entrance to the bay, but it never saw a battle or cannon fire and was abandoned in

1900. Today, Fort Point offers some of the most spectacular views of the Golden Gate Bridge – a view Hitchcock fans will remember from the 1958 film *Vertigo*, which was filmed all over San Francisco. The triple-tiered brick fortress is off Marine Dr, just below the Golden Gate Bridge (see The Bay later in this chapter).

Along the ocean side of the peninsula is **Baker Beach**, the most picturesque of the city's beaches, with craggy rock formations backed up against cliffs. Due to the cold water and currents, it's not much of a swimming beach, but it is popular with sunbathers, with or without swimsuits.

THE RICHMOND (Map 7)

Bordered by the green Presidio to the north and Golden Gate Park to the south, the uniform rectangular blocks of the Richmond District stretch from Arguello Ave all the way to the ocean. The restaurants and shops along busy Clement St make up the heart of the area, and also the heart of New Chinatown.

Cliff House (☎ 415-386-3330; w www .cliffhouse.com), overlooking the Pacific from the north end of Ocean Beach, was originally built in 1863 as an escape from the crowds. After the first was destroyed by fire, the second Cliff House was an impressive, elegant eight-story gingerbread resort built by Adolph Sutro in 1896, which contained art galleries, dining rooms and an observation deck. It survived the 1906 earthquake but was destroyed by fire the following year. The 1909 replacement is nowhere near as grand, but it's still a popular restaurant and lounge with great views, though unexciting food. The Cliff House was due to undergo restoration beginning in 2002, though it won't be closed entirely.

On the deck below the restaurant is a giant **Camera Obscura** (☎ 415-750-0415; admission $2; open 11am-sunset daily), an invention that projects the view from outside the building onto a parabolic screen inside. It was built in 1946 by a local engineer, based on diagrams originally drawn by Leonardo da Vinci. After some debate about its future, it was added to the National Register of Historic Places in 2001. It's definitely worth seeing.

The equally superb and unique **Musée Mécanique** (☎ 415-386-1170) is a one-of-a-kind collection of over 160 arcade games,

risqué Mutoscope motion pictures ('See what the belly dancer does on her day off!') and player pianos, all in working order, from the late 19th and early 20th centuries. Unfortunately, it was kicked out of its longtime home in the Cliff House basement in 2002 due to renovations to Cliff House. At the time of writing there were plans to relocate it temporarily to Pier 45 in Fisherman's Wharf, and to eventually build it a new permanent home back at Cliff House.

The ruins in the cove just north of the Cliff House are all that remain of the **Sutro Baths**, the magnificent six-pool, 3-acre indoor swimming-pool palace Sutro built in 1896. The baths never made money, however, and the building burned down in 1966 amid rumors of insurance fraud.

There's a fine walking path along this surprisingly rugged stretch of coast from Cliff House to **Lands End**, where there are terrific views across the Golden Gate. It starts by the remains of Sutro Baths and passes through **Lincoln Park**, which was established by Golden Gate park keeper John McLaren.

Off 34th Ave, within Lincoln Park, is the **California Palace of the Legion of Honor** (☎ 415-863-3330; adult/child $8/5, free Tues; open 9:30am-5pm Tues-Sun), one of San Francisco's premier art museums, with a world-class collection of medieval to 20th-century European art. A MUNI bus transfer gets you $2 off adult admission; from downtown, take bus No 1, 2 or 38.

GOLDEN GATE PARK (Map 7)

San Francisco's biggest park stretches almost halfway across the peninsula. An 1870 competition to design the park was won by 24-year-old William Hammond Hall; in 1871 he began the task of turning 1017 acres of dunes into the largest developed park in the world, and by the 1880s the park had become the city's most popular attraction. John Laren took over the park's management in 1887 and stayed on as administrator for the next 56 years, until his death at age 97.

Apart from gardens, lakes, sporting facilities and trails, the park also hosts museums and other indoor attractions. Park information is available from lovely **McLaren Lodge** (☎ 415-831-2700; park entrance Fell & Stanyan Sts).

The **Conservatory of Flowers**, the oldest building in the park, was brought from

Ireland for millionaire James Lick's estate, but he died before it could be rebuilt and it went up instead in Golden Gate Park in 1878. Heavily damaged by storms in 1995, the glass-paned conservatory is being remodeled; the projected reopening date is in 2003.

The **California Academy of Sciences** (☎ 415-750-7145; W www.calacademy.org; adult/student $8.50/5.50, free 1st Wed of month; open 10am-5pm daily Oct-May, 9am-6pm June-Sept) is a large natural-history museum with a planetarium and a fun earthquake simulator. Also inside is **Steinhart Aquarium**, highlighted by a mesmerizing 'fish roundabout,' where viewers are surrounded by a 100,000-gallon tank. Show a current MUNI transfer and get $2.50 off the admission price. The academy is currently planning to begin major renovations of its facilities in 2004, when it will temporarily relocate to a new location.

The nearby **MH de Young Memorial Museum** (☎ 415-863-3330) will reopen in 2005 in a new facility at the same location.

The popular **Japanese Tea Garden** (☎ 415-831-2700; adult/child $2/1; open 9am-6:30pm daily summer, 8:30am-6pm winter) was originally the Japanese Village exhibit at the 1894 Midwinter Fair, held in Golden Gate Park. Today it features a pagoda, gates, bridges, statues and a pleasant teahouse where you can enjoy green tea and fortune cookies for $2. It's claimed fortune cookies were actually invented here, back in 1909.

The **Strybing Arboretum & Botanical Gardens** (☎ 415-661-1316) encompasses a number of smaller gardens within its 70 acres, including the Garden of Fragrance, the California Collection of Native Plants and the Japanese Moon-Viewing Garden. Free tours take place daily; stop by the bookstore just inside the arboretum entrance for details.

The park is packed with sporting facilities, including 7½mi of bicycle trails, untold miles of jogging trails, 12mi of equestrian trails, an archery range, baseball and softball diamonds, fly-casting pools, a challenging nine-hole golf course, lawn bowling greens, *pétanque* courts (a French game similar to lawn bowling), four soccer fields and 21 tennis courts. Rowboats and pedal boats can be rented from the **Stow Lake boathouse** (☎ 415-752-0347; open 10am-4pm daily) for $13 to $17 an hour.

On Sunday some roads in the park are closed to traffic, allowing hordes of in-line skaters, bicyclists and street hockey players to buzz around free from obstructing autos. See Bicycling and Running & Skating later in this chapter to find out where to rent bicycles and in-line skates.

THE SUNSET & TWIN PEAKS

South of Golden Gate Park, the city's hilly terrain makes two final skyward lunges at Twin Peaks and Mt Sutro, then rolls westward in block after uniform block to the ocean. Originally known as El Pecho de la Chola (the Breasts of the Indian Girl), the two summits of the appropriately named **Twin Peaks** (922ft and 904ft) offer a superb view of the Bay Area, especially at night. You can drive to Twin Peaks by heading southwest on Market St as it climbs steeply uphill (it becomes Portola Ave) and then turning right on Twin Peaks Blvd.

The area south of Golden Gate Park down to Sloat Blvd and from about 16th Ave to the ocean is known as the Sunset District, a mostly residential area filled with pastel-colored stucco homes built between the 1930s and 1950s. The Inner Sunset, centered on 9th Ave at Irving and Judah Sts, has a collection of decent restaurants, bars and shops only a block or two from Golden Gate Park.

Ocean Beach stretches for miles along the coast, from Cliff House to the cliffs of Fort Funston. On sunny days, you'll find a classic California beach scene: sunbathers, surfers and picnickers. Unfortunately, sunny days are few and far between.

San Francisco Zoo (Map 1; ☎ 415-753-7080; W www.sfzoo.org; Sloat Blvd & 45th Ave; adult/concession $10/7; open 10am-5pm daily) is transforming into a more conservation-friendly outfit. The Lemur Forest opened in 2002, with large, new African savanna and ape exhibits due in coming years.

One mile south, **Fort Funston** is a beautiful windswept area of cliffs, trails and beach: a great place to spend an afternoon watching the hang gliders float above the cliffs.

THE BAY

San Francisco Bay is the largest on the California coast, stretching about 60mi in length and up to 12mi in width. It's fed by the Sacramento and San Joaquin Rivers, mingling with the sea through the Golden Gate. The bay is, however, very shallow, averaging only 6ft to 10ft deep at low tide.

Golden Gate Bridge

Commenced in January 1933 and opened in May 1937, the beautiful Golden Gate Bridge links San Francisco with Marin County and remains the symbol of the city. The bridge, designed by Joseph B Strauss, is nearly 2mi in length, with a main span of 4200ft. When the bridge was completed, it was the longest suspension bridge in the world. Its name comes from the entrance to the harbor, the Golden Gate, but also inadvertently alludes to its 'international orange' paint scheme. Painting the bridge is a never-ending job – a team of 25 painters adds 1000 golden gallons every week.

A prime starting point for bridge appreciation is the Fort Point Lookout at the southern end of the bridge. The lookout offers excellent views and has a gift center, a statue of Strauss and a sample of the 3ft-thick suspension cable. MUNI buses No 28 and 29 run to the toll plaza. There are even better views from the lookout at Vista Point, on the north side of the bridge.

On weekends, pedestrians can walk across the bridge on the east side, while bicyclists can zoom along on the ocean side (see the boxed text 'Hiking & Biking the Bridge' in the San Francisco Bay Area chapter). During the week they share the east side. The bridge toll (southbound only) is $5 per car.

Bay Bridge

The vehicle-only Bay Bridge is considerably longer than the Golden Gate Bridge, carries far more traffic and predates it by six months, but it has never enjoyed the same iconic fame. The Bay Bridge actually consists of three separate parts: a double suspension bridge that leads from San Francisco to the mid-bay **Yerba Buena Island**; a tunnel that cuts straight through the rocky island; and a series of latticework spans that connect Yerba Buena Island to Oakland. There's a $2 toll westbound.

The 1989 earthquake caused a 50ft section of the Yerba Buena–Oakland span to collapse. Though repaired, it served as a wake-up call; that half of the bridge is now being replaced, with construction projected to finish by 2007.

Alcatraz

From 1933 to 1963 the rocky island in the middle of San Francisco Bay was home of the most notorious prison in the United States. The 12-acre Alcatraz became the prison of choice for serious offenders for a simple reason – 'the Rock' was believed to be escape-proof, until the Anglin brothers and co-conspirator Frank Morris floated away in a self-made raft in 1962 and were never seen again. That enigmatic escape was made famous by the 1979 movie *Escape from Alcatraz*, starring Clint Eastwood. Though Alcatraz is only 1½mi from the mainland, they are 1½ very cold miles swept by the bay's often ferocious currents, not to mention the occasional shark.

After the prison's closure, the island was more or less forgotten for six years until 1969, when it was taken over by Native Americans, who claimed Indian peoples' ownership of the land and conducted a 19-month protest sit-in to bring national attention to their causes. The event sparked a wave of Native American activism in the US.

Blue & Gold Fleet (☎ *415-773-1188 for information, 415-705-5555 for reservations*) runs ferries to the island from Pier 41 at Fisherman's Wharf. It's wise to book or pick up tickets well in advance, especially in summer. Departures to the island are from 9:30am to 2:15pm daily (until 4:15pm in summer). The round-trip fare is $13, plus $2 for phone orders; the price includes an excellent audio tour featuring first-hand narratives by former guards and inmates. Guided 'Alcatraz After Dark' tours are also given twice daily from Thursday to Sunday (adult/child $21/18). The **park ranger station** (☎ *415-705-1042*) has information on the island and its history.

BICYCLING

Despite the hilly challenges of many San Francisco streets, cycling is actually fun and popular here. Good places to head to are Golden Gate Park and the Presidio (though in the Presidio, take note that park police frequently ticket cyclists for not stopping at stop signs and other traffic violations). You can also try biking across the Golden Gate Bridge to Sausalito, the Headlands or Mt Tam, the latter being the Bay Area's supreme mountain-biking challenge (see the San Francisco Bay Area chapter).

Bike lanes are more frequent in town nowadays, and bike signs point the way to parks and assist in avoiding the most suicidal of hills. Contact the **San Francisco Bicycle Coalition** (☎ 415-431-2453; **W** www.sfbike .org) for information about rights and rules, advice and schedules of group rides. The coalition also publishes the helpful *Safe Bicycling in San Francisco* brochure.

If you're under 18, California law says you must wear a helmet, and every cyclist must have a light when pedaling at night. And of course, always carry a good lock; bike theft is all too common in the city.

For rentals, try **Avenue Cyclery** (*Map 7;* ☎ 415-387-3155; 756 Stanyan St), right by Golden Gate Park in the Upper Haight, which has bikes starting at $5 per hour, $25 per day. Near Fisherman's Wharf is **Blazing Saddles** (*Map 4;* ☎ 415-202-8888; 1095 Columbus Ave), where rentals cost $7 per hour and $28 per day. It also has a second location on Pier 41, which is super convenient if you're planning to bike across the bridge and return via ferry (maps are provided for this route too).

RUNNING & SKATING
Marina Green has a 2½mi jogging track and fitness course, and there are many running paths through Golden Gate Park. The Presidio is another great park for running, with plenty of routes from the Marina right past the Golden Gate Bridge to Baker Beach.

In-line skating is very popular in Golden Gate Park; you can rent skates at **Skates on Haight** (*Map 5;* ☎ 415-752-8375; 1818 Haight St at Stanyan St) from $6/24 per hour/day and cruise directly into the park.

SAILING & WINDSURFING
Any view of the bay, dotted with sails, shows this is prime sailing country. The bay is tricky territory, though, and only for experienced sailors. **Spinnaker Sailing** (☎ 415-543-7333; **W** www.spinnaker-sailing .com; Pier 40) offers charter boats and lessons (a two-day basic class costs $295).

The bay is also great for windsurfing, but it is not kind to beginners. For more experienced board sailors, the beach off Crissy Field, in the shadow of the Golden Gate Bridge, is a world-class spot. A good place to watch sailboarders is Fort Point, right under the Golden Gate Bridge.

SURFING
Ocean Beach is one of the most challenging and exhausting places to surf in California, especially in winter when the powerful, cold swells can reach 12ft or more. There are no lifeguards, and you should never surf alone or without at least a 3mm full-length wetsuit. For a recorded message on the latest surfing conditions at Ocean Beach, call **Wise Surfboards** (☎ 415-273-1618) or **SF Surfshop** (☎ 415-437-6683), or check **W** www.surfpulse.com.

TENNIS
There are free public tennis courts all over San Francisco. The courts at Mission Dolores Park are popular; for others, call the **San Francisco Recreation & Park Department** (☎ 415-753-7001). The 21 courts in Golden Gate Park charge a fee.

GOLF
San Francisco has three 18-hole public golf courses: **Harding Park** (*Map 1;* ☎ 415-664-4690; Harding & Skyline Blvds), near Lake Merced; **Lincoln Park** (*Map 7;* ☎ 415-750-4653; 34th Ave & Clement St); and, near the Presidio's Arguello Gate, the stunning **Presidio Golf Course** (*Map 7;* ☎ 415- 561-4653). There's also a challenging nine-hole course in **Golden Gate Park** (*Map 7;* ☎ 415-751-8987), near the beach.

WHALE-WATCHING
Mid-October through December is the peak season for whale-watching in the Bay Area, as gray whales make their annual migration south from the Bering Sea to Baja California (see the boxed text 'Gray Whales' in the San Francisco Bay Area chapter). The **Oceanic Society** (☎ 415-474-3385; **W** www .oceanic-society .org) leads whale-watching expeditions from the Yacht Harbor near Marina Green; trips costs between $50 and $70 and run for six to eight hours.

WALKING TOURS
San Francisco lays out a rich feast for those keen on doing their sightseeing on foot. The San Francisco Visitor Information Center (see Information earlier in this chapter) caters to walkers with an excellent line of walking-tour leaflets for Chinatown, Fisherman's Wharf, North Beach, Pacific Heights and Union Square. As for guided tours,

they're often a great way to get grounded in the city during a longer visit, or to just catch a quick but informed glimpse of the city and its famous neighborhoods.

Friends of the San Francisco Public Library (☎ 415-557-4266) leads an eclectic variety of free walking tours led by savvy local historians. Call or stop by the Visitors Information Center or Main Library.

Helen's Walk Tours (☎ 510-524-4544) leads a tour (3½ hours) covering Union Square, Chinatown and North Beach. Tours are given by request, and cost $40 if there are at least four people and $50 if there are only two. Call for reservations.

San Francisco Architectural Heritage (☎ 415-441-3004) offers two-hour walking tours of eastern Pacific Heights every Sunday at 12:30pm ($5).

The **Victorian Home Walk** (☎ 415-252-9485) is a good way for budding architecture buffs to learn more about the city's famous Victorian houses. Tours cost $20 per person and leave daily at 11am from the lobby of the St Francis Hotel in Union Square and last about 2½ hours.

Chinatown is a walker's favorite; you can tag along on a weekly Chinese Heritage Walk ($15) or a Chinese Culinary Walk & Luncheon ($30), departing from the **Chinese Culture Center** (Map 3; ☎ 415-986-1822; Holiday Inn, 750 Kearny St, 3rd floor). Call for reservations.

The Mission is great for walking, especially for seeking out the district's many superb murals. **Precita Eyes Mural Arts and Visitors Center** (☎ 415-285-2287; 2981 Harrison St) conducts a two-hour Mission District Mural Walk (adult/student $12/8) at 1:30pm on Saturday and Sunday.

For the inside line on San Francisco's gay history – from the gold rush days to modern times – and a detailed tour of the Castro District, reserve a spot with **Cruisin' the Castro** (☎ 415-550-8110). The four-hour walk ($40), beginning at 10am from Tuesday to Saturday, includes lunch at a local restaurant.

The **Haight-Ashbury Flower Power Walking Tour** (☎ 415-863-1621) points out the sites of the Human Be-In and the Grateful Dead's former house. The two-hour walk ($15) is on Tuesday and Saturday mornings.

One of San Francisco's best-known walks is the **Dashiell Hammett Tour** (☎ 510-287-9540), led by author Don Herron. The four-

hour tour gumshoes 3mi up and down the streets of the Tenderloin and Union Square. Tours are run on Sunday in May and October only ($10).

SPECIAL EVENTS

In late January and early February, the Golden Dragon Parade is the highlight of the **Chinese New Year** festivities. Contact the **Chinese Chamber of Commerce** (☎ 415-982-3000; 730 Sacramento St) for details.

The country's oldest film festival, **SF International Film Festival**, specializes in a wide spectrum of international titles, some of which you'd be hard-pressed to find anywhere else. Organized by the **SF Film Society** (☎ 415-561-5000; W www.sffs.org), the two-week festival happens every April and/or May, with screenings at the Kabuki in Japantown, the Castro Theatre and other Bay Area cinemas.

On the third Sunday in May, more than 100,000 joggers make their way from the Embarcadero to the ocean in **Bay to Breakers**. Many are in crazy costumes…or no costume at all. Phone ☎ 415-359-2800 for details and entry forms.

Held on Memorial Day weekend at the end of May, **Carnaval** is celebrated with music, a huge parade and dancing in the streets of the Mission. For information phone ☎ 415-920-0125.

June is **Pride Month**, a celebratory month for San Francisco's gay community, with the Gay and Lesbian Film Festival (☎ 415-703-8650; W www.frameline.org) and, on the last Sunday in June, the lively and outrageous Lesbian, Gay, Bisexual and Transgender Pride Parade, attracting hundreds of thousands of people. The evening before is the Pink Saturday party on Castro St. For information call ☎ 415-864-3733 or check W www.sfpride.org.

In July, the cable car drivers compete to be the loudest or most tuneful in the **Cable Car Bell-Ringing Championship**. Phone ☎ 415-923-6217 for details.

For two days in late September, bands, blues legends and R&B artists jam outdoors on Fort Mason's Great Meadow in the **Blues Festival**. Phone ☎ 415-979-5588 for details.

Starting on Labor Day weekend, **Shakespeare Festival** presents free performances of a different play each year, in Golden Gate Park and other Bay Area parks (see the boxed text 'Free & Outdoors' under Entertainment later in this chapter). Phone ☎ 415-422-2221 for details.

Pretty much every neighborhood in San Francisco hosts an annual **street fair**. Two of the most popular are the Folsom St Fair in late September (loaded with leather accouterments and naked strutting), and the massive Castro St Fair in early October. For arts and crafts mixed with blues or jazz, try the Polk St Fair and the Fillmore St Fair, both in the summer months. North Beach hosts a Columbus Day Fair, and the popular Haight St Fair goes all out in early June. For more fairs, check out ⓦ www.sfstreetfair .com or phone the Visitors Information Center.

In mid to late October and into November, you can catch the **Jazz Festival**, featuring performances by legendary and up-and-coming artists throughout the city. For schedule and locations, contact the **SF Jazz Festival store** (☎ *415-788-7353;* ⓦ *www.sfjazz.org; 3 Embarcadero Center).*

With hundreds of thousands of costumed revelers taking to the streets – particularly Castro St (you've never seen more drag queens in once place) and around Civic Center – **Halloween** (October 31) is the city's craziest night of the year. The **Exotic-Erotic Halloween Ball** (☎ *415-567-2255)* at the Concourse Exhibition Center is one of the highlights.

PLACES TO STAY

Deciding on a place to stay in San Francisco requires two decisions: where do you want to stay and what do you want to stay in? The decisions are interrelated: if you want a romantic B&B, you won't end up in the Financial District, and if you want a luxury hotel, you'll probably wind up on Nob Hill or around Union Square. The Visitors Information Center (see Information earlier in this chapter) has a reservation line (☎ 888-782-9673), or check its website at ⓦ www.sfvisitor.org.

Hostelling International (HI) has three San Francisco locations (Union Square, Civic Center and Fort Mason).

The recommendations in this chapter are categorized by neighborhood. Some of these neighborhood sections are then subdivided according to price range. No matter where you stay, reservations are a good idea on summer weekends, over holiday periods (for example, Christmas to New Year) and

during the city's bigger festivals (Halloween and the weekend of the Gay Pride Parade, for instance).

Hotel rates in San Francisco fluctuate quite a bit on a weekly or even daily basis, depending on the time of year, the day of the week and whether the place is already booked up or not. Therefore, prices listed below may well be higher (or sometimes even lower) than the actual rates.

Union Square (Map 2)

If you're staying at a downtown hotel without its own parking, it's best to head for a parking garage rather than risk a tow or a ticket on the street. The cheapest overnight option is the **Fifth & Mission Garage** (☎ *415-982-8522; 833 Mission St),* one block south of Market St near Yerba Buena Gardens, which costs $18 for 24 hours. At the **Ellis-O'Farrell Garage** (☎ *415-986-4800; 123 O'Farrell St),* the daily maximum rate is $25, but there's no access from 1am to 5:30am.

Budget The large, well-equipped **HI San Francisco Downtown** (☎ *415-788-5604; 312 Mason St; dorm beds members/nonmembers* $22/25), a stone's throw from Union Square, has over 280 beds, a few dozen private rooms (from $60 per night) and 24-hour access. The closest BART station is Powell St.

Globetrotters Inn (☎*/fax 415-346-5786; 225 Ellis St; dorm beds per night/week* $17/95), in the Union Square/Tenderloin area, is not far from the HI hostel. Accommodations in this smaller hostel are either in four-bed dorms or in private rooms.

Adelaide Hostel (☎ *415-359-1915, 877-359-1915;* ⓦ *www.adelaidehostel.com; 5 Isadora Duncan Lane; dorm beds from $22, private rooms from $60),* off Taylor St between Post and Geary Sts, is a small inn with free Internet access, breakfast and laundry facilities.

Grant Hotel (☎ *415-421-7540, 800-522-0979, fax 415-989-7719; 753 Bush St; doubles $65-75)* is on the way up to Nob Hill and not far from Chinatown. It's a basic low-priced hotel, offering clean and simple rooms, all with private bathroom.

Dakota Hotel (☎ *415-931-7475; 606 Post St at Taylor St; rooms from $85)* is a snug 42-room property. All rooms have private bathroom and some afford impressive city views.

Sheehan Hotel (☎ 415-775-6500, 800-848-1529; 620 Sutter St; rooms $80-125), is a 64-room hotel with fitness facilities and an indoor swimming pool.

Golden Gate Hotel (☎ 415-392-3702; 775 Bush St; rooms with shared/private bathroom $85/115) is another hotel in this price range.

Mid-Range As prices rise, hotels become more charismatic.

Hotel Bijou (☎ 415-771-1200; W www .hotelbijou.com; 111 Mason St; rooms $115-179), a short block from Hallidie Plaza, stands out among the area's strip joints and peep-show parlors. The theme is cinematic, and videos of films set in San Francisco screen nightly in a small Art Deco–style theater just off the lobby.

Inn at Union Square (☎ 415-397-3510, 800-288-4346, fax 415-989-0529; W www .unionsquare.com; 440 Post St; rooms from $119), just a few steps from Union Square, has 30 elegantly old-fashioned rooms and suites, all nonsmoking.

Hotel Beresford Arms (☎ 415-673-2600, 800-533-6533; W www.beresford.com; 701 Post St; rooms from $129) is a well-kept older hotel with a few spacious rooms, many with kitchens. It's great value, with 96 rooms. Its sister hotel, the 114-room **Hotel Beresford** (☎ 415-673-9900; 635 Sutter St; rooms from $145), is a few blocks away.

Commodore Hotel (☎ 415-923-6800, fax 415-923-6804; W www.thecommodorehotel .com; 825 Sutter St; rooms from $135) is a strikingly hip property that plays on the theme of steamship travel. The rooms have private bathroom and are custom furnished and comfortable.

York Hotel (☎ 415-885-6800, 800-808-9675, fax 415-885-2115; 940 Sutter St; rooms with queen/king bed from $159/179) is an elegant hotel. It appeared in the stairway scenes of Alfred Hitchcock's *Vertigo*.

Maxwell Hotel (☎ 415-986-2000, 888-734-6299, fax 415-397-2447; W www.max wellhotel.com; 386 Geary St; doubles from $165) is a smartly restored 1908 hotel, part of the hip Joie de Vivre chain. Prices include limited parking and breakfast.

White Swan Inn (☎ 415-775-1755, 800-999-9570; W www.foursisters.com; 845 Bush St; rooms with queen bed from $195) and its sister, the **Petite Auberge** (☎ 415-928-6000,

800-365-3004; 863 Bush St; rooms with queen bed from $175), are somewhere between hotel and B&B, with traditional charm, quaint comfort and over-the-top romantic decor.

Hotel Triton (☎ 415-394-0500, 800-433-6611, fax 415-394-0555; W www.hoteltriton .com; 342 Grant Ave; standard/deluxe rooms from $139/299) is notable for its 140 exotically designed guest rooms, including the Carlos Santana and Jerry Garcia suites. Decor is modern in a sort of post–New Wave fashion.

Diva Hotel (☎ 415-885-0200, 800-553-1900; 440 Geary St; rooms from $209), with 108 rooms, is cleanly modern in the glass, chrome and black-enamel style. The rooms are all comfortable, though some are quite small.

Top End Rooms at the luxury hotels typically begin at around $200 a night; suites cost significantly more.

Westin St Francis Hotel (☎ 415-397-7000, 800-937-8461, fax 415-774-0124; 335 Powell St; rooms $229-400) occupies the entire west side of Union Square and is one of the city's most famous hotels.

Grand Hyatt San Francisco (☎ 415-398-1234, 800-233-1234, fax 415-403-4878; 345 Stockton St; rooms $179-379) is on the north side of the square.

Clift Hotel (☎ 415-775-4700, 800-652-5438, fax 415-931-7417; 495 Geary St; rooms from $220) is an old San Francisco classic now owned by Ian Schraeger, featuring an upscale, contemporary Phillipe Starck redesign.

Sir Francis Drake Hotel (☎ 415-392-7755, 800-227-5480, fax 415-391-8719; 450 Powell St; rooms from $289) is an opulently decorated luxury hotel with beefeater-costumed doormen. Rates depend on the season, and package deals can sometimes bring prices down.

Civic Center (Map 2)

Budget One of the city's largest hostels, **New Central Hostel** (☎ 415-703-9988; 1412 Market St; dorm beds $17, rooms from $40) has a couple of hundred dorm beds and four private rooms. The location is convenient – take any BART or MUNI train to Civic Center Station, or take the F-Market streetcar up Market St.

HI San Francisco City Center (☎ 415-474-5721, fax 415-776-0775; 685 Ellis St; dorm rooms $25, private rooms $69) is the newest HI facility in town, with 262 beds and 11 private rooms in an old seven-story Tenderloin hotel. The surrounding area is grungy, especially at night, but there are cheap restaurants and cool clubs to be explored. It has 24-hour check-in and access.

Central YMCA Hotel (☎ 415-885-0460; 220 Golden Gate Ave at Leavenworth St; dorm beds $26, singles/doubles $44/62) is not the best address in town, but this Tenderloin hotel offers simple, clean rooms with shared bathroom. Both men and women are welcome, and there are discounts for students with ISIC cards.

Aida Hotel (☎ 415-863-4141, 800-863-2432, fax 415-863-5151; 1087 Market St; doubles $70), between 6th and 7th Sts, is neat and tidy and excellent value, with 174 rooms.

Embassy Hotel (☎ 415-673-1404; 610 Polk St; singles/doubles from $49/59), on the edge of the Tenderloin, offers plain but clean rooms.

Days Inn (☎ 415-441-8220; 895 Geary St; rooms from $122) is a basic motel with free parking.

Mid-Range Dating back to 1925, the **Abigail Hotel** (☎ 415-861-9728, 800-243-6510, fax 415-626-6580; W www.abigailhotel.com; 246 McAllister St; rooms from $99) is now owned by the Howard Johnson chain. The 61 guest rooms, furnished with antiques, are reasonably priced, and the lobby opens up to lovely Millennium, the city's most renowned vegan restaurant.

Phoenix Motel (☎ 415-776-1380, fax 415-885-3109; 601 Eddy St; king beds from $145) is in the Tenderloin, but it's become a hip place to stay thanks to its rock-and-roll reputation (lots of touring bands stay here, so expect late-night partying). It's a recycled 1950s motor lodge with boxy rooms facing an arty swimming pool. Ultrahip club and restaurant Backflip (see Bars & Clubs under Entertainment later in this chapter) occupies the former coffee shop. Free parking and a continental breakfast make the rooms better value.

South of Market (Map 6)
Globe Hostel (☎ 415-431-0540, fax 415-421-3286; 10 Hallam St; dorm beds $18, private doubles $50), set in a surprisingly quiet location off Folsom St, between 7th and 8th Sts, is well run and friendly. US citizens need a passport to stay. Dorm rooms sleep five, and each room has a private bathroom. Private doubles are available only in the off-season. The hostel has a laundry, TV room and microwave, but no kitchen.

San Francisco International Student Center (☎ 415-487-1463; 1188 Folsom St; dorm beds $15), near the Globe Hostel, is an aging hostel with small dorms that sleep three to five people. Rates fluctuate with season and availability.

Mosser's Victorian Hotel (☎ 415-986-4400, 800-227-3804, fax 415-495-7653; 54 4th St off Market St; rooms from $99) has simple rooms that cost much more if there's a convention in town.

Reneson Hotel Group runs three hotels on the same block of 7th St between Mission and Howard Sts. Each offers standard motel rooms, parking and shuttle service to Union Square. These include the **Hotel Britton** (☎ 415-621-7001, 800-444-5819, fax 415-626-3974; W www.renesonhotels.com; 112 7th St; rooms from $129), the **Americania** (☎ 415-626-0200; 121 7th St; rooms from $119) and the **Carriage Inn** (☎ 415-552-8600; 140 7th St; rooms from $139). The latter two are a bit more deluxe with a pool, Jacuzzi and some rooms with fireplace.

Hotel Griffon (☎ 415-495-2100, 800-321-2201, fax 415-495-3522; W www.hotelgriffon.com; 155 Steuart St; rooms from $175) has a great location at the waterfront, close to the Embarcadero Center and the Ferry Building. The 59 rooms are modern and comfortable, and rates include a continental breakfast. Rooms with a view cost more.

Harbor Court Hotel (☎ 415-882-1300, 800-346-0555, fax 415-882-1313; 165 Steuart St; rooms $115-279), adjacent, is a larger establishment with 130 recently redecorated rooms. Guests can use the gym facilities at the health club next door.

Financial District (Map 2)
Pacific Tradewinds Guest House (☎ 415-433-7970, 800-486-7975, fax 415-291-8801; W www.hostels.com/pt; 680 Sacramento St; dorm beds $24) is a well-maintained, friendly 4th-floor hostel with free DSL Internet access, a fully equipped kitchen and no curfew or chore requirements. It's a great

place to meet other travelers. The nearest BART station is Embarcadero.

Mandarin Oriental San Francisco (☎ 415-885-0999, 800-622-0404, fax 415-276-9304; W www.mandarinoriental.com; 222 Sansome St; standard rooms from $500) is one of the plushest and most expensive hotels in town, ideal if you're on a limitless expense account! Its 158 rooms are on the 38th to 48th floors of the third-highest building in the city, and the views are spectacular.

Hyatt Regency (☎ 415-788-1234, 800-233-1234, fax 415-291-6538; 5 Embarcadero Center; rooms $354), with 800 rooms, is architecturally memorable for its backward-leaning, 20-story atrium. Weekend rates are sometimes cheaper.

Nob Hill (Map 2)

Nob Hill Inn (☎ 415-673-6080; 1000 Pine St at Taylor St; singles/doubles from $125/165) is in a small, pleasant, old Edwardian house. Suites with kitchen facilities cost more.

Nob Hill is topped by four of the city's oldest and classiest hotels: **Fairmont Hotel** (☎ 415-772-5000, 800-527-4727, fax 415-772-5013; 950 Mason St; rooms $170-380); **Huntington Hotel** (☎ 415-474-5400, 800-525-4800, fax 415-474-6227; 1075 California St; rooms from $310); **Renaissance Stanford Court Hotel** (☎ 415-989-3500; 905 California St; rooms from $409) and **Mark Hopkins Inter-Continental** (☎ 415-392-3434, 800-662-4455, fax 415-616-6907; 999 California St; standard rooms from $350). Even if you can't afford an overnight stay, their cocktail lounges are worth a stop (see Bars & Clubs under Entertainment later in this chapter).

Chinatown (Map 3)

Obrero Hotel (☎ 415-989-3960; 1208 Stockton St; rooms from $55), between Pacific St and Broadway, has just 12 rooms with shared bathroom and rock-bottom prices.

Grant Plaza (☎ 415-434-3883, 800-472-6899, fax 415-434-3886; 465 Grant Ave; singles/doubles from $63/76) is just a block from the Chinatown gateway and the California St cable car. The rooms, all with private bathroom, are neat and tidy.

North Beach (Map 3)

Green Tortoise Hostel (☎ 415-834-1000; 494 Broadway; dorm beds $21, private rooms $54)

is a medium-sized place run by the same people who operate the funky Green Tortoise buses (see Organized Tours in the Getting There & Away chapter). It has dorm beds and a few single and double rooms. Prices include breakfast, and kitchen and laundry facilities are available. Bus No 15 from the Transbay Terminal will get you there.

Washington Square Inn (☎ 415-981-4220, 800-388-0220; 1660 Stockton St; rooms $145-245) is a quaint 15-room hotel. Prices include breakfast and afternoon wine and appetizers.

Hotel Bohème (☎ 415-433-9111, fax 415-362-6292; 444 Columbus Ave; rooms $164-174), right in the heart of North Beach, is small and very stylish. All the doubles have private bathroom.

Fisherman's Wharf (Map 4)

HI Fisherman's Wharf (☎ 415-771-7277, fax 415-771-1468; Bldg 240, Fort Mason; dorm beds $23), on a hill just west of Aquatic Park, trades downtown convenience for a quiet setting with kitchen and laundry facilities. To get there, take MUNI bus No 42 from the Transbay Terminal to the stop at Bay St and Van Ness Ave. Bus Nos 30 and 47 also stop there.

San Remo Hotel (☎ 415-776-8688, 800-352-7366, fax 415-776-2811; 2237 Mason St; rooms from $55), tucked on a quiet street near North Beach, is a lovely old-fashioned hotel in an early-20th-century building with small but beautifully appointed rooms, all but the penthouse with shared bathroom. It's one of the city's nicest accommodations for the money.

Dockside Boat & Bed (☎ 415-392-5526; W www.boatandbed.com; office: C Dock, Pier 39; boats nightly per couple $125-340) offers guests a choice of 13 yachts to sleep on. Rates vary depending on the boat.

The streets close to Fisherman's Wharf are overrun with chains and standard tourist motels such as **Radisson Fisherman's Wharf** (☎ 415-392-6700, 800-333-3333; 250 Beach St; rooms $169-279).

The Marina & Cow Hollow (Map 4)

This is the real motel quarter of San Francisco. South of the Golden Gate Bridge, Lombard St (Hwy 101) is nearly wall-to-wall with older, neon-emblazoned motels and mid-range chains. It's a good spot to troll for a room if you arrive by car without a reservation. The neighboring streets are brimming with shops, restaurants and the city's biggest assemblage of pick-up bars.

Marina Motel (☎ 415-921-9406, 800-346-6118, fax 415-921-0364; 2576 Lombard St; summer rate $119) a pleasant 1930s place, is a good place to try.

Travelodge (☎ 415-673-0691, 800-578-7878, fax 415-673-3232; 1450 Lombard St; rooms from $119), near the corner of Van Ness Ave, is another option.

Best Inn (☎ 415-776-3220, fax 415-921-7451; 2850 Van Ness Ave; rooms around $125), around the corner, has a quieter location than the motels right on busy Lombard St.

Head south down Van Ness Ave to find more motels, generally at slightly higher prices, such as the **Comfort Inn** (☎ 415-928-5000, 800-228-5150, fax 415-441-3990; 2775 Van Ness Ave; rooms from $119).

Pacific Heights & Japantown

Pacific Heights has a scattering of pleasant places, including **El Drisco Hotel** (☎ 415-346-2880, 800-634-7277, fax 415-567-5537; 2901 Pacific Ave; doubles from $245). Renovations, though, have turned this 1903 Edwardian hotel into a drastically overpriced option.

Best Western Miyako Inn (☎ 415-921-4000, 800-528-1234, fax 415-923-1064; 1800 Sutter St at Buchanan St; summer rate $125) adds Japanese trimmings to the Best Western formula.

Radisson Miyako Hotel (☎ 415-922-3200, 800-333-3333, fax 415-921-0417; 1625 Post St; summer rate $239), at the eastern end of the Japan Center complex, is a larger and more expensive deluxe hotel with *shoji* screens (rice-paper screens) on the windows and deep Japanese bathtubs in the bathrooms.

The Haight

Metro Hotel (Map 5; ☎ 415-861-5364, fax 415-863-1970; 319 Divisadero St; rooms with full/queen bed $66/77), between Oak and Page Sts, faces a very busy street on the edge of the scruffy Lower Haight. It has cheap and clean rooms, all with private bathroom, plus a garden patio and overnight parking.

Stanyan Park Hotel (Map 7; ☎ 415-751-1000, fax 415-668-5454; W www.stanyan park.com; 750 Stanyan St; rooms $130-185), near Haight St, is right by Golden Gate Park in a fine old Victorian building.

Red Victorian B&B (Map 5; ☎ 415-864-1978, fax 415-863-3293; W www.redvic.com; 1665 Haight St; doubles $86-200), between Cole and Clayton Sts, lets you relive your hippie glory days in trippy, garish digs such as the Flower Child Room, the Sunshine Room or even the Summer of Love Room. Rates for longer stays are cheaper.

Other B&Bs in the area include the **Victorian Inn on the Park** (☎/fax 415-931-1830; W www.victorianinnonthepark.com; 301 Lyon St; rooms $159-199), where rooms in the 1897 'Clunie House' include private bathroom and a continental breakfast.

Alamo Square, north of Lower Haight towards Japantown, is also famous for its Victorians (known as Painted Ladies). Here you'll find pleasant **Alamo Square Inn** (☎ 415-922-2055, fax 415-931-1304; W www.alamoinn.com; 719 Scott St; rooms from $130), which occupies a pair of mansions, and the **Archbishop's Mansion** (☎ 415-563-7872, 800-738-7477, fax 415-885-3193; W www.thearchbishopsmansion.com; 1000 Fulton St; rooms $129-200), which was built in 1904 for the city's archbishop. Prices for both include parking, breakfast and afternoon wine.

The Castro (Map 5)

Twin Peaks Hotel (☎ 415-863-2909, fax 415-863-1545; 2160 Market St; rooms from $49) is basic and cheap; rooms with private bathroom cost a bit more.

Perramont Hotel (☎ 415-863-3222; 2162 Market St; rooms $55), adjacent, has rooms with shared bathroom.

Beck's Motor Lodge (☎ 415-621-8212, 800-227-4360; 2222 Market St; summer rate $129) is a bland 57-room motel.

While same-sex couples are likely to feel at home at almost any San Francisco hotel, a few places in the Castro make an extra effort. The following are lovely inns where anyone's parents would probably feel at home too.

Willows Inn (☎ 415-431-4770, fax 415-431-5295; W www.willowssf.com; 710 14th St; singles/doubles from $100/120), just off Market St, is a comfortable B&B with shared bathrooms, antiques and friendly staff.

24 Henry (☎ 415-864-5686, 800-900-5686, fax 415-864-0406; W www.24henry.com; 24 Henry St; rooms with shared/private bathroom from $65/109) is a five-room Victorian in the quiet Duboce Triangle neighborhood, just a few blocks from the Castro. The same folks also run the **Village House** (4080 18th St; rooms from $80), located right in the thick of the Castro District action.

The Mission (Map 5)

Considering the Mission's become such a popular destination, it's surprisingly lacking in cheap accommodations beyond fleabags and flophouses.

Easy Goin' Hostel (☎ 415-552-8452, fax 415-552-8459; W www.easygo.com; 3145 Mission St; dorm beds from $18, doubles from $40), formerly in the Haight and now on the south side of Cesar Chavez St near Bernal Heights, is working to change the situation. The surrounding neighborhood's charming and safe, with great restaurants, cafés and vibrant clubs. Easy Goin' runs a second hostel South of Market, but all processing is done through this location.

Inn San Francisco (☎ 415-641-0188, 800-359-0913, fax 415-641-1701; 943 S Van Ness Ave; rooms with shared/private bathroom from $95/135; deluxe rooms $215-255), at the other end of the price scale, is a grand Victorian B&B. The deluxe rooms have a hot tub, spa or fireplace.

Airport Area

There are lots of hotels around the airport, many with free direct-dial phones at the airport's baggage-claim area and free shuttle buses that pick up and drop off guests outside the terminals.

There are numerous chains in Millbrae and Burlingame, just south of the airport along Hwy 101. Still more are to the north in South San Francisco, including the always lovely **Motel 6** (☎ 650-877-0770; 111 Mitchell Ave; rooms $69); take the South Airport Blvd exit.

PLACES TO EAT

San Francisco has more restaurants per capita than any other city in the US, but the city's culinary distinction is by no means based on sheer quantity. San Francisco's true strength is the diversity of its influences: Afghan, Burmese, Cambodian, Cajun, Ethi-opian, Filipino, Greek, Indian, Korean, Lebanese, Moroccan, Spanish, Thai, Turkish and more, including the Bay Area's own invention, California cuisine, in which 'fresh,' 'seasonal,' 'light' and 'creative' are key words.

The city's culinary landscape is quickly shedding its boundaries: don't think you must go to North Beach for Italian food, Chinatown for Chinese food or the Mission for Mexican food. Otherwise you're likely to miss out on excellent restaurants elsewhere in the city – and ignore some surprising gems in each of those parts of town.

At most mid-range and top-end restaurants, reservations are recommended on weekdays and are nearly mandatory on Friday and Saturday nights.

Union Square (Map 2)

Budget & Mid-Range Eternally popular, **Sears Fine Foods** (439 Powell St; breakfast from $6; open daily 6:30am-2:30pm) is an old-school breakfast joint right off the square, famous since 1938 for its silver-dollar (Swedish) pancakes.

Café de la Presse (352 Grant Ave; snacks & meals under $10), right across from the Chinatown Gate and near Hotel Triton, sells an international selection of newspapers and magazines to accompany its breakfast dishes, sandwiches and burgers.

Borobudur (700 Post St; dinner from $10), named after a famous Javanese Buddhist temple, has reasonable lunch specials and serves a variety of Indonesian specialties.

Café Claude (☎ 415-392-3505; 7 Claude Lane; dinner mains $12-14) is a justly popular French bistro with outdoor seating, jazz on weekends and romance to spare.

Grand Café (☎ 415-292-0101; 501 Geary St; dinner mains $17-25), at the Hotel Monaco, is truly dazzling to look at, and such grandeur makes for an elegant dining experience. The Petit Café has a more casual menu of sandwiches and pizzas.

Top End Some of the city's most renowned (and expensive) restaurants are around Union Square.

Postrio (☎ 415-776-7825; 545 Post St; dinner mains from $25), downstairs at the Prescott Hotel, has been among the city's prime exponents of California cuisine since celebrity chef Wolfgang Puck opened the place in 1989. Puck's famous pizza ($12 to $16) is available at the bar until midnight.

Masa's (☎ 415-989-7154; 648 Bush St; tasting menus $65-110) is known for its stuffy, formal atmosphere and seriously *haute* and highly acclaimed French cuisine.

Farallon (☎ 415-956-6969; 450 Post St; lunch mains from $12, dinner from $28), next to the Inn at Union Square, has Mark Franz's outstanding 'coastal cuisine' and kooky but intriguing under-the-sea decor by Pat Kuleto. If you can't afford dinner, beach yourself at the beautiful 'jelly bar.'

Fleur de Lys (☎ 415-673-7779; 777 Sutter St) is an internationally renowned French restaurant with a luscious interior draped in lovely hand-printed fabric.

Civic Center & Hayes Valley (Map 2)

Budget The Tenderloin's best place for breakfast is **Dottie's True Blue Cafe** (522 Jones St; breakfast under $10). On weekends there's a line out the door for solid standards such as eggs, pancakes and chicken sausages.

Vicolo (201 Ivy St; slices around $4) serves deep-dish, cornmeal-crust pizza with unusual toppings such as gorgonzola, eggplant and corn by the slice. Paired with a salad, one hefty slice is usually enough.

Powell's Place (511 Hayes St; dinners about $10) has long been popular for its superb fried chicken. Stick with the chicken (also available by the piece from a take-out window), as other Southern dishes on the menu are very hit or miss. Definitely avoid the mashed potatoes (instant) and the green beans (from a can).

Mid-Range Dinners at stylish **Suppenküche** (% 415-252-9289; 601 Hayes St; mains $8-15) focus on Germanic comfort food such as sautéed venison with *spaetzle* (German noodles) and smoked pork chops with sauerkraut – food that pairs well with the excellent German and Belgian beer selections.

Caffè delle Stelle (cnr Gough & Hayes St; dinner mains $8-15) is an upbeat neighborhood Italian place offering pasta dishes and other satisfying meals at humane prices.

Zuni Cafe (☎ 415-552-2522; 1658 Market St; mains $15-25) has been around a couple decades already, but it remains an attractive,

reliable spot for mesquite-grilled meats, brick-oven pizzas and people-watching from the bar.

Top End Once owned by chef Jeremiah Tower (an innovator in California cuisine), **Stars** (☎ 415-861-7827; 555 Golden Gate Ave; mains from $20) continues to shine and attract the glitterati. Despite the prices, it's a fun and lively place and not as formal as you'd imagine.

Jardinière (☎ 415-861-5555; 300 Grove St; appetizers $10-15, mains $20-30) offers French-California cuisine, and its downstairs circular bar is popular with the symphony-saturated crowd.

Millennium (☎ 415-487-9800; 246 McAllister St; dishes $12-18), off the lobby of the Abigail Hotel (see Places to Stay earlier in this chapter), is the city's best vegan restaurant, taking its meatless and dairy-free menu to fine-dining heights far beyond any hippie dishes you might have experienced. Expect organic produce and creative tempeh-, seitan- and tofu-based dishes that blend Asian, North African and Mediterranean flavors.

South of Market (Map 6)

Budget & Mid-Range Don't be put off **Tu Lan** (8 6th St; meals under $10) because of its unsavory location. The fantastic Vietnamese food and bargain prices make a trip to this cramped, humid hole-in-the-wall well worth the effort.

Caffe Centro (102 South Park; breakfast & lunch $4-7), near Bryant and 3rd Sts, is a pleasant, popular café offering good coffee, iced tea, breakfast items, salads and inexpensive sandwiches, served either inside or at outdoor tables.

Yank Sing (49 Stevenson St • 101 Spear St, Rincon Center; dishes $3-4) serves dim sum that many San Franciscans feel is the best this side of Hong Kong.

South Park Cafe (☎ 415-495-7275; 108 South Park; dinner mains $13-18), in business nearly two decades, has well-respected French cuisine, a friendly chef-owner, a charming location and reasonable prices.

LuLu (☎ 415-495-5775; 816 Folsom St; dinner mains $15-22), a stylish converted auto-repair shop that's frequently loud and busy, has an open kitchen with several flaming ovens for rotisserie meats and pizzas.

Julie's Supper Club (☎ 415-861-0707; 1123 Folsom St; mains $12-18), a cornerstone of the SoMa scene since 1987, is a swinging, kitsch-filled restaurant-bar with an interesting comfort-food menu that borrows freely from California, Asian, Italian and Cajun cuisines.

Top End Crowded and popular **Fringale** (☎ 415-543-0573; 570 4th St; dinner mains $15-25) boasts very French waiters and a French-Basque chef who has built his reputation on dishes such as mashed-potato cake studded with shredded duck confit.

Boulevard (☎ 415-543-6084; 1 Mission St; dinner mains from $25), in the pre-quake Audiffred Building, was designed by Pat Kuleto to look like a Belle Époque Parisian salon. Chef Nancy Oakes has a fine way with pork loins, buttery mashed potatoes and crab cakes. Last-minute diners can eat at the excellent bar.

Hawthorne Lane (☎ 415-777-9779; 22 Hawthorne Lane; dinner mains $25) is housed in a stylishly converted warehouse and offers a well prepared, seamless blend of Mediterranean, Asian and California cuisines.

Bacar (☎ 415-904-4100; 448 Brannan St; mains $15-35) is one of the city's newer fine-dining establishments, boasting a bistro-fusion cuisine and a massive, top-notch wine list, which is really the star here. Try one of the 100-plus wines by the glass in the casual downstairs bar, more comfortable than the dining room.

Fifth Floor (☎ 415-348-1555; 12 4th St; dinner mains from $30, tasting menu $85), in the Palomar Hotel above Old Navy, mixes the stately vibe of an exclusive club with a few hip, modern touches. The food is fabulous, which is why it's consistently rated among the city's finest restaurants.

Financial District (Map 2)

Although the Financial District is deathly quiet at night, there are a few interesting restaurants along its borders with the waterfront and North Beach. Many of these places are closed on Sunday.

Kearny St is packed with busy weekday lunch places. **Tomato & Basil** (305 Kearny St; lunch around $5), is a tiny take-out place that makes excellent roast chicken sandwiches.

Palio Paninoteca (505 Montgomery St; sandwiches from $5) is a café that makes excellent coffee and focaccia sandwiches.

Café Bastille (☎ 415-986-5673; 22 Belden Place; lunch from $10, dinner from $15), the focal point of the French ghetto's annual Bastille Day celebration, is the most popular spot on hip, restaurant-jammed Belden Place. Standard bistro fare, such as steak with chips, along with savory crepes and live jazz, keep Bastille lively all week.

Plouf (☎ 415-986-6491; 40 Belden Place; meals from about $15) is another popular and reliable French bistro, famous for its excellent mussels and *pommes frites* (french fries), not to mention tasty wines, sandwiches and seafood mains.

Sam's Grill and Seafood Restaurant (☎ 415-421-0594; 374 Bush St; mains from $10) is one of the city's oldest restaurants, dating from 1867. It hasn't changed a bit since moving to its present location in 1946. Stick to the fresh-fish offerings.

Redwood Park (☎ 415-283-1000; 600 Montgomery; mains from $28) is at the base of the Transamerica Pyramid. Meals are prepared under the guidance of former Fifth Floor executive chef George Morrone. The bar is inviting for just drinks and (pricey) appetizers.

Aqua (☎ 415-956-9662; 252 California St; mains from $30), an elegant and expensive option that's among San Francisco's finest, has its emphasis squarely on seafood. French traditions (with subtle California twists) underlie many of the dishes.

Rubicon (☎ 415-434-4100; 558 Sacramento St; mains $22-32) continues to draw fans to its loft-like interior for the exemplary food and superb wine list, courtesy of renowned sommelier Larry Stone. Owners include Robert DeNiro, Robin Williams and Francis Coppola, for what that's worth.

Nob Hill & Polk (Map 2)

Cordon Bleu (1574 California St; meals $5-7) is a hole-in-the-wall Vietnamese diner serving massive chicken dinners for way-cheap prices. It's conveniently located next to the Lumière Theatre.

Swan Oyster Depot (1517 Polk St; meals $10-20), between California and Sacramento Sts, is an unadorned, old-fashioned seafood bar serving beer, clam chowder, shrimp cocktails and sourdough bread to eager fans. It's definitely among the city's best seafood spots.

Hyde Street Bistro (☎ 415-292-4415; 1521 Hyde St; mains around $15), a neighborhood spot in the heart of Nob Hill, has a cozy atmosphere and a menu featuring simple French bistro fare.

Chinatown (Map 3)

Not surprisingly, Chinatown is packed with Chinese restaurants – from tiny hole-in-the-wall places with cheap eats to cavernous but equally economical dim-sum houses to pricey restaurants serving the latest Chinese *haute cuisine*.

Dol Ho (808 Pacific Ave; dishes $2-4) has dishes that, although smaller than those served in most dim sum houses, are fresh to the core.

Lucky Creation (854 Washington St; mains $5-7) is an excellent Chinese vegetarian restaurant, serving tasty rice and noodle dishes.

House of Nanking (919 Kearny St; mains $5-12), a highlight of Chinatown dining, is popular with tourists and locals alike. The line stretching outside (reservations are not accepted) is a genuine reflection of the good food coming out of the busy kitchen.

DPD (901 Kearny St; mains $4-7), somewhat of a dive, surpasses expectation with delicious noodle soups and thick Shanghai noodles. Other Chinatown restaurants are more highly acclaimed, but this place is the real deal.

Sam Wo's (813 Washington St; mains $4-8) has always been popular for the tongue-in-cheek rudeness of the waiters (rather than the greasy food). You have to make your way through the kitchen and proceed upstairs to feast at this legendary eatery.

Far East Cafe (631 Grant Ave; lunch specials $5), Chinatown's most historic restaurant, draws people more for the carved cherry-wood booths in this dark cavern than its fare, although the price of the lunch specials means you aren't getting reamed for the atmosphere.

Gold Mountain (644 Broadway; dishes $3-4) is an enormous multilevel dining hall where convoys of fresh dim-sum carts file through the aisles during the day. It's always worth asking what seafood items are fresh.

R&G Lounge (631 Kearny St; mains $8-15), one of Chinatown's most celebrated eateries, serves capably prepared Cantonese food at reasonable prices.

Empress of China (☎ 415-434-1345; 838 Grant Ave; dinners from $18) is a complete contrast to Chinatown's cheap dives, with its plush, elegant surroundings, nice views and displays of Han Dynasty art. Stick to the basic mains, though.

North Beach (Map 3)

North Beach is *the* neighborhood for choice Italian food and drinks, whether you're seeking an espresso to kick-start your morning or a plate of pasta to satisfy a late-night hunger. Even as North Beach's Italian population has dwindled – and despite the throngs of tourists – the neighborhood has

Dim Sum

San Francisco rivals Hong Kong in the popularity and quality of its dim sum restaurants. In the Canton province of China, where dim sum originated, the act of eating dim sum is called *yum cha*, or 'drink tea,' because the snacklike dishes first appeared in teahouses.

Typically, dim sum consists of pastrylike items filled with pork, shrimp, taro root or vegetables and then steamed, fried or baked. Steamed vegetables and hearty congee soups (rice porridge with ingredients such as shrimp, fish and peanuts) are commonly offered as well. The best way to enjoy as many different dishes as possible is to dine with a group of people.

In a typical dim sum parlor, waiters roll carts between crowded tables that are crammed from wall to wall in a cavernous dining room. Some of the flashier waiters have a distinctive call that rises above the steady cacophony to advertise the contents of their cart (for non-Cantonese speakers, they lift the lids of their containers to reveal what's inside). Patrons simply select the plates they'd like from the passing carts, usually costing $2 to $4 each. A running tab is kept at your table.

In San Francisco, you can find good dim sum in many parts of town, but for a real experience go to Chinatown. Dim sum is popular every day; on weekends, Chinatown restaurants become noisy circus tents filled with a constant murmur (to some ears it's a roar) of Cantonese voices.

maintained a reasonably authentic European atmosphere, largely thanks to its sidewalk cafés and neighborhood eateries.

Budget A traditional neighborhood delicatessen, **Molinari** *(373 Columbus Ave; sandwiches $5-7)* turns out some of the best sandwiches in North Beach. It has few tables, but Washington Square is just a few blocks away.

Golden Boy Pizza *(542 Green St; slices $2-3)* is a grungy joint with a punkish attitude, serving thick slabs of excellent pizza. A slice or two and a draft beer makes a quick, filling meal.

Liguria *(1700 Stockton St; focaccia $3)* is a no-frills bakery that produces one thing and one thing only: focaccia (with tomato sauce or without). Get there for an early lunch.

Stella Pastry *(446 Columbus Ave; pastries $1-2)* is a good place to start your day with a cappuccino and an Italian pastry. It's a nice little café for breakfast or a snack later in the day.

Mario's Bohemian Cigar Store *(566 Columbus Ave; meals $6-10)* no longer sells cigars. Instead this relaxed café-bar, a classic North Beach spot, serves tasty focaccia sandwiches, strong espresso and rich tiramisu.

Mid-Range A real gem is **L'Osteria del Forno** *(☎ 415-982-1124; 519 Columbus Ave; mains $6-12)* – it's romantic, small (10 tables) and run by two pleasant Italian women who craft tasty thin-crust pizzas and sophisticated antipasti.

Caffè Macaroni *(☎ 415-956-9737; 59 Columbus Ave; mains $9-16)* may not look like much, but this tiny café with sidewalk tables is a lively spot that churns out some of the neighborhood's best Italian food. A second branch called **Macaroni Express** *(124 Columbus Ave)*, across the intersection, features cheaper à la carte items. Credit cards and reservations are not accepted.

Ideale *(☎ 415-391-4129; 1309 Grant Ave; mains $10-18)* is the place to head for Italian fare that's superior to the food in most places in the neighborhood. Stick to the traditional dishes, and don't forget the tiramisu.

Helmand *(430 Broadway; mains $10-16)* serves excellent Afghan food – try the *kaddo borawni* (baked pumpkin with a light yogurt sauce) and the *aushak* (ravioli filled with leeks in a minty yogurt sauce). The vegetarian special, a sampler of several vegetarian dishes, is a good deal.

Capp's Corner *(☎ 415-989-2589; 1600 Powell St; dinners $15-17)*, dating from 1960, is found in a dark and memorabilia-filled room full of crusty regulars and wide-eyed tourists with tickets to *Beach Blanket Babylon* next door. A visit here is more about atmosphere than food – though its simple, trend-bucking meals are actually pretty good.

Top End The ever popular **Rose Pistola** *(☎ 415-399-0499; 532 Columbus Ave; mains $10-27)* fuses updated Beat-pop style (jazz combos play in the evening) with creative regional Italian dishes. Dinner reservations are recommended.

Enrico's *(☎ 415-982-6223; 504 Broadway; mains $12-25)* is the city's oldest sidewalk café, offering delicate pizzas, unique antipasti and traditional seafood and meat dishes. Evening jazz combos add spice to the dining.

Fior d'Italia *(☎ 415-986-1886; 601 Union St; mains $14-26)*, on Washington Square, claims to be the oldest Italian restaurant in the country (it was founded in 1886). The extensive menu requires careful decision making: order conservatively and you'll make out all right, but expect to drop at least $25 per person.

Zax *(☎ 415-563-6266; 2330 Taylor St; mains $18-24)*, near the corner of Columbus Ave and Chestnut St, is a well-kept secret. This California-Mediterranean bistro serves its cosmopolitan crowd stupendous food from a small menu that changes weekly.

Bix *(☎ 415-433-6300; 56 Gold St; mains $14-32)* serves highly regarded cuisine in a lovely room with high ceilings and swanky, old-world ambience. Jazz combos lend an air of supper-club cool, though a bustling bar area (superb martinis) on weekends means it's hardly an intimate affair. You'll find it tucked on a tiny street near the Transamerica Pyramid.

Russian Hill (Map 4)

I Fratelli *(☎ 415-474-8240; 1896 Hyde St at Green St; mains $11-20)* offers wonderful Italian fare and glasses of Chianti in a friendly, inviting atmosphere.

Zarzuela *(☎ 415-346-0800; 2000 Hyde St at Union St; tapas $4-8, meals $10-15)* is an authentic Spanish tapas place where the prices are reasonable and the crowds are often thick.

Le Petit Robert (☎ 415-922-8100; 2300 Polk St; mains $16-19) is a lovely, relatively new spot serving tasty French country bistro meals such as rabbit, duck and steak.

Fisherman's Wharf (Map 4)

Fresh seafood is a Fisherman's Wharf specialty, from the take-out food stalls to expensive waterfront restaurants – although better quality can be found in other parts of the city. If you're here during the mid-November to June crab season, enjoy Dungeness crab and sourdough bread – about as San Francisco as you can get. Try **Alioto's** (☎ 415-673-0183; 8 Fisherman's Wharf) or **Tarantino's** (☎ 415-775-5600; 206 Jefferson St), both with great views and mains from $13 to $25.

Buena Vista Café (☎ 415-474-5044; 2765 Hyde St; dishes $5-12), a historic eatery near the Hyde St cable car turnaround, is primarily a classic bar with a few tables and a menu offering breakfast and burgers. This establishment introduced Irish coffee to the US, so naturally it would be wise to partake of that tradition while you're there.

Ana Mandara (☎ 415-771-6800; 891 Beach St; mains $14-28), in Ghirardelli Square, is one of the loveliest restaurants in San Francisco. Never mind that it's part-owned by Don Johnson and Cheech Marin: the Vietnamese cuisine (head for the seafood) and inventive cocktails are generally excellent.

Gary Danko (☎ 415-749-2060; 800 North Point St; tasting menu $55-74), near Ghirardelli Square, is definitely among the city's (if not the nation's) top restaurants. Danko's French, Mediterranean and American influences mix to create a serious culinary experience (and splurge). The cheese cart is legendary.

The Marina & Cow Hollow (Map 4)

Mel's Drive-In (2165 Lombard St; meals $5-15) is an old San Francisco standby that is one of Lombard St's few fast-food eateries in the Marina. It's an authentic '50s diner that played a significant supporting role in the George Lucas film American Graffiti.

Home Plate (2274 Lombard St; dishes $5-10) is popular for breakfast for good reason.

The pancakes are fluffy, the eggs benedict are delectably rich, and the little scones given as starters are nuggets of joy.

Bistro Aix (☎ 415-202-0100; 3340 Steiner St; dinner $15) has a reasonable fixed price dinner on weeknights. Crispy roast chicken and buttery mashed potatoes are the kind of down-home fare that makes this a popular neighborhood place.

A few blocks south, up the hill, is the Cow Hollow neighborhood, with dozens of restaurants along Union St, from Fillmore St east to Laguna St.

Betelnut (☎ 415-929-8855; 2030 Union St; mains $12-17), near Buchanan St, dishes up a veritable kaleidoscope of southeast Asian cuisines. Reservations are a must. Its streetside bar, the **Dragonfly Lounge**, is jammed most nights with the young, toned and tanned.

Greens (☎ 415-771-6222; Building A; mains $14-19), over at Fort Mason Center, is one of the city's best-known vegetarian restaurants.

Pacific Heights & Japantown

The restaurant stretch of Fillmore St between Sutter and Jackson Sts, just north of Japantown, blends Japanese restaurants with other cuisines.

Jackson Fillmore (☎ 415-346-5288; 2506 Fillmore St; mains $10-18) is a popular eatery set in an old-fashioned room that's always bustling. It serves superb southern Italian food at reasonable prices. Reservations are required for three or more people only.

Elite Cafe (☎ 415-346-8668; 2049 Fillmore St; mains $17-28) is a remarkably well-preserved 1920s restaurant. The Cajun and Creole seafood is good but expensive.

The three interconnected shopping centers of Japan Center – the Tasamak Plaza, Kintetsu Restaurant Mall and the Kinokuniya Building – are packed with restaurants.

Isobune (☎ 415-563-1030; 1737 Post St; dishes $2-5), in the Kintetsu Mall, is a floating sushi bar. These are very popular in Japan. The sushi chef stands in the center of the bar, and selections float past the patrons on wooden boats. It's fun and cheap, and the sushi is delicious.

Mifune (☎ 415-922-0337; 1737 Post St; soups $4-8), also in the Kintetsu Mall, is popular for its big, tasty bowls of noodles at moderate prices.

The Haight

The '60s may be long gone but the Haight is still a young slacker zone, and the emphasis here is definitely on cheap eats in a decidedly hip setting.

Breakfast, especially weekend brunch, is a big deal in the Haight. Try the **Crescent City Cafe** (1418 Haight St; breakfast $5-10), near the intersection of Haight and Ashbury Sts, which has spicy Cajun and Creole vittles and tasty crab cakes. The nearby **Pork Store Cafe** (1451 Haight St; breakfast $5-10) can satisfy carnivorous instincts.

In the Lower Haight, worthwhile brunch and lunch spots include **Kate's Kitchen** (471 Haight St; meals $5-10) and the **Squat & Gobble Cafe** (237 Fillmore St; meals $5-10), the latter serving cheap and tasty crepes.

Magnolia (1398 Haight St; sandwiches $8-10, mains $9-15), in an old Victorian building, is a friendly brewpub with a Grateful Dead–inspired decor that you can either absorb or ignore. It dishes out sandwiches, fries, dinner plates and great craft-brewed ales, many naturally carbonated and served via a British-style hand pump (its specialty). A limited menu is served until midnight (until 11:30pm on Sunday).

Kan Zaman (☎ 415-751-9656; 1793 Haight St; mains $7-12), near Shrader St, features decent and reasonably priced Middle Eastern food, funky Arabian Nights decor and the opportunity to smoke from a hookah; on some weekend nights there's a belly-dancing performance.

Cha Cha Cha (1801 Haight St; tapas $4-8, mains under $15), lively, loud and extremely popular, offers spicy Caribbean tapas and main dishes. It doesn't take reservations, so most nights you'll have to wait up to an hour for a table.

Massawa (☎ 415-621-4129; 1538 Haight St; mains $6-12), near Ashbury St, serves East African, Eritrean and Ethiopian food.

Thep Phanom (☎ 415-431-2526; 400 Waller St; mains $8-12), near Haight St in the Lower Haight, is a reliable and worthwhile Thai restaurant.

Eos (☎ 415-566-3063; 901 Cole St; mains $17-26), in Cole Valley, is one of the city's most highly regarded East-West fusion restaurants. Impressively designed starters get the palate warmed up for Eric Arnold Wong's inventive main courses. It runs a nice wine bar next door too.

The Castro (Map 5)

People-watching is always a popular pastime in the Castro, so naturally, the most happening restaurants tend to be places with good vantage points.

Cafe Flore (cnr Market & Noe Sts; meals under $10) is a Castro institution that tops the list in this respect; it's a popular coffee-house with a large outside patio that is packed on sunny days.

California Harvest Ranch Market (2285 Market St; lunch $4-8) is a gourmet and organic grocery store with a large, excellent salad bar and deli. It doesn't have tables inside, but outdoor benches provide a perfect spot to take a break and to dig into your healthy purchases.

Bagdad Cafe (2295 Market St; meals $5-10), open round the clock, is a good place to head to if you crave a hot turkey sandwich or pancakes in the wee small hours.

2223 Market (☎ 415-431-0692; 2223 Market St; mains $10-25) sits in the lap of the Castro District, loved and cherished, but nameless. The ever-changing menu is small but interesting. Dress is casual, and reservations are recommended.

Chow (☎ 415-552-2469; 215 Church St; mains $6-10), a few doors off Market St, is a remarkably affordable place that serves tasty pizzas, pastas and grilled and roasted meats. It also offers a smattering of Asian noodle dishes. Chow is a popular late-night hangout.

Café Cuvée (☎ 415-621-7488; 2073 Market St; dinner mains $13-16) is a casual café serving salads and sandwiches over the counter at lunchtime. In the evening, it dims the lights and puts California and New American cuisine on the table.

Mecca (☎ 415-621-7000; 2029 Market St; mains $14-29) is as much a nightclub as it is a restaurant, but the kitchen turns out respectable mains. The menu ranges from fish to quail to grilled pork, all served in classic California style, with plenty of exotic greens and fresh vegies. Reservations are recommended.

Home (☎ 415-503-0333; cnr Market & Church Sts; mains under $12) serves top-notch comfort foods from all over the globe. The gnocchi, chili verde and braised pot-roast meals you'll get at this Home, though, probably ain't like it was back on the farm.

The Mission (Map 5)

During the late 1990s, this district exploded as *the* trendy spot for eating and drinking. Expensive restaurants sprouted alongside *taquerías* (places serving tacos), and grungy Mission St became inundated with Land Rover drivers demanding valet parking. The dot-com decline has lessened the yuppie impact, but the neighborhood shows little signs of cooling off, and great places to chow down linger on nearly every block.

Budget Italian, Vietnamese, East-West fusion and tapas have all established a presence in the Mission, but the neighborhood's signature food remains the burrito. Every San Franciscan has a favorite *taquería* – a regular source of debate – but several Mission *taquerías* receive consistently high ratings. In all the following places, burritos range from $4 to $6 on average.

La Taquería (*2889 Mission St*), just south of the 24th St BART station, serves absolutely amazing *carne asada* (steak) and *carnitas* (roast pork) burritos and tacos. There's no rice (which means less post-burrito bloat), and they're a little pricier than average, but are well worth it.

Taquería Can-Cun (*2288 Mission St at 19th St*) is one of the most popular purveyors of big, bold burritos in the city, and it's open after midnight. The tortillas are grilled, not steamed, and you can get whole avocado as an option. Both the beef and the vegetarian burritos are justifiably lauded.

Pancho Villa (*3071 16th St*) is a burrito lovers' staple, and the constant line out the door means the ingredients stay fresh.

Sit-down Mexican restaurants, specializing in dinner plates, margaritas and colorful atmospheres, are also peppered throughout the neighborhood.

Puerto Alegre (*546 Valencia St; meals $6-12*) is popular more for its margaritas than its food. Either way it usually has a line out the door.

Roosevelt Tamale Parlor (*2817 24th St; meals $6-12*), east of Mission St along colorful 24th St, has cheap, tasty *tamales* (ground meat rolled in cornmeal, wrapped in corn husks and steamed) and other specialties, and usually less of a wait for a table.

If you don't want a burrito, head to the restaurant-packed block of 16th St at Valencia St and simply start walking.

Truly Mediterranean (*3109 16th St; meals $4-6*) is a tiny place serving excellent take-out falafel and shwarma.

Pakwan Pakistani Indian Restaurant (*3180 16th St; meals under $10*) is proof that Indian food in San Francisco isn't always pricey. Order at the counter, take a number and then dig into some well-prepared (and very spicy) dishes. Don't expect serenity, though, as the place feels hectic even when not packed.

We Be Sushi (*538 Valencia St • 1071 Valencia St; dishes $3-6*) doesn't serve the most amazing sushi in town, but it is fresh and tasty, and the low-key, friendly atmosphere keeps the place constantly buzzing.

Herbivore (*983 Valencia St; meals $5-15*), next to a small natural foods market on 21st St, is a vegan restaurant. The interior of efficient architectural lines is appropriately reflected in its clean and tasty meatless dishes and rich, dairyless desserts.

Saigon Saigon (*1132 Valencia; dinner mains $6-10*), too often taken for granted, has tasty, reliable dishes and some pretty great prices. The lunch specials (around $5 and served 11:30am to 2pm daily) are among the neighborhood's best bargains.

Liberties (*cnr 22nd St & Guerrero; meals from $10*), nearby, is an Irish pub-restaurant serving a nice pint alongside crispy fish and chips and, on weekends, one of the city's best brunch menus (if you want a traditional Irish breakfast, this is a great place to get it).

St Francis Fountain (*2801 24th St*), east along 24th St, is a magnificent authentic soda fountain and candy counter dating from 1918.

Excellent home-made ice cream can also be found south of Cesar Chavez Blvd at **Mitchell's** (*688 San Jose Ave*), family-owned since 1953, where mango and avocado (!) are among the top flavors.

Great burgers – including turkey, vegie and hormone-free Niman Ranch beef – are turned out at Mission favorites **Burger Joint** (*807 Valencia St; meals $5-8*), **Big Mouth Burger** (*3392 24th St; meals $5-8*) and tiny **Jay's Cheese Steak** (*3285 21st St; meals $5-8*). The latter also, as the name implies, makes tasty cheese steaks.

Joe's Cable Car (*4320 Mission St; meals $5-10*), further south on Mission in the Excelsior, is the Holy Grail of burgers where (as you'll read on signs, napkins, the menu, everywhere) 'Joe grinds his own fresh chuck daily' (and he does a damn good job of it too).

Mid-Range & Top End Highfalutin' restaurants (and some cool ones too) came into the Mission with the dot-coms and have been fixtures ever since.

Ti Couz (☎ 415-252-7373; 3108 16th St; crepes and salads $4-10) is an authentic Breton creperie that turns out a huge variety of delicious sweet and savory crepes (you may be surprised how filling they are). The salads are equally fresh and fabulous.

Walzwerk (☎ 415-551-7181; 381 S Van Ness Ave; dinner mains $10-15) is a small, super-friendly German restaurant serving hearty, flavorful meals you might not have imagined existed behind the former Iron Curtain. The German beer selection is impressive too.

Once a standard-issue 1940s Italian joint, **Bruno's** (☎ 415-550-7455; 2389 Mission St; meals $10-20) is now a hip and swank bar-restaurant-nightclub sporting snazzy vinyl booths and alluring exotica-inspired decor. The venue's ownership, and its menu, seem to change frequently, but the last we heard it was dipping back into its roots with straightforward but high-quality Italian dishes. Whatever it serves, this martini-perfect place is a treasure.

Blue Plate (☎ 415-282-6777; 3218 Mission St; mains $12-18) offers American comfort food done to near-perfection in a homey, friendly and thankfully non-yuppie atmosphere. The meatloaf and thick-cut pork chop are both dreamy.

Slanted Door (☎ 415-861-8032; 584 Valencia St; lunch mains $5-13, dinner mains $8-18), near 17th St, is a Vietnamese restaurant that helped ignite the neighborhood's current culinary boom. Lunches can be surprisingly affordable; dinners are more elaborate but still reasonably priced. Be sure to make a reservation for dinner. (Note that due to renovations, the restaurant may still be temporarily relocated downtown, at 100 Brannan St.)

Delfina (☎ 415-552-4055; 3621 18th St; mains $8-18) is not Italian in the classic sense, but this trendy spot's simple but creative menu is Italian inspired. Be sure to snag a reservation before entering.

The Richmond (Map 7)

When you're looking for great food in San Francisco, do not overlook the Richmond. The neighborhood's easy to reach without a car, as bus No 38 runs up and down Geary St all night long.

One block north of Geary St is Clement St; the stretch between Arguello and Park Presidio Blvds is 'New Chinatown,' lined with a slew of shops and Chinese, Thai, Korean, Vietnamese, Indonesian and other Asian restaurants.

Taiwan Restaurant (445 Clement St; meals under $15) has some very cheap lunch specials, along with handcrafted noodles and dumplings made in the restaurant's glassed-in kitchen.

Bok Choy Garden (1820 Clement St; meals under $15) is a great vegetarian and vegan Chinese restaurant.

Mai's Authentic Vietnamese Kitchen (316 Clement St; meals under $15) has good, inexpensive lunch and dinner plates.

Burma Super Star (309 Clement St; mains $5-10) serves Burmese cuisine, which shares similarities with that of India, China and Thailand. Rich curries and crunchy samosas are worthwhile, and while the interior's nondescript, the meals are cheap and satisfying.

King of Thai Noodle House (639 Clement St; meals $5-8) is more diner-like than Thai places most Westerners know. Never mind the plain decor, though, as the noodle plates and soups will leave you humming for days.

A couple of excellent neighborhood French restaurants are also found out here – a little cheaper than downtown and well worth the journey.

Clementine (☎ 415-387-0408; 126 Clement St; mains $15-18) is gem of a bistro, offering graceful ambience, a cheerful staff and sublime dishes.

Chapeau! (☎ 415-750-9787; 1408 Clement St; mains $16-25) is a family-run restaurant with nonstop charm and a genuine passion for its food.

Geary Blvd, parallel to Clement St, also has a variety of good restaurants.

Angkor Wat (4217 Geary Blvd; mains $9-14) has terrific Cambodian food at inexpensive prices.

Kabuto (5116 Geary Blvd; sushi $3-6, mains $11-20), near 15th Ave, has inspired more than a few sushi enthusiasts to proclaim that it has the best sushi bar in the city. There's a good vegetarian selection too.

Tommy's Mexican Restaurant (5929 Geary Blvd; meals under $15), between 23rd and 24th Aves, specializes in Yucatán cuisine. Its fresh-squeezed lime margaritas are among the best in town. The tequila selection at the bar is truly unbeatable.

Khan Toke Thai House (☎ 415-668-6654; 5937 Geary Blvd; meals $10-20), in the same block as Tommy's Mexican Restaurant, is one of the best Thai restaurants in town. It has a beautifully romantic yet still very casual atmosphere. Wear clean socks, as you'll be asked to remove your shoes and sit at low tables.

La Vie (☎ 415-668-8080; 5830 Geary Blvd; mains $6-16) is one of the city's best Vietnamese restaurants. Try the catfish in pineapple and tamarind broth.

The Sunset (Map 7)

The Sunset District, south of Golden Gate Park, has a large collection of budget ethnic restaurants, particularly along Irving St from 5th Ave all the way to 25th Ave. The Inner Sunset, concentrated around the intersection of 9th Ave and Irving St, has a healthy mix of traditional neighborhood establishments and fashionable new eateries.

Einstein's Cafe (1336 9th Ave; lunch $5) is a low-key, budget-friendly café serving huge bowls of salad and large sandwiches. The backyard patio makes a nice respite on sunny days.

Park Chow (☎ 415-665-9912; 1240 9th Ave; mains $6-12), offering tasty pastas and other comfort dishes, is just as easygoing and satisfying as its sister restaurant near the Castro District.

PJ's Oyster Bed (☎ 415-566-7775; 737 Irving St; meals $15-25) is a fun Cajun-Creole seafood eatery that prepares dishes both exotic and ordinary, such as alligator fillets and crab cakes. It's a longstanding favorite for good reason.

Ebisu (☎ 415-566-1770; 1283 9th Ave; meals $15-25) is a highly regarded Japanese restaurant and sushi bar that usually has long lines of eager eaters waiting to get in.

Ganges (☎ 415-661-7290; 775 Frederick St; meals under $20), close to Haight St, is a popular but relaxed Indian vegetarian restaurant.

ENTERTAINMENT

San Francisco's nightlife doesn't hinge on huge, hyperfashionable nightclubs but rather on its eclectic bars, dance clubs and cutting-edge concert spaces. The city also has a number of theater venues, a renowned opera house, a symphony, a ballet company and numerous modern-dance companies.

The *San Francisco Chronicle*, especially its Sunday Datebook entertainment supplement, has good movie and theater listings. The city's most extensive run-down on entertainment possibilities is found in the free weeklies, the *San Francisco Bay Guardian* and the *SF Weekly*.

TIX Bay Area (☎ 415-433-7827; 251 Stockton St; ticket booth open 11am-6pm Tues-Thur, 11am-7pm Fri & Sat), in Union Square, sells half-price tickets to select musical performances, opera, dance and theater, on the day of the performance. It accepts cash only and charges a small service fee.

For tickets to the theater shows and big-name concerts, call **Ticketmaster** (☎ 415-421-8497) or **BASS** (☎ 415-478-2277).

Cafés

Most San Francisco neighborhoods are loaded with coffeehouses and cafés of all forms and functions. Quite a few coffee-centric businesses also serve beer, wine, snacks and even light meals, and some offer evening music or readings. The following listings are essentially cafés where you go to sip coffee, be it drip or espresso, and do a whole lot of hanging out. Many are open late. Remember that smoking is banned in all cafés, bars and restaurants.

Café de la Presse (Map 2; 352 Grant Ave) is a popular, European-style café with an international selection of newspapers and magazines.

Cup-A-Joe (Map 2; 896 Sutter St), closer to Nob Hill, is a funky coffee shop that also provides Internet access ($2 per 15 minutes).

Momi Toby's Revolution Cafe (528 Laguna St), in Hayes Valley, is a small but airy room with wood-frame windows and a marble-top bar. Coffee, beer, wine, pizzettas and focaccia sandwiches draw you in; the place's vibe makes you want to stay.

Imperial Tea Court (Map 4; 1411 Powell St), in Chinatown, has birdcages hanging above antique tables. Some precious tea varieties are extremely expensive (exceeding $100 per pound), but a others cost just a few dollars.

North Beach (Map 4) is where you'll find the city's best espressos and cappuccinos.

Caffe Trieste (601 Vallejo St) deserves its accolades as one of the finest cafés in the city. The character-filled business opened in 1956, and it harks back to the Beat days.

Caffè Greco (423 Columbus Ave) prepares a superior espresso, but the place is small and almost too popular. You're more likely to find a table a few doors down at **Caffe Puccini** (411 Columbus Ave).

Steps of Rome (348 Columbus Ave), across the street from Caffe Puccini and down a block, is easily the most Italian (and touristy) of North Beach's cafés, with a flirtatious staff and a see-and-be-seen energy.

Caffè Malvina (1600 Stockton St) has old-world elegance; windows along two sides keep it well lit during the day.

The Upper Haight (Map 5) is surprisingly devoid of coffeehouses. **People's Cafe** (1419 Haight St), near Masonic Ave, serves quality coffee and snacks. Lower Haight offers better caffeination options. Hipster (aka slacker) hangout **Horse Shoe** (556 Haight St) is a sprawling venue between Steiner and Fillmore Sts; or there's neighborhood stalwart **Cafe International** (508 Haight St at Fillmore St), which draws a quieter clientele and serves salads, sandwiches and light Middle Eastern meals.

Cafe Flore (Map 5; 2298 Market St), in the Castro, is a wood-framed hothouse with a glassed-in patio. The clientele is a mix of gay and straight, and everyone loves it for people-watching on a warm afternoon.

CHAT Cafe (Map 5; cnr 18th & Sanchez Sts) offers free high-speed Internet access to customers who make a food or beverage purchase.

Orbit Room Café (Map 5; 1900 Market St) is a postindustrial jazz-age space at the corner of Market and Laguna Sts. The crowds are quiet during the day but increasingly lively come nightfall.

The Mission District (Map 5) is another neighborhood with more than enough coffeehouses to satisfy rampant java urges.

Cafe Macondo (3159 16th St) is a model bohemian literary environment, with old couches and leftist Latin-American political posters.

Red Dora's Bearded Lady Cafe and Gallery (485 14th St), near Guerrero St, is a lesbian coffeehouse that doubles as a gallery and performance space.

Cafe La Bohème (3318 24th St) is a longstanding neighborhood gathering spot near the 24th St BART station, attracting a sometimes ragged crowd of up-and-coming hipsters and ageing has-beens.

Cafe Que Tal (cnr Guerrero & 22nd Sts) is a relaxing and relatively quiet spot a block off busy Valencia St. The coffee's not terribly strong, but the atmosphere's plenty inviting.

Bars & Clubs

Downtown is home to some of the city's most classic lounges – good places to go if you're after a serious martini. South of Market has the biggest concentration of live music venues and dance clubs, some with after-hours parties. The Mission District and the Haight are also nightlife hotspots, both neighborhoods littered with bars attracting trendy types and a few regular folks too.

Admission to dance clubs varies by club and event, but regularly hits $10 or even $20 at the glitzier venues. Live music prices range from $5 or $6 for a local act to $20 or $30 for a big-name touring artist at clubs such as Slim's, Bimbo's and the Fillmore.

Remember that smoking is banned inside all bars, clubs, coffeehouses and restaurants; some bars have smoking patios, but in most cases, smokers tend to congregate right outside the door.

Union Square & Financial District (Map 2)

The atmospheric **Compass Rose** (335 Powell St), in the St Francis Hotel, is one of the city's most romantic and historic bars.

Harry Denton's Starlight Room (450 Powell St), on the 21st floor of the Sir Francis Drake Hotel, has amazing views but about the cheesiest middle-aged crowd you could imagine.

Redwood Room (496 Geary St) was once a classic Art Deco lounge in the Clift Hotel. Thanks to its Phillipe Starck makeover, however, it's now an übertrendy yuppie hangout, the crowd slick and rich (or at least trying to look that way).

Blue Lamp (561 Geary St) is a faded but noble Tenderloin bar with vintage decor blues and rock bands most nights.

Red Room *(827 Sutter St)*, a tiny, trendy spot at the Commodore Hotel, is an extravagant study in reds – red vinyl, red bottles, red lights and red martinis.

John's Grill *(63 Ellis St)* has overpriced food that's not that great, but the dark and moody atmosphere makes this 1908 haunt cool for a cocktail. It plays up the Dashiell Hammett connection to extremes (Sam Spade ate here in the *Maltese Falcon)*. Avoid the 'Bloody Brigid' and take your liquor neat.

Biscuits & Blues *(☎ 415-292-2583; 401 Mason St)* is a dependable blues club with nightly music and decent down-home Southern meals.

Pied Piper Bar *(cnr New Montgomery & Market Sts)*, a moody space inside the opulent Sheraton Palace Hotel, is worth visiting to see the huge 1909 Maxfield Parrish painting after which it is named.

For killer views from way up high, the two places to head to are the **Carnelian Room** *(555 California St)*, on the 52nd floor atop the Bank of America Building, and **Equinox** *(5 Embarcadero Center)*, a circular bar atop the bay-front Hyatt Regency that rotates a full 360 degrees.

Civic Center & Tenderloin (Map 2)

Formerly a bordello and a dance hall, the well-loved **Great American Music Hall** *(☎ 415-885-0750; 859 O'Farrell St)* now hosts an excellent roster of rock, jazz, country and blues artists. The over-the-top baroque interior adds to the character and experience.

Edinburgh Castle *(950 Geary St)* has British ales on tap, greasy fish and chips and a pub quiz every Tuesday.

Backflip *(601 Eddy St)*, in the Tenderloin's rock-band-friendly Phoenix Hotel, is a trendy place popular with the fashionable crowd, who come to drink and dance to throbbing electronica.

Hemlock Tavern *(1131 Polk St)*, north of Civic Center on Polk St, is a good, straightforward bar with a heated smoking patio and bands in the back room most nights (for which there is a separate cover charge).

Place Pigalle *(520 Hayes St)*, in Hayes Valley, is forgiven its hipster snobbishness thanks to the many good beers on tap and the comfy couches on which to enjoy them.

Hayes & Vine *(377 Hayes St)* is a sophisticated wine bar that is a must-visit for devotees of the grape.

Martuni's *(cnr Market & Valencia Sts)*, in the direction of the Castro, is a swank and gay-friendly cocktail lounge where you can get fabulous martinis. Thanks to the frequent piano playing and singing, it feels like a cabaret.

South of Market (Map 6)

Most of SoMa's dance and live-music clubs are scattered along Folsom and 11th Sts. There are a few good spots near downtown too.

Slim's *(☎ 415-621-3330; 333 11th St)* is a boxy club with a crisp sound system; an impressive string of rock, blues, country and R&B artists pass through. It's partly owned by rock star Boz Scaggs.

Hotel Utah Saloon *(☎ 415-421-8308; cnr 4th & Bryant Sts)*, housed in a 1908 building, is a funky place with a nice bar and a small music room hosting local and touring acts of all kinds.

Covered Wagon Saloon *(☎ 415-974-1585; 917 Folsom St)* has live punk bands several nights a week, with a heavy metal showcase, 'Lucifer's Hammer,' every Tuesday.

1015 Folsom *(1015 Folsom St)* is the city's foremost dance club, generally featuring the best in local and visiting DJ talent and hosting a rotating roster of popular club nights.

Endup *(995 Harrison St)* is a SoMa institution that attracts gays and straights alike for its throbbing house music and lively crowds. Fag Fridays and all-day Sunday 'T' dances are legendary. Things often run past 4am.

111 Minna *(111 Minna St)* is a gallery by day and trendy nightclub come darkness. It's a cool space that draws a smart SoMa crowd.

The Stud *(cnr 9th & Harrison Sts)* is the elder statesman of SoMa dance clubs, having been around close to 40 years. Straights do frequent it, but it remains first and foremost a gay hot spot.

DNA Lounge *(375 11th St)*, another longstanding SoMa club, was recently reborn with a high-tech attitude and a snazzy new sound system.

Kate O'Brien's *(579 Howard St)* is a comfortable Irish pub that frequently gets crowded with Guinness swillers and clubbers teetering to techno on the upstairs dance floor each weekend.

The Eagle *(cnr 12th & Harrison Sts)* is a quintessential gay leather bar, with an excellent, heated outdoor patio, friendly staff and occasional live bands.

El Bobo *(1539 Folsom St)* is a good spot to sink a few between clubs – or to just hang out.

Annie's Cocktail Lounge *(15 Boardman Place)* is a hip and friendly bar tucked in an alley across from the Hall of Justice.

Nob Hill (Map 2) Atop the Mark Hopkins Hotel is **Top of the Mark** *(999 California St)*, an upscale bar and dance floor. The view is among the finest in town.

Tonga Room *(cnr Mason & California Sts)*, downstairs at the Fairmont Hotel, is a kooky tourist-friendly tiki lounge where rainstorms blow through twice an hour and cheesy bands play on a raft in the artificial lagoon.

North Beach (Map 3) Looking across Jack Kerouac Alley to City Lights Bookstore is **Vesuvio Cafe** *(255 Columbus Ave)*. Vesuvio's history as a Beat hangout may make it a tourist attraction, but it continues to be a popular neighborhood bar.

Two other historic bars sit directly across Columbus Ave: Tosca Cafe and Specs.

Tosca Cafe *(242 Columbus Ave)* is a classic spot dating from 1919 and loaded with old-world character, not to mention a famous jukebox loaded with opera records.

Specs *(12 William Saroyan Place)*, a trip and stumble away from Tosca's, is a dearly loved dive with a gruff veneer (we would not want it any other way) and a remarkable hodgepodge of memorabilia culled, it appears, from ports around the globe.

The Saloon *(1232 Grant Ave)*, founded in 1861, is the city's oldest bar,. The landmark venue has a regular roster of local blues stalwarts including the unstoppable Johnny Nitro.

Blind Tiger *(787 Broadway)*, on the edge of Chinatown, is a hip Asian-influenced dance club with a moody interior, hectic dance crowds and DJs determined to keep pulses pounding.

Bimbo's 365 Club *(Map 4;* ☎ *415-474-0365; 1025 Columbus Ave)*, near Chestnut St, one of the city's swankiest nightclubs, features everything from live swing and rockabilly to alternative rock, country and soul.

Fisherman's Wharf (Map 4) Near the cable car turnaround, **Buena Vista Cafe** *(2765 Hyde St)* is so popular you may have to wait in line to get in.

Lou's Pier 47 *(300 Jefferson St)* is a restaurant and bar that books live music seven days a week.

Steelhead Brewing Company *(353 Jefferson St)*, in the Anchorage Shopping Center, is a cavernous brewpub serving a full roster of hearty and quite tasty microbrews.

The Marina & Cow Hollow (Map 4) Union St, where many of the watering holes are concentrated, is singles-bar central. Expect a loud, frat-party crowd and an unavoidable, sometimes nasty pick-up scene at almost any bar in these two neighborhoods, which lie on either side of Lombard St.

Perry's *(1944 Union St)* is a bona-fide cruising spot, as it was when Armistead Maupin wrote it into his *Tales of the City* novels. Other major meat markets include **Bus Stop** *(1901 Union St)* and the **Comet Club** *(3111 Fillmore St)*.

If you need relief from the madness, try the sports bar **Final Final** *(2990 Baker St)* or neighborhood stalwart **Liverpool Lil's** *(2942 Lyon St)*, near the Presidio.

The Haight (Map 5) Curious **Zam Zam** *(1633 Haight St)*, in the Upper Haight between Belvedere and Clayton Sts, achieved cult status due to late owner-bartender Bruno Mooshei, the 'martini nazi,' who kicked patrons out on a whim, including for ordering the 'wrong' drink. Now the Persian-influenced atmosphere's brighter and attitudes are much nicer.

Club Deluxe *(1509 Haight St)* is a retro venue where well-dressed Frank Sinatra fans still come to worship. Live bands, from swing to rockabilly, keep the place hopping.

In the Lower Haight, the three blocks of Haight St between Pierce and Webster Sts are home to a jumping enclave of noisy bars where young crowds pass the evening hours.

Toronado *(547 Haight St)* is the Holy Mother Church of All Things Craft Brewed, thanks to its broad and ever-changing draft selection, easily the best in town.

Mad Dog in the Fog *(530 Haight St)* is a popular English pub with dartboards, good beer, soccer on TV and tasty pub grub.

Noc Noc *(557 Haight St)* has a wacky cavelike interior that often draws comparisons to the Bedrock home of the Flintstones.

Nickie's BBQ *(460 Haight St)* and **The Top** *(424 Haight St)* are two noisy joints packed most nights of the week. At the Top, the DJ's music of choice is punk and reggae; at Nickie's, the tunes range from hip-hop and world music to deep, thick 1970s funk.

Justice League *(☎ 415-289-2038; 628 Divisadero St)*, several blocks north of Haight St, is the only live music venue whose chief focus is hip-hop acts.

North from Haight St in Japantown is the famous **Fillmore** *(☎ 415-346-6000; cnr Geary & Fillmore Sts)*, still a superb concert venue, with a big stage and a world-famous pedigree dating back to the city's psychedelic heyday. Check local papers to see who's playing.

The Castro & Upper Market St (Map 5) Cruising the Castro is a time-honored activity for the city's large gay community. The neighborhood is directly serviced by numerous MUNI trains and buses.

Café *(2367 Market St)* has a young, ethnically mixed population of gays, lesbians and straights. This may be the only dance floor in the Castro, and the long deck overlooking Market St is a good place to cool off – or eyeball passing fancies in the street below.

Detour *(2348 Market St)* has the city's longest happy hour (2pm to 8pm), a superior sound system, chain-link urban playground decor, go-go dancers and a crowd out for a good time.

Badlands *(4121 18th St)*, sporting a slick redesign, still holds its Sunday beer bust (4pm to 9pm), attracting lines halfway down the block. The diverse gay crowd includes leather men, businessmen and punky kids.

Bar on Castro *(456 Castro St)* is a friendly place with a generally professional crowd of mixed ages.

Metro *(3600 16th St)*, opposite Cafe Flore, is a semi-upscale venue on whose balcony patrons gather.

Twin Peaks Tavern *(401 Castro St)* was allegedly the city's first gay bar to have windows. Today's it's sedate and mature, pleasant for a post-movie cocktail alongside an older gay crowd.

The Mint *(1942 Market St)*, attached to a hamburger joint, draws a diverse karaoke-loving crowd. It's open all day, but things only get interesting after 9pm, when the karaoke gets started (and these people are serious).

Cafe du Nord *(2170 Market St)* is a below-the-street-level, '30s-style former speakeasy that features live jazz, rockabilly, West Coast blues and salsa acts.

The Mission (Map 5) The Mission's bars are, like almost everything else about this neighborhood, a funky mix of the trendy and the everyday. A suburban crowd looking to 'slum it' for a night packs the hottest places on weekends; midweek, though, many of the same venues can be casual and calm. It's easy to get here via BART, but the service shuts down shortly after midnight.

The neighborhood's two hippest dance clubs are on some of the grungiest blocks. **Liquid** *(2925 16th St)*, near South Van Ness Ave, is a stark, deeply urban venue where adventurous DJs keep the electronica scene moving. Further south is **26 Mix** *(3024 Mission St)*, where youthful hipsters groove to edgy blends of hip-hop and house.

Make-Out Room *(☎ 415-647-2888; 3225 22nd St)* is a spacious venue with high ceilings, cheap drinks and rotating art on the walls. DJs spin several nights a week and, usually on Sunday and Monday, the stage hosts an eclectic selection of live bands, from indie-rock to jazz to honky tonk.

Casanova Lounge *(527 Valencia St)* is grungy and cool with an excellent jukebox. Like most Valencia St bars, it can get mighty crowded and noisy, especially on weekends.

Dalva *(3121 16th St)* is a dimly lit venue that feels like the stage design of a Spanish alley.

Kilowatt *(3160 16th St)*, up the street from Dalva, is in a converted firehouse and draws a hip Mission crowd.

Esta Noche *(3079 16th St)* is a Latino gay bar especially popular with cross-dressers.

Zeitgeist *(cnr Valencia & Duboce Sts)*, three blocks north of 16th St, is a popular spot for San Francisco's urban biker scene, from bike messengers to motorcyclists. The beer selection's good, and the back patio is huge and a great place to spend a warm afternoon.

Lexington Club *(3464 19th St)*, a small, friendly and always-busy corner dive, is the only full-time lesbian bar in the city.

Lone Palm *(3394 22nd St)* has a romantic *Casablanca*-like setting.

Latin American Club *(3286 22nd St)*, just east of Valencia St, is a low-key, funky and fun local hangout. Same goes for **Doc's Clock** *(2575 Mission St)*, near 22nd St, a restored local dive known for its stiff drinks and down-to-earth attitude.

Bruno's (2389 Mission St), a swank bar-restaurant, is the perfect retro setting for a classy cocktail. It also books a regular schedule of jazz, indie-rock and other interesting performers. The music room requires a cover charge, but you can sit at the bar (and listen via speakers) for just the price of a beverage.

El Rio (3158 Mission St), at Cesar Chavez St, is an upbeat club that draws a diverse, down-to-earth crowd to its two indoor rooms and large backyard. Live bands play on Saturday, there's world-beat dancing on Friday, and the Sunday afternoon salsa parties are always happening affairs.

Bottom of the Hill (☎ 415-621-4455; 1233 17th St), east of the Mission in Potrero Hill, is a live music venue bringing a steady stream of top-notch indie-rock acts to its small but vibrant room.

The Richmond (Map 7) At the western end of Golden Gate Park, across from Ocean Beach, **Beach Chalet Brewery & Restaurant** (1000 Great Hwy) is a bustling bistro in a historic building. The food is overpriced, but the house-brewed beers are quite good, as are the evening sunsets.

Comedy & Cabaret

A number of bars occasionally feature comedy nights, but for the real thing, San Francisco has two immensely popular comedy clubs: the **Punch Line** (☎ 415-397-4337; 444 Battery St), in Maritime Plaza in the Financial District; and **Cobb's Comedy Club** (Map 4; ☎ 415-928-4320; 2801 Leavenworth St), in the Cannery at Fisherman's Wharf. Both clubs usually have two performances nightly, one around 8pm or 9pm and the other around 11pm. Cover charges range from $7 to $20, plus a two-drink minimum.

Beach Blanket Babylon is an everlasting extravaganza along comedic lines in North Beach (see Theater under Performing Arts later in this section more information).

Cinema

Forget those slick multiscreen theaters because San Francisco boasts some excellent rep houses and lovingly restored, vintage single-screen theaters loaded with cinematic charm. Ticket prices range between $6 and $10 for evening shows.

Castro Theatre (Map 5; ☎ 415-621-6120; 429 Castro St) undoubtedly tops the list for cinemas. The building is as interesting and beautiful as the mix of independent, foreign

---

Free & Outdoors

Free outdoor entertainment abounds in San Francisco, especially in summer, when many of the city's big performance companies – and some of its smaller ones – sponsor events in the open air.

On summer Sundays the **Stern Grove Festival** (☎ 415-252-6252) presents free performances in the Stern Grove Amphitheater, at Sloat Blvd and 19th Ave in the Sunset. The grove's open-air amphitheater is a beautiful spot to enjoy a picnic while listening to music performed by the San Francisco Symphony or big-name jazz artists.

One of the city's most popular outdoor events is **Shakespeare in the Park** (☎ 415-422-2222). Each year one play is performed in parks throughout the Bay Area, and in September it comes to Golden Gate Park. It's free and starts at 1:30pm, but the grove, just across Conservatory Dr from the Conservatory of Flowers, fills up much earlier.

On the second Sunday in September, also in Golden Gate Park, is **Opera in the Park**, a free, non-costumed concert celebrating the opening of the opera season. It runs from 1:30pm to 3:30pm and draws huge crowds. It's held in Sharon Meadow, at the eastern end of the park near Stanyan St.

The **San Francisco Mime Troupe** (☎ 415-285-1717) performs at parks throughout San Francisco and Northern California all summer. Don't expect any silent, white-faced mimes – this is political musical theater in the commedia dell'arte tradition. It's big, it's fun and it's free.

The Market Street Association presents free concerts called **People in the Plazas** (☎ 415-362-2500) at noon each weekday in July, August and September. Performers run from rockabilly to jazz to Latin, and shows take place at various downtown plazas including 101 California St (Monday) and Yerba Buena Gardens (Thursday).

and classic films. A magnificent Wurlitzer organ is played before evening screenings.

Roxie Cinema *(Map 5; ☎ 415-863-1087; 3117 16th St)*, in the Mission, with its eclectic and adventurous programming of new independent, art and classic genre films – including many impressive and rare film noir pictures – is another local treasure.

San Francisco Cinematheque *(☎ 415-822-2885)* is a world-class avant-garde and experimental film organization screening a challenging mix of shorts and features at different venues, including **Yerba Buena Center for the Arts** *(Map 6; cnr Mission & 3rd Sts)* and the **San Francisco Art Institute** *(Map 4; 800 Chestnut St)*. There's no program in summer.

Balboa *(☎ 415-221-8184; 3630 Balboa St)*, a renovated Art Deco gem in the outer Richmond District, has been operating since 1926 and screens thoughtfully paired double features.

Clay Theatre *(2261 Fillmore St)*, in business since 1913, has been in continuous operation longer than any cinema in the city. It shows foreign and art-house fare, as do fellow theaters in the **Landmark** *(☎ 415-352-0810)* chain, the **Lumière** *(1572 California St)*, the **Bridge** *(3010 Geary Blvd)*, the **Opera Plaza** *(cnr Van Ness & Golden Gate Aves)* and the **Embarcadero** *(1 Embarcadero Center)*.

Red Vic Movie House *(☎ 415-668-3994; 1727 Haight St)*, a repertory venue in the Upper Haight, screens popular cult films and other interesting oldies and re-releases.

The city hosts the **Asian American Film Festival** *(☎ 415-863-0814)* in March at Japantown's **Kabuki 8 Theater** *(1881 Post St)*; the popular **San Francisco International Film Festival** *(☎ 415-561-5000; ⓦ www.sffs.org)* in April and May (mainly at the Kabuki and the Castro); the **Gay and Lesbian Film Festival** *(☎ 415-703-8650; ⓦ www.frameline.org)* in June (mainly at the Castro Theatre); and the **Jewish Film Festival** *(☎ 925-866-9559)* in July and August (at the Castro).

Performing Arts

Theater San Francisco is not a cutting-edge city for theater, but it has one major company, the **American Conservatory Theater** *(ACT; ☎ 415-749-2228)*, which puts on performances at a number of theaters in the Union Square area, including the **Geary Theater** *(450 Geary St)*; the **Marines Memorial Theatre** *(609 Sutter St)*; and the **Stage Door Theatre** *(420 Mason St)*.

Magic Theatre *(Map 4; ☎ 415-441-8822)*, at Building D in Fort Mason Center, is probably the city's most adventurous large theater.

The big spectacular shows – such as the Andrew Lloyd-Webber musicals – play at the **Curran Theatre** *(445 Geary St)*, between Mason & Taylor Sts; the **Golden Gate Theatre** *(1 Taylor St at Golden Gate Ave & Market St)*; and the **Orpheum Theatre** *(cnr Market & Hyde Sts)*. Call ☎ 415-512-7770 for tickets for all three.

Club Fugazi *(Map 3; ☎ 415-421-4222; 678 Green St; tickets $25-62)*, in North Beach, features **Beach Blanket Babylon**, San Francisco's longest-running comedy extravaganza, now into its third decade and still packing them in. Many of the jokes will go straight over non-San Franciscans' heads. There are shows Wednesday to Sunday and cleaned-up matinee performances on weekends (audience members must be over 21 years of age, except at matinees).

San Francisco also has many small theater spaces, such as the **Marsh** *(Map 6; ☎ 415-826-5750; 1062 Valencia St)*, **Intersection for the Arts** *(Map 5; ☎ 415-626-3311; 446 Valencia St)*, **Theater Artaud** *(☎ 415-621-7797; 450 Florida St)* and **Theatre Rhinoceros** *(☎ 415-861-5079; 2926 16th St)*, that host solo and experimental shows. Check listings in the city's newspapers.

Classical Music & Opera The San Francisco Symphony, whose musical director is the popular Michael Tilson Thomas, performs September to May in **Davies Symphony Hall** *(Map 2; ☎ 415-864-6000; cnr Grove St & Van Ness Ave)*. Tickets typically cost from about $25 to over $50.

Herbst Theatre *(☎ 415-392-4400; 401 Van Ness Ave)*, in the Veterans Building, also hosts some classical performances, as well as lectures.

San Francisco Conservatory of Music *(☎ 415-759-3475; 1201 Ortega Ave)* puts on a variety of performances at Hellman Hall.

War Memorial Opera House *(Map 2; ☎ 415-864-3330; 301 Van Ness Ave)* hosts performances of the acclaimed **San Francisco Opera** from early September to mid-December. For only $20, students with a valid ID can sit in the $100 orchestra section; these tickets go on sale two hours before curtain up. Standing-room tickets, available for some shows, are $8 and also go on sale two hours before performances.

Dance The **San Francisco Ballet** (☎ 415-865-2000) performs at the opera house and at the **Yerba Buena Center for the Arts** (Map 6; ☎ 415-978-2787; cnr Howard & 3rd Sts).

San Francisco also has a large and diverse modern dance scene.

ODC Theater (Map 5; ☎ 415-863-9834; 3153 17th St) has modern dance nearly every weekend. The Yerba Buena Center and **Theater Artaud** (☎ 415-621-7797; 450 Florida St) also frequently have dance performances. Beyond these venues, most modern dance is in small performance spaces scattered throughout the Mission District. Check the weekly newspapers for listings.

SPECTATOR SPORTS

San Francisco 49ers (☎ 415-656-4900), San Francisco's National Football League team, is one of the most successful teams in league history, having brought home no fewer than five Super Bowl championships. Home for the 49ers is cold and windy Candlestick Park (currently dubbed 3Com Park), off Hwy 101 in the southern part of the city.

The **San Francisco Giants** (☎ 415-972-2000), the city's National League baseball team, moved here in 1958 from its original home, the Polo Grounds in Brooklyn, New York. Since 2000, the Giants have been drawing big crowds to their new downtown digs, Pacific Bell Park (Map 6), and in 2002 they thrilled fans by making it all the way to the World Series.

SHOPPING

San Francisco's shopping, like its nightlife, is best when the words 'small,' 'odd' and 'eccentric' come into play. Sure, there are big department stores and international name-brand boutiques, but quirky and cool places lining the streets of the Haight, Castro, Hayes Valley and the Mission are much more fun.

Union Square is where you'll find the city's biggest stores, such as **Macy's** (☎ 415-397-3333) and **Neiman-Marcus** (☎ 415-362-3900), as well as its largest concentration of brand-name, high-fashion boutiques. Nearby on Market St, **Nordstrom** (☎ 415-243-8500) occupies the top several floors of the stylish **San Francisco Shopping Centre** (cnr Market & 5th Sts), and a huge new **Bloomingdale's** is going into the old Emporium building next door (due to open in 2003).

Fisherman's Wharf, of course, is saturated with junky souvenir and garish 'gift' shops, most notably in and around claustrophobic **Pier 39**. The Cannery and Ghirardelli Square offer a slightly less frenetic experience. More tourist trinkets can be found throughout **Chinatown**, though adventurous types can explore Chinatown's back streets and alleys for bargain-priced cookware and unusual herbal pharmaceuticals.

Union St in **Cow Hollow** is dotted with designer boutiques and upscale gift shops. Only a few blocks north toward the bay is Chestnut St in the **Marina**, with a host of chain stores. Both neighborhoods cater to a yuppie crowd.

The section of Hayes St between Franklin and Laguna Sts, near the Civic Center, is a trendy little enclave known as **Hayes Valley**. The boutiques and stores are smaller and more cutting edge than ones you'll find downtown, often featuring local designers.

Haight St tries hard to sustain its role as a youth-culture mecca. While tie-dye just won't die, the overall trends these days are more about punk chic and platform shoes than hippie beads and sandals. Shopping here is particularly good for vintage clothing and music, especially secondhand CDs and vinyl. The Upper Haight can get very crowded on weekends, and parking is maddening (instead, from downtown take MUNI's N-Judah line or bus No 6, 7 or 71).

The **Castro** has men's clothing stores, good bookstores and fun novelty stores, all aimed to one degree or another at an affluent gay crowd. Come as much for the vibe and the people-watching as for what's in the stores.

South of the Castro, over a high hill, lies **Noe Valley**. The main drag is 24th St, between Diamond and Church Sts, and it's easily reached via MUNI's J-Church streetcar. The area's packed with young parents with baby strollers, who seem to be constantly browsing the numerous good clothing boutiques, bookstores, gourmet food and wine shops, and kids' stores.

In the **Mission District**, Valencia St continues to be a hot spot for vintage shops, locally designed clothing, secondhand furniture and Mexican folk art. You'll also find unique stores such as **Botanica Yoruba** *(Map 5; cnr Valencia & 21st Sts)*, an African gift shop with supplies for various Caribbean and West African religions, including an amazing selection of candles, herbs and incense; Dave Eggers' kooky **826 Valencia** *(Map 5; 826 Valencia St)*, which sells strange pirate supplies and items relating to his journal *McSweeney's*, and also holds free writing workshops for local kids; and everyone's favorite, **Good Vibrations** (see the boxed text 'Adults Only'). South along 24th St you'll find the excellent Mexican art-gift-activist shop **Galeria de la Raza** *(☎ 415-826-8009; cnr 24th & Bryant Sts)*.

The Richmond shouldn't be overlooked for its wealth of curious shops along busy Clement St, including numerous Asian gift and grocery emporiums, a couple of good record shops and the city's biggest and best used bookstore, Green Apple Books (see Bookstores under Information earlier in this chapter). Get here via bus No 2 or 38.

Cameras
Adolph Gasser *(Map 6; ☎ 415-495-3852; 181 2nd St)*, in SoMa between Mission and Howard Sts, has a huge range of new and used photographic and video equipment and also processes film.

Also check out **Photographer's Supply** *(Map 6; ☎ 415-495-8640; 436 Bryant St)* for professional equipment, high-quality film and often some of the city's best prices.

Brooks Camera *(☎ 415-362-4708; 125 Kearny St)*, downtown between Post and Sutter Sts, sells new cameras and does repairs and rentals.

Fashion
San Francisco is a stylish city, but the great thing is that the style spectrum is far-ranging and diverse – in San Francisco, anything goes, from sharp tailored suits to vintage dresses to drag extravagance.

Outlets East of Potrero Hill, the factory outlet of **Esprit** *(☎ 415-957-2540; 499 Illinois St at 16th St)* is a big warehouse offering 30% to 50% discounts on apparel by the San Francisco–based clothing retailer.

Jeremy's *(Map 6; ☎ 415-882-4929; 2 South Park)*, in SoMa, has all sorts of big-name designer seconds at bargain prices.

Designer Clothing Downtown, MAC *(Modern Appealing Clothing; ☎ 415-837-0615; 5 Claude Lane)* has a fabulous men's shop filled with designer and retro gear. MAC's North Beach branch *(☎ 415-837-1604; 1543 Grant Ave)* focuses on hip women's apparel.

Favorite boutiques in Hayes Valley include **Manifesto** *(☎ 415-431-4778; 514 Octavia St)*, a small shop with a retro-chic vibe run by a pair of local designers; and **Asphalt** *(☎ 415-626-5196; 551 Hayes St)*, which boasts a large selection by local designers.

Another good neighborhood for fashion strolling is the Mission, especially along Valencia St. Here you'll find **Dema** *(Map 5; ☎ 415-206-0500; 1038 Valencia St)*, a hip and stylish shop owned and operated by local designer Dema Grim, who specializes in 1960s-influenced designs.

In nearby Noe Valley, **Rabat** *(☎ 415-282-7861; 4001 24th St)* has a great selection of hip shoes and sumptuous women's clothing. **Ambiance** *(☎ 415-647-7144; 3985 24th St ● ☎ 415-552-5095; 1458 Haight St)*, with stores in Noe Valley and the Upper Haight, has casual and dressy women's clothing plus vintage-style hats and jewelry.

Busy Haight St is jam-packed with designer clothing boutiques such as **Behind the Post Office** *(☎ 415-861-2507; 1510 Haight St)* residing side-by-side with kitschy joints selling rock T-shirts and tie-dyed wonderments.

Vintage Clothing & Thrift Shops Haight St has bumper-to-bumper retro clothing shops, including **Held Over** *(☎ 415-864-0818; 1543 Haight St)* and **La Rosa** *(☎ 415-668-3744; 1171 Haight St)*; the latter showcases high-quality (and quite pricey) vintage suits, shirts, dresses and slacks.

The Wasteland *(Map 5; ☎ 415-863-3150; 1660 Haight St)* is a big store with a snotty, hipper-than-thou attitude (I don't *think* so), but since it's loaded with goodies from the past few decades, it's still worthwhile. Also stop into **Buffalo Exchange** *(Map 5; ☎ 415-431-7733; 1555 Haight St)*, a western US chain with a second city store at 1800 Polk St.

Guys and Dolls *(☎ 415-285-7174; 4789 24th St)*, in Noe Valley, is a hidden gem with lots of clothes and accessories from the 1930s and 1940s.

Adults Only

In the heart of the Mission, sexy types will dig the tasteful and bright **Good Vibrations** (Map 5; ☎ 415-974-8980; **w** www.goodvibes.com; 1210 Valencia St). A women-owned, sex-positive shop with a hip and healthy attitude, it's full of vibrators, toys, condoms, books, videos and other fun-filled accouterments.

A bit kinkier is the **Foxy Lady Boutique** (Map 5; ☎ 415-285-4980; 2644 Mission St), specializing in sex-industry chic, including shiny thigh-high stiletto boots and feather underwear.

If you're into leather, do your shopping in the Castro or SoMa. **Image Leather** (☎ 415-621-7551; 2199 Market St) is a hard-core leather and fetish gear shop; descend into the 'dungeon' where there's a museum – of sorts. SoMa's **Stormy Leather** (☎ 415-626-1672; 1158 Howard St) sells leather and PVC intimate apparel, as well as whips, paddles and collars.

American Rag (☎ 415-474-5214; 1305 Van Ness Ave) is a huge store with shoes and new and recycled clothes for probably too much money.

Clothes Contact (Map 5; ☎ 415-621-3212; 473 Valencia St), in the Mission, sells clothes by the pound ($8).

The Mission also has several large thrift stores, which are quite popular – don't think you're the first person to sift through those racks of polyester and piles of wrinkled cotton. The biggest are **Thrift Town** (☎ 415-861-1132; 2101 Mission St); the **Salvation Army Thrift Store** (☎ 415-643-8040; cnr Valencia & 26th Sts); and the **Community Thrift Store** (☎ 415-861-4910; 625 Valencia St).

Food & Wine

On the waterfront, the **Embarcadero farmers market** (open 8am-1:30pm Sat & 10:30am-2:30pm Tues) makes a great morning excursion for its fresh, organic produce, good coffee and pastries, and bustling atmosphere. The Saturday market happens at Market and Green Sts; the Tuesday market is at Justin Herman Plaza, in front of the Ferry Building at the foot of Market St.

Other farmers markets are held Wednesday and Sunday on United Nations Plaza, in the Civic Center, though they're not as exciting.

Boudin Bakery (156 Jefferson St), in Fisherman's Wharf, is a good place to find classic sourdough bread. Other branches are scattered throughout the city, including inside Macy's and at Ghirardelli Square.

Ghirardelli is the big name in chocolate in this town. Packaged Ghirardelli treats are available throughout the city, but **Ghirardelli Chocolate Shop & Caffè** (☎ 415-474-1414), in Ghirardelli Square, sells them on the site of the company's old factory.

For overseas visitors, taking back a couple bottles of Napa Valley or Sonoma Valley wine is a great idea.

Napa Valley Winery Exchange (☎ 415-771-2887; 415 Taylor St), downtown, stocks small-production and specialist wines.

K&L Wines and Spirits (☎ 415-896-1734; 766 Harrison St), near the Moscone Center, has a wide range of Californian wines.

Wine Club (☎ 415-512-9086; 953 Harrison St) has discounted prices on a huge selection of wines, as well as a help-yourself wine-tasting bar.

Music

Amoeba Records (Map 5; ☎ 415-831-1200; 1855 Haight St), near Stanyan St, is the best place for interesting new and used records in all genres. This huge emporium, formerly a bowling alley, will keep you occupied for hours.

Streetlight Records (☎ 415-282-3550; 3979 24th St), in Noe Valley, is another place to look for used records, CDs and tapes.

Of the stores specializing in vinyl, try **Flat Plastic Sound** (Map 7; ☎ 415-386-5095; 24 Clement St), which stocks classical and rare pop vinyl, and **Grooves** (☎ 415-436-9933; 1797 Market St), which has all sorts of vinyl and offers a free search service.

Jack's Record Cellar (Map 5; ☎ 415-431-3047; cnr Scott & Page Sts), in the Lower Haight, is the city's longest-running record store, with a large collection of 78-rpm discs.

Aquarius Records (Map 5; ☎ 415-647-2272; 1055 Valencia St), in the Mission, is a friendly, helpful neighborhood store specializing in hard-to-find indie-rock, electronica, metal, experimental and other unique sounds. Stop in and sign up to receive its excellent biweekly email catalog.

Discolandia (☎ 415-826-9446; 2964 24th St), deep in the Mission, is the oldest Latin-music store in the Bay Area.

Outdoor Gear

Many of these stores sell not only clothing but the necessary equipment for outdoor adventure, including travel guides. They can give good advice, and they have bulletin boards full of information. There are also some great outdoor stores in Berkeley (see under Berkeley in the San Francisco Bay Area chapter).

North Face makes high-quality outdoor and adventure gear, some of which is discounted at its **factory outlet store** (☎ 415-626-6444; 1325 Howard St) between 9th and 10th Sts in SoMa.

Patagonia (☎ 415-771-2050; 770 North Point St), in the Fisherman's Wharf area, is another respected name in outdoor gear, though its products sure aren't cheap.

G&M Sales (☎ 415-863-2855; 1667 Market St) is a large, generalized store with camping, hiking and other outdoor gear.

SFO Snowboarding (☎ 415-386-1666; 618 Shrader St), in the Upper Haight, has state-of-the-art snowboards. **FTC Skateboarding** (☎ 415-386-6693), its sister shop, is next door.

Piercings & Tattoos

Numerous body-piercing professionals will pierce parts of your body nowhere near your ears. Nipples, navels and tongues are all popular, and the genitals are certainly not off limits for many discerning gentlemen and women. Don't worry, these shops are clean, sterile and generally quite friendly.

Cold Steel (Map 5; ☎ 415-431-3133; 2377 Market St at Castro St), in the Castro, handles both piercings and tattoos.

For more piercing options try **Anubis Warpus** (☎ 415-431-2218; 1525 Haight St) in the Haight; **Body Manipulations** (Map 5; ☎ 415-621-0408; 3234 16th St) in the Mission; and **Nomad Body Piercing** (Map 5; ☎ 415-563-7771; 252 Fillmore St), north of the Panhandle, which has a lush tropical decor.

Lyle Tuttle Tattooing (Map 3; ☎ 415-775-4991; 841 Columbus Ave), in North Beach, is probably the city's best-known and longest-running tattoo studio. It also has a small museum.

Black & Blue Tattoo (Map 5; ☎ 415-626-0770; 483 14th St) is a tattoo, piercing and branding shop in the Mission owned and operated by women.

GETTING THERE & AWAY

Air

The Bay Area has three major airports: San Francisco International Airport (SFO), on the west side of the bay; Oakland International Airport, only a few miles across the bay on the east side; and San Jose International Airport, at the southern end of the bay. The majority of international flights use SFO. All three airports are important domestic gateways, but travelers from other US cities (particularly West Coast ones) may find cheaper flights into Oakland, a hub for discount airlines such as Southwest.

SFO (☎ 650-876-7809) is on the Peninsula, 14mi south of downtown San Francisco, off Hwy 101. It has undergone massive renovations in recent years, one result being a brand-new international terminal; another is a much-anticipated BART extension directly to the airport, which should be up and running by the time you're reading this.

The airport is structured like a semicircle, and it's a long walk from one end to the other. The north terminal is where American, Canadian and United Airlines are based; the south terminal is home to numerous other domestic airlines. Short-term parking is in the center. The international terminal is now a separate building, home to all international flights (except for the Canadian ones).

All three terminals have ATMs and **information booths** on the lower level, with computer consoles to help if the booth isn't staffed. **Travelers' Aid information booths** (open 9am-8pm daily) are on the upper level. If you need further assistance, the airport paging and information line is staffed 24 hours; call from any white courtesy phone.

Bus

All bus services arrive at and depart from the **Transbay Terminal** (Map 2; 425 Mission St at 1st St), two blocks south of Market St. You can take **AC Transit** (☎ 510-839-2882) buses to the East Bay; **Golden Gate Transit** (☎ 415-932-2000) buses north to Marin and Sonoma counties; and **SamTrans** (☎ 800-660-4287) buses south to Palo Alto and along the coast.

Greyhound (☎ 415-495-1575, 800-231-2222; w www.greyhound.com) also leaves from the Transbay Terminal, with multiple buses daily to Los Angeles ($42, eight to 12 hours) and other destinations.

Train
CalTrain (☎ 800-660-4287) operates down the Peninsula, linking San Francisco with Palo Alto (Stanford University) and San Jose. The CalTrain terminal is south of Market St at the corner of 4th and Townsend Sts. MUNI's N-Judah streetcar line runs to and from the CalTrain station.

The nearest **Amtrak** (☎ 800-872-7245) terminals are in Emeryville and Oakland (see the San Francisco Bay Area chapter).

GETTING AROUND
To/From the Airport
Bay Area Rapid Transit (BART; ☎ 415-989-2278) is starting a direct train service to San Francisco airport in 2003. When this is up and running, it will be the easiest and most efficient way to reach the airport.

SamTrans (☎ 800-660-4287) also serves the airport. Express bus No KX ($3) takes about 30 minutes to reach San Francisco's Transbay Terminal, running 6am and 1am Monday to Friday. On weekends and late at night, take bus No 397 ($1.10), which leaves on the quarter hour. If BART isn't running yet, look for express bus BX ($1.10), which brings you to the Colma BART station in 20 minutes.

Airport transport buses include the **SFO Airporter** (☎ 415-641-3100), which operates every 20 minutes from each of the three terminals to a variety of downtown hotels. The fare is $12 each way.

Door-to-door shuttle vans are cheaper than cabs, and they'll pick you up from any San Francisco location. Call for a reservation. From the airport, reservations are not necessary, and vans leave from the departures level outside all terminals. Companies include **Super Shuttle** (☎ 415-558-8500), **Lorrie's** (☎ 415-334-9000), **Quake City** (☎ 415-255-4899) and **American Airporter Shuttle** (☎ 415-202-0733, 800-282-7758). Fares are generally $17 each way, although it's cheaper ($12.50) to get dropped off or picked up at any hotel.

Public Transportation
MUNI San Francisco's principal public transportation system is the **San Francisco Municipal Railway** (☎ 415-673-6864; **W** www.sfmuni.com), known as MUNI, which operates nearly a hundred bus lines (many of them electric trolley buses), Metro streetcars, historic streetcars and the famous cable cars. The detailed *Street & Transit Map* costs $2 and is available at newspaper stands around Union Square. A free timetable, worth having if you're riding a line with irregular service, is available at Metro stations and displayed at some bus stops. Don't expect your bus necessarily to be on time.

Standard MUNI fares are $1 for buses or streetcars and $2 for cable cars. Transfer tickets are available at the start of your journey, and you can then use them for two connecting trips within about 90 minutes or so. However, they are *not* transferable to cable cars.

A **MUNI Pass**, available in one-day ($6), three-day ($10) or seven-day ($15) versions, allows unlimited travel on all MUNI transportation (including cable cars). Passes are available from the Visitors Information Center at Hallidie Plaza, the half-price tickets kiosk on Union Square, and some hotels and businesses that display the MUNI Pass sign in their window. A cheaper **Weekly Pass** (valid from Monday to Sunday only) costs $9 and allows free bus and MUNI railway travel and discounts on cable car rides.

BART The **Bay Area Rapid Transit system** (BART; ☎ 415-989-2278) is a subway system linking San Francisco with the East Bay. BART opened in 1972 and is convenient, economical and generally quite safe to use, although caution is required around some BART stations at night and the system shuts down around midnight. Four of the five lines pass through the city. Southern termination points have traditionally been Daly City or Colma, but the line is currently being extended south to San Bruno, South San Francisco, Millbrae and the San Francisco airport.

Downtown, the route runs beneath Market St. The Powell St station is the most convenient to Union Square. From downtown, it's a quick 10-minute ride to the Mission District; take any train heading south.

One-way fares are generally $1.10 within San Francisco, and between $2 and $5 from downtown to various outlying areas. From San Francisco BART stations, half-price transfers ($1 for a round-trip ride) are available for MUNI bus and streetcar services. You can buy them (with quarters) from the white MUNI ticket machines before you exit the BART paid area.

Car & Motorcycle

A car is the last thing you want in downtown San Francisco – it's a nightmare of negotiating the hills and battling for parking spaces, not to mention traffic. Remember, on hill streets (with a grade as little as 3%) you must curb your wheels so that they ride up against the curb – toward the street when facing uphill, toward the curb on a downhill. Failure to do so can result in daunting fines. The **AAA** (☎ 415-565-2012; emergency road service & towing ☎ 800-222-4357; 150 Van Ness Ave) can help members with roadside service.

Some of the cheaper downtown parking garages are the **Ellis-O'Farrell Garage** (123 O'Farrell St; ☎ 415-986-4800); the downtown **Sutter Stockton Garage** (☎ 415-982-7275; cnr Sutter & Stockton Sts); and the **Fifth & Mission Garage** (☎ 415-982-8522; 833 Mission St), near Yerba Buena Gardens. The parking garage under Portsmouth Square in Chinatown is reasonably priced for shorter stops; ditto for the St Mary's Square Garage on California St near Grant Ave, under the square.

Parking restrictions in San Francisco are strictly enforced. Parking in bus stops and blue wheelchair spots can leave you with fines of $250 or more; and blocking a rush-hour lane, a downtown loading zone (yellow) or a driveway can result in a costly tow.

Beware also of street-cleaning days and signs in residential neighborhoods indicating a residential permit system (tickets are $25 or $30). If you suspect your car has been towed, call **City Tow** (☎ 415-621-8605; 850 Bryant St, Room 145).

All major car-rental operators are represented at the airports. Downtown offices are

Alamo (☎ 415-882-9440, 800-327-9633) 687 Folsom St
Avis (☎ 415-885-5011, 800-331-1212) 675 Post St
Budget (☎ 415-928-7864, 800-527-0700) 321 Mason St
Dollar (☎ 866-434-2226, 800-800-4000) 364 O'Farrell St
Hertz (☎ 415-771-2200, 800-654-3131) 433 Mason St
Thrifty (☎ 415- 788-8111, 800-367-2277) 520 Mason St

Taxi

If you need to call a cab, some of the major companies are **Luxor Cab** (☎ 415-282-4141), **De Soto Cab** (☎ 415-970-1300) and **Yellow Cab** (☎ 415-626-2345). Fares start at $2.50 for the first mile and cost 40¢ per fifth of a mile thereafter.

Bicycle

For most visitors, bikes will not be an ideal way of getting around the city, because of the traffic and hills, but the Bay Area is a great place for recreational bike riding. Bicycles are allowed on BART, but there are restrictions. During morning commute hours (about 7am to 9am), bikes are allowed in the Embarcadero Station only for trips to the East Bay. During evening commute hours (about 4:30pm to 6:45pm), bicyclists are not allowed on trains to the East Bay; bicyclists traveling from the East Bay into San Francisco in commute hours must exit at the Embarcadero Station (see the *BART Trip Planner* and the *All About BART* brochure).

Ferry

The opening of the Bay Bridge (in 1936) and the Golden Gate Bridge (in 1937) virtually killed the city's ferries, although in recent years they have enjoyed a modest revival for both commuters and tourists.

The main operator is the **Blue & Gold Fleet**, which runs the **Alameda-Oakland Ferry** (☎ 510-522-3300) from the Ferry Building at the foot of Market St, and on some runs from Pier 41 at Fisherman's Wharf, to Alameda and Oakland. Transfers are available to and from MUNI and AC Transit buses. Blue & Gold's popular ferries to Alcatraz and Angel Island (☎ 415-705-5555, 415-773-1188) leave from Pier 41 at Fisherman's Wharf. To take the ferry to Sausalito or Tiburon in Marin County, board at Pier 41. (During commute hours, there are a few ferries between Tiburon and the Ferry Building in San Francisco.) Blue & Gold also operates the **Vallejo Ferry** (☎ 415-773-1188), which goes to Vallejo from the Ferry Building on weekdays and from Pier 39 at Fisherman's Wharf on weekends and holidays. It also offers a variety of bay cruises and connections to the Six Flags Marine World theme park in Vallejo. **Golden Gate Ferries** (☎ 415-923-2000), part of Golden Gate Transit, has regular services from the Ferry Building in San Francisco to Larkspur and Sausalito in Marin County. Transfers are available to MUNI buses, and bicycles are permitted.

San Francisco Bay Area

To leave San Francisco without exploring the surrounding Bay Area would be an unforgivable oversight. There are day trips to cater to all tastes and budgets, and transportation is generally convenient thanks to the regional bus systems and the Bay Area Rapid Transit (BART) and CalTrain rail systems.

North of San Francisco, Hwys 1 and 101 provide easy access to the Bay Area's prime outdoor playgrounds: the Marin Headlands, Angel Island, Mt Tamalpais, Muir Woods and Point Reyes National Seashore.

The chief attractions in the East Bay, just across the Bay Bridge from San Francisco, are underappreciated Oakland, a culturally and economically diverse community, and off-kilter Berkeley, the setting for an infamous branch of the University of California. South of San Francisco, via Hwy 101 or I-280, are Palo Alto, home to Stanford University; San Jose, the self-styled 'Capital of Silicon Valley'; and laid-back beach towns such as Half Moon Bay and Santa Cruz.

Marin County

If there's a part of the Bay Area that consciously tries to live up to the California dream, it's Marin County. Just a short drive across the Golden Gate Bridge from San Francisco, the region is a mixture of wealthy and laid-back – the so-called 'Marin County hot tubber(s)' that drove former president George Bush Sr crazy. The county's full of folks who eat organic and vote democratic, yet it's rife with sports utility vehicles (SUVs) and expensive houses.

That aside, it's also a region of lush, fog-shrouded mountains, towering redwoods, crashing surf and an abundance of hiking and biking trails in such awe-inspiring parks as Point Reyes, Muir Woods and Mt Tamalpais. All this is why Marin County makes such an excellent (and popular) day trip from San Francisco.

Orientation

Busy Hwy 101 heads north from the Golden Gate Bridge, spearing through Marin's

Highlights

- Angel Island – where you can walk, bike and camp within sight of San Francisco
- Mt Tamalpais State Park – the birthplace of mountain biking
- Historic Oakland – Paramount Theatre, Preservation Park & Jack London's favorite bar
- Bolinas – a secretive coastal town worth finding
- Berkeley – cappuccino, subversion, soapbox preaching and California cuisine
- Santa Cruz – where the big trees meet the big waves

San Francisco Bay Area
page 161

Marin County
pages 162-163

Berkeley
page 187
Central Berkeley
page 190

Downtown Oakland
page 178

San Jose & The South Bay
page 204

The Peninsula
page 197

Downtown
Palo Alto
page 198

Downtown
San Jose
page 202

Around
Santa Cruz
page 214

Santa
Cruz
page 212

middle; quiet Hwy 1 winds along the sparsely populated coast. In San Rafael, Sir Francis Drake Blvd cuts across west Marin from Hwy 101 to the ocean. Tank up before heading toward the coast – from Mill Valley, the closest gas stations are in Olema and Point Reyes Station.

Hwy 580 comes in from the East Bay over the Richmond-San Rafael bridge ($2 toll for westbound traffic) to meet Hwy 101 at Larkspur.

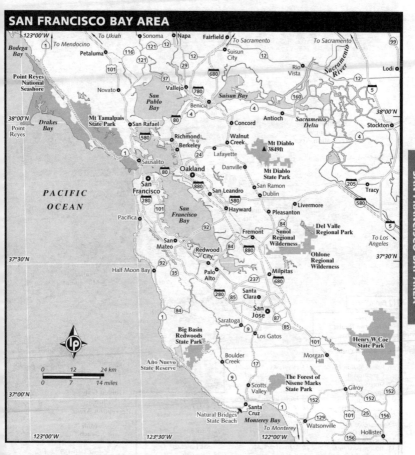

SAN FRANCISCO BAY AREA

Information

Marin County Convention & Visitors Bureau
(☎ 415-499-5000; Ⓦ www.visitmarin.org; 1013 Larkspur Landing Circle; open 9am-5pm Mon-Fri), in Larkspur, handles tourist information for the entire county. Information is also available from visitors centers in Sausalito and Mill Valley.

MARIN HEADLANDS

The headlands rise majestically out of the water at the north end of the Golden Gate Bridge, their rugged beauty all the more striking given the fact that they're only a few miles from San Francisco's urban intensity. A few forts and bunkers are left over from a century of US military occupation – which is, ironically, the reason they're protected

parkland today and free of development. Hiking and biking trails, beaches and isolated campgrounds are all nestled within these rolling coastal hills.

Orientation & Information

After crossing the Golden Gate Bridge, exit immediately at Alexander Ave, then dip left under the highway and head out west for the expansive views and hiking trailheads. Conzelman Rd snakes up into the hills, where it eventually forks: Conzelman Rd continues west, becoming a steep, one-lane road as it descends to Point Bonita; from there it continues to Rodeo Beach and Fort Barry. McCullough Rd heads inland, joining Bunker Rd toward Rodeo Beach.

SAN FRANCISCO BAY AREA

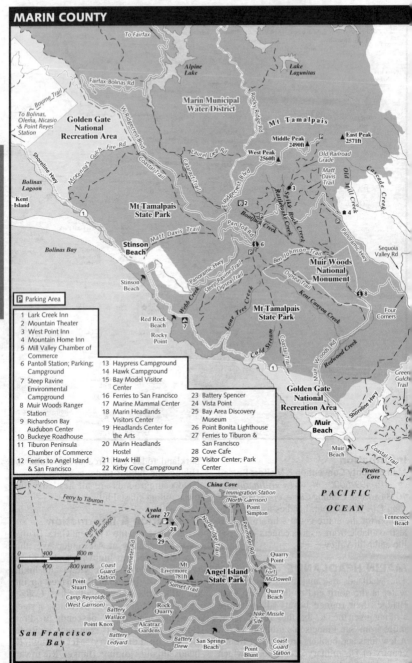

MARIN COUNTY

P Parking Area

1 Lark Creek Inn
2 Mountain Theater
3 West Point Inn
4 Mountain Home Inn
5 Mill Valley Chamber of Commerce
6 Pantoll Station; Parking; Campground
7 Steep Ravine Environmental Campground
8 Muir Woods Ranger Station
9 Richardson Bay Audubon Center
10 Buckeye Roadhouse
11 Tiburon Peninsula Chamber of Commerce
12 Ferries to Angel Island & San Francisco
13 Haypress Campground
14 Hawk Campground
15 Bay Model Visitor Center
16 Ferries to San Francisco
17 Marine Mammal Center
18 Marin Headlands Visitors Center
19 Headlands Center for the Arts
20 Marin Headlands Hostel
21 Hawk Hill
22 Kirby Cove Campground
23 Battery Spencer
24 Vista Point
25 Bay Area Discovery Museum
26 Point Bonita Lighthouse
27 Ferries to Tiburon & San Francisco
28 Cove Cafe
29 Visitor Center; Park Center

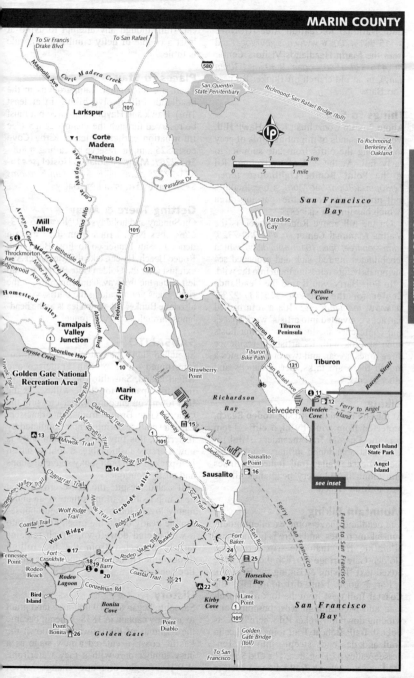

MARIN COUNTY

To Sir Francis Drake Blvd

To San Rafael

Magnolia Ave

Corte Madera Creek

580

San Quentin State Penitentiary

Richmond–San Rafael Bridge (toll)

Larkspur

101

To Richmond, Berkeley & Oakland

Corte Madera

▼ 1

Tamalpais Dr

Camino Alto

Paradise Dr

San Francisco Bay

Arroyo Corte Madera Del Presidio

Mill Valley

5 ⓘ

Throckmorton Ave

E Blithedale Ave

101

Paradise Cay

Miller Ave

Edgewood Ave

131

Homestead Valley

Paradise Cove

Redwood Hwy

Almonte Blvd

● 9

Tiburon Peninsula

Tiburon Blvd

Tamalpais Valley Junction

1

Shoreline Hwy

Tiburon Bike Path

San Rafael Ave

131

Tiburon

Coyote Creek

Miwok Trail

▼ 10

Strawberry Point

Golden Gate National Recreation Area

Marin City

Richardson Bay

ⓘ 11

🚲

🚉 12 Ferry to Angel Island

Belvedere

Belvedere Cove

Tennessee Valley Rd

Oakwood Trail

Bridgeway Blvd

🏛 15

Bobcat Trail

Caledonia St

Sausalito Point

Angel Island State Park

Angel Island

🚗 13

Marincello Trail

Miwok Trail

Chaparral Trail

🚗 14

Gerbode Valley

SCA Trail

Sausalito

🚉 16

see inset

Tennessee Valley Trail

Wolf Ridge Trail

Miwok Trail

Bobcat Trail

Rodeo Valley Trail

Bunker Rd

Tunnel

Ferry to San Francisco

Coastal Trail

Wolf Ridge

● 17

Fort Cronkhite

18 ● 19 Fort Barry

20

Tunnel

Fort Baker

24

🏛 25

Tennessee Point

Rodeo Beach

Rodeo Lagoon

ⓘ ●

Coastal Trail

Conzelman Rd

☀ 21

🚗 22

● 23

Horseshoe Bay

East Rd

Ferry to San Francisco

Bird Island

Bonita Cove

Kirby Cove

Lime Point

San Francisco Bay

Point Bonita 🏛 26

Golden Gate

Point Diablo

1

101

Golden Gate Bridge (toll)

To San Francisco

0   1   2 km
0   .5   1 mile

Information is available from the **Golden Gate National Recreation Area** (*GGNRA;* ☎ *415-561-4700;* **w** *www.nps.gov/goga*) and from the **Marin Headlands Visitors Center** (☎ *415-331-1540; open 9:30am-4:30pm daily*), in an old church off Bunker Rd near Fort Barry.

Things to See
About 2mi up Conzelman Rd is **Hawk Hill**, where thousands of migrating birds of prey soar along the cliffs from late summer to early fall. At the end of Conzelman Rd is the **Point Bonita Lighthouse** (*open 12:30pm-3:30pm Sat-Mon*), a breathtaking half-mile walk from the parking area (which has limited spaces).

On the hill above Rodeo Lagoon is the **Marine Mammal Center** (☎ *415-289-7325; admission free; open 10am-4pm daily*), which rehabilitates injured, sick and orphaned sea mammals before releasing them into the wild.

In Fort Barry, you'll find the **Headlands Center for the Arts** (☎ *415-331-2787;* **w** *www.headlands.org*). It's a refurbished barracks converted into artists' work spaces and conference facilities. The center hosts open studios with its artists-in-residence three times a year, and two or three times a month there are talks, performances and other events.

Hiking
At the end of Bunker Rd sits **Rodeo Beach**, protected from wind by high cliffs. From here the **Coastal Trail** meanders 3½mi inland, past abandoned military bunkers, to the **Tennessee Valley Trail**. It then continues 6mi along the blustery headlands all the way to Muir Beach.

Mountain Biking
The headlands have some excellent mountain-biking routes, and there is no more exhilarating ride than the trip across the Golden Gate Bridge to reach them (see the boxed text 'Hiking & Biking the Bridge').

For a good 12mi dirt loop, take the **Coastal Trail** west from the fork of Conzelman and McCullough Rds, bumping and winding down to Bunker Rd where it meets **Bobcat Trail**; Bobcat Trail joins **Marincello Trail** and descends steeply into the Tennessee Valley parking area. The **Old Springs Trail** and the **Miwok Trail** take you back to

Bunker Rd a bit more gently than the Bobcat Trail, though any attempt to avoid at least a couple of hefty climbs on this ride is futile.

Places to Stay
There are three small campgrounds in the headlands (all involve hiking in at least 1mi). **Hawk** and **Haypress** are free but must be reserved through the visitors center (see Information earlier). Sites at **Kirby Cove** costs $25 a night; reserve by calling ☎ 800-365-2267. **Marin Headlands Hostel** (☎ *415-331-2777; dorm beds $15, family rooms $45*), run by HI, is in Fort Barry.

Getting There & Away
On Sunday and holidays **MUNI** (☎ *415-673-6864*) bus No 76 runs from the CalTrain depot in San Francisco to Fort Barry and Rodeo Beach. By car, take the Alexander Ave exit just after the Golden Gate Bridge and dip left under the freeway. Conzelman Rd, to the right, takes you up along the bluffs; you can also take Bunker Rd, which leads to the headlands through a one-way tunnel.

SAUSALITO
Stretched along the water's edge, with uninterrupted views of San Francisco and Angel Island, Sausalito (population 7825), from the Spanish for 'little willow,' is the first town you encounter after crossing the Golden Gate Bridge from San Francisco. Once a small seafaring center populated by fisherfolk, this tiny bayside community is now fiercely fashionable, a tourist haven jam-packed with both junky souvenir shops and costly boutiques.

It's also, despite the dense crowds and near-impossible parking situation, an undeniably lovely location. Picturesque houses tumble neatly down the green hillside into a well-heeled downtown, which remains largely protected from the fog rolling through the Golden Gate due to the ridgeline behind it.

History
Sausalito began as a 19,000-acre land grant to an army captain in 1838. When it became the terminus of the railway line down the Pacific coast, it entered a new stage as a busy lumber port with a racy waterfront. WWII brought dramatic changes when

Sausalito became the site of Marinship, a huge shipbuilding yard. After the war a new bohemian period began, with a resident artists' colony living in 'arks' (houseboats moored along the bay).

Orientation & Information

Commercial Sausalito is essentially one street, the waterfront Bridgeway Blvd. Humboldt Park and the ferry terminal mark the town center. The **Sausalito Visitor Center** (☎ 415-332-0505; 780 Bridgeway Blvd; open 11:30am-4pm Tues-Sun) has local information; there's also an information kiosk at the ferry terminal.

Things to See

Sausalito's bayside setting is reason enough to visit, though there are some other sites.

Plaza de Viña Del Mar Park, near the ferry terminal, has a fountain flanked by 14ft-tall elephant statues from the 1915 Panama-Pacific Exposition in Golden Gate Park. Opposite Johnson St, **Ark Row** has a number of houseboats, which were once common on the bay.

One of the coolest things in town, fascinating to both kids and adults, is the Army Corps of Engineers' **Bay Model Visitor Center** (☎ 415-332-3871; 2100 Bridgeway Blvd; admission free; open 9am-4pm Tues-Fri, 9am-5pm Sat-Sun). Housed in one of the old Marinship warehouses, it's a 1.5-acre hydraulic model of the San Francisco Bay and the delta region. Self-guided tours take you over and around it as the water flows.

Just under the north tower of the Golden Gate Bridge, at East Fort Baker, the **Bay Area Discovery Museum** (☎ 415-487-4398; admission $7; open 9am-4pm Tues-Fri, 10am-5pm Sat-Sun) is a hands-on museum specifically designed for children. Permanent exhibits include an underwater sea tunnel, a ceramic studio and a science lab.

Boating

On a nice day, Richardson Bay is almost irresistible. Kayaks can be rented from **Sea Trek** (☎ 415-488-1000), in Schoonmaker Marina near the Bay Model Visitor Centre, for $15 per hour. No experience is necessary; lessons and group outings are also available.

Numerous Sausalito companies also offer bay cruises and rent sailboats. The Sausalito Visitor Center has a list.

Biking

Sausalito is great for bicycling, whether just a leisurely ride around town, a trip across the Golden Gate Bridge (see the boxed text 'Hiking & Biking the Bridge'), a coastal jaunt or a tour of other Marin County towns. From the ferry terminal, an easy option is to head south on Bridgeway Blvd, veering left onto East Rd toward the Bay Area Discovery Museum. Another nice route heads north along Bridgeway Blvd, then crosses under Hwy 101 to Mill Valley. At Blithedale Ave, you can veer east to Tiburon; a bike path parallels parts of Tiburon Blvd.

For details on routes, regulations and group rides, contact the **Marin County Bike Coalition** (☎ 415-456-3469; W www.marinbike.org), publisher of the *Marin Bike Route Map*. The **SF Bike Coalition** (☎ 415-431-2453; W www.sfbike.org) is another great resource.

Sausalito Cyclery (☎ 415-332-3200; 1 Gate 6 Rd), at the north end of Bridgeway Blvd near Hwy 101, rents mountain bikes for $12/40 per hour/day.

Hiking & Biking the Bridge

Walking or bicycling across the Golden Gate Bridge to Sausalito is a fun way to avoid traffic, get some great ocean views and bask in that refreshing Marin County air as you work a few muscles. It's actually a fairly easy journey, mostly flat or downhill when heading north from San Francisco (biking back to the city involves one big climb out of Sausalito). Once you're in Sausalito, walk around, have a meal and when you're ready to head back, simply hop on a ferry (see Getting There & Away later).

The trip is about 4mi from the south end of the bridge and takes less than an hour. Pedestrians have access to the bridge's east walkway between 5am and 9pm daily. Cyclists generally use the west side, except on weekdays between 5am and 3:30pm, when they must share the east side with pedestrians (who have the right of way). After 9pm, cyclists can still cross the bridge, on the east side through a security gate.

For more information on rules and rides, contact the **San Francisco Bicycle Coalition** (☎ 415-431-2453; W www.sfbike.org).

Places to Stay

Accommodation in Sausalito is limited and expensive.

Alta Mira Hotel *(☎ 415-332-1350; 125 Bulkley Ave; rooms $95-220)*, a block back from Bridgeway Blvd, is known for its magnificent views.

Hotel Sausalito *(☎ 415-332-4155; 16 El Portal St; rooms from $145)* is a 1915 building downtown, close to the ferry terminal.

Casa Madrona *(☎ 415-332-0502, 800-288-0502; 801 Bridgeway; rooms from $195)* was built in 1885 as a private residence and has been a hotel since 1905. It is a charming place.

Places to Eat

Bridgeway Blvd is packed with both moderately priced cafes and expensive restaurants, all catering to tourists.

Ondine *(☎ 415-331-1133; 558 Bridgeway Blvd; meals over $30)* is right on the bay in an old yacht club, its romantic bar and restaurant surrounded by windows and sporting impressive views. The Mediterranean menu gets high marks too.

Sushi Ran *(☎ 415-332-3620; 107 Caledonia St; items $4-15)*, though pricey, is claimed by many Bay Area residents to be the best sushi spot around. A wine and sake bar next door eases the pain of the long wait for a table.

Guernica *(☎ 415-332-1512; 2009 Bridgeway Blvd; dinners $11-15)* has been serving filling Basque meals in a comfortable atmosphere for over a quarter of a century.

Arawan *(47 Caledonia St; mains under $10)* has reasonably priced Thai food.

Caffe Tutti *(12 El Portal Dr)* has strong cappuccinos, excellent French pastries and sit-down meals. Good coffee's also found at **Caffe Trieste** *(1000 Bridgeway Blvd)*, a branch of the landmark North Beach coffeehouse.

Entertainment

A cocktail on the heated terrace of the **Alta Mira Hotel** *(125 Bulkley Ave)*, the entire bay stretched out in front of you, is almost obligatory.

Despite the town's gentrification, down-home company and occasional live bands are still found at the **No Name Bar** *(757 Bridgeway Blvd)*, supposedly a former Beat generation hangout.

Getting There & Away

Golden Gate Transit *(☎ 415-923-2000)* bus Nos 10 and 50 run daily to Sausalito from San Francisco; the one-way fare is $2.50. Catch them at 1st and Mission Sts outside the Transbay Terminal.

Driving to Sausalito from San Francisco, take the Alexander Ave exit (the first exit after the Golden Gate Bridge) and follow the signs into Sausalito. There are free municipal parking lots in town, which are worth using, as street parking restrictions are strictly enforced.

The ferry is a fun and easy method for getting to Sausalito. **Golden Gate Ferries** *(☎ 415-923-2000)* operates to and from the San Francisco Ferry Building for $5.60 each way. The ferries operate up to 10 times daily and the trip takes 30 minutes. The **Blue & Gold Fleet** *(☎ 415-773-1188)* sails to Sausalito from Pier 41 at Fisherman's Wharf in San Francisco daily year-round. The one-way fare is $6.75, and you can transport bicycles for free.

TIBURON

On a peninsula pointing out into the center of the bay, Tiburon (population 8900) is a bay community that, much like Sausalito, is noted for its gorgeous views. The name comes from the Spanish Punta de Tiburon (Shark Point). It's connected by ferry with downtown San Francisco and is also a popular jumping-off point for nearby Angel Island (see Angel Island later in this chapter).

Orientation & Information

The central part of town is comprised of Tiburon Blvd, with Juanita Lane and charming Main St arcing off. Main St, also known as Ark Row, is where the old houseboats have taken root on dry land and metamorphosed into classy shops and boutiques.

Visitor information is available from the **Tiburon Peninsula Chamber of Commerce** *(☎ 415-435-5633; w www.tiburonchamber.org; 96B Main St; open 8am-4pm Mon-Fri)*.

Things to See & Do

Take the ferry from San Francisco, browse the shops on Main St, grab a bite to eat and you've seen Tiburon. There are great views from the lovely hillside surrounding **Old St Hilary's Church** *(☎ 415-435-1853;*

201 Esperanza; open 1pm-4pm Wed-Sun Apr-Oct), a fine 19th-century example of Carpenter Gothic.

The Angel Island–Tiburon Ferry offers **sunset cruises** (*☎ 415-435-2131*) on Friday and Saturday evenings from May to October for $10. Reservations are recommended.

Back toward Hwy 101 the **Richardson Bay Audubon Center** (*☎ 415-388-2524; 376 Greenwood Beach Rd; open 9am-5pm Sun-Fri)*, off Tiburon Blvd, is home to a huge variety of water birds.

Places to Stay & Eat
Tiburon Lodge and Conference Center (*☎ 415-435-3133, 800-762-7770; 1651 Tiburon Blvd; rooms $159-345)* is a modern upscale hotel with bizarre spa rooms with names such as 'Purple Harem' and 'Red Licorice.'

Sam's Anchor Cafe (*☎ 415-435-4527; 27 Main St; meals from $10)* has had an unbeatable view since 1920. Stop by for seafood or burgers, or just have a cocktail on the deck. Check current weather via Sam's 24-hour webcam (**w** www.samscafe.com).

Guaymas (*☎ 415-435-6300; 5 Main St; mains $10-18)* is another popular waterfront hangout, where fans flock for Mexican meals and bayside margaritas on the patio.

Sweden House (*37 Main St; meals under $10)* is a bakery and café offering coffee, pastries, sandwiches and salads.

Getting There & Away
Golden Gate Transit (*☎ 415-923-2000)* bus No 10 runs from San Francisco ($3.10) and Sausalito ($1.50) via Mill Valley to Tiburon. During the week, commute bus No 8 runs direct between San Francisco and Tiburon.

On Hwy 101, look for the off-ramp for Tiburon Blvd, E Blithedale Ave and Hwy 131; driving east, it leads into town and intersects with Juanita Lane and Main St.

Blue & Gold Fleet (*☎ 415-773-1188)* sails daily from Pier 41 at Fisherman's Wharf in San Francisco to Tiburon; ferries dock right in front of the Guaymas restaurant on Main St. The one-way fare is $6.75, and you can transport bicycles for free. Weekdays, during commute hours, the ferries also operate to and from Tiburon and San Francisco's Ferry Building. From Tiburon, ferries also connect regularly to nearby Angel Island.

ANGEL ISLAND
Angel Island State Park (*☎ 415-435-1915)*, which occupies the entire 750-acre Angel Island, is a short ferry ride from either San Francisco or Marin. With a mild Mediterranean climate and fresh ocean breezes, it is a popular place for walking, biking and even camping.

Originally, Miwok Indians used the island as a hunting and fishing ground. More recently it's been an infantry camp, immigration station, WWII internment camp and Nike missile base. The surviving forts and bunkers reveal these darker chapters of the island's colorful and troubled history.

Things to See & Do
There are 12mi of roads and trails around the island, including a hike (no bikes) to the summit of **Mt Livermore** and a 5mi perimeter trail that offers a 360-degree panorama of the bay. In **Ayala Cove**, the sheltered harbor on the Tiburon side of Angel Island, a small beach backs up to picnic lawns fringed by forest.

The **Immigration Station** operated from 1910 to 1940 as a checkpoint for Chinese, Russian, Japanese and other Asian immigrants, who were often detained for long periods and treated like prisoners. During WWII it was used to intern Japanese Americans. You can learn more from the docents who staff it on weekends and holidays.

Camp Reynolds, on the island's western side, was built as a US Army defense post in 1863 during the Civil War. **Fort McDowell**, on the island's eastern side, was built in 1898 during the Spanish–American War. Both forts offer guided tours. At 1pm and 2pm, a Civil War cannon is fired from the shore near Camp Reynolds.

On Sunday between May and October, **Sea Trek Ocean Kayaking** (*☎ 415-488-1000)* offers guided kayaking excursions around Angel Island. The all-day trip costs $130 per person; the 2½-hour trip is $75 per person. Both include equipment and instructions, and the day-long trip includes lunch.

The island has nine hike-in **campsites** (*☎ 800-444-7275 for reservations; campsites in high/low season $10/7)*. You need to reserve months in advance. For meals, bring a picnic. If you're desperate, however, there is a snack bar, the **Cove Cafe** (*open weekends only in spring & fall, closed in winter)*, near the ferry dock.

Getting There & Around

From San Francisco, take a **Blue & Gold Fleet** (☎ 415-773-1188) ferry from Pier 41. From May to September, there are three ferries a day on weekends and two on weekdays; the rest of the year the schedule is reduced. Round-trip tickets cost $10.50 for adults and $5.50 for children.

From Tiburon, take the **Angel Island–Tiburon Ferry** (☎ 415-435-2131), which costs $5.50 for the round-trip; add $1 for bicycles. Departures are hourly between 10am and 3pm weekdays, and between 10am and 5pm weekends. From October to April, the weekday schedule is reduced.

You can rent bicycles at Ayala Cove for $10/30 per hour/day, and there are **tram tours** (☎ 415-897-0715) around the island from March to November ($11.50).

MILL VALLEY

Nestled under the redwoods at the base of Mt Tamalpais, tiny Mill Valley (population 14,100) is one of the Bay Area's most picturesque hamlets. It was originally a logging town, the name stemming from an 1830s sawmill that was the first in the Bay Area to provide lumber. Though the 1892 Mill Valley Lumber Company still greets you on Miller Ave, the town's a vastly different place today, packed with wildly expensive homes, fancy cars and pricey boutiques.

Mill Valley also served as the starting point for the scenic railway that carried visitors up Mt Tam (see Mt Tamalpais State Park later in this chapter). The tracks were removed in 1940, and today the Depot Bookstore & Cafe (see Places to Eat later) occupies the space of the former station.

Mill Valley visitor information is available from the **chamber of commerce** (☎ 415-388-9700; w www.millvalley.org; 85 Throckmorton Ave; open 10am-4pm Mon-Fri).

Things to See

Several blocks west of downtown along Throckmorton Ave is **Old Mill Park**, perfect for a picnic. Here you'll also find a replica of the town's namesake sawmill. Just past the bridge at Old Mill Creek, the **Dipsea Steps** mark the start of the Dipsea Trail.

Said to have been founded by 35 Mill Valley ladies determined to preserve the local environment, the private **Outdoor Art Club** (cnr W Blithedale & Throckmorton Aves) is housed in a landmark 1904 building designed by Bernard Maybeck.

Most of the downtown shops and galleries are for those with disposable incomes only, though amid the antiques and bath products is the longstanding record store **Village Music** (9 E Blithedale Ave); the walls plastered with memorabilia give it the feel of a museum.

Each October the **Mill Valley Film Festival** (☎ 415-383-5256) presents an innovative, internationally regarded program of independent film.

Hiking

Tennessee Valley Trail, in the Marin Headlands, offers beautiful views of the rugged coastline and is one of the most popular hikes in Marin (expect crowds on weekends). It offers easy, level access to the beach and ocean and is a short 3.8mi, though it can get windy. From Hwy 101, take the Mill Valley–Stinson Beach–Hwy 1 exit and turn left onto Tennessee Valley Rd from the Shoreline Hwy; follow it to the parking lot and trailhead.

A more demanding option is the 7mi **Dipsea Trail**, which climbs over the coastal range and down to Stinson Beach, cutting through a corner of Muir Woods. The trail starts at Old Mill Park with a climb up 676 steps in three separate flights, and includes a few more steep ups and downs before reaching the ocean.

Places to Stay

Just off Hwy 101, you can't miss the big signs of the **Fireside Motel** (☎ 415-332-6906; 115 Shoreline Hwy; singles/doubles $55/75) and its similarly priced neighbor the **Fountain Motel** (☎ 415-332-1732; 155 Shoreline Hwy; singles/doubles $59/79). Both are decent older properties with roadside character.

Mill Valley Inn (☎ 415-389-6608; 165 Throckmorton Ave; rooms from $170), in town, is an elegant place with 25 rooms, some with views of the redwoods. Rates include breakfast on the terrace.

Places to Eat

Depot Bookstore & Cafe (87 Throckmorton Ave; meals under $10), smack in the town center, serves cappuccinos, sandwiches and light meals. The bookstore sells lots of local publications, including trail guides.

Avatar's Punjab Burritos (15 Madrona St; burritos from $5) is worth trying. Its specialty is cheap, tasty and filling Indian-style burritos.

El Paseo (☎ 415-388-0741; 7 El Paseo Ave; meals over $25), a small, charming restaurant specializing in French cuisine, is worth the splurge.

Buckeye Roadhouse (☎ 415-331-2600; 15 Shoreline Hwy; meals from $15), in a large, lodge-like building at the Shoreline Hwy entrance to Hwy 101 south, serves hearty American meals that routinely win critical praise.

Entertainment

Sweetwater (☎ 415-388-2820; 153 Throckmorton Ave) is one of the most intimate music venues in the Bay Area, attracting the likes of JJ Cale, Chris Smither and Maria Muldaur. When there's no music it's still a comfortable pub.

Getting There & Away

From San Francisco or Sausalito, take Hwy 101 north to the Mill Valley–Stinson Beach–Hwy 1 exit. Follow Hwy 1 (here called the Shoreline Hwy) to Almonte Blvd (which becomes Miller Ave), then follow Miller Ave into downtown Mill Valley.

From the north, take the E Blithedale Ave exit from Hwy 101, then head west into downtown Mill Valley.

Golden Gate Transit (☎ 415-923-2000) bus No 4 runs from San Francisco to Mill Valley ($2.50) on weekdays; on weekends take bus No 10, which also stops in Sausalito and Tiburon.

LARKSPUR, SAN ANSELMO & CORTE MADERA

Clustered around Hwy 101 and Sir Francis Drake Blvd are the small inland towns of Larkspur, Corte Madera, Kentfield, Ross, San Anselmo and Fairfax.

In **Larkspur**, you can window-shop along Magnolia Ave or explore the redwoods in nearby Baltimore Canyon. On the east side of the freeway is the hulking mass of **San Quentin State Penitentiary**, California's oldest and second-most famous prison, founded in 1852. Johnny Cash recorded an album here in 1969.

San Anselmo has a cute, small downtown area, including several antiques shops, along San Anselmo Ave. **Corte Madera** is home to

one of the Bay Area's best bookstores, **Book Passage** (☎ 415-927-0960; 51 Tamal Vista Blvd), in the Market Place shopping center. It has a strong travel section, plus frequent author appearances.

Lark Creek Inn (☎ 415-924-7766; 234 Magnolia Ave, Larkspur; mains $20-35) is one of Marin's finest dining experiences. It's housed in an old-style Victorian building tucked away in a redwood canyon. The adjacent bar has a less-formal menu.

Marin Brewing Company (☎ 415-461-4677; 1809 Larkspur Landing Circle; sandwiches & pizzas $7-12) is a popular hangout with reliable craft-brewed beer, pub food and a sometimes rowdy crowd.

Golden Gate Transit (☎ 415-923-2000) offers a daily ferry service from the Ferry Building in San Francisco to Larkspur Landing on E Sir Francis Drake Blvd, directly east of Hwy 101. The trip takes 50 minutes and costs $5.60. You can take bicycles on the ferry.

SAN RAFAEL

San Rafael (population 54,800), the oldest and largest town in Marin, is less upscale than most of its neighbors. Just north of San Rafael, Lucas Valley Rd heads off west to Point Reyes Station, passing George Lucas' Skywalker Ranch (oddly enough, Lucas Valley Rd is not named after the creator of Star Wars).

Orientation

Fourth St, San Rafael's main drag, is lined with cafés and shops. If you follow it west out of downtown San Rafael, it meets Sir Francis Drake Blvd and continues west to the coast.

Things to See & Do

The town began with **Mission San Rafael Arcángel** (☎ 415-454-8141; 1104 5th Ave; museum open 11am-4pm daily), founded in 1817. The present building is a replica dating from 1949.

Designed by Frank Lloyd Wright, the **Marin County Civic Center** (☎ 415-472-3500) is a long, beautiful structure blending into the hills directly east of Hwy 101; exit on N San Pedro Rd, 2mi north of San Rafael. The **gift shop** (open 10am-4pm Mon-Fri) on the 2nd floor is worth checking out for its Wright-inspired items and local literature. Tours begin here Wednesday at

10:30am; reserve by calling ☎ 415-499-6646. The center hosts regular concerts and events, including the Marin County Fair each July and a **farmers market** every Thursday and Sunday morning.

China Camp State Park (☎ *415-456-0766*) is a pleasant place to stop for a picnic or short hike. From Hwy 101, take the N San Pedro Rd exit and continue 3mi east. The name comes from the remains of a Chinese fishing village here, one of many Chinese shrimp-fishing encampments once prevalent around San Francisco Bay.

Rafael Film Center (☎ *415-454-1222; 1118 4th St*), a restored downtown cinema run by the Film Institute of Northern California, offers innovative art-house programming in state-of-the-art surroundings.

Places to Stay & Eat

China Camp State Park (☎ *415-456-0766, 800-444-7275 for reservations; campsites $12*) has 30 walk-in campsites.

Panama Hotel (☎ *415-457-3993; fax 415-457-6240; 4 Bayview St; rooms with shared/private bathroom from $75/100*) is a 16-room B&B dating from 1910, with charm, history and style.

San Rafael Inn (☎ *415-454-9470; 865 E Francisco Blvd; singles/doubles $79/99*) is a simple property.

Las Camelias (*912 Lincoln Ave; meals under $20*) is a favorite for home-made Mexican meals.

Lotus Cuisine of India (*704 Fourth St; mains $10-18*) is another popular local spot. The lunch buffet ($7.45) is a bargain.

Getting There & Away

Numerous **Golden Gate Transit** (☎ *415-923-2000*) buses operate between San Francisco and the San Rafael Transit Center at 3rd and Hetherton Sts. Bus No 40 is the only service that takes bicycles across the Golden Gate Bridge.

MT TAMALPAIS STATE PARK

Standing guard over Marin County, majestic Mt Tamalpais (Mt Tam) has breathtaking 360-degree views of ocean, bay and hills rolling into the distance. The rich, natural beauty of 2571ft Mt Tam and the surrounding area is inspiring – especially considering that it lies within an hour's drive from one of the state's largest metropolitan areas.

Mt Tamalpais State Park was formed in 1930, partly from land donated by Congressman and naturalist William Kent (who also donated the land that became Muir Woods National Monument in 1907). Its 6300 acres are home to deer, foxes, bobcats and many miles of hiking and biking trails.

Mt Tam was a sacred place to the coastal Miwok Indians for thousands of years before the arrival of European and American settlers. By the late 19th century, San Franciscans were escaping the bustle of the city with all-day outings on the mountain, and in 1896 the 'world's crookedest railroad' (281 turns) was completed from Mill Valley to the summit. Though the railroad was closed in 1930, Old Railroad Grade is today one of Mt Tam's most popular and scenic hiking and biking paths.

Orientation & Information

Panoramic Hwy climbs from Mill Valley through the park to Stinson Beach. **Pantoll Station** (☎ *415-388-2070; 801 Panoramic Hwy*) is the park headquarters. Detailed park maps are sold here for $1.

Things to See

From Pantoll Station, it's 4.2mi by car to **East Peak Summit**; take Pantoll Rd and then panoramic Ridgecrest Blvd to the top. Parking is $2 and a 10-minute hike leads to the very top and the best views.

The park's natural-stone, 4000-seat **Mountain Theater** (☎ *415-383-1100*) hosts the annual 'Mountain Play' series on six Sundays between mid-May and late June. Free shuttles are provided from Mill Valley. Free astronomy programs also take place here each summer around the new moon; for information call ☎ 415-455-5370.

Hiking

The $1 park map is a smart investment, as there are a dozen worthwhile hiking trails in the area. From Pantoll Station, the **Steep Ravine Trail** follows a wooded creek to the coast (about 2.1mi each way). For a longer hike, veer right (northwest) after 1½mi onto the **Dipsea Trail**, which meanders through the trees for 1mi before ending at Stinson Beach. Grab some lunch, then walk north through town and follow signs for the **Matt Davis Trail**, which leads 2.7mi back to Pantoll Station, making a good loop. The Matt

Davis Trail continues on beyond Pantoll Station, wrapping gently around the mountain with superb views.

Another worthy option is the **Cataract Trail**, which runs along Cataract Creek from the end of Pantoll Rd; it's about 3mi to Alpine Lake. The last mile is a spectacular rooty staircase as the trail descends alongside Cataract Falls.

Mountain Biking
Bikers must stay on fire roads (and off the single-track trails) and keep speeds under 15 mph (24 km/h). The rangers take these rules seriously, and a ticket can result in a steep fine.

The most popular ride is the **Old Railroad Grade**; for a sweaty, 6mi, 2280ft climb, start in Mill Valley at the end of W Blithedale Ave and bike up to East Peak. It takes about an hour to reach the **West Point Inn** from Mill Valley. For an easier start, begin partway up at the Mountain Home Inn (see Places to Stay later) and follow the **Gravity Car Grade** to the Old Railroad Grade and the West Point Inn. From the latter, it's an easy half-hour ride to the summit.

West Point Inn, by the way, hosts **pancake breakfasts** monthly during the summer, a hearty reward for all those switchbacks. Call ☎ 415-388-9955 for dates.

From just west of Pantoll Station, bikers can either take the **Deer Park fire road** through giant redwoods to the main entrance of Muir Woods or the southeast extension of the **Coastal Trail**, which has breathtaking views of the coast before joining Hwy 1 about 2mi north of Muir Beach. Either option requires a return to Mill Valley via Frank Valley/Muir Woods Rd, which climbs steadily (800ft) to Panoramic Hwy and then becomes Sequoia Valley Rd as it drops toward Mill Valley. A left turn on Wildomar and two right turns at Mill Creek Park leads to the center of Mill Valley at the Depot Bookstore & Cafe.

For further information on bike routes and rules, contact the **Marin County Bike Coalition** (415-456-3469; **W** www.marinbike.org).

Places to Stay & Eat
Pantoll Station (☎ 415-388-2070; campsites $12) has 16 campsites available on a first-come, first-served basis.

Steep Ravine Environmental Campground (campsites $7, cabins $15), just off Hwy 1 about 1mi south of Stinson Beach, has six beachfront campsites and several rustic five-person cabins overlooking the ocean. Both options are booked out months in advance and reservations are mandatory; call ☎ 800-444-7275.

Mountain Home Inn (☎ 415-381-9000; 810 Panoramic Hwy; rooms from $175) is situated on the east side of the mountain. With awesome views of the East Bay, this is also a great spot for a lunch or dinner; reservations are recommended.

Getting There & Away
To reach Pantoll Station, take Hwy 1 to the Panoramic Hwy and look for the Pantoll signs. On weekends and holidays you can take **Golden Gate Transit** (☎ 415-923-2000) bus No 63 from the Marin City transfer station to Pantoll Station and the Mountain Home Inn.

MUIR WOODS NATIONAL MONUMENT
The old-growth redwoods at Muir Woods (☎ 415-388-2595; day-use fee $3; open 8am-sunset daily, to 5pm in winter) were initially eyed by loggers. Then Redwood Creek, as the area was known, seemed perfect for a dam. Those plans were halted when Congressman and naturalist William Kent bought a section of Redwood Creek and, in 1907, donated 295 acres to the federal government. President Theodore Roosevelt made the site a national monument in 1908, the name honoring John Muir, naturalist and founder of environmental organization the Sierra Club.

Surrounded on all sides by Mt Tamalpais State Park, Muir Woods is the closest redwood stand to San Francisco, so it can get quite crowded, especially on weekends. Try to come midweek, early in the morning or late in the afternoon, when tour buses are less of a problem. Even at busy times, a short hike will get you out of the densest crowds and onto trails with huge trees and stunning vistas.

Hiking
An easy walk is the 1mi **Main Trail Loop**, leading alongside Redwood Creek to the 1000-year-old trees at Cathedral Grove; it returns via **Bohemian Grove**, where the tallest tree in the park stands 254ft high.

The **Dipsea Trail** is a good 2mi hike up to the top of aptly named Cardiac Hill.

You can also walk down into Muir Woods by following trails from the Panoramic Hwy (such as the Bootjack Trail from the Bootjack picnic area) or from Mt Tamalpais' Pantoll Station campground (via the Ben Johnson Trail).

Getting There & Away

Muir Woods is just 12mi north of the Golden Gate Bridge. Driving north on Hwy 101, exit at Hwy 1 and continue north along Hwy 1/Shoreline Hwy to the Panoramic Hwy (a right-hand fork). Follow that for about 1mi to Four Corners, where you turn left onto Muir Woods Rd (there are plenty of signs). There are no direct buses to Muir Woods – a fact that's seriously silly since parking and traffic are constant problems.

THE COAST
Muir Beach

The turnoff to Muir Beach from Hwy 1 is marked by the longest row of mailboxes on the North Coast. Muir Beach is a quiet little town with a nice beach, but it has no direct bus service. Just north of Muir Beach there are superb views up and down the coast from the **Muir Beach Overlook**; during WWII, watch was kept from the surrounding concrete lookouts for invading Japanese ships.

Pelican Inn (☎ 415-383-6000; 10 Pacific Way; rooms from $200), ever popular and very English looking, is the only commercial establishment in Muir Beach. It also has a pleasant restaurant and pub, perfect for pre- or post-hike nourishment.

Green Gulch Farm & Zen Center (☎ 415-383-3134, fax 415-383-3128; 1601 Shoreline Hwy) is a Buddhist retreat in the hills above Muir Beach. The center's **Lindisfarne Guest House** (singles/doubles from $75/125) offers a quiet overnight stay with buffet-style vegetarian meals.

Stinson Beach

Stinson Beach, 5mi north of Muir Beach, flanks Hwy 1 for about three blocks and is densely packed with galleries, shops, eateries and B&Bs. The beach itself is often blanketed with fog; when it's sunny, it's blanketed with surfers, families and gawkers. Nevertheless it's nice, with views of Point Reyes

and San Francisco on clear days, and it's long enough for a vigorous stroll.

Three-mile-long **Stinson Beach** is a popular surf spot, but swimming is advised from late May to mid-September only; for updated weather and surf conditions call ☎ 415-868-1922. The beach is one block west of Hwy 1.

About 1mi south of Stinson Beach is Red Rock Beach. It's a popular clothing-optional beach, but it attracts smaller crowds, as it requires a steep hike down from Hwy 1.

About 3½mi north of town on Hwy 1, in the hills above the Bolinas Lagoon, the **Audubon Canyon Ranch** (☎ 415-868-9244; donations requested; open 10am-4pm Sat, Sun & holidays mid-Mar–mid-July) is a major nesting ground for great blue herons and great egrets.

Stinson Beach Motel (☎ 415-868-1712; w www.stinsonbeachmotel.com; 3416 Hwy 1; rooms $85-225) is a remodeled 70-year-old motel surrounded by gardens. It's two blocks from the beach.

Sandpiper Motel (☎ 415-868-1632; 1 Marine Way; rooms $115-195), closer to the beach, has standard rooms with gas fireplaces as well as some restored cottages with full kitchens.

Sand Dollar Restaurant (☎ 415-868-0434; 3458 Hwy 1; dinner from $15) is a longstanding local restaurant with a full bar, nightly dinners and a sunny outdoor patio.

Parkside Cafe (☎ 415-868-1272; 43 Arenal Ave; breakfast $7-9, dinner mains $15-21) is famous for its hearty breakfasts and lunches, but it also serves top-notch (if pricier) dinners. Reservations are recommended.

From Hwy 101, take the Hwy 1 exit and continue north along Hwy 1/Shoreline Hwy. After about 2mi, you'll come to a fork (both roads eventually join up in Stinson Beach). The left-hand fork (the continuation of Hwy 1/Shoreline Hwy) goes past Muir Beach and then swings northwest along the coast to Stinson Beach. The right-hand fork winds its way through Mt Tamalpais State Park before dropping down into Stinson Beach. The roads are equally long, equally beautiful and equally curvy. From San Francisco it's nearly an hour's drive, though on weekends plan for long traffic delays.

Golden Gate Transit (☎ 415-923-2000) bus No 63 runs to Stinson Beach, weekends only, from the Marin City transfer center.

Bolinas

Known as Jugville during the gold rush days, the sleepy beachside community of Bolinas is most famous for its disappearing direction signs, removed from Hwy 1 by locals in a successful campaign to save the town from development (and from marauding tourists). The highway department finally agreed to leave Bolinas to its own devices.

Since the 1970s, Bolinas has been home to the original Niman Ranch. Fine restaurants nationwide clamor for the company's beef, pork and lamb, raised on sustainable lands with natural feed and without the use of growth hormones.

The free monthly *Pacific Coastal Post* gives an interesting perspective on local and world events.

Things to See & Do For a town so plainly unexcited about tourism, Bolinas offers some fairly tempting attractions.

Bolinas Museum (☎ 415-868-0330; 48 Wharf Rd; open 1pm-5pm Fri, noon-5pm Sat & Sun) has exhibits showcasing local artists as well as highlighting the region's history.

There are tide pools along some 2mi of coastline at **Agate Beach**, around the end of Duxbury Point. The **Point Reyes Bird Observatory** (☎ 415-868-1221; open 9am-5pm daily), off Mesa Rd west of downtown, has bird-banding and netting demonstrations, monthly guided walks, a visitors center and a nature trail. Banding demonstrations are in the morning every Tuesday to Sunday from May to late November and on Wednesday, Saturday and Sunday the rest of the year.

Beyond the observatory is the Palomarin parking lot and access to various walking trails, including the easy (and popular) 2mi trail to lovely **Bass Lake** and, beyond it, Alamere Falls and Wildcat Beach.

Places to Stay & Eat Although Bolinas residents are famously unenthusiastic about outsiders, there are accommodations here.

Smiley's Schooner Saloon & Hotel (☎ 415-868-1311, fax 415-868-0502; 41 Wharf Rd; rooms $74-84) is a crusty old place dating back to 1851, with simple but decent rooms. The bar has live bands on weekends and is frequented by plenty of salty dogs and grizzled Deadheads.

Blue Heron Inn (☎ 415-868-1102; 11 Wharf Rd; rooms $125) has two pleasant rooms. Prices include breakfast. There is also a small dinner house; mains cost under $20 and are made with local ingredients, including Niman Ranch meats.

There are several other small B&Bs in town, including **Thomas' White House Inn** (☎ 415-868-0279; 118 Kale Rd; rooms from $100), overlooking Duxbury Reef.

Getting There & Away By car, follow Hwy 1 north from Stinson Beach. The turnoff for Bolinas (it's not signposted, remember) is the first past Audubon Canyon Ranch, on the left. Parking in town is scarce.

Olema & Nicasio

About 10mi north of Stinson Beach near the junction of Hwy 1 and Sir Francis Drake Blvd, Olema was the main settlement in West Marin in the 1860s. There was a stagecoach service to San Rafael and there were *six* saloons. In 1875, when the railroad was built through Point Reyes Station instead of Olema, the town's importance began to fade. In 1906, it gained distinction again as the epicenter of the Great Quake.

About 1mi west of Olema, on Sir Francis Drake Blvd, starts the **Bolinas Ridge Trail**, a 12mi series of ups and downs for hikers or bikers with great views.

About a 15-minute drive inland from Olema, at the geographic center of Marin County, is Nicasio, a tiny town with a low-key rural flavor and a cool saloon and music venue. It's at the west end of Lucas Valley Rd 10mi from Hwy 101.

Olema Ranch Campground (☎ 415-663-8001; camping for two people $23, $3 per extra person), near Hwy 1 and Sir Francis Drake Blvd, has over 200 sites, a gas station and mountain bike rentals ($12/30 per hour/day).

Samuel P Taylor State Park (☎ 415-488-9897; campsites $12), 6mi east of Olema on Sir Francis Drake Blvd, is a much nicer camping option, with secluded campsites in redwood groves.

Rancho Nicasio (☎ 415-662-2219; mains from $16), in the town center, is a rustic saloon serving daily dinners and weekend brunches. It's also a venue for local and national blues, rock and country performers.

On weekends and holidays, **Golden Gate Transit** (☎ *415-923-2000*) bus No 65 runs to Olema and Samuel Taylor Park from the San Rafael Transit Center.

Point Reyes Station

Though still relatively small, Point Reyes Station is the hub of West Marin thanks mostly to the railroad, which ran here until 1933. Dominated by dairies and ranches, the region was invaded by artists in the '60s. Today it's an interesting blend: art galleries and tourist shops, a rowdy saloon and the occasional smell of cattle on the afternoon breeze.

The weekly *Point Reyes Light* has local news and helpful listings of events, restaurants and lodgings.

Sir Francis Drake

Sir Francis Drake was an extraordinary character: a self-made man, fearless, resourceful, clever, ruthless and very lucky. In 1577 he set off from England in a fleet of five small ships. His mission was exploration and adventure, to be financed by what could best be described as piracy, with the hated Spanish the intended victims.

In 1579 the *Golden Hind* was alone off the California coast. Two of the ships, brought only to carry supplies, had been abandoned. The third ship had sunk with all hands during the rounding of Cape Horn, and the fourth had lost contact and turned back to England. Drake and his crew had found rich pickings at the expense of the Spanish, but the *Golden Hind* was in sorry shape. Somewhere along the Marin County coast, possibly at Drakes Beach near Point Reyes, Drake put in to a sheltered bay, ran his ship aground at high tide and tipped it on its side to repair the ravaged hull. He stayed there for five weeks, trading with the local Indians and exploring inland, with one of his crew noting that the land was much more welcoming than it appeared from the sea.

Eventually Drake sailed off on a trip that would carry him right around the world and bring him back to England as a phenomenally wealthy and famous explorer. He cemented his fame by helping defeat the Spanish Armada in 1588.

The only budget choice is the hostel at the nearby Point Reyes National Seashore (see that section later). Cute little cottages, cabins and B&Bs are plentiful in and around Point Reyes, though they're not cheap. The **West Marin Chamber of Commerce** (☎ *415-663-9232*; Ⓦ *www .pointreyes.org*) has numerous listings.

Holly Tree Inn (☎ *415-663-1554, fax 415-663-8566; rooms from $130*), on Silverhills Rd off Bear Valley Rd, has four rooms and three private cottages.

Station House Cafe (*11180 Shoreline Hwy; dinner mains $10-20*) needs help with the decor, but the food is quite good. It uses Niman Ranch meats and there are some vegetarian options too.

Bovine Bakery, also on Shoreline Hwy, has great coffee and even better home-made pastries.

Tomales Bay Foods and Cowgirl Creamery (*80 Fourth St*) is a local market in an old barn. Picnic items, including gourmet cheeses and organic produce, are available.

Dance Palace (☎ *415-663-1075; 503 B St*) has weekend events, movies and live music.

Western Hotel (*cnr Shoreline Hwy & 2nd St*) is a rustic 1906 saloon with occasional live bands.

Hwy 1 becomes Main St in town, running right through the center. On weekends and holidays, Golden Gate Transit bus No 65 runs to Point Reyes Station from the San Rafael Transit Center ($5).

Inverness

This tiny town, the last outpost on your journey westward, is spread along the west side of Tomales Bay. It's got good places to eat and, among the surrounding hills and picturesque shoreline, multiple rental cottages and quaint B&Bs. Several great beaches are only a short drive north.

Blue Waters Kayaking Tours & Rentals (☎ *415-669-2600; 12938 Sir Francis Drake Blvd*), at the Golden Hinde Inn, offers various Tomales Bay cruises, or you can rent a **kayak** (*$30 for 2 hours; $50 per day*) and paddle around secluded beaches and rocky crevices on your own; no experience necessary.

From Hwy 1, Sir Francis Drake Blvd leads straight into Inverness. On weekends and holidays, Golden Gate Transit bus No 65 makes its final stop here from San Rafael.

Manka's Inverness Lodge (☎ 415-669-1034; rooms from $195) was built as a hunting lodge in 1917. It's tucked up the hill on Argyle St, which is just north of town (look for signs off Sir Francis Drake Blvd). It's beautifully rustic and the rooms are comfortable and elegant. The restaurant serves fabulous prix fixe meals (around $50) focusing on wild, local ingredients and meats roasted on an open fire.

Inverness Valley Inn (☎ 415-669-7250; 13275 Sir Francis Drake Blvd; rooms from $130), about 1mi past downtown, is a pleasant, tucked-away property.

Gray Whale Pizza (☎ 415-669-1244; meals from $6), downtown along Sir Francis Drake Blvd, is great for reasonably priced pizzas, pastas and sandwiches, with several vegetarian options.

Point Reyes National Seashore

Point Reyes National Seashore has 110 sq mi of pristine ocean beaches, wind-tousled ridges and diverse wildlife. The enormous peninsula, with its rough-hewn beauty, has excellent hiking and camping opportunities. Be sure to bring warm clothing, however, as even the sunniest days can quickly turn cold and foggy.

The **Bear Valley Visitor Center** (☎ 415-663-1092; Bear Valley Rd; open 9am-5pm Mon-Fri, 8am-5pm Sat & Sun), near Olema, is the park headquarters. It has a great deal of information and maps. There are two additional visitors centers: at the **Point Reyes Lighthouse** (see Things to See & Do later) and the **Ken Patrick Center** (☎ 415-669-1250; open 10am-5pm weekends & holidays) at Drakes Beach.

Things to See & Do Of all the trails at Point Reyes, one of the most awe-inspiring is the **Earthquake Trail** from the park headquarters at Bear Valley. On the trail you can view a 16ft gap between the two halves of a once-connected fence line, a lasting testimonial to the power of the 1906 earthquake that was centered in this area. Another trail leads from the visitor center a short way to **Kule Loklo**, a reproduction of a Miwok village.

Limantour Rd, off Bear Valley Rd about 1mi north of the Bear Valley Visitor Center, leads to the Point Reyes Hostel and to **Limantour Beach**. At the beach there's a trail that runs along Limantour Spit, with Estero de Limantour on one side and Drakes Bay on the other. The **Inverness Ridge Trail** heads from Limantour Rd up to 1282ft Mt Vision, which has spectacular views of the entire national seashore. You can drive almost to the top of Mt Vision from the other side.

Gray Whales

Gray whales may be seen at various points along the California coast, and the Point Reyes Lighthouse is a superb viewpoint for observing these huge creatures on their annual 6000mi migration. During the summer, the whales feed in the Arctic waters between Alaska and Siberia. Around October, they start to move south down the Pacific coast of Canada and the USA to sheltered lagoons in the Gulf of California, by the Mexican state of Baja California.

The whales, led by the pregnant cows, pass Point Reyes in December and January. They're followed by pods of females and courting males, usually in groups of three to five, and then by the younger whales. The whales spend about two months around Baja California, during which time the pregnant whales give birth to calves 15ft or 16ft long and weighing 2000lb to 2500lb. The newborn whales put on 200lb a day, and in February the reverse trip begins.

Gray whales live up to 50 years, grow to 50ft in length and weigh up to 45 tons. Spotting whales is a simple combination of patience and timing. Spouting, the exhalation of moist, warm air, is usually the first sign that a whale is about. A series of spouts, about 15 seconds apart, may be followed by a sight of the creature's tail as the whale dives. If you're lucky, you may see whales spy-hopping (sticking their heads out of the water to look around) or even breaching (leaping clear out of the water). Bring binoculars; whales are typically a quarter- to a half-mile out to sea, though they're closer to shore on the southbound leg of the journey.

Bay Adventures (☎ 415-331-0444) leads whale-watching expeditions during migration seasons. Trips run up the coast to Point Reyes or out to the Farralon Islands. Reservations are required.

About 2mi past Inverness, Pierce Point Rd splits off to the right from Sir Francis Drake Blvd. From here you can get to two nice swimming beaches on the bay: Marshall Beach requires a mile-long hike from the parking area, while Hearts Desire, in **Tomales Bay State Park**, is directly accessible by car.

Pierce Point Rd continues to the huge windswept sand dunes at **Abbotts Lagoon**, full of peeping killdeer and other shorebirds. At the end of the road is Pierce Point Ranch, the trailhead for the 3½mi Tomales Point Trail through the **tule elk reserve**. The elk are an amazing sight, standing with their big horns against the backdrop of Tomales Point, with Bodega Bay to the north, Tomales Bay to the east, and the Pacific Ocean to the west.

The **Point Reyes Lighthouse** (☎ 415-669-1534; open 10am-4:30pm Thur-Mon) is at the very end of Sir Francis Drake Blvd. This spot, with its wild terrain and ferocious winds, feels like the end of the earth and offers the best **whale-watching** on the coast. The lighthouse sits below the headlands; to reach it requires descending (then ascending) over 300 stairs. Nearby **Chimney Rock** makes an excellent short hike especially in spring, when the wildflowers are blossoming. A nearby viewing area allows you to spy on the park's **elephant seal colony**.

If you're intrigued by the surf crashing onto exposed North Beach and South Beach, make sure you keep back from the water's edge, as people have drowned, due to the frequent rogue waves.

On weekends during good weather, from late December through mid-April, the road to Chimney Rock and the lighthouse is closed to private vehicles. Instead you must take a shuttle ($2.50) from **Drakes Beach**, a safe place to wade or swim.

Places to Stay & Eat Just off Limantour Rd is **Point Reyes Hostel** (☎ 415-663-8811; dorm beds $14), an HI property in a beautiful, secluded valley 2mi from the ocean and surrounded by lovely hiking trails.

Point Reyes has four hike-in **campgrounds** (☎ 415-663-1092; campsites $10) with pit toilets, untreated water and tables (no wood fires). Permits are required; reserve at the Bear Valley Visitor Center or by calling ☎ 415-663-8054. Each of the four remote camps requires a 2mi to 6mi hike.

If you're looking for a hotel or B&B, see Inverness and Point Reyes Station earlier in this chapter.

Johnson's Drakes Bay Oysters (☎ 415-669-1149; open 8am-4:30pm Tues-Sun) has fresh, cheap oysters. Look for the sign halfway from Inverness to the Point Reyes Lighthouse.

Getting There & Away By car you can get to Point Reyes a few different ways. The curviest is along Hwy 1, through Stinson Beach and Olema. More direct is to exit Hwy 101 in San Rafael and follow Sir Francis Drake Blvd all the way to the tip of Point Reyes. For the latter route, take the Central San Rafael exit and head west on 4th St, which turns into Sir Francis Drake Blvd. By either route, it's about 1½ hours to Olema from San Francisco.

Just north of Olema, where Hwy 1 and Sir Francis Drake Blvd come together, is Bear Valley Rd; turn left to reach the Bear Valley Visitor Center. If you're heading to the further reaches of Point Reyes, follow Sir Francis Drake Blvd through Point Reyes Station and out onto the peninsula, about an hour's drive.

On weekends and holidays, **Golden Gate Transit** (☎ 415-923-2000) bus No 65 stops at the Bear Valley Visitor Center, Olema, Point Reyes Station and Inverness ($5).

East Bay

Linked to San Francisco by the Bay Bridge, the East Bay mostly consists of dense suburbs that range from poor neighborhoods on the bayside flats to exclusive enclaves high in the hills. Gritty Oakland and opinionated Berkeley, each with a distinct personality, dominate the East Bay, which was originally known as Contra Costa (Spanish for 'Opposite Coast'), a name that still applies to one of the East Bay's counties.

Somewhat surprisingly, miles of woodsy parkland cover the ridgeline above Berkeley and Oakland, and Mt Diablo towers in the background.

OAKLAND

Oakland (population 402,100) is a city on the rise. Despite having a long, colorful history, including a remarkable degree of racial and economic diversity and a vibrant arts scene, the city's admittedly been through some tough times in recent decades. Buildings began falling apart, residents abandoned the city center, crime went on the rise. These days, however, Oakland feels alive all over again. On weekdays, downtown is bustling; at night, the club and restaurant scenes are thriving. Downtown buildings have been renovated, and the hills east of town are home to numerous parks. It's still one of the most diverse cities in the USA. And as for weather, Oakland's almost always warmer and less foggy than San Francisco.

History

The Oakland area's earliest inhabitants were Ohlone Indians. In 1820 the area was included in the enormous rancho granted to Mexican soldier Luis Maria Peralta, but in 1850 three US citizens 'leased' what is now downtown Oakland and Jack London Square from the Peralta family. They sold the land off in lots, and Oakland was born.

The city took off in 1869, with the completion of the first transcontinental railway. As the railroad's West Coast terminus, Oakland grew rapidly into a business and industrial center and a busy port. Things remained that way through the 1920s, until the Great Depression, which hit Oakland hard. Gertrude Stein, who had lived in Oakland during her school years, returned to her old neighborhood in 1934 and was distraught over its dissolution. Her words of despair at the loss of her old home – 'There is no *there* there' – have become the most misquoted phrase ever attached to the city of Oakland.

The completion of the Bay Bridge in 1936 provided a needed boost, as did WWII-era industries such as shipbuilding. The 1940s saw a lively blues scene take shape in Oakland, vestiges of which are still hanging on. In the 1960s, the city was the scene of some violently repressed draft riots, as well as the founding of the Black Panther Party for Self-Defense. In more recent years, as San Francisco's shipping traffic has declined, Oakland's has strengthened. Today, Oakland is the fourth-largest container port in the country. The huge container cranes hovering threateningly above the Oakland docks are said to have inspired the Imperial Walkers that George Lucas dreamed up for *The Empire Strikes Back*.

Parts of downtown Oakland are, admittedly, still forlorn, and in the evenings the whole area empties out. Other sections of the city remain in the grip of urban decay, plagued by drugs, gangs and economic depression. Nonetheless, as a whole, the city is alive and growing, and it's well worth taking time to explore.

Orientation

The two main freeways through Oakland are I-880 and I-580, which parallel each other. Both split off from I-80 at the east end of the Bay Bridge and head south. The Bay Bridge lets you off in West Oakland, a heavily industrial area with residential pockets and housing projects. Downtown and Lake Merritt are southeast of there.

On an island south of downtown is Alameda, home to a former navy base and neighborhoods full of Victorian and Craftsman houses. At the north end of the city are the hip (and more upscale) Piedmont and Rockridge areas. East Oakland spreads southeast toward San Leandro and Fremont. Generally speaking it's best avoided, unless you're heading to the Oakland Coliseum or the airport. Definite destinations, though, are the large regional parks rising into the hills along the city's eastern border.

Broadway is the backbone of downtown Oakland, running from Jack London Square at the waterfront all the way north to Piedmont and Rockridge. Telegraph Ave branches off Broadway at 15th St and heads straight to Berkeley; running east from Broadway is Grand Ave, leading to the Lake Merritt commercial district. San Pablo Ave was formerly US Route 40 (and before that the Lincoln Hwy); it heads north from downtown into Berkeley.

Downtown BART stations are on Broadway at both 12th and 19th Sts; other stations are near Lake Merritt and in Rockridge.

Information

The **Oakland Convention & Visitors Bureau** (☎ 510-839-9000; ⓦ www.oaklandcvb.com; *475 14th St, Suite 120; open 8:30am-5pm Mon-Fri*) is between Broadway and Clay St. There's another information booth in Jack London Square, underneath the Barnes & Noble near Broadway and Embarcadero.

There are **post offices** downtown at 1446 Franklin St and in Piedmont at 195 41st St.

DOWNTOWN OAKLAND

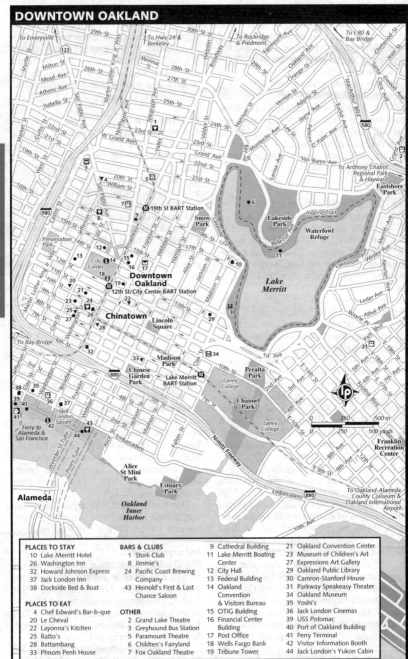

PLACES TO STAY
10 Lake Merritt Hotel
26 Washington Inn
32 Howard Johnson Express
37 Jack London Inn
38 Dockside Bed & Boat

PLACES TO EAT
4 Chef Edward's Bar-b-que
20 Le Cheval
22 Layonna's Kitchen
25 Ratto's
28 Battambang
33 Phnom Penh House

BARS & CLUBS
1 Stork Club
8 Jimmie's
24 Pacific Coast Brewing Company
43 Heinold's First & Last Chance Saloon

OTHER
2 Grand Lake Theatre
3 Greyhound Bus Station
5 Paramount Theatre
6 Children's Fairyland
7 Fox Oakland Theatre
9 Cathedral Building
11 Lake Merritt Boating Center
12 City Hall
13 Federal Building
14 Oakland Convention & Visitors Bureau
15 OTIG Building
16 Financial Center Building
17 Post Office
18 Wells Fargo Bank
19 Tribune Tower
21 Oakland Convention Center
23 Museum of Children's Art
27 Expressions Art Gallery
29 Oakland Public Library
30 Camron-Stanford House
31 Parkway Speakeasy Theater
34 Oakland Museum
35 Yoshi's
36 Jack London Cinemas
39 USS *Potomac*
40 Port of Oakland Building
41 Ferry Terminal
42 Visitor Information Booth
44 Jack London's Yukon Cabin

Oakland's many fine new and used bookstores include **Walden Pond** (☎ 510-832-4438; 3316 Grand Ave), **Pendragon** (☎ 510-652-6259; 5560 College Ave) and **Diesel** (☎ 510- 653-9965; 5433 College Ave). If you're interested in African-American literature or history, check out **Marcus Bookstore** (☎ 510-652-2344; 3900 Martin Luther King Jr Way).

The *Oakland Tribune* is Oakland's daily newspaper. The free weeklies *East Bay Express* and *Urban View* have good Oakland and Berkeley listings.

Downtown

Oakland's downtown is full of historic buildings and a growing number of colorful local businesses. With such easy access from San Francisco via BART and the ferry, it's worth spending a day exploring here – and nearby Chinatown and Jack London Square – on foot.

From May through October, the City of Oakland runs free 90-minute **walking tours** (☎ 510-238-3234) of historic downtown streets, City Hall and Preservation Park at 10am Wednesday and Saturday. Reservations are recommended.

The pedestrianized **City Center**, between Broadway and Clay St, 12th and 14th Sts, forms the heart of downtown Oakland. The twin towers of the Ronald Dellums Federal Building (named in honor of the former US Congressman) are on Clay St, just behind it. Highlighting the skyline is the 1923 **Tribune Tower** (13th & Franklin Sts), an Oakland icon that is home to the *Oakland Tribune* newspaper. The beautiful, refurbished 1914 beaux arts **City Hall** (14th & Clay Sts) is another urban gem.

Washington St between 8th and 10th Sts is now called **Old Oakland**; many historic buildings dating from the 1860s to the 1880s have been renovated (check out the Victorian buildings on 9th St), and the neighborhood's economy has reawakened with a growing number of restaurants, condos and galleries. The latter includes funky **Expressions Art Gallery** (815 Washington St), near the corner of 8th St, and the **Museum of Children's Art** (☎ 510-465-8770; 538 9th St; admission free; open 10am-5pm Tues-Sat, noon-5pm Sun), where exhibits are created by children. The area also hosts a lively **farmers market** every Friday morning – a great time to visit.

For a more tranquil taste of Oakland's past, walk over to **Preservation Park** (☎ 510-874-7580), on Martin Luther King Jr Way between 12th and 14th Sts. The park is a refuge for historic buildings which were relocated here, some previously doomed by the construction of I-980. Today, the 16 restored Victorian buildings, dating from 1870 to 1911, are arranged to approximate a late-19th-century Oakland neighborhood, and they currently house nonprofit organizations and small businesses.

North of the center, where Telegraph Ave angles off Broadway, stands the 1913 flatiron **Cathedral Building**. The **Paramount Theatre** (2025 Broadway) is a restored 1931 Art Deco masterpiece. Tours ($1) are given at 10am on the first and third Saturdays of the month (for performance information, see Entertainment later).

Downtown Oakland has plenty of other buildings adorned with Art Nouveau or Art Deco details; unfortunately, many stand empty and in need of care, especially the further you get from the City Center. One particular jewel is the 1928 **Fox Oakland Theatre** (Telegraph Ave & 19th St; ⓦ www.foxoakland.org), once the largest cinema west of Chicago; it's currently closed and awaiting (with crossed fingers) restoration. Wander the streets off Broadway and you'll come across other impressive, but empty, buildings.

East of Broadway, **Chinatown** centers on Franklin and Webster Sts, as it has since the 1870s. It's also home to Vietnamese, Korean, Cambodian and other Asian cultures. Though smaller than San Francisco's Chinatown, it's still one of the country's largest – and it's far less touristy and kitschy. It's a busy place, in fact, bustling with activity every day of the week; and, of course, it has many good restaurants.

The **Ebony Museum** (☎ 510-763-0141; 1034 14th St; admission from $2.50; open 11am-6pm Tues-Sat) has exhibits on African-American art and heritage.

Jack London Square

The waterfront where writer and adventurer Jack London once raised hell now bears his name. It's hardly a roughshod district anymore, but a tourist-oriented shopping mall dotted with chain restaurants, chain stores and cute little gift shops. The waterfront location is lovely, though, and for that reason it's worth a stroll – especially on Sunday, when a weekly **farmers market** takes over from 10am to 2pm.

Another worthwhile stop is **Heinhold's First & Last Chance Saloon** (☎ *510-839-6761*), allegedly a favorite haunt of London and other Oakland notables. The tiny, quake-shaken building, which has been in continuous operation since 1883, is packed with history and stocks plenty of ice-cold Anchor Steam.

Much cheesier is a replica of Jack London's **Yukon cabin**, across from the saloon and next to a parking lot (talk about out of place). It's supposedly built from the timbers of a cabin London lived in during the Yukon gold rush…though only *half* those timbers.

Since its mid-1990s revitalization, the area also boasts the popular **Jack London Cinemas** (☎ *510-433-1320; 100 Washington St*) and swanky nightclub Yoshi's, which books world-class jazz artists (see Entertainment later).

The 165ft **USS Potomac** (☎ *510-627-1215; admission $5; open 10am-1:15pm Wed & Fri, noon-3:15pm Sun*), Franklin D Roosevelt's 'floating White House,' is moored at Clay and Water Sts by the ferry dock. Two-hour history cruises are also held several times a month from March to November ($30); call for reservations.

Lake Merritt

Lake Merritt is an urban jewel and a popular place to stroll or go running (a 3½mi track circles the lake). Once a tidal marsh teeming with waterfowl, it became a lake in 1869 with the damming of an arm of the Oakland Estuary. The following year, the state legislature designated Lake Merritt a wildlife refuge, the first in the USA. The lake still supports some migratory waterfowl, and it's still connected to the estuary, meaning its 155 acres are saltwater. Like many other Bay Area parks, Lake Merritt is fine during the day, but be cautious at night.

Near the southern end of the lake is the **Oakland Museum** (☎ *510-238-2200; 1000 Oak St; adult/student $6/4; open 10am-5pm Wed-Sat, noon-5pm Sun*), which has rotating exhibitions on artistic as well as scientific themes, not to mention three worthwhile permanent galleries. These are dedicated to the state's diverse ecology; its history, from its

native past to the suburban present; and California art, from lavish 19th-century landscapes to edgy contemporary works. The Lake Merritt BART station is a block away.

Lakeside Park, at the northern end of the lake, includes **Children's Fairyland** (☎ *510-452-2259; admission $6; open 10am-4pm daily summer, Wed-Sun spring & fall, Fri-Sun winter*), which dates to 1950 and has wacky fairy-tale-themed rides and displays to delight kids and parents alike. For a jaunt on the lake, the **Lake Merritt Boating Center** (☎ *510-238-2196*) rents canoes, rowboats, kayaks, pedal boats and sailboats between 10:30am and 4pm daily; hourly charges are from $6 to $12.

In the late 19th century, Lake Merritt was lined with fine homes, only one of which remains: the 1876 **Camron-Stanford House** (☎ *510-444-1876; 1418 Lakeside Dr*). You can take a tour each Wednesday (11am to 4pm) and Sunday (1pm to 5pm) for $4, but the best aspect of the house is really its wonderful lakeside setting and the hint it gives of how Oakland looked in its Victorian heyday.

The two main commercial streets skirting Lake Merritt are **Lakeshore Ave** on the eastern edge of the lake and **Grand Ave**, running along the north shore. Both have some nice spots for meals, cocktails and coffee – see Places to Eat and Entertainment later.

Piedmont & Rockridge

North of downtown Oakland, Broadway becomes a strip of car dealerships so lengthy the city gave it a name: Broadway Auto Row. Just past that is Piedmont, where you'll find lovely residential streets, a spacious cemetery with great views of the bay, and, along Piedmont Ave, wall-to-wall antique stores, coffeehouses, fine restaurants and an art cinema.

Another popular shopping district is Rockridge, one of the East Bay's trendiest neighborhoods. It's centered on College Ave, which branches north off Broadway just past Piedmont. College Ave runs into Berkeley, and the whole length of the avenue is lined with clothing boutiques, good bookstores, a vintage record shop, several pubs and cafés, and quite a few upscale restaurants – maybe the largest concentration in town. You could easily spend a satisfying afternoon or evening browsing, eating and drinking here. Exiting BART at the Rockridge station puts you in the thick of things.

Gertrude Stein & Jack London

Neither of Oakland's two most famous writers was actually born here. Gertrude Stein, daughter of a wealthy stockbroker, was born in 1874 in Pennsylvania, then lived in Vienna and Paris before coming to Oakland for her school years. After college she moved to Paris, where she lived until her death just after the end of WWII. Stein was famous mainly for being famous, and she courted and encouraged many of the seminal artists and writers of her era, most notably Picasso and Hemingway. Her attempts to emulate cubist art in her writing ensured she would be an unread writer, and her best-known book is probably *The Autobiography of Alice B Toklas*, which is actually her own autobiography, not that of Toklas, her long-term partner.

Born in San Francisco in 1876, Jack London was the son of a spiritualist (mom) and an Irish astrologer (dad, who soon deserted the family). London began to turn his life into an adventure story while still a teenager, poaching oysters in San Francisco Bay with his own boat (the *Razzle Dazzle*), working on a ship to Japan, riding freight trains around the USA as a hobo and enthusiastically embracing socialism. Self-educated, he entered the University of California, Berkeley, but soon quit to join the 1897 Klondike gold rush.

Back from Alaska, and still broke, he threw himself into writing with spectacular energy, turning out everything from songs to horror stories. His first book, *The Son of the Wolf*, was published in 1900, and for the next 16 years he averaged three books a year. London soon became the highest-paid writer in the USA, but he burned through the cash even faster. In 1910, he turned to farming in the Sonoma Valley (see the Wine Country chapter) and, in 1916, died in somewhat mysterious circumstances, officially from kidney disease but quite possibly from a drug-overdose suicide.

The Oakland Hills

East of downtown and the I-580, the streets become convoluted, winding through exclusive communities such as Montclair before reaching the ridgeline, where a series of parks edges the hills.

The main attractions here are several large East Bay parks, which are ideal spots for day hiking. Information is available from the **East Bay Regional Parks District** (☎ 510-562-7275; 2950 Peralta Oaks Court). The district manages 59 regional parks, preserves and recreation areas in Alameda and Contra Costa counties, which contain some 1000mi of trails.

Off Hwy 24, the **Robert Sibley Volcanic Regional Preserve** is the northernmost of the Oakland Hills parks. It has great views of the Bay Area from its Round Top Peak (1761ft), an old volcano cone. From Sibley, Skyline Blvd runs south past **Redwood Regional Park** and the adjacent **Joaquin Miller Park** to **Anthony Chabot Regional Park**. A hike or mountain-bike ride through the groves and along the hilltops of any of these sizable parks will make you forget you're in an urban area. At the southern end of Chabot Park is the enormous Lake Chabot, with an easy trail along its shore and canoes, kayaks and other boats for rent from the **Lake Chabot marina** (☎ 510-582-2198).

Opened in 2000, the **Chabot Space & Science Center** (☎ 510-336-7300; 10000 Skyline Blvd; adult/youth $8/5.50; open 10am-3pm Tues-Fri, 10am-5pm Sat-Sun) is a science and technology center in the Oakland Hills just north of Joaquin Miller Park, with loads of exhibits on subjects such as space travel and eclipses. The center's also open Friday and Saturday evenings for planetarium shows and – check it out – free viewing through a 20-inch refractor telescope (weather permitting).

AC Transit bus No 53 runs daily from the Fruitvale BART station to the Chabot Center and Joaquin Miller Park. Bus No 46 runs from the Coliseum BART along Skyline Blvd, during weekday commute hours.

East Oakland

East Oakland, beginning south of downtown Oakland, goes on and on before finally blending into San Leandro. Most visitors simply pass through East Oakland on the way to or from the airport or Coliseum; there are some interesting businesses and cheap restaurants along International Blvd (also known as E 14th St and Foothill Blvd).

Oakland-Alameda County Arena and Network Associates Coliseum (☎ 510-569-2121) sits alongside I-880 and is home to the Oakland A's baseball team, the Golden State Warriors basketball team and the

Oakland Raiders football team (see Spectator Sports later).

If you're traveling to or from Oakland International Airport, consider a brief stop at the **Western Aerospace Museum** (☎ 510-638-7100; admission $4; open 10am-4pm Wed-Sun). From Hegenberger Rd, turn north onto Doolittle Dr. The museum's collection includes a Lockheed Electra (like the one Amelia Earhart was flying when she disappeared back in 1937) and a four-engined British Short Solent flying boat.

Places to Stay

Oakland has a few nice hotel options downtown and in the hills, but budget choices – at least clean ones in safe, secure neighborhoods – are less plentiful. You might be better off looking in San Francisco or Berkeley.

A good option to consider, though, is a B&B. The **Berkeley and Oakland Bed & Breakfast Network** (☎ 510-547-6380; w www.bbonline.com/ca/berkeley-oakland) has listings of 20 private homes that rent rooms, suites and cottages; prices start at $90 or so per night. Reservations a week or two in advance are recommended.

What the East Bay has over San Francisco, lodging-wise, is campsites. There are 75 of them in **Anthony Chabot Regional Park** (☎ 510-639-4751; tent/RV sites $15/20), a few miles south of Oakland off I-580. Reservations are possible (for a $6 service charge) by calling ☎ 510-562-7275.

A strip of cheap, older motels survives on MacArthur Blvd between San Pablo Ave and Broadway; their condition isn't bad, but it's not the greatest neighborhood. If you're intrigued, try the **Imperial Inn** (☎ 510-653-4225; 490 W MacArthur Blvd; singles/doubles $55/65).

Newer chain motels are clustered near the airport on Hegenberger Rd, and along I-880 between the coliseum and downtown. Options run from the simple **Motel 6** (☎ 510-638-1180; 8480 Edes Ave; rooms $66) to the **Courtyard By Marriott** (☎ 510-568-7600; 350 Hegenberger Rd; rooms $89).

Howard Johnson Express (☎ 510-451-6316; 423 7th St; singles/doubles $79/89), downtown, is only six blocks from the 12th St BART station and adjacent to Chinatown.

Jack London Inn (☎ 510-444-2032, 800-549-8780; 444 Embarcadero West; rooms $99) is an affordable 1950s-style motor lodge in Jack London Square, with clean, simple rooms.

Washington Inn (☎ 510-452-1776, fax 510-452-4436; 495 10th St; rooms from $108), one of the city's most charming hotels, is right in the midst of Old Oakland. Recently remodeled, it has 47 rooms, a bar and a restaurant.

Lake Merritt Hotel (☎ 510-832-2300, 800-933-4683, fax 510-832-7150; 1800 Madison St; rooms $179-289) is a stately 1927 Art Deco property overlooking the lake.

Dockside Boat & Bed (☎ 510-444-5858; fax 510-444-0420; 57 Clay St; boats per couple $125-400) rents out yachts moored in the square's marina for a true on-the-water experience. Rates include breakfast.

Claremont Resort and Spa (☎ 510-843-3000, 800-551-7266, fax 510-843-6239; 41 Tunnel Rd; rooms from $270), near Rockridge, is top of the heap if you're looking to indulge. Inside this glamorous white 1915 building are classy restaurants, a fitness center, swimming pools, tennis courts and a full-service spa (room/spa packages are available).

Places to Eat

Downtown If you want to eat outside on a sunny day, grab a sandwich from **Ratto's** (821 Washington St; sandwiches from $5), a vintage Oakland grocery (since 1897) with a deli counter that attracts a devoted lunch crowd.

Le Cheval (1007 Clay St; dishes $5-9), between 10th and 11th Sts, popular for both lunch and dinner, serves Vietnamese food in a spacious downtown room with a curious, contemporary decor.

Oakland's Chinatown may be less picturesque than San Francisco's, but it's just as busy. **Phnom Penh House** (251 8th St; meals under $10) and **Battambang** (850 Broadway; meals under $10) are excellent Cambodian restaurants. The lunch buffet ($6.95) at all-vegetarian **Layonna's Kitchen** (358 11th St; dishes $6-10) has plenty to choose from too.

Heading north on San Pablo Ave are several great old barbecue joints. The Piggly Wiggly sandwich at tiny **Chef Edward's Bar-b-que** (1998 San Pablo Ave; meals from $5) is a fabulous treat, and the service is equally sweet.

Lake Merritt On a commercial strip just north of MacArthur Blvd is **Arizmendi**

(3265 Lakeshore Ave), a bakery co-op selling gourmet pizza by the slice, along with hearty pastries and breads.

Spettro *(3355 Lakeshore Ave; mains $12-16)* has a quirky decor and friendly attitude that keeps fans coming back for its homespun, culturally mixed cuisine.

Autumn Moon Cafe *(3909 Grand Ave; meals $8-16)*, in an old house northeast of the Grand Lake Theatre, serves creative breakfast and lunch dishes, and hearty dinners. The French toast is a classic.

Piedmont and Rockridge Some of the East Bay's finest (and trendiest) restaurants are in these two hopping shopping areas along College and Piedmont Aves. Reservations are recommended for the first four.

Bay Wolf *(☎ 510-655-6004; 3853 Piedmont Ave; mains $18-21)*, founded in 1975 by chef Michael Wild, is a classy yet comfortable restaurant that consistently gets high marks for its inventive, ever-changing Mediterranean cuisine.

Oliveto Cafe & Restaurant *(☎ 510-547-5356; 5655 College Ave; mains $14-30)* is another East Bay favorite, specializing in rustic northern Italian dishes. There's a downstairs café and more formal dining room upstairs.

If you're in the mood for French food, try **Citron** *(☎ 510-653-5484; 5484 College Ave; mains $16-30)*, a simple, elegant bistro in Rockridge, or **Jojo** *(☎ 510-985-3003; 3859 Piedmont Ave; mains $16-20)*, a small country-French place run by veterans of Chez Panisse and Oliveto.

Simpler and more down-home is **Red Tractor Cafe** *(5634 College Ave; meals $5-10)*, a cheery and aromatic eatery serving affordable comfort food such as roast turkey and meatloaf (a meatless version is also available).

Zachary's Pizza *(5801 College Ave; pizzas $12-16)* serves scrumptious but heavy-duty Chicago-style pizza featuring an array of fresh ingredients. Expect a college crowd and a long wait for a table. There's a second location in Berkeley at 1853 Solano Ave.

Entertainment

Bars & Clubs Right in the heart of Old Oakland is the **Pacific Coast Brewing Company** *(906 Washington St)*, serving full meals alongside its own tasty brews (try the Gray Whale Ale).

Oakland Blues

When thousands of blacks moved to the Bay Area in the 1940s to work in the shipyards and other wartime industries, they brought the blues with them. From the mid-1940s to the 1950s, Oakland – specifically West Oakland – was home to a thriving blues scene. Clubs peppered 7th St, Union St and Grove St (now Martin Luther King Jr Way), and most of the era's blues musicians spent time in the clubs' smoky environs. Lowell Fulsom and Jimmy McCracklin are two bluesmen whose enduring music is closely associated with Oakland blues. Ivory Joe Hunter got his start in Oakland.

Unlike Chicago blues, which included the harmonica and could trace its roots to Mississippi, Oakland blues originated in Texas and Louisiana, resulting in 'a slow, draggier beat and a kinda mournful sound,' in the words of Bob Geddins, the man credited with defining and nurturing the style.

In the 1960s, the blues faded from favor. When the popularity of rock threw the spotlight back on the genre, it was the Chicago style, not the Oakland style, that enjoyed a renaissance. West Oakland's underground blues clubs hung on, but in the 1970s the sound began to evolve, incorporating the harmonica and other elements. You can still find blues clubs in Oakland, but no longer are they dominated by the historic Oakland blues sound.

Yoshi's *(☎ 510-238-9200; 510 Embarcadero West)*, at Jack London Square, is the Bay Area's finest jazz club, booking world-class acts each week. Having dinner at the adjacent sushi restaurant is pricey but assures you decent seating.

Kimball's East *(☎ 510-658-2555; 5800 Shellmound St)*, in Emeryville, northwest of Oakland, books big-name jazz and R&B artists. The club's in the Emerybay Public Market; from I-80 take the Powell St exit.

Jimmie's *(1731 San Pablo Ave)* is a large club and restaurant offering a mixture of blues, R&B and (on Sunday) live jazz.

Eli's Mile High Club *(3629 Martin Luther King Jr Way)*, near 37th St, is a surviving relic from Oakland's blues heyday. Local bands and DJs keep the place hopping most nights.

It's not in the best neighborhood, though, so consider a cab.

Stork Club (2330 Telegraph Ave) is a funky dive catering to the East Bay's indie-rock scene with an eclectic lineup of punk, experimental, lo-fi, spoken word, country and other performers.

White Horse (6551 Telegraph Ave) purports to be the oldest gay bar in California; straights are welcome too.

Alley (3325 Grand Ave), near Lake Merritt, is a rustic old tavern with a pub menu and a piano bar. It has been presided over by Rod Dibble since 1960.

5th Amendment (3255 Lakeshore Ave) is a lively Lake Merritt venue that books local jazz and blues bands and has a friendly, flirty atmosphere.

For beer fans, a couple of bustling spots with large selections of microbrews, plus pub food, are **Ben & Nick's** (562 College Ave) in Rockridge and, in Piedmont, **Cato's Alehouse** (3891 Piedmont Ave).

Hotel Ibiza (☎ 510-393-9888; 10 Hegenberger Rd), near the airport, is a renovated 1950s motel that doubles as a designer dance club. Yes you can sleep over, but don't expect quiet.

Theaters & Cinemas The massive Art Deco **Paramount Theatre** (☎ 510-465-6400; 2025 Broadway; [W] www.paramounttheatre.com) shows classic films a few times each month – an amazing experience. The theater is also home to the **Oakland East Bay Symphony** (☎ 510-446-1992) and the **Oakland Ballet** (☎ 510-465-6400) and periodically books big-name concerts.

Grand Lake Theatre (☎ 510-452-3556; 3200 Grand Ave), in Lake Merritt, is another beauty, but unfortunately it has been carved into a multiplex and shows mostly Hollywood releases.

Parkway Speakeasy Theater (☎ 510-814-2400; 1834 Park Blvd), two blocks east of Lakeshore Ave, is a great, laid-back movie-going experience. It shows quality second-run films in a comfy setting and serves beer, wine, sandwiches and pizza.

Spectator Sports

The **Golden State Warriors** (☎ 888-479-4667) are the Bay Area's only NBA basketball team. They play at what's currently called the Network Associates Coliseum (also known as the Oakland-Alameda County Arena and Network Associates Coliseum).

The **Oakland A's** (☎ 510-638-4900), the Bay Area's American League baseball team, play at the Oakland Coliseum's outdoor stadium.

The **Raiders** (☎ 510-864-5000) are Oakland's NFL team, attracting a particularly rabid brand of fan.

You can book game tickets through **BASS** (☎ 510-762-2277), but expect a heavy booking charge (euphemistically called a 'convenience' fee). A's tickets start at $7 for bleacher seats and $20 for infield seats. For most baseball games, it's no problem to just turn up and save the booking fee. Tickets to Warriors and Raiders games, however, often sell out well in advance.

Getting There & Away

You can arrive in Oakland by air, bus, Amtrak, BART or even ferry. From San Francisco by car, cross the Bay Bridge and enter Oakland via one of two ways: I-580, which leads to I-980 and drops you near the City Center; or I-880, which curves through West Oakland and lets you off near the south end of Broadway. I-880 then continues to the coliseum, the Oakland International Airport and, eventually, San Jose.

Air The smaller **Oakland International Airport** (☎ 510-577-4000) is directly across the Bay from San Francisco International Airport. Arriving or departing the Bay Area through Oakland can make good sense, as it's usually less crowded. Note that **Southwest Airlines** (☎ 800-435-9792) flies into Oakland, not San Francisco.

Bus Regional company **AC Transit** (☎ 510-839-2882) runs a number of convenient buses from San Francisco's Transbay Terminal, at Mission and 1st Sts, to downtown Oakland and Berkeley and between the two East Bay cities. A score of buses goes to Oakland from San Francisco during commute hours ($2.50), but only the 'O' line runs both ways all day and on weekends; you can catch the 'O' line at the corner of 5th and Washington Sts in downtown Oakland.

If you are out late at night and looking for to go between between San Francisco and Oakland, the 'A' line runs once an hour between the Transbay Terminal and the corner of 14th St and Broadway.

Between Berkeley and downtown Oakland ($1.35) take bus No 15, which runs from downtown Oakland into Berkeley via Martin Luther King Jr Blvd; or bus No 40, which travels up and down Telegraph Ave between the two city centers. Bus No 51, which runs along Broadway in Oakland and then along College Ave in Berkeley, is less direct but has some handy stops, including Rockridge, the UC Berkeley campus and the Berkeley Marina.

Greyhound (☎ 510-834-3213; 2103 San Pablo Ave) operates direct buses from Oakland to Vallejo, San Francisco, San Jose, Santa Rosa and Sacramento (the San Francisco terminal has many more direct-service options). The station is pretty seedy.

Train Oakland is a regular stop for Amtrak trains operating up and down the coast. From Oakland's **Amtrak station** (☎ 510-238-4306; 245 2nd St) in Jack London Square, you can catch AC Transit bus No 58, 72 or 73 to downtown Oakland, or take a ferry across the bay to San Francisco.

Amtrak passengers with reservations through to San Francisco need to disembark at the **Emeryville Amtrak station** (☎ 510-450-1081; 5885 Landregan St), one stop prior to Oakland; from there, an Amtrak bus will shuttle you to San Francisco's Transbay Terminal.

BART Within the Bay Area, the most convenient way to get to Oakland and back is by **BART** (☎ 415-989-2278, 510-465-2278). Trains run on a set schedule from 4am to midnight on weekdays, 6am to midnight on Saturday, and 8am to midnight Sunday. There are five different routes, operating at 15- or 20-minute intervals on average.

To downtown Oakland, catch a Richmond- or Pittsburg/Bay Point-bound train. Fares to the 12th or 19th St stations from downtown San Francisco are $2.20.

For Lake Merritt ($2.20) or the Oakland Coliseum/Airport station ($2.75), you need to take a BART train headed for Fremont or Dublin/Pleasanton. Rockridge ($2.50) is on the Pittsburg/Bay Point line.

Between Oakland and downtown Berkeley you can also catch a Fremont–Richmond train ($1.10).

A BART-to-Bus transfer ticket, available from white AC Transit machines near BART station exits, costs $1.15.

Ferry Ferries are the slowest and most expensive, but undoubtedly the most enjoyable, way of traveling between San Francisco and Oakland. From San Francisco's Ferry Building, the **Alameda/Oakland ferry** (☎ 510-522-3300) sails to Jack London Square about 12 times a day on weekdays, six to nine times a day on weekends. The trip takes about 30 minutes, and the one-way fare is $4.50; buy tickets on board. Ferry tickets include a free transfer, which you can use on AC Transit buses from Jack London Square.

Getting Around
A taxi from the Oakland International Airport to downtown Oakland costs about $25, to downtown San Francisco about $40. **SuperShuttle** (☎ 800-258-3826) is one of many door-to-door shuttle services operating out of Oakland International Airport. One-way service to San Francisco destinations costs about $30 for the first person and $8 for the second. East Bay service destinations are also served. Call to reserve.

A cheap, easy transportation option is BART. Air-BART buses run between the airport and the Coliseum BART Station every 10 minutes. Tickets cost $2 and can be purchased from machines at the BART station or in airport terminals. AC Transit Bus No 58 also operates between Oakland International Airport and Jack London Square (stopping at the Coliseum BART Station); the local fare is $1.35.

AC Transit (☎ 510-839-2882) has a comprehensive bus network within Oakland. Bus No 13 will take you from 14th St downtown to Lake Merritt and Lakeshore Ave. From Broadway downtown, bus No 58 goes to Grand Ave; bus No 59 runs from Jack London Square to the Piedmont district; and bus No 51 heads to Rockridge and UC Berkeley. Fares are $1.35 and exact change is required.

Weekdays between 11am and 2pm, the **Broadway Shuttle** provides free transportation along Broadway between the Kaiser Center (Webster and 20th Sts) and Jack London Square.

BERKELEY

Even some four decades after the heyday of the Free Speech Movement, Berkeley (population 102,750) is still a bastion of serious liberalism. Bizarre characters continue to haunt its streets, and activist politics are still thrust into everyday life. The huge campus of the University of California, Berkeley (UCB) dominates the town, though by no means is the student sector all there is to Berkeley. Sure, Telegraph Ave is as full of freaks and geeks as ever before – earnest students, street vendors crammed side-by-side and 'colorful' local characters walking, weaving and crawling in-between it all. But Berkeley has a life beyond the university, as proven by the popularity of the 4th Street shopping district, a revitalized downtown and a food-focused section of North Berkeley dubbed the 'Gourmet Ghetto.'

Orientation

About 13mi east of San Francisco, Berkeley is bordered by the bay to the west, the hills to the east and Oakland to the south. I-80 runs along the town's western edge, next to the marina; from here University Ave heads east to the campus and downtown.

Shattuck Ave crosses University Ave one block west of campus, forming the main crossroads of the downtown area. To the north is North Berkeley, including the Gourmet Ghetto; to the south is the downtown shopping strip and the central Berkeley BART station.

San Pablo Ave is another major thoroughfare, crossing University Ave several blocks east of I-80. Heading north, San Pablo leads to Albany, El Cerrito, Richmond and other towns. To the south it takes you straight into downtown Oakland (about 5mi).

If driving, the biggest navigational difficulties are the numerous barriers set up to prevent traffic from clogging residential streets; traversing these areas often leads to backtracking and frustration. Parking isn't easy, either, especially near the campus or downtown. Try the city garages on Durant Ave near Telegraph Ave, or on Center St just west of Shattuck Ave.

Information

The helpful **Berkeley Convention & Visitors Bureau** (☎ 510-549-7040, 800-847-4823; W www.visitberkeley.com; 2015 Center St; open 9am-5pm Mon-Fri) is near the downtown BART station. It has free visitors packets and also sells the useful book 41 Walking Tours of Berkeley ($5). For 24-hour recorded information call ☎ 510-549-8710.

Campus maps and information are available from the university's **Visitor Services Center** (☎ 510-642-5215; W www.berkeley .edu; 101 University Hall, 2200 University Ave). Free campus tours are given at 10am Monday to Saturday and 1pm Sunday.

The **Berkeley Historical Society** (☎ 510-848-0181; 1931 Center St) offers occasional but excellent walking tours with different themes ($10).

University of California, Berkeley

The Berkeley campus of the University of California (called just 'Cal' by many students and locals) is the oldest university in the state. The decision to found the college was made in 1866, and the first students arrived in 1873; today UCB has over 30,000 students, more than 1000 professors and more Nobel laureates than you could point a particle accelerator at.

From Telegraph Ave, enter the campus via Sproul Plaza and Sather Gate, a center for people-watching, soapbox oration and pseudotribal drumming. Alternatively, enter from Center and Oxford Sts, near the downtown BART station.

Interesting campus sights include the **Museum of Paleontology** (☎ 510-642-1821; W www.ucmp.berkeley.edu; admission free; atrium open 8am-9pm Mon-Fri, 8am-5pm Sat & Sun) in the ornate Valley Life Sciences Building. This research museum is mostly closed to the public, but you can peek at exhibits in the atrium, including a Tyrannosaurus rex skeleton.

To the east of the museum, the **Bancroft Library** (☎ 510-642-3781; W http://bancroft .berkeley.edu/; open 9am-5pm Mon-Fri) houses, among other gems, a copy of Shakespeare's First Folio and the records of the Donner Party (see the boxed text 'The Donner Party' in the Sierra Nevada chapter). Its small public exhibits of historical Californiana include the surprisingly small gold nugget that sparked the 1849 gold rush. You must register to use the library, and to do so, you need to be 18 (or to have graduated from high school) and present two forms of

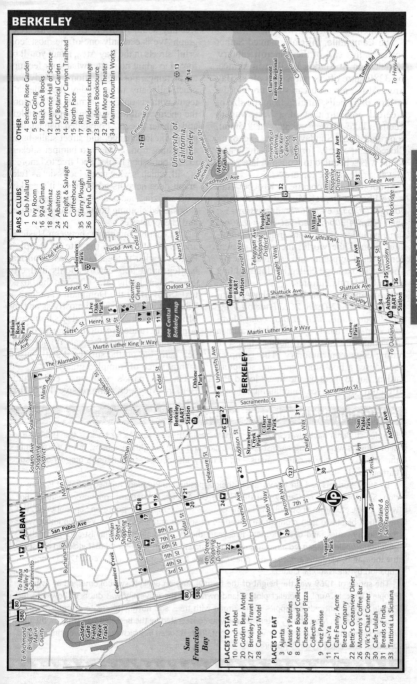

SAN FRANCISCO BAY AREA

BERKELEY

OTHER
4 Berkeley Rose Garden
5 Easy Going
7 Black Oak Books
12 Lawrence Hall of Science
13 UC Botanical Garden
14 Strawberry Canyon Trailhead
15 North Face
17 REI
19 Wilderness Exchange
23 Builders Booksource
32 Julia Morgan Theater
34 Marmot Mountain Works

BARS & CLUBS
1 Club Mallard
2 Ivy Room
16 924 Gilman
18 Ashkenaz
24 Albatross
25 Freight & Salvage Coffeehouse
35 Starry Plough
36 La Peña Cultural Center

PLACES TO STAY
10 French Hotel
20 Golden Bear Motel
27 Berkeley Travel Inn
28 Campus Motel

PLACES TO EAT
3 Ajanta
6 Masse's Pastries
8 Cheese Board Collective; Cheese Board Pizza Collective
9 Chez Panisse
11 Cha-Ya
21 Cafe Fanny; Acme Bread Company
22 Bette's Oceanview Diner
26 Montero's Coffee Bar
29 Vik's Chaat Corner
30 Cafe Tululah
31 Breads of India
33 Trattoria La Siciliana

identification (one with a photo). Stop by the registration desk on your way in.

The **Campanile**, officially named Sather Tower, is just east of the Bancroft Library. Modeled on St Mark's Basilica in Venice, the 328ft spire offers fine views of the Bay Area. At the top, you can stare up into the carillon of 61 bells, ranging from the size of a cereal bowl to that of a Volkswagen. Recitals take place weekdays at 7:50am, noon and 6pm, Sunday at 2pm and 6pm. Closed temporarily for repairs, the Campanile was scheduled to reopen in late 2002. Elevator rides to the top are $2.

South of the Campanile in Kroeber Hall is the **Phoebe Hearst Museum of Anthropology** (☎ 510-643-7648; admission $2; open 10am-4:30pm Wed-Sat, noon-4:30pm Sun), includes items from indigenous cultures around the world, including ancient Peruvian, Egyptian and African items. There's also a large collection highlighting native California cultures.

Across the street, the **UC Berkeley Art Museum** (☎ 510-642-0808; 2626 Bancroft Way; adult/student $6/4, free on Thur; open 11am-7pm Wed-Sun) has 11 galleries showcasing a huge range of works from ancient Chinese to cutting-edge contemporary. The complex also houses a bookstore, café and sculpture garden, not to mention the much-loved Pacific Film Archive (see Entertainment later).

South of Campus

Heading south from the UC campus, Telegraph Ave is certainly one of the most 'colorful' streets in the Bay Area, a fact you'll be forced to admit no matter what your feelings on piercings, pot legalization or tie-dye. At practically any time of day the sidewalk teems with visionaries, vagrants and vendors, the energy wafting between hippie nostalgia and hipster sneers. Ponytailed panhandlers press you for change, and street stalls hawk everything from crystals to bumper stickers to self-published books. Feel free to ignore it at will, which is what many locals do, as Telegraph does have its advantages: it's packed with amazing bookstores, gargantuan record shops, used clothing boutiques, coffeehouses and cheap eateries.

Just east of Telegraph, between Haste St and Dwight Way, is the site of **People's Park**, a marker in local history as a political battleground between residents and city government in the late '60s (see the boxed text 'Subverting the Dominant Paradigm'). The park has since served mostly as an (unofficial) residence for Berkeley's homeless. A publicly funded restoration spruced it up a bit, and occasional festivals do still happen here, but on the surface it's still just a mangy patch of trampled grass.

On the park's southeast end stands Bernard Maybeck's impressive 1910 **First**

Subverting the Dominant Paradigm

Berkeley students have always been passionate about their beliefs. As far back as the 1930s, student activists were rallying against social injustice and human rights violations, but it wasn't until the '60s that the city became famous – or, to many, infamous – as the nation's premier domestic battleground.

By 1964 students had already vocalized their opposition to President Kennedy's Bay of Pigs invasion, Senator Joseph McCarthy and the House Un-American Activities Committee hearings. But when a peaceful sit-in at Sproul Hall on the campus was disrupted by police on September 30, the revolution began to gain momentum. Freedom of speech and anti–Vietnam War sentiment were the primary issues, and over the next five years the UC Regents (the administration) and then-governor Ronald Reagan led a harsh campaign of violent antiprotest reprisal that included arrests in the thousands, veritable armies of riot police, multiple tear-gas assaults and even a 17-day-long occupation by the National Guard.

The spring of 1969 was the height of the turmoil, and an unlikely symbol emerged at its heart: People's Park. In April, a derelict plot of land owned by the university was dubbed 'Power to the People Park.' Hundreds of hippies came armed with trees and flowers to create a center for their counterculture. In May, shortly after the land was consecrated by the Berkeley Free Church, the university seized the land, erecting fences overnight. Riots resulted in which hundreds were injured and one man was killed by stray gunfire.

Church of Christ Scientist (☎ 510-845-7199; 2619 Dwight Way; open Sun services), which uses concrete and wood in its blend of Craftsman, Asian and Gothic influences. Maybeck was a professor of architecture at UC Berkeley and designed San Francisco's Palace of Fine Arts, plus many homes in North Berkeley. Free tours are given the first Sunday of every month at 12:15pm.

To the southeast of the park is the beautifully understated, redwood-infused 1910 **Julia Morgan Theatre** (☎ 510-845-8542; 2640 College Ave), a performance space (formerly a church) created by Bay Area architect Julia Morgan, who designed numerous Bay Area buildings and, most famously, the Hearst Castle. South on College Ave is the **Elmwood District**, a charming nook of shops and restaurants that offers a calming alternative to the frenetic buzz around Telegraph Ave. Continue further south and you'll be in Rockridge (see Oakland earlier in this chapter).

Downtown

Berkeley's downtown, which centers on Shattuck Ave between University Ave and Dwight Way, has far fewer traces of the city's tie-dyed reputation. The area has undergone loads of renovation in recent years, emerging as a bustling area with numerous shops and restaurants, restored public buildings and a burgeoning (or so the city council hopes) arts district. At the center of that district are the acclaimed thespian stomping grounds of the Berkeley Repertory Theatre (see Entertainment later) and the **Aurora Theatre Company** (2081 Addision St); nearby are several good movie houses (two, the California and the Fine Arts, were undergoing upgrades at the time of writing) and concert venue **Berkeley Community Theatre** (cnr Allston Way & Milvia St).

North Berkeley

Just north of campus is a neighborhood filled with lovely homes, parks and some of the best restaurants in California. The popular **Gourmet Ghetto** stretches along Shattuck Ave north of University Ave for several blocks. Food is the main attraction here, of course, with numerous restaurants, including the deified Chez Panisse, bakeries, coffee bars and grocery stores. Northwest of here, **Solano Ave**, which

crosses from Berkeley into Albany, is lined with lots of funky shops, more good restaurants and a couple of movie theaters.

North Berkeley is also chock-full of magnificent homes. You can see many examples of Bernard Maybeck's superb architecture, including 1515 La Loma Ave and at 2704, 2711, 2733, 2751, 2754 and 2780 Buena Vista Way. Wander these and other streets to examine the elaborate gardens and Asian-influenced front gates that are a feature of this neighborhood.

On Euclid Ave just south of Eunice St is the **Berkeley Rose Garden** and its eight terraces of Technicolor explosions. Here you'll find quiet benches and a plethora of almost perpetually blooming roses.

The Berkeley Hills

In the hills east of town is Berkeley's crown jewel, **Tilden Regional Park** (☎ 510-562-7275). The 2077-acre park has more than 30mi of trails of varying difficulty, from paved paths to hilly scrambles, including part of the magnificent Bay Area Ridge Trail. Other attractions include a miniature steam train ($1.75), children's farm, botanical garden, 18-hole **golf course** (☎ 510-848-7373) and environmental education center. Lake Anza is a favorite area for picnics. From spring through late fall you can swim in Lake Anza for $3 (children $2). AC Transit bus No 67 runs to the park from the downtown BART station.

The **Lawrence Hall of Science** (☎ 510-642-5132; Centennial Dr; adult/child $8/6; open 10am-5pm daily), near Grizzly Peak Blvd, is named after Ernest Lawrence, who won the Nobel prize for his invention of the cyclotron particle accelerator. He was a key member of the WWII Manhattan Project, and he's also the name behind Lawrence Berkeley and Lawrence Livermore laboratories. As for the Hall of Science, it has a huge collection of exhibits on subjects ranging from lasers to earthquakes and, outside, a 60ft model of a DNA molecule. AC Transit buses No 8 and No 65 run to the hall from the downtown BART station; you can also catch the university's Bear Transit shuttle (H line) from the Hearst Mining Circle.

Another great find in the hills is the **UC Botanical Garden** (☎ 510-643-2755; 200 Centennial Dr; adult/child $3/1, free Thur; open 9am-5pm daily), in Strawberry Canyon,

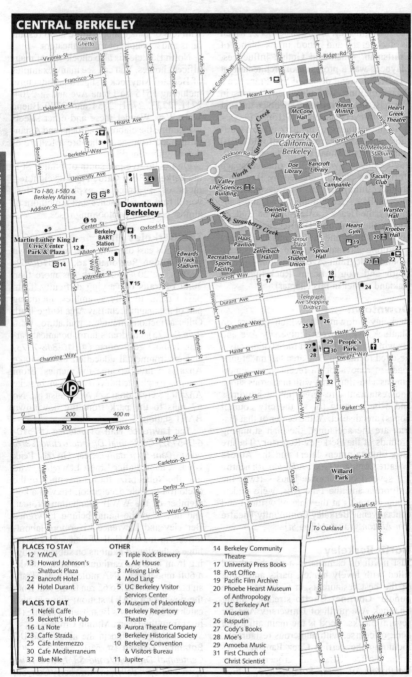

CENTRAL BERKELEY

below the Hall of Science. With over 13,000 species of plants, the garden is one of the most varied collections in the USA. It too can be reached by the Bear Transit shuttle H line.

The nearby fire trail is a woodsy walking loop around Strawberry Canyon that has great views of town and of the off-limits Lawrence Berkeley National Laboratory. Enter at the trailhead at the parking lot on Centennial Dr just southwest of the Botanical Garden; you'll emerge near the Lawrence Hall of Science.

West of Shattuck Ave

Hidden within an industrial area near I-80 lies a three-block area known as the **4th St Shopping District**, offering shaded sidewalks for upscale shopping, or just strolling, and a few good restaurants too. Take heed, it's often very hard to park in this area, especially on weekends.

At the west end of University Ave is the **Berkeley Marina**, frequented by squawking seagulls, silent types fishing from the pier and, especially on windy weekends, lots of colorful kites. Construction of the marina began in 1936, though the pier has much older origins. It was originally built in the 1870s, then replaced by a 3mi-long ferry pier in 1920. Part of the original pier is now rebuilt, affording visitors sweeping bay views.

San Pablo Ave was formerly US Route 40, the main thoroughfare from the east before I-80 came along. The area north of University Ave is still lined with a few older motels, diners and vintage dive bars with impressive neon signs. South of University Ave are pockets of trendiness, such as the short stretch of restaurants, gift shops and clothing stores around Dwight Way.

Places to Stay

The Berkeley Convention & Visitors Bureau (see Information earlier) can recommend local hotels. The **Berkeley and Oakland Bed & Breakfast Network** (☎ 510-547-6380; W www.bbonline.com/ca/berkeley-oakland) has listings of private homes offering lodging, from rooms to secluded garden cottages.

Around Campus & Downtown The best budget option, and compensating for the fact Berkeley doesn't have an official hostel, is the **YMCA** (☎ 510-848-6800; 2001 Allston Way; singles/doubles $46/60), in the heart

of downtown. Rates for the small rooms include use of the sauna and pool. Advance bookings are recommended.

Howard Johnson's Shattuck Plaza (☎ 510-845-7300, fax 510-644-2088; 2086 Allston Way; rooms $79-125), also downtown and close to the BART station is a step up. Recently renovated by the Howard Johnson chain, the 174-room facility was originally called the Hotel Shattuck and dates from 1910.

French Hotel (☎ 510-548-9930; 1538 Shattuck Ave; rooms $95) is right in the Gourmet Ghetto. The modern brick building has 18 very straightforward rooms. Downstairs is a popular café.

Bancroft Hotel (☎ 510-549-1000, 800-549-1002, fax 510-549-1070; W www.bancrofthotel.com; 2680 Bancroft Way; rooms $99-129), across from campus with 22 comfortable rooms, is a favorite with visiting parents. The Craftsman building dates from 1928 and was originally a women's club.

Hotel Durant (☎ 510-845-8981, 800-238-7268, fax 510-486-8336; W www.hoteldurant.com; 2600 Durant Ave; rooms from $160), a block from campus and Telegraph Ave, is a classy 1928 hotel with 140 nice rooms and a popular bar downstairs.

West of Shattuck University Ave is dotted with budget motels. It's not the tidiest part of Berkeley, but many accommodations have been remodeled and are perfectly adequate and safe for overnighters.

Campus Motel (☎ 510-841-3844; 1619 University Ave; singles/doubles from $70/80), near California St, is a small, simple, well-kept establishment with genuine 1950s character. Nearby is the equally acceptable **Berkeley Travel Inn** (☎ 510-848-3840; 1461 University Ave; singles/doubles $65/90), another simple, 1950s-era place with a neat and clean appearance.

Golden Bear Motel (☎ 510-525-6770; W www.goldenbearinn.com; 1620 San Pablo Ave; singles/doubles $99/119), a few blocks north of University Ave, is a clean and modernized 1940s motel. Cafe Fanny (see Entertainment later) is right across the street.

Places to Eat

Telegraph Ave is packed with cafés, pizza counters and cheap restaurants. Many more

SAN FRANCISCO BAY AREA

SAN FRANCISCO BAY AREA

restaurants can be found downtown along Shattuck Ave near the BART station. The section of Shattuck Ave north of University Ave is the 'Gourmet Ghetto,' home to a whole other batch of eating establishments, including California cuisine landmark Chez Panisse.

Around Campus Great for quick, filling meals, **Cafe Intermezzo** (2442 Telegraph Ave; meals $5) holds the title for the biggest and best sandwiches and salads; the bread's home-made too.

Blue Nile (2525 Telegraph Ave; mains under $10) serves great Ethiopian food in a peaceful, pleasant setting.

Trattoria La Siciliana (2993 College Ave; mains $8-16) is an Italian hotspot south of campus among the restaurants of the charming Elmwood District.

North Berkeley Presided over by chef Alice Waters since 1971, **Chez Panisse** (☎ 510-548-5525; 🌐 www.chezpanisse .com; 1517 Shattuck Ave; prix fixe meal $45-75, à la carte mains $10-19) is the holy mother church of California cuisine. The menu changes daily but always revolves around fresh, seasonal, organic vegetables, meats and fish. Formal prix fixe meals are served downstairs, the price rising as the week progresses. Upstairs is the café, offering some of the same dishes à la carte for lunch or dinner; many fans find this casual setting equally satisfying. Reservations are accepted up to a month in advance.

Cha-Ya (1686 Shattuck Ave; dishes $5-9) is loved by vegetarians for its inventive Japanese cuisine including noodle plates, soups and vegetable-based sushi.

Cheese Board Collective (1504 Shattuck Ave) offers a vast selection of gourmet cheeses and home-made breads, enabling you to put together a fantastic lunch. Or head next door for a take-out slice of pizza at the equally popular **Cheese Board Pizza Collective** (1512 Shattuck Ave).

Downtown & West Berkeley Downtown, **La Note** (2377 Shattuck Ave; meals from $5) is a casual country-French restarant serving superb ham-and-Gruyère omelettes, rich French toast and other fabulous breakfast and lunch items.

Beckett's Irish Pub (2271 Shattuck Ave; meals $7-16), nearby, serves hearty Irish meals and ales in a cozy but spacious and beautifully restored French-provincial building dating from 1925.

Berkeley has quite a few excellent Indian restaurants. **Breads of India** (2448 Sacramento St; meals under $10) frequently tops fans' lists. The decor and service aren't fancy, but the food, including inventive naan (bread) choices, is great. Other recommendations include **Ajanta** (1888 Solano Ave; mains $11-15) and the frequently crowded **Vik's Chaat Corner** (724 Allston Way; dishes from $4), the latter serving tasty southern Indian snack-type plates in a large, stark warehouse space.

Cafe Tululah (2512 San Pablo Ave; dishes $5-10) is a hip, friendly place serving inventive and delicious breakfast and lunch dishes. It's a few blocks south of University Ave, amid a handful of shops in a developing neighborhood.

Bette's Oceanview Diner (1807 4th St; $5 and up), where the fancified diner food is tasty, is hugely popular, but table waits can be long.

Entertainment
Cafes Hankering for that classic 'radical Berkeley' vibe? Find it at **Caffe Mediterraneum** (2475 Telegraph Ave), in business since the 1950s. Many patrons haven't changed much (or moved from their tables) since then.

Caffe Strada (2300 College Ave), is a popular, student-saturated hangout with an inviting shaded patio and strong espressos.

Nefeli Caffe (1854 Euclid Ave), a small place in North Berkeley, is a subdued but relaxing spot for a coffee.

Masse's Pastries (1469 Shattuck Ave) makes excellent, inventive cakes and buns.

Montero's Coffee Bar (1401 University Ave) serves strong and superb organic house coffee from its walk-up window. It's ideal for those staying in University Ave motels or just passing by.

Cafe Fanny (1603 San Pablo Ave; breakfast & lunch $4-8), north of University Ave, is owned by Alice Waters. As you'd expect, it serves excellent cafés au lait, home-made pastries and poached-egg dishes. An added bonus is the amazing **Acme Bread Company** next door.

San Francisco cable car descends the hill on Hyde St

Chinatown, San Francisco

San Francisco's Golden Gate Bridge welcomes all visitors to the city

A gilded mime in Union Square

The famous 'Painted Ladies' of Steiner St, San Francisco

Historic Angel Island offers great beach walks and sublime views of the San Francisco skyline

Santa Cruz surfing memorial

In Berkeley, Telegraph Avenue vendors sell it all

The Pacific Coast Highway (Highway 1) north of San Francisco

Bars & Clubs Opened in 1986, **Triple Rock Brewery & Ale House** *(1920 Shattuck Ave)* was one of the country's first brewpubs. The house beers are quite good and there's pub food too. The same owners also run **Jupiter** *(2180 Shattuck Ave)*, a downtown pub with loads of regional microbrews, a beer garden, good pizza and occasional live bands. Both places are popular with students.

Albatross *(1822 San Pablo Ave)*, a block north of University Ave, is one of the most inviting, comfortable pubs in the entire Bay Area. The interior of this British-style pub is spacious, the attitude friendly, the beer selection large and the martinis strong.

Further north on San Pablo Ave are several vintage watering holes, including **Club Mallard** *(752 San Pablo Ave)*, which has outdoor seating, tiki torches and hourly pool tables; and the **Ivy Room** *(860 San Pablo Ave)*, boasting live country, blues and rockabilly bands and an excellent jukebox of classic 45s.

Speaking of live music, Berkeley has lots to offer. Cover charges range from $5 to $20, depending on who's playing.

Freight & Salvage Coffeehouse *(☎ 510-548-1761; 1111 Addison St)*, just off San Pablo Ave, has great traditional folk and bluegrass bands but, be warned, no alcohol.

Ashkenaz *(☎ 510-525-5054; 1317 San Pablo Ave)* is a 'music and dance community center' attracting activists, hippies and fans of folk, swing and world music who love to dance (lessons offered).

924 Gilman *(☎ 510-525-9926; 924 Gilman St)* has been attracting underage fans to its punk shows in West Berkeley since 1986.

La Peña Cultural Center *(☎ 510-849-2568; 3105 Shattuck Ave)*, near the Ashby BART station, offers live music, comedy, theater and poetry with a Latin American flavor.

Starry Plough *(☎ 510-841-2082; 3101 Shattuck Ave)*, next door, is a comfy Irish pub with a varied lineup of local and touring rock, jazz, country and blues bands.

Cinemas Cineastes should seek out the **Pacific Film Archive** *(☎ 510-642-1124; 2575 Bancroft Way; admission $7)*, a world-renowned film center with an ever-changing schedule of international and classic films, many near-impossible to see anywhere else.

Theater & Dance Downtown is home to the **Berkeley Repertory Theatre** *(☎ 510-647-2949; 2025 Addison St)*, a highly respected company that has produced bold versions of classical and modern plays since 1968.

On the south end of campus near Bancroft Way and Dana St, **Zellerbach Hall** *(☎ 510-642-9988)* features dance events, concerts and performances of all types by national and international groups. Call for tickets or check the adjoining **Cal Performances Ticket Office**.

Spectator Sports

Memorial Stadium, which dates from 1923, is the university's 76,000-seat sporting venue. This is the site (in alternating years) of a famous football frenzy between the UC Berkeley and Stanford teams. Call the **Cal Athletic Ticket Office** *(☎ 800-462-3277)* for ticket information on all UC Berkeley sports events, and keep in mind that some sell out weeks in advance.

Shopping

Telegraph Avenue offers everything for the urban hippie, from hand-made sidewalk-vendor jewellery to head-shop paraphernalia. Most appealing are, irrefutably, its terrific book and music stores.

Another strip of shops is along College Ave in the Elmwood District; and on 4th St north of University Ave you'll find upscale clothing, kitchen supply, book and gift stores.

Books Venerable **Cody's Books** *(☎ 510-845-7852, 800-995-1180; 2454 Telegraph Ave)* has a huge selection of new books and almost daily appearances by top authors. There's a great magazine rack too. There's a second location at 1730 Fourth St.

Moe's *(☎ 510-849-2087; 2476 Telegraph Ave)*, a longstanding local favorite, offers four floors of new, used and remaindered books for hours of browsing.

University Press Books *(☎ 510-548-0585; 2430 Bancroft Way)* stocks works by UC Berkeley professors and from other academic and museum publishers.

Black Oak Books *(☎ 510-486-0698; 1491 Shattuck Ave)* is an excellent store in North Berkeley, with new and used selections and a full calendar of author appearances.

Easy Going (☎ 510-843-3533, 1385 Shattuck Ave) is an excellent travel bookstore that also hosts readings.

Builders Booksource (☎ 510-845-6874; 1817 Fourth St) has a fine collection of landscape, gardening and architectural books.

Music If you're a music junkie you might plan on spending a few hours at the original Berkeley branch of **Amoeba Music** (☎ 510-549-1125; 2455 Telegraph Ave), packed with massive quantities of new and used CDs, DVDs, tapes and records (yes, lots of vinyl).

Rasputin (☎ 510-848-9004; 2401 Telegraph Ave), nearby, is another large store full of new and used releases.

Mod Lang (☎ 510-486-1880; 2136 University Ave), downtown, specializes in hard-to-find music imports, indie releases and electronica.

Down Home Music (☎ 510-525-2129; 10341 San Pablo Ave), north of Berkeley in El Cerrito, is a world-class store for roots, blues, folk, Latin and world music.

Outdoor Gear At the intersection of San Pablo Ave and Gilman St are several outdoor stores, including a large and busy **REI** (☎ 510-527-4140; 1338 San Pablo Ave), and the **Wilderness Exchange** (☎ 510-525-1255; 1407 San Pablo Ave), selling new and used gear. A few blocks west is an outlet for **North Face** (☎ 510-526-3530; cnr 5th & Gilman Sts), a well-respected Berkeley-based brand of outdoor gear.

Marmot Mountain Works (☎ 510-849-0735; 3049 Adeline) has climbing, ski and backpacking equipment.

Getting There & Away

Bus Regional company **AC Transit** (☎ 510-839-2882) runs a number of buses from San Francisco's **Transbay Terminal** (Mission & 1st Sts) to the East Bay. The F line runs from the Transbay Terminal to the corner of University and Shattuck Aves approximately every half-hour ($2.50, 30 minutes).

Between Berkeley and downtown Oakland, take AC Transit bus No 15, which runs along Martin Luther King Jr Way, or bus No 40, which travels up and down Telegraph Ave ($1.35). Bus No 51 runs along Broadway in Oakland and then along College Ave in Berkeley, past the UCB campus and down to the Berkeley Marina.

BART The easiest way to travel between San Francisco, Berkeley, Oakland and other East Bay points is on **BART** (☎ 510-465-2278). Trains run approximately every 10 minutes from 4am to midnight on weekdays, with limited service from 6am on Saturday and from 8am on Sunday.

To Berkeley, catch a Richmond-bound train to one of three BART stations: Ashby (Adeline St and Ashby Ave), downtown Berkeley (Shattuck Ave and Center St) or North Berkeley (Sacramento and Delaware Sts). The fare is $2.50 to $2.80 between Berkeley and San Francisco and $1.10 between Berkeley and downtown Oakland. After 8pm on weekdays, 7pm on Saturday and all day Sunday, there is no direct service from San Francisco to Berkeley; instead, catch a Pittsburg/Bay Point train and transfer at 12th St station in Oakland.

A BART-to-Bus transfer ticket, available from white AC Transit machines near BART station exits, reduces the connecting bus fare to $1.15.

Train Although **Amtrak** (☎ 800-872-7245) does stop in Berkeley, the shelter (University Ave and 3rd St) is not staffed and direct connections are few. Far more convenient is the nearby **Emeryville Amtrak station** (☎ 510-450-1081; 5885 Landregan St), a few miles south of the Berkeley stop. Note that Amtrak passengers with reservations through to San Francisco need to disembark in Emeryville, where Amtrak buses continue on to San Francisco's Transbay Terminal.

To reach the Emeryville station from downtown Berkeley, catch AC Transit bus No 51.

Car & Motorcycle With your own wheels you can approach Berkeley from San Francisco by taking the Bay Bridge and then following either I-80 (for University Ave, downtown Berkeley and the UCB campus) or Hwy 24 (for College Ave and the Berkeley Hills).

The city runs two parking garages (see Orientation earlier), and UCB runs one on Bancroft Way between Telegraph Ave and Dana St (around $1 to $2 per hour). The situation improves in the evenings and on weekends, when the other university lots open to the public (check times carefully; fees vary).

Getting Around

Public transport and your feet are the best options for getting around crowded central Berkeley. For instance, walking from the Berkeley BART station to Telegraph Ave takes about 10 minutes.

Berkeley Transit, Ride Sharing & Parking *(TRiP;* ☎ *510-643-7665)* is a good resource for public-transport information. Its **Commute Store** *(2033 Center St)* is near the downtown Berkeley BART station.

AC Transit operates public buses in and around Berkeley (see Getting There & Away earlier). UC Berkeley's **Bear Transit** *(*☎ *510-642-5149)* runs a shuttle from the downtown BART station to various points on campus (25¢). From its stop at the Hearst Mining Circle, the H Line runs along Centennial Dr to the higher parts of the campus (50¢).

Missing Link *(*☎ *510-843-4763; 1961 Shattuck Ave)* rents mountain bikes for about $35 per day.

OTHER ATTRACTIONS

North of Berkeley, the Richmond–San Rafael Bridge links the East Bay with Marin County. Heading north, I-80 is lined with oil refineries, malls and housing developments. Just before reaching Vallejo, I-80 crosses the narrow Carquinez Straits, which lead to Suisun Bay and the Sacramento Delta (see the Sacramento Valley chapter). Towns along the Carquinez Straits, such as Benicia, and Port Costa had a brief boom in the gold rush era.

Heading east from Berkeley and Oakland, Hwy 24 leads into the Caldecott Tunnel; on the other side is seriously suburban Contra Costa County. The climate changes too, as the east side of the Berkeley Hills is generally hotter in summer, colder in winter. BART runs through the hills to Walnut Creek, Pleasant Hill, Concord and Pittsburg/Bay Point. East of Pittsburg in Antioch, Hwy 160 heads north into the Sacramento Delta. The towns of Contra Costa County aren't much of a draw, but the area does have parks and museums worth visiting if you have time – or long to escape the San Francisco fog.

County Connection buses *(*☎ *925-676-7500)* serve Walnut Creek, Concord and beyond. The fare is only 50¢ with BART-to-Bus transfer tickets, issued free at BART stations.

Mt Diablo State Park

Mt Diablo (3849ft) is over 1000ft higher than Mt Tamalpais in Marin County. On a clear day (early on a winter morning is a good bet) the views from Diablo's summit are huge and sweeping. To the west you can see over the bay and out to the Farallon Islands; to the east you can see over the Central Valley to the Sierra. The **state park** *(*☎ *925-837-2525; day-use fee $2; open 8am-sunset)* has 50mi of hiking trails (beware of the poison oak), which can be approached from Walnut Creek or Danville. You can also drive to the top if you wish, where there's a **visitors center** *(open Wed-Sun 11am-5pm summer, 10am-4pm winter)*. The park office is at the junction of the two entry roads. Simple **campsites** cost $12 per night (register at Southgate only); reserve by calling ☎ 800-444-7275.

Danville

Set in the shadow of Mt Diablo, Danville is the archetype of the perfect upper-middle-class Californian suburb. The only real reason to come here is to check out the surprisingly impressive automobile collection in the **Blackhawk Museum** *(*☎ *925-736-2277; adult/student $8/5; open 10am-5pm Wed-Sun)*. The museum includes six different galleries, two of which are devoted to cars – about 100 of them all told, including many one-of-a-kind models. There are also galleries devoted to science and natural history, a 'Discovery Room' for kids and an ongoing series of rotating exhibits curated by the Smithsonian Institution.

The museum is adjacent to The Shops at Blackhawk, a pretentious, upscale retail center, situated at the corner of Crow Canyon Rd and Camino Tassajara, 5mi from the Sycamore Valley Rd exit on I-680.

Eugene O'Neill National Historic Site *(*☎ *925-838-0249)* is an interesting stop too. The famed playwright built Tao House with his 1936 Nobel prize money and wrote *The Iceman Cometh, Long Day's Journey into Night* and *Moon for the Misbegotten* while living here between 1937 and 1944. Free tours are given Wednesday to Sunday at 10am and 12:30pm. You must book in advance, because you have to be picked up by shuttle from downtown Danville. Apparently the residents don't want tourists parking in their neighborhood.

John Muir National Historic Site

Less than 15mi north of Walnut Creek, sleepy Martinez (population 37,050) was the birthplace of baseball slugger 'Joltin' Joe DiMaggio and is also supposedly where the martini was invented (or so some stories go). Before hitting the cocktail lounges you can check out the former **John Muir residence** (☎ 925-228-8860; 4202 Alhambra Ave; admission $3; open 10am-5pm Wed-Sun, daily summer). Built by his father-in-law in 1882, it's the house where the pioneering conservationist and Sierra Club founder lived from 1890 until 1914. The property reflects his in-laws' tastes and lifestyle more than his own; still, the Muir history, the lovely countryside and the view inside his study are worthwhile. The grounds include the 1849 Martinez Adobe, part of the ranch on which the house was built. The park is just north of Hwy 4.

Vallejo

For one week in 1852 Vallejo (population 114,700) was officially the California state capital – until the legislature changed its mind. It tried Vallejo out a second time in 1853, but after a month moved on again (to Benicia). That same year, Vallejo became the site of the first US naval installation on the West Coast (Mare Island Naval Shipyard, now closed). The **Vallejo Naval & Historical Museum** (☎ 707-643-0077; 734 Marin St; admission $2; open 10am-4:30pm Tues-Sat) tells the story.

The town's biggest tourist draw, though, is **Six Flags Marine World** (☎ 707-643-6722; adult $43, child under 48in $27, parking $10; open 10am-8pm Fri-Sun spring & fall, 10am-10pm daily summer), a modern theme park offering mighty coasters and other rides alongside animal shows featuring sharks, killer whales, dolphins, seals and sea lions. Exit I-80 at Marine World Parkway, 5mi north of downtown Vallejo.

Blue & Gold Fleet (☎ 415-773-1188, 707-643-3779) runs ferries from San Francisco's Pier 41 at Fisherman's Wharf to Vallejo for $9 each way.

The Peninsula

San Francisco is the tip of a 30mi peninsula, sandwiched between the Pacific Ocean to the west and San Francisco Bay to the east.

San Francisco, with all its style, attitude and edge, disappears almost as soon as you start driving south on Hwy 101: city gives way to suburbia that continues to San Jose and beyond. Down Hwy 101, Palo Alto and Stanford University are the first real reasons to stop after leaving San Francisco. The alternative north–south route, scenic I-280, has a few further places of interest.

Hwy 1 runs down the Pacific coast via Half Moon Bay and a string of beaches to Santa Cruz. Hwy 101 and I-280 both run to San Jose, where they connect with Hwy 17, the quickest route to Santa Cruz. Any of these routes can be combined into an interesting loop or extended to the Monterey Peninsula (see the Central Coast chapter).

SAN FRANCISCO TO PALO ALTO

South of the San Francisco peninsula, I-280 is the dividing line between the densely populated South Bay area and the rugged and lightly populated Pacific coast. With its sweeping bends, I-280 is a more scenic choice than gritty, crowded Hwy 101. Unfortunately, these parallel north–south arteries are both clogged with traffic during the weekday commute.

Daly City is a bland residential suburb that served as inspiration for 1960s-era singer-songwriter Malvina Reynolds' composition 'Little Boxes.' Immediately south is **Colma** (population 1290), the graveyard for San Francisco ever since cemeteries were banned within the city limits. San Franciscans like to joke there are more dead people here than living – and they might be right.

Filoli (☎ 650-364-2880; adult/student $10/5; open 10am-2:30pm Tues-Sat) is a 654-acre English-style country estate 30mi south of San Francisco. The mansion was built between 1915 and 1917 by William Bowers Bourn II and his wife Agnes, owners of the Empire Gold Mine in Grass Valley. The name comes from the words 'Fight, Love, Live.' If the Georgian mansion looks familiar, you may have been watching too much TV; this was the mansion in *Dynasty*. The formal 16-acre garden is as much an attraction as the house, and both are surrounded by undeveloped, gently rolling countryside – perhaps the property's most luxurious asset. Attitudes here can be snooty and uptight, and the admission fee isn't cheap, but for fans of historic country estates, Filoli is worth visiting.

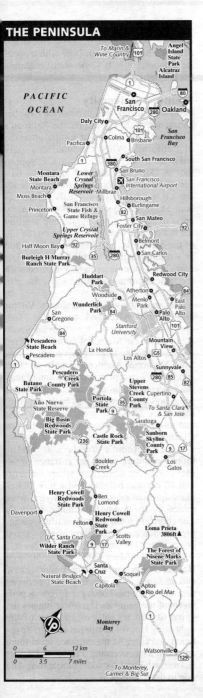

THE PENINSULA

Guided tours and nature hikes are available with advance reservation. To reach the estate, take the Edgewood Rd exit from I-280 and turn north up Cañada Rd.

Right on the bay at the northern edge of San Mateo, 4mi south of San Francisco International Airport, is **Coyote Point Park** *(day-use $4)*. The main attraction is the **Coyote Point Museum** *(☎ 650-342-7755; adult/child $4/2; open 10am-5pm Tues-Sat, noon-5pm Sun)*, with innovative exhibits for kids and adults concentrating on ecological and environmental issues. Exit Hwy 101 at Coyote Point Dr.

PALO ALTO

At the south end of the Peninsula, Palo Alto (population 61,500) is the home to the Bay Area's other internationally renowned educational establishment, Stanford University. This expansive, sylvan campus, covering 8200 leafy acres, dominates Palo Alto in the same way that the UCB campus dominates Berkeley. Yet, Palo Alto is a far glossier, more affluent city than Berkeley; it also lacks Berkeley's wacked-out alternative edge – maybe because Palo Alto is a major high-tech center and home to computer companies such as Hewlett-Packard.

Orientation

Palo Alto is bordered by Hwy-101 on its northeast edge and I-280 to the southwest. In between it's bisected by El Camino Real, which also divides the town from the campus. University Ave is Palo Alto's main street and continues, with a name change to Palm Dr, straight into the heart of the Stanford campus. The extensive Stanford Shopping Center is on El Camino Real just north of campus. East Palo Alto, on the east side of Hwy 101, is best avoided.

Palo Alto means 'Tall Tree' in Spanish, and the town's namesake timber is beside the San Francisquito Creek, where the railway line crosses it, at the junction of Alma St and Palo Alto Ave.

Information

The **chamber of commerce** *(☎ 650-324-3121; 325 Forest Ave; open 9am-5pm Mon-Fri)* dispenses information. For entertainment listings get a copy of the free *Palo Alto Weekly* newspaper, or check the website at **w** www.paloaltoonline.com.

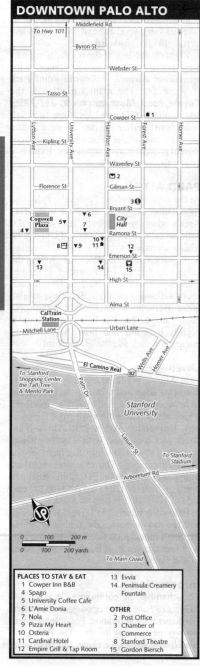

DOWNTOWN PALO ALTO

PLACES TO STAY & EAT
1 Cowper Inn B&B
4 Spago
5 University Coffee Cafe
6 L'Amie Donia
9 Pizza My Heart
10 Osteria
11 Cardinal Hotel
12 Empire Grill & Tap Room
13 Evvia
14 Peninsula Creamery
   Fountain

OTHER
2 Post Office
3 Chamber of
   Commerce
8 Stanford Theatre
15 Gordon Biersch

In nearby Menlo Park, **Kepler's Bookshop** (☎ 650-324-4321; 1010 El Camino Real) is a bright, modern store with a popular adjacent café. It's open until midnight Friday and Saturday.

Stanford University

Leland Stanford was a notorious robber baron, one of the Central Pacific Railroad's 'Big Four' founders and a former governor of California. When the Stanfords' only child died of typhoid during a European tour in 1884, they decided to build a university in his memory. Stanford University opened in 1891, just two years before Leland Stanford's death, but the university grew to become a prestigious and wealthy institution. The campus was built on the site of the Stanfords' horse-breeding farm, and as a result, Stanford is still known as 'The Farm' (not, of course, to be confused with the famous commune of the same name in Summertown, Tennessee).

The main booth for Stanford's **Visitor Information Services** (VIS; ☎ 650-723-2560; open 8am-5pm Mon-Fri, 9am-5pm Sat & Sun) is in the lobby of Memorial Auditorium. Free one-hour walking tours of the campus depart from Memorial Auditorium daily at 11am and 3:15pm, except during the winter break (mid-December through early January) and some holidays. Parking can be a real pain. Meters are $1.50 per hour, and if carrying that much change sounds unwieldy, buy an all-day parking permit ($12) from VIS.

Auguste Rodin's *Burghers of Calais* bronze sculpture marks the entrance to the **Main Quad**, an open plaza where the original 12 campus buildings, in a mix of Romanesque and mission revival styles, were joined by the **Memorial Church** in 1903. The church is noted for its beautiful mosaic-tiled frontage, stained-glass windows and organ with 7777 pipes.

East of the Main Quad, the 285ft-high **Hoover Tower** (open 10am-4:30pm daily, except during final exams, breaks between sessions & some holidays) offers superb views of the campus. The tower houses the university library, offices and part of the right-wing Hoover Institution on War, Revolution & Peace. At the entrance level there are exhibits concerning President Herbert Hoover, who was a student at Stanford. The ride to the top costs $2.

The collection at the **Cantor Center for Visual Arts** (*☎ 650-723-4177; 328 Lomita Dr; admission free; open 11am-5pm Wed-Sun, to 8pm Thur*) is a large museum originally dating from 1894; its collection spans works from ancient civilizations to contemporary art, sculpture and photography.

Immediately south is the open-air Rodin Sculpture Garden, with a large collection of sculpture by Auguste Rodin, including reproductions of his towering *Gates of Hell*. Dotted around the campus is more sculpture, all detailed in the free *Guide to Outdoor Sculpture* leaflet, available at the museum or at **w** www.stanford.edu/dept/ccva. Tours of the garden, on the first Sunday of the month, leave from the Main Quad at 2pm.

The **Red Barn** (*open daily*), part of Leland Stanford's original farm, stands just west of campus. It's here that Eadweard Muybridge, under patronage of Leland Stanford, photographed moving horses in a study that led to the development of motion pictures. Hiking and biking trails lead from the barn into the foothills west of campus.

Stanford Linear Accelerator Center

Few drivers speeding along I-280 realize that things are speeding by beneath them at far higher velocities. The **Stanford Linear Accelerator Center** (*SLAC; 2575 Sand Hill Rd*), run by the university for the US Department of Energy, goes right under the freeway. Positrons (positively charged subatomic particles) hurtle down a straight 2mi path in a 4-inch diameter linac (an accelerator beam tube), on their way to high-speed impacts at the other end of the tube. Experiments at SLAC have determined the existence of further subatomic particles, including quarks, and have gained the facility three Nobel prizes so far. Visitors can have a look inside during the free two-hour tours conducted several times a week. Advance reservations are required; call ☎ 650-926-2204. SLAC is about 2mi west of campus, east of I-280.

NASA-Ames Research Center

A few miles south of Palo Alto, the NASA-Ames Research Center (*☎ 650-604-6497; admission free; open 8am-4:30pm Mon-Fri*) sits at the north side of Moffett Field (see the boxed text over the page). It has conducted research into hyper-velocity flight, and its

Silicon Valley

Don't look for Silicon Valley on the map – it doesn't exist. Silicon is the basic element used to make the silicon chips that form the basis of modern microcomputers. Since the Santa Clara Valley – stretching from Palo Alto down through Mountain View, Sunnyvale, Cupertino and Santa Clara to San Jose – is thought of as the birthplace of the microcomputer, it's been dubbed 'Silicon Valley.' Not only does the valley not exist on the map, it's pretty hard to define even at ground level. The Santa Clara Valley is wide and flat, and its towns are essentially a string of shopping centers and industrial parks linked by a maze of freeways. It's hard to imagine that even after WWII this was still a wide expanse of orchards and farms.

There's very little to see in Silicon Valley; the cutting-edge computer companies are secretive and not keen on factory tours. Their anonymous-looking buildings – expanses of black glass are an architectural favorite – are bland and uninviting. The Tech Museum in San Jose gives some of the valley's technological flavor, as does Santa Clara's Intel Museum (see San Jose later in this chapter). Since the computer business is famed for its garage start-ups, enthusiasts may want to also drive by 367 Addison Ave, just five blocks south of University Ave in downtown Palo Alto. This is the garage where William Hewlett and David Packard started computer giant Hewlett-Packard.

gigantic wind tunnel is still used for advanced aerospace research. Turn off Hwy 101 at the Moffett Field exit and turn left immediately in front of the main gate to reach the visitors center. A one-third scale model of a space shuttle is out front. Inside is a Mercury capsule, a moon rock, and other items and exhibits related to space exploration. Even more interesting is a tour of the actual research facilities. These are also free but must be booked four to six weeks in advance by calling ☎ 650-604-6274. The two-hour tour involves a 2mi walk and may include visits to the wind tunnel, flight simulation facilities or the centrifuge.

Places to Stay

Hidden Villa (*☎ 650-949-8648; 26870 Moody Rd; dorm beds $15-18; closed early*

Moffett Field's Airship Hangar

Driving south on Hwy 101 from Palo Alto you soon pass former naval station Moffett Field on the left, where you're met with the sight of a massive, strangely shaped building that looks as if it was designed for a spaceship. Well, that's sort of close to the truth. In the 1920s and '30s, the US Navy had a small fleet of dirigibles (airships), the biggest crewed by up to 100 men and carrying five fighter planes that could be launched and retrieved while in flight.

In 1933, just eight days before 1100ft-long, 198ft-tall Hangar One was to be dedicated, the USS *Akron* crashed in a storm off New Jersey, killing 73 crew members, including Rear Admiral Moffett, the Navy's visionary of lighter-than-air crafts. The USS *Macon* had been flying out of Moffett Field for over a year when in 1935 it too, crashed, this time into the sea off Big Sur. There's a model of the *Macon* in the NASA-Ames displays, though you must go to the Maritime Museum in Monterey (see the Central Coast chapter) for information about the crash and the recent discovery of the wreckage.

June-early Sept) is an HI hostel tucked away in a calm, pastoral setting in Los Altos Hills, 2mi west of I-280. This 1937 hostel, among the country's oldest, is part of Hidden Villa Ranch, an organic farm and environmental educational center. It's closed when a kids' summer camp takes over. The location is stellar, with many hiking trails, but there's no public transport nearby.

Cardinal Hotel *(☎ 650-323-5101, fax 650-325-6086; w www.cardinalhotel.com; 235 Hamilton Ave; rooms with shared bath $70-80, with private bath $90-155, suites $195-225)* is a centrally located, restored, 1924 property with an elegant, old-fashioned feel.

Cowper Inn B&B *(☎ 650-327-4475; 705 Cowper St; rooms with shared bathroom $80 & $100, with private bathroom $150)* has 14 rooms, two with shared bathroom. Prices include breakfast.

Hotel California *(☎ 650-322-7666, fax 650-321-7358; w www.hotelcalifornia.com; 2431 Ash St; beds $80-95)*, two blocks from the California Ave train station, has 20 non-smoking rooms and free DSL.

For further budget accommodations, there are loads of motels along El Camino Real north and south of Palo Alto.

Stanford Arms *(☎ 650-325-1428; 115 El Camino Real; rooms $60)* is an older property with 14 rooms immediately northwest of both the campus and the Stanford Shopping Center.

Coronet Motel *(☎ 650-326-1081; 2455 El Camino Real; rooms $75)*, just north of Page Mill Rd, is fairly close to the campus' south side. It can be a bit noisy, but it's good value.

Glass Slipper Inn *(☎ 650-493-6611; fax 650-493-4421; 3941 El Camino Real; singles/doubles $55/65)* has a wacky, castle-meets-ski-lodge exterior, a pool and a couple of dozen rooms.

Country Inn Motel *(☎ 650-948-9154; fax 650-949-4190; 4345 El Camino Real; singles/doubles $69/89)*, south of Charleston Rd and tucked behind a few trees, is a friendly place

Places to Eat

There are dozens of good restaurants, from cheap eats to elegant bistros, in the compact blocks of downtown Palo Alto – mainly on University Ave between Cowper and Emerson Sts.

Peninsula Creamery Fountain *(☎ 650-323-3131; 566 Emerson St)*, wonderfully authentic, was founded in 1923 but looks as if yesterday was the opening day. It's famous for its frothy milkshakes.

University Coffee Cafe *(☎ 650-322-5301; 271 University Ave; snacks from $5)* serves fresh-roasted coffee, microbrewed beer, wine and some great sandwiches in a central location.

Pizza My Heart *(☎ 650-322-8100; 220 University Ave; large pepperoni $15)* is a popular spot buzzing nightly to at least midnight. It used to be known as Pizza a Go Go.

Empire Grill & Tap Room *(☎ 650-321-3030; 661 Emerson; mains $10-16)* is a quite popular yuppie hangout that got play in Po Bronson's novel *The First 20 Million*. You can get meals in the garden or a Belgian ale inside.

Nola *(535 Ramona St; mains from $15)* cultivates a wacked-out New Orleans vibe with its Cajun/Creole cuisine and blustery Hurricane cocktails. The decor inside and on the patio is deliberately boisterous and funky.

Mas Sake Freestyle Sushi (☎ 650-321-1556; 260 S California Ave; dishes from $4), which is attached to the dance club Icon (see Entertainment later), gives hip and trendy treatment to classic sushi dishes.

Palo Alto also has quite a few excellent top-tier places, though prices may push you into cardiac arrest. Reservations are a must.

Evvia (☎ 650-326-0983; 420 Emerson; mains from $20) serves superb gourmet Greek food in romantic surroundings. (It has a sister restaurant in San Francisco, Kokkari Estiatorio.)

Osteria (☎ 650-328-5700; 247 Hamilton Ave; mains from $15; open lunch Mon-Fri, dinner Mon-Sat) is hugely popular (meaning, often crowded) thanks to its stellar Tuscan cuisine.

L'Amie Donia (☎ 650-323-7614; 530 Bryant St; meals from $25; open dinner only Tues-Sat) is one of Palo Alto's most pleasant French restaurants, its casual elegance blending smoothly with the country-French cuisine.

Spago (☎ 650-833-1000; 265 Lytton Ave; dinner mains from $20), owned by celebrity-chef Wolfgang Puck (and presided over by Michael French), offers inventive California cuisine in a flashy, contemporary atmosphere, attracting the requisite big spenders.

Entertainment

For what it's worth, Palo Alto is home to the original link in the **Gordon Biersch** (640 Emerson St) chain of brewpubs. The German-style lagers are actually good, though the thick crowds are more stockbroker-geek than hipster-chic.

Antonio's Nut House (321 S California Ave) is a grubbier beer-and-peanuts sort of place, where said nuts are dispensed from a huge mechanical gorilla, so watch out.

Icon (☎ 650-289-0222; 260 S California Ave), formerly rock club the Edge, is a trendy spot for drinks and dancing Tuesday, Friday and Saturday nights; it also hosts local and national rock, jazz and R&B performers. Next door is Mas Sake Freestyle Sushi (see Places to Eat earlier).

Palo Alto Bowl (☎ 650-948-1031; 4329 El Camino Real) is the real deal if you hanker to knock a few back (meaning pins). Adding a trendy twist, on Friday and Saturday nights students and singles take over the lanes until 1am.

Stanford Theatre (☎ 650-324-3700; 221 University Ave) screens vintage Hollywood gems and international classics, accompanied by a 'mighty' Wurlitzer organ.

Getting There & Around

Palo Alto is about 30mi south of San Francisco and 15mi north of San Jose. The easiest way to get here from either end of the Peninsula is via **CalTrain** (☎ 800-660-4287, 650-817-1717), which stops in Menlo Park, Palo Alto and Stanford. Departures are every 30 or 60 minutes on weekdays, hourly on Saturday and every two hours on Sunday. San Francisco to Palo Alto takes about an hour and costs $4.50. Palo Alto to San Jose takes half an hour and costs $3. Palo Alto's CalTrain Station is beside Alma St, just north of University Ave.

Buses arrive and depart Palo Alto at the Transit Center, adjacent to the CalTrain station. From Palo Alto, **SamTrans** (☎ 800-660-4287, 650-817-1717; w www.samtrans.com) bus No 390 runs to the Daly City BART station ($2.20), and bus No KX goes to San Francisco's Transbay Terminal via San Francisco International Airport ($3); both operate about every half-hour daily.

The **Santa Clara Valley Transportation Agency** (VTA; ☎ 800-894-9908, 408-321-2300) serves Palo Alto and the Santa Clara Valley. Bus No 300 (weekdays only) runs between Stanford University, Palo Alto and San Jose ($2), while the No 22 (daily) runs from Palo Alto to San Jose ($1.25).

Marguerite (☎ 650-723-9362) is Stanford University's free public shuttle, providing service from CalTrain's Palo Alto and California Ave stations to the campus. Trains run about every 15 minutes during the day, every half-hour between 8pm and midnight.

There's free two-hour car parking all over town, or you can park all day for $1.50 at CalTrain stations. See under Stanford University earlier for information about parking on campus.

The **Bike Connection** (☎ 650-424-8034; 2011 El Camino Real) rents bikes for $20 to $25 per day. There's a network of bicycle routes around town.

SAN JOSE

Many San Franciscans – and those passing by on the freeways – are quick to turn up their noses at sprawling South Bay neighbor

San Jose (population 923,600) due to its glossy, suburban exterior, which feels more LA than Bay Area. It is the unofficial capital of Silicon Valley and the third-largest city in California. Industrial parks, high-tech computer firms and look-alike housing developments have, in the past few decades, come to dominate the city's landscape, taking over where farms, ranches and open spaces once spread between the bay and the surrounding hills. Well too bad for those naysayers, because by ignoring San Jose they're missing out on a culturally diverse city that's packed full of historic buildings, excellent museums and an impressive number of fine restaurants, and funky old bars. All that and a whole lot of sunny summertime weather.

San Jose, California's oldest Spanish civilian settlement, was founded in 1777 as El Pueblo de San José de Guadalupe; surviving remnants of that era include Plaza de Cesar Chavez and the Peralta Adobe. Between 1849 and 1851 the state's first capital was in San Jose, where the governing body became known as the 'Legislature of a Thousand Drinks.' 'Let's have a drink, let's have a thousand drinks' was the alleged rallying cry at the end of the day. The capital shifted places several more times before settling in Sacramento in 1854.

Speaking of tomfoolery, at History Park stands a replica of the 1881 Electric Light Tower, a harebrained scheme to light all of downtown. And elements of the Old West are still tucked away in the city's corners,

DOWNTOWN SAN JOSE

PLACES TO STAY
7   Hotel De Anza;
    Hedley Club
20 Sainte Claire Hotel
31 Ramada Limited
33 City Center Motel

PLACES TO EAT
5   Tied House
6   White Lotus
8   Blake's Steakhouse
9   La Taqueria
10 Waves Smokehouse
    & Saloon
21 Original Joe's
24 Cafe Matisse
25 Agenda
26 Eulipia
27 Palermo
32 Emile's

BARS & CLUBS
1   Trials Pub
29 Cactus Club
30 The Usual

OTHER
2   Fallon House
3   Post Office
4   Peralta Adobe
11 Greyhound Station
12 San Jose Museum of
    Art
13 Pavilion Shopping
    Center
14 San Jose Repertory
    Theatre
15 Tech Museum of
    Innovation
16 Center for the
    Performing Arts
17 Camera 3; Camera
    Cafe
18 San Jose Public Library
19 Visitor Information
    & Business Center
22 Fox California Theatre
23 Camera One
28 Children's Discovery
    Museum

from the Almaden Feed & Fuel, a one-time stagecoach stop south of town near the former New Almaden quicksilver mine, to Wave's Smokehouse and Saloon downtown on a street formerly known as El Dorado and once home to the city's red-light district.

The city's chief entertainment district is on a stretch of 1st St south of San Carlos St dubbed SOFA (South of First Area), which includes numerous nightclubs, restaurants, galleries and the historic 1927 Fox California Theatre. Another neighborhood to explore is the burgeoning business district along The Alameda, home to restaurants, cafés and the Towne 3 Theatre (see Entertainment later).

And if you see a jet flying close overhead, don't be alarmed. Those are just planes approaching a runway at San Jose International Airport, just north of downtown.

Orientation

Downtown San Jose is at the junction of Hwy 87 and I-280. Hwy 101 and I-880 complete the box. Running north–south the length of the city, from the old port town of Alviso on the San Francisco Bay all the way downtown, is 1st St; south of I-280, the name changes to Monterey Hwy.

San Jose State University is immediately east of downtown. The San Jose International Airport is at the intersection of Hwys 87 and 101.

Parking is free in city-owned lots and garages downtown after 6pm midweek, and all day on weekends.

Information

The helpful **Visitor Information & Business Center** (☎ 408-977-0900, 888-726-5673; W www.sanjose.org; 150 W San Carlos St; open 8am-5pm Mon-Fri, 11am-5pm Sat & Sun) is inside the San Jose Convention Center. Ask for the useful *Historical Walking Tour* leaflet. To find out what's happening and where, try the **Event Information Hotline** (☎ 408-277-3900), the free weekly *Metro* newspaper (W www.metroactive.com), bi-weekly *The Wave* or the Friday 'Eye' section of the daily *San Jose Mercury News*.

Plaza de Cesar Chavez

This leafy square in the center of downtown, part of the original plaza of El Pueblo de San José de Guadalupe, is the oldest public space in the city. It's named after Cesar Chavez – founder of the United Farm Workers, who lived part of his life in San Jose – and surrounded by museums, theaters and hotels.

At the top of the plaza is the **Cathedral Basilica of St Joseph** (80 S Market St), the pueblo's first church. Originally built in adobe in 1803, it was replaced three more times due to earthquakes and fire; the present building dates from 1877.

Tech Museum of Innovation

This excellent technology museum (☎ 408-294-8324; W www.thetech.org; 201 S Market St; museum or IMAX theater admission $9, both $16; open 10am-5pm daily), opposite Plaza de Cesar Chavez, examines subjects from space exploration to the human body to microchip production. The museum also includes an IMAX dome theater, which has shows daily on the hour from 11am to 4pm.

San Jose Museum of Art

The city's centrally located art museum (☎ 408-294-2787; 110 S Market St; admission free; open 11am-5pm Tues-Sun, until 10pm Fri) is one of the Bay Area's finest, with a strong permanent collection of 20th-century works and a variety of imaginative changing exhibits. The modern wing was added in 1991 to a building that started life as the post office in 1892, was damaged by the 1906 earthquake and became an art gallery in 1933.

Children's Discovery Museum

This downtown tech museum for kids (☎ 408-298-5437; 180 Woz Way; admission $7; open 10am-5pm Tues-Sat, noon-5pm Sun) has hands-on science and space displays, plenty of nifty toys and some cool play-and-learn areas such as the kooky 'Alice's Wonderland.' The museum is on Woz Way, which is named after Steve Wozniak, the co-founder of Apple and now a fifth-grade teacher.

Peralta Adobe & Fallon House

These historic San Jose houses represent two very different early architectural styles, sitting across the road from each other near San Pedro Square. Buy tickets for both at the **visitor center** (☎ 408-993-8182; 175 W St John St).

The Peralta Adobe, the city's oldest building, dates from 1797 and is the last survivor from the original Spanish pueblo. The building is very basic, and the two rooms have been furnished as they might have been during their occupation by the Gonzales and Peralta families. Luis Maria Peralta came to the Bay Area at age 16 and died an American citizen and a millionaire, the owner of a large chunk of the East Bay.

Thomas Fallon married the daughter of an important Mexican landowner, built this fine Victorian house in 1854–55 and went on to become mayor of San Jose. There are 15 furnished rooms.

Tours take place between noon and 5pm Saturday and Sunday and cost $6, or you can pay $10 for a joint ticket that includes admission to History Park.

History Park

Historic buildings from all over San Jose have been brought together at this open-air museum (☎ 408-287-2290; www.history sanjose.org; 1650 Senter Rd; admission $6, or $10 including Peralta Adobe & Fallon House; open noon-5pm Tues-Sun), 3mi southeast of the city center in Kelley Park. The center-piece is a half-scale replica of the 237ft-high 1881 **Electric Light Tower**. The original tower was a pioneering attempt at street lighting, in-tended to illuminate the entire town center. It was a complete failure but, lights or not, was left standing as a central landmark until it toppled over in 1915 due to rust and wind. Other buildings include an 1888 **Chinese temple** and the Pacific Hotel, which has ro-tating exhibits inside. The **Trolley Restoration Barn** restores historic trolley cars to operate on San Jose's light-rail line. The trolleys are also run on the park's own short line.

Tours are given on weekends between 12:30pm and 2:30pm; the grounds are open Tuesday to Friday, but many buildings are closed.

Rosicrucian Egyptian Museum

The Rosicrucian Order has a large center in **Rosicrucian Park** (cnr Naglee & Park Aves), west of downtown San Jose, which is devoted to the study of mysticism and metaphysics. The centerpiece is the exten-sive Egyptian Museum (☎ 408-947-3636; adult/student $9/7; open 10am-5pm Tues-Fri,

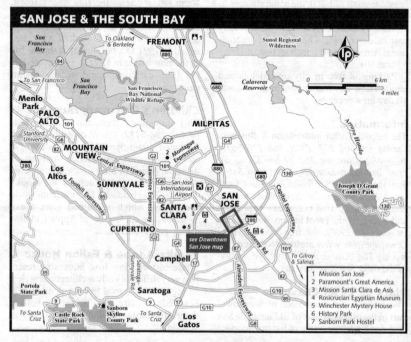

SAN JOSE & THE SOUTH BAY

San Francisco Bay
To Oakland & Berkeley
FREMONT
Sunol Regional Wilderness

To San Francisco
San Francisco Bay
San Francisco Bay National Wildlife Refuge
Calaveras Reservoir

Menlo Park
PALO ALTO
Stanford University

MILPITAS

MOUNTAIN VIEW
Central Expressway
Lawrence Expressway
Montague Expressway

Los Altos
Foothill Expressway

SUNNYVALE
San Jose International Airport

Joseph D Grant County Park

SANTA CLARA

SAN JOSE

CUPERTINO

Capitol Expressway

see Downtown San Jose map

Monterey Rd

Campbell

To Gilroy & Salinas

Portola State Park

Saratoga Sunnyvale Rd

Saratoga

Almaden Expressway

Sanborn Skyline County Park

To Santa Cruz
Castle Rock State Park

To Santa Cruz

Los Gatos

1	Mission San José
2	Paramount's Great America
3	Mission Santa Clara de Asís
4	Rosicrucian Egyptian Museum
5	Winchester Mystery House
6	History Park
7	Sanborn Park Hostel

11am-6pm Sat & Sun), with an extensive collection that includes statues, household items and mummies. There's even a two-room, walk-through reproduction of an ancient subterranean tomb.

Winchester Mystery House
The real mystery here is how anybody managed to build such a ridiculous house, which is little more than a hodgepodge of silly rooms all jammed together like a child's build-a-house game. Sarah Winchester inherited the Winchester rifle fortune, then spent the next 38 years building this sprawling mansion because the spirits of those killed by her husband's guns told her to do so.

The house (☎ 408-247-2101; 525 S Winchester Blvd) is 10mi west of central San Jose, just north of I-280. Most people shell out $16.95 for the 65-minute guided introductory tour, which includes a self-guided romp through the gardens and entry to an exhibit of guns and rifles. The 50-minute 'Behind the Scenes' tour is for diehards willing to pay $13.95 to see the house's basement, plumbing facilities and other underwhelming features. A combined tour is $23.95. All tours are offered every 30 minutes or so from 9:30am to 5pm daily, until 7pm in summer.

Hiking & Biking
There are several parks in the hills around San Jose, each laced with a network of hiking and biking trails.

Almaden Quicksilver County Park (☎ 408-268-8220) is south of town at the site of the old New Almaden mercury mine. Don't eat fish from the reservoirs, but do check out the trails, spring wildflower displays and mining museum, open Friday to Sunday. From San Jose, head south via the Almaden Expressway.

West of San Jose lies **Castle Rock State Park** (☎ 408-867-2952; parking $2), where hiking trails are alternately lush and sun-drenched, providing beautiful ocean vistas. The park is on Hwy 35 in the Santa Cruz mountains, just south of the intersection with Hwy 9.

About a 45-minute drive southeast is 87,000-acre **Henry Coe State Park** (☎ 408-779-2728; parking $2), with 250mi of hiking and biking trails, a large wilderness area, a visitors center (hours vary) and a small campground. From downtown, head south on Hwy

101 for 15mi to Morgan Hill, then east on E Dunne Ave, a narrow, winding road.

Places to Stay
The cheapest lodging options are the HI hostel and camping in Henry Coe State Park. There's a string of older motels south of downtown on Monterey Hwy; the motels along The Alameda are generally in better shape. More are found on N 1st St near the airport. Hotels downtown are busy year-round, thanks to San Jose's copious conventions and trade shows. Because the city is a hotbed of business travelers, midweek rates are often higher than weekends (generally considered Friday to Sunday).

Henry Coe State Park (campsites $7), southeast of San Jose near Morgan Hill, has 20 drive-in campsites. To reserve call ☎ 800-444-7275 at least two days in advance.

Sanborn Park Hostel (☎ 408-741-0166; 15808 Sanborn Rd; beds $10-12) is an HI hostel in an amazingly beautiful 1908 log building among dense redwoods in 3600-acre Sanborn County Park, 12mi west of San Jose. The setting is incredible, and few locals even know it exists. Bring all your food and supplies, as the nearest shops and restaurants are 4mi away in Saratoga. From Saratoga, drive west on Hwy 9 and look for signs to Sanborn County Park. If you don't have a car, the hostel will pick you up from downtown Saratoga; call before 9pm. With a car, from downtown San Jose, follow N 1st St north for approximately 2mi. It's on the north side of I-880 but south of Hwy 101.

Executive Inn (☎ 408-453-1100, 800-877-1331; fax 408-453-1892; 1310 N 1st St; rooms from $89) is near the airport, right across from a light-rail stop.

A few blocks away is the equally basic **Airport Inn International** (☎ 408-453-5340, 800-453-5340, fax 408-453-5208; 1355 N 4th St; weekend rates from $69, midweek from $109). Both offer free airport shuttle service.

Motels line The Alameda between downtown and Santa Clara University; from the city center head west on Santa Clara St, which becomes The Alameda. **Arena Hotel** (☎ 408-294-6500; 817 The Alameda; rooms from $79) is one of the nicer choices.

Heading south of I-280, S 1st St turns into Monterey Hwy (Hwy 82), which is lined with interesting old signs and businesses. There are numerous motels, some crusty and decaying but others still acceptable; try the **Travelers Rest Motel** (☎ 408-297-2641; 1315 S 1st St; rooms from $55). Keep in mind that Monterey Hwy is right under an airport flight path, so expect some jets overhead.

City Center Motel (☎ 408-998-5990; cnr 2nd & E Reed Sts; singles/doubles $55/66), within stumbling distance of the SOFA district, is modest but clean.

Ramada Limited (☎ 408-298-3500; 455 S 2nd St; rooms from $74 weekends, $100 midweek) is within walking distance of the convention center and SOFA, and has a fitness center.

Sainte Claire Hotel (☎ 408-295-2000; fax 408-977-0403; 302 S Market St; rooms from $99 weekends, $159 midweek) was built in 1926 overlooking Plaza de Cesar Chavez. It was renovated in 1992 and is now part of the Hyatt group.

Hotel De Anza (☎ 408-286-1000, 800-843-3700, fax 408-286-0500; 233 W Santa Clara St; rooms from $129 weekends, $179 midweek), downtown, is a restored Art Deco beauty, and its prices match its plush comforts. Weekend rates include breakfast.

Places to Eat

There are plenty of places to choose from along S 1st St and on San Pedro St by San Pedro Square. Vietnamese restaurants are gathered along E Santa Clara St from 4th to 12th Sts. San Jose's small Japantown, around Jackson St and its intersections with 4th, 5th and 6th Sts, has some good mid-range Japanese restaurants.

Original Joe's (☎ 408-292-7030; 301 S 1st St; mains from $12) is a San Jose landmark serving standard Italian dishes in a chrome-and-glass dining room loaded with 1950s charm. Expect a wait, though.

Palermo (394 S 2nd St; mains from $14) has won raves from the local press for its Sicilian meals and is visually striking.

La Taqueria (15 S 1st St; items from $3) serves burritos and tacos just as fabulous as those at its sister restaurant in San Francisco.

Waves Smokehouse & Saloon (65 Post St; dinner $15-20) serves barbecue platters and burgers in an Old West–style saloon and former brothel dating from 1873. If you're not hungry, a drink in the historic bar, where stained glass and dark wood prevail, will take you back to a time when Post St bustled with all manner of sin and commerce. At night there's music, dancing and karaoke.

Tied House (65 N San Pedro St; dishes from $8), near San Pedro Square, is a microbrewery with good house beer, sports on TV and a standard burgers-and-the-like menu.

Vegetarian House (520 E Santa Clara Ave; mains $6-10) serves an international assortment of vegetarian cuisine in an airy room with a juice bar and homages to spiritual master Ching Hai.

White Lotus (☎ 408-977-0540; 80 Market St; meals under $10) is an unpretentious vegetarian restaurant offering Asian stir-fry and noodle dishes.

Emile's (☎ 408-289-1960; 545 S 2nd St; mains $25-35, prix-fixe dinner $38) is San Jose's best-known splurge, run by Swiss-born chef Emile since 1973. The setting is romantic and the California-European cuisine fabulous.

Agenda (☎ 408-287-3991; 399 S 1st St; mains $15-25) serves meat, fish and pasta dishes in the brick-and-wood dining room of a 1908 building. There's also a lovely lounge upstairs and dancing in the cellar.

Eulipia (☎ 408-280-6161; 374 S 1st St; mains $15-25), a former jazz club named after a Rahsaan Roland Kirk composition, serves a mixed New American menu of meat and pasta dishes.

Blake's Steakhouse (☎ 408-298-9221; 17 N San Pedro St; mains $20-30) serves seafood, chops, prime rib and classic cuts of top-shelf steak.

For caffeine, check out **Cafe Matisse** (415 S 1st St), a spacious coffeehouse with a pleasant, laid-back atmosphere, and the **Camera Cafe** (288 S 2nd St), conveniently attached to the Camera 3 Cinema.

Entertainment

If you seek a well-poured pint in a supremely comfortable atmosphere, **Trials Pub** (265 N 1st St), north of San Pedro Square, has many excellent ales on tap (try a Fat Lip), all served in a warm, friendly room with no TVs. There's good pub food too.

Waves Smokehouse & Saloon (65 Post St), downtown, has a mix of DJ dancing, live music and karaoke.

Hedley Club (233 W Santa Clara St), also downtown inside the elegant 1931 Hotel De Anza, is a good place for a quiet drink in Art Deco surroundings.

The biggest conglomeration of clubs is along S 1st St, aka SOFA.

Agenda *(399 S 1st St)* is a bar and restaurant that also serves up live jazz and swing upstairs and house music in the cellar. A happy-hour cocktail in the lovely upstairs bar makes a pleasant start to the evening.

The Usual *(400 S 1st St)* has live rock shows and regular DJ dance nights, as does the nearby **Cactus Club** *(417 S 1st St)*.

If you've been hiking all day in Almaden Quicksilver County Park, stop for a bite and a beer at the **Almaden Feed & Fuel** *(18950 Almaden Rd)*, a funky, century-old joint that was once a stagecoach stop. It's about 10mi south of town, just off the Almaden Expressway.

San Jose Repertory Theatre *(☎ 408-367-7255; 101 Paseo de San Antonio; tickets $20-44)* offers a full season of top-rated productions in a new, 525-seat venue downtown.

Fox California Theatre *(S 1st St)* is undergoing a $70 million renovation; the estimated opening is 2004, when it will be home to Opera San Jose and an ongoing classic film series. The city's annual film festival, **Cinequest** *(☎ 408-995-5033; late Feb-early Mar)* may land there too.

Camera Cinemas *(☎ 408-998-3300)* shows independent and foreign films at three San Jose theaters: the original single-screen **Camera One** *(366 S 1st St)*; the modern, triple-screen **Camera 3** *(288 S 2nd St)*; and the **Towne 3 Theatre** *(1433 The Alameda)*, west of downtown and home to classics and revivals.

Spectator Sports

The San Jose Sharks, the city's NHL team, play at the **Compaq Center** *(cnr Santa Clara & Autumn Sts; tickets $25-107)*, a massive glass-and-metal stadium. The NHL season runs from September to April.

Major League soccer team the San Jose Earthquakes (formerly the Clash) play at **Spartan Stadium** *(cnr 7th & Alma Sts; tickets $10-40)* from late March to mid-October.

Tickets for either team are available from the Compaq Center box office (☎ 408-999-5721) or, for a surcharge, through **Ticketmaster** *(☎ 408-998-8497)*.

Getting There & Away

The quickest and most convenient connection between San Jose and San Francisco is with CalTrain, a commuter rail service that operates daily up and down the Peninsula.

Air Two miles north of downtown, between Hwy 101 and I-880, is the **San Jose International Airport** *(☎ 408-277-4759)*. The airport has grown busier as the South Bay gets more crowded, with numerous domestic flights at two terminals and a new Interim International Arrivals Facility. Expansion is in the works.

Bus & BART Buses to San Francisco ($5, 90 minutes) and Los Angeles ($40, seven to nine hours) are operated by **Greyhound** *(☎ 408-295-4151; 70 Almaden Ave)*.

To reach the BART system in the East Bay, the **Santa Clara Valley Transportation Agency** *(VTA; ☎ 408-321-2300, 800-894-9908)* bus No 180 runs daily between the Fremont BART station and downtown ($2).

Train Between San Jose and San Francisco, **CalTrain** *(☎ 800-660-4287)* makes over three dozen trips (fewer on weekends); the 90-minute journey costs $6 each way. San Jose's main **CalTrain station** *(65 Cahill St)* is just south of The Alameda.

The Cahill St CalTrain station doubles as the **Amtrak** *(☎ 800-872-7245)* station, serving Seattle, Los Angeles and Sacramento.

VTA runs a weekday shuttle from the station to downtown (known as the DASH or Downtown Area Shuttle; route No 804).

Car & Motorcycle San Jose is right at the bottom end of the San Francisco Bay, about 40mi from Oakland (via I-880) or San Francisco (via Hwy 101 or I-280). Expect lots of traffic at all times of day on Hwy 101, especially in the South Bay. Although I-280 is slightly longer, it's much prettier and usually less congested. On the East Bay side, I-880 – another ugly, hugely congested highway – runs between Oakland and San Jose, and I-680 comes in from Contra Costa County.

Getting Around

Every 10 minutes, a free shuttle runs from both terminals to the Metro/Airport Light Rail station, where you can catch the San Jose light rail to downtown San Jose ($1.25).

Super Shuttle *(☎ 408-225-4444)* offers door-to-door bus service to most Silicon Valley destinations; fares start at $17.

The main **San Jose light-rail line** runs 20mi north–south from the city center. Heading south gets you as far as Almaden and Santa Teresa. The northern route runs to the Civic Center, the airport and Baypointe, where it connects with another line that heads west past Great America to downtown Mountain View.

San Jose's historic trolley cars, dating from 1903 to 1928, operate on a 1.5mi loop through downtown San Jose. These vintage vehicles operate on weekends from April to September, and also during the Christmas season.

VTA buses run all over Silicon Valley. Fares for buses (except express lines) and light-rail trains are $1.25 for a single ride and $3 for a day pass. For information and schedules call ☎ 408-321-2300 or ☎ 800-894-9908.

AROUND SAN JOSE
Mission San José

Founded in 1797, the Mission San José was the 14th California mission. Its large Indian population and fertile agricultural lands made it one of the most successful, until a major earthquake struck in 1868, virtually leveling the mission's original 1809 church, which was replaced by a wooden one. In 1979, the wooden church was sold and moved to San Mateo. The adobe church seen today is a reasonably faithful reconstruction of the 1809 structure. A statue of St Bonaventure, in a side altar, dates from around 1808. The adjacent living quarters, now housing a small mission museum, are original.

The mission *(☎ 510-657-1797; 43300 Mission Blvd; museum & church open 10am-5pm daily, mass 8am Mon-Fri)*, in Fremont, is at the foot of Mission Peak Regional Preserve. From I-880 or I-680, take the Mission Blvd exit to Washington Blvd.

Santa Clara

Mission Santa Clara de Asís, the eighth mission in California, is on the Santa Clara University campus, several miles west of downtown San Jose. The mission started life in 1777, on the Guadalupe River. Floods forced the first move; the second site was only temporary; the third church burned; while the fourth church, a substantial adobe construction, was finished in 1784, but an earthquake in 1818 forced the move to the present site. That church, the fifth, was completed in 1822, but in 1926 it burned down, so the present church – an enlarged version of the 1822 church, completed in 1928 – is the sixth church on the fifth site.

Many of the roof tiles came from the earlier buildings, and the church is fronted by a wooden cross from the original mission of 1777. The only remains from the 1822 mission are a nearby adobe wall and an adobe building. The first college in alifornia was opened at the mission in 1851. The college grew to become Santa Clara University, and the mission church is now the college chapel. Santa Clara University is within walking distance of the Santa Clara CalTrain station.

If you're in Santa Clara visiting the mission and have extra time, stop by the **De Saisset Museum** *(☎ 408-554-4528; 500 El Camino Real; admission free; open 11am-4pm Tues-Sun)*, across the old mission plaza; it houses art and history collections.

Intel Museum *(☎ 408-765-0503; 2200 Mission College Blvd; admission free; open 9am-6pm Mon-Fri, 10am-5pm Sat)* has displays on the birth and growth of the computer industry with special emphasis, not surprisingly, on Intel's involvement.

Paramount's Great America *(☎ 408-988-1776; Great America Parkway; adult/child $44/34; open daily June-Aug, Sat, Sun & holidays spring & fall)*, off Hwy 101 in Santa Clara, is a large amusement park that throws you into 50-or-so rides such as Meteor Attack, Star Trek and Stealth, the flying coaster.

Raging Waters

This water theme park *(☎ 408-238-9900; cnr Tully Rd & Capitol Expressway; adult/child $25/20; open May-Sept)*, east of town at Lake Cunningham Regional Park, features slides, pools and high-adrenaline water rides.

SAN FRANCISCO TO HALF MOON BAY

One of the real surprises of the Bay Area is how fast the urban landscape disappears along the rugged and largely undeveloped coast. In the 70mi from San Francisco to Santa Cruz, the coast road, winding Hwy 1, passes beach after beach, many of them hidden from the highway. Most beaches along Hwy 1 are buffeted by wild and unpredictable surf, making them more suitable for sunbathing than swimming. The state beaches along the coast don't charge an access fee, but parking can cost a few dollars.

A cluster of isolated and supremely scenic HI hostels, at Point Montara (22mi south of San Francisco) and Pigeon Point (36mi), makes this an interesting route for cyclists, though narrow Hwy 1 itself can be stressful, if not downright dangerous, for inexperienced cyclists.

Pacifica & Devil's Slide

Pacifica and Point San Pedro, 15mi from downtown San Francisco, signal the end of the urban sprawl. South of Pacifica is Devil's Slide, an unstable cliff area through which Hwy 1 winds and curves. Drive carefully, especially at night and when it is raining, as rock and mud slides are frequent. Heavy winter storms often lead to the road's temporary closure. A tunnel is planned to bypass this problem roadway.

Collecting a suntan or catching a wave are the attractions at **Rockaway Beach** in Pacifica and the more popular **Pacifica State Beach**.

Gray Whale Cove to Miramar Beach

Just south of Point San Pedro is **Gray Whale Cove State Beach** (☎ 415-330-6300), one of the coast's popular 'clothing optional' beaches. There's a bus stop with steps down to the beach and a parking lot ($5). **Montara State Beach** is just a half-mile south.

From the town of **Montara**, 22mi from San Francisco, trails climb up from the Martini Creek parking lot into **McNee Ranch State Park**, which has hiking trails aplenty.

Point Montara Lighthouse HI Hostel (☎ 650-728-7177; cnr Hwy 1 & 16th St; dorm beds $18, private rooms $48) started life as a fog station in 1875, after two steamers wrecked on the shallow ledge offshore. The hostel is adjacent to the current lighthouse, which dates from 1928. This very popular hostel has a living room, kitchen facilities, an outdoor hot tub and an international clientele. There are a few private rooms for couples or families. Reservations are a good idea anytime, but especially on summer weekends. SamTrans bus No 294 will let you off at the hostel if you ask nicely.

Montara has a number of B&Bs too, including **Goose & Turrets** (☎ 650-728-5451,

fax 650-728-0141; 835 George St; rooms $110-165) and the **Farallone Inn** (☎ 650-728-8200; 1410 Main St; rooms $95-195).

South of the lighthouse, the **Fitzgerald Marine Reserve** (☎ 650-363-4020) at Moss Beach is an extensive area of natural tidal pools. Feel free to walk out and explore the pools at low tide, though be careful, as it's slippery. Also, it's illegal to remove any creatures, shells or even rocks – this is a marine reserve, after all. From Hwy 1 in Moss Beach, turn west onto California Ave and drive to the end. Samtrans bus No 294 stops along Hwy 1.

Moss Beach Distillery (☎ 650-728-5595; cnr Beach Way & Ocean Blvd; meals from $15) is a 1927 landmark overlooking the ocean, and it's great for a meal or just soaking up the view on the deck under a blanket. The restaurant even has a ghost, the 'Blue Lady.' Follow the signs from Hwy 1.

South of here is a stretch of coast called Pillar Point. Fishing boats bring in their catch at the Pillar Point Harbor, some of which gets cooked up in seafront restaurants at Princeton such as **Barbara's Fishtrap** (281 Capistrano Rd), off Hwy 1.

If you want to catch your own, there are quite a few outfits working out of Pillar Point Harbor offering trips in search of salmon, rockfish or tuna. Try the **Huck Finn Sportfishing Center** (☎ 650-726-7133), which offers day-long salmon-fishing trips for about $60 per person.

At the west end of Pillar Point is **Mavericks**, a serious surf break that attracts the world's top big-wave riders to battle its huge, steep and very dangerous waves. The annual Quiksilver/Mavericks surf contest is held between December and March, depending on conditions.

Harbor View Inn (☎ 650-726-2329; 51 Alhambra Ave; rooms midweek/weekends from $96/140), right near Pillar Point Harbor, has ocean-view rooms.

HALF MOON BAY

Half Moon Bay (population 11,300) is the main town between San Francisco (28mi north) and Santa Cruz (40mi south). San Jose (43mi) is east across the Santa Cruz Mountains, via Hwy 92. Half Moon Bay developed as a beach resort back in the Victorian era. The long stretches of beach still attract weekenders and a few hearty surfers.

Half Moon Bay spreads out along Hwy 1 (called Cabrillo Hwy in town), but despite the development it's still relatively small. The main drag is a five-block stretch of Main St lined with shops, cafés, restaurants and a few upscale B&Bs. Visitor information is available from the **Half Moon Bay Coastside Chamber of Commerce** (☎ 650-726-8380; W www.halfmoonbaychamber.org; 520 Kelly Ave; open 9am-4pm Mon-Fri).

Things to See & Do

Pumpkins are a major crop around Half Moon Bay, and the pre-Halloween harvest is celebrated in the annual **Art & Pumpkin Festival** (☎ 650-726-9652). The mid-October event kicks off with the World Championship Pumpkin Weigh-Off, where the bulbous orange beasts can bust the scales at over 1000lb.

Inland **Purisima Creek Preserve** has a small but worthwhile set of trails for cyclists and hikers; follow Higgins-Purisma Rd from Hwy 1.

Seahorse (☎ 650-726-2362), about 1mi north of the Hwy 92 junction, offers daily horseback rides along the beach. A two-hour ride is $50; early-bird specials start between 8am and 9am and cost just $30.

Places to Stay & Eat

Half Moon Bay State Beach (☎ 650-726-8820; campsites $12), just west of town on Kelly Ave, is a cheap overnight option, with 57 spartan campsites available on a first-come, first-served basis.

San Benito House (☎ 650-726-3425; 356 Main St; rooms from $127) is one of the more moderately priced Half Moon Bay B&Bs.

Old Thyme Inn (☎ 650-726-1616; 779 Main St; rooms $130-300) is a cute Victorian-era Queen Anne–style building, circa 1899, located a few blocks south of the main shopping strip.

Flying Fish Grill (cnr Hwy 92 & Main St; items from $3) has excellent, fresh cod or salmon tacos, along with other seafood plates, which you can take out or eat in.

M. Coffee (522 Main St; lunch $5-7) has espresso drinks, ice-cream cones and lunchtime sandwiches and salads.

Cameron's Restaurant & Inn (☎ 650-726-5705; 1410 S Cabrillo Hwy; rooms from $99, meals from $8), a couple miles south of the Hwy 92 junction, is an English-style pub in a century-old building, with a large selection of beer and food. If you don't mind barroom noise there are three large, comfortable rooms over the pub.

Getting There & Away

SamTrans (☎ 800-660-4287) bus No 294 operates from the Hillsdale CalTrain station to Half Moon Bay, and up the coast to Moss Beach and Pacifica, daily until about 6pm ($1.10). Bus No 15 runs from Half Moon Bay south to San Gregorio and Pescadero on weekdays only.

HALF MOON BAY TO SANTA CRUZ

More beaches lie south of Half Moon Bay, starting with **San Gregorio State Beach**, 10mi to the south. It has a clothing-optional stretch to the north, but the beach can get so chilly that only polar bears would find the idea appealing.

Pomponio and Pescadero state beaches are further down the coast, on the way to the pleasant little town of **Pescadero**. In mid-August, Pescadero hosts the annual Arts & Fun Fest. At other times of the year stop for sandwiches and fresh, hot garlic-herb bread at **Norm's Market** (287 Stage Rd), or a sit-down meal at **Duarte's Tavern** (cnr Stage & Pescadero Rds; dinner from $16); the latter is an 1894 saloon and restaurant serving the best artichoke soup and ollalaberry pie you're likely to taste.

Bird-watchers enjoy **Pescadero Marsh Reserve**, across the highway from Pescadero State Beach, where numerous species feed year-round. **Butano State Park**, about 5mi south of Pescadero, is good for day hikes.

Pigeon Point Lighthouse Hostel (☎ 650-879-0633; 210 Pigeon Point Rd; dorm beds $18, private rooms $51), an HI facility at Pigeon Point, 5mi south of Pescadero on Hwy 1, is based in the old lighthouse keeper's quarters. The 110ft lighthouse, one of the tallest in America, was built in 1872. The hostel is such a pleasant place that, especially on weekends and throughout the summer, advance reservations are essential.

Inland, large stretches of the hills are protected in a patchwork of parks that, just like the coast, remain remarkably untouched despite the huge urban populations only a short drive to the north and east. Heading east toward Palo Alto, Hwy 84 winds through thick stands of trees. Along the way is the tiny township of **La Honda**, 9mi east of San Gregorio State Beach, and several local parks with hiking and mountain-biking opportunities. La Honda's **Apple Jack's Inn** (☎ 650-747-0331), housed in an old blacksmith's shop, is a rustic, down-home bar offering live music on weekends and lots of local color.

Big Basin Redwoods State Park (☎ 831-338-8860; day-use $3) encompasses 25 sq mi of the largest redwoods in the Southern Coastal Mountain Range, as well as rivers and streams, wildlife and hiking trails. The old-growth forests contain stands of fir, cedar, bay, madrone and oak. Big Basin was California's first state park, signed into law in 1902 after a heated battle between local conservationists and logging interests. Many of the redwoods here are over 1500 years old.

You can access some park trails from Hwy 1, but the main entrance is on Hwy 236; which connects with Hwy 9 about 15mi north of Santa Cruz. The park has 146 family **campsites** (☎ 800-444-7275 for reservations; campsites $12). There are also 36 tent cabins, each equipped with two double-bed platforms and wood-burning stoves ($49); reserve by calling ☎ 800-874-8368.

Año Nuevo State Reserve

A visit to the elephant seal colony on Año Nuevo Beach is a wonderful experience, but in the mid-winter peak season, you must plan well ahead. The beach is 5mi south of Pigeon Point and 27mi north of Santa Cruz.

Elephant seals were just as fearless two centuries ago as they are today, but unfortunately, club-toting seal trappers were not in the same seal-friendly category as camera-toting tourists. Between 1800 and 1850, the elephant seal was driven to the edge of extinction. Only a handful survived around the Guadalupe Islands off the Mexican state of Baja California. With the availability of substitutes for seal oil and the conservationist attitudes of more recent times, the elephant seal made a comeback, reappearing on the Southern California coast from around 1920. In 1955, they returned to Año Nuevo beach, and today the reserve is home to thousands in the peak season.

The peak season is during the mating and birthing time, December 15 to the end of March, when visitors are only allowed on heavily booked guided tours. For the peak

Elephant Seals

Elephant seals follow a precise calendar: between September and November young seals and the yearlings, who left the beach earlier in the year, return and take up residence. In November and December, the adult males return and start the ritual struggles to assert superiority; only the largest, strongest and most aggressive 'alpha' males gather a harem. From December through February, the adult females arrive, pregnant from last year's beach activities, give birth to their pups and, about a month later, mate with the dominant males.

At birth an elephant seal pup weighs about 80lb and, while being fed by its mother, puts on about 7lb a day. A month's solid feeding will bring the pup's weight up to about 300lb, but around March, the females depart, abandoning their offspring on the beach. For the next two to three months the young seals, now known as 'weaners,' lounge around in groups known as 'pods,' gradually learning to swim, first in the rivers and tidal pools, then in the sea. In April, the young seals depart, having lost 20% to 30% of their weight during this prolonged fast.

period, mid-January to mid-February, it's recommended you book eight weeks ahead. Although the **park office** (☎ 650-879-0227) can advise on your chances of getting a place, bookings can only be made by calling ☎ 800-444-7275. Tours cost $4, plus $2 for parking. From the ranger station it's a 3mi to 5mi round-trip hike to the beach, and the visit takes two to three hours. If you haven't booked, bad weather can sometimes lead to last-minute cancellations. The rest of the year, advance reservations aren't necessary, but visitor permits from the entrance station are required; arrive before 3pm.

SANTA CRUZ

A popular weekend escape from San Francisco 70mi to the north, Santa Cruz (population 56,000) is a lovely seaside town with a happening nightlife and warm, pleasant summertime weather. Where its neighbor Monterey (40mi to the south; see the Central Coast chapter) has an upscale sheen, Santa Cruz retains a more authentic 'beach town'

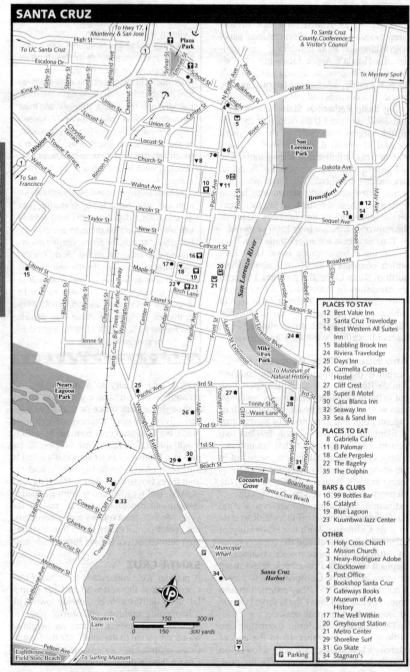

SANTA CRUZ

PLACES TO STAY
12 Best Value Inn
13 Santa Cruz Travelodge
14 Best Western All Suites Inn
15 Babbling Brook Inn
24 Riviera Travelodge
25 Days Inn
26 Carmelita Cottages Hostel
27 Cliff Crest
28 Super 8 Motel
30 Casa Blanca Inn
32 Seaway Inn
33 Sea & Sand Inn

PLACES TO EAT
8 Gabriella Cafe
11 El Palomar
18 Cafe Pergolesi
22 The Bagelry
35 The Dolphin

BARS & CLUBS
10 99 Bottles Bar
16 Catalyst
19 Blue Lagoon
23 Kuumbwa Jazz Center

OTHER
1 Holy Cross Church
2 Mission Church
3 Neary-Rodriguez Adobe
4 Clocktower
5 Post Office
6 Bookshop Santa Cruz
7 Gateways Books
9 Museum of Art & History
17 The Well Within
20 Greyhound Station
21 Metro Center
29 Shoreline Surf
31 Go Skate
34 Stagnaro's

vibe. For one thing – and for better or for worse – Santa Cruz has far more crunchy hippies than wealthy yuppies. This is, after all, where Ken Kesey held his first 'acid test' at a friend's house in the nearby hills (with the Warlocks, aka the Grateful Dead, as the house band). The town is also famous for its strong surfing culture, not to mention being home to more than 13,000 left-of-center students at the University of California, Santa Cruz (UCSC), on a lovely wooded stretch of land above the town.

San Francisco got much of the attention following the 1989 Loma Prieta earthquake, but it did a huge amount of damage to Santa Cruz, because the epicenter was only about 10mi northeast of town. The Pacific Garden Mall was decimated, and a number of people were killed. Today, though, things are basically back to 'normal,' which here means serene much of the year – save for roving bands of students, street punks and genuine crazies – and jam-packed on summer weekends, when crowds swarm the beaches and the boardwalk at Santa Cruz beach.

Orientation

Santa Cruz stretches for a long way along the coast, blending into Capitola, a slightly lower-key beach resort. Santa Cruz itself can be a little confusing, with roads winding uphill and downhill and disappearing then reappearing as they cross San Lorenzo River. Pacific Ave is the main street of downtown Santa Cruz, with Front St one block east.

The University of California campus is about 2½mi northwest of the center.

Information

Santa Cruz County Conference & Visitors Council (☎ 831-425-1234; W www.santacruz .org; 1211 Ocean St; open 9am-5pm Mon-Sat, 10am-4pm Sun) has brochures, maps and accommodation information.

Metro Santa Cruz (W www.metroactive .com/cruz), the town's free weekly newspaper, has event, film and restaurant listings.

Bookshops include the big **Bookshop Santa Cruz** (☎ 831-423-0900; 1520 Pacific Ave) and the equally mammoth **Gateways Books** (☎ 831-429-9600; 1531 Pacific Ave).

Santa Cruz Beach Boardwalk

The 1906 **boardwalk** (☎ 831-423-5590; W www.beachboardwalk.com) is the oldest beachfront amusement park on the West Coast. Its most famous rides include the half-mile-long Giant Dipper, a wooden roller coaster built in 1924, and the 1911 Looff carousel – both National Historic Landmarks.

The boardwalk is open daily from June to August, and on weekends and some holidays in winter; it is closed most of December. Admission is free, but individual rides cost between $2 and $4, or you can buy an all-day pass for $23.95.

From June to August, the boardwalk also hosts free Friday night 'classic rock' concerts, starring the likes of Hermin's Hermits and Gary Puckett.

The adjacent 1907 **Cocoanut Grove** (☎ 831-423-2053) hosts private functions and occasional dance concerts in its ornate Grand Ballroom. It shares the building with the Casino Fun Center video arcade.

Municipal Wharf

You can drive right onto the wharf, where seafood restaurants and gift shops compete for attention. A few shops rent poles and fishing tackle, in case you're keen to join fisherfolk along the wharf waiting patiently for a bite. Most days, noisy pods of sea lions sunbathe beneath the wharf.

Mission Santa Cruz

Mission Santa Cruz (Mission of the Holy Cross), founded in 1791, gave the town its name. The 12th of the California missions, Santa Cruz was isolated from the comings and goings along El Camino Real and had an uneconomically small Ohlone Indian population (missions needed Indians to Christianize and to do the hard work). Worse, the mission was too close to a Spanish settlement – sad experience had proven that settlements and missions did not mix. The mission fell apart after secularization, and earthquakes in 1840 and 1857 destroyed the church. Today the **Holy Cross Church** stands on the original site.

Santa Cruz Mission State Historic Park (☎ 831-425-5849; 144 School St; open 10am-4pm Thur-Sun), one block off Mission Plaza, includes one original structure, the 1791 **Neary-Rodriguez Adobe**. The **mission church** (cnr High & Emmet Sts) was rebuilt in 1931 as a half-size replica; inside is a **gift shop** (☎ 831-426-5686).

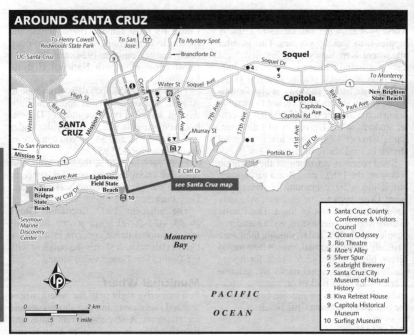

AROUND SANTA CRUZ

1 Santa Cruz County Conference & Visitors Council
2 Ocean Odyssey
3 Rio Theatre
4 Moe's Alley
5 Silver Spur
6 Seabright Brewery
7 Santa Cruz City Museum of Natural History
8 Kiva Retreat House
9 Capitola Historical Museum
10 Surfing Museum

Museums

The small **Museum of Art & History** (☎ 831-429-1964; 705 Front St; adult/student $4/2; open 11am-5pm Tues-Sun, to 7pm Thur) is worth a look for its exhibits exploring local history and highlighting contemporary artists.

A large, cement gray whale fronts the worthwhile **Santa Cruz City Museum of Natural History** (☎ 831-420-6115; 1305 E Cliff Dr; donation requested; open 10am-5pm Tues-Sun) on the east side of the San Lorenzo River. Inside, the natural history collection includes an ancient sea-cow fossil and a touch-friendly tidepool.

The tiny **Surfing Museum** (☎ 831-420-6289; admission free; open noon-4pm Thur-Mon), at Lighthouse Point on W Cliff Dr, overlooks Steamer Lane, the most popular surfing break in Santa Cruz. Inside are displays on surfing, surfers and surfboards.

University of California, Santa Cruz

Established in 1965 in the hills above town, the University of California, Santa Cruz (UCSC) has over 13,000 students and a rural campus dotted with interesting buildings and

fine stands of redwoods. Campus buildings include two galleries, a renowned arboretum and a number of structures from the Cowell Ranch of the 1860s, on which the campus was built. **Seymour Marine Discovery Center** (☎ 831-459-3800; near Delaware Ave & Swift St; adult/student $5/3; open 10am-5pm Tues-Sat, noon-5pm Sun), west of town near Natural Bridges, is part of UCSC's Long Marine Laboratory. The collection includes aquariums and a blue whale skeleton.

Natural Bridges State Beach

This scenic beach is west of Santa Cruz at the end of W Cliff Dr. Besides the beach, there are tidal pools and leafy trees where monarch butterflies hibernate in big bunches from November to March; monarch butterflies can also be seen in the trees behind the natural-history museum. Unfortunately, the eponymous natural bridge has washed away.

Spas

Santa Cruz's New Agey spas are ideal places to unwind. An hour in a private tub at **The Well Within** (☎ 831-458-9355; 417 Cedar St) costs from $22 to $27 per couple.

Riding the Big Tree

The arrival of the Southern Pacific Railway put Victorian-era Santa Cruz on the tourist map. The first railroad line was built in 1875 and carried freight from the Santa Cruz wharf 7mi up the San Lorenzo River Canyon to Felton. The spectacular route, and the Big Trees redwood grove near Felton, soon attracted tourists as well as freight. In 1880, a narrow-gauge line across the Santa Cruz Mountains linked San Francisco, Oakland and San Jose, bringing visitors to Felton and then down to the beach. In 1940, a severe storm washed out the line from the Bay Area to Felton, and the line was never repaired. Afterwards the short Santa Cruz-Felton line reverted to freight use. A plan to build a second rail line to San Francisco, known as the Ocean Shore Railroad, was plagued by the difficult and unstable terrain (just as Hwy 1 is today), and it never consisted of more than random stretches connected by ferry services. The 1906 earthquake finished the line off.

In 1985 passenger services restarted as the **Santa Cruz, Big Trees & Pacific Railway** (☎ 831-335-4400). The short, slow, scenic trip between Santa Cruz's boardwalk and Roaring Camp, a re-creation of an 1880s logging town outside Felton, takes two hours. From mid-June to early September trains operate twice daily; the rest of the year they run on weekends and holidays. The round-trip costs $17/12 for adults/children. From Roaring Camp, you can take a second railway trip on the narrow-gauge steam locomotives of the **Roaring Camp & Big Trees Railroad**. The 75-minute round-trip to the Big Trees redwood stand costs $15.50 for adults and $10.50 for children. This route operates daily in summer, and on weekends and holidays year-round. It's possible to drive to the Roaring Camp depot and catch a train from there; take Hwy 17 to Scotts Valley, exit at Mt Herman Rd and follow that west for 3½mi, turn left on Graham Hill Rd and continue for half a mile.

At **Kiva Retreat House** (☎ 831-429-1142; 702 Water St), a private tub for two people is $20 per hour, and the communal tub costs $16 for unlimited use.

Swimming, Surfing & Diving

The north side of Monterey Bay is warmer than the south, which is cooled in summer by water from the Monterey Canyon. As a result, beach activities are much more feasible in Santa Cruz than at Monterey.

Surfing is popular in Santa Cruz, especially at Steamer Lane. Other favorite surf spots are Pleasure Point Beach, on E Cliff Dr toward Capitola, and Manresa State Beach, beyond Capitola. You can rent surfboards and surfing gear at **Go Skate** (☎ 831-425-8578; 601 Beach St; $10 per day) or **Shoreline Surf** (☎ 831-458-1380; 125 Beach St; $25 per day).

Want to learn to surf? **Club Ed** (☎ 831-459-9283) or **Richard Schmidt Surf School** (☎ 831-423-0928) will have you standing and surfing the first day out. Both charge $80 for either a two-hour group lesson or a one-hour private lesson (recommended for novices); all equipment is included.

If you're interested in diving in the area, **Ocean Odyssey** (☎ 831-475-3483; 860 17th Ave) offers chartered trips and a full range of lessons to bring you up to speed.

Whale-Watching & Harbor Cruises

Whale-watching trips, harbor cruises and fishing expeditions depart year-round from the municipal wharf. **Stagnaro's** (☎ 813-427-2334) is a longstanding operator with a kiosk on the wharf. Whale-watching trips run from December to April, though there's plenty of marine life to see on a summer bay cruise too. Expect to pay between $20 and $30 per person for a three-hour tour. One-hour scenic tours are under $10. Fishing trips cost between $45 and $55 per person, and beginners are welcome.

Biking & Hiking

The hills behind Santa Cruz offer many interesting walks and rides. **Henry Cowell Redwoods State Park** is a particularly popular getaway. In town, a pleasant, easy trip follows winding W Cliff Dr and the coastline. From the boardwalk it's 1mi to Lighthouse Point and 3mi to Natural Bridges State Beach. It's especially nice toward sunset.

Places to Stay

One thing to note immediately is that accommodations in Santa Cruz are not cheap. This is a popular tourist destination, so even shabby budget places can cost a bundle when the weather's nice. And that's another thing – room rates here often vary wildly depending on both the season and day of the week. Be sure to call ahead and check not only availability but also a specific night's price.

Camping is clearly a cheaper option, and there are several good choices in the area. But if you're determined to get that seaside view on a midsummer Saturday from a clean, well-cared-for room, you'd better warm up your credit card.

Camping & Hostels There are many campsites in the mountains and on the beach, and at $12 per tent site they're your best bet for a cheap night's sleep. Call ☎ 800-444-7275 for reservations at Big Basin Redwood State Park (see Half Moon Bay to Santa Cruz earlier in this chapter); at Henry Cowell Redwood State Park near Felton; at New Brighton State Beach in Capitola; or at Sunset State Beach in Watsonville.

Santa Cruz KOA Kampground *(☎ 831-722-0551; campsites $41)* is 12mi south of Santa Cruz, 5mi north of Watsonville and 1mi from the beach. It's pricey, but, hey, there's mini golf, a game room and a pool. The 250 sites fill up fast in summer, so reserve early.

Budget travelers love HI's respectable **Carmelita Cottages Hostel** *(☎ 831-423-8304; 321 Main St; dorm beds $20, private doubles $45)*. Not only is its garden setting lovely, it's just two blocks from the beach and five blocks from downtown. Check-in is open from 5pm to 8pm, so call if you'll be later, and keep in mind that there's an 11pm curfew. Advance reservations are advised.

Hotels & Motels Good areas to hunt for motels include the streets running back from the boardwalk (though some places here are real dives); along Riverside Ave; and along Ocean St on the other side of the San Lorenzo River.

Super 8 Motel *(☎ 831-426-3707; 338 Riverside Ave; rooms midweek/weekends $79/129)* is a typical, predictable motel not far from the beach.

Days Inn *(☎ 831-423-8564, 800-325-2525; 325 Pacific Ave; rooms midweek/weekend $88/165)*, in the no-man's land between downtown Santa Cruz and the waterfront, has standard rooms and friendly staff.

Best Value Inn *(☎ 831-426-7766; 522 Ocean St; rooms midweek/weekends from $69/129)*, formerly the Islander Motel, is an acceptable no-frills option.

Santa Cruz Travelodge *(☎ 831-426-2300; 525 Ocean St; rooms midweek/weekends from $70/100)* and the **Riviera Travelodge** *(☎ 831-423-9515; 619 Riverside Ave; rooms midweek/weekends from $59/99)* both have swimming pools that come in handy for a swim on hot days.

Seaway Inn *(☎ 831-471-9004; fax 831-471-0239; 176 W Cliff Dr; rooms midweek/weekends from $99/169)* is a pleasant, very friendly option.

Best Western All Suites Inn *(☎ 831-458-9898; 500 Ocean St at Soquel Ave; rooms midweek/weekends from $110/175)* is a comfortable property; every room is a suite.

Sea & Sand Inn *(☎ 831-427-3400; 201 W Cliff Dr; rooms with queen/king beds from $149/179)* is a neat and tidy establishment removed from the noisy boardwalk area and perched pleasantly on a cliff; every room looks onto the ocean. If you're going to shell out the bucks for an overnight experience, you might as well do it right.

Casa Blanca Inn *(☎ 831-423-1570, 800-644-1570; 101 Main St at Beach St; rooms from $150)* is one of the nicer beachside motels, with a little more character. Most of its 39 uniquely furnished rooms have unobstructed ocean views, though rooms overlooking Beach St can be noisy. Rates vary according to room size, view and season.

Brookdale Lodge *(☎ 831-338-6433, fax 831-338-3066; Ⓦ www.brookdalelodge.com; 11570 Hwy 9; rooms midweek/weekends from $87/109)*, 14mi north in the Santa Cruz mountains, is a historic getaway dating from 1890, with 46 rooms and a few cottages. It hosts live bands on weekends and offers dinner in a unique creekside setting.

B&Bs Close to the beach and boardwalk, **Cliff Crest** *(☎ 831-427-2609; fax 831-427-2710; 407 Cliff St; rooms winter/summer from $125/195)* is an attractive Victorian-era Queen Anne–style mansion with five rooms.

Babbling Brook Inn *(☎ 831-427-2437; 1025 Laurel St; rooms $170-250)* is not near the beach but it does have 13 attractive rooms and a garden complete with a stream and waterfall. Most rooms have a gas fireplace, spa and deck.

Places to Eat

For organic fruits and vegetables you'd be hard pressed to find better shopping than at the year-round **farmers market** *(cnr Lincoln & Center Sts; open 2:30pm-6:30pm Wed)*. If you crave burgers, pizza slices or Mexican food, browse the downtown storefronts along Pacific Ave and Front St.

Silver Spur *(2650 Soquel Dr; meals under $10)*, 1mi north of Hwy 1 on the east side of town, is well worth the drive. Hearty, home-made breakfasts get no better than the ones served up at this super-friendly place.

The Bagelry *(320A Cedar St; meals under $5)*, near the corner of Maple St, is another popular breakfast spot, open very early every morning.

Cafe Pergolesi *(418 Cedar St; coffee & snacks under $5)* is a student coffeehouse and Santa Cruz landmark, with a balcony overlooking the street, great cakes and pies, and beer on tap.

Seabright Brewery *(519 Seabright Ave; meals from $8)* has decent pub food, tasty microbrewed beer, occasional live bands and a loud and crowded patio.

While most of the seafood joints on the municipal wharf have great views but inflated prices, **The Dolphin** *(☎ 831-426-5830; mains from $14)*, way out at the end, is the notable exception. It's a small, diner-style restaurant with seats inside, a take-out window outside and fresh-off-the-boat seafood either way.

Gabriella Cafe *(☎ 831-457-1677; 910 Cedar St; mains $14-19)* is a tranquil candlelit restaurant with a menu featuring pasta, seafood and local wines.

El Palomar *(☎ 831-425-7575; 1336 Pacific Ave; mains $10-22)*, consistently popular, serves Mexican staples along with more inventive dishes – either way it's fresh and tasty. There's a large tequila selection too.

Entertainment

Kuumbwa Jazz Center *(☎ 831-427-2227; 320 Cedar St)* has been one of the best live music venues in town since 1975, attracting big-name performers to its intimate room.

Catalyst *(☎ 831-423-1338; 1011 Pacific Ave)*, with an 800-seat capacity, is a major Santa Cruz music venue; over the years it's hosted national acts from Gillian Welch to Black Uhuru to Nirvana. When there's no music, the upstairs pool room is still open.

Rio Theatre *(☎ 831-423-8209; 1205 Soquel Ave at Seabright Ave)* is a restored 1949 movie theater that now hosts top-name bands and comedians, theater productions and film events.

Moe's Alley *(☎ 831-479-1854; 1535 Commercial Way)* has a patio, a full bar and a schedule packed with nationally renowned blues artists.

Blue Lagoon *(923 Pacific Ave)* is a dance club popular with students, the local gay crowd and fans of hip-hop, trance, techno and retro sounds.

99 Bottles Bar *(110 Walnut Ave)* is a straightforward bar with, you guessed it, a whole lot of beer to choose from, including more than 40 on tap.

Getting There & Away

Without your own wheels, the easiest way to reach Santa Cruz is on a Greyhound bus. There are no commuter train services to or from Santa Cruz.

Greyhound *(☎ 831-423-1800; 425 Front St)*, next to the Metro Center, has daily buses to San Francisco ($11, three hours), Monterey ($11, 70 minutes) and Los Angeles ($40, 10 hours). On weekdays during commute hours, the **Santa Clara Valley Transit** *(VTA; ☎ 800-894-9908)* and **Santa Cruz Metro Transit** *(☎ 831-425-8600)* jointly operate Hwy 17 express buses from Santa Cruz to downtown San Jose and the CalTrain station ($3). **Santa Cruz Airporter** *(☎ 831-423-1214, 800-497-4997)* runs shuttle buses to the airports at San Jose ($40) and San Francisco ($45).

Santa Cruz is 40mi north of Monterey via Hwy 1 and 35mi west of San Jose via curvy, crowded Hwy 17. From San Francisco, 70mi north, the main scenic route down the coast along Hwy 1 is worth the extra time. Those running late can take I-280 to San Jose and continue south on Hwy 17.

Getting Around

Santa Cruz Metropolitan Transit *(☎ 831-425-8600)* operates from the **Metro Center** *(920 Pacific Ave)*. Useful services include bus No 3B to Natural Bridges State Beach; No 35 to Felton and then on up to Ben Lomond and Boulder Creek; No 40 (limited service) to Davenport and the north coast beaches; and the No 69 to the Capitola Transit Center. One-way trips cost $1; a day pass costs $3.

AROUND SANTA CRUZ
The Mystery Spot

A fine old-fashioned tourist trap, the **Mystery Spot** (☎ 831-423-8897; Branciforte Dr; admission $5; open 9am-7pm daily) has scarcely changed since the day it opened in the 1940s. On this steeply sloping hillside, compasses point crazily, mysterious forces push you around and buildings lean at silly angles. It's clean, harmless fun. It's located 3mi north of town; take Water St to Market St, turn left and continue up into the hills.

Capitola

About 5mi east of Santa Cruz is the little seaside town of Capitola, founded as a 19th-century vacation resort and incorporated in 1949. Nestled quaintly between bluffs along Soquel Creek, it's quieter than Santa Cruz, and the crowds are more affluent and less apt to hold drum circles on the beach. Downtown, you'll find plenty of shops, galleries, B&Bs, restaurants and cute homes. Keep in mind, though, that the streets can get crowded and parking isn't easy; it's best to leave the car in the metered lot behind City Hall, off Capitola Ave at Riverview Dr.

The **Capitola Chamber of Commerce** (☎ 831-475-6522; W www.capitolachamber .com) has local tips and lodging information. It is also the contact for the **Capitola Art and Wine Festival**, held in mid-September. Another useful website is W www.capitola.com.

The **Begonia Festival** (☎ 831-476-3566), on Labor Day weekend, features a parade of flowered floats on Soquel Creek.

The **Capitola Historical Museum** (☎ 831-464-0322; 410 Capitola Ave; open noon-4pm Fri-Sun) hosts two-hour walking tours on Saturday during summer; call to reserve.

SAN JUAN BAUTISTA

In pleasantly sleepy San Juan Bautista, California's 15th mission – the chief reason for visiting – is fronted by the only original Spanish plaza in the state. It's also perched right on the edge of the San Andreas Fault. Some of the climactic scenes in Alfred Hitchcock's Vertigo were shot at the mission.

San Juan Bautista is on Hwy 156 about 2mi east of Hwy 101, between San Jose and Salinas on the way to Monterey. San Juan Bautista has many attractive old buildings, a few motels and a string of restaurants and cafes along 3rd St.

Mission San Juan Bautista

The mission (☎ 831-623-4528; $2 donation requested; church open 9:30am-4:45pm daily) was founded in 1797, and construction of its church started in 1803. The interior, completed in 1816, was painted by American sailor Thomas Doak, who jumped ship in Monterey and is allegedly California's first US settler. The church was built with three aisles, but at some point the outer aisles were walled off. They were destroyed in the 1906 earthquake and were not repaired until the 1970s, when the inner archways were opened up to make this the largest of California's mission churches. The bell tower was also added at that time. Note the footprints of bears and coyotes on the red-tiled floor.

In the Spanish era, the area had a large Indian population and over 4000 are buried in the old **cemetery** beside the mission. The ridge along the north side of the church is the actual line of the San Andreas Fault.

North of the cemetery, a section of the old El Camino Real (King's Highway) can be seen. This Spanish road, built to link the missions, was the state's first. In many places Hwy 101 still follows the original route.

The Plaza & Town

The buildings around the old Spanish plaza are part of the **state historic park** (☎ 831-623-4526; admission $2; open 10am-4:30pm daily). The **Plaza Hotel** started life as a single-story adobe building in 1814 and was enlarged and converted into a hotel in 1858. The adjacent **Castro House** was built for José Maria Castro, who led two successful revolts (in 1836 and 1848) against unpopular governors. In 1848, the house was bought by the Breen family, survivors of the Donner Party (see the boxed text 'The Donner Party' in the Sierra Nevada chapter). The large blacksmith shop and the **Plaza Stable** hint at San Juan Bautista in its heyday, when as many as 11 stagecoaches a day passed through. The railroad bypassed the town in 1876, and San Juan Bautista has remained sleepy ever since.

AROUND SAN JUAN BAUTISTA

Gilroy, 14mi north of San Juan Bautista via Hwy 101, claims to be the garlic capital of the world, and celebrates this achievement with the annual **Gilroy Garlic Festival** (☎ 408-842-1625), attracting over 125,000 people on the last full weekend in July.

Wine Country

Nearly 60% of California's 850 wineries are in the parallel Sonoma and Napa Valleys, the traditional heart of California's 'Wine Country.' The majority of these wineries are small and consumer focused and sell fewer than 10,000 cases each year, accounting for less than 10% of the state's total output.

California's wholesale wines – the bulk stuff, aka Interstate 5 plonk – generally come from industrial operations in the heavily agricultural Central Valley, with less-than-famous provenances such as Fresno, Madera and Tulare (these California counties alone produce eight times more wine than Napa and Sonoma).

The Wine Country's tradition of high-quality batch production dates back to 1857, when Hungarian count Ágoston Haraszthy established the state's first commercial winery, Buena Vista, in rural Sonoma Valley. Yet it wasn't until the mid-1970s that the region's wineries began to gain worldwide acclaim.

The turning point was a blind wine-tasting competition in France in 1976, when two Napa Valley entries – Chateau Montelena's 1973 chardonnay and a '73 cabernet sauvignon from Stag's Leap – outscored a venerable collection of French Bordeaux. These days Napa and Sonoma are distinctive imprimaturs that attract visitors eager to tipple quality wine in rustic settings. Many of California's high-quality wines are still produced in the Napa and Sonoma Valleys, though in recent years there's been an explosion of topflight wineries throughout the state.

The two valleys, Napa and Sonoma, are about two hours by car from San Francisco. Napa Valley, the further inland of the two, has more than 230 wineries and attracts the greatest number of visitors (expect heavy road traffic on weekends). Sonoma Valley, with about 170 wineries, is far less commercial and marginally less congested than Napa. If you have time to visit only one valley, Sonoma is a good choice.

That said, both offer the same rustic beauty of vineyards, wildflowers and golden hills. The valleys can be covered on a hectic day trip from San Francisco, but to do them each justice allow two full days for exploring and wine tasting.

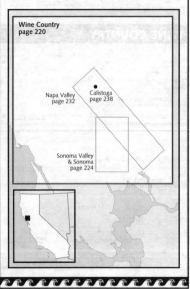

Highlights

- Sunrise, champagne and hot air – the valleys look great from a balloon
- Mud bath Calistoga style – pamper yourself!
- Valley of the Moon, Wellington and Kenwood – three top-quality Sonoma winemakers
- PlumpJack – one of Napa's finest 'undiscovered' wineries
- Yountville's French Laundry – California cuisine at its best

Wine Country
page 220

Napa Valley
page 232

Calistoga
page 238

Sonoma Valley
& Sonoma
page 224

Spring and fall are the best times to visit. Summers tend to be hot and dusty, as well as decidedly crowded. Fall combines fine weather with the grape harvest and the 'crush,' when the wine-making season gets under way with the pressing of the grapes.

History
Wine grapes were introduced to California in the 1760s by Father Junípero Serra, who planted the so-called 'mission' variety (a descendant of Sardinian vines brought to North

America by the conquistadores) at the San Diego Mission. European vines were first introduced by Hungarian count Ágoston Haraszthy, who established a commercial vineyard in Sonoma Valley in 1857 and is credited with founding California's modern wine industry. By the late 1860s there were already 50 vintners in the Sonoma and Napa Valleys.

Later in the century things started to go badly for winemakers, a double assault from cheap imports and the arrival of the deadly root louse phylloxera, fresh from devastating the vineyards of Europe. The wine business was still stumbling from these attacks when Prohibition was enacted in 1919, forcing the closure of all but a handful of vineyards dedicated to the production of sacramental wines.

Prohibition ended in 1933, but it was not until the 1960s that wine production regained its momentum. The wine produced in the Napa and Sonoma Valleys received a crucial vote of confidence at that 1976 blind-tasting competition in France; in recent years the region's wineries have helped fuel an industry that contributes $33 billion each year to the California economy.

Though there's no single wine associated with the Wine Country, typical whites include fumé blanc, Riesling, gewürztraminer, chenin blanc and California chardonnay. Reds include pinot noir, merlot and Beaujolais; the robust cabernet sauvignon and peppery zinfandel are the premier California reds. Ports and sweet muscats are also gaining popularity among local vintners.

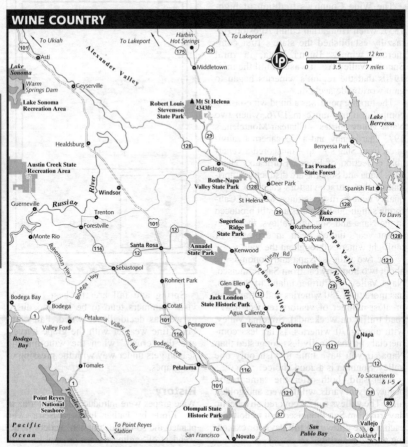

WINE COUNTRY

Wine Tasting

These days few Napa Valley wineries offer free tastings (officially known as 'flights'). If you want to sample the wines, you'll have to pay, usually $3 to $10 for a flight of four to eight varieties; sometimes a complimentary wine glass is included. In Sonoma Valley free tastings are the rule rather than the exception, except at the larger vineyards. Wineries in both valleys generally refund tasting fees if you purchase a bottle.

In any case, you don't want to do *too* much tasting – visiting five or six wineries in a day, sampling four to eight wines at each spot, is enough to give you a dreaded zinfandel zinger (aka a lousy hangover). Note that wineries will not serve alcohol to anyone under the age of 21. And it goes without saying that drinking and driving is absolutely discouraged, not the least because the narrow and curvy roads can be dangerous.

Wineries generally sell a small selection of their own wines, but don't come looking for bargains. Bottles and cases are usually on sale at full retail price and can often be found cheaper at liquor stores and supermarkets. Of course, wines from some of the smaller boutique vineyards, as well as special vintages or reserves, will be available only from the wineries themselves or from a very restricted list of outlets.

Most wineries are open daily from 10am or 11am to 4:30pm or 5pm for tastings, but call ahead if you absolutely, positively don't want to miss a tasting or tour.

There are hundreds of wineries in the valleys, so those mentioned in this chapter are just a sampling of both the better-known larger places and the more interesting smaller places.

Also note that there are topflight wineries in the Alexander Valley and surrounding the nearby towns of Healdsburg and Geyserville (see Healdsburg in the North Coast chapter).

Flying & Ballooning

Glider flights cost $115 to $180 for one person, or $155 to $260 for two people, and last between 20 and 40 minutes. Contact **Crazy Creek Soaring** (☎ 707-987-9112), which operates from the gliderport in Middletown, off Hwy 29 about 10mi north of Calistoga.

The **Vintage Aircraft Company** (☎ 707-938-2444; 23982 Arnold Dr) in Sonoma charges $120/170 for one/two adults for 20-minute biplane tours of the region.

Glassy-Winged Nightmare

California's winemakers have been living under a dark cloud for the last few years. They fear watching their $33 billion industry decimated by a leaf-hopping insect called the glassy-winged sharpshooter.

The insect itself is harmless. What worries winemakers is the fatal bacteria – known as Pierce's disease – that is spread by sharpshooters when they feed on grapevines. The California wine industry has battled Pierce's disease since the 1880s, when the state was attacked by blue-green sharpshooters (a distant relative of the glassy-winged variety). Blue-green sharpshooters have also been blamed for devastating the wine industry in Southern California in the 1900s and the Central Valley in the 1940s.

To the horror of modern winemakers, the glassy-winged sharpshooter is even more effective at spreading Pierce's disease than its blue-green predecessors. It's estimated that it would take two adult insects only a few days to infect an entire acre of grapes.

Since finding its way from southeastern US states to California in the 1980s, the glassy-winged sharpshooter has destroyed vineyards and fruit plants in Southern California and has been detected as far north as Santa Cruz and San Jose. Napa and Sonoma Valley have been spared so far, but winemakers wonder how long their luck will hold.

California's governor has recognized the dangers to the state's fifth-largest export and has allocated millions of dollars to sharpshooter eradication efforts (Pierce's disease itself is incurable).

Many strategies have been developed to control the insects' spread. One of the few strategies that's proven effective is the targeted release of small stingerless wasps, which feed on sharpshooter eggs. It's worked so far, yet local grape growers and winemakers are understandably nervous about betting their economic futures on a small stingerless wasp.

Hot-air balloon flights usually take off early in the morning (around 6am or 7am), when the air is coolest; sometimes they include a champagne breakfast after you land. The cost is $185 to $200 per person, and advance reservations are strongly recommended. Call **Balloons above the Valley** (☎ 707-253-2222) or **Napa Valley Balloons** (☎ 707-944-0228), both in Yountville.

Wine Train

A popular way to explore the Wine Country is on the **Napa Valley Wine Train** (☎ 707-253-2111, 800-427-4124; **w** www.winetrain .com; 1275 McKinstry St, Napa), which conducts tours with brunch ($60), lunch ($70 to $100) and dinner ($80 to $110) throughout the year, in vintage Pullman dining cars that travel from Napa to St Helena and back. The 36mi round trip takes three hours, and it's a beautiful ride. The train leaves Napa from McKinstry St near 1st St.

Bicycling

Touring the Wine Country by bicycle is a memorable experience, although it's best to stick to the quieter back roads when possible. Through Sonoma Valley take Arnold Dr rather than Hwy 12, and through Napa Valley take the Silverado Trail rather than Hwy 29.

Each valley is fairly flat and cycle-friendly, and pedaling between wineries is not too demanding. Crossing from one valley to the other is far more challenging, particularly if you travel via the steep Oakville Grade and Trinity Rd (between Oakville and Glen Ellen).

Bicycles, if transported in a box, can be brought to the Wine Country on Greyhound buses for $15. You can also transport bicycles on Golden Gate Transit buses, most of which have exterior bike racks available for free on a first-come, first-served basis.

Golf

In Sonoma you can tune up at the public nine-hole **Los Arroyos Club** (☎ 707-938-8835; 500 Stage Gulch Rd) for $14 on weekends. Or you can play a full 18 holes at **Oakmont – East** (☎ 707-538-2454; 565 Oak Vista Court) or **Oakmont – West** (☎ 707-539-0415; 7025 Oakmont Dr), two public courses located side by side on the outskirts of Santa Rosa. Green fees are $32 to $40.

Napa has a half-dozen 18-hole courses. Notables include the public **Chardonnay Golf Club – The Vineyards** (☎ 707-257-1900 ext 2244; 2555 Jameson Canyon Dr), off Hwy 12; and the **Napa Golf Course at Kennedy Park** (☎ 707-255-4333; 2295 Streblow Dr), just west of the Napa–Vallejo Hwy. Fees at both are $30 to $50.

Motor Racing

There are year-round events – from Nascar's Winston Cup to the American Le Mans and Superbike tours – at **Sears Point Raceway** (☎ 800-870-7223; **w** www.searspoint.com), at the intersection of Hwys 37 and 121, at the southern end of Sonoma Valley.

Organized Tours

Bicycling Guided group tours are offered by **Getaway Adventures** (☎ 707-763-3040, 800-499-2453), with locations in Petaluma and Calistoga. It offers single- and multi-day trips that typically include meals, lodging, gear and pampering. Prices range from $95 to $900-plus per person.

In Napa, a better option for single-day treks is **Napa Valley Bike Tours** (☎ 707-255-3377; 4080 Byway East). It has a selection of guided trips starting at $105 per person, including lunch and tasting fees.

Bus Bus tours from San Francisco are operated by **Gray Lines** (☎ 415-558-9400, 800-826-0202), which has a daily 9am departure from the Transbay Terminal, at 1st and Mission Sts. This 10-hour, $55 tour (reservations required) covers both Napa and Sonoma Valleys. It includes visits to two or three wineries plus a stop to shop and lunch on your own.

Limousine Fancy a drive in a 1947 Packard convertible limousine? In Napa, **Antique Tours Limousine** (☎ 707-226-9227; 2205 Loma Heights Rd) runs winery tours and more for $90 per hour (minimum four hours).

Beau Wine Tours (☎ 707-257-0887, 800-387-2328) charges $200 and up for four-hour winery tours in stretch limousines; they'll throw in gourmet picnic lunches for an extra $20 per person.

Getting There & Around

From San Francisco, public transportation can get you to the valleys, but it's not the ideal way of working your way around the wineries. Amtrak goes to Martinez (south of Vallejo), and from there you can catch a connecting bus to the main Napa Valley centers.

Bus For door-to-door service ($35 each way) to or from San Francisco's SFO airport contact **Sonoma Airporter** (☎ 707-938-4246, 800-611-4246).

Greyhound (☎ 800-231-2222) runs twice daily from San Francisco's Transbay Terminal up through Napa Valley to Calistoga ($14 one way, three hours) via Oakland, Vallejo, Oakville and St Helena. Call for services north past Calistoga and to Sonoma.

Napa Valley Transit (☎ 800-696-6443) operates buses from the Vallejo Ferry Terminal through Napa Valley to Calistoga; the buses are labeled Route 10, and the fare to Calistoga is $2.10. The **Vine** (☎ 707-255-7631, 800-696-6443) is Napa Valley's local bus network, with a daily service between Calistoga, St Helena, Yountville and downtown Napa.

Golden Gate Transit (☎ 707-541-2000, 415-923-2000) bus No 90 runs from San Francisco to Sonoma ($2); catch it at 1st and Mission Sts, just across from the Transbay Terminal.

Once you're there, **Sonoma County Transit** (☎ 707-576-7433, 800-345-7433) has buses around the Sonoma Valley. Numerous buses run between Santa Rosa and Sonoma, stopping at Kenwood and Glen Ellen along the way.

Car & Motorcycle From San Francisco, take Hwy 101 north across the Golden Gate Bridge and continue to the Hwy 37 Vallejo/Napa exit in Novato. Follow Hwy 37 northeast for a few miles to Hwy 121 and continue north to the junction of Hwys 12 and 121.

For Sonoma Valley, take Hwy 12 north; for Napa Valley,take Hwy 12/121 east. Plan on a 60- to 70-minute drive if the traffic is light, two hours or more during morning and afternoon commute times.

Highway 12/121 splits just before the town of Napa: Hwy 121 turns left (north) and joins up with Hwy 29 (also known as the St Helena Hwy), while Hwy 12 merges with the southbound extension of Hwy 29. If you drive from San Francisco, keep in mind that

Hwy 29 backs up daily between 4pm and 7pm, which will slow your return.

From the East Bay, take Hwy 80 east to reach Hwy 29. From Santa Rosa, take Hwy 12 east to access the northern end of Sonoma Valley. From Petaluma and Hwy 101, take Hwy 116 east toward Sonoma.

Sonoma Valley

'Slow-noma,' the locals' term for their relaxing, livable wine town, hints at the low-key charms of the 17mi-long Sonoma Valley. With its family-owned wineries and quiet rural back roads, the 'Valley of the Moon' (Jack London's literary name for the region) can be a more enjoyable place to wander around than the larger and more crowded Napa Valley.

The town of Sonoma, at the southern end of the valley, is surrounded by wineries and has a fascinating history. Santa Rosa, at the northern end, is the valley's workaday urban center. The main road through the valley is the Sonoma Hwy (Hwy 12), but make an effort to explore some of the quiet lanes and roads just off the highway.

If you have excess energy after visiting the Sonoma Valley wineries, you can drive northwest to the small, high-quality wineries around Healdsburg and Geyserville, and along the Russian River near Guerneville (for more details, see Russian River in the North Coast chapter).

SONOMA VALLEY WINERIES

The wine is just as good as Napa Valley's, but the wineries in Sonoma Valley are generally less crowded, and free tastings are still the norm. If you don't have a car, the town of Sonoma makes a good base, as there are several wineries within easy bicycling distance of the town center.

You can purchase winery maps and load up on discount coupons at the southern branch of the **Sonoma Valley Visitors Bureau** (☎ 707-935-4747; open 9am-5pm daily), off Hwy 121 on the grounds of the Viansa winery.

The following wineries are listed in south–north order, beginning a few miles south of the town of Sonoma. Give yourself at least five hours to visit the valley from bottom to top.

SONOMA VALLEY & SONOMA

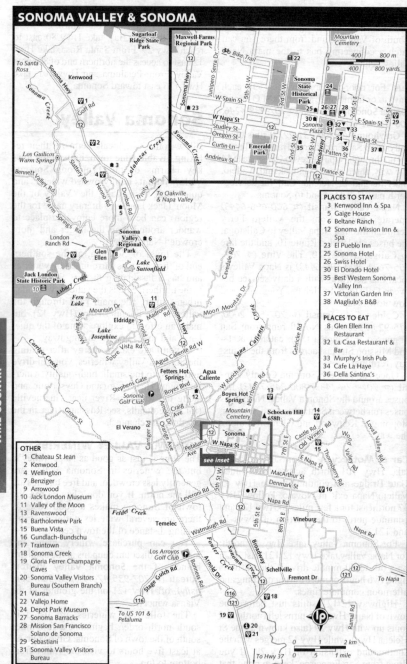

PLACES TO STAY
3 Kenwood Inn & Spa
5 Gaige House
6 Beltane Ranch
12 Sonoma Mission Inn & Spa
23 El Pueblo Inn
25 Sonoma Hotel
26 Swiss Hotel
30 El Dorado Hotel
35 Best Western Sonoma Valley Inn
37 Victorian Garden Inn
38 Magliulo's B&B

PLACES TO EAT
8 Glen Ellen Inn Restaurant
32 La Casa Restaurant & Bar
33 Murphy's Irish Pub
34 Cafe La Haye
36 Della Santina's

OTHER
1 Chateau St Jean
2 Kenwood
4 Wellington
7 Benziger
9 Arrowood
10 Jack London Museum
11 Valley of the Moon
13 Ravenswood
14 Bartholomew Park
15 Buena Vista
16 Gundlach-Bundschu
17 Traintown
18 Sonoma Creek
19 Gloria Ferrer Champagne Caves
20 Sonoma Valley Visitors Bureau (Southern Branch)
21 Viansa
22 Vallejo Home
24 Depot Park Museum
27 Sonoma Barracks
28 Mission San Francisco Solano de Sonoma
29 Sebastiani
31 Sonoma Valley Visitors Bureau

Springtime brings color to the fertile Sonoma wine country

Chardonnay grapevines, Napa Valley

Napa Valley wine ready for export

A sunrise balloon ride is a magical way to see the Napa Valley

Waterfall outside Mendocino

Wildflower explosion along the rugged Sonoma coastline

Harbor seals, North Coast

The water may be cold in Bodega Bay, but hey, surf's up!

Viansa

Whether you're headed to Sonoma or Napa, this is the first major winery on the road north from San Francisco. As a result, this small hilltop winery (☎ 707-935-4700; 25200 Arnold Dr) overlooking Hwy 121 is flooded with visitors on summer weekends. Still, the views are idyllic and the wines and Italian marketplace are worth stopping for. Guided vineyard tours ($5; reservations advised) leave at 11am and 2pm daily.

Gloria Ferrer Champagne Caves

The inspirations at Gloria Ferrer (☎ 707-996-7265; 23555 Hwy 121, Sonoma) are Spanish and Catalan culture, in addition to sparkling chardonnay and pinot wines. The Ferrer family came from Barcelona to Sonoma in 1982 and opened this location in 1986. The tasting room operates more like a wine bar, with glasses ($4 to $7) and full bottles ($18 to $50) that you can enjoy on the sunny hilltop patio.

Sonoma Creek

This is the archetypal no-frills family-run winery. Sonoma Creek (☎ 707-938-3031; 23355 Millerick Rd, Sonoma) puts a higher premium on quality wines than on elaborate displays, and is rarely overcrowded. The tasting room is open from 10am to 4pm on weekends, April to September only. There aren't many signs from the highway; look for Millerick Rd where Hwys 12 and 121 converge.

Gundlach-Bundschu

One of the valley's oldest and most pleasant wineries, Gundlach-Bundschu (☎ 707-938-5277; 2000 Denmark St, Sonoma) was founded by a Bavarian immigrant, Jacob Gundlach, in 1858. It's not surprising, then, that Rieslings and gewürztraminers are the signature varietals. The 1999 cabernet franc is also recommended.

The winery is reached by a winding road and has a peaceful lake and sedate hiking trails. Free tastings are offered daily between 11am and 4:30pm.

Buena Vista

California's oldest premium winery (☎ 707-938-1266; 18000 Old Winery Rd, Sonoma) dates back to 1857, when it was purchased by the pioneering Hungarian vintner Count Ágoston Haraszthy. It has a fine old building

with art displays and is set in shady wooded surroundings. Tastings ($5) are offered between 10:30am and 5pm daily. The free self-guided tour is recommended; guided tours leave most days at 11am and 2pm (reservations advised).

Bartholomew Park

The wines here are as good as any (tastings $3). What makes Bartholomew Park (☎ 707-935-9511; 1000 Vineyard Lane off Castle Rd, Sonoma) stand out is the 3.5mi loop hike through the vineyard grounds. The Palladian Villa at the winery's entrance is a turn-of-the-20th-century replica of Count Haraszthy's original residence; you can visit it between 10am and 4pm on Wednesdays and weekends.

Ravenswood

'No Wimpy Wines' is the official slogan at this low-key winery in the hills above Sonoma (☎ 707-933-2332; 18701 Gehricke Rd off Lovall Valley Rd, Sonoma). Zinfandels are what Ravenswood is famous for, including the superb 1999 Sonoma County zinfandel. Tastings are $4.

Sebastiani

There are regular guided tours of this venerable old winery in the heart of the town of Sonoma (☎ 707-938-5532; 389 4th St E). It was founded by monks in 1825 and purchased in 1904 by Samuele Sebastiani. Free tastings are offered between 10am and 5pm daily.

WINE COUNTRY

Valley of the Moon

There are few wineries immediately north of Sonoma town until you reach this modern, relaxed winery (☎ 707-996-6941; 777 Madrone Rd, Glen Ellen), which is just far enough off busy Hwy 12 to escape heavy traffic. The winery building is not much to look at, but the merlot, zinfandel and vintage port are superb. Free tastings are offered between 10am and 4:30pm daily.

Arrowood

Back on Hwy 12, Arrowood (☎ 707-938-5170; 14347 Hwy 12, Glen Ellen) is a small boutique winery whose founder, Richard Arrowood, helped to establish Chateau St Jean. Though the Arrowood tasting room is nondescript, the quality of its hand-crafted wines is undeniable. Tastings cost $5 ($10 for reserve wines) and are offered between 10am and 4:30pm daily.

Benziger

On the road up to Jack London State Historic Park, this interesting and educational winery (☎ 707-935-3000, 888-490-2739; 1883 London Ranch Rd, Glen Ellen; open 10am-5pm daily) includes a do-it-yourself walk and a 45-minute tram tour through the grapevines (reservations advised). There's also a picnic area. Unfortunately, not all the free tasting wines are up to snuff – it's worth paying $5 to sample the reserve collection.

Wellington

There are no gimmicks at this small workaday operation (☎ 707-939-0708; 11600 Dunbar Rd, Glen Ellen) just off Hwy 12. A quality selection of wines are served free, with no fuss, between 11am and 5pm daily. Wellington is known for its ports (including a sweet white variety) and cabernet sauvignons.

Kenwood

Since its founding in 1970, Kenwood (☎ 707-833-5891; 9592 Hwy 12, Kenwood) has gained a reputation as a quality small-scale operation. Free tastings are offered between 10am and 4:30pm daily, though it's worth the $5 fee to sample from the reserve list. Notables include the 1998 Massara merlot and the stellar 1997 Artist Series cabernet sauvignon.

Chateau St Jean

There's a short self-guided tour of this beautiful, sprawling winery (☎ 707-833-4134; 8555 Hwy 12, Kenwood), which is noted for its whites (the gewürztraminer is especially good) and for its pleasant picnic area. Free tastings are offered between 10am and 5pm daily. The chateau itself dates from 1923 and, thanks to its postcard-perfect features, attracts large crowds of admirers on summer weekends.

Matanzas Creek

Though it's not worth a detour in itself, this winery (☎ 707-528-6464; 6097 Bennett Valley Rd, Santa Rosa) is recommended if you're driving to Sonoma from Santa Rosa and would rather travel via back roads than on busy Hwy 12. The grounds – including a fragrant lavender garden – are serene. Merlots and syrahs are Matanzas' strengths. Tastings ($5) are offered between 10am and 4:30pm daily.

SONOMA

The small town of Sonoma (population 9350) makes an excellent base for exploring the surrounding vineyards. The town can be oppressively crowded on summer weekends, when traffic clogs the otherwise peaceful streets that border green and leafy Sonoma Plaza. This plaza – plus the adjacent mission and 19th-century barracks – loudly proclaims the town's Mexican heritage.

Sonoma has celebrations, cook-offs, concerts and wine auctions throughout the year. Check with the visitors bureau for details.

History

Believe it or not, Sonoma was the site of a second American revolution, this time against Mexico. In 1846, California was an uneasy place. Mexico had neither the resources nor the energy to effectively manage far-flung centers such as Sonoma, and the growing number of American settlers was leading to increased tension.

General Mariano Guadalupe Vallejo, the last Mexican governor of California, suggested that an American takeover was in the best interests of the region. Sensing an opening, American frontiersmen occupied the lightly guarded Sonoma presidio and declared independence. They dubbed California the Bear Flag Republic, after the battle flag they had fashioned. The unfortunate Vallejo was thereafter bundled off to imprisonment in Sacramento.

Despite its early success, the republic was short-lived. Only a month later the Mexican-American War broke out and California was taken over by the US government. The abortive revolt did, however, give California its state flag, which features a bear and still proclaims 'California Republic.'

Vallejo, whose name pops up all over the town, was soon back in Sonoma and continued to play a major role in the development of the region. He was elected to the first state senate in 1850 and was mayor of Sonoma from 1852 to 1860.

Orientation & Information

The Sonoma Hwy (Hwy 12) runs through the center of town. The spacious **Sonoma Plaza**, laid out by General Vallejo in 1834, is the heart of the small downtown area. It's lined with hotels, restaurants and shops.

The helpful **Sonoma Valley Visitors Bureau** (☎ 707-996-1090; **W** www.sonoma valley.com; 453 1st St E; open 9am-5pm daily), on the east side of the plaza, arranges accommodations (no booking fee) and has a wealth of information on local festivals and events, most of which is also available at its website.

Sonoma Plaza & Around

Smack in the middle of the plaza, the mission revival–style **City Hall** (1906–08) has identical facades on all four sides. It's said this was because businesses around the plaza all demanded that City Hall face in their direction. In the northeast corner of the plaza, the **Bear Flag Monument** marks Sonoma's brief moment of revolutionary glory.

Interesting buildings around the plaza include the **Sebastiani Theatre** (476 1st St E), a fine example of a 1934 mission revival cinema that still screens first-run films. Just off the plaza, the **Blue Wing Inn** (139 E Spain St) is thought to have been built by General Vallejo around 1840 to house visiting soldiers and travelers. It later served as a hotel, saloon and stagecoach depot.

The north side of the plaza is lined with some interesting buildings. Next to the Sonoma Barracks, the **Toscano Hotel** (20 E Spain St) started life as a store and library in

the 1850s and became a hotel in 1886. Today you can peek into the lobby 10am to 5pm daily. Free guided tours are given 1pm to 4pm on weekends and Mondays.

Vallejo's first Sonoma home, **La Casa Grande**, was built around 1835 on this side of the plaza, but most of it burned down in 1867. La Casa Grande had a variety of uses after the Vallejo family moved to its new home. Today, the only remains are of the servants' quarters, where the general's Native American servants were housed.

Sonoma State Historical Park

The mission, the nearby Sonoma Barracks and the Vallejo Home are all part of Sonoma State Historical Park (☎ 707-938-1519; combined admission $1; all buildings open 10am-5pm daily).

The **Mission San Francisco Solano de Sonoma** (E Spain St), at the northeast corner of the plaza, was built in 1823, in part to forestall the Russian colony on the coast at Fort Ross from moving inland. The mission was the 21st and final California mission to be founded and the only one built during the Mexican period (the rest were founded by the Spanish). It marks the northernmost point on the El Camino Real (for more information, see the boxed text 'The Missions' in the Facts about California chapter). Five rooms of the original mission remain. The mission's chapel – the highlight of a visit – dates from 1841.

The adobe **Sonoma Barracks** (E Spain St) were built by Vallejo between 1836 and 1840 to house Mexican troops. They later became American military quarters before starting a long and varied civilian life. Now a museum, the barracks show displays on life during the Mexican and American periods.

A half mile northwest of the plaza, the **Vallejo Home**, otherwise known as Lachryma Montis (Latin for 'Tears of the Mountain'), was built in between 1851 and '52 for General Vallejo. It took its name from the spring on the property; the Vallejo family later made a handy income piping this water supply down to the town. The property remained with the Vallejo family until 1933, when it was purchased by the state of California. It still retains many original pieces of Vallejo furniture. A bike path leads to the house from the town center.

WINE COUNTRY

Depot Park Museum

Hidden away two blocks north of the plaza, the Depot Park Museum (☎ 707-938-1762; admission free; open 1pm-4pm Wed-Sun) has art and historical exhibits. The adjacent park hosts a farmers market every Friday from 9am to noon.

Traintown

At Traintown (☎ 707-938-3912; 20264 Broadway; open 10am-5pm daily summer, Fri-Sun only mid-Sept–late-May), 1mi south of the plaza, a miniature steam engine makes 20-minute trips for $3.75. There's also a Ferris wheel ($1.50), merry-go-round ($1) and petting zoo. Kids love it here.

Activities

Bicyclists can get trail maps and solid advice at **Sonoma Valley Cyclery** (☎ 707-935-3377; 20093 Broadway), which also rents bicycles for $6 per hour or $25 per day.

If you're into horseback riding, you can choose from a variety of trails with the **Sonoma Cattle Company** (☎ 707-996-8566), which operates year-round. Two-hour rides through Jack London State Historic Park or Sugarloaf Ridge State Park are $55 per person. Reservations are required.

Tennis fans can use the courts at the Sonoma Valley High School (☎ 707-933-4010; 20000 Broadway) after 5pm weekdays and on weekends.

Places to Stay

Camping The nearest campground is the 50-site **Sugarloaf Ridge State Park** (☎ 707-833-5712; reservations 800-444-7275; 2605 Adobe Canyon Rd; sites $15), just north of Kenwood.

Hotels & Motels There are few true budget options in the town of Sonoma.

El Pueblo Inn (☎ 707-996-3651, 800-900-8844; 896 W Napa St; rooms midweek/weekends from $95/140), six long blocks west of the plaza, is an above-average motel with clean rooms and a swimming pool.

Best Western Sonoma Valley Inn (☎ 707-938-9200, 800-334-5784; 550 2nd St W; rooms midweek $115-145, weekends $170-205), two blocks southwest of the plaza, has a pool and rooms that are clean and comfortably functional.

There are a number of stylish older hotels right on the plaza. **Swiss Hotel** (☎ 707-938-2884; 18 W Spain St; rooms midweek $100-120, weekends $120-180) is a fine old property that has just five elegant rooms, all different and all with wavy floors and walls to show just what a historic place it is.

The **Sonoma Hotel** (☎ 707-996-2996; 110 W Spain St; rooms $110-225) occupies a grand old 1880s building that was completely (and tastefully) renovated a few years ago.

El Dorado Hotel (☎ 707-996-3030; 405 1st St W; rooms midweek/weekends $165/205) is equally appealing. Most rooms have balconies, and there's a pool.

B&Bs The four-room **Magliulo's B&B** (☎ 707-996-1031; 681 Broadway; rooms midweek/weekends with shared bath $95/110, with private bath $105/135) is comfortable enough and just a short walk south of Sonoma Plaza.

Victorian Garden Inn (☎ 707-996-5339; 316 E Napa St; rooms $120-205) has a fragrant back garden and a swimming pool. The rooms themselves are fairly plain and functional. There's a two-night minimum stay on weekends.

There are some good options north of town, in Glen Ellen. The plantation-style **Beltane Ranch** (☎ 707-996-6501; 11775 Sonoma Hwy; rooms $125-165) occupies a serene, wooded property. There are five rooms in the ranch house plus a secluded two-room cottage ($220).

Another recommended spot in Glen Ellen is **Gaige House** (☎ 707-935-0237; 13540 Arnold Dr; rooms $175-295), ideal for a romantic weekend getaway. The grounds are peaceful, there's a pool and some of the 15 rooms have working fireplaces.

Spa Hotels The perfect spot for an indulgent (and expensive) weekend getaway is **Sonoma Mission Inn & Spa** (☎ 707-938-9000, 800-862-4945; 18140 Hwy 12; rooms $185-950), a pampering pink retreat a few miles north of Sonoma. Facilities include a justly famous spa and a championship 18-hole golf course. Nonguests can use the spa facilities on weekdays and Sunday afternoons.

Kenwood Inn & Spa (☎ 707-833-1293; 10400 Hwy 12; rooms $250-395), north of Glen Ellen, has a reputation for luxury without attitude. With only a dozen rooms you can expect plenty of peace and quiet. The onsite spa is free for guests ($35 for nonguests).

Places to Eat

Sonoma Cheese Factory (☎ 707-996-1931), right on Sonoma Plaza, is the place to stock up for a picnic. It's the 'Home of Sonoma Jack Cheese' and has everything you'll need, including free cheese tastings.

Complete your picnic preparations at the local **farmers market**, held every Friday 9am to noon at Depot Park and, in summer, every Tuesday 5pm to 8pm right on the plaza.

Cafe La Haye (☎ 707-935-5994; 140 E Napa St; open Tues-Sun) is great for breakfast ($5 to $10) and light lunches ($7 to $15).

La Casa Restaurant & Bar (☎ 707-996-3406; 121 E Spain St), an inexpensive favorite near the mission, serves respectable Mexican fare from hefty burritos ($5 to $7) to chipotle salmon ($15) and chicken mole ($11).

Popular **Della Santina's** (☎ 707-935-0576; 133 E Napa St; dishes $7-20) is a small trattoria that cooks up delicious Tuscan food.

Murphy's Irish Pub (☎ 707-935-0660; 464 1st St E), in an alley off the plaza, has good pub grub like shepherd's pie ($9) and fish and chips ($9.50), beer and live music.

Even if you're not staying at the **Swiss Hotel** (☎ 707-938-2884; 18 W Spain St; dishes $10-20), the restaurant is recommended for its peaceful back patio and Italian cuisine with California accents.

Glen Ellen Inn Restaurant (☎ 707-996-6409; 13670 Arnold Dr; mains $15-30) is an excellent place to sample California cuisine in Glen Ellen.

Santé (☎ 707-938-9000; 18140 Hwy 12; dishes $15-40), at the Sonoma Mission Inn & Spa, is one of Sonoma Valley's 'in' places, and advance reservations are a must. The food is classic California cuisine. It's easier to get a table at **Big 3 Diner**, the spa's less expensive bistro.

JACK LONDON STATE HISTORIC PARK

Napa Valley has Robert Louis Stevenson, but Sonoma has Jack London. This park (☎ 707-938-5216; off Hwy 12; admission free, parking $3; open 9:30am-sunset daily) traces the last years of Jack London's short life (1876–1916).

Shuffling occupations from Oakland fisherman to Alaska gold prospector to Pacific yachtsman – and of course, novelist on the side – London finished by taking up farming. He bought Beauty Ranch in 1905 and moved there permanently in 1910; today, he would have been called an organic farmer. With his second wife, Charmian, he lived and wrote in a small cottage while his huge mansion, Wolf House, was being built. On the eve of its completion in 1913 it burned down. The disaster was a devastating blow, and although London toyed with the idea of rebuilding, he died before construction got under way.

After her husband's death, Charmian built the House of Happy Walls, which is now preserved as a Jack London **museum**. It's a half-mile walk from there to the remains of Wolf House, passing London's **grave** along the way. Other walking paths wind around the farm to the cottage where he lived and worked. Trails, some of them open to mountain bikes, lead further into the park. Be warned that thickets of poison oak await those who wander off the trails.

SANTA ROSA

Sprawling Santa Rosa (population 147,595) is the Wine Country's major population center and offers reasonably priced accommodations and easy access to Sonoma's wineries.

The city claims a world-famous cartoonist and a horticulturist as adopted sons, and there's enough in the way of museums and shops to keep you busy for an afternoon. Otherwise there's not much to detain travelers unless you're here in late July during the annual **Sonoma County Fair** (☎ 707-545-4200; **W** www.sonomacounty fair.com), held at the fairgrounds on Bennett Valley Rd.

Orientation & Information

The **Santa Rosa Visitors Bureau** (☎ 707-577-8674, 800-404-7673; 9 4th St; open 9am-5pm weekdays, 10am-3pm weekends) is in the railroad depot on the west side of Hwy 101, a few blocks from downtown (take the downtown Santa Rosa exit off Hwy 12 or Hwy 101).

The main shopping stretch is along 4th St, which abruptly ends at Hwy 101 but

WINE COUNTRY

reemerges on the other side in the historic **Railway Square** area. There are a number of downtown parking lots with free parking for the first 1½ hours.

Luther Burbank Home & Gardens

Luther Burbank (1849–1926), a pioneering horticulturist, developed many of his hybrid plant and tree species at his 19th-century Greek Revival home, at the corner of Santa Rosa and Sonoma Aves. The extensive gardens (*☎ 707-524-5445; admission free; open 8am-5pm daily*) are open to the public.

The house and adjacent **Carriage Museum** (*admission $3; open 10am-4pm Tues-Sun Apr-Oct*) have displays on Burbank's life and work.

Charles M Schulz Museum

Charles Schulz, creator of the Peanuts cartoon strip, was a long-term Santa Rosa resident. Schulz was born in 1922, published his first drawing in 1937, introduced the world to Snoopy and Charlie Brown in 1950 and continued producing Peanuts cartoons until a few months before his death in 2000.

This new museum (*☎ 707-579-4452; 2301 Hardies Lane; admission $8; open noon-5:30pm Mon, Wed-Fri, 10:30am-5:30pm Sat & Sun*) was under construction at the time of research and was scheduled to open in fall of 2002; call for hours and admission fees.

Snoopy's Gallery & Ice Arena

Just down the street from the Schulz museum, this commercial gallery and gift shop (*☎ 707-546-3385; 1667 W Steele Lane; admission free; open 10am-6pm daily*) has an awesome collection of Peanuts paraphernalia and products. It's 2½mi north of downtown off Hwy 101.

The adjacent **Redwood Empire Ice Arena** (*☎ 707-546-7147; admission $9, including skates*), formerly owned and deeply loved by Charles Schulz, is open to the public most afternoons (call for schedules).

Places to Stay

Scenic **Spring Lake Regional Park** (*☎ 707-539-8092, reservations 707-565-2267; 5585 Newanga Ave; sites $15*) has 29 campsites

that can be reserved for $7; you need to make the reservation between 10am and 3pm on weekdays. The campground is open daily from May to September; it's open weekends only from October to April. The park itself is open daily year-round. From downtown Santa Rosa, go east on 4th St, turn right on Farmer's Lane, go past the first Hoen St and turn left on the *second* Hoen St, go straight for a bit and then turn left on Newanga Ave. In total it's a 4mi drive.

Rooms are plain, simple and cheap at the **Astro Motel** (*☎ 707-545-8555; 323 Santa Rosa Ave; doubles $45-75*), beside Julliard Park and very close to downtown. If this place is full, there are plenty more motels and chain hotels to choose from on Santa Rosa Ave.

Hotel La Rose (*☎ 707-579-3200; 308 Wilson St; doubles $175*) is a historic hotel in the Railroad Square area.

Vintners Inn (*☎ 707-575-7350; 4350 Barnes Rd; doubles $175-195*) is in the same price range but is a few miles from downtown and surrounded by gardens rather than shopping malls.

Places to Eat

Almost any appetite can be satisfied downtown along 4th St, where there are also a number of bookstores and coffee bars.

The Cantina (*☎ 707-523-3663; 500 4th St; mains $5-8*) is a big and bright Mexican eatery with reasonable prices plus a Tuesday Taco Night with $2 margaritas and 25¢ tacos.

Creekside Bistro (*☎ 707-575-8839; 2800 4th St*) is a funny old place – at breakfast and lunch (6am to 2pm) the menu is all-American with most dishes under $8, while in the evenings (5pm to 9pm) the place becomes a popular French bistro with prices to match (confit of duck $17, fillet of salmon $16).

MiXX (*☎ 707-573-1344; 135 4th St at Davis St; dishes $14-20; closed Sun*), a pricier option, has an eclectic menu (lots of fish) and a wide choice of local wines.

For a change of pace, **Annapurna** (*☎ 707-579-8471; 535 Ross St; mains under $12*), off Mendocino Ave a few blocks north of 4th St, serves delicate curries, stews and other Indian and Nepalese delights, including vegetarian options.

Getting There & Away

Golden Gate Transit (☎ 707-541-2000, 415-923-2000) has daily buses from San Francisco's Transbay Terminal to Santa Rosa ($7, two hours) via Petaluma (Nos 72, 74 and 80).

Sonoma County Transit (☎ 707-576-7433, 800-345-7433) has local bus routes up the Sonoma Valley.

Greyhound (☎ 800-231-2222) has services from San Francisco to Santa Rosa and further north along Hwy 101.

Napa Valley

Napa Valley is longer than Sonoma Valley (around 30mi long), lies further inland and has more wineries.

Two roads run from north to south along the valley: Hwy 29 (the St Helena Hwy) and the more scenic Silverado Trail, just a mile or two east. If you're driving, it's worth the effort to get away from these main arteries – in particular, the congestion on Hwy 29 can be unbearable on weekends in summer and fall.

The roads that link the Silverado Trail with Hwy 29 – including the Yountville, Oakville and Rutherford crossroads – are generally bucolic and carry less vehicle traffic, while still providing access to wineries. If it's pure scenery you're after, the Oakville Grade and rural Trinity Rd (which leads southwest to Hwy 12 in Sonoma Valley) are curvaceous and beautiful. Mt Veeder Rd leads through pristine countryside scenery west of Yountville.

The city of Napa, at the valley's southern end, is the region's main economic hub but is of minimal interest. Better places for a pause are St Helena, Yountville and, at the northern end of the valley, Calistoga – a name famous for mineral water rather than wine.

NAPA VALLEY WINERIES

Many of the more than 230 wineries in Napa Valley are small operations without the facilities or desire to welcome visitors. Wineries that do offer tastings (called 'flights') are usually open from 10am or 11am to 4pm or 5pm daily. While many wineries in Sonoma Valley offer free tastings, Napa's wineries typically charge $5 for a flight of general-release wines and $10 for a flight of reserve wines.

The following wineries are listed in south–north order.

Domaine Carneros

This 137-acre estate (☎ 707-257-0101; 1240 Duhig Rd at Hwy 12/121, Napa; open 10am-6:30pm daily) is partly owned by French champagne maker Taittinger and is housed in an exotic-looking chateau. The winery itself is in the Carneros region, southwest of Napa and halfway to Sonoma Valley. There's a tasting room and visitor center. Tours are offered frequently throughout the day, year-round, and reservations are not required.

Hess Collection & Winery

Wine and art merge in this decidedly top-end winery (☎ 707-255-1144; 4411 Redwood Rd, Napa; open 10am-4pm daily), with a wonderful but expensive art gallery spread over three floors. Tastings are $3 (don't miss the cabernet sauvignon), and self-guided estate tours are free.

Domaine Chandon

French champagne maker Moët-Hennessey has several 'New World' wineries which make 'sparkling wine' (rather than champagne, as the French insist that champagne is only champagne when it comes from the Champagne region of France). The winery (☎ 707-944-8844; 1 California Dr, Yountville; open 10am-6pm daily), just off Hwy 29, has interesting displays, an informative tour, tastings ($8) and an exquisite restaurant (see Yountville Places to Eat later in this chapter).

Clos du Val

This winery (☎ 707-259-2200; 5330 Silverado Trail, Yountville) is not much to look at, but a visit is highly recommended if you enjoy quality zinfandels and cabernet sauvignons. Tastings ($5) are offered 10am to 5pm daily.

Stag's Leap

It was a Stag's Leap cabernet sauvignon that bested the French back in 1976, and they continue to produce exceptional wines. The winery (☎ 707-265-2441; 5766 Silverado Trail, Yountville) also makes an internationally acclaimed chardonnay. Tastings ($7 for general release, $30 for estate reserves) are offered 10am to 4:30pm daily.

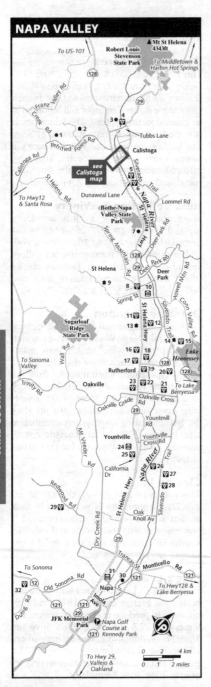

NAPA VALLEY

PLACES TO STAY		21	PlumpJack
2	Triple-S-Ranch	22	Opus One;
9	White Sulphur		Turnbull
	Springs Resort	23	Robert Mondavi
13	Harvest Inn	25	Domaine Chandon
14	Auberge de Soleil	26	Pine Ridge
		27	Stag's Leap
WINERIES		28	Clos du Val
4	Chateau Montelena	29	Hess Collection &
5	Clos Pegase		Winery
6	Sterling Vineyards	32	Domaine Carneros
8	Beringer		
11	Prager Port Works	OTHER	
12	V Sattui; Heitz	1	Petrified Forest
	Cellars	3	Old Faithful Geyser
15	Rutherford Hill	7	Bale Grist Mill State
16	Niebaum-Coppola		Historic Park
	Estate	10	Silverado Museum
17	Grgich Hills Cellar	24	Napa Valley
18	Beaulieu		Museum
19	Cakebread Cellars;	30	Napa Valley Wine
	St Supéry		Train
20	Villa Mt Eden	31	Copia

Pine Ridge

This is a small, low-key winery (☎ 707-253-7500, 800-575-9777; 5901 Silverado Trail, Yountville) noted for its merlots and cabernet sauvignons. Tastings are offered 11am to 5pm daily. It's $5 to sample the current releases, $10 for the reserve vintages. Guided winery tours are offered at 10:15am, 1pm and 3pm daily (reservations required).

PlumpJack

This superb winery (☎ 707-945-1220; 621 Oakville Cross Rd, Oakville) benefits from being just off the beaten path, on a crossroad linking the Silverado Trail with Hwy 29. PlumpJack's 2000 syrah is one of the best in the valley. Tastings ($5) are offered 10am to 4pm daily. The burgeoning Plump-Jack empire also includes restaurants in San Francisco and Lake Tahoe's Squaw Valley.

Robert Mondavi

This is a big commercial winery (☎ 888-766-6328; 7801 Hwy 29, Oakville) with a mission-style design, fronted by a Beniamino Bufano statue. Despite its size, and the sometimes oppressive crowds, it puts on informative tours of the wine-making process ($10), as well as tours that include catered picnics ($60), cheese tastings ($50), evening music and more – call for schedules and reservations.

Opus One

From Hwy 29 the winery building is hard to miss, looking like an Aztec pyramid or a crashed spaceship, depending on your disposition. Opus One (☎ 707-944-9442; 7900 Hwy 29, Oakville) is a partnership between Robert Mondavi and Baron Philippe de Rothschild, proprietor of Château Mouton Rothschild in France's Bordeaux region. This place is not for the financially challenged: it costs $25 to sample the award-winning reds and whites. Tasting rooms are open 10am to 4pm daily. The free winery tour is excellent and departs at 10:30am daily (reservations required).

Turnbull

Turnbull (☎ 800-887-6285; 8210 Hwy 29, Oakville) is a small boutique winery noted for its cabernet sauvignons – the 1997 and 1998 vintages are especially good. The winery has also received glowing reviews for its 2000 sauvignon blanc. The winery itself is unexceptional, but what Turnbull lacks in gimmicks it makes up for in quality. Tastings ($5) are offered between 10am and 4:30pm daily.

Cakebread Cellars

This lesser-known winery (☎ 707-963-5222; 8300 Hwy 29, Rutherford) produces some of the valley's finest whites, including its signature chardonnay and sauvignon blanc. There are no tours. Tastings ($5; $10 for reserve wines) are offered between 10am and 4:30pm daily.

St Supéry

The historic 1882 Atkinson House fronts this modern winery (☎ 707-963-4507, 800-942-0809; 8440 Hwy 29, Rutherford; open 9:30am-5pm daily), which has some of the most innovative winemaking displays in the valley. The guided tour is equally notable – it's easily one of the region's best. Tours cost $5 and depart at 11am, 1pm and 3pm daily; reservations are not required. Tastings are $5, or $10 for reserve wines.

Niebaum-Coppola Estate

The former Inglenook estate (☎ 707-968-1100; 1991 Hwy 29, Rutherford) was purchased by filmmaker Francis Ford Coppola in the mid-1980s, and since then it has consistently produced some of the valley's finest reds. An added bonus is the movie memorabilia from Coppola's films *The Godfather* and *Dracula*. Tastings ($7.50) are offered between 10am and 5pm daily.

Grgich Hills Cellar

This winery (pronounced **girr**-gich) has an unpretentious tasting room; it may be small, but these may be the wines with which you compare all the rest. Tours of the cellar (☎ 707-963-2784, 800-523-3057; 1829 Hwy 29, Rutherford; open 9:30am-4:30pm daily) are by appointment.

Beaulieu

Beaulieu, French for 'beautiful place' and named after an area in France, was founded in 1900 by a French immigrant. It is now one of the largest Napa wineries (☎ 707-967-5200; 1960 Hwy 29, Rutherford). Tastings are free at the visitor center, but cost $18 for five glasses at the reserve cellar. Both are open between 10am and 5pm daily.

Don't Screw with Perfection

Ask most folks in the Wine Country about corks, and you'll get a surprisingly passionate response: don't mess with them.

Nobody likes it when corks fail and turn fine wine into vinegar, or when they break apart upon opening, disintegrating into hard-to-extract crumbs. But consumers, it seems, are no less fond of the solutions offered by some wineries, namely, screw tops and synthetic corks. Portuguese oak bark has been used for centuries to stopper wines. Anything else strikes people as classless, more fitting for cheap bulk wines than for $120 premium vintages.

Napa Valley's PlumpJack winery made a splash in 2000 by releasing a few hundred cases of its premium wines with screw-top caps. But even the winery admits this was more of a publicity stunt than a long-term commitment to shifting away from natural cork.

This battle will ultimately be decided by economics rather than by nostalgia. It's estimated that 8% to 10% of all natural wine corks fail over a 10-year period, and wineries are fearful of losing customers who blame the winery rather than the cork producers for failed seals and tainted wines.

Villa Mt Eden

This winery (☎ 707-963-9100; 8711 Silverado Trail, Oakville) is small, which means that it's less crowded and a bit more down-to-earth than most Napa wineries. Free tastings are offered between 10am and 4pm daily. The winery itself is in a fine old building.

Rutherford Hill

Just past the Auberge de Soleil resort (see Rutherford later in this chapter), this hilltop winery (☎ 707-963-1871; 200 Rutherford Hill Rd, Rutherford) offers good views, shady picnic areas and a fine selection of general release ($5) and reserve ($10) wines to sample between 10am and 5pm daily. Walk-through tours of the cellars ($10) leave at 11:30am, 1:30pm and 3:30pm daily.

V Sattui

This 19th-century winery in an old stone building (☎ 707-963-7774; 1111 White Lane, St Helena; open 9am-5pm daily) loudly encourages picnicking: its deli sells great breads, cheeses and, of course, wine. Tastings are free; try the muscat or Madeira if they're on offer.

Heitz Cellars

When visiting Heitz (☎ 707-963-3542; 436 Hwy 29, St Helena) you're actually visiting only the small, elegant tasting room rather than the vineyards themselves. The 1996 Bella Oaks and 1997 Martha's Vineyard cabernet sauvignon are Heitz's signature releases, but don't ignore the fabulous Grignolio and Ink Grade ports. Tastings are offered between 11am and 4:30pm daily.

Prager Port Works

Eccentricity reigns at Prager (☎ 707-963-7678; 1281 Lewelling Lane, just off Hwy 29, St Helena; open 10am-4:30pm daily), with a tasting room that feels like an afterthought, a wall papered with foreign money and a window intentionally overrun by spider webs. Grab a tasting glass ($10) and sample the award-winning tawny and white ports, or a sweet golden muscat.

Beringer

Fronted by the regal 1883 Rhine House, Beringer (☎ 707-963-7115; 2000 Main St, St Helena) is the oldest continuously operating winery in Napa. It was founded by German brothers Jacob and Frederick Beringer in 1876 and survived Prohibition by manufacturing sacramental and medicinal wines. The free tour includes a visit to the extensive tunnels that burrow into the hill behind the winery. Tastings ($5) are offered between 9:30am and 4:30pm daily.

Sterling Vineyards

The gimmick at Sterling (☎ 707-942-3344; 1111 Dunaweal Lane, Calistoga; open 10:30am-4:30pm daily) is a gondola ride that carries you to the hilltop, which has superb views across the valley. The winery itself – modeled after a white-washed Greek villa – is architecturally interesting. A $6 ticket includes a tour and tasting.

Clos Pegase

This well-respected winery (☎ 707-942-4981; 1060 Dunaweal Lane, Calistoga) combines architecture, art and wine and is one of Napa Valley's highlights. Interesting sculptures dot the grounds of the 1987 Michael Graves–designed buildings, and modern art graces the visitor center. There are free tours at 11am and 2pm and tastings ($5) between 10:30am and 5pm daily.

Chateau Montelena

At the north end of the valley, Chateau Montelena (☎ 707-942-5105; 1429 Tubbs Lane, Calistoga; open 10am-4pm daily) has a beautiful lake with Chinese-style bridges and pavilions, a fine stone chateau and picnic grounds for winery customers. The tasting fee is $10; the estate cabernet sauvignons are especially notable.

NAPA

Napa (population 72,500) is the valley's workaday urban hub. There are interesting old buildings in the small downtown, plus a few good restaurants. But the main reasons to stop are more practical: rent a bike, visit the Copia wine center or perhaps board the Napa Valley Wine Train.

Orientation & Information

Napa's main drag, 1st St, is lined with shops and restaurants.

Napa is sandwiched between the Silverado Trail and the St Helena Hwy (aka Hwy 29).

Coming from San Francisco on Hwy 12/121, continue past the turnoff for Sonoma Valley and turn left (north) onto Hwy 29 (confusingly labeled Hwy 121/29 within the town limits). To reach the downtown area, exit at 1st St and follow it east.

The **Napa Valley Visitors Bureau** (☎ 707-226-7459; 1310 Napa Town Center; open 9am-5pm daily), hidden in a shopping mall between 1st and Pearl Sts, two blocks west of Main St, is the biggest and most active information center in the valley. The staff will make room reservations for you.

Things to See & Do
The main attraction is **Copia** (☎ 707-259-1600; W www.copia.org; 500 1st St; day passes $12.50; open 10am-5pm, closed Tues year-round & Wed Oct-Apr), a $50 million wine, food and cultural center that has brought a much-needed boost to Napa's downtown area. Day passes include access to the extensive organic gardens, art exhibits and wine programs. Tickets for film screenings, cooking classes, outdoor concerts and more are sold separately.

Napa Valley Bike Tours (☎ 707-255-3377; 4080 Byway East), just off Hwy 29, rents bicycles for $6/25 per hour/day. When business isn't too busy, the staff also offer one-way rentals: for an extra $25 you can ride to Calistoga, for example, and they will pick you up and return you and the bike to Napa.

Places to Stay
A central budget option is trusty **Travelodge** (☎ 707-226-1871; 853 Coombs Sts at 2nd St; rooms midweek/weekends $75/90).

The plain **Discovery Inn** (☎ 707-253-0892; 500 Silverado Trail; doubles $45-65), southeast of the town center on Hwy 121 is even cheaper.

John Muir Inn (☎ 707-257-7220, 800-522-8999; 1998 Trower Ave; rooms midweek/weekends $95/145), one of the nicer motel options, is at the corner of Trower Ave and Hwy 29.

Silverado Country Club (☎ 707-257-0200; 1600 Atlas Peak Rd; rooms $280-450) is the place to head if money is no object. This swank resort is in the hills 3½mi east of Napa. The resort has two golf courses, tennis courts and myriad swimming pools. From Hwy 29 turn right (east) on Trancas St

(which becomes Monticello Rd) and go left at Atlas Peak Rd.

Places to Eat
Downtown Joe's (☎ 707-258-2337; 902 Main St; breakfast $6-9, dinner $14-16), on the riverbank at the end of 2nd St, incorporates a microbrewery and restaurant, and operates from breakfast (pancakes and hefty omelets) to dinner (rosemary chicken $14).

Bistro Don Giovanni (☎ 707-224-3300; 4110 Hwy 29; mains $9-17) is a stylish Italian spot with a good wine list, delicious wood-oven-cooked pizzas and stellar risottos. Reservations are advised.

Vintner's Court (☎ 707-257-0200; 16 Atlas Peak Rd; meals around $30) is at the Silverado Country Club. If romance is called for and you're feeling flush, make advance dinner reservations here. The setting and service are impeccable, and the kitchen excels at creative California cuisine with strong Pacific Rim influences.

YOUNTVILLE
Yountville (pronounced **yawnt**-vill; population 2916), one of the larger towns in the valley, is 9mi north of Napa and 21mi south of Calistoga. Yountville straddles Hwy 29 (the St Helena Hwy), though most of its restaurants and shops are on Washington St, which runs parallel to and just east of the highway.

Yountville has banks, markets, a handful of places to stay and plenty of famous top-end restaurants, but otherwise St Helena and Calistoga, further north, make better bases.

Yountville's modernist 40,000-sq-ft **Napa Valley Museum** (☎ 707-944-0500; 55 Presidents Circle; admission $4.50; open 10am-5pm Wed-Mon) chronicles Napa's cultural history and showcases local paintings. It's off California Dr.

The **Napa Valley Tourist Office** (☎ 707-944-1558; 6488 Washington St) has all the usual maps and accommodation pamphlets.

Places to Stay
Yountville is a pricey place to stay.

Napa Valley Lodge (☎ 707-944-2468; 2230 Madison St; rooms $280-350), at the corner of Madison and Washington Sts, is a popular resort with terrace rooms and suites with fireplaces.

Equally nice but slightly less expensive, **Maison Fleurie** (☎ 707-944-2056; 6529 Yount St; rooms $115-250) has 13 rooms, a pool and a spa.

The 112-room **Villagio Inn & Spa** (☎ 707-944-8877; 6481 Washington St; rooms $210-450) has tennis courts, swimming pools and full health spa facilities.

Places to Eat

Live music, outdoor tables and a relaxed crowd are the hallmarks of **Pacific Blues Cafe** (☎ 707-944-4455; 6525 Washington St). It's not fancy, but then again, sometimes all you want is a hamburger ($8) and a beer.

Ristorante Piatti (☎ 707-944-2070; 6480 Washington St; pastas & pizzas $9-15), a branch of the popular California chain, features high-quality Italian fare.

Domaine Chandon (☎ 707-944-2892; 1 California Dr; mains $12-25), just off Hwy 29, is a recommended splurge, with delicious California cuisine served at tables set on a leafy patio. The restaurant is closed Tuesdays and in January. Reservations are strongly recommended.

French Laundry (☎ 707-944-2380; 6640 Washington St at Creek St) is an elegant Yountville eatery at which it's nearly impossible to get reservations. If you succeed, prepare yourself for a superb prix-fixe lunch ($115) or dinner ($135). The menu features traditional French dishes with a distinct California twist.

OAKVILLE

The tiny settlement of Oakville (population 300) is just a few miles north of Yountville. Though it has no sights to speak of, Oakville is well endowed with wineries (10 and counting).

It also has the **Oakville Grocery & Cafe** (☎ 707-944-8802; 7856 Hwy 29; sandwiches $5-8), just north of Oakville Cross Rd. It's one of the best gourmet delis in the Napa and Sonoma Valleys, with delicious sandwiches and a large selection of salads, breads and cheeses.

RUTHERFORD

Like Oakville, Rutherford (population 525) is neither a town nor a village but rather a loose-knit collection of wineries, private homes, and roadside antique and gift shops.

It also has one of the valley's most popular restaurants, **Auberge de Soleil** (☎ 707-963-1211; 180 Rutherford Hill Rd), off the Silverado Trail. This is a quintessential Wine Country dining experience – French with a California twist – and is priced accordingly. Other facilities include private cottages ($525 and up) carved into the hillside, a spa and swimming pool, tennis courts and an outside sculpture garden.

ST HELENA

Hwy 29 runs right through the small town of St Helena (pronounced ha-**lee**-na) and is called Main St in town. St Helena (population 6000) has many interesting old buildings and plenty of restaurants, but it can get uncomfortably busy on summer weekends.

The **chamber of commerce** (☎ 800-799-6456; 1010 Main St, Suite A; open 10am-5pm weekdays, 10am-3pm Sat) can help with information.

The **Silverado Museum** (☎ 707-963-3757; 1490 Library Lane; admission free; open noon-4pm Tues-Sun) has a fascinating collection of Robert Louis Stevenson memorabilia. In 1880 the famous author – at that time sick, penniless and unknown – stayed in an abandoned bunkhouse at the old Silverado Mine with his new wife, Fanny Osbourne. His novel *The Silverado Squatters* is based on his time there. To reach Library Lane, turn east off Hwy 29 at the Adams St traffic lights and cross the railway tracks.

Places to Stay

El Bonita Motel (☎ 707-963-3216; 195 Main St; rooms $110-160) boasts a swimming pool and pleasant grounds, and is a step above the average motel.

Hotel St Helena (☎ 707-963-4388; 1309 Main St; rooms $145-195), right in the center of town, dates from 1881 and has 18 rooms (some with private bathrooms).

Harvest Inn (☎ 707-963-9463, 800-950-8466; 1 Main St; rooms $240-550) is the classiest – and most expensive – choice in St Helena. It offers rooms and suites in a grand Tudor-style building and has two pools, well-tended gardens and lots of luxuries.

White Sulphur Springs Resort (☎ 707-963-8588; 3100 White Sulphur Springs Rd; rooms midweek $85-100, weekends $100-140, private cottages midweek/weekends $135/160), California's oldest resort, is a peaceful place, with hot springs, a swimming pool and a redwood grove.

Places to Eat
The **Model Bakery** (☎ 707-963-9731; 1357 Main St; closed Mon) serves great scones, muffins and coffee.

Armadillo's (☎ 707-963-8082; 1304 Main St; mains $7-12) is a bright Mexican restaurant with reasonable prices.

Tra Vigne (☎ 707-963-4444; 1050 Charter Oak Ave; mains $18-25), on the southern edge of town, just off Main St, is a stylish Italian restaurant with a reputation for some of the best food in the valley.

Cantinetta, in Tra Vigne's walled garden patio, is a deli and wine shop that serves quicker, less expensive meals than the main restaurant.

Wine Spectator Greystone Restaurant (☎ 707-967-1010; 2555 Main St; mains $16-28) is run by the renowned Culinary Institute of America. The menu is pure California, with a broad selection of wines and microbrews from Northern California.

CALISTOGA
Calistoga (population 5190) is probably the most attractive town in Napa Valley. It has numerous places to stay and eat and retains a 'small town' feel that is authentic, rather than forced.

'Calistoga' is synonymous with the bottled water that brandishes its name (Guiseppe Musante began bottling Calistoga mineral water here in 1924), and these natural hot springs have spawned a collection of spas where you can indulge in the local specialty, a hot mud bath.

It is said the town's curious name came from tongue-tied Sam Brannan, who in 1859 founded the town with the heartfelt belief that it would emulate the New York spa town of Saratoga, perhaps as the 'Calistoga' of 'Sara-fornia.'

Orientation & Information
Calistoga's shops and restaurants are strung along **Lincoln Ave**, stretching from the St Helena Hwy (Hwy 29/128) across to the Silverado Trail.

The **Chamber of Commerce & Visitors Center** (☎ 707-942-6333; 1458 Lincoln Ave; open 10am to at least 4pm daily) is behind the Old Railroad Depot.

Sam Brannan
Born in Maine in 1819, Sam Brannan was a larger-than-life character who roamed the US working in printing and newspapers. In 1845 he headed to California to found a Mormon colony. His passion for religious pioneering quickly faded, however, and in 1847 he founded San Francisco's first newspaper, The California Star. It was Sam Brannan who, in 1848, announced to the world that gold had been discovered in the Sierra foothills, sparking the gold rush. The healthy properties of Calistoga's spas and springs were his next discovery. His luck ran out toward the end of his colorful life, and he died penniless in 1888.

Things to See & Do
The small **City Hall**, on Washington St, was built in 1902 as the Bedlam Opera House. Today it houses administrative offices.

Across the street, and created by an ex-Disney animator, the **Sharpsteen Museum** (☎ 707-942-5911; 1311 Washington St; admission free; open 11am-4pm daily) has exhibits from the town's colorful history, and features a restored cottage from Brannan's original Calistoga resort. (The only Brannan cottage still at its original site is at 106 Wapoo Ave, near the Brannan Cottage Inn.)

Calistoga has a collection of **hot-spring spas** and **mud-bath emporiums** where you can be buried in hot mud and emerge much better for the experience.

Mud-bath packages take 60 to 90 minutes and cost $50 to $65. You start semisubmerged in hot mud, then take a shower, then soak in hot mineral water. An optional steam bath and a cooling towel-wrap follow. The treatment can be extended to include a massage, pushing the cost up to $120 or more.

Baths can be taken solo or, in some establishments, as couples. Variations can include thin mud baths (called 'fango' baths), herbal wraps, seaweed baths and all sorts of exotic massages. Discount coupons are sometimes available from the visitor center. It's wise to book ahead, especially on summer weekends.

The following spa centers in downtown Calistoga offer one-day packages. A few of them also offer accommodation (see Spa Hotels under Places to Stay).

WINE COUNTRY

Indian Springs (☎ 707-942-4913) 1712 Lincoln Ave

Nance's Hot Springs (☎ 707-942-6211) 1614 Lincoln Ave

Golden Haven Hot Springs (☎ 707-942-6793) 1713 Lake St

Lincoln Avenue Spa (☎ 707-942-5296) 1339 Lincoln Ave

Dr Wilkinson's Hot Springs (☎ 707-942-4102) 1507 Lincoln Ave

Getaway Adventures (☎ 707-942-0332, 800-499-2453; 1117 Lincoln Ave) rents bicycles for trips around the town and surrounding area for about $25 per day.

Bikes can be rented at similar rates from **Palisades Mountain Sports** (☎ 707-942-9687; 1330-B Gerrard St), behind the post office on Washington St.

CALISTOGA

To Silverado Trail & Robert Louis Stevenson State Park

Fischer Ave.

Wapoo Av

Grant Rd

Brannan St

To Napa County Fairgrounds

Stevenson St

Lake St

4th St

3rd St

2nd St

1st St

Fair Way

Napa River

Washington St

Gerrard St

Franklin St

Calistoga Gliderport

Berry St

Cedar St

Pioneer Park

To Petrified Forest, Old Faithful Geyser & Foothill House

Spring St

Myrtle St

Lincoln Ave

Hazel St

Pine St

128

29

Foothill Blvd

To St Helena & Napa

0   100   200 m
0   100   200 yards

PLACES TO STAY	OTHER
2 Comfort Inn	1 Golden Haven Hot Springs
4 Brannan Cottage Inn	6 Dr Wilkinson's Hot Springs
5 Nance's Hot Springs	7 Old Railroad Depot
11 Mount View Hotel; Catahoula	8 Chamber of Commerce & Visitors Center
12 Roman Spa Motel	9 Laundry
22 The Elms B&B	13 City Hall
23 Calistoga Inn & Brewery	16 Sharpsteen Museum
	17 Lincoln Avenue Spa
PLACES TO EAT	19 Palisades Mountain Sports
10 Puerta Vallarta	20 Post Office
14 Wappo Bar & Bistro	21 Bus Depot
15 Checkers	25 Getaway Adventures
18 Bosko's Trattoria	
24 Pacifico	

Places to Stay

Camping The **Napa County Fairgrounds** (☎ 707-942-5111; 1435 Oak St; tent/RV sites $12/20) is a few blocks northwest of the town center.

Bothe-Napa Valley State Park (☎ 707-942-4575, reservations 800-444-7275; Hwy 29; sites $15), 3mi south of Calistoga, offers slightly better scenery.

Hotels The creekside **Calistoga Inn & Brewery** (☎ 707-942-4101; 1250 Lincoln Ave; rooms midweek/weekends $75/100) is a historic hotel right in the center of town, with 18 simple rooms with shared bathroom. The attached restaurant and brewery are popular local hangouts.

Comfort Inn (☎ 707-942-9400; 1865 Lincoln Ave; rooms midweek/weekends from $70/110) is a bland but functional 55-room motel just north of the town center.

Triple-S-Ranch (☎ 707-942-6730; 4600 Mt Home Ranch Rd; open Apr-Dec), off Petrified Forest Rd about 3mi northwest of town, is a good budget option. Simple rustic cabins start at $65, which includes use of the swimming pool.

B&Bs Next to Pioneer Park, **The Elms B&B** (☎ 707-942-9476; 1300 Cedar St; rooms weekdays $120-155, weekends $125-185) has seven comfortable and well-equipped rooms, plus a front porch perfect for passing time on leisurely summer afternoons.

Brannan Cottage Inn (☎ 707- 942-4200; 109 Wapoo Ave; rooms $115-175) is on the National Register of Historic Places; reservations can be hard to come by.

Foothill House (☎ 707-942-6933, 800-942-6933; 3037 Foothill Blvd; rooms $150-325, cottage $250), a few miles north of town on Hwy 128, has a mix of comfortable inn rooms and a private two-bedroom cottage.

Spa Hotels One of Calistoga's longest running resorts – looking not unlike a Florida retirement community – **Indian Springs** (☎ 707-942-4913; 1712 Lincoln Ave) offers mud baths ($75), mineral baths ($65), massages ($50 and up) and a battalion of facials, masks and exfoliation regimes. Accommodation is in stand-alone bungalows for two ($265/295 midweek/ weekends), four ($315/360) or six ($450/ 500) people.

Elegant **Mount View Hotel** (☎ 707-942-6877; 1457 Lincoln Ave; rooms weekdays $150, weekends from $185) is a popular option that combines historic style with modern facilities (mud baths and swimming pool). Book early to reserve the cottage with private outdoor Jacuzzi ($325).

Nance's Hot Springs (☎ 707-942-6211; 1614 Lincoln Ave; rooms midweek/weekends $75/120) has rooms with kitchenettes in a white-washed building that mixes Spanish ranchero style with 1950s film noir. The Nance's Works treatment ($85) includes a mud bath, mineral bath, blanket wrap and 30-minute massage.

Roman Spa Motel (☎ 707-942-4441; 1300 Washington St; rooms midweek/weekends $95/135) has tranquil gardens, mineral pools and an outdoor swimming pool, but the rooms are plain. The onsite spa is known as **The Oasis** (☎ 707-942-2212).

Places to Eat

Trendy **Pacifico** (☎ 707-942-4400; 1237 Lincoln Ave; open 10am-10pm Mon-Fri, 11am-10pm Sat & Sun; mains $8-14) has excellent and reasonably priced Mexican food, including a tasty weekend brunch ($9 to $14).

More humble, but equally good, Mexican food is served at no-frills **Puerta Vallarta** (1473 Lincoln Ave).

Calistoga Inn & Brewery (☎ 707-942-4101; 1250 Lincoln Ave; mains $6-14) offers tasty microbrews and moderately priced California cuisine, as well as live music on summer weekends.

Checkers (☎ 707-942-9300; 1414 Lincoln Ave; pizzas $8-14, mains $9-15) is part gourmet pizzeria and part Italian bistro, with a good local wine list.

Bosko's Trattoria (☎ 707-942-9088; 1364 Lincoln Ave) is a popular pizzeria and pasta spot.

At **Wappo Bar & Bistro** (☎ 707-942-4712; 1226-B Washington St; mains $8-19; closed Tues) you can dine on an open-air patio, perfect for warm summer evenings. The menu is a mix of Asian, French, South American and California cuisines, all delicious.

Catahoula (☎ 707-942-2275; 1457 Lincoln Ave; mains $12-20), in the Mount View Hotel, is an upscale eatery offering hearty Cajun fare. The best seats are those at the bar (which has a less expensive dinner

menu), where you can watch owner-chef Jan Birnbaum, a native of Louisiana, at work.

AROUND CALISTOGA
Bale Grist Mill State Historic Park
There are good picnicking opportunities at this small state park (☎ 707-963-2236;

A Harbin Memoir

If you're looking for a nontraditional spa experience, consider a trip to Harbin Hot Springs. My one and only experience at Harbin started when I signed up for a Water Dance massage, mostly because the name sounded so mysterious. I was directed to the communal mineral pool, where I met a tall Swedish man with long flowing hair who was stark naked. We shook hands politely. He asked me to undress. Um, did he mean right there?

Conquering my modesty, I disrobed and eased into the pool, where a dozen other naked people paid me little attention. I began wondering what sort of massage I had gotten myself into.

For the next hour the Swedish man and I engaged in something not unlike a naked water ballet. My body was contorted, and I was grabbed, pulled, whisked and plunged under and through the warm water. My initial nervousness turned into stoic acceptance, which in turn became relaxation. By the end I was honestly enjoying this underwater pummeling, despite the odd looks from a friend who wondered why I was dancing in the pool with a naked man.

Harbin Hot Springs (☎ 707-987-2477, massage appointments 707-987-0422) is about 4mi beyond Middletown, which in turn is 12mi directly north of Calistoga, beyond the Robert Louis Stevenson State Park. Run by the Heart Consciousness Church, it offers all the usual spa stuff in 'clothes optional' pools. There's also a simple vegetarian restaurant (for spa guests only).

Dorm accommodations cost $35 to $50, and you must bring your own linen. Camping facilities are also available, as are rooms with shared bathroom (midweek/weekends $95/140), rooms with private bathroom ($110/165) and fully equipped cabins ($155 and up).

Scott McNeely

WINE COUNTRY

admission $2; open 10am-5pm daily), which features a 36ft wheel, dating from 1846, that once ground local farmers' grain to flour. In early October a 'living history' festival, Old Mill Days, is celebrated on the grounds. There's also a mile-long hiking trail that leads to the adjacent **Bothe-Napa Valley State Park**.

The mill and park are on Hwy 29/128 midway between St Helena and Calistoga.

Old Faithful Geyser

Calistoga's slightly smaller version of Yellowstone's Old Faithful spouts off on a fairly regular 45-minute cycle, shooting boiling water 60ft into the air.

The geyser (*☎ 707-942-6463; 1299 Tubbs Lane; admission $6; open 9am-6pm daily summer, 9am-5pm winter)* is about 2mi north of town, off the Silverado Trail. Local newspapers often have discount coupons.

Petrified Forest

Three million years ago a volcanic eruption at nearby Mt St Helena blew down a stand of redwood trees between Calistoga and Santa Rosa. The trees all fell in the same direction, pointing away from the center of the blast, and were covered in ash and mud.

Over the millennia the trunks of these mighty trees were turned into stone and gradually the overlay eroded away to expose the trunks. The first stumps were discovered in 1870, and a monument marks the visit by Robert Louis Stevenson in 1880. He described his visit in *The Silverado Squatters*.

The forest (*☎ 707-942-6667; 4100 Petrified Forest Rd; admission $4; open 10am-6pm daily summer, 10am-5pm winter)* is 5mi northwest of town off Hwy 128.

Robert Louis Stevenson State Park

The volcano cone of Mt St Helena, long-extinct, closes off the end of the valley, 8mi north of Calistoga, in this undeveloped state park (*☎ 707-942-4575; admission free)* at the end of Hwy 29.

It's a tiring 5mi climb to the peak's 4343ft summit, but clear weather will reward walkers with superb views. The park includes the site of the old Silverado Mine where Stevenson and his wife, Fanny, honeymooned in 1880.

North Coast

From Bodega Bay and the beautiful Russian River area up to the Oregon border, California's rugged North Coast holds some of the state's most dramatic scenery, from forests of old-growth redwoods to a rocky, brooding coastline still being carved by crashing waves. Other highlights are quaint historic towns and an individualistic, bohemian culture very different from that of the big cities.

North of San Francisco's Golden Gate Bridge, the Pacific Coast Hwy (Hwy 1) and Hwy 101 fork. Heading north Hwy 1 snakes along the coast past tiny coastal towns and magnificent scenery – rocky, windswept beaches; craggy cliffs punctuated by coves, bays, rivers and quiet estuaries; grasslands that are green in winter, golden in summer and full of wildflowers in spring; and ancient forests of redwood trees. Meanwhile, Hwy 101 heads north through a series of fertile inland valleys sprinkled with vineyards before rejoining Hwy 1 at Leggett, then winding along the Redwood Coast up into Oregon.

Summer on the coast tends to be pleasantly cool and fresh but often foggy. Winter is usually cold and rainy. Spring can be windy. Autumn is an ideal time to trek northward, when the sky is clear and the weather balmy.

Russian River

Less than two hours' drive from San Francisco, the lower Russian River region has magnificent scenery, with water coursing through a hilly landscape of vineyards, tiny towns and coastal redwood forest. Named for early-19th-century sea otter pelt hunters and settlers, the Russian River begins in the mountains north of Ukiah and Hopland then, just south of Healdsburg, it makes a sharp turn west, toward the ocean.

The entire valley offers plentiful outdoor recreation and a slower pace of life, even when crowded during summer. Towns near the lower river reaches include Guerneville, a predominantly gay getaway, little Rio Nido, Forestville, Monte Rio and Duncans Mills. Further away from the river are Occidental, 7mi south of Monte Rio via the Bohemian Hwy, and Sebastopol, a thriving

Highlights

- Redwood National Park – awe-inspiring ancient forests of the tallest trees on Earth
- Russian River Valley – lazy days of cycling, canoeing and kayaking through the wine country
- Mendocino Coast – beaches, lighthouses and towns tenaciously hugging windswept bluffs
- Kinetic Sculpture Race – an amphibious race featuring the quirkiest vehicles you'll ever see

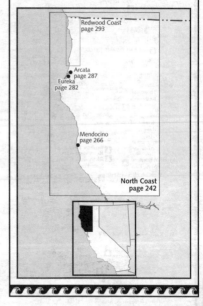

farm town and gateway to the region, off Hwy 101 just 55mi north of San Francisco.

Getting There & Around

River Rd, connecting Hwy 101 just north of Santa Rosa with Hwy 1 on the coast at Jenner, is the main artery of the lower Russian River region. Hwy 116, coming northwest from Cotati through Sebastopol and on to Guerneville, is another principal route.

Sonoma County Transit (☎ 707-576-7433, 800-345-7433) has a daily bus No 20

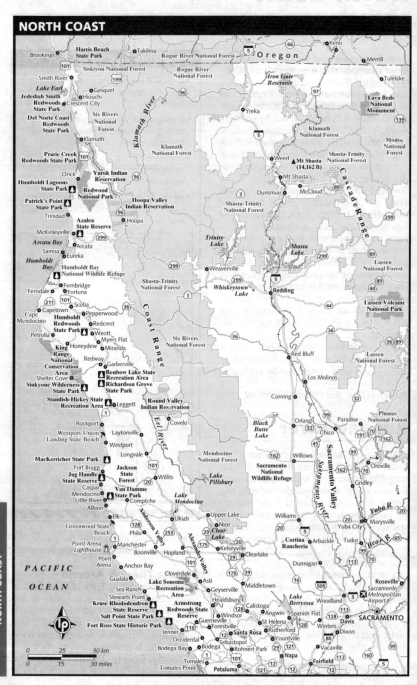

connecting Santa Rosa and the Russian River area, plus route No 28 serving Guerneville, Rio Nido, Monte Rio and Duncans Mills Monday to Friday. On Saturday and Sunday in summer, route No 29 travels from Santa Rosa via Sebastopol and Freestone to Bodega Bay, then heads north on Hwy 1 to Jenner and runs inland along Hwy 116 past Guerneville and other small river towns.

Mendocino Transit Authority *(MTA; ☎ 707-462-1422, 800-696-4682)* has a daily South Mendocino Coast No 95 bus that comes down from Point Arena, turning inland south of Bodega Bay, stopping at Bodega town, Freestone and Sebastopol en route to Santa Rosa. It goes south every morning and returns every afternoon. Be sure to flag this bus down at smaller stops along the designated route.

SEBASTOPOL

In a countryside of rolling hills, vineyards and apple orchards, Sebastopol (population 8100) is famous for its antiques, wineries and Gravenstein apples. Where Hwys 116 and 12 meet is Sebastopol's major intersection. Hwy 116 is called Main St in the middle of town, where it is the primary commercial street; southbound highway traffic uses Main St, and northbound traffic uses Petaluma Ave, one block to the east. At the north end of Main St, the road makes a 90° turn and becomes Healdsburg Ave, continuing north out of town, where it's called Gravenstein Hwy N, toward Forestville and Guerneville. At the south end of town, Main St becomes Gravenstein Hwy S and heads southeast toward Hwy 101.

The **Sebastopol Area Chamber of Commerce & Visitors Center** *(☎ 707-823-3032, 877-828-4748; W www.sebastopol.org; 265 S Main St; open 9am-5pm Mon-Fri)* provides maps and information and, next door, has some historical exhibits. Annual events include the mid-April Apple Blossom Parade, Gravenstein Apple Fair in August and Celtic Festival in late September.

Things to See & Do

Sebastopol Fine Wine Co *(☎ 707-829-9378; 6932 Sebastopol Ave; open 11am-7pm Mon-Fri, 10am-6pm Sat, 10am-4pm Sun)* is a congenial wine shop and tasting room on the plaza.

East of the plaza, **Sebastopol Center for the Arts** *(☎ 707-829-4797; 6780 Depot St; admission free; open 10am-5pm Mon-Fri, 1pm-4pm Sat & Sun)* hosts exhibitions of work by California artists and free Art Walks on the first Thursday of each month.

Salmon – King of the Sea

From late summer through autumn, the rivers of Northern California host thousands of salmon swimming up from the ocean to spawn in the river where they were hatched. After spawning, when a female may lay up to 17,000 eggs, the adult salmon die. The eggs lie buried in gravel, hatching within a few months. The orphaned baby salmon stay hidden in the gravel even longer, receiving nourishment from a yolk sac.

Some species may spend up to three years in freshwater before making the trip out to sea. Upon reaching the ocean, the salmon range far and wide, some migrating thousands of miles and living for anywhere from six months to seven years. When their time comes, they return to the river where they were hatched, swim upstream to spawn and die, and the cycle begins anew.

Of the six Pacific species of salmon, two are predominant in Northern California: chinook (also called 'king' or 'spring' salmon) and coho (also called 'silver' salmon). Chinook are the world's largest species of salmon, reaching 80lb or even 100lb.

Salmon numbers have declined drastically in recent years in most of Northern California's rivers due to a combination of factors, including destruction of their natural habitat. Haphazard logging and the construction of dams both pollute and obstruct traditional migration routes, threatening the salmon's ability to survive.

Hatcheries play an important role in salmon restoration efforts, releasing thousands of young salmon into rivers and streams each year. Fish ladders have been constructed beside many dams to allow the fish to swim upstream to spawn. Sadly, human intervention may not be enough to undo the damage humans have already caused.

Outlying vineyards include **Taft Street Winery** (☎ 800-334-8238; 2030 Barlow Lane; tastings 11am-4pm Tues-Fri, 11am-4:30pm Sat & Sun), off Occidental Rd, and **Sebastopol Vineyards** (☎ 707-829-9463; 8757 Green Valley Rd; tastings 11am-4pm Thur-Mon), off Hwy 116 heading toward Guerneville.

Ace Cider (☎ 707-829-1223; cnr Hwy 116 & Graton Rd) brews its own fruit ciders and imports European beers for its little **Ace-in-the-Hole Pub** (open 11am-7pm Sun-Wed, 10am-9pm Thur-Sat). It often hosts live music on weekends.

Places to Stay

Vine Hill Inn (☎ 707-823-8832, fax 707-824-1045; w www.vine-hill-inn.com; 3949 Vine Hill Rd; rooms $150), off Hwy 116, is a Victorian farmhouse set beside vineyards, north of town. An extra bonus is the spa mineral bath.

Raccoon Cottage (☎ 707-545-5466, fax 707-577-7448; 2685 Elizabeth Court; rates around $95-110) is a private country cottage off Vine Hill Rd, amid oaks, fruit trees and English gardens; rates depend on the length of stay.

Avalon B&B (☎ 707-824-0880, 877-328-2566, fax 707-824-0990; w www .avalonluxuryinn.com; 11910 Graton Rd; rooms $195-320) is a luxury Tudor-style lodge, nestled at the end of its own redwood forest drive. It serves hot breakfasts and afternoon tea, and guests also enjoy a natural swimming hole, sundeck and outdoor hot tub.

Places to Eat

A **farmers market** (cnr Petaluma & McKinley Aves; open 10am-1:30pm Sun Apr–mid-Dec) takes place at the downtown plaza. Got a sweet tooth? Try **Screamin' Mimi's** (☎ 707-823-5902; 6902 Sebastopol Ave) homemade ice cream or the **Sebastopol Cookie Co** (☎ 707-824-4040; 168 N Main St).

Slice of Life (☎ 707-829-6627; 6970 McKinley St; meals under $10; open 11am-9pm Tues-Sun) is a psychedelic vegetarian kitchen and all-natural pizzeria, hidden at a strip mall.

East West Cafe (☎ 707-829-2822; 128 N Main St; meals $6-12; open 7:30am-4pm Mon-Fri, 8am-8pm Sat & Sun) is a peachy place for imaginative and healthy dishes, such as salmon tacos or grilled eggplant sandwiches.

Lucy's Cafe (☎ 707-829-9713; 6948 Sebastopol Ave; lunch $5-11.50, dinner $12-20; open 8:30am-2pm & 5:30pm-9pm daily) cooks up mouth-watering organic California food – anything from ricotta pancakes to rib-eye steaks. You can nosh on baked goods at sunny plaza-side tables.

Pasta Bella (☎ 707-824-8191; 796 Gravenstein Hwy S; meals $8-16; open 11:30am-9pm daily) dishes up heaped plates of inventive, sophisticated yet family-friendly Italian food, and pours impeccable wines by the glass.

Chez Peyo (☎ 707-823-1262; 2295 Gravenstein Hwy S; mains $8-20; open 10am-2pm Sun & 5pm-9:30pm Wed-Sun), 2mi south of downtown, is favored for French country cuisine.

K&L Bistro (☎ 707-823-6614; 119 S Main St; lunch $9-18, dinner $15-23; open 11:30am-3pm Tues-Sat, 5pm-10pm Tues-Sun), downtown Sebastopol's finest restaurant, is a sleek Cal-French affair with a well-stocked wine bar.

Entertainment

Main Street Theatre (☎ 707-823-0177; 104 N Main St) presents repertory and new drama.

Jasper O'Farrell's (☎ 707-823-1389; 6957 Sebastopol Ave) is a traditional Irish-style bar with decent pub grub and live music or other entertainment nightly.

Coffee Catz (☎ 707-829-6600; 6761 Sebastopol Ave) roastery and café, east of the plaza inside historic Gravenstein Station, displays vintage railway cars. There's live acoustic music most weekends.

Powerhouse Brewing Company (☎ 707-829-9171; 268 Petaluma Ave; pub meals $9-15; kitchen open Wed-Sun, pub open daily) is a microbrewery with a sociable outdoor deck. Live bands perform on occasions, when there's a cover charge of $2 to $12.

Shopping

Downtown you'll find **Copperfield's Books** (☎ 707-823-2618; 138 N Main St), boasting a full calendar of literary events; and legendary **Incredible Records** (☎ 707-824-8099; 112 N Main St).

There are antique and collectibles shops strung out along Gravenstein Hwy S toward Hwy 101.

Sebastopol Antique Mall (☎ 707-823-1936; 755 Petaluma Ave; open 10am-5pm daily) houses Asian importers and varied antique dealers.

Midgley's Country Flea Market (☎ 707-823-7874; 2200 Gravenstein Hwy S; open 6:30am-4pm Sat & Sun), opposite Chez Peyo, is the region's largest flea market.

The *Sonoma County Farm Trails* booklet, available at the visitor center, has maps to dozens of nearby farms selling everything from apple jam to gourmet mustard. **Kozlowski Farms** (☎ 800-473-2767; 5566 Gravenstein Hwy N; open 9am-5pm Mon-Fri, 8am-5pm Sat & Sun) gives free tastings.

OCCIDENTAL
Originally a 19th-century logging town, Occidental (population 500) today has touristy artisan shops, splendid eateries and quiet places to lay your head. No matter which way you come, whether you drive or cycle, the unspoiled country roads through vineyards and redwood-forested hills are among the highlights of western Sonoma County.

A 15-minute drive southeast of town in Freestone, **Osmosis Enzyme Bath & Massage** (☎ 707-823-8231; w www.osmosis .com; 209 Bohemian Hwy; open 9am-9pm daily) indulges spa patrons with dry enzyme baths using aromatic cedar fibers (bath and blanket wrap $65 to $75), plus outdoor massages in pagodas.

Union Motel (☎ 707-874-3635; 3731 Main St; rooms $50-65) offers basic motel lodging and free overnight RV parking (but no hookups for RVs) for dinner patrons of the Union Hotel.

Negri's Occidental Hotel (☎ 707-874-3623, 877-867-6084; 3610 Bohemian Hwy; doubles $50-130), at the south end of town, has more inviting motel-style rooms, kitchen suites and a swimming pool.

Inn at Occidental (☎ 707-874-1047, 800-522-6324, fax 707-874-1078; w www .innatoccidental.com; 3657 Church St; rooms $195-320) is a downtown Victorian B&B with lively-looking rooms and gourmet breakfasts.

Howard Station Cafe (☎ 707-874-2838; 75 Main St; meals under $10; open 6:30am-2:30pm Mon-Fri, 6:30am-3pm Sat & Sun) cooks up soul-satisfying comfort fare, equally pleasing to vegetarians and carnivores; its juice bar is simply stupendous.

Negri's (☎ 707-823-5301; 3700 Bohemian Hwy; lunch $8, dinner $16) and the **Union Hotel** (☎ 707-874-3555; lunch $8, dinner $16), opposite one another on Main St, have been dishing out ample family-style Italian meals since the 1930s. The Union Hotel also has a **bakery café** and a **saloon** that dates from 1879. Look for live music at either place on weekends.

GUERNEVILLE & AROUND
Guerneville (population 7000) has the liveliest ambience of all the Russian River resort towns. Four miles downriver, Monte Rio boasts a riverside beach and a handful of places to stay. Continuing further west, idyllic little Duncans Mills is home to only a few dozen souls, but has restored historic buildings, shops and fine eateries. Heading upriver east of Guerneville, Rio Nido has rustic lodgings and Forestville is strewn with vineyards and restaurants.

Winery maps and information are available from the **Russian River Chamber of Commerce** (☎ 707-869-9000, 877-644-9001; w www.russianriver.com; 16209 1st St, Guerneville; open 9:30am-6pm Mon-Thur, 9:30am-7pm Fri, 10am-7pm Sat, 10am-4pm Sun May-Sept; shorter hours Oct-Apr) and the **Russian River Region Visitor Information Center** (☎ 707-869-4096; open 10am-3:45pm daily) at Korbel Champagne Cellars.

Annual events include the Stumptown Days Parade, Rodeo & BBQ and Russian River Blues Festival, both held in June, and Jazz on the River in September. Primarily for lesbians and liberal-minded grrrls, Women's Weekends (w www.russianriver womensweekends.com) are organized in late spring and early autumn.

Armstrong Redwoods State Reserve
Two miles north of Guerneville, this 805-acre park (☎ 707-869-2015; 17000 Armstrong Woods Rd; day-use fee $2 per vehicle) shelters a magnificent stand of virgin redwood forest set aside by Colonel Armstrong, a 19th-century lumber magnate. You can park at the entrance and walk or cycle in for free – the amazing grove of giant trees is a quick walk from the parking lot. Short interpretive nature trails lead further into the forest, where miles of backcountry hikes and campgrounds await. **Armstrong Woods Pack Station**

(☎ 707-887-2939; W www.redwoodhorses
.com) operates year-round, offering 2½-hour
trail rides ($50), full-day rides and overnight
treks. Reservations are required, especially
for longer rides.

Wineries
Pinot noir vintages are famous here.

Korbel Champagne Cellars (☎ 707-824-
7000; 13250 River Rd, Guerneville; tastings
9am-4:30pm daily) was founded by an immigrant from southern Bohemia ('korbel'
means goblet in Czech). It makes sparkling
wines, brandies and microbrewed beer, and
features lavish rose gardens and an 1876 train
station. It runs tours from 10am to 3pm daily.

Topolos at Russian River Vineyards
(☎ 707-887-1575; 5700 Gravenstein Hwy N;
tastings 11am-5:30pm daily) is a family-
owned vineyard, off Hwy 116 and near
Forestville, with a popular Greek-inspired
restaurant (☎ 707-887-1562), which is open
daily in summer).

Iron Horse Ranch Vineyards (☎ 707-
887-1507; 9786 Ross Station Rd; tastings
10am-3pm daily), off Hwy 116, makes
award-winning chardonnay and pinot noir
favored by top chefs and the White House.

Activities
Sandy **beaches** and **swimming holes** are
found all along the banks of the Russian
River. There's also year-round **fishing**.
Most activity outfitters operate from mid-
May to early October only.

Johnson's Beach (☎ 707-869-2022; end
of Church St, Guerneville) rents inner tubes,
canoes, paddle boats and other watercraft at
reasonable rates.

King's Sport & Tackle (☎ 707-869-2156;
16258 Main St, Guerneville) is the local
nerve center for fishing gear and advice; it
also rents kayaks.

Burke's Canoe Trips (☎ 707-887-1222;
W www.burkescanoetrips.com; 8600 River
Rd, cnr Mirabel Rd, Forestville) arranges
multi-day trips down the river. One-day
canoe rental includes a shuttle back to
your starting point for $42, plus $9 per
person if you'd like to camp in its riverside
redwood grove.

Guerneville also has free public **tennis
courts.** A **mini-golf course** and **kiddie
amusement park** are opposite each other on
Neeley Rd, just south of the Hwy 116 bridge.

Places to Stay
The Russian River Valley has few budget
sleeps, but discounts may be available midweek. On weekends and holidays, always
book ahead.

Camping Reached via a steep, winding
mountain road out of Armstrong Redwoods
State Reserve, **Bullfrog Pond** (campsites $12)
has forested campsites with cold water, but
no showers. Primitive hike-in and equestrian
backcountry campsites (campsites $10) are
scattered. All sites are first-come, first-
served, and open year-round.

Johnson's Beach Resort (☎ 707-869-2022;
16241 1st St; tent/RV sites from $10/15, cab-
ins per night $40-45, per week $200-225), on
the river in downtown Guerneville,
doesn't offer much besides a central location.

Casini Ranch (☎ 707-865-2255, 800-451-
8400; 22855 Moscow Rd; campsites $20, RV
sites $24-27) is in quiet Duncans Mills. Beau-
tifully set on riverside ranchlands, it's quite
popular with families. Amenities include hot
showers and watercraft rental.

The Willows (campsites $18), **Creekside
Inn** (RV sites $21), and **Fifes Guest Ranch**
(campsites $25) also offer camping (see the
following sections for more details).

If all these are full, try **Schoolhouse
Canyon Campground** (☎ 707-869-2311;
12600 River Rd) or gay-friendly **Faerie Ring
Campground** (☎ 707-869-2746; 16747 Armstrong Woods Rd), just outside Guerneville.

Motels, Cottages & Resorts In central
Guerneville, **Riverlane Resort** (☎ 707-869-
2323, 800-201-2324, fax 707-869-1954;
W www.riverlaneresort.com; 16320 1st St;
cabins in summer/winter from $65/52) offers
a range of comfortable housekeeping cabins
with fully equipped kitchens. There's a private beach, heated pool and hot tub.

Fifes Guest Ranch (☎ 707-869-0656, 800-
734-3371, fax 707-869-0658; W www.fifes
.com; 16467 River Rd, Guerneville; cabins
$80-135, 2-room suites $135-165) offers
lodging, for gay men, beneath the redwoods
and on the river, just west of downtown.

Fern Grove Cottages (☎ 707-869-8105,
fax 707-869-1615; W www.ferngrove.com;
16650 River Rd; cabins with breakfast $80-
210) has 1920s cabins in the redwoods near
Fife's, some with Jacuzzis and fireplaces. It's
a family-run establishment.

Creekside Inn & Resort (☎ 707-869-3623, 800-776-6586, fax 707-869-1417; W www.creeksideinn.com; 16180 Neeley Rd; B&B rooms $80-100, cottages & suites $130-235) is another country favorite with cozy fireplaces and a swimming pool. It's across the bridge from central Guerneville, off Hwy 116.

Huckleberry Springs Country Inn & Spa (☎ 707-865-2683, 800-822-2683; W www .huckleberrysprings.com; 8105 Beedle Rd, Monte Rio; cottages $145-225) is an inviting mountaintop retreat. Each of only four modern cottages has skylights; the spa, swimming pool and deck share panoramic views. Chef-designed, organic multi-course meals are served in the solarium.

Village Inn (☎ 707-865-2304; W www .village-inn.com; 20822 River Blvd; rooms $85-150, with kitchenette $160-185) is a quiet old-fashioned resort hotel nestled in the redwoods, under the bridge in Monte Rio.

B&Bs Check W www.russianriver.com for a sampling of other hideaways.

The Willows (☎ 707-869-2824, 800-953-2828, fax 707-869-2764; W www.willows russianriver.com; 15905 River Rd; rooms $80-140), yet another popular gay resort, is in a beautiful riverside spot on the east side of town. It offers rooms in an early 1940s redwood lodge with a fully-equipped kitchen, library and grand piano. Free canoes and kayaks are available to guests.

Rio Inn (☎ 707-869-4444, 800-344-7018, fax 707-869-4443; W www.rioinn.com; 4444 Woods Rd; rooms $120-150), just off River Rd in Rio Nido, is a peaceful Tudor-style lodge filled with antiques and towered over by redwoods.

Applewood Inn (☎ 707-869-9093, 800-555-8509; W www.applewoodinn.com; 13555 Hwy 116; rooms $155-295), east of central Guerneville, is a luxurious and romantic country inn with a library, elegant restaurant and river-rock fireplaces.

Santa Nella House (☎ 707-869-9488, 800-440-9031; W www.santanellahouse.com; 12130 Hwy 116; rooms $120-160), past the Applewood Inn, is furnished with antiques and wood-burning fireplaces. Sit on the veranda, or take an upstairs room overlooking the redwood grove. Evening port and dessert are complimentary.

Farmhouse Inn (☎ 707-887-3300, 800-464-6642; W www.farmhouseinn.com; 7871 River Rd; rates $160-275), north of downtown Forestville, rents faux cottage suites each with a fireplace, Jacuzzi and sauna. Guests share the gardens and swimming pool, and can elect to have breakfast in bed.

Raford House (☎ 707-887-9573, 800-887-9503; W www.rafordhouse.com; 10630 Wohler Rd; rooms $125-185) is a restored 1880 Victorian summerhouse on a knoll overlooking a lovely vineyard. It's off River Rd, heading toward Healdsburg.

Places to Eat

Guerneville is not an epicurean paradise, but other, smaller river towns do turn up culinary treasures.

Guerneville There's usually a taco truck parked outside Safeway grocery store on Main St.

Coffee Bazaar (☎ 707-869-9706; 14045 Armstrong Woods Rd; snacks under $5; open 6am daily), a perky local hangout in the Cinnabar building, has light salads, sandwiches, pastries and quiche.

Cousin Wood's Smokehouse (☎ 707-869-0705; meals $6-14; open 5pm-9:30pm Wed, noon-9:30pm Thur-Sun) is at the Stumptown Brewery.

Sparks Restaurant (☎ 707-869-8206; 16248 Main Street; mains $10-15; open 10am-3pm Sat & Sun, 5:30pm-9pm Thur-Mon) offers 'electrifying' organic vegetarian and vegan fare.

Main Street Station (☎ 707-869-0501; 16280 Main St; meals $6-18; open 7am-10pm Mon-Fri, 9am-10pm Sat & Sun) is a family-friendly Italian pizzeria and restaurant with a cabaret ambience.

Fifes Roadhouse Restaurant (see Places to Stay earlier; mains $14-20; open 5pm-9pm Wed-Sun winter, 5pm-10pm daily rest of year) offers tempting gourmet dining, both indoors and on the deck overlooking the pool. It's often open for brunch and lunch too, but hours vary so call first.

Applewood Inn Restaurant (☎ 707-869-9093, 800-555-8509; W www.applewoodinn .com; 13555 Hwy 116; mains $20-30; open 6pm-9pm Tues-Sat), across the Guerneville Bridge, wins rave reviews for its fresh seafood and game in imaginative sauces. Reservations are advised.

Forestville Downtown Forestville's **Tin Pony** (☎ 707-887-1242; 6566 Front St; meals $7.50-12; open 11:30am-8:30pm Wed-Sun) serves Mexican food inside near the bar, or outside in a lovely Spanish-style courtyard.

Chez Marie (☎ 707-887-7503; 6675 Front St; mains $13-20; dinner from 6pm Wed-Sun) is a heart-warming dinner house with country French and Cajun-Creole menus. Reservations are essential; ordering dessert is highly recommended.

Farmhouse Inn (☎ 707-887-3300; 7871 River Rd; mains $25-30; open for dinner Thur-Sun), north of Forestville, has won accolades for its seasonal cooking, often featuring Sonoma lamb, wild salmon or rabbit.

Monte Rio Tucked away beneath the bridge, **Village Inn** (☎ 707-865-2304; 20822 River Blvd; mains $12.50-20; open dinner Wed-Sun) has a jovial wine bar and Californian restaurant.

Duncans Mills Owned by the chef, **Cape Fear Cafe** (☎ 707-865-9246; 25191 Hwy 116; breakfast & lunch $7-13, dinner $14-20; open 9am-3pm & 5pm-9pm daily) is a little eatery focusing on assertive seafood, sirloin and sandwiches. Hiding behind it is the **Fearless Ice Cream** shop.

Wine & Cheese Tasting of Sonoma County (☎ 707-865-0565; 25179 Hwy 116; tastings $6-12; open 11am-5:30pm daily, happy hour until 7pm or later Fri) offers tastes of the region's finest wines, breads, cheeses at a handful of alfresco tables or indoors around the bar.

Blue Heron Restaurant (☎ 707-865-9135; 25300 Steelhead Blvd; lunch $5-15, dinner $10-20; open daily), a casual spot across the river, grills seafood and pub grub that you can down with local microbrews. The **West Sonoma Farmers Market** (open 1pm-6pm Sat May-Sept) happens out back.

Entertainment

Rio Theater (☎ 707-865-0913; cnr Bohemian Hwy & Hwy 116, Monte Rio) shows first-run movies inside an old Quonset hut by the river.

Most of the area's nightlife happens in Guerneville. **Main Street Station** (☎ 707-869-0501; 16280 Main; cover $2-6) has live jazz, blues, acoustic and cabaret acts almost nightly. **Coffee Bazaar** (☎ 707-869-9706;

14045 Armstrong Woods Rd) occasionally has live music.

Club FAB (☎ 707-869-5708; 16135 Main St; cover free-$10) has DJs and live music, drag shows and also film screenings some nights.

Rainbow Cattle Company (☎ 707-869-0206; 16220 Main St) is a popular gay men's bar, occasionally drawing a mixed crowd of lesbians. **Fifes Roadhouse Bar** (☎ 707-869-0656; 16467 River Rd) sees a predominantly male patronage.

Stumptown Brewery (☎ 707-869-0705; 15045 River Rd; open noon-2am daily) has microbrews, billiards and a straighter crowd.

Getting Around

Russian River Bikes (☎ 707-869-1455; 14070 Mill St), beside the Guerneville post office, rents street cruisers, full-suspension mountain bikes and trailercycles.

Inland Highway 101

North of Santa Rosa, Hwy 101 heads north through a series of fertile valleys along the upper Russian River, until it joins the Pacific Coast Hwy at Leggett. Although it may not look as enticing as the coastal route, the roads are faster and less tortuous, leaving you more time along the way to detour into the Sonoma and Mendocino County wine regions, explore the timeless Anderson Valley, splash about Clear Lake or soak at hot springs resorts outside Ukiah. Whew.

Mendocino Transit Authority (MTA; ☎ 707-462-1422, 800-696-4682) operates a South Coast bus No 75, Monday to Friday, that heads north from Gualala to the Navarro River junction, then turns inland on Hwy 128, goes through the Anderson Valley to Ukiah, and returns. At Navarro junction, it connects with a North Coast route to Albion, Little River, Mendocino and Fort Bragg. MTA bus No 65 travels daily on the Mendocino-Fort Bragg-Willits-Ukiah-Santa Rosa route in the morning, returning in the afternoon. A service between Ukiah, Redwood Valley and Willits runs Monday to Saturday, while bus No 54 connects Ukiah and Hopland Monday to Friday.

Greyhound (☎ 800-231-2222; w www .greyhound.com) operates a daily northbound and southbound bus on Hwy 101.

HEALDSBURG

Healdsburg (population 10,750), surrounded by vineyards and wineries, is at the heart of northern Sonoma County wine country. When you add in the natural delights of Lake Sonoma and the Russian River, is it surprising that this affluent town attracts over a million visitors every year? The shady town plaza, bordered by Healdsburg Ave and Center, Matheson and Plaza Sts, buzzes with activity, especially on weekends.

Stop by the **Healdsburg Chamber of Commerce & Visitors Bureau** (☎ 707-433-6935, 800-648-9922; 217 Healdsburg Ave; open 9am-5pm Mon-Fri, 10am-2pm Sat & Sun), a few blocks south of the plaza, for winery maps and information on hot-air ballooning, golf and tennis, spas, farm trails and more. Major annual events include the Russian River Wine Road Barrel Tasting, in March; the Healdsburg Jazz Festival, held around Memorial Day; and the Healdsburg Harvest Century Bicycle Tour, in mid-July.

Things to See

A few block east of the plaza, the **Healdsburg Museum** (☎ 707-431-3325; 221 Matheson St; donation requested; open 11am-4pm Tues-Sun) has a collection of Native American baskets from the local Pomo and Wappo people, and excellent exhibits on northern Sonoma County history. You can obtain a **walking tour** pamphlet to Healdsburg's historic homes from the museum bookshop.

Free summer **concerts** are held outside on Sunday afternoons at the plaza, where art galleries, antique shops, wine tasting rooms and eateries abound. **Toyon Books** (☎ 707-433-9270; 104 Matheson St) sells local guidebooks and maps. The community-driven **Plaza Arts Gallery** (☎ 707-431-1970; ⓦ www.healdsburgarts.org; 130 Plaza St; open 11am-6pm Sun-Thur, 10am-8pm Fri & Sat) spotlights California artists.

Wineries Click to ⓦ www.alexandervalley .org for a calendar of special winery events, including **First Weekend** happenings each month and autumn harvest festivals. The **Sonoma Country Wine Library** (☎ 707-433-3772; cnr Piper & Center Sts; open 9:30am-6pm daily) is inside Healdsburg's public library.

Simi Winery (☎ 800-746-4880; 16275 Healdsburg Ave; tastings 10am-5pm daily),

north of downtown, gives tours of the 19th-century stone cellars inside. **Rabbit Ridge** (☎ 707-431-7128; 3291 Westside Rd; tastings 11am-5pm daily) is a talented small winery.

Hop Kiln Winery (☎ 707-433-6491; 6050 Westside Rd; tastings 10am-5pm daily) has a historic tasting room and a picnic area by a pond. **Clos du Bois** (☎ 707-857-3100, 800-222-3189; 19410 Geyserville Ave, Geyserville; tastings 10am-4:30pm daily) is a major Californian label.

Chateau Souverain (☎ 888-809-4637; Hwy 101, exit Independence Lane, Geyserville; tastings 10am-5pm daily) estate winery boasts a fine country **French restaurant** (mains $10-20; reservations advised).

Dry Creek Vineyard (☎ 800-864-9463; 3770 Lambert Bridge Rd, off Dry Creek Rd; tastings 10:30am-4:30pm daily) was the first area vineyard established after Prohibition ended.

Ferrari-Carano Vineyards & Winery (☎ 800-831-0381; 8761 Dry Creek Rd; tastings 10am-5pm daily) conducts winery tours, or you can wander the gardens instead. **Lake Sonoma Winery** (☎ 707-473-2999; 9990 Dry Creek Rd; open 10am-5pm daily) and microbrewery has sunny outdoor tables with sweeping valley views.

Activities

WC 'Bob' Trowbridge Canoe Trips (☎ 707-433-7247, 800-640-1386, fax 707-433-6384; ⓦ www.trowbridgecanoe.com; 20 Healdsburg Ave) has canoe and kayak rental at half day $45 and full-day $55, plus $3 shuttle transport, from around April until October.

Getaway Adventures (☎ 707-763-3040, 800-499-2453; ⓦ www.getawayadventures .com) offers a morning of vineyard cycling, followed by an alfresco lunch and canoeing or kayaking on the Russian River for $130 per person.

Places to Stay

Camping See also the Around Healdsburg section later.

Alexander Valley Campground (☎ 707-431-1453, 800-640-1386; 2411 Alexander Valley Rd; campsites per person $10; open April-Oct), 2mi east of Healdsburg Ave, has grassy campsites set soporifically between vineyards; discounts are available to Trowbridge Canoe Trips customers.

Cloverdale Wine Country KOA (☎ 707-894-3337, 800-368-4558; W www.wine countrykoa.com; 26460 River Rd, Cloverdale; tent/RV sites from $30/36, 1-bedroom/2-bedroom cabins $50/60) feels far from Healdsburg, but it's only about 6mi from the Central Cloverdale exit off Hwy 101. A sign along the access road encourages the weary driver: 'Don't despair, you're almost there!' The all-star amenities here include hot showers, a swimming pool and hot tub, nature trails, laundry, paddle boats and bicycle rentals.

Motels & Hotels Older, family-owned motels are found several blocks south of the plaza. The **Fairview Motel** (☎ 707-433-5548; 74 Healdsburg Ave; rooms midweek $65, weekends $90-110) and spacious **L&M Motel** (☎ 707-433-6528; 70 Healdsburg Ave; rooms midweek $65, weekends $90-110) both have swimming pools, but the L&M also has barbecue grills, benches and picnic lawns.

Healdsburg Travelodge (☎ 707-433-0101, 800-499-0103; 178 Dry Creek Rd; rooms $70-150) and **Best Western Dry Creek Inn** (☎ 707-433-0300, 800-222-5784; 198 Dry Creek Rd; rooms $70-150) are north of downtown, at the Dry Creek exit off Hwy 101.

Hotel Healdsburg (☎ 707-431-2800, 800-889-7188, fax 707-431-0414; W www.hotel healdsburg.com; 25 Matheson St; rooms $205-425), a posh luxury property right on the plaza, has hip modern decor, a swimming pool and day spa. Breakfast in bed is included.

B&Bs The town is well supplied with Victorian B&Bs, most within walking distance of the plaza.

Healdsburg Inn on the Plaza (☎ 707-433-6991, 800-431-8663, fax 707-433-9513; W www.healdsburginn.com; 110 Matheson St; suites $145-285) has first-rate suites, mostly with fireplaces and tubs for two, and a solarium upstairs inside a century-old building. An afternoon wine tasting is included.

Piper Street Inn (☎ 707-433-8721, 877-703-0370, fax 707-433-1322; W www .piperstreetinn.com; 402 Piper St; rooms $95-145, garden cottage $185) is the most affordable Victorian lodging in town.

Camellia Inn (☎ 707-433-8182, 800-727-8182; W www.camelliainn.com; 211 North St; rooms $90-180) is an elegant 1869 Italianate

town house with a swimming pool and parlor fireplaces. It's two blocks from the plaza.

George Alexander House (☎ 707-433-1358, 800-310-1358, fax 707-433-1367; W www.georgealexanderhouse.com; 423 Matheson St; rooms $145-235) is a historic 1905 Queen Anne Victorian house, east of the plaza.

Haydon Street Inn (☎ 707-433-5228, 800-528-3703, fax 707-433-6637; W www .haydon.com; 321 Haydon St; rooms from $110, cottage suites $250), another Queen Anne Victorian, advertises midweek and off-season discounts.

There are a few more B&Bs in the surrounding countryside.

Belle de Jour Inn (☎ 707-431-9777, fax 707-431-7412; W www.belledejourinn.com; 16276 Healdsburg Ave; rooms $185-250, suites $250-300), opposite Simi Winery, promises every luxury, from hammocks and sun-dried sheets to whirlpool suites.

Madrona Manor (☎ 707-433-4231, 800-258-4003, fax 707-433-0703; W www .madronamanor.com; 1001 Westside Rd; rooms & suites $175-445) is an over-the-top Victorian mansion and carriage house with a swimming pool. It's a mile west of Hwy 101 near a selection of wineries. Candlelight dinners in the romantic restaurant are available to nonguests by reservation.

Places to Eat
Foodies will think they've died and gone to heaven in Healdsburg.

Weekly **farmers markets** (☎ 707-431-1956) set up at Healdsburg Plaza (open 4pm-6pm Tues June-Oct) and at the municipal parking lot (cnr Vine & North Sts; open 9am-noon Sat May-Nov).

Worthy local bakeries include the **Downtown Bakery & Creamery** (☎ 707-431-2719; 308A Center St; open from 7am daily) and **Costeaux French Bakery & Cafe** (☎ 707-433-1913; 417 Healdsburg Ave; open 6:30am-6pm Tues-Sat, 6pm-5pm Sun), which makes boxed lunches.

Oakville Grocery (☎ 707-433-3200; 124 Matheson St; sandwiches around $5; open 9am-7pm Sun-Thur, 9am-8:30pm Fri-Sat summer) should be everyone's first stop for smoked fish, gourmet sandwiches and salads, caviar and picnic fixings, or to indulge in a glass of wine on the plaza terrace.

Center St Deli & Cafe (☎ 707-433-7224; 304 Center St; breakfast & lunch $5-10; open 6:30am daily) is a vintage spot for a bewildering variety of comfort food, from sweet potato pancakes to N'orleans muffaletta.

Little **Ravenette** (☎ 707-431-1770; 117 North St; lunch $7-12; open 11:30am-2:30pm Wed-Sun), beside the Raven Theatre, and **Ravenous Cafe** (☎ 707-431-1302; 420 Center St; mains $15-25; open from 5pm Wed-Sun) serve imaginative American bistro fare.

Felix & Louie's (☎ 707-433-6966; 106 Matheson St; brunch $11-16, dinner $16-22; open 5pm-8:30pm or 9pm Mon-Fri, 10am-3pm Sun) is a swank newcomer on the plaza, a combination Italian ristorante, pizzeria and nightspot.

Dry Creek Kitchen (☎ 707-431-0330; 317 Healdsburg Ave; lunch $13-20, dinner mains $22-35; open noon-2:30pm & 5pm-9:30pm daily) by star chef Charlie Palmer is a hot spot for fresh Californian cuisine, an all-Sonoma wine list and beautiful people-watching.

Zin (☎ 707-473-0946; 344 Center St; lunch $10-15, dinner $13-25; open 11:30am-2pm & from 5pm daily; Thurs-Mon only in winter) boasts a wine bar, open kitchen and provocative California cuisine.

Geyser Smokehouse (☎ 707-857-4600; 21021 Geyserville Ave; meals $6-12; open 11:30am-9pm daily), a 10-minute drive from Healdsburg in rural Geyserville, fires up an authentic Texas barbecue; don't miss the whiskey pudding or the stocked saloon.

Santi (☎ 707-857-1790; 21047 Geyserville Ave, Geyserville; lunch $9-13, dinner $13-25; open 11:45am-2pm Tues-Sat & 5:30pm-9pm Tues-Sun), next door to a charming rural wine-tasting room, is an Italian country kitchen that dishes up seasonal classics. Its cooking classes are very well regarded.

Entertainment

Raven Theater & Film Center (☎ 707-433-5448; 115 N Main St) has concerts, cultural events and first-run movie screenings.

Bear Republic Brewing Company (☎ 707-433-2337; 345 Healdsburg Ave; open 11:30am-late daily) features handcrafted award-winning ales, a pub-style grill menu and live music on weekends.

There's also jazz on Wednesday evenings and during Sunday brunch at **Felix & Louie's** (☎ 707-433-6966; 106 Matheson St), on the plaza.

Getting There & Around

Sonoma County Transit (☎ 707-576-7433, 800-345-7433) has a daily local bus route connecting Santa Rosa with Healdsburg, Geyserville and Cloverdale.

Healdsburg Spoke Folk Cyclery (☎ 707-433-7171; 201 Center St) rents all types of bicycles and has free touring maps.

LAKE SONOMA

Formed by Warm Springs Dam in 1983, beautiful Lake Sonoma has two major arms, 4mi and 8mi long, and many smaller coves. The dam, 319ft high and 3000ft long, is at the east end of the lake. From Hwy 101, take the Dry Creek Rd exit north of Healdsburg and head northwest for 11mi through beautiful Dry Creek Valley's vineyards.

The **visitor center** (☎ 707-433-9483; open 9am-4pm daily) has historical exhibits, as well as maps and information for fishing, boating, camping and hiking on over 40mi of trails. Behind the center is a **fish hatchery**. Two miles further in, the **marina** (☎ 707-433-2200) rents every type of water craft you can think of, from canoes to houseboats.

Liberty Glen Campground (reservations ☎ 877-444-6777; W www.reserveusa.com; campsites $12) has hot showers, panoramic vistas and is rarely crowded. **Primitive campgrounds** (campsites $10) are dotted around the lake, for campers who can boat in or hike in.

HOPLAND

Wonderful Hopland (population 80), just a little three-block town on Hwy 101, is the gateway to Mendocino County wine country. Hops were first grown here in 1866, but Prohibition brought the industry to a halt. In 1983, the Mendocino Brewing Company opened the first brewpub licensed in California since Prohibition, and it put Hopville back on the map.

Besides visiting the **antique shops** that line Hwy 101, you could also taste for free the products of the local vineyards. **Brutocao Cellars** (☎ 800-433-3689; Schoolhouse Plaza, 13500 S Hwy 101; tastings 10am-5pm daily) has a restaurant, wine bar and six full-sized bocce courts (rental $20 per hour). **Fetzer Vineyards** (☎ 800-846-8637; 13601 Eastside Rd; tastings 9am-5pm daily) has a deli and gardens for picnicking; it also stocks Bonterra label organic varietals and offers tours

NORTH COAST

in season. **Jepson Vineyards** (☎ 800-516-7342; 10400 S Hwy 101; tastings 10am-5pm daily) estate winery makes brandy and champagne, and offers tours by appointment.

Drop by **Real Goods Solar Living Center** (☎ 707-744-2100; W www.realgoods.com; 13771 S Hwy 101; open 10am-6pm daily) to learn about alternative energy. Self-guided tours of the fascinating 12-acre site, on the southern outskirts of town, are available anytime during opening hours. There are guided tours at 11am and 3pm Friday to Sunday. The **Sol Fest Summer Solstice Celebration**, held each year on the closest weekend to summer solstice, features well-known speakers, live music, vendor booths and workshops on sustainable living, solar and wind power, organic gardening and other topics.

Other annual events include the **Hopland Women's Festival**, taking place around Memorial Day.

Places to Stay & Eat

Hopland Inn (☎ 707-744-1890, 800-266-1891, fax 707-744-1219; W www.hoplandinn .com; 13401 S Hwy 101; rooms & suites $95-175) is a charming, beautifully restored 1890 Victorian hotel. Fine country meals are served in its downstairs **restaurant** (lunch around $10, dinner $14-25); call ahead for hours and reservations.

Fetzer Vineyards (☎ 707-744-7413, 800-846-8637, fax 707-744-2159; 13601 Eastside Rd; room/suite/cottage from $140/175/200) operates a vineyard B&B.

Munchies (☎ 707-744-1600; 13275 S Hwy 101; sandwiches around $5; open 8am-2pm Mon-Thur, 9am-5pm Fri-Sun) has freshly squeezed juice, Italian gelato and espresso. For quick bites, custom sandwiches and picnic baskets, it can't be beat. It also rents bicycles.

Phoenix Bread Co (☎ 707-744-1944; 13325 S Hwy 101; meals from $7.50; open 10am-7pm Wed-Sun) bakes handcrafted loaves and wood-fired pizzas. Around dinnertime, stop by for barbecue take-out.

Bluebird Cafe (☎ 707-744-1633; 13340 S Hwy 101; breakfast & lunch $5-10, dinner $10-15; open daily) is a simply beloved American diner.

Mendocino Brewing Company (☎ 707-744-744-1015; 13351 S Hwy 101; meals around $12; kitchen closes 8pm, bar open later), one of Northern California's best-

known brewpubs, is famous for its award-winning Red Tail Ale and occasionally has live music. It runs the **Hopland Brewery Tavern Restaurant** on the same premises.

Zemolini's Wine & Coffee Bar (☎ 707-744-9463; 13420A S Hwy 101; open 6am-10pm Mon-Fri, 8am-midnight Sat) has live bluegrass, rock and folk music that draws folks from as far away as Ukiah.

CLEAR LAKE

Just south of Mendocino National Forest, this laidback recreational lake has a shoreline more than 100mi long and boasts the cleanest air in all of California. Mt Konocti, towering over the water at 4200ft, is classified as a dormant volcano, and the lake itself is of volcanic origin. In late summer, thriving algae sometimes gives the waters a murky green appearance; the algae also makes the lake a great habitat for fish, especially bass, and it's home to a variety of birds.

You'll often hear the terms 'upper lake' (the northwest portion) and 'lower lake' (the southeast portion), as the lake narrows in the middle to form two sections. **Lakeport** (population 4800), on the northwest shore off Hwy 29, is the Lake County seat, and is less than an hour's drive east of Hopland. **Clearlake** (population 13,200), off the southeastern shore on Hwy 53, is home to more people than any other lake town, and 40mi from the I-5 freeway via Hwy 20, which links all the north shore hamlets. **Middletown**, another sizable Lake County town, is about 20mi south of Clearlake at the junction of Hwy 175 and Hwy 129, only 40 minutes north of Calistoga.

The **Lake County Visitor Information Center** (☎ 707-263-9544, 800-525-3743; W www.lakecounty.com; 875 Lakeport Blvd, Lakeport; open 8:30am-5:30pm Mon-Fri, 10am-4pm Sat, noon-4pm Sun summer; winter hours reduced), atop a vista point off Hwy 29, has information on absolutely everything around the lake.

Things to See & Do

In Lakeport, the 1871 **Old County Courthouse** (255 N Main St) is a state historic landmark. Inside, the small but interesting **Lake County Museum** (☎ 707-263-4555; open 10am-4pm Tues-Sat, noon-4pm Sun) has Pomo Indian artifacts and other historical exhibits.

Six miles from Lakeport, **Clear Lake State Park** (☎ 707-279-4293; 5300 Soda Bay Rd, Kelseyville), on the lake's southwest shore, has hiking trails, fishing, boating and camping. There's also a **visitor center** with interpretive exhibits on the area's geology, natural history and Native American culture. The **Taylor Planetarium & Observatory** (☎ 707-279-8372 after 3pm; 5727 Oak Hills Lane, Kelseyville; adult/child $3/1) offers star-viewing programs throughout the year, usually Saturday at 7pm.

In Lower Lake, **Anderson Marsh State Historic Park** (☎ 707-994-0688; 8825 Hwy 53) has hiking trails and bird watching, a Pomo Indian archaeological site and a historic ranch house open for tours. Free nature and bird-watching walks, sponsored by the **Redbud Audubon Society** (☎ 707-994-1545), are held at 9am the first Saturday of each month. The **Lower Lake Historical Schoolhouse Museum** (☎ 707-995-3565; 16435 Morgan Valley Rd; open 11am-4pm Wed-Sat) is a restored 19th-century classroom with historical displays.

The **Clear Lake Queen** (☎ 707-994-5432), docked in Lucerne on the north shore, is an elegant three-story paddle wheel steamboat offering sightseeing cruises on the lake, with dining, a bar and live music. A two-hour cruise costs $16 to $25 and a three-hour cruise is $18 to $33; reservations required.

Boats can be rented from a number of places including **On the Waterfront** (☎ 707-263-6789; 60 3rd St, Lakeport), **Blue Fish Cove** (☎ 707-998-1769; 10573 E Hwy 20, Clearlake Oaks), **Blue Heron Kayaks** (707-272-0419) at Clear Lake State Park and the Konocti Harbor Resort marina (see Places to Stay).

A few wineries around the lake have tasting rooms and some offer tours by appointment: **Wildhurst Vineyards** (☎ 800-595-9463; 3855 Main St, Kelseyville; tastings 10am-5pm daily); **Red Hill Wine Tasting** (☎ 707-277-9433; 9710 Broadmoor Way, at Soda Bay Rd, Kelseyville; tastings 11am-7pm Wed-Sun); **Steele Wines** (☎ 707-279-9475; 4350 Thomas Dr, Kelseyville; tastings 11am-7pm Fri-Sun); **Ployez Winery** (☎ 707-994-2106; 1171 S Hwy 29, Lower Lake; tastings 11am-5pm daily); and **Guenoc & Langtry Estate Vineyards** (☎ 707-987-2385 ext 200; 21000 Butts Canyon Rd, Middletown; tastings 11.30am-5pm daily).

Day-trippers are welcome at **Harbin Hot Springs** (see Places to Stay), located outside Middletown.

Places to Stay & Eat

Everything from campgrounds to lavish resorts and B&Bs, and from snack shacks to fine dinner houses are found all around the lake. In summer and on weekends, make reservations.

Lakeport & Kelseyville Clear Lake State Park has four **campgrounds** (seasonal reservations ☎ 800-444-7275; W www.reserve america.com; campsites $12) with hot showers, some open year-round.

Waterfront motels with boat slips include sweet, cottage-style **Mallard House** (☎ 707-262-1601, fax 707-263-4764; W www.mallardhouse.com; 970 N Main St; rooms $50-100), **Anchorage Inn** (☎ 707-263-5417; 950 N Main St; rooms in summer $60-145, in winter $45-95) and **Clear Lake Inn** (☎ 707- 263-3551, 888-800-8002; 1010 N Main St; singles/doubles summer $79/89, winter $55/59).

Arbor House Inn (☎ 707-263-6444; W www.arborhousebnb.com; 150 Clear Lake Ave; B&B rooms $80-100, suites $120) is a late 19th-century house near the lakeshore, with gardens including a koi pond, grape arbor, whirlpool and a barbecue area. Gourmet 3-course breakfasts and afternoon wine with refreshments are complimentary.

Konocti Harbor Resort & Spa (☎ 707-279-4281, 800-660-5253, fax 707-279-9205; W www.konoctiharbor.com; 8727 Soda Bay Rd; rooms $49-130, apartments & beach cottages $110-210, suites $160-375), on Konocti Bay about 4mi from Kelseyville, is the most developed resort on the lake. Its gargantuan grounds comprise a sauna, spa, fitness center, tennis courts, miniature golf and a marina.

Dutch Treat (☎ 707-262-0631; 150 N Main St, Lakeport; light meals around $6; open 6.45am-5pm Mon-Fri, 7.30am-5pm Sat, 7.30am-3pm Sun) is a European-style coffeehouse with coffee and pastries in the morning, and light lunches of fresh salads and sandwiches. Not only that, but the owners are sweethearts.

Park Place (☎ 707-263-0444; 50 3rd St, Lakeport; dinner mains $10-22; open 11am-9pm daily) is justifiably popular, specializing in homemade pasta dishes, fresh seafood and steaks, with a deck overlooking the lake; reservations suggested.

A **farmers' market** *(open 8am-noon Sat May-Oct)* sets up in Kelseyville at Steele Wines.

Sicilian Country Steakhouse *(☎ 707-279-0704; 5685 Main St, Kelseyville; dinner mains $12-25; open lunch & dinner daily)* is popular for its authentic Italian cuisine.

North Shore & Middletown In Glenhaven, **Lake Place Resort** *(☎ 707-998-3331, fax 707-998-4550; w www.lakeplaceresort.com; 9515 Harbor Dr; RV sites $25-30, cottages $30-115)*, on the lake shore, has waterfront cottages with kitchens, plus a hot tub, kayak rental, and boat launching and mooring.

Kristalberg B&B *(☎ 707-274-8009; w www.kristalbergbb.com; off Hwy 20, Lucerne; rooms $60-90, suites $125-150)*, with panoramic views of Mt Konocti, is a sumptuous affair, with decor ranging from 18th-century Italian to soft Victorian style. Rates include gourmet organic breakfasts, afternoon cheese and wine tasting and after-dinner sherry. German, French and Spanish are spoken.

Featherbed Railroad Co *(☎ 707-274-8378, 800-966-6322, fax 707-274-1415; w www.featherbedrailroad.com; 2870 Lakeshore Blvd, Nice; cabooses $102-180)* is a unique B&B. All rooms are inside converted railroad cabooses, most with Jacuzzis for two!

Guenoc & Langtry Estate Vineyards *(☎ 707-987-2385 ext 200; w www.guenoc.com; 21000 Butts Canyon Rd, Middletown; rates per person $120-150)* offers overnight lodging and wine dinners on the former estate of Victorian actress Lillie Langtry.

Harbin Hot Springs *(☎ 707-987-2377, 800-622-2477; w www.harbin.org; Harbin Hot Springs Rd, Middletown; camping $24, dorm bed midweek/weekend $35/50, singles $55/80, doubles from $80/115)* is a historic place to soak up some peace and quiet. Originally a 19th-century health spa and pleasure resort, today the retreat center has a New-Age spiritual bent. Guests enjoy hot- and cold-spring pools, massage, yoga, clothing-optional sunbathing and holistic health workshops, and 1160 acres for hiking. Accommodations are in renovated Victorian buildings and share a common

kitchen. Organic and health-conscious foods are available at the grocery store, café and restaurant. Day rates for spa visits are the same as for camping, or $6 per six-hour visit before 6pm.

The springs are about 3mi off Hwy 175; from Middletown, take Barnes St, which becomes Big Canyon Rd, then head left at the fork.

Entertainment

Konocti Harbor Resort & Spa *(☎ 800-225-2277; w www.konoctiharbor.com; 8727 Soda Bay Rd)* presents headline entertainment (recently Lyle Lovett and Ray Charles) in its outdoor amphitheater and indoor concert hall.

Library Park, on the lakeshore in downtown Lakeport, has a gazebo where free summer concerts are held every Friday evening, anything from blues, ska and rockabilly to tribute bands.

Harbin Hot Springs (see Places to Stay) has an unbelievable line-up of world music and 'sock hops with soul.'

From the Vine *(☎ 707-263-5787; 307 N Main St, Lakeport; open Fri evenings)* is a wine bar and tasting room, serving complimentary hors d'oeuvres.

John Henry's Irish Pub *(☎ 707-994-1790; 16195 Main St, Lower Lake)* is a toasty, out-of-the-way place.

Mount St Helena Brewing Co *(☎ 707-987-3361; 21167 Calistoga Rd, Middletown)*, an award-winning microbrewery, also has a decent pub menu of pasta, pizza, seafood and ribs.

There are also a few bowling alleys, cinemas and casinos around the lake.

Getting There & Around

Driving time between San Francisco and Clear Lake is about 2½ to three hours.

Greyhound *(☎ 800-231-2222; w www.greyhound.com)* has a daily San Francisco–Lakeport bus that makes 14 stops and takes six hours. There is no depot in Lakeport, but the bus will make a flag stop anywhere on Main St. **Lake Transit** *(☎ 707-263-3334, 707-994-3334)* runs weekday routes, connecting all the major lake towns. Buses between Middletown and Calistoga connect through to Santa Rosa on Thursday.

In Lakeport, the **Bicycle Rack** *(☎ 707-263-1200; 302 N Main St)* rents bicycles.

ANDERSON VALLEY

This beautiful agricultural valley is rich with vineyards, apple orchards, sheep pastures, oak trees and redwood groves. Travelers come here primarily to visit the backwoods wineries, but hiking, cycling, fishing, canoeing and kayaking are also popular pursuits.

Tiny **Boonville** (population 700) and **Philo** (population 400) are the valley's principal towns. From south of Ukiah, Hwy 253 heads southwest for 20mi to Boonville. Equally panoramic Hwy 128 makes 60mi of twists and turns between Cloverdale on Hwy 101, south of Hopland, and Albion on Hwy 1 at the coast.

Pick up information in Ukiah or by contacting the **Anderson Valley Chamber of Commerce** (☎ 707-895-2379; W www .andersonvalleychamber.com). Annual celebrations include the Boonville Beer Festival, California Wool & Fiber Festival and Pinot Noir Festival, all happening in May, followed by the Wild Iris Folk Festival in early June.

The **Anderson Valley Historical Society Museum**, housed in a little, old red schoolhouse on Hwy 128 just west of Boonville, has exhibits of photos and artifacts from the valley's history. **Anderson Valley Brewing Co** (☎ 707-895-2337; 17700 Hwy 153), just east of the crossroads at Hwy 128, crafts award-winning beers in a Bavarian-style brewhouse. There are usually tours at 1:30pm and 4pm daily, but always call ahead to check the schedule.

Most of the valley's dozen or so small **wineries** (W www.avwines.com) are outside Philo. Many are family-owned and offer tastings; some offer tours. **Husch Vineyards** (☎ 800-554-8724; 4400 Hwy 128; tastings 10am-6pm daily summer, 10am-5pm rest of year) and **Navarro Vineyards** (☎ 707-895-3686; 5601 Hwy 128; tasting 10am-6pm daily) are respected names.

Accommodations fill up fast, especially on summer weekends.

Hendy Woods State Park (☎ 707-937-5804, seasonal reservations ☎ 800-444-7275; W www.reserveamerica.com; campsites $12, cabins $20), bordered by the Navarro River on Hwy 128 just west of Philo, has hiking trails, picnic areas and a forested campground with hot showers.

Wellspring Renewal Center (☎ 707-895-3893; W www.wellspringrenewal.org; Ray's Rd; campsites $14, cabins from $32) and

Shenoa Retreat Center (☎ 707-895-3156; W www.shenoasprings.com; Van Zandt Rd; cottages $89, with kitchen $160) outside Philo both cater mainly to groups, but accept individual travelers on a space-available basis. Call ahead.

Other Philo lodgings include the **Anderson Valley Inn** (☎ 707-895-3325; 8480 Hwy 128; motel rooms $55, 2-room suites $90); **Philo Pottery Inn** (☎ 707-895-3069; W www .philopotteryinn.com; 8550 Hwy 128; rooms $110-150), a cozy redwood B&B dating from 1888; and the **Pinoli Ranch Country Inn** (☎ 707-895-2450; 3280 Clark Rd; rooms $115-125), north of town.

In Boonville there's the historic **Boonville Hotel** (☎ 707-895-2210; 14040 Hwy 128; rooms $85-225) or the **Anderson Creek Inn** (☎ 707-895-3091, 800-552-6202, fax 707-895-9466; W www.andersoncreekinn.com; 12050 Anderson Valley Way; rooms $120-180), a gracious guest ranch 2mi west of Hwy 128.

A **farmers market** (open 9:45am-noon Sat June-Oct) takes place outside the Boonville Hotel. Nearby **Boont Berry Farm** (☎ 707-895-3576; 13981 Hwy 128) is a natural foods store with a delicious deli and bakery.

Buckhorn Saloon (☎ 707-895-3369; 14081 Hwy 128; lunch $7-10, dinner $11-16; open 11am-9pm daily, 11am-9pm Thur-Mon winter) is one of several well-known places to eat dotted around the valley. It's family-friendly and occasionally hosts live music. The menu is American grill, with a bar serving local wines and microbrews.

The **Boonville Hotel** (mains $16-25; restaurant open 6pm-9pm Thur-Mon, bar *from 3pm daily)* serves hearty gourmet fare in a genteel setting. Menu highlights are locally-caught salmon and rib-eye steaks. Reservations recommended.

UKIAH

Settled in the fertile Yokayo Valley and surrounded by orchards and vineyards, Ukiah (population 15,500) is the Mendocino County seat. That said, it's still the kind of small town where teenagers cruise the streets because there's simply nothing else to do after dark.

Although Ukiah may not have many tourist attractions, its plentiful and affordable places to stay and eat make it an ideal base for hopping between outlying wineries, hot springs and nature reserves.

Running north–south a few blocks west of Hwy 101, State St is Ukiah's main drag, and that's where you'll find most motels and restaurants. The **Greater Ukiah Chamber of Commerce** (☎ 707-462-4705; 200 S School St; open 9am-5pm Mon-Fri), one block west of State St, has information on Ukiah, Hopland and the Anderson Valley.

The **Bureau of Land Management** (BLM; ☎ 707-468-4000; 2550 N State St) has maps and information for backcountry camping, hiking and mountain biking in wilderness areas. There's also an office of the **AAA** (☎ 707-462-3861; 601 Kings Court).

While in town, visit the **Sun House-Grace Hudson Museum** (☎ 707-467-2836; w www .gracehudson.org; 431 S Main St; admission by donation of $2; open 10am-4:30pm Wed-Sat, noon-4:30pm Sun), one block east of State St. Mainstays of the collection are paintings by Grace Hudson (1865–1937), whose sensitive depictions of Pomo Indian subjects complement the ethnological work and Native American baskets collected by her husband, John Hudson. Guided tours of their 1911 Craftsman-style redwood bungalow, next door, depart on demand.

Heading north from downtown toward the fairgrounds, the Union 76 gas station maintains the modest **Redwood Tree Service Station Museum** (859 N State St; admission free; open daily), full of historical photographs and memorabilia.

Special events around town include the Redwood Empire Fair, held on the second weekend of August, and Ukiah Country PumpkinFest in late October, with an arts and crafts fair, children's carnival and fiddle contest.

Places to Stay & Eat

For camping and other accommodations, see Around Ukiah later.

Motel 6 (☎ 707-468-5404, 800-466-8356; 1208 S State St; rooms from $40) is about the cheapest motel.

Other options closer to downtown are the **Economy Inn** (☎ 707-462-8611; 406 S State St; rooms $55-60) and **Days Inn** (☎ 707-462-7584, 800-329-7466; 950 N State St; rooms $60-110), which has more amenities.

Discovery Inn Motel (☎ 707-462-8873, fax 707-462-1249; 1340 N State St; rooms & suites $75-100) has a 75ft heated swimming pool and faux-tropical grotto Jacuzzis. Rates include continental breakfast.

Sanford House B&B (☎ 707-462-1653, fax 707-462-8987; w www.sanfordhouse.com; 306 S Pine St; rooms $75-150), in a quiet neighborhood close to downtown, offers gourmet breakfasts and lodgings in a Queen Anne Victorian house.

The **Ukiah Farmers Market** (cnr School & Clay Sts; open 3pm-6pm Tues June-Oct • cnr Orchard Ave & Perkins St; open 8:30am-noon Sat June-Oct) has fresh local produce, arts and crafts, and live entertainment.

The **Coffee Critic** (☎ 707-462-6333; 476 N State St; snacks $3-6; open 6am-8pm Mon-Thur, 7am-7pm Fri, 7am-10pm Sat & Sun) serves specialty coffees and teas from around the world, plus gelato, ice cream and rich baked desserts.

Moore's Flour Mill & Bakery (☎ 707-462-6550; 1550 S State St; open from 7:30am Mon-Fri) stocks natural foods, fresh-baked breads and groceries.

Ellie's Mutt Hut (☎ 707-468-5376; 732 S State St; meals around $6.50; open 6:30am-8pm Mon-Fri, 6:30am-3pm Sat) serves a varied menu of tasty vegetarian dishes on a flower-bedecked outdoor patio.

Maple Restaurant (☎ 707-462-5221; 295 S State St; meals $5-8; open 7am-1pm Mon-Fri, 7am-3pm Sat & Sun) is an old-fashioned coffee shop serving breakfasts and lunches; try the fruit pancakes and specialty omelettes.

Schat's Courthouse Bakery & Cafe (☎ 707-462-1670; 113 W Perkins St; snacks $2-5; open 6:30am-8:30pm Mon-Sat) is a cheerful place with checkered tablecloths.

Dish *(☎ 707-462-5700; 109 S School St; dishes $8-11; open 9am-5:30pm Mon-Fri, 10am-2pm Sat)* cooks up new American comfort fare. Boxed meals are available to go.

El Sombrero *(☎ 707-463-1818; 131 E Mill St; lunch $7-9, dinner $10-15; open 11am-9pm Tues-Sat, 3pm-8pm Sun)*, near the Sun House museum, lets seafood and authentic Mexican dishes dominate the menu.

Angelo's Italian Restaurant *(☎ 707-462-0448; 920 N State St; lunch $7-10, dinner $11-16; open 11am-2:30pm Mon-Fri, 4pm-9:30pm daily)* serves home-style Italian food, with plenty of vegetarian dishes. The 'Bud & Spaghetti' neon sign really says it all.

Entertainment

Mendocino Community College *(☎ 707-468-3000)* puts on theater, dance and music concerts.

Ask at the chamber of commerce about other performing arts and cultural events, including Sunday summer concerts at Todd Grove Park and local square dances.

Ukiah Brewing Co *(☎ 707-468-5898; 102 S State St; cover $5)* is an unpretentious brewpub that fills up on weekends with live music, anything from reggae to psychograss to new American Folk.

The lively upstairs **cantina** *(El Sombrero, 131 E Mill St)* occasionally has live music, as does **The Coffee Critic** *(476 N State St)*.

Ukiah has plenty of dive bars, scruffy cocktail lounges and Western-style saloons: just head north on State St. Some have billiards and darts, or even country-and-western line dancing.

AROUND UKIAH

Wineries

For a map to nearly three dozen local vineyards, some of which offer tours by appointment, swing by the Ukiah Chamber of Commerce.

Dunnewood Vineyard s *(☎ 800-624-0444; 2399 N State St; open daily)* has an in-town winery tasting room. **Parducci Wine Estates** *(☎ 888-362-9463; 501 Parducci Rd, exit at Lake Mendocino off Hwy 101; tastings 9am-5pm daily)* makes exuberant, fruity vintages.

Redwood Valley Cellars *(☎ 707-485-0322; 7051 N State St, Redwood Valley; tastings 9:30am-5pm daily)*, 7mi north of Ukiah, sells organic wines and cabernet port.

Vichy Hot Springs Resort

Opened in 1854 and named after the world-famous Vichy Springs in France, this is the oldest continuously operating mineral springs spa in California. Around the turn of the 20th century, the springs were a popular day-trip from San Francisco, as literary luminaries, including Mark Twain, Jack London and Robert Louis Stevenson, all came here for the restorative properties of the waters.

Today the resort *(☎ 707-462-9515, fax 707-462-9516; **W** www.vichysprings.com; 2605 Vichy Springs Rd; open from 9am daily)* has the only warm, naturally carbonated mineral baths in North America. Unlike some hot springs on the West Coast, this one requires swimsuits (rentals $1.50) and is extremely commercialized. Spa entry is $22 for two hours or $35 for a full day.

Facilities include a heated outdoor mineral hot tub, 10 indoor and outdoor tubs with natural 100°F (38°C) waters, and a grotto with a ladle for sipping the effervescent waters. Massages are available. Spa entry includes use of the 700-acre grounds – hiking trails go to the old Cinebar mine shaft and to a 40ft waterfall up Grizzly Creek.

The suite and two cottages here, built in 1854, are the three oldest structures standing in Mendocino County. Breakfast and spa privileges are included in overnight accommodation rates *(RV sites $20, lodge singles/doubles $115/150, creek-side rooms $195, cottages $255)*. RV parking doesn't include breakfast or spa entry.

From Hwy 101, take the Vichy Springs Rd exit and follow the state landmark signs east for about 3mi. All told, it takes just five minutes to get there from Ukiah.

Orr Hot Springs

A clothing-optional haven loved by backpackers, locals and drive-through tourists, Orr Hot Springs *(☎ 707-462-6277; 13201 Orr Springs Rd; spa entry Mon $15, Tues-Sun $22; open 10am-10pm daily)* offers a communal redwood hot tub, outdoor tile-and-rock heated pool, four individual porcelain tubs, cold swimming pool, sauna, steam room, massage room and gardens.

Overnight **accommodation** *(camping & dorm futon beds per person $45, singles/doubles $100/135, cottages $185)* includes spa use and access to a communal kitchen. Rates drop 10% Monday to Wednesday.

From Hwy 101, take the N State St exit and go north a quarter mile to Orr Springs Rd, then head west for 9mi. The steep, winding mountain road to the springs takes at least 25 minutes to drive; watch out for blind curves.

Montgomery Woods State Reserve

Two miles west of Orr Springs, this modest 1140-acre preserve (☎ 707-937-5804) protects five groves of old-growth redwoods. A 2mi loop trail traverses the creek, winding through the redwood groves, starting from near the picnic tables and toilets. This is a day-use park; no camping.

Lake Mendocino

Set in rolling hills just 5mi northeast of Ukiah, this 1822-acre artificial lake fills a valley that was the ancestral home of the Pomo Indians. On the north side of the lake, the **Pomo Visitor Center** (☎ 707-485-8285; Marina Dr; usually open 9am-5pm Wed-Sun summer) is modeled after a Pomo roundhouse, with exhibits on tribal culture and the dam. In summer boat rentals are available at the nearby **marina** (☎ 707-485-8644).

Coyote Dam, 3500ft long and 160ft high, is on the lake's southwest corner; the east part of the lake is a 689-acre protected wildlife habitat. The **US Army Corps of Engineers** (☎ 707-462-7581; 1160 Lake Mendocino Dr; open 7:40am-4:30pm Mon-Fri) built the dam and manages the lake, and provides information on camping, hiking and other recreational activities. However, its office is inconveniently located on the Lower Lake.

The lake has over 300 varied campsites spread across multiple **campgrounds** (☎ 877-444-6777; W www.reserveusa.com; campsites $8-18), most with hot showers. Reservations are possible for some, others are first-come, first-served. There are also primitive **boat-in sites** (campsites $5).

For the Upper Lake, turn east from Hwy 101 onto Hwy 20, a few miles north of Ukiah. Before long you'll see the lake on your right, then turn right onto Marina Dr and follow the signs to the visitor center, main campgrounds and marina.

WILLITS

Just over 20mi north of Ukiah, Willits (population 5000) is an average little town with a NoCal bohemian attitude. Ranching, timber and industrial manufacturing are the mainstays of its economy. For visitors, Willits' greatest claim to fame is as the eastern terminus of the Skunk Train. If you're driving to or from Fort Bragg, 35mi away on the Mendocino coast, allow about an hour of driving via winding Hwy 20.

Just south of where Hwy 20 crosses Hwy 101, the Willits Arch boasts that Willits is the 'Gateway to the Redwoods' and the 'Heart of Mendocino County.' Both claims are a bit of a stretch really. The arch originally towered over Reno, Nevada, until it was re-erected here in the 1990s.

North of the arch, Hwy 101 becomes Main St and wanders past motels and psychic readers, steakhouses and smoke shops, by way of the **Willits Chamber of Commerce** (☎ 707-459-7910; W www.willits.org; 239 S Main St; open 10am-4pm Mon-Fri).

The depot for the 120-year-old **Skunk Train** (☎ 707-459-5248, 800-777-5865) is on E Commercial St, three short blocks east of Hwy 101. The train runs daily on a scenic track between Willits and Fort Bragg, on the coast (for details, see Fort Bragg later).

The not-to-be-missed **Mendocino County Museum** (☎ 707-459-2736; 400 E Commercial St; admission by donation; open 10am-4:30pm Wed-Sun) has imaginative exhibits on the area's history and culture. You could easily spend an hour or two perusing the Pomo and Yuki Indian basketry and artifacts, or reading about local scandals and countercultural movements. Outside the museum, the **Roots of Motive Power** exhibit has occasional demonstrations of steam logging and historic machinery, plus lumberjack handcar races every September.

Set among giant redwood trees, **Brooktrails Golf Course** (☎ 707-459-6761; 24860 Birch St), off Sherwood Rd, 2mi north of downtown, is one of the most picturesque nine-hole public golf courses in Northern California. Green fees are $10 to $16. **Jackson Demonstration State Forest**, 15mi west of Willits on Hwy 20, offers day-use recreational activities, including educational forest trails for hiking and mountain biking (the Jackson Demonstration State Forest head office in Fort Bragg is the place to pick up maps, trail guides and other useful information – see that section later in this chapter).

The **Celtic Renaissance Faire**, held in May, features traditional Highland Scottish games, food, music, dancing, jugglers, arts and crafts. Dating from 1926 and held during the first week in July, the **Willits Frontier Days & Rodeo** is billed as 'the oldest continuous rodeo in California.'

Places to Stay
Less than 2mi west of Hwy 101, **Willits KOA Resort** (☎ 707-459-6179, 800-562-8542; Hwy 20; camp & RV sites $28-37, cabins $48-50) sells Skunk Train tickets and has a swimming pool, hiking trails, children's playground and family-oriented activities.

Jackson Demonstration State Forest (☎ 707-964-5674; campsites free), further west along Hwy 20, has campsites with barbecue pits, picnic tables and pit toilets, but no running water. Camping permits are available from the on-site camp host.

Hidden Valley Campground (☎ 707-459-2521; 29801 N Hwy 101; tent/RV sites $17.50/23), 7mi north of Willits, has fairly crowded sites, but just enough greenery.

Motels along Hwy 101 vary in quality, so choose carefully. Ask about Skunk Train packages.

The **Pine Cone Motel** (☎ 707-459-5044; 1350 S Main St; rooms $45-65) and **Pepperwood Motel** (☎ 707-459-2231; 452 S Main St; rooms $30-55, with kitchen extra $10) are safe budget bets.

Holiday Lodge Motel (☎ 707-459-5361, 800-835-3972; 1540 S Main St; rooms $50-110) has a swimming pool, remodeled rooms and rates include continental breakfast. Free Skunk Train pick-up and delivery may be available.

Old West Inn (☎ 707-459-4201, 800-700-7659; 1221 S Main St; rooms $85-150) is a kitsch Wild West motel and a fun place to stay.

More upmarket motels with full amenities on Hwy 101 include **Baechtel Creek Inn** (☎ 707-459-9063, 800-459-9911; 101 Gregory Lane; rooms $70-100) and **Super 8 Motel** (☎ 707-459-3388, 800-800-8000; 1119 S Main St; rooms $80-110).

Willits Creek Cabin (☎ 707-456-0201; e willitscreekcabin@softhome.net; 190 Bittenbender Lane; singles/doubles $85/100) is a 1930s mill worker's cottage within walking distance of downtown. It has a loft, gas fireplace and barbecue grill, and can sleep six people.

Places to Eat
Fresh produce is available at the **farmers market** (cnr Humboldt & State Sts; open 3pm-6pm Thur May-Oct), a block off Hwy 101.

South of downtown, keep your eyes peeled for **Yde's Brewed Awakening**, a drive-thru espresso shack on the east side of Hwy 101.

Mariposa Market (☎ 707-459-9630; 600 S Main St; open 9:30am-6:30pm Mon-Fri, 10am-6pm Sat, 11am-4pm Sun) has natural and organic groceries.

Ardella's Kitchen (☎ 707-459-6577; 35 E Commercial St; meals $5-8; open 6am-noon Tues-Sat), a half-block east of Hwy 101, is a local favorite for breakfast, with plenty of good food and conversation.

Gribaldo's Cafe (☎ 707-459-2256; 1551 S Main St; open 24hr daily) is 'the home of the $2.99 breakfast anytime.' Dinner specialties include beef ribs, and it has a salad bar and buffet earlier in the day.

The Purple Thistle (☎ 707-459-4750; 50 S Main St; mains $12-18; dinner from 4:30pm daily) serves nontraditional Japanese and 'Mendonesian' cuisine, primarily organic. Prices are sky-high and service neglectful, although that doesn't seem to stop the place from filling up nightly – go figure.

You'll get much better value at the colorful, super-fresh **Burrito Exquisito** (☎ 707-459-5421; 42 S Hain St; meals around $6; open 11am-9pm daily), next door, or try the old-fashioned **steakhouse** down the street.

Entertainment
Shanaghie Pub (☎ 707-459-9194; 50B S Main St; closed Sun), beside the Purple Thistle restaurant, has DJs or live entertainment almost nightly.

Willits Community Theatre (☎ 707-459-0895; 212 S Main St) stages award-winning plays, poetry readings and comedy acts year-round.

Coastal Highway 1

Appropriately known as the Pacific Coast Highway, Hwy 1 snakes along the ocean until it turns inland and finally meets Hwy 101 at Leggett, 150 slow miles north of Bodega Bay. If you think patience is not virtuous, turn around now. Otherwise highlights that await you include lonely, windswept Fort Ross, artsy Mendocino village, many fine state parks, the popular Skunk Train between Fort Bragg and Willits, and of course, the rugged beauty of the coastline itself.

Beaches range from wide swaths of windswept dunes to secluded rocky coves. You're more likely to need a warm jacket or windbreaker than shorts and suntan oil. Instead of swimming and sunbathing, the main attractions are walking on the sand, exploring tidepools, searching for unusual shells and driftwood, gazing at the horizon and catching the sunsets.

Other pursuits include surfing, surf fishing, deep-sea fishing, river fishing, crabbing and abalone diving. Tidepools are a special treat at low tide, when you can see starfish, mussels, sea urchins, anemones, hermit crabs and other marine creatures go about their business.

Whale-watching is quite popular from December to April, when gray whales migrate along the Pacific coast. You can spot whales from almost any point or headland, or on cruises from Bodega Bay and Fort Bragg. Harbor seal colonies can be seen at Jenner, by the mouth of the Russian River, and MacKerricher State Park near Fort Bragg.

The coast is usually cool and foggy in summer, cold and rainy in winter. From Memorial Day to Labor Day and on autumn weekends, accommodations all along the coast fill up, so reservations are practically a necessity, even for campgrounds. Try visiting during spring or autumn, especially September and October when the fog lifts, the ocean sparkles blue, and summer tourists have mostly gone home.

Getting There & Away

The **Mendocino Transit Authority** (MTA; ☎ 707-462-1422, 800-696-4682) operates several coastal bus routes. MTA bus No 65 travels the Mendocino–Fort Bragg–Willits–Ukiah–Santa Rosa route every morning, then returns in the afternoon. A daily South Mendocino Coast No 95 bus goes from Point Arena to Santa Rosa and back, via Jenner, Bodega Bay and Sebastopol.

Monday to Friday, a South Coast No 75 bus heads north from Gualala to the Navarro River junction at Hwy 128, then runs inland through the Anderson Valley to Ukiah, returning every afternoon. At the Navarro junction, transfers are available to the North

Coast route passing through Albion, Little River, Mendocino and Fort Bragg Monday to Friday.

In Santa Rosa, you can connect with **Golden Gate Transit buses** (☎ 707-541-2000) operating to and from San Francisco and the Bay Area; **Sonoma County Transit buses** (☎ 707-576-7433, 800-345-7433) connects with other points in Sonoma County, including the Russian River and Sonoma; and **Greyhound** (☎ 800-231-2222; w www.greyhound.com) for points further afield, including along Hwy 101.

BODEGA BAY

Bodega Bay (population 950) is almost always breezy and fresh, even when it's hot and sticky inland. The bayside fishing village gets merrily overrun by visitors who amble along the beaches, peer into tidepools, watch whales off Bodega Head, fish, surf and enjoy the fresh seafood for which Bodega Bay is famous.

Long inhabited by Pomo Indians, the bay takes its name from Juan Francisco de la Bodega y Quadra, captain of the Spanish sloop *Sonora,* which entered the bay in 1775. The area was then settled by Russians in the early 19th century, and farms were established to grow wheat for the Russian fur-trapping empire that stretched from Alaska all the way down the coast to Fort Ross. The Russians pulled out of the area in 1842, abandoning the fort and their farms, and American settlers moved in.

Hwy 1 runs along the east side of Bodega Bay. You can get to Bodega Head peninsula by turning seaward from Hwy 1 onto Eastshore Rd, then turning right at the stop sign onto Bay Flat Rd. Opposite the Tides Wharf complex, the **Sonoma Coast Visitor Information Center** (☎ 707-875-3866; w www.bodegabay.com; 850 Hwy 1; open 10am-6pm Wed-Thur, noon-8pm Fri-Sat, 11am-7pm Sun) provides information for the Bodega Bay area north to Fort Ross.

The **Bodega Bay Fishermen's Festival** held in April is the big event of the year, attracting thousands of visitors; activities include the blessing of the fishing fleet, a flamboyant parade of decorated vessels, an arts and crafts fair, kite-flying, feasting and more fun. Another favorite is the great **crab feed**, held in February or March.

The tiny town of Bodega, a few miles inland from Bodega Bay, was the setting for Alfred Hitchcock's film *The Birds*.

Activities

Landlubbers can find **hiking** at Bodega Head, where there are several good trails, including a 3¾mi trail to the Bodega Dunes Campground. **Candy & Kites** (☎ 707-875-3777; *1415 Hwy 1*) sells a wide variety of single-line and dual-line sport kites; 'Blowdega Head' is usually windy.

Chanslor Riding Stables (☎ 707-875-3333; *2660 Hwy 1*) offers horseback riding on the beach and along Salmon Creek (trail rides $25 to $50). On the oceanfront, **Bodega Harbour Golf Links** (☎ 707-875-3538) is an 18-hole Scottish-style golf course designed by Robert Trent Jones, Jr. Green fees are $40 to $90.

Bodega Bay Surf Shack (☎ 707-875-3944; *1400 Hwy 1*) rents surfboards, boogie boards, windsurfing gear, sea kayaks, bicycles and wet suits, and also offers **surfing** lessons. **Bodega Bay Kayak** (☎ 707-875-8899; *1580 Eastshore Rd*) has kayak rentals and guided coastal tours. **Bodega Bay Pro Dive** (☎ 707-875-3054; *1275 Hwy 1*) offers diving instruction, gear rentals and dive trips.

Make reservations in advance for **sportfishing** charters and, between December and April, **whale-watching** cruises, as the trips are quite popular. **Wil's Fishing Adventures** (☎ 707-875-2323; *1580 Eastshore Rd*) and the **Bodega Bay Sport Fishing Center** (☎ 707-875-3344; *1500 Bay Flat Rd*), beside the Sandpiper Cafe, organize harbor cruises, fishing trips and whale-watching excursions. Bait, tackle and fishing licenses are available at the Bodega Bay Sport Fishing Center or at **The Boathouse** (☎ 707-875-3495; *1445 Hwy 1*), which also schedules fishing trips and serves fish and chips.

See also Sonoma Coast State Beaches, on the following page.

Places to Stay & Eat

Campgrounds here are often full.

Sonoma County Regional Park (*information ☎ 707-875-3540, reservations ☎ 707-565-2267; campsites $16, with reservation $23*) operates **Doran Park** (*201 Doran Beach Rd*) and **Westside Regional Park** (*2400 Westshore Rd*), both with beaches,

hot showers, fishing and boat ramps. Doran Park is on a narrow, windy spit of land between the bay and the ocean. Westside Regional Park campground, on the bay side of Bodega Head, is also exposed.

Bodega Harbor Inn (☎ 707-875-3594; ⓦ *www.bodegaharborinn.com; 1345 Bodega Ave; rooms $60-82, vacation houses $90-160*), half a block uphill from Hwy 1, is the most economical motel in town. It's furnished with antiques.

Chanslor Guest Ranch (☎ 707-875-2721; ⓦ *www.chanslorranch.com; 2660 Hwy 1; rooms $80-150*), about a mile north of Bodega Bay, offers horseback riding, on-site massage, wood-burning fireplaces and a wonderful variety of cozy country B&B rooms.

Bodega Bay Lodge & Spa (☎ 707-875-3525, 800-368-2468; ⓦ *www.bodegabaylodge.com; 103 Hwy 1; rooms $210-285*) is an atmospheric place, popular with golfers. It has indulgent amenities, such as evening wine tastings and an ocean-view swimming pool, whirlpool spa and fitness club. Ask about getaway packages.

Tides Wharf & Restaurant (☎ 707-875-3652; *835 Hwy 1; breakfast & lunch $7-18, dinner $15-35*) and further south **Lucas Wharf Restaurant & Bar** (☎ 707-875-3522; *595 Hwy 1; meals $10-40*) both specialize in seafood and sit right on the waterfront, with big picture windows affording a view of the catch being unloaded at the docks. Although it boasts a well-stocked gourmet food store, Tides is designed for tour buses, while more charming Lucas Wharf has a wonderfully long bar and a take-out deli.

Sandpiper Dockside Cafe & Restaurant (☎ 707-875-2278; *1410 Bay Flat Rd; meals from $10*) is smaller, cheaper and more popular with locals. It cheerfully dishes up fresh seafood and has a fine view of the pier, the marina and the bay. To get there, turn seaward from Hwy 1 onto Eastshore Rd and go straight at the stop sign to the marina.

Duck Club (☎ 707-875-3525; *103 Hwy 1; brunch $7.50-12, mains $18-28*) is a respected restaurant at the Bodega Bay Lodge, overlooking Bodega Head. It serves divinely inspired Cal-French cuisine in an upscale dining room with wrought-iron candelabra.

SONOMA COAST STATE BEACHES

With over a dozen state beaches, this 17mi stretch of rocky coast heading from Bodega Bay to Jenner is collectively known as the **Sonoma Coast State Beach** (☎ 707-875-3483).

Some are tiny beaches tucked away in little coves, others wide expanses of tawny sand. From south to north, notable beaches include the **Bodega Dunes**; 2mi-long **Salmon Creek Beach**; sandy **Portuguese & Schoolhouse Beaches**; **Duncan's Landing**, where small boats unload; **Shell Beach** for tidepooling and beachcombing; and scenic **Goat Rock**, with its harbor seal colony at the mouth of the Russian River, all south of Jenner. Coastal **hiking trails** connect nearly all of the beaches.

A mile north of Bodega Bay, **Bodega Dunes Campground** (campsites $12) has high sand dunes and hot showers. Another 5mi further north, year-round **Wright's Beach Campground** (reservations ☎ 800-444-7275; w www.reserveamerica.com; campsites $12) has popular beachside sites without much privacy.

On Willow Creek Rd, running inland from Hwy 1 on the south side of the Russian River Bridge, are two first-come, first-served environmental campgrounds, **Willow Creek** and **Pomo Canyon** (campsites $10); parking is about 500yd away. Willow Creek has no water; Pomo Canyon has cold water faucets. Both are open April to November, depending on weather.

JENNER

This seaside town (population 160) is perched on the hills at the mouth of the Russian River. Hwy 1 turnouts just north of town provide views of the **harbor seal colony** at the river mouth; pups are born March to August. Staying in Jenner gives travelers quick access to the coast *and* the Russian River area (see that section, earlier).

Jenner Inn & Cottages (☎ 707-865-2377, 800-732-2377; w www.jennerinn.com; Hwy 1; creekside rooms $88-238, ocean-view rooms $158-258, cottages $158-378), in the center of town, is Jenner's most prominent building and landmark. Rates include a vegetarian breakfast. There's also a wine bar and fireside lounge.

River's End (☎ 707-865-2484, fax 707-865-9621; 11048 Hwy 1; rooms & cabins $120-180) has a handful of divine cottages and a fine seafood **restaurant** (lunch $10-20, dinner $23-28; open noon-3:30pm & 5pm-9pm Thur-Mon), all with a splendid river view. It's worth stopping by the intimate bar just for drinks.

FORT ROSS STATE HISTORIC PARK

In March 1812, a group of 25 Russians and 80 Native Alaskans (including members of the Kodiak and Aleutian tribes) arrived here, near the site of a Kashaya Pomo Indian village, and began to build a wooden fort. The southernmost outpost of the 19th-century Russian fur trade on America's Pacific coast, Fort Ross was established as a base for sea otter hunting operations, trade with Alta California, and for growing wheat and other crops to supply Russian settlements in Alaska. The Russians dedicated the fort in August 1812, and occupied it until 1842. It was abandoned because the sea otter population had been all but eliminated, and the agricultural production was never as great as hoped.

Today, 11mi north of Jenner, Fort Ross State Historic Park (☎ 707-847-3286; 19005 Hwy 1; admission per vehicle $2; open 10am-4:30pm daily) presents an accurate reconstruction of the Russian fort. Most of the original buildings were sold, dismantled and carried away to Sutter's Fort in California's Central Valley during the gold rush. The **visitor center** (☎ 707-847-3437) has dated historical displays, but an excellent bookshop with volumes on Californian history, nature and other topics. Ask about hiking to the old Russian cemetery and orchard.

On Living History Day, the last Saturday in July, costumed volunteers bring the fort's history back to life; check the website (w www.parks.ca.gov) for other special events, held frequently, or call the visitor center first.

Reef Campground (☎ 707-847-3286; campsites $10; open Apr-Oct), within the park, about 2mi south of the fort off Hwy 1, has first-come, first-served campsites (cold running water, no showers) nestled into a sheltered seaside gully.

Stillwater Cove Regional Park (☎ 707-847-3245, reservations ☎ 707-565-2267;

22455 N Hwy 1; campsites $16), 2mi north of Timber Cove, has campsites, hot showers and hiking trails under Monterey pines.

Sea Coast Hideaways (☎ 707-847-3278; Hwy 1; campsites with/without hookups $21/19), at Timber Cove, about 3mi north of Fort Ross, offers camping on a bluff overlooking the sea and a private, secluded beach in a little cove. Amenities include hot showers, an outdoor hot tub, boat rentals, scuba gear rentals, fishing bait and tackle, and more. It also rents private homes and cabins in the area, from $195 to $650 for two nights.

Timber Cove Inn (☎ 707-847-3231, 800-987-8319, fax 707-847-3704; 21780 N Hwy 1; rooms midweek/weekends from $78/110) is a luxurious lodge and restaurant. Some rooms, which face either the ocean or a Japanese-style pond, have skylights, fireplaces or sunken Roman tubs.

SALT POINT STATE PARK

This 6000-acre coastal park (☎ 707-847-3221; day-use fee per vehicle $2) has hiking trails, picnic areas, tidepools, pygmy forest and one of California's first underwater parks, **Gerstle Cove Marine Reserve**, great for diving and tidepooling. A short distance inland is **Kruse Rhododendron State Reserve**. Growing abundantly in the filtered light of the redwood forest, the rhododendrons reach heights of 30ft or more, with a magnificent display of pink blossoms in spring, usually around mid-April to late May. To get there, turn east off Hwy 1 onto Kruse Ranch Rd, then follow the signs for about a half-mile to a parking area.

Two campgrounds, **Woodside** and **Gerstle Cove** (reservations ☎ 800-444-7275; w www .reserveamerica.com; campsites $12), both signposted from Hwy 1, offer campsites under Monterey pines with cold running water, but no showers. Walk-in **environmental campsites** (campsites $10) are about a half-mile from the parking area, on the east side of Woodside campground.

SEA RANCH

The planned village of Sea Ranch spreads itself along the coast, south of Gualala. Public through-ways onto many private beaches have been mandated by law, after years of litigation against the ranch corporation. **Hiking trails** now lead from signposted roadside

parking lots down to the sea, and all along the tops of the bluffs. The **Shell Beach** trail (turn off Hwy 1 at mile-marker 55.24) has a wooden staircase, making the coast more easily accessible.

Sea Ranch Lodge (☎ 707-785-2371, 800-732-7262, fax 707-785-2917; w www .searanchlodge.com; 60 Sea Walk Dr; rooms $205-395) has its main building, store and post office at mile-marker 50.60, on the ocean side of Hwy 1. Naturalistic rooms have ocean views, and some have hot tubs and TVs. Also on-site is a restaurant, sundries store and golf course.

North of the lodge, be sure to have a laugh at the eccentric-looking **chapel** on the inland side of Hwy 1.

GUALALA

The tiny coastal settlement of Gualala (population 585) was founded as a lumber mill town by the 1860s. Stop by **Dolphin Arts Gallery** (☎ 707-884-3896; 39225 Hwy 1; open 10am-5pm Wed-Mon, noon-4pm Tues) for maps and tourist information; it's hidden at the mall behind the historic Gualala Hotel.

Inland along old State Rd, at the south end of town, the **Gualala Arts Center** (☎ 707-884-1138; open 9am-4pm Mon-Fri, noon-4pm Sat & Sun) has changing gallery exhibitions and organizes the annual **Art in the Redwoods Festival** on the 3rd weekend in August. Further along that same road, **Gualala River Redwood Park** (☎ 707-884-3533; campsites $15, RV sites $32-38; open Memorial Day to Labor Day) is a redwood grove campground.

Gualala Point Regional Park (☎ 707-785-2377, camping reservations 707-565-2267; 42401 Hwy 1; campsites $12), about a mile south of town, offers camping with hot showers in a redwood grove beside the Gualala River. Hiking trails go along the river, beside the beach and out to coastal bluffs, including Whale Watch Point.

St Orres Inn (☎ 707-884-3303, fax 707-884-1840; w www.saintorres.com; 36601 Hwy 1; B&B rooms $80-95, cottages $110-210), on the northern outskirts of town, is a Russian-looking inn, architect designed with rough-hewn redwood timbers and gardens overlooking the sea. Its fine **dining room** (reservations ☎ 707-884-3335; mains $40) serves inspired North Coast cuisine.

NORTH COAST

POINT ARENA

Point Arena (population 440) is a small fishing town close to a windswept point where a lighthouse has stood for nearly a century. The **Point Arena Lighthouse** (☎ 707-882-2777; adult/child $4/1, hikers & cyclists free; open 10am-4:30pm daily Apr-Sept, 11am-3:30pm Mon-Fri, 10am-3:30pm Sat & Sun Oct-Mar), 2mi north of town, is the second lighthouse to stand on this spot. The original, built in 1870, was toppled by the 1906 earthquake. Visitors can check the museum, and climb 115ft up to the top of lighthouse, where a docent explains the workings.

Several former US Coast Guard homes (think tract housing) nearby are rented by the nonprofit **Point Arena Lighthouse Keepers** (☎ 707-882-2777, 877-725-4448, fax 707-882-2111; homes from $140).

Rollerville Junction (☎ 707-882-2440, fax 707-882-3049; 22900 Shoreline Hwy; tent/RV sites $26/32, cabins/cottages $38/95), back at the turnoff from Hwy 1, has hot showers, a convenience store, laundry and seasonal hot tub.

A mile west of town at Arena Cove, overlooking Point Arena's small pier, the historic **Wharfmaster's Inn** (☎ 707-882-3171, 800-932-4031, fax 707-882-4114; w www.wharfmasters.com; 785 Port Rd; rooms $95-175, suites $225-250) is a restored 1862 Victorian house, offering midweek and off-season discounts.

Downtown are a couple of motels and B&Bs, but there's no reason to stick around. Refuel at budget-minded **El Burrito** (☎ 707-882-2910; 165 Main St; open 7:30am-7pm daily), or further uphill at soulful **Pangaea** (☎ 707-882-3001; 250 Main St; mains $16-22; open from 6pm Wed-Fri, from 5pm Sat & Sun), which serves bold, eclectic Californian cuisine and decadent desserts.

Arena Cinema (☎ 707-882-3456; 214 Main St) shows mainstream, foreign and art films. Stop by the rainbow-mural **coffeehouse** across the street for billiards.

MANCHESTER STATE BEACH

Seven miles north of Point Arena, just north of the tiny town of Manchester, another turnoff from Hwy 1 leads to Manchester Beach, a long, wild stretch of sand. **Ross Ranch** (☎ 707-877-1834), at Irish Beach another 5mi north, offers two-hour horseback rides on the beach ($60) and in the mountains ($50) – call for reservations.

Mendocino Coast KOA (☎ 707-882-2375, 800-562-4188; w www.manchesterbeachkoa.com; tent/RV sites from $29/36, cabins $48-58) has campsites spread among Monterey pines, a cooking pavilion, hot showers, hot tub, swimming pool, hiking trails and rental bicycles.

A half-mile further toward the coast, **Manchester State Park** (☎ 707-882-2463; campsites $7) has a grassy campground with cold running water (no showers). Ten **environmental campsites** (campsites $5) are hidden in the dunes, a 1½mi walk from the parking area; these have untreated creek water. All sites are first-come, first-served.

ELK

Elk (population 250) is another blink-and-you-miss-it coastal town. At the south end of town, **Greenwood State Beach** (☎ 707-877-3458) has picnic tables, but no camping; its **visitor center** (open 11am-1pm Sat & Sun mid-Mar–Oct) has exhibits on the town's logging past. Call **Force 10** (☎ 707-877-3505) for ocean kayaking; two-hour guided trips cost $95.

Several upmarket B&Bs take advantage of the quiet beauty of the coast.

Griffin House at Greenwood Cove (☎ 707-877-3422; w www.griffinn.com; 5910 S Hwy 1; garden/oceanfront cottages from $100/150) has wood-burning stoves.

Greenwood Pier Inn (☎ 707-877-9997, fax 707-877-3439; w greenwoodpierinn.com; 5928 S Hwy 1; suites $130-300), next door, boasts gardens by the sea and friendly innkeepers. All rooms have fireplaces and ocean-view decks. The healthy gourmet **café** (meals under $20) has live music most Saturday nights.

Sandpiper House (☎ 707-877-3587, 800-894-9016; w www.sandpiperhouse.com; 5520 S Hwy 1; rates $140-260) is a grey 1916 seaside home on the outskirts of town.

Elk Cove Inn (☎ 707-877-3321, 800-275-2967, fax 707-877-1808; w www.elkcoveinn.com; 6300 S Hwy 1; rooms/cottages from $100/240, spa suites $300-350) has a cocktail bar.

The **Harbor House Inn** (☎ 707-877-3203, 800-720-7474, fax 707-877-3452; w www.theharborhouseinn.com; 5600 S Hwy 1; cottages $300-425), a Craftsman-style lodge, offers squeezed-together cottages with ocean-view clawfoot tubs. Rates include full breakfast and a four-course dinner.

Queenie's Roadhouse (☎ 707-877-3285; dishes $5-8; open 8am-3pm Thur-Mon), a quaint café serving light fare, stands opposite the state beach, beside a deli and gas station.

Bridget Dolan's Irish Pub & Dinner House (☎ 707-877-1820; 5910 S Hwy 1; meals $8-18; open 5:30pm-9pm Sun-Thur, 5:30pm-9:30pm Fri & Sat) serves bangers and mash, vegetarian lasagna and more.

VAN DAMME STATE PARK

Three miles south of Mendocino, this state park is best known for its unusual **pygmy forest**, where a combination of acidic soil and an impenetrable layer of hardpan just below the surface create a natural bonsai forest with decades-old trees growing only a few feet high. A raised wheelchair-accessible boardwalk provides easy access to the forest.

To get there, turn east from Hwy 1 onto Little River Airport Rd, a half-mile south of the Van Damme State Park entrance, and go 3mi. Or you can hike up from the campground on the 3½mi **Fern Canyon Scenic Trail**, which crosses back and forth over Little River. The **visitor center** (☎ 707-937-4016; open 10am-4pm daily summer, 10am-4pm Sat & Sun rest of year) has nature exhibits, videos and interpretive programs; a half-hour marsh loop trail starts nearby. For sea-cave kayaking tours ($45) and kayak rentals ($20), contact **Lost Coast Kayaking** (☎ 707-937-2434).

If you park by the beach and walk into the park, there's no day-use fee. There are two **campgrounds** (seasonal reservations ☎ 800-444-7275; w www.reserveamerica.com; campsites $12) with hot showers, one just off Hwy 1 and another in a highland meadow. Another 10 **environmental campsites** (sites $12) are a 1¾mi hike up Fern Canyon from the parking lot inside the park.

MENDOCINO

A village perched on a bluff overlooking the Pacific, Mendocino (population 1000) was built as a lumber mill town by transplanted New Englanders in the 1850s. It thrived late into the 19th century, with ships transporting redwood timber from Mendocino Bay to San Francisco. The mills shut down in the 1930s, and the town slept until it was

Star of the Silver Screen

Over 50 films for TV and the silver screen have been shot around tiny Mendocino village, starting with *The Promise*, a 1916 silent film about a train wreck. Some of the best-known movies made here include *East of Eden* (1954) and *Rebel without a Cause* (1955), both starring James Dean; *The Island of the Blue Dolphins* (1964), filmed on the south Mendocino coast; and the *Murder, She Wrote* TV series (1984–96), starring Angela Lansbury. Most recently, *The Majestic* (2001) with Jim Carrey included scenes shot at Point Cabrillo Lighthouse and Fort Bragg's Skunk Train depot.

rediscovered by artists in the 1950s and became a bohemian haven.

The entire town, with its Cape Cod and Victorian buildings all lovingly restored, is on the National Register of Historic Places. So many tourists come for the art galleries, restaurants and B&Bs that, at times, Mendocino seems like a caricature of itself. That said, most locals deal with the stampede graciously. Outside of peak summer season, the ambience is more relaxed and the natural beauty of the region is inexhaustible. Camping along the coast or staying up in Fort Bragg can help you avoid the crowds.

Sneak a virtual peek at w www.gomendo .com, or drop by the **Ford House Visitor Center & Museum** (☎ 707-937-5397; 735 Main St; admission by donation $1; open 11am-4pm daily) for maps, books and information about Mendocino and nearby state parks, and to see the natural and cultural history exhibits. Hot cider and videos are always available. Outside on a bluff are picnic tables and public restrooms. Look across Main St to see one of the town's famous **water towers**.

Things to See

With a nationally recognized program of over 200 art classes, the **Mendocino Art Center** (☎ 707-937-5818, 800-653-3328; w www.mendocinoartcenter.org; 45200 Little Lake St; gallery open 10am-5pm daily) also puts on exhibitions, arts and craft fairs, and live theater. Other **art galleries** around town hold special events between April and December, on the second Saturday evening of each month.

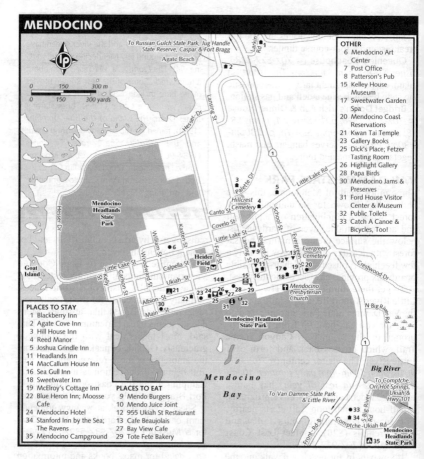

MENDOCINO

To Russian Gulch State Park, Jug Handle State Reserve, Caspar & Fort Bragg

Agate Beach

OTHER
6 Mendocino Art Center
7 Post Office
8 Patterson's Pub
15 Kelley House Museum
17 Sweetwater Garden Spa
20 Mendocino Coast Reservations
21 Kwan Tai Temple
23 Gallery Books
25 Dick's Place; Fetzer Tasting Room
26 Highlight Gallery
28 Papa Birds
30 Mendocino Jams & Preserves
31 Ford House Visitor Center & Museum
32 Public Toilets
33 Catch A Canoe & Bicycles, Too!

Mendocino Headlands State Park

Goat Island

Hillcrest Cemetery
Evergreen Cemetery

Heider Field

Mendocino Presbyterian Church

Mendocino Headlands State Park

Mendocino Bay

Big River

To Comptche, Orr Hot Springs, Ukiah & Hwy 101

To Van Damme State Park & Little River

Mendocino Headlands State Park

PLACES TO STAY
1 Blackberry Inn
2 Agate Cove Inn
3 Hill House Inn
4 Reed Manor
5 Joshua Grindle Inn
11 Headlands Inn
14 MacCallum House Inn
16 Sea Gull Inn
18 Sweetwater Inn
19 McElroy's Cottage Inn
22 Blue Heron Inn; Moosse Cafe
24 Mendocino Hotel
34 Stanford Inn by the Sea; The Ravens
35 Mendocino Campground

PLACES TO EAT
9 Mendo Burgers
10 Mendo Juice Joint
12 955 Ukiah St Restaurant
13 Cafe Beaujolais
27 Bay View Cafe
29 Tote Fete Bakery

The **Kelley House Museum** (☎ 707-937-5791; 45007 Albion St; admission $2; open 1pm-4pm daily June-Sept, 1pm-4pm Fri-Mon Oct-May), inside an 1861 home, has a research library and changing displays about early California and the local area. Another historic building is the 1852 **Kwan Tai Temple** (45160 Albion St), where you can peer in the window to see the old Chinese altar.

The newly restored 1909 **Point Cabrillo Lighthouse** (☎ 707-937-0816; Point Cabrillo Dr; admission free; open 11am-4pm Fri-Mon Mar-Oct) stands on a 300-acre wildlife preserve north of town, midway between Russian Gulch and Caspar Beach. Between May and September, guided ecology and history walks start at 11am on Sunday.

Activities

Sweetwater Gardens Spa (☎ 707-937-4140, 800-300-4140; 955 Ukiah St; open 1pm-10pm Mon-Thur, noon-10pm Fri & Sun, noon-11pm Sat) offers massage and bodywork. A one-hour private tub and sauna session costs $15, but entry to the common public spa is less than half this rate at $8.50 ($6 on Wednesday).

Mendocino Headlands State Park, surrounding the village, is crisscrossed by trails, with walks overlooking the bluffs and rocky coves. On weekends, free **spring wildflower walks** and **whale-watching walks** are given in season, December to March; the Visitor Center has details, and can arrange guided history walks upon request.

Catch A Canoe & Bicycles, Too! (☎ 707-937-0273, 800-320-2453; Comptche-Ukiah Rd) rents mountain bicycles, as well as kayaks and outrigger canoes for self-guided trips up the 8mi-long Big River tidal estuary, the longest undeveloped estuary in Northern California. There are no highways or buildings, only beaches, forests, salt marshes, stream beds, abundant wildlife and historic logging sites, including century-old train trestles, wooden pilings and log dams.

The tiny town of **Albion**, hugging the north side of the Albion River mouth, about 5mi south of Mendocino, provides a navigable river and an ocean bay for kayaking.

Special Events

Mendocino celebrates a number of special events. In late January and early February the **Mendocino Crab & Wine Days** has wine tasting, cooking classes, whale-watching and crab cruises. The **Mendocino Whale Festival** is held on the 1st weekend in March and has wine and chowder tasting, whale-watching walks and strolling musicians.

Mendocino Music Festival (W www.mendocinomusic.com) is held in mid-July and there are orchestral and chamber music concerts on the headlands, with children's matinees and some rehearsals open to the public.

Mendocino Wine & Mushroom Festival is held over 12 days in early November and has guided mushroom tours and a symposium.

In December, the **Mendocino Coast Christmas Festival** has candlelight inn tours, music and more.

Places to Stay

If you don't fancy staying in a Victorian B&B, you may be out of luck here. Keep in mind that accommodations in Fort Bragg, just 10mi up the coast, are typically more affordable.

Mendocino Coast Reservations (☎ 707-937-5033, 800-262-7801, fax 707-937-4236; W www.mendocinovacations.com; 1000 Main St; open 9am-5pm daily) arranges vacation homes, cottages and B&Bs.

Sweetwater Spa & Inn (☎ 707-937-4076, 800-300-4140; W www.sweetwaterspa.com; rooms & cottages $60-200) owns a bewildering variety of accommodations, both in town and at Little River. Rates for cozy B&B rooms, ocean-view cottages and

fanciful water-tower units all include spa privileges.

Camping & Cabins Just uphill from Hwy 1, rustic **Mendocino Campground** (☎ 707-937-3130; Comptche-Ukiah Rd; campsites $19; open Apr-Oct) has hot showers and forest nature trails nearby. It's peaceful.

Russian Gulch State Park (reservations ☎ 800-444-7275; W www.reserveamerica.com; campsites $12), 2mi north of town, has a shady campground with hot showers and rocky headlands, a sandy beach, small waterfall and Devil's Punch Bowl, a collapsed sea arch.

Caspar Beach RV Park (☎ 707-964-3306, fax 707-964-0526; 14441 Cabrillo Dr; campsites $22, RV sites $25-30), another 3mi north of Mendocino, is in a sheltered gully beside Caspar Beach.

About 5mi south of town, Albion has two campgrounds, **Schooner's Landing Campground** (☎ 707-937-5707; campsites $24-29.50) and **Albion River Campground** (☎ 707-937-0606; tent/RV sites $19/27).

Motels & Hotels North of the village, **Blackberry Inn** (☎ 707-937-5281, 800-950-7806; W www.mendocinomotel.com; 44951 Larkin Rd; rates $95-145) has quirky but comfy Old West–theme accommodations.

Hill House Inn (☎ 707-937-0554, 800-422-0554, fax 707-937-1123; W www.hillhouseinn.com; 10701 Palette Dr; rooms $150-225) is a huge motel styled to look like a country inn, with ocean views and tasteful furnishings. Check for Internet booking specials.

Mendocino Hotel (☎ 707-937-0511, 800-548-0513; W www.mendocinohotel.com; 45080 Main St; rooms with/without bath from $120/95, suites $275) is an 1878 Victorian hostelry overlooking the sea, with garden rooms and suites in back.

B&Bs Perhaps the best known of Mendocino's many Victorian B&Bs, **Joshua Grindle Inn** (☎ 707-937-4143, 800-474-6353; W www.joshgrin.com; 44800 Little Lake Rd; rooms $130-245) pampers its guests with gourmet breakfasts and, upon arrival, free cookies and locally made wine. Ask about water-tower rooms.

MacCallum House Inn (☎ 707-937-0289, 800-609-0492; W www.maccallumhouse.com;

NORTH COAST

45020 Albion St; rooms $100-195) dates from 1882. Some cottages have old-fashioned stoves, while other rooms have stone fireplaces.

Other places right in town include **Mc-Elroy's Cottage Inn** *(☎ 707-937-1734, 888-262-3576;* **w** *www.mcelroysinn.com; 998 Main St; rooms $70-115),* an early 1900s Craftsman-style home; the Cape Cod–style **Blue Heron Inn** *(☎ 707-937-4323; 390 Kasten St; rooms $95-115)*; and the **Headlands Inn** *(☎ 707-937-4431, fax 707-937-0421;* **w** *www.headlandsinn.com; cnr Albion & Howard Sts; rooms $110-195),* a cozy saltbox. Lookout rooms at the **Sea Gull Inn** *(☎ 707-937-5204, 888-937-5204; 44960 Albion St; rooms $80-165)* are also worthwhile.

Agate Cove Inn *(☎ 707-937-0551, 800-527-3111, fax 707-937-0550;* **w** *www. agatecove.com; 11201 Lansing St; rooms $130-250, ocean-view cottages $190-290)* has farmhouse rooms and 100-year-old cypress trees.

Stanford Inn by the Sea *(☎ 707-937-5615, 800-331-8884, fax 707-937-0305;* **w** *www .stanfordinn.com; Comptche-Ukiah Rd; rooms with fireplaces $245-285)* is a masterpiece of a lodge with a small working organic farm. Each impeccable room has either a four-poster or sleigh bed, plus a wood-burning fireplace. Guests enjoy gourmet breakfast, complimentary wine and a greenhouse swimming pool and spa. Pets welcome.

Mendocino Farmhouse *(☎ 707-937-0241, 800-475-1536;* **w** *www.mendocinofarmhouse .com; Comptche-Ukiah Rd; rooms $95-145)* is a low-key rural retreat, not far outside town, serving hearty breakfasts and surrounded by meadows and redwood forests.

Old Mill Farm School of Country Living *(☎ 707-937-0244),* on a rolling ridgetop adjacent to Big River, 7mi inland from Mendocino, allows visitors to experience a small, self-sustaining organic farm. The land has hiking trails, a swimming hole, forests, gardens and other natural beauties. Call for details about programs.

Places to Eat

Tote Fete Bakery *(☎ 707-937-3383; 10450 Lansing St),* perfect for a quick nosh or stocking picnic baskets, has a garden out back.

Mendo Burgers *(☎ 707-937-1111; 10483 Lansing St; meals under $5; open 11am-5pm daily),* at the rear of Mendocino Bakery & Cafe, is an old-fashioned lunch counter. This being Northern California, menu options include veggie, chicken, turkey and fish burgers.

Mendo Juice Joint *(☎ 707-937-4033; 10418 Lansing St; snacks $3-6; open from 6:30am daily)* is a funky, laid-back local hangout, mixing up organic juices, smoothies and espresso, plus home-baked pastries and savory goodies.

Bay View Café *(☎ 707-937-4197; 45040 Main St; breakfast & lunch under $10, dinner $10-15; open 8am-4:30pm Sun-Thurs, 8am-10pm Fri & Sat)* is aptly named, with an upstairs dining room and outdoor deck. It's especially known for its good breakfasts.

Mendocino Hotel *(☎ 707-937-0511; 45080 Main St; mains $18-35)* has an elegant Victorian restaurant where you can dine on continental cuisine. Breakfast and lunch are served daily in the hotel's **Garden Bar & Cafe**.

Reservations are recommended for other top-end restaurants, all beloved by foodies.

Cafe Beaujolais *(☎ 707-937-5614; 961 Ukiah St; mains $18-25; open 5:45pm-9pm daily)* is probably Mendocino's most famous restaurant, inside an 1893 Victorian farmhouse. Serving haute California cuisine, the menu features organic produce, seafood and meat from humanely raised animals.

MacCallum House Restaurant *(☎ 707-937-0289, 45020 Albion St; café dishes $6-12, mains $20-32; open from 5:30pm daily),* at the inn of the same name, is also renowned for its fresh regional cuisine, with the chef-owner choosing many ingredients by hand.

955 Ukiah St Restaurant *(☎ 707-937-1955; 955 Ukiah St; mains $15-25; dinner from 6pm Wed-Sun),* back along the garden path, is another respected spot for West Coast cooking, perhaps red snapper with pesto baked in filo pastry.

Moosse Cafe *(☎ 707-937-4323; 390 Kasten St; lunch around $10, dinner $16-22; open 11am-3:30pm & 5:30pm-9:30pm daily),* at the Blue Heron Inn, is an intimate eatery for creative comfort food and original desserts.

The Ravens *(☎ 707-937-5615, Comptche-Ukiah Rd; breakfast $8-13, mains $14-28; open from 8am Mon-Sat, noon-2:30pm Sun, 5:30pm-8:30pm daily),* at Stanford Inn by the Sea, is an outstanding vegetarian restaurant drawing chefs from around the world. It offers prix-fixe vegan dinners with weekly specials, and simply yummy breakfasts.

Entertainment

Mendocino Theatre Company (☎ *707-937-4477;* **W** *www.1mtc.org; 45200 Little Lake St*) performs at the Mendocino Art Center.

You can have cocktails at the **Mendocino Hotel** or the **Grey Whale Bar** at the Mac-Callum House Inn (see Places to Stay, earlier). Locals get toasty at **Dick's Place** (☎ *707-937-5643; 45080 Main St*) and **Patterson's Pub** (☎ *707-937-4782; 10485 Lansing St*), an Irish-style bar with big-screen TVs and an appealing pub menu of sandwiches, seafood and salads, all under $10.

Shopping

Gallery Bookshop (☎ *707-937-2665; 319 Kasten St; open 9:30am-6pm Sun-Thur, 9:30am-9pm Fri-Sat*) has endless shelves of volumes on history, nature and travel, as well as Bookwinkles, for children's books.

Highlight Gallery (☎ *707-937-3132; 45052 Main St*) sells high-quality handcrafted wood carvings, furniture, glass, pottery and jewelry.

Papa Birds (☎ *707-937-2730, 800-845-0522; 45040 Albion St*) has birdhouses and all things avian; call to ask if Saturday morning bird walks along the Mendocino Headlands are being offered again.

Fetzer Tasting Room (☎ *707-937-6190; 45070 Main St; open 10am-6pm daily*) and **Mendocino Jams & Preserves** (☎ *707-937-1037; 440 Main St*), a genuine cottage industry, both offer free tastings.

JUG HANDLE STATE RESERVE

About halfway between Mendocino and Fort Bragg, this stunning reserve has an 'ecological staircase' that you can see on a 5mi **self-guided nature trail.** Five wave-cut terraces ascend in steps from the seashore, each about 100ft and 100,000 years removed from the one before it. Each terrace has its own distinct geology and vegetation; on one level is a pygmy forest, similar to the better-known one at Van Damme State Park. Other features of the reserve include headlands strolls, whale-watching points and a sandy beach in a lovely little cove. Pick up trail guides from the parking lot, just off Hwy 1.

Annie's Jughandle Beach B&B Inn (☎ *707-964-1415, 800-964-9957, fax 707-961-1473;* **W** *www.jughandle.com; Hwy 1; rooms & suites $100-230*), opposite the reserve, is a hospitable place serving Cajun-inspired breakfasts. Cheery rooms inside this 1880s Victorian farmhouse are furnished with antiques; some also have Jacuzzis and fireplaces.

FORT BRAGG

Far less touristy than Mendocino, windy Fort Bragg (population 7025) makes an excellent alternative base for exploring the area's natural coastal delights. The fort established here in 1857 was named for Colonel Braxton Bragg, a veteran of the Mexican War; ostensibly used to 'supervise' local Pomo Indians, it was abandoned a decade later. In 1885, a lumber company was established on the old fort site, and in the same year, the California Western Railroad, later nicknamed the 'Skunk Train,' was built to get the giant redwood trees out of the forest and down to the coast.

Fort Bragg is basically a 'Main Street' town, Main St being Hwy 1. Most everything is on or just off this 2mi main drag; the movie theater and post office are on Franklin St, which runs parallel one block east. Fort Bragg's wharf district, with its fishing boat docks and seafood restaurants, lies at Noyo Harbor, at the mouth of the Noyo River, on the south side of town. The access road is just north of Hwy 20 as you head east to Willits.

The **Fort Bragg-Mendocino Coast Chamber of Commerce** (☎ *707-961-6300, 800-726-2780;* **W** *www.fortbragg.com, www.mendocinocoast.com; 332 N Main St; open 9am-noon & 12:30pm-5pm Mon-Fri, 9am-noon & 12:30pm-3pm Sat*) has a wealth of information about Fort Bragg, Mendocino and the surrounding area. For high-speed Internet access ($10 per hour, minimum $1), visit **Chocolate Divine** (☎ *707-964-7099; 260 N Main St; open daily*).

Things to See & Do

Fort Bragg's pride and joy is the vintage **Skunk Train** (☎ *707-964-6371, 800-777-5865;* **W** *www.skunktrain.com; half-day trips per child/adult $18/25, full-day trips $31/45*). The train got its nickname in 1925 when passenger service was established using stinky gas-powered steam engines. Today, the historic steam and diesel locomotives are odorless, making runs between Fort Bragg and Willits, about 40mi away, through beautiful redwood-forested mountains and along rivers, crossing 30 bridges and passing through two deep mountain tunnels. Departures are from both ends of the line, you can take the train round-trip or one-way in either direction, or go just to Northspur, the halfway point. The depot in Fort Bragg is at the foot of Laurel St, one block west of Main St, in the center of town.

The **Guest House Museum** (☎ 707-964-4251; 343 N Main St; admission $2; open 10am-4pm Thur-Sun winter, 10am-4pm Wed-Sun rest of year), a majestic Victorian house built in 1892, holds historical photos and relics of Fort Bragg's logging history. Entirely a different affair, the **Triangle Tattoo & Museum** (☎ 707-964-8814; 356B N Main St) stands opposite among the Main St art galleries and gourmet food shops. **Northcoast Artists** (☎ 707-964-8266; 362 N Main St) is a co-op gallery, while **The Outdoor Store** (☎ 707-707-964-1407; 247 Main St) carries wilderness gear. Antique shops line **Franklin St**, one block east.

At the north end of town, **Glass Beach** is named for the sea-polished glass found lying on the sands. It's reached by a short headlands trail leading toward the sea from Elm St, off Main St. The nearby **North Coast Brewing Co** (☎ 707-964-2739; 455 N Main St) offers brewery tours Monday to Saturday, but call ahead to check.

A number of small boats at Noyo Harbor offer coastal and **whale-watching cruises** and deep-sea **fishing trips**. At Noyo Harbor, **Noyo Pacific Outfitters** (☎ 707-961-0559; ⓦ www.noyopacific.com; 32400 North Harbor Dr) offers kayak rentals, snorkeling and abalone diving packages.

South of town, family-friendly **Mendocino Coast Botanical Gardens** (☎ 707-964-4352; 18220 N Hwy 1; adult/child $6/3; open 9am-5pm daily Mar-Oct, 9am-4pm daily Nov-Feb) displays native Northern Californian flora over 47 acres of seafront land and coastal bluffs. Main trails are wheelchair-accessible.

Special Events

Fort Bragg has a number of special events. The **Fort Bragg Whale Festival**, held on the 3rd weekend in March, has microbrewed-beer tasting, crafts fair and whale-watching trips. The **Rhododendron Show** is in late April to early May.

The **World's Largest Salmon BBQ** is held in Noyo Harbor on the Saturday closest to 4th of July. **Paul Bunyan Days Labor Day** weekend celebrates California's logging history with a logging show, square dancing, parade and arts fair.

Places to Stay

Like Mendocino, much of Fort Bragg's accommodation is Victorian B&Bs, but there are also plenty of affordable motels along Hwy 1. On weekends and holidays, everything fills up quickly, so reserve ahead.

For more accommodation options, see the MacKerricher State Park and Mendocino sections elsewhere in this chapter.

Pomo RV Park & Campground (☎ 707-964-3373; 17999 Tregoning Lane; tent/RV sites $22/28), about a mile south of town, is set back from Hwy 1 among brilliant flowers. Amenities include laundry and free cable TV hook-ups. Gates close at 11pm.

The **Department of Forestry** (☎ 707-964-5674; 802 N Main St; open 8am-noon & 1pm-5pm Mon-Fri) has maps, permits and information about camping in Jackson Demonstration Forest, east of Fort Bragg, toward Willits.

The family-run **Colombi Motel** (☎ 707-964-5773; 647 Oak St; rooms $35-85), five blocks east of Hwy 1 in a quiet residential area, has the cleanest lodgings in town, next door to a Laundromat. Spacious kitchenettes and family rooms are available; check in at the deli across the street.

Coast Motel (☎ 707-964-2852; 18661 Hwy 1; off-season rooms from $40), just south of Hwy 20, has just about the cheapest rooms.

Surf Motel (☎ 707-964-5361, 800-339-5361; cnr Hwys 1 & 20; rooms $68-78, suites in summer $135) sits above the harbor. Family suites with kitchen sleep six.

The Wharf Restaurant (☎ 707-964-4283, fax 707-964-0254; ⓦ www.wharf-restaurant.com; 32260 N Harbor Dr; motel rooms $40, apartments with kitchen from $95) offers economy lodging, but nothing fancy.

Seabird Lodge (☎ 707-964-4731, 800-345-0022; ⓦ www.seabirdlodge.com; 191 South St; rooms $60-110) is an enormous motel, a notch above the usual standard. It has a heated indoor pool and rooms are set back from the road.

Beach House Inn (☎ 707-961-1700, 888-559-9992, fax 707-961-1627; 100 Pudding Creek Rd; rooms $60-150), on the far north bank of Pudding Creek, is a lovely motel made up of detached buildings with well-appointed rooms; some rooms have fireplaces, ocean views and two-person tubs.

North Cliff Hotel (☎ 707-962-2500, 866-962-2550; w www.fortbragg.org; 1005 S Main St; rooms in summer/winter from $170/100) is an unbeatable choice. All-modern rooms have fireplaces, whirlpool tubs and unobstructed ocean views.

All of the following B&Bs are centrally placed.

Rendezvous Inn (☎ 707-964-8142, 800-491-8142; w www.rendezvousinn.com; 647 N Main St; rooms $70-95) has a fine restaurant. In keeping with the atmosphere of relaxation, the simple rooms have no TV or telephone.

Country Inn B&B (☎ 707-964-3737, 800-831-5327, fax 707-964-0289; w www.beourguests.com; 632 N Main St; rooms $65-145) offers rose gardens, an outdoor hot tub and Skunk Train packages.

Grey Whale Inn (☎ 707-964-0640, 800-382-7244, fax 707-964-4408; w www.greywhaleinn.com; 615 N Main St; rooms/suites $75/200) has two penthouse suites offering sweeping views, one with a double Jacuzzi and another with tropical bamboo furniture.

Avalon House (☎/fax 707-964-5555, 800-964-5556; w www.theavalonhouse.com; 561 Stewart St; rooms $80-145), a beautifully restored Craftsman-style home, has soothing skylights, antique furnishings and modern conveniences.

Weller House Inn (☎ 707-964-4415, 877-893-5537; w www.wellerhouse.com; 524 Stewart St; rooms $95-165), in a historic 1886 Victorian home nearby, is close to Glass Beach. Its reconstructed water tower enjoys the highest vantage point in Fort Bragg – and has a hot tub up top!

At the south end of town, **Lodge at Noyo River** (☎ 707-964-8045, 800-628-1126; w www.noyolodge.com; 500 Casa del Norte Dr; rooms $85-175) is a 19th-century lumber baron's house on a bluff overlooking the harbor.

Places to Eat

A **farmers market** (cnr Laurel & Franklin Sts; 3:30pm-6pm Wed late-May–Oct) takes place downtown. It's not far from the **Mendocino Cookie Company** (☎ 964-0282; 303 N Main St) and **Cowlick's** (☎ 962-9271; 250B Main St) ice-cream parlor.

Eggheads (☎ 707-964-5005; 326 N Main St; meals $8-13; open 7am-2pm Thur-Tues) can't be beaten. At breakfast, homemade cinnamon French toast and over 50 varieties of omelettes appear, some made with locally caught Dungeness crab. It also makes an equally bewildering variety of fresh sandwiches and burgers.

Headlands Coffeehouse (☎ 707-964-1987; 120 E Laurel St; dishes $4-8), just east of Main St, shouldn't be missed. It's a musical place for enjoying coffee, homemade soups, baked goods, veggie-friendly light meals and scrumptious desserts.

Old Coast Hotel Bar & Grill (☎ 707-961-4488; 101 N Franklin St; dishes $5-15; open noon-3pm Fri-Sun, 4pm or 5pm-9:30pm Thur-Tues) may not look like much more than a hard-drinkin' pub, but its fresh seafood and casual California cuisine are better than might be expected, especially dishes made with herbs from its own garden.

North Coast Brewing Co (☎ 707-964-3400; w www.northcoastbrewing.com; 444 N Main St; lunch/dinner under $10/20; open 11:30am-8:30pm daily) is an award-winning brewpub that cooks seafood and American fare.

Rendezvous Inn (☎ 707-964-8142; 647 N Main St; mains $16-23; open from 5:30pm Wed-Sun) offers European-inspired cuisine with excellent wine pairings created by a former chef of Mendocino's Cafe Beaujolais. Reservations are recommended.

Noyo Harbor has several good seafood restaurants, but also some disappointing ones. Choose carefully. Expect to pay around $10 at lunch, twice that at dinner. Gold stars go to **The Wharf Restaurant & Lounge** (☎ 707-964-4283; 32260 N Harbor Dr; open 11am-10pm daily summer), **Sharon's by the Sea** (☎ 962-0680; 32096 N Harbor Dr) and Thai-flavored **Harbor Cafe** (☎ 707-964-8281; 32150 N Harbor Dr; open 5:30pm-8:30pm Tues-Sun).

Entertainment

Caspar Inn (☎ 707-964-5565; 14957 Caspar Rd; cover $5-8, Wed free; live entertainment Wed-Sat), about 5mi south of Fort Bragg off Hwy 1, has live local rock, R&B, world beat and open-mic nights. It's always worth the drive.

Headlands Coffeehouse (☎ 707-964-1987; 120 E Laurel St) has live acoustic music most evenings – it's often classical. Drop by the low-key **North Coast Brewing Company** *(444 N Main St)* or **Old Coast Hotel** *(101 N Franklin St)* bar to taste local microbrews.

Footlighters Little Theater *(☎ 707-964-3806; 248 E Laurel St)* features 1890s-style musicals, comedy and melodrama on Wednesday and Saturday evenings in summer.

Gloriana Opera Company *(☎ 707-964-7469; w www.gloriana.org; 721 N Franklin St)* stages operettas and musicals year-round. **Opera Fresca** *(☎ 707-937-3646, 888-826-7372; w www.operafresca.com)* performs at various venues.

Getting Around

Mendocino Transit Authority *(MTA; ☎ 707-462-1422, 800-696-4682)* runs local No 5 'BraggAbout' buses between Noyo Harbor and Elm St, north of downtown, but be aware that the route doesn't always parallel Main St (Hwy 101).

Fort Bragg Cyclery *(☎ 964-3509; 579 S Franklin St; open 10am-6pm Tues-Fri, 10am-4pm Sat)* and **Ocean Trail Bikes & Rental** *(☎ 707-964-1260; 1260 N Main St)* both rent bicycles.

MacKERRICHER STATE PARK

Only 3mi north of Fort Bragg, this state park *(☎ 707-964-9112)* preserves the rugged coastline from Pudding Creek in the south to Ten Mile River in the north. Features include beaches, sand dunes, coastal bluffs, tidepools and a gentle coastal hiking trail.

The **visitor center** *(11am-3pm Sat & Sun, 10am-6pm daily in summer)* is next to the reconstructed whale skeleton at the park entrance. **Lake Cleone** is a tiny freshwater lake, good for fishing and birding. At nearby **Laguna Point**, an interpretive boardwalk overlooks harbor seals and, from about December to April, migrating whales. **Ricochet Ridge Ranch** *(☎ 707-964-7669; 24201 N Hwy 1)* offers horseback rides through the redwoods and along the beach. A 90-minute trail ride costs $40.

Popular park **campgrounds** *(seasonal reservations ☎ 800-444-2725; w www .reserveamerica.com; campsites $12)*, nestled in the redwoods, have hot showers and potable water. Ten more secluded walk-in sites *(campsites $12)*, just 50 yards from the parking area, are first-come, first-served.

WESTPORT

Westport is a tiny village of around 200 souls, clinging to a coastal bluff. In the late 1800s and early 1900s, it was an important shipping port, with the longest logging chute in California. Today, there's almost nothing here except for romantic, windswept ocean views and abundant peace and quiet.

Wages Creek Beach Camp *(☎ 707-964-2964; 37700 N Hwy 1; tent/RV sites $18/25; usually closed winter)* has hot showers. Another 1½mi north of town, **Westport-Union Landing State Beach** *(☎ 707- 937-5804; campsites $12)* is on a coastal bluff, with exposed sites. A rough **hiking trail** connects the two campgrounds via tidepools and streams, passable only at low tide.

Simple and charming accommodations back in town include **Lost Coast Lodge** *(☎ 707-964-5584; 38921 N Hwy 1; B&B rooms $70-90)*, an inn and restaurant; **Westport Inn** *(☎ 707-964-5135; 37040 N Hwy 1)* motel; and the shingled **Seagate Guest House** *(☎ 707-964-5595; 36875 N Hwy 1)*.

Westport House *(☎ 707-937-4007; summer rate $200)* built c.1832, is a vacation rental overlooking the surf. There's a five-day minimum stay, except during winter when it offers three nights for $500. Don't worry, it's worth every penny.

Refreshing rural retreats are found further north of town.

De Haven Valley Farm *(☎ 707-961-1660, 877-334-2836, fax 961-1677; w www.de haven-valley-farm.com; 39247 N Hwy 1; rooms $90-120, cottages $135-145)*, an 1875 Victorian manor house, has a hillside hot tub.

Howard Creek Ranch *(☎ 707-964-6725, fax 707-964-1603; w www.howardcreek ranch.com; 40501 N Hwy 1; rooms $75-125, suites $105-160)* is a national historic site turned working farm.

From Fort Bragg, it's a slow, winding 15mi to Westport, then another 22mi along Hwy 1 to Leggett at a pace that even snails might find slow.

The Redwood Coast

Heading north by an inland route, Hwy 101 leaves Leggett and 90mi later meets the sea at Eureka on Humboldt Bay, California's largest bay north of San Francisco. From Arcata, just a few miles further north, the highway hugs the coast nearly all the way from Trinidad Bay to Crescent City, another 75mi away.

Along the way, Hwy 101 passes awe-inspiring ancient groves of virgin redwoods, notably at Humboldt Redwoods State Park, with its famous Avenue of the Giants, and Prairie Creek Redwoods State Park, especially along the unforgettable Newton B Drury Scenic Parkway. Both are definitely worth a detour.

Eureka, a fishing and former lumber camp on Humboldt Bay, is the largest town on California's far north coast. It's known for its many fine old Victorian buildings, and delicious fresh seafood. Arcata is a youthful university town showing 1960s counter-cultural flare. Both Humboldt and Arcata bays are good for bird-watching, with several wildlife refuges.

Heading up into Oregon, you can follow along the ocean on Hwy 101, which continues as the coast highway in Oregon, or head inland on Hwy 199, called the Smith River National Scenic Byway.

Highways crossing the Coast Range connect the Pacific with the interior. They are uniformly slow, winding and scenic, mostly snaking through the mountains via river canyons. Hwy 299 between Arcata and Redding, dubbed the Trinity Scenic Byway, has over three hours of mountainous curves; it's a beautiful drive and the primary connection between the coast and the interior (see the Northern Mountains chapter).

Getting There & Around

Greyhound (☎ 800-231-2222; W www .greyhound.com) operates two northbound and two southbound buses daily on Hwy 101, stopping at major cities and many smaller towns, including Trinidad, Orick, Klamath and Klamath's Redwood Hostel.

Redwood Transit System (☎ 707-443-0826) operates buses Monday to Saturday between Scotia in the south and Trinidad in the north, with stops at Eureka, Arcata and little towns along the way. **Redwood Coast Transit** (☎ 707-464-9314) runs between Crescent City, Klamath and Redwood National Park, with many stops along the way; this bus makes two runs a day, Monday to Saturday.

LEGGETT

The tiny settlement of Leggett (population 200), lazing beside the Eel River, is where you'll get your first glimpse of the ancient redwood forests.

Chandelier Drive-Thru Tree Park (☎ 707-925-6363; Drive-Thru Tree Rd; admission per vehicle $3; open 8am-dusk daily) has 200 acres of virgin redwood forest with picnic areas and nature walks. And yes, there's a giant redwood tree with a square hole carved out, which cars can drive through. Only in America.

Another mile or two north of town, 1000-acre **Standish-Hickey State Recreation Area** (☎ 707-925-6482; 69350 Hwy 101; day-use fee per vehicle $2) has picnic areas, swimming holes, fishing in the Eel River and hiking trails in virgin and second-growth redwood forest. Riverside **campgrounds** (☎ 800-444-7275; W www.reserveamerica .com; campsites $12) with hot showers are open year-round, but in summer phone for reservations. Avoid noisy, cramped sites close to the highway.

Continuing north along Hwy 101, redwood tourist traps reign supreme. About 10mi past Leggett, **Confusion Hill** (☎ 707-925-6456; adult/child $3/2; mountain train ride $3/2; open 8am-7pm daily summer, 11am-4pm or 5pm winter) has a gravity house, water running uphill and other artificial oddities. Look for kitsch chainsaw sculptures outside the snack bar.

Redwoods River Resort (☎ 707-925-6249, fax 707-925-6413; W www.redwoodriver resort.com; 75000 Hwy 101; tents $18, RV sites $22-28, cabins with/without kitchen $68/30, A-frame lodge rooms with kitchenette $63-78), opposite Confusion Hill, is a family place in riverside redwood forest.

There are a couple of diners and cafés on Drive-Thru Tree Rd, north of that namesake attraction. Greyhound buses stop opposite Standish-Hickey reserve at **Price's Peg House** (☎ 707-925-6444; 69501 Hwy 101; open 8am-9pm daily), a country grocery store and deli.

RICHARDSON GROVE STATE PARK

About 15mi north of Leggett, this 1400-acre park (Hwy 101; day-use fee per vehicle $2) contains a lovely virgin redwood grove, where many trees are older than 1000 years and some over 300ft tall, and a portion of the Eel River. In summer, rangers lead interpretive nature walks and campfire programs. The **visitor center** (☎ 707-247-3318; open 9am-2pm daily) sells nature books and gifts. It's inside the 1930s Richardson Grove Lodge along with a convenience shop.

The park has three **campgrounds** (summer reservations ☎ 800-444-7275; W www.reserveamerica.com; campsites $12) with hot showers, with some sites open year-round.

BENBOW LAKE

On the banks of the Eel River, 2mi south of Garberville, the 1200-acre **Benbow Lake State Recreation Area** (summer ☎ 707-923-3238, winter ☎ 707-923-3318; day-use fee $2) has a dam that forms 26-acre Benbow Lake in summer, usually from mid-June to mid-September. Annual events include summertime jazz and Shakespeare festivals and special holiday celebrations from Thanksgiving to New Year's Day.

Across Hwy 101, the riverside **campground** (summer reservations ☎ 800-444-7275; W www.reserveamerica.com; tent/RV sites $12/17) is open year-round, but subject to bridge closures due to flooding. There is only one shower and sites endure much highway noise.

Benbow Inn (☎ 707-923-2124, 800-355-3301, fax 707-923-2897; W www.benbowinn.com; 445 Lake Benbow Dr; rooms $100-245, cottage $325) is a large Tudor-style country inn with gardens overlooking the lake. A national historic landmark, it opened in 1926. Hollywood elite once frolicked in the lobby, which is now filled with flickering lamps, antiques and jigsaw puzzles. The inn's world-class **restaurant** (breakfast & lunch $9-15, dinner mains $15-30) serves afternoon tea and Sunday champagne brunch in summer.

GARBERVILLE

The town of Garberville and its sister Redway, 2mi west of Hwy 101, became famous on the underground grapevine in the 1970s for the sinsemilla (a highly potent, seedless marijuana) grown in the surrounding hills. You'll still see marijuana farmers, back-to-landers and other quirkier types hanging around on Redwood Dr, which is the main drag through both towns. Today Garberville (population 1800) is a pint-sized whistle stop on Hwy 101 with basic services, but this is the 'town' for the surrounding rural areas.

The **Garberville-Redway Area Chamber of Commerce** (☎ 707-923-2613, 800-923-2613; W www.garberville.org; 773 Redwood Dr, cnr Church St; open 10am-5pm Mon-Fri, sometimes 11am-3pm Sat summer), inside Jacob Garber Square, has heaps of information. Tune in to Redwood Community Radio (KMUD 91.1FM) for eclectic music, environmental news and provocative local broadcasting.

Treats (☎ 923-3554; 764 Redwood Dr; open from 7am Mon-Fri, 9am Sat & Sun) is an ice-cream and espresso shop with an Internet terminal ($0.10 per minute).

Reggae on the River (☎ 707-923-4583; W www.reggaeontheriver.com), held on the first weekend in August at French's Camp, in Piercy about 10mi to the south, is the major event of the year, drawing huge crowds for reggae, world music, arts and craft fairs, camping and swimming on the Eel River. Three-day festival passes ($112) go on sale March 1 and sell out quickly; no single tickets.

Other annual events include the **Avenue of the Giants Marathon**, in May; the **Harley Davidson Redwood Run** and **Garberville Rodeo**, both in June; the **Hemp Fest** every November; and **Winter Arts Fair** in mid-December.

Places to Stay

There's **camping** at nearby Benbow Lake and along the Avenue of the Giants.

River Rose Cottage (☎ 707-923-3500; off Sprowel Creek Rd, Garberville; doubles $65, extra person $10) is a private riverside cottage with an outdoor clawfoot tub. It's off to the west of Hwy 101.

Several motels line Redwood Dr in Garberville and also Redway, 2mi further west. Try the **Lone Pine Motel** (☎ 707-923-3520; 912 Redwood Dr, Garberville), which has impeccably clean rooms, the next-door **Motel Garberville** (☎ 707-923-2422; 948 Redwood Dr) or the average **Brass Rail Motel** (☎ 707-923-3931; 3188 Redwood Dr) Redway. All offer rooms for $40 to $60.

Best Western Humboldt House Inn (☎ 707-923-2771, 800-528-1234; 701 Redwood Dr; rooms in summer/winter $99/79) is top-of-the-line for Garberville. Seriously.

Places to Eat

For groceries, stop by **Chautauqua Natural Foods** (☎ 707-923-2452; 436 Church St), behind the tourist office.

Nacho Mama (☎ 707-923-4060; 375 Sprowel Creek Rd, at Redwood Dr; meals under $6) is an organic Mexican fast-food stand.

Woodrose Cafe (☎ 707-923-3191; 911 Redwood Dr; meals $6-10; open 6am-2:30pm Mon-Fri, 6:30am-1pm Sat & Sun) is a much-loved local diner, serving delicious organic food since 1977.

Eel River Cafe (☎ 707-923-3783; 801 Redwood Dr; dishes $2-5; open 6am-2pm daily) is another country-style diner, one that cooks up amazing blueberry pancakes.

The Galaxy (☎ 707-923-2664; 849 Redwood Dr; meals $5-8; open 11am-10pm daily) coffeehouse inside a converted gas station offers honest grill fare with vegetarian options. There's almost nothing *not* on the menu, even California date shakes.

Calico's Deli & Pasta (☎ 707-923-2253; 808 Redwood Dr) is a superb café with chilled-out vibes, imaginative salads, daily soups and a full menu of fresh Italian delights.

Brass Rail Inn (☎ 707-923-3188; 3188 Redwood Dr, Redway; mains $15-35; open dinner 5pm-9:30pm daily), a historic redwood roadhouse (once a brothel!) has excellent steak and seafood dinners. Cocktail hour starts at 4pm.

Mateel Cafe (☎ 707-923-2030; 3342-44 Redwood Dr, Redway; lunch $7-11, dinner $15-32; open 11:30am-9pm Mon-Sat) is famous for casual California bistro fare by chef Pierre Gaude. Stone-baked pizzas and organic salads get rave reviews.

Entertainment

Garberville Theatre (☎ 707-923-3580; 766 Redwood Dr) shows first-run movies and art flicks.

Sicilito's (☎ 707-923-2814; 445 Conger St; meals $6-14; open 11:30am-10pm daily), behind the Best Western, is a popular hangout for microbrews, frat-boy food and sports on big-screen TVs.

Voodoo Lounge (Redwood Dr, Redway; usually open 9:30pm-1:30am Tues & Thur-Sat; cover varies) has DJs and live local bands.

The Riverwood Inn (☎ 707-943-3333; 2828 Avenue of the Giants, Phillipsville; bar open till late) is another musical haunt (see the Avenue of the Giants section, next).

Getting There & Away

Greyhound buses stop at **Singing Salmon Music** (432 Church St), half a block east of Redwood Dr.

AVENUE OF THE GIANTS & HUMBOLDT REDWOODS STATE PARK

This incredible 32mi stretch of scenic highway winds through 80-sq-mi Humboldt Redwoods State Park (☎ 707-946-2409), which holds some of the world's most magnificent old-growth redwood forests. As you revel in the drive, say a few thanks to the Save-the-Redwoods League, who purchased the first memorial grove here in 1921. You'll find free **driving guide** pamphlets available from roadside signboards at both the avenue's southern entrance, 6mi north of Garberville, and its northern entrance, a few miles south of Fortuna; there are also several other access points off Hwy 101.

Just south of Weott, a volunteer-staffed **visitor center** (☎ 707-946-2263; open 9am-5pm daily summer, 10am-4pm winter) shows free videos and sells excellent field guides, hiking maps and books. Don't bypass its small, but excellent **museum** housing the historic 1917 'Travel Log.'

Many of the park's most spectacular specimens have been named, including the world-champion coast redwood, called **Giant Tree** (hey, we didn't say they were *imaginatively* named) in **Rockefeller Forest**, found about 4½mi west of the avenue along Mattole Rd. That honor was formerly held by the **Dyerville Giant**, in **Founders Grove**, just north of the visitor center, until it was knocked over in 1991 by another falling tree. A walk along the gargantuan 370ft length, with its wide trunk towering high over your head, helps you appreciate how huge these ancient trees are. Also in Rockefeller Forest, visit the **Tall Tree** and fallen **Flatiron Tree**.

Elsewhere the park has more than 100mi of trails for hiking, mountain biking and horseback riding. Easy walks include the short **nature trails** in Founders Grove and Rockefeller Forest and the **Drury-Chaney Loop Trail** (with fresh berry picking!). More challenging treks include the popular **Grasshopper Peak Trail**, starting from south

NORTH COAST

of the visitor center, which climbs to the fire lookout at 3379ft. **Happy Horse Hill** (☎ 707-943-3008; 1989 Elk Creek Rd, Myers Flat) offers one-hour horseback rides through the forest for $20 per person; children are welcome, and reservations are appreciated.

Places to Stay & Eat

The state park runs three developed **campgrounds** (summer reservations ☎ 800-444-7275; w www.reserveamerica.com; campsites $12) with hot showers, as well as two environmental camps, five trail camps, a hike/bike camp and an equestrian camp. Of the developed ones, **Burlington Campground** is open year-round beside the visitor center, near several hiking trailheads. **Hidden Springs Campground**, about 5mi south of the visitor center, and **Albee Creek Campground**, on Mattole Rd past Rockefeller Forest, are usually open mid-May to early autumn.

Several tiny towns along the Avenue of the Giants also offer simple lodgings and diners. **Giant Redwoods RV & Campground** (☎ 707-943-3198, fax 707-943-3359; w www.giantredwoodsrvcamp.com; 455 Boy Scout Camp Rd, Myers Flat; tent/RV sites from $20/28) has hot showers and recreational activities.

Redcrest Resort (☎ 707-722-4208, fax 707-722-4403; 26459 Avenue of the Giants, Redcrest; tent & RV sites $25, teepees $25, motel rooms & cabins $50-100) is further north.

Madrona Motel & Resort (☎ 707-943-1708; 2907 Avenue of the Giants, Phillipsville; rooms & kitchenettes $55-100) is a quaint, old-fashioned place that's simply peachy and set on a shady hillside.

Miranda Gardens Resort (☎ 707-943-3011, fax 707-943-3584; w www.mirandagardens.com; 6766 Avenue of the Giants, Miranda; rooms $75-55, cottages $110-225), right on the Eel River, has a heated swimming pool, children's playground and summer campfires. The two-bedroom cottages have kitchens, whirlpools and fireplaces.

Myers Country Inn B&B (☎ 707-943-3259, 800-500-6464, fax 707-943-1800; w www.myersinn.com; 12913 Avenue of the Giants, Myers Flat; rooms $125-150) is a shabby-chic inn inside a historic stagecoach stop, all lovingly refurbished.

The Riverwood Inn & El Rio Mexican Restaurant (☎ 707-943-3333; 2828 Avenue

of the Giants, Phillipsville; open 4pm-late Mon-Fri, 11am-10pm Sat & Sun, bar open late), near Garberville, is a long-standing roadhouse for live blues, folk and rock music. It also has rooms for rent.

The little town of Miranda has the most eateries, including a **bakery café** for hot and cold lunches, a **steakhouse** next door and an organic **coffeehouse** further north, at the Giant Redwoods campground turnoff.

SCOTIA

Established in 1887, Scotia (population 1200) is a rarity in modern times: it's one of the last 'company towns' left in California, entirely owned and operated by the Pacific Lumber Company (Palco), which runs the largest redwood lumber mill in the world. The **Scotia Museum & Visitors Center** (☎ 707-764-2222 ext 247; w www.palco.com; cnr Main & Bridge Sts; open 8am-4:30pm Mon-Fri summer) is at the south end of town.

Free **self-guided tours** of the lumber mill are available from 7:30am to 10:30am and 11:30am to 2pm Monday to Friday. In summer, when the museum is open, stop by to pick up your free permit for the self-guided tour; the rest of the year, permits are available at the guard shack at the mill entrance. Give yourself an hour to see everything from giant trees being debarked through to their metempsychosis into board lumber.

An educational **fisheries exhibit** (open 8:30am-4:30pm Mon-Fri), at the mill's visitor parking lot, has Chinook salmon and steelhead fish ponds, and exhibits about the company's various stream enhancement projects. About 4½mi south of Scotia is Palco's **demonstration forest** (open 8am-4:30pm daily summer), with a picnic area and nature trail.

There's no compelling reason to linger here but if you want to stay, the **Scotia Inn** (☎ 707-764-5683, 888-764-2248; w www.scotiainn.com; 100 Main St; rooms/suites from $70/165) is a comfortable historic inn. Drop by the inn's steak-and-potato **pub** (dinners $8-17; open 5pm-9pm daily) or antique-furnished **Redwood Dining Room** (mains $17-26; open 5pm-9pm Wed-Sun, lunch Mon-Fri & brunch Sun in summer) for game cuisine and an extensive wine list.

Hoby's Market (105 Main St), opposite the inn, sells hot deli sandwiches, fresh salads and general provisions. Otherwise there are

Tree-Hugger

For over two years, Julia 'Butterfly' Hill, a preacher's daughter from Jonesboro, Arkansas, lived on an 8ft platform in a 200ft-tall, 1000-year-old redwood named Luna, near the tiny town of Stafford.

Why? She ascended the tree on 10 December, 1997, resolving to stay in it to prevent the Pacific Lumber Company (Palco) from logging this, the largest old-growth tree in a grove of ancient redwoods slated for cutting. Butterfly remained in the tree through storms, taunts, threats, nearby helicopter salvage logging and attempts by the lumber company to forcibly remove her, and vowed that her feet would not touch earth again until she had made a difference in saving the ancient redwood forests.

Earth First! activists provided her with food and contact with the outside world. Communicating by cellular telephone and walkie-talkie, she gave interviews to national media, with the object of drawing attention to the plight of the old-growth redwood forests and the need to preserve them.

In the end, her efforts did save this tree – at the cost of $50,000, paid by Palco, and a guarantee that she would come back down to earth – but Palco went ahead and cut all the other trees on the hillside, leaving Luna standing alone. Then in November 2000, a horrible act of chainsaw vandalism damaged the tree irrevocably. It is still standing, however, thanks to metal bracing supports installed by Palco, the same corporation that wanted to cut the tree down the year before.

You can read all about the saga in Butterfly's book *Legacy of Luna*, or look for local screenings of the documentary 'Butterfly' (W www.butterflyfilm.net) by Doug Wolens.

several **motels** and **diners** in Rio Dell, across the river bridge from Scotia.

Redwood Transit System (☎ *707-443-0826*) buses stop at Hoby's Market and Rio Dell City Hall.

LOST COAST

California's 'Lost Coast,' from where Hwy 1 turns inland north of Rockport up to its northern border around Ferndale, became 'lost' when the state's highway system was put in place early in the 20th century. The steep, rugged King Range, rises to over 4000ft less than 3mi from the coast, with near vertical cliffs plunging into the sea. High rainfall (averaging over 100 inches per year) exacerbates the unstable soil and rock conditions. Together these conditions made the building of a coastal highway here next to impossible, so the Pacific Coast Hwy was routed inland and, in time, legislation was passed to protect the region from development.

Today, the Lost Coast is one of California's most pristine coastal areas. The southern part is composed of King Range National Conservation Area and Sinkyone Wilderness State Park. The area north of the King Range is more accessible, but the scenery is not as dramatic. The only sizable community on the Lost Coast is Shelter Cove, an isolated settlement 25mi west of Garberville.

An ideal time to visit the Lost Coast is in autumn, when there's some chance of clear, if somewhat cool, weather. If you'll be doing any hiking along the coast, late spring (around late April and early May) could be good, as not only might the weather cooperate, but migrating California gray whales may be visible off the coast. That said, if staying warm and dry are your priorities, come between June and August. Be warned, though, that the weather could quickly become lousy at any time of year.

Shelter Cove

Shelter Cove, a seaside resort with beautiful vacation homes on a windswept cove just above Point Delgada, is surrounded by the King Range National Conservation Area. It's a remote settlement, with just one access route: a 23mi paved road winding west over the mountains from Redway, near Garberville; it takes a good 45 minutes to drive.

Shelter Cove RV Park, Campground & Deli (☎ *707-986-7474; 492 Machi Rd; tent/ RV sites $16/27*), right in town, offers hot showers and outdoor tables on an ocean-view deck; fish and chips is their kitchen specialty.

Shelter Cove Motor Inn (☎ *707-986-7521, 888-570-9676;* W *www.sheltercovemotorinn .com; 205 Wave Dr; suites in summer $88-120*) is a delightful place, boasting all ocean-front mini-suites. Downstairs is the **Lost Coast Coffee Company** (☎ *707-986-7888*).

Other lodgings include the **Shelter Cove Beachcomber Inn** (☎ *707-986-7551, 800-718-4789; 412 Machi Rd; rooms $55-95*) and plain **Marina Motel** (☎ *707-986-7595; 533 Machi Rd; rooms $60-85*).

Northern California Properties (☎ *707-986-7346; 101 Lower Pacific Dr*) handles vacation rentals.

Chart Room Restaurant (☎ *707-986-9696; 210 Wave Dr; meals $12-20; open 9am-9pm daily*), opposite the Shelter Cove Motor Inn, has a wonderful ocean view from its chalet porch. Fare is average American stuff, but it has a bar.

In Briceland, on the way to Shelter Cove from Garberville, stop by the **Grass Shack** for organic snacks, juice and espresso.

King Range National Conservation Area

Covering 35mi of virgin coastline, with ridge after ridge of steep King Range mountains plunging almost vertically into the surf, this 60,000-acre wilderness has its highest point at King's Peak (4087ft).

About 9mi east of Shelter Cove, the **Bureau of Land Management** (*open 8:30am-4:30pm daily*) has maps and directions for hiking trails and campsites, which are posted outside after-hours; staff run interpretive programs at Shelter Cove during summer. Information is also available from the BLM office in Arcata (see that section later), which administers the conservation area.

One of the area's most alluring features is the **Lost Coast Trail**, following 24mi of coast from the Mattole Campground on the north end, near Petrolia, to Black Sands Beach at Shelter Cove on the south end. The prevailing northerly winds make it best to hike the trail from north to south; plan on taking three or four days from end to end. For information on backpacker shuttle services to trailheads, call the **Shelter Cove Campground Store** (☎ *707-986-7474*).

Trail highlights include an abandoned lighthouse at Punta Gorda, remnants of old shipwrecks, tidepools and a great abundance of marine and coastal wildlife including sea lions, seals and more than 300 bird species. The trail is mostly level, passing along beaches and over rocky outcrops; consult tide tables, as some rocky outcroppings are passable only at low tide.

A good, shorter **day hike** along the northern stretch of the Lost Coast Trail, with beautiful tidepools along the way, can be made by starting at the Mattole Campground trailhead and hiking 3mi south along the coast to the Punta Gorda lighthouse and back again. The Mattole Campground is easy to reach; it's at the ocean end of Lighthouse Rd, 4mi from the intersection with Mattole Rd, southeast of Petrolia.

From the southern terminus of the Lost Cost Trail at Black Sands Beach, a 5mi uphill walk from Shelter Cove along a paved highway brings you to Chemise Mtn Rd. Here the **Hidden Valley Trail** and **Chemise Mountain Trails**, two steep ridge trails lead 1½mi uphill from Wailaki and Nadelos recreation sites, and connect with another section of the Lost Coast Trail through Sinkyone Wilderness State Park (see the next section). Also in the King Range is the 10.5mi **King Crest Trail**, a fairly easy trek along the main coastal ridge, starting at the end of unpaved King Peak Rd, east of Shelter Cove.

Wailaki and Nadelos both have **developed campgrounds** (*campsites $5-7*). There are also four other campgrounds scattered across the range, plus multiple primitive walk-in sites. For camping outside developed campgrounds, you'll need a free campfire permit, available from the BLM office.

Sinkyone Wilderness State Park

This 7367-acre wilderness park, named for the Sinkyone Indians who once inhabited the area, is another pristine stretch of coastline. The **Lost Coast Trail** continues here for another 22mi, starting from Whale Gulch and heading south to Usal Beach Campground, taking at least three days to hike. Near the north end of the park, the **Needle Rock Ranch House** (☎ *707-986-7711*) serves as a visitor center where you can check in, register for a campsite and get maps and trail guides. Upstairs in the ranch house are two unfurnished bedrooms available for 'indoor camping'; reservations can be made up to nine weeks in advance.

To get to Needle Rock, drive west from Garberville and Redway on Briceland Rd for 21mi through Whitethorn to Four Corners, where you turn left (south) and continue another 3½mi down a very rugged road to the ranch house; it takes about 1½ hours. There's also road access to Usal Beach Campground at the south end of the park from Hwy 1. About 3mi north of Rockport, unpaved County Rd 431 takes off from the highway at milepost 90.88 and goes 6mi up the coast to the campground. These roads are not maintained during rainy months and quickly become impassable.

North of the King Range

The northern section of the Lost Coast is accessible year-round via Mattole Rd, which is paved. It takes about three hours to drive the 68mi from Ferndale in the north, out to the coast at Cape Mendocino and then cut inland again to reach Humboldt Redwoods State Park and Hwy 101. Don't expect redwood forests like those found on Hwy 101: the vegetation here is mostly grassland and pasture, with scattered cattle ranches.

You'll pass through three tiny towns: **Capetown**, **Petrolia** (site of California's first oil well) and **Honeydew**. The only gas station is at the Honeydew post office/market/hangout, but it's open sporadically and can't be counted on; be sure to fill your gas tank before you start the drive. Allow plenty of time, as the road is slow going. Though the drive is pleasant enough, the wild, spectacular scenery of the Lost Coast is not here, but further south in the less accessible regions.

There's camping at the **AW Way County Park** (☎ 707-445-7651; Mattole Rd; campsites per vehicle $12), 6mi southeast of Petrolia, between Petrolia and Honeydew.

FERNDALE

Twenty miles south of Eureka (see later in this chapter), this idyllic little dairy-farming community (population 1400) is a state and national historic landmark. Here century-old Victorian buildings are cheerfully painted and lovingly tended by their inhabitants. Main Street, just a few blocks long, is full of art galleries and antiquarian bookshops, quaint emporiums and soda fountains. But rest assured, Ferndale is not just a tourist trap, it's an authentic, old-fashioned and charming village thriving in an otherwise too-busy modern world.

The **Ferndale Chamber of Commerce** (☎ 707-786-4477; w www.victorianferndale .org/chamber) has no staffed visitor center. Pick up a *Victorian Village of Ferndale* map and visitors' guide, available from tourist brochure racks around town, or a free

---

Crazy Contraptions

The Kinetic Sculpture Race was born in 1969 when Ferndale artist Hobart Brown decided to spruce up his son's tricycle to make it more interesting, creating a wobbly, five-wheeled red 'pentacycle.' Initially, five odd contraptions raced down Main St on Mother's Day, and a 10ft turtle sculpture won. The race was expanded in the early '70s and has now blossomed into a three-day, amphibious event with contraptions competing over 38mi from Arcata to Ferndale. Held over Memorial Day weekend, the race attracts thousands of spectators and usually at least a few dozen entrants (one year there were 99). Cities around the world have followed in Ferndale's footsteps, with far-flung places like Perth, Australia now holding their own kinetic races.

A few of the race rules are as bizarre as the entrants, including 'It is legal to get assistance from the natural power of water, wind, sun, gravity and friendly extraterrestrials (if introduced to the judges prior to the race)' and the Mom Rule, which states that 'If a Pilot is pregnant and in labor, that Pilot may be excused for a reasonable length of time (an hour or so) without penalty. However, the Pilot must return with a gloss 8 x 10 color photo for publicity purposes. The baby may then be carried as a passenger in the Barnacle Category for one leg of the course.'

---

souvenir edition of the *Ferndale Enterprise* newspaper. Check for copies at the Kinetic Sculpture Museum or **Golden Gait Mercantile** (☎ 707-786-4891; 421 Main St), where you can lose hours browsing through the shelves of yesteryear's goods. Mildly eccentric **Hobart Gallery** (☎ 707-786-9259; 393 Main St) also dispenses information.

Things to See & Do

As the original Ferndale settlers began to grow wealthy from the successful dairy farms they operated, some built large, ornate Victorian mansions known as 'butterfat palaces.' The **Gingerbread Mansion** (400 Berding St), a fancy 1898 Queen Anne-Eastlake Victorian mansion, is the most photographed building in town. The **Shaw House** (703 Main St), now a B&B, was the first permanent structure to be built in

Ferndale; the town's founder, Seth Shaw, started building the gabled Carpenter Gothic Victorian home in 1854, though it was not completed until after his death in 1872. The house, called 'Fern Dale' for the 6ft-tall ferns that grew here, housed the new settlement's first post office, of which Shaw was the postmaster – hence the town's name, Ferndale. The 1866 **Fern Cottage** (☎ 707-786-4835; Centerville Rd), a few miles west of town, is open for tours by appointment.

The **Ferndale Museum** (☎ 707-786-4466; cnr Shaw & 3rd Sts; admission by donation; open 11am-4pm Tues-Sat, 1pm-4pm Sun June-Sept; closed Tues rest of year), one block west of Main St, is jam-packed with hundreds of artifacts and historical exhibits.

Nearby the **Kinetic Sculpture Museum** (580 Main St; open 10am-5pm Mon-Sat, noon-4pm Sun) houses the fanciful, astounding kinetic sculptures used in the annual races from Arcata to Ferndale (see the boxed text 'Crazy Contraptions' on the previous page).

Half a mile from downtown (take Bluff St), 110-acre **Russ Park** is a place for short tramps through fields of wildflowers, past ponds, redwood groves and eucalyptus trees.

Special Events
Look out for the **Tour of the Unknown Coast** bicycle race in May; the **Scandinavian Mid-Summer Festival**, with folk dancing and feasting in June; the **Humboldt County Fair**, which takes place over 10 days in mid-August; **Victorian Village Oktoberfest & Harvest Day**; and elaborate Christmas celebrations during December, including a lighted tractor parade, carriage rides, craft fairs, holiday concerts and theater.

Places to Stay
The **Humboldt County Fairgrounds** (☎ 707-786-9511; 1250 5th St; tent/RV sites $5/15) offers camping on the fairground lawns; turn west onto Van Ness St, and go a few blocks down. At least there'll be some grazing sheep to keep you company.

Ferndale Laundromat & Motel (☎ 707-786-9471; 632 Main St; units $50) has two units, each with two bedrooms, kitchen and private bath.

Francis Creek Inn (☎ 707-786-9611; 577 Main St; rooms $60-70) has four comfortable motel-style rooms, next door to a liquor store.

Ferndale's elegant Victorian houses are naturals for B&Bs and boutique hotels.

Victorian Inn (☎ 707-786-4949, 888-589-1808; w www.a-victorian-inn.com; 400 Ocean Ave; rooms $85-175), above a gemologist's shop, dates from 1890. It's furnished with antiques and serves hot breakfasts on weekends.

Hotel Ivanhoe (☎ 707-786-9000; w www .hotel-ivanhoe.com; 315 Main St; rooms $95-160), catty-corner from the Victorian Inn, is a grand historic hotel that served as the town's original stagecoach stop. Some rooms have sleigh beds, velvet-covered rocking chairs and clawfoot tubs.

Shaw House (☎ 707-786-9958, 800-557-7429, fax 707-786-9758; w www.shawhouse .com; 703 Main St; rooms $80-185) has sweet interiors of stained glass and gabled ceilings, with clawfoot tubs and fireplaces in most rooms. Breakfasts are heavenly.

Gingerbread Mansion Inn (☎ 707-786-4000, 800-952-4136; w www.ginger bread-mansion.com; 400 Berding St, cnr Brown St; rooms & suites $150-385), one block east of Main St, is a four-star romantic B&B offering the utmost in service, including afternoon tea and evening turndowns.

Other B&B accommodations are slightly further from downtown.

Collingwood Inn B&B (☎ 707-786-9219, 800-469-1632; 831 Main St, rooms from $99, suites $245), inside the historic Hart House, has assumed gracious new ownership.

Grandmother's House (☎ 707-786-9704; 861 Howard St, off Main St; rooms $75) is a modest 1901 Queen Anne Victorian beside pastoral fields. This B&B accepts children.

Stewart Inn & Gallery (☎ 707-9687; 1099 Van Ness Ave; rooms $110-135) is an 1895 Victorian farmhouse beside a creek, offering full breakfast, evening appetizers and complimentary espresso or chai. Original artwork fills the rooms.

Places to Eat
You won't starve in Ferndale. Inexpensive bakeries, cafés, old-fashioned lunch counters and even candy-making shops line Main St.

Ferndale Meat Co (☎ 707-786-4501; 376 Main St; sandwiches $5; open 8am-5pm daily) has honest-to-goodness sandwiches loaded with cheeses and smoked meats.

Curley's Grill (☎ 707-786-9696; 400 Ocean Ave; dishes $6-18; open 11:30am-

9pm daily, breakfast from 8am Sat & Sun) is a combination bar and restaurant. Servers are chatty – with locals anyway. Even if the California cuisine is just average, the stellar beer and wine lists make stopping by worthwhile.

Hotel Ivanhoe *(☎ 707-786-9000; 315 Main St; mains $10-20; open 5pm-8:30pm Wed-Sat, 5pm-9pm Sun)* has a northern Italian restaurant that jumpstarts the cocktail hour at 4pm.

Angelina Inn *(☎ 707-725-3153; 281 Fernbridge St, Fernbridge; bar menu under $10, dinners $17-25; bar open 4pm, dinner from 5pm Fri-Tues)*, near the Ferndale turnoff from Hwy 101, offers hearty Italian dining and sometimes dancing.

Entertainment

Ferndale Repertory Theatre *(☎ 707-786-5483; 447 Main St)*, a top-quality theater company, has productions year-round; if you're in town, don't miss it – this is Ferndale's pride and joy.

HUMBOLDT BAY NATIONAL WILDLIFE REFUGE

At the south end of Humboldt Bay, this refuge *(☎ 707-733-5406; open sunrise-sunset daily)* is an important one for more than 200 species of birds migrating on the Pacific Flyway each year. Peak season for most species of water birds and raptors is from September to March, while peak season for black brant geese and migratory shorebirds is from mid-March to late April.

Many birds can be seen year-round, including gulls, terns, cormorants, pelicans, egrets and herons. The refuge also harbors seals. Refuge maps showing two short interpretive trails, each taking about a half-hour, are available from Eureka and Arcata tourist offices, or sometimes at the refuge entrance. Turn west from Hwy 101 at the Hookton Rd exit, about 11mi south of Eureka, and follow the signs.

Southport Landing *(☎ 707-733-5915, fax 707-733-5215; 444 Phelan Rd, Loleta; rooms $90-125)* is an 1890 Early Colonial Revival mansion at the end of a country lane on the shore of Humboldt Bay, overlooking the refuge. The turnoff is about 3½mi west of the refuge entrance along Hookton Rd.

EUREKA

Eureka (population 25,600) hugs the shores of Humboldt Bay, the state's largest bay and seaport north of San Francisco, and the base for a significant fishing fleet. At first glance, when you drive into town on Hwy 101, Eureka may not impress: a thunder of traffic, gas stations, chain motels and fast-food joints all crowd the highway. But if you venture into Old Town, just a couple of blocks away, you'll see beautiful Victorian homes, a few museums and a refurbished waterfront commercial district.

Finding addresses downtown is a snap, as most streets are all laid out on a grid, with numbered streets crossing lettered streets. As you enter town from the south, the **Eureka Chamber of Commerce** *(☎ 707-442-3738, 800-356-6381; 2112 Broadway; open 8:30am-5pm Mon-Fri, 10am-4pm Sat & Sun)* has visitor information and maps for Eureka, Arcata and all of Humboldt County. The **Six Rivers National Forest Headquarters** *(☎ 707-442-1721; 1330 Bayshore Way; open 8am-4:30pm Mon-Fri)*, off Broadway opposite Applebee's, has maps and information about the forest.

Lost & Found

Although various early European explorers had long plied the coast of California, the narrow entrance to Humboldt Bay kept it from being 'discovered' until 1806, when Captain Jonathan Winship of the US vessel *O'Cain*, which was chartered to the Russian-American Fur Company sailed into the bay, searching for sea otters. The bay was not settled at that time, however, and it seems to have been forgotten – except, of course, by the Wiyot Indians who called it home. Legend or history – it's hard to tell which, as accounts differ – relates that it was rediscovered, and the town founded, when whaler James T Ryan sailed into the bay in spring of 1850, shouting, 'Eureka!' (Greek for 'I've found it!').

It was a popular expression at the time, especially among gold miners, and this was not the only place to be named Eureka. Nevertheless, the name stuck. Later on, when the first state congress met, 'Eureka' was adopted as California's motto and still appears today on the state seal.

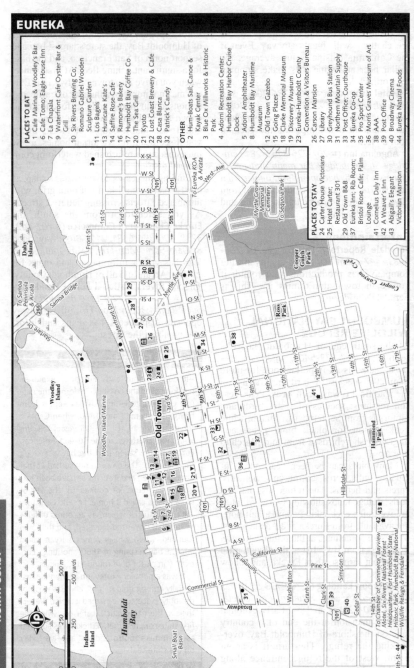

EUREKA

PLACES TO EAT
1 Cafe Marina & Woodley's Bar
6 Cafe Tomo; Eagle House Inn
7 La Chapala
9 Waterfront Cafe Oyster Bar & Grill
10 Six Rivers Brewing Co; Romano Gabriel Wooden Sculpture Garden
11 Los Bagels
13 Hurricane Kate's
14 Saffire Rose Cafe
16 Ramone's Bakery
17 Humboldt Bay Coffee Co
20 The Sea Grill
21 Kyoto
22 Lost Coast Brewery & Cafe
28 Casa Blanca
32 Patrick's Candy

OTHER
2 Hum-Boats Sail; Canoe & Kayak Center
3 Blue Ox Millworks & Historic Park
4 Adorni Recreation Center; Humboldt Bay Harbor Cruise Dock
5 Adorni Amphitheater
8 Humboldt Bay Maritime Museum
12 Old Town Gazebo
15 Going Places
18 Clarke Memorial Museum
19 Discovery Museum
23 Eureka-Humboldt County Convention & Visitors Bureau
26 Carson Mansion
27 Library
30 Greyhound Bus Station
31 Northern Mountain Supply
33 Post Office; Courthouse
34 Eureka Co-op
35 Pro Sport Center
36 Morris Graves Museum of Art
38 AAA
39 Post Office
40 Broadway Cinema
44 Eureka Natural Foods

PLACES TO STAY
24 Carter House Victorians
25 Hotel Carter; Restaurant 301
29 Old Town B&B
37 Eureka Inn; Rib Room; Bristol Rose Cafe; Palm Lounge
41 Cornelius Daly Inn
42 A Weaver's Inn
43 Abigail's Elegant Victorian Mansion

NORTH COAST

Downtown, the central **Eureka-Humboldt County Convention and Visitors Bureau** (☎ 707-443-5097, 800-346-3482; 1034 2nd St; open 9am-noon & 1pm-5pm Mon-Fri) can help. There's also an office of the **AAA** (☎ 707-443-5087; 707 L St).

Travel-oriented **Going Places** (☎ 707-443-4145; 328 2nd St) is one of several excellent bookstores in Old Town.

Things to See

Eureka has many fine old Victorian houses, the most famous of all being the ornate **Carson Mansion**, home of lumber baron William Carson in the 1880s. It's said that 100 men took a full year to build it. Today the mansion is occupied by the private Ingomar Club for men, and is not open to the public (or women either, for that matter). The pink house at 202 M St, opposite Carson Mansion, is an 1884 Queen Anne Victorian designed by the same architects and built as a wedding gift for Carson's eldest son.

The **Blue Ox Millworks & Historic Park** (☎ 707-444-3437, 800-248-4259; w www .blueoxmill.com; adult/child $7.50/3.50; open 9am-4pm Mon-Sat), at the bay end of X St, uses antique tools and mills in the production of gingerbread trim and other decoration for old Victorian buildings. This is one of few places in the world where you can see this being done; a one-hour self-guided tour takes you through the entire mill and other historical buildings.

The free *Eureka Visitors Map*, available at the tourist offices, shows suggested **walking tours** and **scenic drives**, focusing on architecture and history. **Old Town**, along 2nd and 3rd Sts from C St to M St, was once Eureka's down-and-out area, but now has been refurbished into a pedestrian district of distinctive shops, art galleries, cafés and restaurants.

A relic of Eureka's more recent past is the **Romano Gabriel Wooden Sculpture Garden** (315 2nd St), enclosed by a glass case, just off the sidewalk between D and E Sts. For 30 years the brightly painted folk art in Gabriel's front yard delighted locals. After he passed away in 1977, the city moved the collection here to preserve it.

Many of Eureka's minor museums are nearby, but they're strictly for aficionados. The **Clarke Memorial Museum** (☎ 707-443-1947; 240 E St; admission by donation; open noon-4pm Tues-Sat), in the former 1912

Bank of Eureka building, has Native American artifacts and thousands of items pertaining to early Humboldt County history. Also in Old Town are the small **Humboldt Bay Maritime Museum** (☎ 707-444-9440; 423 1st St; admission free; open noon-4pm most days) and the **Discovery Museum** (☎ 707-443-9694; 517 3rd St; admission $3; open 10am-4pm Tues-Sat, noon-4pm Sun), a hands-on museum for kids.

Across Hwy 101, the **Morris Graves Museum of Art** (☎ 442-0278; 636 F St; admission by donation; open noon-5pm Wed-Sun) has modest exhibitions of California artists inside a three-story, 1904 Carnegie Library.

Fort Humboldt State Historic Park (☎ 707-445-6567; 3431 Fort Avenue; admission free; open 9am-5pm daily) is off Broadway, on the south side of town; turn inland onto Highland Ave and you'll see the entrance gate. The fort was established in 1853, on a high bluff affording a view of Humboldt Bay. Steam engine rides are given the third Saturday of each month in summer.

Sequoia Park (☎ 707-442-6552; 3414 W St; admission by donation; open 10am-7pm Tues-Sun May-Sept, 10am-5pm Oct-Apr), in a beautiful redwood grove, has bicycle and hiking trails, a duck pond, children's playground, picnic areas and a small non-profit zoo.

Activities

One of Eureka's most delightful activities is the **Humboldt Bay Harbor Cruise** (☎ 707-445-1910; dock at foot of L St; 75min narrated cruise adult/child $10.50/6.50; daily departures Tues-Sun May-Oct) on the MV *Madaket*, the oldest passenger vessel in continuous use in the USA. The vessel has served in Humboldt Bay ever since being built and launched here in 1910. It ferried workers to the lumber mills and passengers to other places around the bay for many years before the Samoa Bridge was built in 1972. Phone for reservations and schedules. Boats dock at the Adorni Recreation Center.

Hum-Boats (☎ 707-443-5157; Startare Dr), at Woodley Island Marina, offers kayak and sailboat rentals, instruction and tours, ecotours, a water taxi, sailboat charters, sunset sails and full-moon kayak rides.

Northern Mountain Supply (☎ 707-445-1711; 125 W 5th St) sells canoes, hard-shell and inflatable kayaks and camping and backpacking gear. **Pro Sport Center** (☎ 707-443-6328; 508 Myrtle Ave) sells scuba and abalone diving gear, inflatable boats, skiing, snowboarding, camping gear and bicycles. Call to ask about rental possibilities.

Special Events
Annual celebrations include the **Redwood Coast Dixieland Jazz Festival** in early April, followed by the **Rhododendron Festival** later that same month. Summer concerts are held in Sequoia Park from June to August. The summer **Humboldt Arts Festival** and **Blues by the Bay** in July feature concerts, plays and art exhibits. Also check out the Ferndale section earlier in this chapter for details on the Kinetic Sculpture Race, which passes through Eureka.

Places to Stay
Eureka is a great place to base yourself, with the northern Redwood Coast and Trinity Scenic Byway (see the Northern Mountains chapter) all within easy reach. More budget accommodations are found in Arcata, just 20 minutes away by car. Rates quoted here are for peak summer season.

Camping Midway toward Arcata, **Eureka KOA** (☎ 707-822-4243, 800-562-3136; 4050 N Hwy 101, at KOA Dr; tent/RV sites $18/25, cabins & cottages $40) offers a heated pool, convenience store, laundry, playground and bicycle rentals. Ask about weekly and monthly discounts.

There's also camping on the Samoa Peninsula (see that section later).

Motels Dozens of motels line Hwy 101 through town, but you'll get a more peaceful sleep well away from the highway noise.

Downtowner Motel (☎ 707-443-5061, 800-862-4906; 424 8th St; rooms $60) has an outdoor heated swimming pool, indoor sauna and hot tub, and spacious rooms that are clean, quiet and comfortable. Rates include continental breakfast.

Bayview Motel (☎ 707-442-1673, 866-725-6813, fax 707-268-8681; w www.bayviewmotel.com; 2844 Fairfield St; rooms in summer/winter $80/67, with fireplace & Jacuzzi $150/127; 2-room suites $120/107), just off Henderson St at Broadway on the southern outskirts of town, is an upmarket

boutique motel perched on a high bluff overlooking the bay.

B&Bs Eureka's elegantly restored Victorian homes easily lend themselves to B&Bs; most offer discounts in winter.

Old Town B&B Inn (☎ 707-443-5235, 888-508-5235; 1521 3rd St; rooms $110-130) is a restored 1871 Victorian house that was the original home of William Carson.

A Weaver's Inn (☎ 707-443-8119, 800-992-8119, fax 707-443-7923; 1440 B St; rooms/suites $65/125) is an 1883 Queen Anne Victorian home with extensive gardens, cozy wicker furniture and croquet on the lawns.

Cornelius Daly Inn (☎ 707-445-3638, 800-321-9656; w www.dalyinn.com; 1125 H St; rooms $85-125, suites $150) is a 1905 Colonial Revival mansion with generous grounds, Victorian gardens and a fishpond.

Abigail's Elegant Victorian Mansion (☎ 707-444-3144; w www.eureka-california.com; 1406 C St; rooms $95-195) is a delightful national historic landmark that's almost a living history museum, and justly famous for the friendly hospitality of its hosts. Rates for its four guest rooms include a horseless carriage ride around Eureka in your choice of a 1929 Model A Ford coupe with a rumble seat, a 1925 Chevrolet touring car or a 1928 Ford touring car.

Operated by the Hotel Carter, the **Carter House Victorians** (rooms $190-360) offer B&B rooms at three restored buildings all in a row; guests can enjoy the hotel restaurant's sumptuous breakfasts across the street. Accommodations include the luxurious Carter Cottage, a honeymoon hideaway costing $500 per night, and rooms inside the early 1900s Bell Cottage, which has a fully-stocked guest kitchen.

Hotels Eureka boasts two elegant hotels.

Eureka Inn (☎ 707-442-6441, 800-862-4906, fax 707-442-0637; w www.eurekainn.com; 518 7th St; rooms $100-130, suites $130-300) is a luxurious 1922 Tudor-style property on the National Register of Historic Places. It has every amenity, including a heated swimming pool, sauna and hot tub, fine restaurants and a pub.

Hotel Carter (☎ 707-444-8062, 800-404-1390, fax 707-444-8067; w www.carterhouse.com; 301 L St; rooms $140-210, suites

$250-325$) has deservedly won numerous accolades for best inn, best restaurant, best breakfast and so on. Suites have in-room whirlpools, marble fireplaces and marina views. Rates at this hospitable hostelry include a fabulous breakfast, plus wine and hors d'oeuvres each evening.

Places to Eat

Visit the **Eureka Co-op** (☎ 707-443-6027; cnr 5th & L Sts) or **Eureka Natural Foods** (☎ 707-442-6325; 1626 Broadway) for groceries and deli food. Also check out the **farmers market** (Old Town Gazebo; open 10am-1pm Tues June-Oct and old-fashioned **Patrick's Candy** (☎ 707-442-0382; 537 F St).

Los Bagels (☎ 707-442-8525; 403 2nd St; bagelwiches $2.50-6; open 7am-5pm Mon & Wed-Sat, 8am-3pm Sun) offers simpler fare. It's pricey, but the smoked fish with cream cheese is scrumptious.

Ramone's Bakery (☎ 707-442-6082; 209 E St; meals under $10; open 7am-6pm Mon-Sat, 7am-4pm Sun) is another locally owned café, dishing up light lunches of soups, salads and sandwiches.

Saffire Rose Cafe (☎ 707-441-0805; 525 2nd St; lunch $6-10; open 8:30am-8pm Mon-Thur, 8:30am-midnight Fri, 10am-midnight Sat & 11am-6pm Sun), at the historic Vance Hotel, serves simple Italian fare. There's live jazz on Friday and Saturday nights.

La Chapala (☎ 707-443-9514; 201 2nd St; meals $5.50-13.50; open 11am-9pm daily), a family-run kitchen for authentic Mexican food, has murals adorning the interior. Don't miss out on its strong margaritas or homemade flan.

Six Rivers Brewing Co (☎ 707-268-3893; 325 2nd St; pub grub $5-10, mains $8-16; open 11am-10pm daily) serves surprisingly good seafood and plates piled high with hearty grill fare. Enjoy a casual microbrew or two in the open wood-beamed dining room.

Naturally, Eureka has many fine seafood restaurants, many of which have views of Humboldt Bay.

Waterfront Cafe Oyster Bar & Grill (☎ 707-443-9190; 102 F St; mains $10-16; open 9am-9pm daily) in Old Town is popular for fresh catch of the day and of course oysters.

Cafe Marina & Woodley's Bar (☎ 707-443-2233; Hwy 255; mains $10-16; open from 6am daily), with decks for a view over-looking Woodley Island marina, is where you may just see grizzled old sea captains downing a pint.

The Sea Grill (☎ 707-443-7187; 316 E St; seafood dinners $12-20; open 11am-2pm Tues-Fri, 5pm-9pm Mon-Sat) has a genteel parlor atmosphere, and an antique mahogany bar brought round the Horn in the 1880s.

Kyoto (☎ 707-443-7777; 320 F St; mains $15-25; 6pm-9pm Wed-Sat), with bamboo screens and attentive service, is a sushi bar and Japanese dinner house in Old Town.

Also look out for the new **Cafe Tomo** (☎ 707-443-5338; 139 2nd St), at the Eagle House Inn, and **Tomo Deli** (☎ 707-444-3318; 2120 4th St), both branches of popular Tomo's Japanese Restaurant in Arcata.

Hurricane Kate's (☎ 707-444-1405; 511 2nd St; lunch $10, dinner mains $16-22; open 11:30am-3pm & 5pm-10pm Tues-Sat) cooks up a whirlwind of fusion cuisine, including wood-fired specialties. At lunch, heart-warming sandwiches come with sweet potato fritters.

Eureka's finest hotels also have renowned restaurants, for which you'll need to make advance reservations.

Restaurant 301 (☎ 707-445-1390; 301 L St; breakfast $16, multi-course dinners $38-45, à la carte mains $18-26; open 7:30am-10am & 6pm-8:45pm daily), at the Hotel Carter, has won national and international awards. Its famous breakfasts consist of a four-course meal and lavish buffet; prix-fixe dinners of New American cooking can be ordered either vegetarian or meat-and-fish. All of this culinary creativity is augmented by fresh herbs from the inn's own gardens, and the 50-page wine list is inspiring.

Eureka Inn (☎ 707-442-644; 518 7th St) offers elegant dining in its **Rib Room** (mains $25-40; open 5:30pm-10pm daily), which specializes in prime rib. Breakfast and lunch are served in the simpler **Bristol Rose Cafe**.

Entertainment

The **Morris Graves Museum of Art** (see Things to See & Do earlier) hosts performing arts events between September and May, usually on Saturday evenings.

Broadway Cinema (☎ 707-444-3456; Broadway, near 14th St) is a first-run movie house.

Humboldt Bay Coffee Company (☎ 707-444-3969; 211 F St), an alternative-type coffee lounge, has live music on Friday and Saturday nights.

Six Rivers Brewing Co (☎ 707-268-3893; 325 2nd St; bar open until 2am) is Eureka's newest brewpub, and it's a big ol' friendly place with darts, big-screen TVs and vintage video games. On weekends there's often live music and dancing.

Lost Coast Brewery (☎ 707-445-4480; 617 4th St) is another popular microbrewery, famous for its Downtown Brown Ale and serving pub fare from 11am until midnight.

Eureka Inn (☎ 707-442-6441; 518 7th St) has live music in the distinguished **Palm Lounge** Thursday to Sunday nights; downstairs, **Mirrors** is a quieter bar.

If you're looking for hip alternative bars and DJ clubs, you may turn something up by poking around the backstreets of Old Town – or then again, you might only find strip clubs. Good luck.

Getting There & Around

The Arcata-Eureka Airport, about 20mi north of Eureka, is served by two airlines: **Horizon Air** (☎ 800-547-9308) and **United Express** (☎ 800-241-6522).

The **Greyhound bus station** (☎ 707-442-0370, 800-231-2222; 1603 4th St) is central. **Redwood Transit System** (☎ 707-443-0826) buses make a number of stops along 4th and 5th Sts as they pass through Eureka. Local city buses are operated by **Eureka Transit Service** (☎ 707-443-0826), with service Monday to Saturday.

Pro Sport Center (☎ 707-443-6328; 508 Myrtle Ave) rents bicycles.

SAMOA PENINSULA

A windswept natural beauty, the 7mi-long, half-mile-wide Samoa Peninsula is the north spit of Humboldt Bay. It's said that the name derives from a resemblance to Pago Pago Harbor, on the South Pacific island of Samoa. The shoreline road is a back-door route between the towns of Eureka and Arcata – an alternative to taking Hwy 101 around the east side of Humboldt Bay. Anywhere along the peninsula you can access the beach by walking west through the dunes.

At the south end of the peninsula, **Samoa Dunes Recreation Area** (☎ 707-825-2300; open sunrise-sunset) offers picnic areas and opportunities for fishing. For good wildlife viewing, head to **Mad River Slough &**

Dunes; to get there from Arcata, go west on Samoa Blvd for about 3mi, then turn right at Young St, the Manila turnoff. Follow the road to the community center parking lot, from where a trail passes mudflats, salt marsh and tidal channels. Over 200 species of bird can be seen here around the year, with migrating waterfowl in spring and autumn, songbirds in spring and summer, shorebirds in autumn and winter, and abundant wading birds year-round.

The 475-acre **Lanphere Dunes Preserve** is one of the finest examples of dune succession on the entire Pacific coast. These undisturbed sand dunes can reach heights of over 80ft. Because the environment is fragile, access is by guided tour only. A couple of miles south of Lanphere Dunes, the 100-acre **Manila Dunes Recreation Area** (☎ 707-445-3309) is open to the public, with access from Peninsula Drive.

Friends of the Dunes (☎ 707-444-1397; W www.friendsofthedunes.org) leads 2½-hour walks through Lanphere Dunes on the first and third Saturday of each month, rain or shine, departing at 10am from the Pacific Union School parking lot at 3001 Janes Rd, Arcata. It also offers guided Manila Dunes walks on the second and fourth Saturday of each month, 10am to noon, rain or shine, departing from the community center. Bring a jacket and soft-soled shoes. Volunteer restoration workdays are scheduled on alternate Saturdays. Call first, or check the website for details.

Samoa Cookhouse (☎ 707-442-1659; off Samoa Blvd; breakfast/lunch/dinner $8/9/13; open 7am-3:30pm & 5pm-10pm Mon-Sat, 7am-10pm Sun) is the 'last surviving cookhouse in the West' and has a **museum** in one part of the building. The whole place is like a slice out of Eureka's lumber camp past. Diners are seated all together at long tables covered with checkered cloths, then served course after course of hearty, all-you-can-eat dishes. Kids eat for half price. It's just a few minutes northwest of Eureka, over the Samoa Bridge; follow the signs. You can also get there from Arcata via Samoa Blvd.

There's camping at the **Samoa Boat Ramp County Park** (☎ 707-445-7651; campsites $10), on the bay side of the peninsula, about 4mi south of the Samoa Bridge. There's not much there – basically just some picnic tables and a toilet block beside a parking lot – but it has relaxing views and an on-site camp host.

Samoa Airport B&B (☎ 707-445-0765; w www.northcoast.com/airbb; 900 New Navy Base Rd; rooms $75-95), a few miles south of the cookhouse, has rooms inside a refurbished military house, dating from WWII when the private Eureka Municipal Airport was a US Navy blimp base.

ARCATA

Only 5mi north of Eureka, overlooking Arcata and Humboldt bays, Arcata (population 16,500) has a youthful, laid-back ambience reminiscent of the 1960s. When it was founded by the Union Timber Company in 1850, Arcata was called Union Town. Originally a base for the Trinity gold fields in the

mountains to the east and for nearby lumber camps, Arcata grew and became a lumber town with a number of mills. In the late 1850s, popular author Bret Harte worked in Arcata as a journalist; the town became the setting for some of his Gold Rush–era stories. Today Humboldt State University (HSU), the northernmost campus in the state university system, is especially strong on environmental studies and forestry, and has redefined Arcata as a college town.

Orientation & Information

Arcata slopes downhill toward Humboldt Bay. Like Eureka, the town is laid out on the grid system, with numbered streets crossing lettered streets. Downtown is centered on Arcata Plaza, between G and H Sts, the

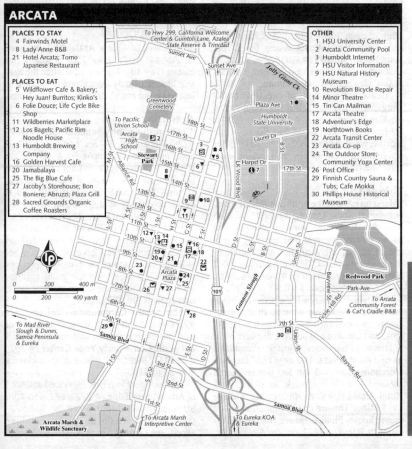

ARCATA

PLACES TO STAY
4 Fairwinds Motel
8 Lady Anne B&B
21 Hotel Arcata; Tomo Japanese Restaurant

PLACES TO EAT
5 Wildflower Cafe & Bakery; Hey Juan! Burritos; Kinko's
6 Folie Douce; Life Cycle Bike Shop
11 Wildberries Marketplace
12 Los Bagels; Pacific Rim Noodle House
13 Humboldt Brewing Company
16 Golden Harvest Cafe
20 Jambalaya
25 The Big Blue Cafe
27 Jacoby's Storehouse; Bon Boniere; Abruzzi; Plaza Grill
28 Sacred Grounds Organic Coffee Roasters

OTHER
1 HSU University Center
2 Arcata Community Pool
3 Humboldt Internet
7 HSU Visitor Information
9 HSU Natural History Museum
10 Revolution Bicycle Repair
14 Minor Theatre
15 Tin Can Mailman
17 Arcata Theatre
18 Adventure's Edge
19 Northtown Books
22 Arcata Transit Center
23 Arcata Co-op
24 The Outdoor Store; Community Yoga Center
26 Post Office
29 Finnish Country Sauna & Tubs; Cafe Mokka
30 Phillips House Historical Museum

major one-way thoroughfares connecting with Hwy 101 at the north end of town near HSU. Heading west out of town, Samoa Blvd connects through the Samoa Peninsula to Hwy 255, making an alternate scenic route into Eureka.

Two miles north of town, off Giuntoli Lane on the west side of Hwy 101, the **Arcata Chamber of Commerce & Visitor Information Center** (☎ 707-822-3619; w www .arcatachamber.com; 1635 Heindon Rd; open 9am-5pm daily) is inside the **California Welcome Center**, serving all of Humboldt County, Del Norte County and the state. Be sure to pick up a free fold-out *Official Map Guide to Arcata.* Next door, the **Bureau of Land Management** (BLM; ☎ 707-825-2300; 1695 Heindon Rd) has information on the Lost Coast and the King Range National Conservation Area.

Humboldt Internet (☎ 707-825-4638; 750 16th St; open 10am-1:30pm & 3:30pm-5pm Mon-Fri) offers Internet access for $2 per hour. Nearby **Kinko's** (☎ 707-822-8712; 1618 G St; open 7am-11pm Mon-Fri, 9am-6pm Sat & Sun) charges $0.20 per minute.

Arcata has a couple of excellent bookstores, with many hard-to-find books. The **Tin Can Mailman** (☎ 707-822-1307; 1000 H St) has used volumes on two floors, while **Northtown Books** (☎ 707-822-2384; 957 H St) handles new books and periodicals, travel maps and guides.

Things to See

Taking up most of the northeast side of town, **Humboldt State University** (HSU; ☎ 707-826-3011) has a large, attractive campus with an art gallery, cultural and sporting events and more; see the Activities and Entertainment sections later. The off-campus **HSU Natural History Museum** (☎ 707-826-4479; 1315 G St; adult/child $1/0.50; open 10am-4pm Tues-Sat) has a few kid-oriented exhibits including fossils, live animals of the north coast, an observation beehive, a tidepool tank, and tsunami and seismic displays.

Historic buildings cluster downtown around **Arcata Plaza**. The large 1857 **Jacoby's Storehouse** (cnr H & 8th Sts) is a registered national historic landmark, as is the 1915 **Hotel Arcata** (cnr G & 9th Sts). The vintage 1914 **Minor Theatre** (1013 10th St) is now a movie house. **Phillips House Historical Museum** (☎ 707-822-4722; cnr 7th & Union Sts; admission by donation; open noon-4pm Sun & by appointment) is an 1854 home open for guided tours, if you're keen.

At the east end of 11th and 14th Sts, **Redwood Park** is lovely, with redwood trees and picnic areas. Adjoining the park is the sizable **Arcata Community Forest**, a beautiful 575-acre redwood forest crisscrossed by 10mi of trails, with dirt roads and paved roads good for hikers and mountain bikers.

On the shores of Humboldt Bay, the **Arcata Marsh & Wildlife Sanctuary** is great for birding and has 5mi of walking trails. The **Redwood Coast Audubon Society** (☎ 707-826-7031) offers guided walks every Saturday at 8:30am, rain or shine; they leave from the parking lot at the south end of I St. Friends of Arcata Marsh give guided tours every Saturday at 2pm starting from the **Arcata Marsh Interpretive Center** (☎ 707-826-2359; 600 South G St; open 9am-5pm daily).

Northeast of Arcata, **Azalea State Reserve** (☎ 707-488-2041; Hwy 200) is found 2mi east of Hwy 101. It's beautiful when the azaleas bloom, usually from around late April to late May, but not so dramatic at other times.

Activities

The **Finnish Country Sauna & Tubs** (☎ 707-822-2228; cnr 5th & J Sts; open noon-10pm Sun-Thur, noon-midnight Fri & Sat) offers blissfully private redwood hot tubs open to the stars, and two saunas in a lovely garden. It costs from $7.65 per half-hour and it books up quickly at night and on weekends, so phone ahead for same-day reservations.

HSU Center Activities (☎ 707-826-3357; open 7.30pm Mon-Thur, 10am-6pm Fri), on the 2nd floor of the University Center, beside the clock tower on campus, sponsors myriad activities, workshops, group outings, sporting-gear rentals and consignment sales; nonstudents are welcome.

The **Arcata Community Pool** (☎ 707-822-6801; 1150 16th St) also boasts hot tubs, an exercise room and more. Or chill out at the **Community Yoga Center** (☎ 707-440-2111; 890 G St), where drop-in classes cost $5 to $10.

Outdoor gear is rented, serviced and sold at **Adventure's Edge** (☎ 822-4673; 650 10th St) and **The Outdoor Store** (☎ 707-822-0321; 876 G St) on the plaza. For bike shops, see Getting There & Around later.

Special Events
Arcata's most famous event is the three-day **Kinetic Sculpture Race** to Ferndale (for details, see the boxed text under Ferndale earlier). Other annual festivals include the **Arcata Bay Oyster Festival** and **Bebop & Brew**, both in June, and the **North Country Fair** in mid-September.

Places to Stay
Arcata, with its affordable lodgings and prime bayside location, makes an excellent base for exploring both Eureka and the giant redwoods further north.

The nearest camping is at **Eureka KOA** (see Eureka Places to Stay earlier), and there are several commercial campgrounds in Trinidad, as well as public camping at Patrick's Point State Park and Clam Beach, near Trinidad, all just a short drive north of Arcata. See the relevant sections later in this chapter for details.

Fairwinds Motel (☎ 707-822-4824, fax 707-822-0568; 1674 G St; rooms $40-55) has OK rooms, but the noise from Hwy 101, just a few feet behind the motel, is loud. Other motels are 2mi north of town at Hwy 101's Giuntoli Lane exit, including **Motel 6** (☎ 707-822-7061, 800-466-8356; singles/doubles from $42/46); **Best Western Arcata Inn** (☎ 707-826-0313, 800-528-1234; standard rooms $65-75), which offers deluxe continental breakfast; and **North Coast Inn** (☎ 707-822-4861, 800-406-0046; 4975 Valley West Blvd; rooms from $65), offering free airport transfers and an on-site restaurant.

Hotel Arcata (☎ 707-826-0217, 800-344-1221; 708 9th St; rooms $70-85, suites $90-140), on the north side of the plaza, is a beautifully restored 1915 hotel with charming, comfortable rooms, all with private bath and clawfoot tubs. A continental breakfast is complimentary.

Cats' Cradle B&B (☎ 707-822-2287, fax 707-822-5287; 815 Park Place; rooms $65-80, suites $105) overlooks town, within walking distance of Redwood Park.

Lady Anne B&B (☎ 707-822-2797; 902 14th St; rooms with bathroom $80-105), in an 1888 Queen Anne Victorian mansion, also manages a vacation rental in Trinidad.

Places to Eat
In the warmer months, there's a **farmers market** (open 9am-1pm Sat Apr-Nov) on Arcata Plaza, and another (open 3pm-6pm Tues June-Oct) sets up outside Wildberries Marketplace.

Wildberries Marketplace (☎ 707-822-0095; 747 13th St; open 7am-11pm daily) is a health-conscious grocery store with an award-winning deli, bakery and juice bar.

Arcata Co-op (☎ 707-822-5947; cnr 8th & I Sts; open 6am-10pm daily) is another huge natural-foods supermarket.

Bon Boniere (☎ 707-822-6388; 791 8th St), inside Jacoby's Storehouse, is an old-fashioned candy shop and ice-cream parlor.

Los Bagels (☎ 707-822-3150; 1061 I St; bagelwiches $2.50-6; open 7am-6pm Mon & Wed-Fri, 7am-5pm Sat, 8am-3pm Sun) is an Arcata original; the over-priced sourdough rounds are nevertheless brilliant.

Wildflower Cafe & Bakery (☎ 707-822-0360; 1604 G St; dishes $5-8; open 8am-8pm Mon-Sat, 9am-1pm Sun) offers baked goods and tasty, wholesome and inexpensive organic vegetarian meals.

Golden Harvest Cafe (☎ 707-822-8962; 1062 G St; breakfast $4-8) serves toothsome breakfasts that will delight carnivores and grazers alike. Bottomless cups of coffee surely don't hurt.

The Big Blue Cafe (☎ 707-826-7578; 846 G St; breakfast & lunch $4-7; open 7am-4pm daily) serves lighter café fare. Citrus salads and ginger beef sandwiches are just a taste of what you'll find.

Pacific Rim Noodle House (☎ 707-826-7604; 1021 I St; dishes $3.25-6.50; open 11am-7pm Mon-Sat) is a popular take-out kitchen, dishing up an eclectic mix of Pacific Rim foods, with tables outside.

Hey Juan! Burritos (☎ 707-822-8433; 16421/2 G St; open 11am-11pm daily) and **Philly Cheese Steak Shoppe** (☎ 707-825-7400; cnr 18th & G Sts; open 11am-late daily) are ever-popular with hungry HSU students strapped for cash.

Arcata also has several more substantial restaurants. Dinner reservations help.

Jambalaya (☎ 822-4766; 915 H St; mains $13-21; open 5pm-9pm Tues-Sat) takes its seafood seriously enough to fly in live Maine lobster once a week. The restaurant's equally fresh thinking on American bistro cuisine has won it many awards; try the Humboldt Bay oysters with smoked chipotle aioli.

Abruzzi (☎ 707-826-2345; enter off H St; mains $12-20; open 5:30pm-9pm daily) is a long-running Italian dinner house downstairs inside the historic Jacoby's Storehouse building. Upstairs, the same folks run the lively **Plaza Grill** (☎ 707-826-0860; sandwiches $7-10, mains $13-20; open 5pm-11pm nightly), which specializes in steak and seafood.

Tomo Japanese Restaurant (☎ 707-822-1414; 708 9th St; lunch $8-11, dinner $14-17; open 11:30am-2pm Mon-Fri & 5:30pm-9:30pm daily), in the Hotel Arcata, is always busy slicing sushi and mixing up intriguing sake cocktails and vegetarian/vegan salads.

Folie Douce (☎ 707-822-1042; 1551 G St; mains $16-26; open 5:30pm-9pm Tues-Thur, 5:30pm-10pm Fri-Sat) is as good as it gets, with new American bistro fare and a wine list that qualifies as a piece of art. And oh, how intoxicating are the spices and aroma of freshly baked gourmet pizzas wafting out the door!

Entertainment
Center Arts (☎ 707-826-4411, tickets 707-826-3928) is a HSU entity that sponsors performances, concerts, international music and more.

Arcata Theatre (☎ 707-822-1220; 1036 G St) also hosts cultural events.

Minor Theatre (☎ 707-822-3456; 1013 H St) shows first-run movies and classic films. Come for bargain matinees at this historic Arcata venue.

Humboldt Brewing Company (☎ 707-826-2739; 856 10th St; pub grub $5-10; open 4pm-midnight Tues, noon-midnight Wed-Sat) serves delicious buffalo wings and fish tacos with its respectable homemade brews. There's live music Thursday to Saturday nights.

Jambalaya (☎ 822-4766; 915 H St) hosts live jazz, blues and other music, plus weekly jam nights and poetry nights; the schedule is posted at the door.

A warm, friendly place for drinks is **Plaza Grill** (☎ 707-826-0860), in the Jacoby's Storehouse building. Dive bars and cocktail lounges are nearby, on the plaza's north side.

Arcata is also awash in coffeehouses. **Sacred Grounds Organic Coffee Roasters** (☎ 707-822-0690; 686 F St; open 7am-11pm Sun-Wed, 7am-midnight Thur-Sat) has live music on weekends, chess boards and shade-grown organic brews.

At Finnish Country Sauna & Tubs, **Café Mokka** (☎ 707-822-2228; cnr 5th & J Sts) is

worth checking out for mellow live acoustic music (usually European folk) on weekend evenings. With just a few tables, some international newspapers and good conversation, the atmosphere is truly Bohemian. Whatever you do, try the hot chai.

Getting There & Around
See the Eureka Getting There & Around section for airport information. **Greyhound** (☎ 800-231-2222) buses travel along Hwy 101, **Redwood Transit System** (☎ 707-443-0826) regional buses and Arcata city buses (☎ 707-822-3775) stop at the **Arcata Transit Center** (☎ 707-825-8934; 925 E St).

Revolution Bicycle Repair (☎ 707-822-2562; 1360 G St) and **Life Cycle Bike Shop** (☎ 707-822-7755; 1593 G St) rent, service and sell bicycles.

TRINIDAD
About 12mi north of Arcata, this affluent, windy hamlet (population 400) on Trinidad Bay always looks freshly painted. Attractions include hiking on Trinidad Head and at beautiful Trinidad State Beach, surfing at Luffenholtz Beach, visiting the museum and old lighthouse, and dining on fresh seafood.

The town and bay also have a long history. Originally settled by Tsurai Indians, Trinidad Bay was 'discovered' by European explorers several times, beginning in 1595. Spanish sea captains Hezeta and Bodega anchored here on 9 June 1775 and named the bay 'La Santisima Trinidad' (the Holy Trinity). However, it wasn't until the 1850s that Trinidad became the site of a booming settlement, after Josiah Gregg and seven companions tramped over the mountains from the Klamath and Trinity gold fields in 1849. Searching for a convenient sea transport link to the mining regions, they rediscovered Trinidad Bay. Like Eureka and Arcata, Trinidad became an important base and supply port for the inland gold fields, with schooners bringing supplies up from San Francisco and returning with redwood lumber from the North Coast forests.

Orientation & Information
The town is small and it's easy to get your bearings. Taking the Trinidad exit from Hwy 101 brings you to the town's major intersection, the corner of Main St, Patrick's Point Drive and Scenic Drive. From this

crossroads, Patrick's Point Drive heads north along coastal bluffs past motels, campgrounds and B&Bs to Patrick's Point State Park. Scenic Drive heads south to Luffenholtz Beach. If you go straight ahead on Main St toward the lighthouse, you'll pass the turnoff to Trinidad State Park.

The **Trinidad Chamber of Commerce** (☎ 707-667-1610; W www.trinidadcalifcham ber.org) has no visitor center, but there's an **information kiosk** at the main crossroads stocked with the free *Discover Trinidad* brochure, which provides an excellent town map. Annual events include the **Trinidad Fish Festival** in June, which is one of the few times the lighthouse opens to visitors.

Things to See & Do

The **Trinidad Memorial Lighthouse** (cnr Trinity & Edwards Sts), a replica of an 1871 lighthouse, sits on a breezy bluff overlooking Trinidad Bay. Half a block inland from the lighthouse, **Trinidad Museum** (☎ 707-677-3883; 529B Trinity St; open noon-3pm Fri-Sun May-Sept) has simple exhibits on the area's natural and human history.

HSU Telonicher Marine Laboratory (☎ 707-826-3671; Edwards St; admission free; usually open 9am-5pm Mon-Fri, 10am-5pm Sat), two blocks further down Edwards St toward Trinidad Head, has a touch tank, several aquariums (look for the 8ft giant Pacific octopus in residence), an enormous whale jaw and a three-dimensional map of the ocean floor.

The free town map from the information kiosk shows several attractive **hiking trails**. The Trinidad Head Trail, with a fine view of the coastline and excellent whale-watching in season, starts from the harborside parking lot. Trinidad State Beach has walking trails on an exceptionally beautiful cove; picnic areas are for day-use only.

True to its name, **Scenic Drive** twists along the coastal bluffs south of Trinidad, passing several tiny coves with views back toward Trinidad Bay. After 2mi, it opens onto the long, broad expanse of **Luffenholtz Beach**, called Little River State Beach and then Clam Beach County Park further south. Scenic Drive doesn't connect all the way through, however, forcing you to detour onto Hwy 101 to reach the county park.

Trinidad is famous for its good fishing, both from the shore and by boat. Sportfishing

trips can be arranged through **Salty's Surf & Tackle Tours** (☎ 707-677-0300; Saunders Shopping Center, 332 Main St) and **Trinidad Bay Charters** (☎ 707-839-4743, 800-839-4744). The harbor is at the bottom of Edwards St, at the foot of Trinidad Head. A five-hour trip will cost about $65 per person.

The long, regular waves at Luffenholtz Beach make it a popular surfing beach; there's also surfing at Trinidad State Beach. Visit the surf shop next to the information kiosk back in town for the low-down.

North Coast Adventures (☎ 707-677-3124; W www.northcoastadventures.com) offer sea and river kayaking lessons and guided eco-trips around Trinidad Bay and further up the coast. Two-hour tours cost from $45, full-day tours from $80.

Places to Stay & Eat

Clam Beach (☎ 707-445-7491; campsites per vehicle $8), south of town off Hwy 101, has excellent camping. Primitive sites are basically anywhere you choose to pitch your tent in the dunes (look for natural windbreaks). Facilities include pit toilets, a few cold water faucets, picnic tables and fire rings.

Trinidad Bay B&B (☎ 707-677-0840, fax 707-677-9245; W www.trinidadbaybnb .com; 560 Edwards St; rooms $125-170), opposite the lighthouse, overlooking the harbor and Trinidad Head, is a fetching Cape Cod–style home.

On Patrick's Point Drive, heading north along the coast, there are several commercial campgrounds and lodgings. See the Patrick's Point State Beach section later for more camping.

Emerald Forest (☎ 707-677-3554, fax 707-677-0963; W www.cabinsintheredwoods .com; 753 Patrick's Point Dr; tent & RV sites $19-25, cabins $75-180) has shady camping and rustic cabins – some with kitchenettes.

Bishop Pine Lodge (☎ 707-677-3314, fax 707-677-3444; W www.bishoppinelodge .com; 1481 Patrick's Point Dr; studio cottage singles/doubles from $80/90, duplex units with shared Jacuzzi $95, 2-bedroom cottage from $105, kitchen units extra $10) is a peaceful, old-fashioned place.

View Crest Lodge (☎ 707-677-3393; 3415 Patrick's Point Dr; tent/RV sites $16/20, cottages $85-135) has campsites and adorable cottages surrounded by trees. Some cottages have a private hot tub.

NORTH COAST

Motels are also along Patrick's Point Dr, a few miles from the town center.

Trinidad Inn *(☎ 707-677-3349;* **w** *www.trinidadinn.com; 1170 Patrick's Point Dr; rooms $65-120)* is sparklingly clean; kitchens are available upon request.

Less appealing are the **Sea Cliffe Motel** *(☎ 707-677-3485; 1895 Patrick's Point Dr; rooms & kitchenettes $45-65)* and **Patrick's Point Inn** *(☎ 707-677-3483; 3602 Patrick's Point Dr; rooms $50-90)*, which has no views.

Turtle Rocks Oceanfront Inn *(☎ 707-677-3707;* **w** *www.turtlerocksinn.com; 3392 Patrick's Point Dr; rooms $120-185, suites $145-210)* has spacious rooms, all with glass-paneled decks and ocean views. A harbor seal colony lives off-shore.

Lost Whale Inn *(☎ 707-677-3425, 800-677-7859;* **w** *www.lostwhaleinn.com; 3452 Patrick's Point Dr; rooms $170-200)*, perched on a cliffside, is another contemporary house, with skylights and hardwood floors. Ask about vacation rentals; children are welcome.

For vacation rentals, **Trinidad Retreats** *(☎ 707-677-1606;* **w** *www.parteehouse.com; daily/weekly rates from $90/550)* is an agency that handles a number of properties.

Kelly's Smokehouse & Fishmarket *(Edwards St; open 9am-6pm daily)*, uphill from the marine laboratory, vends all kinds of smoked, steamed, fried and fresh fish.

Trinidad Bay Eatery & Gallery *(☎ 707-677-3777; cnr Trinity & Parker Sts; most meals $5-8, seafood specials $10-16; open 7:30am-3pm Mon-Thur, 7:30am-8pm Fri-Sun)*, opposite the museum, cooks up heaping, hot breakfast and lunch plates.

Seascape Restaurant *(☎ 707-677-3762; (Main St; breakfast & lunch $7.50-10, dinner $11-22; open 7am-10pm daily, until 8:30pm winter)*, at the harbor since 1940, serves myriad varieties of fresh seafood, plus omelettes and blackberry pancakes for breakfast.

Larrupin' Cafe *(☎ 707-677-0230; 1658 Patrick's Point Dr; dinner $18-22; open 5pm-9pm Thur-Mon)*, north of town, is Trinidad's most famous restaurant; people drive from miles around just to dine here. The hospitable country ambience complements a creative international menu featuring mesquite-grilled savory specialties. Reservations are recommended.

At the time of writing, the **café** above Luffenholtz Beach, with gorgeous sunset views, had closed temporarily.

PATRICK'S POINT STATE PARK

Five miles north of Trinidad, this beautiful 640-acre state park *(☎ 707-677-3570; 4150 Patrick's Point Dr; day use $2)* sits on a coastal bluff jutting out into the Pacific. **Sumêg**, an authentic reproduction of a Yurok Indian village, has hand-hewn redwood buildings where Native Americans gather to hold traditional ceremonies. Look for a native California plant garden nearby.

Other park features include long, broad **Agate Beach**, where people collect sea-polished agates on the sand. There are colonies of seals and sea lions, and extensive tidepools. The **Rim Trail**, a 2mi walk along the bluffs, goes round the edge of the point, with access to rocky outcrops excellent for whale-watching in season. Other **nature trails** lead around unusual rock formations like **Ceremonial Rock** and **Lookout Rock**.

The park has three **campgrounds** *(summer reservations ☎ 800-444-7275;* **w** *www.reserveamerica.com; campsites $12)*, all with attractive, secluded sites. Penn Creek and Abalone campgrounds *(open May-Sept 15)* are more sheltered than Agate Beach *(open year-round)*. Both of the latter have hot showers.

HUMBOLDT LAGOONS STATE PARK

Stretching for miles along the coast, this park *(☎ 707-488-2041)* has long sandy beaches and two large coastal lagoons – Big Lagoon and Stone Lagoon – both excellent for birdwatching. The **Stone Lagoon Visitor Center** *(Hwy 101; usually open 10am-3pm daily June-Sept)* opens seasonally when there are volunteers. About a mile north of the Stone Lagoon Visitor Center, **Freshwater Lagoon** is also good for birding.

All public campsites are first-come, first-served. The state park operates two **environmental campgrounds** *(campsites $7)*: Stone Lagoon, with six boat-in environmental campsites, and Dry Lagoon, off Hwy 101, with six walk-in campsites. Both are open April to October, with check-in at the visitor center. **Humboldt County Parks** *(☎ 707-445-7652; campsites $12)* operates a cypress grove campground beside Big Lagoon, a mile off Hwy 101, with flush toilets and cold water, but no showers.

Redwood Trails RV & Campground *(☎ 707-488-2061; Hwy 101; tent/RV sites*

$15/25), opposite the turnoff to Dry Lagoon, offers a general store and bakery, video game arcade, horseback rides and, if you're lucky, elk lazing in the meadow outside.

ORICK

The small town of Orick (population 340) is pretty unremarkable. However, the **Redwood National & State Parks Information Center** (*☎ 707-822-7611 ext 5265; Hwy 101; open 9am-5pm daily*), sitting beside the beach a mile southwest of town, is a highly recommended stop for those heading north. At the very least, make time for an excellent 12-minute introductory video on redwood forests; you can also pick up your permit to visit Tall Trees Grove here. Some of the parks' most attractive features, including Lady Bird Johnson Grove, Tall Trees Grove and Fern Canyon, are all near Orick.

Freshwater Lagoon Spit (*camping per vehicle $10, hikers & bikers per person $3*), immediately south of the visitor center, is a long strand of gravel RV pull-outs along the highway, with tent sites at the southernmost access point. It's far more scenic than it sounds, and the ocean views and breezes here are lovely.

Rolf's Park Cafe (*☎ 707-488-3841; Hwy 101; motel rooms from $45; breakfast & lunch $6-12, dinner $10-20; open 8am-7pm Wed-Mon, 5pm-7pm Tues, closed Jan & Feb*), at the corner of Davison Rd 2mi north of town, is a German family-run establishment. People travel far out of their way to come and eat here; the food is hearty and generously apportioned, with a menu encompassing many unusual ingredients, including elk, buffalo and wild boar, plus a variety of seafood dishes. At breakfast, the farmer's omelette (a veritable mountain of food) will keep you going all day long.

REDWOOD NATIONAL PARK

Awe-inspiring **Lady Bird Johnson Grove**, reached via a gentle, accessible nature loop trail, is about 2mi down Bald Hills Rd, off Hwy 101; look for the signposted turnoff north of Rolf's Park Cafe.

About 5mi further along the same road is **Redwood Creek Overlook** and immediately after that appears the gated turnoff to the remarkable **Tall Trees Grove**, home to several of the world's tallest redwood trees. Only 50 vehicles are allowed to visit the grove each

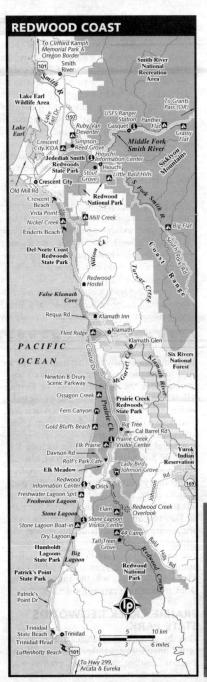

REDWOOD COAST

Coast Redwoods: The Tallest Trees on Earth

Though they once covered much of the northern hemisphere, redwood trees now grow only in China and two areas of California. Coast redwoods *(Sequoia sempervirens)* are found in a narrow, 450mi long strip along California's Pacific coast between Monterey and southern Oregon. They can live for 2200 years, grow to 367.8ft tall (the tallest tree ever recorded) and achieve a diameter of 22ft at the base, with bark up to 12 inches thick.

The structure of coast redwoods has been compared to a nail standing on its head. Unlike most trees, coast redwoods have no deep taproot and their root system is shallow in relation to their height – only 10ft to 13ft deep and spreading out 60ft to 80ft around the tree. The trees sometimes fall due to wind, but they are very flexible and sway in the wind as if they're dancing.

What gives these majestic giants their namesake color? It's the redwoods' high tannin content, which also makes their wood and bark resistant to insects and disease. The thick, spongy bark also has a high moisture content that insulates them even further, enabling the ancient trees to survive many naturally occurring forest fires.

Coast redwoods are the only conifers in the world that can reproduce not only by seed cones, which grow to about the size of an olive at the ends of branches, but also by sprouting from their parents' roots and stumps, using the established root systems. Often you'll see a circle of redwoods standing in a forest, sometimes around a wide crater; this 'fairy ring' is made up of offspring that sprouted from one parent tree, which may have deteriorated into humus long ago. Burls, the large bumpy tissue growths on trunks and fallen logs, are a third method of reproduction.

Four parks, all with spectacular redwood forests – Redwood National Park and the Prairie Creek Redwoods, Del Norte Coast Redwoods and Jedediah Smith Redwoods state parks – are managed cooperatively as the Redwood National & State Parks. Together these parks have been declared an International Biosphere Reserve and a World Heritage Site.

---

day, although usually not that many do; pick up a free permit with the gate lock combination from the visitor center in Orick. Allow three to four hours for the whole trek, which includes a 6mi trip down a rough dirt road (speed limit 15mph), then a steep 1.6mi hike each way to the grove.

Several longer hiking trails include the beautiful 8mi **Redwood Creek Trail**, also allowing access to Tall Trees Grove. A free backcountry permit, available at the park visitor center, is required to hike and camp this trail. It can only be done from Memorial Day to Labor Day, when summer footbridges are in place; outside this season, the bridges are down and water levels fluctuate. You can also come on horseback. Limited **primitive camping** is also available elsewhere in the park; ask the rangers at the Orick information center for details.

PRAIRIE CREEK REDWOODS STATE PARK

This 23-sq-mi park features the beautiful Fern Canyon, many miles of wild and untouched coastline and beaches, prairies with herds of large Roosevelt elk, over 70mi of hiking trails and some spectacular scenic drives. The **Prairie Creek Visitor Center** (☎ 707-464-6101 ext 5300; *open 9am-5pm daily Mar-Oct, 10am-4pm daily Nov-Feb*) is at Elk Prairie, 6mi north of Orick.

The famous 8mi **Newton B Drury Scenic Parkway** runs parallel to Hwy 101, passing through beautiful virgin redwood forests – it's well worth the detour, and it's free. From frequent turnouts along the way, hiking trails branch off for endless explorations through the forest. **Cal Barrel Rd** is a popular 3mi scenic drive that intersects the parkway just north of the Prairie Creek Visitor Center. A little further north, **Big Tree** is just 100 yards down a paved path from the roadside parking area.

Other scenic drives in the park include the **Coastal Drive**, reached by turning west from Hwy 101 onto Davison Rd at Rolf's Park Cafe (see the Orick section earlier). Follow a graded, mostly gravel road for 3½mi to the **fee station** (*admission per vehicle $2*), then head along the coast past Gold Bluffs Beach campground for another mile to an informal parking area. An easy half-mile trail takes you to enchanting **Fern Canyon**, with sheer

Teddy Roosevelt's Elk

Found west of the Cascade Mountains, the Roosevelt elk are the largest of their kind, with males weighing up to 1000 pounds and carrying massive antlers that 'crown,' or branch.

They are named in honor of US President Teddy Roosevelt, who established the national wildlife refuge system in the early 1900s, and made Washington's Olympic National Park into a protected habitat for the endangered elk. By 1925, there were only 25 left, although the population today stands at over 1000 animals. The elks' biggest threats are now from poachers and reckless drivers.

The best places to view these beasts in their velvety glory are all near Orick: along Davison Rd, west of Hwy 101; in Elk Prairie, on the Newton B Drury Scenic Parkway; and at Gold Bluffs Beach, near Fern Canyon. Try to visit in the early morning and late evening, when the herds come out to feed.

Although the elk are about year-round, their most active period is during autumn 'rut' (late August to early October), when mature bulls dramatically challenge each other for the right to a harem. Late May and early June, when calves are born, is another busy time, but newborns are kept well hidden in the tall grasslands until they're ready to keep up with the herd. The elk can be especially unpredictable and dangerous at these times – always keep a safe distance from these powerful creatures.

60ft high walls covered with several species of ferns. The trail continues up into the redwoods, connecting to longer trails.

There are 28 hiking and mountain biking trails through the park, from simple to strenuous. The Prairie Creek Visitor Center has maps and information on trail conditions. Several **short nature trails** start nearby, including the Five-Minute Trail, Revelation Trail, Nature Trail and Elk Prairie Trail. At the north end of the park, the **Ah-Pah Interpretive Trail** covers a recently reforested logging road: you'll be surprised to see how quickly the forest grows back. Notable treks include the 11½mi-long **Coastal Trail** and 3½mi **South Fork-Rhododendron-Brown Creek Loop**, which is especially wonderful in spring when the rhododendrons and other wildflowers are in bloom. Approach it from the Brown-Creek-to-South-Fork direction – unless you adore tramping uphill.

Elk Prairie Campground (*summer reservations* ☎ *800-444-7275;* **w** *www.reserveamerica.com; campsites $12*) is set attractively in the redwoods beside the visitor center at Elk Prairie, where herds of Roosevelt elk are often seen. It has hot showers.

Gold Bluffs Beach (*campsites $12*) is on a remote ocean beach south of Fern Canyon. The campground is open and exposed, but windbreaks have been erected around many of the sites. Hot showers are available; sites are first-come, first-served year-round.

The park also has two backcountry campsites (*campsites per person $3*) and one environmental campsite (*campsite per person $7*).

KLAMATH

Klamath (population 1420) has its most noticeable landmark at the Klamath River Bridge, where golden California bears stand sentry duty at the southern limits of town.

Various **hiking trails** and **scenic drives** in the rural Klamath area wind through Redwood national and state parks; the park map shows where they are. Fishing is also good on the river. The **Salmon Festival** takes place in August, featuring traditional Yurok tribal dances, arts and crafts, and a salmon barbecue. Call the **Klamath Chamber of Commerce** (☎ *800-200-2335*) for information.

Klamath River Jet Boat Tours (☎ *707-482-7775, 800-887-5387;* **w** *www.jetboattours.com; Hwy 101*) offers fully narrated trips (adult $22 to $35, child $11 to $17) between May and October. Boats make plenty of stops for photos of the remarkable views and the abundant wildlife, including bears, elk, deer, otters, mink, eagles, osprey and hawks, and seals and sea lions at the river mouth. Look for the office about 2mi north of the bridge, before a string of salmon jerky shops and RV parks.

It's hard to miss the giant talking statue of Paul Bunyan and Babe the Blue Ox towering over the parking area at the **Trees of Mystery** (☎ *800-638-3389; 15500 Hwy 101; trail admission adult/child $15/8; open 8am-5:30pm daily, winter hours vary*), a shameless tourist trap 5mi north of the bridge. The featured attraction is a gondola ride through the redwood canopy, hardly worth the price of admission. The **End of the Trail Museum** (admission free; open 8am-6:30pm daily summer), hidden at the back of the gift shop, has an outstanding collection of Native American arts and artifacts. It's adjacent to Trees of Mystery, but you don't have to pay for an entry ticket to see the museum.

Places to Stay & Eat

HI Redwood Hostel (☎ 707-482-8265, 800-909-4776, fax 707-482-4665; w www.norcal hostels.org; 14480 Hwy 101; dorm bunks $14-16, private rooms $38; check-in 7:30am-10am & 4:30pm-9:30pm, hostel closed 10am-4:30pm), about 7mi north of Klamath Bridge, off Wilson Creek Rd, this rambling hostel is inside the 1908 pioneer DeMartin House. Overlooking fearsome and moody False Klamath Cove, it adjoins a couple of fine hiking trails. Greyhound buses along Hwy 101 stop right outside. Make reservations, as it's often completely booked.

Mystic Forest RV Park (☎ 707-482-4901; 15875 Hwy 101; tent/RV sites $16/18), about 4mi north of the bridge, offers hot showers, a swimming pool, spa and recreational activities.

Camp Marigold (☎ 707-482-3585, 800-621-8513; 16101 Hwy 101; tent/RV sites $10/15, cabins from $40, lodge rooms $165) is a charming, relaxed and old-fashioned little resort, with hot showers. Cabins are cheaper off-season or weekly.

There are also a few more **campgrounds** on the south bank of the Klamath River, 2mi west of Hwy 101 along Klamath Beach Rd, all bordered by Redwood National Park.

Motel Trees (☎ 707-482-3152, 800-848-2982; 15495 Hwy 101 S; rooms from $50), opposite Trees of Mystery, has theme rooms, a tennis court, and the friendly, family-style **Forest Cafe** (☎ 707-482-5585; breakfast & lunch $5-10, dinner $13-17; open 7:30am-9pm daily May-Sept, 8am-8pm Thur-Mon Mar-Apr & Oct-Dec).

Historic Requa Inn (☎ 707-482-1425, 866-800-8777; w www.klamathinn.net; 451 Requa Rd; rooms $69-105), west of Hwy 101 on the north bank of the Klamath River, is a renowned country inn with an eventful history. Most of the town, including the original 1885 Klamath Inn, was rebuilt after the great fire of 1914. Over the years, all the surrounding buildings succumbed to fires, floods etc. But this one building has survived; it's still there, about a mile from the ocean,

in a wonderfully serene environment. Some cozy rooms have clawfoot tubs. Breakfast is served in the fine dining room, also open by reservation for dinner to guests (and occasionally the general public too); call to check hours.

DEL NORTE COAST REDWOODS STATE PARK

This 6400-acre park (day-use vehicle fee $2) contains beautiful redwood groves and 8mi of unspoiled coastline. Over 15mi of hiking trails range from easy to strenuous. Maps and information are available at the Redwood National & State Parks Headquarters in Crescent City or the Orick information center. At the north end of the park, **Enderts Beach** is accessible from Enderts Beach Rd off Hwy 101, and via the Crescent Beach Trail (north) or Coastal Trail (south). It has magnificent tidepools at low tide. So does **Hidden Beach**, about 2mi south of False Klamath Cove, accessible by the Coastal Trail or the Hidden Beach Trail.

Mill Creek Campground (summer reservations ☎ 800-444-7275; w www.reserve america.com; campsites $12; open May-Sept) is in a redwood grove, 2mi east of Hwy 101, about 7mi south of Crescent City. It has hot showers.

CRESCENT CITY

On a crescent-shaped bay, Crescent City (population 8800) is the only sizable coastal town north of Arcata. Like the rest of the North Coast, it is often socked in by fog during summer and winters are cold and wet, with about 75 inches of rain fall annually.

Crescent City was founded in 1853 as a port and supply center for inland gold mines, but it has very few old buildings, as half the town was destroyed by a tsunami (tidal wave) in 1964. It has since been completely rebuilt. The local economy depends on fishing (especially for shrimp and crab), and on the Pelican Bay maximum security prison, just outside town.

After passing the harbor on the south side of town, Hwy 101 continues up along the east side of Crescent City, with southbound traffic on L St and northbound traffic on M St. If you turn off onto Front Rd, heading west toward the lighthouse, you pass a well-stocked visitor center, the **Crescent City-Del Norte County Chamber of Commerce**

(☎ 707-464-3174, 800-343-8300; **W** www .northerncalifornia.net; 1001 Front St; open 9am-6pm Mon-Fri, 9am-5pm Sat summer; closed Sat rest of year). Crescent City's tiny 'downtown' commercial area is centered along 3rd St. **Redwood National & State Parks Headquarters** (☎ 707-464-6101; 1111 2nd St, cnr K St; open 9am-5pm daily) has information about all four parks under its jurisdiction.

Things to See & Do
The 1856 **Battery Point Lighthouse** (☎ 707-464-3089), at the south end of A St, is still in operation out on a tiny, picturesque island that you can easily walk to at low tide. From April to September, the lighthouse is open as a **museum**, but hours vary, depending on tides and weather. Phone for tour ($2) schedules, or at least check the notice board in the beach parking lot before walking over.

Skip the Ocean World aquarium on Hwy 101, and instead visit the **North Coast Marine Mammal Center** (☎ 707-465-6265; 424 Howe Dr; admission by donation; open 10am-5pm daily), just east of the lighthouse, where injured seals, sea lions and dolphins recuperate after being rescued.

The **Del Norte Historical Society Museum** (☎ 707-464-3922; 577 H St, at 6th St; admission $1.50; open 10am-4pm Mon-Sat May-Sept), inside a 1926 jailhouse, has collections of local Tolowa and Yurok Indian artifacts and minor historical exhibits on Del Norte's pioneer past, the '64 tsunami and a giant lens from St George Reef lighthouse.

You can observe cheese being made at the 1921 **Rumiano Cheese Company** (☎ 707-465-1535; cnr 9th & E Sts; open 8am-5pm Mon-Fri summer, hours vary rest of year). There's a cheese-tasting room, where fresh hot curds sell out quickly between 11am and 2pm.

Special Events
Annual celebrations include the **World Championship Crab Races**, on the third weekend of February; in April, the **State of Jefferson Championships** in white-water kayaking; the **Del Norte County Fair**, in early August; and **Drums on the Beach**, a Native American festival and salmon barbecue, held in September.

Crescent City's Great Tsunami

On March 28 1964, most of downtown Crescent City was destroyed by a great tsunami (tidal wave). At 3:36am a giant earthquake occurred on the north shore of Prince William Sound in Alaska – at 8.5 on the Richter scale, it was the most severe earthquake ever recorded in North America. The first of the giant ocean swells created by the earthquake reached Crescent City a few hours later.

The third wave came up almost into the town. By this time, residents were awake, had heard about the Alaska earthquake and were fearful of what might happen. When the third wave receded, some residents rejoiced, thinking the danger was over. Then a very eerie thing happened: the water receded until the entire bay was empty of water, leaving boats that had been anchored offshore sitting in the mud. When the fourth wave surged in, the frigid water rose all the way up to 5th St, knocking buildings off their foundations, carrying away cars, trucks and anything that wasn't bolted down, and even a lot of things that were. By the time the wave receded, it had destroyed 29 blocks of the town, damaging or displacing more than 300 buildings, and five bulk gasoline storage tanks exploded. Eleven people were killed and three were never found.

Many old-timers are still remembered for their heroic acts during and after the wave, helping to save their neighbors and later rebuild the town. The modern little downtown shopping center that replaced many of the town's older businesses has an unusual but very appropriate name – Tsunami Landing.

Places to Stay
Crescent City is not a place to linger, except as a base for extended visits to nearby Redwood National & State Parks (where you'll also find good camping).

Crescent City Redwoods KOA (☎ 707-464-5744, 800-562-5754; 4241 Hwy 101 N; campsites $20-22, RV sites $23-27, cabins $39-46; often closed Jan & Feb), about 5mi north of town, has 10 acres of redwoods; amenities include hot showers, nature trails and much more.

Del Norte County operates three basic **campgrounds** (☎ 707-464-7230), all with running water and flush toilets, but no showers. Closest to Crescent City, **Florence Keller Park** (*3400 Cunningham Lane; campsites $10*) has picnic areas in a beautiful redwood grove; to get there, take Hwy 101 north to Elk Valley Cross Road and follow the signs. **Ruby Van Deventer Campground** (*4705 N Bank Rd; campsites $10*) is in a tiny redwood grove on the Smith River, off Hwy 197. **Clifford Kamph Memorial Park** (*15100 Hwy 101 N; campsites $5*), is on an appealing little beach (no windbreaks), 1½mi south of the Oregon border.

Lighthouse Cove B&B (*☎ 707-465-6565; 215 S A St; suites $130*) has a glassed-in oceanfront sitting room and sprawling outdoor deck. Next door, **Cottage by the Sea B&B** (*☎ 707-464-9068, 707-464-4890, 877-642-2254; w www.waterfrontvacation .net; A St; suite with kitchen $125*) also offers vacation rentals. Both B&Bs are near the lighthouse.

There are a few budget motels along Front St, near the chamber of commerce. A great many other motels line Hwy 101 south of town, often with rooms experiencing lots of highway noise.

Crescent Beach Motel (*☎ 707-464-5436; 1455 Hwy 101 S; rooms in summer/winter $82/55*), set on a peaceful beach 2mi south of town, has relaxing rooms, mostly with ocean views and decks.

Curly Redwood Lodge (*☎ 707-464-2137, fax 707-464-1655; w www.curlyredwood lodge.com; 701 Hwy 101 S; rooms in summer/ winter from $60/39*) was built entirely from the lumber of one redwood tree that was struck down by lightning. Across from the harbor, only half a mile south of downtown, it's an older motel with spacious rooms.

Super 8 Motel (*☎ 707-464-4111, 800-800-8000; 685 Hwy 101 S; rooms $60/45 summer/winter*) has quieter rooms facing away from the highway.

Other mid-range motels near the harbor include the **BayView Inn** (*☎ 707-465-2050, 800-446-0583; 310 Hwy 101 S*) and **Anchor Beach Inn** (*☎ 707-464-2600, 800-837-4116; 880 Hwy 101 S*).

Quiet places further up the coast, near the Oregon border, include **White Rock Resort Cabins** (*☎ 707-487-1021, 888-487-4659, fax 707-487-1063; w www.whiterockresort.com; 16800 Hwy 101 N; rates $110-160*), which offers cottages with ocean views and hot tubs.

Places to Eat

Good Harvest Cafe (*☎ 707-465-6028; 700 Northcrest Dr, cnr Hwy 101; dishes $3-7; open breakfast & lunch daily*) serves healthy food and rich espresso – well worth a detour on the northern side of town.

Glen's Restaurant & Bakery (*☎ 707-464-2914; 722 3rd St; meals under $10; open 5am-6:30pm Tues-Sat*), one of the town's long-time favorites, is an old-fashioned, friendly diner. It was situated at 1238 2nd St from 1947 until 1964, when the big tidal wave moved it to its present location.

If it's seafood you're after, you could sniff out the restaurants and casual eateries alongside the harbor, one long block west of Hwy 101, at the southern edge of town.

About 20mi north of town, just south of the Oregon border, the **Nautical Inn** (*☎ 707-487-5006; 16850 Hwy 101 N; mains $15-20; open from 5pm Tues-Sun*) has jaw-dropping views of the Pacific. Chefs here cook up top-notch seafood dishes draped in whimsical sauces, plus rack of lamb and other surf-and-turf classics. Make reservations.

Getting There & Away

North of town, tiny Crescent City airport is served by **United Express** (*☎ 800-241-6522*).

The **Greyhound bus station** (*☎ 707-464-2807; 500 E Harding Ave*) is just east of Northcrest Dr, about a mile north of the downtown area via Hwy 101. **Redwood Coast Transit** (*☎ 707-464-9314*) buses also stop here.

Consult Lonely Planet's *Pacific Northwest* travel guide if you're heading up into Oregon. From Crescent City, two routes head north over the border. Hwy 101, the Coast Highway, crosses into Oregon about 20mi north of Crescent City and continues up toward Brookings, Gold Beach and Coos Bay. Hwy 199 branches off from Hwy 101 about 3mi north of Crescent City, then takes an inland route northeast into Oregon toward Grants Pass, where it intersects the I-5 freeway, for trips south to Mt Shasta (see the Northern Mountains chapter).

LAKE EARL WILDLIFE AREA

Two miles north of Crescent City, reached via Northcrest Dr (which becomes Lake Earl Dr), this wildlife area (*☎ 707-464-6101 ext 5151; open sunrise-sunset daily*) covers 10,000 acres of varied terrain, comprising beaches, sand dunes, marshes, meadows, wooded hillsides and two lakes – Lake Earl and smaller Lake Tolowa, connected by a narrow waterway.

Over 250 bird species can be seen in the wildlife habitat area, with resident as well as migrating birds. Deer, coyote and raccoons, as well as sea lions, seals and migrating gray whales, are also spotted here. Cutthroat trout can be caught in the lakes. Wildflowers are a special attraction in spring and early summer. The park also has about 20mi of hiking and horseback trails, most of them level and sandy. You can get information from the Crescent City Chamber of Commerce or the Redwood National & State Parks Headquarters, also in Crescent City (see that section, earlier).

There are two primitive **campgrounds** *(campsites $7)*; a walk-in environmental campground, where you must provide your own water; and a walk-in and equestrian campsite, with well water (not drinkable). Both are first-come, first-served. To register for camping in summer, you must go to Jedediah Smith Redwoods State Park, or Del Norte Coast Redwoods State Park's Mill Creek Campground. Campfire wood is provided in summer.

JEDEDIAH SMITH REDWOODS STATE PARK

On Hwy 199, about 10mi northeast of Crescent City and 5mi of Hwy 101, Jedediah Smith Redwoods *(day-use fee per vehicle $2)* is the northernmost of California's redwood state parks. Deemed a World Heritage Site and Biosphere Reserve, it is named after the first non-Native American explorer of Northern California's interior wilderness areas.

A few miles inland, at the confluence of the Smith River and Mill Creek, this park is often sunny in summer, when Crescent City is foggy. There's a fine **swimming hole** and **picnic area** near the entrance. An easy ½mi **nature trail**, departing from the far side of

the campground, crosses the Smith River via a summer-only footbridge and takes you to the park's most famous stand of redwoods, **Stout Grove**. Also inside the campground, the volunteer-staffed **Jedediah Smith State Park Visitor Center** *(☎ 707-464-6101 ext 5113; open 9am-5pm daily late May-Sept)* sells hiking maps, nature guides and coastal driving audio cassette guides.

The popular **campground** *(summer reservations ☎ 800-444-7275; ⓦ www.reserve america.com; campsites $12)* sits in a beautiful redwood grove beside the Smith River, about 5mi east of Hwy 101. There are hot showers and you'll have plenty of company here, as it's always very busy.

More maps and information about the park are available just east of the campground on Hwy 199, at the **Hiouchi Information Center** *(☎ 707-464-6101 ext 5067; open 9am-5pm daily mid-June–mid-Sept)*. Families can ask to borrow free **activity backpacks** stuffed with entertaining projects designed to keep little ones busy during their visit. Information and maps are also available at the Redwood National & State Parks Headquarters in Crescent City.

Hiouchi, on Hwy 199 about a mile east of the park, is another useful stop. **Lunker Fish Trips** *(☎ 707-458-4704, 800-248-4704; 2095 Hwy 199)* rents inner tubes, rafts and inflatable kayaks and mountain bikes in summer. In fall, winter and spring it offers guided wilderness and fishing trips on nearby rivers. Simple accommodations are available at the **Hiouchi Motel** *(☎ 707-458-3041, 866-446-8244; 2097 Hwy 199; singles/doubles $55/60)*, just opposite **Hiouchi Hamlet RV Resort** *(☎ 707-458-3321, 800-722-9468; tent/RV sites $15/20)*.

For information about the Smith River National Scenic Byway into Oregon along Hwy 199, which follows the middle fork of the Smith River through Smith River National Recreation Area, stop by the **Gasquet ranger station** *(☎ 707-457-3131)*, a few miles east of Hiouchi.

Northern Mountains

Rugged, natural beauty – in fact, some of California's most wild and majestic places – are the attraction here. This chapter covers stunning Mt Shasta, Lassen Volcanic National Park and Lava Beds National Monument, not to mention countless pristine mountain lakes, untamed national forests and wilderness areas. Many Californians will never see these places, thinking them too remote. You can find all the services and accommodation you need here, without having to compete with the thousands of other visitors that crowd Lake Tahoe or Yosemite National Park. All that's required to get off that beaten track is a modicum of pioneer spirit.

Wanderlust helps, as direct routes between favored destinations are few. The I-5 freeway is the main north–south route, but this chapter moves all over the map, starting from mountainous Lassen and Plumas Counties, east of the Sacramento Valley, then heading west over to Redding and finally straight up I-5 to Mt Shasta (the town *and* the mountain) and the Oregon border, making a little detour into the northeastern part of California near Nevada. Then there's a jump across to rural Trinity County, hedged between the Coast Mountains and the North Coast (see the previous North Coast chapter).

The geographical area covered here is vast, and public transport options are few. For camping reservations in all wilderness areas managed by the US Forestry Service, call ☎ 877-444-6777 or check out ⓦ www.reserveusa.com.

Lassen & Plumas Counties

Tourism in these two counties (covering the territory east of Redding and Red Bluff all the way to the Nevada border) revolves around Lassen Volcanic National Park and Lake Almanor, in Lassen National Forest. After a short detour up to McArthur-Burney State Falls, this chapter basically follows the 187mi **Lassen Scenic Byway**, which takes about five hours to drive. From Lassen Volcanic National Park, the route heads east past Lake Almanor, Chester, Westwood and

Highlights

- Mt Shasta – 'Lonely as God, white as a winter moon'
- Lassen Volcanic National Park – a living lesson in volatile, boiling landscapes
- Rambling scenic byways – unspoiled mountain lakes, verdant forests, historic villages and natural hot springs
- Lava Beds National Monument – lava tube spelunking, ancient petroglyphs and the eerie labyrinth of Captain Jack's Stronghold
- Spring and fall migrations – birds filling the air at the Klamath Basin National Wildlife Refuges

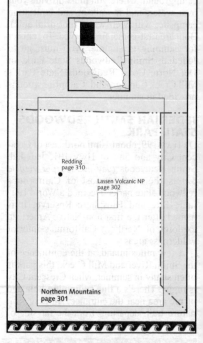

Redding
page 310

Lassen Volcanic NP
page 302

Northern Mountains
page 301

Susanville, then turns south and passes through Hallelujah Junction (only 25mi from Reno), circling back through Quincy to Lake Almanor again. If you're approaching from the south via Lake Tahoe or Truckee, you'll join the loop at Portola, near Plumas-Eureka

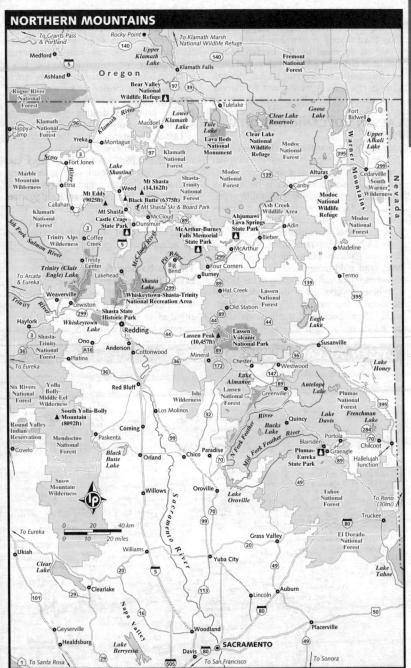

State Park. If you're not feeling quite so ambitious, Lake Almanor has a smaller scenic loop drive around its own shoreline.

A bus, operated by **Mt Lassen Motor Transit** (*☎ 530-529-2722*) between Red Bluff and Susanville, stops on the way at Mineral, Chester (for Lake Almanor) and Westwood. It operates from Monday to Saturday.

LASSEN VOLCANIC NATIONAL PARK

This 106,000-acre national park (**W** *www.nps .gov/lavo; 7-day entry vehicles/hikers/cyclists $10/5/5*) is a living lesson in volcanic landscapes. The park also contains boiling hot springs and mud pots, steaming sulfur vents, fumaroles, lava flows, cinder cones, craters and crater lakes. In earlier times, the region was a summer encampment and meeting point for Native American tribes, who hunted deer and gathered plants for basket-making here, until gold miners and pioneers established emigrant trails beginning in the 1850s.

Wherever you enter the park, you'll be given a free map with general information. More specialized publications about the park's history and natural features and topographic maps are available at the **Manzanita Lake Visitor Center & Loomis Museum** (*☎ 530-595-4444, ext 5180; open 9am-5pm daily mid-June–mid-Oct*), just past the entrance fee station inside the park's northern boundary. There are exhibits and an orientation video inside the museum; during summer, rangers and volunteers lead interpretive programs dealing with geology, wildlife, astronomy and cultural topics.

Lassen Chalet (*open 9am-6pm daily June-Sept, off-season hours vary*), about a mile north of the park's southern entrance station, houses the Southwest Information Station and also has a snack bar, bookstore and gift shop. Otherwise, **park headquarters** (*☎ 530-595-4444; 38050 Hwy 36; open 8am-4:30pm Mon-Fri*) is about a mile west of the tiny town of Mineral, the nearest stop for refueling and supplies.

Things to See & Do

Lassen Peak, the world's largest plug-dome volcano, rises 2000ft over the surrounding landscape to 10,457ft above sea level. Classified as an active volcano, its most recent eruption took place in 1915, when it blew a

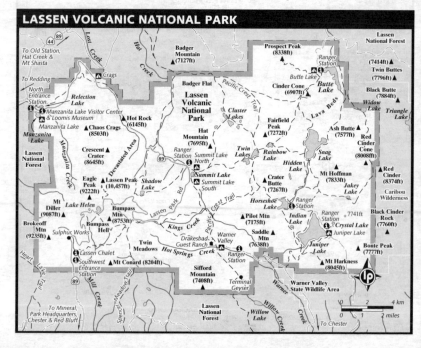

LASSEN VOLCANIC NATIONAL PARK

giant cloud of smoke, steam and ash 7mi into the atmosphere. The national park was created the following year to protect the newly formed landscape. Some areas destroyed by the blast, including the aptly named **Devastated Area**, northeast of the peak, are recovering impressively.

Hwy 89, the road through the park, wraps around Lassen Peak on three sides and provides access to the geothermal areas, lakes, picnic areas and hiking trails. It's only possible to drive through the park in summer, usually around June to October. There have even been times when the road has been closed by snow (as much as 40ft of it) well into July.

In total, the park has 150mi of **hiking trails**, including a 17mi section of the Pacific Crest Trail. Experienced hikers can attack the Lassen Peak Trail, if you have at least 4½ hours to make the 5mi return trip, and early in the season you'll need snow and ice climbing equipment to reach the summit. Near Lassen Chalet, a gentler 2¼mi trail leads through meadows and forest to reach Mill Creek Falls. Further north on Hwy 89, the roadside **Sulfur Works** have bubbling mud pots, a hissing steam vent, fountains and fumaroles. At **Bumpass Hell**, a moderate 1½mi trail and boardwalk leads to an active geothermal area, with weirdly colored pools and billowing clouds of steam. You can go fishing and boating on **Manzanita Lake**.

Places to Stay
The park has eight **developed campgrounds** *(sites $10-14)*, with many more in the surrounding Lassen National Forest. Campgrounds in the park are open from around late May to late October, depending on snow conditions. Manzanita Lake is the only one with hot showers, but both Summit Lake campgrounds, about midway through the park, are also popular. All sites are first-come, first-served.

Drakesbad Guest Ranch *(☎ 530-520-1512, ext 120;* **w** *www.drakesbad.com; Warner Valley Rd; lodge, cabin & bungalow rooms $115-160; open June-early Oct)*, 17mi northwest of Chester, is a wonderfully secluded place inside the park's southern boundary. Guests, many of whom are faithful repeat visitors, use the hot-springs-fed swimming pool or go horseback riding. There's no electricity here (think kerosene lamps and

campfires). Rates include country-style meals (vegetarian cuisine available) and campfire barbecues every Wednesday; ask about weekly discounts.

There are various lodges, cabins and small resorts outside the park, especially between Hat Creek and Old Station, north along Hwy 89. A full list is published in the park's free newspaper, *Peak Experiences*.

Childs Meadow Resort *(☎ 530-595-3383, 888-595-3383;* **w** *www.childsmeadowresort .com; 41500 Hwy 36E, Mill Creek)*, 9mi outside the southwest entrance to the park, is one of many such old-fashioned, rustic places.

Mt Lassen KOA *(☎ 530-474-3133, 800-562-3403; 7749 KOA Road, off Hwy 44; tent sites from $20/25, cabins $40-65)*, in Shingletown almost 20mi west of the park, has a swimming pool, children's playground, deli and laundry facilities.

Red Bluff, Redding and towns around Lake Almanor make reasonable bases for visits to the park.

Getting There & Away
The park has two entrances. The north entrance, at Manzanita Lake, is 45mi east of Redding via Hwy 44. The south entrance is reached via a 5mi access road that turns off from Hwy 89, about 5mi west of Mineral. From the turnoff, it's 48mi west to Red Bluff, 25mi east to Chester, 60mi east to Susanville and 65mi southeast to Quincy.

Mt Lassen Transit *(☎ 530-529-2722)* buses between Red Bluff and Susanville run by Mineral, which is the stop closest to the park. There's no public transport within the park or on the 5mi between Hwy 36 and the park entrance.

LASSEN NATIONAL FOREST
This vast forest (**w** www.r5.fs.fed.us/lassen) surrounds Lassen Volcanic National Park and covers 1.2 million acres (1875 sq mi) of wilderness in an area called 'The Crossroads,' where the granite Sierras, the volcanic Cascades, the Modoc Plateau and the Central Valley meet.

The forest contains 460mi of **hiking trails**, including 120mi of the Pacific Crest Trail, the 12mi Spencer Meadows National Recreation Trail and the 3½mi Heart Lake National Recreation Trail. Special points of interest include a 600yd walk through the **Subway Cave** lava tube; the 1½mi volcanic **Spattercone**

Crest Trail; **Willow Lake** and **Crater Lake**; 7684ft **Antelope Peak**; and the 900ft-high, 14mi-long **Hat Creek Rim** escarpment.

The forest also contains three wilderness areas. The Caribou Wilderness and Thousand Lakes Wilderness are best visited from mid-June to mid-October; the Ishi Wilderness, at a much lower elevation in the Central Valley foothills east of Red Bluff, is more comfortable in spring and fall, as summer temperatures often climb to over 100°F (37°C).

The **Lassen National Forest Supervisor's Office** is in Susanville (see Susanville later in this chapter). Other district ranger offices include **Eagle Lake Ranger District** (☎ 530-257-4188), **Hat Creek Ranger District** (☎ 530-336-5521; *Fall River Mills*), and **Almanor Ranger District** (☎ 530-258-2141; *Hwy 36*), about a mile west of Chester.

McARTHUR-BURNEY FALLS

Six miles northwest of Four Corners, the crossroads where Hwy 89 from Lassen Volcanic National Park intersects Hwy 299 from Redding, is **McArthur-Burney Falls Memorial State Park** (☎ 530-335-2777; **w** *www.burneyfalls.com; day-use fee per vehicle $2*). Fed by a spring, the 129ft falls run with the same amount of water and at the same temperature, 42°F (5°C), year-round. Clear, lava-filtered water comes surging not only over the top, but also from springs in the rocks right across the 129ft waterfall's face, adding up to some 100 million gallons flowing over the falls each day.

There's a lookout point beside the parking lot, with trails going up and down the creek from the falls. A nature trail heading downstream brings you to Lake Britton. Other hiking trails include a portion of the Pacific Crest Trail. The park's **campgrounds** (*summer reservations* ☎ 800-444-7275; **w** *www.reserveamerica.com; drive-in sites $12*) have hot showers and are open year-round, even when there's snow on the ground.

About 10mi northeast of McArthur-Burney Falls, the 6000-acre **Ahjumawi Lava Springs State Park** is known for its abundant springs, aquamarine bays and islets, and for jagged flows of black basalt lava. It can only be reached by boats that are launched at Rat Farm, 3mi north of the town of McArthur along a graded dirt road. Arrangements for **primitive camping** can be made by calling McArthur-Burney Memorial State Park.

PLUMAS NATIONAL FOREST

Enclosing 1.2 million acres in the northern Sierra Nevada, this forest (**w** *www.r5.fs.fed.us/plumas*) extends roughly from Lake Oroville in the southwest, to Lake Almanor in the northwest, to Lake Honey in the northeast, and to Frenchman and Davis Lakes in the southeast. The mountains are covered with evergreen forest, mostly ponderosa and sugar pine, and Douglas, red and white fir. The forest contains more than 100 lakes and some 1000mi of rivers and streams, including the **Feather River Canyon**, through which you can travel for miles on Hwy 70. The forest also has more than 300mi of **hiking trails** and over 50 **campgrounds**.

The **Plumas National Forest Supervisor's Office** is in Quincy (see that section later), sharing space with the **Mt Hough Ranger District Office**. You can also pick up maps and information at the **Beckworth Ranger District Office**, west of Blairsden (see Around Portola later in this chapter), or **Feather River Canyon Ranger Station** in Oroville (see the Sacramento Valley chapter).

LAKE ALMANOR AREA

Lake Almanor, south of Lassen Volcanic National Park on Hwys 89 and 36, is ideal for relaxing in nature year-round. It takes about an hour to drive around the lake's 52mi shoreline. **Chester** (population 2200) is the main town near the lake.

The **Chester-Lake Almanor Chamber of Commerce** (☎ 530-258-2426, 800-350-4838; **w** *www.chester-lakealmanor.com; 529 Main St; open 9am-4pm Mon-Fri*) and **Lassen National Forest Almanor Ranger Station** (☎ 530-258-2141; *Hwy 36; open 8am-4:30pm Mon-Fri*), about a mile west of town, have information about every type of lodging and recreation in, on and around the lake, in the surrounding Lassen National Forest and in nearby Lassen Volcanic National Park.

Boats and water sports equipment can be rented at many places around the lake. **Bodfish Bicycles & Quiet Mountain Sports** (☎ 530-258-2338; *152 Main St, Chester*) rents bicycles, cross-country skis and snowshoes and sells canoes and kayaks. It's a great source of mountain-biking and bicycle touring advice. **Sports Nut** (☎ 530-258-3327; *108 Main St*) also deals in outdoor gear.

Places to Stay & Eat
Around the Lake There's plenty of camping about, including at **federal campgrounds** (*reservations* ☎ *877-444-6777;* **w** *www.reserveusa.com*) in the surrounding Lassen and Plumas National Forests, both of which have sites on the lake's southwest shore.

North Shore Campground (☎ *530-258-3376;* **w** *www.northshorecampground.com; tent/RV sites $21/24*), 2mi east of Chester on Hwy 36, is right by the water.

Knotty Pine Resort & Marina (☎ *530-596-3348, fax 530-596-4404;* **w** *www.knottypine .net; 430 Peninsula Dr; weekly RV sites $150, 2-bedroom cabins with kitchen $120/720 per day/week*) and **Little Norway Resort** (☎ *530-596-3225; 432 Peninsula Dr; cabins from $70/420 daily/weekly*), at Big Cove on County Rd A-13, are 7mi east of Chester. Both places rent boats, kayaks and canoes.

Plumas Properties (☎ *530-596-3203;* **w** *www.almanor.com; 425 Peninsula Dr; rates from $560/week*) offers lakeside vacation rentals.

St Bernard Lodge (☎ *530-258-3382;* **w** *www.stbernardlodge.com; doubles $50*), 10mi west of Chester at Mill Creek, has old-world ambience, and B&B rooms with shared bathrooms (one has a clawfoot tub).

Chester This place has its fair share of budget motels, lodges and B&Bs.

Seneca Motel (☎ *530-258-2815; 545 Martin Way; rooms from $45*) is quieter than other places right on the highway. It has a corrugated iron roof, picnic and barbecue areas, and a communal kitchen.

Timber House Lodge (☎ *530-258-2729; 501 Main St at First St; motel rooms from $55*) has a family-style restaurant, known for its steak, prime rib and seafood, and a bar.

Bidwell House B&B (☎ *530-258-3338; 1 Main St;* **w** *www.bidwellhouse.com; rooms $80-155, cottage $170*) has cheery antique-furnished rooms inside the relocated summer home built by John and Annie Bidwell.

Cinnamon Teal Inn (☎ *530-258-3993; 227 Feather River Dr; B&B rooms $65-85, suite $95*) is a shady house, set a half-block back from Main St.

Knotbumper Restaurant (☎ *530-258-2301; 274 Main St; meals $6-8; open 11am-8pm Mon-Sat*) is a cozy café with a generous deli menu, including tamale pies, shrimp salad sandwiches and other zany items.

Cynthia's Homemade Bakery & Café (☎ *530-258-1966; 278 Main St; lunch $5-10, dinner $10-17; open 11:30am-2pm Tues-Sat, dinner from 5:30pm Fri & Sat*) is above Northwoods Gallery, serving artisan (handmade) breads, gourmet pizzas and boxed lunches.

Benassi's Restaurant (☎ *530-258-2600; 159 Main St; lunch $5-8.50, dinner $10-15; open 11am-2pm & 4:30pm-9pm daily*) serves northern Italian cuisine.

WESTWOOD
A few miles east of Chester, this tiny speck of a town marks the start of the **Bizz Johnson Trail**, which runs for 25½mi between Westwood and Susanville. Once part of the old Southern Pacific right-of-way, it can now be traveled by foot, mountain bike, horseback or cross-country skis (no motorized vehicles are permitted).

It's easiest to do the trail in the Westwood-to-Susanville direction, as it's mostly downhill that way; the 18mi segment between Susanville and Westwood Junction averages a 3% gradient, except at steep Devil's Corral, which runs underneath Hwy 36. Trail guides are available at the chamber of commerce in Chester, the Susanville Railroad Depot and at the trail terminus.

Buffalo Chip's Pizza (☎ *530-256-2412; 322 Birch St; sandwiches $6, pizzas $10-20; open daily until late*) has been baking brick-oven pizzas for over two decades.

SUSANVILLE
On a high desert plateau, Susanville (population 17,150) feels remote from the rest of the world. At the junction of Hwy 36 and Hwy 139 (4mi off US-395 to Alturas), it's just 35mi east of Chester and Lake Almanor, and 85mi northwest of Reno. Although primarily a gathering place for the surrounding cattle and timber districts, the town experienced a jump in economic activity (and population) in 1992, when an expansion of the state prison began here. It is also the Lassen County seat.

Susanville is not a tourist destination, but it offers basic services if you happen to be traveling through this part of California en route to Nevada. The **Lassen National Forest Supervisor's Office** (☎ *530-257-2151; 55 S Sacramento St at Main St; open 8am-4:30pm*

NORTHERN MOUNTAINS

Mon-Fri) has maps and outdoors recreation information. The **Lassen County Chamber of Commerce** (☎ *530-257-4323;* **w** *www.lassen countychamber.org; 84 N Lassen St; open 9am-5pm Mon-Fri)* also helps visitors with tourist information.

Historic **Susanville Depot**, south of Main St off Weatherlow St, operates a **visitor center** (☎ *530-257-3252; 601 Richmond Rd; open 9am-5pm daily May-Oct)* and rents bicycles at reasonable rates. It sits beside the terminus of the Bizz Johnson Trail (see Westwood earlier); staff have brochures on other **mountain biking trails** in the area.

The town's oldest building is named after Susanville's founder, Isaac Roop. **Roop's Fort** was a trading post on the Nobles Trail, a California emigrant route, in 1853. Beside the fort is the tame **Lassen Historical Museum** (☎ *530-257-3292; 75 N Weatherlow St; donation requested; open 10am-4pm Mon-Fri May-Oct)*.

Places to Stay & Eat
Mountain View RV Park (☎ *530-251-4757; 3075 Johnstonville Rd; tent/RV sites $17/26)* is on the east side of town. It's newer than the competition.

Motels along Main St, none of them exceptional, average $40 to $60 per night. Try **River Inn Motel** (☎ *530-257-6051; 1710 Main St)*, the **Susanville Inn** (☎ *530-257-4522; 2705 Main St)* or **Super 8 Motel** (☎ *530-257-2782, 800-800-8000; 2975 Johnstonville Rd)*.

Roseberry House B&B (☎ *530-257-5675, fax 530-257-8739;* **w** *www.roseberryhouse.com; 609 N St; room/suite $80/100)*, two blocks north of Main St, is a sweet 1902 Victorian house where children are welcome.

Pioneer Café (☎ *530-257-2311; 724 Main St)*, a combination bar, billiards room and inexpensive café, has a plaque outside testifying that a saloon has been operating on this site since 1862, and that this is the oldest established business in northeastern California.

Other historic, moderately priced cafés on Main St include the **Grand Café** (☎ *530-257-4713; 730 Main St; open 7am-2pm Mon-Sat)*, established in 1909, and the **Champion Steakhouse** (☎ *530-257-4820; 830 Main St at South Union St; open 5:30pm-8:30pm Mon-Wed, 5:30pm-9:30pm Thur-Sat)*, at the Old St Francis Hotel.

AROUND SUSANVILLE
Eagle Lake
About 15mi northwest of Susanville, this is one of California's largest natural lakes. It attracts visitors from late spring until fall, who come to swim, fish, boat and camp.

On the south shore, you'll find a 5mi **recreational trail** and several **campgrounds** *(sites $14-28; all sites open May-Oct, some year-round)* administered by **Lassen National Forest** *(camping reservations* ☎ *877-444-6777;* **w** *www.reserveusa.com)* and the **Bureau of Land Management** *(BLM;* ☎ *530-257-5381)*. Nearby **Eagle Lake Marina** (☎ *530-825-3454)* offers hot showers, laundry and boat rentals.

Eagle Lake RV Park (☎ *530-825-3133; 687-125 Palmetto Way; RV sites/cabins $25/75)* and **Mariners Resort** (☎ *530-825-3333; Stones Landing; RV sites $28-30, hillside cabins $85-95, lakeside cabins $115-125)*, on the quieter shore, both rent boats.

PORTOLA
Straddling the Middle Fork of the Feather River, Portola's pride and joy is the **Portola Railroad Museum** (☎ *530-832-4131; 700 Western Pacific Hwy; admission $2; open 10am-5pm daily May-Sept, grounds open 10am-7pm Apr-Nov)*, with 39 locomotives and almost 100 freight and passenger cars and cabooses. The **Feather River Rail Society** (☎ *530-832-4532)* offers train rides on summer weekends, or you can drive a locomotive with the help of one of the instructors. Adult/family all-day ride passes cost $2/5 and lessons are $95 to $125 per hour.

On the eastern outskirts of town sits the **Eastern Plumas County Chamber of Commerce** (☎ *530-832-5444, 800-995-6057;* **w** *www.easternplumaschamber.com; 424 Sierra Ave; open 10am-4pm Mon-Fri summer, 10am-2pm rest of year)* and its tiny **historical museum**.

Budget motels line Hwy 70, called Sierra Ave through town. Decent options include the **Sierra Motel** (☎ *530-832-4223; 380 E Sierra Ave; rooms $50-65)* and **Sleepy Pines Motel** (☎ *530-832-4291; 74631 Hwy 70; rooms $55-75, with kitchen extra $10, cabins $110)*, west of town.

Pullman House B&B Inn (☎ *530-832-0107, 800-996-0107; 256 Commercial St; rooms $70-85)*, a fetching 1910 boarding house, is right downtown.

Nicole's Café (☎ 530-832-5659; 239 Commercial St; meals $5-10; open 7am-3pm Mon-Fri) is a friendly little eatery, next to the Ponderosa Bowl. Expect ample portions of good country food, like 'mountain-high' sandwiches and Belgian waffles.

Log Cabin (☎ 530-832-5243; 64 E Sierra Ave; mains $12-18; open 5pm-9:30pm Wed-Mon) is a local landmark specializing in hearty German food. Its bar is made of Tamarack wood, brought from the Grand Tetons by rail in the 1940s.

AROUND PORTOLA

About 7mi north of Portola, inside Plumas National Forest, **Lake Davis** is good for camping, mountain biking, snowmobiling and fishing year-round. **Frenchman Lake** is also popular, but it's further away. Go southeast toward Reno on Hwy 70 for 20mi to the turnoff at Chilcoot, then 8½mi north on Hwy 284 to the lake.

Blairsden & Graeagle

A 20-minute drive west of Portola, the one-street village of **Blairsden** is off Hwy 89, just south of Hwy 70. Less than 2mi further south, **Graeagle** is famous for its four championship-caliber golf courses. Consider staying here rather than in Portola, as not only does this bring you closer to year-round outdoors recreational possibilities, but also because the environs are so soothing.

River Pines Resort (☎ 530-836-2552, 800-696-2551; W www.riverpines.com; 8296 Hwy 89; motel singles/doubles from $70/75, with kitchen add $10-20, 1 & 2-bedroom suites $150-270, housekeeping cottages $90-115), a half-mile north of Graeagle toward Blairsden, is within walking distance of the Feather River. Winter and weekly discounts are available. Guests have access to a swimming pool, hot tub and the popular **Coyote Bar & Grill** (☎ 530-836-2002; open 5pm-9pm Tues-Sun, closed Jan & Feb).

There are many options for vacation rentals in and around Graeagle. All the golf courses offer lodging.

Plumas Pines Realty (☎ 530-836-0444, 800-655-4440, fax 530-836-1627; W www.graeagle.com; 307 Poplar Valley Rd) manages vacation home rentals, with lower rates for longer stays. Ask about special golf packages.

Grizzly Grill (☎ 530-836-1300; 330 Bonta St, Blairsden; early-bird dinners $12-15, mains $12-20, kids menu under $10; open from 5:30pm daily; closed Mon & Tues winter) boggles the mind with its diverse, flavorful menu, from deep-fried rock shrimp with honey-mustard vinaigrette to pepper steak in cognac sauce. With all the smoky warmth of a mountain lodge, this restaurant is worth the drive from Portola or even Quincy. Make reservations in advance, or come early for cocktails around the antique bar.

Plumas-Eureka State Park

Within Plumas-Eureka State Park, some 30mi southeast of Quincy, is **Johnsville**, an Old West mining town still inhabited today. Gold was discovered here in March 1851, and mining continued until WWII. **Eureka Peak** (elevation 7450ft), originally named Gold Mountain, is still the site of an estimated 62mi of mining shafts and air vents. You can also see the mining camp where more than $8 million worth of gold was processed. An old stamp mill, restored miner's home and other historical features have been preserved.

Near the park entrance, 5mi west of Hwy 89 from Graeagle via County Rd A-14, the **visitor center** (☎ 530-836-2380) doubles as a mining history **museum** (admission $1). In summer, hiking and fishing are popular and rangers lead history tours, nature walks and other interpretive programs. **Graeagle Stable** (☎ 530-836-0430) offers guided trail rides ($26-45) and pony rides ($8).

In winter, there's cross-country and downhill **skiing** in the park. The nonprofit **Ski Gold Mountain** (☎ 530-836-2317, 800-446-5368; W www.skigoldmountain.org) runs lifts on the old-fashioned ski bowl, with a 675ft vertical drop. Full-day lift tickets cost $24. Its off-beat atmosphere is relaxing, good for beginner and intermediate skiers. Opening months depend on snow conditions. Cross-country skis can be rented at **Blairsden Mercantile** (☎ 530-836-2589; 282 Bonta St) in Blairsden.

Upper Jamison Creek Campground (drive-in sites $12; usually open May–mid-Oct), set back deep inside the park, has hot showers and a dozen walk-in sites; everything is first-come, first-served. The **Beckworth Ranger District Office** (☎ 530-836-2575; 23 Mohawk Hwy Rd), off Hwy 70 west of Blairsden, has details on other camping nearby in Plumas National Forest.

Lakes Basin Recreation Area

Containing dozens of pristine lakes, many accessible only by hiking and horse trails, this unspoiled region is reached by Gold Lake Rd (Hwy 24), which runs north–south from Hwy 89, south of Graeagle, to Hwy 49, north of Sierra City. Gold Lake Rd is not snowplowed in winter, making it popular for cross-country skiing and snowmobiling.

The Pacific Crest Trail and many other **hiking trails** traverse the area. The Round Lake Loop, a 3.5mi (three-hour) trail, starts from the parking lot of Gold Lake Lodge. The lodge is just north of the region's largest lake, **Gold Lake**, which has a boat landing. **Gold Lake Stables** (☎ 530-836-0940) offers trail rides ($27-98) and overnight pack trips.

Both Tahoe and Plumas National Forests have organized **campgrounds** in the area (Tahoe, ☎ 530-288-3231; Plumas, ☎ 530-836-2575), or you can backpack and camp freely anywhere. Rustic accommodations and dining are available at several old-fashioned lakeside lodges; click to **w** www.lakes basin.com, or pester the Plumas County Visitors Bureau in Quincy for recommendations. Some of the lodges are booked up a year in advance, so you must reserve early.

QUINCY

Quincy (population 5000) is nestled in a valley in the northern High Sierra, southeast of both Lassen Volcanic National Park and Lake Almanor via Hwy 89. Quincy is also the Plumas County seat. If you're driving up from the Sacramento Valley on Hwy 70, which joins with Hwy 89 as it goes through the town, you'll pass through the magnificent Feather River Canyon along the way.

Once in town, Hwy 70/89 splits into two one-way streets, with traffic on Main St heading east, and traffic on Lawrence St heading west. Jackson St, running parallel to (and one block south of) Main St, is another main artery. Most everything you need is on, near, or between these three streets, making up Quincy's low-key commercial district.

The **Plumas County Visitors Bureau** (☎ 530-283-6345, 800-326-2247; **w** www .plumas.ca.us; 550 Crescent St; open 8am-5pm Mon-Fri, also 8am-6pm Sat summer) is half a mile west of town. For maps and outdoors recreational information, visit the **Plumas National Forest Headquarters** (☎ 530-283-2050; 159 Lawrence St; open 8am-4:30pm Mon-Fri) or the **Mt Hough Ranger District Office** (☎ 530-283-0555; 39696 Hwy 70; open 8am-4:30pm Mon-Fri), 5mi further west.

Things to See & Do

The large 1921 **Plumas County Courthouse** at the west end of Main St has huge interior marble posts and staircases and a 2000lb bronze-and-glass chandelier in the lobby.

In the block behind the courthouse, the **Plumas County Museum** (☎ 530-283-6320; 500 Jackson St at Coburn St; admission $1; open 8am-5pm Mon-Fri; also 10am-4pm Sat, Sun & holidays May-Sept) has flowering gardens and exhibits of hundreds of historical photos and relics from the county's pioneer and Maidu Indian days, its early mining and timber industries and construction of the Western Pacific Railroad.

Ask at the visitors bureau for free walking and driving tour pamphlets, if you're keen on seeing more historical buildings or the surrounding **American Valley**. In summer, the icy waters of the county namesake, the **Feather River** (*plumas* is Spanish for feathers), are popular for swimming, kayaking, fishing and floating about in old inner tubes. There are also a lot of winter activities in the area, especially at Bucks Lake (see Around Quincy later in this chapter). Cross-country ski gear and snowshoes can be rented at **Sierra Mountain Sports** (☎ 530-283-2323; 501 W Main St), across from the courthouse.

Places to Stay & Eat

There's plenty of **camping** near Quincy in the Plumas National Forest and at Bucks Lake.

Pine Hill Motel (☎ 530-283-1670, 866-342-2891; 42075 Hwy 70; single/double duplex rooms & cabins $60/65, with kitchen $65/70), a mile west of Quincy, is a rustic, relaxing place.

Ranchito (☎ 530-283-2265; 2020 E Main St; singles/doubles $55/60), on woodsy 3-acre grounds by a brook, is also at the west end of town. Kitchen units are extra.

Other basic **motels** line Hwy 70 at the west end of town, where the highway is also called Crescent St. **Gold Pan Motel** (☎ 530-283-3686, 800-804-6541; 200 Crescent St) and the **Lariat Lodge** (☎ 530-283-1000,

800-999-7199; 2370 E Main St) have rooms in the $40 to $60 range.

The Feather Bed (☎ 530-283-0102, 800-696-8624; 542 Jackson St at Court St; B&B rooms & cottages $90-150) is an 1893 Queen Anne home furnished with antiques just behind the courthouse. Hosts make afternoon tea with cookies and guests can borrow bicycles.

Feather River Lodging (☎ 530-283-1234, fax 530-283-5769; W www.featherriver lodging.com; 300 Golden Eagle Ave; 1-/2-bedroom dorm units $40/50, deluxe units with kitchen $65/80; open June-Aug), 2mi west of town, offers college student housing as summer vacation rentals and is not bad value. Weekly discounts are available.

Greenhorn Guest Ranch (☎ 530-283-0930, 800-334-6939, fax 530-283-4401; W www.greenhornranch.com; 2116 Greenhorn Ranch Rd; adult/junior/child all-inclusive daily lodging $204/131/72) leads horse rides through Plumas National Forest. Daily scheduled activities include square dancing, evening bonfires, cookouts and even frog races. All lodge rooms and cabins are heated. Weekly discounts are available.

Quincy Natural Foods (☎ 530-283-3528; 30 Harbison St) is a market just off Main St.

Courthouse Café (☎ 530-283-3344; 525 Main St; meals under $10; open 7am-2pm daily) serves delicious sandwiches on fresh-baked bread.

Morning Thunder Café (☎ 530-283-1310; 557 Lawrence St; meals $5-8; open 6am-2pm daily) is good for country breakfasts and lunches. It boasts an espresso bar, vegetarian menu and live entertainment on occasion.

Moon's (☎ 530-283-0765; 497 Lawrence St; mains $9-20; open for dinner Tues-Sun), a welcoming little chalet with tempting aromas and charming ambience, fires up choice steaks and refreshing Italian-American fare.

Ten-Two Dinner House (☎ 530-283-1366; 8270 Bucks Lake Rd; open from 5pm Thur-Mon) is a small, moderately priced place in Meadow Valley on the road to Bucks Lake, about an 8mi drive from Quincy. In summer you can sit outside by the creek. It serves superb food with all-natural ingredients and has a changing menu with great specials. Reservations are recommended. Winter hours vary.

AROUND QUINCY
Bucks Lake

About 17mi southwest of Quincy, via Bucks Lake Rd (Hwy 119), this clear mountain lake surrounded by pine forests is popular for fishing and boating. There are good **hiking trails**, including the Pacific Crest Trail passing through the adjoining 21,000-acre Bucks Lake Wilderness in the northwestern part of Plumas National Forest. **Bucks Lake Stables** (☎ 530-283-1147) offers trail rides ($25-60) and overnight pack trips. In winter, the last 3mi of Bucks Lake Rd are closed by snow, making it ideal for cross-country skiers and snowmobiles.

Most campgrounds and services are open from around June to September. Ask at the Plumas National Forest Headquarters or ranger station in Quincy for details on **public campgrounds** with basic facilities.

Bucks Lake Marina (☎ 530-283-4243; 16469 Bucks Lake Rd) offers boat and kayak rentals, camping and cabins.

Bucks Lakeshore Resort (☎ 530-283-6900; W www.buckslake.com; 1100 Bucks Lake Rd, Meadow Valley; cabins $60-115) is a full-service lakeshore lodge with a restaurant, bar and country store. In summer it operates a campground, cabins and boating marina; in winter, it's a cross-country skiing resort. Ask about special packages.

Bucks Lake Lodge (☎ 530-283-2262, 800-481-2825; 16525 Bucks Lake Rd; motel rooms/cabins from $75/85; open year-round) has boat rentals and fishing tackle in summer and cross-country skiing in winter. The restaurant at the lodge is known for good food; locals often drive out from Quincy for dinner.

Haskins Valley Inn (☎ 530-283-9667; e nelsons@inreach.com; B&B $115-135) offers antique-furnished rooms, some with Jacuzzi, fireplace and deck.

Interstate-5 to Oregon

The mammoth I-5 freeway zips through this region, winding from Redding in the south up north past Mt Shasta and Yreka and into Oregon. **Greyhound** (☎ 800-231-2222; W www.greyhound.com) and regional bus services connect most of the main towns.

Odds are that somewhere along the line, you'll encounter **Shasta-Trinity National Forest**, which covers 2.1 million acres, in several separate patches from Six Rivers National Forest in the west all the way to Modoc National Forest in the east. It covers many of Northern California's prime recreational attractions, including a posse of mountain lakes near Redding. A 154mi section of the Pacific Crest Trail passes through the forest, as does the 9mi Sisson-Callahan National Recreation Trail. Castle Crags Wilderness, Mt Shasta Wilderness, Trinity Alps Wilderness, Chanchelulla Wilderness and part of Yolla Bolly-Middle Eel Wilderness all fall within its boundaries.

REDDING

At the north end of the Sacramento Valley, shadowed by mountain ranges on three sides, peaceful Redding (population 80,900) makes an easy base for day trips to Lassen Volcanic National Park, Shasta State Historic Park, Weaverville, nearby lakes and other mountain wilderness destinations.

The area was originally called Poverty Flat by miners, because there wasn't much here. When the railroad came north, Poverty Flat was chosen for the railroad terminus, and a new town was laid out there around 1872. It was named after Benjamin B Redding, who was a land agent for the railroad. For nearly a decade, Redding remained the railroad terminus, while track construction labored over the difficult push northward into the Sacramento Canyon. When politicians later tried to change the town's name to Reading, in honor of Major BP Reading, upon whose land the town had been built, railroad officials stubbornly refused to recognize the change. So Redding it remains.

Downtown is bordered by the Sacramento River on the north and east, with the major thoroughfares being Pine St and Market St. The **Redding Convention & Visitors Bureau** (☎ 530-225-4100, 800-874-7562; W www.visitredding.org; 777 Auditorium Dr; open 8am-6pm Mon-Fri, 10am-5pm Sat) is near Turtle Bay. The **Shasta-Trinity National Forest Headquarters** (☎ 530-244-2978; 2400 Washington St; open 7:30am-4:30pm Mon-Fri, until 5pm summer), off Park Marina Dr, has maps and free camping permits for all seven national forests in Northern California.

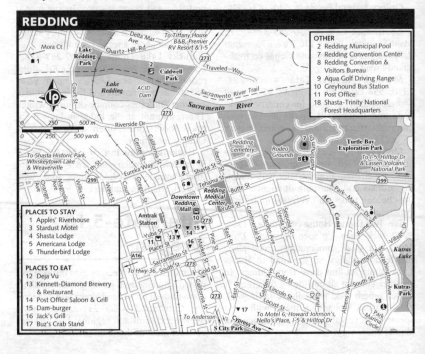

REDDING

OTHER
2 Redding Municipal Pool
7 Redding Convention Center
8 Redding Convention & Visitors Bureau
9 Aqua Golf Driving Range
10 Greyhound Bus Station
11 Post Office
18 Shasta-Trinity National Forest Headquarters

PLACES TO STAY
1 Apples' Riverhouse
3 Stardust Motel
4 Shasta Lodge
5 Americana Lodge
6 Thunderbird Lodge

PLACES TO EAT
12 Deja Vu
13 Kennett-Diamond Brewery & Restaurant
14 Post Office Saloon & Grill
15 Dam-burger
16 Jack's Grill
17 Buz's Crab Stand

In Anderson, about 10mi south of Redding, the **Shasta Cascade California Welcome Center** (☎ 530-365-1180, 800-474-2782; W www.shastacascade.org; 1699 Hwy 273; open 9am-6pm Mon-Sat, 10am-6pm Sun) is at the south end of the Prime Outlets Mall.

Ambitious 300-acre **Turtle Bay Exploration Park** (☎ 530-243-8850, 800-887-8532; W www.turtlebay.org; 800 Auditorium Dr; adult/child $11/6; open 9am-6pm daily summer, 9am-5pm Tues-Sun Oct-May) is intended to be an artistic, cultural and scientific center for visitors of all ages, with an emphasis on the Sacramento River watershed. The complex houses art and natural sciences museums, interactive exhibits for kids focusing on forest ecology, extensive arboretum gardens, a butterfly house and 22,000-gallon, walk-through river aquarium. Eventually it will be connected to the north bank of the river by the spectacular Sundial Bridge, designed by renowned Spanish architect Santiago Calatrava.

Further west in Caldwell Park are the new **Redding Aquatic Center** and the 8mi **Sacramento River Trail**, a paved walking and cycling path.

In summer people go rafting and canoeing on the river. You can even hit golf balls into the river if you swing by **Aqua Golf Driving Range** (☎ 530-244-4653; 2275 Park Marina Dr). **Redding Sports Ltd** (☎ 530-221-7333; 950 Hilltop Dr, off I-5) sells outdoors recreation equipment for every season.

Places to Stay

There are plenty of **RV parks** on the outskirts of town. For more **tent camping** visit Whiskeytown Lake or Shasta Lake (see those sections later).

Premier RV Resort (☎ 530-246-0101, 888-710-8450; 280 N Boulder Dr; tent/RV sites $20/26, 4-person yurts $35), north of downtown off Hwy 273, offers weekly discounts.

Motels downtown include the **Thunderbird Lodge** (☎ 530-243-5422; 1350 Pine St), **Stardust Motel** (☎ 530-241-6121; 1200 Pine St), **Shasta Lodge** (☎ 530-243-6133; 1245 Pine St) and **Americana Lodge** (☎ 530-241-7020; 1250 Pine St). All have cool vintage neon signs and charge $35 to $55 per night.

A couple of 'motel rows' are near I-5 at the south end of town. On Bechelli Lane, just west of the freeway near the Cypress Ave exit, are **Motel 6** (☎ 530-221-0562, 800-466-8356; 2385 Bechelli Lane; rooms $40-55), with quiet rooms facing away from the highway, and **Howard Johnson's** (☎ 530-223-1935, 800-446-4656; 2731 Bechelli Lane; rooms $40-80). On the east side of the freeway, Hilltop Dr has a number of larger, more upmarket hotels and motels.

Tiffany House B&B Inn (☎ 530-244-3225; W www.sylvia.com/tiffany.htm; 1510 Barbara Rd; rooms & cottage $85-135), an elegant Victorian property, has a swimming pool, upright piano and grand views from the end of its quiet residential road, west of Hwy 273, a mile north of the river.

Apples' Riverhouse (☎ 530-243-8440; W www.applesriverhouse.com; 201 Mora Court; rooms $95), on the Sacramento River Trail west of Caldwell Park, pampers guests with evening wine and cheese tastings, a hot tub, chocolates and free rental bicycles.

Places to Eat

Dam-burger (☎ 530-241-0136; 1320 Placer St; burgers & sodas $2-5; open 9am-5pm Mon-Fri, 10am-3pm Sat, 11am-3pm Sun) is a charming, old-fashioned burger joint and soda fountain with a 1930s atmosphere.

Deja Vu (☎ 530-244-4272; 1590 California St; meals under $10; open 7am-3pm daily) should be your first and only stop for breakfast. We dare you to clean your plate when, after ordering an omelette, you also get hash browns and a side stack of pancakes with apricot syrup.

Buz's Crab Stand (☎ 530-243-2120; 2159 East St; meals $5-20; open 11am-9pm daily) is a down-to-earth place favored by locals, with outdoor seating. It serves sourdough bread and seafood dishes fresh daily.

Jack's Grill (☎ 530-241-9705; 1743 California St; mains $10-25; open 5pm-11pm Mon-Sat), moving upmarket, has a solid-gold reputation for choice steaks. They don't take reservations, so you may have a long wait for a table, but it's worth it. Cocktails start at 4pm.

Nello's Place (☎ 530-223-1636; 3055 Bechelli Lane; mains $15-25; open 5pm-9:30pm Tues-Sat), a Redding landmark, is a casual Italian dinner house, southeast of Hartnell Ave.

Post Office Saloon & Grill (☎ 530-246-2190; Downtown Redding Mall) is a genteel place for pub-style lunches or a beer. Across the street, **Kennett-Diamond Brewery & Restaurant** *(1600 California St)*, should have reopened by the time you read this.

Getting There & Around

The unstaffed **Amtrak station** *(☎ 800-872-7245; w www.amtrak.com; 1620 Yuba St)* is one block west of the Downtown Redding Mall. For the north–south *Coast Starlight*, you need to advance reservations by phone or via the website, then pay the conductor when you board the train. Alternatively, visit a travel agency.

The **Greyhound bus station** *(☎ 530-241-2531; 1321 Butte St)* never closes. **Redding Area Bus Authority** *(RABA; ☎ 530-241-2877)* has a dozen city routes operating until around 6pm Monday to Saturday. Fares start at $1 (exact change only).

AROUND REDDING
Shasta State Historic Park

On Hwy 299, 6mi west of Redding, this historic park *(grounds open sunrise-sunset)* preserves the ruins of an 1850s gold-rush mining town called Shasta (not to be confused with the town of Mt Shasta covered later in this chapter). When the gold rush was at its height, everything and everyone had to pass through Shasta. But when the railroad bypassed it to set up in Poverty Flat, poor Shasta lost its reason for being.

An 1861 courthouse now houses an excellent **museum** *(☎ 530-243-8194; admission $1; open 10am-5pm Wed-Sun)*, with a mighty fine gun collection and a gallows out back. Pick up walking tour pamphlets from the visitor information desk here. Trails pass by the Catholic cemetery, brewery ruins and many other historic sites. The Masonic lodge, two stores and a bakery are still functioning buildings, and several private homes are still lived in.

Whiskeytown Lake

Two miles further west on Hwy 299, Whiskeytown Lake *(☎ 530-242-3400; w www.nps.gov/whis/; day-use fee per vehicle $5)* takes its name from an old mining camp. When the lake was created in the 1960s by the construction of a 263ft dam, designed for power generation and Central Valley irrigation, the few remaining buildings of old Whiskeytown were moved and the site was submerged. Today, people descend upon the lake's 36mi of shoreline to engage in a range of activities, including swimming, sailing, gold panning, hiking and mountain biking.

The **visitor center** *(☎ 530-246-1225; open 9am-6pm daily summer, 10am-4pm winter)*, on the northeast point of the lake just off Hwy 299, offers free maps and information about Whiskeytown and the other two units that comprise the Whiskeytown-Shasta-Trinity National Recreation Area. Look for the schedules of ranger-led interpretive programs and guided walks.

On the southern shore of the lake, **Brandy Creek** is good for swimming and has lifeguards on duty over summer. Just off Hwy 299, on the northern edge of the lake, **Oak Bottom Marina** *(☎ 530-359-2269)* has boats for rent. At the west end of the park, the **Tower House Historic District** has the El Dorado mine ruins and the pioneer Camden House, open for summer tours.

Brandy Creek Campground *(RV sites summer/off-peak season $14/7)* offers RV camping on a first-come, first-served basis (no tents). It's basically a series of asphalt parking spots.

Oak Bottom Campground *(summer reservations ☎ 800-365-2267; tent/RV sites $8/18)*, in a more open lakeside setting, offers off-season discounts.

Various **primitive campsites** *(sites summer/winter $10/5)* are also available around the lake (no reservations).

SHASTA LAKE

About 15 minutes north of Redding, Shasta Lake *(w www.shastalake.com)* is the largest reservoir in California and home to the state's biggest population of bald eagles. It is surrounded on its several arms by hiking trails and campgrounds, and teeming with just about anything that will float – it's popular.

HA

The **ranger station** (☎ 530-275-1589; 14250 Holiday Rd; open 8am-5pm Mon-Sat, 8am-4:30pm Sun summer, 8am-4:30pm Mon-Fri rest of year) offers free maps and information about fishing, boating and hiking. To get here, take the Mountaingate Wonderland Blvd exit off I-5, about 9mi north of Redding, and turn right.

At the south end of Shasta Lake on Shasta Dam Blvd (Hwy 151) is **Shasta Dam**, the second most massive concrete dam in the US, weighing 15 million tons. Its 487ft spillway is as high as a 60-story building, and three times higher than Niagara Falls. The dam was built from 1938 to 1945; Woody Guthrie wrote 'This Land Is Your Land' while he was here working on the dam. The **Shasta Dam Visitors Center** (☎ 530-275-4463; open 8:30am-4:30pm Mon-Fri, 8:30am-5pm Sat & Sun) offers free guided tours, departing from the center at 10am and 2pm daily.

Lake Shasta Caverns (☎ 530-238-2341, 800-795-2283; tours adult/child $17/9) is a network of limestone and marble caves. Tours operate daily and include a boat ride across Lake Shasta to the caves. Bring a sweater, as the temperature inside is 58°F (14°C) year-round. Take the Shasta Caverns Rd exit from I-5, about 15mi north of Redding, and follow the signs for 1½mi.

Places to Stay & Eat

About half of the **US Forest Service campgrounds** (reservations ☎ 877-444-6777; w www.reserveusa.com; sites $6-26) around the lake are open year-round. Free boat-in sites are first-come, first-served. **Primitive camping** outside organized campgrounds requires a campfire permit from May to October, available free from any national forest service office.

If you want to rent a houseboat, reserve one as far in advance as possible – many are booked a full year ahead, especially for the summer months. Expect to pay at least $1100 per week.

Holiday Harbor Resort (☎ 530-238-2383, 800-776-2628; Holiday Harbor Rd; sites $17.50-22.50) has tent and RV camping (mostly RV), houseboat rentals and a busy marina offering parasailing and fishing boat rentals. It's off Shasta Caverns Rd right next to the lake.

Antlers RV Park & Campground (☎ 530-238-2322, 800-642-6849; w www.shasta lakevacations.com; 20679 Antlers Rd; tent/RV sites $13-29; cabins from $85), east of I-5 in Lakehead, at the north end of the lake, has a family-oriented campground with a swimming pool, country store and marina renting watercraft and houseboats.

On the west side of I-5, you'll find several more RV parks, some with cabins available, lining Lakeshore Dr.

Lakeshore Inn & RV (☎ 530-238-2003, 888-238-2003; 20483 Lakeshore Dr; tent/RV sites $20-28, cabins from $80) has a swimming pool, restaurant and tavern.

Houseboats and other watercraft can be rented from **Shasta Marina Resort** (☎ 530-238-2284, 800-959-3359; w www.shasta lake.net; 18390 O'Brien Inlet Rd) and **Jones Valley Resort** (☎ 530-275-7950, 800-223-7950, 877-468-7326; w www.houseboats .com; 22300 Jones Valley Marina Dr).

O'Brien Mountain Inn (☎ 530-238-8026, 888-799-8026, fax 530-238-2027; w www .obrienmtn.com; Shasta Caverns Rd; rates $100-225) has rooms with a musical theme and a tree house with skylights, Jacuzzi, kitchen and fireplace.

Most of the resorts and marinas have snack bars or restaurants. There's an inexpensive little **café** (open 8am-3pm daily) with lakefront deck tables at the Holiday Harbor Resort.

CASTLE CRAGS STATE PARK

A 20-minute drive from Mt Shasta, this glorious state park inside Castle Crags Wilderness Area features soaring spires of ancient granite formed some 225 million years ago, with elevations ranging from 2000ft along the Sacramento River to more than 6500ft at the top of the Crags. The crags are similar to the granite formations of the eastern Sierra, and Castle Dome here resembles Yosemite's famous Half Dome.

Rangers at the **park entrance station** (☎ 530-235-2684; day-use per vehicle $2) have information and maps covering nearly 28mi of **hiking trails**. There's also **fishing** in the Sacramento River at the day-use picnic area, on the opposite side of I-5.

If you drive up past the campground you'll reach **Vista Point**, near the start of the strenuous 2.7mi **Crags Trail**, which rises through the forest past the Indian Springs spur trail, then clambers up to the base of Castle Dome, rewarding you with unsurpassed views of Mt Shasta, especially if you scramble the last hundred yards or so up into the rocky saddle gap. The park also has gentle **nature trails** and 8mi of the **Pacific Crest Trail**, which passes through the park at the base of the Crags.

The **campground** *(summer reservations* ☎ *800-444-7275;* **w** *www.reserveamerica .com; sites $12),* open year-round, has running water and hot showers; sites are shady, but suffer from traffic noise. You can camp anywhere in the Shasta-Trinity National Forest surrounding the park if you get a free campfire permit, issued at park offices.

DUNSMUIR

Six miles north of Castle Crags State Park, this town (population 1900) is nestled into the Sacramento River Canyon and known for its pristine landscapes and good fishing. Built by the Central Pacific Railroad, Dunsmuir was originally called Pusher, for the auxiliary 'pusher' engines that muscled heavy steam engines up a steep grade nearby. Later, city founders renamed the town after local coal baron Alexander Dunsmuir, who gave them a fountain that still stands here today.

Dunsmuir is a soothingly old-fashioned kind of place, and an inexpensive alternative to staying in Mt Shasta town, just 8mi away. Meandering Dunsmuir Ave is the main street, but you'll find quaint restaurants, shops and historic buildings on Sacramento Ave, downhill near the train station one block further east. The **Dunsmuir Chamber of Commerce** *(*☎ *530-235-2177, 800-386-7684;* **w** *www .dunsmuir.com; 4118 Pine St; open 10am-11:30am & 12:30pm-4pm Mon-Sat, noon-4pm Sun summer)* has free maps, walking guide pamphlets and excellent information on outdoors recreation and the **Siskiyou Blues & Heritage Festival** in mid-July.

As you follow winding Dunsmuir Ave north over the freeway, look for the **vintage steam engine** in front of tame, missable Dunsmuir City Park & Botanical Gardens. There's a small waterfall up a forest path from the riverside gardens, but **Mossbrae Falls** is the larger and more spectacular of Dunsmuir's waterfalls. To get there from Dunsmuir Ave, turn west onto Scarlett Way, passing under an archway marked 'Shasta Retreat.' Park by the railroad tracks (there's no sign), then walk north along the right side of the tracks for a half-hour until you reach a railroad bridge built in 1901. Backtracking slightly from the bridge, you'll find a little path going down through the trees to the river and the falls. Be *extremely careful* of trains as you walk by the tracks – the river's sound can make it impossible to hear them coming.

Places to Stay & Eat

Railroad Park Resort *(campground* ☎ *530-235-0420, motel* ☎ *530-235-4440, reservations* ☎ *800-974-7245;* **w** *www.rrpark.com; 100 Railroad Park Rd; tent/RV sites $16/24, caboose & boxcar suites $75-100),* about a mile south of town, offers unique accommodation inside vintage railroad cars. The deluxe boxcars are furnished with antiques and clawfoot tubs.

Railroad Park Dinner House *(Railroad Park Resort; mains $11-17; open from 5pm Thur-Sun)* offers California cuisine and a cocktail lounge inside its vintage railroad cars.

Cave Springs Resort *(*☎*/fax 530-235-2721, 888-235-2721; 4727 Dunsmuir Ave; RV sites $15, cabins with kitchen $36-52, motel rooms $45-65),* overlooking the Sacramento River north of downtown, has family-friendly recreational amenities. It's popular, so book ahead. Weekly discounts are given.

Relaxing motels along Dunsmuir Ave include **The Oak Tree Inn** *(*☎ *530-235-2884, 877-235-2884;* **w** *www.oaktreeinn .com; 6604 Dunsmuir Ave; rooms/suites from $55/80)* and the **Cedar Lodge** *(*☎ *530-235-4331, fax 530-235-4000; 4201 Dunsmuir Ave; rooms $40-55),* notable for its exotic bird aviary.

Dunsmuir Inn B&B *(*☎ *530-235-4543, 888-386-7684; 5423 Dunsmuir Ave; rooms with bathroom $65-80)* comes highly recommended by travelers. You can cook in the kitchen or barbecue in the yard.

Diners and cafés line Dunsmuir and Sacramento Aves.

Café Maddalena *(*☎ *530-235-2725; 5801 Sacramento Ave; main $11-17; open 5pm-10pm Thur-Sun summer),* a cheerful place near the train station, serves magnificent Sardinian Italian fare. It's worth the drive from Mt Shasta town just to dine here. Reservations are advised.

Getting There & Away

The unstaffed **Amtrak station** *(*☎ *800-872-7245;* **w** *www.amtrak.com; 5750 Sacramento Ave)* is the only train stop in Siskiyou

County. You can buy tickets for the north–south *Coast Starlight* on board the train, but only after making reservations by phone or via the website.

Greyhound (☎ 800-231-2222; **w** www .greyhound.com) buses stop in front of **Cec- chettini's Books** (5814 Dunsmuir Ave). See the Mt Shasta Getting There & Around section later for regional bus services.

MT SHASTA

You'll probably never forget your first glimpse of towering Mt Shasta. In 1874 nat- uralist and Sierra Club founder John Muir wrote: 'When I first caught sight of it I was 50mi away and afoot, alone and weary. Yet all my blood turned to wine, and I have not been weary since.' About 60mi north of Redding, nowadays the town of Mt Shasta (population 3650; elevation 3563ft) is dwarfed by the mountain.

When European fur trappers arrived in the area in the 1820s they encountered several Native American tribes, including the Shasta, Karuk, Klamath, Modoc, Wintu and Pit River. By 1851, hordes of gold- rush miners had arrived, disrupting the tribes' traditional livelihood. The new rail- road transported logs and workers for a booming lumber industry and, since the town was surrounded by many 'dry' towns, Mt Shasta became a bawdy, good-time place for lumberjacks. Originally called Strawberry Valley for the abundant wild strawberries that grew here, the town was later renamed Sisson, after its principal landowner, innkeeper, mountain guide and philanthropist. In 1924, the name was changed to Mt Shasta.

New Age residents have now replaced the lumberjacks. Many people are attracted by the peak's reputed spiritual dimensions (see the boxed text 'Shasta'). Others come for its sheer beauty and outdoors recreational pos- sibilities, including camping, hiking and mountaineering, soaking in hot springs, ski- ing, mountain biking and boating.

With its modest appeal, the town can be a base for exploring the area's natural won- ders, although the lodgings and restaurants in smaller neighboring communities, such as Weed and Dunsmuir, are better value. Peak tourist season is from Memorial Day through Labor Day and also weekends during ski season (late November to mid-April).

Orientation & Information

Orienting yourself is a snap, with Mt Shasta looming over the east side of town. The downtown area is a few blocks east of I-5. Take the Central Mt Shasta exit, then drive east on Lake St past the visitors bureau up to the town's main intersection at Mt Shasta Blvd, which is the main street.

Shasta

Mt Shasta has been inspiring legends since long before Europeans arrived on the scene. Indigenous peoples viewed the mountain as sacred, climbing its slopes during spiritual quests, healing cere- monies and for shamanic training; some Native Americans believed it belonged to the Great Spirit, whose wigwam was the mountain itself.

Several of the modern legends are – to say the least – a bit unusual, but then again, so are those who believe them. One story was that a race of Lemurians – refugees from the lost continent of Lemuria submerged beneath the Pacific Ocean – lived in cities inside the mountain, coming down only to trade their gold nuggets for mundane supplies.

Variations on that theme say that a race of invisible people or a mystic brotherhood lives inside the mountain. GW Ballard, founder of Mt Shasta's St Germain Foundation (also known as 'I AM') claims to have had a mystical meeting with St Germain on the mountain in the summer of 1930. The foundation now distributes 'Golden Cities' maps with details on how to locate vortexes and be party to updated prophecies.

Many people still believe that Mt Shasta is a magnet for spiritual energy, or that a mystical- creative vortex is formed by the triangle of Mt Shasta, Mt Eddy and Castle Crags. Spirit-conscious folks, artists and even athletes often report feeling their powers enhanced by spending time on the mountain; in fact, hardly a sunset goes by without some soul being found here strumming a guitar, chanting poetry or simply meditating at its vista points.

Mt Shasta Visitors Bureau (☎ 530-926-4865, 800-397-1519; W www.mtshastachamber.com; 300 Pine St at Lake St; open 9am-5pm Mon-Sat, 9am-3pm Sun summer; 10am-4:30pm Mon-Sat, 10am-4pm Sun winter) has detailed handouts on outdoors recreation and lodging across Siskiyou County.

Mt Shasta Ranger Station (☎ 530-926-4511; 204 W Alma St; open 8am-4:30pm daily), one block west of Mt Shasta Blvd, doles out wilderness and mountain-climbing permits, good advice, weather reports and everything you need for exploring the area, as well as selling topographic maps.

The Mountain

'Lonely as God, white as a winter moon,' wrote Joaquin Miller of Mt Shasta in *Life Among the Modocs*. Dominating the landscape, it is visible for more than 100mi from many parts of Northern California and southern Oregon. Though not California's highest peak (at 14,162ft it ranks only sixth) Mt Shasta is especially magnificent because it rises alone on the horizon, unrivaled by other mountains.

Mt Shasta is part of the vast Cascade volcanic chain that includes Lassen Peak to the south and Mt St Helens and Mt Rainier to the north. The presence of thermal hot springs indicates that Mt Shasta is dormant, but not extinct; smoke was seen puffing out of the crater on the summit in the 1850s, though the last eruption was probably a few hundred years ago. The mountain has two cones: the main cone has a crater about 200 yards across, and the younger, shorter cone on the western flank, called Shastina, has a crater about half a mile wide.

In Mt Shasta town, **Fifth Season Sports** (☎ 530-926-3606; 300 N Mt Shasta Blvd at Lake St) rents mountain climbing, camping and backpacking gear, mountain bikes, skis, snowshoes and snowboards. Ski and snowboard rentals are also available at **Sportsmen's Den Snowboard & Ski Shop** (☎ 530-926-2295; 402 N Mt Shasta Blvd) and **House of Ski & Board** (☎ 530-926-2359; 316 Chestnut St), which rents bicycles as well.

Driving You can drive almost all the way up the mountain via the Everitt Memorial Hwy (Hwy A10), and there are fine views at any time of year. Simply head east on Lake St from downtown, then left onto Washington Dr and keep going. **Bunny Flat** (6860ft), which has a trailhead for Horse Camp and the Avalanche Gulch summit route, is a busy place with parking spaces, informational signboards and a toilet. The section of highway beyond Bunny Flat is only open from about mid-June to October, depending on snows. Trails through **Lower Panther Meadow** connect the campground to a Wintu sacred spring, in the upper meadows near the **Old Ski Bowl** (7800ft) parking area. Shortly thereafter is the highlight of the drive, **Everitt Vista Point** (7900ft), where a short interpretive walk from the parking lot leads to a stone-walled outcropping affording exceptional views of Mt Lassen to the south, the Eddys and Marble Mountains to the west and the whole Strawberry Valley below.

Climbing Reaching the summit is best done between May and September, preferably in spring and early summer, when there's still enough soft snow on the southern flank to make footholds easier on the nontechnical route. Though the round-trip could conceivably be done in one day with 12 or more hours of solid hiking, it's best to allow at least two days and spend a night on the mountain. How long it actually takes to climb up and back depends on the route selected, the physical condition of the climbers and weather conditions (for weather information call ☎ 530-926-9613).

Though the hike to the summit from Bunny Flat is only about 7mi, it is a vertical climb of more than 7000ft, so acclimatizing to the elevation is important. You'll need crampons, an ice axe and a helmet, all of which can be rented locally. Rock slides and unpredictable weather can be hazardous, so novices should contact the Mt Shasta Ranger Station for a list of available guides.

There's a fee to climb the mountain; a three-day pass costs $15; an annual pass is $25. Contact the ranger station for details. You must have a free wilderness permit any time you go into the wilderness, whether on the mountain or in the surrounding area.

Mt Shasta Board & Ski Park On the south slope of Mt Shasta, off Hwy 89 heading toward McCloud, this winter sports park (*snow reports* ☎ 530-926-86868; W www.skipark.com; open 9am-10pm Wed-Sat, 9am-4pm Sun-Tues winter; 10am-4pm Wed-Thur &

Sun, 10am-9pm Fri & Sat late June-early Sept)
provides skiing and snowboarding options;
opening dates depend on snowfall. The park
has a 1390ft vertical drop, over two dozen
alpine runs and 18mi of cross-country trails;
rentals, instruction and weekly specials are
available. It's Northern California's largest
night-skiing operation.

In summer, the park offers scenic chairlift
rides, paragliding flights, a 24ft climbing
tower and frisbee golf. Mountain bikers can
take the chairlift up and come whooshing
back down. Special events, including outdoor
concerts, are regularly scheduled.

The Lakes

There are a number of pristine mountain
lakes near Mt Shasta. Some of them are accessible only by dirt roads or hiking trails
and are great for getting away from it all.

The closest Mt Shasta town is **Lake
Siskiyou** (the largest), 2½mi southwest on
Hwy 26, where you can peer into **Box
Canyon Dam**, a 200ft-deep canyon. Another
7mi up in the mountains, southwest of Lake
Siskiyou on Castle Lake Rd, is **Castle Lake**,
an unspoiled place surrounded by granite formations and pine forest. Swimming, fishing,
picnicking and free camping are popular here
in summer; in winter, people ice-skate on the
lake. **Lake Shastina**, about 15mi northwest of
town off Hwy 97, is another beauty, favored
by short-board windsurfers.

Mt Shasta Town

Most of Mt Shasta's other attractions are in
the surrounding areas but the town has a
few places worth visiting.

The **Mt Shasta Fish Hatchery** (☎ 530-926-
2215; open 7am-sunset daily) and **Sisson Museum** (☎ 530-926-5508; admission free; open
10am-4pm Mon-Sat, 1pm-4pm Sun June-
Sept, 1pm-4pm daily Apr-May & Oct-Dec) are
side by side at 1 Old Stage Rd, a half-mile
west of the freeway. The museum has geology
and history exhibits on the town and the
mountain, while the hatchery offers self-
guided walks around outdoor trout ponds.

At **Mt Shasta City Park** (Nixon Rd), off Mt
Shasta Blvd about a mile north of downtown,
the headwaters of the Sacramento River gur-
gle up from the ground in a large, cool
spring. The park also contains walking trails,
picnic spots, sports fields and courts, and a
children's playground. East of downtown,

Shastice Park (☎ 530-926-2494; cnr Rock-
fellow & Adams Drs) has an ice-skating rink
in winter.

In Weed, 8mi north of Shasta town, docents at the **Weed Historic Lumber Town
Museum** (☎ 530-938-0550; 303 Gilman St;
donation requested; open 10am-5pm daily
summer) will explain absolutely everything
about logging to you, using historic photographs and memorabilia. To get there, take
I-5 north to the Hwy 97/Central Weed exit
and follow Main St. A few blocks past the
Weed Chamber of Commerce (☎ 877-938-
4624), turn right at the museum sign. It's a
20-minute drive.

Activities

Shasta Cove Stables (☎ 530-938-3392,
800-662-3529) has been leading trail rides
and guided overnight trips through Shasta-
Trinity National Forest for over 75 years.

River Dancers (☎ 530-926-3517, 800-
926-5002; W www.riverdancers.com) and
Osprey Outdoors Kayak School (☎ 530-926-
6310; W www.ospreykayak.com) offer
whitewater rafting and kayaking trips. Expect to pay at least $80 per adult per day.

Mt Shasta Resort (☎ 530-926-3052;
1000 Siskiyou Lake Blvd) has a rolling, tree-
lined 18-hole golf course with expansive
views of the mountains and Sacramento
River gorge. Green fees ($35 to $50) are
discounted for twilight play.

A treeless, black volcanic cone on the
north side of the town of Mt Shasta, **Black
Butte** rises almost 3000ft. A 2½mi hiking trail
to the top takes at least 2½ hours return. It's
steep and rocky in many places, and there is
neither shade nor water, so heat can be a
problem in summer. Wear good hiking shoes
and bring plenty of water. Or try the 9mi
Sisson-Callahan National Recreation Trail, a
historic route established in the mid-1800s by
prospectors, trappers and cattle ranchers to
connect the mining town of Callahan with the
town of Sisson, now called Mt Shasta.

Stop by the Mt Shasta ranger station or the
visitors bureau for excellent free trail guides
for these and other hikes, including several
access points along the **Pacific Crest Trail**.

Places to Stay

Make reservations well in advance, especially on weekends or holidays and during
ski season.

Camping The visitors bureau has details on over two dozen campgrounds around Mt Shasta.

Mt Shasta KOA (☎/fax 530-926-4029, 800-562-3617; 900 N Mt Shasta Blvd; tent/RV sites from $18/22, cabins $40-50), off E Hinckley St, a few blocks north of downtown, has a swimming pool. Sites are crowded and there's not nearly enough greenery for shade.

Lake Siskiyou Camp-Resort (☎ 530-926-2618; 4239 WA Barr Rd; tent/RV sites from $18/25, cabins $85-105), on the lakeside at Lake Siskiyou, is a great camping destination. It has a swimming beach and offers kayak, canoe, fishing boat and paddle boat rentals.

Check with the Mt Shasta and McCloud ranger stations about US Forestry Service campgrounds in the area. Of course, the best are on Mt Shasta itself. Two are easily accessible from the Everitt Memorial Hwy. **McBride Springs** (campsites $10) has running water, no showers and pit toilets; it's near mile-marker 4 at an elevation of 5000ft. Another 7mi further up the mountain at 7000ft, mystic **Panther Meadows** (campsites free) has 10 walk-in tent sites at the timberline. Arrive early in the morning to secure a spot at either (no reservations).

Horse Camp ($5/3 per person with/without tent), a 1923 alpine lodge run by the Sierra Club, is a 2mi hike uphill from Bunny Flat at 8000ft. Caretakers staff the hut from May to September only.

As long as you set up your camp at least 200ft from the water and get a free campfire permit from the ranger stations, you can camp beside many mountain lakes. **Castle Lake** has six free tent sites, but no drinking water and it's closed in winter. **Gumboot Lake**, 15mi southwest of Mt Shasta, also has free tent camping (purify your own drinking water). **Toad Lake**, 18mi from Mt Shasta town, is not a designated campground but lovely; you go down an 11mi gravel road (4WD advised) and walk the last quarter-mile.

Motels Many motels offer discount ski packages in winter.

Finlandia Motel (☎ 530-926-5596; 1612 S Mt Shasta Blvd; rooms $45-80) is a good budget bet. Deluxe rooms have vaulted ceilings and mountain views. An outdoor hot tub and authentic Finnish sauna open in winter.

Strawberry Valley Inn (☎ 530-926-2052; 1142 S Mt Shasta Blvd; singles/doubles from $85/110) provides a complimentary breakfast buffet and wine every evening in the parlor. Its equally cute sister property **Strawberry Valley Court** (☎ 530-926-2052; 305 Old McCloud Rd; single/double cabins from $75/90) has a white picket fence and shady brick cabins with private garages. Midweek rates are cheaper.

Several other decent budget motels are spread out along Mt Shasta Blvd at the south end of town. Most have hot tubs and charge from $50 to $70 in peak season. Try the quiet **Swiss Holiday Lodge** (☎ 530-926-3446; 2400 S Mt Shasta Blvd) or atmospheric **Mountain Air Lodge & Ski House** (☎ 530-926-3411; 1121 S Mt Shasta Blvd), boasting a communal kitchen and recreation areas. **Shasta Lodge Motel** (☎ 530-926-2815; 724 N Mt Shasta Blvd) is more central, sitting just north of downtown.

Better deals can sometimes be had in Weed, about 8mi north of Mt Shasta town along the I-5 freeway. The South Weed exits are lined with chain motels, while the Hwy 97/Central Weed exit leads into downtown where a few clean, cheerful and family-owned budget motels stand.

B&Bs & Resorts A few long blocks north of downtown, beautiful **Alpenrose Cottage Guest House** (☎ 530-926-6724; 204 E Hinckley St; bed in shared twin room per day/week $35/180, double private room per day/week $60/360) has a mountainview deck, wood-burning stoves, gardens and a communal kitchen.

Dream Inn (☎ 530-926-1536, 877-375-4744; 326 Chestnut St; room with shared bath $60-70, suite $90-100), close to downtown, is a modest white Victorian home with a lily pond and rose gardens. Full gourmet breakfasts are served until noon (hurrah!).

Mt Shasta Ranch B&B (☎ 530-926-3870; w www.stayinshasta.com; 1008 WA Barr Rd at Ream Ave; carriage house single/double rooms with shared bath and kitchen from $45/60, main house singles/doubles with private bath $90/110, cottages $115-160) is an enormous place west of the freeway, with fireplaces, billiards and ping-pong tables. Breakfast is included, except for cottage guests.

Mt Shasta Resort (☎ 530-926-3030, 800-958-3363; 1000 Siskiyou Lake Blvd; 1-bedroom/2-bedroom chalets from $155/205) is nestled above the lakeshore west of town on the way to Lake Siskiyou. The Craftsman-style chalets have kitchens and gas fireplaces. Lodge rooms near the golf course are not such a good deal.

Places to Eat
You can make your own meals with groceries from natural food markets like **Berryvale Grocery** (☎ 530-926-1576; 305 S Mt Shasta Blvd) or **Mountain Song** (☎ 530-926-3391; Mt Shasta Shopping Center, 134 Morgan Way) off Lake St.

Bagel Café & Bakery (☎ 530-926-1414; 315 N Mt Shasta Blvd; snacks & light meals $3-7; open 6am-5pm Mon-Fri, 7am-4pm Sat, 8am-4pm Sun) is an amiable place to hang out, and the menu has plenty of healthy selections, including smoothies and salads.

The Pasta Shop (☎ 530-926-4118; 418 N Mt Shasta Blvd; most meals around $6; open 8am-7pm daily) cooks up pizza, calzone, daily soups and pasta, all fresh and painstakingly homemade (don't expect lightning-fast service).

Poncho & Lefkowitz (☎ 530-926-1102; 107 Chestnut St; meals under $10) offers cheap Mexican food, gourmet hot dogs and local microbrews, with tables overlooking Mt Shasta Blvd.

Mt Shasta is inexplicably overrun with retro 1970s Italian dinner houses. All are pretty much overpriced for what you get, except for **Michael's Restaurant** (☎ 530-926-5288; 313 N Mt Shasta Blvd; open 11am-2:30pm & 5pm-9pm Tues-Fri, noon-9pm Sat) right downtown.

Lily's (☎ 530-926-3372; 1013 S Mt Shasta Blvd; breakfast, lunch $8-11, dinner mains $14-20; open breakfast 7am-10am, lunch 11am-4pm & dinner from 4pm, Mon-Fri, brunch 7am-2:30pm and dinner from 4pm Sat-Sun) delivers more ambience than quality California cuisine. Still, the food is passable, and outdoor tables overhung by flowering trellises are almost always full, especially for breakfast.

Trinity Café (☎ 530-926-6200; 622 N Mt Shasta Blvd; mains $15-22; open 5pm-9:30pm Wed-Sun), at the north end of town, has an intimate, home-like atmosphere and serves wonderfully flavored gourmet fare,

for the same price as mediocre cooking at downtown restaurants.

Serge's (☎ 530-926-1276; 531 Chestnut St; mains $13-19; open 5pm-9pm Wed-Sun), one block east of Mt Shasta Blvd, specializes in continental and French-inspired cuisine, offering seating on the mountain-view terrace or indoors.

You'll find a lot more appealing diners and cafés in old-fashioned Weed, a 20-minute drive north of Mt Shasta town along I-5. **Espresso Bakery** (☎ 530-938-1041; 79 S Weed Blvd; open 7am-4pm daily) sells deadly espresso chocolate candies, as well as yummy fresh pastries and simple deli sandwiches.

Entertainment
Mt Shasta Cinemas (☎ 530-926-1116; Mt Shasta Shopping Center, 118 Morgan Way) shows first-run films.

Has Beans Coffeehouse (☎ 530-926-3602; 1011 S Mt Shasta Blvd; open 5:30am-7pm or later daily) serves superb locally roasted coffee and often has live acoustic music.

Vet's Club Bar (☎ 530-926-3565; 406 N Mt Shasta Blvd) has live music (mostly rock and roll) and dancing, usually on weekends.

Shopping
Village Books (☎ 530-926-1678; 320 N Mt Shasta Blvd) and **Golden Bough Books** (☎ 530-926-3228; 219 N Mt Shasta Blvd) carry fascinating volumes about Mt Shasta on topics from geology and hiking to folklore and mysticism, as does the **Sisson Museum** shop (see under Mt Shasta Town earlier).

Art galleries line Mt Shasta Blvd. **Visions Gallery** (☎ 530-926-1189; 201 N Mt Shasta Blvd), in the Black Bear Building, has skylight exhibition spaces and quality crafts.

Getting There & Around
Greyhound (☎ 800-231-2222; ☒ www.greyhound.com) buses heading north and south on I-5 stop opposite the **Vet's Club** (406 N Mt Shasta Blvd) and at the **depot** (☎ 530-938-4454; 628 S Weed Blvd) in Weed.

The **STAGE bus** (☎ 530-842-8295, 800-247-8243) includes the town of Mt Shasta in its local I-5 corridor route, which also serves McCloud, Dunsmuir, Weed and Yreka several times daily. Other buses connect at Yreka (see the Yreka Getting There & Away section later in this chapter).

The **California Highway Patrol** (CHP; ☎ 530-842-4438) recorded report gives weather and road conditions for all Siskiyou County roads.

For bicycle rental, see The Mountain section, earlier in this chapter.

McCLOUD

The historic mill town of McCloud (population 1600) sits on the north side of Hwy 89, some 10mi east of I-5 freeway, at the foot of the south slope of Mt Shasta. The closest settlement to Mt Shasta Ski & Board Park, it's worth a visit for itself and for very quiet recreation in the surrounding area.

The **McCloud Ranger District Office** (☎ 530-964-2184; Hwy 89; open 8am-4:30pm Mon-Fri year-round, also Sat Memorial Day to mid-Oct), a quarter-mile east of town, has detailed informational handouts on camping, hiking and all kinds of recreation. Or try the **McCloud Chamber of Commerce** (☎ 530-964-3113; w www.mccloudchamber.com; 205 Quincy Ave; open 10am-4pm Mon-Fri).

You can saunter down to see some square dancing at **McCloud Dance Country** (☎ 530-964-2578; cnr Broadway & Pine Sts; admission couple $12), a 1906 dance hall. Summer dances are held almost every Friday and Saturday evening, starting at 7pm.

The **Shasta Sunset Dinner Train** (☎ 530-964-2142, 800-733-2141) offers open-air diesel train rides on some summer afternoons, from June to September. One-hour excursions cost $10/5 per adult/child. Opposite the depot, there's a tiny **historical museum** (open 11am-3pm Mon-Sat, 1pm-3pm Sun).

The **McCloud River Loop**, a 6mi partially paved road along the Upper McCloud River, begins at Fowlers Camp, 5½mi east of town, and emerges onto Hwy 89 about 11mi east of McCloud. Along the way you'll pass turnoffs to three waterfalls, a riparian habitat for bird-watching in Bigelow Meadow, and a hiking path. The loop can easily be done by car, bicycle or on foot.

Other good hiking trails include the **Squaw Valley Creek Trail** (not to be confused with the ski area near Lake Tahoe), an easy 5mi loop trail south of town, with options for swimming, fishing and picnicking. Sections of the Pacific Crest Trail are accessible from Ah-Di-Na campground, off Squaw Valley Rd, and also up near Bartle Gap, which offers head-spinning views. The ranger district

office has a free pamphlet outlining these routes and directions to trailheads.

Fishing and swimming are popular on remote **Lake McCloud** reservoir, 9mi south of town on Squaw Valley Rd, which is signposted as Southern Ave in town off Hwy 89. You can also go fishing on the Upper McCloud River (stocked with trout) and at Squaw Valley Creek. **Friday's RV Retreat** (☎ 530-964-2878; Squaw Valley Rd), 6mi south of McCloud near Squaw Valley Creek, has a fly-fishing school.

Places to Stay

Of about a half-dozen **US Forestry Service campgrounds** nearby, Fowler's Camp is the most popular. Campgrounds have a range of facilities and charge fees of up to $12 per site, while others are free but more primitive (no running water). Ask the rangers for details.

McCloud Dance Country RV Park (☎ 530-964-2252, fax 530-964-2083; 480 Hwy 89 at Southern Ave; tent/RV sites $14/18-22) is central. Then again, it's right on the highway and chock-full of RVs.

Stoney Brook Inn (☎ 530-964-2300, 800-369-6118, fax 530-964-2930; w www.stoney brookinn.com; 309 W Colombero Dr; singles/ doubles from $36/62) was once the Park Hotel, dating from 1922. This quiet retreat features a hot tub with Finnish sauna, barbecue and picnic area, winter ski packages and a variety of airy rooms, some with kitchenettes.

McCloud B&B Hotel (☎ 530-964-2822, 800-964-2823, fax 530-964-2844; w www .mccloudhotel.com; 408 Main St; rooms $75-115, suites with Jacuzzi $125-165), also in the town center, is a registered historic landmark. This 1916 grand hotel has been lovingly restored to a luxurious standard and takes breakfast very seriously.

McCloud River Inn (☎ 530-964-2130, 800-261-7831; w www.riverinn.com; 325 Lawndale Court; rooms with private bath $70-145), also on the National Register of Historic Places, is an imposingly large, buttercup-yellow Victorian, just off Main St.

McCloud Century House Inn (☎/fax 530-964-2206; w www.mccloudcenturyhouse .com; suites $80-100) is a cozy retreat at the west end of town, offering suites with full kitchens. It's a very private place and reservations are essential.

McCloud Vacation Rentals (☎ 530-964-2443; W www.mccloudrentals.com; 213 Quincy Ave) rents affordable vacation homes.

Places to Eat

McCloud Soda Shoppe & Café (☎ 530-964-2747; 245 Main St), in the Old Mercantile Building, is an old-fashioned little soda fountain serving snacks.

Raymond's Ristorante (☎ 530-964-2099; 424 Main St; dinner $14-25; open 11:30am-2pm Wed-Sat, dinner from 5pm Wed-Mon) is a long-running Italian dining room. Homemade gnocchi appears among the country house specialties.

Briarpatch Family Restaurant (☎ 530-964-2700, 140 Squaw Valley Rd, off Hwy 89; open 11:30am-9pm Mon-Fri, 9am-9pm Sat & Sun, live music 9pm-1am Fri & Sat) is a boisterous Mexican-American restaurant beside the RV park.

Shasta Sunset Dinner Train (☎ 530-964-2142, 800-733-2141; W www.shastasunset.com; Main St; 3hr ride with multi-course dinner $80, plus tax & tip) offers a diverting dinner opportunity inside 1916-vintage restored dining cars. In summer, the train boards at 5:30pm Thursday to Saturday, with several routes going west and east from McCloud; trips are scaled back the rest of the year.

STEWART MINERAL SPRINGS

Set in a forested canyon, Stewart Mineral Springs (☎ 530-938-2222, fax 530-938-4283; W www.stewartmineralsprings.com; 4617 Stewart Springs Rd; sauna & mineral baths $15-20, sauna only $10; open 10am-10pm Thur-Sat May-Sept; 10am-6pm daily rest of year) was founded in 1875 by one Henry Stewart, after Native Americans brought him here to heal when he was near death. He attributed his recovery to the healthful properties of the mineral waters, said to draw toxins out of the body.

Today you can soak in a clawfoot tub in a private room, emerging periodically to run to the sauna down the hall. Other services include massage, body wraps, a meditation room, Native American sweat-lodge purification, and a sunbathing deck above a mountain stream. Dining and overnight **accommodation** (tent & RV sites $15, teepees $24, apartments $45-80) are available. To reach the springs, go 10mi north of Mt Shasta town on I-5, past Weed to the Edgewood exit, then head west for 4mi and follow the signs.

YREKA

About 35mi north of Mt Shasta, making it inland California's northernmost city (population 7100), Yreka (pronounced wy-ree-kah) plainly has its roots in the gold rush era. Although most travelers only pass by en route to Oregon, it makes a good spot to stretch, eat and refuel before heading out into the hinterlands of the Scott Valley or the northeastern California wilderness.

Most places of interest are along Main St and Miner St, which intersect in downtown Yreka. For information, drop by the **Yreka Chamber of Commerce** (☎ 530-842-1649, 800-669-7352; W www.yrekachamber.com; 117 W Miner St; open 9am-5pm daily summer, winter hours vary). The **Klamath National Forest Supervisor's Office** (☎ 530-842-6131; 1312 Fairlane Rd at Oberlin Rd; open 8am-4:30pm Mon-Fri), at the south edge of town, has the lowdown on outdoor recreation and camping in the National Forest. There is also an office of the **AAA** (☎ 530-842-4416; 1876 Fort Jones Rd).

Things to See & Do

Fondly known as the Blue Goose, the **Yreka Western Railroad** (☎ 530-842-4146, 800-973-5277; W www.yrekawesternrr.com; 300 E Miner St) is a 1915 Baldwin steam engine

Yreka: What's in a Name?

You may ask yourself, 'Why Yreka?' When, in 1851, Abraham Thompson discovered gold in nearby Black Gulch, there was no town to name. Only six weeks later, more than 2000 prospectors were on hand, raising a tent city with a few rough shanties and cabins thrown in. Originally known as Thompson's Dry Diggings, the settlement expanded to its present site, beside what is now Yreka Creek, and was renamed Shasta Butte City. In 1852, when Siskiyou County was formed, the town won the title of county seat by only one vote over Deadwood, in Scott Valley. To avoid confusion with Shasta town near modern-day Redding, its name was changed again to Wyreka, later Yreka, a Native American word for Mt Shasta meaning 'white mountain.'

pulling both covered and open-air cars. It chugs at 10mph through the Shasta Valley to the tiny town of Montague, with Mt Shasta looming in the distance. Excursion rides cost from $12.50/6 per adult/child. Call for departure times and reservations, especially for in-demand seats in the caboose or engine cars, which cost more. The Yreka depot is on Foothill Dr, just east of I-5 (take the Central Yreka exit).

The **Siskiyou County Courthouse** (311 4th St) downtown was built in 1857 and has a collection of gold nuggets in the foyer. Many blocks further south, the exceptionally well-curated **Siskiyou County Museum** (☎ 530-842-3836; 910 S Main St; admission $1; open 9am-5pm Tues-Sat) brings together pioneer and Native American history. An outdoor section has several historic buildings brought from around the county. Behind the museum is the **Yreka Creek Greenway**, where walking paths wind through the trees.

Places to Stay & Eat

Klamath National Forest operates several area **campgrounds**; the supervisor's office has information. There are several **RV parks** on the outskirts of town.

Comfortable motels are found up and down Main St, including the **Ben Ber Motel** (☎ 530-842-2791; 1210 S Main St) and **Klamath Motor Lodge** (☎ 530-842-2751; 1111 S Main St), which has a swimming pool. All charge around $40 to $60 in summer, with winter discounts.

Best Western Miner's Inn (☎ 530-842-4355; 122 E Miner St; singles/doubles $49/54), at the Central Yreka exit, offers a bit more luxury. It has two heated swimming pools.

More **budget motels** are found south of town, at the Fort Jones exit off I-5.

There are many inexpensive to moderately priced eateries around town, including a few **Chinese restaurants** with cocktail lounges.

Poor George's (☎ 530-842-4664; 108 Oberlin Rd at Main St; full meals $5-8; open 6am-7:45pm Mon-Fri, 7am-1:45pm Sat & Sun), at the south end of town, boasts large portions and a friendly, hometown atmosphere.

Nature's Kitchen (☎ 530-842-1136; 412 S Main St; dishes around $5; open 8am-3pm Mon-Sat), further north along Main St, is a natural foods store and bakery serving healthy vegetarian dishes, fresh juices and good espresso.

Grandma's House (☎ 530-842-5300; 123 E Center St; breakfast & lunch $5-7, dinner $8-15; open 6am-10pm daily, winter hours vary), east of downtown between Main St and I-5, is another place popular for its home-style cooking. Look for the restaurant's cutesy gingerbread-house exterior.

Getting There & Away

Greyhound (☎ 800-231-222; w www.greyhound.com) buses northbound and southbound along I-5 stop at the **Greyhound depot** (☎ 530-842-3145; 115 Miner St).

STAGE (☎ 530-842-8295, 800-247-8243) buses run from a few different stops in Yreka throughout the region, including several times daily along the I-5 corridor to Weed, Mt Shasta, McCloud and Dunsmuir. Other buses depart daily for Fort Jones, Greenview and Etna in the Scott Valley and on Monday and Friday only, out to Klamath River and Happy Camp.

About 25mi north of Yreka on I-5, Siskiyou Summit (elevation 4310ft) catches many storms in winter and closes often – even when the weather is just fine on either side. Check the recorded information line of the **CHP** (☎ 530-842-4438) for road conditions before you travel up to the border.

The easiest route between Yreka and the coast is following I-5 north through the Oregon towns of Ashland, Medford and Grant's Pass, then heading back south on Hwy 199 to Crescent City. Watch out for speed traps as soon as you cross the Oregon border. Hwys 96 and 299 will also get you to the border; they are scenic, but extremely slow and winding.

KLAMATH NATIONAL FOREST

With 1.7 million acres, Klamath National Forest (w www.r5.fs.fed.us/klamath) covers a large portion of California's far north. It's bordered on the west by Six Rivers National Forest, by Trinity Alps Wilderness on the south and by the Oregon border on the north. Its various districts extend in a patchwork pattern, mostly west of Yreka but with one district east of Yreka extending to Lava Beds National Monument.

The forest includes three major rivers – the Klamath, Salmon and Scott – providing opportunities for everything from slow, lazy canoeing and inner-tubing to challenging

State of Mind

Just south of Yreka, on the east side of I-5, you can't miss the barn painted with the yellow sign, 'State of Jefferson,' in 12ft-high letters, or the gigantic cow sculpture mascot guarding the fields nearby. Bumper stickers and license plate holders all attest to existence of this odd 51st state, if only in the minds of local activists.

With an independence movement dating back to the 1940s, the State of Jefferson declared its opposition to its future being determined by big-city voters, whose numbers overwhelmed the small rural population. For example, construction of new backcountry roads vital to the survival of local timber and mining industries was something that had been largely ignored by California state politicians.

Although pundits originally suggested the new entity be called the 'State of Discontent,' the name picked was a tribute to Thomas Jefferson, who authored the Declaration of Independence and later, as US president, sent explorers Lewis and Clark on their way to Oregon, opening the American West. If not for the bombing of Pearl Harbor, which focused attention on national unity instead of political protest, Jefferson may well have been another US state.

No-one can say exactly what the Jefferson boundaries would have been, but modern-day secessionists range from southern Oregon down through Siskiyou and Trinity Counties. The Jefferson State Seal is a gold pan with two X's, symbolizing how it has been double-crossed at every turn. This rebellious ethos is provoked, they say, by excessive taxation and legislation handed down by Sacramento without regard for local needs. Although secession may not be a real possibility at this late date, as a political platform for raising consciousness (and a few eyebrows), the Jeffersonians may yet succeed.

Class V white-water rafting and kayaking. Rafts, canoes and kayaks can be rented, and a number of tour companies offer organized river trips; the ranger stations can provide details.

The forest also incorporates parts of five wilderness areas. The 237,500-acre **Marble Mountain Wilderness**, just west of Scott Valley, has close to 100 lakes and part of the Pacific Crest Trail, and it's relatively easy to get to. The 500,000-acre **Trinity Alps Wilderness,** north of Weaverville, features Alpine terrain, lakes, streams and a 400mi system of trails. The 12,000-acre **Russian Wilderness** includes high, craggy granite formations and more than 20 lakes. The 153,000-acre **Siskiyou Wilderness**, on the west side of the forest, is rugged and seldom visited. A small portion of the **Red Buttes Wilderness** also lies within the forest, though most of it is in the Rogue River National Forest across the Oregon border.

Topographic maps and advice on current conditions for all of these wilderness areas are available at the Klamath National Forest Supervisor's Office in Yreka, or the following ranger stations:

Goosenest Ranger District (☎ 530-398-4391)
  Macdoel, on Hwy 97 northeast of Weed
Happy Camp Ranger District (☎ 530-493-2243)
  Happy Camp, on Hwy 96 about 30 miles west of Yreka

Scott-Salmon River Ranger District (☎ 530-468-5351) Etna, on Hwy 3 southwest of Yreka
Ukonom Ranger District (☎ 530-627-3291)
  Orleans, on Hwy 96 south of Happy Camp

SCOTT VALLEY

Southwest of Yreka, Hwy 3 passes through Scott Valley, a pristine agricultural area nestled between towering mountains, where the Scott Bar Mine operated for 110 years.

At the valley's northern end is Fort Jones, just 18mi from Yreka. There is a **visitor center** (☎ 530-468-5442; 11943 Main St; open 10am-5pm Tues-Sat, noon-4pm Sun) at the back of the Guild Shop mercantile, and a small **museum** (☎ 530-468-5568; 11913 Main St; donation requested; open Mon-Sat summer) of Native American artifacts down the street.

Another 12mi brings you to Etna, known for its tiny **Etna Brewing Company** (☎ 530-467-5277; 131 Callahan St; free brewery tours by appointment, pub open 11am-6pm Wed-Sun). If you're sticking around, try the **Motel Etna** (☎ 530-467-5338; 317 Collier Way; singles/doubles $35/40). If you're hungry, they serve food at the Etna Brewing Company pub, and old-fashioned ice cream sodas at **Scott Valley Drug** (☎ 530-467-5335; 511 Main St; closed Sun).

Continuing south, Hwy 3 passes over Scott Mountain Summit (5401ft) and joins the Trinity Heritage National Scenic Byway, passing Trinity Lake and finally arriving at Weaverville. For details on this route, see Trinity County later in this chapter.

Northeastern California

Where the high desert plateaus of Modoc and Lassen counties give way to the mountains of the northern Sierras, life seems to proceed at a slower pace. Folks seem genuinely happy to greet a traveler, even if they're a bit uncertain as to why you've come here. In fact, so far removed is this corner of the state from big-city living that many Californians never see it.

If you want to get off the beaten path, it's worth taking the time to visit these spectacular, yet little-known areas. Heavy snows may be a deterrent if you don't like winter sports, but otherwise traveling here is a breeze, especially considering the lack of all-too-typical California traffic congestion and smog.

LAVA BEDS NATIONAL MONUMENT

Lava Beds National Monument (W *www.nps .gov/labe; 7-day entry cars/hikers/bikers $5/3/3*), off Hwy 139 immediately south of Tule Lake National Wildlife Refuge, is a remarkable 72-sq-mi landscape of volcanic features – lava flows, craters, cinder cones, spatter cones, shield volcanoes and remarkable lava tubes.

Lava tubes are formed when hot, spreading lava cools and hardens on the surfaces exposed to the cold air. The lava inside is thus insulated and stays molten, flowing away to leave an empty tube of solidified lava. Nearly 400 such tubular caves have been found in the monument, and many more are likely to be discovered. About two dozen or so are currently open for exploration by visitors.

On the south side of the park, near the **visitor center** (☎ *530-667-2282, ext 230;* W *www.nps.gov/labe; open 8am-6pm daily summer, 8am-5pm rest of year*), a short one-way loop drive provides access to many lava tube caves with names like Labyrinth, Hercules Leg, Golden Dome and Blue Grotto. In **Mushpot Cave**, the one nearest

the visitor center, lighting and informative signs have been installed. The visitor center provides free flashlights for cave explorations; you can buy a special caver's 'bump hat' for a nominal price. It's essential you use a high-powered flashlight, wear good shoes (lava is sharp) and not go exploring alone. The visitor center also has free maps, activity books for kids and information about the monument and its volcanic features and history. Rangers lead summer interpretive programs, including campfire talks and guided cave walks.

Other notable features of the region include the tall black cone of **Schonchin Butte** (5253ft), where there's a magnificent outlook accessed via a steep one mile hiking trail (once you reach the top, you can visit with fire lookout staff between June and September); **Mammoth Crater**, the source of most of the area's lava flows; and ancient, faded **petroglyphs** at the base of a high cliff at the far northeastern end of the monument. A leaflet explaining the origin of the petroglyphs and their probable meaning is available in the visitor center, and it's really not worth visiting without it. Look for the hundreds of birds' nests in holes high up in the cliff face, which provide shelter for birds observed at the wildlife refuges nearby.

Also at the north end of the monument, **Captain Jack's Stronghold** is worth seeing. A brochure will guide you through the Stronghold trail; allow plenty of time to be halted in your tracks, meditating on the history and the labyrinthine landscape. The brochure and other books about the Modoc War (see the boxed text 'Captain Jack's Stronghold') are available at the visitor center.

Indian Wells Campground (*sites $10*), near the visitor center at the south end of the park, has water and flush toilets. A couple of **motels** are on Hwy 139 in the nearby town of Tulelake (see the next section).

KLAMATH BASIN NATIONAL WILDLIFE REFUGES

Of the six national wildlife refuges in this group, Tule Lake and Clear Lake refuges are wholly within California, Lower Klamath refuge straddles the California-Oregon border, and the Upper Klamath, Klamath Marsh and Bear Valley refuges are across the border in Oregon. Bear Valley and Clear Lake (not to be confused with the Clear Lake just east

Captain Jack's Stronghold

The labyrinth fortress of lava formations known as Captain Jack's Stronghold, at the north end of Lava Beds National Monument, is the site of an important episode in American history, the Modoc War. Here Modoc subchief Kientpoos, known as Captain Jack, led a band of about 150 Modoc men, women and children in fighting off a six-month-long siege by a US Army force that eventually numbered over 600. As the Modoc War dragged on it became a great shame to the US Army – a sort of Vietnam War for its era.

Prior to the siege, conflicts between the Modocs and early white settlers had led to efforts to confine the tribe on a reservation near Upper Klamath Lake, 70mi north of the lava beds. This ignored the fact that the Modocs and Klamath Indians had long been bitter enemies. After experiencing hardships and harassment on the reservation, Captain Jack had led his followers back home to the Lava Beds area.

Fighting erupted when soldiers sent from Fort Klamath came to arrest Captain Jack and return his people to the reservation. Using the natural cover of the stronghold, the Modocs were able to fight the army to a standstill throughout the rough winter of 1872–73. In the end, the Modocs were defeated and Captain Jack and three of his followers were sold out by their own comrades, then hanged at Fort Klamath – a tragic end to a tragic conflict.

of Ukiah) are closed to the public to protect their delicate habitats, but the rest are open daily during daylight hours.

These refuges provide habitats for birds migrating along the Pacific Flyway; some stop only briefly, while others stay longer to mate, make nests and raise their young. There are always birds here, and during the spring and fall migrations, there can be hundreds of thousands of waterfowl.

The **Klamath Basin National Wildlife Refuges Visitor Center** (☎ 530-667-2231; w www.klamathnwr.org; 4009 Hill Rd; open 8am-4:30pm Mon-Fri, 10am-4pm Sat & Sun) is on the west side of the Tule Lake refuge, about 5mi west of Hwy 139 near the town of Tulelake. Follow the signs from Hwy 139 or from Lava Beds National Monument. The center has a nonprofit bookstore and interesting video program about the birds and the refuges, as well as maps, books, information on recent bird sightings and updates on road conditions.

The spring migration peaks in March, and in some years more than a million birds fill the skies. In April and May, songbirds, waterfowl and shorebirds arrive, some to stay and nest, others to build up their energy before they continue north. In summer, ducks, Canada geese and many other water birds are raised here. The fall migration begins in early September, and by late October peak numbers of birds have departed. In cold weather, the area hosts the largest wintering concentration of bald eagles in the lower 48 states, with sometimes more than 1000 in residence from December to February; Tule Lake and Lower Klamath refuges are the best places to see eagles, as well as other raptors.

The Tule Lake and Lower Klamath refuges attract the largest numbers of birds year-round, and **auto trails** ($3 per vehicle) have been set up; a free pamphlet from the visitor center shows the routes. Self-guided **canoe trails** have been established in three of the refuges. Those in the Tule Lake and Klamath Marsh refuges are usually open 1 July to 30 September; no canoe rentals are available. Canoe trails in the Upper Klamath refuge are open year-round; canoes can be rented at **Rocky Point Resort** (☎ 541-356-2287), on the west side of Upper Klamath Lake.

There's camping nearby at Lava Beds National Monument. A couple of RV parks and budget motels are on Hwy 139 near the tiny town of Tulelake, including the friendly **Ellis Motel** (☎ 530-667-5242; 2238 Hwy 139; doubles with/without kitchen $50/45).

Osborne's Winema Lodge (☎ 530-667-5158; e osbornelodge@cot.net; 5212 Hill Rd) has camping, guest rooms and bunkhouse rooms close to Tule Lake refuge.

MODOC NATIONAL FOREST

This national forest (w www.r5.fs.fed.us/modoc) covers almost 2 million acres of California's northeast corner. Fourteen miles south of Lava Beds National Monument on the western edge of the forest, **Medicine Lake** is a stunning crater lake surrounded by pine forest, campgrounds and volcanic formations. Several flows of obsidian (shiny, black volcanic glass) came out of the volcano that formed Medicine Lake, which is in a caldera,

The Avian Superhighway

California is on the Pacific Flyway, a migratory route for hundreds of species of birds heading south in winter and north in summer. There are birds to see year-round, but the most spectacular views are to be had during the spring and fall migrations. Flyway regulars include everything from tiny hummingbirds, finches, swallows and woodpeckers, to eagles, swans, geese, ducks, cranes and herons.

In Northern California, established wildlife refuges mostly safeguard wetlands used by migrating waterfowl. There are few hiking trails in the refuges, as management prefers people to be as unobtrusive as possible by staying on defined driving routes or in canoes. Rangers can supply information about wildlife in their own refuge and also in other refuges nearby.

The **Klamath Basin National Wildlife Refuges** are all within about an hour's drive of one another. About 1½ hours southeast of the Tule Lake refuge is **Modoc National Wildlife Refuge,** 3mi southeast of Alturas. Another detour brings you to **Ash Creek Wildlife Area**, near the junction of Hwys 299 and 139, about an hour southwest of Alturas.

Other wildlife refuges are just over the border in Nevada and Oregon, including the large **Sheldon National Wildlife Refuge**, about a 1½-hour drive from Alturas, into Nevada; **Hart Mountain National Antelope Range** in Oregon, about two hours from Alturas or Sheldon; and the **Malheur National Wildlife Refuge** in southeastern Oregon, a 1½-hour drive from Hart Mountain.

or collapsed volcano. Pumice eruptions were followed by flows of obsidian, as at **Little Glass Mountain**.

Roads are closed by snow from around mid-November to mid-June, but the area is still popular for winter sports, and accessible by cross-country skiing and snowshoeing. Other notable geologic features of the area, such as lava caves and tubes, are part of a self-guided **roadside geology driving tour**, best done in summer or early fall. You can pick up detailed tour pamphlets from the McCloud ranger station (see the Interstate 5 to Oregon section earlier).

The **Warner Mountains**, on the east side of the forest, are a spur of the Cascade Range. Weather on the Warners is extremely changeable, and snowstorms have occurred there at all times of year, so always be prepared. The range divides into the North Warners and South Warners at Cedar Pass (elevation 6305ft), east of Alturas. **Cedar Pass Snow Park** (☎ 530-233-3323; w cedarpasssnow park.com; open 10am-4pm Sat, Sun & holidays during ski season) offers downhill and cross-country skiing. The **South Warner Wilderness** contains 77mi of hiking and riding trails; the best time to use them is from July to mid-October.

Maps, campfire permits and information are all available at the **Modoc National Forest Supervisor's Headquarters** (☎ 530-233-5811, 800 W 12th St; open 8am-5pm Mon-Fri) in Alturas, a small town that

provides basic services, motels, coffee shops and family-style restaurants.

Trinity County

Weaverville is the seat of Trinity County, a mountain and forest area that's 75% federally owned. With its almost 3300 sq mi, the county is roughly the size of Delaware and Rhode Island together, yet has a total population of only 13,000, not one traffic light or parking meter, and no incorporated towns. In fall, the vibrant colors of changing leaves attract people to the Trinity Scenic Byway and the Trinity Heritage National Scenic Byway.

Starting in Redding and heading west, Hwy 299, known as the **Trinity Scenic Byway**, winds through scenic, rugged mountains for 150mi to Arcata, on the Pacific coast near Eureka. From Redding it goes west past Shasta State Historic Park and Whiskeytown Lake (see the Around Redding section earlier), follows the meandering Trinity River and winds through the Shasta-Trinity and Six Rivers National Forests.

At Weaverville, Hwy 299 intersects with Hwy 3 and the **Trinity Heritage National Scenic Byway**. Heading north, this 105mi scenic drive goes over 9025ft Mt Eddy, before passing Stewart Springs and finally meets I-5 just north of Weed, near Mt Shasta. It takes all day to do this 105mi scenic drive with stops, or a few hours driving straight through, say locals who know the road. Of course, everything depends on the weather. The section beyond Coffee Creek is made impassable by snow in winter; still, there's plenty of lodging in that town if you get stuck. Heading north, the byway branches off onto Hwy 17 (also known as International Paper Road); otherwise, if you keep driving on Hwy 3, you'll eventually reach the Scott Valley (see that section earlier). Around Trinity Divide, the byway intersects with various **hiking trails**, including the historic Sisson-Callahan National Recreation Trail and the Pacific Crest Trail, which you can take southeast from the road for a pleasant 3mi day hike of easy grade into Deadfall Lakes Basin, or challenge yourself by continuing to the summit of 9025ft Mt Eddy. After passing Stewart Springs, the byway finally meets I-5 just north of Weed, near Mt Shasta.

THE LAKES
Lewiston Lake
Twenty-six miles west of Redding, about 5mi off Hwy 299 on Trinity Dam Blvd, Lewiston (population 1300) makes a pleasant rest stop. It's right beside the Trinity River, where there's good fishing below the dam. About 1½mi north, tiny Lewiston Lake is a peaceful alternative to the other area lakes because of its 10mph boat-speed limit. The water is kept at a constant level, providing a nurturing habitat for fish and waterfowl. It is a stopover for a number of migrating bird species – early in the evening you may see ospreys and bald eagles diving for fish.

Places to Stay & Eat Several commercial campgrounds are spaced around the lake. For information on **US Forestry Service campgrounds**, contact the ranger station in Weaverville (see that section, following).

Lakeview Terrace Resort (☎ 530-778-3803, fax 530-778-3960; W www.lake viewterraceresort.com; RV sites $18-21, trailers/cabins from $50/60), a lovely facility 5mi north of Lewiston, offers boat rentals and weekly discounts.

Pine Cove Marina & RV Park (☎ 530-778-3770, 800-778-3838; 9435 Trinity Dam Blvd), the only marina on the lake, offers free information about the lake and its wildlife, plus boat and canoe rentals, potluck dinners and guided off-road tours.

Back near town are a few quiet places.

Old Lewiston Bridge RV Resort (☎ 530-778-3894, 800-922-1924; Rush Creek Rd at Turnpike Rd; tent/RV sites $14/24) offers camping beside the river bridge.

Lewiston Valley Motel (☎ 530-778-3942, fax 530-778-3943; 4789 Trinity Dam Blvd; RV sites $20, motel singles/doubles $45/55) is a tidy place with a swimming pool and RV park, all next to a gas station and convenience store.

The Old Lewiston Inn B&B (☎ 530-778-3385, 800-286-4441; W www.theoldlewis toninn.com; Deadwood Rd; singles/doubles $85/95), an 1875 house in the middle of town on the river, serves country-style breakfasts. Enjoy the hot tub, or ask about all-inclusive fly-fishing and romantic getaway packages.

Lewiston Hotel (☎ 530-778-6800; Deadwood Rd; bar open from 4pm, restaurant 5pm-9pm Wed-Sat), also in the center of town, was built in 1862. Although it is no longer a functioning hotel, this is a hangout with a lot of character, serving excellent drinks and dinners. If you're lucky, they may have live music and dancing.

Trinity (Clair Engle) Lake
North of Lewiston Lake, Trinity Lake is California's third-largest reservoir. It attracts multitudes, who come for swimming, fishing and other water sports. The west side of the lake, accessible off of Hwy 299 via Hwy 3, has most of the campgrounds, RV parks, motels, boat rentals and restaurants.

Pinewood Cove Resort (☎ 530-286-2201, 800-988-5253; W www.pinewoodcove.com; 45110 Hwy 3; tent/RV sites $20/26, A-frame/loft cabins $80/110; campground open Apr 15-Oct 31) is a popular place to stay. **Trinity Alps Marina** (☎ 530-286-2282, 800-824-0083; W www.trinityalpsmarina.com; houseboats from $600/week) rents fishing boats as well as houseboats.

The east side is quieter, with more secluded campgrounds, some accessible only by boat. The Weaverville Ranger Station has information on **US Forestry Service campgrounds**.

WEAVERVILLE
On Hwy 299, at the foot of the spectacular Trinity Alps, 45mi west of Redding and 100mi east of Eureka, Weaverville (population 3300) is a small gem of a town on the National Register of Historic Places.

You can spend a pleasant hour or two just strolling around town, visiting art galleries, museums and other historic structures. Plaques on the outsides of the buildings tell when they were built and what they were.

The **Trinity County Chamber of Commerce** (☎ 530-623-6101, 800-487-4648; **w** www.trinitycounty.com; 211 Trinity Lakes Blvd; open 9am-noon & 1pm-4pm Mon-Fri, sometimes Sat & Sun in summer) has lots of useful information.

Weaverville Ranger Station (☎ 530-623-2121; 210 N Main St; open 8am-4:30pm Mon-Fri) has maps, information and permits for all the lakes, national forests and wilderness areas in and near Trinity County, with specifics on hiking trails, camping areas and recreation sites.

Joss House State Historic Park (☎ 530-623-5284; cnr Hwy 299 & Oregon St; admission $1; open 10am-5pm Sat in winter; 10am-5pm Wed-Sun rest of year), in the center of town, holds the oldest continuously used Chinese temple in California – it dates from the 1870s. Its Taoist shrine features an ornate altar, more than 3000 years old, that was brought here from China. Tours depart from 10am until 4pm on the hour. Next door, the **JJ Jackson Memorial Museum & Trinity County Historical Park** (☎ 530-623-5211; 508 Main St; donation requested; open 10am-5pm daily May-Oct, noon-4pm Apr & Nov) has gold-mining and cultural exhibits, plus vintage machinery, amazing memorabilia and an old miner's cabin outside.

Weaverville Rexall Drug Store (☎ 530-623-4343; 219 Main St; open 10am-6pm Mon-Fri, 11am-3pm Sat) proclaims itself 'California's Oldest Pharmacy.' Established in 1852, it's a living museum as well as a functioning business.

Six Pack Packers (☎ 530-623-6314) leads hunting, fishing and scenic horse pack trips into the Trinity Alps Wilderness. There's **river rafting** at Willow Creek, 55mi west of Weaverville. Outfitters include **Big Foot Rafting Company** (☎ 530-629-2263, 800-722-2223; **w** www.bigfootrafting.com), which leads guided trips and also rents rafts and kayaks, and **Aurora River Adventures** (☎ 530-629-3483, 800-562-8475; **w** www .rafting4fun .com). Contact them for trip information.

Places to Stay
The ranger station has information on many US Forestry Service campgrounds in the area, especially around Trinity Lake. Commercial RV parks, some with tent sites, are dotted along Hwy 299 all the way to Arcata.

Red Hill Motel & Cabins (☎ 530-623-4331, fax 530-623-4341; Red Hill Rd; motel singles/doubles $30/35, duplex doubles $45, cabins with/without kitchen from $50/40) is a quiet place at the west end of town. It's just off Main St, opposite the ranger station. Rates are higher for family units.

Several other inexpensive to mid-range motels are on Hwy 299, called Nugget Lane on the east side of town. Ask at the chamber of commerce if the historic 1861 **Weaverville Hotel** has reopened its doors.

Places to Eat & Drink
A weekly **farmers market** (open 4:30pm-7:30pm Wed May-Oct) sets up shop on Main St in the warmer months.

Mountain Marketplace (☎ 530-623-2656; 222 S Main St; open 9am-6pm Mon-Fri, 10am-5pm Sat) is a natural foods grocery store with a juice bar and vegetarian deli.

Trinideli (☎ 530-623-5856; 201 Trinity Lakes Blvd at Center St; sandwiches $5-7; open 6:30am-5:30pm daily) prepares decadent deli sandwiches, stuffed with all kinds of fresh goodness, with good vibes all around. You'll be salivating over thoughts of what you ate here long after you've left the county.

Mamma Llama (☎ 530-623-6363; 208 N Main St; open 7am-6pm Mon-Sat, 8:30am-3pm Sun) is a bookstore and espresso shop that occasionally has live acoustic music.

La Grange Café (☎ 530-623-5325; 315 N Main St; lunch $7-14, dinner mains $9-22; open 11:30am-9:30pm Mon-Thur, 11am-4pm & from 5pm Fri-Sun) has award-winning continental food and a friendly atmosphere, both in the pub and salon dining room.

At the time of writing, the Pacific Brewery, a fine historic building, had closed to make way for **Red Dragon**, a Chinese restaurant. For places to eat and drink that stay open late, check out Nugget Lane, east of downtown along Hwy 299.

Getting There & Away
From Monday to Friday, a local bus makes a Weaverville–Lewiston loop via Hwy 299 and Hwy 3. Another local bus runs between

Weaverville and Hayfork, a small town about 30mi to the southeast on Hwy 3. **Trinity Transit** *(☎ 530-623-5438)* can provide details.

Coast Mountains

North of the Central Valley, the Coastal Range fans out into other mountain ranges: the Cascades, the Siskiyou Mountains, the Trinity Alps, the Salmon Mountains, the Marble Mountains and the Scott Bar Mountains.

SIX RIVERS NATIONAL FOREST

Hugging the west side of the Klamath and Trinity National Forests and the Siskiyou and Trinity Alps Wilderness Areas, Six Rivers National Forest is a long, narrow green swath. It extends north from at the Oregon border and going south all the way to the Yolla Bolly-Middle Eel Wilderness on the north end of Mendocino National Forest. The six rivers for which the forest is named are (from north to south), the Smith, Klamath, Trinity, Mad, Van Duzen and Eel.

The forest has over a dozen campgrounds, but you can camp anywhere in the forest with a free campfire permit. The Six Rivers National Forest Headquarters in Eureka (see the North Coast chapter) has maps and information on camping, hiking and outdoors recreation. So do the four ranger district stations (from north to south):

Smith River NRA (☎ 707-457-3131), Hwy 199, Gasquet
Orleans Ranger District (☎ 530-627-3291), Hwy 96 at Ishi Pishi Rd, Orleans
Lower Trinity Ranger District (☎ 530-629-2118), 580 Hwy 96, Willow Creek
Mad River Ranger District (☎ 707-574-6233), Hwy 36, Bridgeville

MENDOCINO NATIONAL FOREST

Sixty-five miles long from north to south and 35mi wide, this national forest *(w www.r5.fs .fed.us/mendocino)* comprises more than 1 million acres of forested mountains and canyons, with elevations ranging from the Sacramento Valley foothills on the eastern side up to 8092ft South Yolla Bolly Mountain in the north.

Two wilderness areas are within the forest: the 37,000-acre **Snow Mountain Wilderness**, with its 52mi of hiking trails, and part of the **Yolla Bolly-Middle Eel Wilderness**, with its 40mi of hiking trails. The forest also has three national recreation trails: the 8mi **Ides Cove Loop Trail** in the Yolla Bolly Wilderness, the 3½mi **Travelers Home Trail** at the Middle Fork of the Eel River and the **Sled Ridge Motorcycle Trail** beginning at Middle Creek Campground. What it does *not* have is a single paved road, although almost all of the roads have been graded and are now accessible to two-wheel-drive vehicles.

The **Mendocino National Forest Headquarters** *(☎ 530-934-3316, information line ☎ 530-934-2350; 825 N Humboldt Ave, Willows)* has a 24-hour recorded recreation report.

Several recreation areas, including Lake Pillsbury, Middle Creek-Elk Mountain, Letts Lake, Fouts, Eel River and Plaskett Meadows, have **campgrounds**. You can also camp anywhere for free with a campfire permit.

Lake Pillsbury is probably the forest's most visited spot. It attracts hikers, campers, boaters and anglers, but being rather remote (it's reached by driving 11mi up a gravel road), it's still uncrowded.

Sacramento Valley

The Sacramento Valley follows the middle section of the Sacramento River, a powerful, 375mi-long body of water that originates near Mt Shasta, travels south past towns like Red Bluff, Chico and Sacramento, and meanders through the delta region before finally unloading into San Francisco Bay. 'Sacramento' is the Spanish name for 'Holy Sacrament,' and it was given to the river during the early 1800s.

Running north from Sacramento to Red Bluff, the valley may seem unexciting at first, but peer closer and you'll find rich history and a subtle beauty. The area forms part of what is commonly called the Great Central Valley. Along with the San Joaquin Valley to the south, it's the work engine for the state, the overly cultivated landscape packed with fruit and nut orchards, olive trees, rice fields and other agricultural goods. Orchard blossoms produce colorful spectacles in springtime, fall brings bright yellow leaves, and with the Pacific Flyway overhead, the region teems with thousands of migrating birds during winter. Summer can be brutally hot, but it's also fun, with shady oak trees, rivers and creeks offering refreshment.

This chapter mostly follows Hwys 70 and 99, which travel north from Sacramento, meeting up with I-5 in Red Bluff. See the Northern Mountains chapter for points further north.

SACRAMENTO

Sacramento (population 406,000) was named for the Sacramento River, which passes through town on its way to San Francisco Bay. The town was originally called New Helvetia by its founder, John Sutter, in 1839 in honor of his Swiss lineage. Today it sprawls in all directions from its historically bountiful center.

As the state's capital, Sacramento is a lively, get-things-done city filled with politicians, political aides and conventioneers. The downtown area is surprisingly compact, and at night it nearly empties out. Instead, tourists and residents alike head for historic but tacky Old Sacramento, which faces the river, or the restaurants and clubs in Midtown, Sacramento's small but increasingly trendy neighborhood directly east of downtown.

Highlights

- California State Capitol – where the decisions get made
- California State Railroad Museum – renowned nationally for its classic locomotives and memorabilia
- Oroville's Chinese Temple – a tribute to the community's proud past
- Chico – university nightlife blends with small-town spirit

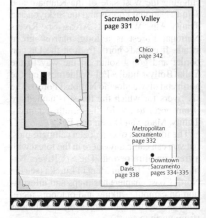

Sacramento Valley
page 331

Chico
page 342

Metropolitan
Sacramento
page 332

Davis
page 338

Downtown
Sacramento
pages 334-335

Ninety miles east of San Francisco and 130mi west of Reno, Sacramento sits at the intersection of busy I-80, I-5 and Hwy 99. During rush hour, highway travel can be a frustrating, backed-up mess. If you're stuck passing through at such a time, a good place to cool your head is at one of the city's vintage ice-cream parlors.

History

In 1839 Swiss immigrant John Sutter arrived in California and proposed to build an outpost north of San Francisco for the Mexican government. The government gave Sutter 76 sq mi of land around the confluence of the American and Sacramento Rivers where, with the aid of local Miwok tribes, Sutter built an adobe fort, planted crops and ran cattle. As the only outpost between San Francisco and Vancouver, British Columbia, Sutter's Fort became a bastion of security and general rendezvous.

When James Marshall discovered gold in the tailrace of Sutter's lumber mill near Coloma in 1848, hundreds of thousands of people flocked to California, most traveling through Sutter's Fort. Sam Brannan built several structures west of the fort, along the Sacramento River, to benefit from the new influx of miners. (See the boxed text 'Sam Brannan' in the Wine Country chapter.) Sutter gave his fort to his son, who christened the newly sprung town 'Sacramento.' Though plagued by fires and flood, the riverfront settlement prospered and became the state capital in 1850.

The transcontinental railroad was conceived in Sacramento by a quartet of local merchants known as the 'Big Four' – Leland Stanford, Mark Hopkins, Collis P Huntington and Charles Crocker. Together they founded the Central Pacific Railroad, which began construction in Sacramento in 1863 and connected with the Union Pacific in Promontory, Utah in 1869.

Orientation

Sacramento sits at the confluence of the Sacramento and American Rivers, roughly halfway between San Francisco and Lake Tahoe. The Sacramento River runs along the western edge of downtown.

Four main highways cross through Sacramento. Hwy 99 and I-5 enter the city from the south; I-80 skirts downtown on the city's northern edge, heading west to the Bay Area and east to Reno; and Hwy 50 runs along downtown's southern edge (where it's also called Business Route 80) before heading east to Lake Tahoe.

Downtown, numbered streets run from north to south, lettered streets run east to west (with Capitol Ave replacing M St). One-way J St is a main drag east from downtown to Midtown. The Tower District is south of downtown at the corner of Broadway and 16th St.

Cal Expo, the site of the California State Fair every August, is east of BR 80 from the Cal Expo exit (see the Metropolitan Sacramento map).

Information

Old Sacramento Visitor Center (☎ 916-442-7644; 1101 2nd St; open 10am-5pm daily) and the **Convention & Visitor's Bureau**

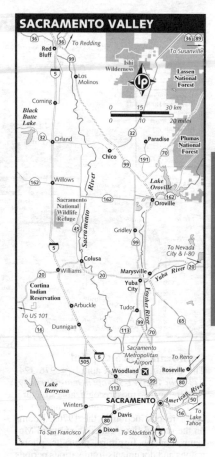

SACRAMENTO VALLEY

(☎ 916-264-7777; W www.sacramentocvb.org; 1303 J St; open 8am-5pm Mon-Fri) both have local information, including event and bus schedules.

Another helpful website to check is W www.cityofsacramento.org/webtech/activities/visit.htm.

The downtown branch of the **post office** (☎ 916-556-3415; 801 I St) is three blocks north of the capitol.

Good bookstores include **The Avid Reader** (☎ 916-443-7323; cnr 10th & L Sts), across from the capitol, and **Beer's Books** (☎ 916-443-9148; 1431 L St), the latter full of used books and local titles.

The **UC Davis Medical Center** (☎ 916-734-2011; 2315 Stockton Blvd) is on the east side of town, south of Hwy 50.

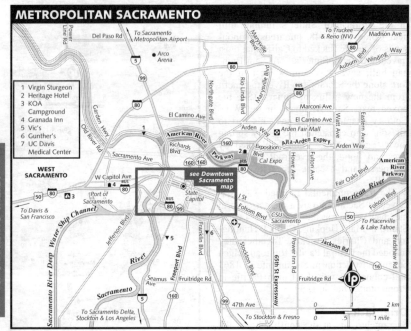

METROPOLITAN SACRAMENTO

1 Virgin Sturgeon
2 Heritage Hotel
3 KOA Campground
4 Granada Inn
5 Vic's
6 Gunther's
7 UC Davis Medical Center

California State Capitol

The California State Capitol (☎ 916-324-0333; cnr 10th & L Sts; open 9am-5pm daily) is Sacramento's most recognizable structure. Built in the late 19th century, it underwent major reconstruction in the 1970s. Rooms on the ground floor, called the Capitol Museum, contain furniture, portraits, photographs and documents from various periods of California history. Free tours leave hourly between 9am and 4pm from the tourist information office in the basement. Also in the basement are great murals, a free video and a **bookstore** (open 9:30am-4pm Mon-Fri, 10:30am-4pm Sat & Sun).

The 40 acres surrounding the capitol make up the **Capitol Park**, with trees from all over the world – a nice place to picnic or escape summer's heat. In the east end is a powerful Vietnam War memorial.

North of the Capitol is the **Governor's Mansion State Historic Park** (☎ 916-323-3047; cnr 16th & H Sts; admission $1; open 10am-4pm daily), built in 1877 and acquired by the state in 1903 (no, the current governor does *not* live there). Guided tours are given hourly from 10am to 4pm daily.

Old Sacramento

Once a bustling river port filled with hopeful gold seekers, Old Sacramento (Old Sac) boasts California's largest concentration of buildings on the National Register of Historic Places. It's interesting, but unfortunately the area has also become a cheap tourist haunt, the cute cobblestone streets littered with saltwater-taffy stores, T-shirt shops, party bars and overpriced restaurants.

At Old Sac's north end is the excellent **California State Railroad Museum** (☎ 916-445-6645; W www.csrmf.org; cnr 2nd & I Sts; adult/child $3/free; open 10am-5pm daily), near where the notorious 'Big Four' masterminded the transcontinental railroad. The museum is the nation's largest of its kind with an impressive collection of rail cars, locomotives, toy models and memorabilia. Tickets include entrance to the restored Central Pacific Passenger Depot, across the plaza from the museum entrance. From here, on weekends from April to September, you can board a steam-powered passenger train ($6) for a 40-minute jaunt along the riverfront.

Old Sac's other great feature is its riverfront setting. The **Spirit of Sacramento**

(☎ 916-552-2933, 800-433-0263), an 1842 paddle wheeler, makes one-hour sightseeing tours of the Sacramento River worth the $10 ticket. There are also cocktail and dinner cruises. The boat leaves several times daily in summer from the L St dock.

Next door to the railroad museum, the **Discovery Museum** (☎ 916-264-7057; 101 I St; admission $5; open 10am-5pm Tues-Sun Sept-May, 10am-5pm daily Jun-Aug) has hands-on exhibits and gold rush displays.

Crocker Art Museum

Housed in the Victorian-style home of Margaret and Judge Edwin B Crocker (tycoon Charles Crocker's brother) – which is a piece of art in itself – this museum (☎ 916-264-5423; 216 O St; adult/student $6/3, free Sun morning; open 10am-5pm Tues-Sun, 10am-9pm Thur) holds the first publicly displayed art collection in the western US. It also houses an extensive show of California art after 1945 and hosts traveling exhibits.

Midtown

Spreading along J St from 16th to 28th St, and also along Capitol Ave east of the State Capitol, Midtown is a growing strip of shops, restaurants and bars that's become the Sacramento hipster crowd's focal point. You'll also find lovely residential neighborhoods and some key cultural and historic sites.

Sutter's Fort State Historic Park

Strangely located amidst a slew of contemporary development, Sutter's Fort State Historic Park (☎ 916-455-4422; cnr 27th & L Sts; admission $1; open 10am-5pm daily), built by John Sutter, was once the only trace of white civilization for hundreds of miles. The fort is restored to its 1850s appearance, complete with original furniture and equipment. It's not a huge thrill, but it does give a comprehensive rundown of the area's European history. About once a month (call for a schedule) staff and volunteers dress in period costume and re-enact village life of the 1850s, adding a festive air to the place.

California State Indian Museum A

necessary antidote to touring Sutter's Fort, is a trip to the adjacent California State Indian Museum (☎ 916-324-0971; 2631 K St; admission $1; open 10am-5pm daily). It's actually more interesting too, as here the gold

rush is not as glorified as everywhere else in Sacramento, but instead explained as an 'invasion' of white settlers who carelessly destroyed native lands, cultures and, yes, people. Exhibits on native lifestyles and handicrafts complement the history displays.

Tower District

The Tower District consists of a small stretch of shops, bars and ethnic restaurants, centered on the landmark **Tower Theatre** (☎ 916-442-4700; cnr 16th St & Broadway), a beautiful 1938 Art Deco movie palace. The nationwide chain **Tower Records** started here and the original sign survives on the theater (the current store, small by today's standards, is across the street). The **Tower Cafe** (1518 Broadway), at the base of the theater, makes for a pleasant respite before or after a film.

Activities

The **American River Parkway**, a 23-mile river system on the north bank of the American River is one of the most extensive riparian habitats in the continental US. The park's network of trails and picnic areas is accessible from Old Sacramento by taking Front St north until it becomes Jiboom St and crosses the river, or by taking the Jiboom St exit off I-5/Hwy 99.

The parkway includes a nice walking/running/bicycling path called the **Jedediah Smith National Recreation Trail** that's accessible from Old Sacramento at the end of J St. Rent bicycles at the waterfront from **Bike Sacramento** (☎ 916-444-0200; cnr Front & J Sts) for $6/20 per hour/day.

Places to Stay

Sacramento's **KOA Campground** (☎ 916-371-6771; fax 916-371-0622; 3951 Lake Rd W; camping $25-36), near the W Capitol Ave exit off I-80, in West Sacramento, has a few grassy tent sites and recreational vehicle (RV) spaces.

Within walking distance of the capitol, Old Sac and the train station, you'll find the **Sacramento HI Hostel** (☎ 916-443-1691; 925 H St; dorm beds $21; office hours 7:30am-9:30am & 5pm-10pm daily). It attracts an international crowd and is a useful place to find rides to San Francisco and Lake Tahoe.

Unless you're paying to stay in a high-class place, the motel options in Sacramento are rather bleak.

SACRAMENTO VALLEY

DOWNTOWN SACRAMENTO

The best thing about the basic **Quality Inn** (☎ 916-444-3980; 818 15th St; singles/doubles $74/84) is its central location a few blocks from the capitol.

Directly across from the Governor's Mansion is the **Clarion** (☎ 916-444-8000; fax 916-442-8129; 700 16th St; rooms from $99); it's a lot more attractive, which is why you'll also pay more. Further motels are found north of here along 16th St, but the area begins to feel pretty shabby.

If you have a car, **Heritage Hotel** (☎ 916-929-7900; 1780 Tribute Rd; rooms from $69), near Cal Expo, is probably the city's finest budget option. It looks like a 1980s college dorm but has clean, quiet and spacious, if rather bland, rooms.

There are more cheap motels in West Sacramento along W Capitol Ave, a part of town that, in all truth, is probably best avoided. If you're stuck, though, try the **Granada Inn** (☎ 916-372-2780; 4751 W Capitol Ave; singles/doubles $49/57), part of a small chain of truckers' motels.

If price isn't a concern, then it's hard to beat the experience of sleeping aboard the **Delta King** (☎ 916-444-5464, 800-825-5464; w www.deltaking.com; 100 Front St; midweek/weekend rooms from $119/169), a paddle wheeler docked in Old Sacramento.

There are a few B&Bs in town, in lovely residential neighborhoods close to Midtown. The 1906 **Hartley House** (☎ 916-447-7829, 800-831-5806; fax 916-447-1820; cnr 22nd & G Sts; rooms from $161) is on a quiet street full of old Victorian houses. Several blocks south is **Amber House** (☎ 916-444-8085, 800-755-6526; fax 916-552-6529; 1315 22nd St; rooms from $169). Rooms are in several nicely renovated buildings, including an 'artist's retreat' and a Mediterranean-style home.

Places to Eat

The tourist joints in Old Sacramento are over-priced and overrated, while Midtown and the Tower District have a growing number of hip, creative and affordable restaurants.

Cafe Bernardo (2726 Capitol Ave; mains from $6) is a Midtown favorite serving practically everything from coffee and pastries to pasta and wine. There's outdoor seating area and an adjacent martini bar that's popular around happy hour.

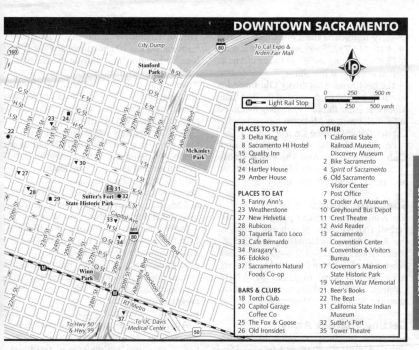

DOWNTOWN SACRAMENTO

M═ Light Rail Stop

PLACES TO STAY	OTHER
3 Delta King	1 California State
8 Sacramento HI Hostel	Railroad Museum;
15 Quality Inn	Discovery Museum
16 Clarion	2 Bike Sacramento
24 Hartley House	4 Spirit of Sacramento
29 Amber House	6 Old Sacramento
	Visitor Center
PLACES TO EAT	7 Post Office
5 Fanny Ann's	9 Crocker Art Museum
23 Weatherstone	10 Greyhound Bus Depot
27 New Helvetia	11 Crest Theatre
28 Rubicon	12 Avid Reader
30 Taqueria Taco Loco	13 Sacramento
33 Cafe Bernardo	Convention Center
34 Paragary's	14 Convention & Visitors
36 Edokko	Bureau
37 Sacramento Natural	17 Governor's Mansion
Foods Co-op	State Historic Park
	19 Vietnam War Memorial
BARS & CLUBS	21 Beer's Books
18 Torch Club	22 The Beat
20 Capitol Garage	31 California State Indian
Coffee Co	Museum
25 The Fox & Goose	32 Sutter's Fort
26 Old Ironsides	35 Tower Theatre

SACRAMENTO VALLEY

Paragary's (cnr 28th & N Sts; dinner mains $12-21), the flagship of local restaurateur Randy Paragary (who also owns Cafe Bernardo), is well loved for its wood-fired pizzas, hand-cut pastas, great wine list and quality meat and fish.

Rubicon (2004 Capitol Ave; sandwiches $6-8) is by far the city's best brewpub for its fresh, well-balanced ales (try the IPA and Hefeweizen) and inviting atmosphere.

You'll find lots of good, affordable ethnic restaurants in the Tower District along Broadway, including **Edokko** (1724 Broadway; meals from $7), a popular Japanese place serving sushi, tempura and lots of rice and noodle dishes.

The best health-food option is the excellent deli at the **Sacramento Natural Foods Co-op** (cnr S St & Alhambra Blvd; lunch $5-7), which even has a small dining area.

On the other end of the spectrum is **Fanny Ann's** (1023 2nd St; food from $5), a kitschy and cluttered old bar that, if you must eat in Old Sacramento, serves a decent burger.

Almost a classic, the **Virgin Sturgeon** (☎ 916-921-2694; 1577 Garden Hwy; dinner $10-20), west of I-5, is in an old barge on the north bank of the Sacramento River dishing up fresh fish and splendid views, the latter the main reason to visit.

For hearty, strong coffee, top choice is **Weatherstone** (812 21st St), which has a lovely patio and great pastries. The outdoor seating and old brick building make **New Helvetia** (1215 19th St) another nice option.

Sacramento gets plenty hot in summer, so cooling off with a refreshing milkshake or ice-cream cone is worth the splurge. Both **Vic's** (3199 Riverside Blvd; shakes $4) and **Gunther's** (2801 Franklin Blvd; shakes $4) are beautiful vintage soda fountains that make their own excellent ice cream. They're both south of Broadway and Hwy 50.

Entertainment

Pick up a copy of the free weekly Sacramento News & Review for a list of current happenings around town or stop by **The Beat** (☎ 916-446-4402; cnr 17th & J Sts), a good new and used record store and ticket venue at the center of Midtown.

The **Tower Theatre** (☎ 916-442-4700; 16th St & Broadway) shows classic, foreign and alternative films as well as some new releases.

Another classic old movie house that's been lovingly restored is the 1949 **Crest Theatre** (☎ 916-442-7378; W www.thecrest.com; 1013 K St), hosting indie and foreign films as well as occasional live music.

The cool, somewhat crusty **Old Ironsides** (cnr 10th & S Sts) hosts some of the best indie bands that come through town. Another good indie-rock venue is Midtown hipster magnet **Capitol Garage Coffee Co** (cnr 15h & L Sts).

For blues bands, check out the **Torch Club** (904 15th St). And **The Fox & Goose** (1001 R St) is a spacious old pub with good beer on tap and more live music.

Spectator Sports

The Kings, Sacramento's professional basketball (NBA) team, play home games at the **Arco Arena** (information ☎ 916-928-6900, tickets ☎ 916-649-8497) from November to May. From May to August, Arco Arena is also home to games by WNBA (Women's National Basketball Association) team the Sacramento Monarchs.

Getting There & Away

The small but busy **Sacramento International Airport** (☎ 916-929-5411), 15mi north of downtown off I-5, is serviced by all major airlines and offers some direct flights to Europe.

Greyhound (☎ 916-444-6858; cnr 7th & L Sts), near the capitol, has numerous daily buses to San Francisco ($13, two hours), Los Angeles ($42, nine hours), Reno ($20, three hours) and Seattle ($68, 17 hours).

From Sacramento's **Amtrak Station** (cnr 4th & I Sts), between downtown and Old Sac, trains leave daily for Seattle ($91, 20 hours), Los Angeles ($51, 15 hours) and Oakland ($17, two hours).

Getting Around

The regional **Yolobus** (☎ 916-371-2877) No 42 costs $1.25 and runs hourly between the airport and downtown (take the clockwise loop) and also reaches West Sacramento, Woodland and Davis. Local **Sacramento Regional Transit** (RT; ☎ 916-321-2877) buses cost $1.50 per ticket or $3.50 for a day pass. RT also runs the **Downtown Area Shuttle (DASH)** trolley between Old Sacramento and downtown, and Sacramento's **light-rail system**, which is mostly used for commuting to outlying communities.

THE SACRAMENTO DELTA

The Sacramento Delta, directly southwest of Sacramento, has 1000mi of waterways. It's a beautiful region that surrounds the place where the Sacramento and San Joaquin Rivers join on their way toward San Francisco Bay. In the 1930s the Bureau of Reclamation issued an aggressive water redirection program – the Central Valley and California State Water Projects – that dammed California's major rivers and directed 75% of their supply through the Central Valley for agricultural use and also for use in Southern California. The siphoning has affected the Sacramento Delta, its wetlands and estuaries, and has been a source of environmental, ecological and political debate ever since.

Before the Shasta, Folsom, Oroville and Friant dams were built, most of this water flowed naturally from the rivers into the Pacific through San Francisco Bay. A natural annual flood cycle purged the delta of impurities that settled and saltwater that encroached during the dry season, and the waterways stayed pretty healthy.

After WWII, agricultural production in the San Joaquin Valley grew enormously, and the use of chemical pesticides and fertilizers became commonplace. Simultaneously, dams appeared on many of the delta's tributaries, stopping the annual floods and redirecting the flow that once took all the harmful buildup out to sea. Soon afterward, the Sacramento River had to be redirected into a peripheral canal to avoid being contaminated by the delta's backflow. Water is let back into the delta from control points along the canal and further redirected to supply 40% of California's drinking water and 45% of its irrigation.

While still a major part of California's political and environmental arena, the delta is also a favorite place for boating, water skiing and duck hunting (the river's woes aren't apparent when you're sitting on the deck of a houseboat drinking margaritas).

Hwy 160, which runs south from Sacramento to Antioch, follows the Sacramento River levee and is the delta's main drag. Along the way you'll encounter lush landscapes and curious towns. **Isleton** has an interesting main street lined with a few shops, restaurants, bars and old buildings, some hinting at the town's Chinese heritage. Isleton's Crawdad Festival, at the end of June, draws people from all over the state.

Locke, the delta's most fascinating town, was built by Chinese farmers after a fire wiped out Walnut Grove's Chinatown in 1912. Tucked below the highway and levee, it feels like a Western ghost town, with dilapidated buildings leaning into each other over the town's single street. Shops and galleries are worn by age and proximity to the water, yet quite picturesque in their decrepitude. Locke's unlikely centerpiece is **Al the Wop's** *(meals $16-20)*, a grungy, memorabilia-filled bar where a rowdy but friendly crowd comes to drink heavily and eat steak dinners ($16-20). Keeping the town's heritage alive is the dusty but worthwhile **Dai Loy Museum** *(☎ 916-776-1661;* **w** *www.locketown.com; admission $1.25; open 11am-4:30pm Thur-Fri, 11am-5pm Sat-Sun)*, an old gambling hall filled with photos and relics. **Rio Vista** has a public beach and boat launch facility. From there, Hwy 12 heads east to I-80.

DAVIS

Davis (population 61,363) is an attractive college town centering on the University of California at Davis (UCD), one of the top schools in the US for agriculture, viticulture and enology and veterinary medicine. The city is a progressive outpost amid the conservative agricultural towns of Sacramento Valley. In addition to a well-educated citizenry, it boasts more bikes per capita than any other town in the US. The student population and year-round community have a mutual respect for each other and together support a vibrant café, pub and arts scene.

Orientation

I-80 skirts the south edge of town, with the Davis/Olive St exit giving the easiest access to downtown, via Richards Blvd and 1st St. UCD lies southwest of downtown, bordered by A St, 1st St and Russell Blvd. The campus' main entrances are from I-80 via Old Davis Rd or from downtown via 3rd St. East of the campus, Hwy 113 heads north 10mi to Woodland, where it intersects with I-5. Another 28mi north it connects with Hwy 99.

Information

The **Davis Conference and Visitor Bureau** *(☎ 530-297-1900;* **w** *www.davisvisitor.com; 130 G St; open 8:30am-4:30pm Mon-Fri)* has free maps and brochures. Another useful website to peruse is **w** www.davis411.com.

For entertainment and event information, check bulletin boards in cafés, bookstores and campus buildings. UCD's campus **information line** *(☎ 530-752-2222)* connects you to any department on campus.

Good bookstores include the **Avid Reader** *(☎ 530-758-4040; 617 2nd St)*, **Bogey's Books** *(☎ 530-757-6127; 223 E St)*, between 2nd and 3rd Sts, and the **UC Davis Bookstore** *(☎ 530-752-6846)* in the student union building.

Things to See & Do

The one-room, nonprofit **Pence Gallery** *(☎ 530-758-3370; 212 D St; open noon-4pm Tues-Sat)* has exhibits of contemporary California art and hosts lectures. It's also one of many galleries in town that participates in the **Art Walkabout**, a free event held evenings on the second Friday of every month. Pick up a list and map at **The Artery** *(☎ 530-758-8330; 207 G St; open 10am-6pm Mon-Sat, 10am-9pm Fri, noon-5pm Sun)*.

Daily **UC Davis campus tours** are free but reservations are required. Contact the **Buehler Alumni & Visitors Center** *(☎ 530-752-8111; cnr Mrak Hall Dr & Old Davis Rd)*. Tours are available in Spanish if you prefer. The visitor center also has campus maps.

For a short hike, a scenic, paved 2mi trail runs through the **UC Davis Arboretum**. And Tuesday evenings the **Equestrian Center** *(☎ 530-752-2372)* offers hour-long trail rides for $23; reservations required.

The **Davis Farmers Market** *(cnr 4th & C Sts)* features food vendors, street performers and live bands from 8am to noon on Saturday, and from 4:30pm to 8:30pm (2pm to 6pm October to March) on Wednesday.

Cycling is popular here, probably because the only hill around is the bridge that crosses over the freeway. A favorite destination is to Lake Berryessa, around 30 miles west. See Getting Around for bike rental information.

Places to Stay & Eat

Like most university towns, Davis' hotel rates are generally stable, except during graduation or special campus events, when they rise high and sell out fast.

University Park Inn *(☎ 530-756-0910, fax 530-758-0978; 1111 Richards Blvd; singles/doubles $75/85)* is clean, standard-issue establishment with a pool on the south side of I-80.

Econo Lodge (*☎ 530-756-1040, 800-424-4777; 221 D St; singles/doubles $59/65*) has rooms that are a little worn but they're still functional.

Aggie Inn (*☎ 530-756-0352, fax 530-753-5738; 245 1st St; rooms from $95*), across from UCD's east entrance, has homey rooms, a Jacuzzi and free coffee and pastries.

Facing the campus, **Davis Bed & Breakfast Inn** (*☎ 530-753-9611, 800-211-4455, fax 530-753-9611; ⓦ www.davisbedandbreakfast.com; 422 A St; rooms from $79*) features an old-fashioned living room, full breakfasts and cozy rooms with private baths.

At nearby **University Inn Bed and Breakfast** (*☎ 530-756-8648, fax 530-756-8016; 340 A St; rooms with/without breakfast from $73/63*) the full breakfast is optional

but all rooms have private baths, phones and cable TV.

Places to Eat

Davis Food Co-op (*cnr 6th & G Sts; open 8am-10pm daily*) has bulk items, local organic produce and a good deli.

Espresso Roma (*231 E St*), between 3rd and 2nd Sts, is a laid-back spot to get your caffeine fix.

Woodstocks (*☎ 530-757-2525; 219 G St; large pizzas around $15*) has Davis' most popular pizza, sold also by the slice ($1.75) for lunch.

Osaka Sushi (*630 G St; sushi $1.50-3.50*) has sushi to rival San Francisco's best, plus excellent sashimi, tempura and teriyaki dinners. It also has a floating sushi bar, where

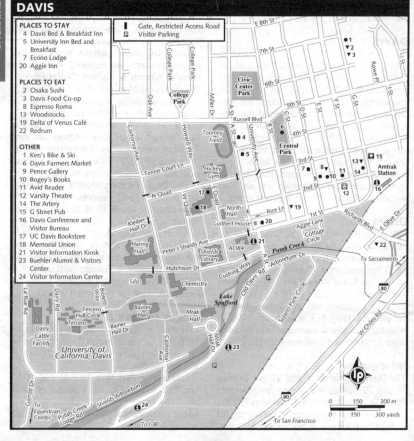

DAVIS

PLACES TO STAY
4 Davis Bed & Breakfast Inn
5 University Inn Bed and Breakfast
7 Econo Lodge
20 Aggie Inn

PLACES TO EAT
2 Osaka Sushi
3 Davis Food Co-op
8 Espresso Roma
13 Woodstocks
19 Delta of Venus Café
22 Redrum

OTHER
1 Ken's Bike & Ski
6 Davis Farmers Market
9 Pence Gallery
10 Bogey's Books
11 Avid Reader
12 Varsity Theatre
14 The Artery
15 G Street Pub
16 Davis Conference and Visitor Bureau
17 UC Davis Bookstore
18 Memorial Union
21 Visitor Information Kiosk
23 Buehler Alumni & Visitors Center
24 Visitor Information Center

Gate, Restricted Access Road
Visitor Parking

you serve yourself from colored plates going around on boats.

Delta of Venus Cafe *(122 B St; meals from $5)* has breakfast items, salads, soups and sandwiches, including some vegetarian and vegan options. It serves beer and wine too.

Near I-80, **Redrum** *(978 Olive Dr; meals from $5)*, formerly known Murder Burger, is popular with students and travelers alike for its fresh, made-to-order beef, turkey and ostrich burgers, thick espresso shakes and excellent curly fries.

Entertainment

Major theater, music, dance and other performances take place at the brand-new **Mondavi Center for the Performing Arts** *(☎ 530-757-3199; w www.mondaviarts.org)* on the UC Davis campus. Further performances, including many UC Davis events, happen at the **Varsity Theatre** *(☎ 530-759-8724; 616 2nd St)*. For tickets and information on shows at either the Varsity or the Mondavi Center, you can also call the **UC Davis Ticket Office** *(☎ 530-752-1915, 866-823-2787)*.

Sudwerk *(2001 2nd St; meals around $10)*, east of downtown, serves excellent craft-brewed German-style lagers along with a German/American menu of bratwurst, steaks, burgers and large salads. The atmosphere's clean and the patio's great on nice days. In winter you can indulge in its strong yet smooth *Doppelbock*.

G Street Pub *(228 G St)* is a bar with pool tables, a pub menu and live bands Thursday to Saturday nights.

After 27 years, well-loved music venue **Palm's Playhouse** *(w www.palmsplayhouse .com)* closed in 2002 to make way for housing development. The good news is that the Palms has reopened in new digs, about 12mi west of Davis, in the town of Winters. Shows now take place in the historic **Winters Opera House** *(☎ 530-795-1825; 13 Main St)*.

Getting There & Away

Across from the student store in UCD's Memorial Union is a ride board where students who need or are willing to give rides (usually to the Bay Area) post notices.

Yolobus *(☎ 530-666-2877)* route No 42 loops between Davis and the Sacramento airport from 5am to 11pm daily and costs $1.25. The route also connects Davis with Woodland and downtown Sacramento.

Davis' **Amtrak station** *(☎ 530-758-4220; 840 2nd St)* is on the southern edge of downtown. Trains serve Sacramento ($6, 30 minutes), Reno ($11, five hours) and Oakland ($15, 1¾ hours) daily.

Getting Around

Nearly every street has a bike lane with its own stoplight. When driving around – especially when pulling out from a parking space – be aware of bike traffic, it's the primary mode of transportation here. **Ken's Bike & Ski** *(☎ 530-758-3223; 650 G St)* rents basic bikes for $10 per day; serious road and mountain bikes cost more.

If you're not biking, student-run **Unitrans** *(☎ 530-752-2877)* shuttles people around town and campus for $0.75. Many buses are red double-deckers. Night service runs to 11:30pm Monday to Thursday only.

OROVILLE

Oroville (population 13,100) is a pleasant town along the Feather River, its small historic district removed from busy Hwy 70 a few miles to the west. At the eastern border of Sacramento Valley, it's a gateway to the gorgeous Feather River Canyon and the rugged northern reaches of the Sierras (see the Northern Mountains chapter). Gold was discovered near here in 1848 by John Bidwell, at a site along the Feather River known as Bidwell Bar (it's now beneath Lake Oroville). The town boomed quickly and was originally called Ophir (Gold) City.

Today the town's about more than just its gold rush past. Oroville was where Ishi, the last surviving member of the local Yahi tribe, was 'found' back in 1911 (see the boxed text 'Ishi' on the following page). It was also home to a Chinese community that at one time numbered over 10,000.

The region is probably best known, though, as a summertime destination, thanks to Lake Oroville, which sits 9mi northeast of town behind Oroville Dam. The surrounding Lake Oroville State Recreation Area attracts boaters, campers, swimmers, bicyclists, backpackers and fishing folk.

Stop at the friendly, helpful **Oroville Area Chamber of Commerce** *(☎ 530-538-2542, 800-655-4653; w www.oroville-city .com/chamber; 1789 Montgomery St; open 9am-4:30pm Mon-Fri)* for information on

Ishi

In the early morning of 29 August, 1911, a frantic barking of dogs woke the butchers sleeping inside a slaughterhouse outside Oroville. When they came out, they found their dogs holding a man at bay – a Native American clad only in a loincloth, who was starving, exhausted, afraid and spoke no English.

They called the sheriff, who took the man to the jail until something could be decided. Newspapers declared a 'wild man' had been discovered, and people thronged in, hoping to see him. Local Indians came and tried to communicate with him in Maidu and Wintu, but to no avail; his language was different from those of the surrounding tribes.

Anthropologists from the University of California, Berkeley, Professors Alfred L Kroeber and Thomas Talbot Waterman, read the accounts in the news. Waterman took the train to Oroville and, using lists of vocabulary words of the Yana Indians who once lived in this region, discovered that the man belonged to the Yahi, the southernmost tribe of the Yana, which was believed to be extinct.

Waterman took 'Ishi,' meaning 'man' in the Yahi language, to the museum at the university, where he was cared for and brought back to health. Ishi spent his remaining years there, telling the anthropologists his life story and teaching them his tribal language, lore and ways.

Ishi's tribe had been virtually exterminated by settlers before Ishi was born. In 1870, when he was a child, there were only about 12 or 15 Yahi left, hiding in remote areas in the foothills east of Red Bluff. Ishi, his mother, sister and an old man were all that were left of the Yahi by 1908. In that year, the others died and Ishi was left alone. On 25 March, 1916, Ishi died of tuberculosis at the university hospital, and the Yahi disappeared forever.

The book *Ishi in Two Worlds: A Biography of the Last Wild Indian in North America*, by Theodora Kroeber, Professor Kroeber's wife, tells Ishi's story. In Oroville, you can drive to the site where he was found (east of town along Oro-Quincy Hwy at Oak Ave), though all that stands is a small monument. Part of the Lassen National Forest in the foothills east of Red Bluff, including Deer Creek and other areas where Ishi and the Yahi lived, is now called the Ishi Wilderness. If you go to Berkeley, you can also see the exhibit on Ishi at the university museum.

local history and outdoor activities. The office of the USFS **Feather River Ranger District** (☎ 530-534-6500; 875 Mitchell Ave; open 8am-4:30pm Mon-Fri) has maps and brochures about the nearby Plumas National Forest. For road conditions phone ☎ 800-427-7623.

Things to See & Do

Downtown are several antique stores and a few historic buildings, most notably the **Chinese Temple** (☎ 530-538-2496; 1500 Broderick St; adult/child $2/free; open noon-4pm Thur-Mon, 1pm-4pm Tues-Wed). The population of Oroville's Chinese community fell to less than 40 in 1970, and the beautifully preserved building, on a quiet street near the river, is a grand tribute to the community's proud past. Built in 1863, it was one of a series of Chinese temples and shrines that spanned from Vancouver to San Diego. It's definitely worth a stop to see the garden, chapels and artifacts.

Between September and November watch chinook salmon jump the fish ladder at the **Feather River Fish Hatchery** (☎ 530-538-2222; 5 Table Mountain Blvd; open sunrise-sunset daily).

From downtown, follow Oroville Dam Rd or Olive Hwy (Hwy 162) to the **Lake Oroville State Recreation Area**, home to numerous outdoor activities and 770ft Oroville Dam. Completed in 1967, it's the tallest earthen dam in the US. The **Lake Oroville State Recreation Area Visitor Center** (☎ 530-538-2219; 917 Kelly Ridge Rd; open 9am-5pm daily) has exhibits on the California State Water Project and local Indian history, plus a viewing tower and loads of recreational information.

The **Freeman Bicycle Trail** is a 41mi off-road loop that takes cyclists to the top of Oroville Dam, then follows the Feather River back to the Thermalito Forebay and Afterbay, storage reservoirs west of Hwy 70. The ride can be broken into segments if desired; while it's mostly flat, the dam ascent is steep. Get a free map of the ride from the chamber of commerce or **Greenline Cycles** (☎ 530-533-7885; 1911 Montgomery St; closed Sun), which also rents bikes for $5/20 per hour/day.

The afterbay also abuts the **Oroville Wildlife Area**, located along the Pacific Flyway and a great place for bird-watching. Serious birders might also head to the **Sacramento National Wildlife Refuge** (☎ 530-934-2801), during winter, where the migratory waterfowl are a spectacular sight. The **visitor center** (open 7:30am-4pm Mon-Fri) is off I-5 near Willows; driving ($3) and walking trails are open daily.

The area surrounding Lake Oroville is full of hiking trails, and a favorite is the 7mi round-trip walk to 640ft **Feather Falls**, which takes about four hours.

Highways 162 and 70 head northeast from Oroville into the mountains and on to Quincy (see the Northern Mountains chapter). Hwy 70 snakes along the magnificent **Feather River Canyon**, an especially captivating drive during the fall.

Places to Stay & Eat

The chamber of commerce, USFS office and the Lake Oroville visitor center have details about campgrounds in the area, including some unusual floating, boat-in campsites. Make reservations by calling ☎ 800-444-7275.

Houseboats and other watercraft can be rented at **Bidwell Canyon Marina** (☎ 530-589-3165, 800-637-1767), on the south end of the lake. Summertime prices start around $1400 for three nights.

Several budget motels are on Feather River Blvd, which runs east of Hwy 70 and south of Montgomery St. The **Sunset Inn** (☎ 530-533-8201, fax 530-533-7515; 1835 Feather River Blvd; singles/doubles $47/55) is simple, clean and decent.

Jean's Riverside B&B (☎ 530-533-1413; W www.oroville-city.com/jeans; 1142 Middlehoff Lane; rooms $85-145) has 10 rooms, some with lovely views and Jacuzzis, along the Feather River west of Hwy 70.

Cornucopia Restaurant & Pie Shop (515 Montgomery St; meals from $6; open 24hr), just off Hwy 70, is a diner-style place serving eggs, sandwiches, burgers and chicken-fried steaks.

Downtown, **The Lunchbox** (1442 Myers St; meals from $5) has fresh-made sandwiches and salads so big you'll be hard-pressed to finish them.

Getting There & Away

Greyhound buses stop at **Tom's Sierra Chevron** (☎ 530-533-1333; cnr 5th Ave & Oro Dam Blvd), a few blocks east of Hwy 70.

CHICO

As a sizable university town, Chico (population 64,581) is a social hub for the region, with good restaurants, coffeehouses, nightclubs, bars and other cultural and entertainment options. It's got something of a party reputation, thanks to CSU's 16,000 students; during summertime, though, Chico heats up in a different way, with temperatures easily surpassing 90°F (32°C). The swimming holes in shady Bidwell Park help take the edge off; and after the air cools at night, downtown takes on an almost idyllic small-town charm.

Chico was founded in 1860 by John Bidwell, who came to California in 1841 and proceeded to make himself one of its most illustrious early pioneers. In the late 1840s, he purchased 40 sq mi here, called the Rancho del Arroyo Chico. In 1868, after a term as a California congressman in Washington, DC, he married Annie Ellicott Kennedy, daughter of a prominent Washington official. They moved to the new mansion he had built, now the Bidwell Mansion State Historic Park. After John died in 1900, Annie continued as a philanthropist there until her death in 1918.

Orientation & Information

Chico is flat and easy to get around. Downtown is west of Hwy 99, most easily reached via Hwy 32 (8th St). Main St and Broadway are the central downtown streets; from there, Park Ave stretches southward and tree-lined The Esplanade heads north.

The **Chico Chamber of Commerce & Visitor Center** (☎ 530-891-5559, 800-852-8570; W www.chicochamber.com; 300 Salem St; open 9am-5pm Mon-Fri, 10am-3pm Sat) shows off the community's spirit and offers more than enough local information.

For more entertainment options, pick up the free weekly *Chico News & Review*.

There's a **post office** (cnr 5th & Broadway Sts) opposite the City Plaza.

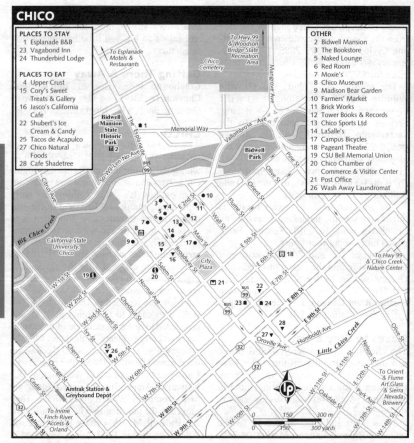

CHICO

PLACES TO STAY
1 Esplanade B&B
23 Vagabond Inn
24 Thunderbird Lodge

PLACES TO EAT
4 Upper Crust
15 Cory's Sweet
    Treats & Gallery
16 Jasco's California
    Cafe
22 Shubert's Ice
    Cream & Candy
25 Tacos de Acapulco
27 Chico Natural
    Foods
28 Cafe Shadetree

OTHER
2 Bidwell Mansion
3 The Bookstore
5 Naked Lounge
6 Red Room
7 Moxie's
8 Chico Museum
9 Madison Bear Garden
10 Farmers' Market
11 Brick Works
12 Tower Books & Records
13 Chico Sports Ltd
14 LaSalle's
17 Campus Bicycles
18 Pageant Theatre
19 CSU Bell Memorial Union
20 Chico Chamber of
   Commerce & Visitor Center
21 Post Office
26 Wash Away Laundromat

The Bookstore *(118 Main St)* has tons of quality used books. Nocturnal hours at **Tower Books & Records** *(211 Main St; open until midnight Sat & Sun)* make browsing a popular nighttime activity in Chico.

Things to See

Chico's most prominent Victorian home and central landmark is **Bidwell Mansion State Historic Park** *(☎ 530-895-6144; 525 The Esplanade)*, built between 1865 and 1868 as the opulent home of Chico's founders John and Annie Bidwell. Tours ($1) are given on the hour between noon and 4pm Wednesday to Sunday. **Chico Museum** *(☎ 530-891-4336; cnr Salem & W 2nd Sts; admission free; open noon-4pm Wed-Sun)*, in the former 1904 Carnegie Library, contains a historical mu-

seum, a re-creation of an old Taoist temple altar (see the boxed text 'Joss Houses') and rotating exhibits.

Ask for a free map of the **Chico State University (CSU)** campus, or inquire about campus events and tours, at the **CSU Information Center** *(☎ 530-898-4636; cnr Chestnut & W 2nd Sts)*, on the main floor of Bell Memorial Union. The attractive campus is infused with sweet floral fragrances in spring, and there's a nice rose garden at its center.

Internationally renowned glass art is made at **Orient & Flume Art Glass** *(☎ 530-893-0373; 2161 Park Ave; showroom open 10am-5pm Mon-Sat)*, a couple of miles south of downtown. Out behind the showroom is a spot where the public can watch the glass being blown; viewing times are

Joss Houses

'Joss,' which in pidgin English means 'deity,' is a corruption of the Portuguese word *deus* (god) – a term used by early navigators to describe idols they found in the East Indies. Joss houses were the principal places of worship for Chinese miners and often the only public symbol of Chinese culture in mining towns.

The exterior of a joss house was usually very simple, while the interior was decorated with rich and symbolic ornamentation. The main images represented were the 'God of Somber Heavens,' 'God of War,' 'God of Medicine' and 'God of Wealth,' combining characteristics of Buddhism, Taoism and Confucianism. Men came to the joss house to ask special favors of a god, or to offer prayers and supplication.

The rituals required in order to 'talk' with a god were very formal. A man entered the joss house, bowed with clasped hands, lit the appropriate candles and incense, knelt on a mat and called the god by name three times. He then took two semi-oval blocks of wood called 'Yum Yeung Puey' and tossed them into the air. If both blocks landed in the same position it was an unfavorable omen. If one block faced up and the other faced down, it meant that the god had to be persuaded.

The worshipper then knocked his head on the ground three times, offered his petition and then shook a cylindrical pot of numbered bamboo slips until one of the slips fell out. The priest or joss-house keeper checked the number before looking up the omen in an ancient text. The priest then beat drums and rang the joss-house bells while the worshipper burned paper money as final payment. At last, the fortune was told.

A few joss houses still survive in California. The Chinese Temple in Oroville is open for tours daily. The Bok Kai Temple in Marysville is open only once a year, during the Bok Kai Festival. The Nevada County Historical Society Museum (see the Gold Country chapter) has a reconstructed altar from an 1860s joss house and an extensive collection of related Chinese relics. In Chico, the Chico Museum holds an impressive re-creation of an old Taoist temple altar. In Weaverville, the Joss House State Historic Park holds an ornate altar, sent from China, that's more than 3000 years old (see the Northern Mountains chapter).

from around 9am until about 12:30pm Monday to Thursday.

One of the best-known, and finest, craft breweries in the country (too big to officially qualify as a 'microbrewery') is **Sierra Nevada Brewery** (☎ 530-893-3520; 1075 E 20th St), which makes many excellent brews, most notably Sierra Nevada Pale Ale. Free tours are given at 2:30pm daily, and continuously from noon to 3pm Saturday. There's also a pub and restaurant (see Places to Eat).

The historic 1894 **Honey Run Covered Bridge** is the only covered bridge in California whose roof consists of three separate sections. Take the Skyway exit off Hwy 99 on the southern outskirts of Chico, head east about a mile, turn left onto Honey Run-Humbug Rd; the bridge is 5mi along, in a small park.

Activities

Starting right downtown, 3670-acre **Bidwell Park**, the nation's third-largest municipal park, stretches 10mi northwest along Chico Creek. Several classic movies have been shot here, including *The Adventures of Robin Hood* and parts of *Gone with the Wind*.

In the park, the **Chico Creek Nature Center** (☎ 530-891-4671; suggested donation $1; open 11am-4pm Tues-Sun) has a living animal museum. The park is full of hiking and mountain biking trails and swimming spots. You'll find pools at One-Mile and Five-Mile recreation areas and swimming holes in Upper Bidwell Park, north of Manzanita Ave, including Bear Hole, Salmon Hole and Brown Hole; expect some skinny-dipping.

In summer **tubing** on the Sacramento River is popular; inner tubes can be rented at places along Nord Ave (Hwy 32). Tubers enter at the Irvine Finch Launch Ramp, on Hwy 32, a few miles west of Chico, and come out at the Washout off River Rd.

CSU Adventure Outings (☎ 530-898-4011) organizes a wide variety of fun adventure outings, which are open to students and nonstudents alike.

Special Events

Chico's chock-full of community spirit and pride, which surfaces most visibly during the numerous family-friendly outdoor events held each summer. The **Thursday**

Night Market takes over several blocks of Broadway every Thursday evening from April to September. At City Plaza you'll find free **Friday Night Concerts** starting in May. **Shakespeare in the Park** (☎ 530-891-1382), at Cedar Grove in lower Bidwell Park, runs from mid-July to the end of August.

Places to Stay

For a pleasant campground with 46 tent and RV sites on a riverbank, head to **Woodson Bridge State Recreation Area** (☎ 530-839-2112, 800-444-7275; camping $12). It's about 25mi north on Hwy 99, then west toward Corning.

There are also campgrounds in nearby **Lassen National Forest** (☎ 530-257-2151), northeast of Chico along Hwy 32.

The biggest collection of budget motels is found along The Esplanade north of downtown. You can also look beside Hwy 99 at the Cohasset Rd exit. Since this is a campus town, graduation and homecoming ceremonies (in May and October respectively) can fill up hotels and raise the price.

Matador Motel (☎ 530-342-7543; 1934 The Esplanade; singles/doubles $46/50) is a pleasant courtyard motel not far from downtown. The rooms are simple but still have some old-fashioned character.

Further north you can also try the no-frills **Town House Motel** (☎ 530-343-1621; 2231 The Esplanade; singles/doubles $42/55) and the **Safari Garden Motel** (☎ 530-343-3201; 2352 The Esplanade; singles/doubles $45/55), which, tucked back in the trees, is quiet and secure.

If you want a budget choice that's smack in the middle of downtown, the **Vagabond Inn** (☎ 530-895-1323; 630 Main St; singles/doubles $45/55) and the nearby **Thunderbird Lodge** (☎ 530-343-7911; 715 Main St; singles/doubles from $40/55) are a little grungy but still acceptable.

Esplanade B&B (☎ 530-345-8084; 620 The Esplanade; rooms $75-95), opposite the Bidwell Mansion, is the closest B&B to downtown.

Tucked in a nearby residential neighborhood is **The Grateful Bed** (☎ 530-342-2464; 1462 Arcadian Ave; rooms from $85); despite the unfortunate name it's a lovely stately 1905 Victorian home.

About a mile west of downtown you'll find **Johnson's Country Inn** (☎ 530-345-7829;

3935 Morehead Ave; rooms $80-125) in an attractive almond orchard.

East of Hwy 99 is **Music Express Inn** (☎ 530-891-9833, fax 530-893-5321; 1091 El Monte Ave; rooms $61-125), which is directly off Hwy 32.

Places to Eat

An outdoor **farmers market** is held in the city parking lot at the corner of Wall and E 2nd Sts. It's open from 7:30am to 1pm Saturday year-round.

Chico Natural Foods (818 Main St) is one of several natural food supermarkets.

Sierra Nevada Taproom & Restaurant (☎ 530-345-2739; 1075 E 20th St; meals $8-15), at the Sierra Nevada Brewery, has decent pub food and fresh, superb ales and lagers on tap, some not available anywhere else.

Tacos de Acapulco (429 Ivy St; meals under $5) is your best bulk-up budget option; its burritos are huge, pretty good and plenty popular with students.

Cory's Sweet Treats & Gallery (230 W 3rd St; $7 and up) isn't a candy shop but a friendly, spacious restaurant with a grown-up atmosphere, art on the walls and satisfying meals. The huge breakfast menu is a worthwhile splurge.

A safe bet for a simple, sit-down meal is **Jasco's California Cafe** (cnr Broadway & W 3rd St; meals from $8), upstairs in the Phoenix Building.

Vegetarians and their friends will dig **Cafe Shadetree** (817 Main St; mains $6-10) for its friendly, relaxed atmosphere and entirely meatless menu (with some vegan entries) that includes tamales, sandwiches and stir-fry dishes. The weekends also bring live bluegrass, jazz and acoustic music.

Just north of downtown is the swanky **Red Tavern** (☎ 530-894-3463; 1250 The Esplanade; dinner mains from $15), one of Chico's pricier places, serving inventive meat and fish dishes to an urban, upscale crowd.

For coffee and excellent baked goods check out **Upper Crust** (130 Main St; meals $3-6), which also serves lunch Monday to Saturday.

Shubert's Ice Cream & Candy (178 E 7th St) is a beloved Chico landmark; they've made delicious homemade ice cream and chocolates for more than 60 years.

Entertainment

Red Room *(126 2nd St)* is a small bar that's red all over but thankfully lacking in attitude. The local beer on tap is as cool and tasty as the music they choose to play.

Next door, the **Naked Lounge** *(118 2nd St)* is where hipsters hang out who prefer a laid-back coffeehouse atmosphere.

Another attractive coffeehouse is **Moxie's** *(128 Broadway)*, which has jazz, acoustic and other low-key sounds several nights a week.

A classic, spacious student hangout is the venerable **Madison Bear Garden** *(316 W 2nd St)*, a funky saloon and burger bar in an interesting old building at the corner of Salem St.

LaSalle's *(☎ 530-893-1891; 229 Broadway)* and the **Brick Works** *(☎ 530-895-7700; cnr Wall & E 2nd Sts)* are open nightly for hip-hop, Top 40 and retro dance nights and live bands from reggae to hard rock.

The **Pageant Theatre** *(☎ 530-343-0663; 351 E 6th St)* screens international and alternative films; Monday is bargain night, with all seats just $2.50.

For theater, films, concerts, art exhibits and other cultural events at the CSU campus, contact the **CSU Box Office** *(☎ 530-898-6333)* or the **CSU Information Center** *(☎ 530-898-4636)* in the Bell Memorial Union.

Getting There & Around

The Chico airport is small and flights are expensive; if you must fly, head to Sacramento instead.

Greyhound *(☎ 530-343-8266)* buses stop at the **Amtrak station** *(cnr W 5th & Orange Sts)*. The train station is unattended; purchase tickets in advance from travel agents.

Butte County Transit *(BCT; ☎ 530-342-0221, 800-822-8145; 70¢)* has buses to Paradise, Oroville and Gridley, while **Chico Area Transit** *(CATS)* serves the local area for $0.75.

Notices from people offering or seeking shared rides are posted on the **ride board** in CSU's Bell Memorial Union. It's on the main floor, just to the right of the bookstore.

Bicycles can be rented from **Campus Bicycles** *(☎ 530-345-2081; 330 Main St)* where mountain bikes cost $35/20 for a full/half day or from **Chico Sports Ltd** *(☎ 530-894-1110; 240 Main St)* where the rates are from $5/15 per hour/day.

RED BLUFF

From I-5, Red Bluff (population 13,147) looks like a sleepy cowtown populated by ranchers and farmers and used by RV drivers as a refueling stop. But beneath its surface of mediocrity, the town has a subtle, surprisingly pleasant appeal.

Red Bluff sprouted from a simple town site laid out by Peter Lassen in 1847 and grew into an important navigational center on the Sacramento River. The town now boasts pleasant tree-lined neighborhoods full of restored 19th-century Victorian mansions, and a business district lined with old storefronts. Cowboy culture is strong here; catch it in action the third weekend of April at the **Red Bluff Round-Up** *(☎ 530-527-1000; w www.redbluffroundup.com)*, a major rodeo event dating back to 1921. It's held east of downtown at the Tehama District Fairgrounds.

The town itself is fairly flat, though nearby mountain peaks (including the Trinity Alps to the northwest and snow-topped Mt Lassen to the east) edge into the sky from almost every direction, adding a comforting beauty and making the little town all the more attractive. It's hot as all get-out come summertime, but it's not hard to find relief in shaded river-side picnic spots and ample water recreation opportunities.

Orientation & Information

Downtown Red Bluff is on the west bank of the Sacramento River, just to the west of I-5. The town's main intersection is at Antelope Blvd and Main St. The historic Victorian neighborhood is in the blocks west of Main St.

Historically, Hwy 99 divided into east and west segments at Red Bluff on its way south to Sacramento. The current, modern Hwy 99 is reached by taking Antelope Blvd east from downtown. Heading south from downtown, however, Main St becomes a narrow, scenic stretch of historic Hwy 99W, which parallels I-5 and leads to the farm towns of Corning, Orland and Willows.

Restaurants and antique stores line busy Main St. A few blocks south of downtown is the small **Red Bluff-Tehama County Chamber of Commerce** *(☎ 530-527-6220, 800-655-6225; 100 Main St; open 8:30am-4pm Mon, 8.30am-5pm Tues-Thur, 8.30am-4:30pm Fri)*.

SACRAMENTO VALLEY

Things to See & Do

The chamber of commerce offers free maps and brochures on Red Bluff's many Victorian homes. Top of the heap is the **Kelly-Griggs House Museum** (☎ 530-527-1129; 311 Washington St; admission by donation; open 1pm-4pm Thur-Sun), a classical Victorian home with period exhibits.

Set on a beautiful, shaded piece of land overlooking a languorous section of the Sacramento River, the **William B Ide Adobe State Historic Park** (☎ 530-529-8599; 21659 Adobe Rd) preserves the original adobe home and grounds of pioneer William B Ide, who 'fought' in the 1846 Bear Flag Revolt at Sonoma (see Facts about California) and was named president of the short-lived California Republic. To get to the park, head about a mile north on Main St, turn east onto Adobe Rd and go another mile, following the signs.

The **Red Bluff Lake Recreation Area**, on the east bank of the Sacramento River, is a spacious park full of trees, birds and meadows, and it offers numerous picnicking, swimming, hiking and camping opportunities. It has interpretive trails, bicycle paths, boat ramps, a wildlife viewing area with excellent birding, a fish ladder (in operation May to September) and a two-acre native and drought-tolerant plant garden. The visitor center, called the **Sacramento River Discovery Center** (☎ 530-527-1196; open 11am-4pm Tues-Sun) has kid-friendly displays about the river, questionable propaganda on the benefits of cattle grazing and information on the Diversion Dam just outside its doors. From mid-May to mid-September, the dam diverts water to irrigation canals and in the process creates Red Bluff Lake, a popular swimmers' destination.

Places to Stay & Eat

Sycamore Grove Camping Area (☎ 530-824-5196; camping $10), beside the river in the Red Bluff Lake Recreation Area, is a quiet, attractive USFS campground. Campsites are on a first-come, first-served basis. It also has a large group campground, Camp Discovery,

where cabins are available and reservations are required.

Motels are found beside I-5 and south of town along Main St.

Cinderella Motel (☎ 530-527-5490; cnr Rio St & Antelope Blvd; singles/doubles from $45/50), on the west side of the Sacramento River, is attractive and has a pool and some rooms with riverfront views. Across the river is the **Travel Lodge** (☎ 530-527-6020; 38 Antelope Blvd; singles/doubles $59/65).

Slightly south of downtown, the **Lamplighter Lodge** (☎ 530-527-1150; 210 S Main St; singles/doubles $44/46) is one of several no-frills choices.

A few Victorian homes east of the business district have been turned into B&Bs, including the massive 1881 **Jeter Victorian Inn** (☎ 530-527-7574; 1107 Jefferson St; rooms $65-140), which has five rooms and a separate cottage, and the **Faulkner House** (☎ 530-529-0520, 800-549-6171; 1029 Jefferson St; rooms $75-100).

Green Barn (cnr Antelope Blvd & Chestnut Ave; dinner mains from $9) is a long-established family restaurant serving American fare for lunch and dinner.

Downtown, the dark and moody **Palomino Room** (723 Main St; beef plates from $8), on the site of the historic Tremont Hotel, has tasty steaks and burgers and a cool cowboy ambience. A couple of blocks north is the equally intriguing **Peking Restaurant** (860 Main St; meals from $5), offering lots of typical, affordable and good Chinese dishes.

A bit pricier is **Raging Fork Riverfront Grille** (500 Riverside Way; mains $12-20), just south of Antelope Blvd and one block east of Main St. It has a beautiful dining room, bar and deck overlooking the river.

If the heat is raging, grab a root-beer float from **Hal's Eat 'Em Up** (158 Main St), a drive-in just south of downtown.

Getting There & Away

The **Greyhound station** (☎ 530-527-0434; 22825 Antelope Blvd) is east of town at the corner of Hwy 36 E.

Gold Country

California's 'Gold Country,' also known as the 'Mother Lode,' extends 300mi along Hwy 49 (named in reference to the year the big rush to this area occurred) through the western Sierra Nevada foothills. Besides beautiful scenery and an abundance of opportunities for outdoor recreation, the area has a wealth of restored mining towns and an up-and-coming wine industry that people liken to the Napa Valley of 30 years ago.

Most places to stay and eat – especially in well-preserved towns such as Nevada City and Sutter Creek – are on the expensive side since they cater to (or are owned by) escapees from the San Francisco or Sacramento area who are used to more than pre-ground coffee and doughnuts. Cheaper motel accommodations are found in service towns such as Auburn, Jackson and Grass Valley.

The main routes from the Bay Area to Hwy 49 are the I-80 and US-50. For a quick glance of what the Gold Country has to offer, visit Auburn, Placerville or even Nevada City, which are close (relatively close in the case of Nevada City) to these routes. If you have more time, drive south of Placerville and explore the area around Murphys and Angels Camp. For camping and recreational opportunities, the North Yuba River can't be beat. Sonora is a good stop for people traveling to or from Yosemite National Park (see the Sierra Nevada chapter).

Snow is common from December to February, but doesn't usually close roads within towns. The I-80 and US-50 are open year-round, but most other roads that go from Hwy 49 into and across the Sierra are closed from around mid-November to mid-May. Unfortunately, it's virtually impossible to travel the region without a car: Nevada City, Grass Valley, Auburn and Placerville are the only places served by public transportation.

History

California's gold rush started in 1848 when James Marshall was inspecting the lumber mill he was building for John Sutter near present-day Coloma. He saw a fleck of gold in the mill's tailrace water and pulled out a gold nugget 'roughly half the size of a pea.' Marshall consulted Sutter, who tested the gold by methods described in an encyclopedia,

Highlights

- Amador County vineyards – Napa Valley wishes it looked so good
- Calaveras Big Trees State Park – the trees are big, the crowds are not
- Downtown Murphys – the definition of charming
- Empire Mine State Historic Park – equipment, buildings and a mine owner's home

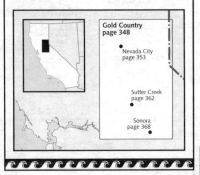

Gold Country
page 348

Nevada City
page 353

Sutter Creek
page 362

Sonora
page 368

and the two men found the piece to be of high quality. Sutter, however, wanted to finish his mill and thus made an agreement with his laborers that they could keep all the gold they found in their spare time if they kept working. Before long, word of the find leaked out.

Sam Brannan, for example, went to investigate the rumors just a few months after Marshall found his nugget. He went to Coloma (the little town by Sutter's Mill – see later in this chapter) to investigate. After finding 6oz of gold in one afternoon, he returned to San Francisco and paraded through the streets, gold dust in hand, proclaiming, 'There's gold in the Sierra foothills!' Convinced that there was money to be made, he bought every piece of mining equipment in the area – from handkerchiefs to shovels. When gold seekers needed equipment for their adventure, Brannan sold them goods at a 100% markup and was a rich man by the time the first folks hit the foothills. (See the boxed text 'Sam Brannan' in the Wine Country chapter for what happened after that.)

By the time construction of the mill was finished, in the spring of 1848, gold seekers

GOLD COUNTRY

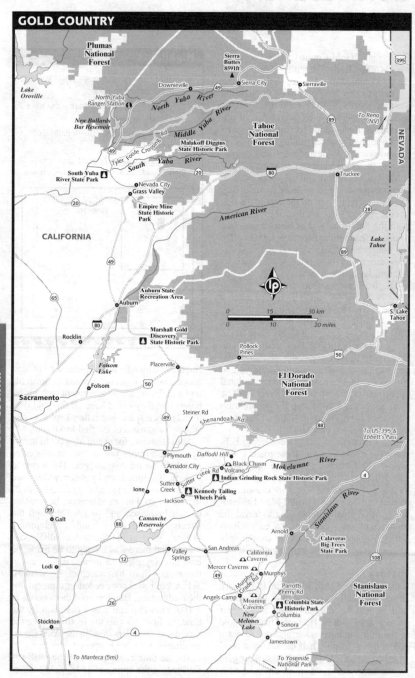

GOLD COUNTRY

had begun to arrive. The first wave came from San Francisco. The new miners found gold so easily that they thought nothing of spending (or gambling away) all they had in one night, knowing that they could find just as much again the next day. They spread the word boastfully, thinking there was plenty of gold for all. By the end of 1848, San Francisco was nearly depleted of able-bodied men, while towns near the 'diggins' – as the mines were called – swelled with thousands of people. News spread to Oregon, the East Coast and South America, and by 1849, more than 60,000 people migrated to California to find the mother lode – the big deposit that miners believed was the source of all the gold found in the streams and riverbeds. (Since then, geologists have discovered that the kind of mother lode that miners dreamed of does not and cannot exist.)

Most prospectors didn't stick around after the initial diggings petered out. In 1859 when the Comstock Lode was found on the eastern side of the Sierra in Virginia City, Nevada, many left. Those who did stay signed on with large operations, such as the Empire Mine in Grass Valley, which were financed by businesses or private fortunes. Gold-extraction processes became increasingly complex and invasive, culminating in the practice of hydraulic mining, by which miners drained lakes and rivers to power their water cannons and blast away entire hillsides (see the boxed text 'Getting the Gold' over the page). After

various environmental and agricultural battles ensued at Malakoff Diggins (see Malakoff Diggins State Historic Park later in this chapter), operators found the price of extraction too great to justify staying in business.

Currently, specimen gold – gold that is still attached to a piece of quartz, making it ideal for museum display – fetches higher prices than gold ore. The largest piece ever found is owned by Kautz-Ironstone Vineyards in Murphys (see Things to See & Do in the Murphys section). Several large-scale, open-pit mines, primarily owned by out-of-state corporations, still exist. Locals will tell you (though guardedly) that there's still plenty of gold in the hills – most easily found in rivers and streams after a heavy rain.

NORTH YUBA RIVER

The northernmost segment of Hwy 49 follows the North Yuba River through some remote, stunning parts of the Sierra Nevada. There are many trails (including part of the Pacific Crest Trail) for hikers, mountain bikers and skiers. The best source of trail and camping information is the **North Yuba Ranger Station** (☎ 530-288-3231; 15924 Hwy 49; open 9am-4:30pm Mon-Sat, closed Sat winter), in Camptonville.

Sierra City

Sierra City (population 282; elevation 4187ft) is the primary supply station for people headed to the **Sierra Buttes**, probably

Gold prospectors poured into California's Gold Country after gold was first discovered in 1848 in the Sierra foothills near present-day Coloma

Getting the Gold

There are essentially two types of gold in the California hills: lode and placer. Lode is the most difficult and costly to reach because it's buried deep within the earth's rock-hard bowels. First a tunnel is blasted, either vertically or horizontally, then an elevator shaft or railroad is built to carry miners in and gold out. The rock – called ore – containing the gold is then crushed to bits in a stamp mill and washed through a sluice box. Gold is heavier than dirt and debris, so it settles into the riffles of a sluice box as water washes away everything else.

Until it was banned in 1884 (see the section on Malakoff Diggins State Historic Park later in this chapter), hydraulic mining was also used to mine lodes. In that process, water cannons blasted entire hillsides away and miners sluiced the debris that came washing down.

Mining placer gold uses the same principles but is easier because Mother Nature has done all of the work already, bringing the gold to the surface through erosion and weathering. A miner simply dips the pan into a streambed that contains gold, swirls it around and lets the sand and dirt wash away. If there's gold at the bottom of the pan, then the miner is a lucky one!

the closest thing to the Alps you'll find in California without hoisting a backpack. There's a vast network of trails here, ideal for backpacking as well as casual hikes. Get the *Lakes Basin, Downieville – Sierra City* map ($1.50) from the **Sierra Country Store** (☎ 530-862-1181; Hwy 49; open 10am-6pm Mon-Sat, 9am-7pm Sun summer; 10am-3pm Sun rest of year).

To get into the Buttes, and the many lakes and streams nearby, take Gold Lake Hwy north from Hwy 49 at Bassetts, 9mi northeast of Sierra City. There are signs indicating numerous campgrounds and hiking trails in the area. Recommended for camping are USFS campgrounds **Salmon Creek**, 2mi north of Bassets, and **Snag Lake**, 5mi north of Bassets, both on Gold Lake Hwy. Each has vault toilets, running water and first-come, first-serve sites ($13). An excellent hiking trail leads 1.5mi to **Haskell Peak** (8107ft) where you

can see from the Sierra Buttes to Mt Shasta and beyond. To reach the trailhead, turn right from Gold Lake Hwy at the sign to Haskell Peak Rd (Forest Rd 9) and follow it 8½mi to the trailhead.

Places to Stay Going east from Sierra City along Hwy 49 are **USFS campgrounds** (sites $13): called Wild Plum, Sierra, Chapman and Yuba Pass. They have vault toilets and running water (Sierra has river water only, purify before drinking) and first-come, first-serve sites. Locals concur that Wild Plum (47 sites) is the most scenic.

Buttes Resort (☎ 530-862-1170, 800-991-1170; Hwy 49; cabins from $75), in the heart of Sierra City, occupies a lovely spot overlooking the river. Most cabins have a private deck and barbecue and some have full kitchens.

Old Sierra City Hotel (☎ 530-862-1300; 212 Main St; rooms $70) was built in 1862 and remodeled in 2001. Each of the four rooms has a private bath and nice trimmings, but no phone or TV.

Yuba River Inn (☎ 530-862-1122; W www.yubariverinn.com; Hwy 49; cabins $50-140), a half mile north of town, has a variety of cabins on the river. Reservations should be made far in advance.

Downieville

This charming little gold rush town (population 347; elevation 2899ft) once had a population of 5000 and was known for being rough – its first justice of the peace was also the local saloon keeper, and the first woman to hang in the Mother Lode did so from Downieville's gallows. Nowadays the town is known as a launch pad for climbers, hikers and mountain bikers. The Downieville Downhill, a mountain-bike course that descends 5000 vertical feet in 12.4mi is consistently rated among the best downhill routes in the USA by bicycle magazines.

For groceries, maps and the local scoop, stop in at **Downieville Grocery** (☎ 530-289-3596; open 7:30am-7:30pm daily, 7:30am-9pm Sun-Thur summer, 7:30am-10pm Fri-Sat). **Downieville Outfitters** (☎ 530-289-0155; W www.downievilleoutfitters.com), in the heart of Downieville, spends all summer renting bikes ($40 to $100 per day), shuttling people to different trails ($15 to $20), taking people on guided rides ($30/45 half/full day) and making bike repairs.

Favorite hikes in the area include the Chimney Rock Trail and Empire Creek Trail. Both are a bit tricky to reach, so pick up a map or trail guide at the North Yuba Ranger Station or the USFS Headquarters in Nevada City.

Places to Stay West of Downieville, Hwy 49 passes numerous campgrounds and trailheads in the Tahoe National Forest. **Carlton Flat, Fiddle Creek, Indian Valley, Rocky Rest** and **Ramshorn** campgrounds all have vault toilets, running water and first-come, first-served sites ($13) along the Yuba River.

Sierra Shangri-La (☎ 530-289-3455; midweek/weekend rooms $85/100, cabins $110-150), 3mi east of Downieville on Hwy 49, serves families that return year after year. In July and August the cabins are usually booked with standing reservations, but rooms – each with a balcony overlooking the river and breakfast brought to the door – are available.

Downtown Downieville has some great places to stay.

Riverside Inn (☎ 530-289-1000; 206 Commercial St; midweek/weekend rooms from $62/70) has rooms with balconies overlooking the river and offers a light breakfast in the morning. There's a TV and bathroom, but no phone, in the rooms and a screen door lets you keep the main door open and listen to the river run by.

Downieville Motor Inn (☎ 530-289-3243; 111 Main St; rooms $59-79) has kitchenettes in most rooms, along with a TV, phone and bathroom. Staff operate a shuttle for mountain bikers for $10 and are helpful in suggesting places to ride.

Carriage House Inn (☎ 530-289-3573; w www.downievillecarriagehouse.com; 110 Commercial St; midweek/weekend rooms from $50/70) has rooms with country-style charm and all the amenities.

SOUTH YUBA RIVER STATE PARK

The California State Park System owns 2000 acres of land along the South Yuba River and leases another 5000 acres from the Bureau of Land Management (BLM). Through the South Yuba River Project, the system hopes to acquire even more river access and connect Malakoff Diggins and South Yuba River state parks with hiking trails. Some of these trails are already in place, including the **Independence Trail**, which starts from the south side of the South Yuba River bridge on Hwy 49 and goes for about a mile.

The longest single-span wood-truss covered bridge in the US, all 251ft of it, crosses the South Yuba River at Bridgeport (not to be confused with an Eastern Sierra town with the same name – see the Sierra Nevada chapter). The bridge – built for private commercial use in 1862 – is indeed interesting, but probably not worth the curvy, 7mi drive (westward off of Hwy 49 on Pleasant Valley Rd). The park does offer gold panning in summer and fall, as well as year-round bird walks on the last Sunday of each month. The hiking and swimming are definitely well worth the trip and can be enjoyed for at least half a day. The Buttermilk Bend trail skirts the South Yuba for 1.4mi, offering river access and wonderful wildflower viewing around April. There's also a 1mi trail to Englebright Reservoir, which has placid waters and several undeveloped campsites.

Maps and information are available from the **state park headquarters** (☎ 530-432-2546) in Bridgeport, or from the Tahoe National Forest USFS Headquarters in Nevada City (see the Nevada City section).

MALAKOFF DIGGINS STATE HISTORIC PARK

Malakoff Diggins, with its restored town site, interesting museum, red stratified cliffs and gigantic mounds of tailings left behind by years of hydraulic mining, is worth a full day's exploration.

The world's first water cannons – designed specifically for hydraulic mining – cut a 200ft canyon through ancient bedrock during the 1850s to unearth rich veins of gold. Rubble washed down from the hillsides, and the tailings dropped back into the Yuba River. This eventually created a problem when the waste reached the flat Sacramento Valley floor: by the 1860s, 20ft mud glaciers blocked the rivers and caused severe flooding each spring during the Sierra snowmelt. After a year of heated courtroom (and barroom) debate between farmers and miners, most hydraulic mining practices were prohibited. North Bloomfield, the small mining community at the center of Malakoff's operation, went bankrupt and fell dormant.

The **Malakoff Diggins State Historic Park Headquarters and Museum** (☎ 530-265-2740; admission per vehicle $5) shows an interesting movie and sells literature and maps. Most of North Bloomfield's structures have been restored to their original condition and now house a few operating stores.

The park has primitive campsites, three developed campgrounds with $14 sites (☎ 800-444-7275 for reservations) and four rental cabins (converted old miners' cabins), plus many picnic areas and a network of hiking trails. There are no RV hookups.

The turnoff for the park, Tyler Foote Crossing Rd, is 11mi north of Nevada City on Hwy 49 and goes northeast for 17mi to the park entrance. The road crosses a 5000ft pass and hits washboard gravel just before the park entrance; a 4WD vehicle is often necessary during winter. Call the park headquarters for road information.

Three miles down Tyler Foote Crossing Rd you'll find **Mother Truckers**, where local folks (of the alternative living persuasion) buy organic groceries and catch up on all the local news.

NEVADA CITY

Nevada City (population 2880; elevation 2525ft) can probably trace its liberal roots to Aaron Sargent, a transplanted New England journalist who helped organize the Republican Party in California and later served in Congress and the Senate. Local history has it that he authored the 19th Amendment (with input from his friend Susan B Anthony, pioneer crusader for women's rights). He introduced a railroad bill in Congress that was signed into law by Abraham Lincoln and led to the construction of the transcontinental railroad. Thanks to the hippies (who arrived in the 1970s) and folks from Los Angeles and the Bay Area (who are still arriving), the town still seems progressive. The arts are a big part of life here – there are three theater companies, two alternative film houses and live music performances almost every night. The downtown area is well preserved and has a quaint feel that makes it one of the best places in the Gold Country to spend a few days. It's an ideal base from which to explore the Yuba River and mining sites near Grass Valley which lies just 5mi south.

Nevada City's streets, often crammed with pedestrians and horse-drawn carriages, are best navigated on foot. Broad St is the main thoroughfare, reached by the Broad St exit off Hwy 49/20. In December the whole town gets decked out in Christmas garb and there are special events every weekend.

Information

Nevada City's **chamber of commerce and Downtown Association** (☎ 530-265-2692, 800-655-6569; 132 Main St), has an immaculate public toilet and many brochures on recreation, lodging, restaurants and entertainment. It's in Ott's Assay Office, where James J Ott assayed the first ore samples from Nevada's Comstock Lode.

The **Tahoe National Forest USFS Headquarters** (☎ 530-265-4531; Hwy 49, open 8am-4:30pm Mon-Sat), at the north end of Coyote St, is a useful resource for trail and campground information from here to Lake Tahoe. A topographical map of Tahoe National Forest is posted in front of the office.

Broad St Books (☎ 530-265-4204; 426 Broad St) has maps and travel guides, history books, bestsellers and a café in which to read them.

Things to See & Do

Housed in Nevada City's original firehouse, the **Nevada County Historical Society Museum** (☎ 530-265-5468; 214 Main St; admission by donation; open 11am-4pm daily Apr-Oct) has an extensive Chinese collection, including the entire altar of an 1862 Joss House (see the boxed text 'Joss Houses' in the Sacramento Valley chapter). It also has a haunted photograph that supposedly houses a living spirit, and attracts parapsychologists by the busload.

Built in 1856, Nevada City's foundry produced the first Pelton waterwheel, which revolutionized hydraulic mining. After WWII, the foundry made Health Master juicers, which became popular with health gurus. Now it's the **Miners Foundry Cultural Center** (☎ 530-265-5040; 325 Spring St), one block off Broad St, and is used for performance art and private parties. You can view the foundry's original equipment on a self-guided tour, which starts at the foundry's entrance. In May the center hosts a jazz jubilee that attracts musicians from around the USA.

The **Nevada City Winery** (☎ 530-265-9463; 321 Spring St; tasting room open

Majestic Mt Shasta, 'Lonely as God, white as a winter moon'

Mammoth Mountain and the Mammoth Basin, a great area for hikers, bikers and skiers

The golden rotunda of the capitol, Sacramento

The State Capitol in Sacramento at night

Fruit boxes in Sacramento's Capitol Museum

Locomotives are the main attraction at the California State Railroad Museum in Old Sacramento

11am-5pm Mon-Sat, noon-5pm Sun) makes award-winning wine (notably syrah and zinfandel) which you can taste for free in its lovely tasting room cum gift shop. Be sure and taste its signature Rough & Ready blend which changes from year to year.

Places to Stay & Eat

Weekend prices are around $10 higher than the weekday prices listed here.

Outside Inn *(☎ 530-265-2233, fax 265-2236; w www.outsideinn.com; 575 E Broad St; rooms $65-105, cabin/cottage $120/140)* is an exceptionally friendly and fun motel, with colorful rooms and a staff that loves the outdoors. Some rooms have a patio overlooking a small creek. It's a 10-minute walk from downtown.

Northern Queen Inn *(☎ 530-265-5824; 400 Railroad Ave; rooms $77-85, cabins $110)* has rooms, as well as chalets that sleep up to five people. Amenities include a heated pool, spa and restaurant, though it's a bit distant from the heart of town. The inn is on the site of Nevada City's Chinese cemetery; legend has it the graves of the cremated bodies are still in the ground, though the grave markers, if there were any, are long gone.

National Hotel *(☎ 530-265-4551; 211 Broad St; rooms $75-119)*, a historic hotel in the heart of downtown, claims to be the oldest continuously operating hotel west of the Rocky Mountains. The building was constructed in the 1850s; the furnishings (1960s vintage) have seen better days.

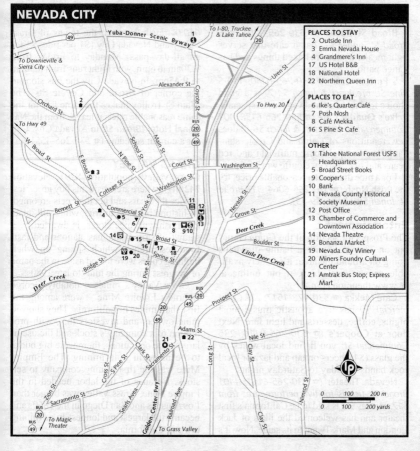

NEVADA CITY

PLACES TO STAY
2 Outside Inn
3 Emma Nevada House
4 Grandmere's Inn
17 US Hotel B&B
18 National Hotel
22 Northern Queen Inn

PLACES TO EAT
6 Ike's Quarter Café
7 Posh Nosh
8 Café Mekka
16 S Pine St Cafe

OTHER
1 Tahoe National Forest USFS Headquarters
5 Broad Street Books
9 Cooper's
10 Bank
11 Nevada County Historical Society Museum
12 Post Office
13 Chamber of Commerce and Downtown Association
14 Nevada Theatre
15 Bonanza Market
19 Nevada City Winery
20 Miners Foundry Cultural Center
21 Amtrak Bus Stop; Express Mart

GOLD COUNTRY

US Hotel B&B (☎ 530-265-7999, 800-525-4525; Broad St; rooms from $95), a few doors up from the National Hotel, has elegantly restored rooms; rates include breakfast and complimentary wine in the evening.

Emma Nevada House (☎ 530-265-4415, 800-916-3662; 528 E Broad St; rooms $100-155), at the top of town, is in the childhood home of 1890s opera star Emma Nevada. It has large and luminous sitting areas and rooms that feel light and airy.

Grandmere's Inn (☎ 530-265-4660; W www.grandmeresinn.com; 449 Broad St; rooms $138-209), in Aaron Sargent's residence of 1856, is centrally located and extremely classy. The decor is subdued, rooms are spacious and clients claim breakfast here is as good as it gets.

Bonanza Market (cnr Broad & Bridge Sts; open 8am-7pm Mon-Sat, 9am-6pm Sun) is a full sized grocery store with a good deli.

Broad St Books (☎ 530-265-4204; 426 Broad St; under $7) has a café that serves light meals, wonderful baked things and has a nice patio.

S Pine St Cafe (☎ 530-265-0260; 110 S Pine St; breakfast & lunch $4-7) is a good choice for breakfast and vegetarian specials.

Ike's Quarter Cafe (☎ 530-265-6138; 401 Commercial St; breakfast & lunch $6-8) does new renditions of Cajun and Creole standards such as po' boys, muffelata and red beans and rice. Turkey etouffe wrap anyone?

For a nice dinner at a reasonable price, try the **Posh Nosh** (☎ 530-265-6064; 318 Broad St; lunch $8, dinner $9-13).

Entertainment

The Prospector section of the Union comes out on Thursday, with a listing of what's going on around the area; it's widely available or you can check it out online at W www.theunion.com.

Café Mekka (☎ 530-478-1517; 237 Commercial St) has live acoustic music most nights, coffee, desserts and light fare. Next door at **Cooper's** (☎ 530-265-0116; 235 Commercial St) you'll find local wines by the glass ($4), beers on tap and jazz or local rock bands Tuesday to Saturday nights.

Nevada Theater (☎ 530-265-6161; 4401 Broad St; tickets for live performances from $17, movies $5) is said to be California's first theater and has welcomed the likes of Jack London and Mark Twain to its stage. Now it's

used for productions of the very good and prolific Foothill Theater Company (☎ 530-265-8587), as well as film festivals and current movie screenings.

Magic Theatre (☎ 530-265-8262; W www.themagictheatrenc.com; 107 Argall Way), south of downtown Nevada City, is probably the smallest, friendliest and most environmentally conscientious movie house in California (management serves popcorn in real bowls, coffee in real mugs and bakes fresh brownies for intermission). It shows films Wednesday to Sunday nights, plus a Sunday matinee for $4.

Getting There & Around

Amtrak runs five buses daily from Nevada City to Sacramento ($13) by way of Grass Valley and Auburn. Buses stop at the **Express Mart store** (301 Sacramento St at Hwy 49).

The **Gold Country Stage** (☎ 530-477-0103) travels between the towns of Grass Valley and Nevada City ($1 per ride, $2 for an all-day pass) Monday to Friday from 7:30am to 6pm, with night runs from 5:30pm to 9:45pm. In Nevada City the bus stops at the corner of Broad and Coyote Sts. The Main St Trolley makes the same trip for the same reasonable rates; it leaves from the **National Hotel** (Broad St) in Nevada City. Call for a current schedule (☎ 530-265-4551).

GRASS VALLEY

Grass Valley (population 8291; elevation 2420ft) is where area residents buy groceries, service their cars and get their pets groomed. Its historic business district, while still intact and flush with nice stores, is dwarfed by a sprawl of strip malls, gas stations and fast-food restaurants, which sprang up when building codes were tossed aside in the name of progress during the mid- to late 1980s.

Grass Valley's mines – notably George Bourne's Empire Mine – were among the first shaft mines in California. They showed mine owners and investors that, with promotion of a company's stock and the use of large-scale operations, there were big bucks to be made in lode mining. The Empire Mine was the first mining company to sell stock. Because of the labor needed in the Empire Mine, Grass Valley was bigger than Los Angeles and San Diego in the 1860s and became the largest and longest-lived mining town in California.

Grass Valley's main thoroughfares are Mill St and W Main St (the heart of the historic business district) and E Main St, which goes north to the shopping centers and mini-malls, continues north as the Nevada City Hwy and heads on into Nevada City as Sacramento St. S Auburn St divides E and W Main St.

On Friday nights in July and August, Mill St is closed to car traffic while food, arts and crafts, and music entertain people in the street.

Information

The **Downtown Association** (☎ 530-272-8315), in the former Mill St home of Lola Montez, has maps and brochures.

The Book Seller (☎ 530-272-2131; 107 Mill St) carries local publications, history books, travel guides and bestsellers. It's a useful place to find out what's going on around town.

Things to See & Do

Situated atop 367mi of mine shafts, which from 1850 to 1956 produced 6 million ounces of gold (about 2 billion modern dollars' worth), **Empire Mine State Historic Park** (☎ 530-273-8522; admission $1; park & visitor center open 9am-6pm daily, 10am-5pm Oct-May) is the Gold Country's best-preserved gold quartz mining operation – worth at least a half-day's exploration. The large mine yard contains head frames, stamp mills, waterwheels and pulleys and is surrounded by the company offices, housed in buildings made of waste rock (rock left over after quartz mining).

The visitor center and museum, well marked at the park entrance on the right side of E Empire St when you're traveling east, shows a worthwhile movie and offers free ranger-led tours every hour. If you miss the tour, be sure to see the color-coded mine system model in the room adjacent to the visitor center. Next to the largest head frame in the mine yard is a stairway that leads 40ft down into the main mine shaft.

On the other side of the visitor center you'll find stately buildings that belonged to the Bourne family, under whose ownership the Empire Mine prospered. You can visit the elegant country club, English manor home, gardener's house and rose garden on a docent-led tour; check the visitor center for the day's schedule.

Hiking trails begin near the old stamp mill in the mine yard and pass abandoned mines and equipment. A trail map is available at the visitor center. The park is 2mi east of Grass Valley via the Empire St exit off Hwy 49.

Grass Valley's Lola Montez

Lola Montez was the 19th-century equivalent to Madonna – beautiful, glamorous and just a bit controversial. Born Eliza Gilbert in Ireland, she took to London's stages as a self-proclaimed Spanish dancer, where she won the heart of Bavarian king Ludwig I, who bestowed on her the title of countess of Landsfeld. During the 1848 revolution against the king, Lola, who had accompanied Ludwig home, was discovered doing her own version of fiddling as Rome burned – sitting in a window seat drinking champagne. Her outrageous behavior led to her forced exodus from Germany.

After dabbling in dancing in Paris with comrades George Sand and Victor Hugo, Lola – who was now over 30 – moved to America, where less sophisticated audiences still applauded her sensual dances and exotic beauty. Always longing to be the center of attention, she moved from New York to Boston to Philadelphia and finally to California, where she felt she was assured a captive audience. By 1853, however, San Francisco and Sacramento already had their share of glamorous entertainers, so Lola went on to settle in Grass Valley, a rough-and-tumble mining town that accepted her with open arms.

Lola stirred controversy by wearing low-cut dresses, smoking Cuban cigars, keeping two grizzly cubs as pets and serving champagne and imported whiskey at her European-style 'salons,' at a time when women were expected to bake bread, keep clothes clean and not have their own wealth. Considered heavenly by the miners and hellish by miners' wives, Lola was Grass Valley's most famous citizen until the Australian gold rush drew her south to fresh audiences that had not had a chance to tire of her shows. Her former home, now the chamber of commerce, is still a Grass Valley landmark.

Grass Valley's **North Star Mine** used the largest Pelton waterwheel ever made. The mine's old stone powerhouse on the west bank of Wolf Creek, at Mill St's south end, is now a **museum** (☎ 530-273-4255; donation requested; open 10am-5pm daily May-Oct) with a small collection of Pelton waterwheels (and their prototypes), mining equipment and artifacts. A few shady, creek-side tables behind the museum make nice picnic spots.

Places to Stay & Eat

Stage Coach Motel (☎ 530-272-3701; 405 S Auburn St; singles/doubles $55/60) is the cheapest you'll find in the area, and not too bad if you don't mind old carpet.

Holbrooke Hotel (☎ 530-273-1353, 800-933-7077, fax 530-273-0434; w www.holbrooke.com; 212 W Main St; rooms $60-145; lunch around $8, dinner $8-15) has Mark Twain's signature in the hotel register and well-appointed rooms. Rates include breakfast. The dining room is a favorite for special occasions and the bar is nothing short of a local institution.

Risky Business B&B (☎ 530-273-6873; w www.riskybusinessonline.com; 318 Neal St; rooms $125-200) has four rooms in a beautifully restored home from 1858. There's a swimming pool and communal spa, plus Jacuzzis in the rooms and it's a block from Grass Valley's historic center.

Tofanelli's (☎ 530-272-1468; 302 W Main St; breakfast & lunch around $8, dinner $8-$13) is where locals go for just about anything from coffee and scones to salads and pastas. Portions are copious, so think about sharing.

Kula Kula (☎ 530-274-2229; 207 W Main St; lunch around $5, dishes $9-15) serves home-style Japanese food and has live piano music on Saturday night.

Getting There & Away

Amtrak buses stop in front of **City Hall** (125 E Main St). There are five buses daily to Sacramento ($11) via Auburn. The **Gold Country Stage**, which runs between Grass Valley and Nevada City, stops in front of the **post office** (E Main St).

AUBURN

In 1856 Auburn (population 12,900; elevation 1255ft) started its own minor railroad to compete with trains running from Sacramento to Folsom by bringing people further north and east, closer to the mines. The Sacramento-Folsom line eventually shut down, while Auburn's railroad became part of Central Pacific's transcontinental route. Interstate 80 follows this route between the Bay Area and Lake Tahoe and is a commuter passage for people who live in Auburn and work in Sacramento. Auburn's proximity to I-80 makes it one of the most visited towns in the Gold Country, though it's mostly a service center town with strip malls, automotive stores and fast-food restaurants. The historic part of town (called Old Town) is nice and can be explored in an hour or so without venturing far from the interstate. Anyone in the area should stop in Auburn on a Sunday when the streets of Old Town are closed to car traffic and a huge flea market, complete with live music and food vendors, takes place from 9am until around 5pm.

Orientation & Information

Auburn lies east of I-80, with the Old Town south of the noticeable Placer County Courthouse (a large yellow building very visible from the freeway) and the new part of town spreading north and east.

Housed in the old Auburn railroad depot at the north end of Lincoln Way, the **Auburn Area Chamber of Commerce** (☎ 530-885-5616; open 9am-5pm Mon-Fri) has museum, lodging and dining guides.

Things to See & Do

A fine few hours could start at the **Placer County Museum** (admission free; open 10am-4pm Tues-Sun), on the first floor of the stately **Placer County Courthouse** (open 8am-5pm daily), and continue with a stroll down to Old Town. Here, the **Shanghai Bar** (☎ 530-8446; 291 Washington St) has been in operation since 1912, right through the Depression and Prohibition. It's a treasure trove of old 'stuff,' worth a look even if you don't imbibe. Live music rocks the place on weekends.

Those who really want to delve into local lore can head to the **Gold Country Museum** (☎ 530-889-6500; High St; admission $1; open 10am-3:30pm Tues-Fri, 11am-4pm Sat & Sun), toward the back of the fairgrounds. The admission is also good for the **Bernhard Museum Complex** (291 Auburn-Folsom Rd;

open 10am-3:30pm Tues-Fri, noon-4pm Sat & Sun), at the south end of High St, built in 1851 as the Traveler's Rest Hotel. The museum has displays depicting the typical life of a 19th-century farm family, including the requisite winery and carriage house.

Places to Stay & Eat

Elmwood Motel (☎ 530-885-5186; 588 High St; singles/doubles $45/50), a slightly shabby property, is the only motel in downtown Auburn. It has an outdoor pool.

Alongside I-80 on Auburn Ravine Rd are a few motels, including the small **Foothills Motel** (☎ 530-885-8444; singles/ doubles $60/65) which has a pool, hot tub and friendly owners. A night here includes breakfast at the coffee shop across the street.

Auburn Best Inn & Suites (☎ 530-885-1800, 800-272-1444, 800-626-1900; rooms from $75) has a spa, pool, work-out room, laundry facility and light breakfast.

Awful Annies (☎ 530-888-9857; 160 Sacramento St; breakfast & lunch $4-8), a local favorite in Old Town, serves breakfast and lunch indoors or outdoors on a deck. Portions are large and desserts are worth saving room for.

Cafe Delicias (☎ 530-888-2050; 1591 Lincoln Way; dishes $5-8) in Old Town is the best place for Mexican food; walk around back to see the tortillas being made by hand.

Bootleggers Old Town Tavern & Grill (☎ 530-889-2229; 210 Washington St; lunch & dinner $8-18) is great for a splurge. It's housed in Auburn's original city hall.

Getting There & Away

Amtrak has one train and eight buses per day to Sacramento ($9, 55 minutes). Northbound busses go to Grass Valley ($7.50, 30 minutes) and Nevada City ($9, 40 minutes). All leave from the **train platform and bus shelter** (277 Nevada St), at the corner of Fulweiler (about 2mi north of the historic part of Old Town). Tickets are sold on board.

Greyhound buses go thrice daily to Sacramento ($9.25, one hour 20 minutes) and Truckee ($14.50, one hour 45 minutes), see also the Sierra Nevada chapter. You'll need to flag the bus from **Flyers Station & Mini Mart** (13461 Bowman Rd) and pay the driver on board.

AUBURN STATE RECREATION AREA

About 4mi south of Auburn, the North and Middle Forks of the American River converge below a bridge on Hwy 49. In summer this is a popular spot for sunning and swimming, though signs clearly warn that the current is strong and dangerous. Numerous trails in the area are shared by hikers, mountain bikers and horses. Boaters have an entire campground and boating trail exclusively for them.

The best place to find maps and information is the **Auburn State Recreation Area California Department of Parks and Recreation office** (☎ 530-885-5648; Hwy 49; open 8am-4:30pm Mon-Fri), halfway between the bridge and Auburn. Trail and campground information is available from a box outside.

One of the most popular trails is the **Western States Trail**, which connects Auburn State Recreation Area to Folsom Lake State Recreation Area and Folsom Lake. It is the site of the annual '100 Miles in One Day' horseback ride, which starts in Soda Springs (near Truckee – see the Lake Tahoe section in the Sierra Nevada chapter) and ends in Auburn. The trail is also the route for the annual Western States 100mi endurance run, held in June.

The **Quarry Trail** makes a level path from Hwy 49, just south of the bridge, along the Middle Fork of the American. There are benches along the way and several side trails that go down to the river.

COLOMA

Originally known for its proximity to Sutter's Mill (site of California's first gold discovery), Coloma (population 1100; elevation 750ft) is now famous for its white-water rafting. Situated on the South Fork of the American River, about 11mi north of Placerville, the 'town' itself consists of a few places to eat strung out along Hwy 49, including the **Coloma Club** (☎ 530-626-6390; 7171 Hwy 49) a bar, restaurant and hangout that comes alive with guides and river rats when the water is high. Other than that, the majority of business is done out of the offices of individual river outfitters, of which there are many, in the area.

Half-day trips usually start upstream at Chile Bar sand bar and end near Marshall Gold Discovery State Historic Park (see the following page). Full-day trips put in at the

GOLD COUNTRY

Coloma Bridge and take out at Salmon Falls, near Folsom Lake. The half-day options start in Class III water and are action-packed to the end (full-day trips start out slowly, then build up to Class III as a climax). The full-day trips include lunch, which is often a gourmet affair. The season is usually from May to mid-October, depending on how wet the winter was and how early the snows start melting. Prices are generally $20 lower Monday to Friday, when crowds are almost nonexistent.

Recommended for its meticulous equipment, knowledgeable guides and tasty food, **Whitewater Connection** (☎ 530-622-6446, 800-336-7238; e raft@whitewaterconnec tion.com) has half-day trips for $89 weekdays ($109/99 Saturday/Sunday), full-day trips for $109 weekdays ($129/119 Saturday/Sunday) and two-day trips starting at $239.

Similar prices and services are offered by **Mother Load River Trips** (☎ 800-427-2387; w www.MaLode.com) which also runs a river conservation trip for parties of six or more at $70 per person, including a talk about river ecology and preservation.

A bigger operation that also runs the Klamath and Kaweah Rivers is **Adventure Connection** (☎ 800-556-6060; w www.raft california.com). Its full-day trips cost $105/135 weekdays/weekends and two-day trips cost $235/285.

A free and enjoyable pastime is watching people navigate the Trouble Maker Rapid, upstream from the bridge next to Sutter's Mill in the state park.

Places to Stay

Most rafting companies own private campgrounds for their guests who do overnight trips. If the campgrounds are not full, however, they often let day-trippers camp for around $15.

American River Resort (☎ 530-622-6700, fax 622-7461; 6019 New River Rd; midweek/weekend camping $20/28, cabins $115-130) is a quarter mile off Hwy 49, just south of the state park, and has a restaurant and bar, a playground, a pond and farm animals. The campsites aren't spectacular, but they are shady and have excellent river access.

As well as tent sites and cabins, **Coloma Resort** (☎ 530-621-2267; 6921 Mt Murphy Rd; tent & RV sites $32, cabins $45) has two bunkhouses that sleep five for $75 (no linen or bedding provided).

Camp Lotus (☎ 530-622-8672; midweek/weekend camping per person $6/8 with $18/24 minimum; open May-Oct), 1mi west of Coloma (take the Lotus Rd turnoff from Hwy 49), has 10 RV spaces but is primarily for tenters. Showers here are hot and the toilets flush. No dogs are allowed.

Golden Lotus B&B (☎ 530-621-4562; 1006 Lotus Rd; rooms $85-120) is highly recommended by locals.

MARSHALL GOLD DISCOVERY STATE HISTORIC PARK

The South Fork of the American River and Hwy 49 run right through Marshall Gold Discovery State Historic Park (admission per car $2; open 8am-sunset daily). Though you can see most of the park by just driving through, its hiking trails, restored buildings and replica of Sutter's Mill warrant a few hours out of the car. The **State Park Visitors Information Center & Museum** (☎ 530-622-3470; Bridge St; open 10am-4:30pm daily), just off Hwy 49, shows a worthwhile movie and has an interesting mining exhibit.

You can make a loop tour by car up to the James Marshall Monument, marked by a statue at the miner's grave site, or hike up the Monument Trail, which passes old mining equipment and a nice designated picnic area (as well as scenic clearings and rock outcroppings that are also fine spots for picnicking).

Panning for gold is a popular recreational pastime here – you can pay $7.50 to pan at Beckeart's Gun Shop (on Hwy 49 across from the visitor center), where you're assured to find some 'color,' as the old-time miners used to call the gold as it appeared in their pans. Or take a chance and try the river's east bank, just across the bridge from the mill replica. Pans are available from the visitor center, and demonstrations are given most weekends from May to September.

PLACERVILLE

'Old Hangtown,' as Placerville (population 9336; elevation 1866ft) is fondly known, has always relied on travelers passing through for its livelihood. Originally it was a destination for gold seekers who reached California by following the South Fork of the American River. In 1857 the first stagecoach to cross the Sierra Nevada linked Placerville to Nevada's Carson Valley – a route that eventually became part of the nation's first transcontinental stagecoach route. Today Placerville is a gas and food stop for people traveling between Sacramento and South Lake Tahoe on Hwy 50. Also the El Dorado County seat, the town has two distinct parts: fast-food restaurants, automotive stores and other chain-owned businesses on Hwy 50 and an active, well-preserved downtown with antique shops, bookstores and bars that could make Hemingway turn teetotaler.

History

Jared Sheldon and William Daylor, who planted the first wheat in the Sacramento Valley, came east during the summer of 1848 to sell some cattle to the miners at Coloma and decided to poke around a previously unmined area about 12mi southeast of modern-day Placerville. They found about $17,000 worth of gold in one week, but they were so dedicated to their farm that they returned to it and hired some Miwok Indians (for 50¢ per day) to do the digging for them. Other miners came to settle here, calling the place 'Dry Diggins,' since the most gold was discovered near the surface of dry streambeds, where it could be extracted with knives, spoons and pointed sticks.

At the peak of the gold rush, gold was found regularly enough to obviate crime, and what crime did occur was dealt with by 'miners' law,' such as tying a criminal to a tree stark naked in the middle of mosquito season. As more people arrived and the gold became harder to find, crime ran rampant and makeshift miners' courts became common.

The courts' sentences increased in severity until, in 1849, five men charged with robbery and attempted murder were met with a unanimous 'Hang them!' In short order, the men were taken to a tree on Main St and strung up. After that event, Dry Diggins was given the name Hangtown. By 1854, when the growing community boasted a church, a temperance union, a theater and several restaurants, and placer mining was supporting an increasing number of miners and their families, the name of the town was changed to Placerville.

Orientation & Information

Main St, the heart of downtown Placerville, runs parallel to Hwy 50 between Canal St and Cedar Ravine Rd. Hwy 49 meets Main St at the west edge of downtown.

The **El Dorado County Chamber of Commerce** (☎ 530-621-5885, 800-457-6279; 542 Main St; open 9am-5pm Mon-Fri) has information on Gold Country and the Lake Tahoe area. **Placerville News Co** (☎ 530-622-4510; 409 Main St) has a wealth of maps, history books, newspapers and magazines of international interest. Banks and several good bookstores are on Main St; the **post office** (Sacramento St) is one block south.

Things to See & Do

Most buildings along Main St date back to the 1850s, including the **El Dorado County Courthouse** (543 Main St), and **Placerville Hardware** (441 Main St), the oldest continuously operating hardware store west of the Mississippi River. An old photograph in front of the store shows early Placerville and the hangman's tree.

Placerville was once a stop on the first transcontinental stagecoach route

Placerville Historical Museum (☎ 530-626-0773; 524 Main St; admission free; open 10am-4pm Wed-Sat, noon-4pm Sun), housed in the Fountain & Tallman Soda Works Building, has a small collection of soda factory relics and Placerville photographs.

One mile north of town on Bedford Ave, **Gold Bug Park** (☎ 530-642-5207; W www.goldbugpark.org; open 8:30am-5pm daily, weather permitting) is on the site of four mining claims that yielded gold from 1849 to 1888. You can visit the Gold Bug Mine and Stamp Mill for $3/1 adults/children (including hard hat) and explore the grounds and picnic area for free.

El Dorado County Historical Museum (☎ 530-621-5865; admission free; open 10am-4pm Wed-Sat, noon-4pm Sun), on the El Dorado County Fairgrounds west of downtown Placerville (exit north on Placerville Drive from Hwy 50), is an extensive complex of restored buildings, mining equipment and re-created businesses.

Places to Stay & Eat

Placerville KOA (☎ 530-676-2267; Hwy 50; tent sites $22, hookups $26, cabins $45-55), 6mi west of Placerville on Hwy 50 (exit north on Shingle Springs Dr), sits on 18 acres of land and has a store, laundry and pool. Tent sites are well shaded, though not grassy.

Cary House Hotel (☎ 530-622-4271, fax 530-622-0696; 300 Main St; rooms from $75), in downtown Placerville, is completely nonsmoking. It has newly restored rooms with decor that reflects its bordello history. Rates include a cold breakfast and weekend wine tasting. Ask for a room in the back to avoid street noise.

Combellack-Blair House B&B (☎ 530-622-3764; 3059 Cedar Ravine Rd; rooms $125), a large place on the National Register of Historic Places, is two blocks south of Main St and has three Victorian-style rooms and a small garden.

Chichester-McKee House B&B (☎ 530-626-1882, 800-831-4008; W www.innlover .com; 800 Spring St; rooms $110-130) was built in 1892 by the head of the local lumber company and features wonderful wood insetting and stained glass windows. Caramel brownies are served in the evening and a full breakfast is provided in the morning.

Fast-food restaurants – well marked and highly visible from Hwy 50 – abound in Placerville, but 'real' food is found downtown.

Gelato D'Oro Cafe (☎ 530-626-8097; 311 Main St; lunch $5-7, dinner around $8) serves crepes, salads and Italian ice cream. Considering the chic but casual atmosphere, it's good value for lunch or dinner.

Z Pie (☎ 530-621-2626; 3182 Center St; pies $5) uses organic ingredients in its salads and savory pot pies that range from traditional chicken to tomatillo vegetable. Combos (lunch or dinner) include a pie, salad and pint of beer for $9, or pie and a pint for $7.50.

Mel's the Original (☎ 530-626-8072) hails from San Francisco and is also good value. Most things on the menu cost $7, from three-egg omelets and large salads to hot beef sandwiches. Ice-cream specialties should be shared by all but the most voracious sweets lover.

Entertainment

Placerville's bars are akin to the neighborhood watering holes in the Midwest: they open at 6am, get an annual cleaning at Christmas and are great for people who want to soak up local color. Marked by vintage signs, the **Hangman Tree** (☎ 530-622-3878; 305 Main St) and **Liars' Bench** (☎ 530-622-0494; 255 Main St) are good for catching the ol' Hangtown scene, as is **Gil's** (☎ 530-621-1402; 372 Main St).

Getting There & Away

Amtrak runs nine buses daily to Sacramento ($13, one hour 40 minutes). Greyhound buses go to Sacramento ($11.25, one hour 35 minutes) four times daily and to South Lake Tahoe ($11.25, one hour 35 minutes) thrice daily. The **Placerville Transit Station** (2964 Mosquito Rd) is a covered bus stop with benches and restrooms; it's about a half mile from downtown, on the north side of Hwy 50.

AROUND PLACERVILLE
Apple Hill

In 1860 a miner planted a Rhode Island greening apple tree on what is the present-day property of the Larsens, and thus began what is now the prolific Apple Hill, a 20-sq-mi area east of Placerville and north of Hwy 50 where there's more than 60 growers. The miner's Rhode Island greening still stands (a major gimmick for the Larsens, who operate a museum) and is flanked by Granny Smiths, pippins, red and yellow delicious, Fujis from Japan and Braeburns from New Zealand. Apple growers sell directly to the public, usually from September to around December.

A decent map of Apple Hill is available at the **Apple Hill Visitors Center** (☎ 530-644-7692; W www.applehill.com) in the Camino Hotel, near the Camino exit off Hwy 50. For a condensed Apple Hill tour, take the Camino exit north onto Barkley Rd until it becomes Larsen Drive. Follow Larsen Drive (which will become Cable and then Mace Rd) until it meets Pony Express Trail back beside Hwy 50. White signs emblazoned with bright red apples mark connecting side roads and byways.

Favorite stops to buy apples, cider, pies and handicrafts are **Larsen's Apple Barn** (2461 Larsen Dr); **Boa Vista Orchards** (2952 Carson Rd); **High Hill Ranch** (2901 High Hill Rd), just off Carson Rd; **Bolsters Hilltop Ranch** (2000 Larsen Dr); and **Argyres Orchard** (4220 N Canyon Rd) (the latter two allow you to pick the apples off the tree!).

Wineries

El Dorado County wines are becoming popular and frequently appear on Bay Area menus. To compete with the Napa and Sonoma markets, area wineries have invested a great deal in their properties, and most offer free tastings on weekends. You can pick up a map at the chamber of commerce or at Wine Smith in Placerville, or from the **El Dorado Winery Association** (☎ 916-967-1299, 800-306-3956; W www.eldoradowines.org; PO Box 1614, Placerville, CA 95667).

Some noteworthy wineries, all north of Hwy 50, are **Lava Cap Winery** (☎ 530-621-0175; 2221 Fruitridge Rd); **Madrona Vineyards** (☎ 530-644-5948; High Hill Rd), just north of Carson Rd; and **Boeger Winery** (☎ 530-622-8094; 1709 Carson Rd). During Passport Weekends, held in March and April, one 'passport' allows entry into seven wineries that offer special tastings and tours.

AMADOR COUNTY WINERIES

The Swiss-born Uhlingers began the wine industry in Amador County by planting the first vines in 1856. The region wasn't really developed until the 1960s, however, when grapes that were traditionally sold to large winemakers for blending started yielding juice and skin of high enough quality to be made into wine on their own.

Amador County is best known for its zinfandel, a peppery wine with hints of berries and black currants. Italian varietals also do well here, so barberas, sangioveses and nebbiolos are common. Tastings at the small, family-run wineries are very laid back, almost always free and can be extremely educational since folks here are willing to discuss just about any aspect of the wine business you're interested in.

Maps are available at the wineries, and from the **Amador Vintners Association** (☎ 209-245-4309, fax 209-267-2298; W www.amadorwine.com). To begin, head east from Plymouth on Shenandoah Rd, which eventually becomes Steiner Rd. Signs indicate where the wineries are and which ones are open (some are closed weekdays). Highly recommended are **Story Winery** (☎ 209-245-6208; W www.zin.com) and **Karly** (☎ 209-245-3922; W www.karlywines .com), both off Shenandoah Rd on Bell Rd; **Shenandoah Vineyards** (☎ 209-245-4455), which has an art gallery in its tasting room; **Vino Noceto** (☎ 209-245-6556; W www. noceto.com), for its sangiovese wine; and **Sobon Estate** (☎ 209-245-6554; museum open 10am-5pm daily), home to the Shenandoah Valley Museum with 12,000-gallon redwood barrels and memorabilia from the area.

Plymouth is the nearest service center, with a grocery store, diner and gas station. The large **Far Horizons 49er Village RV Park and Campground** (☎ 209-245-6981; Hwy 49) isn't a bad place for RVers to spend the night.

AMADOR CITY

Literally a bend in the road (Hwy 49, some 30mi south of Placerville), Amador City (population 250; elevation 620ft) is among the smallest incorporated townships in California. Once home to the Keystone Mine – one of the most prolific gold producers in California – the town lay deserted from 1942 (when the mine closed) until the 1950s, when a family from Sacramento bought the dilapidated buildings and converted them into antiques shops. Now the town has half a dozen shops and the **Amador Whitney Museum** (☎ 209-267-0928; Main St; admission free; open noon-4pm Fri-Sun), which has changing exhibits of local interest.

GOLD COUNTRY

Stop by the Imperial Hotel to pick up a walking-tour map. Behind Amador City's old firehouse (the building with a bright red garage door and bell tower in front) is a stone arastra (a round, shallow pool with a turnstile in the middle used to crush rocks into gravel) once used here to grind gold-laced quartz. The arastra still works and is put to use during the Jose Amador Fiesta in late April.

The **Imperial Hotel** *(☎ 209-267-9172, 800-242-5594; 14202 Main St; rooms midweek/weekend from $95/105; dinner around $30)*, built in 1879, serves gourmet dinners in an elegant dining room. Rooms are decorated with antiques, and rates include full breakfast. Beware that it has officially been certified as haunted, by more than one investigative agency.

SUTTER CREEK

Many travelers consider Sutter Creek (population 2118; elevation 1198ft) their favorite Gold Country town. Its residential areas and the raised, arcaded sidewalks and high-balconied buildings along Main St are excellent examples of 19th-century architecture, and the town is totally intact without any of the sprawl that accompanies so many historic spots.

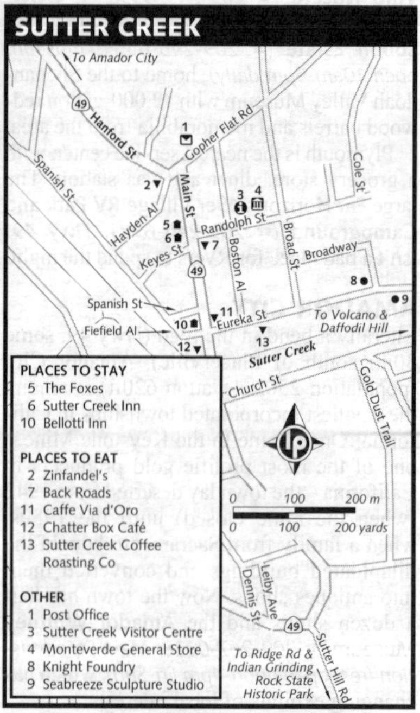
SUTTER CREEK
To Amador City
49
Hanford St
Gopher Flat Rd
Spanish St
Main St
Cole St
Hayden Al
Randolph St
Keyes St
Boston Al
Broad St
Broadway
Spanish St
Fiefield Al
Eureka St
To Volcano & Daffodil Hill
Sutter Creek
Church St
Gold Dust Trail
0 100 200 m
0 100 200 yards
Dennis St
Leiby Ave
To Ridge Rd & Indian Grinding Rock State Historic Park
Sutter Hill Rd
PLACES TO STAY
5 The Foxes
6 Sutter Creek Inn
10 Bellotti Inn
PLACES TO EAT
2 Zinfandel's
7 Back Roads
11 Caffe Via d'Oro
12 Chatter Box Café
13 Sutter Creek Coffee Roasting Co
OTHER
1 Post Office
3 Sutter Creek Visitor Centre
4 Monteverde General Store
8 Knight Foundry
9 Seabreeze Sculpture Studio

In its prime Sutter Creek was the Gold Country's main foundry center, with three foundries operating in 1873 making pans and rock crushers. The **Knight Foundry**, at 81 Eureka St, operated until 1996 as the last water-powered foundry and machine shop in the US. You can still see the workings of the foundry, and on weekends there are volunteers there to explain how everything worked.

Across the street **Seabreeze Sculpture Studio** *(☎ 209-267-5883)* displays the carved stone works of Thomas Baugh in a groovy garden. This is where the artist works and lives, so pieces are sold for even less than wholesale. If they're not there you can choose a piece and put your check or cash in the mail box.

Stop in at the **Sutter Creek Visitor Center** *(25 Eureka St; open 9am-4pm Mon-Fri, 10am-3pm Sat)* for a walking tour map of the town. Next door, **Monteverde General Store** *(☎ 209-267-5155; admission free; open 10am-3pm Sat, 10am-5pm Sun)* has been restored to look just as it did in 1898.

Places to Stay & Eat

Bellotti Inn *(☎ 209-267-5211; 53 Main St; singles/doubles $45/55)* is an exception to the other accommodations in Sutter Creek, which tend toward the expensive. It has musty rooms atop Sutter Creek's oldest bar.

Sutter Creek Inn *(☎ 209-267-5606; w www.suttercreekinn.com; 75 Main St; midweek rooms $80-165, weekend rooms $100-195)* attracts loyal guests year after year. It has 17 rooms that vary in decor and amenities (antiques, fireplaces, swinging beds), an elegant parlor where afternoon sherry is served and a large lawn. Breakfast is served in a cozy kitchen-side dining room.

The Foxes *(☎ 209-267-5882; w www.foxesinn.com; 77 Main St; rooms $140-210)*, next door to Sutter Creek Inn, has seven plush rooms with TVs, VCRs, designer furniture and bathrobes. Breakfasts are of the gourmet variety and afternoon cookies come with tea or a glass of wine.

Sutter Creek's coffeehouses are great for breakfast or lunch. **Back Roads** *(☎ 209-267-0440; 74A Main St; lunch specials around $5)* is a perennial favorite.

Sutter Creek Coffee Roasting Co (☎ 209-267-5550; 20 Eureka St; light meals & coffee $3-6) has a nice patio.

Chatter Box Café (39 Main St; breakfast & lunch around $6) makes all its own bread, buns and pies and serves them with eggs for breakfast or burgers for lunch. The apple pancakes are superb, as are all of its ice-cream specialties.

Zinfandel's (☎ 209-267-5008; cnr Main & Hanford Sts; lunch around $8, dinner $12-20; open Thur-Sun) is said to be the finest restaurant in the area, famous for its eclectic California menu. It's excellent value at lunchtime when many of its signature dishes – roasted tomato polenta, for example – are served at lower prices.

Caffe Via d'Oro (☎ 209-267-0535; 36 Main St; open Wed-Mon) is a bit more casual. It has pastas and pizzas for around $12, interesting salads and an extensive local wine list.

VOLCANO

Volcano (population 100; elevation 2053ft) is a cute-as-a-button bend in the road that feels more like an outpost than a town. It was a Unionist enclave during the Civil War, and these days it is far less developed than other Gold Country towns. Hand-painted signs in front of buildings give amusing insights into Volcano's colorful past. The town lays claim to the first astronomical observation site, the first private law school and the first library in California. Large granitic sandstone rocks line Sutter Creek, which runs through the center of town. The rocks, now flanked by picnic tables, were blasted from surrounding hills by hydraulic processes, then scraped clean of gold-bearing dirt.

Mother Nature's Candle Garden (cnr Constellation & Main Sts; open Thur-Sun) has handmade candles and soaps. The **Hubb Café** (Constellation St) sells local wines by the glass, as well as a variety of foods, and has a great outdoor seating area and live music on weekends.

Things to See & Do

On weekends from April to November, the **Volcano Theatre Company** (☎ 209-223-4663; admission $7-12) produces live dramas in the restored Cobblestone Theater.

Between mid-March and mid-April, **Daffodil Hill**, 2mi northeast of Volcano, is blanketed with more than 300,000 daffodils. The McLaughlin and Ryan families have operated the hilltop farm since 1887 and keep hyacinths, tulips, violets, lilacs and the occasional peacock among the daffodils. The hill is open daily when the flowers are in bloom. There's no fee, but donations toward next year's planting are appreciated.

Indian Grinding Rock State Historic Park (☎ 209-296-7488; Pine Grove-Volcano Rd; admission $2), 2mi southwest of Volcano, is sacred ground for the local Miwok Indians. In it you can see a limestone outcropping covered with petroglyphs – 363 originals and a few modern additions – and mortar holes called chaw'ses used for grinding acorns into meal. The 1185 holes are thought to be the most on any one rock in California.

Adjacent to the rock are replica Miwok structures and the **Regional Indian Museum** (open 11am-3pm Mon-Fri, 10am-4pm Sat & Sun), which has interesting displays about northern Miwok culture and organizes free tours of the park on weekends.

Black Chasm (☎ 888-762-2837; W www .caverntours.com; open 9am-5pm daily), a quarter of a mile east of Volcano on the Volcano-Pioneer Rd, is operated by the same folks who give tours of California Cavern (see San Andreas later) and Moaning Cavern (see Around Columbia State Historic Park). This particular chasm is known for its helictite crystals – rare, sparkling white formations that look like an enlarged snowflake. Guided tours cost $13.

Places to Stay & Eat

The beautiful **campground** (camping $6) at Indian Grinding Rock State Historic Park, has restrooms (no showers) and 21 first-come, first-served sites set among the trees.

St George Hotel (☎ 209-296-4458; W www .stgeorgehotel.com; 16104 Main St; rooms $78-120) has lovely rooms that have been featured in magazines such as *Sunset* and gourmet food which *Gourmet* magazine approves of wholeheartedly. Breakfast is included in the price of a room; patrons with digs elsewhere pay around $8 for breakfast or lunch, $25 for dinner.

Volcano Union Inn (☎ 209-296-7711, fax 269-7733; W www.volcanounioninn.com; 21375 Consolation St; midweek rooms $90-120, weekend rooms $120-160) has four elegant, contemporary rooms with large bathrooms and serves a breakfast buffet that you can eat in your room or take out on the large balcony overlooking the town.

Getting There & Away

Reach Volcano by going northeast from Jackson on Hwy 88 and turning north at Pine Grove, or by the scenic, winding Sutter Creek Rd, which enters the town of Sutter Creek (see earlier) as Church St, near the east end of Main St.

JACKSON

From 1860 to 1920 when the Kennedy and Eureka mines were in full swing, Jackson (population 3800; elevation 1200ft) was the area's primary entertainment center, known for its saloons, gambling halls and bordellos. Businesses geared toward tourism now occupy these historic structures (most of them well preserved), though Jackson – the Amador County seat – is more of a 'take care of business' town than a charming historic village.

It's also where Hwy 88 turns east from Hwy 49 and heads over the Sierra near Kirkwood ski resort (for more information see the boxed text 'Tahoe Ski Areas' in the Sierra Nevada chapter). At the junction there's a 24-hour Safeway supermarket and the **Amador County Chamber of Commerce** (☎ 209-223-0350), which has loads of brochures and the free *Amador County: A County for All Seasons* guide, which has walking tours of most towns in the area. There's a laundry west of the junction on the north side of Hwy 49.

Things to See & Do

Perched on a hill overlooking downtown, the **Amador County Museum** (☎ 209-223-6386; 225 Church St; admission by donation; open 10am-4pm Wed-Sun), two blocks north of Main St, contains general Gold Country history displays, a 1908 baseball uniform and a .32-caliber stealth cane that belonged to the judge who owned the house that is now the museum. Across Church St, a plaque in front of the elementary school marks the site of the first synagogue in the Mother Lode.

A mile from downtown Jackson via North Main St, **Kennedy Tailing Wheels Park** doesn't look like much at first glance, but it's worth closer inspection. It contains four iron and wood wheels, 58ft in diameter (they look like fallen carnival rides), that transported tailings from the Eureka Mine over two low hills into an impounding dam by way of gravity flumes. The wheels aren't very old – they were built in 1914 after the state legislature forbade mining operations to dump toxic tailings into rivers – but they are marvelous examples of engineering and craftsmanship. Be sure to climb to the top of the hill behind the wheels to see the impounding dam.

Mokelumne Hill, which lies 8mi south of Jackson on Hwy 49, was settled by French trappers in the early 1840s. It's a good place to see historic buildings without the common glut of antiques stores and gift shops. *Not* pronounced in French fashion, **Hotel Leger** (☎ 209-286-1401; 8304 Main St; rooms about $70) has a classic bar (established in 1851) with a potbelly stove, ceiling fans and marble tables. The saloon/dining rooms serves burgers, steaks and a variety of sandwiches ($7 to $12) and occasionally hosts live bands on weekends.

Places to Stay & Eat

Jackson's small, inexpensive motels are on the outskirts of town near Hwys 49 and 88.

The **National Hotel** (☎ 209-223-0500, fax 223-4845; 2 Water St; rooms $65-100), downtown, is a historic building with old rooms that are decorated in various themes: John Wayne, Elvis Presley etc. The rooms have access to a balcony that overlooks the town and get plenty of noise on weekends from the lively hotel bar.

Country Squire Motel (☎ 209-223-1657; 1105 N Main St; rooms $45-60, 3-person rooms $82) is between downtown and Kennedy Tailing Wheels State Park. It has a nice lawn, well-worn rooms and a free breakfast of fruit, pastries, juice and coffee.

Amador Inn (☎ 209-223-0970; 12408 Kennedy Flat Rd; midweek/weekend rooms $45/55) has a small garden, outdoor pool and 10 rooms.

Mel's and Faye's Diner Drive-In (☎ 209-223-0853), where Main St meets Hwy 49, is a local institution and favorite stop for travelers. Breakfast begins at 5am, though Mel's is best known for $5 burgers – served in paper-lined baskets with mounds of french fries – and coffee milkshakes.

Teresa's Restaurant (☎ 209-223-1786; 1229 Jackson Gate Rd; meals around $11; open Fri-Tues), a mile out of town, has been dishing up four-course Italian dinners for three generations.

SAN ANDREAS

San Andreas (population 2200; elevation 1008ft), the seat of Calaveras County, has utilitarian businesses concentrated along the highway. The old town, north of Hwy 49 along N Main St, is noteworthy for its county courthouse that houses an art gallery, restored jail and jail yard where notorious stagecoach robber Black Bart awaited trial. Also here is the **Calaveras County Museum** (☎ 209-754-4658; 30 N Main St; courthouse admission $1; open 10am-4pm daily), which has one of the area's best history displays.

In Cave City, 9mi east of San Andreas (take Mountain Ranch Rd to Cave City Rd), are the spectacular **California Cavern** (☎ 888-818-7462; w www.caverntours.com; open 10am-4pm Oct-May, 10am-5pm June-Sept), which John Muir described as 'graceful flowing folds deeply placketed like stiff silken drapery.' Regular tours take 60 to 90 minutes and cost $10. For $95 you can take a Wild Cave Expedition tour, which lasts four hours and includes some serious spelunking.

ANGELS CAMP

Famous as the place where Mark Twain gathered notes for his short story *The Celebrated Jumping Frog of Calaveras County, and Other Sketches*, Angels Camp (population 2380; elevation 1379ft) makes the most of this historic tie. The International Frog Jump Competition is held the third weekend in May and Mark Twain Days are celebrated on Fourth of July weekend. Bronze frogs, imbedded along the sidewalk of Main St, commemorate the International Frog Jumping champions of the past 50 years.

The town was founded by George Angel in 1849 as a service center for surrounding gravel and quartz mines. Hard-rock mining peaked in the 1890s, when 200 stamp mills ran around the clock. Remains of the last mine are visible in Utica Park at the west end of Main St.

Besides antique shops and a fine smattering of buildings from Gold Rush to Art Deco periods, the **Angels Camp Museum** (☎ 209-736-2963; 753 S Main St; open 10am-3pm Mar-Nov) is worth a look. Documents, photographs, relics and 3 acres of old equipment tell of the area's mining heyday.

Calaveras County Visitor Bureau (☎ 800-225-3764; w www.visitcalaveras.org; 1192 S Main St; open 9am-5pm Mon-Sat, 10am-4pm Sun) has a walking tour of Angels Camp, history books and a wealth of information about lodging and recreation throughout the area.

Places to Stay & Eat

Jumping Frog Motel (☎ 209-736-2191; 330 Murphy Grade; rooms $40-56), a block off of Main St towards the center of town, has friendly owners and simple rooms around a courtyard.

Angels Inn Motel (☎ 209-736-4242, 888-753-0226, fax 209-736-6758; 600 N Main St; rooms $69-79) is half a mile from the center of town and has a pool.

Sue's Angels Creek Café (☎ 209-736-2941; 1246 S Main St; breakfast & lunch around $6) is where locals go for pancakes, eggs, hamburgers and hot sandwiches. For a huge deli sandwich, stop at the **Pickle Barrel** (☎ 209-736-2191, Main St). Supermarkets can be found at the north edge of town on Hwy 49.

MURPHYS

Murphys (population 3400; elevation 2171ft), 7mi east of Hwy 49 on Murphys Grade Rd, is named for Daniel and John Murphy, who established a trading post and mining operation on Murphy Creek in 1848, in conjunction with the local Maidu Indians. John was apparently on very friendly terms with the tribe and eventually married the chief's daughter. The town's Main St, which looks like a cross between a Norman Rockwell painting and the set of a John Wayne western, is among the liveliest and most sophisticated in the region. Where you'll find antiques and ice-cream cones in other Gold Country towns, in Murphys you'll find boutiques and wine bars.

Things to See & Do

You'll find several wine-tasting rooms on Main St, including Zucca Mountain, Milliaire Winery and Stevenot Winery (all free and open daily). Nearby is **Murphy's Old Timers Museum** (☎ 209-728-1160; admission by donation; open 11am-4pm Sat & Sun). It has an interesting photo collection and Maidu basket exhibit, and the 'Wall of Relative Ovation,' dedicated by the mostly silly gold rush-era organization called E Clampus Vitus, a

GOLD COUNTRY

men's social organization that still exists today. **Sasha's Reading Room** *(416 Main St)* is a useful source of new and used books, maps and local history guides.

Two miles south of town via Six Mile Rd (next to the Murphys Historic Hotel & Lodge) **Kautz-Ironstone Vineyards** *(☎ 209-728-1251)* is a large winery with beautiful grounds, a small deli and a museum which displays a piece of crystalline leaf gold – weighing in at 44lbs – that was found in Jamestown in 1992. It's one of the most pleasant, well-manicured wineries in the area and crowds are frequent, but the wine-tasting room is spacious. Be sure to taste the 'Symphony' wine, made from a grape hybrid created by a professor from UC Davis.

In the opposite direction, 1mi from downtown on Sheep Ranch Rd, **Mercer Caverns** *(☎ 209-728-2101; admission $7; open 10am-4:30pm Sun-Thur, 10am-6pm Fri & Sat Oct-May; 9am-6pm Sun-Thur, 9am-8pm Fri & Sat June-Aug; 10am-6pm daily Sept)* were discovered in 1885 by Walter Mercer, who, after a long day of gold prospecting, tried to find some water to quench his thirst but found a cool stream of air coming out of the ground instead. A 45-minute guided tour takes you past enormous stalactites, stalagmites and vaulted chambers with names such as 'Chinese Meat Market' and 'Organ Loft.'

Places to Stay & Eat

Most accommodations in Murphys are expensive B&Bs. Check nearby Angels Camp or Arnold for cheaper alternatives.

Murphys Historic Hotel & Lodge *(☎ 209-728-3444, 800-532-7684, fax 209-728-1590; 457 Main St; midweek/weekend rooms $75/85)*, is quite good value considering its location. The restaurant and bar get plenty of local business, and might be considered low brow compared to newer spots in town. It definitely has an old-time Murphys' flavor.

Dunbar House 1880 Bed & Breakfast *(☎ 209-728-2897, 800-692-6006; rooms $175-225)*, on the east end of Main St, has a beautiful garden and four antique-laden rooms. Prices are a bit inflated, but they do include a bottle of local wine, appetizers upon arrival and a big breakfast.

Murphys Inn Motel *(☎ 209-728-1818, 888-796-1800; 76 Main St; midweek/weekend rooms $85/100)*, just off Hwy 4 a half mile from the center of town, has new motel rooms and a pool.

Self-caterers will find all the usual groceries at **Sierra Hills Market**, in the Sierra Hills Center at the junction of Hwy 4 and Main St. For upscale picnic fixings, fancy sandwiches ($7) or a glass of wine and light meal, try **Alchemy Market & Wine Bar** *(☎ 209-728-0700; 191 Main St; open 7am-7pm Sun-Wed, 7am-10pm Thurs-Sat)*.

Grounds *(☎ 209-728-8663; 402 Main St; breakfast & lunch $6-10 daily, dinner around $14 Wed-Sun)* was one of the first 'new' businesses to come to town and is still one of the best. It's an excellent place for a sophisticated meal, or just hanging out with coffee and a book, in a stylish but casual setting.

Murphys Bagel Barn *(☎ 209-728-1511; 140 Main St; open Tues-Sun)* and the **Coffee Roasting Co**, next to each other on the east end of Main St, are great at what they do and have a faithful local clientele.

EBBETTS PASS

Hwy 4 heads northeast from Murphys, passes through Calaveras Big Trees State Park, crosses Ebbetts Pass (elevation 8730ft) and descends to meet Hwy 89, and eventually Hwy 395, on the eastern side of the Sierra. The pass is closed most of the winter but the road is usually plowed up to **Bear Valley Ski Area** *(☎ 209-753-2301)*, a popular resort with 2000ft of vertical rise, 11 lifts, $38 day-tickets and a **cross-country ski center** *(☎ 209-753-2834)*.

Arnold, 18mi east of Murphys and 2mi from the state park, is the biggest community along Hwy 4 and has some affordable accommodations.

Arnold Timberline Lodge *(☎ 209-795-1053; midweek rooms $49-95, weekend rooms $69-145)*, the only place here that gets cable TV, has old but clean rooms with fireplaces.

Ebbetts Pass Lodge Motel *(☎ 209-795-1563; midweek/weekend rooms $47-64)* has raggedy rooms facing the highway, most with kitchenettes and all with nice bathrooms.

Tamarack Pines Inn & Lodge *(☎ 209-753-2080; rooms from $60, cabins from $95)* is a lovely spot with a variety of rooms, a few cabins and cross-country ski trails from its backyard.

Mr B's Diner (☎ 209-795-0601; dishes $4-10) has good, solid, economical all-American food and a friendly atmosphere.

Calaveras Big Trees State Park

This park (W www.sierra.parks.state.ca.us/cbt/cbt.htm; admission $2 per car year-round), at about 5000ft, is a great place to hike and camp among giant sequoia trees. Though small and undeveloped, it is easily accessible (4mi northeast of Arnold on Hwy 4) and not too crowded.

It has two giant sequoia groves, 6000 acres of pine forest and the Stanislaus River and Beaver Creek, which offer excellent trout fishing and great swimming. During winter, the North Grove stays open for snow camping and cross-country skiing.

The **North Grove Campground** is at the park entrance, near the visitor center (open 11am-4pm Sat & Sun, daily in summer), **ranger station** (☎ 209-795-2334) and main parking lots. Less crowded is the **Oak Hollow Campground**, 9mi further on the park's main road.

The **North Grove Big Trees Trail**, a 1mi self-guided loop, begins next to the visitor center and winds along the forest floor past the 'Big Stump' and a tree named 'Mother of the Forest.' A 4mi trail that branches off from the self-guided loop climbs out of the North Grove, crosses a ridge and descends 1500ft to the Stanislaus River.

Not accessible by car, and devoid of any picnic areas or campgrounds, the **South Grove** is a designated nature preserve in the park's most remote reaches. From the Beaver Creek picnic area (half a mile from the visitor center), follow the 9mi **South Grove Trail**. You don't have to hike the whole thing to have a memorable experience.

Reserve campsites through **Reserve America** (☎ 800-444-7275; camping $12).

COLUMBIA STATE HISTORIC PARK

Historically known as the 'Gem of the Southern Mines,' Columbia is an interesting meeting of commercial and historic interests. Four blocks of the town are preserved as a State Historic Park, with people in costume pretending that it's 1849 and horses powering the only nonpedestrian transportation allowed. There is a blacksmith's shop, a wonderful soap and candle company, two old

hotels, a place to pan for gold ($4), plenty of public restrooms and places to picnic or buy food. On the fringe of these blocks are regular homes and businesses that blend in so well that it's hard to tell what's park and what's not. The sum total is a verdant place to see untouched Gold Rush era architecture and keep the pocketbook entertained.

Limestone and granite boulders (they look like whale vertebrae or dinosaur bones) are noticeable around town. These were washed out of the surrounding hills by hydraulic mining and scraped clean by prospectors. There's a fascinating explanation of this kind of mining at the **Columbia Museum** (☎ 209-532-4301; cnr Main & State Sts; admission free; open 10am-4:30pm daily). The museum also has some interesting ore specimens and a slide show about Columbia's history. For written guides and maps, stop in the **Columbia Mercantile** (cnr Main & Jackson Sts; open 9am-6:30pm daily) which also has a wide variety of groceries.

City Hotel (☎ 209-532-1479, 800-532-1479; W www.cityhotel.com; rooms from $105; dinner around $40) has a restaurant run by students of Columbia College's Culinary Arts Program and serves some of the fanciest food in the Gold Country.

Fallon Hotel (☎ 209-532-1470; Washington St; rooms from $70) is home to the Sierra Repertory Theater, whose musical productions draw crowds from near and far. Shows run year-round Wednesday to Sunday and tickets cost $12 to $17. Both hotels were established in 1857 and serve continental breakfasts.

AROUND COLUMBIA STATE HISTORIC PARK
Moaning Cavern

North of a picturesque bridge over the Stanislaus River on Parrots Ferry Rd, Moaning Cavern (☎ 866-762-2837; W www.cavern tours.com; admission $10) is least impressive of the underground chambers in the area but worth the entrance fee if you don't plan on visiting any others. The big attraction here is a 100ft spiral staircase that takes you into the cave, and the chance to rappel 180ft on a three-hour, $95 Adventure Tour.

Between the caverns and the bridge, the Natural Bridge Trail leads down to the Stanislaus River, where the water has carved an immense passage through the hills.

The river actually seems to flow from an immense grotto, a sight well worth the half-mile hike. The trailhead is on a dead-end road (across from an outhouse), well marked from Parrots Ferry Rd; park anywhere along the dead-end road.

SONORA

Settled in 1848 by miners from Sonora, Mexico, this town (population 4800; elevation 1796ft) was, in its heyday, a cosmopolitan center. It had Spanish plazas, elaborate saloons and the Southern Mines' largest concentration of gamblers, drunkards and gold. The Big Bonanza Mine, at the north end of Washington St where Sonora High School now stands, yielded 12 tons of gold in two years (including a 28lb nugget). It's an important town for the area since it holds the administrative offices of Tuolumne County – not to mention a 10-theater movie complex, a Wal Mart and several chain restaurants like Denny's and Applebee's – but it's not the most quaint Gold Country town you'll come across. Its downtown is well preserved and stays lively even after the sun goes down.

Orientation & Information

Two highways cross the Sierra Nevada east of Sonora and connect with US-395 in the Eastern Sierra: Hwy 108 via Sonora Pass and Hwy 120 via Tioga Pass. Note that the section of Hwy 120 traveling through Yosemite National Park is only open in summer (see the boxed text 'Impassable Tioga Pass' in the Sierra Nevada chapter).

The center of downtown Sonora is the T-shaped intersection of Washington and Stockton Sts, with Washington being the main thoroughfare. Businesses on Washington St include banks, bookstores and restaurants.

Tuolumne County Visitors Center (☎ 209-533-4420; ⓦ www.thegreatunfenced.com; 542 Stockton St; open 9am-7pm Mon-Thur, 9am-8pm Fri, 10am-6pm Sat, 10am-5pm Sun summer; 10am-6pm Mon-Sat winter) is helpful with information on recreation, road conditions and lodging. It also has Yosemite National Park information, including maps, current road and weather conditions, and a free phone line to lodgings near the park.

Stop by the **Sierra Nevada Adventure Company** (☎ 209-532-5621; 173 S Washington

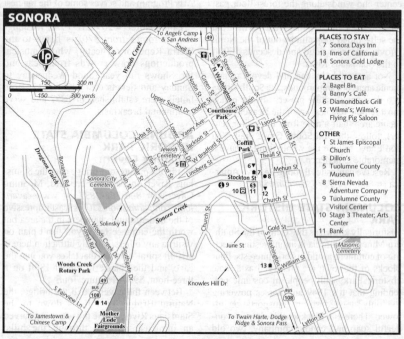

SONORA

PLACES TO STAY
7 Sonora Days Inn
13 Inns of California
14 Sonora Gold Lodge

PLACES TO EAT
2 Bagel Bin
4 Banny's Café
6 Diamondback Grill
12 Wilma's; Wilma's Flying Pig Saloon

OTHER
1 St James Episcopal Church
3 Dillon's
5 Tuolumne County Museum
8 Sierra Nevada Adventure Company
9 Tuolumne County Visitor Center
10 Stage 3 Theater; Arts Center
11 Bank

St) for maps, equipment and friendly advice on where to climb, hike and fish.

Things to See & Do

Housed in the former Tuolumne County Jail, the **Tuolumne County Museum** *(☎ 209-532-1317; 158 W Bradford St; admission free; open 11am-4pm daily)*, two blocks west of Washington St, is an interesting museum with $100,000 worth of gold on display.

Residential neighborhoods, off the north end of Washington St, are lined with restored Victorian houses, and the spooky old **cemetery** at the west end of Jackson St has many graves from that same era. **St James Episcopal Church** *(N Washington St)*, a local landmark north of Elkin St, built in 1860, has been in continuous use since then and is now simply called the 'Red Church.'

Sonora is also a base for white-water rafting: the Tuolumne River is known for its Class IV rapids and its population of golden eagles and red-tailed hawks, while the Stanislaus River is more accessible and better for novice rafters.

Sierra Mac River Trips *(☎ 209-532-1327, 800-457-2580; PO Box 366, Sonora, CA 95370)* has a good reputation and offers a wide variety of trip lengths and destinations. Day trips cost $180, two-day trips are $375. The trips leave from Groveland (a 45-minute drive toward Yosemite), but with enough advance notice the guides can usually arrange transportation from Sonora.

Places to Stay & Eat

Inns of California *(☎ 209-532-3633; 350 S Washington St; singles $60-75, doubles $155)* has a pool, hot tub and motel rooms with all the usual amenities. Ask for a room away from Washington St to avoid traffic noise.

Sonora Days Inn *(☎ 209-532-2400; 160 S Washington St; motel rooms from $73, hotel rooms $80-105)* occupies one of Sonora's oldest and most central hotel structures. It has a rooftop pool and a modern motel addition behind the original hotel.

Sonora Gold Lodge *(☎ 209-532-3952, 800-363-2154; 48 Stockton St; rooms $44-59)* is less central than the other places but has a pool and hot tub.

Wilma's *(☎ 209-532-9957; S Washington St; barbecue dinners $7-11; open 6am-9pm)* is good for local color and for what they call

'just plain good ol' food'; the pies ($3 a slice) and huge breakfasts are famous.

Bagel Bin *(☎ 209-533-1904; 83 N Washington St; open 5am-5pm Mon-Fri)* has bagels and all the fixin's and tasty sandwiches for under $5. For a huge plate of fries, fresh salad, vegetarian sandwich or top-notch burger snuggle in to the **Diamondback Grill** *(☎ 209-532-6661; 110 S Washington St; meals $4-8; open 11am-9pm Mon-Sat, 11am-5pm Sun)*.

Banny's Café *(☎ 209-209-533-4709; 83 S Stewart St; mains $9-14)* does a nice job with chicken, fish and meat and has a very inexpensive, but good, wine list.

Entertainment

The free and widely available weekend supplement of the *Union Democrat* comes out on Friday and lists movies, music, performance art and events for all of Tuolumne County. Many bars and cafés have live music on weekend nights with no cover charge; **Wilma's Flying Pig Saloon** *(☎ 209-532-9957)* and **Dillon's** *(☎ 209-533-1700)*, both on Washington St, are reliable.

Stage 3 Theater *(☎ 209-536-1778; 208 S Green St; admission $8-12)*, in the Arts Center behind the Bank of America at the corner of Washington and Stockton Sts, does off-Broadway and contemporary dramas.

Sierra Repertory Theatre *(☎ 209-532-312; W www.sierrarep.com; 13891 Hwy 108; admission $12-17; shows 8pm Wed-Fri, 2pm Sat & Sun)*, in East Sonora near the Junction Shopping Center, is the same company that performs in the Fallon Hotel (see Columbia State Historic Park earlier in this chapter.

JAMESTOWN

Three miles south of Sonora, just south of the Hwy 49/108 junction, Jamestown (population 540; elevation 1405ft) is affectionately called 'Jimtown' by area residents. Its history developed in waves: the first with Tuolumne County's first gold strike in 1848; the second when the railroad did in 1897; and, lastly, in the 1920s when Jamestown became construction headquarters for dams on the Stanislaus and Tuolumne Rivers. Now, amongst its balconied structures and raised sidewalks, it has some excellent antique stores and a Harley-Davidson shop that attracts weekend bike tours.

The **Emporium** (18180 Main St) has an exceptionally wide selection of Americana bric-a-brac at reasonable prices. The two 'pay $4 get a little gold dust' operations on Main St, can be fun if you want to pretend the Mother Lode is still out there waiting for your magic pan.

Gold Prospecting Expeditions (☎ 209-984-4653, 800-596-0009; 18170 Main St) runs trips that last from a half-hour ($10) to two days ($135) and even offers a three-day college-accredited gold-prospecting course ($595). One of the more popular tours includes a 5mi float down the Stanislaus River ($79 adults, $49 if under 18) with lunch.

Railtown 1897 State Historic Park (☎ 209-984-3953; 5th Ave; admission $6; open year-round), south of Main St, has a 26-acre collection of trains and railroad equipment and was the backdrop for the film *High Noon*. The admission includes a ride on the *Mother Lode Cannon Ball*, a narrow-gauge railroad once used to transport ore, lumber and miners to and from the mines. The train makes a one-hour loop past old mines and equipment. It usually runs Saturday and Sunday from April to October, and Saturday only during winter.

Places to Stay & Eat

If you want to stay in one of Jamestown's historic beauties, make reservations in advance and plan on spending $65 to $135, including breakfast. Good choices are the **Royal Hotel** (☎ 209-984-5271; Ⓦ www.bbonline .com/ca/royalhotel; rooms from $65) which has the feeling of a private home, and the **Jamestown Hotel** (☎ 209-984-3902, 800-205-4901; Ⓦ www.jamestownhotel.com; rooms $80-95), which has spacious rooms, bathrobes and a balcony.

Barendregt's Grocery (18195 Main St; open 8am-8pm Mon-Sat, 9am-6pm Sun) has a vast selection of groceries and a full deli. **Morelia Mexican Restaurant** (☎ 209-984-1432; 18148 Main St; mains $6-9) has a small patio and casual atmosphere. The **Willow Steakhouse** (cnr Main & Willow Sts; mains $12-18) is an old watering hole with a rowdy saloon and dining room that features cheese fondue, at no extra cost, with all of its meals.

San Joaquin Valley

The San Joaquin is the southern half of what's commonly called the Great Central Valley (the northern half being the Sacramento Valley), stretching from Stockton to the Tehachapi Mountains southeast of Bakersfield. It's an arid landscape that traditionally was interspersed with wetlands, tree-lined creeks and riparian ecosystems. The region is fed by rivers such as the Kings, Kern and Merced, which bring water from the snowy peaks of the Sierra Nevada. Tapped today for irrigation, these rivers have made the San Joaquin one of the most agriculturally productive regions in the world. Neat and tidy rows of crops cover nearly every rural acre between the Sierras to the east and the coastal ranges to the west. This is California's own self-contained version of 'the heartland.'

Small family farms are rare here, however. Large corporations dominate the land, producing fruits, nuts, vegetables and dairy items that earn billions in revenue each year, while employing migrant workers at low wages. During the Depression years the fields were populated by 'Okies,' white immigrants from the southern and central Plains; these days the work is performed mostly by laborers from Mexico and Latin America. So while some of the tiny towns scattering the region, such as Gustine and Reedley, retain a classic Main St Americana feel, many more like Cutler and Lamont feel almost entirely Mexican.

For those in a rush, I-5 is the streamlined route between north and south, with virtually no towns or roadside attractions. Traveling Hwy 99 – a road with nearly as long a history as the famous Route 66 – is far more interesting. Following an old wagon route, the highway parallels the railroad between Bakersfield and Sacramento. Historically Hwy 99 ran north into Oregon and Washington, though today I-5 follows that route and Hwy 99's northern terminus is Red Bluff. It connects the region's most important towns, acting as a window into the valley's – and the state's – colorful history.

The San Joaquin contains no sweeping ocean vistas, no jagged, snowcapped peaks. Yet the evening sun streaking its way across the wheat fields, orange groves and vineyards does make a glorious sight.

Highlights

- Kern River rafting – a thrilling white-water ride
- Buck Owens – the country music legend live on stage every week in Bakersfield
- Fresno's Forestiere Underground Gardens – 70 subterranean acres of fruits and flowers

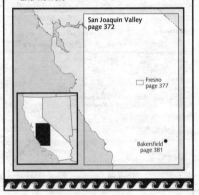

Keep in mind that in midsummer temperatures in the valley often hover around 100°F (37°C) or more.

STOCKTON

It's hard to get around the fact that Stockton (population 243,771) is a pretty run-down city, especially when viewed from downtown, a sort of ghost town where boarded-up buildings and storefronts cry out for renovation. Despite a bleak veneer, Stockton does have real character even in its shabbiest corners, something that comes through in Leonard Gardner's novel *Fat City*, set in Stockton. (Director John Huston later turned that story of two-bit boxers into a superb feature film starring Stacy Keach and Jeff Bridges.) The city's other famous sons include singer Chris Isaak, who regularly sings Stockton's praises, and the alternative-rock band Pavement.

Stockton is also a port city, connecting to San Francisco via a deep-water channel. During the gold rush, it was the main disembarkation point for men and goods headed to the southern mines. More recently the port

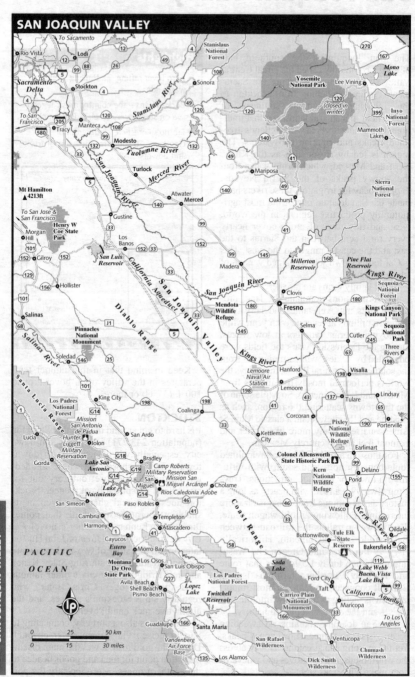

SAN JOAQUIN VALLEY

Tule Fog

Radiation or tule (**too**-lee) fog causes dozens of collisions each year on San Joaquin Valley roads, including Hwy 99 and I-5. As thick as proverbial pea soup, the fog limits visibility to about 10ft, making driving nearly impossible. The fog is thickest from November to February, when cold mountain air settles on the warm valley floor and condenses into fog as the ground cools at night. The fog often lifts for a few hours during the afternoon, just long enough for the ground to warm back up and thus perpetuate the cycle.

Call **Caltrans** (☎ 800-427-7623) to check road conditions before traveling. If you end up on a fog-covered road, drive with your low beams on, keep a good distance from the car in front of you, stay at a constant speed, avoid sudden stops and never try to pass other cars.

served as an important loading and unloading point for San Joaquin Valley agriculture.

A few more areas worth checking out include the architecturally rich Magnolia Historic District and the excellent Haggin Museum.

Orientation & Information

Stockton's main thoroughfares are Pacific Ave (part of which is a shopping district dubbed the 'Miracle Mile') and El Dorado St going north–south, and Park St, Weber Ave and Harding Way going east–west. Maps and information are available at the **Stockton-San Joaquin Convention & Visitors Bureau** (☎ 209-943-1987, 800-350-1987; 46 W Fremont St; open 9am-5pm Mon-Fri), downtown off Center St. On the Miracle Mile is **Maxwell's Books** (2103 Pacific Ave), an independent bookstore dating back to 1939.

Things to See & Do

The **Haggin Museum** (☎ 209-940-6300; 1201 N Pershing Ave; adult/student $5/ 2.50; open 1:30pm-5pm Tues-Sun) has an excellent collection of American landscape paintings, including works by Albert Bierstadt. There are also historical items such as Native American baskets and early Caterpillar tractors, which were developed in Stockton. The museum is surrounded by

Victory Park, a shady picnic spot with a duck pond. Exit I-5 at Pershing Ave and head two blocks north.

About 1mi east of the Haggin Museum, via Acacia St, is the **Magnolia Historic District**, which stands as testimony to Stockton's prosperous past. Eden Park, at Poplar and Acacia Sts, is a good starting point. From here, walk one block north on Hunter to Magnolia St, where most of the beautiful homes – Queen Anne, Craftsman and California Bungalow styles – are located. The visitor bureau has a detailed pamphlet on the history and architecture of this district.

Places to Stay & Eat

Days Inn (☎ 209-948-6151; cnr Weber & Center Sts; singles/doubles $64/75) and **Red Roof Inn** (☎ 209-478-4300; fax 209-478-1872; 2654 W March Lane; rooms from $60) are both centrally located near I-5.

Best Western Stockton Inn (☎ 209-931-3131; fax 209-931-0423; 4219 E Waterloo Rd; singles/doubles $72/86) is just east of Hwy 99.

Ye Olde Hoosier Inn (☎ 209-463-0271; 1537 N Wilson Way; meals from $6) is a well-established 1946 standby decorated with red booths and folksy antiques; it serves breakfast and lunch daily.

Valley Brewing Co (☎ 209-464-2739; 157 W Adams St; meals from $7) opened in 1994 and serves burgers, pizzas and pasta dishes, plus handcrafted ales. The town's original Valley Brewing Company dates back to 1853.

Getting There & Away

Public transportation to and from Stockton is available daily via **Greyhound** (☎ 209-466-3568, 800-229-9424; 121 S Center St) buses and **Amtrak** (☎ 800-872-7245; 735 S San Joaquin St) trains.

MODESTO

Despite sturdy agricultural roots, which include the Ernest & Julio Gallo Winery (founded here in 1933), Modesto (population 190,102) is probably best known as the 'cruising capital of the world,' thanks in great part to hometown boy George Lucas, who immortalized the town, and the tradition, in the movie *American Graffiti*. Cruising, however, was banned by the city in 1993 because of gridlock and violence, though people still show off their hot rods and flashy wheels when and where they can.

Classic car shows are held in 'Graffiti Month' (June); for details, call the **chamber of commerce** (☎ 209-577-5757; 1114 J St).

Another relic from the city's cruising heyday is the vintage **A&W Root Beer Drive-In** (cnr 14th & G Sts), complete with roller-skating carhops.

Downtown sits just east of Hwy 99 (avoid the area west of the freeway), centering on 10th and J Sts, home of a revitalization project that now boasts a flashy multiplex and several chain restaurants. Many historic buildings still survive, though, including the 1934 **State Theatre** (☎ 209-527-4697; 1307 J St), which hosts films and live music. The famous **Modesto Arch** (cnr 9th & I Sts), erected in 1912, stands at what was once the city's main entry point. Its slogan, 'Water Wealth Contentment Health,' was the result of a local contest – though this wasn't the judges' first choice. If they'd had their way, the sign would instead read 'Nobody's Got Modesto's Goat.' From downtown, Yosemite Blvd (Hwy 132) runs east toward Yosemite National Park.

Things to See & Do

Housed in the former city library, the spacious **McHenry Museum** (☎ 209-577-5366; cnr 14th & I Sts; admission free; open noon-4pm Tues-Sun) offers local history, photographs and displays that are well worth a quick look.

One block away the lovely Victorian Italianate **McHenry Mansion** (☎ 209-577-5344; cnr I & 15th Sts; admission free; open 1pm-4pm Sun-Thur, noon-3pm Fri), built in 1883, is the former home of prominent local rancher and banker Robert McHenry.

Places to Stay & Eat

McHenry Ave (Hwy 108), running north from Needham St downtown, has ample budget motels. Near McHenry and Needham is the **Chalet Motel** (☎ 209-529-4370; 115 Downey St; rooms $55), with simple, clean rooms. Downtown, a slightly nicer choice is the **Best Western Town House Lodge** (☎ 209-524-7261; 909 16th St; singles/ doubles $78/83).

DeVa (cnr 12th & J Sts; lunch $7) is an urban coffeehouse with good locally roasted coffee, pastries and sandwiches.

St Stan's Brewery (☎ 209-524-4782; 821 L St; meals $6-15) is a brewpub known for its Altbier, a smooth German style. The food is acceptable albeit mediocre, while the beer's excellent (try the dark).

Tresetti's World Caffe (☎ 209-572-2990; 927 11th St; lunch/dinner from $8/15) is a lovely spot with enticing main dishes, an impressive wine list and a wine retail shop next door.

About a mile east of downtown, the **Falafel Hut** (917 Yosemite Blvd; dishes from $3) makes truly delicious falafels and *shwarmas* (meat off a spit in bread) – a refreshing alternative to highway fast food. Next door is the spacious **India Palate** (915 Yosemite Blvd; mains $8-12), serving tasty Indian meals and a weekday lunch buffet ($5 to $6).

Getting There & Away

Greyhound (☎ 800-229-9424) stops at the Modesto Transportation Center at 9th and J Sts, as do local **MAX** (☎ 209-521-1274) buses. Take bus 34 to the **Amtrak station** (☎ 209-551-2048; 1700 Held Dr), a 40-minute ride from downtown.

MERCED

With its tree-lined streets, historic Victorian homes and magnificent 1875 courthouse, Merced (population 63,893) makes for a pleasant stop whether traveling on Hwy 99 or east to Yosemite National Park via Hwy 140. The downtown business district is active during the day and great for a respite or antique shopping; at night it's less inviting. There are, however, three movie theaters on Main St (two dating from the 1930s), and life around them is lively. The University of California's newest campus is earmarked for the Merced area, though construction has been delayed as a result of environmental arguments.

Newshounds may remember that former US congressman Gary Condit had an office in the federal building here. Condit gained household recognition thanks to his alleged affair with the late Chandra Levy, an intern of his who disappeared in 2001. Condit was voted out of office a year later.

Orientation & Information

Downtown Merced is east of Hwy 99 along Main St, between R St and Martin Luther King Jr Way. Numbered streets run parallel to Hwy 99, with 16th St (the old route of Hwy

99) the main drag. The **California Welcome Center** (☎ *209-384-2791, 800-446-5353; 710 W 16th St*), adjacent to the bus depot, has local maps ($2), information on Merced and Yosemite, and coupon books offering motel discounts.

Check email at **Wired** (☎ *209-386-0206; 450 W 18th St*), a sleek, modern coffeehouse offering Internet access for $5 per hour.

Things to See & Do
Surrounded by a green, serene square, the 1875 **Merced County Courthouse** is the town's architectural patriarch, the last still standing of eight county courthouses designed by Albert A Bennett. Inside is the excellent **Courthouse Museum** (☎ *209-723-2401; admission free; open 1pm-4pm Wed-Sun*), well worth a quick peek.

In Atwater, about 6mi northwest of Merced, the **Castle Air Museum** (☎ *209-723-2178; 5050 Santa Fe Dr; adult/child $7/5; open 10am-4pm daily*) has a field full of restored military aircraft.

During late February and early March, the surrounding orchards come alive with the luxurious scents and sights of almond, peach, apricot and other tree blossoms. Flower fans can follow the **Blossom Tour** along Merced County roads by picking up a map and brochure at the Welcome Center.

Places to Stay & Eat
Merced Home Hostel (☎ *209-725-0407; dorm beds $12-15; closed during the day*) is an eight-bed, family-style hostel in the home of longtime Merced residents who know tons about Yosemite. The hostel fills quickly, especially during summer weekends. Beds must be reserved in advance; call between 5:30pm and 10pm. The hostel doesn't give out its address but it will pick up and drop off guests at the bus and train stations.

Merced has no shortage of budget motels. Among the older, independent establishments close to downtown, the **Slumber Motel** (☎ *209-722-5783; 1315 W 16th St; singles/doubles $35/45*) is clean, safe and relatively quiet.

More budget motels are found on Motel Dr, which runs immediately east of Hwy 99; access it from the Hwy 140 exit. One recommended choice is the **Sierra Lodge** (☎ *209-722-3926; 951 Motel Dr; singles/doubles $39/45*).

For breakfast, it's hard to resist the chatty, small-town-diner scene at **Cinema Cafe** (☎ *209-722-2811; 661 W Main St; meals $4-6*), next door to the **Mainzer** (☎ *209-722-4042*), a stately old movie house.

Several funky, decades-old roadside eateries line 16th St and Main St. One of the most intriguing is the **Branding Iron** (*640 W 16th St; dinner $14 and up*), serving hearty steak platters in a Western atmosphere presided over by 'Old Blue,' a massive stuffed bull's head from a local dairy farm.

Getting There & Away
Yarts (☎ *877-989-2787, 209-388-9589;* **w** *www.yarts.com*) buses depart four times daily for Yosemite Valley from several Merced locations, including the **Merced Transpo Center** (*cnr 16th & N Sts*) and the **Amtrak station** (*cnr 24th & K Sts*). The trip takes about 2½ hours and stops include Mariposa, Midpines and the Yosemite Bug Lodge & Hostel in Midpines. Round-trip adult/child tickets cost $20/14 and include the park entrance fee (quite a bargain!). They can be purchased at the Welcome Center or from the driver.

Greyhound (☎ *800-229-9424*) also operates from the Transpo Center and heads to Los Angeles ($32, 6½ hours) and San Francisco ($27, four hours) numerous times daily.

Amtrak (☎ *209-722-6862, 800-872-7245*) connects Merced with Oakland ($27, 3¼ hours), and Los Angeles ($38, six hours), the latter via a bus connection in Bakersfield.

FRESNO
Bulging like a blister at the hot, dry center of the state, Fresno (population 427,652) is by far the biggest of the San Joaquin Valley towns. Most coastal Californians sniff that it's hardly a destination, only worth passing through on one's way to Yosemite (via Hwy 41), and Kings Canyon and Sequoia National Parks (via Hwy 180). Yet what those travelers don't realize is that, along with Bakersfield, agriculture, politics and even the arts have sturdy roots here.

There's loads of intriguing history in and around this busy Central Valley hub. The old brick warehouses lining the Santa Fe railroad tracks are an impressive sight, as are the many historic downtown buildings such as the 1894 Fresno Water Tower and the 1928 Pantages (Warnors) Theatre. These compete for attention with newer structures such as the sprawling Convention Center and the brand-new ballpark for Fresno's Triple A baseball team, the Grizzlies.

And then there's the Tower District. North of downtown, it boasts the only active alternative-culture neighborhood between Sacramento and Los Angeles, with book and record stores, music clubs and a handful of stylish, highly regarded restaurants.

Like many valley towns, Fresno's also surprisingly diverse. Mexican, Basque and Chinese communities have been here for decades, and, more recently, thousands of Hmong have put down roots in the area. The longstanding Armenian community is most famously represented by author and playwright William Saroyan, who was born, lived and died in this city he loved dearly.

History

The region around present-day Fresno was inhabited by Yokut Indian tribes when John C Fremont, Kit Carson and other explorers arrived here in 1844. In 1872 Fresno became a stop on the Central Pacific Railroad. Winemaker Francis Eisen instigated the US raisin business here in the 1870s after accidentally letting grapes dry on the vine. But raisins became only one of many lucrative Fresno County crops after irrigation turned the arid land into an agricultural goldmine. Between 1954 and 2001, the county was the top agricultural producer in the nation; today it churns out $3 billion annually in commercial commodities such as cotton, cattle and tomatoes. At the same time, though, the area is falling prey to urban sprawl, as more and more farmland gets paved and pollution problems – both in the air and on the ground – skyrocket.

Orientation & Information

Fresno is a large, sprawling city. Downtown lies between Divisadero St, Hwy 41 and Hwy 99. Two miles north, the Tower District sits around the corner of E Olive Ave and N Fulton Ave.

The **Fresno Convention & Visitors Bureau** (☎ 559-237-0988, 800-788-0836; cnr Fresno & O Sts; open 10am-4pm Mon-Fri, 11am-3pm Sat) is inside the Fresno Water Tower.

Things to See & Do

If you see only one thing in Fresno, make it the **Forestiere Underground Gardens** (☎ 559-271-0734; 5021 W Shaw Ave; adult/child $7/4; tours noon & 2pm Sat-Sun) of Sicilian immigrant Baldasare Forestiere, one block east of Hwy 99. Beginning in 1906, Forestiere – whose plans for citrus groves were foiled by the hard soil – dug out some 70 acres beneath the hardpan soil, and, with a unique skylight system, created space for commercial crops and his own living quarters. The property includes bedrooms, a library, patios, grottos and a fish pond, and is now a historic landmark.

In town the **Meux Home** (☎ 559-233-8007; cnr Tulare & R Sts; admission $4; open noon-3:30pm Fri-Sun Feb-Dec) is a good example of 19th-century Victorian architecture. It was the residence of former confederate army surgeon Dr TR Meux.

Grander still is the **Kearney Mansion** (☎ 559-441-0862; 7160 W Kearney Blvd; adult/child $4/2; tours 1pm-3pm Fri-Sun), the only realized portion of the magnificent 'Chateau Fresno' envisioned by raisin baron M Theo Kearney. The mansion is in pleasant Kearney Park (admission $3/car, waived for mansion visitors), 7mi east of downtown via Kearney Blvd – which, lined with palm trees, makes for a beautiful drive.

The **Fresno Art Museum** (☎ 559-441-4221; 2233 N 1st St; adult/student $4/2, free Tues; open 10am-5pm Tues-Fri, noon-5pm Sat & Sun), in Radio Park, has rotating exhibits of contemporary art – including work by local artists – that are among the most intriguing in the valley.

A favorite with children, the **Fresno Metropolitan Museum** (☎ 559-441-1444; 1555 Van Ness Ave; adult/student $7/4; open 11am-5pm Tues-Sun, 11am-8pm Thurs) has hands-on science exhibits, Native American crafts, a large collection of antique puzzles and a William Saroyan gallery.

On Olive Ave just east of Hwy 99, large and shady **Roeding Park** (admission $1/car) is home to the small **Chaffee Zoological Gardens** (☎ 559-498-2671; adult/child $6/4; open 9am-5pm daily Mar-Oct, 10am-4pm Nov-Feb). Adjacent to it are **Storyland** (☎ 559-264-2235; adult/child $3.75/2.75; open 11am-4pm Mon-Fri, 10am-5:30pm Sat & Sun May-Sept, weekends only Oct-Apr), a children's fairy-tale world dating from 1962, and **Playland**, which has kiddie rides and games.

Fresno's **Tower District** began as a shopping mecca during the 1920s, gaining its

FRESNO

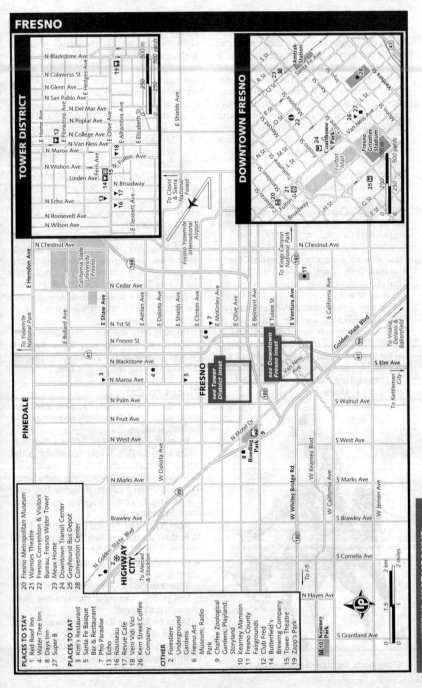

TOWER DISTRICT

DOWNTOWN FRESNO

PINEDALE

HIGHWAY CITY

SAN JOAQUIN VALLEY

PLACES TO STAY
1 Red Roof Inn
4 Water Tree Inn
8 Days Inn
27 Super 8

PLACES TO EAT
3 Kim's Restaurant
5 Santa Fe Basque
   Bar & Restaurant
7 Pho Paradise
13 Echo
16 Rousseau
17 Revue Cafe
18 Veni Vidi Vici
26 Kern Street Coffee
   Company

OTHER
2 Forestiere
   Underground
   Gardens
6 Fresno Art
   Museum; Radio
   Park
9 Chaffee Zoological
   Gardens; Playland;
   Storyland
10 Kearney Mansion
11 Fresno County
   Fairgrounds
12 Club Fred
14 Butterfield's
   Brewing Company
15 Tower Theatre
19 Zapp's Park

20 Fresno Metropolitan Museum
21 Warnors Theatre
22 Fresno Convention & Visitors
   Bureau; Fresno Water Tower
23 Meux Home
24 Downtown Transit Center
25 Greyhound Bus Depot
28 Convention Center

name after the **Tower Theatre** (☎ 559-485-9050; 815 E Olive Ave), which opened in 1939. The theater has since been renovated and turned into a center for the performing arts. Surrounding it are bookstores, shops, high-end restaurants and coffeehouses that cater to Fresno's gay and alternative communities. This is the city's best neighborhood for browsing and kicking back with an iced latte – even if the hipster quotient is tiny by comparison to that of, say, San Francisco's Mission District.

Special Events

On the first Thursday of every month, from 5pm to 8pm, downtown and Tower District studios and galleries open their doors to the public during **ArtHop**, sponsored by the Fresno Arts Council (☎ 559-237-9734).

When at the Convention & Visitors Bureau, pick up a map of the **Fresno County Blossom Trail**, a self-guided tour through local orchards, in bloom during late February and early March.

The newly inaugurated **William Saroyan Festival** celebrates the life and work of Fresno's famous son with readings, performances, exhibits and other events each spring. On the third weekend in April, nearby Clovis hosts the biggest two-day **rodeo** in California. The **Hmong New Year** celebration is held in Fresno in late December.

Clovis hosts the biggest rodeo in California

Places to Stay

Cheap motels line streets adjacent to Hwy 99, and are clearly visible from the highway. Despite the enticement of cool neon signs and cheap rates (several advertise rooms for around $25 per night), most are thoroughly seedy or simply noisy because of freeway traffic.

The options around N Parkway and Olive are the least offensive, notably the **Days Inn** (☎ 559-268-6211; 1101 N Parkway Dr; singles/doubles $47/69), set slightly back from the road.

Close to Hwy 99 but north of downtown is the **Red Roof Inn** (☎ 559-276-1910; 5021 N Barcus Ave; singles/doubles $48/59), just off W Shaw Ave near the Forestiere Underground Gardens.

A better area to troll for lodging is N Blackstone Ave, which runs north from downtown. Numerous choices are found between Shields and Shaw Aves, including the **Water Tree Inn** (☎ 800-762-9071, 559-222-4445; 4141 N Blackstone Ave; singles/doubles $55/65), which has large, clean, comfortable rooms.

If you need to stay downtown near the bus and train station, the very basic **Super 8** (☎ 559-268-0621; 2127 Inyo St; singles/doubles $60/70) will do just fine.

Places to Eat

Believe it or not, Fresno has quite a few upscale eateries with inventive menus and inviting interiors.

Echo (☎ 559-442-3246; 609 E Olive Ave; mains from $20), a lovely restaurant in the Tower District, serves dishes made with local, seasonal and often organic ingredients. The aqua-colored chairs, designed by Frank Lloyd Wright, were salvaged from a funeral home in Delano.

Veni Vidi Vici (☎ 559-266-5510; 1116 N Fulton St; mains from $18), cozy and elegant, is another highly regarded choice with a hopping bar. It's one block south of Olive Ave.

Rousseau (568 E Olive Ave; dinners $7-10) is less pricey, offering a varied menu from pastas to pork chops.

Santa Fe Basque Bar & Restaurant (3110 N Maroa Ave; meals under $15) has been uprooted from its downtown location but is still popular with Fresno's Basque old-timers. Family-style meals include soup, salad, meat, vegetables, bread and dessert. Make sure you come hungry.

Kim's Restaurant *(5048 N Maroa Ave; lunch/dinner $5/8)* serves well-prepared Vietnamese dishes despite its tiny location. More Vietnamese options are scattered along N First St, including **Pho Paradise** *(1848 N First St; lunch $4-6)*, where bowls of the spicy noodle soup are just $4.

Need coffee? **Revue Cafe** *(620 E Olive Ave)* is a friendly Tower District hipster hub; downtown, head for the pleasant **Kern Street Coffee Company** *(2134 Kern St)*, serving soup, sandwiches and smoothies.

Entertainment
In addition to the glorious Tower Theatre, the Tower District has several favorite haunts. Among them are indie-rock hang out **Club Fred** *(1426 N Van Ness Ave)*, divey blues bar **Zapp's Park** *(1105 N Blackstone Ave)* and **Butterfield Brewing Company** *(777 E Olive Ave)*, which serves its own beer and has occasional live music.

Downtown is home to several more classic old theaters, including the stunning 1928 **Warnors Theatre** *(☎ 559-264-6863; 1412 Fulton St)*, which hosts concerts, musicals and other events.

Getting There & Around
Small but growing, the **Fresno Yosemite International Airport** is serviced by about two dozen commercial airlines. The airport is east of Hwy 41, at the east end of Shields Ave. FAX bus 26 runs daily from the airport to downtown.

Greyhound *(☎ 559-268-1829; 1033 Broadway)* connects Fresno to Los Angeles ($22, five hours) and San Francisco ($26, 4¾ hours) from its bus depot in downtown near the new ballpark.

Amtrak *(☎ 559-486-7651, 800-872-7245; 2650 Tulare St)* runs trains to Fresno on the *San Joaquins* route between Oakland ($34, four hours) and Bakersfield ($25, two hours), with bus connections to Los Angeles ($30, 4½ hours).

The local **Fresno Area Express** *(FAX; ☎ 559-488-1122)* has daily bus services to the Tower District (bus 22 or 26), airport (bus 26) and Forestiere Underground Gardens (bus 20, transfer to bus 9) from the downtown transit center at Van Ness Ave and Fresno St. Fares are $1.

HANFORD
Hanford (population 41,000) has a compact, restored downtown that centers on the 1896 **Kings County Courthouse**, the town's crown jewel. The surrounding square is shaded and, like much of the town, great for strolling. Most of Hanford's historic brick buildings along Court and 7th Sts date from the early 1900s; they now house restaurants and shops.

Learn more about the historic buildings at the **Hanford Carnegie Museum** *(☎ 559-584-1367; 109 E 8th St; admission $2; open noon-3pm Tues-Fri, noon-4pm Sat)*. Across from the courthouse is the **Fox Theatre** *(☎ 559-584-7423; 326 N Irwin St)*, an eye-catching Art Deco venue dating from 1929 that regularly hosts live music.

Predating all these buildings is Hanford's **Taoist Temple** *(☎ 559-582-4508; tours by appointment two weeks in advance)*, built in 1893 in **China Alley**, heart of a once-bustling Chinatown. To reach China Alley from downtown, take 7th St east to Green St and turn left; it's immediately on your right.

About 35mi south of Hanford on Hwy 43 is **Colonel Allensworth State Historic Park** *(661-849-3433; admission $2 per car)*. Allensworth was a tiny farm community founded in 1908 by African-American colonel and former slave Allen Allensworth, who hoped to escape racism and bigotry. The unique history, well-preserved buildings and subtle beauty of the surrounding grasslands make for a serene visit.

Places to Stay & Eat
The quiet, shaded campsites ($6) at **Colonel Allensworth State Historic Park** are a rarity in the overly cultivated Central Valley; unless there's a special event, you may be alone.

Downtown Motel *(☎ 559-582-9036; 101 N Redington St; rooms $43-49)* is plain but centrally located in Hanford (between 6th and 7th Sts) and affordable.

Imperial Dynasty *(☎ 559-582-0196; 406 China Alley; dishes $10-30; closed Mon)* sits next to the Taoist Temple but oddly enough serves upscale continental cuisine.

For Chinese food, step across the alley to the friendly **China Cafe** *(420 E 7th St; meals from $4; closed Mon)*.

The Bastille *(☎ 559-585-8599; 113 Court St; lunch/dinner from $8/15)*, housed in the old jail on the courthouse's ground floor, has a cool, dark bar, a pleasant outdoor patio and live music twice weekly. Across the street is **Superior Dairy** (*325 N Douty St*), a vintage 1929 ice-cream parlor; get a cone and sink into one of the pale-pink booths.

Getting There & Away
Amtrak (☎ *559-582-5236, 800-872-7245; 200 Santa Fe Ave, off 7th St*) connects Hanford to Oakland ($39, five hours), Bakersfield ($19, 1½ hours) and Los Angeles ($26, four hours) several times daily.

VISALIA
Visalia (population 96,750) is one of the valley's nicest towns and a good place to stay en route to Sequoia and Kings Canyon National Parks. Bypassed a century ago by the railroad (which goes through Hanford instead), the city is 5mi east of Hwy 99, along Hwy 198. Its downtown – centered on the intersection of Court and Main Sts – has great old buildings and is a popular place to stroll, day or night.

Things to See & Do
The original Victorian and Craftsman-style homes in Visalia are real architectural gems and worth viewing on foot. Get details of a walking tour from the **Visalia Chamber of Commerce and Visitors Center** (☎ *559-734-5876, 877-847-2542;* **w** *www.visaliatourism.com; 720 W Mineral King Ave; open 8:30am-5pm Mon-Fri*). Lovely examples are found north of Main St on both N Willis and Encina Sts.

The gloriously restored 1930 **Fox Theatre** (*cnr W Main & Encina Sts*) hosts assorted concerts and special events.

South of downtown on Hwy 63 (Mooney Blvd), shaded Mooney Grove Park is home to the **Tulare County Museum** (☎ *559-733-6616; park admission $5, museum free; open 10am-4pm Mon, Thurs & Fri, 1pm4pm Sat-Sun*), which has pioneer and Native American memorabilia.

About 7mi east of Visalia is **Kaweah Oak Reserve**, home to 324 acres of valley oak trees, which once stretched from the Sierras to (long-gone) Tulare Lake in the valley. Nice for a short hike, it's also a rare glimpse into the valley's past before orchards and vineyards took over. From Hwy 198, turn north onto Road 182; the park is about a half-mile along on your left.

Places to Stay & Eat
Best Western Visalia Inn (☎ *559-732-4561; 623 W Main St; rooms $72*) has quiet rooms and a downtown location.

A few budget motels are found south of Hwy 198 off the Akers exit. These include the **Marco Polo Motel** (☎ *559-732-4591; cnr Noble & Linwood Aves; singles/doubles $50/60*), which is a friendly place with large rooms.

Despite its plain atmosphere, **Colima** (*111 E Main; meals from $5*) is a favorite Mexican restaurant.

Vintage Press (☎ *559-733-3033; 216 N Willis; mains $20-30*) offers an elegant, upscale dining atmosphere and a spacious bar.

Watson's Veggie Garden (☎ *559-635-7355; 617 W Main St; lunches $4-7*) is a welcome stop for healthy sandwiches and salads.

Main Street has a couple of good coffeehouses, one being **Java Jungle** (*208 W Main St*), where they roast their own beans.

Getting There & Away
Visalia is serviced by **Greyhound** (☎ *559-734-3507; 1927 E Mineral King Ave*), which has daily buses to Los Angeles ($22, 4½ hours) and San Francisco ($42, 6¾ hours). **Amtrak** (☎ *559-582-5236*) shuttles connect with the station in Hanford, by reservation only.

BAKERSFIELD
At the southern end of the San Joaquin Valley lies Bakersfield (population 247,057), one of the valley's biggest towns and key agricultural centers. The region has seen its share of prosperity thanks not only to crops but also to oil. Development of the Kern River oil field began in 1899. It stretches from Oildale, just north of town, to Taft, some 30mi west. It remains one of the biggest oil producers in the nation.

Though some parts of town are rather shabby, downtown is a surprisingly upbeat mix of restored buildings, county offices, restaurants and antique shops, such as the **Five and Dime** (*cnr 19th St & K St*) inside an original Woolworth's building. The 1930 Fox Theater hosts regular performances, and the dusty but still impressive Padre Hotel, though currently closed, is earmarked for redevelopment. Near the freeway, Buck Owens' multimillion-dollar Crystal Palace is a raging success.

In fact, it's amazing how much history there is everywhere you turn. Old Town Kern, east of downtown around Baker and Sumner Sts, is another district that, while currently decaying, was once vibrant and bustling. The Bakersfield Historic Preservation Commission has put together walking tour brochures covering Old Town Kern as well as Bakersfield's historic downtown; call ☎ 661-326-3765 for a copy of either or check the Internet at ⓦ www.ci.bakersfield.ca.us.edcd/historic/index.htm.

History

The Yowlumne branch of the Yokuts lived in a village near what is now 16th and F Sts downtown. In 1776 Friar Francisco Garces arrived, trying to find a route between Sonora, Mexico and Monterey. Gold was discovered near the Kern River in 1853, but not many outsiders settled the valley until the arrival of Colonel Thomas Baker, who in 1863 began reclaiming swamp land and turning what was called 'Kern Island' into an enormous field.

Basques came in the 1890s to tend sheep on 'Baker's field,' followed by oil workers.

During the Depression, Bakersfield became a gathering point for Okie farmworkers, who migrated here from the South and the Great Plains. John Steinbeck wrote about them masterfully in *The Grapes of Wrath*, and the historic labor camp that served as his model still survives south of town near Lamont (see Weedpatch Labor Camp later in this chapter).

The Okies brought their Southern culture with them too, including their love of country music, turning Bakersfield into a hotbed of honky-tonk (see the boxed text 'The Bakersfield Sound' later). The worthwhile Kern County Museum has a small display on the region's musical history.

Orientation & Information

The Kern River flows along Bakersfield's northern edge, separating it from its blue-collar neighbor, Oildale, and a host of unsightly oil fields. Truxtun and Chester Aves are the main downtown thoroughfares; numbered streets run parallel to Truxtun, lettered streets run parallel to Chester Ave.

Both the **Greater Bakersfield Convention and Visitors Bureau** (☎ 661-325-5051; ⓦ *www.bakersfieldcvb.org; 1325 P St; open*

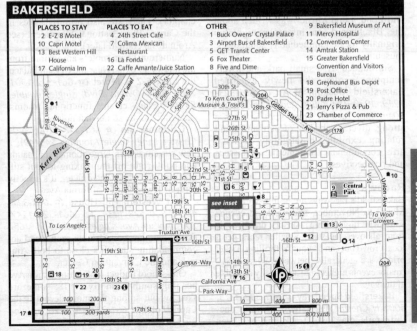

8:30am-5pm Mon-Fri) and the **chamber of commerce** (☎ 661-327-4421; 1725 Eye St; open 9am-5pm Mon, 8am-5pm Tues-Fri) have a detailed city map ($1.50) and loads of brochures, some with discounts to local attractions. Another handy resource is **w** www.bakersfield.com, put together by the *Bakersfield Californian* newspaper. A local monthly, *The Blackboard* (**w** www.the blackboard.knows.it), offers an informative, offbeat perspective.

Museums

The **Kern County Museum** (☎ 661-852-5000; 3801 Chester Ave; adult/child $6/4; open 8am-5pm Mon-Fri, 10am-5pm Sat, noon-5pm Sun), north of downtown, is a worthwhile stop for kids, history buffs and music fans. The pioneer village has over 50 restored and replicated buildings, including a hotel and a wooden oil derrick, spread over 16 shaded acres. A hands-on Children's Discovery Center is designed for the younger set, and for grown-ups, there are exhibits on local history, including the oil industry and the Bakersfield Sound. The latter highlights such local legends as Herb Henson, Tommy Collins and Joe Maphis, whose 1952 hit 'Dim Lights, Thick Smoke and Loud, Loud Music' was written about the Blackboard, an infamous nightclub originally located immediately south of the museum.

Surrounded by a small park and lovely sculpture garden, the newly expanded **Bakersfield Museum of Art** (☎ 661-323-7219; 1930 R St; adult/student $5/2; open 10am-4pm Tues-Fri, noon-4pm Sat) has a strong, diverse schedule of permanent and rotating exhibits, highlighting regional artists but often tackling international issues and perspectives.

Raceways

Bakersfield's raceways are in full swing from March to November, and weekend events, some with high-profile sponsors, draw people from all over the state. Smaller races get a local crowd but can be equally thrilling. Ticket prices are generally between $9 and $12 (major events higher) and are usually available at the gate.

Bakersfield Speedway (☎ 661-393-3373; 5001 N Chester Ave Extension) has a one-third-mile clay oval track and has been hosting races since 1946. Follow Chester Ave north through Oildale.

The area's newest facility is **Buttonwillow Raceway Park** (☎ 661-764-5333), hosting a variety of commercial, club and motorcycle events year-round. It's near the intersection of I-5 and Lerdo Hwy, about 28mi west of Bakersfield via Hwy 58.

The **Famoso Raceway** (☎ 661-399-2210) is a quarter-mile drag strip that hosts vintage and custom events including the Goodguys March Meet, the California Hot Rod Reunion in October and the Fuel & Gas Finals in November. Plenty more racing happens most weekends. The raceway is about 15mi north of Bakersfield. As you head north on Hwy 99, take the Hwy 46 exit, turn right onto Famoso Rd and go east for 4mi.

Home to Nascar events, the **Mesa Marin Raceway** (☎ 661-366-5711) is a half-mile oval where cars do 25 to 100 laps at speeds way over 100mi an hour. Races are held at 7:30pm Saturday nights.

Places to Stay

The area's best camping is about an hour east of town along Hwy 178 in the Lake Isabella region (see Kern River later in this chapter). There are also primitive sites in the Carrizo Plain National Monument (see Around Bakersfield later).

Numerous chain motels are visible from most Hwy 99 exits. Near the Crystal Palace, the busy **E-Z 8 Motel** (☎ 661-322-1901; 2604 Buck Owens Blvd; singles/doubles $39/47) has clean, functional rooms, though it can be somewhat noisy.

California Inn (☎ 661-328-1100; 3400 Chester Lane; singles/doubles $45/49), a new structure with large rooms, spa, sauna and pool (right off the parking lot but still pleasant), is calmer and quieter. It's directly west of Hwy 99 off California Ave.

Best Western Hill House (☎ 661-327-4064, 800-528-1234, fax 661-327-1247; 700 Truxtun Ave; singles/doubles $59/65), downtown, has comfortable rooms and accommodating staff. It's close to both Amtrak and the Convention Center.

Old-school budget motels line Union Ave heading south from Hwy 178; some are sketchy, but among the more decent is the **Capri Motel** (☎ 661-327-3577; 2020 Union Ave; singles/doubles $35/45).

Places to Eat

Bakersfield is blessed with several traditional Basque restaurants, where food is served family-style in a series of courses, including soup, salad, beans and thin slices of tangy beef tongue. All this comes *before* the main course, so you'd better be hungry.

Wool Growers (☎ 661-327-9584; 620 E 19th St; meals $12-18), Bakersfield's oldest Basque restaurant, is a simple eating hall loaded with character. A fried chicken dinner will leave you full for a week, or you can order just the sides, which are more than enough, for $9.

Mexican food is plentiful here too.

Colima Mexican Restaurant (☎ 661-631-1188; 2000 Chester Ave; meals from $5) serves fajitas, mole dinners and other specialties in a lively downtown setting. Cheaper still is **La Fonda** (☎ 661-325-1472; 1230 H St), across from Bakersfield High School, where tasty, fresh tacos are just 65¢ (get three or four, as they're small).

Caffe Amante/Juice Station (☎ 661-864-1081; cnr 18th St & G St; breakfast/lunch $3-5) is a pleasant spot for sandwiches, ice cream, smoothies and espresso.

Trout and eggs is a local favorite at the popular **24th Street Cafe** (☎ 661-323-8801; 1415 24th St; meals $5-8), though expect to wait for a table.

Entertainment

Buck Owens' Crystal Palace (☎ 661-328-7560; w www.buckowens.com; 2800 Buck Owens Blvd), off Hwy 99 at the Rosedale Hwy exit, is a must-stop for country music fans. Looking like it belongs in Branson, Missouri, the flashy, Disney-esque joint is fun nonetheless. It regularly hosts touring country acts, and Buck himself plays here every Friday and Saturday at 7pm ($6, reserve in advance to assure seating). Memorabilia lines the hallways too. The overpriced food is OK but nothing special.

Trout's (☎ 661-399-6700; 805 N Chester Ave at Decatur St), to the north in neighboring Oildale, is a scratchy but still bustling cowboy bar that has survived intact for half a century. Crowds pack the place and dance to the music of Bobby Durham and the great Red Simpson, both onetime Bakersfield Sound hit makers who play there each week.

Downtown the 1930 **Fox Theater** (☎ 661-635-0543; w www.foxtheateronline.com;

The Bakersfield Sound

Country-and-western music has been a major force in Southern California ever since the heyday of the singing cowboys, though the focus then was on Hollywood. As Okie farmworkers migrated to the state, however, they brought their love of country music to rural Central Valley towns as well.

Modesto spawned the Maddox Brothers and Rose; Western swing pioneer Bob Wills opened a club in Sacramento; and Bakersfield became a hotbed of hard-edged honky-tonk country, a style designed to be heard above the din in local nightclubs, of which the town had many.

This so-called Bakersfield Sound thrived here in the 1950s and '60s, thanks to such artists as Tommy Collins, Wynn Stewart, Ferlin Husky, Billy Mize, Red Simpson and Bonnie Owens. The two singers who really put the town on the musical map, though, are Merle Haggard and Buck Owens.

Owens got his start playing in Bill Woods' band at the Blackboard (now sadly torn down). Haggard, who grew up in nearby Oildale, played in Stewart's band before signing to local label Tally. Most also appeared on a popular local TV show, 'Cousin' Herb Henson's *Trading Post*. The Bakersfield Sound faded in the 1970s, but the city's still largely associated with hard-edged country music, which crops up in places like the Crystal Palace and Trout's (for details see Entertainment). The local Kern County Museum also has a display of memorabilia. For more information on Bakersfield's musical history, check out Oildale native Gerald Haslam's excellent *Workin' Man Blues: Country Music in California*.

2001 H St), a restored Art Deco beauty, hosts concerts, live performances and films.

For all-ages punk-rock shows, head to **Jerry's Pizza & Pub** (☎ 661-836-3576; 1817 Chester Ave).

Getting There & Around

Several trains run daily between Bakersfield and Oakland ($42 to $51, 6½ hours) from the new **Amtrak station** (☎ 661-395-3175, 800-872-7245; 601 Truxtun Ave at S St). They follow the route of the *San Joaquins*, which stops in Hanford, Fresno, Merced, Modesto and Stockton, among other cities. Amtrak also runs buses that connect with trains at LA's Union Station ($22, 2½ hours).

Greyhound (☎ 661-327-5617, 800-229-9424; 1820 18th St) connects Bakersfield to Los Angeles ($15, two hours), San Francisco ($34, 8½ hours) and Las Vegas ($38, eight hours) several times each day. The depot is downtown near the Padre Hotel.

Airport Bus of Bakersfield (☎ 800-858-5000, 805-395-0635; 2530 F St) runs a shuttle seven times daily between Bakersfield and the LAX ($27; 2½ hours) at Los Angeles. Call for schedules, and purchase tickets in person a half-hour before departure.

Golden Empire Transit (GET; ☎ 661-869-2438) is the local bus system, and the main downtown transfer station is at Chester Ave and 22nd St. Route 2 runs north on Chester Ave to the Kern County Museum and Oildale; Route 3 runs to Buck Owens Blvd and the Crystal Palace, though service stops at 6:15pm. Fares are 75¢.

AROUND BAKERSFIELD
Weedpatch Labor Camp
In the years following the Depression, Kern County boasted the highest percentage of Okie immigrants in California. Mostly poor white farm laborers from the South and the Great Plains, they came with dreams of a new life in the fields and farms of the Golden State. The majority, though, found only migrant labor jobs and continued hardship.

Dating from 1935, this Farm Security Administration labor camp (the model for 'Weedpatch Camp' in *The Grapes of Wrath*) was one of about 16 in the US set up at the time to aid migrant workers – and it's the only one with any original buildings left. Don't expect much: the original structures are fenced in, awaiting restoration, and newer buildings are still occupied. Despite this, the camp is a fascinating vision into the past – and a wake-up call to the continuing dichotomy between corporate agribusiness and its still-dirt-poor migrant workforce.

From Bakersfield, take Hwy 58 east to Weedpatch Hwy; head south for about 7mi, past Lamont; then turn left on Sunset Blvd, driving another mile. The buildings (the sign reads Arvin Farm Labor Center) are on your right. Please respect the privacy of the residents. **Dust Bowl Days** (W www.weedpatchcamp.com) is a celebration of Okie history held here each October.

Carrizo Plain National Monument
The Carrizo Plain became an official National Monument in January 2001, during Bill Clinton's final hours as president. It's immediately west of the San Joaquin Valley (and I-5), as the land rises into the Caliente Range. Unlike the cultivated San Joaquin, this dry strip of grassland has remained largely undeveloped. The park is traversed by the San Andreas Fault, and at its center is the seasonal Soda Lake. The area is known for springtime wildflower displays, winter bird-watching and numerous endangered wildlife species, including the California condor. Roads are rough and services minimal, but there's a **visitor center** (☎ 805-475-2131; open Dec-May) and free camping year-round. When the visitor center is closed for the season, call the **regional park office** (☎ 661-391-6000) for information. The park is about 45mi west of Bakersfield via Hwy 58.

KERN RIVER
A half-century ago the Kern River originated on the slopes of Mt Whitney and journeyed close to 170mi before finally settling into Buena Vista Lake in the Central Valley. Now, after its wild ride from the high country – where the river drops an incredible 60ft per mile – it's dammed in several places and almost entirely tapped by agricultural interests after hitting the valley floor. Its upper reaches, though, have been declared wild and scenic and are hugely popular with white-water enthusiasts.

About 40mi northeast of Bakersfield, two Kern River dams have created **Lake Isabella**, a recreational hot spot drawing all manner of Southern Californians. Surrounded by chaparral-covered mountains, it lies in the southern Sierra Nevada, and most people access it through Bakersfield via Hwy 178.

Hwy 178 follows the dramatic **Kern River Canyon**, making for a stunning scenic drive through the lower reaches of Sequoia National Forest. East of the lake, Hwy 178 winds another 50mi through a picturesque mixture of pine and Joshua trees before reaching Hwy 395.

Towering redwoods, Sequoia National Park

Dawn over Emerald Bay, Lake Tahoe

Rock climbing in the Sierra Nevada

Ghostly tufa towers rise from the briny waters of Mono Lake

The sheer face of El Capitan, Yosemite National Park

Upper Yosemite Falls

Springtime, Yosemite Valley

Climber, Yosemite National Park

Yosemite's Half Dome, ageless and serene

The town of **Lake Isabella** is a strip of local businesses on the south end of the lake. Here Hwy 155 heads north, around the west side of lake, to **Kernville**, a cute little town straddling the Kern River and *the* hub for rafting on the Kern. Normally serene, the town swarms with visitors on summer weekends. However, there's little protection from the sun, and while the lake is popular for cooling off, note that the river's deceptively strong currents can be extremely dangerous – signs regularly warn visitors to stay out, advice best heeded.

North of Kernville, lies Sequoia National Forest, Giant Sequoia National Monument (which itself sits south of Sequoia National Park – confused yet?). From the east side of the Kern River, follow Sierra Way north alongside the river. The road soon enters dense pine forests interspersed with grassy meadows. The **Kernville Ranger Station** (☎ 760-376-3781; 105 Whitney Rd; open 8am-5pm daily summer, 8:30am-4:30pm Mon-Fri winter) has hiking and camping information on this area, as well as maps ($6.50) and wilderness permits.

Rafting

The Upper Kern and Forks of the Kern (both sections of river north of Kernville) yield Class IV and V rapids during spring runoff and offer some of the most awe-inspiring white-water trips in the country. You'll need experience before tackling these sections, though there are plenty more opportunities for novices. Below Lake Isabella, the Kern is tamer and steadier, its flow controlled by the Army Corps of Engineers.

About six rafting companies operate out of Kernville; all offer competitive prices and run trips from May to August, depending on conditions. Excursions include popular one-hour runs ($18 to $23), daylong Lower Kern trips ($110 to $170) and multiday Forks of the Kern wilderness experiences ($600 to $800). Walk-ups are welcome and experience isn't necessary. Kids aged six and up can usually participate too. Companies include **Sierra South** (☎ 760-376-3745, 800-457-2082; w www.sierrasouth.com); **Whitewater Voyages** (☎ 800-400-7238, 660-376-8806; w www.whitewatervoyages.com); **Mountain & River Adventures** (☎ 800-861-6553, 760-376-6553; w www.mtnriver.com).

Places to Stay & Eat

US Forest Service (USFS) **campgrounds** (☎ 877-444-6777; sites $12-16) line the 10mi stretch between Lake Isabella and Kernville, and several more lie north of Kernville on Mtn 99. The lakeside campsites are frequented by boaters, while those north of Kernville are a bit less crowded and surrounded by trees. Some sites may be reserved.

Lake Isabella has motels, but Kernville's a nicer location and rates here are still reasonable. Many of Kernville's motels have two-day minimum stays on weekends.

River View Lodge (☎ 760-376-6019; 2 Sirretta Rd; rooms $79-99) has remodeled rooms and, yes, a view (though a Recreational Vehicle, RV, park is partly in the way). It's a quaint place, adjacent to the town square.

McCambridge Lodge (☎ 760-376-2288; 13525 Sierra Way; rooms $54-77), on the hill above the square, is a pleasant facility with sweeping lake vistas.

Whispering Pines Lodge (☎ 760-376-3733; 13745 Sierra Way; rooms $99-169), a secluded B&B blending rustic character with luxurious comfort, is just north of town.

For an ice-cold beer or sizzling steak dinner, check out **Ewings** (125 Buena Vista Dr; meals from $14), a spacious lodge dating from 1956 with knockout river views.

SAN JOAQUIN VALLEY

Sierra Nevada

The beauty of the Sierra Nevada has seduced poets, photographers and painters for more than a century. It's an imposing range, over 400mi long and 60mi to 80mi wide, studded by hundreds of jutting peaks, including the highest in the contiguous USA (Mt Whitney, 14,497ft). Three world-famous national parks (Yosemite, Sequoia and Kings Canyon) lie within its boundaries, not to mention eight national forests plus dozens of state parks and wilderness and recreation areas. Between the crest and foothills lies a granite world inter-woven with canyons, rivers, lake basins and meadows – some of California's most majestic and pristine scenery. In other words, the Sierra Nevada is an outdoor enthusiast's dream. Hikers, backpackers and skiers especially will find a playground of near limitless possibilities.

Geology

About 140 million years ago, the Pacific Plate dove beneath the westward moving North American Plate, its surface melting into magma with the intense heat and friction. While some of the magma rose to the surface through volcanoes (like those around Mammoth Lakes), most cooled to form the granite block that would become the Sierra Nevada.

Over the next 50 to 80 million years, this granite block uplifted along faults on its eastern side, tilting westward to form an asymmetrical range. As the mountains rose, the streams draining them became fast-flowing rivers and started carving V-shaped valleys (trending east to northwest) into the western slope.

Glaciers, which covered the higher parts of the range about three million years ago, scraped the V-shaped valleys into U-shaped valleys and as a result left behind the Sierra's most remarkable topography – erratic boulders, scoured peaks and valleys such as Yosemite and Kings Canyon.

Flora

The Sierra's lower western slope, around 2000ft, is covered with California black oak, chaparral, manzanita and high grasses characteristic of its mild climate. Above

Highlights

- Lake Tahoe – hiking, skiing, gambling and 300 days of sunshine
- Mono Lake – meditatively calm volcanic lake with otherworldly tufa formations set against the Sierra peaks
- Yosemite – why John Muir fell in love with the Sierra
- Kings Canyon & Sequoia – off-the-beaten-track parks with smaller crowds, great backpacking and the earth's largest living things

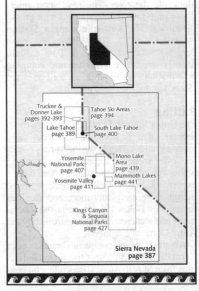

Truckee & Donner Lake pages 392-393

Tahoe Ski Areas page 394

Lake Tahoe page 389

South Lake Tahoe page 400

Yosemite National Park page 407

Mono Lake Area page 439

Yosemite Valley page 411

Mammoth Lakes page 441

Kings Canyon & Sequoia National Parks page 427

Sierra Nevada page 387

2000ft, this foliage gives way to dense conifer forests of pine and fir, meadows and large rock outcroppings. In what is called the High Sierra, above 9000ft, soil was carried away by glacial activity, leaving a polished granite landscape of peaks, basins and ridges where foxtail and white-bark pines, lichen and heather are about all that grow. The Sierra tops out on its eastern side along the Sierra crest, where peaks rise to about 9000ft near Lake Tahoe and get gradually higher in the south, where they reach above 14,000ft.

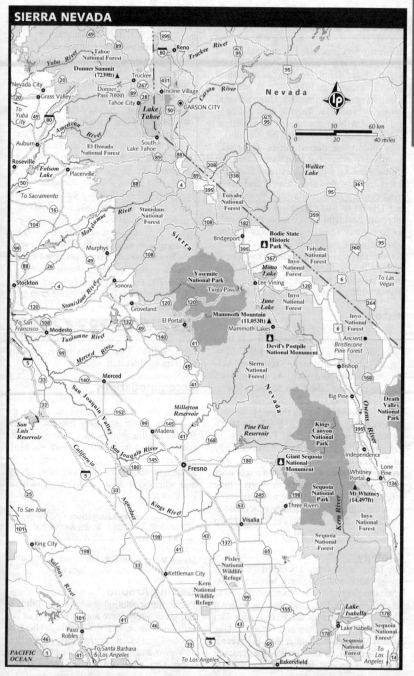

Lake Tahoe

Brilliantly blue, encircled by mountains and bisected by the California-Nevada state line, the Lake Tahoe area is a great destination for those who like to mix outdoor activities and entertainment. Three national forests – Eldorado, Toiyabe and Tahoe – and three wilderness areas – Desolation, Granite Chief and Mt Rose (in Nevada) – offer plenty of opportunities for backcountry exploring. For mountain bikers, the Flume Trail is a prime destination, while skiers have 14 downhill resorts and seven cross-country areas to play in. Emerald Bay and DL Bliss State Park on the western shore are beautiful nature spots that should not be missed. The Nevada side has casinos, especially at Crystal Bay and Stateline.

Lake Tahoe is the second-deepest lake in the USA (up to 1645ft deep) and is 22mi long and 12mi wide with about 72mi of shoreline. Hwy 89 often closes during heavy snowfall.

History

Lake Tahoe was summering grounds for the Washoe Indians long before it was 'discovered' by gold seekers headed from Carson City, Nevada, to the Sacramento Valley during the gold rush. As California's gold petered out, the Comstock Lode was found in Virginia City, Nevada, and fortune hunters crossed back over the mighty Sierra by way of Squaw Valley or along the lake's southern shore. In 1862 the Fish Ferguson Coggins & Smith Company harvested hay on the flatlands of the northern shore, near present-day Tahoe City, and built a schooner to take the hay to the southern shore, where it fetched $250 per ton. The northern shore grew in importance as logging operations sent lumber down the Truckee River to help build the transcontinental railroad.

Geology

The Tahoe Basin formed between the Carson Range (east) and the Sierra Nevada (west) when the Sierra Nevada block uplifted 50 to 80 million years ago. Lava flowing from Mt Pluto, on the northern shore, formed a dam across the basin's outlet and created a lake several hundred feet higher than the present one. Eventually a new outlet, the Truckee River, was eroded from the lava dam; it

---

The Tahoe Rim Trail

The Tahoe Rim Trail is California's newest long-distance trail, wrapping around the Lake Tahoe Basin along lofty ridges and mountaintops for 150mi. Inaugurated in 2001, it took nearly a quarter of a century and a small army of volunteers to complete the trail. Hikers, equestrians and – in some sections – mountain bikers can now enjoy inspirational views of the lake and the snowcapped peaks of the Sierra Nevada while tracing the footsteps of early pioneers, Basque shepherds and the Washoe Indians.

The trail passes through wonderfully rich and diverse terrain, including subalpine meadows, aspen-lined creeks, thick conifer forests, sparkling lakes and wildflower gardens. It takes about two weeks to complete the entire loop (marked with light blue triangles), but even hiking just a short distance will definitely let you sample the stunning panoramas unfolding below you. For more information, contact the **Tahoe Rim Association** (☎ 775-573-0686; W *www.tahoerimtrail.org*).

---

remains Lake Tahoe's only outlet, flowing from its northwestern shore.

Accommodations

Accommodations get booked far in advance around the major holidays and through much of summer. Many motels, hotels, B&Bs, condos and vacation homes may be reserved through central agencies. Most also offer packages that may include lift tickets, meals, casino shows or other offers, and which can be a good deal. The main ones are:

Lake Tahoe Central Reservations (☎ 530-583-3494, 888-434-1262, W www.tahoefun.org)
South Lake Tahoe Visitor's Authority (☎ 800-288-2463, W www.virtualtahoe.com)
Squaw Valley Central Reservations (☎ 800-403-0206, W www.squawvacations.com)

Getting Around

Public transportation around Lake Tahoe is fairly comprehensive and efficient. For details and fares, see the Getting There & Around section under the respective cities.

Year-round bus services are provided by Tahoe City-based Tahoe Area Rapid Transit

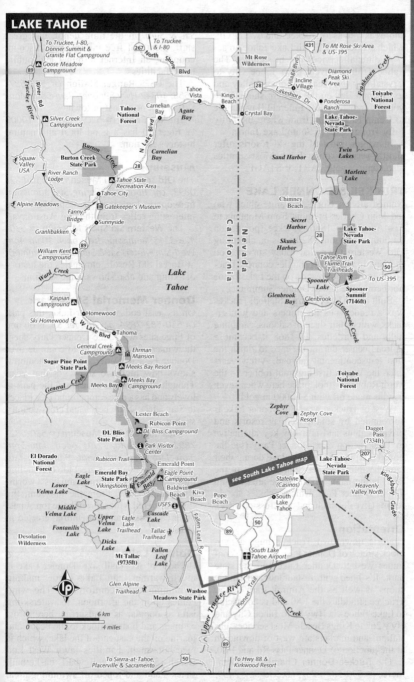

LAKE TAHOE

(TART) along the northern and western shores as well as to Truckee, and by STAGE, which services the South Lake Tahoe area.

Additional services run in summer. The Tahoe Trolley travels from Tahoe City to Crystal Bay (Nevada), to Squaw Valley and to Emerald Bay on the western shore. Here you can transfer to the Emerald Bay Shuttle to Camp Richardson from where the Nifty Fifty Trolley goes to South Lake Tahoe.

In winter, most of the ski resorts offer shuttle service (often free). Most shuttles also connect with TART or STAGE.

TRUCKEE & DONNER LAKE

Named after a Northern Paiute chief who led John Charles Frémont from Montana to Los Angeles in 1846, Truckee (population 13,000; elevation 5820ft) is a charming Old Western town that today survives on tourism. In winter, ski shuttles connect Truckee to most major resorts on the Lake Tahoe northern shore and at Donner Summit.

Built in 1863 as Coburn's Station, Truckee was a rendezvous for miners and lumberjacks, with its fair share of saloons, gambling halls and bordellos. In 1868 it became a railroad center during the race to finish the first transcontinental railroad. A few years later, the West's first big train robbery – the Verdi Robbery – took place here when seven bandits made off with $41,000 in gold.

West of Truckee, via I-80, Donner Lake is surrounded by small, woodsy resorts and private cabins and is a low-key alternative to Tahoe action. The Donner Party (see the boxed text) lodged near the lake during their fateful winter. Donner Summit, west of the lake, is the name given to the area around 7088ft Donner Pass, which includes six ski resorts (five downhill and one cross-country).

Orientation

Historic downtown Truckee hugs a two-block stretch of Donner Pass Rd, which continues west to Donner Lake and the state park. It's lined with restaurants and unique shops as well as the Amtrak train depot. Truckee straddles the I-80 and is connected to Lake Tahoe via Hwy 89 to Tahoe City and Hwy 267 to Kings Beach. Most services, gas stations and markets are west of downtown at the junction of Donner Pass Rd and I-80.

The **Truckee-Donner Chamber of Commerce** (☎ 530-587-2757, fax 530-587-2439;

open 8:30am-5:30pm Mon-Fri, 9am-5:30pm Sat & Sun), in the train depot, has great staff, plenty of free information, discount coupons, an Internet terminal and public toilet facilities.

The **USFS Ranger Station** (☎ 530-587-3558; 10342 Hwy 89; open 8am-5pm Mon-Sat) is 1mi northeast of town.

Truckee Books (☎ 530-582-8302; 10009 W River St) has a good local and natural history selection.

Museums

The **Old Truckee Jail Museum** (☎ 530-582-0893; cnr Jiboom & Spring Sts; admission free; open 11am-4pm Sat & Sun) has some interesting relics from the Old West days.

The **Western Ski Sport Museum** (☎ 530-426-3313; admission free; open 10am-4pm Wed-Sat winter, Sat & Sun only in summer), at Boreal Ski Resort, chronicles the history of skiing and also shows some ski films.

Donner Memorial State Park

On the east end of Donner Lake, this park (☎ 530-582-7894; day-use fee $3) is on one of three sites where the Donner Party spent the winter of 1846 waiting to continue over Donner Pass to Sutter's Fort. A memorial shows how high the snow got that year. Though its history is gruesome, the park is lovely and has a nice campground (see Places to Stay later), sandy beach and cross-country ski trails.

The **Emigrant Trail Museum** (☎ 530-582-7892; adult/child $2/1; open 9am-5pm daily late May-early Sept, 9am-4pm late Sept-early May) does a great job chronicling the Donner Party's journey and has a worthwhile slide show. From the museum, the Emigrant Trail winds through the forest past other cabin sites and a memorial erected in 1918.

Donner Lake

Because of its small size, Donner Lake is much warmer than Lake Tahoe, making swimming quite comfortable. The wind comes up in the afternoon, so waterskiing isn't as popular as windsurfing here. Most campers and boaters flock to the beach and marina on the east end of the lake, which is nice but small. Families favor West End Beach ($3) for its volleyball, basketball, snack stand and roped-off swimming area.

Shoreline Park along the northern shore also gives lake access.

Hiking

There are some great day hikes in the **Granite Chief Wilderness**, south of Truckee and west of Tahoe City. The Five Lakes and Whiskey Creek trails, from the Alpine Meadows parking lot, give steep but immediate access to beautiful alpine lakes and the Pacific Crest Trail. From here you can access backcountry trails, which are good for overnight trips – no wilderness permits are required. The trailhead is about 2mi up Alpine Meadows Rd, which runs west off Hwy 89.

For maps and route suggestions, drop into the USFS ranger station.

Other Activities

Ski resorts around Donner Lake are smaller and less flashy than Squaw Valley but they are still good. For a full rundown, see the boxed text 'Tahoe Ski Areas' later in this chapter.

For guided backcountry tours and skills seminars, **Alpine Skills International** (☎ 530-426-9108, fax 530-426-3063; w www.alpine skills.com), based at Donner Pass, is highly respected.

From about June to September, **Tributary Whitewater Tours** (☎ 530-346-6812, 800-6723 8464; w whitewatertours.com) operates a 7mi, half-day run on the Truckee River from Boca to Floriston (about 6mi northeast of Truckee off the I-80) on Class II to III+ rapids for $64–74.

The Donner Party

In the 19th century, over 40,000 people traveled west along the Overland Trail in search of a better life in California. High drama was common on this arduous journey, but the story of the Donner Party takes the prize for morbid intensity.

The Donner Party left Springfield, Illinois, in April 1846. With six wagons and a herd of livestock, the families of George and Jacob Donner and James Reed intended to make the trip as comfortable as possible. In Independence, Missouri, a large group of emigrants joined them, bringing the party to about 87 people. After Independence, the going was slow, and by July, they were running behind schedule. Eager to save 350mi, most of the group elected to try the Hastings Cutoff, unaware that it had never been used by wagons.

Things soon started to get grim. At one point the group took three weeks to travel 36mi. Arguments and fights broke out among members of the party. James Reed killed a man and was banished in the middle of the desert. Oxen and livestock died of heat exhaustion and dehydration crossing the Great Salt Desert, and wagons were abandoned. By the time the party reached the eastern foot of the Sierra Nevada, many people were walking and provisions were running short.

Snow came early that year, and the party tried and failed three times in November to cross Truckee (now Donner) Pass. Hoping that a break in the weather would reopen the pass, they settled in at Truckee (now Donner) Lake. They had food to last for a month and felt certain that the weather would clear by then. It didn't. Snow fell for weeks, reaching a depth of over 20ft – the most recorded in a century. James Reed, the fellow banished in the desert, made it to Sutter's Fort, California, by mid-October. Fearing that his family was trapped by winter storms, he put together the first rescue party, which arrived at the camps in mid-February. With most livestock and oxen buried in snow, people were surviving on boiled ox hides. Since many were too weak to travel, the rescue party could evacuate only six people.

By the time the second rescue party came in March, people had resorted to cannibalism. Journals and reports tell of 'half-crazed people living in absolute filth, with naked, half-eaten bodies strewn about the cabins.'Again, only a few of the strongest survivors could be rescued. By mid-April, when a final rescue party arrived, the only person remaining at the lake camp was Lewis Keseberg. The rescuers found George Donner's body cleansed and wrapped in a sheet, but no sign of Tasmen Donner, George's wife, who had refused to leave her husband even though she was strong enough to go with earlier rescue parties. Keseberg admitted to surviving on the flesh of those who had died, but denied the accusations that he had killed Tasmen Donner for fresh meat. He spent the rest of his life trying to clear his name. Altogether, only 47 of the 89 members survived.

TRUCKEE & DONNER LAKE

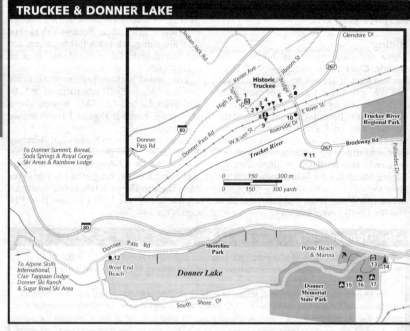

Porter's Ski & Sport (☎ 530-587-1500), in the Crossroads Center at the junction of I-80 and Hwy 89, is one of the best-stocked outfitters and also rents equipment.

Places to Stay

A scenic place to camp is **Donner Memorial State Park** (☎ 530-582-7894, 800-444-7275 for reservations; sites $12), which has three campgrounds, all with flush toilets and hot showers: **Creek Campground** is nicely shaded and near Donner Creek, but sites are close together; **Ridge Campground** is the smallest, with the best access to the campfire center; and **Splitrock Campground** is the largest and most removed from day-use activities.

You'll also find three riverside USFS campgrounds on Hwy 89 south of Truckee: **Granite Flat** (sites $14) is the largest and has flush toilets; **Goose Meadows** (sites $12) is smaller and better protected from highway noise; and **Silver Creek** (sites $10) gets the most crowded because it's closest to Tahoe City. For reservations, call ☎ 877-444-6777.

Right on Donner Pass, you'll find the **Clair Tappaan Lodge** (☎ 530-426-3632, fax 530-426-0742; e clair.tappaan.lodge@sierra club .org; dorm beds members/nonmembers $43/48 Easter-late Nov, $37/41 Dec-Easter), a rustic mountain lodge with hostel-like accommodations. It's operated by the Sierra Club for its members but is also open to nonmembers. Rates include meals, but you're expected to do small chores and bring your own sleeping bag, pillow and towel. From eastbound I-80, take the exit for Soda Springs/Norden and go 2.4mi east on Donner Pass Rd. In winter, a cross-country ski school operates from here.

Truckee's most historic abode, **Truckee Hotel** (☎ 530-587-4444, 800-659-6921, fax 530-587-1599; 10007 Bridge St; rooms without bath $45-135, with bath $105-135) has gone through incarnations as a stage stop, a home for railroad laborers and a lumbermen's boarding house. Now fully restored, it still drips history in both public areas and rooms. Rates include breakfast and afternoon tea.

Donner Lake Village Resort (☎ 530-587-6081, 800-621-6664, fax 530-587-8782; 15695 Donner Lake Rd; condos & suites $80-255) has decent accommodations next to a

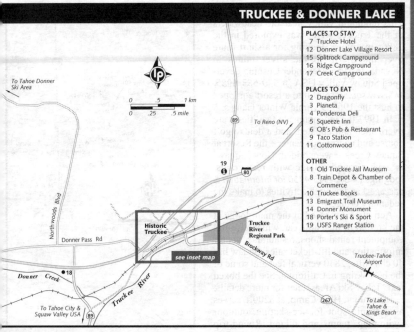

TRUCKEE & DONNER LAKE

PLACES TO STAY
7 Truckee Hotel
12 Donner Lake Village Resort
15 Splitrock Campground
16 Ridge Campground
17 Creek Campground

PLACES TO EAT
2 Dragonfly
3 Pianeta
4 Ponderosa Deli
5 Squeeze Inn
6 OB's Pub & Restaurant
9 Taco Station
11 Cottonwood

OTHER
1 Old Truckee Jail Museum
8 Train Depot & Chamber of
   Commerce
10 Truckee Books
13 Emigrant Trail Museum
14 Donner Monument
18 Porter's Ski & Sport
19 USFS Ranger Station

private beach, marina and pool; snowshoeing and snowmobiling are available in winter.

Rainbow Lodge (☎ 530-426-3871, 800-500-3871, fax 530-426-9221; rooms without/with bath $95/125 summer, $100/145 winter), built in the 1920s, is off I-80 at Royal Gorge Cross Country Ski Resort. It has classic mountain lodge charm, with a huge fireplace and cozy rooms. Access to ski trails is right out the front door.

Places to Eat
Historic Truckee is full of good restaurants, including **Squeeze Inn** and **Ponderosa Deli**, both down-to-earth breakfast and lunch spots where you can fill up for under $10.

OB's Pub & Restaurant (☎ 530-587-4164; 10046 Donner Pass Rd; dishes $4-14) is a throwback to the rough-and-tumble days of Truckee and serves satisfying pub grub. **Taco Station** (10130 W River St; meals under $6), in an old rail car behind the train depot, makes cheap, filling Mexican food.

Dragonfly (☎ 530-587-0557; 10118 Donner Pass Rd; lunch $6-10, dinner $17-21) does California-Asian fusion in its handsomely decorated upstairs space.

Pianeta (☎ 530-587-4694; 10096 Donner Pass Rd; mains $12-25) serves handmade Italian food in a sophisticated setting.

Cottonwood (☎ 530-587-5711; Hwy 267 'Hilltop'; dinner mains $9-24), in a hilltop ex-ski lodge off Hwy 267, is the local 'in' spot with live music most weekends and an interesting menu which is all over the planet. It also has a good bar with inspired appetizers.

Getting There & Around
Amtrak and Greyhound buses both stop at the train depot. Greyhound makes up to five trips daily to Reno ($10.25, 50 minutes) and three to Sacramento ($21.25, three hours) and San Francisco ($37.50, 5½ hours).

Amtrak's *California Zephyr*, which runs between Chicago and Emeryville/San Francisco with a stop in Reno, comes through daily.

The **Truckee Trolley** (☎ 530-587-7451) connects the train depot hourly with Donner Memorial State Park and Donner Lake from around 9am to 5pm. Fares are $1, or $2 for an all-day pass.

To get to Tahoe City, hop on the TART bus at the train depot ($1.25, 45 minutes).

SQUAW VALLEY USA

This mountain valley near the headwaters of the Truckee River was explored in the 1880s by miners looking for a short route over the Sierra to the silver mines in Nevada. In 1955 Alexander Cushing developed Squaw Valley USA (☎ 530-583-6985; W www.squaw.com) into a resort equipped to host the 1960 Olympic Winter Games.

In 1997 the mountainside facilities were overhauled and updated, and a deluxe golf course and conference center – the Resort at Squaw Creek – were added. Now 'Squaw' is a year-round village with restaurants, **lodgings** (☎ 800-545-4350 for information & packages) and enough activities to make the sedentary cringe.

Activities are based at the main lodge at the bottom of the cable car, which also has equipment rental shops, restaurants, visitor information and lift-ticket sales. Squaw has 40 chairlifts, 2830 vertical feet and some of the best skiing in California. See the boxed text 'Tahoe Ski Areas' later for more details.

In summer, **High Camp**, at 8200ft, serves as a scenic spot for ice-skating, outdoor swimming, tennis and hiking. Round-trip rides on the cable car cost $17/5 adult/child ($8/5 after 5pm). Combination tickets are $20/10 ($14/10 after 5pm) for riding and skating; $22/13 ($15/13 after 5pm) for riding and swimming; and $25/17 ($18/15 after 5pm) for all three activities. The cable car operates 9:40am to 10pm from late June through August and until 4pm in early June and from September until mid-October.

Off-mountain activities include horseback riding at **Squaw Valley Stables** (☎ 530-583-7433), on the road leading to the mountain base from Hwy 89. One- and two-hour rides cost $25/45. You can also play golf at the 18-hole **Resort at Squaw Creek** (☎ 530-583-3600), which was designed by Robert Trent Jones; the greens fee is $110.

TAHOE CITY

The largest town on Lake Tahoe's northern shore, Tahoe City (population 2000; elevation 6240ft) has been the lake's primary boating community since Italian and Portuguese fishermen settled here in the 1860s. Its location – at the Hwy 89/28 junction – makes it a much-visited place, though it lacks a real downtown since most busi-

TAHOE SKI AREAS

To Quincy / Reno / To Fallon / 89 / 80 / Mt Rose / 431 / Donner Pass Rd (Old Hwy 40) / Tahoe Donner / To Sacramento / Boreal / 80 / Truckee / Soda Springs / Donner Ski Ranch / 267 / Diamond Peak / Royal Gorge / Squaw Valley USA / Northstar at Tahoe / Sugar Bowl / Alpine Meadows / 28 / Tahoe City / CARSON CITY / Ski Homewood / 89 / Lake Tahoe / 50 / 395 / Nevada / South Lake Tahoe / 88 / Heavenly Valley / 0 15 30 km / 0 10 20 miles / 50 / To Placerville & Sacramento / 89 / Sierra at Tahoe / Kirkwood / 88 / To Stockton / California

nesses are in small shopping centers strung along the lakeshore.

There are several marinas and a nice beach central to town activity (near the Boatworks Mall). On Hwy 89, just south of the Hwy 28 junction, the Truckee River flows through floodgates and passes beneath **Fanny Bridge**, named for the most prominent feature (fanny or rear end) of people leaning over the railings to look at fish.

Orientation & Information

Tahoe City's main drag is Hwy 28, or N Lake Blvd, which starts at the junction with Hwy 89 and skirts the lake's northern and eastern shore as far as Hwy 50.

At the junction of Hwys 89 and 28, next to the Bank of America, the **North Lake Tahoe Resort Association Visitor Information Center** (☎ 530-581-8737, 800-824-348, fax 530-581-4081; 245 N Lake Blvd; open 9am-5pm daily) has lots of maps, lodging, dining, shopping and activities information.

The **Bookshelf** (☎ 530-581-1900; Boatworks Mall) is among the town's best bookstores with a good local section.

Gatekeeper's Museum

South of Fanny Bridge, this museum (☎ 530-583-1762; 130 W Lake Blvd (Hwy 89); admission free; open 11am-5pm Wed-Sun May–mid-June, daily mid-June–early Sept) has a large Washoe basket collection and old Tahoe memorabilia, including ski equipment and photos. The recently re-developed surrounding park is nice for picnicking. The 1908 **Watson Log Cabin** (560 N Lake Tahoe Blvd; admission free; open noon-4pm daily late May-early Sept) is near the public beach.

Activities

A trailhead for the **Tahoe Rim Trail** is just off Hwy 89 (north of Fanny Bridge) on Fairway Dr, across from the Fairway Community Center. The 18½mi stretch from Tahoe City to Brockway Summit is open to **mountain bikers** as well. Expert riders may well be tempted by the 15mi ride up Mt Watson. The route is a bit hard to find and carrying a map is advised.

The Truckee River is gentle and wide as it flows northwest from the lake – perfect for novice **rafters** who like to drag a six-pack behind the boat. **Truckee River Raft Rentals** (☎ 530-583-0123; 185 River Rd) rents boats (adult/child $30/25) for the 5mi float from Tahoe City to the River Ranch Lodge (see Places to Eat), including transportation back to town. For more challenging white-water rafting, see other Activities in the Truckee & Donner Lake section earlier in this chapter.

There are four downhill and one cross-country **ski resorts** in the general vicinity of Tahoe City. See the boxed text 'Tahoe Ski Areas' on the following page for details.

Porter's Ski & Sport (☎ 530-583-2314; 501 N Lake Blvd) is a useful source for trail maps and equipment rentals, including mountain bikes and in-line skates, water skis and alpine/cross-country skis.

Dave's Ski & Boards (☎ 530-583-6415; 620 N Lake Tahoe Blvd), near Grove St, is good for ski and snowboard rentals, while **Back Country** (☎ 530-581-5861; 255 N Lake Blvd) has telemark equipment and snowshoes for rent.

Places to Stay

Just north of town, **Tahoe State Recreation Area** (☎ 530-583-3074, 800-444-7275 for reservations; Hwy 28; sites $16) has flush toilets, showers and 36 sites close to the lake.

There are three USFS campgrounds north-west of town on Hwy 89 (see under Truckee & Donner Lake earlier in this chapter).

William Kent Campground (☎ 530-583-3642, 877-444-6777 for reservations; sites $15), 2mi south of the town on Hwy 89, is another nearby option.

Ensconced in a seven-story high-rise, **Pepper Tree Inn** (☎ 530-583-3711, 800-624-8590; W www.peppertreetahoe.com; 645 N Lake Blvd; rooms $40-200) has spacious rooms with a good range of amenities and views.

Tahoe Marina Lodge (☎ 530-583-2365, 800-748-5650, fax 530-583-2367; 270 N Lake Blvd; condos $115-299) has fully furnished apartments sleeping four to six people. Some have lake views and there's a private beach. There's a two-night minimum, longer around holidays.

River Ranch Lodge (☎ 530-583-4264, 800-535-9900; W www.riverranchlodge.com; Hwy 89 at Alpine Meadows Rd; rooms $85-160) lets you sleep right next to the rushing Truckee River. Rooms have all modern amenities and sport classy lodgepole pine furniture, TV, data ports and river views. Rates include breakfast.

Places to Eat

Blue Agave (☎ 530-583-8113; 425 N Lake Blvd; dishes $4-12.50) is inside the historic Tahoe Inn and serves the best Mexican food in town.

The Bridge Tender (☎ 530-583-3342; 65 W Lake Blvd; dishes $4-8), a local institution near Fanny Bridge, has a wood stove, pool table, daily beer specials and great burgers and rib combos.

Rosie's Cafe (☎ 530-583-8504; 571 N Lake Blvd; breakfast & lunch $5-9, dinner $10-16) and **Jake's on the Lake** (☎ 530-583-0188; lunch $9-14, dinner $16-22), in the Boatworks Mall, are recommended for hearty meals and happy hour appetizer specials.

Wolfdale's (☎ 530-583-5700; 640 N Lake Blvd; dinner mains $18-26) has a creative chef who keeps the menu in flux with seasonal ingredients, including fresh fish and seafood. Most dishes blend the flavors of the Far East with classic Euro touches.

River Ranch Lodge (see Places to Stay; lunch $6-10, dinner $15-26) makes great barbecue lunches in summer and is a popular stop for rafters and bikers. Dinner is a

Tahoe Ski Areas

California's dudes and dudettes never despair when winter chills the Pacific and they put away their surfboards. No, they simply grab other boards (and skis) and head for where the adrenaline of other kinds of 'slopes' calls to them: the Tahoe ski area – nearby, diverse in terrain and world class.

Tahoe has 17 downhill and seven cross-country resorts. The ski season generally runs from November to April, although it can start as early as October with the last storm whipping through in June. In good years, snowfall in higher elevations can reach 35ft or better and the 'deep pow-pow' (powder snow) exerts a frosty sirens' call.

Families will find several resorts that provide a sense of togetherness as all levels of skill are catered to; most have schools training everyone from kids to kamikazes. Prices listed here are for full-day adult/child lift tickets but the definition of 'children' varies by resort and various other packages are available, so call ahead or check the websites.

DOWNHILL SKIING
Truckee/Donner Lake Area

Boreal (☎ 530-426-3666; W www.ride-boreal.com) – good for beginners and intermediate skiers, has some fun terrain parks and half-pipes, and offers free skiing lessons to level 3, night skiing until 9pm; nine lifts, 500 vertical feet; $34/10; 9mi west of Truckee at Donner Summit off I-80.

Donner Ski Ranch (☎ 530-426-3635; W www.donnerskiranch.com) – one of the oldest and cheapest resorts in the area; six lifts, 750 vertical feet; $20/10 (adult $10 midweek); take Soda Springs/Norden exit off I-80, then 3½mi east on Donner Pass Rd.

Soda Springs (☎ 530-426-3666; W www.sodasprings.com) – for not-too-committed skiers and kids, this place has the longest snow-tubing run in the area, plus mini-snowmobiles, snowshoeing, sleds and a Kids X Park; four lifts, 650 vertical feet; $22/10; take Soda Springs/Norden exit off I-80, then follow signs (about 2mi).

Sugar Bowl (☎ 530-426-9000; W www.sugarbowl.com) – a history-rich resort beloved by locals for its steep terrain, abundant snow, deep powder and lively atmosphere. It was allegedly Walt Disney's favorite resort (one of the mountains is named Mt Disney); 11 lifts, one gondola, 1500 vertical feet; $50/12; take Soda Springs/Norden off I-80 exit 10mi west of Truckee, then 3mi east on Hwy 40.

Tahoe Donner (☎ 530-587-9444; W www.tahoedonner.com) – low-key, uncrowded and family-friendly with beginner and intermediate runs only and a ski school; four lifts, 600 vertical feet; $26/12; take Donner State Park exit off I-80 near Truckee.

Tahoe City

Alpine Meadows (☎ 530-581-8374, 800-441-4423; W www.skialpine.com) – laid-back but top-notch, featuring terrain parks with jumps, spines, half-pipes and table tops and some great off-the-beaten-path areas; 14 lifts, 1800 vertical feet; $54/10; 6mi northwest of Tahoe City off Hwy 89.

Northstar-at-Tahoe (☎ 530-562-1010; W www.skinorthstar.com) – good all-around resort with efficient lift system, seven terrain parks, snow-tubing, snowmobiling; sheltered location and still good when windy; 12 lifts, one gondola, 2280 vertical feet; $54/17; off Rte 267 6mi northwest of Lake Tahoe en route to Truckee.

Ski Homewood (☎ 530-525-2992; W www.skihomewood.com) – a huge area and locals' favorite with great lake views, unpretentious ambience and great powder skiing; eight lifts, 1650 vertical feet; $42 ($25 midweek), children under 10 free; 6mi south of Tahoe City on Hwy 89

Squaw Valley USA (☎ 530-583-6985; W www.squaw.com) – vast world-class resort for all levels of expertise, host of 1960 Winter Olympic Games, the most advanced lift system in the USA and

Tahoe Ski Areas

revamped base area, two terrain parks, snow-tubing, ice-skating, free night skiing with lift ticket; 38 lifts, one tram, two gondolas, 2850 vertical feet; $56/5; 5mi northwest of Tahoe City off Hwy 89.

South Lake Tahoe

Heavenly Valley (☎ 775-586-7000; W www.skiheavenly.com) – the biggest resort on the southern shore and the highest in the lake area with the longest descent (5½mi); 27 lifts, one tram, one gondola, 3500 vertical feet; $57/29. There are two parts: Heavenly North (the Nevada side), accessible from Kingsbury Grade north of Stateline off Hwy 50, and Heavenly West at the end of Ski Run Blvd in South Lake Tahoe.

Kirkwood (☎ 209-258-6000, 877-547-9663; W www.skikirkwood.com) – off-the-beaten-path resort set in a high-elevation valley, gets better snow and holds it longer than almost anywhere else; especially good for advanced and extreme skiers; 12 lifts, 2000 vertical feet; $52/11; 35mi southwest of South Lake Tahoe on Hwy 88 (via Hwy 89).

Sierra-at-Tahoe (☎ 530-659-7453; W www.sierratahoe.com) – less crowded than Heavenly Valley and a good choice for day-trippers from the Bay Area; great tree-skiing and snowboard park; 12 lifts, 2212 vertical feet; $50/10; 12mi west of South Lake Tahoe on Hwy 50.

Nevada

Diamond Peak Ski Resort (☎ 775-832-1177; W www.diamondpeak.com) – great views of the lake, with smaller crowds and mostly intermediate and advanced runs; seven lifts, 1840 vertical feet; $41/15; in Incline Village off Rte 28 and Country Club Dr.

Mt Rose Ski Tahoe (☎ 775-849-0704; W www.skirose.com) – Tahoe's highest base ski resort with great views and good snow conditions into spring, great ungroomed powder; five lifts, 1440 vertical feet; $45/12; 22mi south of Reno on Rte 431.

CROSS-COUNTRY SKIING

In addition to the resorts listed here, there are also marked, ungroomed trails at Donner Memorial State Park.

Camp Richardson (☎ 530-542-6584) – ski beside the lake at this resort with 12mi of groomed and 22mi of marked trails; $15/9; on Hwy 89, 2mi north of the 'Y' near South Lake Tahoe.

Clair Tappaan Lodge (☎ 530-426-3632; Donner Summit) – 10mi of trails for beginners and intermediate skiers around a rustic Sierra Club lodge; suggested donation $7/3.50; on old US-40 (Donner Pass Rd) west of Truckee near Donner Summit.

Northstar-at-Tahoe (☎ 530-562-1010) – this resort has 30mi of groomed trails and a skating lane, which are near the downhill slopes; $20/15; 6mi northwest of Lake Tahoe off Hwy 267.

Resort at Squaw Creek (☎ 530-583-6300; W www.squawcreek.com) – 10mi of groomed trails, mostly for novices, also snowshoe rentals; $13; take Hwy 89 to Squaw Valley Rd to Squaw Creek Rd.

Royal Gorge Cross Country Ski Resort (☎ 530-426-3871; W www.royalgorge.com) – the largest cross-country ski resort in the USA, with over 200mi of groomed trails and four surface lifts; $25/12 (adult $21.50 midweek); take Soda Springs exit off I-80, turn right at the lights and follow signs to Summit Station.

Tahoe Cross Country (☎ 530-583-5475; W www.tahoexc.org) – 40mi of quiet trails through the forests near Tahoe City, warming huts, equipment rental and ski school; $17.50; 2mi north of Tahoe City on Dollar Hill off Hwy 28.

Tahoe Donner (☎ 530-587-9484; W www.tdxc.net) – varied terrain with 63mi of groomed trails, and lit trails for night skiing; $19/14; off Donner Pass Rd northwest of Truckee.

gourmet affair, with special nods to the filet mignon, the roasted elk loin and the mushroom ravioli appetizer.

Getting There & Around
Tahoe Area Rapid Transit (*TART;* ☎ *530-581-550-1212, 800-736-6365*) operates buses from Tahoe City along the northern shore as far as Incline Village (in Nevada), along the western shore as far south as Sugar Pine Point, and to Truckee via Hwy 89. Buses run from about 6:30am to 6:30pm daily year-round; tickets cost $1.25 each or $3 for an all-day pass.

From June to early September, TART also operates the **Tahoe Trolley** on three routes: along the northern shore from Tahoe City to Crystal Bay (Nevada); to/from Squaw Valley; and south along the western shore to Emerald Bay. Buses run from 10:30am to 10:30pm and also cost $1.25 per ride.

Also in summer, the free **Tahoe City Trolley** zips people around town from 11am to 6pm, stopping at the malls, the Gatekeeper's Museum and requested destinations.

NORTHERN SHORE
Heading northeast of Tahoe City on Hwy 28 takes you to a string of small, low-key towns, many on superb sandy beaches, with reasonably priced motels and hotels. The lake's northern California-Nevada state line crosses Hwy 28 at Crystal Bay, placing the entire eastern shore in Nevada.

Tahoe Vista
Tahoe Vista (population 1050) has more public beaches (six) than any other town on the lake. Its strip of motels and resorts is quite woodsy and more serene than Kings Beach, the next town up. **North Tahoe Regional Park**, at the end of National St, has hiking, biking, cross-country ski trails and nice picnic facilities.

Beesley's Cottages (☎ *530-546-2448; 6674 N Lake Blvd; rooms $80, cottages from $120; open late May-early Sept*) is a collection of timeworn cottages with cute, cozy and cluttered rooms. The best thing is the grassy setting next to a gorgeous white sandy private beach.

Cedar Glen Lodge (☎ *530-546-4281, 800-500-8246, fax 530-546-2250;* W *www.cedarglenlodge.com; 6589 N Lake Blvd; cottages*

$60-150, rooms $95-160) has personable hosts, newly done-up rooms, and cottages, some sleeping up to six people. Rates include breakfast, and there's a heated outdoor pool, hot tub and sauna and beach access.

Mourelatos Lakeshore Resort (☎ *530-546-9500, 800-824-6381, fax 530-546-2744;* W *www.mourelatosresort.com; 6834 N Lake Blvd; rooms $165-310*), an upscale beach-front property, has great upstairs rooms with vaulted ceilings. Most have lake views and some come with kitchenette, fireplace or Jacuzzi.

Old Post Office (*5245 N Lake Blvd; mains $5-10*), an old-time eatery in Carnelian Bay, a couple of miles south, draws locals with its big breakfasts and lunches.

Spindleshanks (☎ *530-546-2191; 6873 N Lake Blvd; dinner mains $12-23*) is an American bistro with excellent appetizers and lots of wines by the glass.

Kings Beach
Kings Beach (population 2796) is home to many of the Latino folk who work in Lake Tahoe's casinos. Off the highway, the difference in standard of living between those who work in the casinos and those who play in them (and live on the lake's western shore or in Incline Village in the east) is clear. On the highway is a good bunch of affordable motels and popular restaurants.

Besides swimming, kayaking is a popular activity here. **Tahoe Paddle & Oar** (☎ *530-581-3029; 8299 N Lake Blvd*) rents kayaks from $15/70 per hour/day and also runs guided tours.

Sun N' Sand Lodge (☎ *530-546-2515, 800-547-2515; 8308 N Lake Blvd; rooms $50-140*) has been nicely renovated and now even sports a spa with a lake view.

Log Cabin Caffee (*8692 N Lake Blvd*) is *the* place to go for that first coffee jolt in the morning, followed by a big, satisfying breakfast.

Steamers (☎ *530-546-2218; 8290 N Lake Blvd; pizzas $9.50-20*) has a lakeside bar that is popular in summer and serves tasty pizzas in three sizes.

Jason's Beachside Grille (☎ *530-546-3315; 8338 N Lake Blvd; salad bar $8, lunch $5.50-10, dinner $14-22*) has a woodsy interior, a great lake-view patio and classic American fare. The all-you-can-eat salad bar is a vitamin feast.

NEVADA (EASTERN) SHORE

Hwy 28 rolls into Nevada at Crystal Bay, home to a few small casinos, before continuing on to affluent **Incline Village**, gateway to the Diamond Peak Ski Resort (see the boxed text 'Tahoe Ski Areas' earlier). The town's main tourist attraction is **Ponderosa Ranch** (☎ 775-831-0691; adult/child $11.50/6.50; open 9:30am-6pm daily mid-Apr–Oct), a theme park built around the set of the TV classic *Bonanza*. Tours of the Cartwright Ranch include old film clips, a barn full of props and antiques used on the set and a staged gunfight on 'Main Street.'

North of Incline Village off Hwy 431 (Mt Rose Hwy, which connects with US-395 to Reno), Mt Rose has the profile of a woman lying on her back with clasped hands resting on her stomach. An early miner, looking at her from Reno, named the mountain Rose, after his sweetie.

Mt Rose Wilderness lies northwest of Hwy 431, with good access from the Mt Rose Summit and Tahoe Meadows Trailhead, about ½mi west of the summit. Self-register wilderness permits are available at the trailheads, where there are posted maps, rest rooms and free parking. Also here is the Mt Rose ski area (see the boxed text 'Tahoe Ski Areas' earlier).

Much of Lake Tahoe's eastern shore is fringed by the excellent **Lake Tahoe-Nevada State Park**, encompassing beaches, lakes and miles of trails. The highlight here is **Sand Harbor**, a beautiful spot where two sand spits have formed a shallow bay with brilliant turquoise water and white sand beaches. Not surprisingly, the place is intensely popular in summer and often unpleasantly crowded.

At the park's southern end, at the Hwy 50/Hwy 28 junction, **Spooner Lake** has the area's most facilities and the best park information. The lake is stocked with trout, and there are rest rooms, picnic facilities and access to 56mi of groomed cross-country skiing trails.

The 15mi **Flume Trail** is paradise found for experienced mountain bikers. It follows the path of an old flume that carried logs by water to lumber mills and silver mines at Virginia City. The trail heads north from Spooner Lake with the Tahoe Rim Trail, then goes around the western side of Marlette Lake (the Rim Trail goes around the eastern side). Its western side drops straight down to the lake, making it quite treacherous for all but the very expert bikers. There's scenic, first-come, first-served **camping** (sites $7) on the eastern side of Marlette Lake and at Twin Lakes, about 2mi north.

SOUTH LAKE TAHOE

South Lake Tahoe (population 21,650; elevation 6254ft) stretches along the southern shore in a monotonous string of mini-malls and motels along Hwy 50 (here called Lake Tahoe Blvd). The best thing about the town is affordable lodging and dining. The state line divides South Lake Tahoe from Stateline on the Nevada side. This is where most of the 'action' is concentrated, with several boxy casinos looming above the lake and swaths of ski runs looming above the casinos.

The main gap where the lake is visible from Hwy 50 is at South Lake Tahoe State Recreation Area; the best views are from the Heavenly Valley ski area and the top floors of the casinos, and the best beach access is west of town off Hwy 89. The southern shore's concentration of million-dollar homes and boats is in the Tahoe Keys, a network of docks and waterways north of Hwy 50 via Tahoe Keys Blvd.

Orientation & Information

Lake Tahoe Blvd (Hwy 50) wraps around the southern shore of the lake between Spooner Summit (Nevada) and the junction with Hwy 89 (Emerald Bay Rd). Locals refer to this junction as the 'Y'. In winter, Hwy 89 is often closed for snow west of the Tallac Historic Site.

Traffic along Hwy 50 often gets jammed around noon and 5pm Monday to Friday and over weekends; winter Sunday evenings (when skiers head back down the mountain) are the worst. A good alternate route through town is Pioneer Trail, which branches east off Hwy 89/Hwy 50 (south of the 'Y') and reconnects with Hwy 50 at Stateline.

The **South Lake Tahoe Chamber of Commerce** (☎ 530-541-5255; 3066 Lake Tahoe Blvd; open 9am-5pm Mon-Sat) has brochures, maps and jolly staff. For outdoor information, the best stop is at the **USFS Lake Tahoe Visitor Center** (☎ 530-573-2674;

SOUTH LAKE TAHOE

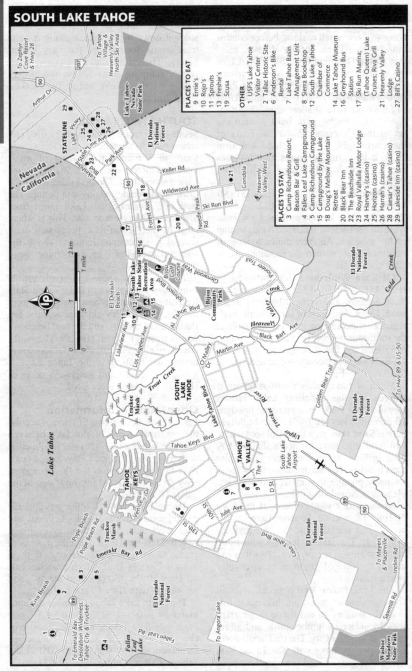

PLACES TO EAT
9 Ernie's
10 Rojo's
11 Sprouts
13 Freshie's
19 Scusa

OTHER
1 USFS Lake Tahoe Visitor Center
2 Tallac Historic Site
6 Anderson's Bike Rental
7 Lake Tahoe Basin Management Unit
8 Sierra Bookshop
12 South Lake Tahoe Chamber of Commerce
14 Lake Tahoe Museum
16 Greyhound Bus Station
17 Ski Run Marina; (Tahoe Queen) Lake Cruises; Riva Grill
21 Heavenly Valley Lodge
27 Bill's Casino

PLACES TO STAY
3 Camp Richardson Resort; Beacon Bar & Grill
4 Fallen Leaf Lake Campground
5 Camp Richardson Campground
15 Campground by the Lake
18 Doug's Mellow Mountain Retreat
20 Black Bear Inn
22 The Beachside Inn
23 Royal Valhalla Motor Lodge
24 Harvey's (casino)
25 Horizon (casino)
26 Harrah's (casino)
28 Caesar's Tahoe (casino)
29 Lakeside Inn (casino)

open 8am-4:30pm daily mid-June–late Sept, Sat & Sun only May & Oct) at the Tallac Historic Site (see later in this section). The **Lake Tahoe Basin Management Unit** *(☎ 530-573-2600; 870 Emerald Bay Rd; open 8:30am-4:30pm Mon-Fri)*, near the 'Y', also has information, but there are plans to move the office in 2003.

The **Sierra Bookshop** *(☎ 530-541-6464; 1072 Emerald Bay Rd)*, in a small mall in the southwestern corner of the 'Y', has a great selection of local history books and guides.

Casinos

Las Vegas it ain't, but there are still plenty of blackjack tables and one-armed bandits here to help you part with your hard-earned cash. **Caesars Tahoe**, **Harrah's** and **Harvey's** are the 'big three' casinos with entertainment, slots and gaming tables, multiple restaurants and resort-like accommodations. **Horizon** and **Bill's** are smaller and less flashy; Bill's is especially friendly for people who don't have gambling experience. About a mile north of the others, **Lakeside Inn** has a local atmosphere and a nice view of the lake. Free gaming guides, which explain casino game rules, are available at all casinos.

Lake Tahoe Museum

Next door to the chamber of commerce, this museum *(☎ 530-541-5458; adult/concession $2/1; open 11am-5pm Tues-Sat mid-June–early Sept)* has a rustic collection of 'stuff' from early settlers, and some nice Native American (mostly Washoe) baskets, jewelry and ceremonial garb.

Tallac Historic Site

About 3mi northwest of the 'Y', on Emerald Bay Rd, the Tallac site encompasses 150 acres and three luxurious estates from the early 1900s. Surrounded by pines and connected by paved hiking/biking paths, the entire area now serves as a big park with beach access and beautiful picnic grounds.

Elias 'Lucky' Baldwin bought Tallac Point in 1880 and built a resort including a hotel, casino, promenade and tennis courts – one of the few and most opulent places on the lake at that time. Eventually, the estate was parceled and sold. Today, three large estate homes still exist.

The **Pope Estate** *(admission $3)* can be toured on summer weekends, while **Heller Estate**, dubbed Valhalla, houses a cultural arts store. The **Baldwin Estate** is home to the **Tallac Museum** *(☎ 530-541-5227; donation requested; open 10am-4pm daily June-Aug & 11am-3pm Sept)*, worth a visit for its Washoe exhibit and old photos of Lake Tahoe.

Desolation Wilderness

This wilderness area, the most heavily used per acre in the USA, spreads south and west from Lake Tahoe, encompassing 100 sq mi of forests, lakes and peaks. Contrary to what its name suggests, the wilderness is vibrantly beautiful and alive with trees, birds, foxes, deer, bears and marmots. Retreating glaciers formed Desolation Valley, sweeping away its soil and leaving huge, polished rock faces in its upper elevations. Trees don't grow in this area, but conifer-like shrubs grow as big as trees, and in late spring wildflowers sprout between the rocks. Camping on these smooth, flat granite surfaces is great, and hiking and climbing is fast and easy.

A favorite day hike destination is the glacier-gouged peak of **Mt Tallac** (9735ft), reached in a strenuous trek from either the Mt Tallac Trailhead (4.6mi each way) or the Glen Alpine Trailhead (5.7mi each way).

There is also good hiking from the Glen Alpine Trailhead at Fallen Leaf Lake, south of Hwy 89 via Fallen Leaf Lake Rd, and from the Eagle Falls Trailhead, found on Hwy 89 at Emerald Bay.

Wilderness permits are required year-round for both day and overnight explorations. Day hikers can self-register at the trailheads, but from late May to late September, a wilderness permit quota system limits overnight camping.

Half of the quota is available in person on a first-come, first-served basis at the USFS Lake Tahoe Visitor Center at the Tallac Historic Site (see Orientation & Information earlier). The other half may be reserved with a major credit card by calling ☎ 530-644-6048, by sending a fax to 530-295-5624 or by sending a check (US banks only) or a money order to 3070 Camino Heights Dr, Camino, CA 95709. Reservations cost $5, camping costs $5 per person for one night, or $10 for two or more nights.

Activities

For an easy spin around town, take the **South Lake Tahoe Bike Path**. It starts at El Dorado Beach, at the northern end of the South Lake Tahoe State Recreation Area, and continues west via Trout Creek, the Upper Truckee River and the Truckee Marsh to Baldwin Beach. A moderate **mountain-bike trail** heads south on Fallen Leaf Rd to Angora Ridge and Angora Lakes with great views of Fallen Leaf Lake and Mt Tallac. Biking is not allowed in the Desolation Wilderness. The USFS Lake Tahoe Visitor Center at Tallac has a list of Lake Tahoe trails and sells good maps.

Anderson's Bike Rental (☎ 530-541-0500; 645 Emerald Bay Rd) rents bikes, skates and scooters, as do several other rental shops along Lake Tahoe Blvd.

El Dorado Beach is a free public beach and picnic area. Along Emerald Bay Rd there are some nice beaches – Pope, Kiva and Baldwin – with good **swimming**, as well as picnic tables and barbecues.

Ski Run Marina, on the lake at the foot of Ski Run Blvd, has several boat rental places. Typical rates are $80 per hour for jet skis, and from $90 per hour for powerboats.

Reminiscent of summer camp, **Camp Richardson Resort** (see Places to Stay), off Emerald Bay Rd, has a nice beach, kayak and canoe rentals ($15 per hour) and a general store.

Zephyr Cove Resort (see Places to Stay), about 4mi northeast of Stateline, is a woodsy resort with a beach swimming area, boat rentals, volleyball courts and an outdoor bar and restaurant. Both resorts (day-use fee $3) swarm with kids in summer.

Touring the lake by boat is worthwhile. The **MS Dixie II** (☎ 775-589-4906) leaves from Zephyr Cove Resort for two-hour cruises to Emerald Bay ($24) and back. Other popular trips are the sunset dinner cruises with live music ($39, including food) and a champagne brunch cruise ($29), which skirts the lake's southern shore.

The **Tahoe Queen** (☎ 530-541-3364), which leaves from Ski Run Marina in town, is slightly cheaper. A popular winter option is its ski package ($78), which includes a high-speed boat trip to the northern shore, a bus ride and lift ticket to Squaw Valley and an après-ski cruise with drinks and music back on shore.

Places to Stay

Camping Campgrounds around South Lake Tahoe open only after the snowmelt.

Fallen Leaf Lake Campground (☎ 530-544-0426, 877-444-6777 for reservations; sites $16), a USFS facility south of Emerald Bay Rd on Fallen Leaf Lake (take Fallen Leaf Lake Rd), has very scenic sites that fill up quickly on weekends.

Campground by the Lake (☎ 530-542-6096; Lake Tahoe Blvd; tents/RV sites $18/25), in a woodsy area behind the chamber of commerce and close to the El Dorado swimming beach, has hot showers and flush toilets. Highway noise is the main detriment.

Camp Richardson Campground (tents $17-25, RV sites $18-26), part of Camp Richardson Resort (see later), has about 300 sites.

Hostels For backpackers, **Doug's Mellow Mountain Retreat** (☎ 530-544-8065; 3787 Forest Ave; dorm beds $15), a small, independent hostel on a quiet side street, is a godsend. Dorms sleep four to six people and there's no curfew.

Hotels, Motels & Resorts Lake Tahoe's southern shore has dozens of lodging options for all wallet sizes. Places cluster near Stateline, along Lake Tahoe Blvd and along Ski Run Blvd. Prices rise by up to 50% on weekends.

Black Bear Inn (☎ 530-544-4451, 877-232-7466, fax 530-544-7315; w www.tahoe blackbear.com; 1202 Ski Run Blvd; rooms $175-475) is a mannered, moneyed and masculine B&B, warmly furnished with stylish Western antiques and immaculately kept and run. Sleep in the lodge or a cabin.

The **Beachside Inn** (☎ 530-544-2400, 800-884-4920, fax 530-544-0600; w www.beach sideinntahoe.com; 930 Park Ave; rooms $75-179) has nice, if gaudy, rooms with microwave and refrigerator. It has an all-day spa and sauna, and its rates include breakfast and afternoon wine and cheese.

Royal Valhalla Motor Lodge (☎ 530-544-2233, 800-999-4101, fax 530-544-1436; w www.tahoeroyalvalhalla.com; 4104 Lakeshore Blvd; rooms $99-119 summer, $65-95 winter) is a sprawling but peaceful complex (with a nice beach) right on the lake. Staff members are quick with a smile, and many of the rooms have balconies. There are two- and three-bedroom units too.

Camp Richardson Resort (☎ 530-541-1801, 800-544-1801, fax 530-541-1802; W www.camprichardson.com; 1900 Jameson Beach Rd, off Emerald Bay Rd; rooms $75-155 summer, $65-95 winter, cabins from $90 per day winter, $565 per week summer) is just 2mi north of the 'Y' but a world apart from the strip mall aesthetic of South Lake Tahoe. It's a busy place with a historic inn and modern hotel, cabins, a campground, plus a beach, marina, riding stables, cross-country ski trails and restaurant.

Zephyr Cove Resort (☎ 775-588-3508, fax 775-588-9627; 760 Hwy 50; tents $20-29, RV sites $25-44, cabins $109-289, $149-359 June-early Sept; open year-round), right on the shore about 4mi north of Stateline, is another family-oriented resort with a pedigree going back to 1919. The sprawling grounds incorporate comfortably furnished cabins with kitchens and cable TV, a campground and RV park, store, restaurant and gift shop. It's right on a swimming beach and near a marina with boat rentals. Tours aboard the MS *Dixie II* launch from here as well (see Activities earlier in this section).

Sorensen's Resort (☎ 530-694-2203, 800-423-9949; W www.sorensensresort.com; Hwy 88; B&B rooms $80-145, 1–2-person cabins $95-165, 2–4-person cabins $105-225, larger cabins & homes $135-450) is a magical year-round resort with woodsy cabins, a cozy dining room and access to cross-country ski and hiking trails as well as good fishing. It's 20mi south of Lake Tahoe, 1mi east of the intersection of Hwys 88 and 89.

Casinos These multilevel 'coin collectors' often have good deals on rooms, which are clean and modern but boring unless you get a suite, which might have a lake view or private Jacuzzi. Nondiscounted rates typically start at $89 but can reach a rather stratospheric $300 during crunch times. Packages including lift tickets, meals and a few gaming tokens are available too.

Harrah's (☎ 775-588-6611, 800-427-7247, fax 775-586-6607) and **Harvey's** (☎ 775-588-2411, 800-745-4320, fax 775-588-6643; W www.harveystahoe.com) have the nicest decor. The American River Café at Harrah's is a good spot for breakfast and lunch.

Caesar's Tahoe (☎ 775-530-3515, 800-367-4554, fax 775-586-2068) has rooms

that are a bit worn, but the nice indoor pool accented with plants and waterfalls is a hoot.

Horizon (☎ 775-588-6211, 800-322-7723, fax 775-588-1344; W www.horizoncasino.com) is the least glamorous of the bunch and therefore usually a bit cheaper.

About 1mi further north on Hwy 50, the **Lakeside Inn** (☎ 775-588-7777, 800-624-7980, fax 775-588-4092; W www.lakesideinn.com) was recently revamped and features surprisingly classy mountain lodge decor.

Places to Eat

Ernie's (☎ 530-541-2161; 1146 Emerald Bay Rd; dishes $3-10; open 6am-2pm) is a classic American hash house near the 'Y', serving gut-busting breakfasts and lunches.

Sprouts (☎ 530-541-6969; 3123 Harrison Ave; dishes around $5), not far from the chamber of commerce, is a natural-foods café bustling with a young and energetic crowd.

Freshie's (☎ 530-542-3630; 3330 Lake Tahoe Blvd; lunch $2.50-9, dinner $10-19), inside the Lakeview Plaza Mall, has Hawaiian decor and a menu sure to please everyone – from vegans to steak-lovers.

Rojo's (☎ 530-541-4960; cnr Lake Tahoe Blvd & San Francisco Ave; lunch $6-9, dinner $14-19) wears the patina of decades of history with pride. Both decor and menu are throwbacks to old Tahoe's mining and lumber days, with plate-bending helpings of ribs, chicken, steak and other grilled grub.

Beacon Bar & Grill (☎ 530-541-0630; Camp Richardson Resort; lunch mains $8.50-13, dinner $10-24) is one of the most beloved places on the southern shore. Enjoy scenic views from the deck or dining room while slurping clam chowder, tucking into a steak or simply sipping the legendary 'Rum Runner' cocktail.

Scusa (☎ 530-542-0100; 1142 Ski Run Blvd; dinner mains $9-20), one of the best Italian places in town, woos diners with whimsical decorations and soul- and palate-pleasing food.

Riva Grill (☎ 530-542-2600; 900 Ski Run Blvd; lunch $10-18, dinner $18-28) serves upscale continental food in a fabulous lakeside setting. A couple of its signature drinks, called 'Wet Woody' (don't ask), will make your eyes glaze over. Breakfasts and Sunday brunches are also served.

Getting There & Around

Greyhound buses make runs several times daily to Sacramento ($21.25, three hours), San Francisco ($28.25, 5½ hours) and other destinations. Buses depart from the **bus station** *(3460 Lake Tahoe Blvd)* at the Ski Run Market. **Tahoe Casino Express** *(☎ 775-785-2424, 800-446-6128; w www.tahoecasino express.com)* connects South Lake Tahoe and Stateline to the Reno-Tahoe International Airport with 14 shuttles daily ($19 one way, 1¾ hours), with stops at the major Stateline casinos. The **South Lake Tahoe Area Ground Express** *(STAGE; ☎ 530-542-6077)* makes frequent stops along Hwy 50 between Zephyr Cove and the 'Y'. It operates year-round from 6am to 1am daily and rides cost $1.25.

In summer the **Nifty Fifty Trolley** *(☎ 530-541-7548)* runs narrated trips along two loop routes, one between Stateline and Zephyr Cove, the other from Stateline to Camp Richardson with onward connections to Emerald Bay ($2 extra). It operates 10am to 10pm daily; an all-day pass is $3.

The main casinos have free shuttles that run until 2am and will stop at any motel/hotel. During ski season, the resorts at Heavenly, Kirkwood and Sierra-at-Tahoe provide free shuttle services daily from numerous hotels and designated roadside stops.

WESTERN SHORE

The western shore of Lake Tahoe, between Emerald Bay and Tahoe City, has the area's nicest state parks and great swimming beaches. The 'towns' along Hwy 89 (called Emerald Bay Rd and, further north, W Lake Blvd) are little more than clusters of cabins and resorts, many of them owned by Bay Area families since the 1920s. In summer the shore is served by the Tahoe Trolley.

Emerald Bay State Park

This long, narrow bay off the southwestern corner of the lake is one of Tahoe's major attractions. It's anchored by the lake's only island – Fanette Island – and has waters that truly justify Emerald Bay's name. Hwy 89 wraps around the bay's southern and western rim, affording great views from pullouts and designated scenic points. The bay can also be explored year-round by boat from South Lake Tahoe (see Activities in that section earlier in this chapter).

One of the park's attractions is **Vikingsholm**, a storybook mansion built by Laura Knight in 1929. It cleverly marries preindustrial craftsmanship with Scandinavian design exemplified by carved wooden ceilings and furniture with Viking motif. Tours ($1) run 10am to 4pm daily June to September.

The mansion is reached by a steep 1mi descent from the Vikingsholm parking lot on Hwy 89. The park's **visitor center** *(☎ 530-541-6498)*, near the mansion, has lots of hiking, historical and other information. The stone ruins atop Fanette Island were once Laura Knight's teahouse.

The 1mi uphill hike from the Eagle Falls parking lot to Eagle Lake is one of the most scenic and popular short hikes on the lake and acts as a teaser to the beauty of Desolation Wilderness. Crowds thin out immediately past Eagle Lake as the trail continues on to the Velma, Dicks and Fontanillis Lakes.

Eagle Point Campground *(☎ 530-525-7277, 800-444-7275 for reservations; sites $12; open mid-June–Sept)* is perched on the tip of Eagle Point, with beach access and views of the bay. Eagle Point is also the southern terminus of the Rubicon Trail (see DL Bliss State Park following).

DL Bliss State Park

If you only have one day on the lake, this park is a good place to spend it. Some of the prettiest sections – Rubicon Point and Lester Beach (also called 'DL Bliss Beach') – boast clear turquoise water and white sand.

Near Calawee Cove Beach, just east of Lester Beach, is the northern trailhead of the **Rubicon Trail**, a scenic lakeside stroll. It offers phenomenal views of shoreline vegetation set off against the sparkling azure waters. The trail meanders south for about 5½mi to Emerald Bay State Park past Emerald Point and the Vikingsholm estate to Eagle Point. You can walk the entire length, but its beauty is easily appreciated in just a mile or so.

Beach and trailhead parking costs $2 and is extremely limited – the lots usually fill up by 10am, in which case it's a 2mi walk from the park entrance to the beach. You can also pick up the trail about halfway along this route near the campground registration office. Check with the visitor center at the entrance *(☎ 530-525-7277)*. The park is generally open from mid-May to September.

DL Bliss Campground (☎ 530-525-7277, 800-444-7275 for reservations; sites $12) has 168 sites with tables and fire pits, plus flush toilets, potable water and hot showers.

Meeks Bay

This sleek, shallow bay with a wide sweep of shoreline gets more light than other spots on the lake, because it has a meadow on its western side that lets in the afternoon sun. It also has warm water by Tahoe standards and is fringed by a beautiful, but busy, sandy beach.

Meeks Bay Resort (☎ 530-525-6946, 877-326-3357; tents/RV sites $20/30, cabins for 2 people from $220, for 6 people $325) was recently purchased by the Washoe Indian tribe, who spruced up the cabins and gave the place an overall face-lift. Day-use parking costs $7.

Meeks Bay Campground (☎ 530-583-3642, 877-444-6777 for reservations; sites $16) is a lovely USFS facility near Meeks Bay Resort. It has flush toilets and potable water but no showers. Day-use beach parking is $3.

Sugar Pine Point State Park

Between Meeks Bay and Tahoma, Sugar Pine Point is a well-run park with tennis courts, a swimming pier and nature center; there's a $5 day-use fee. **Ehrman Mansion** (☎ 530-525-7982), a statuesque late-19th-century estate, provides a glimpse of the lifestyle of Lake Tahoe's rich and famous during that period. In winter there's good sledding on the hills behind the estate. Tours ($2) operate hourly on the hour 11am to 4pm daily from July to early September

The park is also the southern starting point of the **Tahoe Trailways Bike Path**, a popular paved trail traveling north to Tahoe City and then northwest to Squaw Valley.

On the western side of Hwy 89, the park's densely forested **General Creek Campground** (☎ 530-525-7982, 800-444-7275 for reservations; sites $12) has 175 fairly spacious sites shaded by big pine trees.

Tahoma

This has the western shore's greatest concentration of places to stay and eat, as well as a post office and the **PDQ Market** (☎ 530-525-7411; open 6:30am-9pm or 10pm daily), which has a deli and grocery store. In summer the tiny **gas station** (7062 W Lake Blvd) rents kayaks. DL Bliss State Park (see earlier) is a great spot to put in.

Tahoma Meadows B&B Cottages (☎ 530-525-1553, 866-525-1533, fax 530-525-0335; W www.tahomameadows.com; 6821 W Lake Blvd; 2-person cottages $85-159, family cottages $145-265) has darling cottages that are as warm and welcoming as a hug from an old friend. Each has an imaginative decor, thick down comforters, kitchenette and barbecue – some also have hammocks. Fuel up for a day of exploring with one of its hefty and memorable breakfasts.

Norfolk Woods Inn (☎ 530-525-5000; 6941 W Lake Blvd; rooms $110-190) has old-fashioned charm in its plush rooms and rustic cabins. Rates include breakfast, and the restaurant also serves lunch and dinner.

Stony Ridge Cafe (☎ 530-525-0905; dinner mains $18-22) may look like a little roadside shack but in fact it serves gourmet fare using a global roster of ingredients. Breakfast and lunch are available daily, but dinner is served only Thursday to Saturday, though this may change (call ahead).

Chamber's Landing (☎ 530-525-7261) is a great place during summer for lakeside drinks and appetizers. Its signature cocktail is the aptly named 'Chambers Punch', and it also has a fine dining restaurant (mains $18-33).

Homewood

This place revolves around its ski hill in winter and also provides good backcountry ski access to Desolation Wilderness via Black Canyon (marked from Hwy 89). **Tahoe Gear** (☎ 530-525-5233; 5095 W Lake Blvd) is a good spot for trail information and equipment rentals.

Kaspian Campground (sites $14), about 1½mi north of Homewood, is the lake's only campground for cyclists with nine first-come, first-served sites.

Sunnyside

The deck of **Sunnyside Resort** (☎ 530-583-7200; 1850 W Lake Blvd; rooms $100-250) is a fun place to be in summer. It serves lunch (spring to fall), dinner and cocktails around sunset, when most people are just coming off the trails. It offers lakeside accommodations too.

Just north, across the highway, **Cyclepaths** (☎ 530-581-1171; 1785 W Lake Blvd) rents bicycles, in-line skates and other equipment and is a good source of outdoor information of any kind.

Yosemite National Park

Yosemite National Park, a Unesco World Heritage Site, has some of the most exquisite scenery in the USA. More than three million visitors from around the world descend upon the park each year to stand in awe of its glacier-swept beauty. Most make a beeline for Yosemite Valley (also referred to as 'the valley' throughout this chapter), anchored by the humungous monolith of El Capitan and lorded over by the distinctive profile of Half Dome. Waterfalls thunder from granite walls that soar 3000ft above the valley floor, which is draped in meadows and groves and traversed by the Merced River.

Beyond the valley, more than 800mi of trails offer hikers an uncrowded backcountry experience. Yosemite's high country, in the northeastern part of the park, is an alpine wilderness, with flower-filled meadows fringed by conifer forest and threaded by streams, where gem-like lakes shimmer beneath towering pinnacles. Tuolumne Meadows, off the Tioga Rd (open summer only) is the high-country hub beneath the 13,000ft Sierra Crest.

Activity in southern Yosemite – along Hwy 41 – focuses on Wawona, the park's historical center, and the nearby grove of giant sequoias. The northwestern part of the park – the Hetch Hetchy area – gets the least amount of visitors and is a good place to start long hikes into the quiet northern reaches.

History

The Ahwahneechee, a group of Central Valley Miwok and Eastern Sierra Paiute, lived in the Yosemite area for 4000 years before whites set foot in the valley. They survived on black oak acorns and fish from the Merced River and occasionally trapped deer and rabbits. Tribal members spent fall and winter down in the valley before moving into the eastern high country in spring, where they traded with Paiute from the Mono Lake area.

The first group of explorers to glimpse Yosemite Valley arrived in 1833 but they did not descend its steep walls. In the 1850s, as miners settled the Sierra's western foothills, conflict arose between the gold country prospectors and Native Americans who had raided the miners' camps. In 1851 a military expedition – the Mariposa Battalion – was dispatched to punish the Ahwahneechee, eventually forcing the capitulation of Chief Tenaya and his tribe in 1851.

Four years later, San Francisco publisher James Mason Hutchings organized the first tourist party to the valley, which included artist Thomas Ayers. Ayers' sketches of the trip were the first printed publicity advertising Yosemite's scenic wonders.

As visitors increased, Hutchings, Galen Clark, landscape architect Frederick Law Olmsted and other conservationists recognized the importance of protecting Yosemite Valley and the Big Tree Grove (today's Mariposa Grove). In 1864 Abraham Lincoln signed into law the Yosemite Grant, a bill that transferred these two areas to the state of California as a public trust and created Yosemite State Park.

Yosemite *National* Park was established in 1890 with major campaigning led by John Muir and originally included only the areas surrounding the valley and the grove. In 1906, however, the state of California ceded control over both, allowing them to be absorbed into the national park as well.

The US Cavalry managed and administered the park from 1890 to 1914, after which the Department of the Interior took over. The first civilian park rangers were hired in 1898.

Yosemite's popularity as a tourist destination soared throughout the 20th century. By the mid-1970s, traffic and congestion were bad enough to cast a smoggy haze over the valley floor. To alleviate this problem, a General Management Plan (GMP) was developed in 1980. In 1984 the park became a Unesco World Heritage Site.

In 2000 several studies and repeated reviews of and amendments to the GMP eventually resulted in the Yosemite Valley Plan. Its main objectives are to reclaim the park's natural beauty, to allow natural processes to prevail, to promote visitor understanding and enjoyment, and to reduce traffic and crowding. Change, of course, will take years to unfold but will ultimately ensure the survival of Yosemite as one of the world's great natural wonders.

YOSEMITE NATIONAL PARK

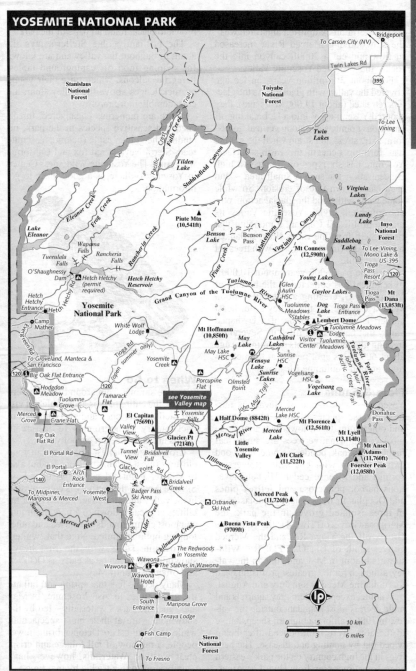

Geology

As the Sierra block uplifted and tilted west, the slow-moving Merced River increased in flow and cut a 3000ft canyon into the rock – the V-shaped Yosemite Valley.

For about 2½ million years, an ice age covered the valley with glaciers . As the glaciers retreated (about 14,000 years ago), they scoured Yosemite's V into a U, breaking off enormous granite slabs along vertical 'joints' formed by stress and strain when the granite was forming beneath the earth's surface. Yosemite has six types of granite – a high concentration for such a small area – and each has its own rate of erosion. So while some walls withstood the glacial action, others crumbled, giving Yosemite Valley its unique profile. El Capitan, a monolith that rises 3593ft from the valley floor, is flanked by rock slides (mostly covered with trees) of weaker granite.

Over the past 6000 years about 10,000ft of sediment has collected in the bottom of Yosemite's U, creating a flat valley floor. Tenaya Canyon, in the valley's northeast corner, is a good example of a U-shaped valley that hasn't been filled in. Several retreating glaciers, remnants of a mini-ice age about 600 years ago, persist at high elevations around Tuolumne Meadows.

Flora & Fauna

Yosemite's wide range of elevations nurtures diverse species of trees, plants, birds and other animals. At lower elevations, the most common native trees are small leaf maple, black oak, ponderosa pine, dogwood (which bloom with big white flowers in spring) and incense cedar. Higher elevations harbor ponderosa and Jeffrey pines and Douglas fir trees. Giant sequoias grow in three isolated groves in the park: the Mariposa Grove, off Hwy 41; the Tuolumne Grove, off the Tioga Rd; and the Merced Grove, south of Big Oak Flat Rd. Wildflowers bloom in May and June in the valley, although for the greatest profusion head to Tuolumne Meadows in July and August.

Wildlife, except Western gray squirrels and mule deer, is most abundant outside the valley. In 1986 California bighorn sheep, native to the area, were reintroduced after being wiped out by hunting and disease. The herd lives in the high country on the park's eastern edge, sometimes seen from Hwy 120. American black bears, which can be golden to dark brown to black, roam all parts of the park.

The brilliantly blue Steller's jays flit about throughout the valley and are known for swiping food off campground tables. Peregrine falcons, which raise their young on rock ledges above the valley floor, are considerably more rare.

There are numerous endangered, threatened and sensitive species in the park, including the golden eagle (below), Yosemite toad, Sierra Nevada red fox and California wolverine. The Yosemite Wilderness Center, in Yosemite Village, is a good place to get information.

When to Go

It's quite simple: from around June to September, the entire park is accessible, all visitor facilities are open and everything from backcountry campgrounds to ice-cream stands are at maximum capacity.

Crowds are smallest in winter but road closures (most notably of Tioga Rd but also of Glacier Point Rd beyond Badger Pass Ski Area) mean that activity is concentrated in the valley and on Badger Pass. Visitor facilities are scaled down to a bare minimum and most campgrounds are closed and other lodging options limited. Note that 'winter' in Yosemite starts with the first heavy snowfall, which can be as early as October, and often lasts until May.

Many people feel that spring and fall are the nicest times to visit Yosemite. In May and June, the park's waterfalls – fed by the snowmelt – are at their most spectacular, while late August to October bring fewer people, a rainbow of fall foliage and crisp, clear weather. Waterfalls, however, have usually slowed to a trickle by that time.

Orientation & Information

There are three primary approaches to Yosemite. From the south, Hwy 41 from Fresno enters at South Entrance – beyond which it becomes Wawona Rd – and passes Wawona and the Glacier Point Rd turnoff. From the southwest, Hwy 140 from Merced (called El Portal Rd within the park) passes El Portal and enters at Arch Rock Entrance. Finally, Hwy 120 from the San Francisco Bay Area and Manteca enters at Big Oak Flat Entrance, where it becomes Big Oak Flat Rd. It then traverses the park as the Tioga Rd before heading east to Lee Vining and Mono Lake (in the Eastern Sierra) via Tioga Pass. Coming from the Eastern Sierra (ie, US-395), Tioga Rd/Hwy 120 is the only access road to Yosemite. This road is only open in the warmer months (see the boxed text 'Impassable Tioga Pass').

Within the park, Yosemite Village has the most facilities, including a large store, an ATM, the visitor center and museums.

For recorded park information, campground availability and road and weather conditions, call ☎ 209-372-0200. For reservations and information about lodging and other types of services (horseback riding, sightseeing tours etc), call ☎ 209-252-4848 or go to the website at W www.yosemitepark.com. The NPS also maintains an excellent and comprehensive website at W www.nps.gov/yose.

Yosemite's entrance fee is $20 per vehicle and $10 for people on foot, bicycle or horseback. It is valid for seven continuous days; a one-year pass to Yosemite is $40. Upon entering the park, you'll receive an illustrated NPS map and copies of the *Yosemite Guide*, a biannual newspaper with park news and useful background information, and the biweekly *Yosemite Today* with current ranger programs, park activities and a shuttle bus map and schedule.

There are gas stations at Wawona, El Portal, the Tioga Rd–Big Oak Flat Rd junction and Tuolumne Meadows. Although the offices usually close after dark, you can get gas anytime by paying at the pump with a credit card. Prices are about 30% higher in the park.

Visitor Centers Information stations at the park entrances in Wawona (☎ 209-375-9531) and Big Oak Flat (☎ 209-379-1899)

Impassable Tioga Pass

Hwy 120, the main route into Yosemite National Park from the Eastern Sierra, climbs through Tioga Pass, the highest pass in the Sierra, at 9945ft. On most maps of California, you'll find a parenthetical remark – 'closed in winter' – printed on the map near the pass. While true, this statement is also misleading. The Tioga Rd is usually closed from the first heavy snowfall in October to May, June or even July! If you're planning a trip through Tioga Pass in spring, you're likely to be out of luck. According to official park policy, the earliest date the road will be plowed is 15 April, yet the pass has only been open in April once since 1980. Call ☎ 800-427-7623 for road and weather conditions before heading for Tioga Pass.

are open spring to fall (closed for lunch), but the **Valley Visitor Center** (☎ 209-372-0299; open year-round) in Yosemite Village is definitely information central for the entire park. Here, you'll find helpful staff, a bookstore, a park concessions courtesy phone and museum-quality exhibits. A beautifully photographed film called *Spirit of Yosemite* screens regularly in the center's West Auditorium Theater (free).

The **Yosemite Wilderness Center** (☎ 209-372-0740; open 8am-5pm daily May-Oct), next to the visitor center, issues wilderness permits and has topographical maps and trip planning guides. In the high country, the **Tuolumne Meadows Visitor Center** (☎ 209-372-0263) has hiking maps and guidebooks. A ranger kiosk, near Tuolumne Meadows Lodge, issues wilderness permits. Both offices are open whenever Tioga Rd is open.

Campfire programs, ranger-led naturalist walks, photography walks, art classes and lots of other activities take place at venues throughout the park. Check *Yosemite Today* for a current schedule.

Money There are ATMs inside the grocery stores at Curry Village, Yosemite Village and Wawona and another just outside the Village Store in Yosemite Village. All major credit cards and traveler's checks (in US dollars) are accepted in the park.

John Muir

Born in Scotland in 1838, John Muir came to America with his father in 1849 and settled near the Fox River in Wisconsin. After studying botany and geology at the University of Wisconsin, he set out on what would be a never-ending journey through the wilds. He accompanied research expeditions to the Arctic and the Yukon and discovered Glacier Bay in Alaska. But more than anywhere else, Muir is synonymous with the Sierra Nevada. He spent most of his life studying the range's geology and plant life and scouting the area between Yosemite Valley and Mt Whitney, where the 200mi John Muir Trail now pays him tribute.

Though he discovered 75 glaciers and mapped much of the Sierra for the first time, Muir is best known for his eloquent writings. His love for the outdoors was so passionate that he spent most of his time in solitude, among trees, cliffs, rocks and waterfalls, using his pen to commune with the environment.

Yosemite was his special love. In *My First Summer in the Sierra* (1911), he wrote about his first view of Yosemite Valley:

'Never before had I seen so glorious a landscape, so boundless an affluence of sublime mountain beauty. The most extravagant description I might give of this view to any one who has not seen similar landscapes with his own eyes would not so much as hint at its grandeur and the spiritual glow that covered it.'

Muir's articles and lobbying efforts were the foundation of the campaign that established Yosemite as a national park in 1890. He died in 1914, one year after losing the battle against the creation of the Hetch Hetchy Reservoir to the city of San Francisco.

Post & Communications The post office in Yosemite Village (closed weekends) accepts general delivery mail; the zip code is 95389. You can send a fax from here but it's very expensive. For free Internet access, go the public library in the Girls' Club Building near the Valley Visitor Center. It keeps erratic hours and limits sessions to 30 minutes.

Books *Yosemite: A Visitors Companion* by George Wuerthner, provides a good general introduction to the park's history, ecology, wildlife, geology and other aspects. Jeffrey P Schaffer's *Yosemite National Park: A Natural History Guide to Yosemite and Its Trails* is a great hiking companion and includes a detailed park map. Also widely available is John Muir's *The Yosemite*, which was reprinted with added photographs by noted nature photographer Galen Rowell. Rowell's tragic death in a private plane crash over the Sierras in August 2002 made headlines around the world. Other Muir books such as *My First Summer in the Sierra* and *The Mountains of California* present the writer at his eloquent, tree-loving best.

Photography Any aspiring Ansel Adams should check out sunrise at Mirror Lake or Yosemite Falls, and sunset from Valley View, Tunnel View or Glacier Point. Another good photo stop is Sentinel Bridge, near Housekeeping Camp, which offers an epic shot of Half Dome.

Free camera walks led by professional photographers leave almost daily; check *Yosemite Today* for what's scheduled during your visit. Slide and print film is widely available and reasonably priced.

Laundry & Showers Housekeeping Camp has a coin-op **laundry** *(open 7am-10pm daily)* and showers ($2). Curry Village, in the valley, also has showers.

Dangers & Annoyances Black bears roam freely throughout Yosemite, where 230 incidents involving these animals were recorded in 2001. If you're driving, you must remove all food, toiletries etc from your car overnight and store it in your room. Campers must use the bear-proof boxes at each site, while backpackers are strongly advised to store their food in bear-resistant food canisters. These may be rented for a few dollars throughout the valley, including where you get your wilderness permits. Also read the boxed text 'Bears, Your Food & You' in the Activities chapter.

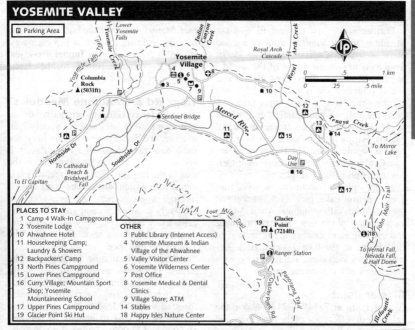

YOSEMITE VALLEY

P Parking Area

Lower Yosemite Falls

Yosemite Village

Columbia Rock ▲(5031ft)

Royal Arch Cascade

0   .5   1 km
0   .25   .5 mile

Sentinel Bridge

Merced River

Tenaya Creek

To Mirror Lake

Northside Dr

Southside Dr

Day Use

To Cathedral Beach & Bridalveil Fall

To El Capitan

Four Mile Trail

John Muir Trail

Glacier Point ▲(7214ft)

Ranger Station

To Vernal Fall, Nevada Fall, & Half Dome

Glacier Point Rd

Panorama Trail

Illilouette Creek

PLACES TO STAY
1 Camp 4 Walk-In Campground
2 Yosemite Lodge
10 Ahwahnee Hotel
11 Housekeeping Camp; Laundry & Showers
12 Backpackers' Camp
13 North Pines Campground
15 Lower Pines Campground
16 Curry Village; Mountain Sport Shop; Yosemite Mountaineering School
17 Upper Pines Campground
19 Glacier Point Ski Hut

OTHER
3 Public Library (Internet Access)
4 Yosemite Museum & Indian Village of the Ahwahnee
5 Valley Visitor Center
6 Yosemite Wilderness Center
7 Post Office
8 Yosemite Medical & Dental Clinics
9 Village Store; ATM
14 Stables
18 Happy Isles Nature Center

Medical Services & Emergency For emergencies, call ☎ 911. The **Yosemite Medical Clinic** (☎ 209-372-4637) and **Dental Clinic** (☎ 209-372-4200) are in Yosemite Valley, on the Ahwahnee Hotel road near Yosemite Village. Hours vary, but emergency care is available around the clock.

Yosemite Valley

The sight of sheer, glacially sculpted granite walls towering above lush meadows and forest really let you *know* you're in Yosemite. Yosemite Village is a good starting point from which to see the valley's star attractions. To avoid traffic and angst, get around by free shuttle bus, bicycle or on foot. Most sights are within a mile or less of each other.

Clearly the valley's main attractions are of the natural kind, but there are also a couple of places of cultural interest.

Next to the Valley Visitor Center (see Visitor Centers earlier), the **Yosemite Museum** (☎ 209-372-0200; *admission free; open at least 9am-4:30pm, closed for lunch*) provides some cultural and historical background on the valley's native Miwok and

Paiute people from 1850 to today. In summer the integrated gallery displays paintings from the museum's permanent collection. Behind the museum, a free self-guided interpretive trail winds through the **Indian Village of the Ahwahnee**, a reconstructed Miwok-Paiute village.

About a quarter mile east of Yosemite Village, the **Ahwahnee Hotel** (see Places to Stay) is a picture of elegance and rustic grace and has been a popular destination for well-to-do tourists since 1927. Built from local granite, pine and cedar, it is splendidly decorated with leaded glass, sculpted tiles and Native American rugs and Turkish kilims. It's worth wandering through even if you aren't staying there.

West of the village, near Yosemite Lodge (see Places to Stay later), a short, easy trail leads to the base of **Yosemite Falls**, whose double-tiered stream is visible from all over the valley. Together, the upper and lower falls cascade 2425ft, making this the tallest waterfalls in North America. Across the valley, the 620ft **Bridalveil Fall** is at its most magical at sunset. The Ahwahneechee call it Pohono (Spirit of the Puffing

Wind), as gusts often blow the falls from side to side.

Further west, just beyond El Capitan Meadow, **Valley View** turnout is a good place to ogle **El Capitan**, which at 3593ft from base to summit is one of the world's largest granite monoliths. Look closely and you'll probably see ropes, haul bags and climbers reckoning with its sheer face.

At the valley's southeastern end, where the Merced River courses around two small islands, **Happy Isles** is the starting point for several popular hikes. The **Happy Isles Nature Center** *(admission free; open May-Oct)* has hands-on nature exhibits.

At the valley's eastern end, a paved trail goes to **Mirror Lake**; pick it up just north of the Yosemite Valley Stables. Ansel Adams took many a photo here, as early morning and evening light catches the reflection of Half Dome in the lake. From here, a 3mi trail makes a loop along Tenaya Creek, with nice views of its U-shaped canyon.

Glacier Point

Glacier Point at 7214ft (3214ft above the valley floor) offers one of the most dramatic viewpoints in the entire park, especially of Half Dome. You can reach it by car via Glacier Point Rd (off Wawona Rd/Hwy 41; usually open May to October), on foot via the Panorama Trail or Four Mile Trail and, in winter, on cross-country skis. The **Glacier Point Hikers' Bus** *(☎ 209-372-1240 for reservations & information)* operates from Yosemite Valley several times daily in summer. Many hikers take the bus one way and hike up or down; the fare is $15 each way. If you're driving, stop at **Tunnel View**, just east of the Wawona Tunnel, for the classic valley panorama.

Tioga Rd & Tuolumne Meadows

Tioga Rd (Hwy 120) was originally built as a mining road in 1882 and is the only road to traverse the park (open summer only; see the boxed text 'Impassable Tioga Pass'). It is 46mi from the Tioga Pass Entrance in the east to the Big Oak Flat Entrance, which is about a two-hour drive. The road travels through superb scenery and gives access to relatively uncrowded campgrounds and excellent day hikes. The only services are in Tuolumne Meadows, about 6mi west of the Tioga Pass Entrance.

At 8500ft, Tuolumne Meadows is the largest subalpine meadow in the Sierra and its wide open fields and clear blue lakes create a dazzling contrast to Yosemite's forested valley. Most of the surrounding granite peaks soar to heights of between 10,000ft and 13,000ft. Temperatures here are 15° to 20°F lower than in the valley. To see the meadows' wild-flowers at their brilliant best, visit in July and August.

The many glacial lakes in this area make for good day-hike destinations. Just west of the Tioga Pass Entrance, the trail to

---

Legendary Half Dome

According to Native American legend, one of Yosemite Valley's early inhabitants went down from the mountains to Mono Lake, where he wed a Paiute named Tesaiyac. The journey back to the valley was difficult, and by the time they reached what was to become Mirror Lake, Tesaiyac had decided that she wanted to go back down to live with her people at Mono Lake. However, her husband refused to live on such barren, arid land with no oak trees from which to get acorns. With a heart full of despair, Tesaiyac began to run toward Mono Lake, and her husband followed her. When the powerful spirits heard quarreling in Yosemite, they became angry and turned the two into stone: he became North Dome and she became Half Dome. The tears she cried made marks as they ran down her face, thus forming Mirror Lake.

Though its origins are mythical, there's no doubt that Half Dome is Yosemite's most distinctive natural monument. It is 87 million years old and has a 93% vertical grade – the sheerest cliff in North America. Climbers come from around the world to grapple with its legendary 'north face,' but good hikers can reach its summit via an 8½mi trail from Yosemite Valley. The trail gains 4900ft in elevation and has cable handrails for the last 200yd. The hike *can* be done in one day, but is more enjoyable if you break it up by camping (Little Yosemite Valley is the most popular spot) one night along the way. For more information, see the special section 'Hiking in Yosemite.'

Gaylor Lakes advances immediately to a high-altitude environment: it's 1mi to Middle Gaylor Lake, another 2mi to the upper lakes. The altitude and steep terrain make this hike quite difficult.

The John Muir Trail (see the boxed text 'Pacific Crest Trail' in the Activities chapter earlier) parallels the Lyell Fork of the Tuolumne River at Tuolumne Meadows, connecting the visitor center, campground and lodge. This is an easy 2mi section with nice swimming holes, meadows and dome views.

Further west along the Tioga Rd, trailheads are well marked for the Cathedral Lakes, Sunrise Lakes and May Lake trails, which are all highly recommended.

In the west of the park, just after the junction of Tioga Rd with Big Oak Flat Rd, are two giant sequoia groves: **Merced Grove,** the park's most serene since it requires a 2mi hike to reach, and **Tuolumne Grove,** the park's smallest, cut through by a 6mi loop road.

From July to early September, the **Tuolumne Meadows Hikers' Bus** (☎ 209-372-1240) connects Yosemite Lodge, in the valley, with trailheads and lodges along Tioga Rd, including Crane Flat, White Wolf Lodge and Tuolumne Meadows Lodge. The fare is $14.50/23 one way/round-trip if traveling the entire distance from Yosemite Lodge to Tuolumne Meadows Lodge, less if you get off in between. There's only one bus in each direction daily.

Also in summer, the free **Tuolumne Meadows Shuttle** travels between the Tuolumne Meadows Lodge and Olmsted Point, including a stop at Tenaya Lake.

Wawona

About 27mi south of Yosemite Valley, along Wawona Rd, Wawona is Yosemite's historical center, home to the park's first headquarters and site of its first tourist facilities. The **Wawona Store** (☎ 209-375-6574) also acts as a post office, deli and bus stop. Nearby is the elegant **Wawona Hotel** (see Places to Stay) and the **Pioneer Yosemite History Center** (admission free; open 24hr), where some of the park's oldest buildings were relocated from various points. It also has a good collection of stagecoaches.

About 6mi south of Wawona (2mi north of the park's South Entrance) lies the **Mariposa Grove of Giant Sequoias,** once John

Muir's favorite grove and home to the 2700-year-old Grizzly Giant. It's about ½mi walk along a well-worn path to this humungous tree, beyond which crowds begin to thin out.

It's well worth taking the time to explore the upper grove, where you'll come across the **Fallen Wawona Tunnel Tree,** the famous drive-through tree that toppled over in 1969. Also here is the **Mariposa Grove Museum** (usually open Sat & Sun only), which helps demystify the ecology of the trees. The grove can also be explored on a one-hour guided tour aboard a noisy open-air tram ($11).

Parking at the grove is limited. From spring to fall, the free **Mariposa Grove Shuttle Bus** loops between the Wawona Store, the South Entrance and the grove.

Hetch Hetchy

After an environmental debate that knocked the wind out of John Muir, the 1913 Raker Bill allowed the city of San Francisco to construct O'Shaughnessy Dam in the Hetch Hetchy Valley, blocking the Tuolumne River to create Hetch Hetchy Reservoir. The 8mi-long reservoir now submerges an area said to be as beautiful as Yosemite Valley, while it supplies the majority of San Francisco's water and hydroelectric power.

In the park's northwestern corner, Hetch Hetchy gets the least amount of traffic yet sports waterfalls and granite cliffs that rival its more famous counterparts. Its relatively low elevation makes it a good destination in spring and fall when much of the high country is still blanketed by ice and snow.

Backpacking

Wilderness permits (free) are required year-round for all overnight trips. A quota system limits the number of people leaving from each trailhead each day. At least 40% of the quota is available on a first-come, first-served basis no earlier than 24 hours before your departure; the remainder may be reserved (☎ 209-372-0740, w www .nps.gov/yose/wilderness/permits.htm) from 24 weeks to two days before your trip for a $5 fee.

Before requesting your permit, know how many people are in your party, your entry and exit dates, your starting and ending trailheads and your principal destination. Permits are issued at the wilderness centers in Yosemite Valley (spring to fall) and

Tuolumne Meadows (summer only), the information stations at Wawona and Big Oak Flat (spring to fall) and the Hetch Hetchy Entrance (summer only).

The best place for camping and backpacking supplies is the **Curry Village Mountain Sport Shop** (☎ 209-372-8396) in the valley. The **Tuolumne Meadows Store** (☎ 209-372-8428; open summer only) also sells equipment and food.

The **Yosemite Mountaineering School** (☎ 209-372-8344), based at Tuolumne Meadows Lodge, has three and four-day guided backpacking trips for $125 to $240 per person, per day depending on the size of the group. The school also rents backpacks, sleeping bags and ground pads ($8/10/3 each per day) and bear canisters ($5 flat fee). It has another branch inside the Curry Village Mountain Sport Shop in Yosemite Valley.

Rock Climbing

With 3000ft granite monoliths and a mild climate, Yosemite is a climber's mecca. Most climbers stay at Camp 4 Walk-In Campground (see Places to Stay later) in the valley, which also has a bulletin board where people looking for climbing partners or equipment post notices. The Curry Village Mountain Sport Shop has equipment, books (climbers recommend the *Yosemite Free Climbs* by Don Reid), maps and a knowledgeable staff.

The Yosemite Mountaineering School (see under backpacking earlier) offers rock-climbing classes for all levels of expertise ($70 to $170, depending on the size of the group) and private guided climbs for one, two or three people ($220/310/405). Equipment is provided, and climbing shoes may be rented by class participants ($8).

The meadow across from El Capitan and the northeastern end of Tenaya Lake (off Tioga Rd) are good for watching climbers dangle from granite (binoculars are needed for a really good view). Look for the haul bags first – they're bigger, more colorful and move around more than the climbers, making them easier to spot.

Biking

Mountain biking is not allowed within the national park, but biking along the 12mi of paved trails is a popular and environment-friendly way to get around the valley. There are **bike rental stations** (☎ 209-372-1208 for

information) at Yosemite Lodge and Curry Village, which are open from spring to fall and charge $5.50/21 per hour/day.

Horseback Riding

Stables are at **Tuolumne Meadows** (☎ 209-372-8427), **Wawona** (☎ 209-375-6502) and in **Yosemite Valley** (☎ 209-372-8348). The season runs from early April to mid-October at Wawona and in the valley, and from May to September at Tuolumne. Rates are $40/55/ 80 for two hours/four hours/all day. No experience is needed for the two- and four-hour rides, but reservations are advised, especially at the Yosemite Valley Stables.

Rafting

From late May to July, floating the Merced River from Curry Village to Sentinel Bridge, is a leisurely way to soak up Yosemite Valley views. **Raft rentals** (☎ 209-372-8319) for the 3mi trip are available at Curry Village for $13.50 per person, including equipment and a tram ride back to the rental kiosk. Rafting above Yosemite Stables or below Cathedral Beach Picnic Area is forbidden.

Winter Activities

Winter can be a magical time in Yosemite. Roads in the valley are plowed, and Hwys 41, 120 and 140 are usually kept open, conditions permitting (Hwy 140 is almost always open). The Tioga Rd/Hwy 120, though, closes with the first snowfall. Be sure to bring snow chains with you, as prices for them double once you hit the foothills.

There is a big outdoor **ice-skating rink** (☎ 209-372-8341; $6.50 per session, rental skates $3.25) at Curry Village, and a free shuttle from the valley to the **Badger Pass Ski Area** (☎ 209-372-1244 for information). Open from around mid-December through early April, this is primarily a beginner and intermediate hill, with five chairlifts, 800 vertical feet, $31/16 adult/child lift tickets, a good ski school and a full-service lodge.

Yosemite offers great terrain for **cross-country skiing**. There are about 350mi of skiable trails, including 25mi of machine groomed track and 90mi of marked trails beginning at Badger Pass. The scenic trail to Glacier Point – 21mi round-trip – also starts from here (see that section earlier).

[Continued on page 422]

HIKING IN YOSEMITE

Yosemite has more than 800mi of trails that go far beyond the beaten tourist path. The best way to enjoy the park's natural splendor is to take to the backcountry, even if it is only 2mi in and only for half a day. Besides the two most popular areas, Yosemite Valley and Tuolumne Meadows, there's good hiking in Hetch Hetchy. Distance mongers should consider hiking between Tuolumne Meadows and the valley floor. There are also trailheads on the Glacier Point Rd, including the Sentinel Dome Trail and the Taft Point Trail, both short and easy hikes ending at fabulous viewpoints. Hikes in the Wawona area are also easy and put you up close to giant sequoia groves. Also see the free newspaper *Yosemite Today*, which you receive when entering the park, for additional hiking suggestions. Detailed maps are available at the visitor centers and stores within the national park.

This section introduces you to some of the most glorious day hikes starting in Yosemite Valley, as well as an extended overnight trip up Half Dome. For more general details about Yosemite National Park, see the main section on the park.

All distances given in the following walks are for the round-trip.

Vernal Fall

Duration: two to three hours
Distance: 2.6mi (4.2km)
Standard: easy to moderate
Start/Finish: Happy Isles

Vernal Fall, which the Miwok people called Pai-wai'-ak, tumbles 317ft over a vertical cliff. The top of Vernal Fall is the easiest of Yosemite's waterfalls to reach, making it one of the valley's most popular day hikes. The wide, once-paved trail, however, has 1000ft elevation gain and another 1000ft elevation loss.

The trailhead is Happy Isles (shuttle bus stop 16), which is near the southern end of Upper Pines Campground. From Happy Isles (4035ft), cross the road bridge over the Merced River and head up its true right (eastern) bank. Opposite the footbridge, which was destroyed by a 1999 flood, join the once-paved trail, which ascends 400ft in 0.7mi to the Vernal Fall footbridge. Along the way you have views of Illilouette Fall (370ft). The very popular footbridge, with a rest room and drinking fountain on its southern side, has photogenic views of Vernal Fall.

Continue beyond the footbridge on the Mist Trail. Expect to get wet, as sheets of water from the fall sprays your path. (On sunny days, the spray dances with rainbows, a truly mesmerizing sight.) It is 0.6mi to the top of Vernal Fall. A final short but steep rock staircase, protected by a railing, brings you to the top of the falls, where you can dry off and enjoy the views and a picnic.

Return to Happy Isles via the same trail, taking care on the often slippery wet rock.

415

Nevada Fall

Duration: four to five hours
Distance: 6.5mi (10.5km)
Standard: moderate
Start/Finish: Happy Isles

In early spring and late fall, portions of the John Muir Trail below Nevada Fall and the Mist Trail near Vernal Fall may be closed. The top of Nevada Fall, however, is usually still accessible.

From Happy Isles, cross the road bridge over the Merced River, turn right, and follow its eastern bank upstream to join the gentle, once-paved pathway that ascends 400ft in 0.7mi to the popular Vernal Fall footbridge. A bit up the path is the junction of the John Muir Trail and Mist Trail. Turn right onto the John Muir Trail.

Follow the gentle switchbacks 1.3mi up the canyon, opposite the southern wall of Sierra Point, through forests of Douglas fir and gold-cup oak to **Clark Point** (5480ft). Continue on a more level trail 1.0mi to the junction with the Panorama Trail. Stay on the John Muir Trail, crossing the footbridge over the Merced River at the top of Nevada Fall (5907ft). Picnic or relax on the granite rocks along the northeastern brink of the falls. A spectacular but often overlooked scenic viewpoint lies a short distance down a spur trail on the river's northern side. The terrace, protected by an iron railing, is at the very edge of the waterfall.

To avoid retracing your steps back to Yosemite Valley, the shorter but steeper Mist Trail leads back to Happy Isles. From the top of Nevada Fall, walk a bit further northeast beyond the footbridge and look for the trail junction near a solar toilet. Turn left onto the Mist Trail beneath Liberty Cap and descend steeply on the 500-step rock staircase alongside Nevada Fall. Cross another footbridge over the Merced River at the **Silver Apron** and continue along Emerald Pool to Vernal Fall on a gentler trail. Below Vernal Fall, descend another short rock staircase and follow the paved pathway from the Vernal Fall footbridge to Happy Isles. To turn this into an overnight trip, continue 1mi beyond Nevada Fall and camp in Little Yosemite Valley along the Merced River.

Yosemite Falls

Duration: five to six hours
Distance: 6.8mi (10.9km)
Standard: moderate to hard
Start/Finish: Camp 4

Cho'lok, or Yosemite Falls, plunges 2425ft in three cascades – the upper falls is 1430ft, the middle 675ft, and the lower 320ft – creating the world's fifth-highest free-leaping waterfall. An excellent trail leads from the valley floor to the top of the falls along the valley's northern rim, but the stiff ascent of 2410ft and equivalent descent makes this a strenuous day hike. When doing the side trip to the spectacular **Yosemite Point**, it's an even stiffer ascent, of almost 3000ft.

This south-facing trail is free from snow earlier than other trails to the valley rim, making it a desirable hike in May and June. At this time, the falls are most powerful. By August the falls can be just a trickle in comparison.

The trailhead is behind Camp 4 (shuttle bus stop 7). From the eastern side of Camp 4 Walk-In Campground (3990ft), go up the slope for a minute to the northside Valley Floor Trail. Head west for a minute to the start of the Yosemite Falls Trail. The trail ascends four-dozen short switchbacks immediately, ascending steeply up a talus slope through gold-cup oaks. After 0.8mi, the trail becomes more gradual and follows switchbacks east to reach **Columbia Rock**, a viewpoint 1mi from the trailhead and 1000ft above the valley floor, with impressive views of Half Dome and Quarter Dome to the east.

In another 0.4mi, the trail approaches **Middle Yosemite Falls**, where breezes may shower you with a cooling mist. After a few more switchbacks, the trail traverses northeast, bending north for views of the upper falls. The trail then makes numerous switchbacks steadily up a rocky cleft in the cliffs to the valley rim. This cleft was once the route of Yosemite Falls, but when the last major glacier receded some 130,000 years ago, it left glacial moraine that blocked the river and shifted its course eastward to the cliff face, forming today's spectacular free-leaping waterfall.

The trail tops out 3.2mi from the trailhead and bends east. At the junction, the trail going straight leads to Eagle Peak. Turn right at this junction and follow the trail to the brink of upper Yosemite Falls at the **Yosemite Falls Overlook** (6400ft). The view of the falls is impressive, but views of El Capitan and Half Dome are obscured. It's also possible to do this hike as an overnight trip. Campsites are in a forested area above Yosemite Creek's true right bank. Return along the same trail, back to Camp 4.

Four Mile & Panorama Trails

Duration: 6½ to eight hours
Distance: 12.6mi (20.3km)
Standard: moderate to hard
Start: Leidig Meadow
Finish: Happy Isles

A great day hike from Yosemite Valley ascends to Glacier Point, traverses the valley's southern rim, and follows the cascading Merced River back to the valley floor. Most of the hike provides a continually changing perspective on the rounded, glacially polished western and southern sides of world-famous Half Dome. Passing alongside three of the valley's major waterfalls, the hike has 7800ft of elevation gain and descent, roughly in equal amounts, making it a demanding yet highly rewarding experience. Much of the trail is forested, providing welcome shade on the big climbs without obscuring the many breathtaking views.

Hikers not inclined to make the steep 3200ft ascent on the Four Mile Trail can instead start the hike from Glacier Point, which is served by the **Glacier Point Hikers' Bus** (☎ 209-372-1240 for reservations & information) from Yosemite Valley. The bus departs from Yosemite Lodge several times daily from June to October, and the fare is $15 each way (1½ hours). Note that the shady, north-facing Four Mile Trail stays closed longer than other trails early in the hiking season due to snow and ice.

Start from Leidig Meadow (4000ft) along Southside Dr at Yosemite Valley's western end. The nearest shuttle bus stop is 7 (Camp 4), from where a short walk west along a paved footpath leads over Swinging Bridge, which is just above sandy Sentinel Beach, to Southside Dr. Walk west along the road for about a minute or two to the Four Mile trailhead. Look for the trailhead sign just before the Yellow Pine/Sentinel Beach picnic area. (Starting from the other end, the trailhead is Happy Isles, shuttle bus stop 16, which is near the southern end of Upper Pines Campground.)

Follow the Four Mile Trail, which is more like 4.6mi, steadily up 2½ to four hours to **Glacier Point** (7214ft), a 3200ft cliff overlooking Yosemite Valley. The trail passes by 2000ft Sentinel Fall and beneath Sentinel Rock (7038ft) as it traverses Yosemite Valley's shady, north-facing wall. It reaches **Union Point** 3mi from the trailhead near a large tree, where the first Half Dome views appear. With impressive views of El Capitan, Cathedral Spires, Three Brothers and Yosemite Falls, and unique perspectives of Royal Arches, Washington Column, North Dome and Half Dome, Glacier Point is a heavily visited spot. Its snack bar and drinking fountain also make it a good rest spot after the long ascent.

From Glacier Point, look for the signed start of the Panorama Trail. Descend the gentle, open, fire-scarred hillside south 2mi to cross a solid footbridge over **Illilouette Creek**, whose shaded banks offer delightful picnic spots. The distant roar from Vernal Fall is audible. As the trail leaves the creek, you have good views of the 370ft Illilouette Fall.

Ascending east to **Panorama Point** and further to the top of **Panorama Cliff** high above the Merced River brings amazing views of the Glacier Point apron, Half Dome, Mt Broderick, Liberty Cap and Mt Starr King. The trail descends to a junction, where the John Muir Trail heads to the left. Follow the trail to the right 0.2mi to the top of **Nevada Fall**, 3.2mi from Illilouette Creek. From Nevada Fall, descend on the Mist Trail via Vernal Fall, or alternatively, descend on the 0.6mi longer and gentler John Muir Trail, to Happy Isles at the eastern end of the valley. See the Nevada Fall hike, earlier.

Half Dome

Duration: two days (or nine to 12 hours)
Distance: 17mi (27.4km)
Standard: hard
Start/Finish: Happy Isles

Rising more than 4800ft above the eastern end of Yosemite Valley, the granite monolith of Half Dome (8842ft) has awed visitors since the park's inception. Its summit was first reached by George Anderson in 1875. These days, rock climbers still tackle the mountain's sheer face, but no technical expertise or equipment are needed for the hike up the main trail. Culminating in 360-degree panoramic views, it skirts two dramatic waterfalls and pretty much follows in Anderson's footsteps.

The rigorous hike is most enjoyable as a two-day trip, although fit hikers can attempt it as a demanding 10- to 12-hour day hike. If you consider this alternative, keep in mind there is a total of 9684ft total elevation change. Day hikers need to start by 6am in order to return before dark; carrying a flashlight is recommended.

Hiking to the top of Half Dome is only allowed when the cable route to the top is open. Depending upon snow conditions, the National Park Service (NPS) puts the cables up as early as late May and takes them down in mid-October. If you're planning an early season or late season trip, it's essential to confirm that the cables are in place. A wilderness permit is required for camping in Little Yosemite Valley. Hikers intent on reaching the top of a Yosemite dome but too intimidated by Half Dome, should consider trudging up to the North Dome (see later). Those with little time or ambition could also head for Sentinel Dome, which is a mere 1.1mi away from the trailhead off the Glacier Point Rd.

Day 1: Happy Isles to Little Yosemite Valley

Duration: three to four hours
Distance: 4mi (6.5km)
Ascent: 2000ft (667m)

From Happy Isles, ascend the paved pathway 0.7mi to the Vernal Fall bridge. Just beyond the bridge, turn right, staying on the John Muir Trail. Follow gentle switchbacks 2mi up to Nevada Fall, 3.4mi from Happy Isles, and cross the footbridge over the Merced River. Continue over a low rise and reach **Little Yosemite Valley** with views of the massive, rounded, golden southern side of Half Dome. Solar composting toilets testify to the popularity of the area's many campsites. Many people camp here to avoid carrying their backpacks higher.

Day 2: Little Yosemite Valley to Half Dome Summit & back to Happy Isles

Duration: six to eight hours
Distance: 13mi (20.9km)
Ascent: 2800ft (934m)
Descent: 4800ft (1600m)

At the eastern end of Little Yosemite Valley, the Merced Lake Trail heads east (right) along the Merced River. Stay on the John Muir Trail, which turns north (left) and climbs steeply through forest 1.3mi to the Half Dome Trail junction.

Turn west (left) onto the **Half Dome Trail**, where a signpost reads 2mi to Half Dome. About 10 minutes above the junction on the left side of the trail is a somewhat hard-to-spot seasonal spring. This trickle is the last source of water on this trail, so fill up your water bottles (make sure you treat the water). Continue for 30 minutes, first up through forest and then up switchbacks to the **northeastern shoulder** (7600ft). Protect your food at all times from varmints scampering around this busy spot.

The exposed route above the northeastern shoulder keeps some hikers from ever going beyond it. A rocky trail snakes 650ft up two-dozen switchbacks in 20 to 30 minutes to a notch at the top of the dome's shoulder and to the base of the **cables**. From here, steel cables bolted to the granite provide handholds, and intermittent wooden cross-boards provide footholds for the final 600ft ascent up an exposed 45-degree rock face. To protect your hands from the steel cables, grab a pair of gloves from the pile at the base. A trip up uncrowded cables takes only 15 minutes, but on crowded cables (or if you are intimidated), it may take 30 minutes or longer. From the relatively flat five-acre expanse on top, enjoy the amazing views of Yosemite Valley – especially from the overhanging northwestern point – Mt Starr King, Clouds Rest (9926ft), the Cathedral Range, Unicorn Peak and the Sierra Crest. Most people spend from 30 minutes to an hour on top. Watch the time carefully to avoid having to descend in the dark.

Camping on top of Half Dome is prohibited for three reasons: to protect the threatened Mt Lyell salamander's habitat, which was being disturbed by people moving rocks to build wind shelters; to reduce human waste left on top; and to protect the last remaining tree, as six of the seven trees previously growing there were illegally cut for camp-fires. Respect the camping ban and protect this fragile ecosystem.

For the descent, retrace your steps to Little Yosemite Valley. At the northeastern brink of Nevada Fall, turn right onto the Mist Trail just before the footbridge, and descend the 500-step rock staircase along-side Nevada Fall. Cross the footbridge above Vernal Fall, and continue to the falls on a gentler trail. Descend another short rock staircase and follow the paved pathway from the Vernal Fall footbridge to Happy Isles.

North Dome

Duration: 4½ to five hours
Distance: 8.4mi (13.5km)
Standard: easy to moderate
Start/Finish: Porcupine Creek trailhead
North Dome is arguably the best vantage point any-where along Yosemite Valley's entire rim. Yet this spectacular spot above the northern rim sees comparatively few hikers. Its perspective on Half Dome, Quarter Domes and Clouds Rest all rising above granite Tenaya Canyon is unrivaled.

The trail has 1000ft of descent but only 422ft of ascent on the way to North Dome, making the round-trip hike a total of 2844ft of elevation change. The side trip to the natural arch on Indian Ridge adds another 480ft of total elevation change. Keep in mind that it's mostly downhill on the way out to North Dome and uphill on the way back, although the gradient is almost never steep. The well-signed Porcupine Creek trailhead (8120ft) is on Tioga Rd (Hwy 120) at road marker T19, 1.3mi east of Porcupine Flat Campground. When camping at Porcupine Flat, walk across Hwy 120 from the campground entrance and follow the footpath that parallels the southern side of Hwy 120 east to reach the trailhead. The **Tuolumne Meadows Hikers Bus** (☎ 209-372-1240) from Yosemite Valley to Tuolumne Meadows passes the trailhead at about 9:30am ($10.50/20 one-way/round-trip). The bus from Tuolumne Meadows to Yosemite Valley passes the trailhead at about 2:45pm ($5/9).

Follow an abandoned road downhill 0.7mi (20 minutes) through red-fir forest. The footpath ends and the trail turns right to cross a creek and then the larger lodge-pole pine-lined Porcupine Creek (7840ft) via a log. Ascend gently and re-enter the open red-fir forest, where you get the first glimpses of Clouds Rest and the Clark Range, and continue 30 minutes to a signed trail junction (7853ft), 1.5mi from the trailhead. The Snow Creek Trail to Yosemite Valley via Mirror Lake turns left (east) here. Continue straight at this junction and go 50ft (0.1mi) further to a second trail junction. At the second junction, take the left fork, which is signed to North Dome.

The trail traverses gently up the forested western slopes of Indian Ridge 10 minutes to an inviting **viewpoint** (7880ft). Granite boulders, open manzanita scrub and a few Jeffrey pines form the foreground to the expansive views across Yosemite Valley to Sentinel Dome and Taft Point. Continue along the ridge's side through an open red-fir forest, where white-flowering manzanitas lie low along the trail; after 15 minutes you'll reach a seasonal creek. A short distance ahead, the trail turns back sharply east (left) and ascends steadily for 10 minutes to gain the ridgeline at the signed Indian Rock trail junction (8120ft), 1.1mi from the previous junction.

From the Indian Rock trail junction (the hike's highest point), the main trail continues south, descending gently for 10 minutes along the open ridge to a spectacular **viewpoint** at the end of the ridge, which makes a fantastic campsite (8000ft). If you decide to spend the night here (or on North Dome), you need to bring water, since none is available nearby. From this viewpoint, directly in front of Half Dome, you also get a view across Yosemite Valley of the hard-to-see Illilouette Fall. North Dome is directly below to the south, and Basket Dome's round granite top (7612ft) is below to the southeast.

At a large, lightning-cropped Jeffrey pine, the trail drops southeast (left) off the ridgeline in the direction of Half Dome and descends for 10 minutes on switchbacks through open Jeffrey pines and manzanitas onto open granite. Cairns mark the route, which leads you a few minutes across the rock to the signed North Dome Trail junction (7560ft), 1mi from the Indian Rock trail junction.

Turn east (left) onto the North Dome Trail for the final 0.5mi. The rough trail descends along a steep granite rib, then through a white-fir forest to a saddle (7400ft) before making the short, easy five-minute ascent over granite to the summit of **North Dome** (7542ft). To the west are the Sentinels, Cathedral Range, El Capitan, the Three Brothers and Yosemite Point; Yosemite Falls are hidden. To the northeast are Basket Dome, Mt Watkins and the distant peaks of the Cathedral Range. Horse Ridge fills the horizon to the south. But looming in front of everything is the sheer northern face of Half Dome. Retrace your steps along Indian Ridge back to the trailhead in two to 2½ hours.

[Continued from page 414]

There are also marked trails at Crane Flat in the backcountry and in the Mariposa Grove of Giant Sequoias in Wawona.

The **Yosemite Cross-Country Ski School** (☎ 209-372-8444) offers learn-to-ski packages ($40), guided tours (from $40 for a half day) and equipment rentals ($16 per day for skis, boots and poles, and $14.25 for snowshoes). The school also runs overnight trips to Glacier Point Ski Hut (one night per person $150 to $180, two nights $225 to $270).

Another hut, the **Ostrander Ski Hut** (☎ 209-372-0740; **w** www.ostranderhut.com), in a gorgeous spot on the bank of Ostrander Lake, is operated by the Yosemite Association. It is staffed throughout winter and open to backcountry skiers and snowshoers for $20 per person, per night. The 10mi (one way) trip requires experience and a high fitness level. Check its website for details.

Organized Tours

While tours are good for covering a lot of ground with someone else in the driver's seat, five of the six tours offered – all from Yosemite Valley – are in big tour buses and make few stops. Most popular is the two-hour **Valley Floor Tour** ($20.50), offered year-round, which stops at major points of interest, including Yosemite Falls, Bridalveil Fall and El Capitan. For other tour options, stop at the information kiosks at Yosemite Lodge or Curry Village, call ☎ 209-372-1240, or check the website at **w** www.yosemitepark.com.

Places to Stay

Camping Campgrounds in Yosemite range from primitive backpacker camps to developed grounds that can accommodate large RVs. All have flush toilets, except for Tamarack Flat, Yosemite Creek and Porcupine Flat, which have vault toilets and are also the only ones without potable water. Sites usually include a picnic table, fire pit and food storage locker. Note that opening dates for campgrounds may vary slightly each year.

For campground reservations in Yosemite National Park call ☎ 800-436-7275. You can make reservations up to five months in advance, beginning the 15th of each month. Don't fret if campgrounds are fully booked. Except during major holidays, you may be able to snag a spot at first-come, first-served campgrounds if you arrive early.

Yosemite Valley has three campgrounds with $18 sites (reservations required). **Upper Pines** (open year-round) has the most trees and nicest sites but is furthest from Yosemite Village. **Lower Pines** (open Mar-Oct) is on the southern shores of the Merced, while **North Pines** (open Apr-Oct) is on the northern bank near the Yosemite Valley Stables.

Camp 4 Walk-In Campground (sites $5 per person; open year-round), near El Capitan, is a first-come, first-served campground popular with climbers. It often fills to capacity by 9am from May to September. Each site holds six people and unless that's the size of your group, expect additional campers to be assigned to your site.

Outside Yosemite Valley, near the park's western entrance, **Hodgdon Meadow** (sites $18; open year-round) makes half of its sites available on a first-come, first-served basis, while at **Crane Flat** (sites $18; open June-Sept), near the junction of Tioga Rd and Big Oak Flat Rd, all sites must be reserved.

Along Tioga Rd, you can camp without a reservation at **Tamarack Flat** (sites $8), **White Wolf** (sites $12), **Yosemite Creek** (sites $8) and **Porcupine Flat** (sites $8). In the east of the park at **Tuolumne Meadows** (sites $18), next to the visitor center, reservations are required for half of the sites. Campgrounds here are usually open from late June to September. If the campgrounds along Tioga Rd are full, try any of the eight USFS campgrounds on Hwy 120 outside the eastern park entrance between Tioga Pass and US-395.

South of the valley, **Bridalveil Creek** (sites $12; open July-early Sept) has no reservation requirements, while at **Wawona** (open year-round) reservations are mandatory from May to September ($18); the rest of the year, it's first-come, first-served ($12).

If you hold a wilderness permit, you may spend one night before and one night after your trip in Yosemite's three backpacker campgrounds at Tuolumne Meadows, Hetch Hetchy and behind North Pines in Yosemite Valley. The cost is $5 per person, per night and reservations are not necessary.

High Sierra Camps Yosemite's High Sierra Camps offer a great way to experience the backcountry without having to carry much food or equipment. The camps are at **Vogelsang, Merced Lake, Sunrise Camp, May Lake** and **Glen Aulin** and are set 6mi to 10mi apart along a loop trail in the park's high country near Tuolumne Meadows. Each has canvas tent cabins sleeping four to six people. Beds have blankets or comforters, but you must bring sheets or sleeping bags and your own towels. Bathrooms have hot showers but water may be limited. The hearty breakfast and dinner are served family style. The rate is $109 per adult, per night, including the two meals. Guided hikes and saddle trips are available too.

A short season (roughly late June to September) and high demand require a lottery for reservations. Applications are accepted from October 15 to November 30, and the lottery is in December. To request an application, call ☎ 559-253-5674 or go online to ⓦ www.yosemitepark.com.

Cabins & Lodges All noncamp accommodations in the park, including cabins and tent cabins, are managed by **Yosemite Concession Services** (YCS; ☎ 559-252-4848, fax 559-456-0542; ⓦ www.yosemitepark .com). Places get snapped up early for the summer months, especially on weekends and holidays, but if you're flexible there's often some space available at short notice, especially midweek. Call ahead to check the availability.

Housekeeping Camp (tent cabins $56; open Apr–Oct) in the valley has 266 canvas tent cabins along the Merced River. Each sleeps up to four people and has a covered outdoor sitting area, fire pit and electrical outlet.

Curry Village (tent cabins $58.50, cabins without/with bath $77/92, standard rooms $112; open year-round), in the valley, has a variety of accommodations. Its canvas tent cabins sleep up to five people but are very close together and don't have heating or a fire pit. Wooden cabins without bath are a bit nicer but still crowded together, while those with bath are spacious and cozy. A few motel-style rooms are also available.

Tuolumne Meadows Lodge (tent cabins $59; open early June–mid-Sept), off Tioga Rd/Hwy 120, offers canvas tent cabins with four beds, a wood stove and candles (no electricity).

White Wolf Lodge (tent cabins $55, cabin with bath $88; open June–mid-Sept), a mile north of Tioga Rd, is in a charming world of its own. The lodge has a great porch and rustic dining room, tent cabins, wood cabins with bath and a lovely campground.

Yosemite Lodge (standard/lodge rooms $112/136; open year-round), in the valley, has modern, motel-like standard rooms and larger lodge rooms with private patio or balcony. All rooms have telephone but no TV.

Wawona Hotel (rooms without/with bath $101/161; open year-round, Fri & Sat nights only from Dec–March), built in 1879, is a graceful mansion with 104 Victorian rooms (some freshly revamped), most of them opening up onto the spacious trademark veranda. About half of the rooms must share facilities.

Ahwahnee Hotel (rooms & cottages $366), a National Historic Landmark built in 1927, is the most luxurious place in the park and has hosted presidents, royals and celebrities. Expect the best.

Tenaya Lodge (☎ 559-683-6555, 800-635-5807, fax 559-683-8684; 1122 Hwy 41; rooms $105-299), about 2mi south of the South Entrance, is a luxurious place to stay, with two pools, a spa and fitness center, three restaurants, woodsy grounds and cozy rooms. Although managed by Yosemite Concession Services, it's outside the park and takes direct reservations.

Non-YCS Accommodations Located about 1½mi east of Hwy 41 in Wawona, **The Redwoods in Yosemite** (☎ 559-375-6666; ⓦ www.redwoodsinyosemite.com; Chilnualna Falls Rd; homes $82-438 per night) rents 125 vacation homes of various sizes and levels of comfort. There's a three-night minimum in summer, two nights otherwise.

Yosemite West Lodging (☎ 559-642-2211; ⓦ www.yosemitewest.com; studios $85-125, homes $155-215) rents homes, cabins and apartment condominiums in a private development just outside park boundaries off Hwy 41 between Wawona and Yosemite Valley. Rates are for two people, but larger units are available also.

Places to Eat

Bringing your own food saves money but can be a hassle because you must remove it all from your car (or backpack or bicycle) and store it in a locker or bear canister overnight. The **Village Store** in Yosemite Village has the best selection for self-caterers, while stores at Curry Village, Wawona Store and Tuolumne Meadows are more limited.

Unless mentioned, eateries here are open year-round.

Curry Village has the cafeteria-style **Dining Pavilion** (*breakfast $10, dinner $12; open mid-Apr–mid-Oct*), serving mediocre all-you-can-eat breakfast and dinner buffets; **Coffee Corner** with pastries and snacks; and the outdoor **Pizza Patio** (*pizza $5-12.50; open spring–fall*).

At Yosemite Lodge, the self-service **Food Court** (*dishes $3-8.50*) is good for breakfast and hot and cold lunches, while the **Mountain Room** (*dinner mains $16-24*) has views of Yosemite Falls and a menu catering to carnivores, though it's a bit overpriced.

The Loft (*pizza from $4.50; open mid-Apr–Oct*), in Yosemite Village, serves generously topped pizza, while **Degnan's Deli** (*sandwiches about $6*) downstairs has freshly made sandwiches.

Ahwahnee Dining Room (*☎ 559-372-1489; breakfast & lunch $10-15, dinner mains $20-25*) requires deep pockets but the baronial setting and gourmet food ensure a memorable experience. Reservations are suggested for all meals and a dress code is in effect at dinner.

Wawona Hotel Dining Room (*lunch $3-8.50, dinner $18-29; open Easter-Oct*) offers another venerable setting with Victorian touches and upscale cuisine.

Entertainment

Ahwahnee Hotel often has evening programs that aren't publicized but are open to anyone; check the marquee in the lobby for the night's offerings.

The park's most noteworthy entertainer is actor Lee Stetson, who does a **one-man show** about the life of John Muir. His wife, Connie, also does a program portraying a 19th-century pioneer woman. One or the other performs almost nightly in the Visitor Center West Auditorium in Yosemite Village. Tickets are $7/3 per adult/child.

Getting There & Around

Yosemite is one of the easiest national parks to reach by public transportation. Buses operated by **Yosemite Area Regional Transportation System** (*YARTS; ☎ 877-989-2787; w www.yarts.com*) meet Amtrak trains and Greyhound buses in Merced (see the San Joaquin Valley chapter) and depart for Yosemite National Park via Hwy 140 up to six times daily year-round. Buses make several stops, including in Mariposa and at the Yosemite Bug Hostel in Midpines, before traveling to Yosemite Valley. Tickets from Merced are $14 each way (2¾ hours). Note that buses may occasionally be delayed or canceled due to road closures caused by heavy snowfall, rock slides or other problems.

In summer YARTS also runs one bus daily in each direction between Yosemite and Mammoth Lakes in the Eastern Sierra via Hwy 120, the Tioga Rd ($20 round-trip, three hours). Fares for either route include the park entrance fee.

Greyhound buses and/or Amtrak trains connect Merced with Los Angeles, Bakersfield and Oakland/San Francisco. Also from San Francisco, **Missing Link Tour Company** (*☎ 800-209-8586; w www.tmltours.com*) runs shuttles to/from the park three times weekly in either direction ($27/50 one way/round-trip, two hours).

In Yosemite Valley, a free shuttle bus operating at frequent intervals makes stops at all day-use parking lots, campgrounds, Yosemite Village, Curry Village, Yosemite Lodge, Ahwahnee Hotel and popular trailheads. Other buses operating in the park are the Glacier Point Hikers' Bus, the Tuolumne Meadows Hikers' Bus, the Tuolumne Meadows Shuttle and the Mariposa Grove Shuttle Bus in Wawona. For details, see the respective sections earlier in this chapter.

YOSEMITE GATEWAYS

The small towns on Yosemite's western and southwestern fringe are mostly old mining towns that now thrive on the park's overflow. These are good places to stay if you arrive without a tent or room reservation. The **Mariposa County Visitor Center** (*☎ 209-966-2456, 800-208-2434; w http://mariposa .yosemite.net; 5158 Hwy 140; usually open until 8pm Mon-Fri mid-May–Sept*) sort of acts as an information hub for the area.

Coming from the east, the nearest town is Lee Vining, 13mi east of the Tioga Pass Entrance (see the Eastern Sierra section later in this chapter).

Oakhurst
Situated at the junction of Hwys 41 and 49, Oakhurst is the last place with normal gas prices, supermarkets, banks and auto-parts stores before you enter the park from the south. While most traffic is Yosemite bound, a fair amount of people pass through Oakhurst en route to **Bass Lake**, a popular fishing and boating spot.

Chain motels are your best bet here, with options including **Shilo Inn** (☎ 559-683-3555; 40644 Hwy 41; rooms $59-149) and **Best Western Yosemite Gateway Inn** (☎ 559-683-2378; 40530 Hwy 41; rooms $54-99), both with swimming pool.

Mariposa
About halfway between Merced and Yosemite Valley, at the Hwy 140/49 junction, Mariposa is the largest and most interesting town near the park. Established as a mining and railroad town during the gold rush, it has a stately courthouse built in 1854 (the oldest in continuous use west of the Mississippi), and a **History Center** (☎ 209-966-2924; open 10am-4pm daily), at the eastern end of town, with mining and railroad exhibits.

The **California State Mining and Mineral Museum** (☎ 209-742-7625; admission $2; open 10am-4pm Wed-Mon Oct-Apr, 10am-6pm daily Mar-Sept), at the fairgrounds a mile south of town off Hwy 49, re-lives the gold rush era. Highlights include a huge gold nugget and a restored mining tunnel that illustrates the harsh life of the miners.

Mother Lode Lodge (☎ 209-966-2521, 800-398-9770; rooms $38-138) and **Mariposa Lodge** (☎ 209-966-3607, 800-966-8819; rooms $48-112), both on Hwy 140, are good places to stay.

Midpines
Yosemite Bug Lodge & Hostel (☎ 209-966-6666, fax 209-966-6667; 6979 Hwy 140; w www.yosemitebug.com; dorm beds $13-16, tent cabins $30-50, rooms without bath $40-70, rooms with bath $55-115), tucked away on a forested hillside about 25mi from Yosemite, is more of a convivial mountain retreat than a hostel. At night, friendly folk of

all ages and from around the globe share stories, music and inexpensive, delicious meals in the woodsy café-lounge before retreating to whatever bed their money can buy: a bunk, a tent cabin, a private room with shared facilities or a uniquely decorated cabin with private bath. Dorm dwellers have access to a kitchen. The Bug rents mountain bikes ($12 to $15 per day) and snowshoes ($8 per day) and it has a local swimming hole as well.

You can usually catch a ride with a fellow hosteler headed for Yosemite; otherwise, you can buy discounted round-trip tickets for the YARTS bus (see Getting There & Around earlier in this section).

The bus also stops at the nearby **KOA Campground** (☎ 209-966-2201, 800-562-9391; tents $21-27, RV sites $31-38, cabins $50-60; open year-round).

El Portal
Just west of the park's Arch Rock entrance, El Portal hugs the Merced River for about 7mi along Hwy 140, and makes for a convenient Yosemite base.

Savage's Trading Post, at its western end where the southern and main forks of the Merced River meet, is a touristy gift shop on the site of a trading post used by miners and Miwok in the 1850s. The adjacent **Red Bug Lodge** (☎ 209-379-2301; rooms $85-125) has funky rooms with odd Art-Deco-meets-Native-American decor.

For better lodging options, continue toward the park.

Cedar Lodge (☎ 209-379-2612, 888-742-4371, fax 209-379-2712; 9966 Hwy 40; rooms $59-149) is an older establishment with adequate rooms.

Yosemite View Lodge (☎ 209-379-2681, 800-321-5261, fax 209-379-2704; 11136 Hwy 140; rates $85-205), closest to the park entrance, is a rambling, modern resort with pools, hot tubs and restaurants. The nicest rooms, some with full, if small, kitchens, overlook the river.

Groveland
From the Big Oak Flat Entrance, it's 22mi to Groveland, an adorable town on Hwy 120 West with restored gold rush-era buildings.

Hotel Charlotte (☎ 209-962-7872, 800-961-7799; Hwy 120; rooms $81, suites $146), in the middle of town, has vintage rooms.

SIERRA NEVADA

Rates include breakfast, and the suites sleep up to four people.

Sugar Pine Ranch *(☎ 209-962-7823; 21250 Hwy 120; rooms $110-150)*, 4mi east of Groveland, is a B&B ensconced on a 60-acre ranch.

Buck Meadows Lodge *(☎ 209-962-5285; 7633 Hwy 120; rooms $69-179)*, about 12mi from the park entrance, has large rooms with old-fashioned furnishings but modern amenities. The restaurant serves American standards for $7 to $15.

Kings Canyon & Sequoia National Parks

South of Yosemite, on the Sierra's western slope, the adjacent Kings Canyon and Sequoia National Parks encompass some of the world's most incredible creations of nature. Giant sequoias stand as the most massive living things on earth, and the awesome canyon of the South Fork of the Kings River rivals any in the Sierra. Despite this superlative world, crowds are sparse thanks to the parks' relative inaccessibility. There's none of the usual amusement park atmosphere. Popular among hikers and backpackers, there are few drive-in sites but loads of trails for all ability levels. Each park has its own history and defining characteristics, but they are administered as one unit.

History

The first people to inhabit these forests were Native American Yokuts. The Monache, or Western Monos, migrated from the area near Mono Lake in the Eastern Sierra and became dominant by the mid-19th century. In 1805 Spanish missionaries, led by Gabriel Moraga, discovered the Kings River, calling it El Río de los Santos Reyes (River of the Holy Kings). A few decades later, the gold rush brought logging and grazing to the Grant Grove area and mining to Mineral King, causing alarm among early conservationists. Visalia journalist George Stewart, called the 'Father of Sequoia National Park,' started a stir in the San Joaquin Valley with newspaper articles about the effects of logging the big trees, which were useless as timber anyway.

In 1890 Sequoia became the second national park in the USA (after Yellowstone). A few days later, the 4 sq mi around Grant Grove were declared Grant Grove National Park. Kings Canyon was designated a national park in 1940, embracing Grant Grove and nearby Redwood Mountain. In 2000, to further convey protection for sequoia groves, more than 327,000 acres of land in the Sequoia National Forest were officially declared Giant Sequoia National Monument.

Flora & Fauna

The parks' low foothills (up to 5000ft) are covered with manzanita, California blue oak and the tall yucca, whose fragrant flowers bloom in early spring. The foothills are usually the only area in which you have to watch for rattlesnakes (see below) while hiking, though occasionally rattlers do appear at higher elevations.

From 5000ft to 9000ft, forests include sugar, ponderosa, Jeffrey and lodgepole pine; fir; and incense cedar. A 200mi stretch north of the Kings River encompasses eight giant sequoia groves, while the remaining 67 are concentrated along a 60mi belt south of the river. Deer and Douglas squirrels are predominant in the area, though coyotes and bobcats also roam these elevations.

In the high country, above 9000ft, forests give way to stark granite landscapes dotted with lakes, and foxtail and white-bark pine.

Black bears are common and proper food storage is required. Check bulletin boards at visitor centers and most parking lots for current instructions (see the boxed text 'Bears, Your Food & You' in the Activities chapter).

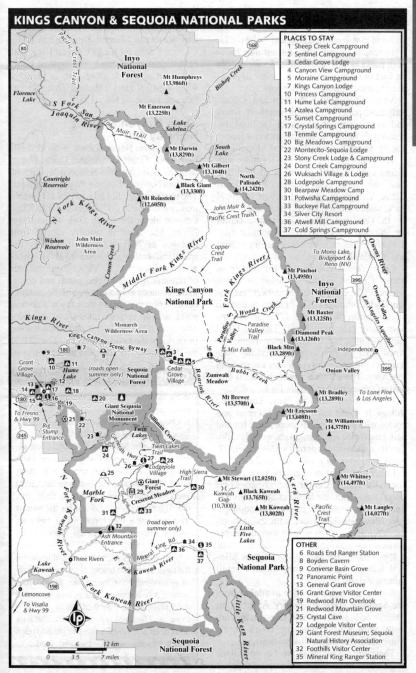

KINGS CANYON & SEQUOIA NATIONAL PARKS

PLACES TO STAY
1. Sheep Creek Campground
2. Sentinel Campground
3. Cedar Grove Lodge
4. Canyon View Campground
5. Moraine Campground
7. Kings Canyon Lodge
10. Princess Campground
11. Hume Lake Campground
14. Azalea Campground
15. Sunset Campground
17. Crystal Springs Campground
18. Tenmile Campground
20. Big Meadows Campground
22. Montecito-Sequoia Lodge
23. Stony Creek Lodge & Campground
24. Dorst Creek Campground
26. Wuksachi Village & Lodge
28. Lodgepole Campground
30. Bearpaw Meadow Camp
31. Potwisha Campground
33. Buckeye Flat Campground
34. Silver City Resort
36. Atwell Mill Campground
37. Cold Springs Campground

OTHER
6. Roads End Ranger Station
8. Boyden Cavern
9. Converse Basin Grove
12. Panoramic Point
13. General Grant Grove
16. Grant Grove Visitor Center
19. Redwood Mtn Overlook
21. Redwood Mountain Grove
25. Crystal Cave
27. Lodgepole Visitor Center
29. Giant Forest Museum; Sequoia Natural History Association
32. Foothills Visitor Center
35. Mineral King Ranger Station

Orientation & Information

For 24-hour recorded information, call ☎ 559-565-3341; w www.nps.gov/seki is the parks' comprehensive website. The entrance fee to both parks is $10 per vehicle, $5 for people on foot or bike; it's valid for seven days. At the entrance station to either park, you'll receive an illustrated NPS map and a quarterly newspaper with phone numbers, hours and descriptions of all visitor facilities, including those in the nearby national forests and the Giant Sequoia National Monument.

The parks have several service hubs with visitor centers, markets and other facilities. The only one open year-round is **Grant Grove Village** in Kings Canyon National Park, which has a market, restaurant, showers ($3) and post office. The **visitor center** (☎ 559-565-4307; open 8am-5pm or 6pm daily) here has an interesting history exhibit and a slide show.

Cedar Grove Village is at the bottom of Kings Canyon (31mi northeast of Grant Grove Village) and has a market, restaurant, lodge, showers ($3); laundry and small **visitor center** (☎ 559-565-3793; open 9am-5pm daily late May-Sept). The road and campgrounds are usually open from late April until the first snowfall (usually September) but other services don't start until late May. There's also a ranger station 6mi east of the village at Roads End.

In Sequoia National Park, **Lodgepole Village** is 4½mi north of Giant Forest and comes with a market, gift shop, snack bar and deli, post office and coin-op showers, laundry facilities and **visitor center** (☎ 559-565-3782; open 9am-5pm daily late May–mid-Oct).

Other information centers include the **Foothills Visitor Center** (☎ 559-565-3135; open 8am-5pm daily June-Sept, shorter hours otherwise), 1mi east of the southern Ash Mountain Entrance, with exhibits on the foothills ecosystem; and a small **ranger station** (☎ 559-565-3768; open 7am-4:30pm daily late May-early Sept) in Mineral King, which has maps and a small mining exhibit.

Books and maps are also available from the **Sequoia Natural History Association** (☎ 559-565-3759; w www.sequoiahistory.org), with a branch at the Giant Forest Museum (see later in this section).

There are ATMs at Grant Grove Village and Cedar Grove Village. Camping supplies are limited. Gas is not available in the parks, although it is sometimes available at Silver City Resort in Mineral King and at Kings Canyon Lodge on Kings Canyon Hwy, both on national forest land. The nearest banks and sporting goods stores are in Reedley, 45mi west off Hwy 180, and Three Rivers, 8mi southwest on Hwy 198.

Kings Canyon & Along Highway 180

Kings Canyon National Park is divided into two areas, Grant Grove and Cedar Grove, with the Giant Sequoia National Monument/Sequoia National Forest wedged in between. The two areas are linked by Hwy 180, which makes a dramatic 2000ft descent into Kings Canyon along the South Fork of the Kings River. The road is usually closed from October or November until Spring. For specifics, call ☎ 559-565-3341 or check w www.nps.gov/seki. Views from the road of massive granite ridges, peaks and domes in the distance give a glimpse of the stunning backcountry that makes the canyon a favorite place among serious hikers and climbers. The road into the valley, and trails leading from it, are the main attractions. The canyon itself is one of the deepest in the lower 48

Giant Sequoias

In the same family as the California coast redwood and Dawn sequoia (recently discovered in China), the giant sequoia (*Sequoiadendron giganteum*) grows only on the Sierra's western slope, between 5000ft and 7000ft. Giant sequoias are the largest living things on earth in terms of volume. They can grow to 300ft tall, 40ft in diameter and live more than 3000 years – the oldest is estimated to be 3500 years old. The main cause of death for the trees is their own size – they topple under their own weight when not adequately supported by their fragile roots.

Sequoia groves might be more abundant if the trees weren't so finicky. They require plenty of groundwater for their wide, shallow root system; a heavy snow pack to trim limbs and dead branches so they won't blow over in a storm; and frequent fires (their thick, soft bark is full of air and very fire resistant) to pop open their tight cones and free the seeds inside.

states at 8200ft. At its western end is an immensity of rust, chartreuse and golden rock sloping down to the river in big chunks and blade-like ridges. Toward its eastern end, near Cedar Grove Village, walls are sheer and further apart, and the valley gains a floor to become U-shaped. Some 6mi past Cedar Grove Village, Roads End is just that, with trailheads, overnight parking and a ranger kiosk that specializes in backpacker information and issues wilderness permits.

General Grant Grove When the bill to create Sequoia National Park was before Congress in 1890, DK Zumwalt, a resident of Visalia, persuaded the bill's sponsor to establish General Grant National Park around the small sequoia grove standing among clear-cut forests. The 4-sq-mi area stood as one of the smallest national parks for 50 years until being absorbed into Kings Canyon National Park in 1940. About 1mi northwest of Grant Grove Village, General Grant Grove encompasses the **General Grant Tree**, estimated to be between 1600 and 1800 years old, and the **Fallen Monarch**, a massive tree which housed early pioneers, sheepherders and US Cavalry horses. An easy self-guided interpretive trail leads through the grove from the parking lot.

Panoramic Point Just north of Grant Grove Village, a steep road travels 2mi to a parking lot from where a short uphill trail leads to Panoramic Point at 7500ft. Below you unfolds a splendid vista taking in a phalanx of snowcapped High Sierra peaks, Kings Canyon and Hume Lake. The road is usually open from late May to September.

Converse Basin Grove About 6mi north of General Grant Grove, and shortly after Hwy 180 enters the Giant Sequoia National Monument, a dirt road heads west from the highway through what John Muir in *The Mountains of California* called 'the northernmost assemblage of Big Trees that may fairly be called a forest.' About five years after Muir's visit, lumbermen turned the forest into a sequoia cemetery. A ½mi loop leads to the **Chicago Stump**, which was cut down, sectioned and reassembled for the 1893 World's Fair in Chicago, where disbelieving Easterners called it a 'California hoax.' A second road goes 2mi north to **Stump Meadow**,

where stumps and fallen logs make good picnic platforms. A marked trail goes to the **Boole Tree**, the only 'monarch' that survived the loggers (2½ hours round-trip).

Boyden Cavern The limestone Boyden Cavern (☎ 209-736-2708 for information), about 11mi west of Cedar Grove along Hwy 180, has whimsically shaped formations – stalagmites, stalactites, domes – near its entrance. While of interest, it can be skipped if you're planning to see Crystal Cave (see later), which is larger and more impressive but requires more walking to see. Tours (adult/child $10/5) run hourly from 11am to 4pm in May and from 10am to 5pm between June and September.

Hume Lake Created in 1900 as a dam for logging operations, Hume Lake is now surrounded by a thick forest of second-growth pine, incense cedar and fir. The Hwy 180 turnoff to the lake is about 8mi north of Grant Grove Village, from where it's another 3mi south to the lake. In summer the lake is popular with swimmers, anglers and boaters.

   Hume Lake Campground (☎ 877-444-6777 for reservations; sites $16) on the lake's northern shore has flush toilets. South of the lake, **Tenmile Campground** (sites $12) has 13 undeveloped sites and is only open in suitable weather.

Generals Highway
Built between 1921 and 1934, Hwy 198 (aka Generals Hwy) connects Grant Grove Village in Kings Canyon National Park with the Giant Forest and the rest of Sequoia National Park. It gives access to the main visitor facilities, campgrounds and, most importantly, the trees everyone comes to see. Along its 46mi between Grant Grove Village and the southern Ash Mountain Entrance, the highway winds from about 6500ft, where the big trees are, to chaparral-covered foothills at around 2000ft. You can drive the full distance in about two hours and totally defeat the purpose of being here. Definitely allow for time out of the car – it's the only way to experience the spectacular grandeur of the trees. Note that from late fall until spring, snow may close Generals Hwy between Grant Grove Village and Lodgepole Village. During those times, Hwy 245 west of the park is the fastest route between the two.

Redwood Mountain Grove About 6mi southeast of Grant Grove Village, this is the most extensive concentration of sequoias and one of the most pristine areas since it's off the beaten path and a bit hard to find. The trees here are dense though not as huge as in Giant Forest (see later). Look for the turnoff to the bumpy dirt road leading to the grove right across from the Quail Flat/Hume Lake junction, about ½mi east of the Redwood Mountain Overlook. After half a mile on the dirt road, you'll reach a parking lot from where you have a choice of two 6mi, a 4mi and a 2mi trail. Some sections skirt **Redwood Creek**, which is flanked by azalea blossoms in May and June. If you have a 4WD, you can also continue driving past the parking lot, although the grove is really best appreciated on foot.

Giant Forest The Giant Forest area, about 2mi south of the Lodgepole Visitor Center, is Sequoia's core and a good destination for first-time visitors to the park. 'Discovered' in 1858 by Hale Tharp and named by John Muir in 1875, these 5 sq mi of redwood groves protect the parks' most massive trees, including **General Sherman** – the largest living tree on earth.

A parking lot gives access to the short trail around the General Sherman Tree, the starting point of the 2mi paved **Congress Trail**, a loop passing by impressive tree groupings such as the 'House' and 'Senate.' To get away from the crowds, continue to the 5mi **Trail of the Sequoias**, which puts you in the heart of the forest.

South of the Giant Forest area, the new **Giant Forest Museum** (☎ 559-565-4480; admission free; open 9am-4pm daily, longer in summer), in a rustic 1928 building, is filled with traditional and hands-on exhibits about sequoia ecology, their life history and their close relationship with fire.

Across from the museum, Crescent Meadow Rd leads east dead-ending after 3mi at **Crescent Meadow**, a lovely area good for picnics. Several easy hikes start from here, including the 1mi trail to **Tharp's Log**, where Hale Tharp, the area's first settler, spent summers in a fallen tree. The road passes **Moro Rock**, a solid granite monolith whose top can be reached via a ½mi carved granite staircase. Views from here are unbeatable, especially at sunset.

Crystal Cave Discovered in 1918 by two fishermen, Crystal Cave (☎ 559-565-3759 for information) extends around 3mi into the earth and has formations estimated to be 10,000 years old. It was carved by an underground river that cut soft marble into large chambers and passageways which filled as the water table rose. Cascade Creek eventually eroded a mouth to the cave, draining the water and exposing the rock to air. Stalagmites and stalactites grew on floors and ceilings in the form of curtains, domes, columns, 'cave bacon' and 'cave popcorn,' all of milky-white marble. The 50-minute tour covers a half mile of chambers and includes detailed interpretation.

Tours (adult/senior/child $8/6/4) run half-hourly from 11am to 4pm between mid-June and early September and less frequently in May and later in September. Tickets are only available at the Lodgepole and Foothills Visitor Centers (not at the cave) and can sell out in summer. The cave itself is northwest of Generals Hwy, up a 7mi-long steep and narrow road; the turnoff is about 15mi north of the Ash Mountain Entrance and 3mi south of the Giant Forest. The ½mi trail from the parking lot to the cave is mostly stairs. Bring a jacket against the chill.

Foothills At about 2000ft, the foothills surrounding the southern end of Generals Hwy have a hot, dry environment compared to the rest of the park. Potwisha Indians lived here until the early 1900s, relying primarily on acorn meal as a staple. A vivid pictograph can be seen at **Hospital Rock** picnic area, once a Potwisha village site, below the sheer face of the rock that dominates the valley. Swimming holes abound along the Marble Fork of the Kaweah River, especially near Potwisha Campground (see Places to Stay); be careful of the powerful current.

Mineral King

Mineral King is a scenic subalpine valley at 7500ft, surrounded by half a dozen smaller valley and mountain passes which reach upward of 11,000ft into more distant backcountry. The area is accessed via the Mineral King Rd, which heads east from Hwy 198, between Three Rivers and the Ash Mountain Entrance at the southern end of Sequoia National Park. Open summer only, it's a twisting, steep and narrow 25mi road that manages to weed out all but those with a mission. Mineral King is Sequoia's backpacking mecca and a good place to find solitude.

The metamorphic rock here is softer than the granite found in other parts of the Sierra, so the valley's walls are sloped instead of sheer and rusty red and purple in color. This odd characteristic led early explorers to think the area was loaded with precious metals. From the 1860s to 1890s, the valley (called Beulah) witnessed heavy silver mining and lumber activity. There are still remnants of old shafts and stamp mills around, though it takes some exploring to find them. Proposals to develop the area into a massive ski resort were thwarted when Congress affixed it to the national park in 1978.

Hiking & Backpacking

With 800mi of marked trails, Kings Canyon and Sequoia National Parks are a backpacker's dream. Cedar Grove and Mineral King offer the best backcountry access, while the USFS Jenny Lakes Wilderness Area (accessible from Big Meadows Trailhead near Big Meadows Campground in the Giant Sequoia National Monument) has pristine meadows and lakes at lower elevations. Trails are usually open by mid-May.

Topo maps and hiking guides are available at all ranger stations and visitor centers. For trail conditions and backcountry information call ☎ 559-565-3341.

Bear-proof canisters for storing your food are mandatory on many trails and may be rented for a few dollars at markets and visitor centers. Check with the visitor centers or ranger stations for the latest regulations.

Wilderness Permits Free wilderness permits are required for all overnight trips and must be obtained from the ranger station or visitor center closest to your trailhead. These are subject to a quota system, with about 75% of spaces open to reservations and the remainder available in person on a first-come, first-served basis. Reserved permits may be picked up after 1pm the afternoon before your departure or before 9am on the day of your hike. Call if you will be delayed. First-come permits are also available after 1pm the day before and more spaces may open up after 9am due to cancellations or no-shows.

Reservations cost $10 and must be received at least three weeks in advance. Fax or mail your request to **Wilderness Permit Reservations** (*☎ 559-565-3708, fax 559-565-4239; HCR 89 Box 60, Three Rivers, CA 93271*). Check the park's website (**w** www.nps.gov/seki) for details.

Kings Canyon You needn't bring a tent to enjoy the canyon's trails. Day-trippers can enjoy numerous gentle paths along the valley floor which offer views of the enticing peaks on all sides. The Cedar Grove day hike map ($2), available at the visitor center and market, is useful for these hikes. The **Zumwalt Meadow Loop** is really nice but often crowded, while the 1mi connecting trail from Roads End to the meadow is less traveled: together they make a good trip.

From Roads End, the **Bubbs Creek Trail** offers a good view but climbs a set of nasty switchbacks before putting you next to the creek, while the **Paradise Valley Trail** follows the river the entire way. (Mist Falls, 4mi from the trailhead, makes a good destination on this trail.) Both connect with the John Muir/Pacific Crest Trail to form the 43mi **Rae Lakes Loop** – a very popular trip. The **Copper Creek Trail** heads north through somewhat lower terrain.

The ranger station at Roads End has a posted map that shows mileages and the location of bear-proof food storage boxes (which may determine where you camp), and a very up-to-date information and message board.

Generals Highway The day-hike map for Giant Forest, available at visitor centers ($2), is useful for making sense of the 40mi of trails concentrated in its 5 sq mi. Trails here are quite gentle, with most of them along meadows and the forest floor. The 5mi **Trail of the Sequoias** passes the most 'famous' named trees along the Congress Trail, then makes its way past Jeffrey pines, rock outcroppings and fern grottoes. With Moro Rock accessible by car, the **Moro Rock Trail** stays uncrowded and offers views of the San Joaquin Valley. **The High Sierra Trail**, from the Crescent Meadow parking lot, is good for views east.

The Lodgepole area offers glacial scenery and some long hikes into high lake basins; trailheads are behind the Lodgepole Visitor

Center at the back of the campground. The short and easy **Tokopah Falls Trail** skirts the Marble Fork of the Kaweah River and ends at a multilevel cascade. The **Twin Lakes Trail** climbs hard for the first mile, mellows out at Cahoon Meadow, then climbs along Clover Creek to the lakes at the foot of Silliman Crest – a good day's adventure.

Mineral King Hiking anywhere from Mineral King involves a steep climb out of the valley along strenuous trails. Be aware of the high elevation, even on short hikes. Enjoyable day hikes go to Crystal, Monarch, Mosquito and Eagle Lakes. For long trips, locals recommend the Little Five Lakes and, further along the High Sierra Trail, Kaweah Gap, surrounded by the sawtooth Black Kaweah, Mt Stewart and Eagle Scout Peak – all above 12,000ft.

Be aware that the Mineral King area is home to a large population of marmots who, mostly in spring, like to chew on hoses, belts and wiring of vehicles to get the salt they crave after their winter hibernation.

Winter Activities

Grant Grove and Giant Forest offer great **snowshoeing** and **cross-country skiing** on marked trails. Since Generals Hwy is not always open between the two areas, you're best advised to choose one or the other as a destination. Its best to bring along a set of tire chains which may be required within the park. Chains are available for rent in Three Rivers south of Sequoia National Park and along Hwy 180, but you're likely to pay a premium.

Trails from Grant Grove connect with those in the Giant Sequoia National Monument and some that are maintained by Montecito Sequoia Lodge (see Places to Stay). Grant Grove Village (including its market and restaurant) is in full swing, with ski and snowshoe rentals, nightly programs at the visitor center, cabin and campground accommodations and naturalist-guided snowshoe walks.

In the Giant Forest area, ski activity focuses on the **Sequoia Ski Touring Center** (☎ 559-565-3435), an excellent day-use facility with rentals, lessons and a retail shop. At Wolverton, 2½mi south of Lodgepole, you'll find a cafeteria, a small market and a snow play area.

Places to Stay

Unless otherwise stated, all accommodations in Kings Canyon are managed by **Kings Canyon Park Service** (*KCPS;* ☎ 559-335-5500, 866-522-6966; ⓦ *www.sequoia-kingscanyon.com*), while **Delaware North Parks Service** (*DNPS;* ☎ *559-784-1500, 888-252-5757;* ⓦ *www.visitsequoia.com*) is in charge of Sequoia. Grant Grove and Wuksachi are the only year-round lodges; all the others close from early October to May.

Free dispersed camping is possible in Sequoia National Forest and Giant Sequoia National Monument; pick up details and a fire permit from a visitor center or ranger station.

NPS campgrounds are first-come, first-served with the exception of Lodgepole and Dorst Creek (reservations ☎ 800-365-2267). Sites have bear-proof boxes, tables and fire pits; most have flush toilets. Campgrounds open around May and close in October.

Kings Canyon & Along Highway 180

On Hwy 180 in the national forest, **Princess Campground** (☎ *877-444-6777 for reservations; sites $14*) has woodsy sites next to a huge meadow. About one quarter are first-come, first-served.

Down in the canyon at Cedar Grove are four NPS campgrounds, each with $14 sites. **Sentinel** and **Sheep Creek** have riverside sites (arrive early on weekends to snag one) and thick incense cedar and pine groves nearby, while **Moraine** and **Canyon View** (*tents only*) are above the river on a steep embankment with sparse ground cover.

The only noncamping facility in the canyon itself is **Cedar Grove Lodge** (*call KCPS for reservations; rooms $99-110*), whose 18 motel rooms have showers and air-con, but they hardly justify the price.

Kings Canyon Lodge (☎ *559-335-2405; rooms $79-109; open mid-Apr–mid-Nov*), a private property in the national forest 17mi east of Grant Grove Village, is better value. Rooms have private bath, and there are cabins that sleep up to six people. The funky restaurant has a Western hunting-lodge feel and a full bar. It even dispenses gas from one of those old-time gravity pumps.

Generals Highway The biggest concentration of NPS campgrounds is in the Grant Grove area. Across from the visitor center,

Sunset has hillside sites, some of which overlook the western foothills and San Joaquin Valley, while sites at **Azalea** are close together; some border a meadow. **Crystal Springs** is the least attractive, with neither ground cover nor privacy. Sites at all these campgrounds cost $14 per night.

Near Lodgepole Village, the fairly secluded **Dorst Creek** (sites $16) is near the small Muir Grove of Sequoias, while **Lodgepole** ($14-16) is an enormous but very nice campground behind the visitor center and market, with sites along the Marble Fork of the Kaweah River. These two are the park's only campgrounds accepting reservations (☎ 800-365-2267).

Azalea and Lodgepole are the only two year-round campgrounds.

In the foothills, **Buckeye Flat** (sites $14) and **Potwisha** (sites $14) have riverside sites near swimming holes. These are good in spring and fall, when the higher elevations get cold, but they get hot and buggy in summer.

USFS-operated campgrounds include **Big Meadows** (sites $12), 6mi northeast of Generals Hwy on a well-marked road, which has vault toilets only. **Stony Creek** (☎ 877-444-6777; sites $16), a bit further south right on the highway, has creekside sites that get the afternoon sun, and flush toilets. Half of its 49 sites are reservable.

Grant Grove Village has the following two lodging options open year-round.

Grant Grove Lodge (call KCPS for reservations; tent cabins $45, cabins with private bath $105-112) has historic cabins with mountain decor. More upscale is the nearby **John Muir Lodge** (call KCPS for reservations; rooms $140, suites $240) with smallish but comfortable rooms and a lobby dedicated to Muir. Ask about its winter specials.

Montecito Sequoia Lodge (☎ 559-565-3388, 800-227-9900, fax 530-967-0540; w www.mslodge.com; rates $69-159 per person) is a beautifully located, family-oriented private resort about 9mi south of Grant Grove Village. In summer it functions as a group vacation camp but from September to May it's open to individual guests. It has a small lake and a heated outdoor pool with superb mountain views. In winter, the resort maintains its own cross-country ski trails. There's a buffet-style restaurant and a stocked kitchen,

where you can prepare your own food. Rates include meals and activities.

Stony Creek Lodge (call KCPS for reservations; rooms $125; open May-Oct), about halfway between Grant Grove Village and Giant Forest, has a big river-rock fireplace in its lobby and worn but adequate motel rooms with private bath.

Wuksachi Village & Lodge (☎ 559-253-2199, 888-252-5757, fax 559-253-5680; rooms $86-177; open year-round), about 4mi north of the Giant Forest, is the park's newest resort. Rooms have telephones and data ports (an exception within the parks), and there's a nice lounge and restaurant in the main building.

From mid-June to early September, DNPS also operates **Bearpaw Meadow Camp** (adult/child $155/75 per night), 11mi east of Giant Forest at 7800ft on the High Sierra Trail, where hikers can stay in tent cabins. Rates include showers, two meals, bedding and towels. This place gets booked up quickly, so reserve early.

Mineral King The two campgrounds on Mineral King Rd are **Atwell Mill** (sites $8), about 5mi west of the ranger station, and **Cold Springs** (sites $8), across from the ranger station, which has two loops along the river and some secluded spots off the road; both have pit toilets.

Three miles west of the ranger station, **Silver City Resort** (☎ 559-561-3223; w www.silvercityresort.com; cabins $70-150, chalets $200-250, 2-night minimum; open late May-Oct) has comfortable, new chalets sleeping four to eight people and more rustic cabins with basic kitchens and shared bathroom facilities. The café serves breakfast (daily) and dinner (Wednesday to Monday), not to mention excellent pies.

Places to Eat

Dining options are limited in both parks. There are markets at Grant, Cedar Grove and Lodgepole Villages, though only the first is open year-round and all are expensive.

Grant Grove Restaurant (meals under $10) has a coffee shop atmosphere with food to match.

There's a self-service restaurant in Cedar Grove Village serving breakfast and dinner. The Kings Canyon Lodge (see Places to Stay) also serves food.

Lodgepole Village has a **snack bar** selling pizza and burgers, and a deli with salads and sandwiches; it also has a nice patio.

The only swank dining place is at **Wuksachi Lodge** (☎ 559-253-2199; breakfast buffet $8.50, mains $13-25), whose menu features chicken, steak, pasta and salads.

Getting There & Away
The parks are only accessible from the south and the west. From the west, Hwy 180 makes a gentle 53mi climb from Fresno to the Big Stump Entrance, 4mi west of Grant Grove Village; from here you can go north into Kings Canyon or south along Generals Hwy. Coming from the south, Hwy 198 runs from Visalia through Three Rivers past Mineral King Rd to the Ash Mountain Entrance at the southern end of Generals Hwy. In winter, Generals Hwy is often closed between Grant Grove and Giant Forest, making Route 245 (west of the park) the best connection.

THREE RIVERS
Right outside Sequoia's Ash Mountain Entrance, Three Rivers stretches for about 12mi along Hwy 198 hugging the Kaweah River. Sierra Dr, the main drag, is lined with motels, stores and artists' studios and galleries. Midway through town, you'll pass a post office, a good pizza parlor and a market for buying supplies.

Naturedome (☎ 559-561-6560; 42249 Sierra Dr) is a geodesic dome (built in harmonious convergence with nature spirits), with a large deck overlooking the Kaweah River. It houses an interesting gift shop featuring local artists' work.

River Envy Iris Farm (☎ 559-561-3630; 43429 Sierra Dr; open to public 1 Apr–4 June) produces a variety of irises, including some genetically engineered to smell like grape juice and orange popsicles! The farm is open to the public during prime blooming season, during which the display grounds bloom with a rainbow of colors, and staff is on hand to answer questions. During the Three Rivers Redbud Festival, held the first weekend in May, artisans set up booths along Sierra Dr, and hundreds of people converge for general merrymaking.

Places to Stay & Eat
The Gateway Lodge (☎ 559-561-4133; rooms midweek/weekends $89/109), about

½mi from the entrance, has tidy and trim motel rooms, and cute cottages above the Kaweah River. Its popular riverside restaurant does casual lunches, while at dinner, choice steaks and seafood are the standard bearers (lunch $7 to $17, dinner $9 to $26).

Sierra Lodge (☎ 559-561-3681, 800-367-879; rooms $38-86), about 3½mi from the park entrance, does not offer much in the character department but is one of the cheapest places in town.

River View (☎ 559-561-2211; 42323 Sierra Dr; lunch $5-9, dinner $11-23) is a roadside restaurant that doubles as the locals' 'living room.' The food screams Americana and portions are giant sequoia–sized.

Eastern Sierra

The Sierra Nevada's jagged crest rises abruptly to almost 2mi above the high desert, with 14 peaks higher than 14,000ft and Mt Whitney as the crown jewel. Many outdoor fans consider this the best side of the Sierra because it offers direct access to alpine scenery, high mountain lakes and lush meadows. Several wilderness areas stretch from north to south for about 250mi. Most trails access at least one of these areas and more than a dozen major passes cross over the Sierra Crest into Yosemite, Kings Canyon and Sequoia National Parks.

The arid Owens Valley lies at the base of the mountains, with the ancient White Mountains, nearly as high but much older than the Sierra, to the east. Once as prosperous as the Central Valley in agriculture, Owens Valley is now a desert-like wasteland, drained by the California Aqueduct to provide water to Southern California.

US-395 parallels the ranges, and paved roads lead west to glassy lakes that teem with trout, drawing scores of anglers. Other roads lead up steep canyons to popular high elevation trailheads. In most of these inviting canyons are USFS recreation areas with campgrounds and private resorts.

Orientation
The Eastern Sierra extends from Bridgeport in the north to the junction of US-395 and Hwy 178 in the south. The mountains are lowest and easiest to access north of Bishop, where Mammoth Lakes serves as a good

destination for hikers, bikers and skiers. South of Bishop, getting into the mountains often requires a long drive up curvy, narrow roads. The easiest access to high dramatic scenery is from Bishop Creek (near Bishop) and Whitney Portal (near Lone Pine).

The little towns along the highway offer accommodations, food, camping, gasoline and supplies. In winter, when traffic thins out, many facilities are closed.

Wilderness Permits

Wilderness permits ($5 per person) for overnight trips are required for all trails in the Ansel Adams, John Muir and Dinkey Lakes Wilderness Areas and for select trails in the Kaiser and Golden Trout Wildernesses. Permits are not needed for day trips.

Trailhead quotas are in effect from 1 May to November for the first three wilderness areas and from the last Friday in June to 15 September for the other two. About 60% of each quota may be reserved in advance by telephone, fax and mail from the **Inyo National Forest Wilderness Permit Office** (☎ 760-873-2483, fax 760-873-2484; 873 N Main St, Bishop, CA 93514). Regulations change on occasion. For up-to-date specifics, check **W** www.r5.fs.fed.us/inyo. For details about trails in the Mt Whitney Zone, see the boxed text 'Climbing Mt Whitney' later in this chapter. For wilderness permits in the Hoover Wilderness, see the Bridgeport section.

Getting There & Around

The Eastern Sierra is poorly served by public transportation and is really best explored under your own steam. From the north, the only way to access the area is on buses operated by Bishop-based **Carson Ridgecrest Eastern Sierra Transit** (CREST; ☎ 760-872-1901, 800-922-1930). Buses make three round-trips weekly between Bishop and Carson City (in Nevada; Tuesday, Thursday and Friday) and three southbound to Ridgecrest (via Lone Pine; Monday, Wednesday and Friday), stopping at all towns in between. Fares depend on distance; the trip from Bishop to Carson City, for instance, is $20 one way.

Carson City is connected by Greyhound buses to San Francisco, Sacramento and other cities and by **Public Rural Ride** (Pride; ☎ 775-888-7466) to Reno.

Traveling between the Eastern Sierra and Los Angeles is possible but cumbersome. From LA, take the Greyhound to Mojave, switch to a Kern Regional Transit bus bound for Ridgecrest and then board the CREST to points north along US-395.

BRIDGEPORT

Bridgeport (population 500; elevation 6500ft) is the first town of any importance between Carson City and Mammoth Lakes. Its main street is as American as apple pie, with classic old storefronts and an impressive 1880 Italianate courthouse trimmed in red and surrounded by a gracious lawn. A few blocks away, in an old schoolhouse, the **Mono County Museum** (☎ 760-932-5281; adult/child $1.50/0.75; open 10am-4pm daily late May-Sept) has one of the better historical collections in the Eastern Sierra.

Bridgeport is famous among anglers who flock to Twin Lakes, Virginia Lakes, the Bridgeport Reservoir, the East Walker River and Twin Lakes Bridgeport for record catches of brown and rainbow trout and perch. The other main attractions here are hot springs – for those who aren't afraid of nudity or washboard roads – and Bodie State Historic Park, one of California's best-preserved ghost towns.

Orientation & Information

US-395 heads east through Bridgeport as Main St, with the turnoff to Twin Lakes at the western end of town and the turnoff to Bridgeport Lake at the eastern end. Hwy 270 to Bodie heads east from US-395 south of the city limits.

The **Bridgeport Ranger Station** (☎ 760-932-7070; open 7:30am-5pm daily July-early Sept, 8am-4:30pm late Sept-July), just south of town on the highway, has posted maps and issues wilderness permits for overnight trips to the Hoover Wilderness. Some trailheads are subject to a quota system from the last Friday in June to mid-September. Half of the quota may be reserved until three weeks before your intended departure date by writing to the ranger station at HCR 1 Box 1000, Bridgeport, CA 93517. The fee is $3 per person.

The best place for fishing information is **Ken's Sporting Goods** (☎ 760-932-7707; 258 Main St), which has lots of maps, plus fishing, hunting and camping gear.

Places to Stay & Eat

All businesses are on Main St.

Bridgeport Inn (☎ 760-932-7380; motel $69-89, hotel $39-99), built as a stagecoach stop on the road to Bodie, has been in operation since 1877. Benign 'spirits' allegedly cruise the halls, though the rooms are purportedly 'ghost free.' The antiques-laden upstairs rooms in the historic hotel are the best. Rooms downstairs have shared facilities. It also has a charming bar and restaurant (mains $13 to $29).

Silver Maple Inn (☎ 760-932-7383; rooms $70-90; open late Apr-Oct) has friendly owners, well-kept grounds and nice rooms.

Walker River Lodge (☎ 760-932-7021, 800-688-3351; ⓦ www.walkerriverlodge .com; rooms $65-170) has a heated pool and spa and is one of only two places open year-round.

Locals drink, play pool and eat pizza at **Rhino's Bar & Grille** (☎ 760-932-7345) in town but they also recommend **Virginia Creek Settlement** (☎ 760-932-7780; mains $12-22), 14mi south of town on US-395, for good steaks and Italian food.

TWIN LAKES

These lakes sit in a beautiful setting, lorded over by the jagged Sawtooth Ridge, including the 12,279ft Matterhorn. This is primarily a fishing resort – revered for its trout and Kokanee salmon – and most businesses are open from May to November only. There are also excellent trails into the Hoover Wilderness and the eastern, lake riddled reaches of Yosemite National Park, for instance from the Barney Lake Trailhead behind Mono Village (see later).

The road to Twin Lakes intersects US-395 at Bridgeport and heads about 12mi through pastures and foothills, past several nice campgrounds on Robinson Creek.

En route, you'll pass **Doc and Al's Resort** (☎ 760-932-7051; tents/RV sites $13/17, rustic cabins $42, trailers $47-60, new cabins $67-98), right on Robinson Creek. Newer cabins sleep four to 10 people and have showers and kitchens; the rustic cabins have shared shower and toilet.

Just before reaching the lower lake, a road goes south to the USFS **Lower Twin Lakes Campground** (☎ 760-932-7070, 800-444-7275 for reservations; sites $13; open May-mid-Oct), with sites on the quiet eastern shore.

Nearby, **Crags Campground** (☎ 760-932-7070, 800-444-7275; sites $13; open May-mid-Oct) is sunnier and more spread out.

At the western end of the upper lake, the road ends at the privately owned **Mono Village** (☎ 760-932-7071, fax 760-932-7468; ⓦ www.monovillage.com; tents/RV sites $11/18, rooms $50-60, cabins $65-125; open late Apr-Oct), a huge resort that offers cheap but fairly cramped lodging, plus boat rental and launch facilities and a greasy-spoon restaurant. The campground has 300 first-come, first-served spaces.

Buckeye Hot Springs

These are the area's best hot springs and some of the hardest to find. The springs surface atop a steep embankment above Buckeye Creek and trickle down into pools outlined with rocks. The largest pool, right next to the creek, is cold when the creek is high. A smaller one, next to a solo tree at the top of the embankment, commands a great view of the surrounding forest. Clothing is optional.

From Bridgeport, follow Twin Lakes Rd west to Doc & Al's Resort, then turn north onto a graded dirt road. After about 3mi, cross Buckeye Creek, then turn right onto Buckeye Hot Springs. Look to your right for an unmarked 'parking lot'. Buckeye Hot Springs Rd continues east back to Hwy 95.

West of the springs, at a bridge spanning Buckeye Creek, a road goes 2mi to the USFS **Buckeye Campground** (sites $11; open May-mid-Oct) with tables, fire grates, potable water and flush toilets. You can also camp for free in undeveloped spots along Buckeye Creek on both sides of the bridge.

BODIE STATE HISTORIC PARK

The combination of its remote location and unrestored buildings makes Bodie (adult/child $2/free; open 9am-7pm late May-Sept, 9am-4pm Oct-early May) one of California's most authentic and best-preserved ghost towns. Gold was discovered along Bodie Creek in 1859, and within 20 years the place grew from a rough mining camp to an even rougher mining town, with a population of 10,000 and a reputation for lawlessness, gambling halls, brothels and no fewer than 65 saloons. More than $100 million worth of ore came from the surrounding hills, but when the gold supply petered out, people petered too, moving on (mostly to the Comstock Lode in Nevada) and leaving Bodie's buildings to the elements. About 5% of them still remain, maintained by the State Park Service, but untainted by restoration.

An excellent **museum & visitor center** (☎ 760-647-6445; open 10am-5pm daily late May-Sept) has historical maps, exhibits and free daily guided tours. Hwy 270, which connects Bodie and US-395 (13mi), is unpaved for the last 3mi and is often closed in winter after heavy snowfall. The grounds of the monument, however, are open year-round, so you can still get to the place using snowshoes or cross-country skis.

VIRGINIA LAKES & LUNDY LAKE
South of Bridgeport, US-395 parallels Virginia Creek until it reaches Conway Summit (8148ft) and drops down into the Mono Basin. The view south from the summit shows the area's topography, with Mono Lake, backed by the Mono Craters, backed by June and Mammoth Mountains – all products of volcanic activity.

Right at Conway Summit, Virginia Lakes Rd climbs west for 6mi along Virginia Creek to a cluster of lakes flanked by Dunderberg Peak (12,374ft) and Black Mountain (11,797ft). A trailhead at the end of the road gives access to the Hoover Wilderness and the Pacific Crest Trail, which continues down Cold Canyon to Yosemite National Park. Another group of lakes, about 2½ to 5mi northwest of the trailhead, are said to have some of the Eastern Sierra's best fishing.

Virginia Lakes Resort (☎ 760-647-6484; cabins $480-1567 per week; usually open mid-May–mid-Oct), at the road's end, is a world of its own. It has snug cabins, a café and a general store that sells fishing tackle and licenses. Cabins are rented by the week and sleep two to 12 people. Nearby, **Virginia Lakes Pack Station** (☎ 760-937-0326) offers trips on horseback.

About 7mi north of Lee Vining, Lundy Lake Rd meanders about 5mi west to Lundy Lake. This is a gorgeous spot, especially when fall foliage lights up the canyon; despite this, it's often uncrowded. The lake is long and narrow, with steep canyons – great for hiking – feeding rivers into its western end. Before reaching the lake, the road parallels a **county campground** (sites $7), with pit toilets and running water.

Lundy Lake Resort (☎ 626-309-0415 for reservations; tents/RV sites $11/15, cabins $55-100; open late Apr-Oct) is a low-key resort popular with anglers and hikers. Its sites are first-come, first-served and it has flush toilets and hot showers. Other facilities include a laundry, boat rentals and a store.

A few miles past the resort, on a good dirt road, is trailhead parking for the Hoover Wilderness with self-register wilderness permits. From here you can head over Lundy Pass to Saddlebag Lake, 2mi north of Tioga Pass and just outside Yosemite National Park.

MONO LAKE
This glistening expanse of alkaline water spreading lazily across the white-hot desert landscape is North America's second-oldest lake. It is an important habitat for millions of migratory and nesting birds. Though the basin and lake are ice age remnants, formed more than 700,000 years ago, the area's most interesting features come from volcanic-related activity. Appearing like dripped sand castles on and near the lake shore, Mono's tufa (pronounced **too**-fah) towers form when calcium-bearing freshwater springs bubble up through alkaline water.

The **Mono Basin Scenic Area Visitors Center** (☎ 760-647-3044; days & hours vary), about 1½mi north of Lee Vining off US-395, has a beautiful view of the lake, good interpretive displays, information, a bookstore and bear canister rentals ($3).

A few miles south, the **Mono Lake Committee Visitor Center** (☎ 760-647-6595; W www.monolake.org; open 9am-5pm daily, 9am-10:30pm late June–mid-Sept), in Lee Vining on the western side of US-395, has Internet access, maps, a great selection of books and a free 30-minute video about the history and geology of the Mono Lake area. You'll find environmental activists here who are passionate about what Mono Lake means. The visitor center also offers interpretive talks, guided hikes, photo excursions and canoe tours of Mono Lake. These operate at 8am, 9:30am and 11am every Saturday and Sunday from mid-June to early September (adult/child $17/7). Reservations are required.

There are examples of tufa towers all around the lake, but the best concentration is

Mono Lake

In 1941 the City of Los Angeles Department of Water and Power (DWP) bought most of the Mono Basin and diverted four of the five streams feeding Mono Lake to the California Aqueduct to provide water to Los Angeles. Over time, the lake level dropped 40ft and doubled in salinity. In 1976 environmentalist David Gaines began to study the concerns surrounding the lake's depletion and found that it would totally dry up within about 20 years. As the major breeding ground for California gulls and habitat for eared grebes and red-necked phalaropes, this was a major threat to California's bird population. Gaines formed the Mono Lake Committee in 1979 and, through numerous campaigns and court battles, managed to win water from the City of LA.

A fluke of nature aided courtroom progress. In 1989 a heavy snow season caused dams to overflow into previously dry spillways, re-watering streams which had not seen water for 10 years. When fish were found in the streams, the courts ruled that although the DWP technically 'owned' water rights, they could not allow the fish to die and thus were obliged to maintain the streams at a level in which fish can survive. In 1994 a landmark ruling by the California State Water Resources Control Board required the DWP to substantially reduce its diversions in order to allow the lake level to rise 17ft to 6392ft above sea level, which is expected to take between 10 and 20 years.

at the **South Tufa Reserve** *(adult/child under 18 $3/free)* on the lake's southern rim. Here a mile-long interpretive trail explains the towers' formation. The best place for swimming is at **Navy Beach**, just east of here, though there are no showers and the salt residue left on your skin can be irritating.

Away from the lakeshore, between the South Tufa Reserve and Hwy 120, is **Panum Crater**, the youngest (about 640 years old) and smallest of the Mono Craters which string south toward Mammoth Mountain. There is a nice panoramic trail around the crater rim (about 30 to 45 minutes), and a short but steep 'plug trail' that puts you at the crater's center among rock formations in shiny black obsidian and pumice stone.

On the northern shore are the **Black Point Fissures**, narrow crags that opened when Black Point's lava mass cooled and contracted about 13,000 years ago. Reaching the fissures requires a substantial – but worthwhile – hike (east of the County Park off US-395 or south of Hwy 167), which is usually hot and very dry. Check in at one of the visitor centers before heading out.

Lee Vining

Lee Vining (population 315; elevation 6780ft) is Mono Lake's utilitarian addition, where you can eat, sleep and gas up. It is also where Hwy 120 heads west over Tioga Pass (open summer only; see the boxed text 'Impassable Tioga Pass' in the Yosemite National Park section earlier) to Yosemite National Park. There are six **USFS campgrounds** *(sites $7)* alongside a creek just off Hwy 120, with pit toilets and running water.

Right in town, **El Mono Motel** *(☎ 760-647-6310; rooms without bath $49-85; open summer only)* has been operating since 1927, but rooms are tiny and rather basic. They come with TV but no phone.

Best Western Lakeview Lodge *(☎ 760-647-6543, fax 760-647-6325; rooms $49-131)* has good-sized modern rooms and friendly front desk staff.

Tioga Lodge *(☎ 760-647-6423, 888-647-6423; w www.tiogalodge.com; rooms $55 winter, $75-95 summer)*, on US-395 about 2½mi north of town, has colorful owners and consists of a cluster of snug historic cabins with a view of Mono Lake; each sports different decor, from rustic to frilly. It also has a restaurant (breakfast $5 to $9, dinner $6 to $16).

Whoa Nellie Deli *(dishes $4-17; open Apr-Nov)* is the Sierra's unlikely gourmet eatery – ensconced inside the Mobil gas station on Hwy 120, near the turnoff from US-395. Chef Matt 'Tioga' Toomey whips up delectable sandwiches big enough to feed a bear, piles of fresh salads and full steak dinners, and even accommodates individual requests whenever possible.

Other good places are **Bodie Mike's Pizza** *(open summer only)*, which specializes in ribs for dinner ($14 to $18.50), and **Nicely's Restaurant** *(meals $5-10)*, which makes hearty breakfasts.

Mono Inn Restaurant *(☎ 760-647-6581; mains $16-26; open dinner only May-Oct)* is

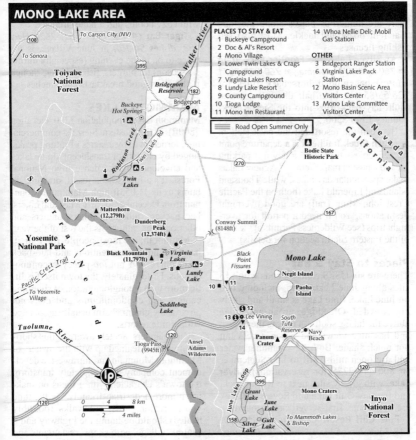

MONO LAKE AREA

PLACES TO STAY & EAT
1 Buckeye Campground
2 Doc & Al's Resort
4 Mono Village
5 Lower Twin Lakes & Crags
   Campground
7 Virginia Lakes Resort
8 Lundy Lake Resort
9 County Campground
10 Tioga Lodge
11 Mono Inn Restaurant

14 Whoa Nellie Deli; Mobil
   Gas Station

OTHER
3 Bridgeport Ranger Station
6 Virginia Lakes Pack
   Station
12 Mono Basin Scenic Area
   Visitors Center
13 Mono Lake Committee
   Visitors Center

Road Open Summer Only

the area's only silver service restaurant where inventive California cuisine pairs up with spectacular views of the lake. Reservations are required.

JUNE LAKE LOOP

Between Mono Lake and Mammoth Lakes, Hwy 158 makes a 16mi loop west of US-395. This scenic route passes Grant, Silver, Gull and June Lakes, flanked by massive Carson Peak and Reversed Peak. The mountains immediately west are part of the Ansel Adams Wilderness, which runs into Yosemite National Park, easily reached by trail.

The area could detain outdoorsy types for a good week, though it's just as easily explored on a nice half-hour detour off US-395. All of the lakes are good for trout

fishing, and Grant and Silver lakes both have free public boat launches. Commercial activity clusters in June Lake Village at the southern end of June Lake. There's an unstaffed information kiosk at the loop's southern end entrance.

Activities

The **June Mountain Ski Area** (☎ 760-648-7733, 888-586-3686 for information) is friendly, smaller and less crowded than Mammoth Mountain (see later in this chapter). Rising 10,135ft above sea level, June Mountain offers 500 acres of skiing with eight lifts, including two high-speed quads and 2600 vertical feet. There are also two terrain parks. Lift tickets cost $47/37/27 adult/teen/child & senior.

In summer **fishing** is hugely popular and there are numerous places along the loop that rent boats and tackle. Most also sell fishing licenses.

At Silver Lake, the **Frontier Pack Train** (☎ 760-648-7701 summer, ☎ 760-873-7971 winter) has guided horseback rides for $25/55/85 one hour/half day/full day and multi-day pack trips into the Sierra backcountry from $500.

Between the resort and the pack station, the **Rush Creek Trailhead** is a departure point for wilderness trips with a day-use parking lot and a posted map. Gem and Agnew Lakes make spectacular day hikes, while Thousand Island and Emerald Lake (both on the Pacific Crest/John Muir Trail) are good overnight destinations. You'll need a permit for overnight trips (see Wilderness Permits at the start of the Eastern Sierra section for details).

Places to Stay & Eat
There are six USFS campgrounds with $13 sites along June Lake Loop, including two on June Lake. **June Lake** is small and shady but crowded. **Oh Ridge**, on an arid ridge above the lake's southern end, is the largest and has nice views and beach access but not much shade. Both have running water and are open mid-April to late September (☎ 800-444-7275 for reservations). **Silver Lake**, with grassy sites next to Rush Creek, and the tiny **Gull Lake** and **Reversed Creek** are first-come, first-served campgrounds.

Pine Cliff Resort Campground (☎ 760-648-7558, tents $11, RV sites $16-20; camping trailers $160-400 per week), next to Oh Ridge, is a private affair and offers a little more comfort, as well as a store and public hot showers ($1).

Boulder Lodge (☎ 760-648-7533; suites, cabins & rooms $65-275), on the shore of June Lake, has large lakefront suites as well as two-bedroom cabins and standard motel rooms. The decor is a bit worn but there's an indoor pool, Jacuzzi and sauna.

Double Eagle Resort & Spa (☎ 760-648-7004, 877-648-7004, fax 760-648-7016; $216-298), near the southern tip of Silver Lake, takes indulgence seriously. The sleek log cabins come with a full set of amenities, wrinkles and worries are soothed away at the swank spa, and fly fisherfolk can hook trout on the grounds. The restaurant (☎ 760-648-7897; breakfast & lunch $6-11, dinner $6.50-

20) has a high ceiling and rustic elegance with cozy booths and a huge fireplace.

Tiger Bar (☎ 760-648-7551; 2620 Hwy 158; dishes $4-15), in June Village, is *the* place to be in the evening (especially during ski season) for burgers, fish and beer, though it also does good breakfasts and lunches.

MAMMOTH LAKES
Mammoth Lakes (population 7200; elevation 7800ft) is the Eastern Sierra's commercial hub, lorded over by a series of jutting peaks, ringed by clusters of translucent alpine lakes and enveloped by the dense Inyo National Forest. It's a four-season resort, drawing ski bums to its 11,053ft-high Mammoth Mountain from December to early May, and hikers, backpackers, mountain bikers, anglers and other outdoor enthusiasts the rest of the year.

Mammoth, as most people refer to it, has a friendly, unpretentious and laid-back atmosphere and not-*too*-pricey accommodations. Unfortunately, the town itself is little more than a conglomeration of shopping centers and condominiums and does not possess the quaint charm usually associated with alpine resorts.

City planners, acutely aware of this shortcoming, have teamed up with the owners of Mammoth Mountain and Intrawest, a development company, to completely transform the town's character, with a focus on making it more pedestrian-friendly. By the time you're reading this, sidewalks (possibly heated) should be lining the highway and a central 'village' with shops, restaurants and upscale lodging is expected to welcome visitors. A gondola will link the village directly with the ski mountain. Long-term plans include the creation of upscale resort facilities and improvements at the mountain itself.

To see what's in store for Mammoth, drop in at the **Intrawest Discovery Center** (6156 Minaret Rd), which has scale models and a saccharine movie outlining the developers' vision. Locals seem to be largely supportive, although some people's enthusiasm is tempered by fear that all this 'progress' will have horrifying effects on the very nature that's always been Mammoth's greatest asset.

History
Believe it or not, Mammoth did not spring to life with the invention of the chairlift. It was originally a mining and lumber town

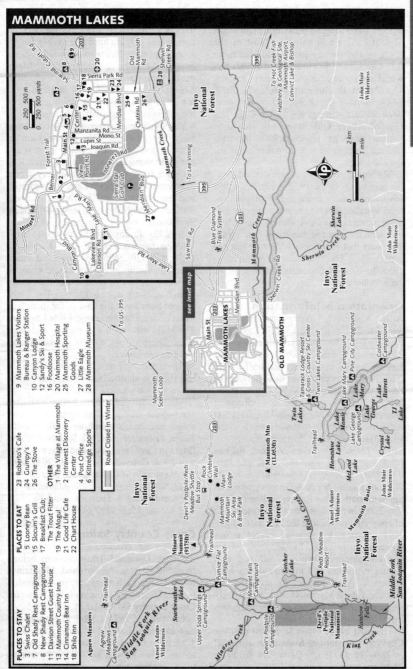

MAMMOTH LAKES

PLACES TO STAY
3 Swiss Chalet
5 Old Shady Rest Campground
7 New Shady Rest Campground
8 Davison Street Guest House
13 Mammoth Country Inn
14 Cinnamon Bear Inn
18 Shilo Inn

PLACES TO EAT
5 Looney Bean
15 Slocum's Grill
17 Breakfast Club;
   The Trout Fitter
19 The Mogul
21 Good Life Cafe
22 Chart House

23 Roberto's Cafe
24 Grumpy's
26 The Stove

OTHER
1 The Village at Mammoth
2 Intrawest Discovery
   Center
4 Post Office
6 Kittredge Sports

9 Mammoth Lakes Visitors
   Bureau & Ranger Station
10 Canyon Lodge
12 Sandy's Ski & Sport
16 Footloose
20 Mammoth Hospital
25 Mammoth Sporting
   Goods
27 Little Eagle
28 Mammoth Museum

Road Closed In Winter

with stamp mills, sawmills, flumes, water-wheels and a rough-and-tumble main street of tent cabins and saloons. Most of the town, on the western end of Old Mammoth Rd, was burned to cinders, but a 14ft fly-wheel and some other old structures remain. The **Mammoth Museum** *(☎ 760-934-6918; 5489 Sherwin Creek Rd; admission free; open 9:30am-4:30pm daily June-Oct)*, just east of where Old Mammoth Rd turns abruptly west, has photographs of the orig-inal settlement and gives out tour maps for the old town.

Mammoth's origin as a ski resort had hum-ble beginnings in the 1930s when just a few adventurous souls made use of simple rope tows installed around the mountain. One of these pioneers was Dave McCoy, who fell in love with the area and eventually built up the ski resort that Mammoth Mountain has be-come today. The first chairlift went up in 1955. In 1986 McCoy also bought adjacent June Mountain.

Orientation & Information
At the Mammoth Lakes turnoff from US-395, Rte 203 heads west for 3mi to Mam-moth Lakes. After the first traffic light, Rte 203 becomes Main St, which continues as Lake Mary Rd past the second traffic light (closed in winter past Twin Lakes). North of the Main St/Lake Mary Rd intersection, Minaret Rd leads past the new village at Mammoth to the Mammoth Mountain Ski Area; in summer, it continues south to the Reds Meadow/Devils Postpile area.

The **Mammoth Lakes Visitors Bureau** *(☎ 760-934-2712, 888-466-2666, fax 760-934-7066; w www.visitmammoth.com; Rte 203; open 8am-5pm daily)* shares space with the **Mammoth Lakes Ranger Station** *(☎ 760-924-5500)* in a building on the northern side of Hwy 203, just before the first traffic light. This one-stop information center issues wilderness permits and has accommodations and campground listings, road and trail condition updates and information on local attractions. A good source for up-to-date in-formation about Mammoth is the free weekly *Mammoth Times* (w www.mammothtimes .com) distributed around town.

The **post office** *(Main St)* is just past the Chevron gas station. **Mammoth Hospital** *(☎ 760-934-3311; 185 Sierra Park Rd)* has a 24-hour emergency room.

Mammoth Mountain Ski Area
This is a true skiers' and snowboarders' re-sort, where playing hard and having fun are more important than who designed your ski anorak. An inactive volcanic peak, **Mam-moth Mountain** *(☎ 760-934-0745, 800-626-6684 for information, ☎ 888-766-9778 for 24hr snow report; w www.mammoth mountain.com)* has 28 chairlifts, two gondolas and enough terrain to keep anyone busy for a week. The combination of tree-line and open bowl skiing is great and the 3100 vertical feet make for some long cruising runs; at the top are very steep, nearly vertical, slopes. Slopes for beginners and advanced skiers account for about 30% each, with the remaining 40% being intermediate runs.

In 2003 all-day lift tickets cost $60/57 weekend/weekday adult, $45/43 child 13 to 18, and $30/29 child 7 to 12 and senior over 65. Multiple-day tickets are cheaper. Expect prices to go up a few dollars every year. Slopes are open 8:30am to 4pm daily.

Four hubs are at the base of the mountain: Main Lodge, Canyon Lodge, Little Eagle and The Mill Cafe – each with parking and ticket sales. There are ski schools at Main Lodge and Canyon Lodge.

Since parking lots fill quickly, it's best to use the free shuttle buses that connect the ski mountain with the town.

Main Lodge and Canyon Lodge both have state-of-the-art equipment rental and repair shops and there's a smaller outfit at Little Eagle. Prices are usually a bit lower at out-fitters in town, including **Footloose** *(☎ 760-934-2400; Gateway Center Mall, 3043 Main St)*, **Mammoth Sporting Goods** *(☎ 760-934-3239; Sierra Center Mall, Old Mammoth Rd)* and **Sandy's Ski & Sport** *(☎ 760-934-7518; Red Rooster Mall, 3499 Main St)*.

Cross-Country Skiing
There's free cross-country skiing along the Blue Diamond Trails System behind New Shady Rest Campground. Maintained by the USFS, trails are mostly ungroomed. A better, if more costly, option is the **Tamarack Cross Country Ski Center** *(☎ 760-934-5293; Lake Mary Rd; tickets adult $18/13/10 full day/afternoon/twilight, senior & youth $13/10/8; open 1st snowfall–mid-Apr)*. Right next to the Twin Lakes, it has 45km of groomed track, skating lanes, marked backcountry

trails and a rustic lodge (see Places to Stay) offering rentals and lessons. Rentals are $19/14 all day/afternoon for adults, $14/11 for seniors and children; lessons start at $38/32 per morning/ afternoon session for adults, $30/26 for seniors and children.

Hiking

There are three main trailheads, all with parking lots and access to good day hikes and longer trails over the Sierra Crest. **Horseshoe Lake**, in Mammoth Basin, is at a high elevation so you needn't hike far to reach alpine scenery; it has a good trail down into Reds Meadow. Also in Mammoth Basin, **Lake Mary** gives easy access to small alpine lakes backed by the impressive Mammoth Crest. Trails from **Agnew Meadows** (toward Devil's Postpile, accessible by shuttle bus) go north along the Pacific Crest/John Muir Trail into the Ansel Adams Wilderness, surrounded by the Minarets, some of the Sierra's most stunning sawtooth peaks, and cirque lakes. In winter many of these trails (especially to Reds Meadow) are popular with backcountry skiers. **Kittredge Sports** (☎ 760-934-7566; 3218 Main St) is a good hiking and backpacking outfitter.

Mountain Biking

Biking is big in the summer months when Mammoth Mountain is transformed into a **Mountain Bike Park** (☎ 760-934-0706), with more than 70mi of groomed singletrack trails. Until 2001, Mammoth was a stop on the NORBA National Championship Mountain Bike Series, one of the top races on the circuit.

Several other trails traverse the surrounding forest. Stop at the visitors bureau for a free map with route descriptions and updated trail conditions. **Footloose** (see under Mammoth Mountain Ski Area earlier) rents bikes for around $10 per hour or $28 to $40 all day.

Fishing

Starting on the last Saturday in April, the dozens of lakes that give the town its name exert their lure to fly and trout fisherfolk from near and far. To join them, you will need a California fishing license, available at sporting goods stores. Mammoth also hosts several fishing derbies, including the Western Outdoor News Double Haul, one of North America's largest fly-fishing

events, on Crowley Lake in September. A good place to rent equipment is **The Trout Fitter** (☎ 760-924-3676, 800-637-6912) in the Shell Mart Center at the corner of Rte 203 and Old Mammoth Rd.

Places to Stay

Mammoth has plenty of accommodations, but prices fluctuate wildly depending on demand, the time of year and whether you're staying midweek or at weekends. Holiday periods command top dollar. In winter, packages including lodging and lift tickets may be the best deal. Check at the visitors bureau.

Camping There are about 20 USFS campgrounds in and around Mammoth Lakes, most of them open from around mid-June to mid-September. Most sites are available on a first-come, first-served basis and cost from $13 to $16. Almost all have flush toilets but no showers. Check at the visitors bureau for a full list of campgrounds, specific opening dates, space availability and public showers.

You can also camp for free on national forest land unless posted otherwise. Check with the visitors bureau for areas that are open to dispersed camping and pick up a free fire permit if you intend to use stoves or charcoal grills.

Some of the nicest campsites are on the shores of **Twin Lakes**, **Lake Mary** and **Lake George**. The campground at **Convict Lake**, south of town off US-395, is open from late April to October.

Rte 203 (Minaret Rd) gives access to six more campgrounds in the **Reds Meadow/Devil's Postpile** area along the San Joaquin River; all offer access to great fishing and hiking.

Less picturesque but closer to town, **New Shady Rest** (☎ 877-444-6777 for reservations) and **Old Shady Rest** (same tel) are two sprawling options right behind the visitors bureau. New Shady Rest is open to tents and RVs from mid-May to October and to tents only for snow camping.

Hostels On a quiet, residential street north of town, you'll find **Davison Street Guest House** (☎ 760-924-2188, 619-544-9093 for reservations; W www.mammoth-guest.com; 19 Davison St; dorm beds $18-27). This friendly, private hostel has five rooms (sleeping a total of 26 people), three bathrooms, a communal kitchen, lounge and sundeck with mountain views. Rates vary slightly by season and day of the week.

Condominiums Mammoth abounds with holiday condominiums, often owned by wealthy Southern Californians as an investment and getaway. Condo stays can be an excellent and affordable option, especially for groups of four or more. Agencies to contact for referrals and availability include **Mammoth Reservation Bureau** (☎ 760-934-2528, ☎ 800-462-5571, fax 760-934-2317; W www .mammothvacations.com) and **Central Reservations of Mammoth** (☎ 760-934-8816, 800-321-3261, fax 760-934-1703; W www .mammothlakes.com).

B&B's & Inns A charming place, **Swiss Chalet** (☎ 760-934-2403, 800-937-9477, fax 760-934-2403; W www.mammothswiss chalet.com; 3776 Viewpoint Rd; rooms $60-75 summer, $80-120 winter) has nicely decorated rooms with TV and telephone. Wind down a day on the slopes in the hot tub or sauna, both with superb mountain views.

Cinnamon Bear Inn (☎/fax 760-934-2873, 800-845-2873; W www.cinnamonbearinn .com; 133 Center St; rooms $89-159) has largish and eclectically furnished rooms. Rates include a full breakfast, afternoon appetizers and use of the communal hot tub.

Mammoth Country Inn (☎ 760-934-2710, 866-934-2710; W www.mammothcountry inn.com; 75 Joaquin Rd; rooms $95-185), a block off Main St, has seven sparkling and recently overhauled rooms (including some with private hot tub), a guest kitchen and good breakfasts.

Shilo Inn (☎ 760-934-4500, 800-222-2244, fax 760-934-7594; 2963 Main St; rates $119-150) offers great value. The spacious mini-suites have microwaves and refrigerators, and rates include a generous continental breakfast. The best part, though, is the large fitness area, complete with gym, indoor pool, hot tub, steam room and sauna.

Tamarack Lodge Resort (☎ 760-934-2442, 800-237-6879, fax 760-934-2281; W www.tamaracklodge.com; cabins $120-350, lodge rooms $82-230), on the shore of Lower Twin Lake, is charming and rustic. The cozy lodge has a fireplace, bar and restaurant. Cabins, some of them brand-new,

sleep up to nine people and come with full kitchen, telephone, private bath, a porch and nice alpine furniture.

Places to Eat
Mammoth has plenty of places to get that morning coffee jolt and fuel up on carbos for a day on the slopes, including **Breakfast Club** (☎ 760-934-6944; 2987 Main St) and **The Stove** (☎ 760-934-2821; 644 Old Mammoth Rd), both favorites with the locals. Also try **Looney Bean** (☎ 760-934-1345; 3280 Main St), a communicative coffeehouse with intensely aromatic coffees and fresh baked goods. It's next to the Chevron gas station.

Roberto's Cafe (☎ 760-934-3667; 271 Old Mammoth Rd; dishes $2-10) makes Mammoth's best Mexican food, has a good tequila selection and a sunny outdoor patio.

Grumpy's (☎ 760-934-8587; 361 Old Mammoth Rd; dishes $4-20) is a busy sports bar with pinball machines, pool tables and video games, plus an energy-restoring menu of American and Mexican fare fit for any budget.

Good Life Cafe (☎ 760-934-1734; Mammoth Mall, Old Mammoth Rd; breakfast & lunch $4.50-9.50) has some selections for the health-conscious, including generously filled wraps and sandwiches and big bowls of salad. In fine weather, the deck tables are the most coveted.

The Mogul (☎ 760-934-3039; 1528 Tavern Rd; dinner mains $10-25), a popular steak and prime rib joint, sports that casual ski-lodge look and ambience. Its all-you-can-eat salad bar is $9.

Slocum's Grill (☎ 760-934-7647; 3221 Main St; dinner mains $10-25) is distinguished by a polished yet lively atmosphere and attracts a more mature crowd. The menu revolves around creative pasta, grilled meat and fish.

Chart House (☎ 760-934-4526; 106 Old Mammoth Rd; mains $14-40) is about as sophisticated as things get in Mammoth. The chef specializes in expertly prepared fish and seafood, but steaks, chicken, prime rib and salads also make an appearance on the menu.

AROUND MAMMOTH LAKES
Devil's Postpile National Monument
The 60ft, multisided columns of blue-gray basalt at this monument are the most conspicuous and interesting products of the

area's volcanic activity. The columns formed when lava, which flowed through Mammoth Pass, cooled and fractured vertically. A glacier came through later to give them their cracked, shiny surface.

The park is usually open from June to September, weather permitting, and visitors are subject to a $5 per person entrance fee. Unless you are camping, you can only get there on foot or aboard a free shuttle bus. These depart every 30 minutes from 7am to 7pm daily from the Gondola Building across from the ski area's Main Lodge and stop at campgrounds, viewpoints and the **Devil's Postpile Ranger Station** (☎ 760-934-2289). From here, it's about a ½mi trail to the columns and 2½mi through fire-ravaged forest to the spectacular Rainbow Falls, a 101ft sheet cascade.

The last stop is at **Reds Meadow Resort** (☎ 760-934-2345, 800-292-7758), which has a café, general store and pack station and campground.

The shuttle bus makes the entire one-way trip in about 45 minutes.

Convict Lake

About 5mi southeast of Mammoth and 2mi west of US-395, this is one of the prettiest lakes in the area, with pellucid emerald water embraced by two massive peaks – Mt Morrison and Laurel Mountain. The lake is named for a group of convicts who only made it this far after a jailbreak. A gentle trail skirts the lake, through aspen and cottonwood trees, and a trailhead on the southeastern shore goes to Genevieve, Edith, Dorothy and Mildred Lakes in the John Muir Wilderness.

Convict Lake Campground (sites $13-15) has terraced sites (on a first-come, first-served basis) and flush toilets, while **Convict Lake Resort** (☎ 760-934-3800, 800-992-2260; cabins $90-695) has cabins with kitchens and bathrooms for all tastes, from rustic to ritzy. Its restaurant (mains $16-26) is one of the few places around here and wows diners with gourmet continental cuisine worthy of a big city.

Hot Creek Fish Hatchery & Geological Site

About 5mi southeast of Mammoth on US-395 a sign signals the turnoff (east) to the Hot Creek Fish Hatchery (open daily), which raises about three million trout each year for stocking lakes and streams in the Sierra.

Continue for about 2mi to the **Hot Creek Geological Site**, which consists of a series of bubbling and steaming hot springs and pools at the bottom of a volcanic basin. Water from the mountains filters through cracks in the earth's crust and gets heated up by magma. The steam vents, creating springs of boiling water in what becomes a natural cauldron. It's possible to soak in the pools, though sections can be scalding. Pay attention to posted signs and take care when bathing.

BISHOP

Bishop (population 3700; elevation 4150) is the largest town south of Mammoth Lakes. Its modest, unpretentious appearance is in stark contrast to the wonderland of nature surrounding it. A major recreation hub, Bishop gives access to excellent fishing in nearby lakes and to the John Muir Wilderness via Bishop Creek Canyon. On Memorial Day weekend, Bishop celebrates 'Mule Days' with mule auctions, mule races, mule parades, a mule rodeo etc – and everyone becomes a cowhand or, at least, a mulehand, for the day. Some 40,000 people descend upon the town on those days.

Bishop is also the northernmost town of the **Owens Valley**, once a fertile agricultural region irrigated by Sierra streams. Since the early 20th century, water from the Owens River has been siphoned off by the Los Angeles Aqueduct, reducing the valley to a wasteland. Owens Lake, once 30ft deep and an important stopover for migrating waterfowl, dried up. On windy days, dry sediment from the exposed lakebed becomes airborne, infusing the air with tiny dust particles that can cause health troubles, especially for people with respiratory problems. To alleviate this situation, the Los Angeles Department of Water & Power is implementing dust control measures by shallow-flooding sections of the lakebed and by planting salt grass to stabilize the soil.

Orientation & Information

Bishop has US-395's sharpest curve, where it meets Hwy 6 (to Benton, Nevada) at a right angle. The town extends south of this junction for about 3mi along Main St.

The **White Mountain Ranger Station** (☎ 760-873-2500; 798 N Main St; open 8am-5pm daily late May-early Sept, shorter hours rest of year) issues wilderness permits and has trail and campground information for the White Mountains, Big Pine, and Rock and Bishop Creek Recreation Areas.

Nearby is the **Bishop Area Visitor Center** (☎ 760-873-8405; W www.bishopvisitor.com; 690 N Main St; open 9am-5pm Mon-Fri, 10am-4pm Sat-Sun).

Laws Railroad Museum

This extensive collection (☎ 760-873-5950; Hwy 6; donation requested; open 10am-4pm daily) of historic buildings, trains and equipment is 4mi northeast of Bishop. The central exhibit is the 1883 Laws railroad depot, a train and passenger depot that serviced the narrow-gauge line used to transport people and agricultural products from near Carson City to just south of Lone Pine through the then-fertile Owens Valley. Other historic buildings, including Bishop's first church, have been moved here and hold antiques and exhibits of all kinds.

Paiute Shoshone Indian Cultural Center

The earliest inhabitants of the Owens Valley were Paiute and Shoshone people who today live on four reservations of which the largest is the Bishop Indian Reservation. This center (☎ 760-873-4478; 2300 W Line St; adult/child $4/1; open 9am-5pm Mon-Fri, 10am-5pm Sat & Sun) acts as tribal headquarters and gathering place. There's also a gift shop and museum displaying basketry, tools, clothing and dwellings, including a sweat house and a cooking shelter.

Mountain Light Gallery

Bishop was the adopted home of the celebrated master of wilderness photography Galen Rowell and his wife Barbara Cushman, a renowned professional shooter in her own right. Both tragically died when their private plane crashed just south of Bishop airport on August 11, 2002. A choice selection of Galen Rowell's most awe-inspiring photos of the Sierra is on view at the **Mountain Light Gallery** (☎ 760-873-7700; 106 S Main St; admission free; open 10am-6pm Sun-Thur, 10am-9pm Fri-Sat), established by the couple.

Activities

The Owens River Gorge, 9mi north of town on the eastern side of US-395, has excellent rock climbing, as do the Buttermilk Hills, west of town on both sides of Hwy 168; the latter are also good for bouldering. Some of the staff at **Wilson's Eastside Sports** (☎ 760-873-7520; 224 N Main St) are experienced climbers who may have good route suggestions; the shop rents equipment and sells maps and guidebooks.

A short drive west of town via Hwy 168 takes you to **Bishop Creek Canyon**, a high sierra alpine playground with pine forests, lakes and streams. The southern fork ends at South Lake, surrounded by jagged peaks. There are several campgrounds and the trailhead for Bishop Pass gives access to countless more lakes in the John Muir Wilderness.

The northern fork of the road ends at Lake Sabrina, with the much smaller North Lake nearby. It's prettiest in fall when the aspen trees turn. **Fishing** is good in all of the lakes (North Lake is the least crowded), and **hiking** trails lead through the John Muir Wilderness to Sequoia National Park.

Horse packing is huge in Bishop with enough business for several outfitters, each offering a variety of tours: **Rainbow Pack Outfitters** (☎ 760-873-8877, 760-872-8803; 600 Main St) at Parchers Resort near South Lake; **Bishop Pack Outfitters** (☎ 760-873-4785, 800-316-4252) at the North Fork of Bishop Creek; and **Rock Creek Pack Station** (☎ 760-935-4493 summer, ☎ 760-872-8331 winter), about a half-hour drive north of Bishop in a lovely canyon.

About 5mi south of Bishop, turn right on Keough Hot Spring Rd, then right on County Rd and start looking for natural **hot springs** (admission free) to your left. Nearby, on Keough Hot Spring Rd, is **Keough's Hot Springs** (adult/concession $7/4), a historic outdoor pool (dating from 1919), which is filled with tepid water from the mineral hot springs.

Places to Stay & Eat

Brown's Town (☎ 760-873-8522; sites $14-19), on the southern edge of town, is a nicely shaded campground with grassy sites, hot showers, laundry and other amenities.

Ten USFS campgrounds along Bishop Creek, 9mi west of town via Hwy 168, are surrounded by trees and are close to fishing and hiking. Most cost $11 and all are first-come, first-served.

Bishop has plenty of roadside motels along US-395, with unexciting rooms from $40. For a little more style and comfort, try the following places:

Matlock House (☎ 760-873-3133; 1313 Rowan Lane; rooms $75-85) is a good-value B&B with decor that harkens back to the 'good old days.'

Comfort Inn (☎ 760-873-4284; 805 Main St; rooms $85-150) is a nicely maintained, big place with a pool, barbecue room and fish-cleaning room.

Best Western Creekside Inn (☎ 760-872-3044, 800-273-3550; 725 N Main St; rooms $109-159) is as upscale as things get in Bishop. The nicely landscaped grounds enclose a heated pool and a spa. Rooms are fully equipped and quite large.

Erick Schat's Bakkery (☎ 760-873-7156; 763 N Main St; sandwiches $6-7), a much-hyped spot, has been making shepherd bread and other baked goodies since 1938. The snack and espresso bar usually crawls with tourists.

Amigos (☎ 760-872-2189; 285 N Main St; dishes $3-10) serves authentic and good Mexican food. Don't be deterred by the plain decor or the plastic cacti in the window.

Bar-B-Q Bills (☎ 760-872-5535; 187 S Main St; meals under $10), an old-fashioned self-service eatery, slow-cooks smoked meat in a delicious barbecue sauce. Noncarnivores will welcome the well-stocked salad bar.

Whiskey Creek (☎ 760-873-7174; 524 N Main St; mains $7-23), in a gabled country inn, serves appetizers and simple dishes in the bar with its mountain-view sundeck and more elaborate meals in the slightly stuffy dining room.

Kava Coffeehouse (206 N Main St) has great coffee and smoothies, an upbeat ambience and Internet access. Hikers often gather here to fuel up on breakfast, baked goods and sandwiches.

BISHOP TO LONE PINE
Big Pine & Big Pine Canyon

The town of Big Pine, 15mi south of Bishop, is little more than a pit stop and launch pad for trips to the Ancient Bristlecone Pine Forest, although its **visitor center** (☎ 760-938-2114; 126 S Main St) has plenty of good information about the entire area.

Several motels hold court along Main St, all with basic rooms costing $30 to $55. Options include **Bristlecone Motel** (☎ 760-938-2067; 101 N Main St), with large, faded rooms with phone and TV, and **Big Pine Motel** (☎ 760-938-2282; 370 S Main St), with pretty grounds and friendly staff.

Big Pine Canyon, 10mi west of Big Pine via Glacier Lodge Rd (Crocker Ave in town), has good fishing and hiking. There's a **campground** (sites $13) with pit toilets and potable water, while **Glacier Lodge** (☎ 760-938-2837; cabins $70-75) has cabins (two-night minimum), public showers and a small store.

Stop at the kiosk at the canyon entrance for information and, if planning an overnight trip, a wilderness permit. The scenery here is not as spectacular as that of canyons further north, but trails lead to the **Palisade Glacier**, the southernmost in the USA and the largest in the Sierra. Glacial runoff turns the lakes below a milky turquoise color that looks great on film. It's about 9mi to the glacier via the North Fork trail. **Glacier Pack Train** (☎ 760-938-2538) offers day rides for $50 and pack trips for $90 per day.

Ancient Bristlecone Pine Forest

The Great Basin bristlecone pines found here are the oldest living things on earth; some of them are over 4000 years old. The oldest trees are squatty and gnarled, with exposed roots and wide-reaching limbs. Soil depletion takes place at a rate of 6in per 1000 years here, revealing the age of those trees whose roots are a few feet above ground.

The forest is in the White Mountains, a dry and stark range that was once higher than the Sierra but is much older and thus heavily eroded. To get here, take Hwy 168 east 12mi from Big Pine to White Mountain Rd, then turn left (north) and follow the curvy road 10mi to Schulman Grove, where there is a **visitor center** (☎ 760-873-2500 for recorded information; usually open late May-Oct) and parking lot. The trip should take no more than one hour. From here self-guided trails lead through different groves.

A second grove – the **Patriarch Grove** – is home of the world's largest bristlecone pine. It's about 12mi from the visitor center via a graded dirt road (popular with mountain bikers). Four miles further on is the Barcroft High Altitude Research Station, the departure point for day **hikes** to the top of White Mountain, at 14,246ft the third-tallest peak in the California and only 251ft lower than Mt Whitney. The round-trip is about 15mi via an abandoned road. Although the route is easy to find, this is no walk in the park due to the high elevations. Allow plenty of time and bring at least two quarts of water per person.

There's free camping at the undeveloped **Grandview Campground** at 8600ft before you reach the visitor center. It has an awesome view but bring your own water.

Independence

This sleepy highway town (population 1000; elevation 3925ft) has been a county seat since 1866 and is home to the **Eastern California Museum** (☎ 760-878-0354; 155 N Grant St; donation requested; open 10am-4pm Wed-Mon), three blocks west of US-395. Although old-fashioned, this is one of the best local history museums in the Sierra. Star displays are a small but poignant exhibit about life at the Manzanar relocation camp as well as a prized Paiute and Shoshone basket collection.

West of town via Onion Valley Rd (Market St in town), Onion Valley has two nice **campgrounds** (sites $11; open mid-March–mid-Oct) and the trailhead for the Kearsarge Pass Trail, an old Paiute trade route, with good day hike possibilities and the shortest backside access to Kings Canyon National Park. The trail to Golden Trout Lakes is strenuous and poorly marked. A herd of California bighorn sheep lives south of Onion Valley around Shepherd Pass.

Back in town is the small but excellent **Winnedumah Hotel** (☎ 760-878-2040; e winnedumah@qnet.com; 211 N Edwards St; rooms $50-85, dorm beds HI members/nonmembers $19.50/22.50). It served as the home away from home for the Hollywood elite filming in the nearby Alabama Hills (see Lone Pine later in this chapter). Today it's a charming inn and is also affiliated with Hostelling International. The beautiful lobby and warm furnishings are welcoming, and there's a peaceful garden as well. Rates include breakfast.

Manzanar National Historic Site

In February 1942 President Roosevelt signed an executive order requiring all West Coast Japanese – most of them American citizens – to be placed in relocation camps. Manzanar was the first of 10 such camps, built among pear and apple orchards, 6mi south of Independence. Between 1942 and 1945, Manzanar interned around 11,000 people in its 500-acre living area, enclosed by barbed wire and guarded by sentry posts.

After the war, the camp was leveled and its dark history was buried underneath the dust of the Owens Valley for decades. Recognition remained elusive until 1973 when the site was given landmark status; in 1992 it became a national historic site. Recent restoration has resulted in reconstructed barbed-wire fencing and the completion of a self-guided auto tour. The primary remaining building, an old high school auditorium, is being converted into an interpretive visitor center.

LONE PINE

Lone Pine (population 2800; elevation 3700ft) is famous for three things: the Alabama Hills, the gateway to Mt Whitney and the turnoff for Death Valley. Founded in the 1800s as a supply post for Owens Valley ranchers and farmers, Lone Pine experienced one boom during the 1850s mining activity, and another century later when movie stars such as Cary Grant, Gary Cooper and Hopalong Cassidy made Westerns in the nearby Alabama Hills. The Lone Pine Film Festival in October commemorates this period.

Lone Pine has plenty of motels, restaurants and stores flanking US-395 (called Main St here). Whitney Portal Rd heads west at the town's one stoplight, while Hwy 136 to Death Valley veers off southeast about 2mi south of town.

The **Interagency Visitor Center** (☎ 760-876-6222; open 8am-5pm daily year-round), 1½mi south of town at the US-395/136 junction, is information central for not only much of the Sierra but also for Death Valley.

The **Mt Whitney Ranger Station** (☎ 760-876-6200; Main St; open 7am-4:30pm May-Oct, later in Jul-Aug), in Lone Pine, issues wilderness permits and has local trail and road conditions posted.

Alabama Hills

West of Lone Pine, the Alabama Hills are an otherworldly landscape where nature has had its weird way with big piles of red boulders, chiseling them into warped shapes that kindle the imagination. If the scene looks familiar, it's because numerous old Westerns, including *How the West Was Won*, were made here. For close-ups of 'movieland',

Climbing Mt Whitney

At 14,497ft, Mt Whitney is the highest point in the contiguous USA and the climb to its peak is among the most popular hikes in the entire country.

The Main Mt Whitney trail leaves from Whitney Portal, about 13mi west of Lone Pine via the Whitney Portal Rd (closed in winter), and climbs about 6000ft over 11mi. Most people in good physical condition can make the climb, although only superbly conditioned, previously acclimatized hikers should attempt this as a day hike. Altitude sickness is a common problem, and rangers recommend spending a day or two camping at the trailhead to adjust. There are two camps along the route, the Outpost Camp at 3½mi and the Trail Camp at 6mi up the trail. If you go for it, get full details from the **ranger station** (☎ 760-876-6200) in Lone Pine before heading out. A recommended guide is *Climbing Mt Whitney* by Walt Wheelock and Wynne Benti, sold at the ranger station for $8.95.

Whitney Portal has two attractive campgrounds tucked into a pine forest along Lone Pine Creek: **Whitney Portal** (☎ 877-444-6777 for reservations; sites $14), about 1mi east of the trailhead, with lovely terraced sites, pit toilets and potable water; and the first-come, first-served **Whitney Trailhead** (sites $6), with the same facilities. Both are usually open from mid-May to mid-October. If they're full, consider the Lone Pine Campground 7mi east of here (see Places to Stay & Eat in the Lone Pine section). The **Whitney Portal Store** sells groceries and snacks and rents bear-resistant food containers. It also has public showers and a café with hot meals.

The biggest obstacle in getting to the top of the mountain is obtaining a wilderness permit, which is required for all overnight trips as well as for day hikes past Lone Pine Lake (about 2.8mi from the trailhead). Due to the trail's popularity, a quota system is in effect from 1 May to 1 November, limiting daily access to 60 overnight and 100 day-hikers. Permits are now distributed via a lottery. Send or fax your application to the **Wilderness Permit Office Info National Forest** (fax 760-873-2484; 873 N Main St, Bishop, CA 93514) anytime between 1 and 28 February. Reservations cost $15 per person. Check **W** www.r5.fs.fed.us/inyo for details.

head west on Whitney Portal Rd. For a quick introduction, turn left at Tuttle Creek Rd (look for the Portagee Joe Campground sign), which takes you on an easy 15-minute loop on a paved road. Bigger and more dramatic formations are accessed via the graded, unpaved Movie Rd. The turnoff is about 3mi west of Lone Pine off Whitney Portal Rd. The Interagency Visitor Center has a history sheet and map for locating the exact spots.

Places to Stay & Eat

Lone Pine Campground (☎ 877-444-6777 for reservations; sites $12; open mid-Apr–mid-Oct), well signed on Whitney Portal Rd west of town, is hot and dry but there's running water and composting toilets.

Best Western Frontier (☎ 760-876-5571; 1008 S Main St; rooms $54-103 mid-Mar–mid-Oct, $39-76 mid-Oct–mid-Mar), south of town, has a variety of pleasant rooms, including some with private Jacuzzi. Rates include a light breakfast.

Alabama Hills Inn (☎ 760-876-8700, 800-800-6468; **W** www.alabamahillsinn .com; 1920 S Main St; rooms $58-109 summer, $45-75 winter) is a newish place whose friendly rooms come with refrigerator and microwave.

Historical Dow Hotel (☎ 760-876-5521, 800-824-9317; **W** www.dowvillamotel.com; 310 S Main St; rooms without/with bath $38/52 summer, $23/39 winter) once lodged movie stars such as John Wayne and Errol Flynn. Built in 1922, the place has been restored but retains much of its charm. The attached **Dow Villa Motel** (same tel nos; rooms $80-115 summer, $64-92 winter) has generic rooms with all modern conveniences.

Locals recommend **PJ's Cafe** (446 S Main St; dishes $4-13; open 24hr) for good coffee shop fare, and **Mt Whitney Restaurant** (dishes $7.50-12) for classic and exotic burgers (buffalo, ostrich, venison) in a 'rock and roll meets the Old West' type of ambience. It has lots of movie memorabilia as well.

Ranch House Cafe (meals $5-15), 20mi south of Lone Pine in **Olancha**, has downhome American food served all day in a rustic space with tall ceilings, big wooden booths and red-checkered tablecloths.

California Deserts

Forget about green. After a while, the starkness of the desert landscape, the clarity of the light and the spaciousness are beautiful in their own way. Sometimes intensely hot, but rarely oppressive, the desert climate has long been regarded as healthy, especially by those from colder, wetter and greener places.

California's deserts are sparsely populated, except for the resort cities around Palm Springs and the irrigated agricultural area of the Imperial Valley. Even the most spectacular areas – Death Valley National Park, Joshua Tree National Park and Anza-Borrego Desert State Park – are not crowded for most of the year. On the long stretches of road between them, solitude and seemingly endless expanses of nothingness are likely to be the real attractions. The harshness and the isolation of the desert can also present real dangers. Visitors should be well prepared and take proper precautions.

Anyone looking to do some hiking should pick up *Hiking California's Desert Parks*, by Bill Cunningham and Polly Burke, or John Krist's *50 Best Short Hikes*, both widely available at bookstores and San Diego area visitor centers.

History

Since prehistoric times people have lived in those corners of the desert where springs, streams or lakes can sustain them. Signs of this ancient occupation are found at several desert sites. For early European explorers, such as Juan Bautista de Anza and Jedediah Smith, the desert was a barrier between the habitable West Coast and the settled areas to the south and east. The trails they pioneered, such as the De Anza Trail and the Spanish Trail, can still be traced. Miners also came and went, establishing towns that died as the minerals played out, leaving their skeletons and stories scattered in the desert.

Permanent European settlements came only with dependable water supplies, first with agricultural communities in the Imperial Valley and Coachella Valley, followed by the health and holiday resorts of Palm Springs. The military took over huge areas for training in WWII and still has 3 million acres of weapons test sites, desert training centers, gunnery ranges, live bombing areas

Highlights

• Joshua Tree National Park – funky trees and fun climbing

• Death Valley National Park – salt flats, sand dunes, spectacular sunrises and sunsets

• Palm Springs Aerial Tramway – from hot desert to cool pine forest in 14 minutes

• Anza-Borrego Desert State Park – palm oases, deep canyons and wide open spaces

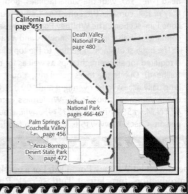

California Deserts page 451
Death Valley National Park page 480
Joshua Tree National Park pages 466-467
Palm Springs & Coachella Valley page 456
Anza-Borrego Desert State Park page 472

and the large Edwards Air Force Base, which is used for aircraft testing and space shuttle landings.

Geography

About one quarter of California is desert. The area roughly south and east of Palm Springs is the 'low desert,' called the Colorado Desert since it's the area around the valley of the Colorado River. It is actually part of the great Sonora Desert, most of which lies in Arizona and Mexico. The area roughly north of Palm Springs, south of Sierra Nevada, and east of Bakersfield is the 'high desert.' Named the Mojave Desert, it extends into northwestern Arizona, southern Nevada and the southeast corner of Utah. The low desert is mostly less than 600ft above sea level (though there are a few peaks over 1000ft), while the high desert averages about 2000ft (though Death Valley, in the middle of the

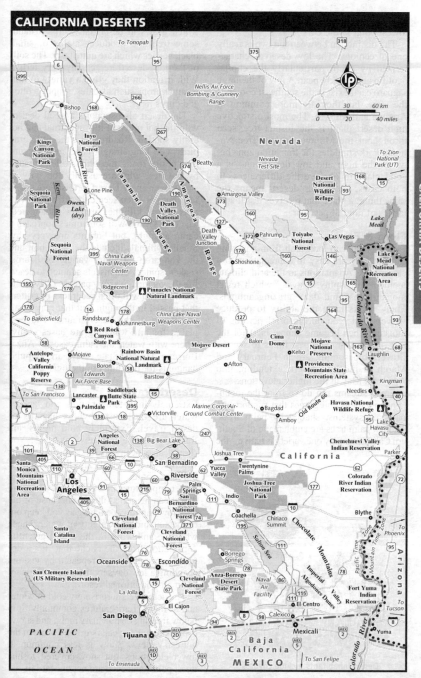

high desert, drops below sea level to the lowest point in the US).

The distinction between the two is really one of ecology. The low desert is characterized by cacti, particularly the cholla, ocotillo and prickly pear. A few of the large saguaro cacti exist in the southeast corner of the state, but they are more common in Arizona and Mexico. The most distinctive high desert plant is the Joshua tree, seen throughout the Mojave. Joshua Tree National Park straddles the transition zone between the high and low deserts and is a good place to observe the differences. In both cases, the word 'desert' means the same thing: a place that receives less than 8 inches of rainfall per year.

Flora & Fauna

Desert plants can look drab from a passing car, but they are easy to appreciate with a closer look. Adaptations to the arid climate include thin, spiny 'leaves,' which resist moisture loss and deter grazing animals. Many plants have the ability to produce flowers and seed during brief periods of moisture, then become almost inert for the rest of the year. The best times to see the flowers blossoming are in February and March in the low desert, extending into April and May at the higher elevations.

Small streams run down from the mountains in valleys and gorges that support tiny oasis ecosystems, shaded by palm trees. Though palm trees are emblematic of Southern California, only one variety is native – the

California fan palm *(Washingtonia filifera)*, which grows in desert oases. It's a handsome tree and produces stalks of small black berries which are quite tasty. The soils of the low desert are actually very fertile. With irrigation they grow a variety of hot-weather crops such as dates, grapes, cotton and citrus trees.

The desert also supports a good deal of wildlife, but much of it is nocturnal and not easily spotted. Roadrunners, the little gray birds with long straight tails, are seen running beside roads, though not often pursued by coyotes, who are usually too wily to show themselves. Desert tortoises are not so fast, but not often seen either; frequent victims of road kill, they are now endangered. The cute kit fox will sometimes approach a camp at night, but bobcats are very shy. Smaller animals include the jackrabbit and the kangaroo rat and a variety of lizards, snakes, spiders and insects adapted to desert life. If you look in sandy patches early in the morning you will often see tracks of critters that passed in the night, but that may be all you'll see of the desert fauna. The best places for bird-watching are oases – anywhere with water; the palm oases of Anza-Borrego Desert State Park are popular hangouts for budding ornithologists.

Desert Travel

Extremely high temperatures and lack of water are the most obvious hazards of desert travel. Extremely cold nights and flash floods are less obvious risks. You should also be aware of some poisonous wildlife, vicious plants and the dangers of old mine shafts.

A temperature of 120°F (48°C) in the desert can be quite tolerable because of the very low humidity – so long as you keep out of the sun and drink plenty of water. Those who live and work in the desert get little consolation from the cliche that 'it's a dry heat,' especially when repeated by visitors spending a few days by the swimming pool of an air-conditioned resort.

The desert gets surprisingly cold in winter and at night. Temperatures commonly drop below freezing on a January night, and snow-capped mountain peaks surround some of the hottest valleys. Snow is less common at lower elevations, but snow-covered Joshua trees, palms and cacti are not unheard of.

Desert inhabitants include coyotes

Water In the desert, it's absolutely essential to drink lots of water. Perspiration and evaporation keep the body cool, but the rate of moisture loss is high. Take regular drinks of water even if you don't feel thirsty and whatever you do, don't ration your water consumption. Beverages with alcohol, caffeine or sweeteners will actually reduce the amount of water available to cool your body. Be sure to drink extra water to compensate for their dehydrating effects, or better still, avoid them altogether, at least during the day.

Allow one gallon of water per person per day, twice that if you're walking, climbing, biking or engaging in any other outdoor activity. Carry an extra gallon of water per person in case you get stuck, as well as a few gallons of radiator water for your car. Always carry water in nonbreakable containers.

There are natural springs in the deserts, but don't rely on them as a water source: their flows change from year to year and the water is usually not potable without purification.

Clothing Wear a hat that shades the head and neck. It's best to wear loose, light-colored clothing that covers most of the body. Shorts, sandals and tank tops leave too much skin exposed to the heating effects of the sun. Thick-soled shoes are necessary to protect your feet from the hot ground. Bring warmer clothing for night wear – at least a sweater, hat and windbreaker – plus extra layers in winter.

Sunburn (caused by UV radiation) is a separate problem, distinct from the heating effects of the sun (which is infrared radiation). To protect against sunburn, use a high SPF sunscreen (don't forget to put it on your ears!), lip balm and quality sunglasses. Small communities and visitor centers often sell these items at higher prices; it's best to pack them with you.

Desert Survival The biggest danger is being stranded in the desert without adequate supplies of water. An interesting back-road drive can become a disaster if a car breaks down or gets stuck in sand. Even a short walk can turn fatal if you get lost or injured.

Sparse vegetation beckons cross-country travel, but natural markers on the landscape are few and often look similar to each other; remember that harsh light and wide open spaces can play tricks on your vision. To avoid getting stuck, take a map and compass and know where you're going. Be sure that your vehicle is in good condition, and don't push it beyond its limits. Never venture alone into remote areas. Always tell someone where you're going and when you'll be back.

If you do get stuck, stay with your vehicle and wait for rescue. A car is easier to spot from a distance than a lone walker. If you become hopelessly lost while walking, seek the closest shady spot and stay put. People walking around in the desert can become exhausted and/or dehydrated very quickly.

CALIFORNIA DESERTS

Desert Protection & Conservation

In October 1994, the California Desert Protection Act was passed by Congress, giving additional environmental protection to millions of acres of California deserts. Death Valley and Joshua Tree were upgraded from national monuments to national parks, and 2031 sq mi was added to the protected area of Death Valley. The act also created the East Mojave National Preserve, which transferred the management of the former East Mojave National Scenic Area from the Bureau of Land Management (BLM) to the National Park Service (NPS).

Though generally welcomed by conservationists, these changes had some controversial features. Existing mining activities were allowed to continue in the extended areas of Death Valley National Park, which was seen as an erosion of the level of protection offered by national park status. Hunting was permitted in the East Mojave National Preserve, though it is not exactly a preservation activity. Then there was the question of funding the land management – the Republican Congress allocated the NPS an additional $1 (yes, just one dollar) per year to manage the 2188-sq-mi East Mojave National Preserve.

Most of California's deserts are recognized as being of international environmental significance. They form part of the UN-designated Mojave & Colorado Deserts Biosphere Preserve.

A few basic emergency supplies can greatly prolong desert survival. Have at least a gallon of water per person in reserve. Take a mirror, matches and maybe some flares so you can signal for help. A tent or groundsheet can provide vital sun protection as well as increase your visibility. A flashlight, pocketknife, first-aid kit and extra food may also be useful.

Flash Floods Flooding can occur after heavy rains, even if the downpour is many miles away. It is unwise to camp or park in streambeds or washes if there is even the slightest chance of rain in any upstream area.

Poisonous Animals Black widows, scorpions, rattlesnakes and centipedes are venomous but unlikely to attack. Be sure to check your shoes before putting them on in the morning, and don't leave your bag unzipped, outside overnight. See Dangers & Annoyances in the Facts for the Visitor chapter for more information.

Pointy Plants Obviously, cacti have spikes. Less obvious are the tiny barbs, which make the spikes difficult to pull out of your skin. Bring strong tweezers or pliers to extract them, and avoid hiking in shorts.

Mines There are hundreds of abandoned mineral mines in the deserts. Watch out for holes or shafts, which can be hard to see and easy to fall into. Old shafts are very dangerous as the supporting timbers have usually deteriorated and the air may contain poisonous gases. Never enter old mines.

Railroads Old rail lines may appear to be abandoned but are often still in use – by mineral extraction companies or private railroad enthusiasts. Never walk on railroad tracks where there is no escape route or where you can't see a half-mile in both directions.

Explosives Much of the desert has been used for military training and testing. Though this is done mostly in well-defined areas, unexploded bombs and shells have turned up in many places and should never be touched. It is unwise to enter any area marked as a live bombing range or to venture off on any unmapped side roads.

Getting Around

The main desert towns are reachable by bus, and some by rail as well, but to get out into the desert itself you really need your own transportation. You can rent cars in the desert towns, but rentals are usually cheaper in the coastal cities. Don't even think about hitching – you could die from the heat just waiting for a lift.

Car Much of California's desert is accessible on paved roads and requires no more than a regular car, driven with care. Many car rental contracts do not allow the vehicle to be driven off normally trafficked roads.

As you travel into more remote areas, it's increasingly important to make sure the car is in good condition and that you have spare gas, oil and coolant. You might also carry a tire pump, a shovel to dig your wheels out

Hot Enough for You?

Temperatures vary with the seasons and the altitude. The hottest temperature ever recorded in the USA was 134°F (56°C) in Death Valley on July 10, 1913. Summer temperatures commonly exceed 120°F (48°C) in the lower elevations of the California deserts. Average daily maximum temperatures in July are 116°F (46°C) in Death Valley and 107°F (41°C) in Palm Springs. It's usually around 10° to 15°F cooler at higher elevations – the July average in Barstow, which is at 2100ft, is 101°F (38°C). A rule of thumb is that temperatures fall by about 1°F for every 300ft of elevation loss.

These figures are not the whole story, however. The reported and commonly quoted figure is the air temperature measured in the shade – a thermometer in the sun can rise rapidly to well over 150°F (65°C) and may literally burst. Sun blazing through the windows will turn a car into a little hothouse; the temperature inside can reach 160°F (70°C) within minutes, which can be fatal for children or pets.

When it's this hot, adhesives soften, boxes disintegrate, pages fall out of books, plastics melt and photographic film can change color. Exposed surfaces reach truly blistering temperatures after a few hours in the sun – the temperature on the desert floor can exceed 200°F (93°C). You can fry an egg on the ground – literally!

and a board or traction mats in case you get stuck in loose sand. For really rough roads a 4WD vehicle is best, but regular cars can travel most unpaved roads if the clearance between the underside of the car and the ground is adequate. Visitor centers usually post current road conditions that tell which roads require a 4WD. Off-road driving is prohibited on all public land, except in areas designated for off-road vehicle use.

When your car is parked, use cardboard, plastic sunshields or towels to cover the steering wheel, dashboard and seats. Even a few minutes parked in the sun can leave the interior too hot to touch. Perishable food should be stored in the trunk.

Check tires before you start a day's hot-weather driving and make sure they are at full pressure – an under-inflated tire can overheat very quickly. Never deflate a tire that has become hot after driving.

Watch the temperature gauge of your car. If it starts to heat up, turn off the air-conditioning. If it continues to get hotter, pull over, face the front of the car into the wind, keep the engine running and dribble water over the front of the radiator (*not* over the engine or fan). Turning the car heater on to the max can also help.

Bicycle In winter, bike touring can be wonderful if you are prepared. Bring extra tires and inner tubes, several gallons of water per day and cold-weather gear for the night. Start early in the morning, rest during the hottest part of the day and start up again when the sun is getting low. The best places for this are where visitor facilities are close together: Anza-Borrego, Death Valley and Palm Springs. You can rent mountain bikes in most desert towns for one-day trips.

Note that bikes must stay on designated roads because their continuous tire-track acts as a waterway, causing more damage than isolated footprints.

Palm Springs & Coachella Valley

The so-called resort cities, which extend the length of the Coachella Valley, are really quite odd. They form an almost continuous sprawl of heavily landscaped housing developments, golf courses and upscale resorts. The thick, green oasis created by this artificial human occupancy is surrounded on all sides by parched desert floor or steep, dry mountains. In the thick of it all, however, people seem to forget that they are not supposed to be comfortable in such a place and thus do a fabulous job of vacationing and living in flamboyant extravagance that tends to be contagious.

Palm Springs, with a population of around 43,000, was traditionally a winter retreat for Hollywood stars. It is still the best-known and most visited area, with a vast gay and lesbian community and excellent examples of modernist architecture from the 1940s and '50s.

Going southeast down the valley, Cathedral City, Rancho Mirage and Palm Desert bleed without much distinction in to one another, though Palm Desert's El Paseo (the Rodeo Drive of the desert) distinguishes it from the others. At the far southern end of the valley, Indio originally serviced the railroad and the surrounding agricultural areas and is currently the hot spot for development.

Most visitors (about 3.5 million per year) come in the cooler months to play golf or just enjoy the desert climate, and thousands of college kids descend on the town for spring break. In the midday heat, there's not much to do except hang around a pool, get up into the mountains via the aerial tramway or head into an air-conditioned place like a museum or shopping center (from which there are plenty to choose).

History

Cahuilla people occupied the canyons on the southwestern side of the Coachella Valley, where permanent streams flowed from the San Jacinto Mountains. They also used the hot springs where the city of Palm Springs now stands. The early Spanish explorers gave the Cahuilla the name Agua Caliente, meaning 'hot water.'

In 1851, the Cahuilla staged a revolt against American authorities and, though it was put down, their land rights were recognized in the 1852 Treaty of Temecula. However, the treaty was not ratified by Congress and was superseded by a new arrangement in 1876.

In order to promote the construction of a railroad from Los Angeles to Yuma, Arizona,

CALIFORNIA DESERTS

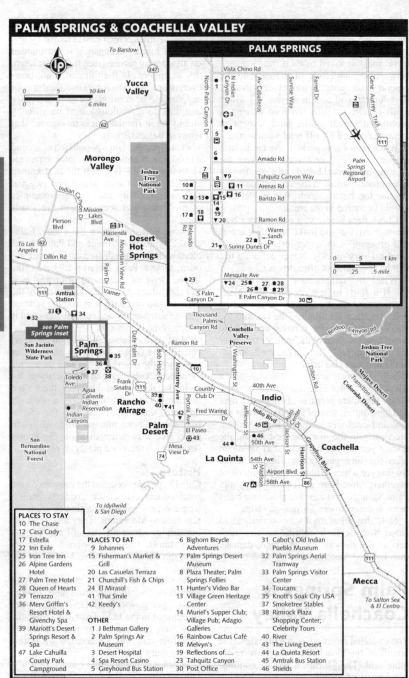

PALM SPRINGS & COACHELLA VALLEY

PALM SPRINGS

PLACES TO STAY
10 The Chase
12 Casa Cody
17 Estrella
22 Inn Exile
25 Iron Tree Inn
26 Alpine Gardens Hotel
27 Palm Tree Hotel
28 Queen of Hearts
29 Terrazzo
36 Merv Griffin's Resort Hotel & Givenchy Spa
39 Mariott's Desert Springs Resort & Spa
47 Lake Cahuilla County Park Campground

PLACES TO EAT
9 Johannes
15 Fisherman's Market & Grill
20 Las Casuelas Terraza
21 Churchill's Fish & Chips
24 El Mirasol
41 Thai Smile
42 Keedy's

OTHER
1 J Bethman Gallery
2 Palm Springs Air Museum
3 Desert Hospital
4 Spa Resort Casino
5 Greyhound Bus Station
6 Bighorn Bicycle Adventures
7 Palm Springs Desert Museum
8 Plaza Theater; Palm Springs Follies
11 Hunter's Video Bar
13 Village Green Heritage Center
14 Muriel's Supper Club; Village Pub; Adagio Galleries
16 Rainbow Cactus Café
18 Melvyn's
19 Reflections of....
23 Tahquitz Canyon
30 Post Office
31 Cabot's Old Indian Pueblo Museum
32 Palm Springs Aerial Tramway
33 Palm Springs Visitor Center
34 Toucans
35 Knott's Soak City USA
37 Smoketree Stables
38 Rimrock Plaza Shopping Center; Celebrity Tours
40 River
43 The Living Desert
44 La Quinta Resort
45 Amtrak Bus Station
46 Shields

the valley was divided into a checkerboard of square-mile sections. The odd-numbered sections were granted to the Southern Pacific Railroad, while the even-numbered sections were given to the Agua Caliente as their reservation. After the railroad was built, the company sold most of its land and the whole valley was developed first as farmland, and later with health spas, hotels and resorts.

It was not until the 1940s that surveys established the exact boundaries of the sections, and by then much of the Native American land had been built on. Though they couldn't sell the land, the Indians were able to charge rent. As the valley has grown more affluent, the several hundred Indians who have established tribal membership have become very wealthy.

At the southern end of the valley, Indio was a construction camp for the railway in the 1870s, and its artesian water was tapped to irrigate the first crops. Date palms from Algeria were introduced in 1890 and have become the major fruit crop of the valley, along with citrus fruits and table grapes. Later, water was brought all the way from the Colorado River.

In Palm Springs, the first hotels were for those who sought the health benefits of the natural hot springs and a desert climate. From the late 1920s it became popular as a resort area and as a winter getaway for Hollywood stars. One of the city's first councilwomen, Ruth Hardy, was responsible for many of the restrictive ordinances that saved Palm Springs from the excesses of uncontrolled development, including bans on two-story houses and large outdoor advertisements.

Orientation

The resort cities extend more than 25mi from Palm Springs to Indio, with most of the communities along Hwy 111, south of I-10. Going up and down the valley, it's often quicker to take the interstate than to follow Hwy 111 through miles of suburbs and dozens of traffic lights.

Palm Springs has a reasonably compact downtown area, centered on about four blocks of Palm Canyon Dr, with shops, banks, restaurants and a few sights. In this area, traffic goes south on Palm Canyon Dr and north on Indian Canyon Dr. Tahquitz Canyon Way divides these streets into north and south.

Restaurants and chain motels are spread out along E Palm Canyon Dr and Hwy 111 from Palm Springs to Cathedral City.

Information

The **Palm Springs Visitor Center** (☎ 760-778-8418; 2781 N Palm Canyon Dr; open 9am-5pm daily), near the turnoff to the aerial tramway, provides free hotel bookings, special interest guides, maps and many tourist publications, including *Play Palm Springs* and *Play Gay Palm Springs* (both free). Fans of modernism can pick up a map, *Palm Springs Modern* ($5), which will guide them to homes – many of them private – designed by Albert Frey, Richard Neutra, Donald Wexler and George and Bob Alexander.

A good website to check is **w** www.palm springs.com, where you'll often find discount coupons for attractions, tours and restaurants. For Internet access go to any public library in the valley; a very nice one is in Rancho Mirage at the corner of Hwy 111 and Bob Hope Dr.

The **Palm Springs post office** (☎ 800-275-8777; 333 Amado Rd) can help with postal requirements. **Desert Hospital** (☎ 760-323-6511; 1150 N Indian Canyon Dr) is the place to get 24-hour emergency care. The *Desert Sun* is the local newspaper.

Palm Springs Desert Museum

This museum (☎ 760-325-0189; 101 Museum Dr; adult/child $7.50/3.50, free 1st Tues of month; open 10am-5pm Tues-Sat, noon-5pm Sun), west of Palm Canyon Dr behind Desert Fashion Plaza, has a small but good modern art collection, including an impressive piece by Seattle glass artist Dale Chihuly. There are also some excellent Cahuilla baskets and large dioramas and displays of desert plants and wildlife.

Palm Springs Air Museum

Adjacent to the Palm Springs International Airport, the Air Museum (☎ 760-778-6262; 745 N Gene Autry Trail; adult/concession $8/6.50; open 10am-5pm daily, 8am-3pm June-Sept) has an exceptionally good collection of WWII aircraft, photos and flight memorabilia, as well as a large theater where movies are shown regularly for no additional charge.

Village Green Heritage Center

This grassy little square (221 S Palm Canyon Dr) in the heart of downtown has some 'heritage' attractions, though most people use it as a place to sit and eat ice cream and fudge, which you can buy at the sweets store next door. The true historic sites surrounding the square include the **Agua Caliente Cultural Museum** (☎ 760-323-0151), which has pictures and artifacts on the tribe's history; **Ruddy's General Store**, a reproduction of a 1930s general store; and the 1884 **McCallum Adobe**, said to be the oldest building in Palm Springs. The buildings are open 10am to 4pm Thursday to Saturday, noon to 3pm Sunday and Wednesday.

The Living Desert

The desert is living all around – a fact that is sometimes hard to remember with pavement and golf greens stretching in all directions. For guaranteed wildlife sightings and interpretive plaques, visit this outdoor museum and botanical garden (☎ 760-346-5694; 47-900 Portola Ave; adult/concession $8.50/4.25; open 9am-5pm daily Sept-May, 8am-1pm June-Aug, last admission 1 hour before closing), south of Hwy 111, Palm Desert. It has a wide variety of desert plants and animals, plus wonderful exhibits on desert geology and Indian culture. Between Thanksgiving and January 1, from 6pm to 9pm, the museum also presents its Wild-Lights show, a light festival featuring lights on the trees and special animal shapes, for an additional $4. Discounts are available.

Palm Springs Aerial Tramway

A real highlight of a visit to Palm Springs is a trip in this revolving cable car (☎ 760-325-1391; W www.pstramway.com), which climbs nearly 6000 vertical feet, from the desert floor up to the San Jacinto Mountains, in about 14 minutes. You ascend through visibly different vegetation zones from the Valley Station (2643ft) to the Mountain Station (8516ft). It's 30°F (1°C) to 40°F (4°C) cooler as you step out into pine forest at the top, so bring some warm clothing – the trip up is said to be the equivalent (in temperature) of driving from Mexico to Canada.

The Mountain Station at the top of the tram has a bar, cafeteria, observation area and a theater showing a short film on the tramway. The views over the valley are brilliant.

It's worth allowing some time (a day or two if you're a backcountry enthusiast) at the top to enjoy the **San Jacinto Wilderness State Park**. There are miles of trails, including a nontechnical route up to San Jacinto peak (9879ft), used for hiking in summer, snowshoeing and skiing in winter. There are also several primitive campgrounds (free). Everyone going into the backcountry (even for a few hours) must register at the ranger kiosk on the ground level of the Mountain Station for rescue purposes. Maps are available ($1 to $7) at the kiosk and, better yet, at the State Park Visitor Information Center at the Mountain Station. Also at the visitor center, ask about the **cross-country ski center**, which operates when there's ample snow. You can rent skis, sleds and snowshoes for around $8/18 per hour/day. The staff are knowledgeable about snow conditions and backcountry routes.

Tramway hours are 10am to 8pm Monday to Friday, 8am to 8pm Saturday, Sunday and holidays. During May to November, the last cable car goes up at 9pm and comes down at 9:45pm. A round-trip costs $20.80 per adult and $13.80 for a senior or child; various discounts are available. A Ride 'n' Dine combination, which includes a buffet dinner at the top, is available after 4pm for $27.80/18.80. It's not a bad dinner for $7 extra, but the deal may not allow enough time for a leisurely look around at the top.

It's also possible to hike to the top of the tram via the Skyline Trail, which starts near the Palm Springs Desert Museum. This is an *extremely* challenging hike, recommended only for the very fit who have a whole day to spend and leave no later than 7am. The reward, besides stellar views and multiple climatic zones, is a free tram ride down.

Indian Canyons

Streams flowing from the San Jacinto Mountains sustain a rich variety of plants in the canyons around Palm Springs. The canyons (admission $6; open 8am-5pm fall & winter, 8am-6pm spring & summer) were home to Indian communities for hundreds of years and are now part of the Agua Caliente Indian Reservation. A walk up these canyon oases, shaded by fan palms and surrounded by towering cliffs, is a real delight. From downtown, go south on Palm Canyon Dr for about 2mi to the reservation entrance. From here,

Alternative Energy

California is a massive consumer of fossil fuels, but it has also established some full-scale projects to exploit alternative sources of energy. The desert regions offer not just an abundant source of strong sunshine, but also excellent sites for wind generators and areas where geothermal energy can be tapped. The wind generators present a quite spectacular sight, with their blades the size of airplane wings, rotating on top of 80ft towers that turn to face the prevailing wind. Thousands of these towers are lined up at locations such as the San Gorgonio Pass near Palm Springs and the Tehachapi Pass west of Mojave, where geographical conditions reliably produce strong winds. As air in the desert heats and rises during the day, cooler air is drawn in from the coastal areas, accelerating as it goes through the narrow passes (the average wind speed in the San Gorgonio Pass is 15mph to 20mph). The older generators (many imported from Denmark) have a capacity of around 40kW to 50kW. But with technology rapidly developing, the newer turbines are much larger and have a capacity of around 500kW.

For more information, call the **Desert Wind Energy Association** (☎ 760-329-1799). **Palm Springs Windmill Tours** (☎ 760-320-1365; adult/child $22/10) will take you on a 1½-hour driving tour of the windmill area, providing volumes of information and stopping for photo opportunities along the way. Tours are at 10am and 2pm Tuesday, Thursday and Saturday, and leave from a parking lot a half mile south of I-10 at Indian Ave (directions are provided when you call to make a reservation).

The potential for geothermal energy also results from geographical circumstances. The Salton Trough, extending from the Gulf of California through the Imperial and Coachella Valleys, was created by massive sections of the earth's crust moving apart. This movement creates fractures and stress points. These not only cause earthquakes but also allow molten magma to work its way close to the earth's surface, heating the groundwater. In some places, this creates natural hot springs, but the heat can also be tapped to provide steam to power generators. Geothermal power plants operate at a number of sites near the Salton Sea, which is the deepest part of the trough, and the thinnest part of the earth's crust.

it's 3mi up to the Trading Post which sells hats, maps, water and knickknacks. At the entrance to each canyon is a trail post with a map and information about that particular hike.

Closest to the entrance gate to the reservation is **Andreas Canyon**, where there's a pleasant picnic area. Nearby are imposing rock formations where you can find Indian mortar holes, used for grinding seeds, and some rock art (see The Beginnings and California's Indians in Facts about California). The trail up the canyon is an easy walk.

About a 20-minute walk south from Andreas Canyon is **Murray Canyon**, which can't be reached by road and is therefore less visited. It's a good place for bird-watching, and bighorn sheep might be seen on the slopes above the canyon.

Following the winding access road to the end brings you to **Palm Canyon**, which is the most extensive of the canyons, some 15mi long, with good trails and a store selling snacks and souvenirs. In the morning, look for animal tracks in the sandy patches.

Tahquitz Canyon

Opened in 1999 after being closed for 30 years, Tahquitz Canyon (☎ 760-416-7044 for information; ⓦ www.tahquitzcanyon .com) is a historic and sacred centerpiece for the Agua Caliente people. It was traditionally home to Agua Caliente ancestors, but was taken over by teenage squatters in the 1960s. Eventually the canyon became a point of contention between the Agua Caliente, local law enforcement agencies and 'hippies' who claimed the right to live in its alcoves and caves. A major clean-up raid rid the canyon of inhabitants, but it took many years to haul trash, erase graffiti and get the area back to its natural state.

It's still off-limits to independent hikers, but for $12.50 you can visit its waterfall, rock art and ancient irrigation system on a guided 2mi, two-hour hike. Tribal rangers lead the hikes, leaving at 8am, 10am, noon and 2pm. The visitor center at the canyon entrance shows a video about the legend of Tahquitz, has exhibits about the canyon and offers a great view over Coachella Valley.

Other Attractions

There are quite a few other attractions in and around the valley, which may be worth a visit if you have the time and a particular interest. One of the quirkiest is **Cabot's Old Indian Pueblo Museum** (☎ 760-329-7610; 67616 E Desert View Ave; admission $2.50; open Sat & Sun only June-Aug; Sat, Sun & most other days mid-Sept–mid-May), in Desert Hot Springs. It's a ramshackle, junk-filled old house built by a rich East Coaster who gave up his fortune to become a desert-loving recluse.

The valley's original hot springs have been part of the Indian-owned **Spa Resort Casino** (☎ 760-325-1461; 100 N Indian Canyon Dr) for over 30 years. Day visitors can use the spa for $17, or choose from a variety of wraps, scrubs and rubs that cost substantially more.

Another piece of living history is **Shields** (☎ 760-347-0996; 80-225 Hwy 111), on the eastern edge of Palm Desert. Since 1924 it has shown visitors a film, 'The Romance and Sex Life of the Date', before selling gift boxes, date cakes and date milkshakes.

Knott's Soak City USA (☎ 760-327-0499, **w** www.oasiswaterresort.com; 1500 S Gene Autry Trail; adult/child $22/15; open daily Mar-Sept, Sat & Sun only Oct) has a wave pool, water slides and misted beaches where you can get way too much sun.

Activities

Golf Golf is huge here, with more than 90 public, semiprivate, private and resort golf courses, and a total of 1733 holes. It takes 1 million gallons of water per day to irrigate the golf courses. There are several big tournaments annually, and the College of the Desert even has a School of Golf Management. Greens fees run from $26 to $215, depending on the course, the season and the day of the week. Most hotels can make arrangements for their guests to play on at least one local course. You can receive substantial savings through **Stand-by Golf** (☎ 760-321-2665; open 6:30am-9pm daily), which can provide guaranteed tee times, at a discount, for same-day or next-day play at 20 courses.

Hiking There are lots of enthusiastic local hikers, and it's a great way to see the canyons, wildlife and vegetation of the region. Most hiking is in the Indian Canyons and from the top of the aerial tramway (see earlier). **Trail**

Discovery Outdoor Guide Service (☎ 760-325-4453; **w** www.palmspringshiking.com) offers guided hiking and running trips locally and in Joshua Tree National Park. It doesn't operate its trips during the hottest times of year, so call for availability and prices.

Palm Springs Desert Museum (☎ 760-325-0189; 101 Museum Dr) conducts short hikes on Friday and Saturday, and visitors may be able to join in; call for information.

Biking Palm Springs and the valley have an excellent network of bike paths that are great for getting around. **Bighorn Bicycle Adventures** (☎ 760-325-3367; cnr Palm Canyon Dr & Amado St; open 9am-5pm daily), in downtown Palm Springs, rents bikes ($10/28/100 per hour/day/week) and leads daily tours of the Indian Canyons. It is a good general resource for biking information.

Horseback Riding Smoketree Stables (☎ 760-327-1372; 2500 Toledo Ave) arranges trail rides, from a one-hour outing to an all-day trek. The cost is about $35 per hour and it takes novice and experienced riders. Rides leave on the hour, but it's suggested you call ahead or arrive 20 minutes early to secure a spot.

Organized Tours

Celebrity Tours About the best way to pick up on the gossip and glamour of Palm Springs is to take a trip with **Celebrity Tours** (☎ 760-770-2700), based at **Rimrock Plaza Shopping Center** (4751 E Palm Canyon Dr). You can do it yourself with a map of the stars' homes from the visitor center ($5.50), but you'll miss out on the amusing commentary and all the juicy gossip. The tours run October to May and cost $17 for an hour, and $23 for the deluxe, 2½ -hour run.

Desert Adventures This very professional operation (☎ 760-324-5337, 888-440-5337) runs guided **jeep tours** to the Indian Canyons, Santa Rosa Mountains, around the Bighorn Sheep Preserve and to other areas that can be hard to get to, even with your own 4WD. The guides/drivers are full of information about the natural environment and Indian lore. Tours cost about $30/75 per hour/half-day.

PS Modern Tours Palm Springs has been an architectural playground since people with money started coming here in the 1920s. Its modern and international-style buildings are becoming increasingly recognized as these two movements take their place *en vogue*. This tour (☎ 760-318-6118, W eps moderntours@aol.com) covers the 1920s to the '70s but pays special attention to the '50s and '60s, when architects such as Frey, Neutra and John Lautner were on the scene. Tour groups leave from downtown Palm Springs at 9:30am and 1:30pm for a 1½-hour ($40) or 2½-hour ($55) tour, which takes in the downtown area and then visits outlying areas by van.

San Andreas Fault Tours People rave about this three-hour tour (☎ 760-322-6029; 11am Mon & Wed, 9am Tues & Thur), which covers 100mi of the San Andreas Fault and costs $25. The tour van makes stops at places of interest, and the guides do an excellent job of interpreting this active fault which is responsible for most of California's earthquakes. Reservations are required.

Sky Watcher Sky Gazing Tours There is really no better place to see the stars than the desert. On Friday and Saturday night from 8pm to 10pm, Sky Watcher Star Gazing Tours (☎ 760-345-2363) holds free 'tours' of the sky at **La Quinta Resort** (☎ 760-564-4111) in La Quinta. Staff have telescopes and binoculars to use and tell stories based on Native American tradition. It's a great way to spend a few hours.

Special Events
There are large-purse, celebrity golf tournaments each month here, and an excellent Dixieland Jazz Festival in March.

Every Thursday from 6pm to 10pm the downtown blocks of N Palm Canyon Dr are closed to traffic for **Villagefest** – a certified farmers market that is joined by musicians, food vendors and purveyors of art and handicrafts.

On the last weekend in April, Indio's Empire Polo Club hosts the **Coachella Music & Arts Festival** (☎ 310-788-7060 for information; tickets around $75 per day), one of the hottest two-day music festivals of its kind. Artists range from indie pop no-names to DJs Sasha & Digweed to pop idols such as Björk. For respite during the noon-to-

midnight event, people play with interactive sculpture and watch films in plastic blow-up lounge chairs.

Places to Stay
Many of the accommodations in Coachella Valley are expensive resort-style hotels. The sheer number of rooms here, however, means that there are some great bargains to be had, notably at small, independent places. You'll find many 'inns' and 'lodges' since the word 'motel' seems to have a bad connotation around here. Air-con rooms, cable TV and swimming pools are the norm. Peak season is December to March, low season is mid-May to the end of August. Taxes add another 10% to these prices.

Camping There are several Recreational Vehicle (RV) parks, but only one place for tent camping.

Lake Cahuilla County Park (☎ 760-564-4712 for reservations; sites $10-15) is 4mi south of La Quinta at the western end of 58th Ave. It has 85 tent and 65 RV sites, showers and picnic facilities. Reservations are recommended in the winter holiday season.

Better spots for camping are Joshua Tree National Park (see that section later in this chapter), which is only an hour away by car, and San Jacinto Wilderness State Park, which has primitive sites, at the top of the aerial tramway (see Palm Springs Aerial Tramway earlier in this chapter).

Inns & Hotels Iron Tree Inn (☎ 760-325-8237, 877-696-9668; 1600 Calle Palo Fierro; rooms from $50; closed 15 June–15 Sept) looks a bit dumpy from the outside, but each room is decorated in light Southwest tones and has a microwave and refrigerator. Its location, south of downtown Palm Springs off East Palm Canyon Dr, is quiet but central.

Alpine Gardens Hotel (☎ 760-323-2231, 888-299-7455; W www.alpinegardens.com; 1586 E Palm Canyon Dr; rooms from $60, $20 less in summer) is in the same neighborhood as the Iron Tree Inn. It's got cozy rooms, floral decorations, a spa and lots of garden space.

Palm Tee Hotel (☎ 760-327-1293, 888-757-7657; W www.palmteehotel.com; rooms from $75, $25 less in summer), across the street from Alpine Gardens, has a bigger pool but not as much landscaping. Its rooms are uninteresting but have a refrigerator and microwave, and rates include a light breakfast.

A bit more money will get you within walking distance to all of the action in the heart of Palm Springs.

Casa Cody (☎ 760-320-9346, fax 760-325-8610; 175 S Cahuilla Rd; rooms from $69, $20 less in summer) is the best value in this area. It has individual, pueblo-like bungalows set amid lush greenery, grills for guests to use and a complimentary breakfast. One drawback might be its two pools, which are quite small and exceedingly quiet.

The Chase (☎ 760-320-8866, 877-532-4273; w www.chasehotelpalmsprings.com; 200 W Arenas Rd; rooms from $59/79/89 summer/Sept-Dec & March–mid-May/winter, $10 more Fri & Sat) is another good choice. It's got a big pool, shuffleboard court, spacious lobby stocked with fruit and magazines, and standard motel-style rooms.

Estrella (☎ 760-320-4117, 800-237-3687; w www.estrellapalmsprings.com; 415 S Belardo Rd; rooms midweek/weekend from $99/119) is a 'sexy' property where modernism meets historic Palm Springs aesthetic. Its rooms' decor is black and white with touches of bold color, the bed and bath linens are superior to most, and two of three pools are 'adult only.'

Resorts A modernist's mecca north of Palm Springs, **Hope Springs Resort** (☎ 760-329-4003; w www.hopespringsresort.com; 68075 Club Circle Dr; rooms from $150) has 10 impeccably stylish rooms, nice views, complimentary breakfast and a natural hot spring that flows through three pools.

Marriott's Desert Springs Resort & Spa (☎ 760-341-2211, 800-331-3112, fax 760-341-1872; 74855 Country Club Dr; rooms & suites $235-2100 Sept-June, large discounts rest of year), in Palm Desert, is perhaps the most over-the-top resort in the valley. Rooms have all modern amenities, the grounds have golf, tennis and various spa facilities, and there are small boats to take you across an artificial lake to the restaurant.

Merv Griffin's Resort Hotel & Givenchy Spa (☎ 760-770-5000, 800-276-5000, fax 760-324-6104; w www.palmsprings.com/merv; 68-900 Frank Sinatra Dr; rooms from $220), near downtown Palm Springs,

has 14 acres and enough French decor to choke even Louis XIV. The price includes transportation to/from the airport and unlimited use of the spa and fitness facilities (which otherwise cost $40 per day), making it a *relative* bargain.

Gay Lodgings There are an increasing number of places that cater expressly to gay and lesbian clientele.

Queen of Hearts (☎ 760-322-5793, 888-275-9903, fax 322-5795; 435 Avenida Olancha; rooms from $110) used to be called the Desert Knight, Palm Springs' first gay-only resort which opened in 1960. Now it's exclusively for women, with lovely rooms (most with kitchens) and robes, a sparkling (as in carbonated) pool and complimentary breakfast.

Terrazzo (☎ 866-837-7996; w www.terrazzo-ps.com; 1600 E Palm Canyon Dr; rooms $105/125 summer/winter) is a men-only place that feeds its guests breakfast and lunch (and afternoon cookies), has a microwave, refrigerator and VCR in each room and a small fitness room to work off all the indulgence.

Inn Exile (☎ 760-327-6413, 800-962-0186; w www.innexile.com; 545 Warm Sands Dr; rooms $87-140 year-round) is another private men's inn where 'clothing is always optional' and guests are fed breakfast, lunch and evening cocktails on the house. It has four pools, two spas, a billiards room and lovely landscaping.

Places to Eat

Most restaurants on Palm Canyon Dr, in downtown Palm Springs, are tourist-focused and overpriced. For really good value and local color, step off the beaten track (even just a block or two). On Palm Desert's El Paseo you'll get more for your money than along Palm Canyon Dr but still have the opportunity to stroll and scope out menus. Outdoor eating areas are sometimes sprayed with a fine mist of water to keep them cool, which is a nice touch.

Las Casuelas Terraza (☎ 760-325-2794; 222 S Palm Canyon Dr; mains $7-12), one of the oldest and most vivacious places on Palm Canyon Dr, is worth going to if people-watching and a margarita sound good.

For more authentic Mexican food go south to **El Mirasol** (☎ 760-323-0721; 140 E

Palm Canyon Dr; mains $8-12). The menu is small but the food is excellent and the ambience is friendly and casual. Nearby **Churchill's Fish & Chips** (☎ 760-325-3716; *665 S Palm Canyon Dr, mains around $7.50)* has a British pub atmosphere and serves jolly good fish and chips for $7.50. It also has shrimp, scallops and clams, as well as Guinness on tap for $2.75.

Fisherman's Market & Grill (☎ 760-327-1766; *235 S Palm Canyon Dr; most meals around $7)* is a block away from the bustle of Palm Canyon Dr in Palm Springs. It grills fresh fish or shellfish, which is served as a salad, sandwich, taco or with coleslaw and rice. Beer is a mere $2.50 and the key lime cheesecake gets rave reviews.

Thai Smile (☎ 760-341-6565; *42-467 Bob Hope Dr; lunch around $6, mains around $5-13)*, in Rancho Mirage, is in a shopping plaza next to the River shopping mall, but you'd never know that from inside. Modern Thai decor and flavorful food, which ranges from standards like pad thai to inventions like grilled eggplant salad, make this place worth seeking out.

Keedy's (☎ 760-346-6492; *73-633 Hwy 111; breakfast & lunch under $5)*, in Palm Desert, serves cheap breakfasts and lunches. The place is old and the ingredients are far from organic, but the eggs, pancakes, hamburgers and milkshakes here are icons of the all-American meal.

There's no shortage of fine dining in the valley. For a casual but elegant and very reasonably priced high-end meal, try **Johannes** (☎ 760-778-0017; *196 S Indian Canyon Dr; mains $11-26)* in Palm Springs. Its dishes are inventive but not fussy, and all ingredients are of the best quality.

Entertainment

Cruising Palm Canyon Dr, downtown Palm Springs, on foot is pretty entertaining on most nights; the warm air and minimal need for clothing make people uncommonly jovial. Stop for a drink at the Jetsons-inspired **Muriel's Supper Club** (☎ 760-325-8839; *210 S Palm Canyon Dr)* or, if it's after 9pm, pay the $10 cover charge to see its live music and dance performance.

A few doors down, the **Village Pub** (☎ 760-323-3265; *262 S Palm Canyon Dr)* is a casual place, with live music, darts and good beer on tap.

A swinging gay and lesbian venue is **Toucans** (☎ 760-416-7584; *2100 N Palm Canyon Dr)*, which has a 'sarongs optional' policy, lots of tropical froufrou and umbrellas in every drink.

Arenas Rd runs perpendicular to Palm Canyon Dr, and two blocks east of their intersection is a concentration of gay and lesbian hangouts. **Hunter's Video Bar** (☎ 760-323-0700; *302 E Arenas Rd)* has a mostly male clientele, lots of TV screens and a fun dance scene. **Rainbow Cactus Café** (☎ 760-325-3868; *cnr Arenas Rd & Indian Canyon Dr)* is a nice lunch/dinner restaurant, with a lively piano bar.

Legal gambling is possible just a few blocks from Palm Canyon Dr, at the **Spa Resort Casino** (☎ 800-258-2946; *100 N Indian Canyon Dr)* – the casino entrance is at 140 N Indian Canyon Dr.

Sunday afternoon jazz is a standard at **Melvyn's** (☎ 760-325-0046; *200 W Ramon Rd)*, in Inngleside Inn. Anyone can join in and there's no cover charge.

The historic **Plaza Theater** (☎ 760-327-0225; **w** www.psfollies.com; *128 S Palm Canyon Dr)*, dating from 1936, hosts a Ziegfeld Follies-style review that includes music, dancing, showgirls and comedy. The twist is that many of the performers are as old as the theater – all are over 50, some up to 80. But this is not the amateur hour. Palm Springs can pull some big names out of its celebrity closet, and the show has been known to feature such stars as Bing Crosby, Doris Day and Jack Benny. At $35 to $70, tickets aren't cheap, but the cast from the past can turn in a great performance. There are evening shows and matinees from November to May; reservations are recommended.

Shopping

Browsing is best on Palm Canyon Dr, in Palm Springs, and El Paseo in Palm Desert. There are quite a few art galleries and antique stores, but unless you have a megabudget, you'll be looking more than buying.

J Behman Gallery (☎ 760-320-6806; *1000 N Palm Canyon Dr)* is part of the main art school in Palm Springs. The work they show tends to be contemporary, though classical pieces sneak in every once in awhile.

Adagio Galleries (☎ 800-288-2230; *193 S Palm Canyon Dr)* in the Village Pub exhibits and sells the work of prominent Southwest artists such as John Nieto and Frank Howell.

Reflections of... (☎ 760-323-3882; 285 S Palm Canyon Dr) has an extensive and whimsical glass art collection that they claim is one of the largest in the USA.

River (71800 Hwy 111) has a number of upscale stores, restaurants and a big movie complex. Lots of stores in downtown Palm Springs sell 'resort wear,' a typical Palm Springs purchase. Another local specialty is dates – the Coachella Valley produces 90% of the US supply.

Getting There & Around

Palm Springs International Airport (☎ 760-318-3800; w www.palmspringsairport.com) is served by Alaska Airlines, American Airlines, America West, American Eagle, Delta Air Lines/SkyWest, Horizon Air and, in winter, Northwest Airlines, Continental Airlines and a Canadian charter carrier, **Canada 3000** (☎ 877-658-3000).

Unless your hotel offers airport transfers, the best option is to take a shuttle or taxi; figure about $12 per person. Reputable companies include **At Your Service** (☎ 760-343-0666, 888-700-7888) and **Prime Time Shuttle** (☎ 760-341-2221).

Greyhound (☎ 760-325-2053; 311 N Indian Canyon Dr; open 8am-6pm daily) has nine buses to LA ($17.25, around three hours) between 6am and 11pm daily (buy your ticket on the bus when the station is closed). Amtrak buses leave from a bus shelter in front of the Palm Springs International Airport and go to Bakersfield, Fresno, Oakland and Stockton. Buy your tickets on board.

Sunline (☎ 760-343-3451), the local bus service, is described by a reader as 'lethargic and unpredictable,' which is basically true. It does, however, service most of the valley from about 6am to 10pm, and the air-conditioned buses are clean and comfortable. Line 111 follows Hwy 111 between Palm Springs and Indio (about 1½ hours). You can transfer to other lines that loop through the various communities. The standard fare is 75¢ (exact change required), plus 25¢ for a transfer. All the buses have wheelchair lifts and a rack for two bicycles.

I-10 from LA (about a two-hour drive) is the main route into and through the Coachella Valley, but Hwy 74, the Palms to Pines Hwy, is the more scenic route and worth a detour.

Car rental companies include **Alamo** (☎ 760-778-6271, 800-327-9633), **Avis** (☎ 760-778-6300, 800-331-1212), **Dollar** (☎ 760-325-7333, 800-800-4000), **Enterprise** (☎ 760-778-0054, 800-325-8007) and **Hertz** (☎ 760-778-5100, 800-654-3131).

Ace Taxi (☎ 760-835-2445) provides 24-hour taxi service. **Palm Springs Taxi** (☎ 760-323-5100) and **American Cab** (☎ 760-775-1477) are also good companies.

Joshua Tree National Park

Joshua Tree National Park straddles the transition zone between the Colorado Desert and the higher, cooler Mojave Desert. The latter supports its distinctive Joshua trees which look like something out of a Dr Seuss book. Wonderfully shaped rock outcroppings (mostly of quartz monzonite) are popular with rock climbers who generally consider 'J-Tree' the best place to climb in California. Backpackers are less enthusiastic about the park since there is no natural water flow, but day hikers and campers enjoy the array of subtle desert colors and the chance to scramble around on big boulders.

The most whimsically dramatic conglomeration of rocks is in the locally called 'Wonderland of Rocks' area, while the biggest trees are near Covington Flats. To see the transition from the high Colorado Desert/Sonora Desert to the low Mojave, drive along the Pinto Basin Rd, which drops from the Twentynine Palms area into the Pinto Basin.

Those who enjoy history and local lore should take a tour of the **Desert Queen Ranch** (☎ 760-367-5555 for reservations; tours 8:30am, 10:30am, 1pm & 3pm daily Sept-Mar, also 5pm April-May, 8:30am & 7pm only June-Aug, adult/concession $5/2), around 12mi northeast of Hidden Valley Campground on a dirt road. Russian immigrant William Keys built a homestead on 160 acres here in 1917 and over the next 60 years established a full working ranch, school, store and workshop which still stand pretty much as they did when Keys died in 1969.

Information

The park headquarters is at the **Oasis Visitor Center** (☎ 760-367-5500; W www.nps .gov/jotr; National Monument Dr; open 8am-5pm daily, 8am-6pm winter) in Twentynine Palms, just outside the park's northern boundary. It has useful information, books and maps. The Oasis of Mara, behind the visitor center, has the original 29 palm trees for which the town is named. The Pinto Mountain Fault (a small relative of the San Andreas Fault) runs through the oasis, which is believed to be charged with psychic energy.

The smaller **Cottonwood Visitor Center** (open 8am-4pm daily) is a few miles inside the park's southern entrance. Vehicle entry, good for seven days, costs $10; walkers and cyclists are charged $5. For emergency assistance, call ☎ 909-383-5651.

Hiking

You really need to get away from your car to appreciate Joshua Tree's funky lunar landscapes and intriguing details. The visitor centers will give you maps and advice about the various short, marked trails that focus on different features of the park, including **Fortynine Palms Oasis**; **Hidden Valley**; **Lost Horse Mine**; **Keys View** and **Inspiration Point**; **Ryan Mountain**; **Cholla Cactus Garden**; and **Lost Palm Oasis**. The 1.7mi **Skull Rock Loop** is an easy, well-marked trail with interpretive panels along the way.

Longer hikes are possible, but are a real challenge because of the need to carry water: at least two gallons per person per day. Anyone going on an overnight hike into the backcountry must fill out a registration card (to aid in census-taking and rescue efforts) and deposit the stub at one of 12 backcountry boards in parking lots throughout the park. Cars left overnight not identified on a registration card may be cited or towed away.

The well-traveled, 16mi **Boy Scout Trail**, on the western side of the park, starts from either the Indian Cove or Keys West backcountry board.

Rock Climbing

From boulders to cracks to multi-pitch faces, there are possibly more routes here than anywhere else in the USA. The longest climbs are not much more than 100ft or so, but there are many challenging technical routes, and most can be easily top-roped for training. Some of the most popular climbs are in the **Hidden Valley** area.

A specialized climbing book, such as *Joshua Tree Rock Climbing Guide* by Randy Vogel, is a must. The kind folks at Coyote Corner, in the town of Joshua Tree, (see later in this section) have climbing books and route diaries that you can thumb through or buy.

For a day of instruction or guiding, contact **Uprising Adventure Guides** (☎ 760-320-6630, 888-254-6266; W www.uprising .com). **Nomad Ventures** (☎ 760-366-4684; cnr Twentynine Palms Hwy & Park Blvd; open 8am-6pm daily, later Sat & Sun winter), in the town of Joshua Tree, is an excellent climbing store.

Biking

Joshua Tree National Park is popular for biking, though bicycles must stay on the roads and trails. A mountain bike or, at minimum, a road bike with fat, knobby tires, is necessary for the many unpaved roads.

Two favorite bicycle routes are the challenging **Pinkham Canyon Rd**, which begins at the Cottonwood Visitor Center, and the **Old Dale Rd**, which starts 6½mi north of there. The **Queen Valley Rds** network is a more gentle set of trails and has bike racks along the way so people can lock up their bikes and go hiking.

Bikes are a great form of transportation out here: hop on your two-wheel steed to get from your campground to any destination and you'll have gorgeous scenery along the way.

Places to Stay

There are nine campgrounds in the park. **Black Rock Canyon** (☎ 800-365-2267; sites $10) and **Indian Cove** (☎ 800-365-2267; sites $10) have sites that must be reserved; campsites at **Hidden Valley**, **Ryan**, **Sheep Pass**, **Jumbo Rocks**, **Belle**, **White Tank** and **Cottonwood** are available on a first-come, first-served basis only. At busy times, during spring and fall, find a site before noon and stake your claim. Water is available at Black Rock Canyon and Cottonwood campgrounds, and close to Indian Cove. Only the three campgrounds with water cost money (sites $10). The other campgrounds are free and have pit toilets, tables and fireplaces, but you have to bring your own water. Jumbo Rocks is especially attractive for its

CALIFORNIA DESERTS

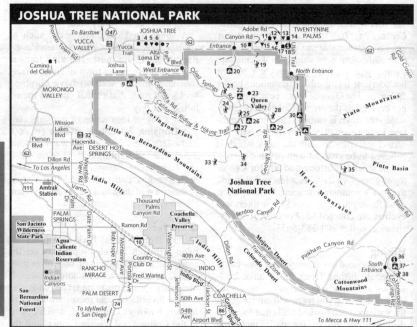

JOSHUA TREE NATIONAL PARK

sheltered rock alcoves that act as perfect sunset/sunrise-viewing platforms.

Backcountry camping is permitted but not less than a mile from the nearest road, or 500ft from the nearest trail, and not in any wash or day-use area. Fires are not permitted anywhere.

AROUND JOSHUA TREE NATIONAL PARK

None of the towns around the park are particularly charming, but they do the trick if you want a motel and a bite to eat. The drive to/from Palm Springs is just over an hour, so people that aren't interested in camping often come to the area on a day trip.

Twentynine Palms

Right by the northern entrance to the national park, Twentynine Palms (population 15,348; elevation 3242ft) is a service town for the park and the nearby Marine Corps Combat Training Center (don't freak out if you hear loud noises every once in awhile). Most of the town is a sprawl, spread along 29 Palms Hwy. Where the highway crosses Adobe Rd is a sort of downtown. Though not particularly attractive, the town has enough inspirational scenery to have inspired the writing and recording of U2's *The Joshua Tree* album (at the Harmony Motel; see later) and keep artist Edward Ruscha, who lives here in relative seclusion, entertained.

Places to Stay & Eat Twentynine Palms has the biggest selection of accommodations near the national park.

Harmony Motel (☎ 760-367-3351; 71161 29 Palms Hwy; singles/doubles $40/46) is a peaceful spot on the western edge of town. It has a small pool, large rooms (several with kitchens), and nice places for sitting or meditating, a favorite pastime of the owner.

Rancho Dolores Motel (☎ 760-367-3528; 73352 29 Palms Hwy; rooms from $55) is a bit more typical for a motel in these parts, with Spanish-style decor, a large pool and rooms with cable TV.

Sunset Motel (☎ 760-367-3484; 73842 29 Palms Hwy; rooms $36) is small and a bit run-down, but generally clean and friendly.

Twentynine Palms Inn (☎ 760-367-3505; 73950 Inn Ave; cabins about $85 midweek

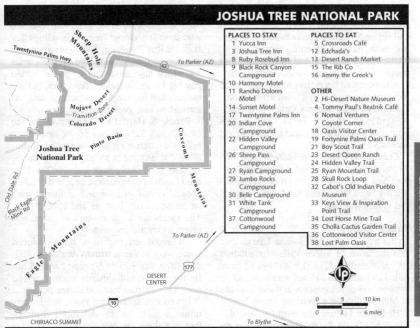

JOSHUA TREE NATIONAL PARK

PLACES TO STAY	PLACES TO EAT
1 Yucca Inn	5 Crossroads Café
3 Joshua Tree Inn	12 Edchada's
8 Ruby Rosebud Inn	13 Desert Ranch Market
9 Black Rock Canyon Campground	15 The Rib Co
10 Harmony Motel	16 Jimmy the Greek's
11 Rancho Dolores Motel	**OTHER**
14 Sunset Motel	2 Hi-Desert Nature Museum
17 Twentynine Palms Inn	4 Tommy Paul's Beatnik Café
20 Indian Cove Campground	6 Nomad Ventures
22 Hidden Valley Campground	7 Coyote Corner
26 Sheep Pass Campground	18 Oasis Visitor Center
27 Ryan Campground	19 Fortynine Palms Oasis Trail
29 Jumbo Rocks Campground	21 Boy Scout Trail
30 Belle Campground	23 Desert Queen Ranch
31 White Tank Campground	24 Hidden Valley Trail
37 Cottonwood Campground	25 Ryan Mountain Trail
	28 Skull Rock Loop
	32 Cabot's Old Indian Pueblo Museum
	33 Keys View & Inspiration Point Trail
	34 Lost Horse Mine Trail
	35 Cholla Cactus Garden Trail
	36 Cottonwood Visitor Center
	38 Lost Palm Oasis

CALIFORNIA DESERTS

low season, from $135 Fri-Sun high season), built on and around the Oasis of Mara, is the most interesting place to stay. The inn has a variety of old adobe-and-wood cabins with names such as Ghost Flower and Hedge Needle.

Desert Ranch Market (cnr 29 Palms Hwy & Adobe Rd; open 7am-10pm daily) has a full selection of produce.

Jimmy the Greek's (☎ 760-367-3456; 73501 29 Palms Hwy; open 7am-6pm Mon-Thur, 7am-9pm Fri, 7am-4pm Sat; dishes $4-10), across the highway, is the locals' call for hot and cold sandwiches and daily specials such as eggplant parmesan or fish and chips.

Edchada's (☎ 760-367-2131; 73502 29 Palms Hwy; open 11am-9pm daily; meals $6-11), nearby, serves big plates of authentic Mexican food and makes good margaritas.

The Rib Co (☎ 760-365-1663; 72183 29 Palms Hwy; mains $7-15; 11:30am-9pm Sun-Thur, 11:30am-10pm Fri & Sat), which also has a location in Yucca Valley, has excellent barbecue sandwiches, burgers, chicken and ribs, plus salads and a few veggie items.

Joshua Tree

The town of Joshua Tree (population 3898; elevation 2728ft), where the access road to the western entrance of the national park branches off Hwy 62, has the most soul of any town near the park. The reason (or result) is that it attracts climbers who stop at **Nomad Ventures** (cnr 29 Palms Hwy & Park Blvd), a well-stocked climbing store, and **Coyote Corner** (cnr 29 Palms Hwy & Park Blvd), purveyor of climbing gear, literature, essential oils, hats and friendly advice.

Joshua Tree Inn (☎ 760-366-1188, 800-366-1444; 61259 29 Palms Hwy; rooms & cottages $75-125) has lots of character and new rooms, and rates include a free breakfast.

For an out-of-the-way respite, call **Ruby Rosebud Inn** (☎ 760-366-4676; w www.rosebudrubystar.com; rooms $155, cabin from $170), which has two guest rooms and a cabin that sleeps up to eight people.

Mohave Rock Ranch (☎ 760-366-8455; w www.mojaverockranch.com; cabins from $185) has lovely fully equipped cabins that are worth considering if you plan to stay in the area for a while. The ranch was constructed completely from local materials (including recycled relics of the past – rocks, fossils, wagon wheels, shells, bones) and set on 55 acres. The two-bedroom cabins each have a sleeping porch, patio, kitchen and bathroom, and sleep one to four people. Call the ranch for directions.

Microbrewed beers, live music and vegan food are also part of this town's attraction.

Tommy Paul's Beatnik Cafe (☎ 760-366-2090; 61597 29 Palms Hwy), is the town's primary coffeehouse; it also offers Internet access $2 per 15 minutes.

Crossroads Café (☎ 760-366-5414; 61715 29 Palms Hwy; dishes under $8; open 7am-9pm Sun-Thur, 7am-11pm Fri & Sat) serves healthy breakfasts, huge sandwiches, salads and dinner specials.

Yucca Valley

To the west, the town of Joshua Tree merges into the town of Yucca Valley (population 19,800; elevation 3279ft), with Hwy 62 (here called 29 Palms Hwy) lined with unattractive commercial developments and the Institute of Mental Physics, a 'spiritual center.'

Hi-Desert Nature Museum (☎ 760-369-7212; 57116 29 Palms Hwy; donation requested; open 10am-5pm Tues-Sun) has a few interesting exhibits on desert flora and fauna – the spring wildflower displays can be good and the scorpions are impressive.

Along or near 29 Palms Hwy you'll find numerous chain motels, supermarkets and fast-food outlets.

Yucca Inn (☎ 760-365-3311, fax 760-228-1509, 800-989-7644; W www.desertgold.com; 7500 Camino del Cielo; singles/doubles $50/60), well-marked off Twentynine Palms Hwy at the western edge of town, offers large rooms, a pool and free breakfast.

Pioneer Town

From the town of Yucca Valley, take the Pioneer Town Rd north 7mi from Hwy 62 and you'll drive straight into the past. Pioneer Town was built as a movie backdrop by Roy Rogers, Dale Evans, Gene Autry and a few other of Hollywood's big time Western folk in 1946 and has hardly changed since. The idea was that actors would have homes here, become part of the set and really live the Wild West life they acted out. The main street (Mane St) is lined with buildings that were used in countless Western movies and TV shows, including *Gunfight at the OK Corral*.

Pioneer Bowl (☎ 760-365-3615; open 4pm-9:30pm Mon-Wed, 11am-late Fri & Sat, 7am-9pm Sun, closed Thur) – a bowling alley built for Roy Rogers in 1947 – is still in use, with original equipment and arcade games for which any good antique hound would pay big bucks. Its saloon sells beer, buffalo burgers and ice-cream concoctions, and has interesting memorabilia strewn about.

Pappy & Harriet's Pioneertown Palace (☎ 760-365-5956; meals $6-15; open from 5pm Thur, 10am Fri-Sun) is a great destination for anyone who enjoys live blues, cowboy hats, cheap beer and *real* Tex-Mex food (such as pinto beans, beef and chicken cooked over mesquite and slathered with barbecue sauce), burgers and cheese fries. The meals are large enough to share, and reservations are recommended.

To avoid driving in a binge-induced coma, stay at **Pioneertown Motel** (☎ 760-365-4879, fax 365-3127; rooms from $38). Its rooms are individually decorated and each has a refrigerator and coffee pot.

If you can spend a bit more, head a few minutes north to the delightful **Rimrock Ranch Cabins** (☎ 760-228-1297, fax 818-956-0268; 50857 Burns Canyon Rd; cabins from $75, 2-night minimum), where time slows down and tensions melt away. Built in the 1940s as the area's first homestead, its four lovingly decorated cabins are a Southern California insider hideaway. Each comes with a full kitchen, TV & VCR (free videos) and a private patio perfect for stargazing.

Chiriaco Summit & General Patton Memorial Museum

Chiriaco Summit is primarily a highway stop with a **motel** (standard rooms $35) and a **diner** (try its 'Desert Training Center Burger' made with Spam, $5.50). It was once important, however, as the 'town' nearest the Desert Training Center, established by General Patton to prepare US troops for the North African campaign in WWII.

The General Patton Memorial Museum (☎ 760-227-3483; admission $5; open 9:30am-4:30pm) has a very thorough exhibit about the career of General George S 'Blood 'n' Guts' Patton, who said of the harsh desert environment that 'if you can work in this country, it will be no difficulty at all to kill the assorted sons of bitches you will meet in any other country.'

Outside the museum is an interesting non-military exhibit, **The Big Map** *(museum admission $3; open 9am-5pm daily)*, a 5½-ton relief map of Southern California, which was used to plan the 242mi aqueduct that brings water from the Colorado River to LA. The old tanks outside can be seen for free.

The Low Desert

The rich agricultural district of the Imperial Valley is a monument to vision and pioneering enterprise, but only those with an interest in irrigation and agribusiness, odd Americana culture or vast expanses of nothingness will find much to see.

The Salton Sea looks intriguing on a map but is uninspiring in reality, though it does attract many water bird species. The most interesting parts for desert lovers are the remote Algodones Dunes, where thousands of people spend the whole winter in colonies of motor homes – a bizarre sight. Calexico, on the border of California and Mexico (get it?), is a good alternative to Tijuana when crossing into Baja California.

IMPERIAL VALLEY

The soil of the Imperial Valley is rich in alluvial deposits from the ancient course of the Colorado River, and its agricultural potential was recognized as early as the 1850s. Because the area is actually below sea level, water flowing down the Colorado River to the Gulf of Mexico was able to be channeled via the Alamo watercourse, through Mexican territory, then back north into the Imperial Valley. This ambitious plan was realized by CR Rockwood, George Chaffey and their California Development Company, and was bankrolled by the sale of water rights to local water companies. The first water flowed in 1901. By 1905 the valley had 67,000 acres irrigated and a population of 12,000. An agreement with the Mexican government in 1904 stipulated that half the diverted water be supplied to Mexico, where much of it was used to grow cotton in the Mexicali Valley by a US company using imported Chinese laborers.

In 1905, the Colorado River flooded, its water flowing uncontrolled through the canals and into the Imperial Valley. The disaster provided impetus for a more effective and centralized water management system.

Local water companies amalgamated to form the Imperial Irrigation District (IID), which initiated US congressional support for large-scale management of the Colorado River. This resulted in the construction of the 80mi-long All-American Canal, which diverts water from the Colorado River at the Imperial Dam and carries it to Calexico, without passing through Mexico, as did the Inter-California Canal that it replaced.

IID water now irrigates more than 500,000 acres. An orderly patchwork of fields produces cattle feed, cotton, tomatoes, sugar beets, melons, strawberries, lettuce and other crops. Some fruits and vegetables are grown in winter to take advantage of higher out-of-season prices. An interesting environmental discussion about agriculture in the Imperial Valley is found in Marc Reisner's *Cadillac Desert: The American West and Its Disappearing Water*.

There are just a few places of interest.

El Centro

Hub and county seat of the Imperial Valley, El Centro (population 24,500) has a moderately imposing courthouse, several shopping centers and the standard array of fast-food restaurants.

Pioneers Park Museum *(☎ 760-352-1165; 373 E Aten Rd; admission $4; open 10am-4pm Tues-Sun)*, at the corner of Hwy 111, is a cut above the average local historical society effort and is well worth a stop. It tells the story of irrigation, inundation and immigration in the Imperial Valley. Particularly interesting are exhibits on a dozen different ethnic groups who settled the valley in the early 20th century.

A number of inexpensive motels can be found near the Hwy 86/4th St exit from I-8. **E-Z 8 Motel** *(☎ 760-352-6431; 455 Wake Ave; singles/doubles $35/43)* is south of I-8. It has typical motel rooms surrounding a parking lot.

Brunner's Motel *(☎ 760-352-6431; 215 N Imperial Ave; rooms from $83)* has a variety of room configurations, all of a high standard. Rates include a full breakfast in the coffee shop.

Salton Sea

The largest lake in California, the Salton Sea is surprisingly unattractive. The only real reason to visit is for bird-watching: migratory

The Salton Sea

In 1905 the Colorado River flooded and overflowed into irrigation channels, nearly inundating the entirety of the Imperial Valley. It took 18 months, 1500 workers, $12 million and half a million tons of rock to put the Colorado River back on its course to the Gulf of Mexico. As a result the previously dry Salton Sink became a lake, 45mi long and 17mi wide. It had no natural outlet and, as evaporation reduced its size, the natural salt levels became more concentrated. The Salton became an inland sea, with its surface actually 228ft below the level of the sea in the Gulf of California and its water over 1½ times as salty.

and endangered birds that stop here include snow geese, mallard, brown pelicans, bald eagles and peregrine falcons. The **Sonny Bono Salton Sea National Wildlife Refuge** (☎ 760-348-5278; 906 W Sinclair Rd; open 7am-3:30pm Mon-Fri) is off Hwy 111 between Niland and Calipatria.

Fishing is popular, though not recommended because of the high concentration of selenium in the fish. There are three boat-launching ramps, and small boats may be launched anywhere round the shoreline.

Swimming is not pleasant – the water is murky with plankton and the salt stings the eyes – nor is it recommended at the southern end of the sea because of pollution.

Due to its warm climate, 'snowbirds' – people from cold climates who migrate to warm environments for the winter – tend to like the area. Most of them congregate in Slab City, south of I-10 and east of Niland, which becomes a veritable urban RV-scape from November to May. One eccentric site worth turning off Hwy 111 to see is **Salvation Mountain**, a 100ft-high hill constructed of concrete and hand-mixed adobe and covered with brightly colored Christian declarations. It's the continual life work of Leonard Knight who has been living behind his mountain and refreshing its acrylic cloak daily, since 1985. Turn east off the highway at Niland and you can't miss it.

If you do want to stay overnight, the Salton Sea State Recreation Area has several undeveloped **campgrounds** (tent/hookup sites $7/19). **Bombay Beach Campground**, south of the visitor center on the eastern shore, is the best of these. Sites are distributed on a first-come first-served basis. The 'beach' here was formed by sinking old vehicles – including buses – into the mud of the Salton Sea. The idea was to create cavernous formations that would grow marsh plant life and help support the birdlife here. If it's going to work at all, it's got a long way to go.

Algodones Dunes

Up to 300ft high, these sand dunes along the eastern edge of the Imperial Valley were once beaches on Lake Cahuilla. The shifting sands were an obstacle for early European explorers and the builders of canals and roads.

When the dunes buried the first trails between the Imperial Valley and Yuma, a wooden road was tried. Sections of heavy timber planks, bound together with steel straps, formed the road's surface. When sand covered a section, it could be dragged to a new position by a mule team. The 'plank road,' continually being moved with the dunes, provided the only link across this strip of desert from 1916 to 1926 when a surfaced highway was built. Remnants of the plank road may be seen from Grays Well Rd, south of I-8, and there's a section in the Pioneer Park Museum near El Centro.

Much of the dunes area is open to 4WD vehicles, but there's also a designated wilderness area near Glamis. If you want to see some undisturbed dune country, try the **Imperial Sand Dunes National Natural Landmark**, north of Hwy 78 and west of Glamis. It's a preserve for desert plants and animals, closed to vehicles but open for walkers.

For a good view of the area, head for the **Osbourne Overlook**, off Hwy 78 about 4mi west of Glamis. For hiking, head north from Glamis on Ted Kips Rd (at the Glamis Store, immediately west of the railroad tracks) and go 2mi to the BLM Watchable Wildlife Area.

The **El Centro Field Office** (☎ 760-337-4400; 1661 S 4th St; open 8am-4pm Mon-Fri), in El Centro, and the **Cahuilla Ranger Station & Visitor Center** (☎ 760-344-3919; Gecko Rd; open 10am-4pm Fri-Sun Sept-May) in Cahuilla, south of Hwy 78, have maps and information. Phones, food and gas are available in Glamis on Hwy 78. Otherwise, there are virtually no facilities at all between the Imperial Valley and the Colorado River.

Places to Stay

The BLM operates free camping at Midway, Gecko and Roadrunner Campgrounds. All three have toilets, but no water or other facilities. You can camp anywhere on undeveloped public land for up to 14 days. Long-term visitor areas (LTVAs) have been established for those who spend the whole winter in motor homes in undeveloped desert areas.

Anza-Borrego Desert

This desert – which contains the 600,000-acre Anza-Borrego Desert State Park – has some of the most spectacular and accessible desert scenery you'll find anywhere. The human history goes back 10,000 years, recorded in ancient Native American pictographs. Spanish explorer Juan Bautista de Anza passed through in 1774, pioneering an immigrant trail from Mexico. The Southern Emigrant Trail was established by Pedro Fages in 1782, used as the mail route to Mexico from 1826 and then traveled by General Kearny and his troops to secure California for the USA in 1846. The Butterfield Stageline followed the same route during the 1840s and '50s, as did many who came to California seeking gold in 1849.

ANZA-BORREGO DESERT STATE PARK

This enormous state park – the largest in the USA outside of Alaska – occupies almost a fifth of San Diego County. It definitely requires a car to navigate, and several trips might be necessary to really get to the know the three different areas of the park: around Borrego Springs, near Blair Valley and near Split Mountain.

If you are short on time or if it's your first visit to the park, head for **Borrego Springs** (population 2989; elevation 590ft), a two-street township with a market and a handful of restaurants and motels. Its excellent visitor center, plus its number of easy-to-reach sights – including Font's Point and Borrego Palm Canyon – make the area fairly representative of the park as a whole.

The desert's southernmost region, south of and including Blair Valley, is the least visited and – aside from those in Blair Valley – has few developed trails and facilities. Attractions here, besides the solitude, include Goat Trestle and the Carrizo Badlands, which has an overlook affording great views. The Split Mountain area, in the desert's southeast, is popular with 4WD vehicles, but also contains interesting geology and spectacular wind caves.

The spring wildflowers in Anza-Borrego can be absolutely brilliant, depending somewhat on the amount of winter rain. Verbena, dune primrose, desert sunflower, brittlebush and desert lily are just some of the varieties to be seen. The flowers start blossoming in late February at the lower elevations and reach their best over subsequent months at successively higher levels. The bloom is such an attraction, it has its own phone line, **Wildflower Hotline** (☎ 760-767-4684), to manage questions about it.

There are several routes to the desert from San Diego: I-8 to S2 is the longest route, but is freeway most of the way. Many people come through Julian, though Hwy 78 through Poway can be quite busy. An extremely pleasant, if curvy, route is Hwy 79 through Cuyamaca Rancho State Park. Plan on 2½ hours of driving, whichever route you take.

Information

The **Anza-Borrego Desert State Park Visitor Center** (☎ 760-767-5311; open 9am-5pm daily, Sat & Sun only June-Oct), 2mi west of Borrego Springs township, is built partly underground and, from the parking lot, it looks just like a low scrubby hill. The walls are faced with local stone and blend beautifully with the mountain backdrop. Around the center is a selection of plants that you'll encounter in the park, all clearly labeled. Inside, a small theater shows a short slide show on the natural history of the park, and there are exhibits on desert flora and fauna as well as a good selection of publications. Staff are helpful and well informed.

A free park-use permit is required for any car leaving the highway to access the park and is good for overnight camping. Fires are permitted in metal containers only; wood gathering is prohibited.

Summers here are extremely hot. The average daily maximum temperature in July is 107°F (41°C) but it can reach 125°F (51°C). It's slightly cooler at higher elevations.

CALIFORNIA DESERTS

CALIFORNIA DESERTS

ANZA-BORREGO DESERT STATE PARK

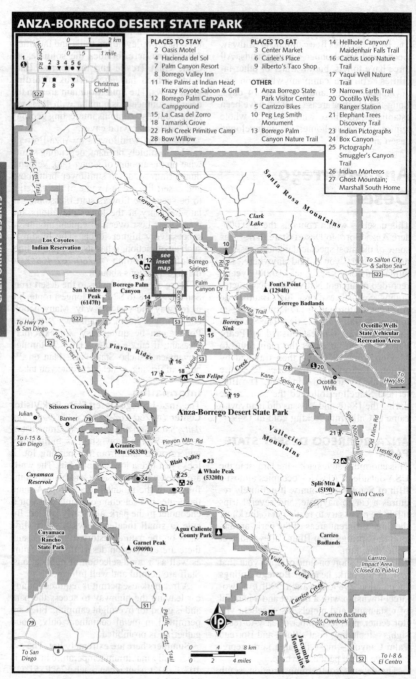

PLACES TO STAY
2 Oasis Motel
4 Hacienda del Sol
7 Palm Canyon Resort
8 Borrego Valley Inn
11 The Palms at Indian Head;
   Krazy Koyote Saloon & Grill
12 Borrego Palm Canyon
   Campground
15 La Casa del Zorro
18 Tamarisk Grove
22 Fish Creek Primitive Camp
28 Bow Willow

PLACES TO EAT
3 Center Market
6 Carlee's Place
9 Jilberto's Taco Shop

OTHER
1 Anza Borrego State
   Park Visitor Center
5 Carrizzo Bikes
10 Peg Leg Smith
   Monument
13 Borrego Palm
   Canyon Nature Trail

14 Hellhole Canyon/
   Maidenhair Falls Trail
16 Cactus Loop Nature
   Trail
17 Yaqui Well Nature Trail
19 Narrows Earth Trail
20 Ocotillo Wells
   Ranger Station
21 Elephant Trees
   Discovery Trail
23 Indian Pictographs
24 Box Canyon
25 Pictograph/
   Smuggler's Canyon
   Trail
26 Indian Morteros
27 Ghost Mountain;
   Marshall South Home

Things to See & Do

Northeast of Borrego Springs, where S22 takes a 90-degree turn to the east, there's a pile of rocks just north of the road. This, the **Peg Leg Smith Monument**, is a monument to Thomas Long 'Peg Leg' Smith – mountain man, fur trapper, Indian fighter, horse thief, liar and Wild West legend. Around 1829, Peg Leg passed through Borrego Springs on his way to LA and supposedly picked up some rocks that were later found to be pure gold. Strangely, he didn't return to the area until the 1850s, when he was unable to find the lode. Nevertheless, he told lots of people about it (often in exchange for a few drinks), and many came to search for the gold and add to the myths.

On the first Saturday of April, the **Peg Leg Liars Contest** is a hilarious event in which amateur liars compete in the Western tradition of telling tall tales. Anyone can enter, so long as the story is about gold and mining in the Southwest, is less than five minutes long and is anything but the truth.

A 4mi dirt road, usually passable without a 4WD (check with the visitor center) goes south of S22 to **Font's Point** (1249ft), which offers a spectacular panorama over the Borrego Valley to the west and the Borrego Badlands to the south. Walking the 4mi to the point is a good way to *really* be amazed when the desert seemingly drops from beneath your feet.

South of Hwy 78 at Ocotillo Wells (where there's a ranger station), paved Split Mountain Rd takes you past the **Elephant Trees Discovery Trail**, one of the few places to see a 'herd' of the unusual elephant tree whose name comes from its resemblance to an elephant's leg. Related to frankincense and myrrh, the trees have a wonderful fragrance not unlike department stores around the holiday season. The trees were thought not to exist in the Colorado Desert until a full-fledged hunt was launched in 1937, during which 75 were discovered in the Fish Creek area.

About 4mi south along Split Mountain Rd is a dirt-road turnoff for Fish Creek Primitive Camp, a further 4mi brings you to **Split Mountain**. The road – very popular with drivers of 4WD vehicles – goes right through Split Mountain between 600ft-high walls created by earthquakes and erosion. The gorge is about 2mi long from north to south. At the southern end, several steep trails lead up to delicate caves carved into the sandstone outcroppings by the wind.

In the west of the park, around 5mi south of Scissors Crossing (where S2 crosses Hwy 78) is **Blair Valley**, known for its Indian pictographs and morteros (hollows in rocks used for grinding seeds). The area also offers nice campgrounds and hiking trails.

A monument at Foot and Walker Pass marks a difficult spot on the Butterfield Overland Stage Route, and in **Box Canyon** you can still see the marks of wagons on the Emigrant Trail. A steep 1mi climb leads to **Ghost Mountain** and the remains of a house occupied by the family of desert recluse Marshall South.

Hiking

The **Borrego Palm Canyon Nature Trail** is a popular self-guided loop trail that goes northeast from the Borrego Palm Canyon Campground. The trail climbs 350ft in 3mi past a palm grove and waterfall, which make a delightful oasis in the dry, rocky countryside.

The **Hellhole Canyon/Maidenhair Falls Trail** starts from the Hellhole Canyon Trailhead, 2mi west of the visitor center on S22, climbs past several palm oases to a thick waterfall that supports bird life and a variety of plants.

In a 3mi round-trip you can see pictographs and a nice view of the Vallecito Valley from the **Pictograph/Smuggler's Canyon Trail**, which starts 3½mi from S2 in Blair Valley.

A variety of other short trails have been laid out, many of them with interpretive signs or self-guiding brochures – different trails highlight different features. The 1mi **Cactus Loop Nature Trail** is a good place to see a variety of cacti. Nearby, the 2mi **Yaqui Well Nature Trail** has many labeled desert plants and passes a natural water hole that attracts a rich variety of birdlife as well as the occasional bighorn sheep in winter. The **Narrows Earth Trail**, 2mi east of Tamarisk Grove, is a short trail that highlights the local geology but also has some unusual chuparosa shrubs, which attract hummingbirds.

The newspaper provided by the visitor center has a useful trail guide and locator map.

Mountain Biking

Both primitive roads and paved roads are open to bikes. Popular routes are Grapevine Canyon, Oriflamme Canyon and Canyon Sin Nombre. The visitor center has a free mountain-bike guide. **Carrizo Bikes** (☎ 760-767-3872; 648 Palm Canyon Dr), in Borrego Springs, rents bikes for $10 per hour or $32 for 24 hours, and also leads guided rides.

Places to Stay

Camping Camping is permitted anywhere in the park as long as you're not within 200 yards of any road or water source. You can't light a fire on the ground, and gathering vegetation (dead or alive) is prohibited.

Borrego Palm Canyon Campground (☎ 800-444-7275 for reservations; tent/RV site $10/16), 2mi northwest of Borrego Springs, has campfire programs, flush toilets and showers.

Tamarisk Grove Campground (☎ 800-444-7275 for reservations; sites $10), 12mi south of Borrego Springs near Hwy 78, is smaller than Borrego Palm Canyon Campground, but has more shelter and similar facilities.

Bow Willow Campground (sites $7), off S2 in the southern part of the park, has only 16 sites, with water, pit toilets, tables and fire pits.

There are several other campgrounds in the park – **Culp Valley, Arroyo Seco, Yaqui Well, Yaqui Pass, Fish Creek** and **Mountain Palm Springs** – which are free but have no water and only minimal facilities. Information about any or all campgrounds can be obtained from any ranger station or visitor center in the park, or online at **w** www.anzaborregostatepark.org.

Motels & Resorts These are in Borrego Springs, 2mi from the park. The summer season, when temperatures are high and room rates are low, is May to September.

Oasis Motel (☎ 760-767-5409; 366 Palm Canyon Dr; rooms around $30/60 summer/ winter, $10 more with kitchenette) is the cheapest place in town. Rooms are a bit rundown, but have all the regular amenities.

Hacienda del Sol (☎ 760-767-5442; 610 Palm Canyon Dr; rooms $60, $95 with kitchenette) is also basic but has fresher rooms with cable TV and in-room coffeemakers.

Better value is **Palm Canyon Resort** (☎ 760-767-5341, 800-242-0044; 221 Palm Canyon Dr; rooms from $70/95 summer/ winter), which has a very nice pool and spa, manicured grounds and a good restaurant.

The Palms at Indian Head (☎ 760-767-7788, 800-519-2624; 2220 Hoberg Rd; rooms $80-160), off Palm Canyon Dr to the north, is an older resort hotel with a popular restaurant (see Places to Eat) and great desert views. It offers greatly reduced rates, depending on availability.

Luxury has two faces here. **La Casa del Zorro** (☎ 760-767-5323, 800-824-1884; 3845 Yaqui Pass Rd; rooms $135-875 winter, from $95 rest of year), southeast of town, has attractive grounds, Southwest architecture, spacious rooms and a formal lobby and dining room.

Borrego Valley Inn (☎ 760-767-0311; **w** www.borregovalleyinn.com; 405 Palm Canyon Dr; rooms $145-$185) has an intimate spa-resort feel, with contemporary architecture. It offers afternoon lemonade, evening cocktails and a healthy breakfast, all included in the rates.

Places to Eat

Ignore the market on Christmas Circle and go to **Center Market** (590 Palm Canyon Dr; open 8:30am-6:30pm Mon-Sat, 8:30am-5pm Sun), in the Center, for a wide selection of good produce.

Jilberto's Taco Shop (659 Palm Canyon Dr; most dishes under $5) serves excellent Mexican food, though the atmosphere lacks charm. Most folks eat at the outdoor tables.

Carlee's Place (☎ 760-767-3262; Christmas Circle at Palm Canyon Dr; mains around $8) is recommended by locals for burgers, salads, pasta, steak dinners and atmosphere. Could it also be the pool table?

Krazy Koyote Saloon & Grill (☎ 760-767-7788; 2220 Hoberg Rd; meals around $11), in The Palms at Indian Head resort, has great Southwest-style food, a fun atmosphere and a terrific view.

The Mojave Desert

The Mojave Desert covers a vast region, from urban areas on the northern edge of LA County to the remote, sparsely populated country of the Mojave National Preserve. Most people just pass through the desert on their way to the Eastern Sierra, Death Valley or Las Vegas, but those with the time will find a lot worth stopping for. It's not really feasible to explore the Mojave without your own vehicle.

Those who want to explore the area will find useful information in *Walking the East Mojave Desert* by John McKinney and Cheri Rae.

EAST MOJAVE NATIONAL PRESERVE

Created as part of the 1994 California Desert Protection Act, this preserve contains 1.6 million acres of sand dunes, Joshua trees, volcanic outcroppings and stunning rock formations – sort of like Death Valley and Joshua Tree National Parks rolled into one, with even fewer people. And where people are absent, desert fauna tends to be more plentiful. Bighorn sheep, desert tortoise and wily coyote are frequently sighted, especially in the evening and early morning. One drawback with the scarcity of visitors is the lack of asphalt: once you're off the major highways, you're almost always on a dirt road.

Strong winds are the norm. Temperatures stay near (or above) 100°F (38°C) from May to September, then hang in around 50°F (10°C) for most of the winter, though occasional winter snow storms are not unheard of.

Information

There are very good information stations, funded by the National Park Service (NPS) in the largest towns nearest the preserve: **Baker** (☎ 760-733-4040; 72157 Baker Blvd; open 9am-5pm daily) and **Needles** (☎ 760-326-6322; 707 Broadway; open 8am-4pm Tues-Sun). Each has interpretive displays, current road and weather information, maps and natural history books. The smaller **Hole-in-the-Wall Ranger Station** (☎ 760-928-2572; open 10am-2pm Sat & Sun) is 19mi north of I-40 at the end of the paved Black Canyon Rd.

Things to See & Do

You can spend an entire day driving around the preserve, taking in its sights and exploring some of them by foot.

Visible to the south from I-15, **Cima Dome** is a 1500ft hunk of granite spiked with volcanic cinder cones and crusty outcroppings of basalt left by lava that flowed from over 7 million years ago to around 10,000 years ago.

Kelbaker Road, which goes south from I-15, is the best place from which to see this anciently charred landscape up close. At one point the number of cones is so great that they are protected as the **Cinder Cones National Natural Landmark**.

Also off Kelbaker Road are the **Kelso Dunes**, fabulously shaped sand dunes that rise up to 600ft and have an unusual pearly hue. They frequently produce a booming or singing noise as sand blows up the windward side of the dunes and then sweeps down the 'slip-face' of the dunes. Hiking around and upon these sand heaps can be a ball and is less taxing than one might imagine, as the sand gets well compressed by the wind.

On the eastern side of Kelbaker Rd, the Providence Mountains create an impressive wall of rocky peaks. Within the mountains, accessible from Essex Road off I-40, are **Mitchell Caverns**, known for their drip-like formations called speleothems.

North of the caverns, at the end of Black Canyon Rd (which extends north from Essex Rd), stands the **Hole-in-the-Wall** formation. These vertical walls of tuff (pronounced 'toof'), which look something like cliffs made of unpolished terrazzo marble, are thought to be from a powerful volcanic eruption that blasted rocks up to 60ft into the air and across the landscape some 18.5 million years ago.

At the viewing point for Hole-in-the-Wall is the ranger station (see Information earlier). A favorite **hike** for people with two cars is to the ranger station from the Mid Hills trailhead, 8mi north – and 1200ft higher – on an unpaved road.

Places to Stay & Eat

Two campgrounds are open year-round, each with pit toilets, running water and first-come, first-served sites ($12). **Hole-in-the-Wall** (4,400ft) has 35 sites surrounded by rocky desert landscape, while **Mid Hills** (5,600ft) has 26 sites among pine and juniper trees. The road to reach it is unpaved but generally well maintained.

Stock up on groceries and water before entering the preserve. You'll find supermarkets and all the requisite fast-food restaurants in Baker and Needles. A favorite place to eat in Baker is the **Greek Restaurant** (dishes $4-7) at the Hwy 127/I-15 junction, right next to the world's largest thermometer.

ANTELOPE VALLEY

The Antelope Valley is dead flat, and it's difficult to see a valley, much less an antelope. Apparently thousands of pronghorn antelopes once roamed the region, spending summers in the mountains and winters down in the warmer desert climate. Today the two main towns here – **Palmdale** and **Lancaster** – have a combined population of about 208,000 and dormitory suburbs that seem to go on forever. Obviously, K-Mart would be missed much more than an antelope in this part of the world these days.

A few things worth seeing are miles away from the urban area. If you need to stay here, you'll find motels off Hwy 14 at Palmdale Blvd and on Avenue K in Lancaster.

Antelope Valley California Poppy Reserve

From mid-March to mid-May, the hills are covered with wildflowers, particularly California's state flower, the golden poppy. The area offers several easy hiking trails. The **interpretive center** (☎ 661-724-1180; admission $5 per car; open daily in blossoming season) has more information. To get here, take the W Avenue I exit from Hwy 14 and continue west for about 13mi.

Antelope Valley Indian Museum

Incongruously housed in a Swiss chalet-style building (constructed by H Arden Edwards in 1928), this museum (☎ 805-942-0662; **w** www.avim.av.org; admission $1; open 11am-4pm Sat & Sun mid-Sept–June) has a very good collection of Indian artifacts from California and the Southwest. There are interactive demonstrations, films and tribal members who come to demonstrate basket weaving, acorn grinding and the like. From Hwy 14 take the E Avenue I exit and go east about 8mi south to Avenue J. Then head east another 9mi to 150th St, south to Avenue M, and lastly east until you see the chalet up among the boulders on your left.

Saddleback Butte State Park

Rising 1000ft above the desert floor, this granite butte has a great view if you make it to the top (and if it's a clear day). The park (☎ 805-942-0662) also has a nice grouping of native Joshua trees and several resident desert tortoise. From Hwy 14 take the E Avenue I exit, go east about 8mi, south to Avenue J,

then east another 10mi; the park is on the right after 170th St. A **campground** (sites $10) with flush toilets and 50 first-come, first-served sites, is a mile south of Avenue J, well signed from 170th St.

VICTOR VALLEY

This area includes the residential communities of Victorville, Hesperia and Apple Valley, with a total population of more than 150,000. Many residents are retirees. Victor Valley was also home to Roy Rogers and Dale Evans, until Roy's death in 1998 and Dale's in 2001.

Roy Rogers–Dale Evans Museum

Roy Rogers (known as the 'King of the Cowboys') made more than 80 movies for the Republic studio between 1938 and 1952, as well as more than 100 half-hour TV shows and a comeback movie in 1976. Many of the shows also featured his wife, Dale Evans 'Queen of the West', and his horse Trigger 'The Smartest Horse in the Movies.'

This museum (☎ 760-243-4547; admission $7, concessions available; open 9am-5pm daily), housed in a building resembling an Old West fort, has a mind-boggling collection of souvenirs, awards, testimonials, photographs and mementoes. Here you'll find Roy's favorite cars and boats; autographed baseballs; dozens of guns; ornate saddles; the stuffed heads of animals killed on hunting trips to Africa, Asia and Alaska; and a framed invitation to Ronald Reagan's inauguration. Trigger himself is here, stuffed and saddled. The museum was established by Roy and Dale, and taken as a whole (including its visitors) is well worth visiting as an authentic and not terribly self-conscious piece of mid-20th-century Americana.

To get here, exit I-15 at Roy Rogers Dr in Victorville and go west. Then take the first left and look for the giant statue of Trigger at the end of Civic Dr. The museum offers discounts for seniors, children and AAA members.

MOJAVE & AROUND

About 70mi north of LA you cross the LA County line and really feel like you are out of the city. The Upper Mojave is harsh, inhospitable country, with sporadic mining settlements and vast areas set aside for weapons and aerospace testing.

The town of Mojave (population 4297; elevation 2757ft) has Hwy 14, or the Sierra Hwy, as its main street, with the railroad on its western side and a commercial strip of motels, shops and eateries on the eastern side. Tourist information is available, sometimes, in the old red railroad caboose in the lot next to Mike's Family Restaurant. Driving through, you might think this town has a huge international airport, but all those airliners are actually in storage, where deterioration is minimal in the dry desert air.

Edwards Air Force Base
Southeast of town, this 301,000-acre base (formerly called Muroc) is a flight test facility for the US Air Force, NASA and civilian aircraft, and a training school for test pilots with the 'right stuff.' It was here that Chuck Yeager flew the Bell X-1 on the world's first supersonic flight, and the first shuttles glided in after their space missions (they still land here when the weather is bad at Cape Canaveral).

At the time of writing, the base was closed to visitors to support the 'primary mission of flight tests and national defense objectives.' Current information can be found online at w www.edwards.af.mil/trip/docs_html/museum.html or by calling ☎ 661-277-8050. If/when it does reopen, the **Air Force Flight Test Center Museum** (☎ 661-277-3510; 405 S Rosamond Blvd; admission free; open 9am-5pm Tues-Sat) is worth a look. Exhibits range from natural history to WWII flight tests to modern, supersonic flight technology.

Boron
Thirty miles east of Mojave, Boron is the site of a huge open-cut borax mine. North of Boron, visible from Hwy 395, is a vast array of solar collectors, part of the Luz Corporation's electricity generating system. Within the town itself is the **Twenty Mule Team Museum & Visitor's Bureau** (☎ 760-762-5810; 26962 Twenty Mule Team Road; admission free), where you can see samples of local rock, learn about the US Borax Company's legendary Twenty Mule Team and pick up information about accommodations in the area.

Red Rock Canyon State Park
This small park (☎ 661-942-0662 for information; day-use fee $2; visitor center open Sat & Sun, closed summer) straddles Hwy 14

about 20mi north of Mojave. Its very striking sandstone cliffs have eroded into weird formations that present a spectacular range of colors at sunrise and sunset; you may recognize it from the opening scenes of *Jurassic Park*. There are some marked hiking trails, where you'll see Indian grinding holes and a variety of desert plants. The **Ricardo Campground** (sites free) has 50 tent sites on a first-come, first-served basis along with drinking water and pit toilets.

BARSTOW
At the junction of I-40 and I-15, Barstow (population 22,470; elevation 2106ft) is about halfway between LA and Las Vegas, and lots of travelers break their journey here. They're not looking for charm, nor will they find any. In fact, this area has been a crossroads for desert travelers for centuries. The Spanish priest Francisco Garcès came through in 1776, and the Old Spanish Trail passed nearby. By the 1860s, settlers on the Mojave River were selling supplies, mostly liquor, to California immigrants. Mines were established in the surrounding hills, but Barstow really got going as a railroad junction after 1886. It still has a big rail freight business and serves a couple of military bases, as well as being the unofficial capital of the Mojave Desert.

Information
The Barstow Rd exit, heading north from I-15, takes you right past the **California Desert Information Center** (☎ 760-255-8760; 831 Barstow Rd; admission free; open 9am-5pm daily, closed for lunch), which has some pretty good exhibits on desert environments and history, plus lots of tourist information on Barstow and the Mojave. A good place to get regional information or find a clean restroom is **Barstow's California Welcome Center** (☎ 760-253-4782; 2796 Tanger Way) in the Tanger Factory Outlet Center, at the Lenwood Rd exit off the I-15.

Things to See & Do
Two blocks north of I-15 via the Barstow Rd exit, **Mojave River Valley Museum** (☎ 760-256-5452; 270 E Virginia Way; admission free; open 11am-4pm daily) concentrates on local history and has some artifacts from the Calico Early Man Archaeological Site (see Around Barstow later in this chapter).

Factory Merchants (☎ 760-253-7342; open 9am-8pm daily), at the Lenwood Rd exit off I-15, just south of town, is a factory outlet center with more than 50 stores selling fashions, footwear and household goods. Look carefully when you're shopping, as some items may be flawed or may have been marked up before being marked down. Real bargains are few and far between.

Places to Stay & Eat

There are perfectly nice budget motels on E Main St. Those with TV, in-room coffee-makers and rooms from $33 include **Stardust Inn** (☎ 760-256-7116; 901 E Main St), **Desert Inn** (☎ 760-256-2146; 1100 E Main St) and **Executive Inn** (☎ 760-256-7581; 1261 E Main St).

For a little more money, you get a little more comfort at **Quality Inn** (☎ 760-256-6891; 1520 E Main St; singles/doubles $59/64) or **Best Western Desert Villa** (☎ 760-256-1781, 800-528-1234; 1984 E Main St; rooms from $70), where rates include breakfast.

Ramada Inn (☎ 760-256-5673; 1511 E Main St; rooms $84/89), probably Barstow's most comfortable accommodations, has a pool, spa and a restaurant.

Apart from the standard, big-name places such as **Carrow's** (1200 E Main St) and **International House of Pancakes** (1441 E Main St) there are some local places of good value.

Golden Dragon (☎ 760-256-1890; 1231 E Main St; dishes $6-8) serves substantial Chinese and Thai dishes and has good dinner specials.

Rosita's (☎ 760-256-1058; 540 W Main St; dishes $6-8), a mile or so south of the main strip, does authentic Mexican food. On the way you'll pass a few of Barstow's bars.

Getting There & Away

Buses and trains both arrive and depart from the historic railroad station, **Casa del Desierto** (☎ 760-256-8757; 681 N 1st St; station open 9am-2pm & 3pm-6pm daily), north of Main St. You'll really need a car to get around Barstow and the surrounding area.

Greyhound has 10 buses a day to LA ($22.25, 2½ five hours) and seven to San Diego ($35.50, five to eight hours). Eight buses per day go east to Las Vegas ($22.25, three hours) and on to Denver.

Amtrak has two buses per day headed for Bakersfield ($21, three hours), from where there are connections going south to LA and north to the San Francisco Bay Area and beyond. One Amtrak train, the *Southwest Chief*, stops at Barstow; it travels between LA ($27, five hours) and Chicago ($248, 41 hours). Buy tickets on board.

AROUND BARSTOW
Rainbow Basin National Natural Landmark

Amazingly colorful layers of sedimentary rock can be seen here, folded and distorted into interesting formations. There's a scenic drive and several short hiking trails. Note that not all roads are good for regular passenger vehicles: obey the signs that read '4WD/High Clearance Vehicles Only.' Many mammal fossils, from 12 to 16 million years old, have been found at the site. The nearby **Owl Canyon Campground** (sites $6) has first-come, first-served sites, pit toilets and water. To get to Rainbow Basin and the campground, take First Ave from Main St in Barstow and turn left on Irwin Rd. After going north for 8mi, take Fossil Bed Rd west for 2mi.

Calico Ghost Town

The mines around here produced millions of dollars worth of silver and borax, but as the ore played out and the price of silver fell, the town died and was virtually abandoned by 1907. There was little left but foundations in 1951 when Walter Knott (of Knott's Berry Farm fame) began to rebuild it. Calico Ghost Town (☎ 760-254-2122, 800-862-2542; w www.calicotown.com; adult/concession $6/3; open 9am-5pm daily) is now a tourist attraction, around one third of which is original. The rest has been reconstructed and offers multiple opportunities to let you help pay for the reconstruction. You pay extra to go gold panning, tour the Maggie Mine, ride a little steam railway, see the 'mystery shack,' or catch a show at the Calikage Playhouse; these attractions cost about $2.25 each. Calico Ghost Town is off I-15 about 10mi north of Barstow.

Calico Campground (☎ 760-254-2122; sites $22/18 with/without hookups, cabins $28) is a red earth parking lot adjacent to the ghost town. A fun option might be to rent the bunkhouse ($12), which sleeps 12 people.

KOA (☎ 760-254-2311; sites $22/18 with/without hookups, cabins $28), near the I-15, has the same prices as Calico Campground but is better.

Calico Motel (☎ 760-254-2419; singles/doubles $24/33), on the southern side of I-15, looks like it hasn't changed since the 1950s, but it's kind of cute.

Calico Early Man Archaeological Site

Artifacts found at the 'Calico Dig', begun in 1964 by Dr Louis Leakey, have been dated back 200,000 years, which doesn't fit with the theory that the first Americans came from Asia some 20,000 years ago. But are these stones really human tools? Some of them just look like rocks with chips in them, and no human bones have yet been found at the site. See for yourself at the visitor center (☎ 760-256-5102; w www.ca .blm.gov/barstow/calico.html; adult/child $5/1; open 12:30pm-4:30pm Wed, 9am-4:30pm Thur-Sun), or on one of the site tours offered at 9:30am, 11:30am, 1:30pm and 3:30pm Thursday to Sunday (afternoons only on Wednesday). The site is north of I-15, 15mi east of Barstow.

Death Valley

The name itself evokes all that is harsh, hot and hellish in the deserts of the imagination, a punishing, barren and lifeless place of Old Testament severity. Historically, though, the valley has not been as deadly as other parts of California, and naturalists are keen to point out that many plants and animals thrive here. Still, the average visitor expecting blazing sunlight, stark scenery and inhuman scale will not be disappointed.

DEATH VALLEY NATIONAL PARK

The actual valley is about 100mi north to south and 5mi to 15mi wide, with the Panamint Range on its western side and the Amargosa Range on its eastern side. Death Valley National Park (admission $10) covers a much larger area – more than 5000 sq mi – which includes several other ranges and valleys to the north. Created as part of the 1994 California Desert Protection Act, the park's primary reason for being is protection, not tourism. You won't find the barrage of services, ranger programs and developed sights common to California's other national parks, and sometimes you'll have to make a concerted effort to pay the entrance fee (especially from April to October).

History

The Timbisha Shoshone lived in the Panamint Range for centuries, visiting the valley from winter to early summer every year to hunt and gather food, particularly mesquite beans. They also hunted waterfowl, caught pupfish in marshes and cultivated small areas of corn, squash and beans. Encroachments made by mining and tourism interests saw the Shoshone become more sedentary, with many taking on paid work, some making baskets for the tourist market. In 1933, the tribe was allocated a village site near Furnace Creek, which they still occupy.

The fractured geology of Death Valley left many accessible minerals. The earliest miners here, in the 1860s, sought gold, silver, copper and lead. A dozen mines were started in the surrounding mountains, each closing as the ore played out. The most sustained mining operation was the Harmony Borax Works, which extracted borate, an alkaline mineral used to make detergents and other products. The stuff was shipped out in wagons pulled by 20-mule teams and hauled 160mi to a railhead at Mojave. By the late 1920s, most of the mining had ceased, though there was a brief resurgence during WWII when minerals such as manganese, tungsten and lead were needed for wartime production.

Tents at Stovepipe Wells in the 1920s were the first tourist accommodations, followed by converted workers' quarters at Furnace Creek. In 1933, the area was designated a national monument, and for the next 11 years units of the Civilian Conservation Corps (CCC) constructed roads, ranger stations, campgrounds and entrance gates. The area under protection was increased in 1994 when Death Valley was designated a national park, becoming the largest national park in the continental USA.

Geology

The rock formations you see today were created by geological events that occurred as long ago as 500 million years. Extensive faulting and fracturing allows some of the

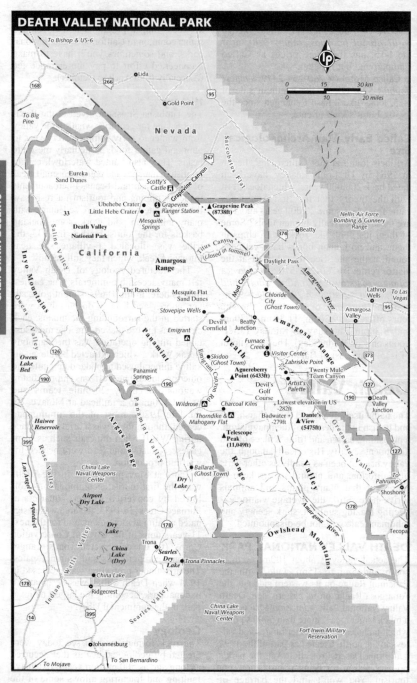

DEATH VALLEY NATIONAL PARK

oldest rocks to be visible on the earth's surface, when normally they would be hidden deep underground.

Limestone and sandstone from the earliest period, seen in the Panamint Range and the Funeral Mountains, were formed on an ancient seabed and slowly lifted by movement in the earth's crust. From 70 million to 250 million years ago, the rock strata were bent, folded and cracked as converging tectonic plates pushed up mountain ranges. These stresses weakened the earth's crust, leading to a period of volcanic activity, distributing ash and cinders that provided much of the rich coloring seen in the valley.

About 3 million years ago, the tectonic plates began to move apart, causing major faults. One of these faults formed on the eastern side of what is now Death Valley, and another formed on the western side of the Panamint Range. The valley floor and the mountain range together form a single geological structure, which is slowly rotating – the valley floor is subsiding while the range is being lifted. At the same time, erosion is carrying material down the mountains and depositing it in the valley. Much of this erosion occurred between 2000 and 10,000 years ago, when the climate was much wetter than at present, so the valley was filling with sediment even as its floor subsided. At Badwater, from where you can walk out to the lowest part of the valley, the sediment layer is some 9000ft deep.

When to Visit

Winter is the peak season, when accommodations can be booked solid, campgrounds are filled before 11am and people wait in line for hours to see Scotty's Castle (see later in this section). Fall is less crowded, while spring is the best time for wildflowers. Death Valley used to be practically empty in summer, but it has become more popular in recent years, especially with European visitors who are keen to experience 120°F (48°C) temperatures. With an air-conditioned car, a summer trip is quite feasible, especially if you do your sightseeing in the early morning and late evening, spending the hottest part of the day by a pool or at the significantly cooler higher elevations.

Orientation & Information

It's not hard to find your way around the valley by car. There are only a few main roads and they're all well marked. Furnace Creek, towards the southern end of the valley, has most of the facilities for visitors, including the **Furnace Creek Visitor Center** (☎ 760-786-3200; w www.nps.gov/deva; open 8am-6pm daily). This excellent facility has a small museum on the natural and human history of the valley, a good selection of books, maps and information, and a moderately interesting slide show every half-hour. The town's other facilities include a well-stocked **general store** (open 7am-9pm daily year-round), a post office, gas station, campground, restaurants and motel rooms.

There's also a smaller store, accommodations and a campground at **Stovepipe Wells**, about 20mi northwest of Furnace Creek; both have public showers ($2). Supplies and gas are expensive in the valley. Food and water are available, and gas is cheaper, in the small towns, such as Panamint Springs in the west and Beatty in the east, on the park's periphery (remember that these towns are an average of 30mi from the park).

If you're passing near Ridgecrest (see Around Death Valley later in this section), it's definitely worth stopping at the Maturango Museum for its free information sheets on the park, including hiking, mountain biking and geology. If you ask, you can also get such sheets at the Furnace Creek Visitor Center.

The national park's entry fee of $10 per vehicle is valid for multiple entries over seven days and includes a good map of the park. Not all entrances have a fee collection station open at all times, but you are still expected to pay at one of the ranger stations. Make a point of doing so – the rangers have better things to do than chase fee dodgers and the NPS needs the funding.

For 24-hour ranger assistance, call ☎ 760-786-3200. For other emergencies dial ☎ 911.

Driving Tour

This tour goes from south to north and back. Even starting outside the valley, you could do it all in a single day if you started very early, which is always a good thing to do in the desert. If you have more time, take one of the side trips listed later in this section.

Start by driving up to **Dante's View** (5475ft), which offers one of the best overall

Death in the Valley

A small party of forty-niners wandered into the valley when they separated from a larger emigrant group crossing western Nevada. Taking what they hoped would be a shortcut to the California gold fields, they entered the valley from the east in December 1849. They crossed the valley floor, but could not get their wagons over the Panamint Range. While most of the party sheltered near a water hole, two young men, Lewis Manly and John Rogers, were sent to scout for a route west over the mountains. The captain of the group explored to the south, but after some days of walking he turned back, dying before he reached the water hole again.

The remainder of the party split up, with one group eventually making their way out over Towne Pass. The others, members of the Bennett and Arcan families, including women and children, waited for the two scouts. Manly and Rogers eventually returned, after 26 days and 600mi in the wilderness, and guided the survivors out of the valley along the route now called Emigrant Canyon. As they left the valley, Ms Bennett reputedly looked back and uttered the words 'Goodbye, death valley.' It's not surprising the name stuck; more remarkable is the fact that 24 of the 25 emigrants actually survived the ordeal.

views of the valley at any time, but the view is absolutely brilliant at sunrise or sunset. Heading down towards the central valley, take a short walk out to **Zabriskie Point**, which is a great place to see lava-capped formations and eroded badlands; you'll have plenty of company on the paved trail leading to the viewing platform. The hiking trail, which is 50 yards to the right of the paved trail and skirts the base of the formations, is usually empty. Then, get in your car and backtrack about 3mi, to go through **Twenty Mule Team Canyon**, a windy one-way loop through an ancient lake bed – it will make you feel like an ant in a quarry.

Continue north to Furnace Creek, where you can have breakfast, take a break and sit in some shade. The **Borax Museum** (admission by donation; open 9am-4pm daily Oct-May), on the Furnace Creek Ranch, will tell you all about the stuff, and there's a big collection of old coaches and wagons out the back. The Furnace Creek Visitor Center, with excellent exhibits on Death Valley, is just up the road. Further north again is a not-so-interesting interpretive trail through the ruins of the Harmony Borax Works.

From Furnace Creek you can drive 50mi straight through to the northern end of the valley or stop for sightseeing on the way. If it's getting hot, go straight through and see the sights on the way back. When you get to the Grapevine Ranger Station you'll have to pay the entry fee if you haven't done so yet (keep your ticket). A few hundred yards after the gate, turn right to Scotty's Castle (see later in this section), which is nearly 3000ft above sea level and noticeably cooler. The large palm-shaded lawn here is one of the most enjoyable places to be in the heat of midday. You can get food here, though it's better to bring a picnic.

Going west after the Grapevine Ranger Station brings you to **Ubehebe Crater**, a ½mi-wide hole caused by the explosive meeting of superheated volcanic lava with cool groundwater. You can take a 1½mi walk around its rim, and a ½mi walk up to the younger and smaller **Little Hebe Crater**.

Head back down the valley, and by the time you get to the scenic loop of the **Mesquite Flat Sand Dunes** the temperature should be more bearable, and the sun will be lower in the sky, making the dunes more photogenic. This is another good place to spend some time out of the car.

Near the road, an old pump marks the site of the original **Stovepipe Wells**, which were tapped by pounding old stovepipes into the sand at a dried-up water hole. Opposite the end of the loop, look for the field of arrow weed clumps called the **Devil's Cornfield**. Nearby is **Stovepipe Wells Village**, with a ranger station, a store, and a pool or showers ($2).

Return to Hwy 190, drive back south through Furnace Creek and branch right at the next junction. Two miles south is **Golden Canyon**, which really glows in the late afternoon. Six miles further is the turnoff for the **Artist's Drive** scenic loop, which is also at its best around sunset – the spot called **Artist's Palette** is particularly colorful. Across to the west, the valley floor is filled with lumps of crystallized salt in what is called the **Devil's Golf Course**; in the middle of this salt pan is the deepest part of the valley. The lowest point accessible by road is accessible from **Badwater** (282ft below sea level), a little further south. Walk out onto the constantly evaporating bed of salty, mineralized water that is the only habitat of the soft-bodied Death Valley snail.

Scotty's Castle

Walter E Scott, alias 'Death Valley Scotty', was the quintessential tall-tale teller that captivated people with his stories of gold. His most lucrative friendship was with Albert and Bessie Johnson, wealthy insurance magnates from Chicago. Despite knowing who Scotty was somewhat of a liar and a freeloader, they bankrolled the construction of this elaborate vacation home which eventually became their main residence.

When Albert Johnson died in 1948, the house was willed to a charity with a provision that Scotty be allowed to stay on until he died (1954). The building isn't much from the outside, but inside there are furnishings imported from Europe, handmade tiles, carved timber and elaborate wrought iron made especially for the house.

To get the full story on Scotty's Castle (☎ 760-786-2392), take one of the guided tours, which leave regularly between 9am and 5pm. They cost $8, and there can be a long wait (or they can sell out completely); call ahead for reservations. If you just want a glimpse of the place and its history, the grounds are free for exploring and the Exhibit Hall has an excellent collection of bits and pieces from the past.

Side Trips

There are many interesting side trips along the edges of the valley and in the surrounding ranges. Detailed information is available from the Furnace Creek Visitor Center (see Orientation & Information, earlier). Before starting out, it's wise to check with the center for information, maps and an update on road conditions.

Emigrant Canyon Rd A scenic road climbs steeply up this canyon to Emigrant Pass (5318ft). On the way, dirt roads turn off to the ghost town **Skidoo** and **Aguereberry Point** (6433ft), which has superb views over Death Valley. Continue along Emigrant Canyon Rd and turn left up

Wildrose Canyon to reach the **Charcoal Kilns**, a line of large, stone, beehive-shaped structures used to make charcoal for smelting silver ore.

The landscape here is subalpine, with forests of piñon pine and juniper, and can be covered with snow in winter. You may need a 4WD to reach the end of the road at Mahogany Flat (8133ft). A trail goes from there to Telescope Peak (see Hiking later in this section).

The Racetrack Large rocks appear to be moving across this mud flat, making long, faint tracks in the sun-baked surface. One theory is that winds push the rocks along when the valley is wet or icy. The Racetrack is 20mi south of Ubehebe Crater, via a dirt road that sometimes requires a 4WD.

Daylight Pass The Daylight Pass Rd (Hwy 374 to Beatty, Nevada) goes east of the valley, past a rough road to the ghost town Chloride City. Off the Daylight Pass Cutoff, another rough road leads to the ruins of the Keane Wonder Mine.

Titus Canyon A 25mi, one-way scenic road goes from the Daylight Pass Rd through this dramatic canyon to the floor of Death Valley. It's usually closed in summer, and may only be passable for 4WD vehicles.

Eureka Sand Dunes Rising up to 680ft from a dry lake bed, these are perhaps the tallest dunes in the country. In the northern end of the valley, near Ubehebe Crater, 44mi of dirt road leads to the dunes. Unless there has been wet weather, the road can be traveled by a regular car.

Hiking

The Furnace Creek Visitor Center has good maps and hiking information, and will encourage you to fill out a backcountry registration form. Rangers regularly conduct guided hikes, except during summer.

In the valley, the most popular hikes are the ones that let you explore the numerous side canyons, such as Mosaic Canyon, Golden Canyon, Natural Bridge Canyon and Titus Canyon Narrows. At higher (and cooler) elevations, hiking trails skirt some of the old mining areas, such as the Keane Wonder Mine and Chloride City. The hike to **Wildrose Peak** (9064ft) from the charcoal kilns is a 8½mi round-trip, with a healthy climb of nearly 3000ft.

The most demanding hiking trail climbs 7mi and 3000ft from Mahogany Flat to the summit of **Telescope Peak** (11,049ft). From here it's possible to see both the highest and the lowest points in continental USA, Mt Whitney and Badwater. Allow six to nine hours for the round-trip, and don't attempt it in winter unless you're equipped for snow and ice climbing. The last 2mi to the trailhead might be too rough for a regular car, so you may have to start walking from the charcoal kilns – this will add about 4mi, and 2000ft, to the trip.

Biking

Bikes are only allowed on roads open to vehicle traffic – not on hiking trails. The visitor center has a list of suggested bike routes.

Horseback Riding

Travel on horseback is the most traditional and probably still the most enjoyable way to see the area. **Furnace Creek Ranch** (☎ 760-786-3339) arranges three rides daily, except during summer. One/two-hour rides cost $35/50.

Places to Stay

Apart from the campgrounds and the elegant Furnace Creek Inn, accommodations in the valley are overpriced, with minimal standards of service. If you want a roof over your head, you get much better value in one of the towns around Death Valley. Panamint Springs, in the west, and Beatty, Nevada, in the east, are the best options.

Camping Campgrounds in the park are not particularly appealing (some are like gravel parking lots with a toilet block), but being out there for the sunset, the stars, the sunrise and the silence is magic. In summer, camping at the lower levels is not really feasible, it's just too hot. In fact, only the Furnace Creek, Mesquite Spring and Wildrose Campgrounds are open year-round. Call ☎ 800-365-2267, or check w http://reservations.nps.gov, to book a site at any one of these campgrounds (booking is possible only from October to April).

Furnace Creek Campground (sites $16 May-Sept, $10 Oct-Apr), with its entrance just south of the visitor center, has 136 sites and is close to the facilities at Furnace Creek. It fills up early during busy times and has very little shade.

Texas Springs (sites $10; open Oct-Apr), between Furnace Creek Visitor Center and the Furnace Creek Inn, has a little more shade and a nice setting, on a hillside slightly above the valley floor.

Sunset Campground (sites $10; open Oct-Apr), near Texas Springs but at a slightly lower elevation, is a large facility that is mainly for RVs.

Stovepipe Wells Campground (sites $10; open Oct-Apr), with very little shade and lots of RVs, is not to be confused with the adjacent RV-only park (sites $20). It's next to the general store, run by Stovepipe Wells Village.

Emigrant Campground (sites free; open Apr-Oct) is a small facility 9mi south of Stovepipe Wells. At 2100ft, it's cooler than the other campgrounds and has nice views down to the valley.

Mesquite Springs (sites $10; open year-round), towards the northern end of the valley, at 1800ft, is one of the more attractive campgrounds. It sits mid-valley and has quite a bit of greenery.

In the Panamint Range, approaching Telegraph Peak, are three free campgrounds which enjoy mild weather in summer but can get snow in winter. **Wildrose** (4100ft) is open year-round (unless it's snowed in), and water should be available in summer. **Thorndike** (7500ft) and **Mahogany Flat** (8133ft) are small campgrounds, open March to November. You may need a 4WD to reach them.

By going into the backcountry, you can camp for free in most parts of the national park, as you're at least 1mi from the nearest road and ¼mi from any water source. The old mining areas are for day-use only; the rangers don't want people in them after dark. It's a good idea to check with the visitor center first and to fill out a backcountry registration form.

Hotels Stovepipe Wells Village (☎ 760-786-2387; w www.stovepipewells.com; patio rooms $50, standard rooms $70, deluxe rooms $92) is in Stovepipe Wells – a pretty unattractive place except for a few trees and a pool. Staff won't tell you about the patio rooms unless you ask, and even then they are reluctant to rent them. Rooms are small, a bit worn and the air-con is noisy, but they're definitely the cheapest rooms in the valley.

Run by Xenterra, **Furnace Creek Ranch** (☎ 760-786-2345; W *www.furnacecreek resort.com; cabins $102, motel rooms from $133 plus $15 per extra adult)* is a ¼mi south of the Furnace Creek Visitor Center near the restaurants and general store. It has pretty ordinary cabins for one or two people as well as motel rooms. Facilities include a large swimming pool, tennis courts and a golf course (the greens fees are $30/55 summer/winter).

Furnace Creek Inn (☎ 760-786-2345; W *www.furnacecreekresort.com; rooms from $235, or $155 mid-May–mid-Oct; open year-round)*, also run by Xenterra, is a top-end place up the hill from the ranch. It has elegant, Spanish-style stone buildings dating from 1927; an attractive, chemical-free, springwater-fed, solar swimming pool; tennis courts; a nice restaurant and bar; and palm-shaded grounds.

Places to Eat

You can find limited grocery items (eggs, cheese, hot dogs) at Stovepipe Wells, and a more balanced selection (including dry goods, some produce and deli sandwiches) at Furnace Creek General Store. Restaurants at the Furnace Creek Ranch include **Forty Niner Cafe** *(breakfast & lunch $6-8, dinner around $10)*; and **Wrangler Steak House** *(buffet breakfast/lunch $6/9, dinner mains $13-21)*, which offers steak and/or seafood dishes for dinner.

Furnace Creek Inn *(lunch around $10, dinner around $15)* has an elegant restaurant, which requires reservations and does not allow diners wearing jeans or T-shirts at dinner time.

Corkscrew Saloon, the bar within Stovepipe Wells Village (see following), provides the only nightlife in town, and it's not a bad place for a drink and game of pool. It makes pizzas to go from 5:30pm to 9:30pm nightly.

Stovepipe Wells Village (☎ 760-786-2387; *breakfast & lunch $5-8, dinner $10-18)* has a comfortable dining room with a full bar which is suitable for the whole family. The bar also serves nachos, fries and chicken wings (around $7) in the afternoon when the restaurant closes between lunch and dinner.

Getting There & Away

There is no regular scheduled service to Death Valley, though some charter buses and tours operate from Las Vegas.

Good roads come into Death Valley from every direction, and all of them offer some spectacular views. Driving west into the valley, from US-95, on either Rte 374 or 267, takes you past high desert scenery that could easily fit into Mongolia or Patagonia; driving out of the valley via Pana-mint Springs, along Rte 190, is breath-taking when you can see the entire Sierra Nevada stretched out in front of you. Gas is expensive in the park too, so fill up before you enter.

AROUND DEATH VALLEY
Ridgecrest

Ridgecrest (population 24,600; elevation 2289ft), southwest of the park, is the last sizable town before Death Valley, and not a bad place to get information, stock up on water, gas and supplies or to spend a night in reasonably priced accommodations.

The town is here because of the China Lake Naval Weapons Center on its eastern edge. Visiting the center was not allowed at the time or writing, due to high security. In peaceful times you can see what this facility does by looking at the **China Lake Exhibit Center** (☎ 760-939-3454, 760-939-8645; *open 7:30am-4:30pm Mon-Fri)*.

The **Maturango Museum** (☎ 760-375-6900; *cnr China Lake Blvd & Las Flores Ave; donation requested; open 10am-5pm daily)* is an excellent resource for the area. It has a great driving-tour guide, *Getting There is Half the Fun*, for people heading to Death Valley, as well as information about hiking, biking, geology, weather, flora and fauna in the park. Museum staff conduct tours of local petroglyph sites, and are knowledge-able about the museums' exhibits. They also have information about and directions to the nearby **Trona Pinnacles**, a site where tufa spires rise out of an ancient lake bed like those at Mono Lake.

Places to Stay & Eat There are several budget motels south of town along China Lake Blvd, including **Budget Inn & Cafe** (☎ 760-375-1351; *831 N China Lake Blvd; singles/doubles $38/42)*, which has kitchens in most units.

The slightly upscale **Carriage Inn** (☎ 760-446-7910; 901 N China Lake Blvd; rooms from $75) has large, clean rooms with cable TV. There is a restaurant in the hotel, and the most lively shopping center in town – with a K-Mart, Borders Books & Music, and movie theaters – is across the street. China Lake Blvd has an almost complete set of the most popular fast-food franchises.

Around 16mi south of Ridgecrest, on Hwy 395 in Johannesburg, you'll find the independent **Death Valley Hostel** (☎ 760-374-2323; Hwy 395; dorm beds $12, private rooms $22 per person; open 7am-9am & 6pm-9pm daily). If you're traveling this way, it's a good stop. It has a fully stocked kitchen, in-house food store, free towels and bed linen. Its friendly staff that can provide information about Death Valley and arrange free tours of the Trona Pinnacles and petroglyphs, Fossil Falls, Red Rock Canyon and more.

Beatty, Nevada

This little one-street Nevada town (population 1623; elevation 3308ft), only 40mi from Furnace Creek, is the best bet for cheap accommodations near Death Valley. It's also a good place to soak in hot springs, look through flea markets and find people to drink beer with.

Eight miles north of town, **Bailey's Hot Springs** (☎ 775-553-2732; sites $15) has five campsites that are a little too near the road, and three natural mineral pools. A soak costs $2, towel rental is $1 and the pools close at 8pm.

The HI-affiliated **Happy Burro Hostel** (☎ 775-553-9130; 100 Main St; dorm beds $15) has cramped rooms that sleep three people and have either a TV or a kitchen. The public space downstairs is cozy, but also cramped.

Burro Inn (☎ 775-553-2225, 800-843-2078; rooms from $45) has clean motel rooms that surround a parking lot, an ATM and a popular bar/restaurant/casino with a $5 all-you-can-eat salad bar.

Exchange Club Motel & Casino (☎ 775-553-2333, 888-561-2333, fax 553-9348; rooms from $48) has similar but slightly larger rooms. Its bar is a good place to belly up, and its restaurant serves large portions (burgers, steaks, sandwiches) for under $10.

A mile north of town, **Stagecoach Hotel & Casino** (☎ 775-553-2419, 800-424-4946, fax 775-553-2548; rooms from $55) is spruced up in garish color. Rooms are nice and the casino is the most popular in town. The restaurant is OK, with standard fare for around $8.

Phoenix Inn (☎ 775-553-2250, 800-845-7401, fax 775-553-2260; rooms $35-38) houses people in double-wide trailers that are adequate but a bit shabby.

For a good, and copious, Mexican meal, hit **Ensenada Grill** (☎ 775-553-2600; mains $6-11). Fish tacos, sopes and chile rellenos are all highly recommended.

Amargosa Valley

About 10mi north of the California-Nevada border on Hwy 373, **Longstreet Inn & Casino** (☎ 775-372-1777, 800-508-9493, fax 775-372-1280; RV sites $21, rooms from $60) is a very lively place where motel rooms are reasonably priced. It has a laundry, store, two OK restaurants, a pool (with a mini-waterfall), a whirlpool, a nine-hole golf course and a place to gamble.

South about 5mi, **Desert Village Motel** (☎ 775-372-1405; cnr Hwy 373 & Mecca Rd; rooms from $45) is a rather drab place that should only be a last ditch option. **Rosa's Mexican Café** (closed Mon), however, is a good place to stop for authentic and cheap Mexican food.

Amargosa Hotel & Opera House

At the junction of Hwys 127 and 190 (marked as Death Valley Junction on the map), 12mi east of the park boundary, is the regionally famous and brilliantly quirky **Amargosa Hotel & Opera House** (☎ 760-852-4441). A creation of the multitalented Marta Becket, the opera house has a trompe l'oeil audience, which joins the sell-out crowd of 150 who regularly come to watch the 75-year old Marta's dance and mime performances. The shows run on Monday and Saturday from October to May, and tickets cost $15/12 for adult/concession. Call first to book and confirm show times (there are no shows June through September).

The opera house is part of an arcaded plaza built by the Borax company in 1924. Now the Mission-style building has 12 totally worn-out hotel rooms that miraculously fetch $45 (with one bed and shower) or $55 (with two beds and bath) during the opera season. The place is worth a visit even if you don't stay or see a show.

Shoshone

The small town of Shoshone (population 70; elevation 1569ft) gives good access to Death Valley by a choice of two scenic routes. It's 57mi via the shorter, northern route from Furnace Creek.

Shoshone Inn (☎ *760-852-4335; singles/ doubles $42/57*) is the only place to stay and not bad at these prices. The rates include access to an old but clean and very relaxing natural hot springs pool.

You'll have a few more choices at Baker, but it's 58mi further south from Death Valley.

Ten miles south of Shoshone and east of Hwy 127 in Tecopa, the **HI Desertaire Home Hostel** (☎ *760-852-4580, 877-907-1265; 2000 Old Spanish Trail Hwy*) charges members/nonmembers $15/18 for a bed in one of two dormitories or in a private room that sleeps up to five people. There is a communal kitchen, dining and living room, sheet and towel rental for $1 each and parking. The folks who watch over the place require that you make a reservation before arriving (even if it's only 10 minutes before) and will give you plenty of information about the local hot springs and other sights of Tecopa.

Nevada

You know you're in Nevada when even the roadside gas station has a slot machine. Brochures enjoin visitors to 'discover both sides of Nevada,' and for many travelers this means driving all night to reach Las Vegas or Reno, a few minutes of pure adrenaline at the gaming tables, and the hangover that ensues after blowing $100 in less than 10 minutes.

The triangle of southern Nevada is part of the Mojave Desert, which extends into California, northwestern Arizona and southern Utah. The main city is, of course, world-famous Las Vegas.

The state's western corner, however, is actually the birthplace of modern Nevada. Reno and its neighbor Sparks started as way stations for emigrants and grew to become centers of rail transport, entertainment, services and education. Virginia City was the scene of the big mining bonanza when the Comstock Lode was discovered in the late 1800s. Carson City, the state capital, emerged from the orderly farming communities of the Carson Valley.

The **Nevada Commission on Tourism** (☎ 775-687-4322, 800-638-2328; **w** www .travelnevada.com) sends free books and maps, as well as information on accommodations, campgrounds and events. For highway conditions, call ☎ 877-687-6237, or log onto **w** www.nvroads.com.

The area code for most of Nevada is ☎ 775. The only exception is Las Vegas, which is ☎ 702.

Except for poker, all gambling pits the player against the house, and the house always has a statistical edge. Some casinos offer introductory lessons in blackjack, roulette and craps. To enter a gambling area you must be at least 18 years old. And speaking of vices, note that prostitution is definitely illegal in Clark County (which includes Las Vegas) and Washoe County (which includes Reno). The legal brothels are in rural counties outside the major cities. Don't expect the romance of an Old West bordello: some are literally just tattered double-wide trailers on the side of a lonesome highway.

Nevada's climate is very dry – this is the desert, remember – and summer temperatures regularly top 100°F (37°C). In Las Vegas these can run even higher. During

Highlights

- Gambling in the Golden Gate – the oldest casino in downtown Vegas
- Valley of Fire State Park – a quiet escape from slot-machine mania
- National Automobile Museum – Dymaxion, Phantom Corsair, Beatnik Bandit and other quirky cars on show in Reno
- Virginia City – home of the Comstock Lode and eccentric, old-time saloons

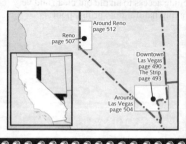

winter, nights are cool in Las Vegas, while Reno's higher elevation means temperatures frequently drop well below freezing.

I-80 runs from Reno to San Francisco (west) and Salt Lake City (east). I-15 takes drivers from Las Vegas to Los Angeles. Two-lane Hwy 95 is the chief north–south artery, connecting Las Vegas with Reno.

Las Vegas

Most people are dazzled by their first sight of the bright lights in Glitter Gulch and along the Strip, and are staggered by the scale and extravagance of it all. Yes, Las Vegas (population 511,246; elevation 2174ft) is an exciting place, and if you like gambling and glitter, you'll love it – at least until your money disappears or the incessant 'ding ding ding' of slot machines and the haggard countenances of down-and-out gamblers wear you down. Kids love it for the pure fun factor. Budget backpackers love it too, for the cheap meals, cheeseball entertainment and, if they spend enough time at the nickel slots, complimentary cocktail or two.

To anyone with cultural pretensions, however, Las Vegas is tasteless, gaudy and crass – a giant coliseum of not just harmless kitsch but screaming commercialism and all-out waste. To environmentalists, the massive lakes, fountains and cultivated golf courses in the middle of the hard-bitten Mojave Desert are a vision of ignorance and blasphemy. It's easiest to pretend otherwise, but all that water comes from very limited sources (shrinking aquifers and the overburdened Colorado River); and the sight of all those lights in the face of rising electrical rates can't help but rouse questions regarding conservation.

Yet despite what one might feel about Las Vegas, it's a rather remarkable place. In just a century it's grown from a remote railroad stop to one of the top destinations in the USA. It attracts over 35 million visitors a year to a fantasy world whose facade is as artificial as a movie set, and whose sprawling existence is based almost entirely on tourism. Las Vegas has made an industry of providing budget-priced glamour and the delusional hope of instant wealth – and the public gobbles it right up.

HISTORY

The only natural feature to account for the emergence of Las Vegas is a spring north of downtown once used by Paiute Indians. In 1829 Rafael Rivera, a scout for a Mexican trading expedition, discovered the spring, after which the area became known to overland travelers as *las vegas* (the meadows), a place with reliable water and feed for horses. Explorer John Frémont literally put the place on the map in 1844. Las Vegas became a regular stop on the Spanish Trail. Mormons built the first structure in 1855, a small mission and fort abandoned by 1858. There was little development until 1902, when much of the land was sold to the San Pedro, Los Angeles and Salt Lake Railroad, later absorbed by its parent, the Union Pacific. Work on the railroad connecting Las Vegas with California began in the summer of 1904, with train operation kicking off in January 1905.

Union Pacific subdivided what is now downtown Las Vegas, and 1200 lots were auctioned off in a single day, May 15, 1905, now celebrated as the city's birthday.

As a railroad town, Las Vegas had machine shops, an ice works and its share of hotels, saloons and gambling houses. In 1920 the population was 2300. The railroad laid off hundreds in the mid-1920s, but one Depression-era development infused new life into the city: the building of Hoover Dam. This huge project, begun in 1931, provided jobs and growth in the short term, and the water and power necessary for the city's long-term growth.

In 1931 Nevada legalized gambling and simplified its divorce laws, but unlike Reno, Las Vegas, dominated by conservative Mormon politics, was not quick to capitalize on these changes. In 1941 Tommy Hull built the first casino on the Strip, the Western-themed El Rancho Vegas, on land opposite the current Sahara (El Rancho burned down in 1960). The next wave of investors, also from out of town, were mobsters such as 'Bugsy' Siegel, cocreator of the Flamingo in 1946. The Flamingo set the tone for the new casinos – big and flashy, with lavish entertainment to attract the high rollers. The underworld connections, if anything, added to the city's burgeoning mystique. Most of its phenomenal development occurred after WWII, when innovations such as air-conditioning and reliable water supply made life in the desert not just bearable, but desirable.

In the 1950s a slew of huge resorts began giving shape to the Las Vegas Strip, with joints such as the Sands (the original Rat Pack's playground) and the Desert Inn, later home to the reclusive Howard Hughes (who came to own numerous Strip casinos). Only a few of the old casinos still exist today, however, including the Sahara, Stardust, Flamingo and New Frontier, although all have undergone multiple face-lifts. A new

NEVADA

The Rat Pack

After Elvis, it's the Rat Pack that has the biggest and most revered legacy in Las Vegas history. Centered on Frank Sinatra, Dean Martin, Sammy Davis Jr, Joey Bishop and Peter Lawford, the Rat Pack were fixtures on the Strip from the late 1950s through the 1960s, and the Sands was their playground. They sang, joked, boozed, womanized and gambled together, and left behind an aura of hipster showmanship and bourbon-saturated, black-tie cool.

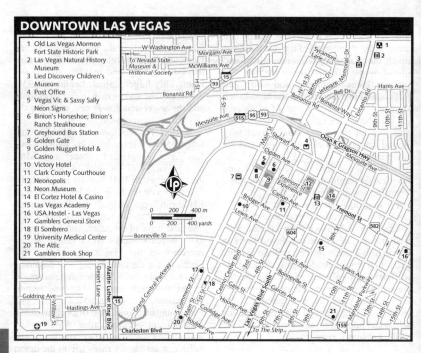

DOWNTOWN LAS VEGAS

1 Old Las Vegas Mormon
   Fort State Historic Park
2 Las Vegas Natural History
   Museum
3 Lied Discovery Children's
   Museum
4 Post Office
5 Vegas Vic & Sassy Sally
   Neon Signs
6 Binion's Horseshoe; Binion's
   Ranch Steakhouse
7 Greyhound Bus Station
8 Golden Gate
9 Golden Nugget Hotel &
   Casino
10 Victory Hotel
11 Clark County Courthouse
12 Neonopolis
13 Neon Museum
14 El Cortez Hotel & Casino
15 Las Vegas Academy
16 USA Hostel - Las Vegas
17 Gamblers General Store
18 El Sombrero
19 University Medical Center
20 The Attic
21 Gamblers Book Shop

growth spurt began in the mid-1980s and
led to the mega-resorts that now grace the
South Strip. Since then the city's population
has nearly doubled.

To keep hotel beds filled during lulls in the
tourist season, Las Vegas also got into the
convention business, with the first center
opening in April 1959. Today, conventions
are big business, flooding the city with
nearly four million conventioneers each year.

ORIENTATION

Two main highways come into Las Vegas: the
I-15 and Hwy 95. For downtown, Hwy 95 is
exited at Las Vegas Blvd and I-15 at
Charleston Blvd. I-15 parallels the Strip – a
3mi stretch of Las Vegas Blvd – so if you're
driving work out which cross street will bring
you closest to your destination. If it's your first
time in Vegas and you're not in a hurry, get off
I-15 at Blue Diamond Rd, just south of the airport, and cruise the length of the Strip from
south to north, right into downtown.

Downtown Las Vegas, the original town
center, is a compact grid. Its main artery,
Fremont St, is now a covered pedestrian
mall lined with older casinos and hotels

(with no shortage of neon). Public buildings, such as the post office and city hall,
are a few blocks north. Keep in mind this is
not a downtown like you're used to: the
business district consists of casinos and
hotels, and there's virtually no shopping,
except for souvenirs.

The blocks around the intersection of
Main St and Fremont St are known as Glitter Gulch and are lorded over by a pair of
grinning neon icons known as Vegas Vic
and Sassy Sally. Heading east, Fremont St
turns into the Boulder Hwy, the old main
route to Hoover Dam. Downtown it's lined
with great old neon signs but also drunks,
fleabag motels and a decrepit veneer.

Between downtown and the Strip is a tatty,
shopworn stretch of Las Vegas Blvd, packed
tight with cheap motels, garish wedding
chapels and sticky-floored sex shops. The
colossal, three-legged Stratosphere tower
marks the northern terminus of the Strip,
which nowadays is unofficially divided into
two segments.

The North Strip, running from the
Stratosphere to the New Frontier, is marked
by a number of somewhat older casinos

that, by today's standards, feel relatively plain, lacking the theatrical flash of the monstrosities to the south.

The South Strip begins with Treasure Island and runs south to Mandalay Bay. This section has the most outrageous and over-the-top casinos; it's the area of Las Vegas most tourists hear about and come to gawk at. Beyond the Mandalay Bay, as you approach the airport, the bright lights peter out and the desert, once more, begins to take over.

More giant casinos are found east of the Strip along Paradise Rd, and just west of I-15 near the intersection of Flamingo Rd and Valley View Blvd.

Traffic is heavy on the Strip around the clock, and near impossible on weekend nights. If you're actually trying to get somewhere, use one of the parallel roads (Industrial Rd or Paradise Rd). If you don't want to deal with driving, which is probably smartest, the local bus system is cheap and reliable.

Beyond the Strip, Las Vegas consists of minimalls, chain stores and plain, residential suburbs. Large and sprawling, it could be anywhere – and it's amazing to think it all exists here because of tourism. North Las Vegas is a pretty tough area. Southeast of Vegas, Henderson is a satellite suburb with some 'real' industries, such as chemical production and metal processing.

Rush hour can be maddening on local freeways and streets, especially Hwy 95 heading north and major westbound roads such as Charleston Blvd (the route to Red Rock Canyon, see Around Las Vegas later in this chapter). Go sit by the pool and wait it out.

INFORMATION
Tourist Offices
The **Las Vegas Visitor Center** (☎ 702-892-0711, fax 702-892-2824; W www.lasvegas24hours.com; cnr Paradise Rd & Convention Center Dr; open 8am-5pm daily) is opposite the Las Vegas Convention Center (enter from Convention Center Dr) and has plenty of brochures, good advice and an excellent historic-photo display depicting Las Vegas in its Rat Pack prime. There is also a reservation service here (☎ 800-332-5333) and free phone connections to local hotels; call as many as you want – it's worth shopping around and comparing prices to get the best deal. If you're parking, you can avoid fees by saying you're just going to the visitor center.

Beware the businesses along the Strip advertising themselves as 'Official Tourist Bureaus;' they're basically low-rent, sometimes even shady, travel agencies pushing overpriced sightseeing trips to the Grand Canyon. If you want to see the canyon, the visitor center can give real advice.

Useful websites on Las Vegas include W www.insidervlv.com and W www.lasvegas.com.

There's an office of **AAA** (☎ 702-870-9171; 3312 W Charleston Blvd; open 8:30am-5.30pm Mon-Fri) in Las Vegas; if you experience car trouble staff can refer you to good local repair shops.

The **Gay & Lesbian Community Center** (☎ 702-733-9800; 953 E Sahara Ave, suite B25) can direct you to gay-friendly hotels and clubs.

A Las Vegas Wedding

Nowhere is getting married as easy as in Nevada. And apparently it's also very popular, with some 115,000 couples exchanging vows in Las Vegas annually (that's about 300 a day, with Valentine's Day and New Year's Eve the most popular).

Part of the appeal is that you can get hitched here in a flash. Other states require residency periods, blood tests and other such time-consuming silliness. In Nevada, all you need is to be over 18, have proof of identity and $50 (in cash) for the license. If either party has been previously married, the divorce must be finalized, and you'll need to give the date and the location of the decree.

In Las Vegas, licenses are doled out at the **Clark County Courthouse** (☎ 702-455-4416; 200 S 3rd St; open 8am-midnight Mon-Thurs, 8am Fri-midnight Sun). Shell out another $50 to get married by the county marriage commissioner at 309 S 3rd St, or find yourself a wedding chapel. The range of chapels (and price packages) is mind-boggling, some with drive-through windows, Elvis impersonators, medieval costumes and all manner of frilly, kitschy pomp. Don't expect much ceremony, though: there's probably another couple, hearts bursting with love, in line right behind you.

Money

Casino cashiers, open 24 hours, exchange traveler's checks and major foreign currencies, but banks will give a better rate. Along the Strip, ATMs are practically nonexistent outside the casinos, where you may be charged higher transaction fees than when withdrawing money from a bank ATM.

Tipping Las Vegas is one of *the* service-job capitals of the world, and most of the staff depend on tips to supplement their meager wages. Drinks are usually complimentary while you're playing the tables, but tip the waiter $1 or so for each round. Dealers expect to be tipped (or 'toked') only by winning players, maybe 10% of a win or with a side bet that the dealer collects if the bet wins. Buffet meals are self-serve, but it's nice to leave a small tip for the person who brings you a drink or cleans your table. Room-cleaners appreciate $2 a day (leave it on the pillow or side table), and while valet parking is generally free, it's a good idea to tip the valets a couple of bucks too.

Post & Communications

General delivery mail comes to the downtown **post office** *(301 Stewart Ave)*.

Bookstores

There's a **Waldenbooks** *(☎ 702-733-1049; 3200 Las Vegas Blvd)* in Fashion Show Mall. The **Gamblers Book Shop** *(☎ 702-382-7555; 630 S 11th St)* has books on every aspect of gambling.

Medical Services

For 24-hour emergency service contact the **University Medical Center** *(☎ 702-383-2000; 1800 W Charleston Blvd)*. **Gamblers Anonymous** *(☎ 702-385-7732)* may be able to help with gambling concerns.

Dangers & Annoyances

Most tourist areas are well lit, populated and pretty safe, especially along the Strip. North Las Vegas is reputed to be an unsafe area, but there's not much reason to go there anyway. Fremont St as it heads east from downtown gets very grungy and may feel threatening; if you're staying at the hostel in that area, you'll feel safer walking in a group. The stretch of Las Vegas Blvd between downtown and the Stratosphere tower is also rather unsavory; best not to walk it at night.

The words 'smoke-free' and 'Las Vegas' are never used in the same sentence: there are ashtrays at every telephone, elevator, pool and shower, in toilets, taxis and at the movies.

CASINOS

Casinos make money when they get the punters through the doors, and in Las Vegas the competition is so intense that casinos go to extraordinary lengths to lure their marks. Cheap booze, food and entertainment are still the prime draws. These days, though, a casino's got to have more than just flashing neon lights to draw the suckers in.

Since the late 1980s the south end of the Strip has become something of a cross between an amusement park (complete with roller coasters) and a shopping mall. For about a 3mi stretch south of the Las Vegas city limits, Las Vegas Blvd is lined with massive all-in-one hotel-casinos that each contain thousands of hotel rooms, vast gaming rooms and an increasing amount of non-gambling entertainment. Luxury is on the rise too, with each hotel competing for the greatest amount of marble in the bathroom and the most luxurious spa treatments.

The lure of giant black pyramids, exploding volcanoes and IMAX rides may draw you in, but once inside, you'll find the gambling scene is pretty much the same at every property. Most casinos are gaudy, noisy and deliberately disorienting. Long rows of slot machines are surrounded by mirrors, lights and more slot machines, all beeping and ringing like demented computer games and rattling the occasional win into a metal trough with as much noise as possible. Listening to a handful of folks winning back a few quarters of their investment leaves you deluded that everyone's raking in a jackpot. The tables for blackjack, craps and roulette are slightly more classy, though they usually require minimum bets of $5 or $10.

If you get lost, look up. Many casinos nowadays have signs pointing to hotel registration, restaurants, shopping malls and other locations. The registration desk is a good place to aim for; you can get your bearings from there. Some casinos may even have a few exit signs. If you're really stuck, ask a security guard or attendant; there are plenty of them around.

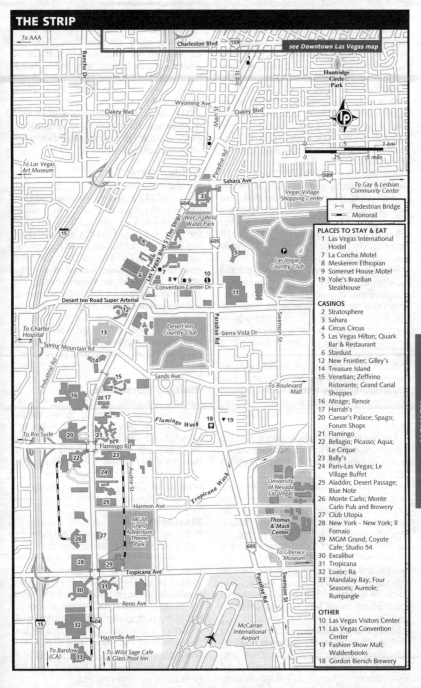

THE STRIP

To AAA

Charleston Blvd

see Downtown Las Vegas map

Huntridge
Circle
Park

Wyoming Ave

Oakey Blvd

Oakey Blvd

Rancho Dr

3rd St

Main St

Paradise Rd

To Las Vegas
Art Museum

Sahara Ave

Vegas Village
Shopping Center

To Gay & Lesbian
Community Center

Wet 'n' Wild
Water Park

Las Vegas
Country Club

Las Vegas Blvd S (The Strip)

Convention Center Dr

Desert Inn Road Super Arterial

To Charter
Hospital

Desert Inn
Country Club

Sierra Vista Dr

Spring Mountain Rd

Swenson St

Sands Ave

To Boulevard
Mall

Industrial Rd

Flamingo Wash

To Rio Suite

Flamingo Rd

Audrie St

Tropicana Wash

University of Nevada
Las Vegas

Harmon Ave

MGM Grand
Adventure
Theme Park

Thomas
& Mack
Center

To Liberace
Museum

Tropicana Ave

Reno Ave

Paradise Rd

Swenson St

To Barstow
(CA)

Hacienda Ave

McCarran
International
Airport

To Wild Sage Cafe
& Glass Pool Inn

| | Pedestrian Bridge |
| | Monorail |

0 — 5 — 1 km
0 — .25 — .5 mile

NEVADA

PLACES TO STAY & EAT
1 Las Vegas International
  Hostel
7 La Concha Motel
8 Meskerem Ethiopian
9 Somerset House Motel
19 Yolie's Brazilian
  Steakhouse

CASINOS
2 Stratosphere
3 Sahara
4 Circus Circus
5 Las Vegas Hilton; Quark
  Bar & Restaurant
6 Stardust
12 New Frontier; Gilley's
14 Treasure Island
15 Venetian; Zeffirino
  Ristorante; Grand Canal
  Shoppes
16 Mirage; Renoir
17 Harrah's
20 Caesar's Palace; Spago;
  Forum Shops
21 Flamingo
22 Bellagio; Picasso; Aqua;
  Le Cirque
23 Bally's
24 Paris-Las Vegas; Le
  Village Buffet
25 Aladdin; Desert Passage;
  Blue Note
26 Monte Carlo; Monte
  Carlo Pub and Brewery
27 Club Utopia
28 New York - New York; Il
  Fornaio
29 MGM Grand; Coyote
  Cafe; Studio 54
30 Excalibur
31 Tropicana
32 Luxor; Ra
33 Mandalay Bay; Four
  Seasons; Aureole;
  Rumjungle

OTHER
10 Las Vegas Visitors Center
11 Las Vegas Convention
  Center
13 Fashion Show Mall;
  Waldenbooks
18 Gordon Biersch Brewery

Black globes in the ceiling have hidden cameras that survey the scene constantly, while the cocktail waitresses cruise among the customers, dressed in fishnet stockings, togas, cowboy boots, grass skirts or other outfits contrived to match the casino theme.

Most of the customers are dressed somewhere between golf-course casual and fast-food sloppy. In special rooms for the real high rollers, the stakes are higher and the people flaunt their wealth by losing hundreds or thousands without flinching.

Angling for a free drink? Plop yourself down at a machine in the path of an oncoming cocktail server, adopt the dull-eyed look of a serious slot addict and drop in a few coins, slowly and carefully (video poker is best as it takes longer to play). Don't call out or rudely tap the waitress on the shoulder; wait for her to come to you.

When parking, you can drive around back to the casino's free lot or multistory garage if you choose. However, this often involves a very long walk to the casino itself. It's easier to leave your car with a parking valet; the service is technically free, though it's customary to leave a $1 or $2 tip with the attendant.

South Strip casinos are the showpieces everyone comes to Las Vegas to see. Here you'll find the pirate battles, fountain shows and erupting volcanoes, not to mention top-shelf restaurants, poncy mall shops and 3-D IMAX shows.

The North Strip is where you'll find the few survivors from the old Rat Pack days – or at least an aging vision of that illustrious past, as by today's standards these casinos are very middle-of-the-road. The towering Stratosphere is the chief exception – and Circus Circus is sort of a strange world unto itself – but most, including the Sahara, New Frontier and Stardust (home of the Wayne Newton Theater) are graying around their edges. They're very clean, though, and they still attract hordes of bus-tour patrons, middle-income families and 20-to-30-somethings who've discovered that the hotel rooms here are among the best bargains in town.

Downtown casinos are the city's oldest, a jumble of blazing neon, red velvet and fading carpet. Though the lights are still outlandishly bright, the casinos themselves are less gimmicky. This part of town feels more like Reno than anything on the Strip, and it attracts a more working-class, down-to-earth crowd intent on gambling. It can be quite a scene for that: grinning and sweating, the players crowd around the craps and card tables, having the time of their lives, if only for a few short moments.

The casinos highlighted below are ordered more or less from downtown to the South Strip. There are plenty more in between and spreading east and west too.

Golden Gate

For those curious as to what Vegas might have been like a century ago, this hotel and casino is the place to head. In fact, unless you're wowed by the outlandishness of the Strip, it's one of the city's most charming casinos. It's also got some serious history, dating back to 1906 (amazing that this town has let anything survive that long), when it opened as the Hotel Nevada. The 106 rooms have been faithfully preserved, and the gaming room retains the feel of an Old West saloon, complete with lovely wood trim, ceiling fans and a live honky-tonk pianist nightly. The tables can get busy, but the old bar's a great place to take a breather.

Binion's Horseshoe

Another venerable downtown casino, the Horseshoe was founded by Benny Binion in 1951. The World Series of Poker has been held here each April and May for over 30 years, and in the basement is one of the city's best-loved coffee shops. The gambling hall has Old Vegas charm in its pressed-tin ceiling, red-velvet wallpaper and rowdy crowd.

Stratosphere

Bob Stupak opened this casino on the north end of the Strip in 1996, right on the site of his previous temple of low-budget tackiness, Vegas World. The Stratosphere is marked by an 1149ft tower (down from the originally planned 1800ft), which has a restaurant, lounge and observation deck on top, along with a couple of thrill rides. High Roller ($9) is a coaster that wraps around the outside of the tower; Big Shot ($11), however, is a terrifying free-fall ride that moves up and down the tower's very tip. Both rides together cost $15.

Circus Circus

One of the original casino-cum-theme parks, dating to 1968, Circus Circus has a variety of free circus acts in the tentlike interior, a 'midway' with carnival attractions and a room of video games. Under the Adventure-dome are a double-loop roller coaster and 15 other rides.

Treasure Island

From the street you'll notice the pirate ship and man-of-war parked in Bucaneer Bay, a man-made lagoon fronting this pirate-themed hotel. Every 90 minutes from 4:30pm to midnight, the hotel stages a pyrotechnic sea battle, with lots of noise, smoke and drama. It's the best free show on the Strip, and kids, of course, dig it. You can also watch it from the Battle Bar inside.

Venetian

This massive property, opened in 1999 on land formerly occupied by the Sands, could be the most luxurious on the Strip. It's beautifully appointed (it better be for costing $1.5 billion) and features numerous nods to its namesake city. The domed lobby is lovely, every room is a suite and all manner of shops line canals that are certainly much cleaner than the originals (see Shopping later in this chapter). Gondoliers push tourists through these turquoise waters (keep in mind this is all on the *2nd floor*), crooning operatically under the artificially lit 'sky' ($12.50). And for those seeking real art, there's some truly serious work in the **Guggenheim Hermitage** and **Guggenheim Las Vegas** (admission to each/both $15/25).

Mirage

Steve Wynn's original Strip casino was the first of the ridiculously theatrical, flash palaces that define modern Las Vegas. Here, in the tropical pond that fronts the place, a fake volcano erupts about once every half hour after dusk; flames rise out of orange-colored water and a deep Sensur-round-style rumble threatens to break windows. It's silly and cheesy, but, well, you'll probably want to see it.

The gaming room is set amid a faux rain forest – not quite tiki-lounge kitsch, so don't get excited. Siegfried & Roy perform here for some serious dough (see Entertainment later in this chapter), but you can see their white tigers, bored and lethargic, for free in a cage near the entrance. Out back is the Dolphin Habitat and the Secret Garden of Siegfried & Roy; a combo pass costs $10.

Caesars Palace

Founded by Vegas pioneer Bob Sarno (who also gave us Circus Circus), this plush hotel-casino is practically a grandfather to the newer Strip properties, dating back to 1966 (though since then it's been reworked and renovated plenty). And as perhaps the most tastefully glamorous of the Strip casinos, it continues to draw in crowds. Attractions here include Race for Atlantis ($10), a 3-D IMAX extravaganza at the Forum Shops (see Shopping later in this chapter), and Magical Empire, a three-hour dinner-theater experience ($75) involving magical wizards and dancing fire.

Bellagio

Catering to upscale tastes and fat wallets, Steve Wynn's luxurious palace, Bellagio, offers lovely architecture and decor; a small **art gallery** (admission $12) with a $300 million collection of paintings by Matisse, van Gogh and others; and, out front, a free fountain show, featuring 1200 water jets that erupt amid a misty spectacle of light and music (beware Lionel Richie) every 15 minutes each evening. Foodwise, Bellagio contains some stellar offerings in Le Cirque, Aqua and Picasso, three of the top-rated (and most expensive) restaurants in town.

Paris-Las Vegas

Play the slots under the huge, metal legs of a 50-story mock Eiffel Tower at this casino, opened in 1999. Rides to the tower's top cost $9. The interior is like a Parisian square, and for a casino it feels surprisingly spacious, pleasantly moody and even rather light.

Aladdin

Opened in 2000, the new Aladdin (on the grounds of the old Aladdin) is the Strip's newest major hotel-casino. It sports an Arabian desert motif with a more modern, vaguely upscale flair. Like most of the Strip casinos it has a shopping mall, the huge Desert Passage (see Shopping later in this chapter). The Aladdin, however, filed for bankruptcy only 13 months after opening, so how it will fare in coming years is a mystery.

NEVADA

New York-New York

This hotel's facade is a microsized version of the Manhattan skyline, with replicas of the Statue of Liberty, Brooklyn Bridge and numerous skyscrapers. Inside are Park Ave shops, a Greenwich Village street scene, with restaurants and false storefronts, and, upstairs, a Coney Island midway. The Manhattan Express ($10.50) is probably the town's most thrilling roller coaster, plunging, twisting and looping in the open air above the Strip.

MGM Grand

With over 5000 rooms, this massive, green-striped structure is one of the world's largest hotels. Its glowing facade conjures up the Emerald City from *The Wizard of Oz*, the hotel's former theme. Major concerts will cost you plenty at the 17,000-seat Grand Garden Arena – home to Barbra Streisand's overhyped Millennium concert – while a visit to the Lion Habitat remains free. There's also a CBS television research facility here, where Joe and Jane Average get to rate potential TV pilots.

Excalibur

This huge hotel, opened in 1990, consists of a surprisingly crude, Disney-like medieval castle situated between two massive hotel towers that together boast some 4000 rooms. Brash and obnoxious, it's nonetheless got a family-fun attitude and is popular with kids. For adults, however, unless the idea of the 24-hour Renaissance Faire is your little slice of heaven, you may want to steer clear –especially if you find yourself on the 2nd floor, where a faux medieval village features strolling magicians, jugglers and singers.

Luxor

The gargantuan steel-and-glass pyramid is a sight in itself, a modern Vegas landmark since opening in 1993. A sphinx and obelisk sit out front, and at night a beam of light points straight up from the pyramid's apex for apparently no reason other than because it can. At the pyramid's hollow center is the world's largest atrium, staggering in its vastness. Attractions here include an IMAX theater ($9) and King Tut's Museum ($5), a replica of the famous pharaoh's tomb.

Las Vegas Hilton

Originally called the International, this white behemoth is found off the Strip, on Paradise Rd near the Convention Center. It's most famous for being the place where Elvis Presley played 837 consecutive sold-out shows during the final eight years of his life. A statue of 'the King' in the lobby commemorates this feat.

These days the Hilton draws thousands of suit-and-tied conventioneers alongside a steady steam of Trekkies, who come for **Star Trek: The Experience** *(admission $25)*, a combination of museum, theatrical presentation and gut-wrenching thrill ride.

There's also the Trek-themed Quark Bar & Restaurant (see Places to Eat later in this chapter) and a cool, space-age gambling area called Spacequest Casino. Pick up a six-pack of Romulan Ale on the way out ($9.95), brewed, curiously enough, in El Salvador.

FREMONT STREET EXPERIENCE

In an effort to inject new life into Las Vegas' aging downtown, a truly strange $70 million canopy has been installed over a four-block section of casino-lined Fremont St, which itself is now a pedestrian mall. After dark the canopy erupts in a dizzying six-minute light-and-music extravaganza that uses more than two million light bulbs and 540,000 watts of sound. The show takes on various themes such as Tropical Fever and Classic Rock, with crazy animation accompanying songs by Led Zeppelin, the Who and goodness knows who else. Cheesy and brash, it's also so totally weird (not to mention loud) that you can't help but stand captivated. Casino lights dim, and some folks actually bring chairs.

At the east end of the Experience is what's called the **Neon Museum**, an outdoor exhibit showcasing vintage signs retrieved from recently leveled hotels such as the Hacienda and the old Aladdin.

Adjacent is **Neonopolis**, a brand-new shopping and entertainment complex designed, like the Experience itself, to update the city's downtown and bring in new crowds. It's basically a mall, yet alongside the cinema, stores and restaurants are several more excellent vintage neon signs, always worth a peek.

MUSEUMS

Not everyone who comes to Las Vegas can handle endless days sitting in front of a clattering bank of slot machines, nursing whiskey sours and Winston 100s. If you're aching for a break back in the outside world, there are some sights and museums around town worth exploring.

Nevada State Museum & Historical Society

This museum (☎ 702-486-5205; 700 Twin Lakes Dr; adult/child $2/free; open 9am-5pm daily), in Lorenzi Park off W Washington Ave, surveys the state's history and environment (there's even a mammoth skeleton). More interesting, though, is the section that examines the role of the Mob in turning the old railroad town into a gambling resort (with a special exhibit on the Flamingo Hotel). Also look for the displays on atomic testing that went on in the state, and marvel at the fact that being near an explosion was once touted as a tourist attraction.

Las Vegas Natural History Museum

Dedicated to wildlife and the natural environment, this museum (☎ 702-384-3466; 900 Las Vegas Blvd N; adult/child $5/3; open 9am-4pm daily) has full-size dinosaur models and a good diorama showing plants and animals of Nevada's deserts.

Old Las Vegas Mormon Fort State Historic Park

Adjacent to the Natural History Museum, this park (☎ 702-486-3511; 908 Las Vegas Blvd N; admission $2; open 8:30am-3:30pm daily) preserves remains of the Las Vegas Mormon fort; it's fairly unspectacular, but this is where non-native settlement started in 1855. An adobe quadrangle provided refuge for travelers along the Mormon Trail. Some of the original walls still stand, and a three-room display shows artifacts and photos from the early days.

Lied Discovery Children's Museum

This hands-on science museum (☎ 702-382-3445; 833 Las Vegas Blvd N; adult/child $6/5; open 10am-5pm Tues-Sun) has exhibits that allow kids to make giant bubbles, be a radio disc jockey or pilot a space shuttle simulator.

The museum is in the same building as the Las Vegas Library (an interesting piece of architecture), about half a mile north of Hwy 95.

Liberace Museum

For the lowdown on high camp, this temple of extravagance (☎ 702-798-5595; 1775 E Tropicana; adult/senior/child $7/5/free; open 10am-5pm Mon-Sat, 1pm-5pm Sun), dedicated to pianist Wladziu Valentino Liberace (1919–87), is the one to see. Memorabilia from his life include the world's largest rhinestone, his glittery outfits, crazy cars and 18 of his 37 pianos; there's even quiet acknowledgment of his homosexuality. Proceeds go to the Liberace Foundation, which sponsors the musical education of talented young people.

HISTORIC BUILDINGS

Unsurprisingly, there aren't many. Not only is this a new city, but many of the original buildings and classic Rat Pack–era casinos have long since been demolished. (The visitor center has a good collection of historic photos.)

Downtown has a few survivors, such as the 1906 **Golden Gate** (originally called the Hotel Nevada) and the **Victory Hotel** (307 S Main St), which dates from 1910 and still attracts some tourists to its simple rooms despite a thoroughly grungy exterior. The 600 block of 3rd St has some surviving railroad-company houses from the same period. The 1930 **Las Vegas Academy** (315 S 7th St) has Art Deco detailing, while nearby, some substantial residences of the same era are built in Spanish mission style.

PLACES TO STAY

With so many mammoth hotels, finding a place to stay in Las Vegas is usually not a problem – except when big conventions are in town. During those times, prices are hiked enormously and places fill up fast. The obverse is true during lulls in convention activity, in summer and around the Christmas holidays, when the same rooms go for rock-bottom rates. At these times, even the big hotel-casinos will try to lure you with attractive deals that may include spa passes, free shows and even airline discounts. In general, prices are lowest Sunday to Thursday. Weekend rates can easily double or more, and they can be higher on Saturday than on Friday.

NEVADA

The visitor center has a toll-free reservation service through which you can get current rates, and free phones from which you can make reservations (see Information earlier in this chapter).

Motel prices are less variable, but they still tend to be higher on Friday and Saturday nights and may have a two-night minimum stay.

With all that in mind, don't take the prices below as gospel, only as a loose guide. Heck, they may even turn out to be cheaper; it's worth a call or online search to find out.

Camping & Hostels
Camping is available in parks east and west of the city (see Around Las Vegas later in this chapter).

Las Vegas International Hostel (☎ 702-385-9955; 1208 Las Vegas Blvd; dorm beds $14) is an independent no-frills place in a grungy area south of downtown, and it's popular with international backpackers; an HI card gets you a slight discount. There's a small kitchen, lounge and laundry. It's pretty clean and well run but gets crowded, so check in early (no reservations). The hostel also runs inexpensive tours to the Grand Canyon, Bryce Canyon and Zion National Parks. There are also semiprivate rooms ($28), though you'll pay almost as much as a motel.

USA Hostel – Las Vegas (☎ 702-385-1150, fax 702-385-4940; 1322 Fremont St; dorm beds from $15, private rooms from $40) is an independent hostel in a nasty area (be careful walking around) a few blocks east of the Fremont St Experience. The facilities, though, are fine and include a pool and Jacuzzi. The staff offer free pick-up from the Greyhound station for those staying two or more nights.

Motels
Inexpensive motels abound in Vegas. Usually they aren't as good value as a casino special, and many are in unsavory parts of town, but they can be cheaper than a casino on weekends.

The decrepit motels east of downtown along Fremont St have some cool neon signs but are not recommended for sleeping. Between downtown and the Strip are lots more choices, though most here, too, are dodgy. Instead, look along the North Strip and the streets leading east from it, or on the south end of the Strip near the airport.

La Concha Motel (☎ 702-735-1255; 2955 Las Vegas Blvd S; midweek/weekends from $48/68), a 1950s classic right in the center of the North Strip near the Stardust, is one of the most visually appealing motels in town. Look for the large arched entryway.

Somerset House Motel (☎ 702-735-4411; 294 Convention Center Dr; midweek/weekends from $33/44) is a simple but friendly motel. It's just east of the Strip for those who need that little bit of distance.

Glass Pool Inn (☎ 702-739-6800, 800-527-7118; 4613 Las Vegas Blvd S; midweek from $39) is a good choice at the far southern end of the Strip. It's famous for its swimming pool, which has big, round windows that allow you to see the pool from below the waterline.

Casinos – Downtown
Downtown's most famous casino is probably **Binion's Horseshoe** (☎ 702-382-1600, 800-237-6537, fax 702-382-5750; W www.binions.com; 128 E Fremont; rooms $30-60), right in the heart of the Fremont St action. The place retains genuine Old Vegas charm, and rooms sometimes are as cheap as $20. Check the website for specials.

El Cortez Hotel & Casino (☎ 702-385-5200, 800-634-6703, fax 702-385-9765; 600 Fremont St; queen beds $27.50), dating from 1941, is the first hotel-casino to be owned by an East Coast organized-crime syndicate. Don't worry, the place is legit these days.

The **Golden Nugget** (☎ 702-385-7111, 800-634-3454, fax 702-386-8362; W www.goldennugget.com; 129 E Fremont St; midweek/weekends from $59/99) has tapped deeply into the bus-tour market and attracts a lot of seniors. Despite all the brass and glitter it's rather bland. This was Steve Wynn's first big casino project (he renovated it in the 1970s) before founding the Mirage and Bellagio.

Casinos – North Strip
The last surviving 1950s-era hotel-casino touting a desert theme, the **Sahara** (☎ 702-737-2111, 800-634-6666, fax 702-737-1017; 2535 Las Vegas Blvd S; midweek/weekends from $30/80) doesn't churn up a whole lot of excitement inside, but it does contain very comfortable rooms for great prices. It's one of the best deals in town, in fact. The 'old' tower is a little cheaper and just fine.

The **Stardust** (☎ 702-732-6111, 800-634-6757, fax 702-732-6257; 3000 Las Vegas Blvd S; midweek/weekends from $54/80) was born in the 1950s and renovated in the '90s. It's a straightforward place, popular with older folks and those seeking a Wayne Newton encounter. The purple-tinted tower is new and shiny, but the lowest room rates may leave you stuck in the 'villa' out back. Still, it's decent value.

Circus Circus (☎ 702-734-0410, 800-634-3450, fax 702-734-2268; 2880 Las Vegas Blvd S; midweek/weekends from $34/89) is a big, family-friendly budget place.

Casinos – South Strip

You want spectacle, you got it: some of the biggest hotels in the world are lined up next to each other on the southern end of the Strip.

Every room at the **Venetian** (☎ 702-414-1000, 877-857-1861, fax 702-414-1100; W www.venetian.com; 3355 Las Vegas Blvd S; midweek/weekends from $159/199) is a suite, and they're among the city's finest. Even the standard rooms are an impressive 650 sq ft, and the biggest suites top out at 1456 sq ft. Rooms with good Strip views cost a bit more.

Caesars Palace (☎ 702-731-7110, 800-634-6661, fax 702-731-6636; W www.caesars palace.com; 3570 Las Vegas Blvd S; rooms from $109) is another of the Strip's ritziest joints, with large, luxurious rooms. Standard rooms are at least 350 sq ft, 'superior' rooms in the newer tower are 525 sq ft. There are three pools and lots of amenities.

Bellagio (☎ 702-693-7111, 888-987-6667, fax 702-693-8546; W www.bellagiolasvegas .com; 3600 Las Vegas Blvd S; rooms from $159) comes with a steep price tag designed to keep riffraff out. Standard rooms are large at 510 sq ft but not nearly as luxurious as one might expect.

Monte Carlo (☎ 702-730-7000, 800-311-8999, fax 702-730-7250; W www .monte-carlo.com; 3770 Las Vegas Blvd S; midweek/weekends from $69/119) is an upscale hotel-casino, with more than 3000 nicely appointed rooms and a slightly more subdued atmosphere than some of its fancy-pants, nose-in-the-air neighbors.

Mandalay Bay (☎ 702-632-7777, 877-632-7000, fax 702-632-7013; W www.man dalaybay.com; 3950 Las Vegas Blvd S; rooms from $149) is an upscale place with a beach-resort theme, an excellent pool and 3220 rooms. That's not including the additional 500 rooms dedicated to the ultra-luxurious **Four Seasons** (☎ 702-632-5000; rooms from $200), occupying the hotel's 35th to 39th floors.

Bally's (☎ 702-739-4111, 800-634-3434; W www.ballyslv.com; 3645 Las Vegas Blvd S; rooms from $59) doesn't have the amusement park–like gimmicks of its neighbors, but it does have 2800 sizable, and often affordable, rooms.

Paris-Las Vegas (☎ 702-946-7000, 888-266-5687, fax 702-946-4405; W www.paris lasvegas.com; 3655 Las Vegas Blvd S; rooms from $79) has nearly 3000 rooms, each at least 450 sq ft. If full, they may be able to quote you rates at Caesars Palace, the Hilton, the Flamingo or Bally's, as they're all also owned by Park Place Entertainment, the gaming division of Hilton.

New York-New York (☎ 702-740-6969, 800-693-6763, fax 702-740-6810; W www .nynyhotelcasino.com; 3790 Las Vegas Blvd; rooms from $65) replicates Big Apple details rather well, right down to the thick accent on the reservation clerk. Inside the 12 towers are 2000 rooms, standard size between 300 and 400 sq ft.

Luxor (☎ 702-262-4000, 800-288-1000, fax 702-262-4454; 3900 W www.luxor.com; Las Vegas Blvd S; rooms from $69), next door to Excalibur, is a hulking glass pyramid with an ancient-Egyptian theme. The rooms in the 30-story pyramid are lined around a massive atrium (vertigo sufferers may want to avoid this place) and are reached via what they call an 'inclinator,' an elevator that follows the incline of the pyramid. Save for the windows, angled to echo the shape of the structure, the rooms are comfortable but not terribly exciting. More rooms are in a tower out back. The spa is excellent, so try to get passes.

MGM Grand (☎ 702-891-1111, 800-929-1111, fax 702-891-1030; W www.mgmgrand .com; 3799 Las Vegas Blvd S; midweek/weekends from $59/89) is the biggest hotel in Las Vegas, with a whopping 5000 rooms spread across four 30-story towers.

PLACES TO EAT
Casino Buffets & Specials

The all-you-can-eat buffet is a Nevada dining institution, and one that can get pretty sloppy as greedy diners pile their plates with mountains of schlock – as if eating $30 worth of overcooked beef at a $5 buffet will recoup the $25 they've just flushed into the slots.

Traditionally, the food quality at these troughs has been substandard. But more recently, a handful of the top-end hotels have polished-up the buffet concept, laying out spreads that are actually impressive. It's not Spago or Le Cirque – both of which have branches in town – but at least the fish is fresh, not frozen, and the vegetables haven't been lingering under a heat lamp since daybreak. Several places feature food stations, where dishes are made to order.

Breakfast is the cheapest meal and dinner the most expensive; weekend brunches are often served. Weekend dinners sometimes feature special menus and cost a few bucks extra.

A good strategy is to hit the buffet for lunch. It's considerably cheaper than dinner, and since most casinos serve lunch until 2pm or 3pm daily, all that shrimp, pork and pasta you just stuffed down your gullet is likely to keep you full well past suppertime.

The best buffet in town is a subject of local debate, but the better spreads definitely include the following.

Bellagio (3600 Las Vegas Blvd S; breakfast/lunch/dinner $12/15/25) is a strong contender for the title of being home to the city's top buffet. The vastness of it all is mind-boggling, and the quality is as good as it gets – fish flown in fresh five times a week, for instance, and lots of crisp fruits and vegies.

Paris-Las Vegas (3655 Las Vegas Blvd S; $12-25) leans heavily on its French theme in both decor and cuisine at its Le Village Buffet, where you can sample bites from every province of France.

Rio Suite Hotel and Casino (3700 W Flamingo Rd; breakfast/lunch/dinner $10/12/17), west of the Strip, pulls in locals and tourists to its Carnival World Buffet, featuring numerous international offerings.

Bally's (3645 Las Vegas Blvd S; brunch $55; 9:30am-2:30pm Sun) offers the Sterling Brunch just once a week, a serious gourmet splurge that's priced accordingly.

Most casinos also advertise special bargain-priced meals; keep your eyes on the billboards and marquees, especially on the North Strip and downtown. The prime-rib dinner at the modest, Western-themed **New Frontier** (3120 Las Vegas Blvd S; meals $8.95), Sunday through Thursday, is one such deal.

For breakfast, the basement coffee shop at **Binion's Horseshoe** (128 E Fremont St; breakfast under $5) has long been famous for its massive ham-and-egg special, not as cheap as it was but the thick meat slab still spills off the plate.

Speaking of cheap, the **Golden Gate** (cnr Fremont & Main Sts) has been dishing out its 99¢ shrimp cocktails since 1959. It also serves a $7.77 porterhouse steak.

Casino Restaurants

For dinner ideas, peruse the free *Las Vegas Weekly*, which has good opinionated reviews and listings. Other free publications such as *Today in Las Vegas* and *What's On* also contain listings and descriptions of casino restaurants.

Star Trek fans and other geek-pretenders should head immediately to the Las Vegas Hilton, home to the surprisingly cool and moody **Quark Bar & Restaurant** (3000 Paradise Rd; meals from $10). Amid a futuristic setting you can indulge in 'little green salads,' 'hamborgers' and other 'exotic' dishes, perhaps even with Klingons in a nearby booth.

Monte Carlo Pub and Brewery (3770 Las Vegas Blvd S; meals from $8) serves good pub food alongside craft-brewed beers, such as the tasty Jackpot Ale. Get there before 9pm, though, when beer prices increase and the bands that play nightly crank up the volume.

Coyote Cafe (3799 Las Vegas Blvd S; dinner from $20), an MGM Grand clone of a popular Santa Fe spot, serves satisfying 'nouvelle southwestern.'

Il Fornaio (3790 Las Vegas Blvd S; dinner from $15) is a reliable Italian eatery along the Greenwich Village street-scene section of New York-New York. The homemade breads are almost the best thing about the place.

Seemingly overnight, Las Vegas went from buffet capital to a magnet for top-end dining and celebrity chefs. The following hot spots are well worth your bucks, if you didn't already blow them at the craps table, and reservations are essential. Some impose a dress code.

Le Cirque (☎ 702-693-7223; 3600 Las Vegas Blvd S; dinner $80-95), inside Bellagio, is a satellite of New York City's famed French restaurant (jacket and tie required for men). Bellagio is also home to **Aqua** (☎ 702-693-7223; mains $30-50), a branch of Michael Mina's top-rated San Francisco seafood palace, and **Picasso** (☎ 702-693-7223; dinner $80), featuring superb Spanish-and French-inspired cuisine.

Renoir (☎ 702-791-7223; 3400 Las Vegas Blvd S; tasting menu $75-100), inside the Mirage, is another serious French restaurant that gets top honors.

Wolfgang Puck's Las Vegas branch of his trendy **Spago** (☎ 702-369-6300; 3500 Las Vegas Blvd S; dinner mains $12-40) brings his trademark California cuisine to the Forum Shops at Caesars Palace. Spago has a casual cafe and a more formal dining room.

Aureole (☎ 702-632-7401; 3950 Las Vegas Blvd S; dinner from $50), at Mandalay Bay, is country cousin of another famous New York institution. It is known for its New American cuisine and stunning four-story wine tower, the latter alone worth a gander.

Zeffirino Ristorante (☎ 702-414-3500; 3355 Las Vegas Blvd; mains from $25), at the Venetian, serves superb Italian cuisine that rivals what you'd get in the mother country itself.

Binion's Ranch Steakhouse (☎ 702-382-1600; 128 E Fremont; dinner from $25), atop Binion's Horseshoe downtown, is an old-school favorite that still gets high ratings for its superb beef and sweeping views.

Other Restaurants

In the Somerset Shopping Center, just east of the Strip, is **Meskerem Ethiopian** (252 Convention Center Dr; meals $4-10), a small, pleasant spot serving Ethiopian meals, including vegetarian mains and Ethiopian-style egg dishes at breakfast. There's espresso too, and a market next-door.

El Sombrero (807 S Main St; dishes under $10) is an old-time, unassuming Mexican restaurant that's been in business since 1951. The portions are huge, simple and delicious.

Yolie's Brazilian Steakhouse (☎ 702-794-0700; 3900 Paradise Rd; prix fixe dinner $27) piles in the out-of-towners to feast on its marinated steaks.

Wild Sage Cafe (☎ 702-944-7243; 600 E Warm Springs Rd; mains from $15) is a top-rated New American–cum-Californian place that, refreshingly, is not found inside a casino and doesn't sport the gleaming face of a celebrity chef.

ENTERTAINMENT

Free papers such as *Today in Las Vegas* and *What's On*, available around town, provide thorough listings of current mainstream happenings. Alternatives to the casino scene are covered in the *Las Vegas Weekly*.

Casinos

The major casinos offer a staggering range of entertainment options. The 'big-room' shows can be concerts by the likes of Tom Jones and Lenny Kravitz, or they can be Broadway musicals or Vegas-style sound-and-light extravaganzas. These usually start around $30 but can run as high as $100 or more a pop; a couple of cocktails are sometimes thrown in.

Elvis impersonators aren't as prevalent these days, and the Rat Pack has passed away, but mediocre lounge singers are everywhere. Some perform on stage and an entry fee is charged, others perform in some bar off the casino floor. The latter are usually free – and so they should be, since they're generally as tacky as you could imagine. (Think Doobie Brothers covers by overly primped performers with no sense of irony; Sammy and Dean are probably rolling in their graves.) If you want the campy cheese factor of Old Vegas, your best bet is to scour the bars and lounges of the older casinos.

The most popular shows often sell out, especially on weekends, so make advance reservations. Following is a sample of some of the best-known venues and shows:

Bally's (☎ 702-739-4567; 3645 Las Vegas Blvd S) books big-name acts in its Celebrity Room; its long-running *Jubilee* ($53 to $70) is a showgirl spectacle.

Bellagio (☎ 702-796-9999; 3600 Las Vegas Blvd S) has the best – and most expensive – show in town: the awe-inspiring *O,* which features Cirque du Soleil performing an aquatic production on, in and above a 1.5 million gallon pool ($90 to $110).

Caesars Palace (☎ 702-731-7333; 3570 Las Vegas Blvd S) is scheduled to open its brand-new Colosseum showroom in 2003, with Celine Dion as the kick off headliner.

Excalibur (☎ 702-597-7600; 3850 Las Vegas Blvd S) runs the *Tournament of Kings,* featuring jousting, jesters, wizards, invading armies and dragons in combat, while spectators feast on a medieval banquet ($42).

Flamingo (☎ 800-221-7299; 3555 Las Vegas Blvd S) has a few different theaters and productions, including singer Gladys Knight in the main showroom ($55 to 65), comedy troupe Second City in Bugsy's Celebrity Theater ($28) and the bawdy revue *Bottoms Up* ($13).

Harrah's (☎ 702-369-5222; *3475 Las Vegas Blvd S*) has singer-bandleader Clint Holmes ($60), topless revue *Skintight* ($40) and rotating comedians at the Improv ($24).

Luxor (☎ 702-262-4400; *3900 Las Vegas Blvd S*) is home to the Blue Man Group ($87), the topless show *Midnight Fantasy* ($33), IMAX films ($9) and several other entertainment options.

Mandalay Bay (☎ 702-632-7777; *3950 Las Vegas Blvd S*) has the music and dance show *Storm* ($55 to $65), as well as the 12,000-seat Events Center, an outdoor island stage and the 1800-seat branch of nightclub chain **House of Blues**.

MGM Grand (☎ 702-891-7777; *3799 Las Vegas Blvd S*) has *EFX Alive*, an over-the-top high-tech extravaganza that in the past has featured pop stars such as David Cassidy and Rick Springfield.

Mirage (☎ 702-792-7777; *3400 Las Vegas Blvd S*) is host to the long-running magic show by Siegfried & Roy, complete with white tigers, whose dinner you'll help finance at a staggering $105 a ticket.

Monte Carlo (☎ 702-730-7777; *3770 Las Vegas Blvd S*) is home to magician Lance Burton ($55 to $60), who has his own $27 million theater.

Stardust (☎ 702-732-6111; *3000 Las Vegas Blvd S*) is where you'll find the Wayne Newton Theater, with Mr Las Vegas himself performing regularly in all his glittery glory ($55). Don Rickles also does his shtick here every couple of months ($50).

Treasure Island (☎ 702-796-9999; *3300 Las Vegas Blvd S*) presents *Mystère*, featuring Cirque du Soleil ($80).

Tropicana (☎ 702-739-2411; *3801 Las Vegas Blvd S*) has been running its classic production *Folies Bergère* for years ($50 to $62). The early show is 'covered,' the late show is the 'adult' version.

Bars & Clubs

Many, though not all, of the fancier dance clubs have a dress code, which usually means no jeans, sneakers or sports attire. Most have a cover charge of $5 to $20, with women and locals often getting a discount.

Across from the Monte Carlo is **Club Utopia** (☎ 702-740-4646; *3765 Las Vegas Blvd S*), a popular dance spot that plays techno, hip-hop and Top 40.

Club Rio (*3700 W Flamingo Rd*) is a flashy dance club found west of the Strip at the glittering Rio. The chic **VooDoo Lounge** is upstairs, overlooking the city from the 51st floor.

Ra (*3900 Las Vegas Blvd*), inside the Luxor, is a supertrendy dance venue with space-age gimmicks such as gigantic statues with laser beams shooting from their eyes.

Studio 54 (*3799 Las Vegas Blvd S*) is a vibrant dance club taking up three floors at the MGM Grand.

Gilley's (*3120 Las Vegas Blvd*) is a country dance hall, saloon and barbecue place inside the New Frontier. It's named after singer Mickey Gilley and his Houston country bar Gilley's, the setting for *Urban Cowboy*.

Rumjungle (*3950 Las Vegas Blvd*), at Mandalay Bay, is a Caribbean restaurant by day, transforming into a hot and saucy nightclub after 11pm.

Gordon Biersch Brewery (*3987 Paradise Rd*), a microbrewery chain originating in Palo Alto, California, has German-style lagers, a clean-cut crowd and local bands.

Blue Note (*3663 Las Vegas Blvd S*), at the Aladdin, pays homage to its famous New York namesake and features quality jazz artists, along with some rock and blues performers.

For a straight-up casino lounge experience, the **Starlight Lounge** at the Stardust feels like a classic Las Vegas hang-out; the **Lagoon Saloon** at the Mirage is like boozing inside a terrarium; and **Houdini's Lounge** at the Monte Carlo, next to the baccarat area, offers dark and comfy respite if you're in dire need of what the country singer Dick Curless called a 'loser's cocktail.'

SHOPPING

Until lately, shopping for anything but cheap souvenirs and your next free drink hasn't really been a chief focus of visitors here. Nowadays, though, the scene has evolved once again. The big Las Vegas casinos have gone from sin palaces to amusement parks to, currently it seems, shopping malls, with vast corridors of shop after shop, some as expensive and snooty as anything in Upper Manhattan or San Francisco's Union Square.

So if you tire of cards and dice, you can take a break to ogle some Cartier or get in a tizzy over Gucci.

The **Grand Canal Shoppes** at the Venetian include over 60 boutiques in an Italian streetscape scene, with 'sidewalk' coffee shops and with singing gondoliers plying the 2nd-floor 'Grand Canal' under a blue-lit 'sky.' Despite being entirely artificial, the atmosphere is surprisingly calming – is this what the 21st century holds in store?

At Caesars Palace, the **Forum Shops** offer an indoor imitation of a Roman street; the painted 'sky' changes from dawn to dusk every three hours, and at the fountain, marble statues come to life and pay homage to self-indulgence. Besides all these shenanigans you'll find some seriously top-end stores.

The Aladdin's **Desert Passage**, despite *Arabian Nights*–like gestures and decor, edges embarrassingly close to a traditional suburban shopping mall. Speaking of which, there's one of those right on the Strip, **Fashion Show Mall** (*3200 Las Vegas Blvd S*), next to Treasure Island.

Downtown has finally entered the mall game, with the opening in 2002 of the $100 million **Neonopolis**. The multistory structure, taking up a full block at the corner of Las Vegas Blvd and Fremont St, contains a multiscreen movie theater, restaurants and shops in a gamble to win more tourists to the area.

For more unique items, try the **Gamblers General Store** (*800 S Main St*), where you can buy your own slot machine (they'll organize shipping) and personalized poker chips.

The Attic (*1018 S Main St*) has a surreal collection of vintage clothing, though better bargains will likely be found in nearby thrift stores or local pawn shops.

GETTING THERE & AWAY
Air
Immediately south of the Strip, **McCarran International Airport** (☎ *702-261-5211;* W *www.mccarran.com*) has direct flights coming from most US cities and a few from Canada and Europe. Arriving via a package that includes airfare and accommodation is increasingly common and often the best deal. Check casino websites for specials, or talk to a travel agent. If you're picking someone up, parking is paid by meters, so bring lots of quarters.

Bus
Downtown, **Greyhound** (☎ *702-384-8009; 200 S Main St*) has regular buses to and from Los Angeles ($34, seven hours), San Diego ($46, 8½ hours) and San Francisco ($67, 15 hours). Package tours to Las Vegas often include bus transportation for little more than the usual cost of accommodations.

Amtrak (☎ *800-872-7245*) runs buses to and from Los Angeles ($34, six hours), as does the backpacker-oriented **Missing Link Tour Company** (☎ *800-209-8586;* W *www.tmltours.com*). Its shuttles run three times weekly in either direction ($39/75 one-way/round trip), with free pickup from area hostels and hotels. The drop-off point for Amtrak is the Greyhound station downtown at 200 S Main St.

Car
Agencies abound and competition keeps car- rental prices fairly low, except during peak times. Besides all the major agencies there are numerous local agencies, including **Brooks** (☎ *702-735-3344; Las Vegas Blvd S Site 6*), **Fairway** (☎ *702-369-7216; 4645 Procyon St Site A*) and **Sav-Mor** (☎ *702-736-1234; 5101 Rent Car Rd*).

GETTING AROUND
To/From the Airport
Many hotels provide free airport shuttle services for guests. If that doesn't suit you, try **Bell Trans** (☎ *702-739-7990*) which will take you to the Strip ($4.25 per person) from outside baggage claim. Taxi fares to Strip hotels are $10 or $12, to downtown about $20.

Bus
Aside from walking, the local bus system **Citizens Area Transport** (CAT; ☎ *702-228-7433*) is the best way to get up and down the Strip (and to other locations around town) without a car. Fares are $2, it's relatively quick (it doesn't battle its way to each casino entryway but stops along Las Vegas Blvd) and it comes every 10 or 15 minutes all day and night. Bus Nos 301 and 302 operate up and down the Strip.

The **Strip Trolley** (☎ *702-382-1404*) operates a loop from Mandalay Bay to the Stratosphere ($1.65) between 9:30am and 1:30am daily. It's generally slower than the bus, though.

NEVADA

Monorail

Four short monorail tracks have been laid out between select Strip casinos, but you could almost walk it in the time you spend finding the station, waiting for the train and trundling along the track (rides are free). A new line being constructed between Bally's, the Hilton and the Sahara promises to be genuinely useful. Fantasies still linger for a monorail between the Strip and downtown, but don't hold your breath.

Taxi

Standard base fares for taxis are $2.30 for the first mile, plus for $1.80 each additional mile. Companies include **Whittlesea** (☎ 702-384-6111) and **Yellow Cab** (☎ 702-873-2000).

Around Las Vegas

RED ROCK CANYON

The contrast between the artificial brightness of Las Vegas and the natural splendor of Red Rock Canyon Conservation Area, a 20mi drive west of the Strip, couldn't be greater. The canyon is actually more like a valley, with the steep, rugged Red Rock escarpment rising 3000ft on its western edge. Red Rock makes an excellent, easy getaway from the madness of the Strip, though because of its proximity, visitors shouldn't expect solitude.

To get here from Las Vegas, head west on Charleston Blvd, which turns into SR 159, for about 30 minutes (don't travel during rush hour, though, when it's horribly clogged). At the canyon there's a 13mi, one-way scenic loop with access to hiking trails.

The excellent **visitor center** (☎ 702-363-1921; open 8:30am-4:30pm daily) has maps and hiking information. The scenic loop is open 8am to dusk, and the park day-use fee is $5. First-come, first-served **camping** (sites $10) is available 2mi east of the visitor center.

LAKE MEAD & HOOVER DAM

It's less than an hour's drive down Hwys 95 and 93 from Las Vegas to Lake Mead and Hoover Dam. They are the most-visited sites within the **Lake Mead National Recreation Area** (☎ 702-293-8907), which encompasses 110mi-long Lake Mead, 67mi-long Lake

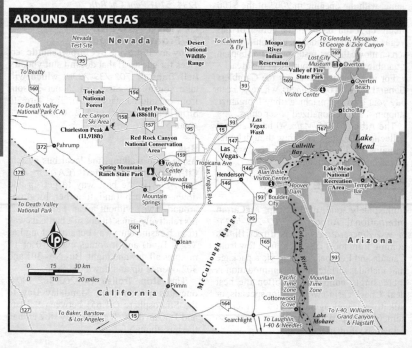

AROUND LAS VEGAS

Mohave and many miles of desert around the lakes.

Lake Mead has 550mi of shoreline surrounded by stunning desert scenery. The **Alan Bible Visitor Center** (☎ 702-293-8990; open 8:30am-4:30pm daily), about 26mi east of Las Vegas on Hwy 93, has information on recreational options, camping and natural history. Northshore Rd makes an excellent scenic drive along the north side of the lake, leading to Valley of Fire State Park. Shore-side campgrounds are at Boulder Beach, Las Vegas Wash, Callville Bay, Echo Bay and Temple Bar (in Arizona).

Boulder Dam (renamed Hoover Dam) was built between 1931 and '35, and was the world's largest dam at the time. It backed up the Colorado River to form Lake Mead, flooding canyons, archaeological sites, wilderness areas and communities. Flood control, irrigation, hydroelectric power and a regulated water supply were the main purposes for Hoover Dam's constr-uction, and they remain the dam's primary functions today.

Tours are self-guided, last about two hours and take place on top of the dam (adult/child $10/4). Tickets are sold at the **visitor center** (☎ 702-294-3524; open 9am-5pm daily). The adjacent parking garage costs $5.

VALLEY OF FIRE STATE PARK

Near the north end of Lake Mead, Valley of Fire State Park (day-use per vehicle $5) is a masterpiece of desert scenery – a fantasy of wonderful shapes carved in psychedelic sandstone. It's similar, in appearance and geology, to the desert landscapes of Utah, Arizona and New Mexico, but just an hour's drive from Las Vegas and largely uncrowded.

The **visitor center** (☎ 702-397-2088; open 8:30am-4:30pm daily) is just off SR 169, which runs through the park. It has excellent exhibits, general information and hiking suggestions. The valley is at its most fiery at dawn and dusk, so staying in one of the two first-come, first-served **campgrounds** (tent sites $8) is worthwhile. The quickest route from Las Vegas is via I-15 and SR 169, though the drive along Lake Mead's Northshore Rd is more scenic; the latter hooks up with Hwy 95 near Henderson, south of Vegas.

Reno

Reno (population 182,818; elevation 4500ft) is a long way from Las Vegas. Not just in distance (445mi) and climate (temperatures are consistently below those of Vegas), but in overall spirit. Both cities are gambling meccas, home to 24-hour casinos, high-rise hotel towers, a huge service industry and many thousands of frantic tourists with dreams of a debt-free lifestyle. But unlike Las Vegas, which is defined more by its fake cityscapes, Reno has managed to preserve a certain small-town charm.

Most people come to Reno for a quick weekend getaway from nearby towns such as Sacramento, Boise or Fresno. And they come to gamble, holing up in a casino just long enough to burn through next month's rent money and take a quick dip into the baby's college fund before hobbling back to their day jobs. If you're up early on a Sunday morning you'll see them out there, stumbling down Virginia St in dizzy wonder, holding their heads, shouting at their spouses, or simply staring into the void of a streetscape that no longer glitters and gleams with shiny promises.

Of course, that's just one side of Reno. Not that it's exactly teeming with cosmopolitan attitude, but unlike its fantasyland cousin down south, Reno is real. Never mind that its hotels aren't as big, its casinos not as tricked out. Where Las Vegas relishes its artificiality, Reno retains the feel of a city that was actually meant to be here.

If you want to gamble, the games inside the casinos are exactly the same as the ones in Las Vegas, and you're just as likely to lose your money. The biggest difference is you're not doing so under a fake New York skyline or beside an artificial Venetian canal. Reno repeatedly reminds you that it's 'The Biggest Little City in the World' – most notably on the famous arch over N Virginia St – and as cheesy as that slogan will always be, there's something refreshing about it too.

Reno has quite a few historic buildings scattered around town, such as the 1911 **Washoe County Courthouse** (117 S Virginia St), where Clark Gable and Marilyn Monroe first meet in John Huston's film *The Misfits*. Sadly, though, while Reno wears its history proudly, it also – like Vegas – appears to find no shame in erasing chunks of it. Years ago, travelers would see interstate billboards advertising 'Harold's Club or Bust' as far as 1000mi away; today that venerable downtown property – and it's neighbor, the Nevada Club – is nothing more than a long entryway into glitzy Harrah's. And the old Mapes Hotel, Nevada's prototypical hotel-casino – a building once on the National Register of Historic Places – is now just a patch of blacktop and dirt used for random civic events.

Probably the most attractive thing about Reno, though, is its convenient location at the border between the Great Basin Desert and the Sierra Nevada mountains. With its cheap eats and plentiful motels, it makes an excellent base for trips into the scenic surrounding areas.

HISTORY

In the 1850s, travelers on the Humboldt Trail to California crossed the Truckee River at Truckee Meadows (where Reno now stands), followed the river up into the mountains north of Lake Tahoe and crossed the Sierra at Donner Pass – basically the route of today's I-80. Several people established river crossings and charged tolls. The most enterprising of them was Myron Lake, who also built a hotel, saloon and several miles of road to steer people to his bridge. After the mining boom started in Virginia City, Lake's crossing became a busy thoroughfare, and Lake became rich, acquiring most of the surrounding land.

When the Central Pacific Railroad came through, Lake offered to donate land for a town if the company would establish a passenger and freight depot. A deal was struck and, in May of 1868, lots were auctioned in a new town named after Jesse Reno, a Union general killed in the Civil War. In 1870 Reno became the seat of Washoe County, and in 1872 the Virginia & Truckee Railroad linked it to the boomtowns of the Comstock Lode. By 1900 Reno was a rough railroad town of 4500 people, though it had acquired a university, thanks to some generous mining magnates.

As the mining boom played out and most of Nevada stagnated, Reno made an economic virtue of social vices. Gambling and prostitution were frontier traditions that became attractions in Reno as they were suppressed in increasingly respectable California. During Prohibition, Reno not only tolerated the speakeasies, but became a place for mobsters to launder their money. The other major 'industry' was that of divorce, easily finalized after the short six-week residency requirement was met.

Irrigation in the Carson Valley, agriculture, light industry and warehousing have since helped to diversify the economy, along with tourism based on gambling, the attractions of Lake Tahoe and the region's history.

ORIENTATION

The main highway to and from Reno is I-80, which heads west to Truckee (32mi) and San Francisco, and east to Sparks (5mi), Elko and Salt Lake City. Hwy 395 runs south through Carson City (30mi) to the Eastern Sierra and on to Southern California.

Reno's main drag, with most of the casinos and millions of watts of electricity, is N Virginia St, between I-80 and the Truckee River. The landmark Reno Arch crosses Virginia St at Commercial Row, with the railroad tracks cutting through the town behind it. South Virginia St runs for several miles south of the river and has motels, malls, casinos and the expanding Reno-Sparks Convention Center. Back downtown, W 4th St is the main east–west roadway. The University of Nevada campus is just north of I-80.

INFORMATION

Reno's downtown **visitor center** (☎ 775-827-7366, 800-367-7366, fax 775-827-7713; **w** www.renolaketahoe.com; 1 E 1st St; open 8am-5pm Mon-Fri) is on the 2nd floor of the Cal-Neva building, adjacent to the Cal-Neva Casino on N Virginia St. It has free state maps and more brochures than you'll know what to do with. The **National Council on Problem Gambling** (☎ 800-522-4700) has a 24-hour help line.

Hospitals with emergency rooms are **St Mary's** (☎ 775-770-3627; 235 W 6th St) and **Washoe Medical Center** (☎ 775-982-4100; 77 Pringle Way), southeast of downtown.

CASINOS

Traveling south from I-80 on N Virginia St, the first big casino you come across is **Circus Circus** (500 N Sierra St), which offers free circus acts every half hour or so and a midway full of carnival games. It's linked by walking bridges to the long-standing **Eldorado** (345 N

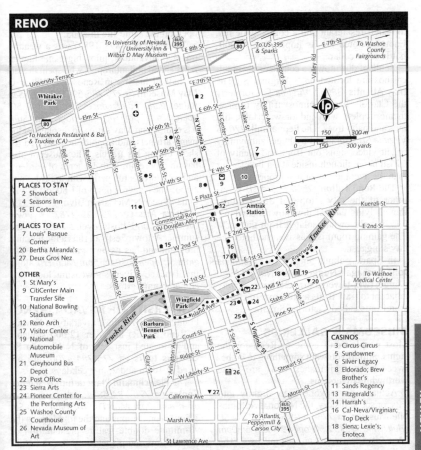

RENO

To University of Nevada,
University Inn &
Wilbur D May Museum

To:US-395
& Sparks

To Washoe
County
Fairgrounds

Whitaker
Park

To Hacienda Restaurant & Bar
& Truckee (CA)

Amtrak
Station

Kuenzli St

Truckee River

To Washoe
Medical Center

Wingfield
Park

Barbara
Bennett
Park

Truckee River

To Atlantis,
Peppermill &
Carson City

PLACES TO STAY
2 Showboat
4 Seasons Inn
15 El Cortez

PLACES TO EAT
7 Louis' Basque
Corner
20 Bertha Miranda's
27 Deux Gros Nez

OTHER
1 St Mary's
9 CitiCenter Main
Transfer Site
10 National Bowling
Stadium
12 Reno Arch
17 Visitor Center
19 National
Automobile
Museum
21 Greyhound Bus
Depot
22 Post Office
23 Sierra Arts
24 Pioneer Center for
the Performing Arts
25 Washoe County
Courthouse
26 Nevada Museum of
Art

CASINOS
3 Circus Circus
5 Sundowner
6 Silver Legacy
8 Eldorado; Brew
Brother's
11 Sands Regency
13 Fitzgerald's
14 Harrah's
16 Cal-Neva/Virginian;
Top Deck
18 Siena; Lexie's;
Enoteca

NEVADA

Virginia St) and the relatively newer **Silver Legacy** *(407 N Virginia St)*, cofounded by the Mandalay Resort Group (formerly Circus Circus Enterprises) and the Eldorado. Dominating the downtown skyline with its bossy, 37-story tower, the Silver Legacy, built around a silver-mining theme, is the closest Reno has to Vegas-like showmanship. Inside its bulbous, 180ft white dome is a massive sky painting and a 120ft-high imitation mining rig, which periodically erupts into a sound-and-light spectacle.

Across the tracks from the Eldorado stands **Fitzgerald's** *(255 N Virginia St)*, an older but still-active property with a dopey and sorely outdated 'lucky leprechaun' theme. Nearby is **Harrah's** *(219 N Center St)*, still one of the biggest and fanciest casinos in town.

Founded by William Harrah, the casino's been at its present location since 1946. It was bought by Holiday Inns Inc in 1980.

Closer to the river is the **Cal-Neva/ Virginian** *(cnr 2nd & N Virginia Sts)*; the Cal-Neva, founded in 1962, took over the only slightly fancier Virginian not long ago, and together they attract an old-fashioned, nondescript gambling crowd. The cheapest meal in town, 99¢ ham and eggs, is found here (see Places to Eat later in this chapter). The low-rent **Sundowner** and **Sands Regency** are three blocks west of Virginia St.

East of S Virginia St and facing the Truckee River sits the city's newest complex, **Siena** *(1 S Lake St)*, a decidedly upscale property built around a Tuscan village theme. More resort than mere gambling hall, it boasts a luxurious health spa, a top-shelf restaurant and a comfy wine bar, Enoteca, noted for its impressive 18,000-bottle wine cellar.

South of downtown, a couple of big hotel-casinos are located on S Virginia St. The ritzy **Atlantis** (*3800 S Virginia St*), formerly the Clarion, has an almost trippy tropical theme, replete with indoor waterfalls, tiki huts and palm trees. The **Peppermill** (*2707 S Virginia St*) is branded by huge, annoyingly bright video signs out front and plenty of garish neon, though inside it's a bit classier than the average downtown property.

The **Reno Hilton** (*2500 E 2nd St*) is another of the city's top-end destinations, though lying east of downtown near Hwy 395, it's somewhat isolated from the pack. The gaming room is massive, the hotel the city's biggest.

In Sparks, about 5mi east of Reno, is **John Ascuaga's Nugget** (*1100 Nugget Ave*), a large, twin-towered property immediately adjacent to I-80. It sits amid a row of cheesy storefronts called Victorian Square.

MUSEUMS & GALLERIES

Most people don't come to Reno for the sights. Still, if you want something to do between casino skirmishes, there are some worthwhile diversions.

Actually, for anyone even slightly into cars, or social history, the **National Automobile Museum** (☎ 775-333-9300; 10 Lake St; adult/child $7.50/2.50; open 9:30am-5:30pm Mon-Sat, 10am-4pm Sun) is a must-see. The collection includes some one-of-a-kind, custom-built and experimental vehicles, such as Buckminster Fuller's 1934 Dymaxion and Ed Roth's 1961 Beatnik Bandit. The museum is on the south bank of the Truckee River, an easy walk from downtown.

To bowling aficionados, Reno's **National Bowling Stadium** (☎ 775-334-2695; 300 N Center St) is definitely worth a pilgrimage. The 363,000-sq-ft facility has a mind-boggling 78 lanes and a 450ft scoreboard – a sight you can take in (for free) from the spectator stage.

You'll find a mix of contemporary art and historical exhibitions at the **Nevada Museum of Art** (☎ 775-329-3333; 160 W Liberty St; adult/child $5/3; open noon-6pm Tues-Sun), founded in 1931 and considered the oldest cultural institution in the state. A

brand-new museum building is scheduled to open on the same site in 2003.

Wilbur May (1898–1982) was a wealthy traveler, adventurer, pilot, big-game hunter, rancher and philanthropist, who spent the latter half of his life in Reno. The **Wilbur D May Museum** (☎ 775-785-5961; Rancho San Rafael Park; adult/concession $4.50/2.50; open 10am-5pm Tues-Sat, noon-5pm Sun) has exhibits on May's life and displays of the many artifacts and trophies he collected (or shot) during his travels. The museum also has an arboretum with 12 acres of gardens, and a children's fun park, with log rides and a zoo. The center is north of I-80, off N Virginia St near N McCarran Blvd.

Sierra Arts (☎ 775-329-2787; w www.sierra-arts.org) hosts events such as the summer Artown Festival, runs a local grants program and has its own **gallery** (17 S Virginia St; open 8:30am-5pm Mon-Fri) along the Truckee River, showcasing local and contemporary artists.

UNIVERSITY OF NEVADA, RENO

Founded in 1874, the University of Nevada at Reno (UNR) has over 12,000 students and is located just east of N Virginia St. **Campus tours** (☎ 775-784-4700) are offered at 10am and 2pm weekdays.

The **Fleischmann Planetarium & Science Center** (☎ 775-784-4811; admission free; open 8am-8pm Mon-Fri, 10:30am-8pm Sat & Sun) is on campus and the highlight is the 90-minute double-feature presentation of 70mm films and planetarium shows (adult/child $7/5). There's also free telescope viewing on clear Friday nights.

Just north of the planetarium, the **Nevada Historical Society Museum** (☎ 775-688-1190; 1650 N Virginia St; adult/child $2/free; open 10am-5pm Mon-Sat) is a great find for anyone interested in Nevada history.

ACTIVITIES

For details on outdoor activities on and around Lake Tahoe – hiking, skiing, mountain biking etc – see the Sierra Nevada chapter. Though it's between a 30- and 60-minute drive from most ski resorts, Reno does work as a skiing 'base camp,' thanks to its cheap and plentiful lodging. Call the visitor center or check the websites of the various casinos (during ski season) for prices of special stay-and-ski packages.

Anglers need to get a license from a sporting goods store. Pyramid Lake, 32mi north of town, is noted for the Lahontan cutthroat trout (see Around Reno later in this chapter).

SPECIAL EVENTS
Like any place courting the tourist and convention trade, Reno has a full calendar of annual events. Some of the most interesting are also the most likely to fill the hotels, so plan your visit accordingly.

The **Reno Rodeo** (☎ 775-329-3877), among the largest and richest of rodeos in the country, fills the **Livestock Events Center** (cnr E 9th St & Sutro St) every June with bucking broncos and bruised cowpokes.

Hot August Nights (☎ 775-356-1956) is the summer's next big happening, with parades and concerts celebrating the cars and music of the 1950s and '60s.

The Livestock Events Center again heats up in late August as the **Nevada State Fair** (☎ 775-688-5767) brings back that good old country-fair fun, with rides, games and livestock events.

The annual **Best in the West Nugget Ribs Cookoff** (☎ 800-647-1177), at John Ascuaga's Nugget, packs the streets of Sparks each Labor Day weekend with thousands of meat fans smeared in tangy sauce.

In mid-September, the **National Championship Air Races** (☎ 775-972-6663) – the world's longest-running air race – happens at Stead Airport, northwest of downtown.

PLACES TO STAY
You can get a pretty cheap room in Reno, though not on weekends (especially Saturday nights) or during special events when accommodations are often booked far ahead. Rates can fluctuate wildly – depending on the day of the week, the season, the week's activities and how booked up the place is by the time you call – so take the figures below only as a loose guide.

Camping
Campgrounds with tent sites are all at least 20mi away from the city. Try **Davis Creek Park** (☎ 775-849-0684; sites $13), south toward Carson City along Hwy 395; or the **Mt Rose Campground** (☎ 877-444-6777; sites $10; open late June-early Sept), on Hwy 431 southwest of Reno and high in the Sierras at nearly 9000ft.

There's also camping on the shores of Pyramid Lake (see Around Reno later in this chapter) and around Lake Tahoe (see the Sierra Nevada chapter).

Hotels & Motels
A number of cheap motels are found along E 5th and W 4th Sts, though keep in mind that some attract unsavory types and have a shady veneer. Others are just fine. You can also look south of downtown along S Virginia St.

El Cortez (☎ 775-322-9161; 239 W 2nd St; singles/doubles midweek $26/29, weekends $34/38), in an attractive 1931 Art Deco building that was once the tallest in town, has spartan rooms that are among Reno's cheapest. It does rent some rooms by the week, but the place is clean and safe. Parking is across the street from the hotel, which is near the Greyhound station.

Seasons Inn (☎ 775-322-6000, 800-322-8588; 495 West St; rooms midweek/Fri/Sat from $42/69/99), behind Circus Circus, is a three-story motel with its own parking lot out front; the block is decent and the rooms are clean and fairly quiet.

Showboat (☎ 775-786-4032, 800-648-3960; 660 N Virginia St; midweek/weekends from $40/70) is similar to Seasons Inn. It has clean, standard rooms and is a couple of blocks north of the downtown casino cluster.

University Inn (☎ 775-323-0321, fax 775-323-2929; 570 N Virginia St; rooms from $55), on the north side of I-80 near the university, is good if you can afford to spend more. It's quiet, friendly and just out of range of the casino frenzy.

A truly wacky way to experience Reno is to stay in one of the 'fantasy' motels, which offer rooms and suites tricked out in cheesy fun themes, from ocean beach to brash bordello, Irish castle to outer space.

Adventure Inn (☎ 775-828-9000, 800-937-1436, fax 775-825-8333; W www.adventureinn.com; 3575 S Virginia St; standard rooms midweek/weekends from $59/99) offers a huge range of themed rooms (the website has lots of photos). All rooms come with a spa and range in size up to 1800-sq-ft superdeluxe suites.

Casinos
Rates at the big hotel-casinos fluctuate with demand, the seasons and whether any big events are going on. As a rule, you get the

NEVADA

best rate Sunday through Thursday; Friday is somewhat higher and Saturday can more than double the midweek rate. Winter rates are usually a bit lower than rates in summer. It's always best to phone ahead and reserve; or call the visitor center for assistance. Also, check the Internet, as some offer lower rates and specials via their websites.

Sundowner (☎ 775-786-7050, 800-648-5490; ⓦ www.sundowner-casino.com; 450 N Arlington Ave; midweek/weekends $35/90), three blocks west of N Virginia St, is consistently one of the cheapest hotel-casinos in town. The 600 rooms aren't fancy, but they're perfectly adequate.

Sands Regency (☎ 775-348-2200, 800-648-3553, fax 775-348-2226; ⓦ www.sands regency.com; 345 N Arlington Ave; rooms midweek/weekends from $42/79), with 800 rooms, is another good budget option; it's just south of the Sundowner and a short walk from N Virginia St. Check the website for even cheaper room specials.

Circus Circus (☎ 775-329-0711, 800-648-5010, fax 775-329-0599; ⓦ www.circus reno.com; 500 N Sierra St; rooms midweek/weekends from $45/89) has garish pink decor, and each of the 1572 rooms still reflect a turn-of-the-century European circus theme. Remodeled not too long ago, they're in better shape than you'd expect.

Eldorado (☎ 775-786-5700, 800-648-5966, fax 775-348-9269; ⓦ www.eldorado reno.com; 345 N Virginia St; rooms midweek/weekends from $65/100) has over 800 rooms in its 25-story tower, plus numerous cafes and restaurants. A two-night minimum stay applies most weekends. The mezzanine level features ceiling murals, arched walkways, columns and the Fountain of Fortune, a bronze-and-marble kitsch fantasy.

Silver Legacy (☎ 775-329-4777, 800-687-8733, fax 775-325-7177; ⓦ www.silverlegacy reno.com; 407 N Virginia St; rooms midweek/weekends from $55/119) is one of the flashiest places in town, taking up two city blocks and boasting a three-tiered, 400ft tower. That aside, the 1720 Victorian-themed rooms are crisp, comfortable and quiet. Rooms with better views cost a bit more.

Harrah's (☎ 775-786-3232, 800-427-7247, fax 775-788-2644; ⓦ www.harrahs .com/our_casinos/ren; 219 N Center St; rooms midweek/weekends from $49/129) is another one of the fancier places downtown,

in a gold-embossed sort of way. The 950 rooms may not have hugely exciting decor, but they're still plenty nice.

Siena (☎ 775-337-6260, 877-743-6233, fax 775-337-6608; ⓦ www.sienareno.com; 1 S Lake St; rooms from $99) is topping the heap for luxury, style and comfort. It's the newest hotel-casino in town, complete with a full-service spa and a friendly atmosphere. The 214 rooms are plush and well appointed, and while prices can fluctuate, they're not as high as you'd expect, making this potentially one of the city's best deals.

Peppermill (☎ 775-826-2121, 800-648-6992, fax 775-698-7348; ⓦ www.pepper millreno.com; 2707 S Virginia St; tower rooms midweek/weekends from $55/109) is south of downtown and hard to miss thanks to its blinding sign out front and some garish neon. Guests have access to a cool outdoor pool, though, with a faux mountainscape and a waterfall. The cheapest rooms are in a motor lodge out back, and are acceptable but dull. Rooms in the main tower are far nicer with a funky, modern attitude.

Reno Hilton (☎ 775-789-2000, 800-648-5080; ⓦ www.renohilton.com; 2500 E 2nd St; rooms midweek/weekends from $59/99) has 2000 rooms, making it the biggest hotel in town. The rooms are spacious and the ambience upscale. The Hilton caters to business types and conventioneers.

PLACES TO EAT

Reno has lots of eateries, though unlike Las Vegas, the options for cutting-edge cuisine are limited. Budget-minded travelers can go crazy at the casinos' all-you-can-eat buffets, or penny-pinch with a prime-rib or late-night steak-and-egg special.

The buffets aren't exactly shoestring bargains anymore, but they are still a good deal if you're really hungry. Keep in mind that cheap isn't always a good thing with buffets; it's worth spending a few bucks more for a better selection and, most importantly, higher quality food. Worthwhile choices include the **Eldorado** (345 N Virginia St; dinner $15-25), **Harrah's** (219 N Center St; dinner $11-23) and the **Peppermill** (2707 S Virginia St; dinner $15-25). Dinner is usually pricier on Fridays and Saturdays, but lunch offers the best value anyway and will keep you full past suppertime.

Cal-Neva/Virginian (cnr 2nd & N Virginia Sts; meals $1 and up) has ham and eggs for a measly 99¢ in its **Top Deck** coffee shop if dirt cheap's what you want. There are other specials too, including all-you-can-eat spaghetti for $2.50 and a $9 prime-rib dinner at the **Copper Ledge**.

Brew Brothers is a large brewpub on the 2nd floor of the **Eldorado** (345 N Virginia St; meals from $7), good for a late-night pizza and one of the eight house-brewed ales, which are surprisingly tasty. The place gets packed and very loud, though, when the nightly rock bands kick in.

Deux Gros Nez (249 California Ave; breakfast & lunch $4-7) offers a welcome respite from the casinos and their cheap and greasy dinners. It is a friendly, low-key and very real coffeehouse with kooky decor; it's located upstairs and behind the Cheese Board. The smoothies, espresso shakes, pastries and pasta dinners are delicious, the atmosphere's down-home and the coffee's strong.

At **Louis' Basque Corner** (☎ 775-323-7203; 301 E 4th St; dinner $18), in business for over 35 years, a full dinner means soup, salad, two courses and side dishes, one glass of wine or nonalcoholic drink and ice cream.

There are many Mexican restaurants in town. A couple of local favorites include **Bertha Miranda's** (336 Mill St; dinner mains around $10) and **El Borracho** (1601 S Virginia St; meals under $10), which wins praises for its guacamole and kitschy decor.

Admittedly, much of the casino food is lowbrow, but a few do have superswanky restaurants serving memorable meals (and at memorable prices). Reservations are recommended.

Lexie's (☎ 775-337-6260, 877-743-6233; 1 S Lake St; dinner mains $10-30), a contemporary Italian restaurant at the Siena, specializes in fresh seafood but serves pasta dishes and organic beef too. Wine freaks with cash to burn may want to book a spot for the 'Tuscan Table'. It's a seven-course meal held in the Siena's downstairs wine bar, **Enoteca**, that's as much a wine seminar as it is a gourmet dinner. It's a pricey $200, wine included, and takes four hours to complete.

White Orchid (☎ 775-826-2121; mains from $27), at the Peppermill, is distinguished by an extensive wine list and a sophisticated menu that includes Maine lobster and Kobe beef.

ENTERTAINMENT

Reno doesn't have the excessively slick glitz of Las Vegas, but there are local venues and civic arts organizations – not to mention plenty of cheesy casino lounge performers – to keep you entertained. Check out the weekly Reno News & Review (**w** www.newsreview.com) for guidance.

At the casinos, you're as likely to see rock bands such as Los Lobos as you are magic shows and golden-throated stalwarts such as Tony Bennett. Venues with major showrooms include the following: **Reno Hilton** (☎ 775-789-2285; 2500 E 2nd St), which holds an outdoor summertime concert series; **John Ascuaga's Nugget** (☎ 775-356-3304; 1100 Nugget Ave, Sparks), which has a 'Stepping Out Package' for shows in the Celebrity Showroom, including dinner, that is a great deal; **Harrah's** (☎ 775-788-3773; 219 N Center St), which has Sammy's Showroom, named in honor of Sammy Davis Jr, who performed here 40 times between 1967 and 1989; and **Silver Legacy** (☎ 775-329-4777; 407 N Virginia St), where shows take place under the garish geodesic dome in the center of town.

Outside the casino circuit, **Hacienda Restaurant & Bar** (☎ 775-746-2228; 10580 N McCarran Blvd) has live rock, salsa DJs and jazz; and the **Great Basin Brewing Company** (☎ 775-355-7711; 846 Victorian Ave), a microbrewery in Sparks, has good beer and live bands.

Reno also has seasons of ballet, orchestral music, opera, jazz and theater. Most performances take place at the **Pioneer Center for the Performing Arts** (☎ 775-686-6600; cnr S Virginia & State Sts).

GETTING THERE & AWAY

Reno-Tahoe International Airport (☎ 775-328-6400) is 5mi southeast of downtown. Airlines serving the Reno area include Alaska, American, American West, Continental, Delta, Frontier, Northwest, Southwest and United.

Greyhound (☎ 775-322-2970; 155 Stevenson St) has daily departures to San Francisco ($34, five hours), Los Angeles ($59, 11 hours) and Las Vegas ($72, nine hours).

Amtrak (☎ 775-329-8638, 800-872-7245; 135 E Commercial Row) has one westbound train daily to Sacramento ($41, 5½ hours) and Oakland ($46, 8½ hours).

NEVADA

If you're driving carry snow chains during winter, especially if you're thinking of driving through the Sierra. For road conditions, call the **Nevada Department of Transportation** (☎ 775-793-1313).

GETTING AROUND

Many hotels offer free shuttle services to and from the airport. The **RTC Citifare bus system** (☎ 775-348-7433), which covers Washoe County, also runs bus No 13 every half hour between the Reno airport and downtown. Routes generally converge at the CitiCenter Main Transfer Site downtown, which also has an information booth. Fares are $1.25 (exact change required) and transfers are free. Other useful routes include bus No 8 (for the university), No 11 (for Sparks) and No 1 (for points along S Virginia St).

Around Reno

PYRAMID LAKE

A beautiful blue expanse in the stark, treeless high desert about 30mi north of Reno, 27mi-long Pyramid Lake is popular for recreation and fishing. The lakeshore was inhabited as early as 11,000 years ago, and the semi-nomadic Paiute Indians visited the lake annually to powwow and to harvest fish congregating for their spawning run up the Truckee River. In 1843, explorer John Frémont named the lake for the small island he thought resembled the Pyramid of Cheops.

The great Paiute chief Winnemucca negotiated treaties with the European settlers as early as 1855, but two bloody conflicts occurred in 1860. In 1874 Pyramid Lake and the surrounding lands were declared an Indian reservation, though settlers and the railroad companies still managed to acquire portions of the best land. Truckee River water, which had always replenished the lake, was also siphoned off for irrigation, lowering the water level by more than 100ft.

For modern anglers, the most prized catch is the Lahontan cutthroat trout, which can grow up to 40lbs and has the honor of being Nevada's state fish. Along with the endemic cui-cui, another remnant from ancient Lake Lahontan, the cutthroat trout has suffered a disastrous decline in numbers because of environmental changes, such as dams interfering with their spawning runs. Since the 1970s, efforts have been made to restore the environment of the lake and to stock it with fish spawned in hatcheries.

The usual entry to the **Pyramid Lake Paiute Indian Reservation** is off Hwy 445 from Sparks; the boundary is near the Pyramid Lake Store, 23mi from Sparks. Some 5mi further north is **Sutcliffe**, where you can get supplies, and permits for camping, fishing and boating from the **ranger station** (☎ 775-476-1155) or **marina** (☎ 775-476-1156).

Camping is allowed in many places around the lake, as long as you have a permit (and rangers do check). Permits cost $5 per person, per night; pick one up from the ranger station.

Across the lake you can see Anaho Island, a sanctuary for the American white pelican, and the Pyramid, the tufa formation that gives the lake its name.

VIRGINIA CITY

Virginia City, about 23mi south of Reno, was a mining boomtown during the late 19th century and the site of the famous Comstock Lode, a monstrous silver bonanza that stands as one of the world's richest strikes. The town grew to around 30,000 residents at its peak, and today it's a National Historic Landmark, overrun with summertime visitors in search of Old West stories and icons.

Main St is a strip of vintage buildings restored into wacky saloons, cheesy souvenir shops and some pretty hokey 'museums.' That aside, Virginia City is actually very picturesque and considerably more authentic at its core than many other overly restored and reconstructed 'historic' towns. The drive into town from Reno via Hwy 341, which offers great views of the mountains, is an experience in itself.

The main drag is C St, where you'll find the **chamber of commerce** (☎ 775-847-0311; W *www.virginiacity-nv.com*) inside an old railroad car. The smart and sassy *Comstock Chronicle*, a local weekly, has visitor information and a good sense of history.

Many of the town's attractions are seriously silly, though some are true gems, such as the **Fourth Ward School** (☎ 775-847-0975; 537 C St), a monumental four-story building that once housed 1025 students.

The quirky **Way It Was Museum** (☎ 775-847-0766; admission $2.50; open 10am-6pm daily), on N C St, gives some good background on mining the lode, as does the half-hour tour of the **Chollar Mine** (☎ 775-847-0155), in May to September ($5), at the south end of F St. Dozens of playd-out miners are buried at the photogenic **Silver Terrace Cemetery**, off Carson St.

If you're thirsty, C St offers plenty of choices, such as the **Delta Saloon**, which has old photos plastered on its walls, and the crusty **Red Dog Saloon** (76 N C St). The Red Dog's been dubbed the 'birthplace of psychedelic rock' because its house band in 1965 was the Charlatans, who after a summer-long stint here went on to help found the psychedelic San Francisco Sound.

The beautiful **Gold Hill Hotel** (☎ 775-847-0111; W *www.goldhillhotel.net*; rooms $45-200), 1mi south of town on Hwy 342, is clean, full of character and claims to be Nevada's oldest hotel. For dinner, the noodle and rice plates at **Mandarin Garden** (30 B St; less than $10) are affordable, delicious and even vegetarian-friendly.

San Diego Area

San Diego County covers 4200 sq mi, extending about 60mi between Orange and Riverside Counties to the north and the Mexican border in the south, and about 70mi from the Pacific seashore over the coastal mountain range to the deserts of Anza-Borrego. The area has a great variety of landscapes, a superb coastline and a near-perfect climate. Its population of more than 2.7 million people is growing at an estimated rate of 11,000 per month.

The metropolitan part of the county includes the city of San Diego (population 2.1 million) and a number of diverse suburban communities.

People looking for a laid-back California lifestyle will find it in San Diego's beach towns (Ocean Beach, Pacific Beach, Mission Beach) and along the North County Coast (see the Around San Diego section), more than in any other part of the state. But while water hounds and lovers of the great outdoors will find San Diego extra inviting, there really is – as corny as it sounds – something for everyone here. Museums, military ships, shopping districts, Mexican restaurants, gay and lesbian venues, beaches and boat excursions may not make San Diego as internationally recognized as LA or as charming as San Francisco, but the sum total creates a place that is extremely pleasant to visit.

San Diego

It's easy to fall in love with San Diego. After all, what's not to like? When much of the USA shivers under blankets of rain and snow, San Diegans still picnic outdoors or slice through waves on surfboards. Its downtown skyline stands sentinel over one of the world's great natural harbors. At the foot of the high-rises, the historical Gaslamp Quarter offers dining and nightlife. Miles of beaches form its western edge, while the Anza-Borrego Desert beckons in the east. Add to that the country's largest urban park and the San Diego Zoo and SeaWorld. Not surprisingly, San Diegans are proud of their hometown and shamelessly yet endearingly promote

Highlights

- Balboa Park – museums galore and animals too

- Cabrillo National Monument – stunning vistas of city and sea

- La Jolla – caves, coves and contemporary art

- Del Mar – shopping, surfing and betting on the horses

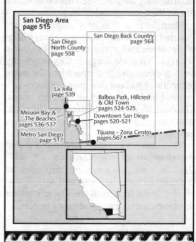

it as 'America's Finest City.' So, what's not to like?

Detractors have pointed to a degree of complacency that all this perfection has inspired. 'Dynamic' and 'San Diego' are rarely mentioned in the same sentence. Still a city shaped by the military, it lacks the urban energy of Los Angeles or San Francisco. As do those two cities, San Diego has a sizable immigrant population, but little cosmopolitan flair. Built by visionaries, it now seems mired in a 'no-growth' and 'no-change' attitude. In the end, though, it's hard to fault San Diego for its smugness. As the saying goes, 'If it ain't broke, don't fix it.' Whether you swim in a cove in La Jolla, watch the city skyline bathed in the glow of the setting sun or quaff a cold one in Pacific Beach, you'll find that America's Finest City is a mighty fine one indeed.

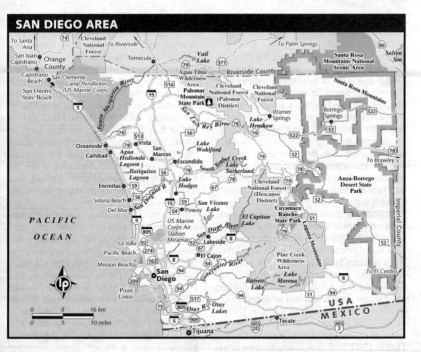

SAN DIEGO AREA

HISTORY

San Diego's coastal area and the periphery of the Salton Sea hold middens (ancient refuse heaps) that date back 20,000 years, making this some of the oldest known human-inhabited land in the USA. The Hokan-speaking Kumeyaay had the largest territory, from the coast to the low desert and from south of what's now the Mexican border to near present-day Oceanside. In the north, the Ute-Aztecan-speaking Luiseño/Juaneño people lived on the coast and the slopes of Mt Palomar (as some of their descendants still do).

Juan Rodríguez Cabrillo sailed into San Diego Bay in 1542, named it San Miguel and continued northwards. The next Spaniard to arrive was Sebastian Vizcaíno in 1602. He entered the bay on the feast day of San Diego de Alcalá and could not resist renaming the place San Diego.

In 1769, under Gaspar de Portolá and Padre Junípero Serra, 40 men founded a military outpost and the first of the California missions on the hill now known as the Presidio. After a tenuous start, missionary activity spread to the north, and other

missions were also established in the San Diego area, including San Luis Rey Francia in 1798 and the *asistencias* (satellite missions) of San Antonio de Pala (1815) and Santa Ysabel (1818).

After the breakup of the missions (around 1833), San Diego became a civilian pueblo. It remained a ramshackle village at the base of the Presidio hill, with only a few hundred residents until the 1850s when William Heath Davis, a former sea captain and San Francisco property speculator, bought 160 acres of bayfront land and erected prefabricated houses, a wharf and warehouses.

Dubbed Davis' Folly, the development was ahead of its time. In 1867 Alonzo E Horton, another San Francisco speculator and businessman, acquired 960 acres of waterfront land and promoted it as 'New Town.' This time the new subdivision prospered, especially after 1872 when a fire devastated much of the settlement near Presidio hill.

The discovery of gold in the hills east of San Diego in 1869 started a frenetic mining boom. In 1884 the rush brought the railroad to San Diego, but after the gold played out, the population fell from 4000 to 2000.

Despite the efforts of the city's boosters, San Diego did not acquire an industrial base in the 19th century.

When San Francisco hosted the Panama-Pacific International Exposition (1914), San Diego, in a burst of self-promotion, held the Panama-California Exposition, which ran for most of 1915 and 1916. In an effort to give the city a distinctive image, exposition buildings were deliberately designed in a romantic, Spanish-Mexican style. To this day, this move contributes more to San Diego's Mediterranean/mission-style architecture and Spanish street names than does the city's actual heritage as a small and remote colonial Spanish outpost.

Around the same time as the exposition, aviation pioneer Glenn H Curtiss began a flight camp in San Diego and helped develop ship-based aircraft on San Diego Bay. When Ryan Airlines built the *Spirit of St Louis* for Lindbergh's transatlantic flight in 1927, and Consolidated Aircraft opened its factory in 1931, San Diego at last had an industry.

Following the bombing of Pearl Harbor in 1941, the headquarters of the US Pacific Fleet was moved from Hawaii to San Diego. The boom in wartime activity transformed the city: the harbor was dredged and landfill islands were built, vast tracts of instant housing appeared, public spaces were turned into training camps, storage depots and hospitals, and the population doubled in a couple of years. The war, the Marines, the Navy and naval aviators were the subjects of films showcasing San Diego (albeit incidentally) from *Guadalcanal* to the *Sands of Iwo Jima*. Its wartime role, more than anything else, put San Diego on the American map.

Postwar San Diego became a booming city in a booming state. The naval and military presence provided an expanding core of activity, employing up to a quarter of the workforce. The climate and a seafront location have also been major factors in the city's growth. Recreation facilities such as Mission Bay help attract visitors, who now contribute a big slice of the county's income. Education and research (especially in biotechnology) are now major activities too, while the San Diego Padres baseball team and the San Diego Chargers football team have both been positive representatives of the city.

ORIENTATION

San Diego is a pretty easy place to find your way around. The airport, train station and Greyhound terminal are all in or near the downtown area, which is a compact grid east of San Diego Bay. The main north–south freeway is I-5, which parallels the coast from the Camp Pendleton Marine Corps Base in the north to the Mexican border at San Ysidro. Also running north to south, I-805 is a detour from I-5, bypassing the downtown area to the east. I-8 runs east from Ocean Beach, up the valley of the San Diego River (called Mission Valley), past suburbs such as El Cajon and on to the Imperial Valley and Arizona.

Waterfront attractions along the Embarcadero are just west of the downtown grid. Balboa Park, with its many museums and famous zoo, is in the northeastern corner of the city, and Old Town, San Diego's original site, is a couple of miles northwest of downtown. Above Old Town, the Presidio hill overlooks Mission Valley, now a freeway and a commercial corridor, and just to the east is Hillcrest, the center of the city's gay and lesbian community (in the heart of Uptown).

Coronado, with its well-known 1888-vintage Hotel del Coronado, is across San Diego Bay, accessible by a long bridge or a short ferry ride. At the entrance to the bay, Point Loma offers great views over sea and city from the Cabrillo National Monument. Mission Bay, northwest of downtown, has lagoons, parks and facilities for many recreational activities. The nearby coast – with Ocean Beach, Mission Beach and Pacific Beach – epitomizes the Southern California beach scene, while La Jolla, a little further north, is a more upscale seaside community and the home of the University of California at San Diego (UCSD).

A good way to see it all in one day is with Old Town Trolley Tours, which allows you to get on and off at Balboa Park, Coronado, Old Town, Horton Plaza and more (see Organized Tours).

INFORMATION
Tourist Offices

The **San Diego Convention & Visitors Bureau** (☎ *619-236-1212;* **w** *www.sandiego.org*) will send a complimentary vacation-planning guide anywhere in the world and offers

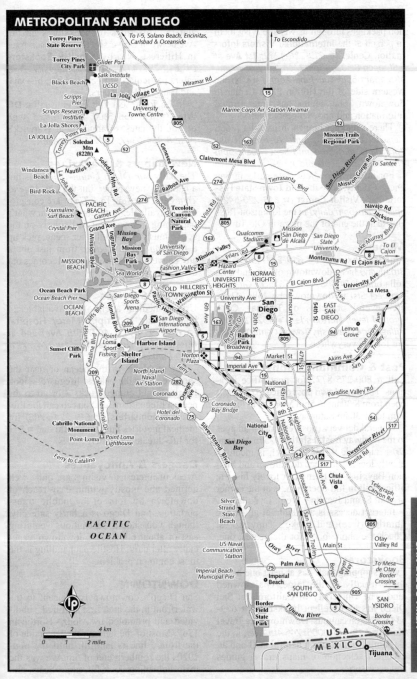

METROPOLITAN SAN DIEGO

Torrey Pines State Reserve
Torrey Pines City Park
Glider Port
Salk Institute
Blacks Beach
UCSD
Scripps Pier
Scripps Research Institute
La Jolla Shores
La Jolla Village Dr
Miramar Rd
To I-5, Solano Beach, Encinitas, Carlsbad & Oceanside
To Escondido
University Towne Centre
Marine Corps Air Station Miramar
LA JOLLA
Soledad Mtn (822ft)
Windansea Beach
Nautilus St
Bird Rock
Clairemont Mesa Blvd
Tierrasanta Blvd
Mission Gorge Rd
To Santee
Mission Trails Regional Park
San Diego River
To El Cajon
Navajo Rd
Jackson Dr
Lake Murray Blvd
Tourmaline Surf Beach
Garnet Ave
PACIFIC BEACH
Crystal Pier
Grand Ave
Tecolote Canyon Natural Park
Linda Vista Rd
Mission San Diego de Alcalá
San Diego State University
Montezuma Rd
El Cajon Blvd
College Ave
University Ave
La Mesa
Mission Bay
Mission Bay Park
University of San Diego
Mission Valley
Qualcomm Stadium
Friars Rd
MISSION BEACH
Sea World
Fashion Valley
Hazard Center
NORMAL HEIGHTS
UNIVERSITY HEIGHTS
El Cajon Blvd
Fairmount Ave
54th St
EAST SAN DIEGO
Ocean Beach Park
Ocean Beach Pier
OCEAN BEACH
San Diego Sports Arena
OLD TOWN
HILLCREST
Washington St
University Ave
San Diego
30th St
Pershing Dr
Balboa Park
Lemon Grove
Lemon Grove Ave
San Diego Trolley
Sunset Cliffs Park
Point Loma Sport Fishing
Harbor Dr
San Diego International Airport
Broadway
Horton Plaza
Market St
47th St
Euclid Ave
Akins Ave
Harbor Island
Shelter Island
North Island Naval Air Station
Coronado
Imperial Ave
National Ave
43rd St
Paradise Valley Rd
Cabrillo National Monument
Point Loma
Point Loma Lighthouse
Ferry to Catalina
Hotel del Coronado
Coronado Bay Bridge
Harbor Dr
8th St
National Blvd
National City
Highland Ave
San Diego Bay
KOA
Sweetwater River
Bonita Rd
Chula Vista
Telegraph Canyon Rd
PACIFIC OCEAN
Silver Strand State Beach
Silver Strand Blvd
San Diego Trolley
Main St
Otay River
Otay Valley Rd
To Mesa de Otay Border Crossing
US Naval Communication Station
Imperial Beach Municipal Pier
Palm Ave
Imperial Beach
SOUTH SAN DIEGO
Beyer Blvd
SAN YSIDRO
Border Field State Park
Tijuana River
Border Crossing
USA
MEXICO
Tijuana

0   2   4 km
0   1   2 miles

SAN DIEGO AREA

online hotel reservations and discount vacation packages through its website. Visit them in person at the **International Visitors Information Center** (*☎ 619-236-1212; 1st Ave at F St; open 8:30am-5pm Mon-Sat year-round, also 11am-5pm Sun June-Aug*) – it's on the western side of the Horton Plaza Center in downtown. The center has free printed information and knowledgeable staff.

There's another branch in **La Jolla** (*7666 Herschel & Prospect, Suite A; open 10am-7pm daily mid-June–mid-Sept, 10am-5pm Thur-Tues mid-Sept–mid-June*).

For information about state parks in San Diego County, go to the **Old Town State Historic Park Visitor Center** (*☎ 619-220-5427; open 10am-5pm daily*) in the Robinson-Rose House at the end of the plaza in Old Town.

Money
American Express (*☎ 619-234-4455; 258 Broadway*) has a downtown office, and a La Jolla branch (*☎ 858-459-4161, cnr Girard & Prospect Sts*) in downtown La Jolla. There are several branches of **Thomas Cook** (*ground level, Horton Plaza • 4525 La Jolla Village Dr • University Towne Center*). ATMs are found everywhere.

Post & Communications
Call *☎* 800-275-8777 for post office locations. The **downtown post office** (*815 E St*) is open from 8:30am to 5pm Monday to Friday, 9am to 11:30am Saturday.

General delivery (post restante) mail goes to the **Midway postal station** (*2535 Midway Dr*) – zip code 92138 – which is inconveniently located between downtown and Mission Bay, just off Barnett. A lovely historic office, still in full operation, is at the corner of Wall St and Ivanhoe Ave in La Jolla.

Internet access is available at all **public libraries** (free) and **Kinko's** copy stores. Check the phone book for the nearest one.

Bookstores
Every shopping mall has at least one bookshop, usually of the large, chain-owned kind. The University of California at San Diego has an excellent **bookstore** (*☎ 619-534-7323*) on campus. Downtown, **Le Travel Store** (*☎ 619-544-0005; 745 4th Ave*), in the Gaslamp Quarter, has a helpful staff and an excellent selection of maps, travel guides and accessories.

Bookhounds should peruse the old, new and rare offerings of bookstores on 5th Ave between University and Robinson Aves in Hillcrest. Nearby, **Obelisk Bookstore** (*☎ 619-297-4171; 1029 University Ave*) caters particularly to gay, lesbian, bisexual and transgender readers.

In La Jolla, seek out the unusual at **DG Wills** (*☎ 858-456-1800; 7461 Girard Ave*), or find the latest of anything at **Warwick's** (*☎ 858-454-0347; 2812 Girard Ave*).

Newspapers & Magazines
The daily *San Diego Union-Tribune* is not a bad daily newspaper, but the *Los Angeles Times* and the *New York Times* are conspicuously available. For information on what's happening in town, and particularly on the active music, art and theater scene, pick up a free *San Diego Reader* from just about any convenience store or café. It comes out every Thursday.

Medical Services
Urgent medical attention is available 24 hours a day at **Scripps Mercy Hospital** (*☎ 619-294-8111; 4077 5th Ave*) and at **Mission Bay Hospital** (*☎ 619-274-7721; 3030 Bunker Hill St*).

For problems in the ocean or near the shore, contact the nearest lifeguard – look for the bright orange trucks – or go to the nearest lifeguard tower. You can call the lifeguard **headquarters** (*☎ 619-224-2708*) for medical inquiries but you should dial *☎* 911 for life-threatening emergencies.

Dangers & Annoyances
Areas of interest to visitors are quite well defined and mostly within easy reach of downtown by foot or by public transportation. San Diego is a fairly safe city, though you should be cautious venturing east of about 6th Ave in downtown, especially after dark. Hostile panhandling is the most common problem.

DOWNTOWN
San Diego's downtown is adjacent to the waterfront in the area first acquired, subdivided and promoted by Alonzo Horton in 1867. Most of the land on the waterside of the trolley line is landfill: until the mid-1920s the southern end of 5th Ave was the main unloading dock for cargo boats, and

junkets and fishing boats used to be tied where the Convention Center now stands.

No longer the combination of uninteresting office developments and creeping inner-urban dereliction it was in the 1960s, downtown still lacks the urban energy of, say, San Francisco or even Seattle. Still, a visit to Horton Plaza and the Gaslamp Quarter – the primary hubs for shopping, dining and entertainment – is an integral part of experiencing San Diego. And the Embarcadero is good for a harbor-side stroll.

In the northwestern corner of downtown, Little Italy is a vibrant Italian-American neighborhood and one of the most pleasant places to stay – handy to the freeway, walking distance to the harbor and close to good eats.

Horton Plaza Center

The centerpiece of San Diego's downtown redevelopment, this huge project involved the leveling of seven city blocks and the construction of a five-level complex with 2300 parking spaces. It has a multiscreen cinema, two live theaters, restaurants, cafés and 140 shops lining an open courtyard. It was designed by Jon Jerde, a controversial California-based urban architect, using the 'festival-marketplace' concept of urban renewal, in which a congregation of vendors with separate facades and entrances set up shop in one unified space. It was completed in 1985 at a cost of more than $145 million.

From the outside the plaza is not very inviting (critics say it 'turns its back on downtown,' which, at the time of construction, was really run-down). Inside, the toy-town arches and balconies typical of postmodernism make it feel slightly as if you're walking through an MC Escher drawing. The top-floor food court is not cheap but has inventive signage and is a great place for people-watching.

The Horton Plaza Center (☎ 619-238-1596; open 10am-9pm Mon-Fri, 10am-7pm Sat, 11am-6pm Sun) is open at the hours shown here, though some shops and restaurants have extended hours. The main pedestrian entrance is on Broadway. Parking is validated with purchase.

Gaslamp Quarter

When Horton first established New Town San Diego in 1867, 5th Ave was its main

---

San Diego in 48 Hours

When I was living in La Jolla a friend of mine from France called: he was coming to visit, for 48 hours. Despite my insistence that there is just too much to see in San Diego to only spend two days, it was all the time he had. I was determined to show him the best of it. Here was our schedule:

Day 1

8am	Breakfast at the Pannikin (La Jolla)
9am–11:30am	Walk through La Jolla, along the Cove, to the Museum of Contemporary Art and down to Windansea Beach
Noon	Lunch at Kono's (Pacific Beach)
1pm–5pm	Rent bikes and ride south, along the boardwalk and over to Ocean Beach; look in tattoo parlors, shop for antiques; have a beer
6pm	Walk around the Gaslamp Quarter and dine at Bandar
8pm	See *Love's Labours Lost* at the Old Globe Theater
11pm	Stop for gelato at Gelato Vero on the way home

Day 2

7:30am	Hike through Torrey Pines State Reserve
9am	Walk through UCSD, look at the Stuart Collection and stop in at the Geisel Library
11:30am	Lunch at Bread & Cie (Hillcrest)
12:30pm	Shop for books and chotzskys in Hillcrest
1pm–4pm	Explore Balboa Park
4:30pm	Have a drink at the Hotel del Coronado
6:30pm	Dinner at Mona Lisa in Little Italy
8pm	See a reggae show at the Belly Up Tavern (Solana Beach)

He didn't see the San Diego Zoo or SeaWorld (next time, with the kids), but man-o-man did he have fun!

Marisa Gierlich

---

street and home to its main industries – saloons, gambling joints, bordellos and opium dens. While more respectable businesses grew up along Broadway, the 5th Ave area became known as the Stingaree, a notorious red-light district. By the 1960s it had declined to a skid row of flophouses and

DOWNTOWN SAN DIEGO

bars, but its seedy atmosphere made it so unattractive to developers that many of its older buildings survived when others around town were being razed. In the early 1980s, when developers started thinking about demolition and rebuilding, local protests and the Gaslamp Quarter Council saved the area.

Wrought-iron streetlamps, in the style of 19th-century gas lamps, were installed, along with trees and brick sidewalks. Restored buildings dating from the 1870s to the 1920s now house restaurants, bars, galleries and theaters. The 16-block area south of Broadway between 4th and 6th Aves is designated a National Historic District, and development is strictly controlled. There's still a bit of sleaze though, with a few adult entertainment shops and some very downmarket

hotels, but they give some character to the area, which might otherwise have become gentrified beyond recognition. An enjoyable time to visit is on a warm evening when people throng the streets and crowd the outdoor tables (see the Places to Eat and Entertainment sections later in this chapter). To get a feel for Gaslamp Quarter architecture and history, it's better to come and walk around during the day.

William Heath Davis House (☎ 619-233-4692; cnr Island St & 5th Ave), one of 14 prefabricated houses that Davis brought from Maine in 1850, contains a small museum with 19th-century furnishings. At 11am each Saturday, the Gaslamp Quarter Historical Foundation offers a two-hour guided walking tour from here (adult/concession $5/3).

DOWNTOWN SAN DIEGO

PLACES TO STAY
6 La Pensione Hotel
23 Inn at the YMCA
26 Hotel Bristol
30 US Grant Hotel
43 USA Hostel San Diego
48 HI San Diego
   Downtown Hostel
53 J Street Inn

PLACES TO EAT
2 Mona Lisa
7 Filippi's Pizza Grotto
8 Mimmo's Italian Village
9 Caffe Italia
12 Star of the Sea
13 Anthony's Fish Grotto
34 Rubio's
36 Bandar
39 Cafe Lulu
40 Star of India
42 Olé Madrid
46 The Cheese Shop
49 Café Sevilla
52 Royal Thai
55 Dick's Last Resort

OTHER
1 Casbah
3 California Rent-a-Car
4 West Coast Rent a Car
5 Waterfront

10 Our Lady of the Rosary
   Catholic Church
11 Firehouse Museum
14 Cruise Ship Terminal
15 Old Columbia Brewery
   & Grill
16 Civic Theatre
17 4th & B
18 Copley Symphony Hall
19 Hornblower Cruises
20 San Diego Harbor
   Excursion
21 Ferry Landing
22 Museum of
   Contemporary Art
   Downtown
24 Post Office
25 Diego Children's
   Museum/Museo de
   los Ninos
27 Greyhound Station
28 Transit Store
29 Spreckels Theater
31 American Express
32 Times Art Tix
33 Grand Theater Horton
35 San Diego Convention
   & Visitors Bureau/
   International Visitors
   Information Center
37 Croce's Top Hat Bar &
   Grille
38 Croce's Restaurant &
   Jazz Bar
41 The Bitter End
44 Le Travel Store
45 Gaslamp 15
47 Gaslamp Books &
   Antiques
50 William Heath Davis
   House
51 The Original Bike Cab
   Co
54 San Diego Chinese
   Historical Museum

Gaslamp Books & Antiques (☎ 619-237-1492; 413 Market St; admission free) doubles as a museum, since the owner displays all sorts of memorabilia that he's collected during his 50-plus years in San Diego. It's worth a look.

The heart of San Diego's China Town has always been on 3rd Ave (although it has spread out considerably in recent years). At the corner of J St, the Chinese Mission Building was designed by Louis J Gill (minimalist San Diego architect Irving Gill's nephew) and houses the **San Diego Chinese Historical Museum** (☎ 619-338-9888; 404 3rd Ave; admission $2; open 11am-3pm Tues-Sun). Built in the 1920s, it's a small, stucco building with red tiles decorating the roofline, hardwood floors and a nice backyard.

Museum of Contemporary Art Downtown

Opposite the train station and adjacent to the San Diego Trolley stop, the MCA (☎ 619-234-1001; 1001 Kettner Blvd; admission free; open 11am-5pm Thur-Tues, closed Wed) is the downtown branch of the La Jolla–based institution that has shown innovative artwork to San Diegans since the 1960s. The ever-changing exhibits of painting and sculpture are publicized widely (see the *Reader* or call the gallery).

San Diego Children's Museum/ Museo de los Niños

Young children enjoy this interactive museum (☎ 619-233-5437; 200 Island Ave; adult/child under 3 $6/free; open 10am-4pm

SAN DIEGO AREA

Tues-Sat). It has giant construction toys, spaces for painting and modeling, and a stage with costumes for impromptu theater, as well as storytelling, music, activities and changing exhibits.

Little Italy

Between Hawthorn and Ash Sts on the north and south, and Front St and the waterfront on the east and west, is San Diego's Little Italy. The area was settled in the mid-19th century by Italian immigrants, mostly fishermen and their families, who created a cohesive and thriving community. They enjoyed a booming fish industry and whiskey trade (which some claim was backed by local Mafia).

When I-5 was completed in 1962, the heart (and, many say, soul) of the area was destroyed. Buildings were condemned and entire blocks were demolished for the freeway's construction. After its completion, increased traffic turned pedestrian streets and harbor access routes into busy thoroughfares. Over the past five years, however, redevelopment has brought exciting contemporary architecture to the area, making Little Italy the hippest place to live and eat in the downtown area. And the area (especially along India St) is still a good place to find imported foods (see the Places to Eat section), Italian newspapers and people from 'da old country.'

Built in 1925, **Our Lady of the Rosary Catholic Church** *(cnr State & Date Sts)* is still a hub of Little Italy activity. Its rich ceiling murals, painted by an Italian who was flown over to do the work, are among San Diego's best pieces of religious art. Across the street in Amici Park, locals play *boccia*, an Italian form of outdoor bowling.

The **Firehouse Museum** *(☎ 619-232-3473; 1572 Columbia St at Cedar St; admission $2; open 10am-2pm Thur & Fri, 10am-4pm Sat & Sun)* preserves a historical collection of firefighting equipment and has exhibits depicting some of San Diego's 'hottest' moments.

EMBARCADERO

San Diego's waterfront, built almost entirely on landfill, is about 500 yards wider than it was in the late 1800s. The result is a well-manicured area geared toward pedestrian pleasure seekers.

Start a harborside stroll at the **Maritime Museum** *(☎ 619-234-9153; 1492 N Harbor Dr; adult/concession $6/4 to all 3 vessels;*

open 9am-8pm daily), just north of Ash St. The 100ft masts of the square-rigger *Star of India* make the museum easy to find. Built on the Isle of Man and launched in 1863, the tall ship plied the England–India trade route, carried immigrants to New Zealand, became a trading ship based in Hawaii and, finally, worked the Alaskan salmon fisheries. It's a handsome ship, but don't expect anything romantic or glamorous on board; this is an old workhorse, not the Love Boat. Also moored here are tall ships the *Berkeley* and the *Medea*. In summer, nautical-type movies are shown aboard the *Star of India*; call the museum for times and information.

Continue south, past where harbor cruise ships are docked (see Organized Tours) to the euphemistically named **Seaport Village** *(☎ 619-235-4014; open 10am-10pm daily summer, 10am-9pm rest of year)*. Neither a port nor a real village, this collection of novelty shops, restaurants and snack outlets has an unconvincing maritime theme with ersatz early-20th-century seafront architecture. It's touristy and twee, but not a bad place for souvenir shopping and a bite to eat.

Wrapping southeast along the **Embarcadero Marina Park** – where there's a public fishing pier and an open-air amphitheater, which presents free concerts on summer evenings – you'll see the 'sails' of the **San Diego Convention Center** *(☎ 619-525-5000)*. Built in a successful attempt to promote the city as a site for major conventions, this unusual-looking complex opened in 1989 and is booked solid more than five years into the 21st century. The design, by Canadian avant-garde architect Arthur Erickson, was said to have been inspired by an ocean liner. It is open most days if you want to have a look inside.

BALBOA PARK

With its museums, gardens and world-famous zoo, Balboa Park tops the list of what to see in San Diego. Maps dating from 1868 show that Alonzo Horton's planned additions to San Diego included a 1400-acre City Park at the northeastern corner of what was to become downtown. Always the businessman, Mr Horton enhanced the value of the land in his subdivision by restricting the areas available for future development. Nice on the map, it was still bare hilltops, chaparral and steep-sided arroyos (water-carved

The Legacy of Kate Sessions

Kate O Sessions graduated with a degree in botany from the University of California at Berkeley in 1881, a time when few women attended college and even fewer studied the natural sciences. She came to San Diego as a schoolteacher but soon began working as a horticulturist, establishing gardens for the fashionable homes of the city's emerging elite. In 1892, in need of space for a nursery, she proposed an unusual deal to city officials: she would have the use of 30 acres of city-owned Balboa Park for her nursery in return for planting 100 trees a year and donating 300 others for placement throughout San Diego. The city agreed to the arrangement, and Kate Sessions more than fulfilled her side of the bargain. Within 10 years, Balboa Park had shade trees, lawns, paths and flower beds. Grateful San Diegans soon began referring to her as 'The Mother of Balboa Park.'

gullies) until 1892 when Kate Sessions started her nursery on the site, paying rent to the city in trees (see the boxed text 'The Legacy of Kate Sessions').

By the early 1900s, Balboa Park had become a well-loved part of San Diego. Its name honors a Spanish conquistador believed to be the first European to sight the Pacific Ocean.

In planning the 1915/16 Panama-California Exposition, Irving Gill's modern, minimalist architecture was rejected in favor of the beaux arts style and baroque decoration of New Yorkers Bertram Goodhue and Carlton Winslow. The exposition buildings were meant to be temporary and were constructed largely of stucco, chicken wire, plaster, hemp and horsehair. They were so popular, however, that many continued to be used. As the originals deteriorated, they were replaced with durable concrete structures. These buildings now house the museums along El Prado, the main pedestrian thoroughfare in the park.

In 1935 the Pacific-California Exposition brought new buildings erected southwest of El Prado around the Pan-American Plaza. Architecturally, the Spanish colonial theme was expanded to include the whole New World, from indigenous styles (some of the buildings had Pueblo Indian and even Mayan influences) through the 20th century. Most of these have been preserved too and now house other exhibits, museums and theaters.

The San Diego Zoo occupies 200 acres in the north of the park, and the eastern third is occupied by the sports facilities of Morley Field, with tennis courts, a swimming pool, a velodrome, nine- and 18-hole golf courses, and even a golf course designed for playing with Frisbees. About a quarter of the original 1400 acres has been given over to the Cabrillo Freeway, the US Naval Hospital and other nonpark uses.

Orientation & Information

If you just want to enjoy the gardens and the atmosphere, you can visit Balboa Park any time and just stroll around, but be cautious after dark. To visit all the museums and attractions would take days, so it's a good idea to plan your visit. The website w www.balboapark.org is a useful tool. Note that many museums are closed Monday, and several per week (on a rotating basis) are free Tuesday.

The Balboa Passport (available at the Information Center) costs $30 and is good for a single entry to 12 of the park's museums for one week; for an additional $25 you also get deluxe admission to the San Diego Zoo. If you come on Tuesday, or only want to see a couple of the museums, the passport is not such a good deal. Most of the museums are open from about 10am to 4:30pm daily. The **Balboa Park Information Center** (☎ 619-239-0512; 1549 El Prado; open 9am-4pm daily) is in the House of Hospitality and has a helpful staff and a good park map.

Balboa Park is easily reached from downtown on bus No 7, 7A or 7B along Park Blvd. By car, Park Blvd provides easy access to free parking areas near most of the exhibits, but the most scenic approach is over the Cabrillo Bridge. From the west, El Prado is an extension of Laurel St, which crosses Cabrillo Bridge with the Cabrillo Freeway 120ft below. Make a point of driving this stretch of freeway (State Hwy 163): the steep roadsides, lush with hanging greenery, look like a rain-forest gorge.

The free Balboa Park Tram stops at various points on a continuous loop through the main areas of the park. (It's actually a bus rather than a tram and is not to be confused with the Old Town Trolley tour bus.) For the most part, however, it's more enjoyable to walk.

BALBOA PARK, HILLCREST & OLD TOWN

Friars Rd

Morena Blvd

San Diego River

Riverwalk
Golf Course

Hotel Circle N

Hotel Circle S

1

2

3

Taylor St

Mission Valley Fwy

8

8

Pacific Hwy

Rosecrans St

Presidio
Park

Presidio Hills
Golf Course

Taylor St

Juan St

M

Congress St

San Diego Trolley

see Old Town inset

Heritage
Park

Lewis St

Fort Stockton Dr

Washington Place

Washington St

University Ave

Eagle St

Falcon St

Albatros St

Jefferson St

Moore St

Hortensia St

California St

Old Town

Washington St

Hawk St

Goldfinch St

Bush St

Hillcrest

Midway Dr

Barnett Ave

5

San Diego Fwy

Pacific Hwy

Sutter St

Andrews St

Wilde St

Kite St

Reynard Way

1st Ave

US Marine Corps
Recruit Depot

M

Washington St

16

17

18

19

20

Chalmers St

Walnut Ave

Union

Horton Ave

Ivanhoe Ave

Dove St

Spruce St
Footbridge

Vine St

Upas St

Thorn St

Sassafras St

Kettner Blvd

India St

Columbia St

State St

San Diego Fwy

California St

Redwood St

Quince St

Palm St

Middletown

Pacific Hwy

OLD TOWN

8

Morena Blvd

Whitman St

Jackson St

26

Presidio
Park

Gaines St

Rosecrans St

Sunset St

27

Presidio Hills
Golf Course

Presidio Dr

Jackson St

Mason St

Sunset St

Presidio
Way

Cosoy
Way

28

Taylor St

Calhoun St

Juan St

Wallace St

29

30

Old Town
San Diego State
Historic Park

San Diego Ave

San Diego Trolley

31

Old Town
Plaza

32

33

34

Heritage
Park

Heritage
Park Row

Congress St

Mason St

Twiggs St

5

35

Conde St

Harney St

37

36

38

39

0   150   300 m
0   150   300 yards

HILLCREST

40

Brant St

Curlew St

Washington St

41

42

43   44

University Ave

45   46

47

3rd Ave

4th Ave

5th Ave

6th Ave

48

Robinson Ave

49

50

51

State St

Columbia St

0   100   200 m
0   100   200 yards

SAN DIEGO AREA

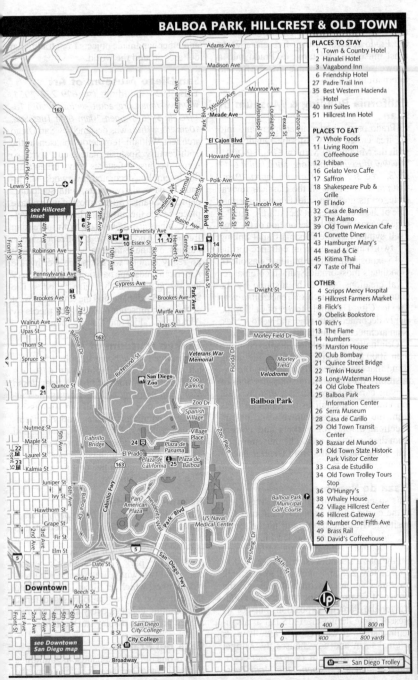

BALBOA PARK, HILLCREST & OLD TOWN

PLACES TO STAY
1 Town & Country Hotel
2 Hanalei Hotel
3 Vagabond Inn
6 Friendship Hotel
27 Padre Trail Inn
35 Best Western Hacienda Hotel
40 Inn Suites
51 Hillcrest Inn Hotel

PLACES TO EAT
7 Whole Foods
11 Living Room Coffeehouse
12 Ichiban
16 Gelato Vero Caffe
17 Saffron
18 Shakespeare Pub & Grille
19 El Indio
32 Casa de Bandini
37 The Alamo
39 Old Town Mexican Cafe
41 Corvette Diner
43 Hamburger Mary's
44 Bread & Cie
45 Kitima Thai
47 Taste of Thai

OTHER
4 Scripps Mercy Hospital
5 Hillcrest Farmers Market
8 Flick's
9 Obelisk Bookstore
10 Rich's
13 The Flame
14 Numbers
15 Marston House
20 Club Bombay
21 Quince Street Bridge
22 Timkin House
23 Long-Waterman House
24 Old Globe Theaters
25 Balboa Park Information Center
26 Serra Museum
28 Casa de Carillo
29 Old Town Transit Center
30 Bazaar del Mundo
31 Old Town State Historic Park Visitor Center
33 Casa de Estudillo
34 Old Town Trolley Tours Stop
36 O'Hungry's
38 Whaley House
42 Village Hillcrest Center
46 Hillcrest Gateway
48 Number One Fifth Ave
49 Brass Rail
50 David's Coffeehouse

SAN DIEGO AREA

A tip for winter visitors: the first Friday and Saturday in December, Christmas on the Prado festival, brings free entrance to most museums and turns El Prado into a showcase of performance art, crafts and international food.

California Building & Museum of Man

El Prado passes under an archway and into an area called the California Quadrangle, with the Museum of Man (☎ 619-239-2001; W www.museumofman.org; adult/child 6-17 $5/3; free 3rd Thur of month; open 10am-4:30pm daily), done in the classical revival style, on its northern side. Figures on either side of the arch represent the Atlantic and Pacific Oceans, while the decoration of the arch itself symbolizes the Panama Canal linking the two. This was the main entrance for the 1915 exposition, and the building was one of Goodhue's most ornate Spanish colonial revival creations, said to be inspired by the churrigueresque church of Tepotzotlán near Mexico City. The single Tower of California, richly decorated with blue and yellow tiles, is an architectural landmark of San Diego.

Originally, the building displayed more than 5000 ethnographic artifacts, including some that were specially made for the exposition – the cast concrete reproductions of Mayan carvings are still on display. The museum now specializes in Indian artifacts from the American Southwest and has an excellent display of baskets and pottery from the San Diego area. The museum shop sells good handicrafts from Central America and elsewhere.

Plaza de Panama

This space, in the middle of El Prado, was at the center of the Panama-California Exposition. The equestrian statue on the southern side is of El Cid, who led the Spanish revolt against the Moors in the 11th century. On the plaza's southwestern corner, next to a rare New Zealand agathis tree (a small, fragrant evergreen with flat leaves), the House of Charm was the Indian Arts building for the Panama exposition, but got its present name during the 1935 fair as a souvenir market. It was recently rebuilt to its original form and now houses the Mingei International Museum (☎ 619-239-0003; adult/student $5/2; open 11am-4pm Tues-Sun), which has an excellent permanent collection of costumes, toys, jewelry, utensils and other handmade objects from traditional cultures around the world.

San Diego Museum of Art

This 1924 building (☎ 619-232-7931; W www.sdmart.org; adult/senior & youth 18-24/child $8/6/3; open 10am-6pm Tues-Sun, 10am-9pm Thur) was designed by San Diego architect William Templeton Johnson in the 16th-century Spanish plateresque style, so named because it features heavy ornamentation resembling decorated silverwork. The facade is particularly ornate, with sculptures depicting Spanish artists (most of whom have pieces inside the museum). Important traveling exhibits are shown here with increasing frequency. The permanent collection has a number of fine European paintings (though no really famous works), some worthwhile American landscape paintings and some very interesting pieces in the Asian galleries. The Sculpture Garden, behind the café to the west of the main museum building, has pieces by Alexander Calder and Henry Moore.

Timken Museum of Art

Distinctive for *not* being in imitation Spanish style, this 1965 building (☎ 619-239-5548; 1500 El Prado; admission free; closed Mon, Sun morning & Sept) houses the Putnam collection. The small but impressive group of paintings includes works by Rembrandt, Rubens, El Greco, Cézanne and Pissarro. There's also a wonderful selection of Russian icons, which will appeal even to those who are not fans of this art form. Don't miss the Timken.

Botanical Building

This building (admission free; open Fri-Wed) looks just lovely from El Prado, reflected in a large lily pond that was used for hydrotherapy in WWII when the Navy took over most of the park. The building's central dome and two wings are covered with redwood lathes, which let filtered sunlight into the collection of tropical plants and ferns. The planting changes every season (there's a great poinsettia display in December).

Casa del Prado

This is one of the most handsome buildings along El Prado, but there is little to draw the visitor inside. It was built as a temporary structure for the 1915 exposition, but an earthquake in 1968 caused so much damage that the building was condemned. It was rebuilt with the support of community arts groups, who now use it for theater and dance performances.

Casa de Balboa

The House of Commerce & Industry was designed by Goodhue in the imitation Spanish colonial style for the 1915 exposition and later used for a variety of purposes until it burned down in 1978. The original building was faithfully reconstructed, including concrete decorations cast from pieces of the original. It now houses three museums (admission $4 per museum), each with its own museum shop and a small café.

The highlight here is definitely the **Museum of Photographic Arts** (☎ 619-238-7559; admission free 2nd Tues of month; open to 5pm daily), expanded fairly recently by La Jolla architect David Singer. International exhibits range from wildlife shots to 'what the heck is that' art pieces.

The **Museum of San Diego History** (☎ 619-232-6203; admission $5, free 2nd Tues of month; open 10am-4:30pm Tues-Sun) covers the American period from about 1848. Downstairs, the **Model Railroad Museum** (☎ 619-696-0199; child under 15 free, all free 1st Tues of month; open 11am-4pm Tues-Fri, 11am-5pm Sat & Sun) has working models of actual railroads in Southern California, both historical and contemporary.

Reuben H Fleet Space Theater & Science Center

One of Balboa Park's most publicized venues, this one features a hands-on science museum and a huge-screen Omnimax theater. The hemispherical, wrap-around screen and 152-speaker sound system create sensations that range from fantastic to OK, depending on what film is showing. The interactive science display was very innovative when this center opened in 1973, but that type of thing has since been done often and better. The theater (☎ 619-238-1233; W www.rhfleet.org; adult/student $9/7.20) has shows from 9:30am to 9pm or 11pm daily. The Science Center (☎ 619-238-1233; adult/child $6.50/5) is included in the theater price but can be visited by itself.

Natural History Museum

A recent face-lift of William Templeton Johnson's 1933 original has brought a beautiful space and giant-screen cinema to this museum at the eastern end of El Prado. The feature movie changes, but always is about the natural world and always gets rave reviews from young viewers. The museum houses lots of rocks, fossils and stuffed animals, as well as an impressive dinosaur skeleton and a California fault-line exhibit. Special children's programs are held most weekends. The museum (☎ 619-232-3821; W www.sdnhm.org; admission $3/12 regular/special exhibits, free 1st Tues of month; open 9:30am-4:30pm daily) also arranges field trips and nature hikes in Balboa Park and further afield.

Spanish Village Art Center

Behind the Natural History Museum is a grassy square with a magnificent Moreton Bay fig tree (sorry, no climbing). Opposite is a group of small tiled cottages, billed by park authorities as 'an authentic reproduction of an ancient village in Spain,' which are rented out as artists' studios. You can watch potters, jewelers, glass blowers, painters and sculptors churn out pricey decorative items, 11am to 4pm daily. North of the Spanish Village is a 1924 **carousel** and a **miniature railroad** (both open 11am-4:30pm Sat, Sun & holidays, daily in summer), which charge $1 per ride.

Spreckels Organ Pavilion

Going south from Plaza de Panama, you can't miss the circle of seating and the curved colonnade in front of this organ, said to be the largest outdoor musical instrument in the world. Donated by the Spreckels family of sugar fortune and fame, the organ came with the stipulation that San Diego must have an official organist. Free concerts are held at 2pm every Sunday, and at 7:30pm Monday from mid-June to August.

Pan-American Plaza

This plaza is now just a large parking lot southwest of the Spreckels Organ. As you approach it, the **United Nations Building** is on your right. Its **Unicef International Gift Shop** (open daily) has a good selection of stationery, jewelry and candy, and gives most of its proceeds back to the artists. Nearby, the **House of Pacific Relations** (☎ 619-292-8592) is actually 15 cottages from the 1915 exposition, inside which you will find furnishings and displays from many countries. The cottages are open free of charge on Sunday afternoon and often have crafts and food for sale.

Also of interest are the Palisades Building with the **Marie Hitchcock Puppet Theater** (☎ 619-685-5045); the **San Diego Automotive Museum** (☎ 619-231-2886), which has a varied collection of more than 60 cars and motorcycles, perfectly restored and well displayed, with helpful staff and classic cars and motorcycles such as a 1933 Duesenberg Roadster and a classic motorcycle by Indian.

The round building at the southern end of the plaza houses the excellent **Aerospace Museum** (☎ 619-234-8291), with an extensive display of aircraft – originals, replicas, models and a lot of Charles Lindbergh memorabilia. Don't miss the planes out front, or the courtyard, where a Phantom jet pursues a Russian MiG-17 between Art Deco lamp standards.

At the adjacent **Starlight Bowl**, the **Starlight Opera** (☎ 619-544-7800) presents a summer season of musicals and light opera.

The Federal Building was built for the 1935 exposition but was recently renovated to hold the **San Diego Hall of Champions Sports Museum** (☎ 619-234-2544; admission $6; open daily), which has exhibits on San Diego sports figures (recently deceased baseball legend Ted Williams, and the Olympic diver Greg Louganis are perhaps the best known), a rock-climbing wall and a 'Center Court', where you might see a mini-Chargers training camp at which actual Charger team members strut their stuff.

Centro Cultural de la Raza

This center for exhibitions of Mexican and Native American art (☎ 619-235-6135; W www.centroaza.com; donation requested; open noon-5pm Thur-Sun) is way out on the fringe of the main museum area (easiest access is from Park Blvd). The round, steel building is actually a converted water tank. Inside, the temporary exhibits of contemporary indigenous artwork can be very powerful.

Marston House

In the far northwestern corner of Balboa Park is the former home of George Marston, philanthropist and founder of the San Diego Historical Society. The house (☎ 619-298-3142; 3525 7th Ave) was designed in 1904 by noted San Diego architects William Hebbard and Irving Gill and is a fine example of the American Arts and Crafts style. The society has restored the interior as a showplace for Arts and Crafts furnishings and decorative objects. The **Historical Society** (☎ 619-232-6203) conducts 45-minute tours of the house ($5/4 adult/concession) and gardens from 10am to 3:30pm Friday, Saturday and Sunday.

Gardens of Balboa Park

Balboa Park includes a number of quite distinct garden areas, reflecting different horticultural styles and environments. A way to learn more about the gardens is to take one of the free weekly Offshoot Tours, conducted by park horticulturists from mid-January to Thanksgiving. The **Park & Recreation Department** (☎ 619-235-1114) has more information. Reservations are not required – be at the front of the Botanical Building by 10am.

If you're exploring on your own, visit the **Alcazar Garden**, a formal, Spanish-style garden; **Palm Canyon**, which has more than 50 species of palms; the **Japanese Friendship Garden** (admission $3, free 3rd Tues of month; open Tues & Fri-Sun); the **Australian Garden**; the **Rose Garden**; the **Desert Garden**, which is best in spring; and **Florida Canyon**, which gives an idea of the San Diego landscape before the Spanish settlement. The **Natural History Museum** (☎ 619-232-3821) runs guided walks in the canyon.

San Diego Zoo

The zoo is one of San Diego's biggest attractions, and anyone at all interested in the natural world should allow a full day to see it. More than 3000 animals, representing more than 800 species, are exhibited in a beautifully landscaped setting, typically in enclosures that replicate their natural habitats. The origins of the San Diego Zoo can be traced to the 1915/16 Panama-California Exposition and the enthusiasm of one local man, Dr Harry Wegeforth. The exposition featured an assortment of animals in cages along Park Blvd. It's now San Diego folklore that Wegeforth, hearing the roar of one of the caged lions, exclaimed, 'Wouldn't it be wonderful to have a zoo in San Diego? I believe I'll build one.' He started his campaign in 1916 in the newspaper and soon formed the

Zoological Society of San Diego. By pulling a few strings, Dr Wegeforth then ensured that quarantine requirements made it almost impossible to remove exotic animals from the county, so the society was able to acquire much of the menagerie left over from the exposition.

As a private organization, the Zoological Society could not be given a site on public land, but in 1921 a nice compromise was reached. The society donated all the animals and facilities to the city, and the city provided 200 acres of Balboa Park to use as a zoo, which would then be administered by the society. Though the site was bisected by canyons and largely barren, these problems were turned to advantage: canyons provided a means of separating different groups of animals to prevent the spread of disease, and they could be individually landscaped to simulate appropriate natural settings.

Wegeforth had a talent for extracting money from wealthy benefactors – John Spreckels, the millionaire sugar king, warned that the wily surgeon would 'cut you off at the pockets.' One of the first big donations was from journalist Ellen Browning Scripps (founder of Scripps College in Claremont, California), who paid for a perimeter fence, which was to enforce the payment of admission fees as much as to keep the animals in.

Local support for the zoo meant that unorthodox ways were often found to add to its collection. San Diegans brought in various finds, such as seals and snakes – rattlesnakes caught in Balboa Park were often profitably traded for animals from other zoos. In one exchange, the zoo provided fleas for a New York flea circus. The US Navy unofficially contributed an assortment of animals that had been adopted as mascots but could no longer be kept on ships. US Marines landing in Nicaragua were offered prizes if they captured beasts for Dr Wegeforth. During the 1930s Wegeforth himself traveled the world, collecting jaguars from Venezuela, orangutans from Borneo and marsupials from Australia. On a trip to India, Wegeforth contracted pneumonia and malaria; he died in 1941. His final contributions to the zoo were three elephants, which arrived in San Diego two months after his death.

By the end of WWII, the San Diego Zoo had a worldwide reputation, and it helped to rebuild the collections of European zoos that had been devastated by the war. The Zoological Society continued at the forefront of zoo management with the introduction of 'bioclimatic' habitats, which allowed a number of different types of animals to share a simulated natural environment. In the 1960s the society started work on an 1800-acre Wild Animal Park, 32 miles north of the city (see the Escondido section), which now provides free-range areas for many large animals.

Information The zoo (☎ 619-234-3153; ⓦ www.sandiegozoo.org; regular admission adult/child $20/12, deluxe admission package $32/20) is in the northern part of Balboa Park and has a large free parking lot off Park Blvd. The No 7 bus will get you there from downtown. Visitors should call for current hours, as they vary according to the time of year. The information booth is just to the left of the entrance as you come in – if you would like to leave the zoo and return, staff will stamp your hand.

The 'deluxe admission package' includes a 40-minute guided bus tour, which otherwise costs $5/3.50, as well as a round-trip aerial tram ride on the Skyfari cable car. Discount coupons for the zoo are widely available from San Diego magazines, weekly newspapers and coupon books at hotels and information centers. A combined ticket to visit both the San Diego Zoo and the Wild Animal Park within a five-day period costs $46.80/31.40.

It's wise to arrive early, as many of the animals are most active in the morning. You could start with a tour in a double-decker bus, which gives a good overview of the zoo and includes an informative commentary. Animal shows are held in the two amphitheaters (no extra charge), and they're usually entertaining, especially for kids. The Skyfari cable car goes right across the park and can save you some walking time, though there may be a line to get on it. From June to September, the zoo is open until 10pm and has special exhibits that focus on nocturnal creatures.

Facilities are provided for disabled visitors; call the zoo (☎ 619-231-1515 ext 4526) for specific information.

Highlights The zoo and the Wild Animal Park share an active program of breeding endangered species in captivity for reintroduction into their natural habitats. This has been done with a number of species, including the

Arabian oryx, the Bali starling and the California condor (below).

The **zoo gardens** are well known. They now include some plants that are used for the specialized food requirements of particular animals.

The zoo has also expanded its entertainment and educational role in the community with the opening of a **children's zoo exhibit** (where youngsters can pet small critters) and of outdoor theaters for animal shows. Both children and adults will enjoy the animal nursery, where you can see the zoo's newest arrivals.

Most visitors will have their own favorites. The **koalas** are so popular that Australians may be surprised to find them a sort of unofficial symbol of San Diego. The **Komodo dragon**, an Indonesian lizard that can grow up to 10 feet long, not only looks fearsome, but strides around the reptile house in a very menacing manner.

Tiger River, a realistic, re-created Asian rain forest, is one of the newer bioclimatic exhibits. **Gorilla Tropics** is an African rain forest. A third bioclimatic environment is the **Sun Bear Forest**, where the Asian bears are famously playful.

The large **Scripps Aviary** and **Rainforest Aviary** are both impressive structures where carefully placed feeders allow some close-up viewing. Finally, don't miss the Chinese **pandas** and **African Rock Kopje** (outcrop), where klipspringers (small antelopes) demonstrate their rock-climbing abilities.

HD

MISSION VALLEY

Although it would often dry up in late summer, the San Diego River was the most reliable source of freshwater for the crops and the livestock of the early missions. The river valley, now called Mission Valley, was frequently flooded until, in the mid-1950s, dams were completed upstream. I-8 now runs its length and is dotted with hotels and shopping centers. Some green, open space remains, but much of it is golf courses and country clubs. The restored Mission San Diego de Alcalá is definitely worth a visit, but Mission Valley's most touted feature now is its triad of shopping centers: Fashion Valley, the Hazard Center and Mission Valley Center.

The San Diego Trolley runs the length of the valley, from downtown to the mission, with stops at Qualcomm Stadium and all the shopping centers. The trolley's route cuts through a scenic corridor of riparian land (and golf courses) not seen from the freeway. You could make a day of trolley-shopping, getting off at each of the big centers. Fashion Valley has specialty stores such as Tiffany & Co, Enzo Antolini and Restoration Hardware, as well as biggies such as Saks Fifth Ave, Macy's and Nordstrom; most are open until 10pm. Mission Valley Center is known for its upscale discount outlets, which include the Nordstrom Rack and Saks Off Fifth Ave; both malls have some good restaurants and multiplex movie theaters.

Mission San Diego de Alcalá

Though the first California mission was established on Presidio hill, Padre Junípero Serra decided in 1773 to move it a few miles upriver, closer to a better water supply and more arable land.

In 1784 the missionaries built a solid adobe and timber church, but it was destroyed by an earthquake in 1803. The church was promptly rebuilt, and at least some of it still stands on a slope overlooking Mission Valley. With the end of the mission system in the 1830s, the buildings were turned over to the Mexican government and fell into disrepair. Some accounts say that they were reduced to a facade and a few crumbling walls by the 1920s.

Extensive restoration began in 1931, with financial support from local citizens and the Hearst Foundation, a philanthropic organization funded by one of California's most influential families (see the Hearst Castle section in the Central Coast chapter). The pretty white church and the buildings you see now are the result of the thorough restoration.

The **visitor center** (☎ 619-281-8449) in the mission has a friendly and informative staff, some good books and some tacky souvenirs. The mission (*Friars Rd; adult/child $3/2; open 9am-5pm daily*) is two blocks north of I-8, between I-15 and Mission Gorge Rd; from the Mission trolley stop, walk two blocks north and turn right onto San Diego Mission Rd.

Conversion & Revenge

The first missionaries visited Indian settlements with gifts and promises, and their first converts, whom they called 'neophytes, were encouraged to move into the mission compound on the Presidio, where they lived and worked and contracted European diseases. The Spanish soldiers in the Presidio garrison abused the mission neophytes and also raided Indian villages. According to Padre Serra's reports, soldiers would chase their victims on horseback and 'catch an Indian woman with their lassos, to become prey for their unbridled lusts.' So, in 1774 the priests left the Presidio and started their new mission near a large Kumeyaay village, away from the influence of the military.

Unfortunately, they were also away from the protection of the military, and in November 1775 the increasingly resentful Kumeyaay made a concerted attack on the mission and burned it to the ground. One of the priests, Luis Jayme, appealed to the attackers with arms outstretched, crying 'Love God, my children!' He was dragged away and beaten to death, becoming California's first martyr. The survivors retreated to the Presidio, and the Spanish authorities captured, flogged and executed the leaders of the attack. After a few months, the missionaries returned to their site in the valley and built a second mission, with a tiled roof to resist the flaming arrows of Indian attacks – this type of roof became a standard feature of mission architecture.

OLD TOWN

Under the Mexican government, which took power in 1821, any settlement with a population of 500 or more was entitled to become a 'pueblo.' Since the Presidio's population was about 600, soldiers from the garrison were able to cultivate and partition the land below Presidio hill and to make it the first official civilian Spanish settlement in California – the Pueblo de San Diego. A plaza was laid out around Casa Estudillo, home of the pueblo's commandant, and within 10 years it was surrounded by about 40 huts and a few houses. This square mile of land (roughly 10 times what is there today) was also the center of American San Diego until the fire of 1872, after which the city's focus moved to the new Horton subdivision.

John Spreckels built a trolley line from Horton's New Town to Old Town in the 1920s and, to attract passengers, began restoring the old district. In 1968 the area became Old Town State Historic Park, archaeological work began and the few surviving original buildings were restored. Other structures were rebuilt, and the area is now a pedestrian district (with parking lots around the edges) with shade trees, a large open plaza and a cluster of shops and restaurants.

In an attempt to emphasize Old Town's historical significance – it has become primarily a shopping and eating destination – the Park Service has hired interpretive rangers to give tours and has expanded the visitor center to include an excellent American-period museum (Indian pieces are in the Museum of Man at Balboa Park). The **visitor center** (☎ 619-220-5422; open 10am-5pm daily) is in the Robinson-Rose House at the southern end of the plaza. The center has a California history slide show, memorabilia and an informative staff. The Robinson-Rose building has some good history books for sale and a diorama depicting the original pueblo.

If you're particularly interested in the historical background, pick up a copy of the *Old Town San Diego State Historic Park Tour Guide & Brief History* ($2), or take a guided tour, which leaves from the visitor center at 2pm daily (there's also an 11am tour if enough people show up).

Across from the center is **La Casa de Estudillo** *(admission free)*, a restored adobe home furnished with original furniture. It's worth a look and has a self-guided tour map, available from a docent at the house's northwestern entrance.

The **Bazaar del Mundo**, just off the plaza's northwestern corner, is a colorful collection of import shops and restaurants, which are open late and definitely worth passing through. Along San Diego Ave, on the southern side of the plaza, is a row of small, historical-looking buildings (only one is authentically old), some of which house souvenir and gift shops. Two blocks from the Old Town perimeter sits **Whaley House** (☎ 619-298-2482; 2482 San Diego Ave; admission $5; open 10am-4:30pm daily, closed Tues in winter), the city's oldest brick building, which was *officially* certified as haunted by the US Department of Commerce in the early 1960s. Displayed here is an excellent

SAN DIEGO AREA

collection of period furniture and clothing from when the house served as courthouse, theater and private residence.

Just north of Old Town, **Casa de Carrillo** dates from about 1820 and is said to be the oldest house in San Diego. It is now the pro shop for the public **Presidio Hills Golf Course** (☎ 619-295-9476).

The Old Town Transit Center, on the trolley line at Taylor St at the northwestern edge of Old Town, is a stop for the *Coaster* commuter train, the San Diego Trolley (orange and blue lines) and bus Nos 4 and 5 from downtown; Old Town Trolley tours stop southeast of the plaza on Twiggs St.

Presidio Hill

In 1769 Padre Junípero Serra and Gaspar de Portolá established the first Spanish settlement in California on Presidio hill, overlooking the valley of the San Diego River. You can walk up from Old Town along Mason St and get excellent views of San Diego Bay and Mission Valley. Atop the hill, **Presidio Park** has a few walking trails and shaded benches. A large cross, made with tiles from the original mission, commemorates Padre Serra. American forces occupied the hill in 1846, during the Mexican-American War, and named it Fort Stockton, for American commander Robert Stockton. A flagpole, cannon, some plaques and earth walls now form the **Fort Stockton Memorial**. The nearby **El Charro Statue**, a bicentennial gift to the city from Mexico, depicts a Mexican cowboy on horseback. Nothing remains of the original Presidio structures, but there are archaeological digs under way.

It would be easy to believe that the **Serra Museum** (☎ 619-297-3258; adult/child $5/2) is a well-preserved Spanish colonial-style structure, but in fact it was designed by William Templeton Johnson in 1929. The museum has a small but interesting collection of artifacts and pictures from the Mission and rancho periods, and gives a good feel for the earliest days of European settlement. Call the museum for current hours.

UPTOWN & HILLCREST

Without being too precise, Uptown is a triangle north of downtown, east of Old Town and south of Mission Valley. In the late 19th century it was fashionable to live in the hills north of downtown – only those who owned

a horse-drawn carriage could afford it. Called Bankers Hill after some of the wealthy residents – or Pill Hill, because of the many doctors – these upscale heights had unobstructed views of the bay and Point Loma before I-5 was built. A few of the ornate Victorian mansions survive, most notably the 1889 **Long-Waterman House** (2408 1st Ave). Easily recognized by its towers, gables, bay windows and veranda, it was once the home of former California governor Robert Waterman. Also notable is the **Timkin House**, one block to the north.

A favorite pastime of residents old and new is crossing the 375ft **Spruce St Footbridge** that hangs over a deep canyon between Front and Brant Sts. The **Quince Street Bridge**, between 4th and 3rd Aves, is a wood-trestle bridge built in 1905 and refurbished in 1988 after its slated demolition was vigorously protested by community activists.

At the corner of Washington and India Sts is a shingled complex once known as the **India Street Art Colony**. Opened in the 1970s by architect and artist Raoul Marquis, the art studios, import shops and theaters that originally occupied it are gone. They have been replaced by an excellent café and some first-rate inexpensive eateries.

At the heart of the Uptown is **Hillcrest** (bus Nos 1, 3 and 25 go to/from downtown along 4th and 5th Aves), the first suburban real-estate development in San Diego. If you drive around, you'll see the work of many of San Diego's best-known architects from the early 20th century, including Irving Gill and William Templeton Johnson. The Mediterranean and Spanish mission styles, and the influence of the Arts and Crafts movement, are also evident. But the real attraction of Hillcrest is its lively street life, due in part to its position as the center of San Diego's gay and lesbian community.

To look around, start at the **Hillcrest Gateway**, which arches over University Ave at 5th Ave. Not far away, on 5th Ave between University Ave and Washington St, is the **Village Hillcrest Center**, with its colorful postmodern architecture. There you will find a **multiplex cinema** (☎ 619-299-2100) and restaurants and shops, as well as News Etc, a newsstand with a great selection. Go east on University Ave to see the 1928 **Kahn Building** at No 535; it is an original Hillcrest commercial building with architectural elements that border on kitsch. Go south on 5th Ave to find a variety of bookstores, many with a good selection of nonmainstream publications.

Hillcrest's **farmers market** *(5th Ave, cnr Normal & Lincoln Sts; open 9am-1pm Sun)* is a fun place to people-watch and buy fresh produce.

POINT LOMA
On the southern tip of Point Loma, the peninsula that seems to hang down across the entrance to San Diego Bay, is **Cabrillo National Monument** *(bus No 26 from downtown; admission $4 per car, $2 by bike or bus; open 9am-5pm daily)*, San Diego's finest place to visit for history and views. It's also the best place in San Diego to see the gray whale migration (January to March) from land. The **visitor center** *(☎ 619-557-5450; open 9am-5:15pm daily)* at the monument has an excellent presentation on Portuguese explorer Juan Rodríguez Cabrillo's exploration, plus very good exhibits on the native inhabitants and the area's natural history. The 1854 **Old Point Loma Lighthouse**, atop the point, is furnished with typical lighthouse furniture from the late 19th century, including lamps and picture frames hand-covered with hundreds of shells – testimony to the long, lonely nights endured by lighthouse keepers. On the ocean side of the point, you can drive or walk down to the **tide pools** to look for anemones, starfish, crabs, limpets and dead man's fingers (thin, tubular seaweed).

San Diego's first fishing boats were based at Point Loma, and in the 19th century whalers dragged carcasses onto its shores to extract the whale oil. Chinese fishermen settled on the harbor side of the point in the 1860s but were forced off in 1888 when the US Congress passed the Scott Act prohibiting anyone without citizenship papers from entering the area. Coming home from a normal day's run outside the international waters boundary (30mi offshore), the Chinese were met by officials who prohibited them from re-entering the harbor. Portuguese fishing families came about 50 years later – around the same time that Italian immigrants settled on the other side of the harbor – and established a permanent community. The **Portuguese Hall** is still a hub of activity and many people living on Point Loma are of Portuguese descent.

The tidal flats of **Loma Portal**, where Point Loma joins the mainland, were used as an airstrip in 1927 by Charles Lindbergh for flight testing the *Spirit of St Louis*. The following year a functioning airport was established; it was named Lindbergh Field. It has expanded considerably and is now known as San Diego International Airport.

OCEAN BEACH
San Diego's most bohemian seaside community is a good place to get tattooed, shop for antiques and go to a restaurant without shoes or a shirt. Newport Ave, the main drag that runs perpendicular to the beach, is a compact zone of bars, surf shops, music stores, used-clothing stores and, in the 4800 and 4900 blocks, antiques consignment stores. Bus No 23 connects OB to downtown.

The half-mile-long Ocean Beach Pier is good for fishing and for a breath of fresh air. Just north of the pier, near the end of Newport Ave, is the beach scene headquarters, with volleyball courts and sunset barbecues. North of here is **Dog Beach**, where dogs can run unleashed and chase birds around the marshy area where the San Diego River meets the sea. A few blocks south of the pier is **Sunset Cliffs Park**, where watching surfers and the sunset is the big attractions.

There are good surf breaks at the cliffs and, to the south, off Point Loma. Under the pier, hot surfers slalom the pilings. Those who are not so hot need to beware the rips and currents, which can be deadly.

If you're here on Wednesday afternoon, stop by the OB **farmers market** *(4pm-7pm Wed, 4pm-8pm June-Sept)* to see street performers and sample fresh food.

CORONADO
Compact and densely populated with 28,500 people, Coronado is a trim combination of military families, retirees and folks who depend on resort hotels for their paychecks. Directly across the bay from downtown San Diego, Coronado is, administratively, a separate city and known for closely guarding its ambience and environmental quality.

A spectacular 2.12mi bridge, Coronado Bay Bridge (opened in 1969), joins Coronado to the Mainland; the Silver Strand, a long, narrow sand spit, runs south to Imperial Beach. Nevertheless, it's often referred to as Coronado Island, and the locals like to call it 'the Rock.' The large North Island Naval Air Station occupies a big chunk of land which was once an island.

In 1888 Elisha Babcock and Hampton Story opened the Hotel del Coronado, the showy centerpiece of a new resort, and by 1900 they were broke. John D Spreckels, the millionaire who bankrolled the first rail line to San Diego, took over Coronado and turned the whole island into one of the most fashionable getaways on the West Coast.

Information

The **Coronado Visitors Bureau** (☎ 619-437-8788; w www.coronadovisitor.com; 1047 B Ave; open 9am-5pm Mon-Fri, 10am-5pm Sat, 11am-4pm Sun) has information and conducts a walking tour ($6), starting from the **Glorietta Bay Inn** (1630 Glorietta Blvd), near Silver Strand Blvd, at 11am Tuesday, Thursday and Saturday. The 90-minute route takes in many of Coronado's most interesting sights.

Cars with driver only pay a $1 toll when coming over the bridge to Coronado, but it's free for vehicles with passengers. Bus Nos 901, 902 and 903 from downtown run the length of Orange Ave to the Hotel del Coronado.

Ferries leave from San Diego's B St Pier every hour on the hour to make the 15-minute trip to Coronado, and return every hour on the half hour ($2). **San Diego Water Taxi** (☎ 619-235-8294) provides on-call transportation to/from the mainland from 10am to 10pm daily ($5 per person). Rent a bike at Coronado's Ferry Landing Marketplace ($5 per hour) or bring one on the ferry for 50¢. Alternatively, use the electric Coronado Shuttle to get around (free). The Old Town Trolley tour stops in front of Mc P's Irish Pub, on Orange Ave at 11th St.

Hotel del Coronado

Commonly known as the Hotel Del (☎ 619-435-6611, 800-468-7337), this place is a much-loved San Diego institution. Architecturally, it's pretty quirky, with its conical towers, cupolas, turrets, balconies and dormer windows. It's an all-timber building, and the cavernous public spaces reflect the background of railroad depot–designing architects James and Merritt Reed. The acres of polished wood do give the interior a warm, old-fashioned feel.

The Del was where Edward (then Prince of Wales) first met Mrs Simpson (then Mrs Spenser) in 1920, though the two did not become an item until some years later. Other hotel guests have included many US presidents and other dignitaries – pictures and mementos are displayed in the hotel's History Gallery. Hotel Del achieved its widest exposure in the 1959 movie *Some Like It Hot*, which earned it a lasting association with Marilyn Monroe. Take a cassette-guided tour ($3) from the Lobby Shop or one of the personally guided tours ($10/15 hotel guests/nonguests), which start at 10am, 11am and 1pm daily except Sunday. There's an interesting resident ghost story too – something about a woman suffering from unrequited love who silently appears on a TV screen in the room where she had her heart broken.

For more details, see the sections on Places to Stay and Places to Eat.

MISSION BAY

In the 18th century, the mouth of the San Diego River formed a shallow bay when the river flowed, and a marshy swamp when it didn't – the Spanish called it False Bay. After WWII, a fine combination of civic vision and coastal engineering turned the swamp into a 7-sq-mi playground, with 27mi of shoreline and 90 acres of public parks. With financing from public bonds and expertise from the Army Corps of Engineers, the river was channeled to the sea, the bay was dredged and millions of tons of sludge were used to build islands, coves and peninsulas. A quarter of the land created has been leased to hotels, boatyards and other businesses, providing ongoing revenue for the city.

The attractions of Mission Bay run the gamut from luxurious resort hotels to free outdoor activities. Kite flying is popular in Mission Bay Park, beach volleyball is big on Fiesta Island, and there's delightful cycling and in-line skating on the miles of smooth bike paths. Sailing, windsurfing and kayaking dominate the waters in northwest Mission Bay, while water-skiers zip around Fiesta Island. For information about equipment rentals, see under Activities later.

You can save adrenaline and still have a perfectly nice time on the bay aboard the **Bahia Belle** (☎ 858-539-7779; 998 West Mission Bay Dr; adult/concession $6/4), a floating bar disguised as a stern-wheeler paddleboat. It cruises between two resort hotels, the Catamaran and the Bahia, on weekends year-round, Wednesday to Sunday in June and daily in July and August. It also offers dinner, sunset and night cruises.

SeaWorld

Undoubtedly one of San Diego's best known and most popular attractions, SeaWorld (☎ 619-226-3901; w www.seaworld.com/sea world/ca; bus No 9 from downtown; adult/child $43/33; open 9am-11pm daily in summer, 10am-6pm daily rest of year) opened here in 1964. Shamu, the SeaWorld killer whale, has become an unofficial symbol of the city. The park is very commercial, but nonetheless entertaining and even slightly educational. Its popularity can be a drawback, causing long waits for some shows and exhibits during peak seasons.

At the regular admission you may have a pretty expensive day. Discount coupons are available, and buying tickets online gives you 10% off, but the extras really add up – parking costs $7, the food is expensive (use the picnic areas at the park entrance to save a few bucks) and not many people escape without spending something on the ubiquitous SeaWorld souvenirs. Ways to get the best value for your ticket include a re-entry stamp, which lets you go out for a break and return later (good during summer when the park is open late); a combination ticket which is also good for Universal Studios (in Los Angeles); and a two-day ticket that costs only $4 more than a regular one.

The highlights of SeaWorld are varied but focus on live shows that feature trained dolphins, seals, sea lions or killer whales. There are numerous aquarium-like installations where you can see and learn about underwater creatures, as well as petting pools where you can touch the slippery surface of a dolphin or manta ray.

The park is easy to find by car – take Sea World Dr off I-5 less than a mile north of where it intersects with I-8. By bus, take No 9 from downtown. Tickets sales end 1½ hours before closing time.

MISSION BEACH & PACIFIC BEACH

Where people pilgrimage daily to watch and cheer as the sun sinks into the sea is a special place. From the South Mission Jetty at the southern tip of Mission Beach to Pacific Beach Point at the northern end of Pacific Beach are 3mi of solid SoCal beach scene. **Ocean Front Walk**, the beachfront boardwalk, can get crowded with joggers, in-line skaters and bicyclists anytime of the year and is one of the best people-watching venues in San Diego. On a warm summer weekend, parking becomes impossible and suntanned bodies cover the beach from end to end. The main north-south road, Mission Blvd, is so crowded that the police often just close it down.

A bike or in-line skates are great ways to get around. Both can be rented from places such as **Hamel's** (☎ 858-488-5050; 704 Ventura Place), near the Giant Dipper roller coaster in Mission Beach, or **Cheap Rentals** (☎ 858-488-9070; w www.cheap rentals .com; 3685 Mission Blvd at Santa Clara St), which has low prices and rents everything from bikes and in-line skates to baby joggers.

Down at the Mission Beach end, many small houses and apartments are rented for the summer season, and the hedonism is concentrated in a narrow strip between the ocean and Mission Bay. Up in Pacific Beach (or PB) the activity spreads inland, especially along Garnet Ave, which is well supplied with bars, restaurants and used-clothing stores. At the ocean end of Garnet Ave, the Crystal Pier is a popular place to fish or watch surfers.

The surf at Mission Beach is a beach break, good for beginners, body boarders and bodysurfers. It's more demanding around Crystal Pier, where the waves are steep and fast. Tourmaline Surfing Park, at the far northern end of the beach, is particularly popular with long boarders. For information on equipment rentals, see the Activities section.

Belmont Park

This family-style amusement park (☎ 858-488-0668; admission free) in the middle of Mission Beach has been here since 1925. When it was threatened with demolition in the mid-1990s, concerted community action saved the the large indoor pool known as the Plunge and the classic wooden roller coaster ($3.50; open from 11am daily). More modern attractions include the Pirates Cove children's play zone and Venturer II, which features

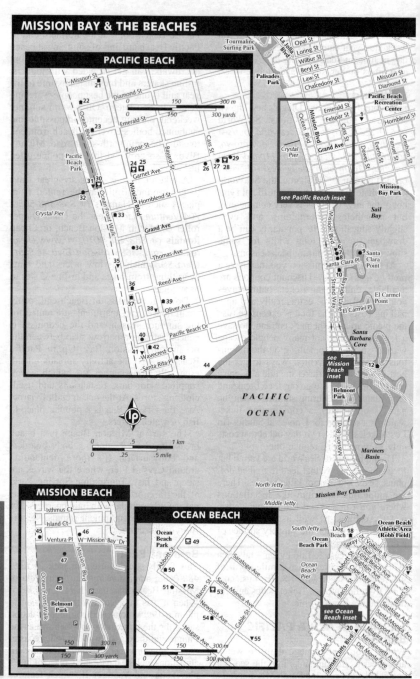

MISSION BAY & THE BEACHES

Garnet Ave
Magnolia St
Garnet Ave (Restaurant Row)
Balboa Ave
Grand Ave
Thomas Ave
Reed Ave
Oliver Ave
Pacific Beach Dr
Lamont St
Morrell St
Noyes St
Olney St
Lee St
Ingraham St
Jewell St
Kendall St
Haines St
Riviera Dr
Crown Point Dr

Mission Bay Dr
Del Rey St
Morena Blvd
Mission Bay Golf Course
N Mission Bay Dr
De Anza Rd
Rose Creek Shore Dr

Mission Bay Park
Mission Bay Park
De Anza Cove

Crown Point

Mission Bay

Fiesta Island

Vacation Rd
Vacation Isle
Ingraham St

Fiesta Island Rd

Mission Bay Park

Dana Basin
W Mission Bay Dr
Quivira Rd
Quivira Basin

Pacific Passage

Sea World

Mission Bay Park

Sea World Dr
Mission Bay Dr

San Diego River

Clairemont Dr
Ingulf St
Milton St
Morena Blvd
Galveston St
E Mission Bay Dr

Friars Rd

Kurtz St

San Diego Sports Arena
Sports Arena Blvd
Midway Dr
Rosecrans St
East Dr

W Point Loma Blvd

Dusty Rhodes Park

Sunset Cliffs Blvd

Collier Park West
Cleator Community Park
Famosa Blvd
Nimitz Blvd

Guizot St
Santa
Venice St

Chatsworth Blvd
Worden St
Tennyson St
Voltaire St

Rosecrans St
Lytton St
Barnett Ave

Midway Dr

Sail Ho Golf Course

US Marine Corps Recruit Depot

Pacific Hwy

P Parking Area

amusement machines that combine video games with virtual reality technology. There are also beachwear boutiques, a bar and some places to eat. It's free to enter Belmont Park; you pay separately for the attractions.

LA JOLLA

Immaculately landscaped parks, white-sand coves, upscale boutiques and a perfect geographical siting atop cliffs that meet deep, clear blue waters make it easy to understand why 'La Jolla' is often translated from Spanish as 'the jewel.' In fact, Indians who inhabited the area from 10,000 years ago to the mid-19th century called the place 'mut la Hoya, la Hoya' – the place of many caves. In any case, it's pronounced 'la **hoy**-ya' and is a great place to spend the day. Bus No 34 connects La Jolla to downtown via the Old Town Transit Center.

The area was subdivided in the 1880s but started developing when Ellen Browning Scripps moved here in 1897. The newspaper heiress acquired much of the land along Prospect St, which she subsequently donated to various community uses. Not only did she support local institutions such as the **Bishop's School** (cnr Prospect St & La Jolla Blvd) and the **La Jolla Woman's Club** (715 Silverado St), she also had them designed by Irving Gill, who set the architectural tone of the community – an unadorned Mediterranean style characterized by arches, colonnades, palm trees, red-tile roofs and pale stucco.

The surrounding area is home to UCSD, several renowned research institutes and a new-money residential area called the Golden Triangle, bounded by I-5, I-805 and Hwy 52. The space-age church in this area, which you see from I-5, is a Mormon Temple, completed in 1993.

Downtown La Jolla

The compact town sits atop cliffs surrounded on three sides by the ocean. Distant views of Pacific blue are glimpsed through windows and from between buildings, but there is little interaction between the heart of downtown and the sea. The main thoroughfares, Prospect St and Girard Ave, are known for the 'three Rs' – restaurants, rugs and real estate. La Jolla is San Diego's best place to go for high-class shopping: galleries sell paintings, sculpture and decorative items, and small boutiques fill in the spaces between Banana

Republic, Armani Exchange and Saks Fifth Avenue, which is on Wall St near Herschel Ave. Alternative health guru Deepak Chopra's **Center for Well Being** (☎ 858-551-7788; 7630 Fay Ave) attracts wellness-conscious people from around the globe.

For a bit of old La Jolla, head northwest along Prospect St. **John Cole's Bookshop** (☎ 858-454-4766; 780 Prospect St) is in a cottage once owned by Ellen Browning Scripps and renovated to Irving Gill's design. Around the corner, the **La Jolla Historical Society** (☎ 858-459-5335; Eads Ave; open noon-4:30pm Tues-Thur) has vintage photos and beach memorabilia – think old bathing costumes, lifeguard buoys and the like. Further northwest on Prospect St, you will find St James Episcopal Church, the La Jolla Recreation Center and the Bishop's School, which were all built in the early 20th century.

The **Museum of Contemporary Art** (☎ 858-454-3541; 700 Prospect St; admission $4; free 1st Tues & 3rd Sun of month; open 11am-5pm in winter, 11am-8pm Mon-Fri in summer & Thur year-round, closed Wed) gets world-class exhibitions. Originally designed by Irving Gill in 1916 as the home of Ellen Browning Scripps, the building has been renovated by Philadelphia-born postmodern architect Robert Venturi and has an Andy Goldsworthy sculpture out front.

Walk east on Silverado St to Girard Ave. Here you'll find the latest from big names in fashion and, at the corner of Wall St, the **Athenaeum Music & Arts Library** – a music and art library where you can see small art exhibits and read daily newspapers from around the globe.

The Coast

Downhill from downtown, the La Jolla coastline is rugged and invigorating. Private properties going right down to the beach restrict access, and parking is very limited at some points, but there is a wonderful walking path that skirts the shoreline for a half-mile.

The path's western end begins at the **Children's Pool**, where a jetty (funded by – you guessed it – Ellen Browning Scripps) protects the beach from big waves.

Originally intended to give La Jolla's youth a safe place to frolic, the beach is now more popular with sea lions and is a great place to view them up close as they lounge on the shore. East of the Children's

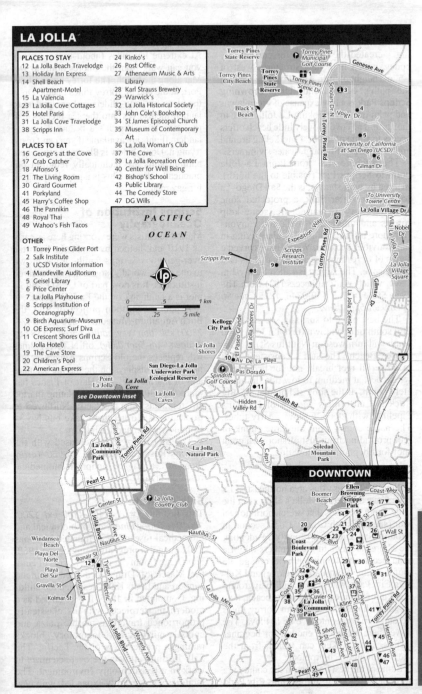

LA JOLLA

PLACES TO STAY
12 La Jolla Beach Travelodge
13 Holiday Inn Express
14 Shell Beach Apartment-Motel
15 La Valencia
23 La Jolla Cove Cottages
25 Hotel Parisi
31 La Jolla Cove Travelodge
38 Scripps Inn

PLACES TO EAT
16 George's at the Cove
17 Crab Catcher
18 Alfonso's
21 The Living Room
30 Girard Gourmet
41 Porkyland
45 Harry's Coffee Shop
46 The Pannikin
48 Royal Thai
49 Wahoo's Fish Tacos

OTHER
1 Torrey Pines Glider Port
2 Salk Institute
3 UCSD Visitor Information
4 Mandeville Auditorium
5 Geisel Library
6 Price Center
7 La Jolla Playhouse
8 Scripps Institution of Oceanography
9 Birch Aquarium-Museum
10 OE Express; Surf Diva
11 Crescent Shores Grill (La Jolla Hotel)
19 The Cave Store
20 Children's Pool
22 American Express

24 Kinko's
26 Post Office
27 Athenaeum Music & Arts Library
28 Karl Strauss Brewery
29 Warwick's
32 La Jolla Historical Society
33 John Cole's Bookshop
34 St James Episcopal Church
35 Museum of Contemporary Art
36 La Jolla Woman's Club
37 The Cove
39 La Jolla Recreation Center
40 Center for Well Being
42 Bishop's School
43 Public Library
44 The Comedy Store
47 DG Wills

PACIFIC OCEAN

Torrey Pines State Reserve
Torrey Pines City Beach
Torrey Pines State Reserve
Black's Beach

Torrey Pines Municipal Golf Course
Genesee Ave
Torrey Pines Scenic Dr
Scholars Dr
Voigt Dr
N Torrey Pines Rd
University of California at San Diego (UCSD)
Gilman Dr
To University Towne Centre
La Jolla Village Dr
Nobel Dr
Villa La Jolla Dr
La Jolla Village Square
Expedition Way
Scripps Research Institute
Torrey Pines Rd
La Jolla Scenic Dr N
Gilman Dr
5

Scripps Pier

Kellogg City Park
El Paseo Grande
La Jolla Shores Dr
La Jolla Shores
Av De La Playa
Pas Dorado
10
San Diego-La Jolla Underwater Park Ecological Reserve
Spindrift Golf Course
11
Ardath Rd
Hidden Valley Rd
Via Capri
Soledad Mountain Park

Point La Jolla
La Jolla Cove
see Downtown inset
La Jolla Caves

Girard Ave
Torrey Pines Rd
La Jolla Community Park
La Jolla Natural Park
Pearl St

La Jolla Country Club

Center St
Draper Ave
La Jolla Blvd
Nautilus St
Nautilus St
La Jolla Mesa Dr

Windansea Beach
Playa Del Norte
Playa Del Sur
Gravilla St
Kolmar St
Bonair St
Nautilus St
Electric Ave
Neptune Pl
Waverly Ave
La Jolla Blvd
12
13

DOWNTOWN

Boomer Beach
Ellen Browning Scripps Park
Coast Blvd
16 17
14 15
19
18
21
22 24 25
26
Wall St
Prospect St
Jenner Blvd
27 28
Herschel Ave
Ivanhoe Ave
29
30
31
32
33
34
35
36
37
Silverado St
Cuvier St
Girard Ave
Coast Blvd
38
39
La Jolla Community Park
40
Kline St
Drury Ave
41
Torrey Pines Rd
Herschel Ave
Bishops Lane
Fay Ave
Eads Ave
Silver
Draper Ave
44
45
46
47
42
43
Pearl St
48
49
Coast Boulevard Park
Wall St

SAN DIEGO AREA

0 .5 1 km
0 .25 .5 mile

Pool, La Jolla's only 'skyscraper' – the infamous mid-'60s-vintage 939 Coast Building – created the impetus for current city codes, which limit new structures west of I-5 to a height of 30ft. Atop Point La Jolla, at the path's eastern end, **Ellen Browning Scripps Park** is a tidy expanse of green lawns and palm trees overlooking La Jolla Cove to the north. The cove's lovely little beach offers access to some of the best snorkeling around and is popular with rough-water swimmers.

The offshore area from Point La Jolla north to Scripps Pier (visible to the north), marked by white buoys, is the **San Diego–La Jolla Underwater Park**, a protected zone with a variety of marine life, some kelp forests and interesting reefs and canyons (for more information, see Scuba Diving in the Activities section). Waves have carved a series of caves into the sandstone cliffs east of the cove. The largest is called Sunny Jim Cave, which you can access ($2) from **The Cave Store** (☎ 858-459-0746; 1325 Cave St; open 9am-5pm daily).

The best place to surf and see surfers is 2mi south of downtown (take La Jolla Blvd south and turn west on Nautilus St) at Windansea Beach. The surf's consistent peak (a powerful reef break, not for beginners) works best at medium to low tide. Immediately south, at the foot of Palomar St, **Big Rock** is California's version of Hawaii's Pipeline, with steep, hollow, gnarly tubes. The name comes from the large chunk of reef protruding from just offshore – a great spot for tidepooling at low tide.

La Jolla Shores

Called 'the Shores,' this area northeast of La Jolla Cove is where La Jolla's cliffs meet the wide, sandy beaches that stretch north to Del Mar (see the North County Coast section in Around San Diego). Primarily residential, the Shores is home to the members-only La Jolla Beach and Tennis Club (its orange tile roof is visible from La Jolla Cove) and Kellogg City Park, whose beachside playground is good for families. To reach the beach, take La Jolla Shores Dr north from Torrey Pines Rd and turn west onto Ave de la Playa. The waves here are gentle enough for beginner surfers, and kayakers can launch from the shore without much problem.

Some of the best beaches in the county are north of the Shores in **Torrey Pines City Park**, which covers the coastline from the Salk Institute up to the Torrey Pines State Reserve. At extreme low tides (about twice a year), you can walk from the Shores north to Del Mar along the beach. The **Torrey Pines Glider Port**, at the end of Torrey Pines Scenic Dr, is the place for hang-gliders and paragliders to launch themselves into the sea breezes that rise over the cliffs. It's a beautiful sight – tandem flights are available if you can't resist trying it. Down below is **Blacks Beach**, where bathing suits are technically required but practically absent. This is a popular hangout for gay men.

Scripps Institution of Oceanography

Marine scientists were working here as early as 1910 and, helped by donations from the ever-generous Scripps family, it has grown to one of the world's largest marine research institutions. It is now part of UCSD, and its pier is a landmark on the La Jolla coast.

A public education project of SIO, the **Birch Aquarium-Museum** (☎ 858-534-3474; 2300 Exhibition Way; adult/concession $8.50/5; open 9am-5pm daily), off N Torrey Pines Rd, replaces the old Scripps Aquarium and has brilliant displays on the marine sciences and of marine life. The Hall of Fishes has more than 30 fish tanks, simulating marine environments from the Pacific Northwest to tropical seas. To get there, take bus No 34 from downtown and La Jolla.

The SIO is not to be confused with the **Scripps Research Institute** (10550 Torrey Pines Rd), a private, nonprofit biomedical research organization.

Salk Institute

This institute (☎ 858-453-4100 ext 1200; 10010 N Torrey Pines Rd) for biological and biomedical research was founded by Jonas Salk, the polio-prevention pioneer, in 1960. San Diego County donated 27 acres of land, the March of Dimes provided financial support and Louis Kahn designed the building. Completed in 1965, it is regarded as a modern masterpiece, with its classically proportioned travertine marble plaza and cubist, mirror-glass laboratory blocks raming a perfect view of the Pacific. The Salk Institute attracts the best scientists to work in a research-only environment. The facilities were recently expanded, with new laboratories designed by Jack McAllister, a follower of Kahn's work. You can tour the Salk Institute with a volunteer guide at 11am and noon Monday to Friday. Bus Nos 41 and 301 go along N Torrey Pines Rd.

Torrey Pines State Reserve

Encompassing the land between N Torrey Pines Rd and the ocean from the Torrey Pines Glider Port to Del Mar, this reserve (☎ 858-755-2063; w www.torreypine.org; open 9am-sunset daily) preserves the last mainland stands of the Torrey pine (Pinus torreyana), a species adapted to sparse rainfall and sandy, stony soils. Steep sandstone gullies are eroded into wonderfully textured surfaces, and the views over the ocean and north to Oceanside are superb, especially at sunset.

The main access road, Torrey Pines Scenic Dr, off N Torrey Pines Rd (bus Nos 41 and 301) at the reserve's northern end, leads to a simple adobe – built as a lodge in 1922 by (drum roll) Ellen Browning Scripps – which now acts as a visitor center (☎ 858-755-2063) with good displays on the local flora and fauna. Rangers lead nature walks from here at 11am and 2pm weekends.

Entry and parking is $2 per car – if the ticket office is closed, get a permit from the yellow machine in the lower parking lot – or free if you walk in. Several walking trails wind through the reserve and down to the beach. If you want to hike, park near the driving range on N Torrey Pines Rd and take the paved path northwest until you reach a box of trail maps at the beginning of the Broken Arrow Trail.

University of California, San Diego

A campus of the University of California, UCSD was established in 1960 and now has more than 18,000 students and an excellent academic reputation, particularly for its math and science programs. It lies on rolling coastal hills in a park-like setting, with many tall and fragrant eucalyptus trees. Its most distinctive structure is the Geisel Library (formerly the Central Library), an upside-down pyramid of glass and concrete whose namesake, children's author Theodor Geisel, is better known as Dr Seuss, creator of the Cat in the Hat. He and his wife have contributed substantially

to the library, and there is a collection of his drawings and books on the ground level.

From the eastern side of the library's second level, an allegorical snake created by artist Alexis Smith winds down a native California plant garden past an enormous marble copy of John Milton's Paradise Lost. The piece is part of the Stuart Collection of outdoor sculptures spread around campus. Other works include Niki de Saint Phalle's Sun God, Bruce Nauman's Vices & Virtues (which spells out seven of each in huge neon letters), Robert Irwin's very blue Fence and a forest of talking trees. Most installations are near the Geisel Library, and details are available from the Visual Arts Building or the Price Center, where the UCSD bookstore (☎ 858-534-7323) has an excellent stock and a helpful staff. In the Mandell Weiss Center for the Performing Arts is the La Jolla Playhouse (☎ 858-550-1010), known for its high-quality productions.

The best access to campus is off of La Jolla Village Dr or N Torrey Pines Rd (bus Nos 41 and 301 from downtown); parking is free on weekends.

Soledad Mountain

For a 360-degree view of La Jolla, take Nautilus St east from La Jolla Blvd, turn left on La Jolla Scenic Dr and follow it to Soledad Mountain Park. The large cross on top was the subject of an unsuccessful lawsuit in the late 1960s – residents objected to the sectarian religious symbol on publicly owned land.

ACTIVITIES

For information on biking, see the Getting Around section later in this chapter.

Surfing

Surfing is the primary reason that a good number of San Diegans are here. The water can get crowded and several spots – Sunset Cliffs and Windansea – are somewhat 'owned' by locals, but in general San Diego is a great place for surfers of any skill level.

Fall offers the best chance to find strong swells and offshore Santa Ana winds. In summer, swells come from the south and southwest, and in winter, from the west and northwest. Spring brings more frequent onshore winds, but the surfing can still be good. For the latest beach, weather and surf reports, call City Lifeguard (☎ 619-221-8824).

Beginners looking to rent equipment should head to Mission Beach or Pacific Beach, where the waves are gentle. North of the Crystal Pier, Tourmaline Surf Beach is an especially good place to take your first strokes. Places such as **Bob's Mission Surf** (☎ 858-483-8837; W *www.missionsurf.com; 4320 Mission Blvd)*, near Garnet Ave, and **Pacific Beach Surf Shop** (☎ 858-488-9575; *747 Pacific Beach Dr)* rent boards ($5 to $8 per hour) and wet suits ($3). **OE Express** (☎ 858-454-6195; W *www.oeexpress.com; 2158 Avenida de la Playa)*, in La Jolla Shores, offers lessons for $75 (reduced rate for two or more people) including equipment. Next door, the wonderful women at **Surf Diva** (☎ 858-454-8273; W *www.surfdiva.com; 2160 Avenida de la Playa)* offer weekend workshops for gals (only) of all ages. The cost is $98, or $115 from May to October.

The best surf breaks, from south to north, are at Imperial Beach (especially in winter); Point Loma (reef breaks which are less accessible, but less crowded; best in winter); Sunset Cliffs in Ocean Beach; Pacific Beach; Big Rock (California's Pipeline); Windansea (hot reef break, best at medium to low tide, but crowded); La Jolla Shores (beach break best in winter); and Blacks Beach (a fast, powerful wave). Further up, in North County, there are breaks at Cardiff State Beach, San Elijo State Beach, Swami's, Carlsbad State Beach and Oceanside.

Body surfing is good at Coronado, Pacific Beach, Boomer Beach near La Jolla Cove (for the experienced only; best with a big swell) and La Jolla Shores. To get into the whomp (the forceful tubes that break directly on shore), know what you're doing and head to Windansea or the beach at the end of Sea Lane (both in La Jolla).

Scuba Diving

Divers will find kelp beds, shipwrecks (including the *Yukon*, a WWII destroyer) and canyons deep enough to host bat rays, octopus and squid off the coast of San Diego County. For current conditions call ☎ 619-221-8824. Some of California's best and most accessible (no boat needed) diving is in the San Diego–La Jolla Underwater Park Ecological Reserve, accessible from the La Jolla Cove. With an average depth of 20ft, the 6000 acres of look-but-don't-touch underwater real estate is great for snorkeling

as well. Ever-present are the spectacular, bright orange Garibaldi fish – California's official state fish and a protected species (there's a $500 fine for hooking one of these). Further out are forests of giant California kelp, which can increase its length by up to 3ft per day, and the 100ft-deep La Jolla Canyon.

Quite a few commercial operators conduct scuba courses, sell or rent equipment, fill tanks and conduct boat trips to nearby wrecks and islands. A snorkel and fins can be had for around $10; scuba gear rentals cost from about $90 to $210 per person, per day. Closest to the water, **OE Express** (☎ 858-454-6195; W *www.oeexpress.com; 2158 Avenida de la Playa)* is in La Jolla Shores.

Fishing

A state fishing license is required for people over 16 years old (see the Activities chapter). A **recorded service** (☎ 619-465-3474) provides fishing information.

The most popular public fishing piers are Imperial Beach Municipal Pier, Embarcadero Fishing Pier, Shelter Island Fishing Pier, Ocean Beach Pier and Crystal Pier at Pacific Beach. The best time of year for pier fishing is from about April to October. Offshore catches can include barracuda, bass and yellowtail. In summer, albacore is a special attraction. A license is not required for fishing off any of these piers.

Many companies run daily fishing trips year-round. All charge around $32/22 adult/concession for a half-day trip (9am to 1pm or 2pm to 6pm), and $90 to $135 for a full day; equipment and a license cost an extra $8 per person. Most also have overnight and three-day trips, plus special charters for large groups. The most reputable are **Islandia Sportfishing** (☎ 619-222-1164; W *www.islandiasport.com; 2803 Emerson St)*; **H&M Landing** (☎ 619-222-1144; W *www.hmlanding.com)* on Shelter Island; **Seaforth Sport Fishing** (☎ 619-224-3383; W *www.seaforthlanding.com)* in Quivira Basin on Mission Bay; and **Point Loma Sport Fishing** (☎ 619-223-1627; W *www.pointlomasportfishing.com; 1403 Scott St)*. Look for discount coupons in the *Reader*.

Boating

Power and sailboats, rowboats, kayaks and canoes can be rented on Mission Bay – try

Mission Bay Sportcenter (☎ 619-488-1004; 1010 Santa Clara Place) or **Adreneline Watersports** (☎ 619-488-2582; w resortwa tersport.com) at the Catamaran Resort Hotel (see Places to Stay).

Ocean kayaking is a good way to see sea life and explore cliffs and caves inaccessible from land. **Southwest Kayaks** (☎ 619-222-3616), near SeaWorld at the Dana Landing, has guided trips and classes, both starting at $35. It's easy to explore the caves and cliffs around La Jolla from the put-in of **OE Express** (☎ 858-454-6195; 2158 Avenida de la Playa), in La Jolla Shores; a two-hour rental costs $35.

Experienced sailors can charter yachts for trips on San Diego Bay and out into the Pacific. Quite a few charter companies are based around Shelter Island, including **Shelter Cove Marina** (☎ 619-224-2471; 2240 Shelter Island Dr); **San Diego Yacht Charters** (☎ 619-297-4555; 1880 Harbor Island Dr); and **Harbor Sailboats** (☎ 619-291-9568; 2040 Harbor Island Dr, Suite 104).

Whale-Watching

Gray whales pass San Diego from mid-December to late February on their way south to Baja California and again in mid-March on their way back up to Alaskan waters. Their 12,000mi round-trip journey is the longest migration of any mammal on earth.

Cabrillo National Monument is the best place to see the whales from land and has exhibits, whale-related ranger programs and a shelter from which to watch for the whales' spouts (bring binoculars). Torrey Pines State Reserve and La Jolla Cove are also good spots for whale-watching.

Half-day whale-watching boat trips are offered by all of the companies that run daily fishing trips (see earlier). The trips generally cost $20/15 adult/concession for a four-hour excursion and the companies will let you come back for free the next day if you don't see anything. Look for coupons and special offers in the *Reader*.

Hang-Gliding

Glider riders hang at **Torrey Pines Gliderport** (☎ 858-452-9858; 2800 Torrey Pines Scenic Dr), in La Jolla, which is famous as a gliding location. Tandem flights in a hang-glider cost $150 per person for 20 minutes.

Experienced pilots can join in if they have a USHGA Hang 4 rating and take out an associate membership of the Torrey Pines Hang Glider Association.

Hot-Air Ballooning

Brightly colored hot-air balloons are a trademark of the skies above Del Mar, on the northern fringe of the metropolitan area. For pleasure flights, contact **Skysurfer Balloon Company** (☎ 858-481-6800; 1221 Camino del Mar).

The *Reader* carries other balloon company listings and frequently contains hot-air excursion discount coupons. Flights are usually at sunrise or sunset. They last an hour (though up to three hours may be required for instruction and transportation) and cost around $130 on weekdays, $150 weekends.

ORGANIZED TOURS

Several companies run narrated tours of the city and surrounding attractions. **Grayline** (☎ 619-491-0011) has four-hour city tours twice daily in summer (once daily in winter) for $25/16 adult/child, and trips to Wild Animal Park, La Jolla, Coronado, and other destinations. It also offers four-hour trips to Tijuana for $26. The tours pick up from various points downtown, including Horton Plaza and several of the bigger hotels.

San Diego Scenic Tours (☎ 858-273-8687; w www.sandiegoscenictours.com) covers the city for similar prices and has a family package that allows two children to go for free with two paying adults. It also offers trips to Tijuana, including a four-hour sightseeing trip for $26, and an eight-hour shopping trip for the same price.

Not to be confused with the Metropolitan Transit System's trolleys, which run on rails, the Old Town Trolley is a green and orange bus done up to resemble an old-fashioned streetcar. **Old Town Trolley Tours** (☎ 619-298-8687) does a loop around the main attractions near downtown and in Coronado, and you can get on or off at any number of stops, staying to look around as long as you wish. Tours start at 9am and run every 30 minutes or so until 7pm. You can start at any trolley stop (they are well marked with orange and are usually next to a regular San Diego Transit bus stop), though the official trolley stand is in the Old Town (which is convenient for parking) on Twiggs St. The tours make quite a good introduction to the city, and the commentary is entertaining. The cost is $25/12 per adult/child, with a 10% discount on tickets purchased online. If you want to get on the water as well, check out its Seal Tour, which includes a trip around Mission Bay in an amphibious vehicle ($30/14 per adult/child).

San Diego's version of a rickshaw is the pedicab – a carriage pulled behind a bicycle which takes up to four people. These are a fun way to get from place to place and a good way to see downtown. The drivers (pedalers?) often have tips on what's happening around town. You can flag an empty pedicab, or call **The Original Bike Cab Co** (☎ *888-245-3222)* and one will pick you up. It operates 10am to midnight weekdays, 10am to 3am weekends, and costs $4 per person to get from the Embarcadero to Horton Plaza. The same company offers bike tours of downtown and other parts of San Diego (from $25), and rents bikes for around $18 per day (they'll deliver the bikes to your hotel for free).

Increased national security has limited the visitation of **military facilities**. When aircraft carriers are in port, however, you can tour them on weekends by appointment; call ☎ 619-545-2427. It's also possible to step aboard a submarine and have a look around; call ☎ 619-553-8643 for details.

Both **Hornblower Cruises** (☎ *619-725-8888;* **W** *www.hornblower.com)* and **Harbor Excursions** (☎ *619-234-4111)* run sightseeing tours from the Embarcadero (near the *Star of India)*. There are around six departures per day and prices are $13/6 adult/child for the one-hour tour and $18/9 for the two-hour one. Both also have nightly dinner-dance cruises for $50/30 per person ($55 on Saturday).

SPECIAL EVENTS
The calendar is full of community, cultural and sporting events. Some of the most interesting and unusual are listed in this section. A more detailed list with up-to-date information can be obtained from the **San Diego Convention & Visitors Bureau** (☎ *619-236-1212)*.

Ocean Beach Kite Festival (March) – kite making, decorating, flying and competitions, at Ocean Beach (☎ 619-531-1527)

San Diego Crew Classic (April) – national college rowing regatta, Crown Point Shores

Del Mar Fair (June 15 to July 4) – a huge county fair with headline acts and hundreds of carnival rides and shows, at the Del Mar Fairgrounds (☎ 619-755-1161)

US Open Sandcastle Competition (end of July) – amazing sand-castle-building competition, in Pacific Beach (☎ 619-424-6663)

Air Show (August) – the right stuff, shown off by the Blue Angels and Top Guns, at the Marine Corps Air Station Miramar

Summerfest Chamber Music Festival (August) – a two-week series with international performers (☎ 619-459-3728)

Old Globe Festival (September) – renowned Shakespearean festival, at the Old Globe Theatre (☎ 619-239-2255) in Balboa Park

San Diego Street Scene (September) – street festival with music on outdoor stages and plenty of food, in the Gaslamp Quarter

Thunderboat Races (September) – unlimited hydroplane championship, on Mission Bay

Christmas on El Prado (December) – crafts, carols and candlelight parade, in Balboa Park (☎ 619-239-0512)

Harbor Parade of Lights (December weekends) – dozens of decorated, illuminated boats, afloat in procession, on the harbor

Old Town Posadas (December) – a traditional Latin Christmas celebration, in Old Town

PLACES TO STAY
Tourism is a major industry in San Diego, and there are more than 45,000 hotel rooms in the county. In the summer season (roughly Memorial Day to Labor Day, ie, late May to early September), accommodations, particularly near the beaches, are heavily booked and prices are higher. Taxes in San Diego County add 10.5% to the bill.

There is also a wealth of summer rentals in the beach areas. If you have a group and want to stay for more than a few days, renting a place can be excellent value. Try calling agents such as **Mission Bay Vacations** (☎ *858-488-6773, 800-882-8626)* or **Penny Realty** (☎ *858-272-3900, 800-748-6704)*, but call early.

Camping
There are several campgrounds around San Diego, but only two allow tent camping.

Campland on the Bay (☎ *619-581-4260, 800-422-9386; 2211 Pacific Beach Dr; sites $30-150)* has more than 40 acres fronting Mission Bay. It has a restaurant, pool, boating facilities and full RV hookups. Site costs vary depending on their proximity to the water. The location is great, but the tent area is not very attractive (too many RVs, not enough trees) and can be crowded. Reservations are a good idea in the warmer months. The RV-only section of Campland is **De Anza Harbor Resort** (☎ 858-273-3211; $30 per night, $190 per week).

KOA (☎ 619-427-3601; 111 N 2nd Ave; tent/RV sites $28/36, cabins $39-47), in Chula Vista, is about 5mi southeast of downtown San Diego.

Hostels

HI San Diego Downtown Hostel (☎ 619-525-1531; 521 Market St; dorm beds $16/19 members/nonmembers; open 7am-midnight daily) is an HI facility centrally located in the Gaslamp Quarter, handy to public transportation and nightlife. It offers basic dorm rooms, and has nice kitchen facilities.

HI San Diego Point Loma Hostel (☎ 619-223-4778; 3790 Udall St; dorm beds $16/19 members/nonmembers), another HI hostel in Loma Portal, is a 20-minute walk from the heart of Ocean Beach and near a market and Laundromat. Bus Nos 23 (from downtown, weekdays only) and 35 (from Old Town, daily) run along nearby Voltaire St.

San Diego's private hostels, intended for international travelers, often allow Americans with proof of out-of-state residency.

USA Hostel San Diego (☎ 619-232-3100, 800-438-8622; ⓦ www.sandiego@usahostels .com; 726 5th Ave; dorm beds $15-19, doubles $44), downtown above Asti's Ristorante, is a Victorian-era hotel refitted with six-bed dorms and some double rooms. Its lounge and kitchen areas are quite nice, and its rates include a hot breakfast. Free shuttles to the beach or area attractions are offered sporadically, as are day tours, in-house parties and beach barbecues. It's right in the Gaslamp Quarter, so can be a bit noisy, but the crowd here doesn't seem to mind.

Ocean Beach International Hostel (☎ 619-223-7873, 800-339-7263; 4961 Newport Ave; dorm beds $15-18, doubles $35-40), only a couple of blocks from the ocean, is a friendly, fun place and has a helpful staff. It's popular with European travelers. Bus No 35 from downtown passes Newport Ave a block east of the hostel.

Banana Bungalow (☎ 858-273-3060; 707 Reed Ave; dorm beds $15-20), right on Mission Beach, has a top location, a beach-party atmosphere and is reasonably clean, but it's pretty basic and can get crowded. A complimentary hot breakfast is served daily. The communal area is a patio, which fronts right on the boardwalk and is a great place for people-watching and beer-drinking.

Motels & Hotels

Downtown Note that some of the cheapest downtown hotels provide what is sometimes called SRO (single room occupancy); they rent basic rooms, by the day, week or month, to people who might otherwise be homeless. Low-budget travelers often stay in these places and find them quite tolerable, though some regular guests can be, well, colorful characters. There are developers who would like to get rid of SROs, especially in the 'improving' areas such as the Gaslamp Quarter, but they serve a useful social function and are a relief from total gentrification. Rates are cheaper by the week, but there is typically a key deposit. In the cheapest rooms, you share a hall bathroom.

Inn at the YMCA (☎ 619-234-5252; 500 W Broadway; rooms $55) is handy to the Amtrak and Greyhound stations and to the trolley to Tijuana. It has rooms with shared bathroom, which are quite OK as a money-saving option.

J Street Inn (☎ 619-696-6922; 222 J St; units from $60 per night, $180 per week) is a postmodern, rather hip choice near the Gaslamp Quarter. All units have kitchenettes.

La Pensione Hotel (☎ 619-236-8000, 800-232-4683; ⓦ www.lapensionehotel.com; 1700 India St; singles/doubles $65/75 year-round) has high-quality rooms and low prices, and is in the heart of Little Italy.

US Grant Hotel (☎ 619-232-3121, fax 619-232-3626; 326 Broadway; singles from $150-180, doubles from $165-200, suites from $295) is the classiest and most historic hotel downtown and the place to go if money is no object. It's not very old (1910), but was built by Ulysses S Grant Jr and named for his father, president Ulysses S Grant. It has housed a host of famous guests, including Charles Lindbergh, Albert Einstein and Harry S Truman. Special packages can be substantially cheaper, so it's worth calling.

Hotel Bristol (☎ 800-662-4477; ⓦ www .hotelbristolsandiego.com; 1055 First Ave; rooms from $130) is your kind of place if it's pop art in the rooms and in the lobby you'd prefer.

SAN DIEGO AREA

Horton Grand Hotel (☎ 619-544-1886, 800-542-1886; 311 Island Ave; rooms from $140) is the place to go for lacey curtains and a gas-fueled fireplace. Ask about special rates before you book.

Old Town Conveniently located near the freeways, **Padre Trail Inn** (☎ 619-297-3291, 800-255-9988; 4200 Taylor St; 1-/2-bed rooms $69/79 summer, $59/69 winter) is pretty cheap. It has a pool, bar and restaurant, and air-conditioned rooms.

Best Western Hacienda Hotel (☎ 619-298-4707, 800-888-1991; 4041 Harney St; suites from $135), more central to Old Town, is a step up in comfort from Padre Trail Inn. It's a suites-only place, with kitchens, a pool, a workout room, Jacuzzi and nightly cocktail hour. Rates can go as low as $89, depending on availability.

Hillcrest The **Friendship Hotel** (☎ 619-298-9898; 3942 8th Ave; rooms $29-45 per night, $125-150 per week), with basic rooms, is a solid budget option in Hillcrest. It's on a quiet side street within walking distance of restaurants and nightlife.

Hillcrest Inn (☎ 619-293-7078; 3754 5th Ave; rooms from $59), with a central courtyard, Jacuzzi and friendly staff, is good value. It welcomes straight and gay guests, but no children.

Inn Suites (☎ 619-296-2101; 2223 El Cajon Blvd; rooms from $107/87 summer/winter) has a large pool and a bit more character than most chain motels.

Mission Valley Hotel Circle North and Hotel Circle South on either side of I-8 have a dozen or so mid-range chain motels, handy to Old Town, shopping centers and the San Diego Trolley line.

The cheapest of these are **Vagabond Inn** (☎ 619-297-1691, 800-522-1555; 625 Hotel Circle S; rooms $65-135) and **Comfort Inn Suites** (☎ 619-291-7700, 800-647-1903; 2485 Hotel Circle Place; singles/doubles from $79/89), both with higher rates in summer.

Town & Country Hotel (☎ 619-291-7131, 800-772-8527; 500 Hotel Circle N; singles/doubles from $125/145) is a popular base for business gatherings as well as the leisure crowd. Price specials often keep rooms filled off-peak.

Hanalei Hotel (☎ 619-297-1101, 800-882-0858; 2270 Hotel Circle N; rooms $79-129, suites $150-250), with an endearingly over-the-top Polynesian-theme, is one of San Diego's best bargains.

Mission Bay The best places on Mission Bay are like tropical resorts, with lush gardens and private beaches. A budget alternative is the **Vagabond Inn** (☎ 619-274-7888; 4540 Mission Bay Dr; rooms from $70-89 summer, $10-15 less in winter) – it's not on the water, but it's handy to I-5.

San Diego Princess Resort (☎ 619-274-4630; 1404 W Vacation Rd; rooms from about $185 summer) is one of the first and finest of the lush variety of hotel. It's in the center of Mission Bay on Vacation Isle. It has several bars, restaurants and pools, plus boat, bike and skate rentals.

Other beautifully landscaped resort hotels include **Bahia Resort Hotel** (☎ 619-488-0551; 998 W Mission Bay Dr); **Catamaran Resort Hotel** (☎ 619-488-1081; 3999 Mission Blvd); and **Hyatt Islandia** (☎ 619-224-1234; 1441 Quivira Rd). Rooms at all of these start at around $155, but can be much cheaper if availability is high. If you want a tropical island type of experience, it's worth calling to see if you can get a deal.

Harbor Island & Shelter Island If you like yachts and harbor views, then you might want to stay on one of these landscaped breakwaters.

Sheraton Harbor Island (☎ 619-291-2900; 1380 Harbor Island Dr; rooms around $165) offers the complete luxury experience.

Humphrey's Half Moon Inn (☎ 619-224-3411, 800-542-7400; 2303 Shelter Island Dr; rooms from $185/150 summer/winter), on Shelter Island, has a tropical island atmosphere and a good jazz club.

Best Western Island Palms Hotel (☎ 619-222-0561; 2051 Shelter Island Dr; rooms from $175/140 summer/winter) is less fancy and usually a bit cheaper than Humphrey's.

Ocean Beach Located in the heart of OB's action, **Ocean Beach Motel** (☎ 619-223-7191; 5080 Newport Ave; rooms from $70) has rooms with ocean views.

Ocean Villa Motel (☎ 619-224-3481, 800-759-0012; 5142 W Point Loma Blvd; rooms without/with kitchenette from $113/140 summer, from $70/87 winter), further north than Ocean Beach Motel but also close to the sea, is a family place ('no pets, no parties'), clean and well run, with a pool and a variety of rooms.

Mission Beach & Pacific Beach Pacific Beach has most of the accommodations along the beach. In Mission Beach try the small **Santa Clara Motel** (☎ 858-488-1193; 839 Santa Clara Place; singles/doubles from $95 summer, $50/55 winter), an ordinary motel just steps away from both ocean and bay beaches. It's good value in the off-season, but the rates surge in summer.

Motels in Pacific Beach can be pretty good value in winter, but in summer prices increase by 30% or more, and rooms can be scarce.

Mission Bay Motel (☎ 858-483-6440; 4221 Mission Blvd; rooms $90-140 summer, $60-90 winter) has rooms that overlook a parking lot and a busy street, but the beach and Garnet Ave are nearby and the hotel staff is very nice.

Pacific View Motel (☎ 858-483-6117; 610 Emerald St; singles/doubles from $47/52 winter) is classic '60s in appearance and close to the beach.

Pacific Sands Motel (☎ 858-483-7555; 4449 Ocean Blvd; rooms $55-60 winter) is also well positioned and well worn. Most rooms have a full kitchen.

Beach Haven Inn (☎ 858-272-3812, 800-831-6323; 4740 Mission Blvd; rooms from $75-165) is a block from the beach, with quite good rooms.

Surfer Motor Lodge (☎ 858-483-7070, 800-787-3711; 711 Pacific Beach Dr; rooms/family units from $85/125 winter, from $100 summer), a bigger place than Beach Haven Inn, is right on the beach with a pool and a restaurant. It has a variety of rooms, all with refrigerator, phone and TV.

Beach Cottages (☎ 858-483-7440; 4255 Ocean Blvd; rooms from $105/65 summer/winter) has motel rooms, apartments and beachfront cottages; weekly and monthly rates available September to April. It's a well-run place, and you have to book early.

Pacific Terrace Hotel (☎ 858-581-3500, 800-344-3370; 610 Diamond St; rooms with ocean view $260-355) has rooms with great views, but the rates are high considering you can get (nearly) the same view from the boardwalk in front of the hotel.

A more unique investment would be renting a cottage on the pier at **Crystal Pier Hotel** (☎ 858-483-6983, 800-748-5894; 4500 Ocean Blvd; original cottages from $130 winter, new cottages up to $250 winter, minimum 2-night stay, $170-280 summer, minimum 3-night stay), one of the most interesting places to stay in San Diego. Dating from 1927, the distinctive arched entrance to the pier is a landmark at the end of Garnet Ave. The original cottages sleep one to four people; some of the newer and larger cottages sleep up to eight people.

La Jolla It's hard to find a room here for under $100. One place to look is across from La Jolla Cove at **Shell Beach Apartment Hotel** (☎ 858-459-4306; 981 Coast Blvd; studios/1-bedroom suites from $65/98, with ocean view $85/118).

La Jolla Cove Travelodge (☎ 858-454-0791; 1141 Silverado St; singles/doubles from $95/120 summer, $50/60 winter), central to downtown La Jolla, charges higher prices than it could in any other location.

Additional 'budget' lodgings can be found on La Jolla Blvd, south of town. **La Jolla Beach Travelodge** (☎ 858-454-0716; 6750 La Jolla Blvd), near Windansea beach, and **Holiday Inn Express** (☎ 858-454-7101; 6763 La Jolla Blvd), across the street from the Travelodge, has rooms starting at around $89 ($145 in summer).

La Valencia (☎ 858-454-0771; 1132 Prospect St; standard rooms $250-550 year-round), with historic charm and unbridled California elegance, is unmatchable. Great views, pink walls, palm trees and Mediterranean-style architecture (designed by William Templeton Johnson) have attracted movie stars and millionaires since it opened in the 1920s.

New movie stars and millionaires tend to prefer **Hotel Parisi** (☎ 858-454-1511, 877-472-7474; 1111 Prospect St; rooms from $255/205 summer/winter), across the street from La Valencia, is a self-conscious, Zen-like boutique hotel.

Scripps Inn (☎ 858-454-3391; 555 Coast Blvd; rooms from $145), tucked behind the San Diego Museum of Contemporary Art, is a relaxed gem with ocean-view rooms. This 13-room place often sells out – book early.

La Jolla Cove Cottages (☎ 858-551-4556; W www.lajollacovecottages.com) are small family units near the cove which would make a good home base for a week or so.

Coronado The cheapest lodging on Coronado is at **El Rancho Motel** (☎ 619-435-2251; 370 Orange Ave; rooms $50-110), but with only eight units, snagging a room here requires some luck – or advance reservations.

Coronado Inn (☎ 619-435-4121, 800-598-6624, fax 619-435-6296; 266 Orange Ave; rooms $85-140) has a pool and rooms with microwaves and refrigerators.

Hotel del Coronado (☎ 619-435-6611, 800-468-3533; 1500 Orange Ave; rooms from $235-595) provides, of course, the true Coronado experience. Apart from the historical ambience, it has tennis courts, a pool, a spa, shops, restaurants and the Pacific Ocean out back. However, nearly half the accommodations are not in the main hotel but in an adjacent seven-story modern building with no historical feel at all. Even the rooms in the original building are pretty ordinary.

PLACES TO EAT
Gaslamp Quarter
More than 65 places here offer everything from a quick breakfast to a gourmet dinner, with quite a range of prices. Some eateries are mainly daytime operations, while others offer entertainment well into the night (see Entertainment later in this chapter). Many change their character and clientele as the day progresses, serving lunch to business-people, light dinner to the theater set and cocktails to a late-night crowd.

Rubio's (☎ 619-231-7731; 901 4th Ave; meals under $7) serves quick, cheap and good Baja-style Mexican food.

Cafe Lulu (☎ 619-238-0114; 419 F St; light meals $4-8; open to 3am) has breezy café decor and an outside terrace; it's a good spot for coffee and light meals.

Star of India (☎ 619-544-9891; 423 F St; buffet lunch $8, dishes $7-12), next door to Cafe Lulu, is a first-class restaurant with North Indian food and a good all-you-can-eat buffet lunch.

The Cheese Shop (☎ 619-232-2303; cnr 4th Ave & G St; snacks $4.50-7) is a daytime deli much loved by locals for its great sandwiches and coffee.

Olé Madrid (☎ 619-557-0146; 751 5th Ave) and **Café Sevilla** (☎ 619-233-5979; 555 4th Ave) are both Spanish tapas restaurants

where the tab can add up to around $25 per person, especially if you stay around to enjoy the sangria (around $15 a pitcher) and live music. Both places stay open till 2am and have dancing.

Dick's Last Resort (☎ 619-231-9100; 345 4th Ave; meals $6-12) is a legendary place with a riotously fun atmosphere. It serves buckets of beer and big helpings of fried food, and has a large patio.

Royal Thai (☎ 619-230-842; cnr 5th Ave & Island St; dishes $5-11, lunch specials $7.50) is an excellent, elegant eatery in a building that has been an Asian restaurant since it opened its doors as Nanking Cafe in 1912. It has another **branch** (☎ 858-551-8424; 757 Pearl St) in La Jolla.

Bandar (☎ 619-238-0101; 825 4th Ave; dishes $6-11) is an exotic Middle Eastern spot that has been showered with awards and accolades. It has sidewalk seating and dishes of magically marinated meat served with fragrant rice.

Embarcadero
Point Loma Seafoods (☎ 619-223-1109; 2805 Emerson St; dishes $4-8), in the Shelter Island Marina, has a market-cum-deli that is one of the liveliest places for seafood. Sushi, sandwiches and seafood platters are made with the freshest fish available, and it sells fresh bread, beer and wine to go with it.

Star of the Sea (☎ 619-232-7408; mains $9-25), built over the water at the end of Ash St, is the classiest and costliest of the various Anthony's outlets on the Embarcadero itself. Anthony's outlets have been serving up seafood for decades.

Anthony's Fish Grotto (☎ 619-232-5103; mains $7-26), right next door to Star of the Sea, offers virtually the same seafood in simpler surroundings and for less money.

Anthony's Fishette, on a veranda south of the Grotto, is cheapest of all. Excellent fish and chips with coleslaw costs around $5 and you can still enjoy the same view over the harbor.

Little Italy
In a cavernous building decorated to the hilt, **Mimmo's Italian Village** (☎ 619-239-3710; 1743 India St; meals under $10) is a deli that serves salads, hot and cold sandwiches and lunch specials (eg, lasagna, eggplant parmigiana).

SAN DIEGO AREA

Filippi's Pizza Grotto (☎ 619-232-5094; 1747 India St; dishes $6.50-12) is about the oldest pizza place in town and still one of the best, with inexpensive pies to eat in or take out.

Mona Lisa (☎ 619-234-4893; 2061 India St; meals $6-11) has hearty meals and a retail market that offers a variety of imported Italian items.

Washington Street

Further north on India St, where it meets Washington St, is a block of well-known casual eateries.

For some of the best food in town under $10, make a beeline to Saffron, which has two separate sections: **Saffron Thai Grilled Chicken** (☎ 619-574-0177; 3731 India St; dishes $5-8), which specializes in charcoal-grilled chicken served with a choice of sauces, a salad and jasmine rice, and **Saffron Noodles & Saté** (☎ 619-574-7737; 3737 India St; mains $4.50-8.75), where you can dig into big bowls of steaming noodle soup or order a plate of stir-fried noodles paired with various ingredients. Both Saffrons close at 9pm Monday to Saturday, at 8pm Sunday.

El Indio (☎ 619-299-0394; 3695 India St; dishes $1.50-3) is known for its tacos ($1.50) and tamales ($2) but has a large menu and excellent breakfast burritos ($3).

Shakespeare Pub & Grille (☎ 619-299-0230; 3701 India St; pub grub around $6) is one of the most authentic English ale houses in town, with darts, a large selection of beers on tap and pub grub such as fish and chips, beef stew, and bangers and mash.

Gelato Vero Caffe (☎ 619-295-9269; cnr Washington & India Sts) has San Diego's best Italian-style ice cream. It stays opens late and displays local artists' work.

Old Town

Mexican and Southwestern flavors dominate in most Old Town eateries. They tend to go for contrived Mexican atmosphere (lots of margaritas and mariachi bands cruising the tables), but the food can be good, their outdoor tables are popular and it all can make for a pleasant evening.

Casa de Bandini (☎ 619-297-8211; 2660 Calhoun St; meals under $10.50) is one of the most established places, serving reasonably priced meals such as *pollo asado* or enchiladas.

Bazaar del Mundo, at the northwestern corner of the Old Town Plaza, has three restaurants with a lively atmosphere and mediocre food (meals are $5 to $11, appetizers around $4) – good, though, for drinks and for people-watching.

The Alamo (☎ 619-296-1112; cnr San Diego Ave & Harney St; dishes under $5), one of the least expensive but most authentic places, is a take-out taquería (taco shop).

Old Town Mexican Cafe (☎ 619-297-4330; 2489 San Diego Ave; dishes around $8) is a favorite among locals. It has a big bar and dining room as well as excellent food; its *machacas* (shredded pork with onions and peppers) are famous in San Diego. You can watch tortillas being made as you wait to be seated.

Hillcrest

Hillcrest offers a good choice of fun and good-value eateries. On Tuesday nights specials are offered at many eateries (from 5pm to 8pm) and can range from a free appetizer to a buy-one-meal-get-one-free.

Taste of Thai (☎ 619-291-7525; 527 University Ave; dishes $6-9) offers food with or without meat, all levels of spiciness.

Kitima Thai (☎ 619-298-2929; 406 University Ave; dishes $6-11), across the street, is definitely a winner in the looks department, and the food – fragrant, light and complex – leaves little to be desired, too.

Corvette Diner (☎ 619-542-1001; 3946 5th Ave; most dishes around $8) is a classic, with its riotous '50s-theme decor and an all-American menu.

Hamburger Mary's (☎ 619-491-0400; 308 University Ave; dishes $5.50-10, Sun buffet $12.95) is a self-consciously gay eatery, with daily specials such as the 'Hunka Hunka Burnin' Love' burger and a famous Sunday champagne brunch buffet. The nicest tables are outdoors amid the plants and flower plots.

Bread & Cie (☎ 619-683-9322; 350 University Ave; sandwiches $3-5.75) has hand-crafted bread that can be made into a sandwich or eaten as a meal in itself.

Whole Foods (☎ 619-294-2800; 711 University Ave), east of 5th Ave, is a huge health-oriented market with grab-and-go goods and a café.

Ichiban (☎ 619-299-7203; 1449 University Ave) has sushi and bento box specials which are a bargain at around $5.

SAN DIEGO AREA

Living Room Coffeehouse (☎ 619-295-7911; 1417 University Ave; light meals around $7; open to midnight daily, later Fri & Sat) is a comfy place offering coffee, pastries and light meals.

Coronado

Coronado Brewing Co (☎ 619-437-4452; 170 Orange Ave; most meals under $10) has a patio, delicious home brew and lots of foods that are good for the soul if not for the waistline (read: pizza, pasta and sandwiches with fries).

Mc P's Irish Pub & Grill (☎ 619-435-5280; 1107 Orange Ave; dishes $6.50-11) is owned by an ex-Navy Seal and consequently is popular with the military set. Typical pub fare, including corned beef and cabbage and mulligan stew, go down well with a pint of Guinness, especially on its lovely 'paddy-o' (its pun). It has nightly entertainment as well.

Chez Loma (☎ 619-435-0661; 1132 Loma Ave; open dinner & Sun brunch only; mains $11-18), where dining takes place in a restored 1899 landmark cottage, has bistro food that's definitely been updated for the 21st century. The emphasis is on fresh fish, but meats and pastas show up on the menu as well. It's pricey, but you can save by coming before 6pm and ordering the three-course fixed-price dinner for $18; later the same will cost $28.

Rhinoceros Cafe & Grill (☎ 619-435-2121; 1166 Orange Ave; daily specials $9-14) serves pastas, sandwiches, salads and daily specials.

The Beaches

Many places along the beach offer inexpensive food and a young, local scene. Garnet Ave has a wide variety of cuisines and numerous bars.

For breakfast, head to **Broken Yolk** (☎ 858-270-9655; 1851 Garnet Ave), where you can try one of the 47 omelet specials; **Kono's** (☎ 858-483-1669; 704 Garnet Ave), where $5 breakfast burritos and blueberry pancakes eaten in view of Crystal Pier are excellent; or **The Eggery** (☎ 858-274-3122; 4150 Mission Blvd), where, according to some, you'll find the best French toast in town.

Lunch or dinner with a view can be had at **World Famous** (☎ 858-272-3100; 711 Pacific Beach Dr) or **The Green Flash** (☎ 619-270-7715; 701 Thomas Ave; dishes $5-10), both with sandwiches, burgers and fresh

seafood dinners. Happy Hour runs from 3pm to 7pm weekdays, and World Famous serves lobster tacos for $1.50 on Wednesday.

Zen 5 (☎ 858-490-0121; 1130 Garnet Ave), where sushi is the star of the show, is a young, energetic restaurant with fast, friendly servers. At dinnertime, if you order at least five selections (priced from $3.50 to $8.95) per table, there is a discount of 50%.

The Mission Café (☎ 858-488-9060; 3795 Mission Blvd; dishes $4-7, dinner specials around $8), down in Mission Beach, serves light breakfasts, excellent salads and sandwiches, dinner specials and famously good coffee.

In Ocean Beach, there are numerous places along Newport Ave where you can eat and drink on a budget. Sit in an old surf mobile as you eat one of the legendary burgers at **Hodad's** (5010 Newport Ave; burgers $5). Fries, shakes and old surf tunes are popular here too (not shoes, however).

Ortega's Cocina (☎ 619-222-4205; 4888 Newport Ave; meals $5-8) is so popular that people stand in line for a spot at the counter. Seafood ($6 to $8) is the specialty, but it also makes great enchiladas, chimichangas, burritos and the like (under $5).

Rancho's Cocina (☎ 619-226-7619; 1830 Sunset Cliffs Blvd; most dishes under $5), two blocks south of Newport Ave, has a healthy twist on Mexican fare and an outdoor patio.

OB People's Market (☎ 619-224-1387; cnr Voltaire & Sunset Cliffs Blvd) is an organic cooperative with bulk foods, fresh soups and excellent pre-made sandwiches, salads and wraps, mostly under $5.

La Jolla

For a caffeine fix and light meals under $10, hit La Jolla's exceptional cafés: **The Pannikin** (☎ 858-454-5453; 7467 Girard Ave), which has been 'wakin' up San Diego since 1964,' and **The Living Room** (1010 Prospect St), which gets an international student crowd from the adjacent language school.

Inexpensive and popular with the surf culture, **Wahoo's Fish Tacos** (☎ 858-459-0027; 637 Pearl St; tacos $2, burritos $4, salads & rice bowls $6) does wonderful things with rice, beans, grilled vegies and meats (or fish). Cold beer and reggae are on tap.

Porkyland (☎ 858-459-1708; 1030 Torrey Pines Rd), with Mexican food, is where folks go to eat themselves silly for under $10.

Alfonso's (☎ 619-454-2232; 1251 Prospect St; dishes from $11) is the upscale standby for margaritas and inventive Mexican fare; it also has a lovely patio.

Harry's Coffee Shop (☎ 858-454-7381; 7545 Girard Ave), worth trying for breakfast or lunch, is a veritable institution that's a favorite with professional athletes and has been reviewed in the *New York Times*. Meals are around $8.

Girard Gourmet (☎ 858-454-3321; 7837 Girard Ave; dishes under $6) is a quality deli with heaped-up sandwiches, hot lunch specials and irresistible pastries for under $6.

Crab Catcher (☎ 858-454-9587; 1298 Prospect St; seafood mains $15-30), in the Coast Walk complex, is a good option for seafood and views. Drinks and appetizers during its nightly happy hour (3pm to 7pm) could make a nice meal for around $10.

George's at the Cove (☎ 858-454-4244; 1250 Prospect St; lunch $25, dinner $45), which requires diners to wear a jacket for dinner, has an award-winning wine cellar and a lovely view. The ambiance is elegant but not pretentious, but you'll need a reservation for dinner.

ENTERTAINMENT

The free weekly *San Diego Reader* and *San Diego Union Tribune*'s Night & Day section hit the stands each Thursday – both have comprehensive listings and reviews of movies, theater, galleries and gigs. The nightlife scene for gay men and lesbians is small but lively, and, predictably, concentrated in Hillcrest.

Call **Ticketmaster** (☎ 619-220-8497) for event information and to book tickets. **Times Arts Tix** (☎ 619-497-5000), in the little Horton Plaza park on Broadway, sells half-price tickets for same-day evening or next-day matinee performances in theater, music and dance, as well as full-price tickets to most major events in the area.

Bars & Clubs

Waterfront (☎ 619-232-9656; 2044 Kettner Blvd) was literally on the waterfront until the harbor was filled and the airport built. San Diego's first liquor license was granted to this place in the 1930s and is still held by its original owner. The bar is still going strong and, besides being full of historic 'stuff,' is one of the best places to spend the

afternoon or evening. It has a big window that opens onto the street, $5 bar food and live music on weekends.

If you like buying your beer at the source, San Diego has a number of microbreweries. Karl Strauss beer, for instance, is available at many bars but is made at **Old Columbia Brewery & Grill** (☎ 619-234-2739; 1157 Columbia St).

Gaslamp Quarter The distinction between eating and entertainment venues can be fuzzy in this lively area.

Croce's Restaurant & Jazz Bar (☎ 619-233-4355; 802 5th Ave) and **Croce's Top Hat Bar & Grille** (☎ 619-232-4338; 802 5th Ave), both run by the Croce family, have extensive food menus ($12 to $15) and nightly jazz, blues and R&B.

The Bitter End (☎ 619-338-9300; 770 5th Ave) is an old brothel that has been turned into an atmospheric watering hole with an extensive tap selection and nightly crowd.

Other interesting downtown venues include **Café Sevilla** (☎ 619-233-5979; 555 4th Ave), which has live Latin American music and dancing most nights (see also Places to Eat), and **Olé Madrid** (☎ 619-557-0146; 751 5th Ave), which often features DJs spinning funk and acid jazz.

Casbah (☎ 619-232-4355; 2501 Kettner Blvd), near Little Italy, is a fun place to see alternative rock bands. It has couches, pinball machines and dimly lit alcoves if you don't feel like dancing.

Old Town Despite the name, **O'Hungry's** (☎ 619-298-0133; 2547 San Diego Ave) is more for drinking than for eating. It serves beer by the yard, and sometimes has live music – it can be a fun place.

Club Montage (☎ 619-294-9590; 2028 Hancock St), just southwest of Old Town, is one of San Diego's hippest cathedrals of dance with a crowd that's young, trendy and good-looking. Wednesday is college night, gays rule Thursday and Saturday, while Friday is mixed.

Club Bombay (☎ 619-296-6789; 3175 India St), in the same neighborhood, is lesbian-owned but also draws its share of gay men. It's famous for Sunday barbecues with cheap burgers and beer. From Thursday to Saturday, local lesbian bands hold the small stage.

Hillcrest The **Brass Rail** (☎ 619-298-2233; 3796 5th Ave), perhaps the city's oldest gay bar, has a different music theme nightly, from Latin to African to Top 40. The Brass Rail also gets its share of straights and has lots of 'toys' to play with, like a pinball machine, pool table and dart board.

Number One Fifth Ave (☎ 619-299-1911; 3845 5th Ave), across the street in the next block, is a tiny neighborhood joint with a patio.

Rich's (☎ 619-497-4588; 1051 University Ave), a few blocks east of Number One, has DJs who shower a mixed crowd with Latin, techno, pop and House from Wednesday to Sunday. Thursday attracts straights and bisexuals, and there's a patio for smoking.

Flicks (☎ 619-297-2056; 1017 University Ave), a few doors down from Rich's, is a conventional video bar dominated by big screens and is mostly a place to hang and nurse a drink. It's kind of like Starbucks with alcohol.

The Flame (☎ 619-295-4163; 3780 Park Blvd) is the city's oldest and most popular lesbian lounge. Recently remodeled, the plush retro decor now features pink padded walls, drapery and red lighting. It has a large dance floor and an indoor cigar bar.

The Beaches In Pacific Beach, there is a number of bars and clubs on and around Garnet Ave and near the beach – most of them pretty down-to-earth. Most open at 4pm weekdays, noon on Friday and Saturday.

Blind Melons (☎ 858-483-7844; 710 Garnet Ave) has mainly blues performers and some rock.

Club Tremors (☎ 858-272-7278; 860 Garnet Ave), a dance club popular with a young crowd, has a low cover charge and cheap snacks.

Moondoggies (☎ 858-483-6550; 832 Garnet Ave), next door to Club Tremors, has a large patio, big-screen TVs, pool tables, good food and an extensive tap selection.

Society Billiard Cafe (☎ 858-272-7665; 1051 Garnet Ave) is billed as San Diego's plushest; it offers 15 full-sized tables, snacks and a **bar** (open 11am-2am daily).

Cannibal Bar (☎ 858-539-8650; 3999 Mission Blvd), in the Catamaran Resort Hotel, is an intimate tropical place that books reggae, Latin and acid-jazz bands.

Winston's (☎ 619-222-6822; 1921 Bacon St), in Ocean Beach, features live reggae most nights.

La Jolla Jazz venues include **Crescent Shores Grill** (☎ 858-459-0541; 7955 La Jolla Shores Dr), atop Hotel La Jolla, and **Torreyana Grille** (☎ 858-450-4571; 10950 Torrey Pines Rd), in the Hilton Torrey Pines.

Karl Strauss Brewery (☎ 858-551-2739; cnr Wall St & Herschel Ave) makes Karl Strauss beer, if you didn't get to the Old Columbia Brewery. Pints are $2 from 4pm to 7pm weekdays.

The Comedy Store (☎ 858-454-9176; 916 Pearl St; open nightly), in La Jolla, is one of the area's most established comedy venues. It serves meals, drinks and chuckles. There's often a cover charge ($6 to $12 on weekends with a two-drink minimum).

North County The **Belly Up Tavern** (☎ 858-481-2282, 858-481-8140; 143 S Cedros Ave; tickets $5-20), in Solana Beach, is worth visiting if there is a show there that interests you. The converted warehouse gets reggae, jazz, blues and local pop bands.

Coffeehouses

Coffeehouses in San Diego are popular hangouts as well as nighttime venues; often they have live music. Try **Cafe Lulu** (☎ 619-238-0114; 419 F St) in the Gaslamp Quarter; Little Italy's **Caffe Italia** (1704 India St); **New Break Coffee** (☎ 619-224-6666; 1959 Abbot St) in Ocean Beach; **Zanzibar** (Garnet Ave) in Pacific Beach; and **The Pannikin** (☎ 858-454-6365; 7458 Girard Ave) in La Jolla.

David's Coffeehouse (3766 5th Ave) is the hub of social activity in Hillcrest. It's open until midnight, has public Internet access and yummy baked things.

Classical Music

The accomplished **San Diego Symphony** (☎ 619-235-0804; 750 B St) presents classical and family concerts at the Civic Center, as well as the innovative Light Bulb Series, an interactive program intended to demystify classical music. In summer the symphony moves outdoors to the **Navy Pier** (960 N Harbor Dr) for its more light-hearted Summer Pops season.

La Jolla Symphony (☎ 619-534-4637) is of very good quality and holds concerts at

UCSD's Mandeville Auditorium from November to May.

High-caliber performances of small orchestral works are the hallmarks of the **San Diego Chamber Orchestra** (☎ 888-848-7326, 760-753-6402), whose season runs from September to April. Venues range from Copley Symphony Hall downtown to the Sherwood Auditorium at the **Museum of Contemporary Art** (700 Prospect St) in La Jolla, and even at the nightclub **4th & B Street** (345 B St).

Cinema

The main downtown cinemas are the **Grand Theater Horton** (☎ 619-234-4661), at Horton Plaza, and Pacific Theater's elegant new **Gaslamp 15** (☎ 619-232-0400; 5th & G Sts); both show current release movies.

Village Hillcrest (☎ 619-299-2100; 5th Ave), in Hillcrest, and **The Cove** (☎ 619-459-5404; 7730 Girard Ave), in La Jolla, show some European and classic movies, as well as current releases.

Theater

Theater thrives in San Diego and is one of the city's greatest cultural attractions. Book tickets from the theater or with one of the agencies listed in the introduction to this section. Venues include:

Civic Theatre (☎ 619-570-1100) 202 3rd Ave at B St, in the Community Concourse
Grand Theatre Horton (☎ 619-234-9583) 444 4th Ave
La Jolla Playhouse (☎ 619-550-1010) UCSD
Lamb's Players Theater (☎ 619-437-0600) 1142 Orange Ave, Coronado
San Diego Junior Theatre (☎ 619-239-8355) Casa del Prado, Balboa Park
San Diego Repertory Theatre (☎ 619-231-3586) 79 Horton Plaza
Spreckels Theater (☎ 619-235-9500) 121 Broadway
Theatre in Old Town (☎ 619-688-2494) 4040 Twiggs St

Worth special mention are Balboa Park's **Old Globe Theaters** (☎ 619-239-2255; w www.theglobetheaters.org; tickets $17-55), where visitors to the 1935/36 Pacific-California Exposition enjoyed 40-minute renditions of Shakespeare's greatest hits. Saved from demolition in 1937, the theaters became home to a popular summer series of Shakespeare plays, which were performed in full. In 1978 the whole complex was destroyed by an arson fire, but was rebuilt in the style of the original 17th-century Old Globe in England. It reopened in 1982, winning a Tony award in 1984 for its ongoing contribution to theater arts. Between the three venues here – Old Globe, Cassius Carter Stage and the outdoor Lowell Davies Festival Theater – there are performances most evenings and matinees on weekends.

Opera

San Diego Opera (☎ 619-570-1100; tickets standing $15, seats $38-115) is known to rival its LA counterpart for high-quality, eclectic programming. It has hosted such stars as Placido Domingo, José Carreras and Cecilia Bartoli. Its season runs from January to May, with performances at the Civic Theatre. Discount tickets are sometimes available from Times Arts Tix, and standing-room tickets are available from the theater just before a performance (arrive an hour early to ensure getting in). With a standing-room ticket you are allowed to take any empty seat once the lights go down.

SPECTATOR SPORTS

The San Diego Padres baseball team and San Diego Chargers football team share **Qualcomm Stadium** (☎ 619-283-4494; 9449 Friars Rd), in Mission Valley (there's a San Diego Trolley stop right in front). It was originally named for sports journalist Jack Murphy, who was instrumental in getting the park built. He also worked to bring the Chargers football team to town in 1961 and the Padres baseball team in 1968.

Baseball season goes from April to September. Tickets ($5 to $24) are usually available at the gate unless it's a game crucial to the standings or the LA Dodgers are in town on a Friday or Saturday night. Football season lasts from August to January, and tickets start at $24.

Buy tickets through Ticketmaster by phone or online or in person (no service charges) at the stadium, Gate C, from 9am to 6pm weekdays, 10am to 4pm Saturday.

The **San Diego Sports Arena** (☎ 619-224-4176; 3500 Sports Arena Blvd) is where the San Diego Sockers play soccer and the San Diego Gulls play ice hockey. It's also the venue for any big rock concerts visiting town.

SAN DIEGO AREA

Be aware that the neighborhood may be a little rough after dark.

SHOPPING

Every museum and visitor attraction has a gift shop, so souvenir hunters might find a stuffed Shamu at SeaWorld, a realistic rubber snake at the zoo or an old photo at the Museum of San Diego History. The Spanish Village area of Balboa Park is a good place to find paintings (mostly watercolors) of the San Diego area. A uniquely San Diegan gift would be anything emblazoned with the logo of a local surf shop. If you make a trip into the Backcountry (see later in this chapter), locally grown dates, avocados, citrus fruit and wine can be had at reasonable prices.

The most expensive shops are in Horton Plaza and downtown La Jolla, while big department stores – **Macy's, Nordstrom, Robinsons-May** etc – are in Fashion Valley shopping center (see Mission Valley earlier in this section) and the **University Towne Centre** (☎ 858-546-8858), east of I-5 in La Jolla.

For swimwear, women should head to **Pilar's Beachwear** (☎ 858-488-3056; 3745 Mission Blvd) in Mission Beach, which has all the latest styles in all sizes.

Gone Bananas (☎ 858-488-4900; 3785 Mission Blvd), not far from Pilar's, also has a large selection of mix-and-match bikinis and one-pieces, including Body Glove, Mossimo, Sauvage and three dozen other brands.

South Coast Surf Shops (☎ 619-223-7017; 5023 Newport Ave), in Ocean Beach, sells beach apparel and surf gear from Quiksilver, Hurley, Billabong and O'Neill.

South Coast Wahines (☎ 858-273-7600; 4500 Ocean Front Blvd), at the foot of the Crystal Pier in Pacific Beach, is similar but caters to women only.

Thrift-loving hipsters regularly scour the racks at the city's vintage clothing stores for that unique look. Most stores buy, sell and trade. One of the largest and oldest is **Aardvark's Odd Ark** (☎ 858-274-3597; 979 Garnet Ave), in Pacific Beach, which sells Hawaiian shirts, suede vests, zoot suits, glamour gowns and other fun stuff.

The Buff (☎ 858-581-2833; 1059 Garnet Ave) has a range of outrageous clothes, many suitable for Halloween costumes, plus hot accessories.

Buffalo Exchange (☎ 858-273-6227; 1007 Garnet Ave) has a more conservative bent and stocks both vintage and contemporary fashions, including name brands.

Adams Ave is San Diego's main 'antique row,' cutting across some of San Diego's less visited neighborhoods. The greatest concentration of shops is in Normal Heights between I-805 and I-15. The area has dozens of shops, including **Retreads** (☎ 619-284-3999; 3220 Adams Ave), specializing in furniture, and **Back from Tomboctou** (☎ 619-282-8708; 3564 Adams Ave), with art and antiques from around the world. For a store directory, check the Adams Ave business association website at **w** www.gothere.com/AdamsAve.

For really cheap stuff, try **Kobey's Swap Meet** (☎ 858-226-0650; open 7am-3pm Fri-Sun), a massive flea market in the parking lot of the San Diego Sports Arena. On sale are new and used items, including sunglasses, clothing, jewelry, produce, flowers and plants, tools and furniture. Admission is 50¢ on Friday, $1 on weekends; parking is free.

GETTING THERE & AWAY
Air

Most flights into **San Diego International Airport-Lindbergh Field** (☎ 619-231-2100), about 3mi west of downtown, are domestic. Coming in from overseas, you'll most likely change flights – and clear US Customs – at one of the major US gateway airports, such as LA, Chicago or Miami. Only British Airways operates a nonstop flight to San Diego from London-Gatwick.

The standard one-way fare between LA and San Diego is about $75. The flight from LA takes only about 35 minutes; the drive is around two hours. Rental car prices are about the same in both cities.

If you're flying to/from other US cities, it's almost as cheap to fly to/from San Diego as it is to LA. Airlines serving San Diego include Aeromexico, America West, American, Continental, Delta, Northwest, Southwest and US Airways.

Bus

Greyhound (☎ 800-231-2222, 619-239-3266; 120 W Broadway) serves San Diego from cities all over North America. The station has luggage lockers ($2 for six hours) and telephones.

The standard one-way/round-trip fare to and from LA is $16/28; buses depart almost every half hour and the journey takes from 2¼ to 3¾ hours, depending on the number of stops en route. There is a bus to Anaheim, the home of Disneyland, which runs nine times per day for the same prices (and about the same trip duration).

Services between San Francisco and San Diego require a transfer in LA and cost $52/87. The journey takes 11 hours, and there are nine departures daily. There are two direct buses to Las Vegas and seven more that require you to change in either LA or San Bernardino. The trip takes from 7½ to 13½ hours and costs $45/80.

Greyhound also offers direct services from San Diego to Tijuana, across the border in Mexico, where you can connect to other buses serving destinations throughout Mexico. Buses leave almost hourly, on the half hour. The trip takes just over an hour and costs $5/8.

There are also seven daily buses to Calexico, inland on the US side of the border, across from Mexicali. The trip takes three hours and costs $22/34. Services from Calexico are limited to two buses a day.

Train

Amtrak (☎ 800-872-7245; **w** www.amtrak .com) trains arrive and depart from the **Santa Fe train depot** (1050 Kettner Blvd) at the western end of C St. The *Pacific Surfliner* makes nine round-trips to LA; four trains continue on to Santa Barbara, and two of these head further north to San Luis Obispo.

Travel to San Francisco is a bit more complicated. You first have to take an Amtrak motor coach to Bakersfield, change to the *San Joaquins* to Emeryville (near Oakland) and from there take another motor coach to downtown San Francisco. Slightly faster but pricier is the trip aboard the *Pacific Surfliner* to LA, where you can catch the *Coast Starlight* to Oakland with onward motor coach service to San Francisco. Services to other parts of the USA also require a change in LA.

Standard coach fares between San Diego and LA are $25 each way and the trip takes 2¾ hours. Fares to San Francisco cost $56 via Bakersfield (14 hours) or $93 via Los Angeles (12 hours). Trips to/from Santa Barbara cost $30 each way (5½ hours).

GETTING AROUND

Many people get around by car, but you can reach most places on public transportation. Metropolitan buses and the trolley lines are run by Metropolitan Transit Service (MTS), and several other bus companies serve surrounding areas. All sorts of local public transportation tickets, maps and information are available from the **Transit Store** (☎ 619-234-1060; 102 Broadway at 1st Ave; open 8:30am-5:30pm Mon-Fri, noon-4pm Sat & Sun). It sells the Day Tripper Transit Pass ($5/12 for one day/four consecutive days), which is good for unlimited travel on local buses, the trolley and bay ferry.

To/From the Airport

Bus No 992 – nicknamed The Flyer – operates at 10- to 15-minute intervals between the airport and downtown ($2). Buses leave between 4:52am and 1:21pm and make several stops along Broadway before heading north on Harbor Dr to the airport.

Several companies operate door-to-door shuttles from all three airport terminals. Per-person fares depend on the distance traveled; figure about $12 to Mission Valley's Hotel Circle, $8 to Old Town or downtown and $14 to La Jolla. For some of the shorter trips, taxis charge only slightly more and may therefore be preferable, especially if there's more than one of you traveling.

If you're going *to* the airport, call the shuttle company a day or so ahead to make arrangements for a pick-up time and location. **Cloud 9 Shuttle** (☎ 619-505-4950, 800-974-8885) is the most established company; others include **Xpress Shuttle** (☎ 619-295-1900), **Airport Shuttle** (☎ 619-234-4403) and **Seaside Shuttle** (☎ 619-281-6451).

Bus

MTS covers most of the metropolitan area, North County, La Jolla and the beaches and is most convenient if you're going to/from downtown and not staying out late at night. Get the free *Regional Transit Map* from the Transit Store (see earlier).

For route and fare information, call ☎ 619-233-3004 or 800-266-6883, where operators are available 5:30am to 8:30pm Monday to Friday, 8am to 5pm Saturday and Sunday. For 24-hour taped information, call ☎ 619-685-4900. For route planning via the Internet, go to **w** www.sdcommute.com.

Fares cost $1.75 for most trips, including a transfer that is good for up to two hours; on express routes it's $2: exact fare is required.

Useful routes to/from downtown include the following:

No 3	Balboa Park, UCSD
No 4	National City
No 5	Old Town, Little Italy
No 7	Seaport Village, Balboa Park
No 25	Mission Valley, Fashion Valley, Hillcrest
No 30	Pacific Beach, University Towne Centre
No 34	Sports Arena, Mission Beach, Belmont Park, Pacific Beach, Stephen Birch Aquarium, UCSD, University Towne Centre
No 35	Ocean Beach
No 901	Coronado

Train

A commuter rail service, the *Coaster*, leaves the Santa Fe train depot and runs up the coast to North County, with stops in Solana Beach, Encinitas, Carlsbad and Oceanside. In the metropolitan area, it stops at the Sorrento Valley station (where there's a connecting shuttle to UCSD) and Old Town. Tickets are available from vending machines at stations and must be validated prior to boarding. Fares range from $3 to $3.75; machines give change.

There are nine daily trains in each direction Monday to Friday; the first trains leave Oceanside at 5:23am and the Santa Fe depot at 6:33am; the last ones depart at 5:28pm and 6:42pm, respectively. On Saturday, there are four trains only.

For information, contact **Regional Transit** (☎ 619-233-3004, 800-266-6883 from North County; w www.sdcommute.com).

Trolley

Two trolley lines run to/from the downtown terminal near the Santa Fe train depot. The Blue Line goes south to the San Ysidro border and north to Old Town, then continues east through Mission Valley as far as the Mission San Diego de Alcalá. The Orange Line goes east, past the Convention Center to El Cajon and Santee. Trolleys run between 4:20am and 2:20am daily at 15-minute intervals during the day, and every 30 minutes in the evening. The Blue Line continues running all night on Saturday.

Fares vary with distance, but peak at $2.50. Tickets are dispensed from vending machines on the station platforms and are valid for three hours from the time of purchase. Machines give change.

Car

All the big-name rental companies have desks conveniently located at the airport, but the lesser-known ones can be cheaper. It's definitely worth shopping around and haggling – prices vary widely, even from day to day within the same company. The western terminal at the airport has free direct-phones to a number of car-rental companies – you can call several and then get a courtesy bus to the company of your choice. Also, car rentals are as cheap or cheaper in LA, so it might be preferable to get one there.

For contact details of the big-name companies, including Avis, Budget and Hertz, see the Getting Around chapter. Some of the smaller, independent companies – such as **California Rent a Car** (☎ 619-238-9999; 904 W Grape St) and **West Coast Rent a Car** (☎ 619-544-0606; 834 W Grape St), both in Little Italy – may have lower rates and more relaxed conditions.

Taxi

Established companies include **American Cab** (☎ 619-292-1111), **Orange Cab** (☎ 619-291-3333), **San Diego Cab** (☎ 619-226-7294) and **Yellow Cab** (☎ 619-234-6161). Fares are around $1.80 to start, and then are about $1.90 per mile.

Bicycle

Some areas around San Diego are great for biking, particularly Pacific Beach, Mission Beach, Mission Bay and Coronado.

All public buses are equipped with bike racks and will transport two-wheelers for free. Inform the driver before boarding, then stow your bike on the rack on the tail end of the bus. Useful routes include: bus No 34 between downtown and La Jolla (via Ocean Beach, Mission Bay, Mission Beach and Pacific Beach); No 41 between Fashion Valley Center and UCSD; No 150 between downtown and University Towne Centre; No 301 between University Towne Centre and Oceanside; and No 902 between downtown and Coronado. For more information call ☎ 619-685-4900.

The following outfits all rent various types of bicycles, from mountain and road bikes to kids' bikes and cruisers. In general, expect to pay about $5 per hour, $10 to $14 per half-day (four hours) and $15 to $25 per day.

Bike Cab Co (☎ 619-232-4700) 523 Island Ave, downtown

Holland's Bike (☎ 619-435-3153) 977 Orange Ave, Coronado

Hamel's Beach Rentals (☎ 858-488-5050) 704 Ventura Place, Mission Beach

Cheap Rentals (☎ 858-488-9070) 3685 Mission Blvd, Mission Beach

Boat

A regular ferry ($1.50) goes between Broadway Pier and Coronado. A **Water Taxi** (☎ 619-235-8294) makes a regular connection between Seaport Village and Coronado, where it stops at the Ferry Landing Marketplace and Glorietta Bay. It also makes on-call trips to Shelter Island, Harbor Island, Chula Vista and South Bay. The cost is $5 per person.

Around San Diego

NORTH COUNTY COAST

The North County extends up the coast from the pretty seaside town of Del Mar to the Camp Pendleton Marine Base. This continuous string of beachside suburban communities resembles the San Diego of 30 years ago, though more and more development (especially east of I-5) is turning North County into a giant bedroom community for San Diego and Orange County. Still, the beaches here are terrific, and the small seaside towns are good places to stay for a few days if, more than sightseeing, you want to soak up the laid-back Southern California scene.

From the south, N Torrey Pines Rd is the most scenic approach to Del Mar, and you can continue along the coast on S21 (which changes its name from Camino del Mar to Pacific Coast Hwy to Old Hwy 101, going north). A quicker route is I-5, which continues to Los Angeles and beyond. Bus No 301, which allows bikes, departs from University Towne Centre and follows the coastal road to Oceanside, while No 800 is a peak hour express service; for information call the **North County Transit District**

(☎ 760-722-6283). Greyhound buses stop at Del Mar, Solana Beach, Encinitas and Oceanside. The *Coaster* commuter train stops in Solana Beach, Encinitas, Carlsbad and Oceanside.

The **San Diego North County Convention & Visitors Bureau** (☎ 760-745-4741, 800-848-3336; W www.sandiegonorth.com; 360 N Escondido Blvd), in Escondido, is an excellent source for further information. Staff will mail out a free visitors guide upon request.

Del Mar

This is the ritziest of North County's seaside suburbs. It has excellent (if pricey) restaurants, unique galleries, high-end boutiques and a horse-racing track, which is the site of the annual county fair. Downtown Del Mar (sometimes called 'the village') extends for about a mile along Camino del Mar. At its hub, where 15th St crosses Camino del Mar, the very tasteful **Del Mar Plaza**, overlooking the water, has terraces, restaurants and quality boutiques. At the beach end of 15th St, **Seagrove Park** overlooks the ocean. This little chunk of well-groomed beachfront is a community hub frequented by locals.

The **Del Mar Racetrack & Fairgrounds** (☎ 858-755-1141; track admission $3) was started in 1937 by a group including Bing Crosby and Jimmy Durante, and its lush gardens and pink, Mediterranean-style architecture are delightful. The thoroughbred racing season runs from mid-July to mid-September.

From mid-June to July 4, the **Del Mar Fair** (☎ 858-755-1161; adult/child/senior $15/8/12) is a major event, with livestock exhibits, carnival shows, rides and big-name performers every night.

Places to Stay & Eat Staying near the beach in Del Mar is nice, and there are plenty of hotels, but it's not cheap.

Del Mar Motel (☎ 858-755-1534, 800-223-8449; W www.delmarmotelonethebeach.com; 1702 Coast Blvd; singles/doubles from $119/139 summer, from $89/109 winter) is right on the beach. It allows up to five people to stay in its double rooms for no extra charge.

If you're going to splurge, there are few places better to do it than at **L'Auberge Del**

SAN DIEGO NORTH COUNTY

1 Mission San Antonio de Pala
2 Mission San Luis Rey Francia
3 California Surf Museum
4 Ruby's
5 Oceanside Visitor Information Center
6 Legoland California
7 Carlsbad Ranch
8 La Paloma Theater
9 Quail Botanical Gardens
10 Self-Realization Fellowship Retreat; Meditation Garden
11 Pipes Café
12 Ki's Restaurant
13 Belly Up Tavern
14 Cedros Ave Design District
15 Del Mar Racetrack & Fairgrounds
16 Del Mar Plaza
17 Seagrove Park

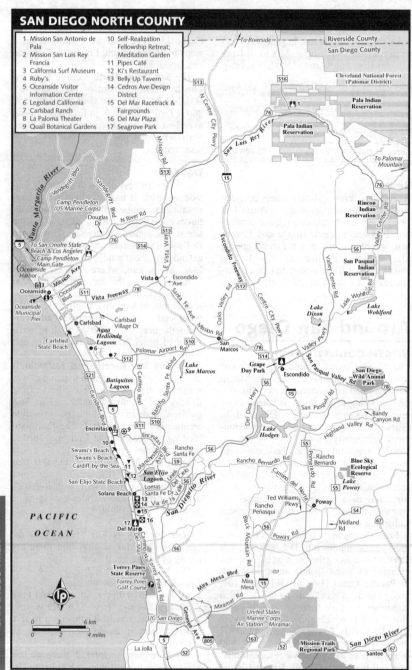

Mar Resort & Spa (☎ 858-259-1515, 800-553-1336; 1540 Camino Del Mar; rooms from $225), right across from Del Mar Plaza. Built on the grounds of the historic Hotel Del Mar – where Charlie Chaplin and Lucille Ball once frolicked (though not with each other) – its reincarnation continues to draw celebrities, including Bonnie Raitt and Mel Brooks.

The patio and restaurants atop Del Mar Plaza have one of San Diego's best vantage points.

Il Fornaio (☎ 858-755-8876; light meals $7.50-10, dinner mains from $16) does upscale Italian and runs the adjacent **Enoteca**, which serves grappa, wine and light meals.

Esmeralda's Books & Coffee (☎ 858-755-2707; snacks under $6), at the top of the plaza over Il Fornaio, has colorful artwork and often gets well-known authors for its weekly readings.

Pacifica Del Mar (☎ 858-792-0476; mains $18-25), also at the top of the plaza, has excellent California cuisine and fresh fish.

For self-catering try the deli at **Good Nature Market** (☎ 858-481-1260), on the Plaza's lower level.

Solana Beach

Solana Beach is the next town north – it's not quite so posh as Del Mar, but it has good beaches and the recently dubbed **Design District** (Cedros Ave), which has unique art and architecture studios, antiques stores and handcrafted clothing boutiques. One of the first businesses here was **Belly Up Tavern** (☎ 858-481-2282, 858-481-8140; 143 S Cedros Ave), a converted warehouse which is still a popular music venue and regularly gets great bands. The cover charge is $5 to $10, or up to $20 for top attractions.

Wild Note Cafe (☎ 858-259-7310; dishes from $6), a new part of the Belly Up, is a good spot for lunch or dinner.

Two long-standing Mexican restaurants are worth looking up – **Fidel's** (☎ 858-755-5292; 607 Valley Ave; meals around $10) and **Tony's Jacal** (☎ 858-755-2274; 621 Valley Ave; meals around $10). Valley Ave goes north of Via de la Valle, just west of I-5.

There are some budget-priced motels along S21, which follows the coast. They are a mixed bag, with a few chain hotels represented as well as some independent, mid-range places.

Cardiff-by-the-Sea

Shortened to 'Cardiff' by most, this stretch of restaurants, surf shops and New Age-style businesses along the Pacific Coast Hwy is good for surfing and is popular with a laid-back crowd. The nearby **San Elijo Lagoon** is a 1000-acre ecological preserve popular with bird-watchers for its abundance of herons, coots, terns, ducks, egrets and about 250 more species. A 7mi network of trails leads through the area.

Pipes Café (121 Liverpool Ave; breakfasts $4-6) is a popular pre-surf fueling point.

Ki's Restaurant (☎ 760-436-5236; 2591 S Coast Hwy 101; meals $4-8) is a hub of activity which, besides having excellent smoothies, health-burgers and salads, also has an ocean view and jazz and blues bands from 8:30pm to 11:30pm Friday (free). Across the road is Cardiff's 'restaurant row,' with upscale seafood restaurants whose windows get washed by the waves.

San Elijo State Beach Campground (☎ 760-753-5091, 800-444-7275 for reservations; tent/RV sites $12/18) overlooks the surf at the end of Birmingham Dr.

At **Cardiff State Beach**, just south of Cardiff-by-the-Sea, the surf break on the reef is mostly popular with long boarders, but it gets very good at low tide with a big north swell. A little further north, San Elijo State Beach has good winter waves.

Encinitas

Yogi Paramahansa Yoganada founded his **Self-Realization Fellowship Retreat & Hermitage** here in 1937, and Encinitas has been a magnet for holistic healers, natural lifestyle seekers and vegetarians ever since. The gold lotus domes of the hermitage – conspicuous on Old Hwy 101 (S21) – mark the southern end of Encinitas and the turnout for **Swami's**, a powerful reef break surfed by territorial locals. There's a parking lot just south of the hermitage, on the western side of Old Hwy 101, which gives a good view of the surf. There is also a great vista from the hermitage's **Meditation Garden** (entrance 215 K St; open to public 9am-5pm Tues-Sat, 11am-5pm Sun); the entrance is west of Old Hwy 101.

The heart of Encinitas is north of the hermitage between E and D Sts. Apart from outdoor cafés, bars and surf shops, the town's main attraction is **La Paloma Theater**

(☎ 760-436-7469; 471 S Coast Hwy 101), built in 1928. La Paloma shows current movies nightly.

The inland hills are used for commercial flower farms, most notably the **Paul Ecke Poinsettia Ranch**, established in 1928. In December there's an enormous poinsettia display at the ranch, and in spring the flowers grow in bands of brilliant color, which look spectacular from I-5.

The 30-acre **Quail Botanical Gardens** (☎ 760-436-3036; adult/child $5/2; open 9am-5pm daily) has a large collection of California native plants and sections planted with flora of various regions of the world, including Australia and Central America. From I-5, go east on Encinitas Blvd to Quail Gardens Dr.

Moonlight Beach Motel (☎ 760-753-0623, 800-323-1259; 233 2nd St; rooms from $80 summer, $60 winter) is large and in a good location.

Carlsbad

Carlsbad (population 68,200) is a good place to stay if you want to be within walking distance of shopping, restaurants and the beach. Rather than being stretched out along the highway like many North County towns, it has a solid downtown of four square blocks between I-5 and Carlsbad Blvd (which run north-south and are connected by Carlsbad Village Dr running east-west). The **Visitor Information Center** (☎ 760-434-6093; 400 Carlsbad Village Dr) is housed in the original 1887 Santa Fe train depot.

The town came into being when the railroad came through in the 1880s. John Frazier, an early homesteader, former sailor and ship's captain, sank a well and found water that had a high mineral content, supposedly the identical mineral content of spa water in Karlsbad (hence the town's name), in Bohemia (now the Czech Republic). He capitalized on the aquatic similarities of the two places and built a grand spa hotel, which prospered until the 1930s. The Queen Anne–style building that was the hotel is now **Neiman's Restaurant & Bar** (☎ 760-729-4131; 2978 Carlsbad Blvd), a place where the atmosphere is appreciably better than the overpriced food.

The long, sandy **beaches** of Carlsbad are great for walking and seashell hunting. Good access is from Carlsbad Blvd, two blocks south of Carlsbad Village Dr, where there's a boardwalk, rest rooms and free parking.

Legoland California Modeled loosely after the original Legoland, in Denmark, Legoland California (☎ 760-918-5346; open 9am-8pm daily mid-June–Labor Day, 10am-5pm otherwise; adult/child 3-16 $34/ 29, two-day tickets $42/37) is an enchanting fantasy environment built entirely of those little colored plastic building blocks that many of us grew up with. There are bicycles to ride around the grounds, a boat tour of some exhibits, and many opportunities to build (and buy) your own Lego structures. It's all rather low-key compared with bigger, flashier parks such as Disneyland and therefore especially suited for younger children (10 and under).

To get to Legoland, take the Legoland/Cannon Rd exit off I-5 and follow the signs. From downtown Carlsbad or downtown San Diego, take the *Coaster* to the Poinsettia Station, from where bus No 344 goes straight to the park.

Carlsbad Ranch From March to May, the 50-acre flower fields of Carlsbad Ranch are ablaze in a sea of carmine, saffron and the snow-white blossom of ranunculus flowers. The fields are two blocks east of I-5; take the Palomar Airport Rd exit, go east, then left on Paseo del Norte Road – look for the windmill. Call ☎ 760-431-0352 for hours, prices or an events schedule.

Batiquitos Lagoon South of Carlsbad, separating it from Encinitas, is this lagoon, one of the last remaining tidal wetlands in California. A self-guided tour lets you explore area plants, including the prickly pear cactus, coastal sage scrub and eucalyptus trees, as well as lagoon birds such as the great heron and the snowy egret. One of the artificial islands in the lagoon is a nesting site for the California least tern and the western snowy plover, both endangered species. The ultra-deluxe Four Seasons Aviara resort and golf course hugs the lagoon's northern edge, while its eastern side is bordered by the equally luxurious La Costa Resort & Spa.

Places to Stay & Eat Three miles south of downtown Carlsbad is **South Carlsbad**

State Park Campground (☎ 760-438-3143, 800-444-7275 for reservations; tent & RV sites $17-22, $1 extra Sat night), which has 222 tent and RV sites.

Motel 6 (☎ 760-434-7135; 1006 Carlsbad Village Dr; from $46 Sun-Thur, from $50 Fri-Sat) is probably the best value; you could also try Surf Motel (☎ 760-729-7961, 800-523-9170; 3135 Carlsbad Blvd; from $129 summer, from $69 winter).

Top-end options include Carlsbad Inn (☎ 760-434-7020, 800-235-393; 3075 Carlsbad Blvd; rooms from $178), on the beachfront, and La Costa Resort & Spa (☎ 760-438-9111; Costa Del Mar Rd; rooms from $325), 2mi east of I-5, with acres of grounds and all sorts of recreational facilities.

Armenian Cafe (☎ 760-720-2233; 3126 Carlsbad Blvd; dishes $6-12), two blocks south of Carlsbad Village Dr, is often chosen by locals for its excellent and authentic Middle Eastern food.

Pizza Port (☎ 760-720-7007; 571 Carlsbad Village Dr; meals $3-16) has salads, pizza and locally brewed beer.

Oceanside

Oceanside (population 72,500) is home base for many of the employees who work on, or for, the big Camp Pendleton Marine Base on the town's northern border. Most attractions of interest to visitors are along the coast, unless you're in the market for automotive parts or a military-style jacket. Amtrak, Greyhound, the *Coaster* and MTS buses all stop at the Oceanside Transit Center (235 S Tremont St).

The Oceanside Visitor Information Center (☎ 760-721-1101; 928 N Coast Hwy) is an easy stop when traveling along the coast. It has coupon books for local attractions as well as maps and information for the greater San Diego area.

The main thing to look at is the wooden Oceanside Municipal Pier, extending more than 1900ft out to sea. It's so long that there's a little golf buggy to transport people to the end (50¢). There are bait and tackle shops, with poles to rent and lights for night fishing, as well as snack bars and the mid-priced, '50s-style Ruby's (☎ 760-433-7829), which, in addition to good burgers and milkshakes, has a full bar. Two major surf competitions – the West Coast Pro-Am and the National Scholastic Surf

Association (NSSA) – take place near the pier in June.

A history of these contests, plus photos, old boards and memorabilia of Duke Kahanamoku (the Olympic gold medal swimmer and surfing pioneer who died in 1968) is on display at the California Surf Museum (☎ 760-721-6876; 223 N Coast Hwy; admission free; open 10am-4pm Thur-Mon).

Very few buildings remain from the 1880s, when the new Santa Fe coastal railway came through Oceanside, but there are still a few left that were designed by Irving Gill and Julia Morgan. The Oceanside Visitor Information Center has a pamphlet describing a self-guided history walk.

At the northern end of the waterfront, the extensive Oceanside Harbor provides slips for hundreds of boats. Helgren's (☎ 760-722-2133; 315 Harbor Dr S) offers a variety of charter trips for sportfishing ($29/55 half/full day) and whale-watching ($18 for a full day). At the southern end of the harbor, Cape Cod Village, a group of shops and restaurants, has a distinctly nautical flavor.

Founded in 1798, Mission San Luis Rey Francia (☎ 760-757-3651; 4050 Mission Ave, Hwy 76; admission $4; open 10am-4pm daily) was the largest California mission and the most successful in recruiting Indian converts. It was known as the 'king of the missions,' and at one time some 3000 neophytes lived and worked here. After the Mexican government secularized the missions, San Luis fell into ruin; the adobe walls of the church, from 1811, are the only original parts left. Inside there are displays on work and life in the mission, with some original religious art and artifacts. The mission is 4mi inland.

Behind the mission, tranquil Heritage Park Village & Museum (☎ 760-966-4545; grounds open 9am-4pm daily, buildings 1pm-4pm Sun only) preserves historic structures from the early 20th century, including a doctor's office, a jail and a blacksmith shop.

Budget motels are not hard to find, but they may fill up on weekends and in summer.

Guesthouse Inn & Suites (☎ 760-722-1904; rooms from $65), close to I-5 off the Coast Hwy exit, formerly the Bridge Motor Inn, has a restaurant and harbor view.

Oceanside Days Inn (☎ 760-722-7661; singles/doubles $59/69) has basic rooms and is near the Oceanside Harbor Dr exit.

SAN DIEGO AREA

San Onofre State Beach

A long and largely undeveloped beach area north of Oceanside, San Onofre is well known to longboarders. It is often called 'old man's' because the older generation likes the gentle waves here. The younger, more aggressive set surfs Trestles, a fast, hollow wave at the northern end of the beach. Access to San Onofre is off I-5 (via Basilone Rd), north of a highly conspicuous nuclear power plant (which is reputed to make the water warmer here). There is a **campground** (☎ 800-444-7275 for reservations; tent & RV sites $20/18 summer/winter) on the bluffs above the beach.

NORTH COUNTY INLAND

The I-15 heads north from San Diego, through Poway, Rancho Bernardo and Escondido to the Riverside County line. The number one attraction is the San Diego Wild Animal Park east of Escondido, but there are also some interesting historical sites, and the area provides access to the scenic backcountry around Palomar (see the San Diego Backcountry section later in this chapter).

Poway

This rural community of 50,000 is best known for its state-of-the-art **Poway Center for the Performing Arts** (☎ 858-748-0505; 1598 Espola Rd), just off I-15. For visitors, perhaps the greatest appeal lies in the town's slow-moving country atmosphere. **Old Poway Park** (☎ 858-679-4313; 14134 Midland Rd; 10am-4pm Sat, 11am-2pm Sun) is an assemblage of historic buildings, including a church, Templars Hall and Nelson House. Kids love the Train Barn, which houses a 1907 steam engine and an 1894 Los Angeles trolley.

Tract homes give way to wilderness the further east you go. **Lake Poway**, at the eastern terminus of Lake Poway Rd, is a major getaway for locals and offers fishing (it is stocked with trout), boating, camping, hiking etc but, ironically, no swimming. A concession stand sells fishing licenses and rents boats (no fishing or boating on Monday and Tuesday and all of October). The lake is surrounded by a wilderness area with access to numerous trails, including the 3mi lake loop and the 2½mi hike to Mt Woodson. The **Blue Sky Ecological Reserve** is a 700-acre protected area that is especially rewarding for birders.

Escondido

This quiet satellite town of 128,000 is the commercial hub of inland North County. Besides the numerous antique shops and two wineries, the main draw is the **California Center for the Arts**, a mixed-use facility anchored by a concert hall, a smaller theater, an art museum and conference center. The **museum** (☎ 760-839-4120; 10am-5pm Tues-Sat, noon-5pm Sun; adult/senior/student $5/4/3) features changing exhibits of 20th-century paintings, sculpture, photography and installations.

Escondido's history is given center stage at the **Heritage Walk** (☎ 760-743-8207; 321 N Broadway; admission free; open 1pm-4pm Thur-Sat), a collection of retired Victorian buildings, including a library, barn, windmill and railroad depot in Grape Day Park.

There's no shortage of places to stay, with all budgets covered.

Escondido RV Resort (☎ 760-740-5000, 800-331-3556; 1740 Seven Oaks Rd; sites $35-40) has 67 sites, a TV lounge, store, heated pool and spa. Tent campers can try **Lake Dixon** (☎ 760-741-3328, 760-839-4680; 1700 La Hondra Dr; tent/RV sites $12/18), which has a pleasant setting.

Among the cheapest motels is **Palms Inn** (☎ 760-743-9733, 800-727-8932; 2650 S Escondido Blvd; singles/doubles $50/60), with rates that include a continental breakfast.

San Diego Wild Animal Park

Since the early 1960s, the San Diego Zoological Society has been developing this 1800-acre, free-range animal park. The main attractions at this park (☎ 760-747-8702; w www.sandiegozoo.org; adult/senior/child 3-11 $26.50/23.85/19.50; gates open 9am-6pm daily in summer, 9am-4pm rest of year) are herds of giraffes, zebras, rhinos and other animals roaming the open valley floor. Visitors take a 50-minute ride around the animal preserves on the Wgasa Bush monorail (actually an electric tram), which gives great views of the animals and includes an interesting commentary. The animals look wonderful in the wide, open spaces, though often you can't get as close to them as you can in a regular zoo.

At the Petting Kraal you can often touch some of the youngest animals in the park. Animal shows are held in a number of areas, starting between 11am and 4:30pm daily. Get a map and a schedule as you enter.

The park has a full range of services, souvenir shops and places to eat. It is just north of Hwy 78, 5mi east of I-15 from the Via Rancho Parkway exit. Bus No 307 will get you there from the Escondido Transit Center, Monday to Saturday, but it's a long, involved process getting back, so you may be better off going by car.

You can stay in the park an hour after the gates close. Admission includes the monorail ride and all animal shows. Discount coupons are widely available. A combined ticket to visit both the San Diego Zoo and the Wild Animal Park within a five-day period costs $46.80/31.40 for adult/child. Parking is $6 extra. For a real safari experience, photo caravan tours go right in among the animals, but they're quite expensive, and reservations are required; there are also night tours available at different times of year – call the main number and ask for guest relations. Facilities are available for disabled visitors; call ☎ 760-738-5067 for information.

Mission San Antonio de Pala

Built in 1810 as an *asistencia* to Mission San Luis del Rey, this was to have been one of a chain of inland missions, but the plan was abandoned, as was the whole mission system a few years later. This mission – on Hwy 76, 7mi east of I-15 – is largely reconstructed and has a small **museum** *(☎ 760-742-3317; admission $2.50; open 10am-4pm Tues-Sun)*. It's on the Pala Indian Reservation in a quiet, rural area and makes for a pleasant stop along Hwy 76.

SAN DIEGO BACKCOUNTRY

Going inland from San Diego, you quickly get into sparsely populated rural areas a world away from the highly developed coast. Much of San Diego County's backcountry is occupied by the Cleveland National Forest, which offers camping, hiking and mountain biking. An excellent book for the trail – or for finding a trail – is Jerry Schad's *Afoot and Afield in San Diego County*, widely available for around $16.

If you are exploring the Cleveland National Forest by car, you must obtain a National Forest Adventure Pass in order to use forest facilities, including hiking trails (see the boxed text 'National Forest Adventure Pass' in the Activities chapter for details).

Hwy 79 is a scenic route through the backcountry, from the wine-producing area near Temecula (in Riverside County), south via Warner Springs and the old gold-mining area of Julian, to Cuyamaca Rancho State Park and I-8. To explore the backcountry, you can go by car, though you can get to most places by buses, which run infrequently (not at all on Sunday and Monday) but are cheap. Call **Northeast Rural Bus System** *(☎ 760-767-4287)* at least a day ahead to make a reservation.

Palomar Mountain

At 6140ft, Palomar Mountain is the centerpiece of three promontories that make up the 25mi-long Palomar Range. It is densely forested with pine, oak, fir and cedar and receives several feet of snow a year. Although there are two self-register, first-come, first-served USFS campgrounds near the top of the mountain (**Fry Creek** and **Observatory**) most people come for the day to see the 200-inch Hale telescope (in use since 1948) at the **Palomar Observatory** *(☎ 760-742-2119; admission free; museum & viewing platform usually open 9am-4pm daily)*, near Palomar Mountain State Park.

Since the California Institute of Technology owns most of the land surrounding the observatory, hiking is limited. There is the 2.2mi **Observatory National Recreation Trail**, which goes from Observatory Campground up to the observatory itself; this is a good one-way trail if you arrange transportation to get yourself back, or it can be done as an out-and-back starting at either end.

To reach the observatory from Hwy 76, take the East Grade Rd (County Hwy S7) or steep and windy South Grade Rd (County Hwy S6) to the junction, where the **Palomar Mountain General Store** *(☎ 760-742-3496; open 11am-5:30pm Mon-Fri, 8:30am-6pm Sat & Sun)* has food and supplies. The observatory is 5mi north, well marked by road signs.

West of the junction, S7 goes to **Palomar Mountain State Park** *(☎ 760-742-3462; day-use fee $2)*. A map is posted at the entrance station, where you pay the day-use fee, waived if you camp at **Doane Valley**

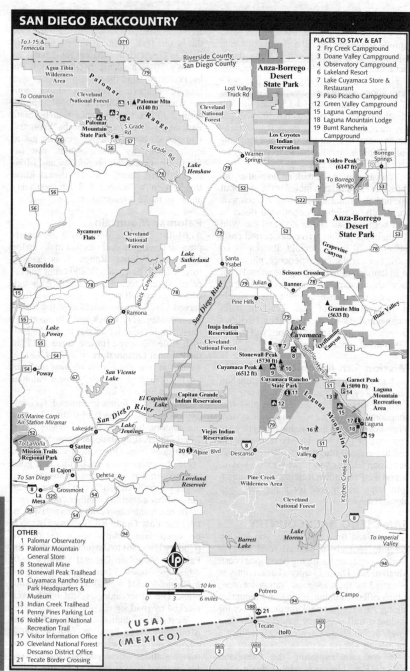

SAN DIEGO BACKCOUNTRY

PLACES TO STAY & EAT
2   Fry Creek Campground
3   Doane Valley Campground
4   Observatory Campground
6   Lakeland Resort
7   Lake Cuyamaca Store & Restaurant
9   Paso Picacho Campground
12 Green Valley Campground
15 Laguna Campground
18 Laguna Mountain Lodge
19 Burnt Rancheria Campground

OTHER
1   Palomar Observatory
5   Palomar Mountain General Store
8   Stonewall Mine
10 Stonewall Peak Trailhead
11 Cuyamaca Rancho State Park Headquarters & Museum
13 Indian Creek Trailhead
14 Penny Pines Parking Lot
16 Noble Canyon National Recreation Trail
17 Visitor Information Office
20 Cleveland National Forest Descanso District Office
21 Tecate Border Crossing

Campground (☎ 800-444-7275 for reservations; tent & RV sites $12). Reservations are recommended.

Julian

The gold rush came to these parts in 1869, when placer deposits were found in a creek near present-day Julian. When quartz gold was discovered, hard-rock mines were started and the town was established in 1870. These days Julian (population 3860) enjoys its position at the crossroads of Hwys 78 and 79, an easy two hours from San Diego and 40 minutes from Anza-Borrego Desert State Park (see the California Deserts chapter). The primary reason people visit its 19th-century main street is to eat apple pie – the trademark product of this largely agricultural region – and, in summer, to enjoy the cool air at 4200ft.

Eagle Mining Company (☎ 760-765-0036) has preserved two of the town's original mines, the Eagle and the High Peak, up C St a few blocks east of Main St. They have displays of minerals and mining machinery and tours of the mines ($7) from 1pm to 3pm daily.

Julian Pioneer Museum (☎ 760-765-0227; 2811 Washington St; admission $2; open 10am-4pm Tues-Sun most of year, Sat & Sun only in winter) has a typical collection of old clothing, tools and photos, but it's worth a short browse. It's a block west of Main St.

Places to Stay & Eat There are a few private campground-RV parks south of town on Hwy 79, but the best camping around is in the Cuyamaca Rancho State Park (see the following section).

Accommodations in Julian are mostly pricey B&Bs. Places fill up on weekends and holidays, and many have a two-night minimum stay. The **Chamber of Commerce** (☎ 760-765-1857; 2129 Main St) has information about many of them.

Julian Hotel (☎ 760-765-0201, 800-734-5854; w www.julianhotel.com; 2032 Main St; rooms from $95/130 midweek/weekends), which dates from 1897, is very central but it's expensive considering most of the rooms don't have bathrooms. Better value is **Julian Lodge** (☎ 760-765-1420, 800-542-1420; midweek/weekends from $85/105) but it's still no bargain.

The two favorite pie purveyors, both on Main St, are **Mom's** and the **Julian Pie Co**, with whole pies for around $10 and slices for $2.50. The tiny **Apple Valley Bakery** (☎ 760-765-2532; 2212 Main St) has a good lunch special: half a sandwich, soup and a slice of pie for $6.60. Otherwise, lunch at any of the indistinguishable diners costs around $7 (without pie). **Bailey's BBQ Pit** (☎ 760-765-9957; cnr Main & A Sts; dishes $7-11), at the northern end of town, offers something different and has live music on weekends.

Cuyamaca Rancho State Park

Delightful for the variety of its landscapes, Cuyamaca Rancho is a lush, cool contrast to both the coastal areas and the deserts. Situated 6mi north of I-8 on Hwy 79, its 33 sq mi embrace meadows with spring wildflowers, forests of oak, willow, sycamore and pine, and wild animals such as deer, raccoons, bobcats and squirrels; there's also rich birdlife.

The genesis of the park was in 1870 when gold was discovered just south of Cuyamaca Lake. By 1872, the town of Cuyamaca had grown up around the Stonewall Mine, and from 1887 to 1891 California governor Robert Waterman developed the area with gusto. When the ore – and Waterman's interest in the mine – petered out, homesteaders tried to make the area into a resort. A Mr Dyars, who was a descendant of a gold rush forty-niner, bought the rancho in 1923 and 10 years later helped create the state park. The Dyars' former home is now the **park headquarters** (☎ 760-765-0755; open 8:30am-4:30pm Mon-Fri), and a **museum** (admission free; open daily in summer, Sat & Sun only in winter) with a good display on local Native Americans.

The park is popular with hikers, mountain bikers and equestrians, and has miles of well-defined trails that start from trailhead parking lots along Hwy 79; maps are posted at each trailhead. Two recommended hikes are the 5½mi (round-trip) climb to Cuyamaca Peak (6512ft), offering a panoramic view, and the 4½mi hike up Stonewall Peak (5730ft) to look over the old mine site. You can also drive to the **mine site**: turn east off Hwy 79 at the 'Los Caballos Campground' sign, 1mi north of Paso Picacho Campground.

There are two drive-in campgrounds in the park, **Green Valley** and **Paso Picacho** (☎ 800-444-7275 for reservations; sites $12); Paso Picacho also has very basic cabins for $15.

Lakeland Resort (☎ 760-765-0736; 14916 Hwy 79; rooms $48-60) is opposite the lake just outside the park's northern boundary. A mile north is Lake Cuyamaca Store & Restaurant (☎ 619-765-0700; meals $6-11), which has limited groceries and a decent restaurant with homemade breakfast goodies, German specialties for lunch and dinner, and a wide selection of German beers.

For maps and information, stop at one of the campground entrance kiosks or (in winter) at the office upstairs in the park headquarters. There's a $5 day-use fee, which you need to put in an envelope when you park.

Laguna Mountains

The Laguna crest lies at the eastern edge of the Cleveland National Forest. From the crest there is a 6000ft drop to the Anza-Borrego Desert below – you can often see the Salton Sea, 60mi away, and the San Jacinto Mountains, which are 2000ft higher than the sea and often snow-covered. The Lagunas are slightly lower and drier than the Cuyamacas – which lie 11mi west – but they support a wonderful array of plant life, including Jeffrey and Coulter pines and the rare Laguna aster (Machaeranthera asteroides lagunesis), which blooms in August and September. Coyotes, mountain lions and foxes are among the four-footed creatures you might see.

The Sunrise Hwy (County Road S1) runs along the highest part of the range, which is designated as the Laguna Mountain Recreation Area from I-8 in the south to Hwy 79 in the north. There are self-service information booths at both ends of the highway, and a visitor information office (☎ 619-473-8547; County Rd S1; open 1pm-5pm Fri, 8am-5pm Sat, 10am-4pm Sun) in the small community of Mt Laguna, about halfway between I-8 and Hwy 79. There's also information at the Cleveland National Forest Descanso District Office (☎ 619-445-6235; open 8am-4pm Mon-Fri, 7:30am-3pm Sat), off I-8 east of Alpine.

Laguna Mountain Lodge (☎ 619-445-2342; rooms $50/60 midweek/weekend, cabins $55/70), in Mt Laguna township, rents rustic, somewhat bare-bones cabins and has a good selection of maps, books and groceries. Two campgrounds in the area, along Sunrise Hwy, are Laguna Camp-ground and Burnt Rancheria Campground (☎ 800-444-7275 for reservations; sites $12).

This area has a number of hiking trails, including a 37mi section of the Pacific Crest Trail and the 10mi Noble Canyon National Recreation Trail. The Penny Pines parking lot, 4mi north of Laguna Mountain Lodge, is a good starting point for several hikes. A 2mi jaunt (on the Pacific Coast Trail) up to Garnet Peak (5090ft) is worthwhile on a clear day – the views from the peak are dizzying. West, across Sunrise Hwy from Penny Pines, the trail to Big Laguna Lake leads through stands of Jeffery pine and a large open meadow. You can also hike over to the Cuyamacas by way of the Indian Creek Trail.

Tijuana, Mexico

Visiting Tijuana is a real experience. As a Mexican city, Tijuana is neither typical nor attractive, but as border towns go, it is almost an archetype, with gaudy souvenir shops, noisy bars and sleazy backstreets. Though more respectable than it once was, it has never completely overcome the 'sin city' image it acquired during US Prohibition. But these days most people can feel comfortable in the main shopping streets, at least until sunset. In fact, the most offensive characters you may run into are young Americans who come here to get legally drunk under age 21.

Tijuana (pronounced tee-hwah-na and sometimes called TJ) has a population unofficially estimated at around 1.2 million. Just across the US border from San Diego's southern suburbs, it's a significant city in its own right, though in some ways the two cities are so interdependent that they can almost be regarded as a single urban area. About 70% of Tijuana's economy is based on 'frontier transactions' such as tourism, and another 15% is from maquiladoras (factories assembling products for the US market).

Meanwhile, San Diego promotes Tijuana as one of its own tourist attractions and depends on the border town for a supply of cheap labor. But beyond the shopping and entertainment precincts, Tijuana does have its own life, with office buildings, factories and housing developments, as well as 10 universities.

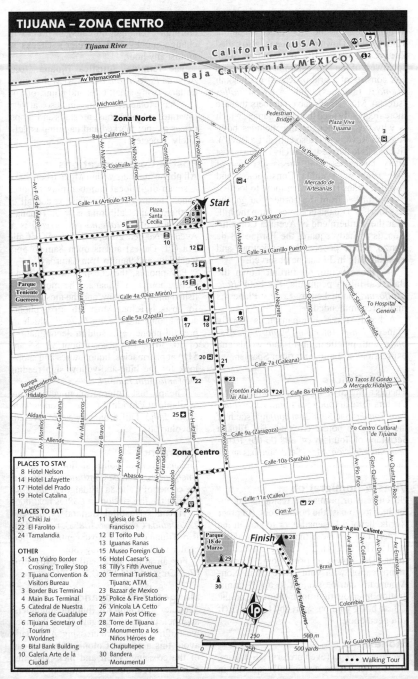

TIJUANA – ZONA CENTRO

Tijuana River

California (USA)

Baja California (MEXICO)

Av Internacional

Michoacán

Zona Norte

Pedestrian Bridge

Plaza Viva Tijuana

Via Poniente

Mercado de Artesanías

Calle Comercio

Start

Calle 1a (Artículo 123)

Plaza Santa Cecilia

Calle 2a (Juárez)

Calle 3a (Carrillo Puerto)

Parque Teniente Guerrero

Calle 4a (Díaz Mirón)

Calle 5a (Zapata)

Calle 6a (Flores Magón)

Calle 7a (Galeana)

Frontón Palacio Jai Alai

Calle 8a (Hidalgo)

To Tacos El Gordo & Mercado Hidalgo

To Hospital General

To Centro Cultural de Tijuana

Calle 9a (Zaragoza)

Rampa Independencia

Hidalgo

Aldama

Zona Centro

Calle 10a (Sarabia)

Calle 11a (Calles)

Cjon Z

Finish

Blvd Agua Caliente

Brasil

Colombia

Parque 18 de Marzo

Torre de Tijuana

Blvd de Fundadores

Av Guanajuato

0   250   500 m
0   250   500 yards

PLACES TO STAY
8 Hotel Nelson
14 Hotel Lafayette
17 Hotel del Prado
19 Hotel Catalina

PLACES TO EAT
21 Chiki Jai
22 El Farolito
24 Tamalandia

OTHER
1 San Ysidro Border Crossing; Trolley Stop
2 Tijuana Convention & Visitors Bureau
3 Border Bus Terminal
4 Main Bus Terminal
5 Catedral de Nuestra Señora de Guadalupe
6 Tijuana Secretary of Tourism
7 Worldnet
9 Bital Bank Building
10 Galería Arte de la Ciudad

11 Iglesia de San Francisco
12 El Torito Pub
13 Iguanas Ranas
15 Museo Foreign Club
16 Hotel Caesar's
18 Tilly's Fifth Avenue
20 Terminal Turística Tijuana; ATM
23 Bazaar de Mexico
25 Police & Fire Stations
26 Vinícola LA Cetto
27 Main Post Office
28 Torre de Tijuana
29 Monumento a los Niños Héroes de Chapultepec
30 Bandera Monumental

••• Walking Tour

SAN DIEGO AREA

ORIENTATION & INFORMATION

Tijuana parallels the US border for about 12mi (19km). Downtown Tijuana (also called Zona Centro) is a 10- to 15-minute walk southwest of the San Ysidro border crossing and consists of a grid pattern of north-south *avenidas* (avenues) and east-west *calles* (streets). Most streets have numbers that are more frequently used than their names, which is why this chapter usually includes both. Avenida Revolución (also called 'La Revo'), five blocks to the west, is the city's main tourist artery; businesses along streets just west of here such as Avenida Constitución and Avenida Niños Héroes cater more to locals.

The further from the border you go, the less touristy Tijuana becomes. Atop the hill, near the southern end of Avenida Constitución, is a shady square, the Parque 18 de Marzo, where people play basketball and everyday life in TJ can be observed.

For those venturing further down the Baja California peninsula, the book *Baja California*, published by Lonely Planet, is highly recommended.

A handy travel companion is Lonely Planet's *Latin American Spanish phrasebook,* with practical, up-to-date words and expressions in Latin American Spanish.

Tourist Offices

There's a branch of the **Tijuana Convention & Visitors Bureau** *(open 9am-5pm Mon-Thurs, 9am-7pm Fri-Sat, 9am-2pm Sun)* just south of the pedestrian border crossing. The **Tijuana Secretary of Tourism** *(☎ 688-05-05; 10am-5pm Mon-Fri, from 11am Sat & Sun)* has an office on Avenida Revolución at Calle 1a.

Visas & Immigration

US citizens or permanent residents not intending to go past the border zone (in other words, beyond Ensenada), or to stay in the border zone for more than 72 hours, don't need a visa or even a passport to enter Tijuana. Do, however, bring some form of identification with your photo on it. Non-Americans can be subject to a full immigration interrogation upon returning to the US, so bring your passport and USA visa (if you need one).

Money

Everyone accepts (even prefers) US dollars, and tourist prices are usually quoted in dollars. There are lots of *casas de cambio* (foreign-exchange bureaus), which will change money and traveler's checks at almost any hour.

The **Terminal Turistica Tijuana** *(1025 Avenida Revolución)* has an ATM that gives dollars. Bring small bills and coins, or you may have to accept change in pesos at very low rates. At most souvenir stalls and shops, prices are not marked and haggling is definitely expected.

Post & Communications

All phone numbers within Mexico consist of a seven-digit local number plus an area code. The area code for Tijuana and all of northern Baja California is ☎ 6. Tijuana's main post office *(oficina de correos)* is at Avenida Negrete 2050, at the corner of Calle 11a (PE Calles) and is open 8am to 5pm weekdays and 9am to 1pm Saturday.

Pay phones, the cheapest way to make calls, abound in Tijuana. The most established phone company, and the most reliable for costs, is Telnor. Most Telnor pay phones accept coins and *tarjetas Ladatel,* which are prepaid phone cards sold in denominations of 30, 50 or 100 pesos (about $3, $5 and $10) at pharmacies, liquor stores and shops: look for the blue-and-yellow sign reading *De Venta Aquí Ladatel.*

Cheap, fast Internet connections are available at **Worldnet** *(Calle 2a; open 9am-11pm daily),* half a block west of Avenida Revolución.

Emergency

Tijuana's **central police station** *(☎ 060 for emergencies; Avenida Constitución 1616)* is at the corner of Calle 8a (Hidalgo) in the Zona Centro; the **fire station** *(☎ 068)* is next door.

Tijuana's **Hospital General** *(☎ 684-09-22; Avenida Centenario 10851),* north of the Río Tijuana, is the most central medical center with an emergency room.

For an ambulance, call the **Cruz Roja** *(Red Cross; ☎ 684-8984).*

Dangers & Annoyances

'Coyotes' and *polleros* (human smugglers) and their clients congregate along the river, west of the San Ysidro crossing. After dark, avoid this area and Colonia Libertad, east of the crossing. Theft and pick-pocketing are not uncommon in Tijuana, nor are short-changing, bill-padding and the addition of 'gringo-tax.'

Car theft is a major problem in Tijuana. Don't leave anything valuable-looking in your car, and park it in a guarded garage or lot rather than on the street (even if you have a car alarm).

THINGS TO SEE & DO

Tijuana's downtown is the city's most historical part, although most of its past has been obliterated by unimaginative storefronts, gaudy advertisements, and terrace bars enveloped in loud music and unfiltered car exhaust. Nowhere is this garish commercialism and utilitarian architecture more in evidence than on **Avenida Revolución**, downtown's main artery and tourist magnet. Virtually every visitor has to experience at least a brief stroll up and down this raucous thoroughfare, popularly known as 'La Revo.'

Walking Tour

This walking tour begins on one of Tijuana's oldest streets and takes in all major sights in the downtown area. It covers 3mi and can take from two hours to all day, if you spend time lingering, or break to eat and shop.

A good place to start is at the **Tijuana Secretary of Tourism Office** on **Plaza Santa Cecilia**, right at the foot of Avenida Revolución. From here, head south for one block to Calle 2a (Juárez), turn right (west) at the **Bital Bank Building** (1929) – among the few surviving architectural gems of Old Tijuana – and walk one block to Avenida Constitución. Here, duck into the tranquil courtyard of Antiguo Palacio Municipal and have a look at local talent in the **Galería Arte de la Ciudad** (Municipal Art Gallery; ☎ 685-01-04).

Continue west on Calle 2a to the imposing **Catedral de Nuestra Señora de Guadalupe**, Tijuana's oldest church, which evolved from an adobe chapel built in 1902. Turn south on Avenida F (5 de Mayo) to emerge next to the **Iglesia de San Francisco**, a single-nave church with an interesting star-vaulted ceiling, walls of modern stained glass and polished wood floors. Next to it is the popular **Parque Teniente Guerrero**, named for a soldier who helped defend Baja California against the Magonistas in 1911. The park has a reputation as

a major after-dark cruising area for gay men. During the daytime, however, it's a popular place for families and a comfortable place to spend a few hours.

Take a stroll around the park before backtracking east along Calle 3a (Carrillo Puerto) to Avenida Constitución, then turn right (south) and look for the entrance to a passageway halfway down the block's eastern side. Turn left into the passageway for a visit to the **Museo Foreign Club** (☎ 666-37-49; admission free; open 7am-5pm daily), a haphazard collection of historical photographs and memorabilia founded by William McCain Clauson, an American who gained international fame as a singer of Mexican folk songs in the 1950s and '60s.

Exit this little alley on Avenida Revolución and turn right – you'll find yourself right at the legendary **Hotel Caesar's**. Built in 1930, the venerable – if somewhat worn – birthplace of the Caesar salad has a fun collection of bullfighting memorabilia.

Further south on La Revo, you'll pass the **Frontón Palacio Jai Alai**. For decades this striking Tijuana landmark hosted jai alai, a fast-moving game of Basque origin, which is kind of a hybrid of squash and tennis. Poor attendance and the game's waning popularity forced its owner to close down in the late 1990s.

Turn right on Calle 10a (Sarabia), cross Avenida Huitzilao (the southern continuation of Avenida Constitución) and turn into Calle Cañon Johnson, where you can rest during a wine tasting at **Vinícola LA Cetto** (pronounced elle-a-**tsche**-tto) (☎ 685-30-31; Calle Cañón Johnson 8151), Tijuana's branch of Mexico's largest winery. Prices at the winery's store are 25% lower than around town and start at $5 for a bottle of wine, $6 for sparkling wine or brandy and $12 for tequila. Tours (US$2) of the winery are offered 10am to 5pm Monday to Friday and 10am and 4pm Saturday.

Backtrack to Avenida Huitzilao, then head uphill (south) to Parque 18 de Marzo with its **Monumento a los Niños Héroes de Chapultepec**, at the foot of a giant Mexican flag, the **Bandera Monumental** inaugurated in 1997 by former president Ernesto Zedillo. Continue downhill along Calle Brasil to Blvd de los Fundadores and the **Torre de Tijuana**, where the tour concludes.

The fastest way back to where you started is straight north on Avenida Revolución.

Centro Cultural de Tijuana (Cecut)

Tijuana's modern cultural center (☎ 684-11-11; cnr Paseo de los Héroes & Avenida Independencia; open 9am-noon & 2pm-5pm Tues-Sat, 10am-8pm Sun) goes a long way toward undermining the city's reputation as a cultural wasteland and is a facility that would be the pride of any city of comparable size in the world. In front of the distinctive complex is a humongous cream-colored sphere – sort of a giant golf ball – known as La Bola (The Ball), which was designed by noted architects Pedro Ramierez Vasquez and Manuel Rosen Morrison.

Inside, a state-of-the-art museum chronicles the history of Baja California from prehistoric times to the present. It provides an excellent introduction to the peninsula and belongs on everybody's must-see list. The exhibits were designed by Mario Vásquez, Mexico's top museum designer, who was also behind Mexico City's famous Museo Nacional de Antropología (National Anthropology Museum), one of the best museums of its kind in the world.

PLACES TO STAY & EAT

Most visitors just come to Tijuana for the day, but there are plenty of accommodations available if you need to stay. Many places are much cheaper and rougher than anything you'll find in San Diego, but mid-range hotels are quite accommodating and less expensive than equivalent lodgings on the other side of the border. The really cheap hotels in the Zona Norte, Tijuana's red-light district, should definitely be avoided.

Hotel Nelson (☎ 685-43-03; Avenida Revolución 721; rooms $45) is a perennial favorite with gringos for its central location and 92 clean, carpeted standard-issue rooms. Inexpensive breakfasts and snacks are available in the coffee shop.

Hotel Lafayette (☎ 685-39-40; Avenida Revolución 325; singles/doubles US$22/28) offers the best value in the budget category. It's a safe, spick-and-span place – but do ask for a room facing away from La Revo.

Hotel del Prado (☎ 688-23-29; Calle 5a 8163; rooms without/with bath US$15/17),

run by a gracious proprietor, is decidedly no-frills, but as clean as a whistle and cheap.

Hotel Catalina (☎ 685-97-48; cnr Calle 6a & Avenida Madero; rooms US$28) is just a little more expensive than Hotel del Prado, but is a notch up in terms of comfort. Owners of this family hotel stress security, and rooms are clean and tidy.

There's a taco stand (or two) on nearly every corner as well as carts that sell roasted corn, fresh fruit and fresh seafood. The tastiest stuff usually comes from the place that's most crowded. Those with testy stomachs should use caution, however, as street food does have a bad track record for giving people the infamous 'Tijuana Trots.'

El Farolito (Calle 7a; breakfast US$3; lunch or dinner US$6), near Avenida Constitución, is a little eatery decked out in a riot of color. You can watch the food being prepared in the open kitchen.

Tamalandia (☎ 685-75-62; Calle 8a 8374; snacks US75¢ each) is a cheery little place selling homemade tamales stuffed with beef, chicken or cheese, plus the dessert-like dulce.

Chiki Jai (☎ 685-49-55; Avenida Revolución 1388; mains US$9), next to the Frontón Palacio Jai Alai, has been packed with patrons since 1947. In the golden days of jai alai (the 1950s and '60s), the most famous players used to hang out here.

Tacos El Gordo (Blvd Sánchez Taboada at Calle Javier Mina; tacos $1; open 24hr), next to Mercado Hidalgo, has cult status among night owls.

ENTERTAINMENT

The rowdy Avenida Revolución is the place to go for ear-splitting live and recorded music at bars and clubs. The upstairs **El Torito Pub** (Avenida Revolución 643) has a large, circular dance floor, two pool tables and even a mechanical bull.

Iguanas Ranas (cnr Avenida Revolución & Calle 3a), not far from El Torito, is similar but is creatively decorated to resemble a circus. You can sit inside a retired yellow school bus that's now part of the facade, but there's a terrace here as well. In the back is a large black-lit room, which is a disco/sports bar with pool tables.

Also popular is **Tilly's Fifth Avenue** (cnr Avenida Revolución & Calle 5a), a smaller, ground-floor establishment that has been around in one form or another since 1927.

SHOPPING
Many Americans make regular trips across the border to purchase prescription drugs and pharmaceutical items, which are significantly cheaper here. Other popular buys in Tijuana are vanilla, Kahlua, tequila and turtle oil lotion.

Each person returning to the USA is allowed to bring $400 worth of goods duty-free back across the border. The symbol 'CH' behind 10k or 14k on a gold product means that it's gold-plated or gold-filled. Real silver products must be stamped '925', and *alpaca* means silver-plated.

Bazaar de Mexico (☎ 638-47-37; cnr Avenida Revolución & Calle 7a) is an excellent showcase of quality arts and crafts from all around Mexico. Quality is high and prices are not as inflated as in other stores.

Mercado Hidalgo is where locals come to buy spices, dried chilies, exotic produce, fresh tortillas and seasonal specialties made from Aztec grains. The easiest way to find the market is to walk east from Avenida Revolución on Calle 9a (Zaragoza) until you reach Avenida Sanchez Taboada, cross the street and continue down Avenida Javier Mina; the market is on the right.

Mercado de Artesanias is the first big outdoor market you'll encounter when coming over the border by foot. Here you'll find TJ's biggest concentration of souvenirs, crafts and curios – bargain hard.

GETTING THERE & AWAY
The San Ysidro border crossing is open 24 hours. Mesa de Otay, about 6mi east of Tijuana, is open from 6am to 10pm and is much less congested.

Air
Flights to other Mexican cities can be substantially cheaper from **Aeropuerto Internacional Abelardo L Rodríguez** (☎ 683-24-18), right on the international border in the suburb of Mesa de Otay, 6mi east of downtown. To US cities, it is better to fly from San Diego, since it is generally cheaper and there are more flights.

Bus
Buses from San Diego's Greyhound station ($5) depart almost hourly between about 5:30am and 12:30am. Greyhound buses heading to San Diego from the Central Camionera also have connections to Los Angeles ($18).

The old **main terminal** (☎ 688-07-52; cnr Avenida Madero & Calle 1a), in the Zona Centro, offers services by Subur Baja to Tecate and Rosarito, Greyhound to the USA, and Elite and TNS to the Mexican mainland.

The terminal is a short taxi ride or about a 10-minute walk from the border and has telephones, fax and photocopy services as well as clean bathrooms (2 pesos).

The **border bus terminal** (☎ 683-56-81) is on the southeastern edge of Plaza Viva Tijuana. From here, ABC operates buses to Ensenada, San Quintín and San Felipe, while Estrellas del Pacífico goes to Mexicali, Guadalajara, Mazatlán and other mainland Mexico destinations.

Mexicoach's Rosarito Beach Express departs from here at 11am and 1pm, 3pm and 5pm Monday to Saturday. The round-trip fare is $6.

Trolley
The trolley runs from downtown San Diego to San Ysidro ($3.25) every 15 minutes from about 5am to midnight. From the San Ysidro stop, take the pedestrian bridge over the road and go through the turnstile into Mexico. You don't need a taxi to get to the middle of town – just follow the blue and white signs reading 'Centro Downtown' through the largely deserted tourist trap of Plaza Viva Tijuana, take another pedestrian bridge across the Río Tijuana and walk another couple of blocks to the northern end of Avenida Revolución.

Car
If you're going to Tijuana for just one day, don't drive your car – the traffic is frenetic, parking is a pain and there may be a long wait to cross back into the USA. It's better to take the trolley or drive to San Ysidro (exit I-5 at the last exit before the border), leave your car in a day parking lot (about $6) and walk across the border. If you want to go further down into Baja California, a car is useful. It's much cheaper to rent a car in San Diego than in Tijuana, but make sure the rental company will let you take it across the border.

Mexican law recognizes only Mexican *seguro* (car insurance), so a US or Canadian policy won't suffice. Driving in Mexico without Mexican insurance is extremely foolish. If you're entering Tijuana from San Diego, you'll find numerous insurance offices right at the Via de San Ysidro and Camino de la Plaza exits off of I-5. Rates are government controlled and fairly standard on both sides of the border: $8 for the first day and $2.50 for each additional day. Most major US insurance companies and the American Automobile Association (AAA) can also arrange coverage.

GETTING AROUND

From the San Ysidro border, take any bus marked 'Centro' to go downtown. Buses stop on the southeastern edge of Plaza Viva Tijuana; there's usually someone with a notebook to steer you toward the right bus to anywhere in town. The fare is 4.50 pesos (which works out at about 50¢). Drivers have no change. Of course, the easiest way to reach La Revo from the border crossing is on foot (for more details, see under Trolley earlier).

Orange County

Few visitors realize that there's more to Orange County than Disneyland. While the region needn't be a priority on the itinerary of first-time visitors to California, it does have a wide range of worthwhile attractions beyond the Mouse Park, including excellent beaches (there are 42mi of coastline), interesting museums and fine entertainment. Although a mosaic of 34 cities with 2.7 million inhabitants, Orange County identifies itself as a 'county' more than any other in Southern California, with countywide publications such as the daily newspaper *Orange County Register*, and the *Orange County Weekly* for entertainment reviews and listings.

Inland towns have large Latino populations whose ancestors came here when orange crops were the main source of income. Both the demographics and the landscape changed in the 1970s and '80s when several major corporations set up headquarters here, starting a trend that has kept Orange County one of the fastest-growing urban centers in the US. In 1995 mismanagement and corruption forced the county to declare bankruptcy, from which it has since recovered. The resident community, however, remains safely within California's highest per capita income brackets and is characterized by its political and social conservatism.

Information
Most of Orange County's cities maintain visitor bureaus (see individual sections for contact details), but for general area information, stop in at the new **California Welcome Center** (☎ 714-667-0400; 2800 N Main St) in the MainPlace mall in Santa Ana off the Main St exit of the I-5, at the intersection with Hwy 22. The office is on the lower level, near the southwest outside entrance.

Getting There & Around
The Amtrak stations in Fullerton, Anaheim, Orange, Santa Ana, Irvine and San Juan Capistrano, all on the Los Angeles–San Diego route, are served by the *Pacific Surfliner* and the Metrolink commuter trains from downtown Los Angeles.

John Wayne-Orange County Airport (☎ 949-252-5200; W *www.ocair.com*) is just off the I-405 in Irvine. Small and convenient,

Highlights

- Disney's California Adventure – an imaginative celebration of the best of the Golden State
- Orange County's beaches – unlimited fun in the sun and the water
- Mission San Juan Capistrano – gorgeous and well-preserved, this is the most popular of the California missions
- Laguna Beach – a breathtakingly beautiful sliver of the California Riviera, with a long tradition in the arts
- Crystal Cathedral – a sparkling house of worship by master architect Philip Johnson

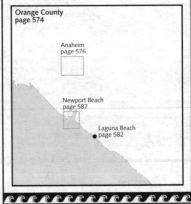

Orange County
page 574

Anaheim
page 576

Newport Beach
page 587

Laguna Beach
page 582

it's growing in popularity as a viable alternative to Los Angeles International Airport (LAX) for domestic flights. Currently, Alaska Airlines, America West, American, Continental, Delta, Northwest, Skywest, Southwest, United and US Airways operate some 300 daily flights out of this airport.

Orange County Transportation Authority (*OCTA;* ☎ 714-636-7433; W *www.octa.net*) buses serve towns and destinations throughout the county. The fare is $1 per ride or $2.50 for a day pass. Both types of tickets are sold aboard and you'll need exact change. Transfers are free. Free OCTA bus system maps and schedules are available at train stations, most chambers of commerce and online.

Many hotels and motels have free shuttles to Disneyland and other area attractions.

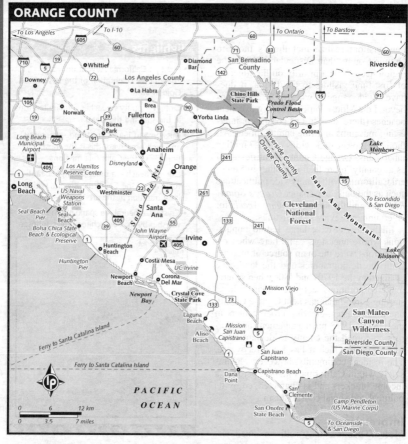

ORANGE COUNTY

ANAHEIM

Anaheim (population 306,000), best known as the home of Disneyland, recently completed a staggering $4.2 billion revamping and expansion. The cornerstone of the five-year effort is the addition of a second theme park, Disney's California Adventure, along with Downtown Disney, an outdoor entertainment mall. Park access roads have been widened and attractively landscaped and the whole area has been given the lofty name 'The Anaheim Resort.'

Anaheim was settled more than a century ago by German immigrants who came to grow grapes and produce wine. The wine industry collapsed in the late 1880s after a blight wiped out the vineyards, but oranges and other crops soon took over and the

town remained an agricultural hotbed until after WWII. Life changed forever in 1955 when Walt Disney first welcomed visitors to Disneyland.

The **Anaheim/Orange County Visitor & Convention Bureau** (☎ 714-765-8888, fax 714-991-8963; w www.anaheimoc.org; 800 W Katella Ave), just south of Disney's California Adventure, has information on countywide lodging, dining and transportation. The staff is also helpful in answering questions over the phone.

Disneyland Resort

When Walt Disney trotted out his famous mouse in 1928, it was the beginning of a commercial bonanza that's been expanding relentlessly ever since. Fueled by the dreams of children worldwide, Disney has become a legend of corporate success – and excess – in virtually every field it has entered: movies, TV, publishing, music and merchandise and, of course, theme parks.

Opened in 1955 by Walt Disney himself, **Disneyland** (☎ 714-781-4565, 213-626-8605; w www.disneyland.com) is 'imagi-neered' to be the 'happiest place on earth,' from the impeccable, pastel sidewalks to the personal hygiene of the roughly 21,000 park employees, called 'cast members' in Disney-speak.

In February 2001, a second park opened adjacent to the original: **Disney's California Adventure** (☎ 714-781-4565, 213-626-8605; w www.disneyland.com), which revolves around the state's most famous natural and human-made landmarks. Together with Downtown Disney and three Disney resort hotels, the parks form the Disneyland Resort.

You'll need at least one day for each park, and more if you want to go on all the rides. Lines are the longest during summer and around major holidays. In general, visiting midweek is better than Friday, Saturday or Sunday, and arriving early in the day is best. Bring a hat, suntan lotion, patience and – if cutting costs is your aim – bottled water. Also keep in mind that many rides have minimum age and height requirements, so avoid tantrums by preparing the kids. Disneyland has a baby-care center, currency-exchange

stations, banks and even a kennel. There's no smoking anywhere in the parks.

Disney recently introduced the free Fast-pass system, which pre-assigns you specific boarding times for selected rides, thereby significantly cutting wait times. Look for ticket machines near the entrances to the rides. Simply show up at the time printed on the ticket and go straight to the Fastpass line instead of the regular line. There may still be a wait but it'll be *much* shorter.

Tickets & Hours One-day admission to either park is $45, or $35 for children aged three to nine. 'Multi-Day Park Hopper Tick-ets' cost $114/90 for three days and $141/ 111 for four days of admission within a two week period. These tickets give you access to both parks, but you can only visit one park per day. Prices increase yearly; check the website for the latest information or to buy tickets. Parking is an additional $8.

Park hours vary pretty much daily and depend upon the marketing department's projected attendance numbers. During peak season – mid-June to early September – hours are usually 8am to midnight, but the rest of the year 10am to 8pm or 10pm is more typical.

Disneyland You enter Disneyland on **Main Street USA**, which is a cheery re-creation of small-town America circa 1900, with myriad shops and the Candy Palace. Have your pic-ture taken with Mickey and Minnie or any of the other jumbo Disney characters that usu-ally hang out around here, then plunge on to the seven Disney 'lands' orbiting Sleeping Beauty's Castle, inspired by a real castle in southern Germany.

Main Street ends in the Central Plaza. Im-mediately on your right is **Tomorrowland**, home to many of the high-tech rides. The best ones are Star Tours, where you find yourself clamped into a StarSpeeder vehicle piloted by a dysfunctional android for a wild and bumpy ride through deep space. Space Mountain will take your head off as you hur-tle into complete darkness at a frightening speed – you *will* scream long and loud.

In **Adventureland**, to the left of Central Plaza, the highlight is the jungle-themed In-diana Jones Adventure. Enormous HumVee-type vehicles lurch off into the wild for spine-tingling encounters in re-creations of

---

Tricky Dick Library

In Yorba Linda, in northeastern Orange County, is the **Richard Nixon Presidential Library & Birthplace** (☎ 714-993-3393; 18001 Yorba Linda Blvd; adult/student & senior over 62/child 8-11 $5.95/3.95/2; open 10am-5pm Mon-Sat, 11am-5pm Sun). Here you can watch a film called Never Give Up: Richard Nixon in the Arena, listen to carefully edited White House tapes from the Watergate era, see the pistol given to Nixon by Elvis Presley and view the telephone used to communicate with Apollo 11 astronauts while they were on the moon. There's also a re-creation of the Lincoln Sitting Room, Nixon's favorite area of the White House. To get to the library, exit east on Yorba Linda Blvd from Hwy 57 and continue straight to the museum.

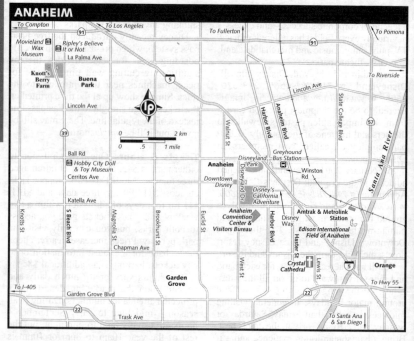

ANAHEIM

themes and stunts from the famous trilogy. Little ones will love climbing the stairways of the nearby Tarzan's Treehouse and imagining what arboreal life would be like.

Just beyond is **New Orleans Square** with such charming offerings as the Haunted Mansion where you'll be beguiled by hokey frights and sights. For relaxation, hop on the subterranean float and sail through the tawdry land of the Pirates of the Caribbean, where buccaneers' skeletons perch atop their mounds of booty.

Next up, **Frontierland** harkens back to the rip-roarin' Old West, when cowboys made their own kind of law and order. This is a low-key area of the park, and even small children will emerge unshaken after a ride on the Big Thunder Mountain Railroad roller coaster.

In the park's center, **Fantasyland** can be approached through Sleeping Beauty's Castle. It's filled with the characters of classic children's stories such as Dumbo the Elephant and Peter Pan. The amazing It's a Small World ride is a float past hundreds of animatronic children from all of the world's cultures singing the theme song of the place. Children are enthralled by this musical

voyage, but be warned: days after you've finished picking Disney popcorn out of your teeth, this song will still be batting around in your head. (The only sure antidote is listening to the entire collection of Led Zeppelin.) Another classic ride is the Matterhorn Bobsleds, a roller coaster that's gentle by today's standards, but fun nonetheless.

At the northern edge of the park, **Mickey's Toontown** is another favorite with the elementary school set. This is where Mickey and Minnie make their home (separate ones, of course; this *is* Disneyland), where Donald keeps his boat, Goofy has a Bounce House, Chip 'n Dale a Treehouse and Roger Rabbit invites you to a Car Toon Spin.

Disney's California Adventure The newest Disney park, right next to the original, may be smaller in size but not in imagination. Essentially paying homage to California, it has a spacious layout divided into three themed sections. After entering beneath a scale replica of the Golden Gate Bridge, you'll find the **Hollywood Studios Backlot** off to the left, while straight ahead is the thematic heart of the park, appropriately called

Moonrise under Cap Rock, Joshua Tree National Park

Joshua Tree National Park

Rugged peaks loom above Harmony Borax Works, Death Valley National Park

Death Valley National Park

Dunes and more dunes, Mesquite Flat, Death Valley National Park

Waxing surfboards in La Jolla

Old Point Loma Lighthouse, San Diego harbour

A 1950s Laguna Beach diner in Orange County

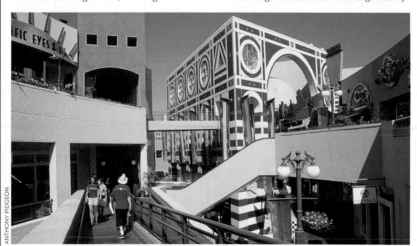

Downtown San Diego's Horton Plaza Center is the post-modern place to shop

Golden State. Beyond here, adjacent to a large lagoon, is **Pacific Pier** where you'll find most of the thrill rides.

The park sits on 55 acres and contains about two dozen attractions and rides, numerous restaurants and shops as well as a wine-tasting bar, sourdough bakery and tortilla factory. The one experience not to be missed is the astonishing Soarin' Over California, a virtual hang-gliding ride sure to give you 'bird-envy' as you float over the state's most beautiful landscapes and sights, including the Golden Gate Bridge and, of course, Disneyland itself.

For more birds-eye views of the park, head to the **Sun Wheel**, a giant Ferris wheel where each of the gondolas pitches and yaws as it makes its grand circuit. The park's wildest ride is aboard the aptly named California Screamin', a roller coaster, built around a Mickey Mouse silhouette.

The best of the shows is It's a Bugs Life, a hilarious yet oddly touching 3D extravaganza with some very tactile surprises. Another highlight is a stop in the **Golden Dreams cinema**, where an eerie embodiment of 'Whoopi Goldberg' takes you on an emotional yet informative journey through California history. Far from saccharine, the movie does not shy away from dark moments, including the exploitation of Chinese railroad workers and other minorities.

Downtown Disney This ¼mi-long walking mall presents a fun, though sanitized, mix of dining, shopping and entertainment venues. Highlights include a **House of Blues** (☎ 714-778-2583) for live concerts and Southern food; the **ESPN Zone** (☎ 714-300-3776), a vast sports and drinking emporium with 175 TV monitors (only dedicated sports fans will be able to tolerate this visual and aural onslaught); and **Y Arriba Y Arriba** (☎ 714-533-8272), a Latin restaurant and nightclub which sizzles with live music and dancing most nights.

Places to Stay
Even though Anaheim gets the biggest chunk of its business from Disneyland tourism, it is also a popular year-round convention destination, and room rates shift around accordingly. Many places offer packages that combine lodging with tickets to Disney and other area attractions.

Budget About S... the town of Fullert... (☎ 714-738-3721, fax ... full@aol.com; 1700 N Ha... beds members/nonmembers S... closed 11am-4pm). It's a clean an... facility in a Mediterranean home w... st 20 beds in three dorms, a nice porch, Internet access and kitchen facilities. Bus No 47 runs to the hostel from the Anaheim Greyhound station; from the Amtrak station, take bus No 111. Bus No 43 to and from Disneyland stops just down the street.

The area around Disneyland – especially Harbor Blvd and Katella Ave – teems with reasonably priced accommodations; all the major chains (Motel 6, Travelodge, Econo Lodge etc) are represented. Rooms here are reliably clean, have basic amenities and cost $70 or less, sometimes even with continental breakfast. Most are within walking distance to Disneyland and/or offer shuttle services to the parks. Prices may be slightly higher between May and October. The **Holiday Inn Express** (☎ 714-772-7755; 435 W Katella Ave) is reasonable.

Independent motels and hotels near Disneyland include **Alamo Inn** (☎ 714-635-8070, 800-378-9696, fax 714-778-3307; 1140 W Katella Ave; rooms $49-99) is generic but pleasant and has decent rates. Amenities include a small pool, indoor spa and free movies.

Tropicana Inn & Suites (☎ 714-635-4082, 800-828-4898; 1540 S Harbor Blvd; rooms $68-98) is large and better than average, very close to Disneyland, with friendly staff and breezy, nicely equipped rooms.

Mid-Range Castle Inn & Suites (☎ 714-774-8111, 800-227-8530, fax 714-956-4736; 1734 S Harbor Blvd; rooms $92-132) is a bit overpriced, but kids love the castle theme complete with gargoyles. The standard rooms are large but surprisingly bland.

Candy Cane Inn (☎ 714-774-5284, 800-345-7057, fax 714-772-5462; 1747 S Harbor Blvd; rooms $87-114) offers some of the best value around here. The welcoming grounds sport a profusion of flowers and, in addition to all mod-cons, rooms have such upscale extras as down comforters and plantation shutters. Free breakfast is provided.

The Anabella (☎ 714-905-1050, fax 714-905-1054; **w** www.anabellahotel.com; 1030

...ena Ave; rooms $79-149) offers a more 'adult' atmosphere. This gorgeous Spanish mission-style property has a classy restaurant, a palm-fringed pool and spa area and soothingly decorated rooms and suites.

Top End Disney's three big resort hotels are right next to the park. For reservations, call ☎ 714-956-6425 or ☎ 800-225-2024 or check w www.disneyland.com. One-night stands are expensive at $190 to $470, but multi-night and vacation packages usually save some money.

The most elegant of the trio is **Disney's Grand Californian Hotel** (☎ 714-635-2300, fax 714-300-7300; 1600 S Disneyland Dr), a beau-tiful place in Craftsman style with custom-made furnishings and a lobby of cathedral proportions. It's next to the California Adventure park and has its own entry gate.

Disneyland Hotel (☎ 714-778-6600, fax 714-956-6597; 1150 Magic Way) is more geared to families, who will enjoy the tropical pool area with a 110ft water slide and a pirate ship. Grown-ups can wind down the day with a cocktail at the Lost Bar lounge.

Disney's Paradise Pier Hotel (☎ 714-999-0990, 714-776-5763; 1717 S Disneyland Dr) has a vibrant flair and colorful decor, but is otherwise the least interesting of the three.

Places to Eat

Eating in the parks is expensive and the quality and service rarely match the price. In the original Disneyland park **Bengal Barbecue** is a snack bar serving chicken, steak and vegetable kebabs for around $3.50. For a bigger meal, one of the nicest places is the candlelit **Blue Bayou** (mains $23-29), where diners sample Louisiana-style cuisine while blending into the backdrop of the subterranean Pirates of the Caribbean voyage.

At Disney's California Adventure, one of the more reasonably priced places is the **Golden Vine Terrace**, which has outdoor seating and gourmet sandwiches and pastas for around $10.

Downtown Disney offers the best restaurant selection around here.

Rainforest Café (☎ 714-772-0413; mains $10-25) maintains a faraway tropical theme but serves a pan-American pastiche, including pizza, pasta, seafood and such.

Catal & Uva Bar (☎ 714-774-4442; bar mains $8-16, mains $16-26) has a chef who

plays competently with Mediterranean flavors and ingredients. The downstairs bar, with outdoor seating, is more casual and cheaper.

Choices are surprisingly slim away from the Disney domain, but here are a few worthwhile places: **Mimi's Café** (☎ 714-956-2223; 1400 S Harbor Blvd; meals $6.50-15) has pretty New Orleans-style decor so perky it might put you off your Prozac. Dig into large portions of inspired coffee shop fare, or get jolted into reality at the espresso bar. There are good pastries too.

Millie's (☎ 714-535-6892; 1480 S Harbor Blvd; mains $7-15) is another family restaurant. Come here if lines at Mimi's are too long. Great banana splits.

Cuban Pete's (☎ 714-490-2020; 1050 W Ball Rd; mains $12-25) may look like a Caribbean witch's castle, but inside it's all woodsy and decorated with photos of Old Havana. The cleverly spiced Cuban food is definitely more suited for grown-ups' palates.

Getting There & Away

The Anaheim Resort is just off I-5 on Harbor Blvd, about 30mi south of Downtown Los Angeles. The **Airport Bus** (☎ 800-772-5299; w www.airportbus.com) runs between LAX and Disneyland area hotels at least hourly ($16/25 one-way/round-trip).

Greyhound (☎ 714-999-1256; 100 W Winston Rd) has frequent departures to/from Downtown LA ($8.25, one to 1½ hours) and to San Diego ($14, 2¼ to three hours).

Amtrak trains stop at the depot next to Edison International Field of Anaheim. Tickets to/from LA's Union Station are $9.50 (45 minutes), to San Diego $20 (two hours).

AROUND ANAHEIM
Knott's Berry Farm

Just 4mi northwest of Disneyland, off the I-5, is this park (☎ 714-220-5200; w www .knotts.com; 8039 Beach Blvd, Buena Park; adult/senior & child 3-11 $40/30, after 4pm on days the park is open past 6pm admission $20/15). It is smaller and less frenetic than the Disneyland parks and is especially suited for families with pre-teen children. The thrill rides are not quite as intense and prices for food and souvenirs are more reasonable. Most people manage to 'do' Knott's on a one-day visit. Some rides have minimum height restrictions. Opening hours vary seasonally so call for specific details. Parking costs $8.

The park opened in 1932, when Mr Knott's boysenberries (a blackberry-raspberry hybrid) and Mrs Knott's fried-chicken dinners attracted crowds of local farmhands. Mr Knott built an imitation ghost town to keep them entertained and eventually hired local carnival rides and charged admission. Mrs Knott kept frying the chicken, but the rides and Old West buildings became the main attraction.

Today, the park still keeps the Old West theme alive at Ghost Town which features buildings brought here from actual historic mining towns in California and other western states. There are staged gun fights, gold-panning demonstrations and steam-train rides. Knott's also acknowledges pre-gold-rush history with Aztec dancers and a California missions exhibit – there's even mariachi music in Fiesta Village.

But it's the thrill rides that draw most people to Knott's. The newest of the bunch is 'Xcelerator', a '50s themed roller coaster that blasts you on a gut-wrenching journey aboard a fin-tailed, flame-emblazoned '57 Chevy, including a hair-raising twist at the top.

One of the best wooden roller coasters around is 'GhostRider', which hurtles you along a neck-breaking 4530ft track, at one time plunging you 108ft with a G-force of 3.14. Unfortunately this ride is insanely popular and lines can be very long.

Another mega-scream on the block is 'Perilous Plunge' which catapults you to a height of 127ft, then drops you down a 115ft water chute at a 75 degree angle. You *will* get soaked on this one. Also popular is 'Supreme Scream' which drops you 30 stories at 50mph with a G-force of 4, bouncing back upward with a G-force of -1.5, all in about 45 seconds.

For a tamer adventure, 'Big Foot Rapids' sloshes down a faux white-water river, leaving you absolutely drenched (unless they turn the waterfalls off, which happens in colder weather). 'Camp Snoopy' is a kiddy wonderland populated by Snoopy, Charlie Brown, Lucy, Linus and all the other Peanuts characters.

In October Knott's hosts what is regarded as Southern California's best and scariest Halloween party. Professional performers in costume haunt the park, special rides and attractions are put up for the occasion, and lights around the park are dimmed or turned off.

There are plenty of eateries within the park but the classic meal is of course a fried chicken and mashed potato dinner at **Mrs Knott's Chicken Dinner Restaurant** *(mains $15-20)*. It's in the California Marketplace, a shopping and dining mall just outside the park's main gate.

Next to Knott's is the affiliated **Soak City USA** *(☎ 714-220-5200; adult/child 3-11 $22.95/15.95, general admission after 3pm $12.95; open summer only)*, a popular water park with high-speed, tube and other slides.

Ripley's Believe It or Not & Movieland Wax Museum

These 'museums', one block north of Knott's, are pretty hokey tourist traps, although they too can be fun if you find yourself in a wacky state of mind. The more interesting of the two is **Ripley's** *(☎ 714-522-1152; 7850 Beach Blvd; adult/senior over 55/child 4-11 $8.95/6.95/5.25; open 11am-5pm Mon-Fri, 10am-6pm Sat & Sun, extended summer hours)*. Adventurer, reporter and collector Robert L Ripley traveled the globe in the 1920s and 1930s in search of curiosities. Some of these pieces of folk memorabilia and documentations of human oddities provide some twisted entertainment.

Movieland Wax Museum *(☎ 714-522-1155; 7711 Beach Blvd; adult/senior over 55/child 4-11 $12.95/10.55/6.95; open 10am-7:30pm Mon-Fri, 9am-8:30pm Sat & Sun, extended summer hours)*, across the street from Ripley's, is the usual dizzying maze of wax figures of celebrities, politicians and religious figures. The last tickets are sold 90 minutes before closing.

Combination tickets to both places are $16.90/13.95/9.75.

Hobby City Doll & Toy Museum

About 2mi south of Knott's, Hobby City is a cluster of 20 specialty art and craft shops, including an American Indian store in a log cabin and the Cabbage Patch Official Adoption Center. The Doll & Toy Museum *(☎ 714-527-2323; 1238 S Beach Blvd; adult/ concession $2/1; open 10am-6pm daily)*, housed in a half-scale model of the White House, offers the best entertainment value here. Along with every type of Barbie doll ever made, the museum has Russian dolls from the 1800s. Its toy replicas of TV, movie and sports personalities, rock stars and presidents present an interesting survey of pop culture in the US over the last 60 years.

Bowers Museum of Cultural Art

In a gracious 1932 mission-style complex in Santa Ana, this exquisite museum (☎ 714-567-3600; 2002 N Main St; permanent exhibit adult/student & child under 18 $5/free, special exhibit adult/senior & student/child 5-18 $14/10/8; open 10am-4pm Tues-Sun) has a rich permanent collection of pre-Columbian, African, Oceanic and Native American art, but gets its biggest crowds with its tantalizing and high-quality special exhibits. Recent examples include 'Egyptian Treasures from the British Museum' and 'The World of the Etruscans.'

Tickets are also good for the Kidseum (☎ 714-480-1520; 1802 N Main St; open 10am-4pm Sat & Sun, noon-5pm Tues-Sun July & Aug), one block south, which keeps youngsters entertained with hands-on exhibits relating to world cultures.

The Bowers has one of the best museum restaurants around. Called Tangata (☎ 714-550-0906; mains $8-15; open lunch Tues-Sun), it features a Mediterranean menu masterminded by Los Angeles star chef Joachim Splichal.

Crystal Cathedral

You needn't agree with televangelist Robert Schuller's teachings or be an 'Hour of Power' fan to appreciate the architecture of the Crystal Cathedral (☎ 714-971-4000; 12141 Lewis St), in Garden Grove, about 2mi southeast of Disneyland. Looking like a cross between a modern office complex and a science fiction movie set, the cathedral is built in the shape of a four-pointed star and boasts 10,661 windows, seating capacity for 3000 and an organ with 16,000 pipes.

Designed by Cleveland-born Philip Johnson, international-style architect turned postmodernist, the church anchors a vast campus of gardens, reflecting pools, fountains and sculpture. You can explore on your own or take a free 30-minute tour (offered regularly from 9am to 3:30pm Monday to Saturday). Don't miss the free-standing modern Gothic prayer chapel on the cathedral's north side; its pillars are made of eight different types of Italian marble and inside is a five-piece lead crystal cross that weighs 200lb.

Schuller's congregation is part of the protestant Reform Church of America, which originally worshipped at the Orange County Drive-In movie theater with Schuller preaching from atop the snack stand. His 'Hour of Power' is now broadcast on TV networks around the world.

The church's productions of the Glory of Christmas and the Glory of Easter are major fund-raisers. These are staged spectacles reenacting these biblical stories using live camels, flying angels and other theatrical gimmicks. For tickets call ☎ 714-544-5679.

Orange

The city of Orange (population 127,000), about 6mi southeast of Disneyland, is home to the mega-sized mall The Block at Orange (see the boxed text 'A Shopper's Paradise' later), but you'll find more charm in the town's historic center, called Old Towne Orange. It was originally laid out by Alfred Chapman and Andrew Glassell who, in 1869, received the 1 sq mi piece of real estate in lieu of legal fees. Here, surrounding a plaza (at the intersection of Chapman and Glassell Sts), is the best and most concentrated collection of antiques, collectibles and consignment shops in Orange County.

Fun places to browse include American Heritage (110 S Glassell St), which hawks Coke memorabilia, vintage gas pumps and old slot machines, and Happiness by the Bushel (128 N Glassell St), which has lots of low-key treasures. Alas, real bargains here and in the other stores are rare and unfortunately some dealers may try to pass off replicas as antiques, so caveat emptor.

The footsore can refuel at several coffee-houses around Plaza Square, including Starbucks and Diedrich Coffee. Next to the latter is Felix Continental Cafe (☎ 714-633-5842; meals $15-25), an Orange institution serving inexpensive Cuban dishes, in an informal ambience with great sidewalk seating.

Citrus City Grille (☎ 714-639-9600; 122 N Glassell St; lunch $8-12, dinner $13-26) is more upscale, chic and pricey, but the California cuisine is inventive and the menu loaded with interesting items.

From the Disneyland area, take OCTA bus No 43 (direction Costa Mesa) to Harbor & Chapman, then switch to bus No 54 to Lemon & Chapman. This will put you right into Old Towne Orange.

Little Saigon

The city of Westminster, southwest of Anaheim near the junction of I-405 and Hwy 22, is home to a large Vietnamese population, which has carved out its own vibrant commercial district around the intersection of Bolsa and Brookhurst Aves. Its heart is the **Asian Garden Mall** *(9200 Bolsa Ave)*, a behemoth of a structure. About 400 ethnic boutiques, including herbalists and jade jewelers, invite browsing on two floors.

One of the best of the many casual eateries here is **Pho 79** *(☎ 714-893-1883; dishes $4-15)*, on the lower level toward the mall's north entrance, which has a great variety of noodle and vegetable dishes. The *pho ga* (chicken noodle soup) is superb.

Glen Ivy Hot Springs

In Corona, technically just east of Orange County in Riverside County, is this lovely bathing complex *(☎ 888-258-2683; 25000 Glen Ivy Rd; admission Mon-Thur $25, Fri-Sun & holidays $35; open 9:30am-6pm during daylight savings time, 9:30am-5pm rest of year)*. Nicknamed 'Club Mud', it has 15 pools and spas filled with naturally heated mineral water and surrounded by 10 acres of landscaped grounds profuse with bougainvillea, eucalyptus and palm trees. You can wallow in the water, lounge in the saunas or steam rooms, take an aqua aerobics class, treat yourself to a massage (extra fee), or swim some laps in a larger swimming pool.

The best part here, though, is the red-clay mud pool. Like some prehistoric animal wandering into the tar pits, you first soak yourself in muck. Then, apply what amounts to a full-body mask by grabbing chunks of clay and smearing them all over your body before lounging in the sun until it's baked on to your skin. Whether this treatment truly has therapeutic effects is debatable, but it's certainly fun. And here's a tip for photos: you can shape the mud on your head into fantastic masks, horns and sci-fi shapes. Bring an old swim suit, though, as the clay does stain a little. Minimum age for entry is 16.

To get there, exit I-15 at Temescal Canyon Rd, turn right and drive 1mi to Glen Ivy Rd, then right again and go straight to the end.

Across the street, the **New Saigon Mall Cultural Court** marries commercialism and spirituality with its impressive display of statues and murals.

Orange County Beaches

The surfers, artists and retirees that inhabit Orange County's beach towns give the coast its own vibe, distinct from the rest of the county. The small communities strung along Pacific Coast Hwy are very relaxed despite the area's fast-paced development. Oil rigs sit about a mile offshore all along the coast and are scattered among the houses and businesses inland, giving the landscape a surreal appearance.

Accommodations get booked far in advance from June to early September, when prices rise and some places impose minimum stays of two or three nights.

Getting Around

An easy way to travel between Orange County's beach communities is aboard OCTA bus No 1 which connects Long Beach (part of Los Angeles; see that chapter for more information) and San Clemente via Pacific Coast Hwy about every 20 minutes midweek. The last northbound bus leaves San Clemente at 7:30pm, and the last southbound bus leaves Long Beach at 8:26pm. On weekends buses operate hourly and stop running one hour earlier.

LAGUNA BEACH

Secluded beaches, low cliffs, glassy waves, waterfront parks and eucalyptus-covered hillsides imbue Laguna Beach (population 23,700) with a Riviera-like feel and make it one of Southern California's most charming seaside resorts. The little town has a strong and long tradition in the arts and is home of several renowned festivals (see the boxed text 'Laguna Arts Festivals' later in this chapter) as well as the highly regarded **Laguna Playhouse** *(606 Laguna Canyon Rd)*. Public art abounds and there are several dozen galleries, a renowned art museum and a popular art walk tour on the first Thursday evening of the month. Laguna swells with tourists on summer weekends,

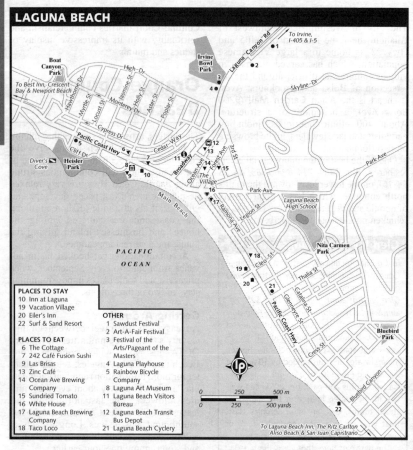

LAGUNA BEACH

PACIFIC
OCEAN

PLACES TO STAY
10 Inn at Laguna
19 Vacation Village
20 Eiler's Inn
22 Surf & Sand Resort

PLACES TO EAT
6 The Cottage
7 242 Café Fusion Sushi
9 Las Brisas
13 Zinc Café
14 Ocean Ave Brewing Company
15 Sundried Tomato
16 White House
17 Laguna Beach Brewing Company
18 Taco Loco

OTHER
1 Sawdust Festival
2 Art-A-Fair Festival
3 Festival of the Arts/Pageant of the Masters
4 Laguna Playhouse
5 Rainbow Bicycle Company
8 Laguna Art Museum
11 Laguna Beach Visitors Bureau
12 Laguna Beach Transit Bus Depot
21 Laguna Beach Cyclery

0   250   500 m
0   250   500 yards

To Laguna Beach Inn, The Ritz Carlton
Aliso Beach & San Juan Capistrano

but away from the Village (the central business district) and Main Beach (where the Village meets the shore), there's plenty of uncrowded sand and water.

History

Laguna's earliest inhabitants, the Ute-Aztecas and Shoshone tribes, called the area 'Lagonas' because of two freshwater lagoons in what is now Laguna Canyon. The name endured until 1904, when it was changed to Laguna. At roughly the same time, San Francisco artist Norman St Claire came to Laguna to paint watercolors of the surf, cliffs and hills. His enthusiasm attracted other artists who were influenced by French impressionism and they were known as the 'plein air' (as in 'outdoors')

school. The Laguna Beach Art Association was founded in 1918, and by the late '20s more than half of the town's 300 residents were artists.

The most lasting development began in Laguna Beach in 1926, when the Pacific Coast Hwy between Newport Beach and Dana Point opened, giving Laguna three access routes. Mary Pickford, Douglas Fairbanks, Mickey Rooney and Bette Davis vacationed here regularly and helped establish the Laguna Playhouse and the Festival of the Arts.

Orientation & Information

Laguna stretches for about 7mi along the Pacific Coast Hwy. Shops, restaurants and bars are concentrated along a ¼mi stretch in

Laguna Art Festivals

Laguna Beach's landmark event is the **Festival of the Arts,** a seven-week juried exhibit of 160 artists whose work varies from paintings to handcrafted furniture to scrimshaw. Begun in 1932 by local artists who needed to drum up buyers, the festival now attracts patrons and tourists from around the world. In addition to the art, there are free daily artists' workshops, a children's art gallery and live entertainment. The grounds at 650 Laguna Canyon Rd are open 10am (closing hours vary) daily July to August; admission for adults is $5, seniors and students $3.

The most amazing aspect of the fair, and a tremendous experience that will leave you rubbing your eyes in disbelief, is the **Pageant of the Masters** *(tickets at ☎ 949-497-6582, 800-487-3378;* W *www.foapom.com; admission $15-65),* where human models are blended seamlessly into re-creations of famous paintings. This also began in 1933 as a sideshow to the main festival. Tickets need to be ordered weeks in advance, though you may be able to pick up last-minute cancellations at the gate. Nightly performances begin at 8:30pm.

In the '60s Laguna Beach artists who did not get into the juried exhibition started their own festival to take advantage of the art seekers passing through town. They set up directly across from the festival (at 935 Laguna Canyon Rd), mocking its formal atmosphere by scattering sawdust on the ground. Thus, the so-called **Sawdust Festival** *(☎ 949-494-3030;* W *www.sawdustartfestival.org; adult/senior/child $6.50/5.50/2; open 10am-10pm)* was born. It is juried now but it still has arts and crafts that are utilitarian and quite affordable.

A third art happening, the **Art-A-Fair Festival** *(☎ 949-494-4514; 777 Laguna Canyon Rd; adult/student & senior $5/3; open 10am-9pm or 10pm)* runs simultaneously. It is a nationally juried show focused mainly on watercolors, pastels and oil paintings, although photography, jewelry, ceramics and other arts and crafts are displayed as well.

the Village, along three parallel streets (Broadway, Ocean and Forest).

The **Laguna Beach Visitors Bureau** *(☎ 949-497-9229, 800-877-1115, fax 949-376-0558;* W *www.lagunabeachinfo.org; 252 Broadway; open 9am-5pm Mon-Fri, 11am-3pm Sat, 11am-3pm Sun July & Aug only)* has helpful staff and lots of pamphlets. The free weekly *Coastline News* is a good source for local news and events.

Parking is a perpetual problem around here. If you're spending the night, leave your car at the hotel and use the bus (see Getting Around). Parking lots in the Village charge $10 or more per entry and fill up quickly in summer.

Laguna Art Museum

This breezy museum *(☎ 949-494-8971; 307 Cliff Dr; adult/concession/child under 12 Wed-Mon $5/4/free, admission Tues free; open 11am-5pm Tues-Sun)* has changing exhibits usually featuring one or two California artists and a permanent collection heavy on California landscapes, vintage photographs and works by early Laguna artists. There are free docent tours at 2pm and an interesting gift shop.

Beaches

Laguna Beach has 30 public beaches and coves. Most are accessible by stairs off Pacific Coast Hwy; just look for the 'beach access' signs. **Main Beach** has volleyball and basketball courts and is best for swimming. Just north, the bluff-top Heisler Park gives access to several coves, including **Diver's Cove**, a deep protected inlet popular with guess who. **Crescent Bay**, north of town, has big hollow waves good for bodysurfing but parking is difficult here; try the bluffs atop the beach.

About 1mi south of the Village, **Victoria Beach** has volleyball courts and La Tour, a Rapunzel's tower-like structure from 1926. Take the stairs down Victoria Dr; there's limited parking on Pacific Coast Hwy. Nearby **Aliso Beach** has a fair amount of parking and is popular with surfers, as is Salt Creek Beach in Laguna Niguel.

Places to Stay

Best Inn *(☎ 949-494-6464, 877-363-7229; 1404 N Coast Hwy; rooms $64-94, in summer $99-159)* is about 1mi northwest of the Village and is a friendly, better-than-average motel.

Laguna Beach Inn (☎ 949-494-5450, 800-504-7678; 2020 S Coast Hwy; rooms $89-99, in summer $129-149) is a well-kept, horseshoe-shaped place with standard rooms about 1¼mi southeast of the Village.

Vacation Village (☎ 949-494-8566, 800-843-6895; w www.vacationvillage.com; 647 S Coast Hwy; rooms & suites $83-251, in summer $92-339), southeast of the Village, is a family-friendly place with 130 units, about half of them with kitchens, plus a pool and spa.

Eiler's Inn (☎ 949-494-3004, fax 949-497-2215; 741 S Coast Hwy; rooms $95-220) is a romantic B&B stuffed with antiques, fluffy pillows and flowery wallpaper. The dozen rooms wrap around a fountain courtyard where wine and cheese are served in the afternoon. Breakfast should keep you fed until the afternoon.

Surf & Sand Resort (☎ 949-497-4477, 800-524-8621, fax 949-494-7653; w www.surfandsandresort.com; 1555 S Coast Hwy; rooms $225-375) sports a natural color scheme and luxurious rooms with all the trappings. Some rooms have views of the private beach and ocean. The new spa beckons with a wide range of soothing treatments.

Inn at Laguna (☎ 949-497-9722, 800-544-4479, fax 949-497-9972; 211 N Coast Hwy; rooms $99-499, in summer $149-529) has rooms of various sizes and views, but all have a fresh, new look complete with French blinds and thick featherbeds. Special amenities include an in-room VCR, CD player, bathrobes and a continental breakfast delivered to your room.

The Ritz-Carlton (☎ 949-240-2000, 800-241-3333, fax 949-240-0829; rooms $395-695), about 4mi south of town in the community of Laguna Niguel, offers lap-of-luxury accommodations in an opulent setting. The most affordable experience here is a drink in the Lobby Lounge – a grand place to watch the sunset.

Places to Eat

Zinc Café (☎ 949-494-6302; 350 Ocean Ave; dishes $2-7) has a hedge-enclosed patio and a healthful breakfast and lunch menu with plenty of meatless selections. It's self-serve.

Taco Loco (☎ 949-497-1635; 640 S Coast Hwy; dishes $3-9) is a self-service sidewalk café that appeals to surfers, the budget-conscious and those wanting a late-night

snack. Mexican fare forms the core of the menu, which also includes the exotic 'hemp' burger and the blackened mushroom and tofu burger.

Las Brisas (☎ 949-497-5434; 361 Cliff Dr; mains $11-20), a Laguna institution with great ocean views, serves Mexican seafood in the dining room and snacks ($7-12) on the patio. The nacho platter easily feeds two. Breakfast, Sunday brunch and the weekday happy hour are popular.

The Cottage (☎ 949-494-3023; 208 N Coast Hwy; breakfast & lunch $5-10, dinner $11-17) has a 'grandma's living-room' look plus a large patio. Breakfast is served until 3pm (try the cranberry-orange pancakes); otherwise it's meaty American classics and pasta.

242 Café Fusion Sushi (☎ 949-494-2444; 242 N Coast Hwy; dinner $18), helmed by a skilled sushi chef, makes some of the best fishy morsels in town.

Sundried Tomato (☎ 949-494-3312; 361 Forest Ave; lunch $5-10, dinner $7-24) pairs a crisp Euro look with a casual patio. The food's all Californian, though, with interesting salads, pastas and sandwiches.

White House (☎ 949-494-8088; 340 S Coast Hwy; lunch $6.50-10.50, dinner $8-23) serves contemporary food and turns into a bar and nightclub after dark, often with live music. More entertainment is provided by Laguna's two microbrewery pubs, the **Laguna Beach Brewing Company** (422 S Coast Hwy) and the **Ocean Ave Brewing Company** (237 Ocean Ave). Both have indoor and outdoor seating and serve decent pub grub.

Getting There & Around

To reach Laguna Beach from the I-405, take Hwy 133 (Laguna Canyon Rd) west. Laguna is served by OCTA bus No 1.

Laguna Beach Transit (☎ 949-497-0746) has its central bus depot on Broadway, just north of the visitors bureau in the heart of the village. It operates three routes at hourly intervals (no service between noon and 1pm and on Sunday). For visitors, the most important is the Blue Line which travels to the hotels and beaches along Pacific Coast Hwy, terminating at the Ritz-Carlton hotel. Each ride is $0.75.

Bicycle rental places include **Laguna Beach Cyclery** (☎ 949-494-1522; 240 Thalia St) and **Rainbow Bicycle Co** (☎ 949-494-

5806; 485 N Coast Hwy). The cost of a 24-hour rental is about $20 for cruisers and $25 to $35 for mountain bikes.

AROUND LAGUNA BEACH

Dana Point is not merely another beach community 8mi south of Laguna Beach, its harbor is also one of the departure points for ferries to Mediterranean-flavored Santa Catalina Island (see the Los Angeles chapter for more information on this island), which beckons about 26mi offshore. The **Catalina Explorer** (☎ 877-432-6276; **W** *www.catalina ferry.com)* shuttles across the channel into Avalon at 9am daily with return trips scheduled to leave at 5pm (adult/child round-trip $41/31, 1¼ hours). Boats operate from Friday to Sunday in April and May and daily from July to mid-September. From June to mid-September, there's also shuttle service from Avalon to Two Harbors, which accesses the island's hinterland (additional $25/15, one hour).

San Juan Capistrano

This little town, about 10mi south and inland of Laguna Beach, is home to the extraordinary **Mission San Juan Capistrano** (☎ 949-234-1300; *31882 Camino Capistrano; adult/concession/child $6/5/4; open 8:30am-5pm daily),* one of California's most visited and most beautiful missions. The charming Serra Chapel – whitewashed and decorated with colorful symbols – is the only building still standing in which Father Junipero Serra said Mass. Serra founded this mission on 1 November, 1776, and tended it personally for many years. With access to San Clemente harbor, and as the only development between San Diego and Los Angeles, this was one of the most important missions in the chain. Like many others, it was largely self-sustaining and had its own mills, granaries, livestock, crops and other small industries.

Plan on spending at least an hour looking at the sprawling grounds – with lush gardens, fountains and courtyards – and mission structures, including the padre's quarters, soldiers' barracks, cemetery and Great Stone Church. The gift shop has materials on early California and mission history.

San Juan Capistrano is also where the legendary swallows return each year to nest – on 19 March, the feast of Saint Joseph – after wintering in South America, just as the song says. The Festival of the Swallows is the highlight of the mission's active year-round events schedule. The birds hang around until 23 October and are best observed at feeding time, usually early in the morning and late afternoon, early evening.

Camino Capistrano, leading up to the mission, is lined with souvenir shops, galleries and restaurants. One block west of here, next to the Capistrano train depot, the **Los Rios Historic District** is a cutesy assemblage of 31 historic cottages and adobes now mostly housing cafés and gift shops. **The Coach House** (☎ 949-496-8930; *33157 Camino Capistrano)* is a well-known live entertainment venue featuring a roster of local and regional rock and alternative bands.

Getting There & Away From Laguna Beach, take bus No 1 south to K-Mart Plaza, then connect to bus No 191/A direction Mission Viejo which drops you near the mission ($2, one hour). The Amtrak depot is one block south and west of the mission. Drivers should exit I-5 at Ortega Hwy and head west for about a ¼mi.

NEWPORT BEACH

Newport Beach (population 72,000) is the largest and most sophisticated of Orange County's beach towns, with one of the biggest pleasure craft harbors in the US as well as some fun shopping in town and at the big Fashion Island mall.

Pacific Coast Hwy passes through the part of Newport that centers around harbor activity, with boat dealerships and charters, yacht clubs and seafood restaurants clustered in buildings that once served as shipping warehouses for the Irvine Ranch (a large sheep-raising and tenant farming operation that was part of the original Spanish land grant on which Irvine was built).

South of Pacific Coast Hwy via Balboa Blvd, the Balboa Peninsula makes a natural 6mi barrier between Newport Harbor and the ocean. Most tourist activity is centered here, including beaches and the Balboa Fun Zone. The two largest harbor islands are Lido Isle, an upscale residential zone, and Balboa Island, which has fun boutiques and eateries along Marine Ave. There's more shopping north of Pacific Coast Hwy at

Fashion Island, a vast mall with multiplex movie theaters and numerous restaurants.

The week before Christmas brings thousands of spectators to Newport Harbor to watch the nightly Christmas Boat Parade, a tradition begun in 1919. The 2½ hour parade of lighted and decorated boats begins at 6:30pm. You can watch it all for free from the Fun Zone or Balboa Island or from a

A Shopper's Paradise

Besides boasting Disneyland and the beaches, Orange County prides itself on being Southern California's shopping capital. The area brims with enormous, attractively designed malls, complete with fountains, restaurants, movie theaters, shops and entertainment.

South Coast Plaza is a snazzy center at 3333 Bristol St (exit I-405 at Bristol) in the town of Costa Mesa that grosses more than any other mall in the US. Price tags at big-name designers such as Chanel, Escada and Prada do their part to establish the record.

Further south, in Newport Beach, **Fashion Island** (550 Newport Center Dr) has a relaxed open-air setting with 200 stores, a multiplex cinema and several good restaurants.

The **Irvine Spectrum Center**, at the confluence of I-5 and I-405 on Irvine Center Dr, is comparatively small but has an IMAX theater and a courtyard inspired by the Alhambra in Granada, Spain.

The megasize **Block at Orange** tries to prove that biggest is best with 800,000 sq ft of open-air promenade, a Gameworks arcade featuring state-of-the-art video games, a skate park and a 30-screen multiplex, plus myriad stores and eateries.

The newest mall is **MainPlace Santa Ana** (2800 N Main St), a complex housing 190 stores plus three department stores; it's connected to hotels in the Disneyland area by a shuttle ($2.50 round-trip).

If all this is too much mall for you, perhaps a visit to **The Lab Anti-Mall**, 2930 Bristol St, Costa Mesa, is in order. Conceived in 1993 to bring 'urban culture' to quintessentially suburban Orange County, it's housed in a refurbished factory occupied by 'alternative,' youth-oriented stores such as Na Na and Urban Outfitters.

passenger boat for about $8 (reservations ☎ 949-673-5245). For general information call ☎ 949-729-4400.

Orientation & Information

Hwy 55 (Newport Blvd) is the main access road from I-405. It intersects with Pacific Coast Hwy, then merges with Balboa Blvd leading to the eastern tip of the Balboa Peninsula. Hwy 73 (the Corona del Mar Fwy) also connects the I-405 with Newport Beach, before continuing as a toll road to Laguna Beach and beyond.

The **Newport Beach Conference & Visitors Bureau** (☎ 949-722-1611, 800-942-6278, fax 949-722-1612; w www.newport beach-cvb.com; 3300 W Pacific Coast Hwy), near the junction of Hwy 55 and Pacific Coast Hwy, has good lodging and dining guides and a detailed map of the town.

Balboa Peninsula & Island

This strip of land, about 6mi long and a ¼mi wide, has a white sand beach on its ocean side and stylish homes, including the 1926 **Lovell House** (1242 W Ocean Front). Designed by Rudolph Schindler, one of Southern California's most seminal modernist architects, it was built using site-cast concrete frames with wood.

Hotels, restaurants and bars cluster around the peninsula's two piers: Newport Pier, near its western end, and Balboa Pier east of here. Near the latter is the **Balboa Fun Zone**, which has delighted locals and visitors since 1936. There's a small Ferris wheel, arcade games, touristy shops and restaurants as well as the landmark 1905 **Balboa Pavilion**, which is beautifully illuminated at night. The Fun Zone is also the place to catch a harbor cruise, fishing or whale-watching excursion, the catamaran to Catalina Island (departs daily at 9am, $37 round-trip) or the ferry to Balboa Island just across the channel.

At the very tip of the peninsula, by the West Jetty, is **The Wedge**, a bodysurfing and knee-boarding spot famous for its perfectly hollow waves that can get up to 30ft high. This is *not* a good place for learning how to handle the currents; newcomers should head a few blocks west for calmer water.

The Balboa Fun Zone is connected to **Balboa Island** via a tiny car and passenger ferry, which operates around the clock

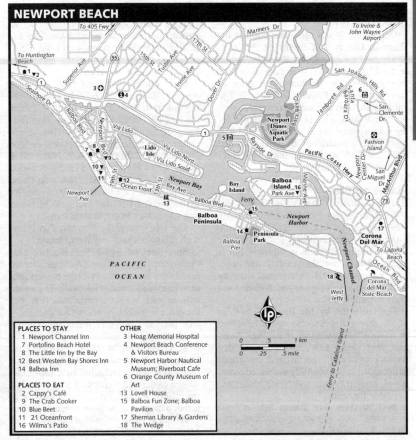

NEWPORT BEACH

To 405 Fwy
To Irvine &
John Wayne Airport
Mariners Dr
To Huntington Beach
San Joaquin Hills Rd
Superior Ave
75th St
Tustin Ave
17th St
Irvine Ave
Dover Dr
San Clemente Dr
Seashore Dr
Balboa Blvd
Via Lido
Via Lido Nord
Via Lido Soud
Lido Isle
Newport Dunes Aquatic Park
Back Bay Dr
Jamboree Rd
Santa Barbara Dr
Fashion Island
Newport Bay
Bayside Dr
Pacific Coast Hwy
Newport Center Dr
San Miguel Dr
MacArthur Blvd
Newport Pier
Ocean Front
Bay Ave
Balboa Blvd
Bay Island
Balboa Island
Park Ave
Marine Ave
Newport Bay
Ferry
Balboa Peninsula
Newport Harbor
Corona Del Mar
To Laguna Beach
Peninsula Park
Balboa Pier
Newport Channel
Ocean Blvd
PACIFIC OCEAN
West Jetty
Corona del Mar State Beach
Ferry to Catalina Island

0   .5   1 km
0   .25   .5 mile

PLACES TO STAY
1 Newport Channel Inn
7 Portofino Beach Hotel
8 The Little Inn by the Bay
12 Best Western Bay Shores Inn
14 Balboa Inn

PLACES TO EAT
2 Cappy's Café
9 The Crab Cooker
10 Blue Beet
11 21 Oceanfront
16 Wilma's Patio

OTHER
3 Hoag Memorial Hospital
4 Newport Beach Conference & Visitors Bureau
5 Newport Harbor Nautical Museum; Riverboat Cafe
6 Orange County Museum of Art
13 Lovell House
15 Balboa Fun Zone; Balboa Pavilion
17 Sherman Library & Gardens
18 The Wedge

($1.25 for car and driver, $0.50 per person). It lands at Agate Ave, about 11 blocks west of Marine Ave, the main drag lined with cutesy stores, cafés and restaurants. For close-ups of the island's many beautiful homes, take a stroll along its shoreline; it's about 1½mi around.

Museums
Near Fashion Island, the **Orange County Museum of Art** (☎ 949-759-1122; 850 San Clemente Dr; adult/concession/child under 16 $5/4/free; open 11am-5pm Tues-Sun) provides a survey of California art and cutting-edge contemporary exhibits. It's supplemented by a sculpture garden, gift shop and a theater screening classic, foreign and art-related films.

The **Newport Harbor Nautical Museum** (☎ 949-673-7863; 151 E Coast Hwy; admission free; open 10am-5pm Tues-Sun), housed in a stern-wheeler, documents the re-gion's maritime heritage through old-timey photographs, ship models, paintings and memorabilia.

Corona del Mar
A ritzy bedroom community with elegant stores and restaurants, Corona del Mar is spread along Pacific Coast Hwy and hugs the eastern flank of the Newport Channel. The beach here lies at the foot of rocky cliffs. Children love the tide pools at Little Corona Beach. There are restrooms and volleyball courts. Parking costs $6 per vehicle, though you may be able to find free

spaces atop the cliffs behind the beach along Ocean Blvd.

Corona del Mar's prize attraction is the **Sherman Library & Gardens** (☎ 949-673-2261; 2647 E Pacific Coast Hwy; adult/child under 12 Tues-Sun $3/free, admission Mon free; gardens open 10:30am-4pm daily, library open 9am-4:30pm Tues-Thur). The gardens are lush and well maintained, with profuse orchids, a koi pond and a garden for the visually impaired. The small research library holds a wealth of California historical documents, as well as paintings by early California landscape artists.

Places to Stay

Newport Channel Inn (☎ 949-642-3030, 800-255-8614, fax 949-650-2666; w www .newportchannelinn.com; 6030 W Pacific Coast Hwy; rooms in winter $59, in summer $79) sits right on the busy highway but is just one block from the beach. It has large, fully-equipped motel-style rooms sleeping from two to seven people and friendly and knowledgeable hosts.

The Little Inn by the Bay (☎ 949-673-8800, 800-438-4466, fax 949-673-4943; w www.littleinnbythebay.com; 2627 Newport Blvd; rooms $79-229) starts your day with a continental breakfast and newspaper delivered to your cheerfully decorated room. Bikes, boogie boards and beach chairs are available for rent.

Best Western Bay Shores Inn (☎ 949-675-3463, 800-222-6675, fax 949-675-4977; w www.thebestinn.com; 1800 W Balboa Blvd; rooms $109-269) has smallish, but nicely equipped rooms with nautical decor. Rates include breakfast, in-room movies and beach gear. Rooms with bay or ocean views are $10 to $30 extra.

Portofino Beach Hotel (☎ 949-673-7030, 800-571-8749, fax 949-723-4370; w www .portofinobeachhotel.com; 2306 W Oceanfront; rooms $130-300) is a small and old-fashioned place right on the beach. Rooms, all with marble baths, are a bit on the stuffy side, especially those with fireplaces; some have ocean views.

Balboa Inn (☎ 949-675-3412, 877-225-2629, fax 949-673-4587; w www.balboainn .com; 105 Main St; standard rooms from $169), in a 1929 landmark building near Balboa Pier, is a lovely hotel with European touches.

Places to Eat

Cappy's Café (☎ 949-646-4202; 5930 W Pacific Coast Hwy; breakfast & lunch $5-13) gets an enthusiastic thumbs up from locals for its scrumptious omelets and other cholesterol-feast breakfasts.

Crab Cooker (☎ 949-673-0100; 2200 Newport Blvd; mains $7-22) has been dishing out fresh, fishy fare since 1951. Tables are always packed at this unpretentious hangout, although environmentalists might cringe at the paper plates and plastic cutlery.

Riverboat Café (☎ 949-673-3425; 151 E Pacific Coast Hwy; mains $13-25) is a nice place for a romantic dinner that won't bust the budget. It's on the same stern-wheeler as the Newport Harbor Nautical Museum and specializes in continental cuisine.

The area around the Newport Pier brims with dining options – casual to fancy.

Blue Beet (☎ 949-675-2338; 107 21st Place; lunch $4-8, dinner $7-19) gets its relaxed vibe from framed vintage posters, big armchairs and a red-brick wall. The menu entices with burgers, pasta and fish, but the place is really best known for its nightly live jazz and blues concerts (occasional cover charge).

21 Oceanfront (☎ 949-673-2100; 2100 W Oceanfront; dinner $20-60) is primo for fish and seafood, including such rarities as beluga caviar and abalone. It's all served in the refined ambience of an overstuffed Victorian dining room with an ocean-view bar.

Wilma's Patio (☎ 949-675-5542; 203 Marine Ave; dishes $6.50-15) is a family-style institution on Balboa Island serving big burgers, roast chicken, pasta and other satisfying classics.

Getting Around

OCTA bus No 71 stops at the corner of Pacific Coast Hwy and Newport Blvd and goes south to the end of the Balboa Peninsula. Bus No 57 goes north to South Coast Plaza in Costa Mesa.

HUNTINGTON BEACH

Ever since Hawaiian-Irish surfing star George Freeth ('imported' by pioneer developer, Henry Huntington) gave surfing demonstrations here in 1914, Huntington Beach (population 189,000) has been one of Southern California's most popular surf destinations. In fact, it earned the title 'Surf City,

USA' from rock and roll surf daddies Jan and Dean. In September the Huntington Beach Pro/Am Surf Series Championship – a landmark event in the sport – takes place just south of the Huntington Beach Pier. Also look for the **Surfing Walk of Fame** at the corner of Pacific Coast Hwy and Main St), which immortalizes mostly local legends.

Huntington is also home to the **International Surfing Museum** (☎ *714-960-3483; 411 Olive St; adult/concession $2/1; open noon-5pm Wed-Sun)*, off Main St. One of the few of its kind in California, it is an entertaining mecca for surf-culture enthusiasts. Exhibits chronicle the sport's history with photos, early surfboards and surf wear, and surf music recordings by the Beach Boys, Jan and Dean and the Ventures. There is also an interesting display about women of surf.

Once the least polished and most low-key of Orange County's beach towns, gentrification has definitely arrived in Huntington. Along lower Main St, old-fashioned surf culture meets sleek new-millennium cookie-cutter architecture enlivened by numerous cafés, bars and casual restaurants. For maps and information, drop in to the **Visitors Bureau** (☎ *714-969-3492, 800-729-6232, fax 714-969-5592;* W *www.hbvisit.com; 417 Main St; open 9am-5pm Mon-Fri)*.

Bolsa Chica State Beach & Ecological Preserve

The 3mi stretch of Pacific Coast Hwy north of Huntington toward Seal Beach is flanked on one side by **Bolsa Chica State Beach**, which has dark and dusty sand facing a monstrous oil rig half mile off shore. On the other side of the highway is the **Bolsa Chica State Ecological Preserve**, which looks rather desolate (especially with the few small oil wells scattered about) but actually teems with bird life. Terns, mergansers, pelicans, pintails, grebes and endangered Belding's Savannah sparrows congregate among the pickleweed and cordgrass in a restored salt marsh. A 1½mi loop trail starts from the parking lot on Pacific Coast Hwy.

Places to Stay & Eat

Colonial Inn Hostel (☎ *714-536-3315, fax 714-536-9585;* W *www.huntingtonbeach hostel.com; 421 8th St; bunks $18, singles/* doubles per person $21)*, in a 1906 home three blocks from the beach, is the area's only hostel, and it's a peach. Dorms sleep three to eight people and communal areas include a nice kitchen, a living room and backyard. There's a laundry, Internet access, and free surfboard and bike rentals.

Sun 'n' Sands Motel (☎ *714-536-2543; 1102 Pacific Coast Hwy; rooms $69-149)* is one of a few budget motels across from the beach. It has nice, clean rooms and a pool.

Quality Inn (☎ *714-536-7500; 800 Pacific Coast Hwy; rooms $80-130)* is a handsome property with dependably clean rooms, each with cable TV, refrigerator and at least a partial ocean view. The rooftop Jacuzzi and free continental breakfast are pleasant touches.

Lower Main St is packed with casual eateries catering to the surfing crowd. Options include the **Sugar Shack** (☎ *714-536-0355; 213 Main St; dishes $5-10)*, a breakfast and lunch institution where local artifacts decorate the walls, and **Wahoo's Fish Taco** *(120 Main St; dishes $2-7)*, where you can fill up cheaply on tasty and healthy Mexican food or rice bowls with various toppings.

SEAL BEACH

Seal Beach (population 25,100) is refreshingly noncommercial, with a great beach and a charming and very walkable downtown area. It stretches along a few blocks of Main St, between Ocean Ave, which skirts the beach, and Pacific Coast Hwy. Along here are several restaurants as well as some interesting antique and consignment clothing stores. The historic **Bay Theater** (☎ *562-431-9988; 340 Main St)* occasionally hosts concerts performed on the theater's Wurlitzer organ.

Main St spills into the **Seal Beach Pier**, jutting out 1885ft over the ocean. The current pier, built in 1985, replaced the 1906 original, which fell victim to winter storms in the early 1980s.

Seal Beach's **chamber of commerce** (☎ *562-799-0179, fax 562-795-5637; 201 8th St, Suite 120)* dispenses lodging and other information but only about its members.

Seal Beach is also home to a huge US naval weapons station and to Leisure World, one of Southern California's first and most exclusive retirement communities.

Los Angeles

LOS ANGELES

Overwhelming. Intimidating. Frightening. Or even, where *is* it? No other city on earth is so talked about, yet so misunderstood. Los Angeles (city population 3.7 million, county population 9.5 million) is feared for its natural disasters, dreaded for its crime and violence, disparaged for its jammed freeways and poor air quality and scorned for what some call a plastic personality.

Here's the deal: LA is not an easy place to grasp. It doesn't feel like any city you've ever known. It's vast and amorphous, with no clearly defined center. But the key to understanding – and appreciating – the place is to throw out the notion that it's a city at all. In fact, it's a conglomeration of 88 independent cities, some of them with quite distinct identities (Santa Monica, Pasadena and Long Beach among them), many others merely nondescript sprawls, blending anonymously into the urban maelstrom.

What makes LA so fascinating is its wealth of human experience, its rich menu of intriguing flavors and textures. Anytime the mood strikes, you can explore a different culture, food, music – or even a historical period – simply by driving a few miles across town. Savor authentic chow mein in Chinatown, top-notch sushi in Little Tokyo, matzo soup in the Fairfax District or California cuisine in Beverly Hills. Dancing? You could don zoot suits and do the jitterbug or go for salsa and merengue, or perhaps just good old-fashioned rock and roll. Watch Pacific Islanders perform in their traditional costumes, jam with jazz greats on Central Ave or wave at celebrities in the Hollywood Christmas Parade. Impressionist paintings at the Getty Center, indigenous pottery at the Southwest Museum, Latino murals in East LA...the choices are endless. One thing's for sure: 'boredom' does not appear in the LA lexicon.

HISTORY

The earliest residents of the LA area were the Gabrielino and Chumash Indians, who arrived between 5000 and 6000 BC. The Gabrielinos were hunter-gatherers who lived inland (their staple food was the acorn, finely ground and made into bread or porridge), while the Chumash lived on the coast as sea trawlers.

Highlights

- Sun, swim and surf at Zuma, Santa Monica or Manhattan Beach

- Feast your eyes on Old Masters and new visions at the Huntington, LACMA, Norton Simon and Getty Center art museums

- Get close up – if not personal – with your favorite sitcom star during a live taping

- Discover LA's 'wild side' during a hike in the Santa Monica Mountains

- Come to the Venice Boardwalk for the ultimate SoCal beach scene

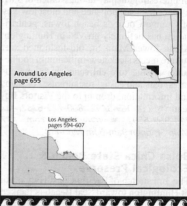

Around Los Angeles
page 655

Los Angeles
pages 594-607

The first European known to have laid eyes upon the Los Angeles Basin was Juan Rodríguez Cabrillo, who sailed the coast in 1542. From Santa Monica Bay, he observed a brown haze over the landscape – from campfires at the Gabrielino village of Yangna – and called the bay Bahia de los Fumos, or 'Bay of Smokes.'

The Mission Period

Greater LA has two missions: Mission San Gabriel Archangel (1771) and Mission San Fernando Rey de España (1797). Both have been restored and can be visited. The Gabrielinos who gathered at these missions had no previous concept of heaven or hell but began trading hard labor for supposed salvation. In the process, they were exposed to a variety of diseases that decimated the tribes.

In 1781 the missions embarked on a plan to create separate agricultural communities to produce food and support the missions' expansion. Forty-four *pobladores* (settlers) were assigned from San Gabriel to establish a new town near the village of Yangna, on the banks of a cottonwood-lined stream about 9mi southwest of the mission. The town they established, El Pueblo de Nuestro Señora la Reina de los Angeles del Río Porciúncula (The Town of Our Lady the Queen of the Angels of the Porciuncula River), was named for a saint whose feast day had just been celebrated.

Los Angeles, as the pueblo became known, grew into a thriving farming community. Taking full advantage of long sunny days, the settlers developed orange and olive groves, vineyards and wheat fields and sustained cattle, sheep and horses.

Rancho Period

Joseph Chapman, a blond Boston millwright-cum-pirate, became the first Yankee Angeleno in 1818; he was known as El Inglés, 'the Englishman.' Others followed slowly; by the mid-1830s, there were still only 29 US citizens in Los Angeles. But these few bought entire shiploads of imported goods from seafarers in exchange for full cargoes of hides. In setting up a system of credit for rancheros, they essentially established California's first banking system.

Jedediah Smith, who established the first overland route to the western states, arrived at Mission San Gabriel Archangel in 1826. Kit Carson, a legend of the American West, helped pave the Santa Fe Trail to Los Angeles in 1832. But most Easterners didn't know much about Los Angeles until 1840, when Richard Henry Dana's *Two Years Before the Mast* gave an account of his mid-1830s experience in the coastal hide-and-tallow trade. 'In the hands of an enterprising people, what a country this might be', Dana wrote of Los Angeles, then with a population of just over 1200.

From Small Town to Big City

With California statehood, LA was incorporated on April 4, 1850. It was an unruly city of dirt streets and adobe homes, of saloons, brothels and gambling houses that thrived on the fast buck. But by 1854, Northern California's gold rush had peaked, and the state was thrust into a depression. As unemployed miners swarmed to LA and other cities, banks and businesses that had harnessed their futures to miners' fortunes closed their doors.

But a bit of wheeling and dealing brought a railroad spur line to LA in 1876, via the San Joaquin Valley. In 1885 the Atchison, Topeka & Santa Fe Railroad directly linked LA across the Arizona desert to the East Coast.

Coinciding with the arrival of the railroad was the establishment of the citrus industry in Southern California. As California oranges found their way onto New York grocery shelves, coupled with a hard-sell advertising campaign, Easterners heeded the advice of crusading editor Horace Greeley to 'Go West, young man.' LA's population jumped from 2300 in 1860 to 11,000 in 1880 and more than 50,000 in 1890. It reached 100,000 in 1900. Never mind that LA didn't have a natural harbor or a supply of fresh water adequate to support even a small town.

The first of these needs was addressed by the construction of a harbor at San Pedro, 23mi south of City Hall. Work began in 1899; the first wharf opened in 1914, the year the Panama Canal was completed, which suddenly made San Pedro 8000mi closer to the Atlantic seaboard. It soon became the busiest harbor on the West Coast.

Bringing drinking water to the blossoming city would require a much more complex solution, as the sporadic flow of the Los Angeles River (as the Río Porciúncula became known) and water from a few artesian wells were clearly insufficient. To find out what happened, see the boxed text 'Water for a Thirsty Giant,' over the page.

Zoom to the Present

LA's population soared to one million by 1920 and two million by 1930, largely because of the discovery of oil, in 1892, by Edward Doheny near Downtown LA. Exporting the oil also caused a boom in shipping and related harbor industries.

During WWI, the Lockheed brothers and Donald Douglas established aircraft manufacturing plants in the area. Two decades later, with another world war brewing, the aviation industry employed enough people to help lift LA out of the Great Depression. By the end of WWII, billions of federal dollars

Water for a Thirsty Giant

The growth of semi-arid Los Angeles into a megalopolis is inextricably linked to water. When the city's population surged to 200,000 people in the early 20th century, groundwater levels were insufficient to support the city's needs, let alone sustain future growth. Water had to be imported, and Fred Eaton, a former LA mayor, and William Mulholland, the city water bureau superintendent, knew just how and where to get it: by aqueduct from the Owens Valley, at the foot of the Eastern Sierra, some 250mi northeast.

The fact that Owens Valley itself was settled by farmers who needed the water for irrigation didn't bother either the men or the federal government, which actively supported the city in acquiring land and securing water rights in the valley area.

Voters gave Mulholland the $24.5 million he needed to build an aqueduct to carry snow-melt from the mountains to the city. Work began in 1908. An amazing feat of engineering – crossing barren desert floor as well as rugged mountain terrain – the aqueduct opened to great fanfare on November 5, 1913. An extension to the Mono Basin in 1940 lengthened it by 105mi. The Owens Valley, though, would never be the same.

With most of Owens Lake drained, the once fertile valley became barren, causing farms to close and businesses to go bust. A bitter feud between valley residents and the city ensued; some foes even used dynamite to sabotage the aqueduct.

To this day, LA's Department of Water and Power (LADWP) owns 307,000 acres in Inyo and Mono Counties and the system still supplies about 75% of the city's water (the remainder comes from dams on the Colorado River, 300mi east). Residents at the water's source still resent the thirsty giant to the south, although the LADWP is now sponsoring efforts to restore the Owens Valley. For more on that subject, see the boxed text 'Mono Lake' in the Sierra Nevada chapter.

had been poured into Southern California military contracts, and thousands of families had moved to the region to work at the plants.

The influx of aviation employees caused a new real estate boom, creating whole new suburbs. At the same time, thousands of African-American workers came to LA from Texas and Louisiana, causing a vibrant community to develop in South Central LA. What had been just a small colony before the war had grown into one of the nation's great black cultural centers by the '50s.

But it is the film industry that has symbolized 20th-century LA. Independent producers were attracted here beginning in 1908 because LA's sunny climate allowed indoor scenes to be shot outdoors and any location, from ocean to desert to alpine forest, could be realized nearby. Studios grew in Culver City and Universal City, but the capital of filmdom was the LA suburb of Hollywood.

But all the while, trouble was brewing in the city. Policy makers had turned a blind eye to growing ethnic friction for decades. In 1965 the city experienced one of the nation's worst race riots: The primarily black neighborhood of Watts exploded with six days of burning and looting. Thirty-four people died in the riots, and more than a thousand were wounded. More race riots occurred in 1979 and 1992. The latter – a direct result of the acquittal of LAPD members charged with beating Rodney King – cost 54 lives and $1 billion in property damage.

In LA history, the 1990s was the decade 'from hell,' and not just because of the riots. Heavy rain in 1992 and in the winter of 1994-95 caused major flooding, mudslides and property damage. Brush fires made many more people homeless in 1993. And then, of course, there was the Northridge earthquake of 1994, which registered 6.9 magnitude and brought down freeways, apartments and nervous systems.

Police brutality continued to stay in the news headlines and, at the end of the decade, became coupled with police corruption in the so-called 'Rampart scandal.' LAPD officers assigned to the Rampart area near Downtown LA, one of the most gang-infested and crime-ridden districts, had employed illegal tactics of violence and planted evidence in order to curtail gang activity. Crime did drop, but the price was the LAPD's integrity.

GEOGRAPHY & GEOLOGY

LA County encompasses geographical extremes, ranging from subtropical desert to 74mi of seacoast and mountains over 10,000ft. It straddles one of the world's major earthquake fault zones, dominated by the great San Andreas Fault. Quakes rated above 6.0 on the Richter scale have wreaked death and destruction in LA five times this century – with epicenters near Long Beach in 1933, in the San Fernando Valley in 1971 (Sylmar) and 1994 (Northridge), and two in 1992 in the Big Bear region.

CLIMATE

LA has a temperate Mediterranean climate, protected from extremes of temperature and humidity by the mountain ranges to its north and east. The average temperature is 70°F (21°C), with summer highs usually in the mid-80s to low 90s and winter lows in the mid-50s to low 60s. Offshore breezes keep beach communities 10° to 15°F cooler than areas inland or in the San Fernando Valley. Morning coastal fog also contributes to the cooling effect. Evenings tend to be cool, even at the peak of summer. Rain falls almost exclusively between November and April, with extended storms raging in January and February.

ORIENTATION

Most first-time visitors to LA are instantly confused, even intimidated, by its vast size and sprawl. Unlike other metropolises like, say New York or Paris, LA is a decentralized hodgepodge with no clearly defined center but many different and quite distinct neighborhoods.

The historic heart of Los Angeles is Downtown, about 12mi east of the ocean, while northeast of here affluent Pasadena is home to the Rose Bowl, Jet Propulsion Laboratory (JPL) and California Institute of Technology (Caltech). Latin American immigrants cluster east of Downtown in East LA but have also moved into such historically African-American neighborhoods as Compton and Watts south of here.

Most areas of interest to visitors are west of Downtown LA. Hollywood encompasses such neighborhoods as bohemian-turned-trendy Silver Lake and fashionable Melrose Ave, while West Hollywood is LA's gay and lesbian epicenter. Most TV and movie studios, though, are actually north of Hollywood in the San Fernando Valley.

Further west, the 'three B's – Bel Air, Brentwood and Beverly Hills – epitomize the 'lifestyles of the rich and famous.' Equally posh are the northernmost beach communities: Malibu, Pacific Palisades and Santa Monica, while coastal towns further south – including Venice Beach, Manhattan Beach and Redondo Beach – are relaxed, middle-class enclaves where beach culture rules. Along with San Pedro, Long Beach, the southernmost beach town, is home to the LA Port. Offshore, thinly populated Catalina Island has a Mediterranean flavor and makes for a nice day trip.

Maps

For navigating within particular neighborhoods, the maps in this book are sufficiently comprehensive. Lonely Planet also produces a laminated Los Angeles map available in bookstores or on W www.lonely planet.com. Detailed street maps are available at gas stations, bookstores or the Automobile Association of Southern California (see the phone book for the branch nearest you).

INFORMATION
Tourist Offices

Maps, brochures, lodging information and tickets to theme parks and other attractions are available through the Los Angeles Convention and Visitors Bureau's (LACVB) **Downtown Visitor Center** (Map 2; ☎ 213-689-8822, fax 213-624-1992; W www.lacvb .com; 685 S Figueroa St; open 8am-5pm Mon-Fri, 8:30am-5pm Sat). At the time of writing, a new branch was scheduled to open in the Hollywood & Highland complex in Hollywood sometime in 2002.

The **California Welcome Center** (Map 4; ☎ 310-854-7616; 8500 Beverly Blvd; open 10am-6pm Mon-Sat, 11am-6pm Sun), on the street level of the Beverly Center mall, has visitor information about the entire state and tickets to local attractions. The staff can also help with hotel reservations.

Hollywood City Pass This is a ticket booklet with coupons good for one-time admission to the following attractions within a 30-day period: Universal Studios Hollywood,

[Continued on page 608]

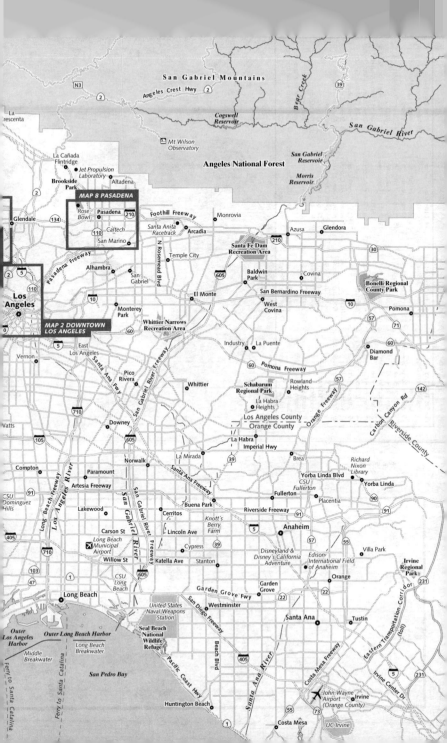

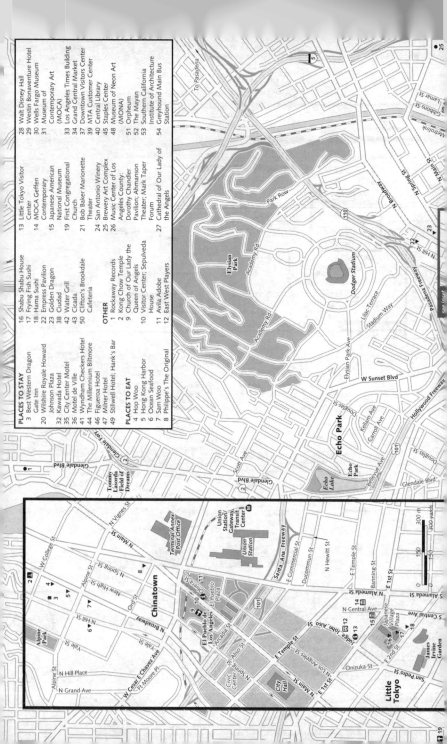

PLACES TO STAY
3 Best Western Dragon
Gate Inn
20 Wilshire Royale Howard
Johnson Plaza
32 Kawada Hotel
35 City Center Motel
36 Motel de Ville
41 Wyndham Checkers Hotel
44 The Millennium Biltmore
46 Figueroa Hotel
47 Milner Hotel
49 Stillwell Hotel; Hank's Bar

PLACES TO EAT
4 Hop Woo
5 Hong Kong Harbor
6 Ocean Seafood
7 Sam Woo
8 Philippe's The Original

16 Shabu Shabu House
17 Frying Fish Sushi
18 Hama Sushi
22 Empress Pavilion
23 Golden Dragon
38 Ciudad
42 Water Grill
43 Cicada
50 Clifton's Brookdale
Cafeteria

OTHER
1 Rockaway Records
2 Kong Chow Temple
9 Church of Our Lady the
Queen of Angels
10 Visitor Center; Sepulveda
House
11 Avila Adobe
12 East West Players

13 Little Tokyo Visitor
Center
14 MOCA Geffen
Contemporary
15 Japanese American
National Museum
19 First Congregational
Church
21 Bob Baker Marionette
Theater
24 San Antonio Winery
25 Brewery Art Complex
26 Music Center of Los
Angeles County;
Dorothy Chandler
Pavilion; Ahmanson
Theater; Mark Taper
Forum
27 Cathedral of Our Lady of
the Angels

28 Walt Disney Hall
29 Westin Bonaventure Hotel
30 Wells Fargo Museum
31 Museum of
Contemporary Art
(MOCA)
33 Los Angeles Times Building
34 Grand Central Market
37 Downtown Visitors Center
39 MTA Customer Center
40 Central Library
45 Staples Center
48 Museum of Neon Art
(MONA)
51 Orpheum
52 The Mayan
53 Southern California
Institute of Architecture
54 Greyhound Main Bus
Station

PLACES TO STAY
1 Hollywood Bungalows
8 Highland Gardens Hotel
9 Magic Castle Hotel
12 Orange Drive Manor Hostel
13 Orchid Suites Hotel
14 Liberty Hotel
19 Student Inn International Hostel
20 Hollywood Roosevelt Hotel
22 Hollywood International Hostel
24 The Gershwin Hollywood Hostel & Hotel
65 USA Hostel

PLACES TO EAT
4 Yuca's
5 Vida
6 Yamashiro
11 Birds
25 Dar Maghreb
32 Old Spaghetti Factory
39 El Conquistador
44 Patina
46 Palermo
47 Fred's 62
50 Vermont
52 Musso & Frank Grill
60 Miceli's
61 Les Deux Café

HOLLYWOOD BLVD

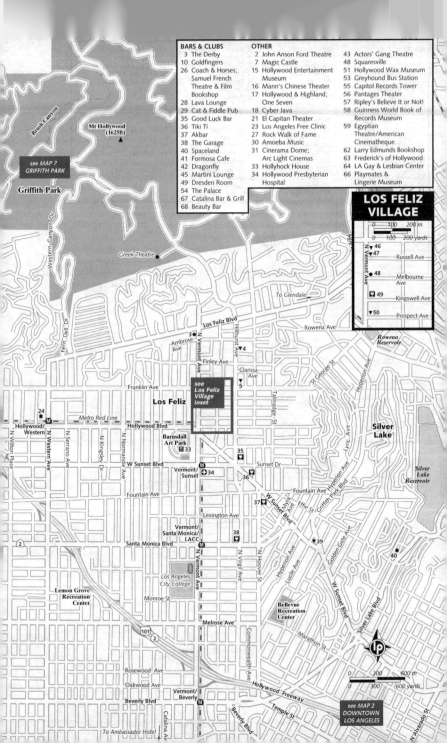

BARS & CLUBS
- 3 The Derby
- 10 Goldfingers
- 26 Coach & Horses; Samuel French Theatre & Film Bookshop
- 28 Lava Lounge
- 29 Cat & Fiddle Pub
- 35 Good Luck Bar
- 36 Tiki Ti
- 37 Akbar
- 38 The Garage
- 40 Spaceland
- 41 Formosa Cafe
- 42 Dragonfly
- 45 Martini Lounge
- 49 Dresden Room
- 54 The Palace
- 67 Catalina Bar & Grill
- 68 Beauty Bar

OTHER
- 2 John Anson Ford Theatre
- 7 Magic Castle
- 15 Hollywood Entertainment Museum
- 16 Mann's Chinese Theater
- 17 Hollywood & Highland; One Seven
- 18 Cyber Java
- 21 El Capitan Theater
- 23 Los Angeles Free Clinic
- 27 Rock Walk of Fame
- 30 Amoeba Music
- 31 Cinerama Dome; Arc Light Cinemas
- 33 Hollyhock House
- 34 Hollywood Presbyterian Hospital
- 43 Actors' Gang Theatre
- 48 Squaresville
- 51 Hollywood Wax Museum
- 53 Greyhound Bus Station
- 55 Capitol Records Tower
- 56 Pantages Theater
- 57 Ripley's Believe It or Not!
- 58 Guinness World Book of Records Museum
- 59 Egyptian Theatre/American Cinematheque
- 62 Larry Edmunds Bookshop
- 63 Frederick's of Hollywood
- 64 LA Gay & Lesbian Center
- 66 Playmates & Lingerie Museum

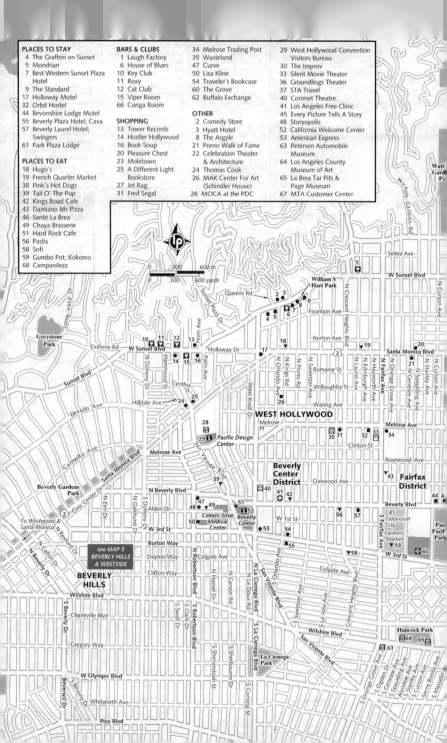

PLACES TO STAY
4 The Grafton on Sunset
5 Mondrian
7 Best Western Sunset Plaza Hotel
9 The Standard
17 Holloway Motel
32 Orbit Hostel
44 Bevonshire Lodge Motel
55 Beverly Plaza Hotel; Cava
57 Beverly Laurel Hotel; Swingers
61 Park Plaza Lodge

PLACES TO EAT
18 Hugo's
19 French Quarter Market
38 Pink's Hot Dogs
39 Tail O' The Pup
42 Kings Road Cafe
43 Damiano Mr Pizza
46 Santé La Brea
49 Chaya Brasserie
51 Hard Rock Cafe
56 Pastis
58 Sofi
59 Gumbo Pot; Kokomo
68 Campanilezz

BARS & CLUBS
1 Laugh Factory
6 House of Blues
10 Key Club
11 Roxy
15 Viper Room
66 Conga Room

SHOPPING
13 Tower Records
14 Hustler Hollywood
16 Book Soup
20 Pleasure Chest
23 Moletown
25 A Different Light Bookstore
27 Jet Rag
31 Fred Segal
34 Melrose Trading Post
35 Wasteland
47 Curve
50 Lisa Kline
54 Traveler's Bookcase
60 The Grove
62 Buffalo Exchange

OTHER
2 Comedy Store
8 Hyatt Hotel
8 The Argyle
21 Porno Walk of Fame
22 Celebration Theater & Architecture
24 Thomas Cook
26 MAK Center For Art (Schindler House)
28 MOCA at the PDC
29 West Hollywood Convention Visitors Bureau
30 The Improv
33 Silent Movie Theater
36 Groundlings Theater
37 STA Travel
40 Coronet Theatre
41 Los Angeles Free Clinic
45 Every Picture Tells A Story
48 Storyopolis
52 California Welcome Center
53 American Express
63 Petersen Automobile Museum
64 Los Angeles County Museum of Art
65 La Brea Tar Pits & Page Museum
67 MTA Customer Center

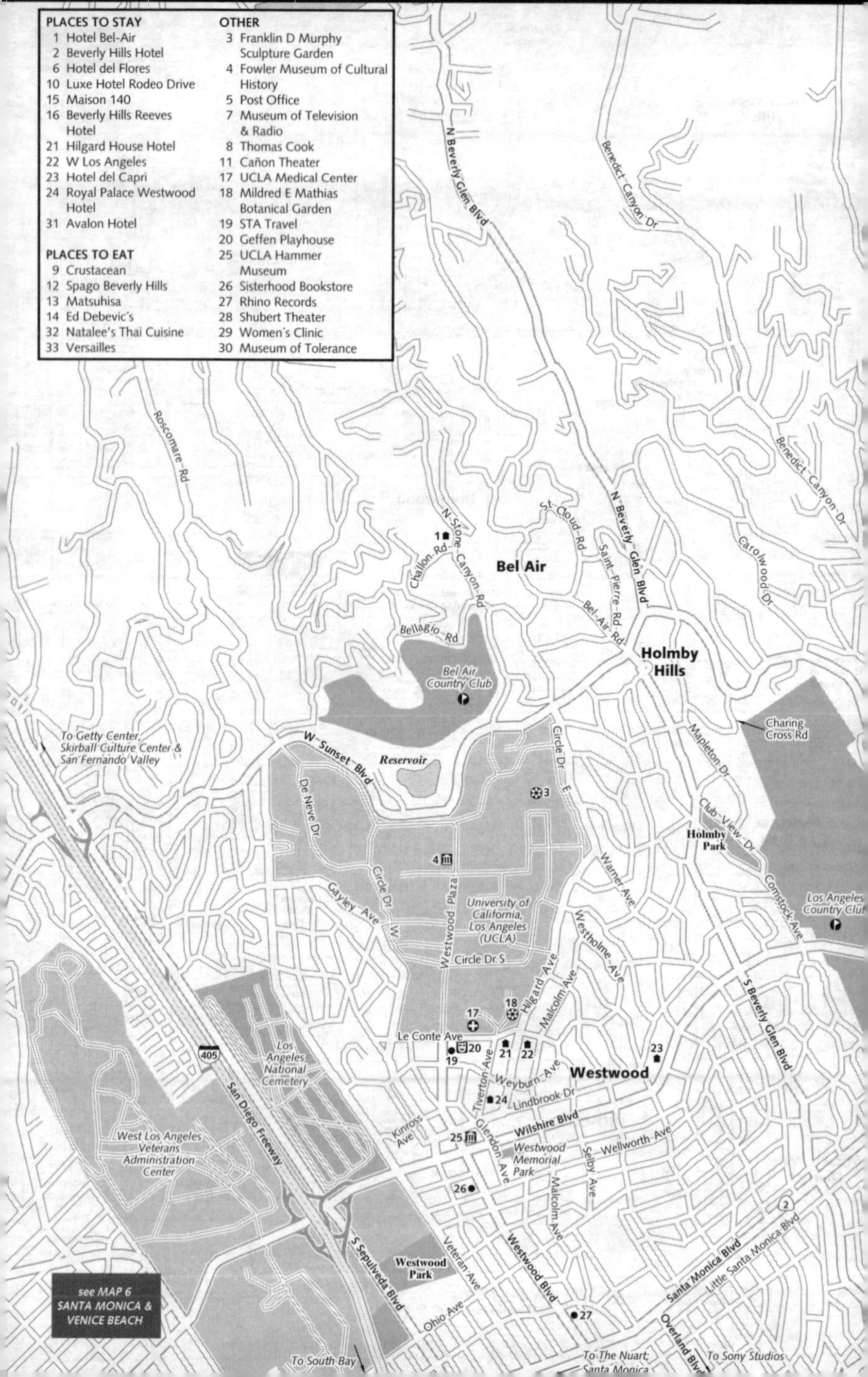

MAP 5 BEVERLY HILLS

PLACES TO STAY
1 Hotel Bel-Air
2 Beverly Hills Hotel
6 Hotel del Flores
10 Luxe Hotel Rodeo Drive
15 Maison 140
16 Beverly Hills Reeves Hotel
21 Hilgard House Hotel
22 W Los Angeles
23 Hotel del Capri
24 Royal Palace Westwood Hotel
31 Avalon Hotel

PLACES TO EAT
9 Crustacean
12 Spago Beverly Hills
13 Matsuhisa
14 Ed Debevic's
32 Natalee's Thai Cuisine
33 Versailles

OTHER
3 Franklin D Murphy Sculpture Garden
4 Fowler Museum of Cultural History
5 Post Office
7 Museum of Television & Radio
8 Thomas Cook
11 Cañon Theater
17 UCLA Medical Center
18 Mildred E Mathias Botanical Garden
19 STA Travel
20 Geffen Playhouse
25 UCLA Hammer Museum
26 Sisterhood Bookstore
27 Rhino Records
28 Shubert Theater
29 Women's Clinic
30 Museum of Tolerance

N Beverly Glen Blvd
Benedict Canyon Dr
Benedict Canyon Dr
Roscomare Rd
Carolwood Dr

Bel Air

Challon Rd
N Stone Canyon Rd
St Cloud Rd
N Beverly Glen Blvd
Saint-Pierre Rd
Bel Air Rd

Holmby Hills

Bellagio Rd

Bel Air Country Club

To Getty Center,
Skirball Culture Center &
San Fernando Valley

W Sunset Blvd
Reservoir

Charing Cross Rd

Mapleton Dr

De Neve Dr

Circle Dr E

Circle Dr W

Warner Ave

Holmby Park

Club View Dr

Comstock Ave

Los Angeles Country Club

Gayley Ave

University of California, Los Angeles (UCLA)

Westwood Plaza

Circle Dr S

Wertholme Ave

Wellworth Ave

S Beverly Glen Blvd

405

Los Angeles National Cemetery

Le Conte Ave

Hilgard Ave

Malcolm Ave

Westwood

Thornton Ave

Weyburn Ave

San Diego Freeway

West Los Angeles Veterans Administration Center

Lindbrook Dr

Glendon Ave

Wilshire Blvd

Westwood Memorial Park

Kinross Ave

Selby Ave

Wellworth Ave

Malcolm Ave

Veteran Ave

Westwood Blvd

S Sepulveda Blvd

Westwood Park

Ohio Ave

Santa Monica Blvd

Little Santa Monica Blvd

2

Overland Blvd

see MAP 6
SANTA MONICA &
VENICE BEACH

To South Bay

To The Nuart,
Santa Monica

To Sony Studios

Laurel Canyon

Hollywood Hills

Lake Franklin Dr

Franklin Canyon Dr

Lower Franklin Reservoir

Coldwater Canyon Park

Greystone Park

Coldwater Canyon Dr

Schuyler Rd

Doheny Rd

Doheny Rd   W Sunset Blvd   Holloway Dr

To Hollywood

Mountain Dr   Loma Vista Dr

Sunset Blvd

Santa Monica Blvd

N Crescent Dr

N Beverly Drive

N Beverly Dr

Lomitas Ave

Will Rogers Memorial Park

Melrose Ave

Pacific Design Center

WEST HOLLYWOOD

N Crescent Dr

Elevado Ave

N Elm Dr

N Maple Dr

N Foothill Rd

Carmelita Ave

Hillcrest Rd

N Arden Dr

N Alta Dr

N Sierra Dr

BEVERLY HILLS

N Rodeo Dr

N Camden Dr

N Bedford Dr

N Roxbury Dr

N Linden Dr

Walden Dr

Sunset Blvd

Whittier Dr

N Alpine Dr

N Rexford Dr

N Canon Dr

N Beverly Dr

Beverly Gardens Park

Santa Monica Blvd

Civic Center Dr

Beverly Center District

N La Cienega Blvd

San Vicente Blvd

Beverly Center

see MAP 4 WEST HOLLYWOOD & MID-CITY

N Beverly Blvd

Alden Dr

Cedars-Sinai Medical Center

N Robertson Blvd

N Elm Dr   N Maple Dr   N Oakhurst Dr

W 3rd St

Burton Way

N Swall Dr   N Clark Dr   N Hamel Dr

Colgate Ave

Beverly Gardens Park

Dayton Way

Clifton Way

Vilshire Blvd

Wilshire Blvd

Charleville Blvd

Gregory Way

S Oakhurst Dr   S Doheny Dr

S Robertson Blvd

La Cienega Park

Moreno Dr

S Santa Monica Blvd

S Lasky Dr

S Linden Dr

S McCarty Dr

S Roxbury Dr

S Bedford Dr

S Peck Dr

S Camden Dr

S Rodeo Dr

S Beverly Dr

S Reeves Dr

S Canon Dr

Beverly Hills High School

Constellation Blvd

Century City Shopping Center

Roxbury Recreation Center

Century City

W Olympic Blvd

S Shenandoah St

S La Cienega Blvd

S Coring St

Roxbury Dr

Whitworth Ave

Century Park W

Avenue of the Stars

Century Park E

20th Century Fox Studios

W Pico Blvd

W Pico Blvd

Hillcrest Country Club

To The Mint

Beverwil Dr

S Beverly Dr

0   300   600 m
0   300   600 yards

2   5   6   7   8   9   10   11   12   13   14   15   16   28   29   30   31   32   33

MAP 6 SANTA MONIC

PLACES TO STAY
13 Hotel California
14 Ocean Lodge
15 Hotel Casa del Mar
16 Bayside Hotel
17 Sea Shore Motel
21 Cadillac Hotel
23 Hostel California
25 Jolly Roger Hotel
28 Ritz-Carlton Marina del Rey
29 Venice Beach House
30 Inn at Venice Beach
31 Foghorn Harbor Inn
34 Share-Tel Apartments
37 Venice Beach Cotel
38 Venice Beach Hostel
41 Cal Mar Hotel Suites
43 Fairmont Miramar Hotel Santa Monica
58 HI-Los Angeles–Santa Monica
59 Georgian Hotel
60 Pacific Sands Motel

PLACES TO EAT
2 Taiko
18 Omelet Parlor
22 Rose Cafe
32 Joe's
33 Lilly's
35 Abbot Pizza
36 Sidewalk Cafe
40 Jodi Maroni's Sausage Kingdom
46 Wolfgang Puck Express
48 Real Food Daily
49 JiRaffe
50 La Serenata di Garibaldi
51 Border Grill
56 Ye Olde King's Head

BARS & CLUBS
5 O'Brien's
6 Temple Bar
7 14 Below
26 Scruffy O'Shea's
42 Toppers
44 The West End
55 Harvelle's

OTHER
1 Dutton's
3 The Nuart
4 Odyssey Theatre Ensemble
8 Bergamot Station; Santa Monica Museum of Art
9 California Map & Travel
10 Pacific Park
11 Carousel; UCLA Ocean Discovery Center
12 International Chess Park; Original Muscle Beach
19 DNA
20 Venice Family Clinic
24 James Corcoran Gallery
27 Route 66
39 LA Louver Gallery
45 Puppet and Magic Center
47 STA Travel
52 Fred Segal
53 Laemmle Theater
54 Hear Music
57 Interactive Cafe
61 Santa Monica Visitor Center

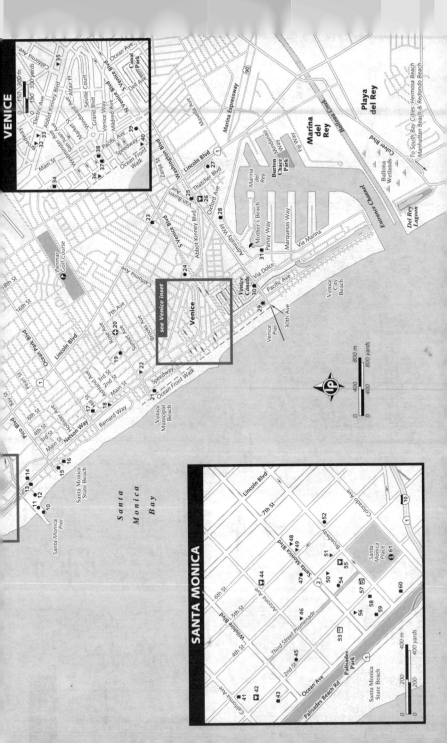

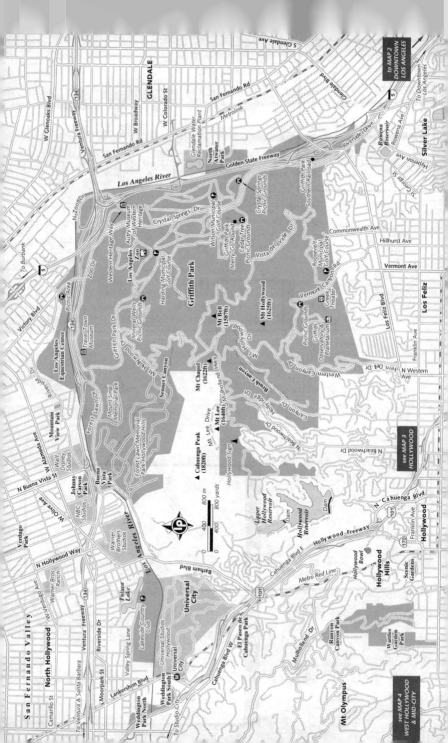

DOWNTOWN

100 200 m
0 100 200 yards

PLACES TO STAY
16 Westway Inn
17 Saga Motor Hotel
21 Pasadena Inn
22 Bissell House
23 Ritz-Carlton Huntington Hotel

PLACES TO EAT
3 Marston's
15 Europane
20 Saladang; Saladang Song
24 Xiomara

OTHER
1 Gamble House
2 Charles Green's Private Residence
4 Public Library
5 Greyhound Bus Station
6 Norton Simon Museum
7 Vista del Arroyo Hotel; Court of Appeals
8 City Hall
9 Paseo Colorado
10 Pasadena Convention & Visitors Bureau
11 Pacific Asia Museum
12 Pasadena Playhouse
13 Vroman's
14 Ice House
18 American Express
19 Wrigley Mansion & Gardens
25 Gordon Biersch Brewery
26 Equator Coffeehouse
27 Distant Lands Bookstore

[Continued from page 593]

American Cinematheque at the Egyptian Theatre, Autry Museum of Western Heritage, Museum of Television & Radio, Hollywood Entertainment Museum and Petersen Automotive Museum. A city tour with Starline Tours is also part of the package. The booklet costs $59/39 adult/child (three to 11) and is available at any of the participating places, at the LACVB visitor centers and online at w citypass.net/hollywood.

Money
Banks are ubiquitous and usually offer the best rates for currency exchange. Los Angeles International Airport (LAX) has currency-exchange offices in all terminals, although exchange rates are not great. You might do better changing your money into dollars or traveler's checks in your home country.

Foreign-exchange brokers include **Thomas Cook** *(☎ 800-287-7362 all branches; Map 4; 806 Hilldale Ave, West Hollywood • Map 5; 421 N Rodeo Dr, Beverly Hills)* and **American Express** *(Map 4; ☎ 310-659-1682;*

8493 W 3rd St, Beverly Center District • Map 8; ☎ 626-449-2281; 269 S Lake Ave, Pasadena).

Post & Communications
No matter where you are in LA, you're never far from a post office branch. You can find out which one is closest by calling ☎ 800-275-8777.

Thanks to the proliferation of electronic communication devices, LA County is now divided into five area codes; all telephone numbers in this book are accompanied by the appropriate area code.

Internet cafés come and go but these have stayed: **Cyber Java** *(Map 3; ☎ 323-466-5600; 7080 Hollywood Blvd, Hollywood)*; **Interactive Café** *(Map 6; ☎ 310-395-5009; 215 Broadway, Santa Monica)*; and **Equator Coffeehouse** *(Map 8; ☎ 626-564-8656; 22 Mills Place, Pasadena).*

Digital Resources
There's no shortage of websites about Los Angeles. Good general sites include w www .at-la.com, with links to more than 70,000

What's Free in LA

Fame may not be free in Los Angeles, but many of the city's museums or attractions don't charge admission or offer it free on certain days and at certain times.

Museums (always free)
Adamson House & Malibu Lagoon Museum (Malibu)
California African American Museum (Exposition Park)
California Science Center (Exposition Park)
Frederick's of Hollywood Lingerie Museum
Getty Center (Westside)
Museum of African American Art (Leimert Park)
Travel Town Museum (Griffith Park)
USC Fisher Gallery (Downtown)
Watts Towers Art Center (South Central)
Wells Fargo History Museum (Downtown)

Historic Sights (always free)
Avila Adobe – Olvera St (Downtown)
Mann's Chinese Theater Forecourt (Hollywood)
Cemeteries – Forest Lawn Memorial Park (Hollywood Hills) and Forest Lawn Cemetery (Glendale), Hollywood Forever Cemetery, Westwood Memorial Park Cemetery
Wrigley Mansion & Gardens (Pasadena)

Museums (sometimes free)
Autry Museum of Western Heritage (Griffith Park) – second Tuesday of the month
Fowler Museum of Cultural History at UCLA (Westside) – all day Thursday
Huntington Library, Art Collection & Botanical Gardens (San Marino/Pasadena) – first Thursday of the month
Japanese American National Museum (Downtown) – 5pm to 8pm first, second and fourth Thursday and free all day every third Thursday
MAK Center for Arts & Architecture/Schindler House (West Hollywood) – 4pm to 6pm Friday
MOCA – Museum of Contemporary Art (Downtown) – 5pm to 8pm Thursday
MOCA Geffen Contemporary (Downtown) – 5pm to 8pm Thursday
MOCA at the PDC (West Hollywood) – 5pm to 8pm Thursday
Museum of Latin American Art (Long Beach) – all day Friday
UCLA Hammer Museum (Westside) – Thursday

Rodeo Drive, Los Angeles

Surfing off Manhattan Beach, Los Angeles

The 1927-vintage Pasadena City Hall lights up the night

Santa Monica's Third Street Promenade

Basketball on Venice Beach

Santa Barbara State Historic Park

Neptune Pool, Hearst Castle

The rugged and splendid Big Sur coastline

Santa Barbara shopping mall

A limpid lily pond reflects the Santa Barbara Mission bell tower

MICHAEL AW

RICHARD CUMMINS

JUDY BELLAH

RICHARD CUMMINS

DAVID TOMLINSON

pages covering everything from arts to tourism; and **w** www.digitalcity.com/losangeles, which has a visitor guide and restaurant and club reviews. For up-to-date events news, check the *Los Angeles Times'* online 'Calendar' section at **w** www.calendarlive.com.

Travel Agencies

Besides American Express mentioned under Money earlier in this section, STA Travel has several branches around town, including one on Melrose Ave in Hollywood *(Map 4; ☎ 323-934-8722; 7202 Melrose Ave)*, another near UCLA in Westwood *(Map 5; ☎ 310-824-1574; 920 Westwood Blvd)* and one in Santa Monica *(Map 6; ☎ 310-394-5126; 411 Santa Monica Blvd)*.

Bookstores

Excellent travel bookstores include **Traveler's Bookcase** *(Map 4; ☎ 323-655-0575; 8375 W 3rd St, Beverly Center District)*, near the Beverly Center; **California Map & Travel** *(Map 6; ☎ 310-396-6277; 3312 Pico Blvd, Santa Monica)*; **Distant Lands** *(Map 8; ☎ 626-449-3220; 56 Raymond Ave, Pasadena)*; and **Nations** *(☎ 310-318-9915; 500-504 Pier Ave, Hermosa Beach)*.

For general interest, head to hip **Book Soup** *(Map 4; ☎ 310-659-3110; 8818 Sunset Blvd)* in West Hollywood, which has an international newsstand and a sizable gay and lesbian section. **Dutton's** *(Map 7; ☎ 310-476-6263; 11975 San Vicente Blvd)*, in Brentwood, caters to a well-read, educated clientele. **Vroman's** *(Map 8; ☎ 626-449-5320; 695 E Colorado Blvd)*, in Pasadena, is Southern California's oldest (since 1894) bookstore.

Medical Services & Emergency

Major hospitals include **Hollywood Presbyterian Hospital** *(Map 3; ☎ 323-660-5350; 1300 N Vermont Ave, Hollywood)*; **Cedars-Sinai Medical Center** *(Map 4; ☎ 310-855-5000; 8700 Beverly Blvd, West Hollywood)*; and **UCLA Medical Center** *(Map 5; ☎ 310-825-9111; 10833 LeConte Ave, Westwood)*. Have your insurance card ready.

If you are uninsured or have a plan with a high deductible, you can keep costs down by going to a state-subsidized clinic where fees are assessed according to your ability to pay. Among the best are the **Los Angeles Free Clinic** *(Map 3; ☎ 323-462-4158; 6043 Hollywood Blvd, Hollywood • Map 4;*

☎ 323-653-1990; 8405 Beverly Blvd, Beverly Center District); the **Women's Clinic** *(Map 6; ☎ 310-203-8899; 9911 Pico Blvd, suite 500, Century City)*; and the **Venice Family Clinic** *(Map 7; ☎ 310-392-8630; 604 Rose Ave, Venice)*.

In a real emergency, call ☎ 911 for assistance from police, fire department, ambulance or paramedics.

Dangers & Annoyances

Much has been written about crime in LA, though overall figures have declined in recent years. If you take ordinary precautions, chances are you won't be victimized.

Walking around in the daytime is generally no problem anywhere, although extra caution should be exercised in East LA, South Central, some sections of Hollywood and the MacArthur Park neighborhood west of Downtown, which are plagued by interracial gang activity, drugs and prostitution. Stay away from these areas after dark or, if you must venture there, use a private vehicle (car or taxi) and don't walk around.

The streets of Hollywood yield dangers from drug addicts and crazed people, and should be avoided after nightfall; ditto for Venice. Exercise a bit of extra caution in Silver Lake and West Hollywood. Westside communities such as Westwood and Beverly Hills, as well as the beach towns (except Venice), are generally among the safer areas, as is Pasadena.

DOWNTOWN (Map 2)

Perennial doubters and incorrigible cynics will never believe it, but LA *does* have a center. Few of the city's areas have as much to offer per square mile as Downtown. It is rich in history (this is, after all, the city's birthplace), architecture, restaurants and cultural institutions. In fact, it's possible to 'travel around the world' in just a day as you make your way from Chinatown to Little Tokyo to the Mexican marketplaces of Olvera St and Broadway, and back to the 21st-cent-ury America of the Financial District.

Getting around Downtown is easy; most places of interest are quickly reached by walking. The foot-weary can ride the DASH minibuses, which operate at five- to 10-minute intervals and cost just 25¢ per ride. Downtown is served by Metro Rail's Red Line subway from Hollywood and Universal Studios, the

Blue Line from Long Beach and the Gold Line from Pasadena (opening in 2003), as well as the Big Blue Bus' No 10 express bus from Santa Monica and many other bus lines from throughout the metropolitan area. Drivers should park on the periphery to avoid the horrendous fees charged in the center.

Financial District

LA's modern business district extends seven blocks south from the Civic Center to 8th St and from I-110 six blocks east to Hill St. At its heart is Bunker Hill, which, a century ago, was a fashionable residential neighborhood flecked with stately Victorian mansions. It deteriorated into a slum after the 1920s and remained in a sorry state until the '60s, when the city opted for razing the historic neighborhood and replacing it with a forest of steel-and-glass high-rises. Also here are large condominium complexes and the futuristic **Westin Bonaventure Hotel**, whose five cylindrical glass towers provide frequent movie locations.

Grand Ave bisects Bunker Hill's two main complexes: the Wells Fargo Center and California Plaza. On the ground floor of the former, the **Wells Fargo History Museum** (☎ 213-253-7166; admission free; open 9am-5pm Mon-Fri) relives the gold rush era with maps, guns, traveling paraphernalia, an original stagecoach and a 2lb gold nugget.

At the northern end of California Plaza is the acclaimed **Museum of Contemporary Art** (MOCA; ☎ 213-626-6222; 250 S Grand Ave; adult/concession $8/5, free after 5pm Thur; open 11am-5pm Tues-Sun, 11am-8pm Thur). Housed in a stunning building by Japanese architect Isozaki Arata, it presents paintings, sculptures and photographs from the 1940s to the present. Tickets are also good for same-day admission at the MOCA Geffen Contemporary (see under Little Tokyo later in this section) and within 30 days at the MOCA at the Pacific Design Center (see the West Hollywood section).

A nice way to descend Bunker Hill is via the **Bunker Hill Steps**, which lead down to 5th St and the **Library Tower**, the city's tallest building. Immediately opposite is the **Central Library** (Map 2; ☎ 213-228-7000; 630 W 5th St), a repository of about 2.5 million books and historical photographs, and two galleries. The building was originally designed in 1922 by Bertram Goodhue and incorporated many

Egyptian motifs, an architectural fad at that time. A modern wing was added in 1993 as was the **Maguire Gardens**, a small and tranquil park of sinuous walkways, pools and fountains and whimsical artwork.

Civic Center

Extending eight blocks east to west from San Pedro to Figueroa Sts, the Civic Center contains most of LA's city, county, state and federal office buildings.

The most distinctive edifice is the 1928 **City Hall** (200 N Spring St), which served as the 'Daily Planet' building in Superman and the police station in Dragnet. A much-needed renovation to bring the building up to par with earthquake and other safety codes was recently completed.

Diagonally across from City Hall is the **Los Angeles Times Building** (☎ 213-237-5757 for reservations; 202 W 1st St), home of western North America's largest daily newspaper. Free 45-minute tours introduce visitors (10 years and older) to the inner workings of this print-media giant. They run at 9:30am, 11am and 1:30pm Monday to Friday; make reservations at least one week in advance.

The complex of three theaters – Dorothy Chandler Pavilion, Ahmanson Theatre and Mark Taper Forum – known collectively as the **Music Center of Los Angeles County** (☎ 213-972-7211, 213-972-7483 for tour reservations; 135 N Grand Ave), dominates the northwestern end of the Civic Center mall, between 1st and Temple Sts. The Chandler Pavilion is the current home of the LA Philharmonic Orchestra and has hosted several Academy Awards ceremonies. Free one-hour tours run from 10am to 1:30pm Tuesday to Saturday.

If all goes according to schedule, the LA Philharmonic will move into the spectacular **Walt Disney Hall** just south of the Music Center sometime in 2003. Designed by Frank Gehry, its exterior is a choreography of dynamically curving and folding walls that seems like an abstract interpretation of a ship caught in a rough sea. The vaguely nautical theme continues inside with a fragmented sail-like ceiling that curves and billows upwards, and tiered and sectioned audience seating that completely wraps around the orchestra pit.

East of the Music Center, on Temple St, looms another new LA landmark, the **Cath-**

edral of **Our Lady of the Angels**, LA's new Catholic cathedral. Spanish star architect José Rafael Moneo has come up with an unapologetically modern design which has no right angles, and features milky alabaster windows, an illuminated cross and a vast bronze door by local sculptor Robert Graham. A generous plaza leads up to the cathedral entrance.

El Pueblo de Los Angeles

This 44-acre state historic park north of the Civic Center commemorates the founding site of LA and preserves many of LA's earliest buildings. Fiestas and lively celebrations take place in the pueblo throughout the year.

The park's main attraction is **Olvera St**, a narrow, block-long passageway which has been an open-air Mexican marketplace since 1930. Volunteers lead free one-hour walking tours of El Pueblo Tuesday to Saturday mornings from the **visitor center** (☎ 213-680-3800), in the Sepulveda House (1877). Also on Olvera St is LA's oldest building, the refurbished **Avila Adobe** (1818), built by a wealthy Mexican ranchero and one-time LA mayor.

Olvera St spills into the Old Plaza, the central square of the original pueblo. West of the plaza is the **Church of Our Lady the Queen of the Angels** (535 N Main St), originally built of adobe by friars and indigenous laborers, between 1818 and 1822.

Southeast of El Pueblo, on Alameda St, is **Union Station** (1939) the last of the great railroad stations built in the USA. Massive chandeliers dangle above a marble-floored waiting room anchored by clunky leather armchairs. You may have seen the station in the movies *Bugsy* and *The Way We Were*.

Chinatown

Fewer than 5% of LA's 170,000 Chinese make their home in the 16 square blocks of Chinatown, but the district north of El Pueblo along Broadway and Hill St is still their social and cultural center.

In February Chinatown's streets become a feast for the senses as giant dragons, decorated floats and lion dancers take part in the **Chinese New Year parade**. On any day of the year you can enjoy fresh Cantonese or Sichuan delicacies at dozens of restaurants, or browse for cheap kitsch, exquisite silk clothing, boxed tea or such culinary oddities as dried sea cucumber and pickled ginseng.

The more touristy section of Chinatown is a plaza of gift shops and restaurants called **Old Chinatown** on the northern end of Broadway. South of here is the **Kong Chow Temple** (2nd floor, 931 N Broadway) above the East West Federal Bank. To enter, ring the bell and someone should come to let you in.

Little Tokyo

Immediately south of the Civic Center is Little Tokyo, a bustling neighborhood first settled by early Japanese immigrants in the 1880s. During WWII, it was effectively decimated by the relocation of US-born Japanese into internment camps. The community took decades to recover but today, Little Tokyo is once again the social, economic and cultural center for nearly 250,000 Japanese Americans. Along the streets and outdoor shopping centers, you'll find sushi bars, temples and traditional Japanese gardens. For maps and information, drop in at the **Little Tokyo Visitor Center** (☎ 213-613-1911; 307 E 1st St; open 10am-5:30pm Mon-Sat).

A good place to start your exploration of Little Tokyo is at the **Japanese American National Museum** (JANM; ☎ 213-625-0414; 369 E 1st St; adult/senior/student $6/5/3, free after 5pm Thur & free every 3rd Thur of month; open 10am-5pm Tues-Sun, 10am-8pm Thur). On view are objects of work and worship, photographs and art relating the history of Japanese emigration to, and life in, the USA during the past 130 years, including the painful chapter of the WWII camps.

Behind the JANM is the **MOCA Geffen Contemporary** (Map 2; ☎ 213-626-6222; 152 N Central Ave; adult/concession $8/5, free after 5pm Thur; open 11am-5pm Tues-Sun, 11am-8pm Thur) in a Frank Gehry–converted warehouse perfect for large-scale installations. Tickets are also good for same-day admission to MOCA at California Plaza and within 30 days at MOCA at the Pacific Design Center.

Arts District

In the dilapidated, industrial section south and east of Little Tokyo has sprung up a lively loft arts district. There are artists' studios and galleries, mostly filled with highly unusual and experimental art. The **Southern California Institute of Architecture** (Sci-Arc; ☎ 213-613-2200; 960 E 3rd St) recently moved its campus here and has an interesting gallery as well. **Brewery Art Complex** *(2100 N Main St)* is a self-contained artist colony northeast of here. Nearby, the **San Antonio Winery** *(☎ 323-223-1401; 737 Lamar St; admission, tasting & tours free; open 10am-6pm Sun-Wed, 10am-7pm Thur-Sat)* is the last remaining winery in the city, founded in 1917 by Italian immigrant Santo Cambianica. Many of San Antonio's wines may be sampled and there are free behind-the-scenes tours (daily on the hour from 11am to 3pm) and a nice restaurant as well.

South Park

The southwestern edge of Downtown LA is still a work in progress. In 1999 the futuristic **Staples Center** *(☎ 877-305-1111, box office ☎ 213-742-7340; 1111 S Figueroa St)*, a state-of-the-art sports and entertainment arena seating up to 20,000 spectators, opened here next to the Los Angeles Convention Center. Developers' hopes that the new home of the Los Angeles Lakers, Los Angeles Clippers and Los Angeles Kings would revitalize the entire area are slowly beginning to pan out as more restaurants are moving into the area and new hotels are on the drawing board as well.

East of the arena, the **Museum of Neon Art** *(MONA; ☎ 213-489-9918; 501 W Olympic Blvd; adult/concession/child $5/3.50/free; open 11am-5pm Wed-Sat, noon-5pm Sun)* is a cool gallery highlighting neon, electric and kinetic art. Permanent installations include a rocking Elvis and a serenely smiling Mona Lisa. It also organizes night-time bus tours. Southeast of here, the **Fashion District** is a 56-block area framed by Broadway and Wall St and 7th St and Pico Blvd. It is LA's clothing manufacturing, wholesale and retail center. For details, see the Shopping section later this chapter.

In the 700 block of Wall and Maple Sts, the **Southern California Flower Market** *(admission Mon-Fri/Sat $2/1; open 8am-noon Mon, Wed & Fri, 6am-noon Tues, Thur & Sat)* is the largest cut-flower market in the country, employing nearly 2000 people and dating back to 1913.

EXPOSITION PARK

Exposition Park, which began as an agricultural fairground in 1872, contains a cluster of museums that are still its main attraction. If you're visiting in summer, be sure to check out the lovely **Rose Garden**, a

groomed sprawl of 15,000 bushes, representing some 150 varieties of the noble blossom. Exposition Park is directly served from Downtown by DASH buses. North of the park is the University of Southern California (USC) and a historical residential district marked by many Victorian, Queen Anne and Art Deco structures.

Natural History Museum of LA County

On the park's northwestern edge sits a baronial 1913 Spanish Renaissance structure, home to the Natural History Museum of LA County *(☎ 213-763-3466; adult/senior/child $8/5.50/2; open 9:30am-5pm Mon-Fri, 10am-5pm Sat & Sun)*. The museum's vast collections chronicle the earth's evolution and showcase the astonishing diversity of natural life. Two habitat halls present African and North American mammals, but it's the Dinosaur Hall that's the most reliable crowd pleaser. Smaller galleries are dedicated to American history from the pre-Columbian era to 1914, and to 400 years of California history. The Gem and Mineral Hall dazzles with 2000 specimens, including 300lb of gold. Kids love the Insect Zoo of local and exotic creepy crawlies, including tarantulas, Madagascan hissing cockroaches and even a giant ant farm. Other exhibits include the Schreiber Hall of Birds and the Marine Life Hall.

California Science Center

If your memory of school science makes you groan, then a visit to the California Science Center *(☎ 213-744-7400; 700 State Dr; admission free; open 10am-5pm daily)* should convince you that, gee, science *can* be fun. This hands-on, interactive, state-of-the-art facility is one of LA's favorite family destinations and presents educational experience in a playful and often humorous environment.

There are three main exhibition areas. The **World of Life** exhibit is based on the concept that all forms of life – from amebas to cacti to Homo sapiens – share the same basic processes, from reproduction to the intake and processing of energy to the disposal of waste. The highlight here is the 'Bodyworks' theater starring a techno-doll named Tess who's billed as '50ft of brains, beauty and biology.'

Especially for Kids

It's easy to keep kids entertained in LA and around. There's plenty to explore on the beach, in the mountains and even in the urban core. Amusement parks such as Disneyland, Knott's Berry Farm and Universal Studios score big with older kids, although none are a bargain.

Here is a short list of alternatives to the amusement parks (see the relevant sections in this chapter for detailed coverage). See also the Activities chapter, earlier in this book, for additional ideas.

Aquarium of the Pacific (Long Beach)
Autry Museum of Western Heritage (Map 7; Griffith Park)
Cabrillo Marine Aquarium (San Pedro)
California Science Center (Exposition Park)
La Brea Tar Pits and Page Museum (Map 4; Miracle Mile District)
Los Angeles Zoo (Map 7; Griffith Park)
Natural History Museum of LA County (Exposition Park)
Queen Mary (Long Beach)
UCLA Ocean Discovery Center (Map 6; Santa Monica)

LA also has several galleries dedicated to children, usually with an active schedule of storytelling, reading and workshops. **Every Picture Tells a Story** (Map 4; ☎ 323-932-6070; 7525 Beverly Blvd, Fairfax District) and **Storyopolis** (Map 4; ☎ 310-358-2500; 116 N Robertson Blvd, Beverly Center District) are both good places to check out.

Generations of Angelenos have grown up with **Bob Baker Marionette Theater** (Map 2; ☎ 213-250-9995; 1345 W 1st St, Echo Park), near Downtown. Since 1963, it has enthralled kids aged two to 12 with its adorable singing and dancing marionettes and stuffed animals that interact with their young audiences seated on a carpet. It's pure magic.

In Santa Monica, the **Puppet and Magic Center** (Map 6; ☎ 310-656-0483; 1255 2nd St) is a 40-seat theater with regularly scheduled performances as well as puppet workshops and a puppet museum.

The Calendar supplement of the Thursday Los Angeles Times as well as the newspaper's Sunday Calendar section have special listings of dedicated children's activities.

Virtual reality games, high-tech simulators, laser animation and other such gadgetry await in the **Creative World** exhibit, whose focus is on the benefits and consequences of human innovations in communication, transportation and structures.

Quite literally 'out of this world' is the new **Air & Space Gallery**, which teaches the principles of flight as well as about space travel and exploration through telescopes, satellites and probes. Exhibits include the Explorer 1, the first satellite to be launched into space from the USA, and the real Gemini 11 space capsule flown into space in 1966.

Adjacent to the Science Center, the **IMAX Theater** (☎ 213-744-2014; adult/student/child $7/5.25/4.25) presents awe-inspiring nature-themed 2-D and 3-D movies.

California African American Museum

This acclaimed museum (☎ 213-744-7432; admission free; open 10am-5pm Tues-Sun), in the park's northeastern corner, presents the complex range of African and African-American art and artifacts, including works by painters of the 1920s Harlem Renaissance. Lectures, theater, music and other cultural programming complement the exhibits. Closed for extensive renovations at the time of writing, it was set to reopen in spring of 2003. Call to confirm.

Los Angeles Memorial Coliseum

In southern Exposition Park, this 106,000-seat stadium (☎ 213-748-6131; 3911 S Figueroa St) was built in 1923 and has hosted not just the 1932 and 1984 Summer Olympic Games, but also the World Series in 1959 and Super Bowls I and VII. The adjacent **Los Angeles Memorial Sports Arena** (☎ 213-748-6136; 3939 S Figueroa St) dates from 1959 and hosts rock concerts, ice shows, circuses and rodeos.

Around Exposition Park

Just north of the park, the **University of Southern California** (USC) is one of the oldest private research universities in the American West. Distinguished alumni include George Lucas, John Wayne, Frank Gehry and Neil Armstrong. Free 50-minute campus walking tours are offered 10am to 3pm daily; call ☎ 213-740-6605 for reservations.

On campus is the **Fisher Gallery** (☎ *213-740-4561; 823 Exposition Blvd; admission free; open noon-5pm Tues-Sat Sept-Apr*), whose permanent collection includes 19th-century American landscapes, British artists and works from the French Barbizon school.

The double-domed Moorish structure on Jefferson Blvd at the northeastern corner of campus is the 1926 **Shrine Auditorium**, which has 6500 seats and is one of the largest theaters in the USA.

EAST LOS ANGELES

Driving into East LA – just beyond the LA River east of Downtown – feels a bit like crossing the border from San Diego into Tijuana. With more than 90% of its one million residents Latino, this area has the largest concentration of Mexicans outside of Mexico.

Life in the barrio is tough but lively. People shop and mill about in the streets lined with bakeries *(panaderías)*, convenience stores *(tiendas)* and stores selling herbal cures *(botanicas)*. Brightly colored murals adorn many facades. But behind the color, life can look pretty grim. The district suffers from high unemployment and crime, low income and poor schools and infrastructure.

In general, East LA is not conducive to tourist visits, although the risk of becoming a victim of crime is still relatively low. It's best to visit in the daytime and to speak at least a few words of Spanish.

Good streets to explore are **Cesar Chavez Ave**, **Mission Rd** and the neon-festooned **Whittier Blvd**, whose section between I-710 and Atlantic Blvd has been dubbed 'East LA's Sunset Strip' for its concentration of clubs, bars and restaurants.

Mariachi Plaza, at the corner of Boyle Ave and 1st St, is where traditional Mexican musicians wait beneath wall-sized murals to be hired for restaurant performances or social gatherings. Nearby is **El Mercado** (*3425 E 1st St*), a wonderfully boisterous and colorful indoor market, where vendors sell everything from tortilla-making machines to mariachi outfits. At the restaurants upstairs, you'll be serenaded with live mariachi music.

Plaza de la Raza (*3540 N Mission Rd*) is a community arts center that provides free or low-cost after-school classes in theater, dance and the fine arts to neighborhood children. Another arts center is **Self-Help Graphics** (☎ *323-264-1259; 3802 Cesar E Chavez Ave*), founded in 1972 by Sister Karen Boccalero, a Franciscan nun with a strong belief in the healing powers of art. Inside are several galleries and a great gift shop.

SOUTH CENTRAL

Gangs, drugs, poverty, high crime and drive-by shootings are just a few of the negative images – not entirely undeserved – associated with this district. Yet pockets of this area are surprisingly appealing, both culturally and historically. Early LA big wigs built grand mansions here, while culture and the arts – especially jazz music – thrived to the point where South Central invited comparison to New York's Harlem.

Most of the area's neighborhoods and commercial strips were hard hit by the 1992 racial riots, as they were by the Watts riots of 1965. While not traditionally a tourist destination, it should not be overlooked by those with an interest in LA's African-American heritage.

Unfortunately, the violent crime rate in sections of this area is rather high. It's unlikely that you will become a target, but it's better to exercise extra caution and to restrict visits to the daytime.

Watts Towers

South Central's main attraction is the intriguing Watts Towers (☎ *213-847-4646; 1765 E 107th St; adult/concession/child under 17 $2/1/free; tours half-hourly 11am-2:30pm Tues-Fri, 10:30am-2:30pm Sat, 12:30pm-3pm Sun*). On the National Register of Historic Places, this curious and unique folk-art monument is the life's work of Italian immigrant Simon Rodia. In 1921 Rodia set out to 'make something big' – and then spent the next 33 years doing just that. Supporting his towers are slender columns containing steel reinforcement, which he tied with wire, wrapped with wire mesh and covered by hand with cement. Incorporated into the facade are glass (much of it's from green 7-Up bottles), mirrors, sea shells, rocks, ceramic tile and pottery. The recently restored towers are considered among the world's greatest works of folk art.

The adjacent **Watts Towers Art Center** (☎ 213-847-4646; admission free) has changing art exhibits by local and national artists. The center also sponsors free art classes, dance and theater workshops, and other programs designed to involve the local community.

Leimert Park

This neighborhood, south of Martin Luther King Jr Blvd and east of Crenshaw Blvd, is a lovely district with quiet streets canopied by towering trees and lined by handsome single-family homes. The action is centered in Leimert Village, a two-block strip of Degnan Blvd between 43rd St and Leimert Park, where you'll find restaurants, coffeehouses, shops and performance spaces.

Nearby is the **Museum of African American Art** (☎ 323-294-7071; 4005 S Crenshaw Blvd; admission free; open 11am-6pm Thur-Sat, noon-5pm Sun), on the 3rd floor of the Robinsons-May department store in the Baldwin Hills Crenshaw Plaza mall. It's noted for its works of Palmer Hayden, a leading painter of the Harlem Renaissance.

HOLLYWOOD (Map 3)

Hollywood is back – well, sort of. For years little more than a decidedly *un*glittering web of grimy streets peopled by teenage runaways, junkies and prostitutes, central Hollywood has of late been subjected to an aggressive revitalization program that may actually be bearing some fruit.

Some of the historic movie palaces – the El Capitan and the Egyptian – have been restored, and the glamorous Pantages Theater is undergoing a renaissance as the city's hottest venue for musicals. The Metro Red Line makes getting here from places such as Downtown or Universal City a matter of minutes. But the most visible change to the streetscape has been the opening of Hollywood & Highland, a vast retail and entertainment complex. While these developments have sparked new interest in the area, the jury is still out on whether the 'new Hollywood' will be just a giant tourist trap or a dynamic urban haven.

To get to Hollywood from Santa Monica, take bus No 4 or 304 to La Brea, then switch to bus No 212 ($1.65, about one hour).

Hollywood Blvd

More than 2000 marble-and-bronze stars are embedded in the sidewalk along the **Hollywood Walk of Fame**, stretching east from La Brea Ave to Gower St and south along Vine St between Yucca St and Sunset Blvd. Each star bears the celebrity's name engraved and an emblem identifying their artistic field – movies, TV, radio, recording or live theater. Induction ceremonies are held once or twice a month. Call the **Hollywood Chamber of Commerce** (☎ 323-489-8311) for the schedule.

Hollywood Entertainment Museum (☎ 323-465-7900; 7021 Hollywood Blvd; adult/senior/child $7.50/4.50/4; open 10am-6pm Tues-Sun) employs state-of-the-art technology to unravel the history and mystery of moviemaking. A few doors down is the 1927 **Hollywood Roosevelt Hotel** (7000 Hollywood Blvd), which hosted the first Academy Awards ceremony in 1929.

The next block is ground zero of Hollywood revitalization in the form of a vast complex called **Hollywood & Highland** for its location at the intersection of these two streets. At first glance little more than a cleverly designed outdoor shopping mall, it also features restaurants, nightclubs, a luxury hotel and the Kodak Theater, a state-of-the-art auditorium that is the new home of the Oscar awards show and other glitzy events. It's all anchored by the circular **Babylon Court,** where a huge, freestanding triumphal arch decorated with neo-Babylonian motifs frames views of the Hollywood Sign. A pair of pompous pachyderms perched on lofty pedestals lords over the scene, which was inspired by the set of DW Griffith's 1916 movie *Intolerance*. The structure literally dwarfs **Mann's Chinese Theater**, the most famous of Hollywood's movie palaces (1927). Leaving one's foot or handprints in wet cement in the forecourt has been a special honor since Douglas Fairbanks, Mary Pickford and Norma Talmadge started the tradition. Across the street, the **El Capitan Theater** (6838 Hollywood Blvd) has an impressively ornate Spanish Colonial facade and a flamboyant East Indian-inspired interior.

Around the corner is the future home of the **Hollywood History Museum** (w www.hollywoodhistorymuseum.com; 1666 Highland Ave) inside the freshly restored Max Factor

Building (1935). The museum, which is set to open in 2003, will chronicle movie history from the silent era to the present. To check on its progress, go to its website. Already open for business is Mel's Drive-In, a 1950s-style diner.

In the next block awaits a trio of well-visited tourist traps: **Ripley's Believe it or Not!** (☎ 323-466-6335; 6780 Hollywood Blvd; adult/child/student $10.95/7.95/9.95; open 10am-midnight Fri & Sat), where you can examine 300 exhibits of the weird and wild; the **Guinness World of Records Museum** (☎ 323-462-8860; 6764 Hollywood Blvd; adult/senior/child $10.95/8.50/6.95; open 10am-midnight Sun-Thur, 10am-1am Fri & Sat) next door; and the **Hollywood Wax Museum** (☎ 323-462-5991; 6767 Hollywood Blvd; adult/senior/child $10.95/8.50/6.95; open 10am-midnight Sun-Thur, 10am-1am Fri & Sat), across the street.

Just beyond these is the **Egyptian Theatre** (☎ 323-466-3456; 6712 Hollywood Blvd), Hollywood's oldest cinema (1922) and now the home of the nonprofit American Cinematheque. Recently revamped, the theater's exotic decor is a glamorous setting for seeing a movie. On most weekends at 2pm and 3:30pm, you can get the inside scoop on Hollywood history by watching the one-hour Forever Hollywood documentary (☎ 323-461-2020, ext 3 for information; tickets $7).

At **Frederick's of Hollywood Lingerie Museum** (☎ 323-466-8506; 6608 Hollywood Blvd; admission free; open 10am-6pm Mon-Sat, noon-5pm Sun), at the back of the undergarment store, you can admire such 'flimsies' as a tasseled bustier worn by Madonna, Joan Crawford's billowy underskirt and Robert Redford's boxers.

The intersection of Hollywood and Vine may be fabled but there's nothing much to look at, except perhaps the **Capitol Records Tower** (1750 N Vine St), designed to look like a stack of records.

Hollywood Sign

This is Hollywood's, and indeed LA's, most recognizable landmark, built in 1923 as an advertising gimmick for a real estate development called Hollywoodland. Each letter is 50ft tall and made of sheet metal. Hiking to the sign is illegal. For good views, head to the Griffith Park Observatory or to the top of Beachwood Canyon Dr.

Paramount Studios

Southeast of central Hollywood, Paramount Studios (5555 Melrose Ave) is the only movie studio still in Hollywood proper. Founded in 1914, this is the home of the original Star Trek TV series and the current Star Trek: Voyager. Its roster of blockbuster movies ranges from the 1921 The Sheik with Rudolph Valentino to the Indiana Jones trilogy and Forrest Gump. Tours of the studios have been suspended because of security concerns but may resume at any time. Call ☎ 323-956-1777 for updates.

Hollywood Forever Cemetery

Just north of Paramount, this cemetery (☎ 323-469-1181; 6000 Santa Monica Blvd; grounds usually open 7am-6pm daily, mausoleum open 8am-5:30pm daily) is crowded with famous 'immortals,' including Rudolph Valentino, Tyrone Power, Jayne Mansfield and Cecil B DeMille. A detailed map ($5) to the stars' graves is available in the flower shop on the right past the entrance. Shop hours vary but are shorter than grounds hours.

Barnsdall Art Park

Occupying an olive-shrouded hill on Vermont Ave between Hollywood and Sunset Blvds (enter from Hollywood Blvd), Barnsdall Art Park is a city-owned cultural and arts center. Its main visitor attraction is the **Hollyhock House**, Frank Lloyd Wright's earliest LA project (1921). It is currently undergoing total rehabilitation and will remain closed until about 2005. An exhibition of photographs, furniture and other items from the house will go on view at the park's **Los Angeles Municipal Art Gallery**, most likely in early 2003. For details, call ☎ 213-473-8455.

WEST HOLLYWOOD (Map 4)

West Hollywood (WeHo) is one of LA's hippest neighborhoods, teeming with nightclubs, restaurants and elegant hotels. Numerous galleries add an artsy touch, and trendy shops cater to celebrities and fashion fanatics from around the world. This is also the heart of LA's gay and – to a lesser extent – lesbian community, which accounts for one third of WeHo's 36,000 residents. During June's Gay Pride Parade and Halloween, Santa Monica Blvd explodes in a partying frenzy.

Design is big here, with more than 150 showrooms (trade only) at the **Pacific Design Center** *(PDC; ☎ 310-657-0800; 8687 Melrose Ave)* alone and dozens more in the surrounding streets (the 'Avenues of Design'). The PDC itself is an architectural landmark nicknamed the 'Blue Whale' for its behemoth dimensions and shiny blue glass facade. In its courtyard you'll find a small branch of the Museum of Contemporary Art (see Downtown earlier in this chapter), called **MOCA at the PDC** *(☎ 310-657-0800; admission $3, free Thur after 5pm; open 11am-5pm Tues-Sun, 11am-8pm Thur).* It presents a lively schedule of work by new and established international artists, with a particular emphasis on architecture and design themes.

Also at the PDC, on the mezzanine level, is the **West Hollywood Convention & Visitors Bureau** *(☎ 310-289-2525, 800-368-*

6020; **W** *www.visitwesthollywood.com),* where you can pick up more information about the town.

Melrose Ave

Starting at the PDC, Melrose Ave is LA's former and once-again epicenter of cool and a good place to pick up eccentric fashions and vintage clothing. Countless boutiques, many of the wacky and unique variety, flank both sides of this thoroughfare. Restaurants, bars and theaters are also part of the eclectic mix, making Melrose one of the most fun places in town to stroll around. The action concentrates in the section between Fairfax and La Brea Aves, but in recent years the area around the PDC has also gained in popularity. Don't even bother showing up before noon on any day, and if you can, come on Saturday for people-watching at its finest.

Schindler House

A couple of blocks north of Melrose Ave is the former home of modernist architect Rudolph Schindler, now the **MAK Center for Art & Architecture** *(☎ 323-651-1510; 835 N Kings Rd; admission $5, free 4pm-6pm Fri; open 10am-6pm Wed-Sun).* The Austrian-born Schindler was a disciple of Frank Lloyd Wright and built his house in 1921. Today, it functions as a think tank supporting current art and architecture issues.

Sunset Strip

The famed Sunset Strip – Sunset Blvd between Laurel Canyon Blvd and Doheny Dr – is lined with nightclubs, restaurants and hotels that collectively are a 'who's who in the zoo' of LA rock history: the Whisky A Go Go, The Roxy, Rainbow Bar & Grill and the former Gazzarri's (now Key Club) are among the legendary haunts where many a career was launched. The Doors, Jimi Hendrix, Bob Marley, Bruce Springsteen and Van Halen are among the many who have performed at these clubs. If you're into Hollywood history, it was at the Rainbow (then the Villa Nova) where actress Marilyn Monroe and baseball star Joe DiMaggio met on a 'blind' date in 1953.

Sunset is also the billboard capital of the world. These enormous and imaginative vanity boards are one-of-a-kind placards for new movies, album releases, wannabe stars and antismoking campaigns.

Gay & Lesbian LA

West Hollywood (WeHo) is the heart of LA's gay and lesbian scene, and there's practically 24/7 action in the bars, restaurants, clubs, coffeehouses and gyms along Santa Monica Blvd. Most cater primarily to gay men, though there are a few for lesbian and mixed audiences.

Beauty reigns supreme in 'Boyz Town' and the intimidation factor can be high unless you're buffed, bronzed and styled. Silver Lake is cruising heaven for the Levi's and leather crowd and also has a few Latino bars. The beach towns have more relaxed, neighborly scenes, while venues in the San Fernando Valley are generally more mundane and mainstream gay. For updates and specifics about the various scenes, check the free gay and lesbian magazines available in bars, restaurants and gay-friendly establishments.

A Different Light Bookstore *(Map 4; ☎ 310-854-6601; 8853 Santa Monica Blvd, West Hollywood)* in West Hollywood, is the city's number one gay bookstore. **Sisterhood Bookstore** *(Map 5; ☎ 310-477-7300; 1351 Westwood Blvd, Westwood)* caters to women, though not exclusively to lesbians. The main branch of the **LA Gay & Lesbian Center** *(☎ 323-993-7400; **W** www.laglc.org; 1625 N Schrader Blvd, Hollywood)* is a one-stop service and health agency.

Further east, you'll find that LA is not only home of the Hollywood Walk of Fame, but also of the **Rock Walk of Fame** *(7425 Sunset Blvd)*. Immortalized in concrete right in the entrance of the Guitar Center store are the hands of such legends as BB King, ZZ Top, Steely Dan, the Doobie Brothers and dozens more.

By the way, LA also has a **Porno Walk of Fame**, but to see this you'll have to travel three blocks south to the gay movie theater **Tomkat** *(7734 Santa Monica Blvd)*. Even those who wouldn't touch a porn movie with a 10-inch pole may have heard of such legendary hard-core studs and divas as Harry Reems and the recently deceased Linda Lovelace. Alas, if you were expecting cement prints of performers' signature body parts, you'll be disappointed: it's PG-rated hands and feet only.

MID-CITY (Map 4)

Mid-City is the area wedged between the Westside and Downtown, north of I-10 but south of Hollywood. Its principal artery is **Wilshire Blvd**, which cuts east–west for 16mi. It passes an eclectic succession of neighborhoods – Koreatown, Hancock Park, the Miracle Mile, the Fairfax District, Beverly Hills, Westwood and finally Santa Monica – before terminating at the Pacific Ocean. Metro Rapid bus No 720 runs along its entire length.

Koreatown

Koreatown is an amorphous area west of Downtown and south of MacArthur Park. Much of it is an undistinguished sprawl of modern shopping malls and housing tracts, but for architecture fans a number of delicacies await along Wilshire Blvd.

The blocks between Western Ave and Hoover St are distinguished by several elaborate churches, most built in the 1920s in a variety of historic styles ranging from Romanesque to baroque. One of the most interesting is the **First Congregational Church** *(Map 2; 540 Commonwealth Ave)*, actually located one block north of Wilshire Blvd.

Further west is the Art Deco **Wiltern Theatre** (1931), which gets its name from its location at the southeastern corner of *Wil*shire and *Wes*tern Blvds. It has the same turquoise facade as the former **Bullocks Wilshire** *(1929; 3050 Wilshire Blvd)*, which is 1mi east. This was the nation's first department store to cater to customers arriving by car. For decades, it was *the* place to shop and have tea in the 5th floor tearoom. The store closed in 1992 and is now occupied by the Southwestern University School of Law, which recently reopened the restored **tearoom** *(open10am-6pm Mon-Thur, 10am-3pm Fri)*.

Between the two buildings is **Ambassador Hotel** *(1922; 3400 Wilshire Blvd)*, once among LA's grandest hotels but now abandoned. It was here that Sirhan Sirhan assassinated Democratic presidential nominee Robert F Kennedy in 1968.

Miracle Mile District

The stretch of Wilshire Blvd between La Brea Blvd and Fairfax Ave earned the epithet 'Miracle Mile' after an entrepreneur, AW Ross, bought previously empty land beside the Rancho La Brea tar pits in 1920 and turned it into the city's first commercial district outside of Downtown. Today, the strip is also known as 'Museum Row.'

La Brea Tar Pits & Page Museum One of the world's premier paleontological sites, La Brea Tar Pits supplied the tar *(brea* in Spanish) used by Native Americans and early settlers to waterproof roofs and boats. In 1906 scientists realized that the bubbling black pools had acted like flypaper, entrapping animal and plant life during the Pleistocene ice age beginning 40,000 years ago. Pit excavations yielded more than a million fossilized skeleton parts, including those of such long-extinct mammals as saber-toothed cats, ground sloths, mammoths and mastodons, along with 200 different bird, reptile, insect and plant species.

Tar pit discoveries are exhibited in the **Page Museum** *(☎ 323-936-2230; ⓦ www .tarpits.org; 5801 Wilshire Blvd; adult/ concession/child 5-12 $6/3.50/2; open 9:30am-5pm Mon-Fri, 10am-5pm Sat & Sun).*

Excavations still continue – usually from July to mid-September – when visitors may observe the process from the **Pit 91 Visitors Station** *(☎ 323-934-7243; admission free; open 10am-4pm Wed-Sun).*

Los Angeles County Museum of Art Just west of the tar pits is the Los Angeles County Museum of Art *(LACMA; ☎ 323-857-6000; ⓦ www.lacma.org; 5905 Wilshire Blvd;*

adult/senior & student/child $7/5/1; open noon-8pm Mon, Tues & Thur, noon-9pm Fri, 11am-8pm Sat & Sun), one of the leading art museums in the USA for its size, scope and depth. The vast collection's main strength lies in European art, including Italian baroque paintings and works by Rembrandt, Degas and Gauguin.

Also on display are ancient and Islamic art spanning eight millennia, with pieces from Egypt, Greece, Rome, Turkey and Iran. The museum's assemblage of Southeast Asian art encompasses stone and bronze sculpture, painting and decorative arts. Its Far Eastern section has works from as early as the Neolithic period (400 to 1800 BC), as well as items from the Imperial and Song dynasties and a replica of a Ming-period scholar's studio. A highlight of the Pavilion for Japanese Art is the collection of rare Shin'enkan temple paintings.

The museum has commissioned Dutch architect Rem Kohlhaas to completely redesign its facilities, a process that is scheduled for completion by 2005. Some galleries may be closed in upcoming years. Check the museum's website for updates.

Petersen Automotive Museum LA's love affair with the automobile is celebrated at the Petersen Automotive Museum *(☎ 323-930-2277; ⓦ www.petersen.org; 6060 Wilshire Blvd; adult/senior/child $7/6/5; open 10am-6pm Tues-Sun)*. Even non-car buffs will enjoy the ground-floor exhibit, which leads you through a mock streetscape of LA in the '20s and '30s and chronicles how inventions such as gas stations, billboards, minimalls, drive-in restaurants and movie theaters were spawned in LA. The upstairs galleries house special exhibits, while the 3rd floor features a 'discovery center', where kids can learn science by way of the automobile.

Fairfax District
The spine of LA's principal Jewish neighborhood is the section of Fairfax Ave between Santa Monica and Wilshire Blvds. It's home to Orthodox and Hasidic Jews, with lots of yeshivas (gender-segregated religious day schools) and delis, kosher butcher shops, furniture stores and other small businesses.

For visitors, the main point of interest is the **Farmers Market** *(☎ 323-933-9211; 6333*

W 3rd St). The 150-plus vendors offer an international array of hot and cold foods as well as fresh produce and unique gift items. Just north of the market looms **CBS Television City** *(☎ 323-852-2624; 7800 Beverly Blvd)*, while east of the market a chic new mega-mall called **The Grove at Farmer's Market** has sprung up. It's an attractively designed open-air space with plenty of upscale stores and a 14-screen movie theater. A trolley shuttles shoppers from the mall to the Farmers Market.

GRIFFITH PARK (Map 7)
Spreading across a rugged mountainous area, Griffith Park is five times the size of New York's Central Park and blanketed by California oak, wild sage and manzanita. The famous Hollywood Sign is atop Mt Lee, on the park's western edge. Within its boundaries are an outdoor theater, an observatory, the city zoo, a major museum, golf courses, tennis courts, playgrounds, bridle paths and hiking trails.

To get to the park from Santa Monica, take the Big Blue Bus No 10 east to Olive and 14th in Downtown, then change to bus No 96 north. From Hollywood, take bus No 181 east to Riverside Dr and Los Feliz Blvd and transfer to bus No 96 here.

Griffith Observatory & Planetarium
Narrow winding roads – or, for the physically adept, trails – lead up to the Griffith Observatory & Planetarium *(☎ 323-664-1191; ⓦ www.griffithobs.org; 2800 E Observatory Rd)*. Clinging to the southern slopes of Mt Hollywood, the snowy white facade and shiny copper domes have been a local landmark since 1935. The view of the city from here is stunning but, alas, off limits until about 2005 while the complex remains closed during a thorough renovation. Check the website for updates.

Los Angeles Zoo
The LA Zoo *(☎ 323-644-6000; 5333 Zoo Dr; adult/senior/child $8.25/5.25/3.25; open 10am-5pm daily)* is home to some 1200 animals representing 350 mammal, bird, amphibian and reptile species. They live in a dozen habitats laid out according to the animals' continental origins: North and South America, Africa, Australia and

Eurasia. A highlight is the chimpanzees of Mahale Mountains (located in Tanzania) exhibit, although the Ahmanson Koala House is also a crowd favorite. A recent addition is a new habitat for the zoo's Komodo dragons, Southeast Asian lizards that can grow up to 10ft long. Adventure Island, an interactive area for children, focuses on animals found in the American Southwest.

Autry Museum of Western Heritage

Anyone interested in the history of the American West will hit the mother lode at this delightful museum (☎ 323-667-2000; W www.autry-museum.org; 4700 Western Heritage Way; adult/senior & student/child 2-12 $7.50/5/3, free 2nd Tues of month; open 10am-5pm Tues-Sun, 10am-8pm Thur). Its 10 galleries skillfully combine scholarship and showmanship to reveal how the West was 'discovered' again and again, by everyone from prehistoric tribes to missionaries. Special exhibits illustrate what made the West so wild, including an 1880s carved mahogany saloon bar, gaming tables, cheating devices and an impressive Colt firearms collection.

The museum also presents concerts, gallery talks, symposia, panel discussions, film screenings and storytelling sessions for children.

Travel Town Museum

Railroad buffs will not want to miss Travel Town (☎ 323-662-5874; 5200 W Zoo Dr; admission free; open 10am-4pm Mon-Fri, 10am-5pm Sat & Sun), an outdoor transportation museum that specializes in pre-WWII railroad antiques. Highlights include steam locomotives (the oldest from 1864, the 'youngest' from 1925), freight and passenger cars (including several sleepers) and cabooses. The best day to visit is on the first and third Sunday of every month when volunteers run free rides (donations appreciated) on a caboose pulled by a diesel engine. A miniature train operates daily.

Other Attractions

Kids' attractions, centered in the park's southeastern corner, include the Griffith Park Southern Railroad (☎ 323-664-6788; operates 10am-4:30pm Mon-Fri, 10am-5pm Sat & Sun), a miniature train ride in operation since 1948. It makes a 1mi loop past

pony rides, through an old Western town and a Native American village.

Generations of Angelenos and visitors have also delighted in riding the richly festooned 1926 merry-go-round (☎ 323-665-3051; rides $1; operates 11am-5pm daily in summer, Sat & Sun only in winter) nearby. To get to this area, follow Crystal Springs Dr along the park's eastern flank.

Forest Lawn Memorial Park – Hollywood Hills

Just west of Griffith Park, this 340-acre cemetery (☎ 323-254-7251; 6300 Forest Lawn Dr; admission free; grounds open 8am-6pm daily) boasts sculpture, mosaics and artwork, plus a fine catalog of dead celebrities, including Lucille Ball, Liberace, Bette Davis and Stan Laurel.

BEVERLY HILLS & WESTSIDE (Map 5)

Throughout the world, the mere mention of Beverly Hills conjures an image of fame and wealth, reinforced by TV and film. The reality of Beverly Hills is not so different from the myth. Stylish and sophisticated, this city-within-a-city is indeed a place where the well-heeled frolic. Rodeo Drive is lined with a veritable who's who of haute couture. Opulent manors face manicured grounds on palm-shaded avenues winding gently uphill on the northern side of Santa Monica Blvd.

You can get maps to the stars' homes at tourist stores or from street-corner vendors, although these are usually hopelessly outdated. A major landmark is the Beverly Hills Hotel (☎ 310-887-2887; 9641 Sunset Blvd), nicknamed the 'Pink Palace,' which has served as the unofficial hobnobbing headquarters of the Hollywood power elite since 1912.

West of Beverly Hills, the quiet, affluent neighborhoods of Bel Air and Brentwood and the Westwood campus of the University of California constitute what is commonly referred to as the Westside.

Museum of Television & Radio

Contrary to its name, the Museum of Television & Radio (MTR; ☎ 310-786-1000; 465 N Beverly Dr; suggested donation adult/senior & student/child $6/4/3; open noon-5pm Wed-Sun, noon-8pm Thur) is not a traditional showcase of artifacts but an enormous archive of original works of two of the 20th-century's breakthrough media. The heart of the museum beats in the Stanley Hubbard Library, a repository of some 100,000 broadcasts spanning 75 years, all available for viewing. There's also a daily changing schedule of screenings, three galleries, a radio listening room with pre-recorded programs, seminars and the occasional live broadcast. Call ☎ 310-786-1025 for a schedule or pick one up at the lobby information desk.

Museum of Tolerance

Run by the Simon Wiesenthal Center, this museum (☎ 310-553-9036; 9786 W Pico Blvd; adult/senior/student & child $9/7/5.50; open 11:30am-4pm Mon-Thur, 11am-5pm Sun year-round; 11:30am-1pm Fri Nov-Mar, 11:30am-3pm Fri Apr-Oct; photo ID required) uses the latest interactive technologies to make visitors confront their own closely held beliefs. The Tolerancenter, which focuses on racism and prejudice, features the 'Point of View Diner,' where you'll be served with the message of personal responsibility, and the 'Millennium Machine,' which educates about human rights abuses throughout the world. The core of the museum, though, is the Holocaust Section, with more information about the subject available in a separate gallery, at the Multimedia Learning Center and from Holocaust survivors who speak to the public at various times during the week.

UCLA

Established in 1919, UCLA (☎ 310-825-4321; 405 Hilgard Ave) has about 36,500 students and is one of the premier institutions of higher learning in the USA. Free student-guided tours (☎ 310-825-8764 for reservations) of the 419-acre campus are given at 10:30am and 1:30pm weekdays by reservation only. The campus grounds are beautifully landscaped and contain several buildings of architectural interest, as well as museums and exhibit spaces.

One campus highlight is the Fowler Museum of Cultural History (☎ 310-825-4361; adult/senior/child & student $5/3/free, free Thur; open noon-5pm Wed-Sun, noon-8pm Thur), which has a world-class collection of art and artifacts from non-Western cultures. Gardens include the quiet and picturesque Franklin D Murphy Sculpture Garden, with 70 works by Rodin, Moore, Calder and

other artists; and the Mildred E Mathias Botanical Garden, with its more than 4000 plant species in the campus' southeastern corner (enter on Tiverton Ave).

UCLA Hammer Museum

In less than a decade, this museum (☎ 310-443-7000; 10899 Wilshire Blvd; adult/senior/child under 17 $5/3/free, free Thur; open 11am-7pm Tues-Wed & Fri-Sat, 11am-9pm Thur, 11am-5pm Sun) graduated from a mere vanity project for its main benefactor, the late industrialist Armand Hammer, to a respected showcase of both contemporary and period art. Changing exhibits draw from Hammer's collections of impressionist and postimpressionist art and lithographs by French caricaturist Honoré Daumier, as well as from the UCLA Grunwald Center for the Graphic Arts. At the time of writing, the museum was expected to close for a major renovation in early 2004, with a reopening planned for 2005.

Westwood Memorial Park

This small, star-studded cemetery (1218 Glendon Ave) is a bit hard to find – from Wilshire Blvd, turn south onto Glendon Ave and look for the driveway immediately to your left. Here you'll find the tombs of Marilyn Monroe, Natalie Wood, Roy Orbison and Frank Zappa (in an unmarked grave).

Getty Center

The Getty Center (☎ 310-440-7300; 1200 Getty Center Dr; admission free; open 10am-6pm Tues-Thur & Sun, 10am-9pm Fri & Sat) hunkers atop a Brentwood hillside like an impregnable postmodern fortress, but once you arrive within its vast courtyards it's a very welcoming place indeed. It took 14 years of planning and construction and $1 billion to build this stunning Richard Meier–designed 110-acre 'campus.' It unites the art collections assembled by oil magnate J Paul Getty with several Getty-sponsored institutes focused on conservation, art research and education.

Four two-story pavilions house the permanent collection, while a fifth presents changing exhibitions. The upper floors of each building focus on paintings, the lower floors on sculptures, illuminated manuscripts, drawings and furniture. Tours, lectures and interactive technology make the art accessible to all. Also take time to admire the architecture, the landscaping and the superb views.

Admission is free, but parking reservations ($5) are mandatory – *except* after 4pm weekdays and all day weekends and for college students. In addition, no reservations are needed to park in the lot on Sepulveda Blvd at Constitution Ave (just north of Wilshire Blvd) with free shuttle service to the Getty. MTA bus No 561 or Big Blue Bus No 14 serve the center.

Skirball Cultural Center

A cluster of galleries, performance and exhibit spaces, the Skirball Cultural Center (☎ 310-440-4500; 2701 N Sepulveda Blvd; adult/senior & student/child under 12 $8/6/free; open noon-5pm Mon-Sat, 11am-5pm Sun) takes visitors on a journey through the history of the Jewish people, showcasing their contributions to the world and to America, often with refreshing irreverence.

Interactive touch screens and video displays add just the right touch of 'tech', and children should delight in the **Discovery Center**, where they become hobby archeologists and can dig into the past – literally – by unearthing ancient artifacts.

There is a free summer outdoor concert series as well as a packed schedule of lectures, concerts and performances (prices vary). **Zeidler's Café** (mains $6 to $10) serves strictly kosher and creative pizzas, pasta, salads and other goodies for lunch, including many choices for vegetarians and the lactose-intolerant.

Sony Pictures Studios

In 1990 the former studio lot of MGM – the most powerful Hollywood studio from 1924 to 1986 – was acquired by Sony Pictures Entertainment (☎ 310-520-8687; 10202 W Washington Blvd). At one time, MGM had so many stars under contract (Spencer Tracy, Katherine Hepburn, Elizabeth Taylor, Jimmy Stewart, to drop just a few names) that its motto became, 'More stars than there are in heaven.'

Despite the historical link, the two-hour walking tour focuses mostly on Sony productions. Highlights include a visit to the *Jeopardy* set and sound stage 27, where you can still see the 'Yellow Brick Road.' Tickets also give access to the commissary (restaurant) and the studio store. The tours cost $20 and run at 9:30am, 11am, noon and 2:30pm weekdays. Reservations are required and children must be 12 or over.

MALIBU

Malibu has been a celebrity enclave since the 1920s, when money troubles forced landowner May Ridge to lease out property west of the Malibu Lagoon. Clara Bow and Barbara Stanwyck were among the first to move to what became the **Malibu Colony**, which today is home to such headliners as Mel Gibson, Sting, Tom Hanks and Barbra Streisand. Stars still prize their privacy in this gated and well-policed community. While it's impossible to get past the gate, it is legal to walk along the beach – as long as you stay below the high-tide mark.

To 'normal' folks, Malibu is best appreciated through its parks and beaches. Lining the coast from east to west over a stretch of about 25mi, some of the best beaches include Las Tunas, Malibu-Surfrider, Point Dume, Zuma and Leo Carrillo.

The rugged mountains that rise abruptly behind Malibu are part of the **Santa Monica Mountains National Recreation Area** and are dotted with state and county parks with access to almost 600mi of **hiking trails**. Popular trailheads include those in Topanga, Will Rogers and Point Mugu State Parks.

Cultural sights include the **Adamson House** (☎ 310-456-8432; 23200 Pacific Coast Hwy), a beautiful 1928 Spanish Colonial villa laced with Moorish elements in enchanting surroundings. The free tours (30 to 45 minutes) operate 11am to 2pm Wednesday to Saturday. The adjacent **Malibu Lagoon Museum** (☎ 310-456-8432; admission free; open 11am-3pm Wed-Sat) is a local history museum. The **J Paul Getty Villa** in Malibu was still undergoing remodeling at the time of writing.

SANTA MONICA (Map 6)

Over the past decade, Santa Monica has undergone an amazing metamorphosis which is the envy of urban planners worldwide. Once a quaint, slightly wacky seaside resort, it has become a glitzy beach town with a cosmopolitan flair. For travelers, Santa Monica is a great destination. It's safe, easily explored on foot, has good air quality, shopping, lodging, dining and entertainment and miles of beach.

LOS ANGELES

For maps, room reservations and general information, visit either branch of the **Santa Monica Visitor Center** (☎ 310-393-7593 for both branches; w www.santamonica.com). The main one (open 10am-4pm daily) is on the 2nd floor of the Santa Monica Place mall (near the corner of 2nd St and Colorado Blvd). A smaller kiosk (open 10am-5pm daily May-late Oct, 10am-4pm daily late Oct-Apr) is at 1400 Ocean Blvd.

The heart of Santa Monica is the **Third Street Promenade**, a pedestrian mall between Broadway and Wilshire Blvd. Here you'll find street entertainment (especially on weekends), restaurants, bars and movie theaters. The southern end of the promenade is anchored by **Santa Monica Place**, a shopping mall designed by Frank Gehry.

Two blocks west of the promenade, Ocean Ave parallels **Palisades Park** atop a bluff overlooking the ocean. Below is the famous **Santa Monica Pier** with restaurants, bars and shops and the quaint 1920 **carousel** that starred alongside Paul Newman and Robert Redford in The Sting. Beneath the carousel is the **UCLA Ocean Discovery Center** (☎ 310-393-6149; admission $3; open noon-4pm daily June-Oct, 11am-5pm Sat-Sun Nov-May), a child-oriented facility dedicated to demystifying the denizens of Santa Monica Bay such as jellyfish and sharks. The pier's main draw is the **Pacific Park**, a small-scale amusement park with a small roller coaster, a solar-powered Ferris wheel, and a host of smaller kiddy rides and arcade games.

South of the pier look for the newly refurbished **International Chess Park** and the site of the **Original Muscle Beach**, where the Southern California exercise craze began back in the 1930s. Brand-new equipment now once again draws a new generation of gymnasts, bodybuilders and other athletes to the historic venue.

Other Santa Monica areas suitable for strolling, shopping and dining are **Montana Ave** in the city's northern section and **Main St** on the southern end of town, near the border with Venice Beach.

Bergamot Station
The nearly 40 galleries berthed within the sprawling industrial grounds of Bergamot Station (☎ 310-453-7535; 2525 Michigan Ave) have been a nexus of the LA arts scene since the complex opened in 1994. Also

here is the **Santa Monica Museum of Art** (☎ 310-586-6488; suggested donation adult/students, seniors & artists $3/2; open 11am-6pm Tues-Sat, noon-5pm Sun), the saucy and irreverent home of changing contemporary art exhibits with an emphasis on new and experimental media.

VENICE BEACH (Map 6)
The quintessential bohemian playground, Venice Beach is famous for its Ocean Front Walk and Muscle Beach, its canals and unique population blend of hippies, New Agers, artists, Industry types and students. It's hard to imagine now that until about a century ago Venice was nothing but dreary swampland. Enter Abbot Kinney (1850–1920), a visionary, dreamer and developer, who drained the marshes, dug a 16mi network of canals and built a promenade, pier and theater. Kinney even imported gondoliers from Italy to pole people through his beachfront paradise, which he dubbed 'Venice of America.' The spectacular opening took place on July 4, 1905. Alas, Hollywood soon eclipsed Venice's star and Kinney's vision was taken over by speakeasies and gambling halls in the Prohibition era.

In 1993 the surviving 3mi of the historic canals were restored and are now lined by picturesque million-dollar-plus homes. The **Venice Canal Walk** threads through this idyllic neighborhood, best accessed from either Venice or Washington Blvds near Dell Ave.

The chief attraction of modern Venice is its **Ocean Front Walk**, also known as the Venice Boardwalk. Bikini-clad bicyclists, chainsaw-juggling entertainers, wannabe Schwarzeneggers, a rollerskating Sikh minstrel, 'meat is murder' activists, henna tattoo artists – it's a freak show that must be seen to be believed. Strolling, biking or skating along this 1½mi stretch between Marine St in the north to the Venice Pier is a great way to spend an afternoon, especially on weekends.

Venice is home to many artists, a presence reflected in the numerous galleries and abundant public art, including Jonathan Borofsky's 34ft **Ballerina Clown** at Rose Ave and Main St. Top galleries include **LA Louver Galleries** (☎ 310-822-4955; 45 N Venice Blvd; open 10am-6pm Tues-Sat) and the **James Corcoran Gallery** (☎ 310-966-1010; 1633 Electric Ave; visits by appointment only), which often showcase local artists.

LOS ANGELES

SAN PEDRO

About 21mi south of Downtown LA, San Pedro is a slow-paced harbor community on the northern fringe of Worldport LA, one of the busiest ports in the world.

Sights include the **Los Angeles Maritime Museum** (☎ 310-548-7618; Berth 84, bottom of 6th St; requested donation $1; open 10am-5pm Tues-Sun) in a Streamline Moderne former car ferry terminal. The 75,000-sq-ft facility contains more than 700 ship models, ship figureheads, navigational equipment and an operating amateur radio station. About 1mi north, at Berth 94, is the **SS Lane Victory** (☎ 310-519-9545; adult/child 5-15 $3/1; open 9am-4pm daily), used during WWII to transport cargo to Allied troops and now a museum.

Just south of the Maritime Museum, Ports O' Call Village is a hopeless tourist trap, supposedly evocative of 19th-century New England seaside towns. It's also the main departure point for harbor tours offered several times daily by **Spirit Cruises** (☎ 310-548-8080) from Berth 77. One-hour narrated tours cost $7.50; 90-minute cruises are $9.

It's a short drive south to the **Cabrillo Marine Aquarium** (☎ 310-548-7562; w www.cabrilloaq.org; 3720 Stephen White Dr; suggested donation adult/child $5/1, parking $6.50; open noon-5pm Tues-Fri, 10am-5pm Sat & Sun). This is a fun and educational place and sure to keep kids entertained. Among the 38 tanks displaying colorful fish and other marine life is one where visitors are encouraged to pick up starfish, sea urchins, sea cucumbers and other denizens of the sea. The museum is undergoing an expansion set to be completed in late 2004, but will remain open in the meantime.

A good way to get around San Pedro is by **Electric Trolley**, which runs Thursday to Sunday at 15-minute intervals; rides cost only 25¢.

LONG BEACH

Long Beach is the southernmost city in LA County and has an easygoing, small-town atmosphere and a couple of flagship attractions. Getting around is made easy by using the Passport, a shuttle bus that circulates to most places of interest (free within downtown, 90¢ otherwise).

The action centers on the three-block stretch of **Pine Ave** between Long Beach Plaza and Ocean Blvd, which teems with restaurants, nightspots and shops. Belmont Shore, about 3mi east of downtown, has interesting shopping and dining along 2nd St. Further on is the elite borough of Naples, a maze of canals that can be explored aboard authentic gondolas (☎ 562-433-9595; 5437 E Ocean Blvd). One-hour tours cost $55 per couple.

Long Beach has a **visitor center** (☎ 562-436-3645, 800-452-7829; w www.visit longbeach.com; One World Trade Center, suite 300; open 8:30am-5pm Mon-Fri) and an **information kiosk** (open 10am-5pm daily May-Sept, 10am-4pm Sat-Sun Oct-Apr) outside the aquarium.

Long Beach Aquarium of the Pacific

In this age of aquariums, when watery zoos are proliferating faster than sea slugs on Viagra, Long Beach has fielded a contender that swims along with the best of them. The Aquarium of the Pacific (☎ 562-590-3100; 100 Aquarium Way; adult/senior/child $18.75/14.95/9.95, parking $6; open 9am-6pm daily) consists of 17 habitats and 30 smaller focus tanks covering three Pacific Rim regions: Southern California and Baja California, Northern Pacific and Tropical Pacific. Presented in an imaginative and informative way, the more than 10,000 fish, mammals and birds from 550 species instill a sense of wonder and awe in visitors of all ages. The newest attraction is the Shark Lagoon, where you literally reach out and touch some of these toothy predators – and quite possibly put lingering nightmares of Jaws to rest. For an extra fee, the aquarium also offers behind-the-scenes tours and ocean boat trips (seasonal).

Queen Mary Seaport

The Titanic may have captured all the headlines, but the Queen Mary (☎ 310-435-3511; 1126 Queens Hwy; adult/child $19/15, parking $8; open 10am-6pm daily) was actually even more luxurious and considerably larger. The 81,237-ton liner was launched in 1934 and made 1001 Atlantic crossings before being retired in 1964 and moored in Long Beach three years later. One of the most luxurious of the luxury liners, it was favored by celebrities and royalty. Part of it is now a hotel.

Basic admission includes a self-guided tour as well as the 'Ghost and Legends of the Queen Mary' special-effects tour. The optional Behind the Scenes Tour and WWII Tour cost an extra $8/5 each.

Moored next to the ocean liner is the **Scorpion** (☎ 562-435-3511; adult/concession $10/9; open 10am-6pm daily), a 1973 Russian submarine whose fascinating – if claustrophobic – interior is open for touring. Combination tickets with the *Queen Mary* are available.

Directly across Queensway Bay from the two vessels is **Shoreline Village**, a shopping-and-dining complex, and departure point for harbor and whale-watching cruises.

Museums

Long Beach is home to two art museums. The exquisite **Museum of Latin American Art** (☎ 562-437-1689; 628 Alamitos Ave; adult/student & senior $5/3, free Fri; open 11:30am-7pm Tues-Fri, 11am-7pm Sat, 11am-6pm Sun) is the only one in the western USA to showcase contemporary Latin American art.

Right on the ocean is the **Long Beach Museum of Art** (☎ 562-439-2119; 2300 E Ocean Blvd; adult/student & senior $5/4; open 11am-5pm Tues-Sun), whose permanent collection is particularly strong in 20th-century European art, California modernism and video art.

SAN FERNANDO VALLEY

Known simply as 'The Valley,' this broad, flat 220-sq-mi region is as well known for its earthquakes as for its seemingly endless commercial strips and tract homes. Car culture was basically invented here, and the Valley takes credit for giving birth not only to the minimall but also to the drive-in movie theater, the drive-in bank and of course the drive-in restaurant.

Framed by mountain ranges that trap the air, the Valley is usually capped by a thick layer of smog and is about 15° to 20°F hotter than the beach. Major communities are Glendale, Burbank, North Hollywood and Studio City.

Now often mocked by outsiders, the Valley was actually quite fashionable among early Hollywood moguls, including Walt Disney and John Wayne, who had their private homes here. In their wake came most of the

major studios. These days, the Valley is also the world capital of the adult-film industry.

Universal Studios Hollywood

Universal Studios (Map 7; ☎ 818-508-9600; 100 Universal City Plaza; adult/child $43/35, ask about special packages; opening hours vary seasonally) is the world's largest movie and TV studio, built by Carl Laemmle in 1915 on the site of a former chicken ranch. Studio tours began in 1964 and have since been experienced by 100 million visitors.

You'll need to devote a full day to Universal. It gets very busy in summer, so prepare yourself for long waits in stifling heat. Bring a hat, suntan lotion, patience and – if cutting costs is your aim – sandwiches and bottled water. Some rides, including the popular Back to the Future and Jurassic Park, have minimum height requirements (usually 42in or 46in).

Universal Studios sprawls across 413 acres, the upper and lower sections connected by a quarter-mile-long escalator. To get your bearings, head straight for the **Backlot Tour**, a 45-minute part-educational, part-thrill ride behind the scenes of moviemaking. A tram whisks you and about 250 other visitors past the studio's maze of 35 soundstages with narration by Ron Howard coming from an audio system and four video monitors. You'll see where scenes from *Jurassic Park* and *Apollo 13* were filmed, rumble past outdoor sets such as Courthouse Square, best known from *Back to the Future*, and the Bates Hotel featured in Hitchcock's *Psycho*. During the thrill portion of the tour you'll face up to an 8.3-magnitude earthquake, a flash flood, a collapsing bridge and encounters with a hokey plastic shark and a roaring, in-your-face King Kong.

Universal doesn't have a huge number of rides, making it possible to experience them all in a single day. Classics include **Back to the Future,** during which you'll free-fall into volcanic tunnels, plunge down glacial cliffs and collide with dinosaurs. **The ET Adventure** is a gentle flight aboard a monorailed 'bicycle' through a charming fantasy world. Top billing goes to **Jurassic Park**, a float through a prehistoric jungle past friendly herbivores before coming face to face with vicious velociraptors and a ravenous Tyrannosaurus rex. The ultimate thrill is...well, let's not spoil the surprise. (Hint: You'll get wet.)

The newest attractions are **Spider-Man Rocks**, a 20-minute musical show with stunts and pyrotechnics based on the Marvel Comics star, and several **Special Effects Stages** where the illusion-making process is demystified.

Adjacent to Universal Studios is **Universal City Walk**, a fantasy environment of shops, restaurants, cinemas and nightclubs. The best time to visit is after dark, when vibrant neon signs transform the promenade into a miniature Las Vegas–style strip. Parking is a painful $7.

Other Studio Tours

For a rare and realistic glimpse behind the scenes of one of Hollywood's oldest movie and TV production facilities, take the two-hour **Warner Bros Studios Tour** (Map 7; ☎ 818-972-8687; 4000 Warner Blvd). You'll visit the museum, the backlot and several soundstages and outdoor sets. The tours cost $32 and run half-hourly 9am to 3pm weekdays. Reservations are required; children under eight are not allowed.

Nearby, the **NBC Studios Tour** (Map 7; ☎ 818-840-3537; 3000 W Alameda Ave) usually takes you to the set of Jay Leno's *Tonight Show* and into such departments as wardrobe, makeup, set construction, special effects and sound effects. The 70-minute tours cost $7.50/4.25 adult/child and run 9am to 3pm daily. Both studios are in Burbank.

Forest Lawn Cemetery

Often cheekily called the 'country club for the dead,' this humongous cemetery (☎ 818-241-4151; 1712 S Glendale Ave, Glendale; admission free; open 9am-5pm daily) is the posthumous destination of such Hollywood legends as Clark Gable, Walt Disney and Carole Lombard. There's plenty of repro art strewn about the grounds, including Michelangelo's David and a stained-glass rendition of Da Vinci's *Last Supper*. Despite the obvious kitsch factor, a visit here is fascinating, if only to catch a glimpse of death culture so powerfully satirized in Evelyn Waugh's *The Loved One* (1948).

Mission San Fernando Rey de España

Founded in 1797, this mission (☎ 818-361-0186; 15151 San Fernando Mission Rd; adult/concession/child under 7 $4/3/free;

open 9am-4:30pm daily) was the second Spanish mission built in the LA area. The highlight is the 1822 convent with 4ft-thick adobe walls and 21 Romanesque arches. Inside is an elaborate baroque altarpiece from Spain. Its museum deals with mission history and displays Native American artifacts. Peacocks strut around the grounds, which are sprinkled with statues. The mission is in the northern Valley, roughly where the I-405 and Hwy 118 meet.

PASADENA & AROUND (Map 8)

The Tournament of Roses and the Rose Bowl may have given Pasadena long-lasting fame, but it's the lively spirit of this stately city that characterizes it today. From its impressive early-20th-century mansions to its fine art museums and culinary pleasures, Pasadena is a happening place.

Approximately a 15-minute drive northeast of Downtown, Pasadena rests in the shadow of the San Gabriel Mountains. Founded in 1873 by Midwestern settlers, it became a haven for writers, painters and especially architects at the turn of the 20th century. In 1891 Amos G Throop founded Throop University, which evolved into the California Institute of Technology. In 1940 Southern California's first freeway opened, the Arroyo Seco Parkway – since designated as the I-110 (Pasadena Fwy). This connected the city with Downtown LA, and ever more commuters settled in Pasadena.

The heart of Pasadena beats in Old Town, a 20-block historic district stretching along Colorado Blvd between Arroyo Parkway and Pasadena Ave. It's chock-a-block with restaurants and coffeehouses, retail chain stores, bookstores, galleries, nightclubs and cinema complexes. East of here is the new **Paseo Colorado**, a nicely designed outdoor shopping mall.

For information, visit the **Pasadena Convention & Visitors Bureau** (☎ 626-795-9311; 171 S Los Robles Ave; open 8am-5pm Mon-Fri, 10am-4pm Sat). Free Pasadena ARTS buses regularly shuttle between Old Pasadena, the Pasadena Playhouse District and South Lake Ave.

If all goes according to schedule, the new light-rail Gold Line will be serving Pasadena from Downtown LA's Union Station starting in late summer 2003.

Norton Simon Museum

The Norton Simon Museum (☎ 626-449-6840; 411 W Colorado Blvd; adult/senior/child under 18 & student $6/3/free; open noon-6pm Wed-Mon, noon-9pm Fri) boasts a superb collection of European art from the Renaissance to the 20th century, and an exquisite sampling of 2000 years of Asian sculpture from India and Southeast Asia. Boticelli, Cézanne, Degas, Goya, Matisse, Monet, Picasso, Raphael, Rembrandt, Renoir, Rubens, Toulouse-Lautrec and van Gogh are just a few of the big-name artists found here. The museum's lighting and display conditions were recently revamped by Frank Gehry, while Nancy Goslee Power turned the outdoor space into a lovely sculpture garden modeled after Claude Monet's at Giverny.

Wrigley Mansion & Gardens

South of the Norton Simon Museum stands the imposing 1914 Wrigley Mansion (☎ 626-449-4100; 391 Orange Grove Blvd; admission free; open year-round), an ornate Italian Renaissance–style villa. Once owned by chewing gum magnate William Wrigley Jr, it is now the headquarters of the Tournament of Roses Association. Free tours run between 2pm and 4pm on Thursday from February through August. At all other times only the lush gardens, ablaze with roses and camellias (in season, of course), are open to the public.

Rose Bowl & Arroyo Seco

Among Pasadena's grandest architectural achievements is the 98,636-seat Rose Bowl stadium (1922; ☎ 626-577-3100; 1001 Rose Bowl Dr), home of the UCLA Bruins football team, and also the site of the Rose Bowl football game played on New Year's Day and a monthly flea market.

The stadium sits in the midst of **Brookside Park**, a broadening of Arroyo Seco that is popular with hikers, cyclists and horseback riders. In the early 20th century, this was the center of 'Arroyo Culture,' an aesthetic movement involving many of the craftsmen, artists and architects behind some of Pasadena's great homes. Dating from that period is the imposing former **Vista del Arroyo Hotel** (1903; 125 S Grand Ave), restored in the 1980s to house the Ninth Circuit US Court of Appeals. Spanning the arroyo is the city's most infamous landmark, the **Colorado St Bridge** (1913). 'Suicide Bridge,' as it has

come to be known, became the area's favorite jumping spot for those hard hit by the stock market crash in 1929 and has since remained popular with forlorn souls.

Gamble House

Gamble House (☎ 626-793-3334; 4 Westmoreland Place; adult/senior & student/child under 12 $8/5/free) is a 1908 design by Charles and Henry Greene and is considered a top example of Craftsman architecture. It features terraces, bedroom porches for outdoor sleeping and overhanging eaves to keep out the sun. It starred as the home of mad scientist Doc Brown (Christopher Lloyd) in the three Back to the Future movies. Guided one-hour tours depart roughly every 20 minutes from noon to 3pm Thursday through Sunday, except major holidays. Other Greene & Greene homes are on nearby Grand Ave and Arroyo Terrace, including **Charles' private residence** (368 Arroyo Terrace).

Pacific Asia Museum & Civic Center

With its upturned roofs, dragon motifs and serene courtyard, the Chinese imperial palace–style museum (☎ 626-449-2742; 46 N Los Robles Ave; adult/senior & student/child $5/3/free; open 10am-5pm Wed-Sun, 10am-8pm Fri) is a bit of an architectural oddity. On display is a fine compilation of five millennia of both rare and common art and artifacts. The museum's strength is in Chinese ceramics from several dynasties as well as in Japanese paintings and drawings by Hiroshige and Hokusai.

Just west of here is Pasadena's **Civic Center**, built between 1927 and 1933, where Italian Renaissance and Spanish Colonial architectural styles meet Beaux Arts. Highlights are the magnificent **Pasadena City Hall** (100 N Garfield Ave), built around a courtyard garden and fountain, and the **Public Library** (285 E Walnut St) north of here.

Pasadena Museum of California Art

A new arrival in the city, the Pasadena Museum of California Art (☎ 626-568-3665; 490 E Union St; adult/senior & student/child under 12 $6/4/free, free 1st Fri of month; open 10am-5pm Wed-Sun, 10am-8pm Fri) focuses its mission on art, architecture, photography and design created by California artists from 1850 to today. Exhibits reveal how the state has always been a breeding ground of the imagination, nourished by a climate of experimentation, cross-cultural influences and a landscape patterned as richly as an Amish quilt.

California Institute of Technology

Twenty-six Nobel laureates and 43 winners of the National Medal of Science are faculty members or alumni of Caltech (☎ 626-395-6327; 551 S Hill Ave), which gives you some idea why it's regarded with awe in academic circles. (Yes, Albert Einstein did sleep here.) General campus tours are offered at 2pm Monday to Friday (except holidays, rainy days and during winter break from mid-December to early January) and include a visit to the seismology laboratory. Reservations are mandatory. Architectural tours are available as well; call for details.

Caltech also operates the **Jet Propulsion Laboratory** (JPL), NASA's main center for robotic exploration of the solar system, in La Cañada just north of Pasadena. Though not open to the public, JPL provides glimpses of its activities on its website at **W** www.jpl.nasa.gov and through an annual 'open house' (usually in June).

Huntington Library, Art Collection & Botanical Gardens

At once a cultural center, a research institution and a relaxing place to spend a day, the former estate of railroad tycoon Henry Huntington (☎ 626-405-2100; 1151 Oxford Rd; adult/senior/student/child 5-11 $10/8.50/7/4, free 1st Thur of month; open noon-4:30pm Tues-Fri, 10:30am-4:30pm Sat & Sun) is one of LA's attractions not to be missed.

The sprawling **botanical gardens** alone – with some 14,000 species of trees, shrubs, flowering and nonflowering plants – are worthy of a visit. Even more impressive is the **library** collection of rare English-language books, maps and manuscripts, including a 1455 Gutenberg Bible, the Ellesmere manuscript of Chaucer's *Canterbury Tales* (1410) and Benjamin Franklin's handwritten autobiography.

The **Huntington Art Gallery**, in the former family mansion, boasts a collection of 18th-century British and French paintings

(among them Thomas Gainsborough's *Blue Boy*); European period sculptures, porcelains and tapestries; and American paintings from the 1730s to the 1930s, including works by Mary Cassatt, Edward Hopper and John Singer Sargent.

Southwest Museum

Just south of Pasadena, this museum (☎ 323-221-2164; 234 Museum Dr; adult/senior & student/child 7-18 $6/4/3; open 10am-5pm Tues-Sun) holds one of the most formidable collections of Native American art and artifacts in the USA. Each of the four halls is dedicated to a native North American culture: the Great Plains, the Northwest Coast, the Southwest and California. This division lets you compare the traditions, rituals, clothing, crafts, religious ceremonies, and social and political organizations that developed in each of these areas. The museum owns one of the largest basket collections in the USA (11,000 items), as well as some 7000 pieces of pottery and 6600 paintings, textiles, religious icons and decorative and folk art from Latin America. A major expansion, under way at the time of writing, was scheduled to be completed by spring 2004.

Heritage Square Museum

Eight vintage Victorian buildings dating from 1865 to 1914 were rescued from the wrecking ball and moved to Heritage Square (☎ 626-449-0193; 3800 Homer St; adult/senior/child 6-12 $6/5/3; open noon-4pm Fri-Sun), an open-air museum just off the Ave 43 exit of I-110.

Highlights include the Italianate Perry House and the Longfellow Hastings Octagon House. The grounds are open for self-guided tours, but to marvel at the interiors you'll have to join a guided tour, which is included in the admission price.

Mission San Gabriel Archangel

Southeast of Pasadena, in the city of San Gabriel, this California mission (☎ 626-457-3048; 537 W Mission Dr; adult/senior/child 6-12 $5/4/2; open 9am-4:30pm daily) was founded in 1771 by Franciscan missionaries as the fourth in the line of 21 missions. Local Indians built the original church from stone, brick and mortar in a capped-buttress design with Moorish elements inspired by the cathedral in Córdoba in southern Spain. It's been destroyed and restored numerous times, most recently in 1993.

Inside the church is a copper baptismal font, an altar made in Mexico City in 1790 and wooden statues of saints. The cemetery harbors, among many others, 6000 Indians who are honored with a memorial. Also on the grounds are soap and tallow vats, fireplaces, fountains and a replica of a kitchen. The museum contains Bibles, religious robes and Indian artifacts.

BEACHES

Beaches beckon all along the LA County coastline. Plenty of sunshine, warm air and lots of activities draw people to the shorefront year-round. Surfing, sailing, swimming, sunbathing, volleyball, beachcombing or simply strolling through the sand are all enjoyed by locals and visitors alike.

Water temperatures become tolerable by late spring and are highest (about 70°F, or 21°C) in August and September, but in winter the Pacific is rather chilly. Most beaches have showers and rest rooms, lifeguards, snack stands and regular clean-up.

Hazards are few but shouldn't be ignored. Swimming is usually prohibited for three days after major storms because of dangerously high pollution levels from untreated runoff. The local nonprofit organization **Heal the Bay** (☎ 310-453-0395; W www.healthebay.org) issues a monthly Beach Report Card, which evaluates ocean water quality based on a grading system from A+ to F. For information, call or check its website. Another element of danger is strong currents, called riptides, which can drag swimmers away from the shore; look for white, frothy water and flat waves.

With miles and miles of wide sandy shores to enjoy, LA's beaches rarely get packed with people. The most popular ones are in Santa Monica, Venice and Manhattan Beach. There's good surfing at Malibu Lagoon State Beach, aka Surfrider Beach, and at the Manhattan Beach pier. Pratte's Reef is an artificial surfing reef at Dockweiler State Beach. Zuma Beach, in the northern county, is one of the most beautiful beaches and has some of the cleanest water; still further north El Pescador, El Matador and La Piedra are often used as movie sets and are popular with nudists.

SANTA MONICA MOUNTAINS

Few LA visitors ever realize that the metropolis actually borders wilderness in the **Santa Monica Mountains National Recreation Area**. Consisting of more than 150,000 acres, it's a playground cherished by locals but often overlooked by visitors. This is a shame because it's an easily accessible sample of the rugged beauty found throughout California. Even a short hike makes for a refreshing break from urban sightseeing and will increase your appreciation of both the city and its natural surroundings. Outdoor activities in the park include **hiking, mountain biking, horseback riding** and **bird-watching**. Almost 600mi of trails crisscross the area, including the popular 65mi Backbone Trail. Several canyon roads cut through the mountains, providing easy access to trails.

Spring, when temperatures are moderate and **wildflowers** are in bloom, is the most pleasant time to visit the park. Avoid midday hikes in summer (the mercury can climb above 100°F, or 38°C). Fall can be nice too, though there's the threat of fire. Winter often brings rain that may result in trail closure. In general, most trails are rugged and require sturdy footwear (sneakers or light hiking shoes are OK). Layer your clothing and bring sunscreen, a hat and lots of water. Look out for waxy, glistening three-lobed leaves that may be poison oak. Other dangers, though rare, come from rattlesnakes and mountain lions (see the Facts for the Visitor chapter for details on what to do if you encounter either of these).

The National Park Service maintains a **visitor center** (☎ 805-370-2300; W www.nps .gov/samo; 401 W Hillcrest Dr; open 8am-5pm Mon-Fri, 9am-5pm Sat & Sun, closed major holidays) in Thousand Oaks in the very western San Fernando Valley. Take the Lynn Rd exit from Hwy 101, head north on Lynn Rd, east on Hillcrest Dr, left on McCloud Ave and turn at the first driveway on your right. The center dispenses information and sells maps, hiking guides and books.

Guided hikes are offered by the **Sierra Club** (☎ 213-387-4287; W www.angeles.sier raclub.org) and the **National Park Service**. Excellent guidebooks with detailed area hikes are John McKinney's *Day Hiker's Guide to Southern California* and *Walking Los Angeles: Adventures on the Urban Edge*, widely available in city bookstores.

LOS ANGELES

ORGANIZED TOURS

Several companies offer essentially the same types of bus tours at roughly the same prices, including the popular city tour and a tour of the stars' homes (both around $40). Theme park tours to Universal Studios, Disneyland, Knott's Berry Farm and Six Flags Magic Mountain cost $60 to $75, admission included; children's discounts are available. Try **Starline Tours** (☎ 800-959-3131), **LA Tours** (☎ 323-937-3361) or **EuroPacific Tours** (☎ 800-303-3005).

Los Angeles Conservancy Tours

The **Los Angeles Conservancy** (☎ 213-623-2489, W www.laconservancy.org) is a non-profit organization with a mission to preserve and raise awareness of the historical buildings in LA. Trained docents conduct a series of entertaining and informative walking tours through the Downtown area. Tours are thematic and, except where noted, meet at 10am, last about 2½ hours and cost $8. Reservations (by phone or online) are required.

Following is a listing of the most popular tours. Call or check the website for a complete schedule.

Angelino Heights (first and third Saturday of the month; $10) – Tours LA's first suburb, with its late-19th-century Victorian homes, including interior visits of two of them

Art Deco (every Saturday) – Spotlights various landmarks built in this jazzy, geometric style en vogue in the 1920s and '30s

Biltmore Hotel (second Saturday of the month at 11am) – The 90-minute tour of this glamorous hotel includes visits to its health club, kitchen and presidential suite

Broadway Theaters (every Saturday) – A tour of the Broadway National Register Historic Theater District takes you inside several theaters, although which ones you'll see depends on accessibility on that day

City Hall (first and fourth Saturday) – Takes you inside the newly restored town hall, with visits to the rotunda, the city council chamber and the public works session room

Union Station (third and fourth Saturday) – Tours the last great railway station built in the USA (1939) as well as the 1993 Transit Gateway addition

---

LA Bike Tours (☎ 323-466-5890, 888-775-2453; W www.labiketours.com) offers guided tours focusing on city neighborhoods, including Venice/Santa Monica and Hollywood; one also explores Topanga Canyon in the Santa Monica Mountains. Tours cost $30 to $75, including snacks, bottled water, bike and helmet.

Companies offering whale-watching, harbor sightseeing or dinner cruises include **Hornblower Cruises** (☎ 310-301-6000; 13755 Fiji Way, Marina del Rey) and **Shoreline Village Cruises** (☎ 562-495-5884; 429 Shoreline Village Dr, Long Beach).

A new company called **Red Line Tours** (☎ 323-402-1074; W www.redlinetours .com) operates walking tours of Hollywood and Downtown. Its affable guides use a clever mix of anecdotes, fun facts and historical and architectural data to keep their charges entertained and educated at the same time. Everyone wears headsets that allow you to hear the guide even over the worst traffic noise. The current schedule features tours of Historic Hollywood, Historic Downtown and Contemporary Downtown. Tours cost $20/18/15 adult/senior and student/child nine to 15.

SPECIAL EVENTS

LA has a packed calendar of special events, with many festivities celebrating the traditions and culture of LA's different ethnic groups. We only have space to list a smattering of what's on, so check with the visitor centers or peruse the *Los Angeles Times* or *LA Weekly* for current goings-on.

Tournament of Roses Parade (☎ 818-419-7673) January
Chinese New Year (☎ 213-617-0396) February
LA Marathon & Bike Tour (☎ 310-444-5544) March
Toyota Grand Prix of Long Beach (☎ 800-752-9524) April
Blessing of the Animals (☎ 213-628-1274) April
Cinco de Mayo Celebration (☎ 213-624-3660) May
Mariachi USA Festival (☎ 213-848-7717) June
Los Angeles Gay & Lesbian Pride Celebration (☎ 323-860-0701) June
Lotus Festival (☎ 213-485-1310) July
Malibu Art Festival (☎ 310-456-9025) July
Central Avenue Jazz Festival (☎ 213-485-2437) August
Nisei Week (☎ 213-687-7193) August

Long Beach Blues Festival (☎ 562-436-7794) September
LA County Fair (☎ 909-623-3111) September
Oktoberfest (☎ 310-327-4384) September
Catalina Island Country Music Festival (☎ 619-458-9586) September
Día de los Muertos (☎ 213-624-3660) November
Doo Dah Parade (☎ 818-449-3689) November
Hollywood Christmas Parade (☎ 323-469-2337) November
Holiday Festival of Lights (☎ 323-913-4688) December
Christmas Boat Parade (☎ 310-821-7614) December
Las Posadas (☎ 213-968-8492) December

PLACES TO STAY

Clearly, where you want to stay in LA will dictate to a great extent how much you'll have to pay. Budget lodgings are scarce in Beverly Hills and West Hollywood but more abundant in Hollywood, Downtown and Pasadena. Hostels cluster in Hollywood and Venice Beach.

Downtown (Map 2)

Budget A touch of 1920s glamour survives at **Stillwell Hotel** (☎ 213-627-1151, 800-553-4774, fax 213-622-8940; W www.stillwell-la.com; 838 S Grand Ave; singles/doubles from $49/59). This historic property has been treated to a comprehensive makeover and now features 250 basic but nicely appointed rooms with TV and air-con.

Milner Hotel (☎ 213-627-6981, 877-645-6377; W www.milner-hotels.com; 813 S Flower St; rooms $60-80) has 177 old-fashioned rooms, a multilingual staff and a restaurant-pub. Rates include a full breakfast and airport pick-up.

A few blocks west of Downtown proper is this pair of characterless but cheap motels: **Motel de Ville** (☎ 213-624-8474; 1123 W 7th St; rooms $40-45) and **City Center Motel** (☎ 213-628-7141, 800-816-6889, fax 213-629-1064; 1135 W 7th St; rooms $40-50).

Mid-Range Combining history with hip is **Figueroa Hotel** (☎ 213-627-8971, 800-421-9092, fax 213-689-0305; W www.figueroahotel.com; 939 S Figueroa St, South Park; rooms $98-185), a quirky 1927 gem. Its lofty lobby evokes a Spanish hacienda but features eclectic decor from around the Mediterranean, especially Morocco. The theme continues in the rooms, which vary

in size and price. It's a popular place and great value for the money.

Best Western Dragon Gate Inn (☎ 213-617-3077, 800-282-9999, fax 213-680-3753; W www.dragongateinn.com; 818 N Hill St; rooms $89-159, child under 18 free) has 52 comfortably furnished rooms with Chinese decorative accents and a good range of amenities.

Kawada Hotel (☎ 213-621-4455, 800-752-9232, fax 213-687-4455; W www.kawadahotel.com; 200 S Hill St; rooms $109-129) is a modern, good-value place orientated toward business travelers, meaning that rates often drop on weekends – ask! In-room extras include VCRs and kitchenettes and there's a restaurant downstairs.

Wilshire Royale Howard Johnson Plaza (☎ 213-387-5311, 800-421-8072, fax 213-380-8174; 2619 Wilshire Blvd; single/double/triple/quad $129/149/159/179 Apr-Sept, $109/129/139/159 Oct-Mar), in the MacArthur area northwest of Downtown, offers modern conveniences in a vintage property. Rooms are warmly furnished and come with lots of amenities.

Top End Downtown's poshest hotel, **The Millennium Biltmore** (☎ 213-624-1011, 800-245-8673, fax 213-612-1545; 506 S Grand Ave; rooms $205-250) has a pedigree going back to 1923. A galaxy of US presidents, celebrities and dignitaries have paraded through its sumptuous public areas, with carved and gilded ceiling, marble floors and grand staircases. Rooms epitomize luxury.

Wyndham Checkers Hotel (☎ 213-624-0000, 800-423-5798, fax 213-626-9906; W www.checkershotel.com; 535 S Grand Ave; rooms $166-228), nearby, is smaller than The Millenium Biltmore but just as exquisite. Marble bathrooms and a rooftop spa are among the special touches you'll find in this European-style hotel. Amenities include free newspaper and shoe shine.

Hollywood (Map 3)

Budget Hollywood is hostel heaven, making it a good place to stay for the slim-wallet crowd. Most hostels offer free or discounted pick-ups from LAX and the Greyhound and Amtrak stations.

Hollywood International Hostel (☎ 323-463-0797, 800-750-6561, fax 323-463-1705; W www.hollywoodhostels.com;

6820 Hollywood Blvd; dorm beds $17, private rooms $40), across from Hollywood & Highland, is clean and has separate floors for men and women/couples, although arrangements can be made for intergender groups traveling together. Dorms sleep three or four people and there's a large lobby with all new furnishings, a pool table and TV, plus a communal kitchen and laundry. Passport or student ID required.

USA Hostel *(☎ 323-462-3777, 800-524-6783; W www.usahostels.com; 1624 Schrader Blvd; dorms $17, private rooms $36-48)* has good-sized rooms with satellite TV and private bathrooms. Guests gather in the modern, well-stocked kitchen or meet during live comedy shows staged here twice weekly. Rates include a free pancake and waffle breakfast.

Student Inn International Hostel *(☎ 323-469-6781, 800-557-7038 in LA only, no fax; W www.studentinn.com; 7038½ Hollywood Blvd; dorm bunks $14.50 per person, dorm queen beds for 2 $11 per person, private rooms $39.50)* has the usual kitchen, lounge and Internet kiosk set-up. Every room has its own bathroom, but the entire place could use an overhaul. International passport or student ID required.

Hollywood Bungalows *(☎ 323-969-9155, fax 323-969-9678; W www.hollywoodbungalows.com; 2775 Cahuenga Blvd; dorm beds $15-22, private rooms with TV $59),* in the former Banana Bungalow space but under new ownership, still has a party atmosphere and a nice pool. Dorms sleep four, six or 10 people and have cable TV, bathroom and lockers. Free or low-cost shuttles and tours help you get around LA. On the downside, the location (near the Hollywood Bowl, next to the freeway) is less than ideal if you depend on public transportation.

The Gershwin Hollywood Hostel & Hotel *(☎ 323-464-1131, 800-446-7835, fax 323-462-8171; W www.gershwinhollywood.com; 5533 Hollywood Blvd; dorm beds $22, private rooms $45-75)* signals that hosteling has come of age in LA. Converted from a rambling old apartment building, the Gershwin sports ultra-cool New Millennium design and 174 dorms and private rooms, all with private bathroom and about half with kitchenettes. It's right outside a Metro Red Line subway station and near a big shopping center and restaurants. It has all the usual hostel facilities, as well as a busy activity schedule with free or low-cost shuttles and tours.

Orange Drive Manor Hostel *(☎ 323-850-0350, fax 323-969-8164; W www.orangedrivehostel.com; 1764 N Orange Dr; dorm beds $19-23, singles $37, doubles without/with bath $42/47)* is a friendly and nonsmoking hostel, just steps from Mann's Chinese Theater. It's housed in a rambling 1920s manor, complete with hardwood floors, steep staircases and high ceilings and recently received a thorough sprucing up. Most dorms sleep four people and come with adjacent bathroom.

Hollywood is also dotted with numerous cheap motels, but some are of questionable repute. Besides the ones listed here, you might also try the string of chains and independents along Sunset Blvd between La Brea Blvd and Vine Ave, where rates are in the $40 to $60 range.

Liberty Hotel *(☎ 323-962-1788, 800-750-6561; 1770 Orchid Ave; rooms from $50, with kitchen from $55),* right behind the Hollywood & Highland complex, is a friendly place with 21 large, bright rooms with TV and private bathroom. Coffee and parking are free, and there's a guest laundry.

Highland Gardens Hotel *(☎ 323-850-0535, 800-404-5472, fax 323-850-1712; W www.highlandgardenshotel.com; 7047 Franklin Ave; rooms $65-75, kitchen suites $85-175)* has comfortable rooms wrapped around a leafy courtyard. It has a guest laundry and pool, and provides a free breakfast. Janis Joplin overdosed in room 105 on October 3, 1970.

Mid-Range & Top End The **Magic Castle Hotel** *(☎ 323-851-0800, 800-741-4915, fax 323-851-4926; W www.magiccastlehotel.com; 7025 Franklin Ave; rooms & suites $69-169)* is one of Hollywood's most popular hotels, and for good reason. Remodeled rooms have kitchens and modern decor and there's a large heated pool as well. Ask about getting into the Magic Castle, a private, fabled magic club nearby.

Orchid Suites Hotel *(☎ 323-874-9678, 800-537-3052, fax 323-467-7649; e info@orchidsuites.com; 1753 N Orchid Ave; rooms $79-119)* is another establishment that doesn't put too much of a squeeze on the wallet. It has a pool and 36 nicely appointed suites with full kitchens; some also have balconies. Breakfast is included, too.

Hollywood Roosevelt Hotel (☎ 323-466-7000, 800-950-7667, fax 323-462-8056; W www.hollywoodroosevelt.com; 7000 Hollywood Blvd; rooms $199-229) is a glamorous Spanish Colonial place dating from 1927, which recently received a top-to-bottom overhaul. Extras include high-speed wireless Internet access in all rooms, free stays for children under 18 with parents and poolside cabanas for extra privacy. Ask about special deals.

West Hollywood & Mid-City (Map 4)
Pickings are slim for the cash-strapped crowd in WeHo but there's a good hostel on Melrose and several affordable motels near the Farmers Market.

Orbit Hostel (☎ 323-655-1510, 877-672-4887, no fax; e reservations@orbithotel.com; 7950 Melrose Ave; dorm beds $15-22, private rooms $45-79) is a great, clean place with boldly colored retro decor, a convivial ambience and a hip location. Dorms sleep four to six people, and private rooms have TV and some even have balconies. All rooms have a full bathroom. There's also an Internet kiosk, a large lounge, outdoor patio and coin laundry and free breakfast; dinner is available for $5. Pick-ups from LAX are free. Passports are required to book a dorm bed.

Park Plaza Lodge (☎ 323-931-1501, fax 323-931-5863; 6001 W 3rd St; rooms $60-65) has generously sized rooms filled with antique-style furniture, refrigerators and air-con.

Bevonshire Lodge Motel (☎ 323-936-6154; 7575 Beverly Blvd; rooms $50-55) is a nondescript but quiet place, whose clean and comfortable rooms come with air-con, TV and phone.

Beverly Laurel Hotel (☎ 323-651-2441, 800-962-3824, fax 323-651-5225; 8018 Beverly Blvd; rooms $80-84, with kitchenette $10 extra) is the best of the bunch. Its largish rooms – wrapped around a pool – have more than a modicum of style, and the attached **Swingers diner** is open all day with nothing costing over $10.

In the heart of WeHo, **Holloway Motel** (☎ 323-654-2454; W www.hollowaymotel.com; 8465 Santa Monica Blvd; rooms $85-105) can get a bit noisy but is otherwise good

value. Rooms have voicemail, data ports and safes. Parking and breakfast are included in the rates.

The Standard (☎ 323-650-9090, fax 323-650-2820; W www.standardhotel.com; 8300 Sunset Blvd; rooms $99-225) is anything but standard. This young, hip hotel has lots of boundary-pushing design surprises. Rooms have CD players, VCRs and platform beds and there's a 24-hour coffee shop as well. In the evenings, the shag-carpeted lobby turns into a lounge with DJ.

Best Western Sunset Plaza Hotel (☎ 323-654-0750, 800-421-3652, fax 323-650-6146; W www.sunsetplazahotel.com; 8400 Sunset Blvd; rooms $109-199) has high-energy, cosmopolitan flair and nicely decorated and spacious rooms. All are fully wired for high-speed communication and have kitchenettes. Rates include breakfast.

The Grafton on Sunset (☎ 323-654-4600, 800-821-3660, fax 323-654-5918; W www.graftononsunset.com; 8462 W Sunset Blvd; rooms $165-300) is a boutique hotel designed with Feng Shui principles in mind. Extras include free shuttle service within 2mi, an extra-sized pool and guest-list privileges at certain area nightclubs.

Beverly Plaza Hotel (☎ 323-658-6600, 800-624-6835, fax 323-653-3464; W http://beverlyplazahotel.com; 8384 W 3rd St; rooms $142-272), near the Beverly Center, has large, fashionably appointed rooms with European flair, and a great restaurant called **Cava** (see Places to Eat). Ask about the hotel's special rates.

Mondrian (☎ 323-650-8999, 800-525-8029, fax 323-650-5215; W www.mondrianhotel.com; 8440 Sunset Blvd; rooms $335-525) is LA's beacon for the beautiful and celebrated. An air of exclusivity reigns at this melodramatically minimalist place, which juxtaposes harsh geometry with playful lighting effects. Rooms – no surprise – are top-notch.

Beverly Hills (Map 5)
'Budget' and 'Beverly Hills' don't normally mix, but there are a few properties even those without a trust fund can probably afford.

Beverly Hills Reeves Hotel (☎ 310-271-3006, fax 310-271-2278; W www.bhreeves.com; 120 S Reeves Dr; rooms $45-85) is an older but spanking clean property on a quiet street. Rooms have microwave, refrigerator and color TV. Rates include breakfast and parking.

Hotel del Flores (☎ 310-274-5115; 409 N Crescent Dr; rooms without/with bath $65/95) has a homey environment and a central location but otherwise a bit of a downtrodden air.

Maison 140 (☎ 310-281-4000, 800-432-5444, fax 310-281-4001; **w** www.maison140.com; 140 S Lasky Dr; rooms $150-215), in silent movie star Lilian Gish's former private villa, redefines value for money. The decor cleverly marries French and Asian temperaments. Its rooms sport boldly patterned wallpaper, eclectic artwork, vintage furnishings and numerous luxury touches. A light breakfast is included in the price.

The *grande dame* of LA caravanserais, **Beverly Hills Hotel** (☎ 310-276-2251, 800-283-8885, fax 310-281-2905; **w** www.the beverlyhillshotel.com; 9641 Sunset Blvd; rooms $345-455, bungalows/suites from $380/745) gives you the utmost in luxury. Mingle with the power players on parade at the pool and in the Polo Lounge.

Luxe Hotel Rodeo Drive (☎ 310-273-0300, 800-468-3541, fax 310-859-8730; **w** www .luxehotels.com; 360 N Rodeo Dr; rooms $255-355, suites $355-455) has a clean, contemporary and uncluttered look and 88 airy rooms replete with luxurious linens and bath accouterments. Days start with a complimentary light breakfast.

Avalon Hotel (☎ 310-277-5221, 800-535-4715, fax 310-277-4928; **w** www.avalon hotel.com; 9400 W Olympic Blvd; rooms $200-250, suites $289-475) is a stylish boutique hotel where mid-century modern meets new millennium amenities. Marilyn Monroe once lived in the building, and Lucy and Desi came and went as well.

Hotel Bel-Air (☎ 310-472-1211, 800-648-4097; **w** www.hotelbelair.com; 701 Stone Canyon Rd; rooms $385-550, suites $700-3000) places the emphasis on privacy, which is why celebrities love the secluded bungalows, fountain courtyards and gardens. Visit, if only to stroll the dreamy grounds or to have a drink.

Westwood (Map 5)

Royal Palace Westwood Hotel (☎ 310-208-6677, 800-631-0100, fax 310-824-3732; **w** www.royalpalacewestwood.com; 1052 Tiverton Ave; rooms $85-139, child under 12

free) is no palace but is still good value with a variety of rooms, including some with Jacuzzi. Assets include free parking, breakfast and cable TV.

Hotel del Capri (☎ 310-474-3511, 800-444-6835, fax 310-470-9999; **w** www .hoteldelcapri.com; 10587 Wilshire Blvd; rooms $100-125, suites $125-155) is a charmer with brightly decorated rooms and suites (with kitchenette) surrounding a terrace and swimming pool. A free shuttle takes guests to Beverly Hills and Westwood.

Hilgard House Hotel (☎ 310-208-3945, 800-826-3934, fax 310-208-1972; **w** www .hilgardhouse.com; 927 Hilgard Ave; singles/doubles $129/139) is a snug boutique hotel with Old World charm and antique-style furnishings.

W Los Angeles (☎ 310-208-8765, 877-946-8357, fax 310-824-0355; **w** www.who tels.com; 930 Hilgard Ave; suites from $320) immediately announces that it's no ordinary hotel: the valets wear headsets, the staircase doubles as a fountain, and the lobby-bar has a game table for playing tic-tac-toe. Rooms are first-rate.

Los Angeles International Airport

All properties listed in this section are within 2mi of the airport and offer free 24-hour shuttle service.

The gregarious, resort-like **LA Adventurer/ Backpackers Paradise Hostel** (☎ 310-672-3090, fax 310-412-9100; **w** www.back packersparadise.com; 4200 W Century Blvd; dorm beds $12, private rooms $39-75) woos guests with made-up beds and fresh towels daily, as well as free trips to Venice Beach and a local shopping mall. Rates include continental breakfast, cookies and tea in the afternoon and a nightly 'champagne party' with food. It also has a pool and restaurant-pub. Pick-ups from Greyhound and Amtrak stations are free, too.

Super 8 Motel (☎ 310-670-2900, 800-800-8000; 9250 Airport Blvd; rooms $55-95) is a suitable choice if you want little more than a roof over your head for a night or two.

Hacienda Hotel (☎ 310-615-0015, 800-421-5900; **w** www.haciendahotel.com; 525 N Sepulveda Blvd; rooms $89-99) is a sprawling good-value place with 630 modern rooms distinguished by quasi-psychedelic carpets, a decent restaurant and a country-and-western lounge.

Expect comfort if not style at **Quality Hotel Airport** (☎ 310-645-2200, 800-228-5151; 5249 Century Blvd; rooms $79-169), which also has a food court with cheap snacks, as well as a fitness center with heated pool.

Barnabey's Hotel (☎ 310-750-0300, 888-239-6295, fax 310-545-8621; W www.barnabeyshotel.com; 3501 Sepulveda Blvd; rooms $99-179) is a homey inn with Victorian flair (think lots of lace and oak). A lovely patio, pub and popular restaurant are on the premises.

Four Points by Sheraton (☎ 310-645-4600, fax 310-649-7047; W www.fourpointslax.com; 9750 Airport Blvd; rooms $89-99) has pleasant landscaping and nicely furnished rooms with lots of amenities. Work out post-flight kinks at the gym or pool.

Upscale airport hotels cater to largely business travelers. Expect to pay between $120 and $200 per room; suites cost a bit more. Options include: **Crowne Plaza LA Airport** (☎ 310-642-7500, 800-255-7606, fax 310-342-7010; 5985 W Century Blvd); **Los Angeles Airport Hilton & Towers** (☎ 310-410-4000, 800-445-8667, fax 310-410-6250; 5711 W Century Blvd); and **Los Angeles Airport Marriott** (☎ 310-641-5700, 800-228-9290, fax 310-337-5358; 5855 W Century Blvd).

Malibu

Leo Carrillo State Beach Campground (☎ 805-488-5223, 800-444-7275 for reservations; 9000 Pacific Coast Hwy; sites $12) is a kid-friendly and extremely popular site near a long sandy beach about 28mi northwest of Santa Monica. It has 138 tent and RV sites, a general store, flush toilets and hot pay showers.

Casa Malibu Inn (☎ 310-456-2219, 800-831-0858, fax 310-456-5418; e casamalibu@earthlink.net; 22752 Pacific Coast Hwy; rooms $129-349) is a lovely beachfront property. Some of the 21 rooms have decks, fireplaces and kitchenettes and rates include a gourmet breakfast.

Malibu Beach Inn (☎ 310-456-6444, 800-462-5428, fax 310-456-1499; W www.malibubeachinn.com; 22878 Pacific Coast Hwy; rooms $209-329, suites $339-399) is a breezy oceanside hideaway near the Malibu Pier. Rooms have a balc... Jacuzzi), ocean views and ... include a continental breakfa...

Santa Monica (Map 6)

The **HI Los Angeles-Santa Mon...** (☎ 310-393-9913, 800-909-4776, fax 310-393-1769; 1436 2nd St; dorm beds $24-29, private rooms $66-72) has a kitchen, courtyard, library, theater, laundry and travel store. Though it's centrally located and has got a lot going for it, some of our readers have reported problems with 'mean staff' and one even called it a 'hostile hostel.' Keep us posted.

Sea Shore Motel (☎ 310-392-2787, fax 310-392-5167; 2637 Main St; rooms & suites $70-100), two blocks from the beach, is clean and well run and popular with Europeans. Renovated rooms have lots of amenities, and breakfast is available at the adjacent café (extra charge).

Pacific Sands Motel (☎ 310-395-6133, fax 310-395-7206; 1515 Ocean Ave; rooms $55-125) is a basic option, where adequately sized rooms have TV and phone.

Bayside Hotel (☎ 310-396-6000, 800-525-4447; W www.baysidehotel.com; 2001 Ocean Ave; rooms $79-139), right by the beach, has rooms with balconies and data port phones. Parking is free.

Ocean Lodge (☎ 310-451-4146, 800-393-6310, fax 310-393-9621; W www.oceanlodgehotel.com; 1667 Ocean Ave; rooms $97-350) is a 1950s hotel with updated and nicely furnished rooms and free high-speed Internet access.

Cal Mar Hotel Suites (☎ 310-395-5555, 800-776-6007, fax 310-451-1111; W www.calmarhotel.com; 220 California Ave; suites $99-159) is a good choice for families or people in need of plenty of space. All suites have full kitchens and surround a swimming pool.

Hotel California (☎ 310-393-2363, 800-537-8483, fax 310-393-1063; W www.hotelca.com; 1670 Ocean Ave; rooms $135-325), just steps from the beach, greets you with whimsical surf-inspired decor. The sunny rooms come with glossy hardwood floors, small refrigerators and data ports, while suites have private patios and kitchenettes.

Fairmont Miramar Hotel (☎ 310-576-7777, 800-866-5577, fax 310-458-7912; W www.fairmont.com; 101 Wilshire Blvd;

oms $269-859) is a classy property anchored by a massive 120-year-old Moreton Bay fig tree. Presidents, royalty and celebrities have all stayed in the luxurious guests rooms or bungalows set among quasi-tropical gardens.

Georgian Hotel (☎ 310-395-9945, 800-538-8147, fax 310-451-3374; W www.geor gianhotel.com; 1415 Ocean Ave; rooms $235-525), in a striking Art Deco landmark overlooking the ocean, has decor so Great Gatsby-esque that wearing a straw-boater wouldn't feel out of place. Rooms are fully equipped with mod cons.

Hotel Casa del Mar (☎ 310-581-5533, 800-898-6999, 310-581-5503; 1910 Ocean Front Walk; rooms $370-595), next to the sand, is a posh new player in historic beachfront digs. Wallow in luxury in Mediterranean-flavored rooms, most of them ocean-facing.

Venice & Marina del Rey (Map 6)

Those with a communal spirit have plenty of hostels to choose from in Venice.

Share-Tel Apartments (☎ 310-392-0325, fax 310-392-9804; e rooms@share-tel.com; 20 Brooks Ave, Venice; dorm beds $20, private rooms $46-50; non-US travelers only), right by the beach, has four- to eight-bed dorms, each with kitchens, bathrooms and safes. Rates include linen, breakfast daily and weekday dinners. The private rooms, alas, are overpriced. Facilities include Internet access, cable TV and coin laundry.

Venice Beach Hostel (☎ 310-452-3052, fax 310-821-3469; W www.caprica.com/ venice-beach-hostel; 1515 Pacific Ave, Venice; dorm beds $15-19, private rooms $50-55) is a convivial, if slightly funky, multistory affair a whiff away from the beach. Dorms (some women-only) sleep four to six people and have private bathrooms. There's a large kitchen and recreational area. Americans are welcome but must present ID.

Venice Beach Cotel (☎ 310-399-7649, fax 310-399-1930; 25 Windward Ave, Venice; dorm beds without/with ocean view $15/17.50, private rooms $35-49) is steps from the beach above a fancy restaurant and welcomes you with a drink. It has dorms sleeping three to six people with private bathroom and ready-made beds with towels and soap. Americans with passports are welcome.

Hostel California (☎ 310-305-0250, fax 310-305-8590; e kschmahle@aol.com; 2221 Lincoln Blvd, Venice; beds in 6-person dorm $20; beds in 30-person dorm $16, private rooms $44) is a 20-minute walk to the beach and has a TV lounge, Internet kiosk, coin-op laundry and a kitchen. Parking, bed linen, lockers and airport pick-ups (by prior arrangement) are free. Americans with out-of-state ID are OK. Prices are a bit lower in winter.

Jolly Roger Hotel (☎ 310-822-2904, 800-822-2904; W www.jollyrgr.com; 2904 Washington Blvd, Venice; rooms $70-80, motel rooms $15 less) is near the beach and trendy Abbot Kinney Blvd. Basic rooms with large bathrooms are great value. More budget-minded? Stay in the motel section.

Cadillac Hotel (☎ 310-399-8876, fax 310-399-4536; W www.thecadillachotel.com; 8 Dudley Ave, Venice; dorm beds $20, rooms $89, suites from $130) is in a charming beachfront Art Deco building. Rooms have ocean views, TV, phone and private bathroom. Guests can also enjoy the gym and sauna, rooftop sundeck and coin-op laundry.

Inn at Venice Beach (☎ 310-821-2557, 800-828-0688, fax 310-827-0289; W www .innatvenicebeach.com; 327 Washington Blvd; rooms $99-159), two blocks from the beach, is a pleasant spot with fresh and cheerful decor. Rooms have high ceilings and amenities such as refrigerators and hair dryers. Rates include breakfast.

Foghorn Harbor Inn (☎ 310-823-4626, 800-423-4940, fax 310-578-1964; e info@ foghornhotel.com; 4140 Via Marina, Marina del Rey; rooms $99-169) sits right next to placid Mother's Beach. Rooms are smallish and fairly plain, but all have marina views and refrigerators. Breakfast is included.

Venice Beach House (☎ 310-823-1966, fax 310-823-1842; 15 30th Ave, Venice; rooms $120-190) is a homey retreat with nine sun-drenched rooms. Charlie Chaplin used to stay here when it was the beach house of a local developer.

Ritz-Carlton Marina del Rey (☎ 310-823-1700, 800-241-3333, fax 310-823-2403; 4375 Admiralty Way, Marina del Rey; rooms $249-569) is a lavish property with its own marina and charter yachts, lighted tennis courts, pool and spa. Rooms come with all the trappings.

LOS ANGELES

South Bay

Chain motels charging $50 or less per room abound along the Pacific Coast Hwy, which barrels through the South Bay communities.

Dockweiler Beach RV Park (☎ 310-322-4951, 800-950-7275; 8255 Vista Del Mar, Playa del Rey; tents/RV sites $15/25 late May–mid-Sept, $12-17 mid-Sept–May) is great if you don't mind camping out near LAX, an oil refinery and a sewage treatment plant. Main assets are a central beach location and low rates.

Surf City Hostel (☎ 310-798-2323; w www.hostels.com/surfcity; 26 Pier Ave, Hermosa Beach; dorm beds $15-18, private rooms $35-45), not far from the beach, is a friendly hostel on Hermosa's 'bar row.' Murals brighten up the hallways leading to the rooms, kitchen and lounges with TV, VCR and Internet kiosk. Some dorms have en suite bathrooms. Call for a free airport pick-up; discounts are available from Amtrak and Greyhound stations. American travelers are OK for short stays. Rates also include a small breakfast.

Sea View Inn (☎ 310-545-1504, fax 310-545-4052; w www.seaview-inn.com; 3400 Highland Ave, Manhattan Beach; rooms $95-225), near the beach, has 31 rooms and suites decked out in fresh colors. Most rooms have ocean views, kitchenette, VCR and voicemail. The 'executive suites,' essentially miniapartments with full kitchen, are great for families.

Grandview Motor Hotel (☎ 310-374-8981, fax 310-374-8983; 55 14th St, Hermosa Beach; rooms $82.50-149) is a safe, quiet and sparklingly clean establishment. Its big rooms come with refrigerator and patio. The lobby is on the 2nd floor – ring the bell to enter.

San Pedro & Long Beach

HI Los Angeles – South Bay (☎ 310-831-8109; 3601 S Gaffey St No 613, San Pedro; dorm beds members/nonmembers $17.10/ 20.10 , private rooms $42), on a windy bluff overlooking the Pacific, gets the top award for scenery. This nicely decorated hostel comes with a big kitchen, game and entertainment equipment, plus a volleyball court. Bunks are in gender-segregated dorms sleeping three to five people.

Inn of Long Beach (☎ 562-435-3791, 800-230-7500, fax 562-436-7510; 185 Atlantic Ave, Long Beach; rooms $65-75, suites $120) is a friendly, central establishment whose rooms face a central courtyard with a heated swimming pool and spa. Local calls and parking are free, as is breakfast.

Dockside Boat & Bed (☎ 562-436-3111, 800-436-2574, fax 562-436-1181; w www .boatandbed.com; Rainbow Harbor, Dock 5, 316 E Shoreline Dr, Long Beach; rooms $175-300) is suited for salty types with a sense of romance. Let yourself be rocked to sleep aboard a private yacht (choices include a 50ft Chinese junk) with a view of the Queen Mary.

Lord Mayor's B&B (☎/fax 562-436-0324, 800-691-5166; w www.lordmayors.com; 435 Cedar Ave, Long Beach; rooms $85-140) is inside a 1904 Edwardian house. Rooms get their character from stylish antique furniture and not from frilly over-decorating; bathrooms have claw-foot tubs, and there's an ample sundeck.

Hotel Queen Mary (☎ 562-435-3511; w www.queenmary.com; 1126 Queens Hwy, Long Beach; rooms $109-219) enables you to stay in the original refurbished staterooms of this former luxury liner. Portholes don't provide much light, but the mood of Art Deco afloat is unmatched. The cheaper rooms are somewhat cramped.

San Fernando Valley

Budget motels cluster along E Colorado St in Glendale. Among them are **Chariot Inn Motel** (☎ 818-507-9600; 1118 E Colorado St; rooms $58-95), which has refrigerators and movies in its 31 good-sized rooms; and **Glendale Lodge** (☎ 818-507-6688; 1510 E Colorado St; rooms $62-82, suites $92-120). Both include a small breakfast in their rates.

Universal City Inn (☎ 818-760-8737, fax 818-762-5159; 10730 Ventura Blvd, Studio City; rooms $79-90) is a flower-festooned place with modern, large and air-conditioned rooms. It's just off busy Hwy 101, within walking distance to Universal Studios.

Safari Inn (☎ 818-845-8586, 800-782-4373, fax 818-845-0054; w http://anabelle-safari.com; 1911 W Olive Ave, Burbank; rooms $109-129, suites $179) sports vintage neon signage but a recent modernization has propelled this motel into the 21st century. Suites have full kitchens and sleep up to five people.

Sportsmen's Lodge Hotel (☎ 818-769-4700, 800-821-8511, fax 818-769-4798;

W *www.slhotel.com; 12825 Ventura Blvd, Studio City; rooms $152-185)* is built around a handsome garden with waterfalls and a swan pond. There's a free shuttle to/from Universal Studios.

Pasadena (Map 8)

Pasadena's 'motel row' is along E Colorado Blvd between Lake Ave and Rosemead Blvd. Dozens of budget-priced motels line this strip, some in better repair than others, including such chains as Comfort Inn, Econo Lodge, Holiday Inn, Ramada and Travelodge.

Westway Inn *(☎ 626-304-9678; 1599 E Colorado Blvd; rooms $62-89)* is a friendly place whose 61 modern rooms sport a refrigerator, coffeemaker and hair dryer; some have a private Jacuzzi.

Saga Motor Hotel *(☎ 626-795-0431, 800-793-7242; 1633 E Colorado Blvd; rooms $63-93)*, next door to Westway Inn, is similar and provides a small breakfast.

Pasadena Inn *(☎ 626-795-8401; 400 S Arroyo Parkway; rooms $55-89)*, about 1mi south of Old Pasadena, is a well-maintained standard affair with a pool. Rooms have cable TV and phones, but refrigerators and microwaves must be rented for an extra fee.

Artists' Inn & Cottage *(☎ 626-799-5668, 888-799-5668, fax 626-799-3678;* W *www .artistsinns.com; 1038 Magnolia St; rooms $115-205)*, in a lovely Victorian farmhouse, is a popular B&B. Each of its nine rooms and suites has decor recalling various artists and periods.

Bissell House *(☎ 626-441-3535, 800-441-3530, fax 626-441-3671;* W *www.bissell house.com; 201 Orange Grove Blvd; rooms $125-175)* is another B&B, with five charming rooms that sport leaded-glass windows and private bathrooms with pedestal sinks and claw-foot tubs.

Ritz-Carlton Huntington Hotel *(☎ 626-568-3900, 800-241-3333, fax 626-568-3700;* W *www.ritzcarlton.com/hotels/huntington; 1401 S Oak Knoll Ave; rooms $245-310)* is a sumptuous 392-room hostelry surrounded by lush, sprawling gardens. Special touches include a covered picture bridge and California's first Olympic-sized swimming pool.

PLACES TO EAT

The folks in San Francisco or New York may scoff, but the fact remains: there's great food in Los Angeles. Why? The number one reason, perhaps, is a willingness to experiment. LA attracts people from around the world – and with them comes their food. Creative chefs take bits and pieces from different traditions and combine them in ways that were unimaginable only a few years ago.

Innovative cuisine is most commonly found in upscale West Hollywood, Beverly Hills, Santa Monica and Pasadena. Mexican, Chinese, Japanese and other cuisines abound throughout the city, but the most authentic places are the various ethnic pockets such as Little Tokyo, Chinatown and East LA. Italian, French and Mexican restaurants are popular everywhere. And there are enough hamburger joints, cafés and hole-in-the-wall diners to suit every pocketbook.

Most restaurants are open daily for lunch and dinner, but specific opening times tend to vary widely and change frequently. Call ahead if you've got your eye on a particular spot. Reservations are a good idea at most mid- and upper-range restaurants.

Downtown (Map 2)

The motley melange of ethnicities, languages and social strata characterizing Downtown LA is also reflected in the variety of its culinary offerings.

Bustling Broadway has a couple of excellent places that are a dream come true for the cash-strapped. **Grand Central Market** *(317 Broadway)* offers plenty of self-serve eateries where you'll fill up for under $5. Good picks include **Maria's Pescado Frito** in the central aisle for fresh fish tacos and *ceviche*; **Sarita's Pupusería** in the north aisle for toothsome Salvadoran *pupusas* filled with cheese, pork or beans; and **Roast to Go** in the central aisle for tacos and burritos. **China Cafe**, on the upper level, has big platters of chow mein, although its bestsellers are the huge, steamy and delicious bowls of noodle soups.

Clifton's Brookdale Cafeteria *(☎ 213-627-1673; 648 S Broadway; meals $3-7)* is an ultra-campy LA institution in business since 1932. After filling your tray, you'll sit down in an 'enchanted forest' with faux trees, squirrels and deer. For spiritual sustenance, duck into the diminutive chapel.

The nearby Financial District brims with high-end places popular with power players.

Cicada *(☎ 213-488-9488; 617 S Olive St; mains $15-32)*, in the historic Oviatt building, is an Art Deco riot with a gilded cathedral ceiling and a menu focused on contemporary Italian fare.

Ciudad (☎ 213-486-5171; 445 S Figueroa St; lunch Mon-Fri $9-18.50, dinner nightly $15-26) regales diners with a pioneering pan-Latino menu. Even the desserts are worth the butt-building indulgence.

Water Grill (☎ 213-891-0900; 544 S Grand Ave; mains $21-34) serves dock-fresh and impeccably prepared seafood and fish. There's also an oyster bar. Try to leave room for the signature chocolate bread pudding.

Little Tokyo is the obvious place for fresh sushi. **Hama Sushi** (☎ 213-680-3454; 355 E 2nd St; sushi combinations $12-15), a pocket-sized bar, is known among connoisseurs from all over town, but **Frying Fish Sushi** (☎ 213-680-0567; 120 Japanese Village Plaza; sushi servings $1.50-4.50) has some of the best prices. For something different, try **Shabu Shabu House** (☎ 213-680-3890; 127 Japanese Village Plaza; regular/large-sized plates $8/9.60 lunch, $11/13.60 dinner), one of the best places for the culinary ritual of *shabu shabu*, the Japanese version of fondue. Lines are guaranteed, but the wait is worth it.

Chinatown restaurants come essentially in two types: the formal banquet hall/dim sum parlor, and the casual eatery where you can chow down on quickly prepared standard dishes (eg, lemon chicken and Mongolian beef) at rock-bottom prices (usually $5 to $8).

Top contenders among the former are **Ocean Seafood** (☎ 213-687-3088; 757 N Hill St), a spacious Hong Kong–style place, and **Empress Pavilion** (☎ 213-617-9898; 988 N Hill St), on the 3rd floor of Bamboo Plaza. A typical lunch at either will set you back about $20, while dinners are around $30. There's also the slightly cheaper **Golden Dragon** (☎ 213-626-2039; 960 N Broadway), with great seafood and smoky *chow fun* (rice noodles).

Chow houses to try include **Hong Kong Harbor** (845 N Broadway), **Sam Woo** (727 N Broadway) and **Hop Woo** (855 N Broadway).

South of Chinatown is **Philippe's The Original** (☎ 213-628-3781; 1001 N Alameda St; meals under $5), in business since 1908 and self-proclaimed 'home of the French Dip sandwich'. Watch retro-clad 'carvers' prepare juicy roast beef sandwiches for dipping into fragrant juice from the roasting pan. Coffee is just 9¢ (no misprint).

Hollywood (Map 3)

Old Spaghetti Factory (☎ 323-469-7149; 5939 W Sunset Blvd; meals $6-11) serves heaps of filling, cheap and actually quite good pasta in a gloriously over-the-top setting blending a Big Red Streetcar, roomy leather booths and 'Dr Seuss–ian' armchairs. All orders come with salad, fresh bread, coffee or tea, and dessert.

Birds (☎ 323-465-0175; 5925 Franklin Ave; meals $6-12) is a hip coffee shop famous for its marinated chicken sent through the rotisserie for that light, crispy tan and paired with tasty dipping sauces, bread and a side dish.

Miceli's (☎ 323-466-3438; 1646 N Las Palmas Ave; lunch Mon-Fri $7-12, dinner nightly $9-17), Hollywood's oldest Italian restaurant (1949), has carved booths and hundreds of empty Chianti bottles dangling from the beamed ceiling. The house wine is a steal at $12 a bottle.

Yamashiro (☎ 323-466-5125; 1999 N Sycamore Ave; mains $18-35), a replica Japanese palace, is seductively perched on a southerly slope of the Hollywood Hills, overlooking the sea of glitter that is the city at night. The food's only so-so, but the views are unforgettable, especially at night.

Musso & Frank Grill (☎ 323-467-7788; 6667 Hollywood Blvd; mains $20-35, open Tues-Sat), already a hit back in the silent film era, still pulls in Industry heavyweights. Service is smooth, and so are the martinis.

Les Deux Café (☎ 323-465-0509; 1638 Las Palmas Ave; mains $24-34) is a French restaurant that draws a swanky crowd heavy on brass, beauty and power. Preferred seating is in the secluded garden around a log-shaped reflecting pool. Enter the restaurant via Grants parking lot.

Dar Maghreb (☎ 323-876-7651; 7651 Sunset Blvd; 7-course meal $37) enables guests to journey from Tinseltown to *A Thousand and One Nights*. As you dig into a mouthwatering feast – served family style and eaten without utensils – you may find the back of your neck tickled by the tassel of a voluptuous belly dancer.

Patina (☎ 323-467-1108; 5955 Melrose Ave; mains $29-39, set dinner $70-80), in a spectacularly redesigned space, is a highlight on every deep-pocketed foodie's map. Chef Joachim Splichal digs deep into his bottomless culinary repertoire to create a

LOS ANGELES

menu that cleverly fuses Californian tastes with European touches.

Silver Lake & Los Feliz (Map 3)

El Conquistador (☎ *323-666-5136; 3701 Sunset Blvd, Silver Lake; mains $9-13.50)* is an eccentric Mexican cantina in a festive indoor garden setting with twinkling lights. The food is delicious, the service friendly and the prices honest.

Fred's 62 (☎ *323-667-0062; 1854 Vermont Ave, Los Feliz; dishes $2.62-13.62)* is an updated '50s-style diner in the heart of Los Feliz Village where polyethnic sandwiches, salads and noodles are dished out around the clock to hungry hipsters on small budgets.

Palermo (☎ *323-663-1178; 1858 Vermont Ave, Los Feliz; mains $7-13; open Wed-Mon)* is a family kind of place that's as welcoming and comfortable as a hug from an old friend. Couples, kids, gays, cops, producers and the impecunious come for generously topped pizzas and big plates of pasta; the small antipasto salad feeds four (as an appetizer).

Vermont (☎ *323-661-6163; 1714 Vermont Ave, Los Feliz; lunch $9-16, dinner $13-30)* is an elegant restaurant with medieval-style vaulted ceilings above plain, concrete floors. The menu is mostly Mediterranean, impeccably prepared with fresh ingredients and usually featuring at least a couple of meatless mains.

Vida (☎ *323-660-4446; 1930 Hillhurst Ave, Los Feliz; dinner $15-28)* is a chichi establishment whose chef often pushes the boundaries of California cuisine. If you appreciate eccentric presentation and like to surprise your taste buds with unusual flavor combinations, you'll find plenty to like here.

Yuca's (☎ *323-662-1214; 2052 Hillhurst Ave, Los Feliz; dishes $3-6)* is a little hut where burritos, tacos and tortas bulging with such Yucatan-style fillings as *machaca* and *cochinita pibil* all fly nonstop through the service window.

West Hollywood & Mid-City (Map 4)

French Quarter Market (☎ *323-654-0898; 7985 Santa Monica Blvd, West Hollywood; dishes $5-13)*, popular with the gay crowd and everyone else, serves casual California fare, including mountains of fresh, delicious salads. Seating is either on the outdoor patio or the New Orleans–inspired interior.

Hugo's (☎ *323-654-3993; 8401 Santa Monica Blvd, West Hollywood; dishes $8-10)* may not look 'Hollywood' but it usually swarms with Industry insiders and wannabes, especially for breakfast. Much of the menu has a wholesome bent (eg, Tantric vegie burgers).

Foodies will have a field day in the Beverly Center district. Places worth trying include the following:

Tail O' The Pup (☎ *310-652-4517; 329 N San Vicente Blvd; meals under $5)* is a hot dog–shaped eatery which is one of the last remaining pieces of mimetic architecture in LA. In business since 1938, it was once a favorite of Orson Welles.

Cava (☎ *323-658-8898; 8384 W 3rd St; tapas $4-13, mains $15-32)*, inside the Beverly Plaza Hotel, sizzles with Spanish/Latin decor and live salsa upstairs on selected nights. For tapas, you can't go wrong with the superb *ceviche* served in a half coconut shell.

Kings Road Cafe (☎ *323-655-9044; 8361 Beverly Blvd; dishes $5-11)* has delicious bistro fare at budget prices. Try the stuffed gourmet panini or tasty pastas. Seating is inside or at sidewalk tables, and there's an international newsstand next door.

Hard Rock Cafe (☎ *310-276-7605; 8500 Beverly Blvd* • ☎ *818-622-7625; Universal City Walk; dishes $7-19)* has branches on the ground floor of the Beverly Center mall and on Universal City Walk.

Chaya Brasserie (☎ *310-859-8833; 8741 Alden Dr; mains $14-28)* has a menu that's as creative as the 'Zen-meets-industrial' dining room. The chef performs miracles with Cal-French cuisine complemented by Asian inflections.

Pastis (☎ *323-655-8822; 8114 Beverly Blvd; mains $16-20)* is a relaxed place where yellow walls bring the sunshine indoors and meals become culinary celebrations that comfortably stretch out for an entire evening. The menu changes frequently but is heavy on southern French classics.

Sofi (☎ *323-651-0346; 8030¾ W 3rd St; mains $12-23)* delivers the enchantment of a Greek taverna on its shaded patio deck canopied by bougainvillea and leafy trees. The rack of lamb is the signature dish, but it also makes a mean moussaka and a satisfying appetizer platter.

At the **Farmers Market** (*6333 W 3rd St)* you can put together a picnic from the cheese, sausage, bread and delicatessen vendors, or grab some takeout and eat it in the central patio. A good place is the New Orleans–style **Gumbo Pot** (☎ 323-933-0358; dishes $5-9), which serves a tasty jambalaya (a spicy rice dish with chicken and sausage). At the hip Art Deco **Kokomo** (☎ 323-933-0773; 6333 W 3rd St; lunch $5-8, dinner $8-15) you can belly up to the Formica counter alongside Industry types from neighboring CBS for big breakfasts and other substantial fare.

Damiano Mr Pizza (☎ 323-658-7611; 412 N Fairfax Ave; slices from $2, full pies from $10, pasta from $5.25), a few blocks north of the market, is a low-key night owls' favorite whose staff fires up New York–style pies until sunrise.

Pink's Hot Dogs (711 La Brea Ave at Melrose Ave; hot dogs $2.35-3.65; open to 2am Mon-Fri, to 3am Sat & Sun), further east, is a landmark 'doggeria,' and also enjoys cult status with the late-night crowd.

Santé La Brea (☎ 323-857-0412; 345 N La Brea Ave; dishes $5-10) makes vegan food that's good for your waistline, heart and spirit and is best consumed in the leafy outdoor patio. Breakfast is served as well.

Campanile (☎ 323-938-1447; 624 S La Brea Ave; lunch Mon-Fri $12-18, dinner Mon-Sat $24-38) has defined 'urban rustic' cooking. Chef Mark Peel comes up with new culinary creations daily, but staples include grilled meats and vegetables. Nancy Silverton reigns as the dessert goddess.

Beverly Hills & Westside (Map 5)

Crustacean (☎ 310-205-8990; 9646 Little Santa Monica Blvd, Beverly Hills; mains $18-38) is a beautiful place where design features include a sunken aquarium where plump koi lazily tumble. Seafood reigns supreme here, with top honors going to the whole roasted Dungeness crab treated to an aromatic balm of 'secret spices.'

Ed Debevic's (☎ 310-659-1952; 134 N La Cienega Blvd, Beverly Hills; dishes under $10) is a flashback to the age of beehives, hula hoops and Elvis. Sassy servers bring burgers, fries and other satisfying goodies to patrons squeezed into sparkly Naughahyde booths fitted with tableside miniature jukeboxes.

Matsuhisa (☎ 310-659-9639; 129 N La Cienega Blvd, Beverly Hills; mains from $20, tasting menu $100-120) is one of LA's top

restaurants. The 25-plus page menu may well be the culinary equivalent of *War and Peace* – epic, intimidating and heroic.

Spago Beverly Hills (☎ 310-385-0880; 176 N Cañon Dr, Beverly Hills; mains $17-32), Wolfgang Puck's flagship restaurant, has a seasonal menu that is best enjoyed on the romantic patio anchored by ancient olive trees. Make reservations early or hope for no-shows.

Natalee's Thai Cuisine (☎ 310-855-9380; 998 S Robertson Blvd • ☎ 310-202-7003; 10036 Venice Blvd, Culver City, Westside; mains $6-10) is a stylish Thai eatery whose kitchen produces all the traditional Thai staples.

Versailles (☎ 310-289-0392; 1415 S La Cienega Blvd, Beverly Hills • ☎ 310-558-3168; 10319 Venice Blvd, Culver City, Westside; mains $6-11) has some of the best Cuban food this side of Havana. The lip-smacking roast garlic lemon chicken will make you cluck with delight.

Malibu

Neptune's Net (☎ 310-457-3095; 42505 Pacific Coast Hwy; meals $5-20), near the Ventura County line, serves superbly fresh seafood in a decidedly unpretentious setting. Come at sunset, sit at the rustic table, look out over the sea, peel a pile of shrimp and wash it all down with a cold beer.

Inn of the Seventh Ray (☎ 310-455-1311; 128 Old Topanga Canyon Rd; lunch $7-15, dinner $19-31, Sunday buffet brunch $22) is a New Age-y place in an idyllic canyon setting. The karmically correct menu features plenty of meat-free and vegan dishes. Seating is inside or on a shaded patio.

Santa Monica (Map 6)

Omelet Parlor (☎ 310-399-7892; 2732 Main St; breakfast & lunch under $7) has been whipping up industrial-weight omelets and solid sandwiches since opening during the 'Summer of Love' in 1967. Expect a line on weekend mornings.

Real Food Daily (☎ 310-451-7544; 514 Santa Monica Blvd; dishes $6-12), one of LA's best organic and vegan restaurants, serves nutritious nosh on two floors of artsy ambience.

Ye Olde King's Head (☎ 310-451-1402; 116 Santa Monica Blvd; dishes $6.50-13) is the unofficial headquarters of the Westside's huge British expat community. Regulars swear they make the best fish and chips in town.

Wolfgang Puck Express (☎ 310-576-4770; 1315 Third Street Promenade; dishes $7-10) gives gourmets on a budget a chance to sample some of Puck's bestsellers such as the Chinese chicken salad and tasty pizzas.

Taiko (☎ 310-207-7782; 11677 San Vicente Blvd, Brentwood; mains $7-22), inside a small mall, is a prim Japanese noodle house serving awfully good and generous bowls of succulently flavored soba and udon, either hot or cold.

La Serenata De Garibaldi (☎ 310-656-7017; 1416 4th St; mains $9-22) makes upscale Mexican fare in a cheerful indoor courtyard setting.

JiRaffe (☎ 310-917-6671; 502 Santa Monica Blvd; lunch $10-12.50, dinner $18-28) has a 'private mansion' feel with walnut furniture, crystal chandeliers and original art, but there's nothing stuffy about it. The Cal-French food is as elegant as the surroundings and the service is attentive yet discrete.

Border Grill (☎ 310-451-1655; 1445 4th St; lunch $7.50-15, dinner $14-25) looks as if it was designed by six year olds but has a decidedly grown-up menu of boldly flavored south-of-the-border dishes.

Venice Beach (Map 6)

Abbot Pizza (☎ 310-396-7334; 1407 Abbot Kinney Blvd; slices $2.50, pizzas from $13.50) is a little walk-in joint that makes habit-forming bagel-crust pizzas with such gourmet toppings as wild mushrooms, barbecue chicken and olive pesto. Possibly one of the best pie places in town.

Jodi Maroni's Sausage Kingdom (2011 Ocean Front Walk; sausages $4), on the boardwalk, has exotically spiced gourmet sausages that are a good fast-food option.

Rose Cafe (☎ 310-399-0711; 220 Rose Ave; café prices under $4, restaurant $6-16) is an old standby with two tree-fringed patios. The café serves yummy baked goods, while the restaurant focuses on California classics.

Sidewalk Cafe (☎ 310-399-5547; 1401 Ocean Front Walk; dishes $8-12) serves big plates of good, old-fashioned American fare to a steady stream of locals and tourists. As a bonus, you'll have front-row seats of the stream of quasi-humanity parading along the Venice Boardwalk.

Lilly's (☎ 310-314-0004; 1031 Abbot Kinney Blvd; mains $10-19) is an unhurried neighborhood bistro with a flowery, secluded courtyard. The best deal is the $10 two-course lunch.

Joe's (☎ 310-399-5811; 1023 Abbot Kinney Blvd; mains $20-22, 4-course prix-fixe menus $38 & $48), next door to Lilly's, is a classic neighborhood eatery serving Cal-French food. Even simple dishes become little flavor bombs that will linger on the palate and in the memory.

South Bay

The South Bay brims with good-value, casual eateries, but has also a few selections for those looking for a sophisticated dining experience.

Great breakfast places include **Uncle Bill's Pancake House** (1305 Highland Ave, Manhattan Beach); the **Back Burner Cafe** (87 14th St, Hermosa Beach) and the **Beach Hut No 2** (14th St, Hermosa Beach) across the street. You can fill up at each of these for under $8, but all close around 2pm.

Good Mexican eateries, all serving combinations for around $7 to $9 and a la carte items from $2.50, include **El Sombrero** (1005 Manhattan Ave, Manhattan Beach), **El Gringo** (2620 Hermosa Ave, Hermosa Beach) and **La Playita** (37 14th St, Hermosa Beach).

Chez Mélange (☎ 310-540-1222; 1716 S Pacific Coast Hwy, Redondo Beach; mains $10-30) serves up reliably good global fare in an elegant, bourgeois dining room. The Cajun meatloaf is a signature dish.

Long Beach

Pine Ave is Long Beach's 'restaurant row' lined mostly with mid-range and upscale places that overflow with patrons on Friday and Saturday nights.

Alegria (☎ 562-436-3388; 115 Pine Ave; tapas $6-10, mains $14-20) has a trippy, Technicolor mosaic floor, trompe l'oeil murals, and spicy and exotic Nuevo Latino cuisine. It has live entertainment nightly. You could make this a budget place by sticking to tapas.

L'Opera (☎ 562-491-0066; 101 Pine Ave; mains $11-29), an Italian gourmet temple, is the kind of place where ambience, food, service and wine collaborate to create a dining experience which will linger on one's mind long after the (sizable) bill has been paid.

King's Fish House (☎ 562-432-7463; 100 W Broadway; mains $14-30) makes fish and seafood for the soul, all impeccably fresh and served in a high-energy setting.

Away from the strip, **Belmont Brewing Company** (☎ 562-433-3891; 25 39th Place; lunch $6-12, dinner $9-25) is an oceanfront brew-pub and restaurant with a large outdoor deck perfect for watching sunsets. The brews, fresh and hand-crafted, go well with the well-priced menu that offers far more than just 'pub grub'.

San Fernando Valley

The recently expanded Universal City Walk now has nearly 30 restaurants, most of them clones of successful eateries around town, including **Jodi Maroni's Sausage Kingdom** (see Venice Beach section) and **Versailles** (see Beverly Hills & Westside section). **Karl Strauss Brewery** (☎ 818-753-2739; dishes $6-15) serves Pan-American food infused with Germanic touches, which goes down especially well with a mug of the house brew.

Some good choices elsewhere in the Valley include the following.

Zankou Chicken (☎ 323-665-7842; 5065 Sunset Blvd, Glendale; dishes $2.60-8) does lip-smacking rotisserie chicken paired with creamy hummus, salad and pita bread. Hard-core fans slather on the garlic sauce.

Poquito Más (☎ 818-563-2252; 2635 W Olive Ave, Burbank; dishes $3.50-7) is a shack-like Mexican eatery serving food that is both fast and healthy. The *ahi* tacos and chicken burritos reach gourmet quality. Also try the tortilla soup.

Bob's Big Boy (☎ 818-843-9334; 4211 Riverside Dr, Burbank; dishes $5-9), a classic coffee shop from the late '40s, offers a genuine slice of Americana. On Saturday and Sunday between 5pm and 10pm, its car-hop service (*sans* the roller skates) lets you catch that *American Graffiti* vibe. Breakfast is served anytime.

Café Bizou (☎ 818-788-3536; 14016 Ventura Blvd, Sherman Oaks; lunch $7-14, dinner $13-19) is a charmer where French food gets the royal treatment at paupers' prices. Add soup or salad to your main course for just $1 more; corkage fee is just $2.

Ca' del Sole (☎ 818-985-4669; 4100 Cahuenga Blvd, North Hollywood; mains $8-17) is a slice of Italy in the midst of suburbia. Diners are wowed by tantalizing,

flavor-intensive northern Italian fare in a setting of curvaceous booths and panoramic windows.

Market City Café (☎ 818-840-7036; 164 E Palm Ave, Burbank; mains $12-17) serves Italian pizza, panini, pasta and salads in their infinite variety, although the best deal may well be the all-you-can-eat antipasto bar for $8 (or $5.25 with main course). It has a nice patio.

Bistro Garden at Coldwater (☎ 818-501-0202; 12950 Ventura Blvd, Studio City; mains $15-30) is the place for romantic dining on inventively prepared seafood, meats and pasta in the Euro-style winter garden.

Pasadena (Map 8)

Europane (☎ 626-577-1828; 950 E Colorado Blvd; dishes $6-9; open 7am-5:30pm, to 2pm Sun) makes buttery croissants, crispy biscotti and everything in between, plus complete sandwiches with inspired fillings.

Marston's (☎ 626-796-2459; 151 E Walnut Ave; dishes $6-11; open Tues-Sat), inside a homey cottage, is a local breakfast and lunch hangout. The French toast has that perfect golden tan, the pancakes are plump and the sandwiches and salads are stuffed with super-fresh ingredients.

Saladang (☎ 626-793-8123; 363 S Fair Oaks Ave; mains $10-21) is a Thai dining shrine where the ordinary becomes extraordinary. To meet demand, the owners also opened Saladang Song, a few doors down, with more traditional fare and even more striking design.

Xiomara (☎ 626-796-2520; 69 N Raymond Ave; lunch $10-20, dinner $18-28) has sleek decor that's a perfect foil for the visual and flavor explosions arriving on your plate. The menu, which has a Nuevo Latino orientation, changes often.

ENTERTAINMENT

To keep your finger on what's hot in LA, your best sources of information are the Calendar section of the daily *Los Angeles Times* (especially the magazine-like Thursday supplement) and the free *LA Weekly*, available at restaurants, shops, pubs etc.

Tickets for most events are available by phone or in person from each venue's box office, usually with no or only a small booking fee. Many venues also allow reservations via the Internet. In some cases, reservations may only be made through **Ticketmaster** (☎ 213-480-3232; w *www.ticketmaster.com*), which collects exorbitant handling fees and service charges in addition to the ticket price.

Music & Dance Clubs

LA's club and live music scene is one of the liveliest in the country and caters to everyone's tastes and expectations, from pale-faced college-age ravers to designer-chic yuppies and ex-hippie baby boomers. No musical era is off-limits, be it '20s jazz, '30s and '40s big band swing, '50s rockabilly, '60s rock and roll, '70s disco, '80s punk and new wave, and techno, house, gothic, industrial, trip hop, hip hop, trance, etc sounds of today.

The line between bars, clubs and music venues often becomes blurred, with many places changing chameleon-like during the week. For the latest information, the *LA Weekly* is your best source.

Downtown (Map 2) Located in a fantastic pre-Columbian–style ex-movie palace, **The Mayan** (☎ 213-746-4287; 1038 S Hill St; open Fri & Sat) has salsa and merengue on the main floor, and hip hop, disco and Spanish rock in the other rooms. It's extremely dressy – definitely no jeans or sneakers.

Hollywood (Map 3) A hipster haven, **Dragonfly** (☎ 323-466-6111; 6510 Santa Monica Blvd; open nightly) has an oddly appealing grungy look and books mostly rock bands. DJs spin a wild musical mix after the live entertainment has wrapped up. The patio is great for bumping into people.

The Derby (☎ 323-663-8979; 4500 Los Feliz Blvd) has been LA's 'Swing Central' since 1993 and was featured in the movie *Swingers*. Some of the best dancers in town jump 'n' jive around the pint-sized dance floor, while stylish retro bands play on. Call to ask about free lessons.

The Garage (☎ 323-662-6802; 4519 Santa Monica Blvd) is the headquarters of Silver Lake's self-styled grunge-meisters. Come here for bands that are often provocatively bizarre and wild – and sometimes even talented.

Goldfingers (☎ 323-962-2913; 6423 Yucca St) has fabulous Liberace-style over-the-top decor and caters to hard-core clubbers with its frenzied mix of funk, glam rock and punk. Great martinis, too.

Martini Lounge (☎ 323-467-4068; 5657 Melrose Ave; open daily) combines a dark lounge with a two-story dance club where the music ranges from rock and roll to electronica. The crowd is young, hip and local.

One Seven (☎ 323-461-2017; Hollywood & Highland complex) appeals to the 'fabulous' between 15 and 20. A spin-off of the popular teen magazine *Seventeen*, this chic, high-energy club has DJ-spun and live music and an alcohol-free 'energy bar'.

The Palace (☎ 323-467-4571; 1735 N Vine St), in a huge, glam Art Deco landmark, has a state-of-the-art sound system and is open to ages 18 and up.

Spaceland (☎ 323-833-2843; 1717 Silver Lake Blvd) is the epicenter of Silver Lake's underground rock scene and is the best place to catch local bands hoping for a career breakout. Put on your thrift-shop finest.

West Hollywood & Mid-City (Map 4) The unpretentious and small **Cat Club** (☎ 310-657-0888; 8911 Sunset Blvd), owned by Slim Jim Phantom of Stray Cats fame, presents mostly multiple acts of solid live rock and roll. It has a lounge and patio for smoking and relaxing your eardrums.

Conga Room (☎ 323-549-9765; 5364 Wilshire Blvd) is a gorgeous Latin dance club with the heady feel of pre-revolution Havana; it's co-owned by Jimmy Smits and Jennifer Lopez. The 'sound-sational' ballroom usually vibrates with hip-shaking gents and twirling ladies in spiky heels.

House of Blues (☎ 323-848-5100; 8430 Sunset Blvd) features the customary faux Mississippi Delta decor and so-so Southern food. Top talent of all stripes, not just the blues, come here and shows often sell out. The Sunday Gospel Brunch is an institution.

Key Club (☎ 323-274-5800; 9039 Sunset Blvd) is an ultrachic club with galactic decor and top-notch sound. Its earlier incarnation, known as Gazzari's, launched the Doors and the Byrds. Today, it has an eclectic schedule of live acts and DJs.

The Mint (☎ 323-954-9630; 6010 W Pico Blvd, Crescent Heights) has been dishing out live blues, rock and jazz to the faithful in a no-nonsense environment that's changed little since 1937.

Roxy (☎ 310-276-2222; 9009 Sunset Blvd), a Sunset fixture since 1973, serves as a launch pad for bands on the verge of stardom.

On most nights, the line-up mixes local and national rock bands, but people like Neil Young or Bruce Springsteen also pop in on occasion.

Viper Room (☎ 310-358-1880; 8852 Sunset Blvd), owned by Johnny Depp, is a small hangout for musicians, celluloid celebs, hyper showbiz types and their hangers-on. Regulars swear the spot peaked long ago, but lines still wrap around the block.

Santa Monica (Map 6) A locals' hangout, **14 Below** (☎ 310-451-5040; 1348 14th St) has two bars and three rooms, plus a fireplace in winter. Bands, mostly from around LA, cover the spectrum from alternative to reggae, rock to ska.

Temple Bar (☎ 310-393-6611; 1026 Wilshire Blvd) is among the most happening hangouts west of Hollywood. The bands are hit-or-miss, but the drinks are strong, the crowd is heavy on the eye candy and the ambience is fairly unpretentious.

The West End (☎ 310-313-3293; 1301 5th St) is Santa Monica's party central. Bring your dancing shoes and get *down* to disco, '80s flashbacks, hip hop, reggae and rock. It has live bands and cheap drinks.

Jazz & Blues
Babe & Ricky's (☎ 323-295-9112; 4339 Leimert Blvd, Leimert Park) is LA's oldest blues club presided over by Mama Laura, aka Laura Mae Gross, for nearly four decades. The Monday night jam session, with free food, often brings the house down.

Catalina Bar & Grill (Map 3; ☎ 323-466-2210; 1640 Cahuenga Blvd, Hollywood) is one of LA's finest jazz venues and draws big name musicians of international stature, including Chick Correa and Branford Marsalis.

Harvelle's (Map 6; ☎ 310-395-1676; 1432 4th St, Santa Monica) is a tiny blues joint which has delighted generations of fans since 1931. Accomplished local groups perform blues, R&B, funk and rock nightly.

Jazz Bakery (☎ 310-271-9039; 3233 Helms Ave, Culver City), inside a former bakery, brings in a mix of heavy hitters on tour and top-notch local talent. Charlie Haden, David Murray and Milt Jackson have all played here.

Lighthouse Café (☎ 310-372-6911; 30 Pier Ave, Hermosa Beach) is a timeless beachside mainstay that's been around since the 1950s.

Blue Café (☎ 562-983-7111; 210 Promenade, Long Beach) is a local institution and a regular stop for prominent jazz and blues talent. It has good drinks and food as well.

Bars & Pubs
No matter where you are in LA, you're never far from a bar. Besides the ones mentioned in this section, many restaurants, hotels and clubs also have bars for sopping up the various LA vibes – and drinks – and for observing the scene.

Downtown In Stillwell Hotel, **Hank's Bar** (Map 2; ☎ 213-623-7718; 838 Grand Ave) is a classic tunnel-shaped watering hole bathed in dungeon-like darkness, seemingly immersing you in a Raymond Chandler novel.

HMS Bounty (☎ 323-385-7275; 3357 Wilshire Blvd) is a barely lit retro tavern in Koreatown, a few miles west of Downtown proper. The Naughahyde booths and stiff drinks at buck-saver prices are currently wooing a new generation of scenesters.

Hollywood (Map 3) In Silver Lake, **Akbar** (☎ 323-665-6810; 4356 W Sunset Blvd) is trendy *sans* the attitude. It's hot with gay men and straight women who come for cocktails, conversation and jukebox music. Complexion-friendly candlelight, Moorish arches and dangling cylindrical wicker lamps add a touch of the exotic.

Good Luck Bar (☎ 323-666-3524; 1514 Hillhurst Ave) ushers you into a Chinese fantasy world of carmine red wallpaper and paper lanterns. The crowd is cool, the jukebox is loud and the drinks seductively strong (Yee Mee Loo Blue and a Chinese herb-based whisky are popular choices).

Tiki Ti (☎ 323-669-9381; 4427 Sunset Blvd) is a garage-sized tropical tavern where showbiz folks, blue-collar types and Silver Lake trendoids jostle up to the bar which is engulfed in wickedly wonderful nautical kitsch. 'Rae's Mistake', the house special, is anything but.

Beauty Bar (☎ 323-464-7676; 1638 N Cahuenga Blvd) is a pint-sized cocktail bar giving new meaning to the word 'retro': it's entirely decorated with hair salon paraphernalia from the Kennedy era. Sip your martini or get your nails done while seated in swivel chairs beneath plastic hair dryers.

Dresden Room (☎ 323-665-4294; 1760 N Vermont Ave) is an old-time place that recaptured the spotlight after being featured in the 1997 movie *Swingers*. The campy singing duo of Marty and Elaine has 'owned' this lounge since 1981 and still pack in an intergenerational crowd of the newly or eternally hip.

Formosa Cafe (☎ 323-850-9050; 7156 Santa Monica Blvd), the one-time watering hole of Bogart, Monroe and Gable, is the place to sop up some Hollywood nostalgia. Smokers will appreciate the roof deck and patio. Mai tais and martinis are beverages of choice. Skip the food.

Lava Lounge (☎ 323-876-6612; 1533 N La Brea Ave) exudes a seductive tropical feel, with its curvaceous booths, tiny tiki lamps, bamboo and palm fronds and live bands. To get that special Maui buzz, order a Blue Hawaiian ($8).

Cool Hollywood pubs include the **Cat & Fiddle** (6530 Sunset Blvd) and the **Coach & Horses** (7617 Sunset Blvd).

Coastal Communities A comfortable Irish entry, **O'Brien's** (Map 6; ☎ 310-829-5303; 2226 Wilshire Blvd, Santa Monica) is popular with the post-college crowd. There's a smoking patio and a long bar in which to make friends over a pint of Guinness.

Scruffy O'Shea's (Map 6; ☎ 310-821-0833; 822 Washington Blvd, Venice) has a happening happy hour, English pub grub and live bands playing reggae, rock, salsa, swing and Irish seven nights a week.

Toppers (Map 7; ☎ 310-393-8080; 1111 2nd St, Santa Monica), at the top of the Radisson Huntley Hotel and reached via a fun exterior elevator ride, has one of LA's best happy hours (4:30pm to 7:30pm daily) and superb ocean sunsets.

Aloha Sharkeez (☎ 310-374-7823; 52 Pier Ave, Hermosa Beach) is a spit-and-saw-dust cantina where the objective is to get drunk as fast as possible, which is why mysterious concoctions such as Lava Flow and Blue Voodoo come in huge pitchers.

Poopdeck (☎ 310-376-3223; 1272 Strand, Hermosa Beach) is another sweaty and smelly boozing institution with nightly drinks specials and cheap beer. Sometimes it feels like you're crashing a frat party.

Yard House (☎ 562-628-0455; 401 Shore-line Village Dr, Long Beach) has bartenders who command an oval bar that looks like a spaceship helm. Some 250 beers are on tap, connected to 5mi of beer lines and 27 pumps. Serious boozers consume their brew from 'yards.'

Pasadena Right in Old Pasadena, **Gordon Biersch Brewery** (Map 8; ☎ 626-449-0052; 41 Hugus Alley) is a microbrewery (with a beer garden) working with original German recipes. It churns out respectable smooth-tasting brews, including a crisp pilsner, the slightly sweet Märzen and the full-bodied Dunkles.

Cinema

Cinemas – usually multiplexes with up to 20 screens – are ubiquitous in the movie capital of the world. First-run films sell out early on Friday and Saturday nights. Shows after 6pm cost around $9.50 (adult), those before are often discounted. Advance credit card bookings can be made by calling ☎ 213-777-3456 or ☎ 310-777-3456, or by logging on to ⓦ www.moviefone.com; there's no surcharge for this service.

Historic theaters include the recently restored Cinerama Dome (now part of the state-of-the-art ArcLight Cinemas movie theater complex), the El Capitan, the Egyptian and Mann's Chinese Theater in Hollywood; the Warner Grand in San Pedro; and the Orpheum in Downtown. You'll find clusters of theaters on Third Street Promenade in Santa Monica, on Colorado Blvd in Old Pasadena and in Westwood Village.

Good revival and art-house cinemas include **The Nuart** (Map 7; ☎ 310-478-6379; 11272 Santa Monica Blvd, Westside), which is famous for its Saturday midnight *Rocky Horror Picture Show* screenings; and the fourplex **Laemmle Theatre** (Map 6; ☎ 310-394-9741; 1332 2nd St, Santa Monica), which shows recent-release non-US films with an offbeat bent. Then there's also the **Silent Movie Theatre** (Map 4; ☎ 323-655-2520; 611 N Fairfax Ave, Fairfax District), where screenings are accompanied by live music.

Theater

Theater has long been a lively and integral part of LA's cultural scene. Choices range from glittery musicals and plays to ensemble shows and independent fringe theater in unconventional venues. LA's theaters are great

Getting into a Studio

To see a particular TV star while in LA, your best bet is to watch a taping of his or her show. Doing so is easy, and tickets are free – but plan well ahead as the top shows (such as *Friends*) fill up early. Production season runs from August to March. All shows have minimum age requirements (usually 16 or 18). On the day of the taping, come to the studio early to guarantee getting a seat, since tickets are distributed in excess of capacity.

The easiest way to get tickets is through **Audiences Unlimited** (☎ *818-753-3470, ext 812;* **w** *www.tvtickets.com*), which handles the distribution for dozens of shows, mostly sitcoms. Tickets may be ordered up to 30 days prior to the show's taping date. If ordered by phone, they'll be mailed to you, but if you go online, orders are processed immediately and you get to print out your own ticket. The company also operates a booth in the Entertainment Center at Universal Studios Hollywood where you can get tickets for shows filming that day or the next day. Sometimes they even provide free shuttle buses to the studio.

For tickets to *The Tonight Show with Jay Leno*, taping at **NBC Television Studios** (**w** *www.nbc.com/nbc/footer/tickets.shtml*), write to: The Tonight Show with Jay Leno/Tickets, 3000 W Alameda Ave, Burbank, CA 91523, at least six weeks in advance. Enclose a self-addressed stamped envelope and specify three alternate dates. Tickets are also available in person at the box office on a first-come, first-served basis starting at 8am on the day of the taping, which starts at 5pm. Tickets to NBC sitcoms are available through Audiences Unlimited (see earlier).

Paramount Studios (☎ *323-956-5575 for recorded show schedule,* ☎ *323-956-1777 for tickets;* **w** *www.paramountshowticket.com*) also offers tickets to some of the shows taping here. Call or check its website for details.

places to catch both the budding stars of tomorrow and see major film and television actors return to their roots as they perform live on stage.

Half-price theater tickets for shows taking place that week are sold on the Internet by **Theatre LA** (**w** *www.theatrela.org*), an alliance of 160 large and small theaters in the LA area. A service fee of $2 to $6 per ticket applies.

Mark Taper Forum *(Map 2;* ☎ *213-628-2772; Music Center, 135 N Grand Ave, Downtown)* is considered the leading theater in Southern California. Its resident ensemble specializes in developing new plays, and many productions go on to Broadway, some even garnering Tony and Pulitzer awards. The Taper has a public rush for last-minute $10 tickets, sold 10 minutes before curtain.

Major venues for touring productions, often lavish musicals, include the **Ahmanson Theatre** *(Map 2;* ☎ *213-972-0700)*, also at the Music Center, the **Shubert Theater** *(Map 5;* ☎ *310-201-1500, 800-447-7400; 2020 Ave of the Stars, Westside)* and the Art Deco **Pantages Theater** *(Map 3;* ☎ *323-468-1770; 6233 Hollywood Blvd, Hollywood)*.

East West Players *(Map 2;* ☎ *213-625-4397; 120 N Judge John Aiso St, Downtown*

LA) is the leading Asian Pacific American ensemble with a repertory ranging from classics to Broadway and plays specific to the community's experience. Alumni have gone on to win Tony and Emmy awards.

Actors' Gang Theatre *(Map 3;* ☎ *323-465-0566; 6209 Santa Monica Blvd, Hollywood)*, co-founded by Tim Robbins, presents daring and offbeat interpretations of classics and new works produced during ensemble workshops.

Celebration Theater *(Map 4;* ☎ *323-957-1884; 7051 Santa Monica Blvd, West Hollywood)* is among the nation's top producers of gay and lesbian plays.

Coronet Theater *(Map 4;* ☎ *310-657-7177; 366 N La Cienega Blvd, West Hollywood)* premiered Bertolt Brecht's *Galileo* here in 1947. Ever since, this little but illustrious venue has hosted a slew of big name actors, including Richard Dreyfuss, Peter Falk and Gwyneth Paltrow. In recent history, the theater expanded its audience with an extended run of the outrageous if hilarious Puppetry of the Penis, a show featuring what's been called 'genital origami.' Go figure.

Cañon Theatre *(Map 5;* ☎ *310-859-8001; 205 Cañon Dr, Beverly Hills)* is usually booked for extended runs of runaway successes such as *Love Letters* by AR Gurney and *The Vagina Monologues* by Eve Ensler, both featuring rotating celebrity casts.

Geffen Playhouse *(Map 6; ☎ 310-208-5454; 10886 Le Conte Ave, Westwood)* puts on cutting-edge productions by leading American playwrights, often featuring a star-studded cast.

Odyssey Theater Ensemble *(Map 7; ☎ 310-477-2055; 2055 S Sepulveda Blvd, Westside)* specializes in innovative productions of modern classics as well as those of non-US playwrights, both living and dead.

A Noise Within *(☎ 323-953-7795; 234 S Brand Blvd, Glendale)* puts the 'class' into 'classical.' Founded by alumni of the American Conservatory Theater in San Francisco, the repertory ranges from Shakespeare to Calderón de la Barca to Noel Coward.

Pasadena Playhouse *(Map 8; ☎ 626-356-7529; 39 S El Molino Ave, Pasadena)*, dating from 1924, has a loyal LA following. Performances are of a high quality and include many West Coast and world premieres.

Classical Music & Opera

The **Dorothy Chandler Pavilion** *(Map 2; ☎ 213-972-7211; Music Center, 135 N Grand Ave, Downtown)* serves as the main venue of the LA Philharmonic Orchestra (until completion of the Walt Disney Hall; see under Civic Center earlier), the LA Opera and the LA Master Chorale.

LA Philharmonic Orchestra *(☎ 213-850-2000)*, under the stewardship of Esa-Pekka Salonen since 1992, has enjoyed a loyal following despite his insistence on programs that focus on works by obscure composers – or obscure works by famous composers.

LA Opera *(☎ 213-972-8001)* is directed by Plácido Domingo, one-third of the Three Tenors, whose focus is on an eclectic but high-quality repertory of both popular and less mainstream operas.

LA Master Chorale *(☎ 213-626-0624, 800-787-5262)* is a critically acclaimed 120-voice chorus that presents stand-alone recitals and also serves as the chorus for the LA Philharmonics and the LA Opera.

Comedy Clubs

On any given night, comedians are exercising their 'chops' in one of LA's many comedy clubs. Reservations are advised. Note that many clubs have a two-drink minimum in addition to the cover charge.

Clubs abound in West Hollywood, where the **Groundlings Theater** *(Map 4; ☎ 323-934-9700; 7307 Melrose Ave)*, an improv school and company, has tickled people's funny bones for more than 20 years. Graduates include Lisa Kudrow, Pee-Wee Herman, Jon Lovitz, Phil Hartman and Julia Sweeney.

Other legendary haunts include **The Improv** *(Map 4; ☎ 323-651-2583; 8162 Melrose Ave)*; the high-tech **Laugh Factory** *(Map 4; ☎ 323-656-1336; 8001 Sunset Blvd)*, which keeps cranking out mainstream comics; and the **Comedy Store** *(Map 4; ☎ 323-656-6225; 8433 Sunset Blvd)*.

Outdoor Venues

One of the great pleasures of the LA summer is spending a mild summer night at a performance in one of the city's historic outdoor venues.

For patrons of the **Hollywood Bowl** *(Map 3 & 4; ☎ 323-850-2000; 2301 N Highland Ave)* the music is just one reason to come to this historic outdoor amphitheater. Most folks start off the evening with a picnic, then relax beneath the starry skies to the sounds of Mozart, Gershwin or The Who with a glass of wine (bring your own). Carry along a pillow and blanket, as it can get a bit chilly.

Equally historic is the nearby **John Anson Ford Theatre** *(Map 3; ☎ 323-461-3673; 2580 E Cahuenga Blvd)*, which presents a far-ranging program of music, dance and family events.

The **Greek Theater** *(Map 7; ☎ 323-665-1927; 2700 N Vermont Ave)*, in a natural bowl in Griffith Park, books top rock and pop bands. Try to get seats close to the stage for better acoustics.

If it's theater-in-the-wild you're after, try the **Will Geer Theatricum Botanicum** *(☎ 310-455-3723; 1419 N Topanga Canyon Blvd, Malibu)*, founded by 'Grandpa Walton' and set in a natural outdoor amphitheater. Shakespeare and more modern playwrights such as Tennessee Williams or Thornton Wilder all feature on the program.

Good clubs elsewhere in town include **Comedy & Magic Club** (☎ 310-372-1193; 1018 Hermosa Ave, Hermosa Beach), where Jay Leno regularly tests out new material for The Tonight Show, and **Ice House** (Map 8; ☎ 626-577-1894; 24 N Mentor Ave, Pasadena), which attracts major professional talents of today and the stars of tomorrow.

SPECTATOR SPORTS

LA's most famous team is arguably its professional men's basketball team, the **LA Lakers**. Led by coach Phil Jackson and star players Shaquille O'Neill and Kobe Bryant, it captured its third national championship in a row in 2002. The Lakers play at the **Staples Center** (Map 2; ☎ 213-742-7340; 1111 S Figueroa St; tickets $22-165) in Downtown LA. Tickets are hard to get and are available through Ticketmaster (see Entertainment earlier).

The Staples Center is also home of the **Los Angeles Sparks** (☎ 877-4477-2757 for information; tickets $7.50-120), the city's professional WNBA women's basketball team, which plays from June to August, and the **Los Angeles Clippers** (☎ 213-742-7500; tickets $11-90), LA's second – and secondary – NBA men's team. The National Hockey League's **Los Angeles Kings** (☎ 213-742-7100, 888-546-4752; tickets $20-100) also plays at this new facility.

LA's National League baseball team, the **Los Angeles Dodgers**, plays at **Dodger Stadium** (Map 2; ☎ 323-224-1448; 1000 Elysian Park Ave; tickets adult $6-21, child 4-12 $4 any seat), just north of Downtown LA. The season runs from April to October and tickets are usually available at the box office on game day.

LA does not have a professional football team, but it does host a major league soccer team – **Los Angeles Galaxy** – which for now plays at the **Pasadena Rose Bowl** (Map 8; ☎ 626-535-8300 or ☎ 877-342-5299 for tickets & information; 1001 Rose Bowl Dr; tickets adult $18-22, child $8-15). In 2003 the team may move to a new sports complex being built on the campus of Cal State Dominguez Hills in the southern LA suburb of Carson.

Horse-racing enthusiasts consider **Santa Anita Racetrack** (☎ 626-574-7223; 285 W Huntington Dr, Arcadia; admission $5), east of Pasadena, to be one of the best tracks

in the USA. **Hollywood Park Race Track** (☎ 310-419-1500; 1050 S Prairie St; admission $7) is in Inglewood, near LAX. Admission to either track is free if under 18 and accompanied by an adult.

SHOPPING

Most Angelenos do their shopping in multistory malls, some of them offering upwards of 200 stores in a single complex. For a less frantic approach to shopping, head for a handful of streets where the people-watching is as much fun as the window browsing.

Where to Shop

There are several neighborhoods to visit for 21st-century funk and cutting-edge design shops. **Melrose Ave** (Map 3) between La Brea and Fairfax Aves has a great concentration of quirky and hip boutiques. Silver Lake and Los Feliz have flurries of funky clubwear stores as well as thrift and vintage clothing shops. Check out **Los Feliz Village** (Map 3) along Vermont Ave as well as the 3000 and 4000 blocks of **Sunset Blvd** (Map 3).

On N Robertson Blvd between Beverly Dr and W 3rd St in the **Beverly Center District** (Map 4) are the boutiques of young upscale designers. Further north near Robertson's Blvd and Melrose Ave, you'll find LA's center for design, with abundant furniture and accessory stores.

In Beverly Hills, **Rodeo Drive** (Map 5) is known the world over for its up-up-upscale designer boutiques and jewelry stores, art galleries and antique shops. Parallel Beverly Dr is packed with mainstream retail stores.

Santa Monica's pedestrianized **Third Street Promenade** (Map 6) is anchored by the Santa Monica Place mall on Broadway. This is where you'll find mainstream fashions, novelties and casual clothing, funky fashions and much more. Other good shopping streets in Santa Monica are **Main St** (Map 6) for galleries, furnishings and fashions, and upscale **Montana Ave** for one-of-a-kind clothing boutiques, specialty gifts and knickknacks for the home.

Cheap and crazy goods are the name of the game along the **Ocean Front Walk** in Venice Beach (Map 6). Need an erotic bronze dancing Shiva icon or a bronze cowbell from Switzerland? A spiked leather hat for your dog or a spiked leather bikini for your sister (or vice versa)? You'll find it here.

Gentrified **Colorado Blvd** (Map 8) in Old Pasadena has plenty of bookstores, boutiques, housewares and specialty stores. Also in Pasadena is **South Lake Ave**, notable for its London-style shopping arcades.

Broadway and **Olvera St** in Downtown LA (Map 2) and **El Mercado** in East LA are good places to find Mexican hand-crafted leather and hand-woven clothing as well as children's toys and piñatas. **Chinatown** has many shops selling imported porcelain, furniture and silk clothing, as well as chopsticks and soapstone Buddhas. Little Tokyo's main shopping center is the **Japanese Village Plaza**, where you can stock up on kimonos and books, and toys and crafts, from origami art to fine spun pottery. For African art – masks, sculptures, paintings and crafts – head to Degnan Ave in **Leimert Village**.

Bargain clothing shoppers flock to the **Fashion District** in Downtown LA (Map 2), a frantic 56-block warren of fashion that is the epicenter of the city's clothing industry. Note that most stores only accept cash and that refunds or exchanges are uncommon. Dressing rooms are rare and designer knockoffs abound.

Fashion

The Place & Co (☎ 310-645-1539; 8820 S Sepulveda Blvd, near LAX) is great for those into logo mania but without a trust fund. It sells barely worn couture at steep discounts.

Fred Segal (Map 6; ☎ 323-651-4129; 8100 Melrose Ave, Hollywood • Map 7; ☎ 310-458-9940; 500 Broadway, Santa Monica) is a classy boutique collective selling eclectic urban clothing to fashionistas such as Cameron Diaz and Helen Hunt.

Curve (Map 4; ☎ 310-360-8008; 154 N Robertson Blvd, West Hollywood) has cutting-edge and sometimes off-the-wall couture by both underground and established designers, alongside the owners' own creations.

Lisa Kline (Map 4; ☎ 310-246-0907; 136 S Robertson Blvd, West Hollywood) caters to

---

Calling All Pack Rats: A Primer on LA's Flea Markets

Flea markets or swap meets: call them what you will, LA has plenty of them. Nourished by a remarkably diverse population with often eclectic tastes, these gatherings can make for the best bargain shopping around. Whether you're hunting for a '57 Chevy hubcap or a Hopalong Cassidy pocket knife, arrive early, bring a bag and small bills and get ready to haggle.

Burbank Monthly Antique Market – About 125 vendors gather at the Pickwick, on Main St and Riverside Dr, to sell antiques, clothing, furniture, art and collectibles on the fourth Sunday of the month, 9am to 3pm. Admission is $3.

Glendale Community College Swap Meet – On Mountain Ave near Verdugo is where over 200 antiques and collectibles dealers set up every third Sunday of the month, 8am to 3pm. Admission is free.

Long Beach Outdoor Antique & Collectible Market – Over 800 antiques and collectibles dealers sell quality stuff at the Veteran's Memorial Stadium, on Conant St between Lakewood Blvd and Clark Ave, every third Sunday of the month, 8am to 3pm. Admission is $5.

Melrose Trading Post (Map 4) – About 120 vendors of hip and bizarre collectibles make the Trading Post, at Fairfax High School on Melrose and Fairfax Aves, one of LA's coolest markets every Sunday, 9am to 5pm. Admission is $2.

Pasadena City College Flea Market (Map 8) – Over 500 vendors selling most used merchandise, including clothes, crafts, jewelry and collectibles, take over the college's parking lots at 1570 E Colorado Blvd on the first Sunday of the month, 8am to 3pm. Admission and parking are free.

Rose Bowl Flea Market (Map 8) – The largest in the land, this market has over 2200 vendors who descend upon the Rose Bowl on the second Sunday of the month, 6am to 3pm. Admission is $20 from 6am to 7:30am, $10 from 7:30am to 9am and $7 after 9am.

Santa Monica Outdoor Antique & Collectible Market – On Airport Ave off Bundy Dr, you'll find Victorian to postmodern wares along with tasty food on the fourth Sunday of the month, 8am to 3pm. Admission is $5.

post-pubescent shoppers with a collection big on both progressive and traditional styles.

DNA (Map 7; ☎ 310-399-0341; 411 Rose Ave, Venice) is jam-packed with a small but choice assortment of hip garb by local and national designers for men and women, much of it with a stylish European flair.

Vintage

Hollywood is the hub of LA's vintage clothing scene.

Squaresville (Map 3; ☎ 323-669-8464; 1800 N Vermont Ave, Los Feliz Village) lets you put together that funky Left Coast look, available here at prices that won't require you to rob a bank.

Buffalo Exchange (Map 4; ☎ 323-938-8604; 131 N La Brea Ave) stocks mainstream types of clothing, with a few Calvins and Versaces thrown into the mix, as well as shoes and accessories.

Jet Rag (Map 4; ☎ 323-939-0528; 825 N La Brea Ave) is a warehouse-sized store with quality retro clothing and accessories. On Sunday, thrifty hipsters do battle in the parking lot foraging for treasure among the bales of used clothing selling for $1 per item.

Wasteland (Map 4; ☎ 323-653-3028; 7428 Melrose Ave) has eye-catching window displays and top-quality vintage and contemporary designer fashions.

Lingerie & Erotica

Tacky to tasteful – whatever is your fancy, in free-wheeling LA there's no shortage of stores to get your nocturnal niceties.

Frederick's of Hollywood (Map 3; ☎ 323-466-8506; 6608 Hollywood Blvd, Hollywood) is one of the oldest lingerie stores and still among the most popular.

Playmates (Map 3; ☎ 323-464-7636; 6438 Hollywood Blvd, Hollywood) is somewhat more hard-core, so to speak, and a favorite of exotic dancers, actresses and ladies of the night.

Hustler Hollywood (Map 4; ☎ 310-860-9009; 8920 Sunset Blvd, West Hollywood), where the motto is 'Relax – it's just sex,' is an emporium of erotica run by the daughter of top porno purveyor Larry Flynt.

Pleasure Chest (Map 4; ☎ 323-650-1022; 7733 Santa Monica Blvd, West Hollywood) is a sexual-hardware store catering to every conceivable fantasy and fetish.

Hollywood Memorabilia

To keep the tinsel glittering a bit longer, pick up a souvenir from these stores, all of which stock a bit more than plastic Oscar statuettes and Hollywood Sign fridge magnets.

It's a Wrap (☎ 818-567-7366; 3315 W Magnolia Ave, Burbank) sells wardrobe previously worn by the stars during shoots. Tags reveal the name of the show and sometimes that of the actor.

Reel Clothes & Props (☎ 818-508-7762; 12132 Ventura Blvd at Laurel Canyon, Studio City) is similar to It's a Wrap, but more into higher-priced collectibles.

Larry Edmunds Bookshop (Map 3; ☎ 323-463-3273; 6644 Hollywood Blvd, Hollywood) is a long-time purveyor of scripts, posters, stills and books about films, theater and TV.

Samuel French Theatre & Film Bookshop (Map 3; ☎ 323-876-0570; 7623 Sunset Blvd, Hollywood) is an amazing repository of filmic, dramatic and musical fare scripts, scores and books.

Moletown (Map 4; ☎ 323-851-0111; 900 N La Brea Ave, Hollywood) is a stage-sized emporium of TV and movie memorabilia, such as mugs, dolls, jackets etc.

Music

For used CDs, the place with the biggest selection is **Amoeba Music** (Map 3; ☎ 323-245-6400; 6400 Sunset Blvd, Hollywood), although **Rockaway Records** (Map 2; ☎ 323-664-3232; 2395 Glendale Blvd, Silver Lake) is also pretty good.

Tower Records (Map 4; ☎ 310-657-7300; 8801 W Sunset Blvd, Hollywood) is where chart hounds, import freaks and classical connoisseurs find their fill. Check the Yellow Pages for other branches around town.

Rhino Records (Map 5; ☎ 310-474-8685; 1720 Westwood Blvd, Westwood) is a legendary store and label founded in the 1970s which specializes in independent labels and promotional overstock.

Hear Music (Map 6; ☎ 310-319-9527; 1429 Third Street Promenade, Santa Monica) is the place to come for quality music from around the world – Celtic to African to Cuban.

GETTING THERE & AWAY
Air

If you're flying to Los Angeles, you'll most likely land at **Los Angeles International Airport** (LAX; Map 1; ☎ 310-646-5252;

W *www.lawa.org)*, 17mi southwest of Downtown LA. Smaller regional airports are Burbank-Glendale-Pasadena, 14mi northwest of Downtown, and Long Beach Airport, 22mi south. Outside LA County are John Wayne-Orange County Airport in Irvine, 40mi southeast, and Ontario International Airport in San Bernardino County, 40mi east.

LAX has eight terminals situated around a two-level, central traffic loop that also provides access to short-term parking garages. Ticketing and check-in are on the upper (departure) level, while baggage claim areas are on the lower (arrival) level. The hub for most international airlines is the Tom Bradley International Terminal (TBIT).

To travel between terminals, board the free Shuttle A beneath the LAX Shuttle sign on islands outside each terminal on the lower level. Hotel courtesy shuttles stop here as well. A free minibus equipped with a wheelchair lift for the disabled can be ordered by calling ☎ 310-646-6402.

Bus

Greyhound connects LA with cities all across North America. The 24-hour **Main Bus Terminal** *(Map 2; ☎ 213-629-8401; 1716 E 7th St at Alameda St)* is in Downtown. The area is a bit rough, but the station itself is safe enough inside. Other LA-area Greyhound stations are **Hollywood** *(Map 3; ☎ 323-466-6381; 1715 N Cahuenga Blvd)*, **Pasadena** *(Map 7; ☎ 626-792-5116; 645 E Walnut St)* and **Long Beach** *(☎ 562-218-3011; 1498 Long Beach Blvd)*.

Greyhound serves San Diego at least hourly ($14, 2¼ to four hours) and has up to 10 buses to/from Santa Barbara ($13, two to 3½ hours). Services to/from San Francisco run almost hourly ($42, 7½ to 12 hours).

Missing Link Tour Company *(☎ 800-209-8586;* W *www.tmltours.com)* operates a shuttle between LA and Las Vegas with three departures weekly in either direction ($39/75 one-way/round-trip, five hours).

Train

Amtrak *(☎ 800-872-7245;* W *www.amtrak .com)* is based at **Union Station** *(Map 2; 800 N Alameda St)* in Downtown. Interstate trains stopping in LA are the *Coast Starlight* to Seattle, the *Southwest Chief* to Chicago and the *Sunset Limited* to Orlando. The *Pacific Surfliner* regularly connects LA with San Diego ($27, three hours), Santa Barbara ($20, 2¾ hours) and San Luis Obispo ($31, 5½ hours).

Car & Motorcycle

If you're driving a car or riding a motorcycle into LA, there are several routes by which you might enter the metropolitan area.

From San Francisco and Northern California, the fastest route to LA (about six hours) is via I-5 through the San Joaquin Valley. Hwy 101 is slower (about eight hours) but somewhat curvier and a bit more picturesque. By far the most scenic – and slowest – route is via Pacific Coast Hwy, or Hwy 1 (allow at least 10 hours).

From San Diego and other points south, I-5 is the obvious route. At Irvine, I-405 branches off I-5 and takes a westerly route to Long Beach and Santa Monica, bypassing Downtown LA entirely and rejoining I-5 near San Fernando. This route is a time-saver if you're headed to the Westside.

If you're coming to LA from Las Vegas or the Grand Canyon, take I-15 south to I-10, then head west. I-10 is the main east–west artery through LA and continues on to Downtown and Santa Monica.

GETTING AROUND

Contrary to popular belief, LA does have a comprehensive and even fairly efficient public transportation system. Nearly all communities are served by buses, and a fast light- and heavy-rail system hits many of the major area attractions, including Hollywood and Universal Studios. Still, the automobile remains by far the area's most popular mode of transportation. Before rushing headlong into the bumper-to-bumper melee, though, consider all of your transportation options.

To/From LAX

Practically all hostels and airport-area hotels have arrangements with shuttle companies for free or discounted pick-ups from LAX. Check with the property when making your reservation or peruse the information kiosks at the airport.

Several companies operate door-to-door shuttles from all terminals; vans stop on the lower level beneath the signs marked 'Shuttle.' If there's just one of you, they're usually cheaper than a taxi and faster than public transportation. Three companies dominate:

Prime Time (☎ 800-473-3743), **Super Shuttle** (☎ 310-782-6600) and **Xpress Shuttle** (800-427-7483). Expect to pay $12 to Downtown, $19 to Hollywood and $14 to Santa Monica. Most shuttles operate 24 hours a day and drop you off right at your destination, but you may have to wait your turn along the route as other passengers are accommodated as well.

The budget-conscious approach is to take the free 24-hour Shuttle C bus, which stops outside each terminal every 10 to 20 minutes, to the **LAX Transit Center** (cnr 96th St & Vicksburg Ave). Here you can connect to public buses that will take you anywhere in the greater Los Angeles area. For Hollywood, take MTA bus No 42 West to Overhill and La Brea and transfer to MTA No 212 ($1.60, 1¼ hours). For Downtown, stay on MTA bus No 42 ($1.35, one hour). Santa Monica, Venice and Westwood (UCLA) are served by the Big Blue Bus No 3 (75¢, one to 1½ hours).

If you're headed for Pasadena, the **Airport-Bus** (☎ 800-938-8933) runs every two hours from 9:15am to 7:15pm and costs $12 each way.

LAX is not directly served by trains but the closest station, a 10-minute bus trip away, is Aviation, on the Metro Rail Green Line. Take the free Shuttle G bus that stops on the lower (arrival) airport level beneath the LAX Shuttle signs. The Green Line runs south to Redondo Beach and northeast to Norwalk. On an eastbound train, you can transfer at the Rosa Parks (Imperial/Wilmington) station to the Metro Blue Line, which will take you north to Downtown LA or south to Long Beach. The fare is $1.35.

Use the courtesy phones in the arrival areas to phone car rental companies for quotes or reservations. Their offices are at some distance from the airport, but each has free shuttles.

Curbside taxi dispatchers will summon a cab for you. Average fares are $20 to $25 to Santa Monica, $25 to $35 to Downtown or Hollywood and up to $80 to Disneyland. A $2.50 airport surcharge is added to your fare. If there are two or three of you to share the expense, a taxi is the fastest and most convenient way to travel.

Bus

The **Metropolitan Transportation Authority** (MTA; ☎ 800-266-6883; w www.mta.net) has the largest fleet of buses. Fares are $1.35 for unlimited travel on a single bus or rail line in one direction; transfers are 25¢ each. Freeway Express buses cost $1.85 to $3.85, depending on the route and distance. Weekly passes are $11 and are issued from Sunday to Saturday. To find out how to get from point A to point B, call MTA's toll-free number or use its website's trip planner. For information in person – including maps, timetables and passes – you could also visit an MTA Customer Center. There are branches in **Downtown LA** (Map 2; Level C, ARCO Plaza, 515 S Flower St; open 7:30am to 3:30pm) and in the **Miracle Mile District** in Mid-City (Map 4; 5301 Wilshire Blvd; open 9am to 5pm).

A great way to get across town is on the express Metro Rapid bus No 720, which travels along Wilshire Blvd from Santa Monica to Downtown and into East LA via Westwood, Beverly Hills, Fairfax and Mid-City.

Santa Monica-based **Big Blue Bus** (☎ 310-451-5444; w www.bigbluebus.com) operates throughout the Westside, including Santa Monica, Venice, Westwood (UCLA), Pacific Palisades and LAX. Bus No 14 goes to the Getty Center. The fare is 75¢ and transfers to another Big Blue Bus are free (those to an MTA bus are 25¢). The express bus No 10 is the fastest way to get to Downtown LA from Santa Monica ($1.75). Bus No 3 serves LAX.

The city of **Los Angeles Department of Transportation** (LADOT; w www.ladottransit.com) operates local shuttle buses, called DASH, in 19 communities, including Downtown, Hollywood, the Fairfax District, Koreatown, Watts and Mid-City. Most buses run frequently from around 7am until about 7pm Monday to Saturday; the fare is 25¢. For more information, call the LA area code you're in, plus ☎ 808-2273. Maps are available from this number, the website, at tourist offices and on DASH buses.

Train

The MTA (see Bus above) also operates Metro Rail, a network of rail lines linking Downtown and Hollywood, North Hollywood, Long Beach, Redondo Beach, Norwalk and, starting in 2003, Pasadena. One-way tickets are $1.35 and are dispensed by coin-operated machines.

For visitors, the Metro Red Line subway is the most useful because it connects three attraction-packed neighborhoods: Downtown, Hollywood and Universal City. The

LOS ANGELES

Blue Line goes from Downtown LA to Long Beach, while the Green Line travels between Norwalk and Redondo Beach. The Red and Blue Lines converge at Downtown's 7th St/Metro Center station, while the Blue and the Green Lines connect at the Rosa Parks (Imperial/Wilmington) stop.

Set to open sometime in the second half of 2003 is the Gold Line, LA's newest light-rail line. It connects Downtown's Union Station with Pasadena in about 33 minutes, with stops in Chinatown, Highland Park and South Pasadena.

Metrolink (☎ 800-371-5465; w www .metrolinktrains.com) is a 416mi system of six commuter train lines, connecting Downtown's Union Station with the four counties surrounding Los Angeles – Orange, Riverside, San Bernardino and Ventura – as well as with northern San Diego County. Most trains run during peak commute hours; some lines offer restricted Saturday services.

Car & Motorcycle

LA sprawls across such a huge geographical area that unless time is no factor – or money is extremely tight – you're going to want to spend some time behind the wheel. The worst thing about driving is the sheer volume of traffic, especially during the morning and afternoon commutes. Accidents can jam up roads for miles and the pretzel-shaped interchanges and access ramps may seem daunting at first, but cars are still the fastest way to get around the city.

Santa Monica, Beverly Hills and West Hollywood have public parking garages where the first two hours are usually free and rates are low thereafter. Parking in business districts such as Century City or Downtown can cost as much as $3.50 for each 20-minute period. In Downtown, this can easily be avoided by choosing a lot on the area's perimeter, which may charge just $3 per day.

Parking at motels and cheaper hotels is usually free, while fancier ones charge anywhere from $5 to $20 per day in addition to the room rate. Valet parking – for a fee, of course – at nicer restaurants and hotels is ubiquitous.

All the main international car-rental agencies have branches throughout LA, although prices tend to be best at the LAX branches, where the competition is greatest.

A great alternative, especially for those under 25, is a company called **Super Cheap Car Rental** (☎ 310-645-3993, fax 310-645-3995; w www.supercheapcar.com; 10212 S La Cienega Blvd; open Mon-Sat). Its cars may not be the latest models, but rates include full insurance (liability and collision with a $400 deductible), taxes and unlimited mileage within certain areas. Cars for use within California and to Las Vegas start at $199 per week; if you need one only to get around LA and Orange County, it's $169. There is a one-week minimum.

For Harley rentals, go to **Eagle Rider Motorcycle Rental** (☎ 310-536-6777, 800-501-8687; 11860 S La Cienega Blvd, El Segundo), 2mi south of LAX, or **Route 66** (☎ 888-434-4473; 4161 Lincoln Blvd, Marina del Rey). Rates range from $75 to $225 per 24 hours, with discounts for longer rentals.

Taxi

You can't just thrust your arm out and expect to hail a taxi in LA. Except for those lined up outside airports, train stations, bus stations and major hotels, cabbies respond to phone calls. Fares are metered; you pay $2 at flag fall, $1.80 per mile. Companies include **Checker** (☎ 800-300-5007), **Independent** (☎ 800-521-8294), **United Independent** (☎ 800-822-8294) and **Yellow Cab** (☎ 800-200-1085).

Bicycle

Many MTA buses are now equipped with bike racks and bikes ride for free, although you must securely load and unload your bike yourself. Bicycles are allowed on Metro Rail trains during nonpeak times provided you have a permit (call ☎ 800-266-6883), and may be taken onto Metrolink trains at no charge anytime, without permits.

Around Los Angeles

SANTA CATALINA ISLAND

Mediterranean-flavored Santa Catalina (population 4000) – called just Catalina locally – is one of the largest of the Channel Islands, a chain of semi-submerged mountains that rise from the ocean floor off the coast of Southern California. Nearly all

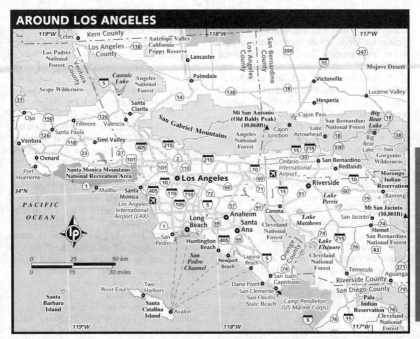

AROUND LOS ANGELES

tourist activity concentrates in the tiny port town of Avalon on the island's southeastern end, which is flooded by as many as 11,000 people on busy summer weekends. The only other settlement is the remote Two Harbors, which occupies an isthmus about 20mi northwest of Avalon.

Discovered by Juan Rodríguez Cabrillo in 1542, Catalina remained relatively untouched until 1811 when the native seafaring Indians were forcibly resettled on the mainland and most of the island fell under private ownership. In 1919 Catalina was purchased by chewing-gum magnate William Wrigley Jr (1861–1932), who also briefly made it the spring training headquarters for his major league baseball team, the Chicago Cubs.

Tourists began flocking to Avalon in the 1930s, but thanks to the conservation-minded Wrigley, Catalina's interior and most of its coastline remained undeveloped. In 1975 the Wrigley family deeded 86% of the island to the nonprofit Catalina Island Conservancy, thus assuring the preservation and restoration of the island's unique ecosystem.

Besides more than 400 plant and 100 bird species – including recently reintroduced bald eagles – deer, goats, boars and the endemic Catalina Island fox inhabit the island. A curiosity are the hundreds of North American bison descended from those brought here in 1924 for the filming of Zane Grey's *The Vanishing American.*

A trip to Catalina is not for the budget-minded. Although easily 'seen' on a day trip, its tranquil ambience is best sampled on an overnight trip. Aside from the boat ride, lodging and eating are quite costly and to truly experience the island, you'll also need to invest in tours or activities.

Avalon

Hotels, restaurants and shops line the shorefront Crescent Ave and its side streets. The **Chamber of Commerce & Visitors Bureau** (☎ 310-510-1520; w *www.catalina.com; open daily*) has a booth on the Green Pier.

Avalon's dominant landmark is the white, circular, Spanish Moderne **Casino** (☎ 310-510-2500; *1 Casino Way*), built for Wrigley in 1929. Despite the name, this has never been a gambling joint but a party venue instead. The top-floor grand ballroom once featured big-band dancing; beneath is a gorgeous Art Deco movie theater with a pipe organ and murals. Visit during first-run movie screenings or join a 50-minute tour ($12). Also here is the **Catalina Island Museum** (☎ 310-510-2414; adult/child $1.50/0.50; open 10:30am-4pm daily), which journeys through 7000 years of island history.

The **Wrigley Memorial & Botanical Garden** (☎ 310-510-2288; 1400 Avalon Canyon Rd; admission $3; open 8am-5pm daily) is about 1½mi inland. A spiral staircase climbs the 130ft tower of the memorial, built in 1934 of blue flagstone and decorative glazed tile. The surrounding 38-acre garden has great cacti groves, succulents and samples of eight plant species endemic to Catalina.

The Interior

Catalina's interior is a nearly deserted, homogeneous sprawl of sunbaked hillsides, valleys and canyons. Although the landscape appears to be barren, it actually teems with flora and fauna; encountering a herd of bison is a memorable experience.

The easiest way to see the interior is on a guided tour (see Organized Tours), but more ambitious types can also explore it on foot or by mountain bike. Both activities require permits available from the **Catalina Island Conservancy** (☎ 310-510-1421; w www.catalinaconservancy.org; 125 Claressa St, Avalon). Hiking permits are free, but those for bicycles cost a rather steep $50 per year, which includes insurance. See Places to Stay for campground information and Getting There & Around for public transportation details.

The only 'village' in the backcountry is Two Harbors, which has a general store, dive center, restaurant, snack bar and the hilltop **Banning House Lodge** (☎ 310-510-0244; rooms $87-253), a B&B dating from 1910.

Water Sports

To truly experience Catalina's charms, you must take to or dive into the water. Most outfitters have booths on the Green Pier in Avalon.

There's **swimming** off the narrow beaches along Crescent Ave, but don't expect much privacy. For smaller crowds (sort of), walk 10 minutes north, past the Casino, to the private **Descanso Beach** (admission $2), where alcohol consumption is allowed.

Snorkelers should head to Lovers' Cove, the bay just east of the boat terminal, or to the **Casino Point Underwater Park**, which is also the best shore dive. Expect to see sunset-colored garibaldi and even the occasional horn or leopard shark (harmless). Snorkeling equipment rents for around $7.50/12 per hour/day from outfitters near the cove and on the pier. Other sites are accessible by boat only. **Snorkel Catalina** (☎ 310-510-3175), near the boat terminal, offers a variety of tours, as does **Catalina Divers Supply** (☎ 310-510-0330).

Kayak rentals are available from **Descanso Beach Ocean Sports** (☎ 310-510-1226, Descanso Beach). Single kayaks cost $11/45 per hour/day, and guided tours start at $28. **Joe's Rent-A-Boat** (☎ 310-510-0330), on the Green Pier, rents kayaks as well as small boats, both good for escaping the crowds in Avalon and for exploring the rugged coastline. Rates start at $35/175 per hour/day.

Organized Tours

The easiest way to see Catalina is on an organized tour, offered by **Discovery Tours** (☎ 310-510-8687) and **Catalina Adventure Tours** (☎ 310-510-2888). Options include explorations of the island interior (from $26) and of Catalina's rich underwater gardens aboard a glass-bottom boat ($9.50). There are also scenic tours of Avalon, harbor cruises, night cruises and others. **Jeep Eco-Tours** (☎ 310-510-2595, ext 0), operated by the Catalina Island Conservancy, runs three-hour backcountry tours for $98 per person.

Places to Stay

Camping Catalina has one campground in Avalon and four in the interior. Camping fees are $12/6 per adult/child from mid-March to mid-November and $6 per person for the rest of the year. If you don't have your own tent, the Hermit Gulch and Two Harbors campgrounds rent two- and four-person tents ($10/16) and tent cabins for up to six people ($30). Camping fees are extra. Reservations can be made by fax (☎ 310-510-7254) or online at w www.scico.com/camping.

Hermit Gulch is in Avalon Canyon, a 1½mi hike inland or a short ride aboard the Avalon Trolley (see Getting Around), and has flush toilets and hot showers.

The main inland campground is the blufftop **Two Harbors** with cold showers, potable water and chemical toilets. **Little Harbor** is 6.8mi from Two Harbors next to two lovely sandy beaches and has the same facilities. **Parson's Landing**, 7mi west of Two Harbors, offers undeveloped sites, chemical toilets and no running water, although a 2½-gallon bottle per person and firewood (available at the campground) are included in the price. **Black Jack** is 9mi from Avalon near the island's highest elevation.

Hotels Catalina's hoteliers depend heavily upon summer business when rates soar and two-night minimum stays are common on weekends. Rates often drop by 50% in winter. Many hotels offer pick-up service from the boat.

Hermosa Hotel (☎ 310-510-1010, 877-241-1313; w www.hermosahotel.com; 131 Metropole St; rooms without bath $35-50, with bath $45-65, cottages $60-100) is as budget as Catalina gets. It offers a variety of lodging options, including cottages with kitchens.

Catalina Beach House (☎ 310-510-1078, 800-974-6835; 200 Marilla Ave; rooms $75-160 summer, $35-105 winter) is a pretty place with good midweek rates and rooms with TV, VCR (free movies), phones, microwave and coffeemaker. Divers are welcome.

Catalina Island Inn (☎ 310-510-1623, 800-246-8134; 125 Metropole Ave; rooms $99-289) has rooms with ocean views and balconies.

Hotel St Lauren (☎ 310-510-2299, 800-645-2471; 231 Beacon St; rooms $40-375), sitting pretty in pink, has the look of a Victorian but was actually only built in 1987. It has a grown-up ambience and a wide range of rooms, from budget to ocean-view suites.

Zane Grey Pueblo Hotel (☎ 310-510-0966, 800-378-3256; 199 Chimes Tower Rd; rooms $135-165 summer, $80-110 winter) is a quiet 16-room adobe inn in the hills. Zane Grey was an American Western writer and this was once his private home. Rooms have no phones but come with the best views around; there's a pool as well.

Places to Eat

For self-catering, drinks and picnic supplies, the **Vons supermarket** (Metropole St) is your best option.

For breakfast, the place to beat is **Pancake Cottage** (☎ 310-510-0726; 118 Catalina St; dishes $4-9; open 6:30am-1pm daily), the cafeteria-style setting notwithstanding. If you like your omelette alfresco, head to **Casino Dock Café** (☎ 310-510-2755; 2 Casino Way; lunch dishes $3-8), which also serves burgers and drinks on a waterfront deck right next to the Casino.

Topless Tacos (Crescent Ave; dishes $5-10) is good for filling up fast on burgers and Mexican food, while **Antonio's** (☎ 310-510-0060; 114 Sumner St; dishes from $7) serves thickly laden pizzas and hot and cold sandwiches at tables draped in red-checkered cloths. **Mr Ning's Chinese Garden** (☎ 310-510-1161; 127 Sumner St; dishes $6-16) also lets you fill up cheaply.

More formal dining options include:

Armstrong's (☎ 310-510-0113; 306 Crescent Ave; lunch $6-14, dinner $15-25) serves dock-fresh fish and seafood and gets long lines of people hoping to snare a table on the waterfront patio.

Channel House (☎ 310-510-1617; 205 Crescent Ave; lunch $8-16, dinner $14-26) offers steaks and seafood in a romantic, candle-lit ambience.

Steve's Steakhouse (☎ 310-510-0333; 417 Crescent Ave; lunch $7-15, dinner $12-25) has similar food to Channel House but has the added value of upstairs seating with harbor views.

Getting There & Around

Catalina Express (☎ 310-519-1212, 800-481-3470) offers the fastest and smoothest ferry service with up to 30 departures daily. Boats leaving from San Pedro, Long Beach's Downtown Landing and from the docks next to the Queen Mary in Long Beach take about one hour, with round-trip tickets costing $40 (discounts for children and seniors). Boats headed straight for Two Harbors depart from San Pedro only (same fare, 90 minutes). There is also a service to Avalon from Dana Point, just south of Laguna Beach in Orange County (see that chapter).

Catalina Flyer (☎ 949-673-5245) runs one catamaran daily from Newport Beach in Orange County to Avalon ($37, 75 minutes).

Fifteen-minute helicopter flights with **Island Express** (☎ 310-510-2525) depart from the boat terminals in San Pedro and next to the Queen Mary and cost $73.50/136 one-way/round-trip.

Taxis, bicycles and golf carts may be rented for travel around Avalon. Public transportation is provided by the **Avalon Trolley** (☎ 310-510-0342), which operates along two routes, hitting all major sights and landmarks, for $1 per ride.

The **Safari Bus** links Avalon with Two Harbors and also stops at the trailheads for the Black Jack and Little Harbors campgrounds. It runs daily from mid-June to early September. Fares depend on distance traveled; Avalon to Two Harbors is $20 each way. Buy tickets at any office **Discovery Tours** (☎ 310-510-8687 for information).

Buses to the island **airport** (☎ 310-510-0143) leave up to seven times daily year-round and cost $15 round-trip.

SIX FLAGS MAGIC MOUNTAIN & HURRICANE HARBOR

For roller coaster fans, the final frontier is Six Flags Magic Mountain (☎ 661-255-4100; 26101 Magic Mountain Parkway, Valencia; adult/senior & child under 4ft $41/27, child under 2 free, parking $7; open 10am daily Mar 31–early Sept; Sat, Sun & holidays only rest of year Sat; closing hours vary 6pm-midnight).

Velocity is king here and you can go up, down, fast and inside out in more ways at Magic Mountain than anywhere else this side of the Space Shuttle. There are 15 coasters among more than 100 rides, shows and attractions in the 260-acre park.

The latest addition is **X**, billed as the 'world's first four-dimensional roller coaster,' where you race in vehicles that spin independently 360 degrees forward and backward on a separate axis, leaving you constantly gasping and aghast.

Other highlights include **Riddler's Revenge**, one of the world's tallest and fastest stand-up roller coasters; and **Batman: The Ride**, which serves up high-speed loops and corkscrews with a 0-gravity spin. **Superman: The Escape** blasts you from 0 to 100mph in seven seconds and then gives you 6½ seconds of weightlessness while you fall back to earth. **Flashback** has six spiral hairpin drops, while **Tidal Wave** has you boating over a 50ft waterfall.

Right next to Magic Mountain is Hurricane Harbor (☎ 661-255-4100; adult/senior & child under 4ft $22/15, child under 2 free; open 10am daily late May–early Sept, Sat & Sun only early May–late Sept, closing hours vary). This water park with a tropical jungle theme is famous for its wicked slides, such as **Black Snake Summit**, a 75ft speed slide, and **Bamboo Racer**, where you go down head first on one of six racing slides. There are also fanciful lagoons and wave pools. Be sure to bring sunscreen.

If you want to visit both Magic Mountain and Hurricane Harbor, get the combo ticket for $53. Tickets can be used on the same day, on consecutive days or for a return visit.

Getting There & Away

From Downtown LA, take I-5 north about 30mi and exit at Magic Mountain Parkway. Getting here by public transportation is cumbersome but not impossible. From Downtown LA's Union Station, take the Metrolink train to the Santa Clarita station, then catch bus No 10 or 20 (every half hour) to the park. Organized tours are also widely available through LA-area hotels.

SAN BERNARDINO NATIONAL FOREST

The 1031 sq mi of the San Bernardino National Forest, about a two-hour drive east of LA, provide great respite from the urban bustle for locals and visitors. Popular summer activities include hiking, mountain biking, horseback riding, water sports and fishing, while in winter several resorts beckon skiers and snowboarders. The forest encompasses half a dozen wilderness areas and just as many peaks above 10,000ft, including **Mt San Gorgonio** (11,502ft), Southern California's tallest.

The 110mi **Rim of the World Scenic Byway** (Hwy 18) traverses the entire range and affords glorious views – at least on clear days. Otherwise, bird's-eye views of the smog-enshrouded urban sprawl below can actually be quite depressing, although you can take comfort in knowing that you've escaped it all.

Towns such as Big Bear Lake and the communities around Lake Arrowhead make for excellent bases to explore the attractions of the forest, while the San Gorgonio Wilderness offers an opportunity for a complete backcountry retreat.

The forest is hugely popular with weekend warriors, but from Monday to Thursday you'll often have trails and facilities to yourself and can also benefit from much lower accommodation prices. Besides the camp-grounds mentioned in this section, free dis-persed (remote) camping is possible in certain areas. Check with the ranger stations about required permits, rules and locations.

Note that black bears do roam the forest, although they're not yet as habituated to humans as they are elsewhere in California, for instance in Yosemite National Park. Be sure to read the boxed text 'Bears, Your Food & You' in the Activities chapter earlier in this book.

For the latest road conditions, call **Caltrans** (☎ 800-427-7623).

Getting There & Around

Those exploring the forest by car must ob-tain a National Forest Adventure Pass (see the boxed text in the Activities chapter). For a list of local vendors, call ☎ 909-884-6634 or see **W** www.fsadventurepass.org.

Mountain Area Regional Transit Authority (MARTA; ☎ 909-584-1111) operates bus services twice daily (except Sunday) to the forest communities from the town of San Bernardino, including from the Greyhound and Metrolink stations there. The fare to Lake Arrowhead is $3; to Big Bear Lake you pay $5.

Greyhound buses from Downtown LA to San Bernardino depart at least hourly ($10.25, 1¼ to 3¾ hours), while Metrolink operates Monday to Saturday only (1½ hours).

Big Bear Lake

Big Bear Lake (population 21,000; eleva-tion 6750ft) is a year-round, family-friendly mountain resort and the most popular get-away in the San Bernardino Mountains. In summer, the lake itself – 7mi long and av-eraging half a mile across – is great for fish-ing, canoeing, boating, water skiing and sailing. Swimming is possible too, but best done away from the shore, which suffers from excessive milfoil growth.

Big Bear gets its biggest crowds on snowy winter weekends when the ski areas of Bear Mountain and Snow Summit exert their frosty siren call. The mountains are taken over by hikers and mountain bikers as soon as the snow melts.

Orientation & Information Most of Big Bear is sandwiched between the lake's southern shore and the mountains. The main road through town is Hwy 18 – here called Big Bear Blvd – which is lined by motels, cabins and restaurants. Tourist activity is concentrated in 'The Village,' while east of here you'll find the access roads to the ski resorts, numerous ski rental places, and more restaurants and lodging options. The lake's northern shore, along Hwy 38 (here North Shore Blvd), is much quieter and is the departure point for many hiking trails.

The **Big Bear Lake Resort Association** (☎ 800-4-244-2327, fax 909-866-8034; **W** www.bigbearinfo.com; 630 Bartlett Rd; open 8am-5pm Mon-Fri, 9am-5pm Sat & Sun) has maps and information about member businesses, and books accommodations for $10 per reservation.

For outdoor information related to the for-est (hiking, mountain biking, camping etc), visit the **Big Bear Discovery Center** (☎ 909-866-3437; open 8am-6pm daily May-Oct, 8am-4:30pm Nov-Apr) on the northern shore. The center has some educational ex-hibits and a gift shop, sells guided tours and the National Forest Adventure Pass and also organizes ranger talks.

Skiing With an 8000ft ridge rising above the lake's southern side, Big Bear usually has snow between mid-December and March or April. When nature fails, snow-making ma-chines pick up the slack. Basic ski, boot and pole rentals start at $13.50 per day (more for high-performance gear; discounts for multi-day rentals), offered by outfitters along Hwy 18 and at ski area lodges.

Both of Big Bear's ski mountains are off Hwy 18: **Snow Summit** (☎ 909-866-5766, 24-hour snow report ☎ 888-786-6481; **W** www.snowsummit.com) has 12 lifts, 1175 vertical ft and $41 adult lift tickets ($32 for half-day and $25 for night tickets, $50 dur-ing holidays). Most of its runs are for inter-mediate and expert skiers and there's night skiing as well. Snow Summit is famous for its freestyle terrain, packed with half- and super-pipes, jumps, rails, banks, boxes and other features. A separate Family Park has easy runs.

Bear Mountain (☎ 909-585-2519, 24-hour snow conditions ☎ 800-232-7686; **W** www.bearmtn.com) has 12 lifts, 1665 vertical ft and $39 tickets ($30 half-day, $49 holiday). Bear Mountain generally gets more snow than Snow Summit and has more runs suitable for beginner and intermediate skiers. Its snowboarding park is popular, too.

Hiking In summer, people trade their ski boots for hiking boots and hit the forest trails. If you only have time for one short hike, make it the **Castle Rock Trail**, which is 2.4mi round-trip and offers superb views. The first half-mile is pretty steep but the trail flattens out somewhat after that. The trailhead is off Hwy 18 on the western end of the lake. Also popular is the moderately difficult **Cougar Crest Trail**, starting near the Discovery Center, which links up with the Pacific Crest Trail (PCT) after about 2mi, and offers views of the lake and Holcomb Valley. For even better vistas, head east for another half mile to the top of **Bertha Peak** (8502ft).

Mountain Biking Big Bear is a mecca of the mountain biking scene and hosts several pro and amateur races each year. About 40mi of roads and trails for all levels of riders crisscross the bike park on Snow Summit. The 13mi **Grandview Loop** is great for getting a feel for the terrain. A chairlift ($10, all-day pass $20) provides easy access to the top. (If you just want to go up for the views or to hike, it's $7, or $10 round-trip.)

Maps, chairlift tickets and bike rentals are available from **Team Big Bear** (☎ 909-866-4565; w www.teambigbear.com) at the mountain base. Rentals are $27/50 half/all day, including helmets.

For more experienced bikers, Holcomb Valley, Delamar Mountain and Van Duesen Canyon off Hwy 38 are popular destinations.

Water Sports In summer, Big Bear Lake provides a cool respite from the heat. Swim Beach, near the Village has lifeguards and is popular with families. The best **swimming**, however, is on the lake's very western end, in a beautiful secluded bay accented by islands made up of piles of boulders and the privately owned China Island. There's no access from the street, so the only way to get there is by boat or jet ski.

Jet skis (for one to three people) rent from $75 to $100 per hour; water skiing is $110 per hour; speed boats (for two to six people) are $65 to $95 per hour, plus gas; pontoon boats (for eight to 10) cost $50/185 per hour/day, plus gas; and sail boats (for two to six people; two-hour minimum) are $25 to $45 per hour.

The lake teems with trout, catfish, bass, carp and other fish, though catching them is not always easy. Those bent on success should sign up with **Cantrell Guide Service** (☎ 909-866-3218), which guarantees prospective fisherfolk their catch – or your money back. You'll need a fishing license, available at sporting stores around town, and $75 per hour for the boat, with a three-hour minimum. John will provide the poles, bait and expertise. If you want to go on your own, fishing boat rentals start at $20 per hour (less per hour for longer rentals) at Big Bear Marina near the Village.

Other Activities The Holcomb Valley, just north of Big Bear, was the site of Southern California's biggest gold rush in the early 1860s. The **Gold Fever Trail** is a 20mi self-guided tour of the gold country along a graded dirt road. It can be traveled by mountain bikes and practically all vehicles in two to four hours, stops included. The Discovery Center (see Orientation & Information) has a free pamphlet describing 12 sites of interest along this route. If you prefer to let someone else do the driving, take the tour offered by **Off-Road Adventures** (☎ 909-585-1036), which costs $50.

Another great backcountry destination is **Butler Peak**, a mountain top crowned by a historic fire tower, from where you have tremendous panoramic views. You'll need a mountain bike or high-clearance vehicle to get there, or join a guided tour offered by the Discovery Center ($30) or **Big Bear Jeep Tours** (☎ 909-878-JEEP; 40977 Big Bear Blvd).

Great for families is the **Alpine Slide** (☎ 909-866-4626; Big Bear Blvd), west of the Village. It involves a placid chairlift ride up Magic Mountain (actually more of a hill), followed by a fun wheeled bobsled ride that hurtles down a concrete track with you at the controls – more or less. Single rides cost $5, five rides are $18. The complex also includes a water slide, go-cart track and miniature golf.

For nine-hole **golf**, sign up for tee time at the **Bear Mountain Golf Course** (☎ 909-585-8002; open Apr-Nov).

Places to Stay Accommodations in Big Bear Lake run the gamut from snug B&Bs

and resort cabins to lodges, hotels, camp-grounds and private homes.

All campgrounds have picnic tables, fire rings and potable water and toilets. Pineknot, Serrano and Hanna Flat accept reservations for half of their sites (☎ 800-444-6777). Note that the actual opening dates depend on the weather.

Pineknot *(sites $18; open May–mid-Oct)*, at the top of Summit Blvd and popular with mountain bikers, has 48 spaces in a fir, pine and oak forest next to the Snow Summit ski area.

Serrano *(tents/RV sites $20/30; open Apr-Nov)*, near the Discovery Center, is the most popular campground in the area and fills up quickly on summer weekends. There are 132 spaces, and it has showers.

Hanna Flat *(sites $17; open mid-May–mid-Oct)*, 2½mi north of Hwy 38, is remote but still accessible by car, making it popular with adventurous families. It has 88 spaces.

More isolated are the 17 sites at **Big Pine Flat** *(sites $12)*, 4mi past Hanna Flat, and the 19 sites at **Holcomb Valley** *(sites $10)*, 4mi north of Hwy 38.

Thanks to the guts and vision of a guy who knows his way up and down the mountains, Big Bear now has its own independent hostel. **Adventure Hostel** *(☎ 909-866-8900, 800-866-5255, fax 425-790-0212;* **w** *www.adventurehostel.com; 527 Knickerbocker Rd; dorm bunks $20, private rooms $60 (1-3 people), $80/100/120 for 4/5/6 people)* is a clean, friendly place in a converted family home on the eastern edge of the Village. Guests share a kitchen, lounge, backyard, dining and games room, and there's free high-speed Internet access as well.

Renting a cabin gives you lots of privacy and independence and is a popular way to overnight in Big Bear. Places range from small and shabby to huge and elegant, but most have kitchens and the better ones sport fireplaces, sundecks and Jacuzzis. Prices vary accordingly, starting at $75 and surging to $400 a night. The Big Bear Lake Resort Association can make referrals, or you might try **Grey Squirrel Resort** *(☎ 909-866-4335, 800-381-5569, fax 909-866-6271;* **w** *www.greysquirrel.com; 39372 Big Bear Blvd)*, which also rents private homes ($150 to $500 per night) right in the woods.

Dozens of lodgings, most independently owned, are strung up along Big Bear Blvd.

Honey Bear Lodge *(☎ 909-866-7825, 800-628-8714, fax 909-866-1958;* **w** *www.honeybearlodge.com; 40994 Pennsylvania Ave; rooms $59-139 midweek, $89-199 weekends)* has rooms for all budgets, many of which still sparkle from a recent makeover. The loft suites and those with in-room spas are charming, but even the economy units have TV, microwave, refrigerator and a fireplace.

Northwoods Resort *(☎ 909-866-3121, 800-866-3121, fax 909-878-2122;* **w** *www.northwoodsresort.com; 40650 Village Dr; rooms $79-169 midweek, $119-209 weekends)*, right in the Village, is a modern mountain resort with heavily decorated, comfortable rooms, a pool, fitness center and a good restaurant (see Places to Eat).

Knickerbocker Mansion *(☎ 909-878-9190, 800-388-4179, fax 909-878-4248;* **w** *www.knickerbockermansion.com; 869 Knickerbocker Rd; rooms $110-155, suites $200-225)* is a B&B in a log home hand-built by Big Bear's first dam keeper in the 1920s. More rooms are in the adjacent converted carriage house.

Places to Eat For self-catering, the **Vons supermarket** on Hwy 38, toward the eastern end of the lake, offers the widest choice and also has a deli and a bakery.

Pinenut Coffee House & Bakery *(535 Pine Knot Ave; dishes under $8)*, a nice spot in the Village, makes healthful wraps and chocolate chip cookies to die for. At night, it's a casual hangout, sometimes with live music.

Stillwells *(☎ 909-866-3121; lunch $8-12, dinner $14-30)*, inside the Northwoods Resort, goes gourmet at night but is a really nice spot for lunch, especially if you can snag a table on the pond-adjacent patio.

About a quarter mile east of the Village is this trio of worthwhile eateries:

Grizzly Manor Cafe *(☎ 909-866-6226; 41268 Big Bear Blvd; breakfast & lunch under $7; open to 2pm daily)* has 'Twin Peak'-ish charm and is famous for its bear-sized breakfasts, including pancakes the size of catchers' mitts. It's an American hash-house icon.

Old Country Inn *(☎ 909-866-5600; 41126 Big Bear Blvd; lunch $7-8.50, dinner $12-22)* puts the accent on hearty German fare, although there's plenty of seafood to accommodate noncarnivores. You'll be dining under the mournful eyes of mounted stags and elk. Good breakfasts, too.

LOS ANGELES

Sonora Cantina (☎ 909-866-8202; 41144 Big Bear Blvd; dishes $5-14), next door to Old Country Inn, brings the cheerful aesthetics of Mexico to the mountains and serves all the staples from burritos to carnitas.

Getting There & Around Big Bear Lake is about 100mi northeast of LA, about a 2½ hour drive. From the I-10, take the Hwy 30 exit in Redlands and follow it to Hwy 330 to Hwy 18. Local MARTA buses (see earlier) operates along Big Bear's southern shore.

Arrowhead

Arrowhead (population 15,000; elevation 5200ft) is not a single town but a cluster of communities orbiting **Lake Arrowhead**, located about 90mi east of LA and 28mi west of Big Bear via Hwy 18. The lake, created in the 19th century, was one of Southern California's first weekend getaway destinations. Today, it is ringed by residences whose owners also possess access rights to the lake, making it practically impossible for the general public to get wet. Officially, the only way to use the lake is by staying at the Lake Arrowhead Resort (see Places to Stay & Eat) or by renting a shoreline cabin or condo. Unofficially, many people ignore the rules and plunge in anyway.

In 1979 developers with heaps of economic foresight but little concern for nostalgia razed Arrowhead's rustic old town center and built Lake Arrowhead Village, a spiffy collection of gift shops and factory outlets surrounding a parking lot on the lake's south shore. A nearby walkway from the parking lot skirts the lake for a hundred yards or so, ending at a promontory covered with a small patch of grass where you can enjoy a picnic.

Orientation & Information Lake Arrowhead Village (the 'Village') is a 2mi drive north on Hwy 173, off Hwy 18. Other Arrowhead communities include Blue Jay, west of the Village via Hwy 189; tiny Agua Fria, just south of Blue Jay and also on Hwy 189; Skyforest on Hwy 18, about 1½mi east of the Hwy 173 turnoff; and Cedar Glen, east of the Village via Hwy 173.

There's a grocery store on the upper level of the Village, but otherwise day-to-day commercial activity centers on Blue Jay, which has a bank, gas station, post office and supermarket. Also in the Village (above the Subway sandwich shop) is the **Lake Arrowhead Chamber of Commerce** (☎ 909-337-3715, 800-337-3716; w www.lakearrowhead.net; open 9am-5pm Mon-Fri, 10am-3pm Sat).

For campground and trail information, maps and the National Forest Adventure Pass, stop by the **Arrowhead Ranger Station** (☎ 909-337-2444; open 8am-4:30pm Mon-Sat) on Hwy 18, about a quarter mile east of the Hwy 173 turnoff.

Lake Arrowhead Village There's little to do in the Village, unless shopping is your thing. To get out on the lake, you can take a narrated 45-minute tour aboard the *Arrowhead Queen*, a miniature paddle wheeler that operates daily year-round ($11/10/7.50 adult/senior/child). Buy tickets at Leroy's Sports on the walkway skirting the lake. Nearby, **McKenzie Waterski School** (☎ 909-337-3814) offers water-skiing lessons and 15-minute rides for $45 each.

Skiing About 13mi east of Lake Arrowhead, on Hwy 18, is the smallish ski mountain of **Snow Valley** (☎ 909-867-2751) and, across the highway, the cross-country resort of **Rim Nordic** (☎ 909-867-2600), with 20mi of groomed tracks through the forest. There's also cross-country skiing at **Green Valley Nordic** (☎ 909-867-2600) at the end of Green Valley Lake Rd; the turnoff from Hwy 18 is about 3mi east of Running Springs. Trail passes are $15 per day.

Hiking Outdoor lovers will probably want to skip the Village entirely and head to the hills. The **Deep Creek** area north of the lake offers good hiking and mountain biking, with access to the Pacific Crest Trail. To get there, take Hwy 173 around the southern shore of the lake and turn east on Hook Creek Rd. Two miles past Cedar Glen, the pavement ends and the country road continues 2mi to the Splinters Cabin trailhead with a parking lot. The **Deep Creek Hot Springs** are a popular destination and reached by following PCT north for about 5mi. You can also access them in a 40-minute hike from Bowen Ranch via Hesperia north of the mountains, but you'll be asked to pay a $4 toll to cross private land. For more information, see the boxed text 'Some Like It Hot – Some, Not.'

More tame and accessible is the **Heap's Peak Arboretum Trail**, a half-mile loop through a lovely garden. The trailhead is 2mi east of the ranger station on Hwy 18. Somewhat more demanding is the 1.7mi **North Shore Recreation Trail**, which starts between sites 10 and 11 on the North Shore Campground (see Places to Stay for directions).

Places to Stay & Eat The Arrowhead area has three USFS campgrounds (☎ 800-444-6777 for reservations).

Dogwood *(sites $20; open May-Nov)*, off Hwy 18 near the Hwy 189 (Blue Jay) turnoff, has 94 beautiful, shaded sites in a dense pine forest. Amenities include flush toilets and new showers.

North Shore *(sites $15; open May-Sept)*, a quarter mile (via Hospital Rd) from Hwy 173, has 27 sites surrounded by oak trees and with access to hiking trails.

Green Valley *(sites $15; open mid-May–mid-Sept)* is near a small fishing lake at the end of Green Valley Lake Rd, off Hwy 18 near Running Springs.

Noncampers have plenty of cabins and lodges to choose from, including:

Arrowhead Tree Top Lodge *(☎ 909-337-2311, 800-358-8733; 27992 Rainbow Dr; rooms $59-141)*, a half-mile south of the Village, has a pool and access to a private dock. The rustic rooms have refrigerator and TV; those facing away from the highway are quieter.

Carriage House *(☎ 909-336-1400, 800-526-5070; 472 Emerald Dr; rooms $95-135)* is a snug and romantic New England-style B&B owned by a world-traveling couple. Rates include an elegant breakfast and afternoon appetizers.

Lake Arrowhead Resort *(☎ 909-336-1511, 800-800-6792; 27984 Hwy 189; forest-view rooms $109-189, lake-view rooms $149-229)*, a luxurious place next to the Village, is great if you can afford the price tag. It has a beautiful lobby with a large fireplace, as well as a pool, hot tub, fitness center and a private beach.

Restaurants in the Village include the lakeside **Belgian Waffle Works** *(☎ 909-337-5222; items $5-8.50)*, which is the place to beat for breakfast. The interior is all frilly Victorian, so you might want to hold out for a table on the lake-view patio. For snacks and even better views, go to **Lake Arrowhead**

Some Like It Hot – Some, Not

As do bus and train stations, unique attractions in nature tend to be magnets for the weird and warped. One of these is the darkly fabled Deep Creek Hot Springs in the mountains near Lake Arrowhead where a series of pools of varying heat – fed by natural springs – has been a popular hiking destination for decades. The vibe can be sinister: 'Good Time Charley' Manson found the place to his liking and a jawbone is all that's left of one local lounger who simply disappeared. There have been assaults, drunken brawls and the inevitable reports of drugs and the behavior they inspire. In the '60's, AWOL soldiers and squalid squatters made their fetid encampments in the surrounds and – these days – park rangers only go there in teams, and armed.

Still the trekkers come and skinny-dip they will, even though access means having to pay $4 for the short-route egress to the pools across the property of an armed, long-haired landowner who cruises his domain on a dirt bike, collecting his fee. Despite all this, there's no question that the pools are a real natural asset. The naked, fortunately, still far outnumber the dead. But before plunging into the heat of Deep Creek, you might want to keep this in mind: 'Caveat Natator' (Bather, beware).

David Peevers

Village Pizza Deli *(items $6-12)*, with a huge terrace on the Village's upper level.

You'll find more eating options in other Arrowhead communities.

Borderline Family Restaurant *(☎ 909-336-4363; Blue Jay; most dishes under $10)* caters to all cravings – burgers to sandwiches to Mexican food.

Avanti's *(☎ 909-336-7790; 28575 Hwy 18, Skyforest; lunch $7-12, dinner $11-18)*, about 1mi east of the Arrowhead Ranger Station, makes the best Italian food around. There's been talk about it moving to the Village, so check with the chamber of commerce if you can't find it.

Casual Elegance *(☎ 909-337-8932; 26848 Hwy 189, Agua Fria; dinner $15-28; open Wed-Sun)*, in a rambling old villa, is a fine dining establishment with crisp table linens and a cozy ambience.

San Gorgonio Wilderness

South of Big Bear via Hwy 38, the San Gorgonio Wilderness is the least developed part of the San Bernardino National Forest and is lorded over by Mt San Gorgonio (11,502ft). Lots of hiking and equestrian trails traverse the area's steep and rugged terrain, which at the low elevations, is arid and hot in the summer and teeming with rattlesnakes. At higher elevations, oak and manzanita are joined by cedar, fir, sugar and lodgepole pines. Black bears, coyotes, deer and squirrels are common, and sightings of bald eagles are frequent in the Heart Bar campground area.

Hwy 38 runs along the wilderness' northern periphery, giving access to trailheads, campgrounds and the few services in the area. A free wilderness permit, required for day hikes and camping, is available from the **Mill Creek Ranger Station** (☎ 909-794-1123; 34701 Mill Creek Rd, Mentone), 10mi east of Redlands via Hwy 38; the **Barton Flats Visitor Center** (open May-Oct) further north of here; and at the **Big Bear Discovery Center** (see the Big Bear Lake section earlier in this chapter). Trail maps are available at these places for $6. Most of the trailheads are in the Barton Flats area.

Places to Stay & Eat Sites at the USFS campgrounds along Hwy 38 are reservable (☎ 877-444-6777).

Barton Flats and **San Gorgonio** (sites $20; open mid-May–Sept) are the best-equipped campgrounds, with flush toilets and showers.

Heart Bar (open mid-May–Sept; sites $15) is the largest, with 94 sites and flush toilets. Sites here are spacious and flat, surrounded by large ponderosa pines that offer beauty but not much privacy.

South Fork (sites $15), a few miles further west, is the most intimate and has secluded, shady sites, but it is subject to highway noise.

The main town around here is Angelus Oaks, which has a general store, cabins and restaurants.

Seven Oaks Mountain Cabins (☎ 909-794-1277; 40700 Seven Oaks Rd; cabins $70) has charming little log cabins beside the Santa Ana River, a volleyball and tennis court and a lodge with games and a big fireplace.

The Lodge at Angelus Oaks (☎ 909-794-9523, fax 909-794-9523; e damionl@ibm.net; 37825 Hwy 38; cabins for 2/4/6 people $45/55/65, $20 more Fri & Sat) is another comfortable getaway.

Oaks Restaurant (☎ 909-794-3611; 37676 Hwy 38; dishes under $10) serves the usual American fare, including a few vegetarian items.

Getting There & Away There's no public transportation to the wilderness. Coming from LA, exit the I-10 at Orange St N in Redlands and follow the signs to Hwy 38.

Central Coast

California's Central Coast stretches from Ventura Harbor to Monterey Bay, 273mi of near unadulterated beauty clinging to the edge of the continent.

Highlights of the southern stretch include Santa Barbara and San Luis Obispo, both lively college towns of great attractiveness to visitors. Just past the latter, the Santa Lucia Range runs north all the way to the Monterey Peninsula, separating the Pacific Ocean from the San Joaquin Valley.

Travel here is either on Hwy 1 (along the coast) or on Hwy 101 (on the eastern side of the mountains). Scenic Hwy 1 – aka the Pacific Coast Hwy – offers one of the most dramatically beautiful drives in the world, skirting spectacular coastline, especially along Big Sur, where wind and water are continually shaping the mountains into cliffs and rocky promontories. Coastal redwoods grow along the Big and Little Sur Rivers, and the Ventana Wilderness supports the Santa Lucia fir which is endemic to the area. Hearst Castle is another major tourist draw.

Hwy 101 follows the route of the old El Camino Real, built to connect California's missions, and passes by rolling fields, pastures and vineyards, as well as the craggy peaks of the Pinnacles National Monument.

Between San Simeon (near Hearst Castle) and Carmel, the narrow, slow and winding Nacimiento-Fergusson Rd (G18) is the only road connecting Hwy 1 and Hwy 101.

VENTURA

Ventura (population 101,000), an agricultural and manufacturing center, may not be the most spectacular kick-off to the Central Coast, but it is not without charm, especially in its historic downtown along Main St, north of Hwy 101 via Seaward Ave. Here, you'll find a terrific assortment of antique and thrift shops as well as the town's **Visitor Center** (☎ *805-648-2075, 800-333-2989; 89 S California St, Suite C; open 8:30am-5pm Mon-Fri, 9am-5pm Sat & 10am-4pm Sun*).

Ventura's mission roots remain in evidence at the **Mission San Buenaventura** (☎ *805-643-4318; 211 E Main St; admission*

Highlights

- Monterey – adobe buildings, Cannery Row, and the stunning Monterey Bay Aquarium, for close encounters of the fishy kind

- Big Sur – a coastal ribbon of velvety hillsides, rugged cliffs and vistas that touch the soul

- Hearst Castle – a fantasy in the sky that teeters between kitsch and cult

- Santa Barbara – a quintessential California beach town, relaxed, friendly and handsome, with lots of nature and history for good measure

- Pinnacles National Monument – remote and small, but with intriguing rock formations and caves

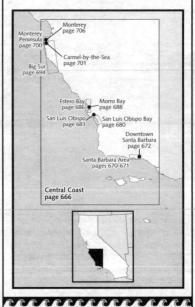

by donation $1; open 10am-5pm Mon-Sat, 10am-4pm Sun), the last one founded by Padre Junípero Serra in 1782. The restored church is still home to an active congregation. A stroll around the complex is a tranquil experience, which leads you through a courtyard and a small museum, past statues

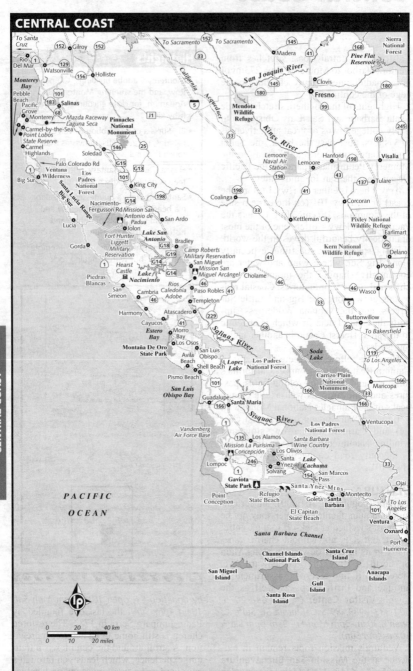

CENTRAL COAST

of saints and 250-year-old paintings of the Stations of the Cross.

The mission's original foundations and related artifacts are among items on display in the nearby **Albinger Archaeological Museum** (☎ *805-648-5823; 113 E Main St; open 10am-4pm Wed-Sun June-Sept)*.

Across the street, the **Ventura County Museum of History & Art** (☎ *805-653-0323; 100 E Main St; adult/senior/child 13-15 $4/3/2; open 10am-5pm Tues-Sun)* has an eclectic mix of exhibits. Highlights include some 300 quarter-life-sized historical figures, dressed in period costumes (by George Stuart), and an exhibit tracing Ventura's history from the Chumash Indians to today.

Ventura Harbor, southwest of Hwy 101 via Harbor Blvd, is where boats depart for the Channel Islands (see the following section). Even if you don't embark on an island adventure, **Channel Islands National Park Visitor Center** (☎ *805-658-5730; 1901 Spinnaker Dr; open 8:30am-5pm daily)* has an interesting natural history display and a three-story lookout from where you can see the islands on a clear day.

Greyhound (☎ *805-653-0164; 291 E Thompson Blvd)* runs up to five buses daily from Los Angeles ($12, 2½ hours) en route to Santa Barbara ($8.25, 40 minutes).

CHANNEL ISLANDS NATIONAL PARK

The Channel Islands are an eight-island chain lying off the coast from Newport Beach to Santa Barbara. The four northern islands – San Miguel, Santa Rosa, Santa Cruz and Anacapa – along with tiny Santa Barbara island 38mi west of San Pedro (see the Los Angeles chapter) comprise the Channel Islands National Park. The islands have unique flora and fauna and extensive tide pools and kelp forests. Here you'll find 145 plant and animal species that are not found anywhere else in the world, which is why the park is sometimes nicknamed 'California's Galapagos.'

Originally inhabited by the Chumash and Gabrielino Indians (who were taken to the mainland missions in the early 1800s), the islands were owned by sheep ranchers and the US Navy until the mid-1970s, when conservation efforts began. San Miguel, Santa Rosa, Anacapa and Santa Barbara Islands are now owned by the **National Park Service**

(NPS; W *www.nps.gov/chis)*, which also owns 20% of Santa Cruz (the other 80% belongs to the Nature Conservancy).

Anacapa, which is actually three separate islets, is the closest to the mainland and offers a nice, easy but memorable introduction to the islands' ecology. A visitor center and picnic area sit atop the island's narrow plateau. Snorkeling, diving, swimming and kayaking are all possible in the rich kelp beds surrounding the island.

Santa Cruz, the largest island, is laced with hiking trails and is probably the best island for exploring on your own. Popular activities include swimming, snorkeling, scuba diving and kayaking.

Beautiful sandy beaches, nearly 200 bird species and the Painted Cave are highlights on **Santa Rosa**, which is the best destination for longer trips.

San Miguel – the most remote of the four northern islands – offers solitude and a wilderness experience, but it's often shrouded in fog and is very windy. Some sections are off-limits to prevent disruption of the fragile ecosystem. There are interesting natural formations (eg, Caliche Forest, made of calcium-carbonate castings of trees) and an elephant seal colony at Point Bennett at various times during the year. Smaller colonies are on Santa Barbara and Santa Rosa Islands.

Santa Barbara is home to the humongous northern elephant seal and is a remote playground for birds and marine wildlife. Facilities include a visitor center and a primitive campground. Hikers, bird-watchers, divers, snorkelers and anglers will all find their fill here.

Beautiful anytime of year, the islands receive most of their visitors between June and September; however, the nicest times to visit are during spring wildflower season (in April and May) and in September and October, when the weather conditions are the most calm.

Places to Stay

All islands have primitive **campgrounds** *(reservations* ☎ *800-365-2267; campsites $10)*, which are open year-round. Each one has pit toilets and picnic tables, but you must take everything in (and out, including trash). Water is only available on Santa Rosa and Santa Cruz Islands. Due to fire danger, campfires are not allowed, but enclosed camp stoves are OK. Be prepared to carry your stuff ½mi to 1½mi to the campground from the landing areas.

The campground on Santa Barbara is large, grassy and surrounded by hiking trails, while the one on Anacapa is high, rocky and isolated. Camping on San Miguel, with its unceasing wind, fog and volatile weather, is only for the hardy. Santa Rosa's campground is sheltered by a canyon with wonderful views of Santa Cruz, whose own site is within a eucalyptus grove. Del Norte, a backcountry campground on Santa Cruz, had just opened at the time of writing. It's in a shaded oak grove, a 3½mi hike away from the landing. For full details about all of the campgrounds, check the NPS website.

Getting There & Away

To get to the visitor center and boat docks when going north on Hwy 101, exit at Victoria Ave, turn left on Victoria, right on Olivas Park Dr to Harbor Blvd; Olivas Park Dr runs straight into Spinnaker Dr. Going south, exit Seaward onto Harbor Blvd, then turn right on Spinnaker Dr.

Two boat and one air operator offer camper transportation and excursions to the islands.

Island Packers (☎ 805-642-1393, recorded information ☎ 805-642-7688; w www.island packers.com; 1867 Spinnaker Dr), adjacent to the visitor center, offers day trips and packages to all the islands. Rates are $37/20 per adult/child for the eight-hour East Anacapa trip and $32/20 for the six-hour East Anacapa trip. Overnight campers pay $48/30; for an extra $6, you can bring along a kayak (for rent from several outfitters in the area; see Island Packers' website for a list). Camping trips to San Miguel Island cost $90/80. For additional fares, call or check the website. The company's nonlanding whale-watching tours cost $24/16 for the 3½-hour gray whale trip (January to March) and $58/47 for the all-day blue and humpback whale-watching trip (July to September).

Truth Aquatics (☎ 805-962-1127; w www .truthaquatics.com; 301 W Cabrillo Blvd), the park's Santa Barbara-based operator, offers similar excursions to Island Packers.

Most trips require a minimum number of participants and may be canceled anytime due to surf and weather conditions. In any case, landing is never guaranteed, again because of changeable weather and surf conditions. Reservations are recommended for weekend, holiday and summer trips, and credit card or advance payment is required.

Those prone to seasickness might want to consider taking a 25-minute flight to Santa Rosa Island with **Channel Islands Aviation** (☎ 805-987-1301) instead. Day trips leave year-round from the airports in Camarillo and Santa Barbara and cost $106 for adults and $84 for children aged two to 12; campers pay $162. There's a three-person minimum per flight; this is also the cost for drop-off and pick-up from the island.

OJAI

About 35mi southeast of Santa Barbara and 14mi inland from Ventura off Hwy 33, Ojai (pronounced oh-hi, meaning 'moon' to the Chumash; population 8000) is a town that has long drawn artists and New Agers. Several spiritual institutes, including the Krishnamurti Foundation and the Krotona Institute of Theosophy, have set up residence here. Ojai is famous for the rosy glow that emanates both from its mountains at sunset – the so-called Pink Moment – and from the faces emerging from spa treatments. In fact, the scenery here is so stunning that Frank Capra felt the Ojai Valley worthy of representing the mythical Shangri-La in his 1937 movie Lost Horizon.

For information, go to the **Ojai Chamber of Commerce** (☎ 805-646-8126, fax 805-646-9762; w www.the-ojai.org; 150 W Ojai Ave; open 9:30am-4:30pm Mon-Fri, 10am-4pm Sat & Sun).

The Arcade Plaza, a maze of mission revival–style buildings on Ojai Ave (the main thoroughfare), contains cutesy shops and art galleries. **Bart's Books** (☎ 805-646-3755; 302 W Matilija St), one block north of Ojai Ave, is worth at least a half-hour browse.

As a resort, Ojai flourished in the 1980s but now parts of it look a tad ragged. The exception is **Ojai Valley Inn & Spa** (☎ 805-646-5511, 800-422-6524; rooms & suites $279-450), on the western end of town, a luxurious golf and spa resort with amazing gardens and nice architecture.

Farm Hostel (☎ 805-646-0311; Hwy 33; dorm beds $15), about 10 minutes from downtown, perfectly reflects the serene and spiritual aura of Ojai. Guests stay in gender-segregated dorms on this working family farm set in a large organic orchard. You can prepare your own meals (vegetarian only) in the communal kitchen, and enjoy such modern amenities as cable TV and Internet access. Reservations are mandatory, smokers need not apply, and proof of international travel is required. Free pickups are available from anywhere in downtown Ventura.

The 9mi **Ojai Valley Trail**, converted from old railway tracks, is popular with walkers, joggers, cyclists and equestrians.

The only direct bus service is from the city of Ventura. Take the Greyhound bus or Amtrak train to Ventura, then board bus No 16 ($1, 45 minutes, once an hour) at Main & Figueroa Sts, which goes straight to downtown Ojai. The bus company is **SCAT** (☎ 805-487-4222).

SANTA BARBARA

Sandwiched between the Pacific Ocean and Santa Ynez Mountains, Santa Barbara (population 90,000) is affluent and pretty, with red-tile roofs, white stucco and a seaside lassitude reminiscent of Mediterranean towns. It's one of the highlights of the Central Coast and a popular weekend getaway for city-weary Southern Californians.

Five colleges in the area, including the University of California at Santa Barbara (UCSB), give the town a youthful vivacity and balance its yachting and retirement communities. Downtown Santa Barbara has outstanding architectural integrity, a masterpiece of a courthouse and noteworthy art and natural history museums. Rising abruptly and majestically to the north, the Santa Ynez foothills offer great hiking and camping.

History

Until about 200 years ago, Chumash Indians thrived in the Santa Barbara area, living in villages along the coast and in the Santa Ynez Mountains. In 1542, Juan Rodríguez Cabrillo entered the channel, put up a Spanish flag and went on his way. Sebastián Vizcaíno, a cartographer for the Duke of Monte Rey, landed in the harbor on December 4, 1602 (the feast day of St Barbara), and literally put Santa Barbara on the map. But being claimed and named by Spain didn't affect Santa Barbara's Chumash until the arrival of missionaries in the mid-1700s.

As elsewhere in California, the padres converted the Chumash, virtually enslaved

them to construct the mission and presidio, and taught them to wear clothing and to change their traditional diet of acorn mush, roots and fish to meat. The Indians contracted European diseases and were decimated, though today the tribe is again very much alive and well.

Easterners started arriving in force with the 1849 gold rush, and by the late 1890s Santa Barbara was an established vacation spot for the rich, famous and creative. The American Film Company, founded at the corner of Mission and State Sts in 1910, was the largest in the world for about three of its 10 years in existence. Thanks to the local film commission, the movie and TV business continues to thrive in the city. Every March, independent US and international films are shown at the Santa Barbara International Film Festival.

Orientation

Downtown Santa Barbara is laid out in a square grid – its main artery is State St, which runs north-south. Lower State St (south of Ortega St) has a large concentration of bars, while upper State St (north of Ortega St) has most of the pretty shops and museums. Cabrillo Blvd hugs the coastline and turns into Coast Village Rd as it enters the eastern suburb of Montecito.

Santa Barbara is surrounded by small affluent communities: Hope Ranch to the west, Montecito and Summerland to the east. UCSB is just west of Hope Ranch in Isla Vista, and most of Santa Barbara's college crowd lives around the campus or in neighboring Goleta.

Information

Santa Barbara's **Visitor Center** (☎ 805-965-3021; w www.santabarbaraCA.com; 1 Garden St; open 9am-5pm Mon-Sat, 10am-5pm Sun Sept-June, 9am-6pm daily July-Aug) has maps, brochures and busy but helpful staff. Another branch (☎ 805-884-1475; 4th floor, Santa Barbara Maritime Museum; open 11am-5pm or 6pm daily) is more outdoor-oriented and dispenses plenty of data about the Channel Islands National Park and the Los Padres National Forest.

Back in town, the private **Hot Spots Visitor Center** (☎ 805-564-1637, 800-793-7666; 36 State St; open 9am-9pm Mon-Sat, 9am-4pm Sun Apr-Nov; shorter hours Dec-Mar) is inside a 24-hour café with Internet access.

SANTA BARBARA AREA

PLACES TO STAY & EAT
4 San Roque Motel
5 Travelers Motel
8 Brown Pelican
9 Cabrillo Inn

To Cold Springs Tavern, Los Padres
National Forest, Chumash Painted Cave State
Historic Park, Lake Cachuma & Wine Country

San Antonio
Tucker's   Canyon County
Grove   Park
Park   Cathedral Oaks Rd   154

Cathedral Oaks Rd
Lake Los
Carneros
Lake Los
Carneros
County Park

El Canto
Heights   101   Goleta   217   Hollister Ave

Fairview Ave
Clarence Ward Memorial Blvd
Patterson Ave
Laguna
Blanca

To Hwy 1,
Solvang
& Lompoc   Hollister Ave

Storke Rd
Los Carneros Rd

Santa Barbara
Municipal Airport

Hidden Oaks
Country Club

Hope Ranch

Ocean Meadows
Golf Course

El Colegio Rd

Devereux
Slough   Isla Vista
University of
California,
Santa Barbara

University of
California,
Santa Barbara

Goleta Beach
County Park

PACIFIC

Coal Oil
Point

Isla Vista
Beach Park

Campus
Beach

Goleta
Point

OCEAN

0   1   2 km
0   .5   1 mile

Banks and ATMs are on State St; nearby is the **main post office** (*836 Anacapa St*).

The Red Tile Tour

This self-guided 12-block walking tour is an excellent way to take in all major downtown sights and historic landmarks, including the Santa Barbara County Courthouse, Museum of Art, Historical Museum and El Presidio (all covered in this section). Pick up a free map from the visitor centers.

Santa Barbara County Courthouse

The 1929 courthouse (*☎ 805-962-6464; 1100 Anacapa St; open 8am-5pm Mon-Fri, 10am-5pm Sat & Sun*) is one sight not to be missed. Built in Spanish-Moorish Revival style, it features hand-painted ceilings, wrought-iron chandeliers and tiles from Tunisia and Spain. You're free to explore it on your own, but the best way to see it is on a free docent-led tour offered at 2pm Monday to Saturday, and at 10:30am Monday, Tuesday and Friday. Be sure to have a look at the mural room, and go up the 80ft clock tower for your panoramic shots of the city.

Santa Barbara Museum of Art

This well-regarded art museum (*☎ 805-963-4364; 1130 State St; adult/senior/student $6/4/3, free Thur & 1st Sun of month; open 11am-5pm Tues-Thur & Sat, 11am-9pm Fri, noon-5pm Sun*) presents European and American hot shots – a la Monet, Matisse, Hopper and O'Keeffe – as well as Asian art, photography and classical sculpture. There's also an interactive children's gallery, a café and store.

Santa Barbara Historical Museum

Located in an adobe complex, this educational museum (*☎ 805-966-1601; 136 E De La Guerra St; admission free; open 10am-5pm Tues-Sat, noon-5pm Sun*) has an exhaustive collection of local memorabilia which ranges from the mundane, such as antique furniture, to the intriguing, such as the intricately carved coffer that belonged to Padre Serra. You can also learn about Santa Barbara's involvement in toppling the last Chinese monarchy, a rather obscure chapter in history. Free guided tours are given at 1:30pm Wednesday, Saturday and Sunday.

SANTA BARBARA AREA

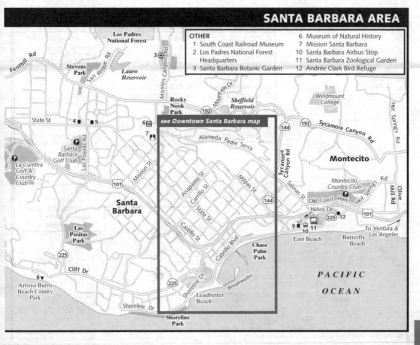

OTHER
1 South Coast Railroad Museum
2 Los Padres National Forest Headquarters
3 Santa Barbara Botanic Garden
6 Museum of Natural History
7 Mission Santa Barbara
10 Santa Barbara Airbus Stop
11 Santa Barbara Zoological Garden
12 Andrée Clark Bird Refuge

El Presidio de Santa Barbara State Historic Park

One of four in California, this 18th-century former Spanish fort (☎ 805-966-9719; admission by donation; open 10:30am-4:30pm daily), on E Cañon Perdido St between Anacapa and Santa Barbara Sts, harbors some of the city's oldest structures, which seem to be in constant need of propping up and restoring. Founded in 1782 to protect the missions between Monterey and San Diego, the presidio also served as social and political hub and as a stopping point for traveling Spanish military. Be sure to visit the chapel, with an interior that explodes in kaleidoscopic color and features some interesting trompe l'oeil effects.

Mission Santa Barbara

Called the 'Queen of the Missions,' Mission Santa Barbara (☎ 805-682-4713; 2201 Laguna St; adult/child $4/free; open 9am-5pm daily) sits on a majestic perch ½mi north of downtown. It was established on December 4 (the feast day of St Barbara) in 1786, as the 10th California mission. Three adobe structures preceded the current stone version from

1820; its main facade integrates neoclassical-style columns. Today, the mission still functions as a Franciscan friary as well as a parish church and museum. The church features Chumash wall decorations, and the gardens in the courtyard evoke tranquility. Behind it is an extensive cemetery with 4000 Chumash graves and elaborate mausoleums of early California settlers.

Museum of Natural History

Visit this museum (☎ 805-682-4711; 2559 Puesta del Sol Rd; adult/senior & teen/child $7/6/4, free last Sun of month; open 9am-5pm Mon-Sat, 10am-5pm Sun), two blocks north of the mission, if only for its beautiful architecture and landscaping. Inside, the Chumash exhibit is worth a look, as is the complete skeleton of a blue whale, though other exhibits are quite mediocre. There's also a planetarium.

Santa Barbara Botanic Garden

A mile north of the Museum of Natural History, this 65-acre botanic garden (☎ 805-682-4726; 1212 Mission Canyon Rd; adult/concession $5/3; open 9am-sunset daily) is

DOWNTOWN SANTA BARBARA

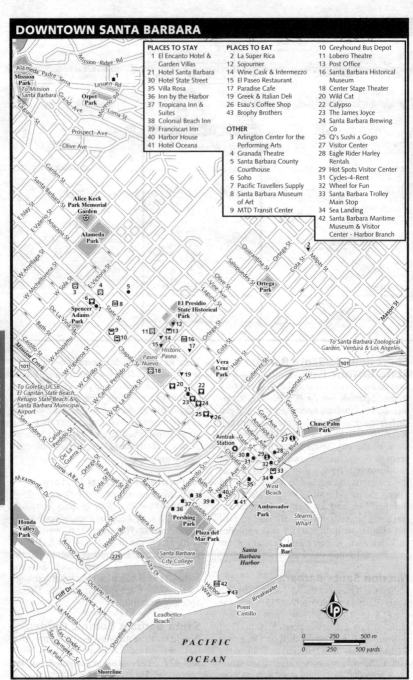

PLACES TO STAY
1 El Encanto Hotel & Garden Villas
21 Hotel Santa Barbara
30 Hotel State Street
35 Villa Rosa
36 Inn by the Harbor
37 Tropicana Inn & Suites
38 Colonial Beach Inn
39 Franciscan Inn
40 Harbor House
41 Hotel Oceana

PLACES TO EAT
2 La Super Rica
12 Sojourner
14 Wine Cask & Intermezzo
15 El Paseo Restaurant
17 Paradise Cafe
19 Greek & Italian Deli
26 Esau's Coffee Shop
43 Brophy Brothers

OTHER
3 Arlington Center for the Performing Arts
4 Granada Theatre
5 Santa Barbara County Courthouse
6 Soho
7 Pacific Travellers Supply
8 Santa Barbara Museum of Art
9 MTD Transit Center
10 Greyhound Bus Depot
11 Lobero Theatre
13 Post Office
16 Santa Barbara Historical Museum
18 Center Stage Theater
20 Wild Cat
22 Calypso
23 The James Joyce
24 Santa Barbara Brewing Co
25 Q's Sushi a Gogo
27 Visitor Center
28 Eagle Rider Harley Rentals
29 Hot Spots Visitor Center
31 Cycles-4-Rent
32 Wheel for Fun
33 Santa Barbara Trolley Main Stop
34 Sea Landing
42 Santa Barbara Maritime Museum & Visitor Center - Harbor Branch

CENTRAL COAST

devoted to California's native flora. About 5½mi of trails meander through cacti, redwoods, wildflowers and past the old mission dam, built by the Chumash to irrigate the mission's fields.

Santa Barbara Zoological Garden

The zoo (☎ 805-962-5339; 500 Niños Dr; adult/senior & child under 12 $8/6; open 10am-5pm daily) has gorgeous gardens as well as 700 animals from around the world, including big cats, monkeys, elephants and giraffes. The 100-year-old vegetation was once part of a palatial estate.

Just east of the zoo, the **Andrée Clark Bird Refuge** (1400 E Cabrillo Blvd; admission free) consists of a lagoon, gardens and a path from which to observe nesting freshwater birds.

The Waterfront

At its southern end, State Street gives way to **Stearns Wharf**, a rough, wooden pier with a few snack and souvenir shops. Built in 1872 by John Peck Stearn, it's the oldest continuously operating wharf on the West Coast. During the 1940s it was owned by Jimmy Cagney and his two brothers. Partly destroyed by a 1998 fire, it has now been restored. Southwest of here, right in the harbor, the newish **Santa Barbara Maritime Museum** (☎ 805-962-8404; 113 Harbor Way; adult/concession $5/3, free 3rd Thur of month; open 11am-6pm Thur-Tues) celebrates the town's briny history with memorabilia and hands-on exhibits, including a big-game fishing chair from which you can 'reel in' a trophy marlin. Elsewhere you can take a virtual trip through the Santa Barbara Channel and peek through a 45ft-tall US Navy periscope.

South Coast Railroad Museum

If you go gaga over trains, don't miss this museum (☎ 805-964-3540; 300 N Los Carneros Rd; admission free; open 11am-4pm Wed-Sun June-Sept, 1pm-4pm Oct-May). It houses a sizable collection of railroad artifacts, old photographs and a 300-sq-ft model railroad. Children get a kick out of riding the miniature train ($1). The museum is ¼mi from the Los Carneros exit off Hwy 101 in a 1901 Southern Pacific Railroad depot in Goleta, 8mi northwest of downtown Santa Barbara.

Activities

East Beach is the long sandy stretch between Stearns Wharf and Montecito; it's Santa Barbara's largest and most popular beach. At its eastern end, across from the Biltmore Hotel, Armani swimsuits and Gucci sunglasses abound at **Butterfly Beach**.

Between Stearns Wharf and the harbor, **West Beach** has calm water and is popular with families and tourists staying in nearby motels. On the other side of the harbor, **Leadbetter Beach** is a good spot for surfing and windsurfing, with access to a grassy picnic area atop the cliffs.

West of Santa Barbara near the junction of Cliff Dr and Las Positas Rd, **Arroyo Burro Beach** (also called Hendry's) has a parking lot, picnic area and restaurant.

The Santa Ynez foothills (part of Los Padres National Forest, see Along Highway 154 later in this chapter) are 20 minutes by car from downtown. The hills are full of **hiking** trails, most of which cut through rugged chaparral and steep canyons offering incredible coastal views. The hike through Rattlesnake Canyon is popular with locals, as is the one along the Tunnel Trail to Inspiration Point. A central place for trail maps is **Pacific Travellers Supply** (☎ 805-963-4438; 12 W Anapamu St).

The Cabrillo Bikeway runs for 3mi along the beachfront between the Andrée Clark Bird Refuge and Leadbetter Beach, while the Goleta Bikeway continues west to UCSB. Wheel for Fun and Cycles-4-Rent are a couple of bike rental outfits near the beach end of State St. Cruisers and inline skates go for about $7 per hour.

Sea Landing (☎ 805-882-0088), on the beach at the foot of Bath St, rents kayaks, jet skis and jet boats and also operates whale-watching excursions to the Channel Islands aboard the Condor Express, a state-of-the-art high-speed catamaran which is stable enough for most stomachs. Trips last about 4½ hours, cost $70 for adults and $40 for children; whale sightings are guaranteed, so if you miss out you can come back for a free trip. For sailboat rental, try **Santa Barbara Sailing Center** (☎ 805-962-2826) in the harbor.

Organized Tours

Santa Barbara Trolley (☎ 805-965-0353; adult/child $12/7) makes a narrated 90-minute loop past Stearns Wharf, the courthouse,

CENTRAL COAST

the art museum and the mission. Tickets are valid all day, allowing you to get off and on as you please. The first trolley leaves from Stearns Wharf at 10am, the last one at 4pm (at 5:30pm from June to September).

Places to Stay

In summer (here meaning about mid-May to mid-September) budget accommodations are practically nonexistent in Santa Barbara. Even a cheap motel room that may cost just $35 in November can soar to as much as $150 in 'season.' In general, midweek rates are lower than Friday and Saturday nights. Some hotels impose a two-night minimum stay. **Santa Barbara Hot Spots** (☎ 800-564-1637; W www.hotspotsusa.com) and **Coastal Escapes** (☎ 800-692-2222; W www.coastalescapes.com) offer free room-reservation services.

Budget There is no campground anywhere near downtown Santa Barbara, but about 17mi and 20mi west of town, respectively, right on the beach off Hwy 101, are **El Capitan State Beach** and **Refugio State Beach** (☎ 805-968-1033, reservations ☎ 800-444-7275; campsites $12). Refugio is a popular surf spot and student hangout, while El Capitan, perched on low bluffs, is more popular with families. Amenities include flush toilets, hot showers, picnic tables and barbecues. There's also camping in the Los Padres National Forest and at Lake Cachuma (see the Along Highway 154 section later in this chapter).

Santa Barbara had no hostel at the time of writing, but a new one – the Santa Barbara International Hostel – was expected to open in late 2002. Call ☎ 805-963-3586 for an update or check W www.bananabungalow.com.

Hotel State Street (☎ 805-966-6586, fax 805-962-8459; e ewtrade@ix.netcom.com; 121 State St; rooms in summer $50-70, in winter $40-55) is one of the best deals in town for those willing to share facilities. The good-sized rooms are spotless and many have big windows, a sink and TV, but no phone. It's only two blocks from the beach but also right next to the train station, so bring ear plugs and ask for the quietest room.

A number of fairly affordable motels, especially in the off-season, cluster along upper State St near Las Positas Rd. Bus Nos 6 and 11 make the trip out here.

Travelers Motel (☎ 805-687-6009; 3222 State St; rooms $39-65) is one of the cheapest options around here and has smallish but clean rooms with TV and phones.

San Roque Motel (☎ 805-687-6611, 800-587-5667; 3344 State St; rooms in summer $69-169, in winter $49-89) is a step up in the aesthetics department and also has a nicely landscaped garden and pool.

Mid-Range & Top End Wrapped around a magnificent palm tree is **Harbor House** (☎ 805-962-9745, fax 888-474-6789; 104 Bath St; rooms in summer $78-158, in winter $68-108), which has stylish rooms that are pretty without B&B-style busy-ness.

Franciscan Inn (☎ 805-963-8845, fax 805-564-3295; 109 Bath St; rooms in summer $105-220, in winter $85-175), across the street, is a delightful place, run with efficiency and charm. It has a nice pool, a spa and guest laundry, and its rates include breakfast and afternoon drinks.

Cabrillo Inn (☎ 805-966-1641, 800-648-6708, fax 805-965-1623; W www.cabrillo-inn.com; 931 E Cabrillo Blvd; rooms $89-169) won't win any design awards but the location right across from East Beach is hard to beat. Rates are for rooms with partial ocean view; add $20 to $30 for the full view.

Villa Rosa (☎ 805-966-0851, fax 805-962-7159; W www.villarosainnsb.com; 15 Chapala St; rooms $125-230) is an intimate inn wrapped around a flower-festooned courtyard with swimming pool and Jacuzzi. The afternoon wine hour and nightcap in the lounge are conducive to meeting people.

Colonial Beach Inn (☎ 805-966-2219, 800-468-1988, fax 805-962-9428; W www.sbhotels.com; 223 Castillo St; rooms $126-188) has extra-sized rooms with decor inspired by the American South; some have kitchenettes. Rates include breakfast. The same owners also operate **Tropicana Inn & Suites** (☎ 805-966-2219; 223 Castillo St) across the street and **Inn by the Harbor** (☎ 805-963-7851; 433 W Montecito St). Rates are similar to the Colonial Beach Inn.

Hotel Santa Barbara (☎ 805-957-9300, 888-259-7700; W www.hotelsantabarbara.com; 533 State St; rooms $129-229) marries easy-going Euro flair with American amenities. A spacious lobby gives way to quiet rooms with flowery curtains, bedspreads and thick carpets.

Hotel Oceana (☎ 805-965-4577, 800-965-9776, fax 805-965-9937; **w** www.hotel oceana.com; 202 W Cabrillo Blvd; rooms Sun-Thur $175-275, Fri-Sat $225-350, suites $325-400) is a sprawling oceanfront refuge which has morphed from four drab motels into one stylish enclave with breezy and beautifully appointed rooms. If beachin' isn't bitchin', you can also relax at two pools, wallow in the Jacuzzi or work off tensions in the gym. Rooms in the back are quieter.

El Encanto Hotel & Garden Villas (☎ 805-687-5000, 800-346-7039, fax 805-687-0903; **w** www.elencantohotel.com; 1900 Lasuen Rd; rates $229-800), long considered *the* hotel in Santa Barbara, sits on a hill above the mission with a great view of downtown and the ocean. Its secluded cottages with private patios are nestled among 10 acres of lush gardens.

Places to Eat

Santa Barbara has great culinary offerings for everyone from the gourmet to the discerning diner looking for a good deal.

La Super Rica (622 N Milpas St; dishes under $7) is food guru Julia Child's favorite Mexican restaurant and who are we to argue? Order from the window, then join local families at the picnic-style tables for some authentic *comida* (food).

Esau's Coffee Shop (403 State St; dishes under $7) is a no-nonsense, no-attitude local institution with orange booths, wacky decor and a satisfying menu of classic American breakfasts and lunches.

Greek & Italian Deli (cnr State & Ortega Sts; dishes $5-8) makes great hot and cold sandwiches, gyros and deli salads, and also sells cold cuts, cheeses and other items good for putting together that beach picnic.

Sojourner (☎ 805-965-7922; 134 E Cañon Perdido; dishes $4-12), a friendly and upbeat café, gets creative with vegetables, tofu and tempeh, rice and seeds and other healthful and wholesome ingredients.

Brown Pelican (☎ 805-687-4550; 2981½ Cliff Dr; breakfast & lunch $6-13.50, dinner $12-29), at Hendry's Beach (bus No 5 from the transit center), doesn't get any closer to the ocean. The fare at this informal café ranges from cleverly spiced fish tacos to satisfying fish and chips, and healthful heaps of salads.

Paradise Cafe (☎ 805-962-4416; 702 Anacapa St; dishes $5-20) is the quintessential California café, with mouthwatering oak-grilled burgers, inventive salads, light pastas, seafood and steak, all best consumed on the outdoor patio (no smoking).

Brophy Brothers (☎ 805-966-4418; Breakwater; mains $7-18) is beloved for its superbly fresh fish and seafood, its bubbly atmosphere and its salty setting right in the marina. Favorites include the clam chowder and *cioppino* (seafood stew), all served with chewy sourdough bread.

Intermezzo (☎ 805-966-9463; 813 Anacapa St; mains $9-15), the more casual cousin of the Wine Cask (see later in this section), has the sleek sophistication of a European bistro and a menu to match. It serves three meals a day but doesn't take reservations.

Wine Cask (☎ 805-687-4417; 813 Anacapa St; lunch $10-15, dinner $20-35) is a local dining shrine canopied by a gold-leafed beamed ceiling. Alternatively, pick a table in the flowery courtyard for dining on classic American cuisine while sipping stellar wines.

To stock up on fresh produce, visit the **farmers market**, held Tuesday late afternoons on the 500 block of State St between E Haley and E Cota Sts, and Saturday mornings at the corner of Santa Barbara and Cota Sts.

Entertainment

The free *Independent* is published on Thursday and has thorough events listings and reviews. The *Santa Barbara News-Press* has a daily events calendar and a special Friday supplement called 'Scene.'

Santa Barbara's after-dark scene revolves around lower State St and Ortega St. Most places have happy hour and college nights, when the booze is cheap and the atmosphere rowdy.

The James Joyce (☎ 805-962-2688; 513 State St) does well in bringing the ambience of a Dublin pub to California, with a neat carved ceiling, dart boards and a crackling fireplace. On Saturday night, the house band heats up the crowd with Dixieland jazz.

Santa Barbara Brewing Co (☎ 805-730-1040; 501 State St) has about a dozen homemade concoctions on tap. The shiny copper and steel brewing vats form part of the decor.

Calypso (☎ 805-966-1388; 514 State St) plays energetic dance music as does

Q's Sushi a Gogo (☎ 805-966-9177; 409 State St), which also has billiards tables and a sushi bar. Wild Cat (☎ 805-962-7970; 15 W Ortega St), looking like a cross between a warehouse and a love den, is a 1970s revival lounge, with a diverse crowd and a good mix of music.

Soho (☎ 805-962-7776; 1221 State St), above McDonald's, has live bands nightly and only charges admission for weekend and big-name shows.

El Paseo (☎ 805-962-6050, 10 El Paseo), back in the Historic Paseo, is a colorful Mexican restaurant with a touristy touch but it has one of the town's best happy hours with honest margaritas and a free big buffet.

Santa Barbara supports a variety of companies and historic venues. Lobero Theatre (1873; ☎ 805-963-0761; 33 E Cañon Perdido St), one of California's oldest theaters, presents ballet, modern dance, chamber music and special events, often featuring internationally renowned top talent. Granada Theatre (☎ 805-966-2324; 1216 State St), built in 1930, focuses on musicals and operettas, while Arlington Center for the Performing Arts (☎ 805-963-4408; 1317 State St) is home to the Santa Barbara Symphony and also contains a movie theater. For live theater, visit Center Stage Theater (☎ 805-963-0408) in Paseo Nuevo mall.

Shopping
Shops along State St feature clothing, knickknacks, antiques and books. Paseo Nuevo, between Cañon Perdido and Ortega Sts, is a charming outdoor mall anchored by Nordstrom and Robinsons-May department stores, plus various retail chains such as Gap and Victoria's Secret.

La Arcada (1114 State St), near Figueroa St, is an historical red-tile passageway designed by Myron Hunt (builder of the Rose Bowl in Los Angeles), which is filled with boutiques, restaurants and whimsical public art. Another lovely, flower-festooned courtyard is the Historic Paseo, opposite Paseo Nuevo.

Getting There & Away
The small Santa Barbara Municipal Airport (☎ 805-683-4011; 500 Fowler Rd), in Goleta some 8mi west of downtown off Hwy 101, has scheduled flights to/from Los Angeles,

San Francisco, Denver, Phoenix and other US cities.

Santa Barbara Airbus (☎ 805-964-7759, 800-423-1618) shuttles between Los Angeles International Airport (LAX) and Santa Barbara ($37, $69 round-trip, 14 a day).

Greyhound (☎ 805-965-7551; 34 W Carrillo St) has up to nine daily buses to Los Angeles ($12, 2¼ to three hours) and up to seven to San Francisco ($32, 8½ to 10 hours).

The Amtrak depot (lower State St) has direct train and coach services to Los Angeles ($20) and San Luis Obispo ($22).

Santa Barbara is bisected by Hwy 101. For downtown, take the Garden St or Cabrillo Blvd exits. Parking on the street and in any of the 10 municipal lots is free for the first 90 minutes (all day Sunday). Eagle Rider (☎ 805-963-2453, 866-345-7437; 52 Helena Ave) rents Harleys for $90 to $145 per day.

Getting Around
The Downtown-Waterfront Shuttle bus runs every 10 to 15 minutes from 10:15am to 6pm along State St to Stearns Wharf. A second route travels from the zoo to the yacht harbor at 30-minute intervals. The fare is $0.25 per ride; transfers between routes are free.

Buses operated by Santa Barbara Metropolitan Transit District (MTD; ☎ 805-683-3702) cost $1 per ride and travel all over town and adjacent communities, including Goleta and Montecito. The Transit Center (1020 Chapala St) has details on routes and schedules.

ALONG HIGHWAY 154
Highway 154 is a scenic route veering north of Santa Barbara through the Los Padres National Forest. It bisects the Santa Barbara Wine Country and the Santa Ynez Valley before joining up with Hwy 101 north of Los Olivos.

Chumash Painted Cave State Historic Park
This small state park (☎ 805-968-3294; open dawn-dusk daily) shelters vivid pictographs painted by the Chumash about 200 years ago. The cave is protected by a metal screen, so a flashlight is helpful for getting a good view. Look for the turnoff to Painted Cave Rd, about 8mi north of Santa Barbara; the last stretch of the road is narrow and steep and not suited for RVs (Recreational Vehicles).

Los Padres National Forest

Los Padres National Forest covers about two million acres of coastal mountains in various pockets stretching from the Carmel Valley (see later this chapter) to the western edge of Los Angeles County. It's great for hiking, camping, horseback riding, mountain biking and other outdoor pursuits. For information, check with the Santa Barbara Visitor Center in the Maritime Museum (see Information under Santa Barbara earlier in this chapter) or with the **Forest Headquarters** (☎ 805-968-6640; 6755 Hollister Ave, Suite 150; open 8am-4:30pm Mon-Fri) in Goleta. If you are traveling by car, you must have the National Forest Adventure Pass in order to park in the forest (see the boxed text in the Activities chapter).

Paradise Rd, which crosses Hwy 154 north of San Marcos Pass, offers the best access to developed facilities in the forest. About 4mi up the road is a ranger station with posted maps and information. There are three **campgrounds** (campsites $12) before the ranger station and one just past it. At Red Rocks (clearly marked from the ranger station), the Santa Ynez River deeply pools among rocks and waterfalls, creating a great swimming and sunning spot. Many hiking trails radiate out from here.

Paradise Rd also gives access to a great slice of Americana: **Cold Spring Tavern** (☎ 805-967-0066; 5595 Stagecoach Rd), a legendary stagecoach stop which is still a popular watering hole and restaurant. A rough-hewn plank floor connects a warren of dimly lit rooms decorated with an odd assortment of Western memorabilia and framed photographs and newspaper articles. The food, alas, is mediocre and overpriced. The turnoff to Stagecoach Rd is about ¼mi north of the junction of Paradise Rd and Hwy 154. Follow it for about 3mi to the tavern, passing underneath the amazing San Marcos Bridge.

Lake Cachuma County Park

Lake Cachuma is a haven for anglers and boaters and also has a large **campground** (☎ 805-686-5054; tent/RV sites $16/22) with picnic tables, barbecues, flush toilets and hot showers. Sites are on a first-come, first-serve basis and fill quickly on weekends. You can also rent a 'yurt', basically a tent cabin on a redwood deck, for $35 to $55 per night (reservations ☎ 805-686-5050). Park admission is $5 per vehicle.

Santa Barbara Wine Country

Highway 154 travels straight through the Santa Ynez Valley, the heart of the Santa Barbara Wine Country. Fog and ocean breezes flowing into the valley create microclimates well suited for growing grapes. About three dozen wineries, mostly family-run, produce Chardonnays as well as Pinot Noir, Merlot, Cabernet Sauvignon and other varietals. Most have lovely picnic grounds, are open for touring and operate tasting rooms. The visit or centers in Santa Barbara distribute free maps with brief descriptions of each winery, including tasting room hours.

Worthwhile stops include **Sunstone** (☎ 805-688-9463; 125 Refugio Rd), just off Hwy 246, and **Foley** (☎ 805-688-8554; 1711 Alamo Pintado Rd), south of Hwy 154. A great place to put together a picnic is **El Rancho Market**, on Hwy 246, about ¼mi west of Refugio Rd.

SOLVANG

In 1911, three Danish farmers established the Atterdag College folk school in the Santa Ynez Valley to pass on their Danish traditions to future generations. The small town that grew up around the school was named Solvang (Sunny Field; population 5300) and today looks like a Scandinavian theme park, complete with windmills, gas-lit street lamps and 'gingerbread' houses. Its diminutive lanes are lined by bakeries, gift shops and galleries. Stop in at the **Visitors Bureau** (☎ 805-688-6144, 800-468-6765; 1511 Mission Dr) for maps and information.

Elverhøj Museum (☎ 805-686-1211; cnr 2nd St & Elverhoy Way; admission by donation; open 1pm-4pm Wed-Sun), housed in a replica 18th-century Jutland farmhouse, is the town's local history museum. Its collection of papierklip (paper cutout) art, period clothes and furniture, farm tools and old photographs is worth a look.

The **Hans Christian Andersen Museum** (☎ 805-688-2052; 1680 Mission Dr; admission by donation; open 10am-5pm daily) has a collection of Andersen's books, manuscripts, letters and photographs, plus paper cutouts created by the author himself.

Easy Rider fans may want to stop in at **Vintage Motorcycle Museum** (☎ 805-686-9522;

320 Alisal Rd; admission $5; open 11am-5pm Sat & Sun), which has classic bikes, including a 1955 Matchless G640 and a 1936 BMW.

Old Mission Santa Inés (☎ 805-688-4815; *1760 Mission Dr; adult/child under 16 $3/free; open 9am-5:30pm daily, 9am-7pm June-Sept)* was founded at the height of missionary prosperity in 1804. Today it contains a collection of vestments, church records and Chumash artifacts.

The cheapest place to stay is **Hamlet Motel** (☎ 805-688-4413, 800-253-5033; *1532 Mission Dr; rooms $50-120)*, which is nothing special but gives you a small free breakfast. For further immersion into all things wee and cute, check in at **Chimney Sweep Inn** (☎ 805-688-2111, 800-824-6444; *1564 Copenhagen Dr; rooms $80-250)*, which has frilly rooms with fireplaces, and loft suites.

Solvang brims with restaurants and bakeries. Locals recommend **Birkholms** (*1555 Mission Dr)* for its shortbread cookies and pastries. Also good is **Solvang Restaurant** (*1672 Copenhagen Dr; meals under $8)*, which serves *aebleskivers* (ball-like pancakes dusted with powdered sugar) as well as 'normal' American breakfasts and lunches.

From June to October, the **Pacific Conservatory of the Performing Arts** (*information* ☎ 800-468-6765) presents outdoor theater – of the light, entertaining kind – almost nightly.

Solvang is on Hwy 246, just east of Hwy 101. Amtrak motor coaches make the trip out here from Santa Barbara several times daily ($13, 50 minutes).

LOMPOC

If one were to describe Lompoc (pronounced **lohm**-poke; population 41,000), the largest town along Hwy 1 as it winds between Pismo Beach and Santa Barbara, in four words, they would be: mission, military, murals and flowers.

Vandenberg Air Force Base, about 13mi north on the coast, supports this sprawling city characterized mostly by long stretches of undistinguished commercial development. Lompoc's old town, though – roughly where H St meets Ocean Ave – sports a number of historic buildings and antique stores and is worth a quick stroll. Also here is the **Lompoc Chamber of Commerce** (☎ 805-736-4567; *111 South I St)*, which has maps and a self-guided tour pamphlet. But even without it, you can't help noticing the many colorful

murals – some naive, some quite accomplished – that brighten this area. In a neoclassical-style villa at 200 S H St, the **Lompoc Museum** (☎ 805-736-3888; *admission free; open 1pm-5pm Tues-Fri, 1pm-4pm Sat & Sun)* is worth a quick look for its collections of Chumash and regional artifacts.

Lompoc is embedded in a valley carpeted with **flower fields** (larkspur, sweet peas, delphinium and many others), which erupt in a profusion of color, especially between June and August. These are grown to be sold as cut flowers, but while still flowering they're free to enjoy for all. Most of the fields cluster in the western section of town, west of Bailey Ave between Central and Ocean Aves.

Mission La Purísima Concepción

About 3mi northeast of Lompoc's old town this beautiful mission (☎ 805-733-3713; *park admission per car $2; open 9am-5pm daily)* was completely restored in the 1930s by the Civilian Conservation Corps (CCC). Its buildings are fully intact and decorated as they were during the mission period – right down to blankets on the cots and grindstones in the courtyard. The mission fields still support livestock, and the gardens are planted with medicinal plants and trees once used by the Chumash. Also here are fountains and ground-level troughs where women did the wash – one for the Indians and one for the mission women. The original mission was actually 3mi south but was rebuilt here, by Chumash Indians, after a major earthquake in 1812.

Surrounding the mission are 15mi of hiking and horse trails. At the park entrance is a museum and bookstore with a good selection of local history books and a free trail map.

The mission is just off Hwy 246; look for the turnoff to Purisima Rd on the northern side of the highway and follow it for about 1mi. From Old Town Lompoc, follow Ocean Ave east, which turns into Hwy 246.

SAN LUIS OBISPO BAY

The Pacific Coast Hwy (Hwy 1) rejoins Hwy 101 in San Luis Obispo Bay, which is bordered by a string of laid-back, little towns: Oceano, Grover Beach, Pismo Beach, Shell Beach and Avila. The main industry here is tourism and there's plenty of opportunity for outdoor recreation, including fishing, bicycling, swimming and even clamming. Public buses operated by **South County Area Transit** *(SCAT;* ☎ *805-773-5400)* ply between the communities on a fixed schedule year-round. The fare is $0.75 (exact change required).

Oceano

The southernmost of the bay communities, Oceano (population 4800) is the gateway to the **Oceano Dunes State Vehicular Recreation Area** *(recorded information* ☎ *805-473-7223;* w *www.ohv.parks.ca.gov; day-use fee $4; open 6am-11pm daily)*, a 6mi-long stretch of sand where off-road warriors can have a field day. The only California beach where vehicles are allowed, it is often used as a movie set *(The Sheik* with Rudolph Valentino was one of the earliest films shot here). Access is via Pier Avenue off Hwy 1.

BJ's ATV Rentals *(*☎ *805-481-5411; 197 Grand Ave)*, in Grover Beach, the next town up, rents various bikes from $20 to $50 per hour or $80 to $250 per day, depending on the size.

Oceano is home to three campgrounds. **Oceano Dunes SVRA Campground** *(*☎ *805-473-7220, reservations* ☎ *800-444-7275; campsites $6)* offers undeveloped camping right in the sand. It's popular with dune warriors and not a good choice if you're not one of them.

Oceano County Campground *(494 Air Park; campsites $19-23)* is cramped but well maintained and next to a duck pond. It has 22 spaces with hookups available on a first-come, first-served basis.

Oceano Campground *(*☎ *805-489-2684, reservations* ☎ *800-444-7275; tent/RV sites $12/18)* has 82 sites on nicely kept grounds shaded by eucalyptus trees.

Pismo Beach

Pismo Beach (population 8000), the largest of the bay towns, is a conglomeration of tourist shops and restaurants around Pismo Pier, along a wide sandy beach. The town is still called the 'Clam Capital of the World' because the tasty mollusks were once found in abundance on Pismo's beaches. These days, the beach is pretty much clammed out, although there always seem to be people out there trying their luck in the muck.

No instruments are needed: Just twist your foot into the wet sand to about ankle level and feel with your toes for something hard. You can keep up to 10 clams, provided they're at least 4½ inches in diameter and you have a California fishing license (available at sport shops and liquor stores). The **Clam Festival** in mid-October celebrates the beloved clam with an arts and crafts fair, and music and food booths.

These days, though, butterflies have supplanted clams as Pismo's most prevalent animal attraction. Tens of thousands of migrating monarch butterflies descend upon the town between late November and March, making their winter home in the secluded **Monarch Butterfly Grove**. Forming dense clusters in the tops of eucalyptus and pine trees, these beautiful, dark orange creatures perfectly blend into the environment and are easily mistaken for leaves. Free access to the grove is via the North Beach Campground, south of town off Hwy 1.

For area information visit the **Pismo Beach Chamber of Commerce** *(*☎ *805-773-4382, 800-443-7778;* w *www.pismocha-ber.com; 581 Dolliver St; open 9am-5pm Mon-Sat, 10am-4pm Sun)*.

Places to Stay & Eat About 1mi south of the Pismo Pier, off Hwy 1, **North Beach Campground** *(*☎ *805-489-2684, reservations* ☎ *800-444-7275; campsites $12)* has 103 nicely spaced, grassy sites, in the shade of eucalyptus trees. It offers easy beach access, flush toilets and hot showers but no hookups.

Pismo Beach has dozens of motels, but rooms fill up quickly and prices skyrocket between May and September and during the Clam Festival. Midweek rates are usually lower.

Ocean Breeze Inn *(*☎ *805-773-2070, 800-472-7873;* w *www.surfinn.net; 250 Main St; rooms $89-159; suites with kitchen $89-199)* is a block from the beach. Rates include a small breakfast and use of the heated pool. Some of its kitchen suites sleep up to six people.

Dolphin Cove Lodge *(*☎ *805-773-4706, fax 805-773-4214; 170 Main St; rooms $70-100, suite $130-180)*, right next to the beach with views of the Pismo Pier, is a friendly, nonsmoking property. Rates include a small continental breakfast. A bit of gossip: James Dean enjoyed trysting with Pier Angeli in room No 8.

North of town, toward Shell Beach, several upscale resorts squat atop scenic bluffs. A

SAN LUIS OBISPO BAY

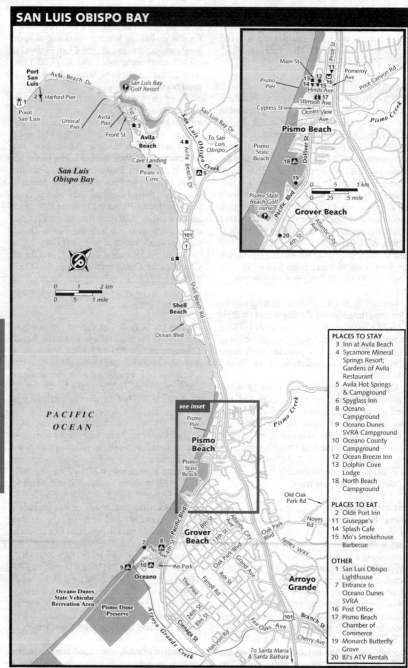

Port San Luis

1 Point San Luis

Avila Beach Dr

2 Harford Pier

Unocal Pier

Avila Pier

Front St

1st St

3

Avila Beach

San Luis Bay Golf Resort

San Luis Bay Dr

To San Luis Obispo

Cave Landing

Pirate's Cove

4

Avila Beach Dr

San Luis Obispo Creek

5

San Luis Obispo Bay

101

1

6

Shell Beach Rd

Shell Beach

Ocean Blvd

0   1   2 km
0   .5   1 mile

PACIFIC OCEAN

see inset

Pismo Pier

Pismo Beach

Pismo State Beach

Pismo Creek

Old Oak Park Rd

Noyes Rd

Grover Beach

7
8
Pier Ave
9   10
Oceano
Air Park

Pacific Blvd
8th St
13th St
Atlantic City Blvd
Oak Park Blvd
Grand Ave
Farroll Rd
Ash St
The Pike
James Way
Oak Park Blvd

Arroyo Grande

101

Branch St

Cherry Ave

To Santa Maria & Santa Barbara

Oceano Dunes State Vehicular Recreation Area

Pismo Dune Preserve

Arroyo Grande Creek

Cienaga St
24th St
Elm St
Halcyon Rd
Fair Oaks Ave

Inset (Pismo Beach)

Main St
Price St
Pismo Pier
Pismo Ave
13 12 11
14 15
Pomeroy Ave
Price Canyon Rd
16
17
Hinds Ave
Stimson Ave
Cypress St
Ocean View Ave
Pismo Beach
Pismo State Beach
18
Dolliver St
19
Pacific Blvd
Pismo State Beach Golf Course
Grover Beach
20
4th St
Atlantic City Ave
Pismo Creek

0   .5   1 km
0   .25   .5 mile

PLACES TO STAY

3 Inn at Avila Beach
4 Sycamore Mineral Springs Resort; Gardens of Avila Restaurant
5 Avila Hot Springs & Campground
6 Spyglass Inn
8 Oceano Campground
9 Oceano Dunes SVRA Campground
10 Oceano County Campground
12 Ocean Breeze Inn
13 Dolphin Cove Lodge
18 North Beach Campground

PLACES TO EAT

2 Olde Port Inn
11 Giuseppe's
14 Splash Cafe
15 Mo's Smokehouse Barbecue

OTHER

1 San Luis Obispo Lighthouse
7 Entrance to Oceano Dunes SVRA
16 Post Office
17 Pismo Beach Chamber of Commerce
19 Monarch Butterfly Grove
20 BJ's ATV Rentals

CENTRAL COAST

good stop is **Spyglass Inn** (☎ 805-773-4855, 800-824-2612, fax 805-773-5298; w www .spyglassinn.com; 2705 Spyglass Dr; rooms $79-199), which has freshly remodeled rooms (many with ocean views), a spa and pool and a restaurant with a heated ocean-view deck.

You'll find several casual cafés and restaurants along Pomeroy Ave, directly up from the pier.

Splash Cafe (☎ 805-773-4653; 197 Pomeroy Ave; dishes $1.75-7.75) is a buzzing hole-in-the-wall that makes award-winning clam chowder and great grilled ahi tuna sandwiches for $4.50.

Mo's Smokehouse Barbecue (☎ 805-773-6193; 221 Pomeroy Ave; meals $6-19) offers a taste of the American South with a Pacific Ocean breeze. Ribs, sandwiches, chicken platters, all doused in secret sauce, are finger-lickin' good.

Giuseppe's (☎ 805-773-2870; 891 Price St; lunch $8-12, dinner $16-24), a few blocks inland, is a top-ranked Italian restaurant serving tasty meat and seafood specialties in addition to sandwiches, salads, pizza and pasta.

Shell Beach

Technically part of Pismo Beach, Shell Beach is a residential community, which winds north roughly from where Hwy 101 meets the ocean. Businesses, including motels and hotels, stretch along Shell Beach Rd. Ocean Blvd, lined with a grass parkway and picnic tables, gives access to the rocky beach with teeming tide pools.

Avila Beach

Avila Beach (population 1250) is a survivor. In the late 1990s, this once lovely beach town was all but wiped off the map by a massive, protracted oil spill courtesy of the nearby Unocal refinery. A costly clean-up, which required replacing the contaminated soil, tearing down structures and moving much of the population, was completed in 2001. The 'New Avila' comes with a redesigned waterfront and a once-again clean and white sandy beach. Infrastructure, however, is still in its infancy as people are returning slowly to this tiny town whose south-facing location keeps it mostly fog-free.

At the time of writing, there was just a single hotel, **Inn at Avila Beach** (☎ 805-595-2300, fax 805-595-9560; 256 Front St; rooms midweek $79-129, weekends $99-199), and it's a nice one. The decor is a cheerful mix of Mediterranean, Southwestern and Mexican styles, with vibrant colors, lots of hand-painted tiles, wrought iron and wood. Not all rooms are created equal, so check before you commit.

About 1mi north of Avila Beach is **Port San Luis**, a working fishing harbor. Enjoy panoramic bay views from the rickety Harford Pier, home to an excellent fish restaurant called **Olde Port Inn** (☎ 805-595-2515; mains $6-26). Its clam chowder and *cioppino* are standouts, and you can watch the sea lions laze beneath the pier through special glass-bottom tables.

Just south of Avila Beach, **Cave Landing** is a 150ft promontory that was used as a dock for large ships in the early 1900s. A rocky trail from the parking lot's southern end leads down to the cave and to **Pirate's Cove**, a beautiful sandy beach where clothing is optional. Locals recommend that women do not go alone unless there are plenty of people around. High tides, responsible for the cove's interesting rock formations, will sweep your stuff out to sea if you don't put it near the cliffs.

The road out to Avila, a lovely sycamore- and maple-lined glen, meanders past the upscale **Sycamore Mineral Springs Resort** (☎ 805-595-7302; 1215 Avila Beach Dr; rooms $127-177, suites $219-308), where guests melt away tensions in private hot mineral spas. **Gardens of Avila** (☎ 805-595-7365; lunch $7-13, dinner $20-28), the resort's sophisticated restaurant, serves Pacific Rim cuisine best enjoyed on the lush rock-walled patio (dinner reservations advised).

Even if you're not staying at the resort, you can treat yourself to a luxuriant soak in one of 20 private redwood **hot tubs** (open 24 hr), discreetly scattered over a woodsy hillside. It costs $12.50 per hour per person and towels are available for a fee. Reservations are advised.

Cheaper but less atmospheric is the communal pool at the nearby **Avila Valley Hot Springs** (☎ 805-595-2359; 250 Avila Beach Dr; admission $7.50; open 8am-8pm Sun-Thur, 8am-9pm Fri-Sat), in operation since 1907. The adjacent **campground** (campsites $30, partial/full hookups $35/40) has flush toilets and hot showers; rates include two pool admissions.

SAN LUIS OBISPO

San Luis Obispo (SLO; sun loo-**iss** obispo; population 43,700), about 8mi inland from the bay, is a lively yet low-key town with a high quality of life and vibrant community spirit. Like so many California cities, it grew up around a mission founded in 1772 by Padre Serra, which is still an active parish today. SLO is also home to the California Polytechnic State University (Cal Poly), which is renowned for its 'learning by doing' approach to education. Its 17,000 students inject a healthy dose of hubbub into city streets, pubs and cafés during the school year and less so in summer when the year-round population of ranchers and oil refinery employees is more visible.

The best day to visit SLO is Thursday, when the famous **farmers market** turns Higuera St, the main drag, and adjacent lanes into a giant street party from 6pm to 9pm. Barbecues belching smoke, strolling families and live music and entertainment make this one of the liveliest evenings you'll have anywhere in California.

SLO also has a small **wine country** with just five wineries. It's a few miles southeast of town and specializes in buttery chardonnays and elegant pinot noirs.

SLO's reasonably priced accommodations and proximity to beaches, state parks and Hearst Castle (45mi north), make it a good Central Coast inland hub.

Orientation & Information

SLO's compact downtown is bisected by the main commercial arteries of Higuera St, which travels one way going southwest, and Marsh St, parallel to Higuera St, running one way northeast. Hotels and motels cluster along the northeastern end of Monterey St, one block north of Higuera St. San Luis Creek, once used to irrigate mission orchards, flows through downtown parallel to Higuera St. The best exits from Hwy 101 are Marsh St and Monterey St. Parking is free for the first hour in several downtown parking garages.

SLO's **chamber of commerce** (☎ 805-543-1255, 800-676-1772; W www.visitslo.com; 1039 Chorro St; open 10am-5pm Sun & Mon, 8am-5pm Tues & Wed, 8am-8pm Thur & Fri, 10am-8pm Sat) has plenty of free printed matter and a useful city map ($2.95). You can use the free telephone to check for room availability at local hotels and motels. The **SLO Visitors & Conference Bureau** (☎ 805-541-8000, 800-634-1414; W www.sanluisobispocounty.com; 1037 Mill St; open 8am-5pm Mon-Fri) is another source of information.

Banks are along Higuera and Marsh Sts, near the **main post office** (☎ 805-541-3062; cnr Marsh & Morro Sts).

SLO County General Hospital (☎ 805-781-4800; 2180 Johnson Ave) is ½mi southeast of Monterey St.

Things to See

SLO's attractions cluster around **Mission Plaza**, a shady oasis with restored adobes and an amphitheater overlooking San Luis Creek, right in the heart of downtown.

The plaza is lorded over by the **Mission San Luis Obispo de Tolosa** (☎ 805-543-6850; church admission free, museum admission by donation $2; open 9am-5pm daily Apr-Oct, 9am-4pm Nov-Mar) on Monterey St between Chorro and Broad Sts. The fifth of the California missions, it was established in 1772 and named for a French saint. Often called the 'Prince of the Missions,' its church has an unusual L-shape with a flat open-beam ceiling and white-washed walls decorated with the Stations of the Cross. Mass is celebrated regularly (check times). An adjacent building contains an endearingly old-fashioned museum about daily life during the Chumash and mission periods.

For a more comprehensive survey of local history, drop into the **San Luis Obispo County Historical Museum** (☎ 805-543-0638; 696 Monterey St; admission free; open 10am-4pm Wed-Sun), just southwest of the mission. It's housed in the 1904 Carnegie Library, an imposing stone structure.

Mission Plaza is bounded by the gentle San Luis Creek, which is lined with public art and is a nice spot for respite or a picnic. It leads straight to the **San Luis Obispo Art Center** (☎ 805-543-8562; 1010 Broad St; admission free; open 11am-5pm Tues-Sun), a showcase for local artists as well as visiting exhibits from around California.

One block southwest of here, the **Children's Museum** (☎ 805-544-5437; 1010 Nipomo St; adult/child under 2 $5/free; open 11am-5pm Tues-Sat, noon-4pm Sun) has hands-on activities and interactive displays teetering between being educational and fun.

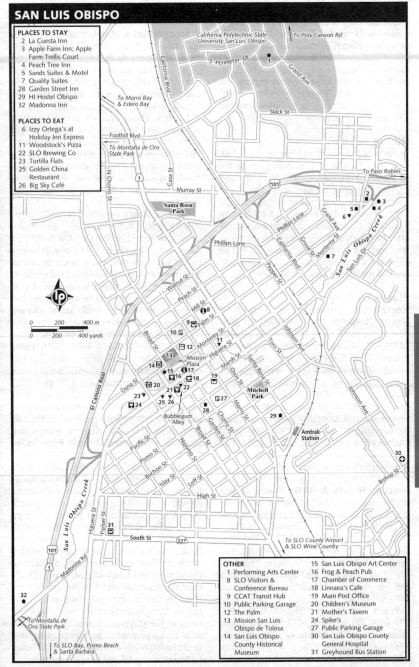

SAN LUIS OBISPO

PLACES TO STAY
2 La Cuesta Inn
3 Apple Farm Inn; Apple
  Farm Trellis Court
4 Peach Tree Inn
5 Sands Suites & Motel
7 Quality Suites
28 Garden Street Inn
29 HI Hostel Obispo
32 Madonna Inn

PLACES TO EAT
6 Izzy Ortega's at
  Holiday Inn Express
11 Woodstock's Pizza
22 SLO Brewing Co
23 Tortilla Flats
25 Golden China
  Restaurant
26 Big Sky Café

OTHER
1 Performing Arts Center
8 SLO Visitors &
  Conference Bureau
9 CCAT Transit Hub
10 Public Parking Garage
12 The Palm
13 Mission San Luis
  Obispo de Tolosa
14 San Luis Obispo
  County Historical
  Museum
15 San Luis Obispo Art Center
16 Frog & Peach Pub
17 Chamber of Commerce
18 Linnaea's Cafe
19 Main Post Office
20 Children's Museum
21 Mother's Tavern
24 Spike's
27 Public Parking Garage
30 San Luis Obispo County
  General Hospital
31 Greyhound Bus Station

CENTRAL COAST

The prize for SLO's 'most bizarre sight' unquestionably goes to **Bubblegum Alley**, a narrow walkway blanketed with thousands of wads of discarded chewing gum. The origin of this local fetish may be murky, but the result bears a vague resemblance to modern art (Jackson Pollock comes to mind) and is both impressive and repulsive. Look for the entrance to the alley between 733 and 737 Higuera St.

Hiking

There are plenty of good hikes around SLO, many of which start from Poly Canyon Rd on the Cal Poly campus. Hiking maps and parking information are available at the booth on the right as you enter the campus. Other popular day hikes lead to Bishop Peak and Cerro San Luis Obispo, which offer panoramic views of San Luis Obispo Bay and the surrounding ranch land. The chamber of commerce has a hiking map and descriptive hiking handout sheet.

Places to Stay

Hostels On a lovely tree-lined street, **HI Hostel Obispo** (☎ 805-544-4678, fax 805-544-3142; 1617 Santa Rosa St; dorm beds $17.50-20, private rooms $40-60; check-in 7:30am-10am & 4:30pm-10pm daily, hostel closed 10am-4:30pm) is a well-kept 20-room facility in a converted Victorian, which gives it a bit of a B&B feel. It's just one minute from the Amtrak station and a 10-minute walk from downtown. Amenities include Internet access, a nicely equipped kitchen and a lounge area with fireplace. For breakfast, host Tom whips up complimentary sourdough pancakes. Parking is free.

Motels, Hotels & B&Bs Motels cluster on the northern end of Monterey St. Smoking is a no-no at most SLO establishments, so check ahead if this is important to you.

La Cuesta Inn (☎ 805-543-2777, 800-543-2777, fax 805-544-0696; w www.lacuesta inn.com; 2074 Monterey St; rooms $89-149) is a 72-room charmer with a pool and Jacuzzi and free continental breakfast, afternoon tea and local calls.

Peach Tree Inn (☎ 805-543-3170, 800-227-6396, fax 805-543-7673; w www.peach treeinn.com; 2001 Monterey St; rooms $60-175) is friendly and folksy, with a flowery lobby. Rates include a hearty breakfast with homemade breads. The creekside rooms are the nicest.

Sands Suites & Motel (☎ 805-544-0500, 800-441-4657, fax 805-544-3529; 1930 Monterey St; rooms Oct-Apr $59-119, May-Sept $129-169) has spacious rooms swathed in a natural color scheme and endowed with a slew of mod-cons. Rates include free continental breakfast and local calls.

Garden Street Inn (☎ 805-545-9802; 1212 Garden St; rooms $90-160) is a lovingly restored 1887 Victorian B&B with 13 theme rooms and suites. Rates include a big breakfast served in a stylish room with original stained-glass windows. In the afternoon, guests gather for complimentary wine and cheese.

Quality Suites (☎ 805-541-5001, 800-228-5151, fax 805-546-9575; 1631 Monterey St; rooms $129-195 Oct-Apr, $169-250 May-Sept), a hacienda-style place, is an excellent bet, with its flower-intense courtyard area, pool and spa. Suites sport refrigerator, microwave, VCR, stereo system and TV. A full cooked-to-order American breakfast and a happy hour with free drinks and snacks are included in the rates.

Apple Farm Inn (☎ 805-544-2040, 800-374-3705, fax 805-546-9495; 2015 Monterey St; rooms $179-399) is SLO's primo in-town facility, even though it's right next to the freeway entrance. It's a flowery Victorian country inn with an antique mill house and a popular restaurant. Rates include free afternoon tea, local calls and newspaper. Slightly cheaper rooms are available at the attached **Apple Farm Trellis Court** (☎ 805-544-2040; rooms $99-279).

Madonna Inn (☎ 805-543-3000, 800-543-9666, fax 805-543-1800; 100 Madonna Rd; rooms $137-330) is a wonderfully over-the-top 'only in America' landmark right off Hwy 1/101. It's worth a stop even if you're not spending the night. Behind the gingerbread exterior awaits a quirky fantasyland Barbie would love: scarlet plastic booths, synthetic flower arrangements, undulating chandeliers and heart-shaped chairs. Don't miss the waterfall urinal in the men's restroom, which is activated when you...activate it. At night, you can discover your inner beast in the Caveman Room (carved from solid rock), pretend to be European royalty in the lavish Austrian Room or live out other fantasies in any of 109 unique rooms.

Places to Eat

SLO has a good range of restaurants, most of them casual establishments. Vegetarians should feel well catered to.

Big Sky Cafe (☎ *805-545-5401; 1121 Broad St; dishes $6-16*) is a hip and friendly spot which serves New Millennium cuisine with a down-home touch. Tuck into such global fare as blackened chicken salad or the popular Big Sky noodle bowl while seated at sturdy tables in the lofty dining room that doubles as a gallery. It serves good breakfasts too.

Golden China Restaurant (☎ *805-543-7354; 685 Higuera St; all-you-can-eat lunch/dinner buffet $6.95/10.95, mains $7-19*) woos those with big appetites and small wallets. If the huge buffet doesn't appeal, you can also order à la carte.

Izzy Ortega's (☎ *805-543-3333; 1850 Monterey St; mains $9-15*), inside the Holiday Inn Express, is a lively place with a pleasing south-of-the-border selection.

SLO Brewing Co (☎ *805-543-1843; 1119 Garden St; dishes $6-10*) is a popular brewpub whose homemade beers go well with its burgers, grilled meats and fish and large salads. There's billiards downstairs and live music Thursday to Saturday.

Tortilla Flats (☎ *805-544-7575; 1051 Nipomo St; mains $8-15*) is a sprawling cantina which is as famous for its special meal deals (like the lunchtime all-you-can-eat taco and fajita bar for $6.95) as it is for its 80 different tequilas and raucous happy hours.

Woodstock's Pizza (☎ *805-541-4420; 1000 Higuera St; slices $1.75, pizzas from $14.25*) is SLO's landmark pizza joint – fast, greasy and always crowded. Pizzas come on white or whole-wheat crust. From 11am to 3pm Monday to Friday, $6 buys all the pizza you can eat.

Entertainment

Frog & Peach Pub (☎ *805-595-3764; 728 Higuera St*) wears the patina – and smell – of an old-style British pub with pride. Come for a pint of ale, a game of darts or the live music on weekends.

Mother's Tavern (☎ *805-541-3853; 729 Higuera St; pub meals $3.50-6.50*), across the street, gets enthusiastic thumbs up from locals for its fun decor, live entertainment and honest prices. Its pub grub menu (burgers, nachos, salads and the like) is excellent value.

Linnaea's Cafe (☎ *805-541-5888; 1110 Garden St*), a friendly coffeehouse, goes for the low-key crowd. It has an artsy vibe and a serene back patio anchored by a little fish pond. Folk and acoustic guitarists sometimes take to the stage.

Spike's (☎ *805-544-7157; 570 Higuera St*) is a beer-lover's dream, with around 40 different brews available (25 on tap). If somehow you manage to guzzle one of each, you get a wall plaque to commemorate what's left of your liver. The bar is part of The Creamery, a historic complex converted into an art gallery space.

The Palm (☎ *805-541-5161; 817 Palm St; admission Tues-Sun $6.50, Mon $4*) is an old-style independent movie house showing foreign and classic films nightly.

Performing Arts Center (☎ *805-756-2787, 888-237-8787; 1 Grand Ave*), a state-of-the-art facility on the Cal Poly campus, is the town's main cultural venue and presents an eclectic schedule of concerts, theater, dance and other events.

Getting There & Away

The small **SLO County Airport** (☎ *805-541-1038*), 3mi south of downtown between Hwy 1/101 and Broad St, is served by America West, American Airlines and United Airlines, with scheduled services to Los Angeles, San Francisco and Phoenix (Arizona).

Greyhound (☎ *805-543-2121; 150 South St*) runs six daily buses to Los Angeles ($26.25, four to six hours) via Santa Barbara ($18, two to three hours), and up to eight to San Francisco ($40.50, 5½ to seven hours).

Regional buses operated by **Central Coast Area Transit** (CCAT; ☎ *805-541-2228*) travel north to Morro Bay, Cambria and San Simeon and south to the SLO Bay communities, including Pismo Beach. Another route goes to Paso Robles. There are stops throughout town, but lines converge at the **transit hub** (cnr Palm & Osos Sts). Fares depend on distance, and unlimited day passes cost $3; drivers don't make change. Schedules are available at the chamber of commerce.

SLO is the northern terminus of Amtrak's *Pacific Surfliner*, with daily services to destinations such as Santa Barbara, Los Angeles and San Diego. The *Coast Starlight* between Seattle and Los Angeles (via Sacramento) also stops at SLO daily. The Amtrak station is at the southern end of Santa Rosa St.

CENTRAL COAST

Getting Around

SLO's downtown is best explored on foot, though the foot-weary can hop on the free **SLO Trolley** *(noon-5pm daily, to 9pm Thur during farmers market)*, which loops around Marsh, Higuera, Nipomo, Monterey and Palm Sts.

SLO Transit (☎ *805-541-2277)* operates local buses, including regular trips to the Cal Poly campus. Fares are $0.75. An excellent service is provided by the nonprofit **Ride-On Transportation** (☎ *805-541-8747)*, which offers 'Safe Rides' within SLO for just $2 between 9pm and 3am Thursday, Friday and Saturday night. Just call ☎ 235-SAFE (☎ 235-7233) when you need them. Ride-On also runs tours to Hearst Castle for $40/30 per adult/child, including admission, on selected days.

ESTERO BAY

Estero Bay is a long, shallow, west-facing bay with Cayucos at its northern end and Montaña de Oro State Park at its southern end. Morro Bay, a deep inlet guarded by Morro Rock and separated from the ocean by a 12mi-long sand spit, sits about halfway between the two and has most of Estero Bay's services and tourist activity. Morro Rock is the bay's unmistakable landmark, used as a navigation marker since the Portolá expedition in 1769.

Getting Around

Central Coast Area Transit (see Getting Around in the San Luis Obispo section) bus No 12 travels up Hwy 1 from San Luis Obispo as far north as San Simeon, with stops in Los Osos, Morro Bay, Cayucos and Cambria. The fare depends on the distance traveled but tops out at $2.25 each way.

Montaña de Oro State Park

About 6mi southwest of Morro Bay, Montaña de Oro State Park covers about 13,000 acres of undeveloped mountain and seaside terrain. Its coastal bluffs are a favorite spot for hiking, mountain biking and horseback riding. The northern half of the park includes a row of sand dunes (some 85ft high) and the 4mi-long sand spit that separates Morro Bay from the Pacific. The park's southern section consists of finger-like bluffs and an ancient marine terrace, which after seismic uplifting is now a series of 1000ft

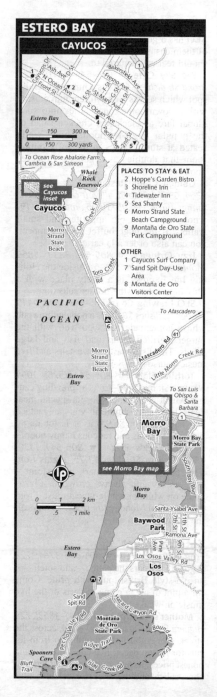

ESTERO BAY

CAYUCOS

PLACES TO STAY & EAT
2 Hoppe's Garden Bistro
3 Shoreline Inn
4 Tidewater Inn
5 Sea Shanty
6 Morro Strand State
   Beach Campground
9 Montaña de Oro State
   Park Campground

OTHER
1 Cayucos Surf Company
7 Sand Spit Day-Use
   Area
8 Montaña de Oro
   Visitors Center

peaks. In spring the hills are blanketed by bright poppies, wild mustard and other wildflowers that give the park its name, meaning 'mountain of gold' in Spanish.

The park's **Visitor Center** (☎ 805-528-0513; open 11am-3pm daily Apr-Aug, 11am-3pm Thur-Sun Sept-Mar), about 3mi south of the park boundary, does triple duty as a ranger station and natural history museum. It sits right above **Spooners Cove**, once used by smugglers and now a beautiful sandy beach and picnic area. Several **hiking trails**, including the Bluff Trail, which skirts the cliffs and has beach access points, start from here. To get to the sand dunes, turn off onto Sand Spit Rd from the main park road to the **Sand Spit Day-Use Area**, about 1.8mi north of the visitor center.

A short walk east of the visitor center is the lovely **Montaña de Oro State Park Campground** (☎ 805-528-0513, reservations ☎ 800-444-7275; campsites $7) with 50 sites, each near the creek or against the hillside. Fees include use of picnic tables, fire pits and pit toilets and drinking water, but no showers.

The park is about 7mi from Hwy 1. Exit at South Bay Blvd and follow the signs, which will lead you through the towns of Los Osos and Baywood Park.

Morro Bay

Still home to a large commercial fishing fleet, the biggest claim to fame of Morro Bay (population 9700) is its namesake **Morro Rock**, a 578ft peak that juts dramatically from the ocean floor just offshore. It's part of a chain of nine such volcanic rocks stretching between here and San Luis Obispo, which formed some 21 million years ago. Unfortunately, panoramic views of the bay and rock are compromised by a trio of cigarette-shaped smokestacks of a coal power plant, which inexplicably squats at the bay's northern end.

The bay itself is a giant estuary inhabited by two dozen threatened and endangered species, including the brown pelican, sea otter and steelhead trout. Morro Rock is home to peregrine falcons. In winter, about 120 migratory bird species make the bay their home.

Leading south from Morro Rock is the **Embarcadero**, a fairly scruffy waterfront walkway lined with touristy shops and restaurants. It's the launching area for boat tours (see Activities later) and the main stage of

the popular Morro Bay Harbor Festival in October. Also here is the **Morro Bay Aquarium** (☎ 805-772-7647; admission $2; open 9:30am-5:30pm daily, 9:30am-6pm May-Sept), a sad marine life exhibit entered through a gift shop. There are captive seals and ancient, cramped tanks that will undoubtedly have animal rights activists recoiling in horror.

Three blocks inland from the Embarcadero is the much more pleasant Main St with interesting shopping and the local **chamber of commerce** (☎ 805-772-4467, 800-231-0592, fax 805-772-6038; w www .morrobay.com; 880 Main St; open 8am-5pm Mon-Fri, 10am-3pm Sat).

Morro Bay State Park This 1965-acre state park incorporates an 18-hole golf course, a marina with kayak rentals and a campground. Also here is the **Museum of Natural History** (☎ 805-772-2694; adult/ child $3/1; open 10am-5pm daily), which was being overhauled at the time of writing. New exhibits will examine the impact of oceanic, atmospheric, geologic and human forces on the environment and shed light on how living things adapt to changes.

Just north of the museum is a eucalyptus grove that harbors the **Heron Rookery State Reserve**, one of the last remaining great blue heron rookeries in California; from late February to May, you can spot them feeding their young.

Activities The paddle wheeler **Tiger's Folly II** (☎ 805-772-2257; 1205 Embarcadero) makes trips around the harbor daily from May to September and on weekends in winter; check-in at Harbor Hut Restaurant (see Places to Stay & Eat). The one-hour cruises cost $10/5 adult/child.

For views of kelp forests and schools of fish, take a spin on **Seaview** (☎ 805-772-9463; 699 Embarcadero No 8), a semi-sub which plies the waters daily; it departs from the Embarcadero at the bottom of Pacific St. Tours cost $12.50/5.50 adult/child.

If you'd rather explore the area under your own steam, rent a canoe or kayak from **Canoe 2 U** (☎ 805-772-3349; 699 Embarcadero No 9) next door. Rentals start at $4 per person per half-hour or $19.50 per half-day.

Salty types ready to try their hand at sportfishing could book a trip with **Virg's**

MORRO BAY

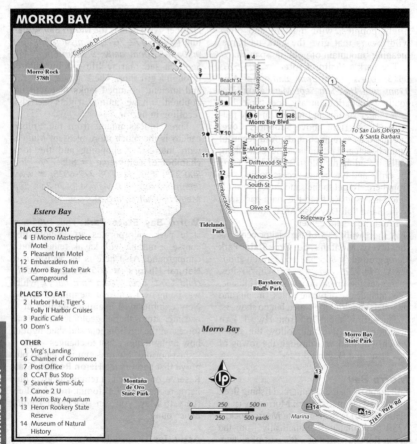

Morro Rock
578ft

Coleman Dr

Embarcadero

Beach St

Dunes St

Harbor St

Morro Bay Blvd

Pacific St

Marina St

Driftwood St

Anchor St

South St

Olive St

Ridgeway St

Market Ave

Monterey St

Shasta Ave

Bernardo Ave

Kern Ave

To San Luis Obispo
& Santa Barbara

Morro Ave

Main St

Embarcadero

Estero Bay

Tidelands
Park

Bayshore
Bluffs Park

Morro Bay

Montaña
de Oro
State Park

Morro Bay
State Park

State Park Rd

Marina

PLACES TO STAY
4 El Morro Masterpiece
   Motel
5 Pleasant Inn Motel
12 Embarcadero Inn
15 Morro Bay State Park
   Campground

PLACES TO EAT
2 Harbor Hut; Tiger's
   Folly II Harbor Cruises
3 Pacific Café
10 Dorn's

OTHER
1 Virg's Landing
6 Chamber of Commerce
7 Post Office
8 CCAT Bus Stop
9 Seaview Semi-Sub;
   Canoe 2 U
11 Morro Bay Aquarium
13 Heron Rookery State
   Reserve
14 Museum of Natural
   History

0   250   500 m
0   250   500 yards

Landing (☎ *805-772-1222, 800-762-5263; 1215 Embarcadero*). Daily trips cost \$28/ 40 half/full day; poles rent for \$6/8. An open ocean license is required and can be purchased at Virg's.

Places to Stay & Eat North of town, Morro Strand State Beach Campground (☎ *805-772-8812, reservations ☎ 800-444-7275; campsites \$12*) has 81 sites behind the sand dunes. There are flush toilets and cold showers but no hookups.

Morro Bay State Park Campground (☎ *805-772-7434, reservations ☎ 800-444-7275; tent/RV sites \$12/18*), about 2mi south of town, has beautiful sites fringed by eucalyptus and cypress trees. It has hot water, and trails leading to the beach.

Motels cluster along Main and Harbor Sts. Rates drop in the off-season, but make reservations in summer and in the Harbor Festival.

Pleasant Inn Motel (☎ *805-772-8521, 888-772-8521, fax 805-772-1550; w www .pleasantinnmotel.com; 235 Harbor St; rooms \$49-90*) is a flower-festooned place which does justice to its name. It has a B&B-type flair and 10 prettily appointed rooms, some with kitchens.

El Morro Masterpiece Motel (☎ *805-772-5633, 800-527-6782, fax 805-772-1404; w www.masterpiecemotel.com; 1206 Main St; rooms \$69-325*) sports the look of a Mediterranean castle and is decorated with framed art throughout. The staff are friendly and rooms are good-sized with a relaxed European-style ambience.

Embarcadero Inn (☎ 805-772-2700, 800-292-7625, fax 805-772-1060; w www.emb arcaderoinn.com; 456 Embarcadero; rooms $95-225) makes for a friendly Morro Bay base. Most of the large rooms have balconies with views of 'The Rock' and all feature upscale baths, VCRs and refrigerators. Some also have gas fireplaces. Rates include continental breakfast and daily newspaper.

Going strong since 1942, **Dorn's** (☎ 805-772-4415; 801 Market Ave; breakfast $4.50-11, lunch $7.50-16, dinner $9-25) is famous for its clam chowder, fresh fish and extensive wine list. The decor is elegant, but anything goes attire-wise.

Harbor Hut (☎ 805-772-2255; 1205 Embarcadero; lunch $8-17, dinner $15-34) has tropical tiki looks, a casual ambience and a menu heavy on steaks and seafood.

Pacific Café (☎ 805-772-2965; 1150 Embarcadero; dinner $12-17) is a locals' favorite, with a congenial owner/chef who's a master at classic Mediterranean fare and a wine connoisseur to boot.

Cayucos

At the bay's northern end, small and slow-paced Cayucos (ki-**you**-kiss; population 3400) preserves the look and feel of an old Western town. It's cheaper and less commercial than Morro Bay, but even here times are a-changing; simply take a look at the grand new homes fringing the broad white beach.

The town developed around the mouth of Cayucos Creek and a wharf and warehouse built by Captain James Cass in 1867. Ocean Ave, which parallels Hwy 1, is the main thoroughfare with historic storefronts and most of the hotels and restaurants. At the town's northern end is the long pier, built in 1875, from which you can fish without a license.

Cayucos' gentle waves are good for beginner surfers. **Cayucos Surf Company** (☎ 805-995-1000; 95 Cayucos Dr), just a few steps north of the pier, rents surfboards for $10/20 half/full day, and other gear as well.

Places to Stay & Eat Just half a block from the beach, **Tidewater Inn** (☎ 805-995-3670, 800-965-2699; 20 S Ocean Ave; rooms midweek $55-65, weekend $75-85) is a small motel sporting spiffy, newly renovated rooms sporting flowery decor.

Shoreline Inn (☎ 805-995-3681; 1 N Ocean Ave; rooms mid-Sept–mid-May $75-95,

suites $95-134; rooms mid-May–mid-Sept $105-123, suites $105-150), right on the beach near the pier, offers excellent value. All rooms have balconies with ocean views, but the suites are a bit bigger and have more modern furnishings.

Hoppe's Garden Bistro (☎ 805-995-1006; 78 N Ocean Ave; lunch $8-14, dinner $12-28) is a California-French gourmet eatery offering big-city sophistication at small-town prices.

Sea Shanty (☎ 805-995-3272; 296 S Ocean Ave; dishes $4-18) is unpretentious, funky and eccentric, and offers a down-home diner menu plus a slew of tantalizing desserts. There's a supermarket across the street.

Ocean Rose Abalone Farm

Pretty it ain't, this milky-white, glutinous mollusk named abalone. Yet it's prized as the ultimate delicacy – not to mention aphrodisiac – by culinary connoisseurs around the world. Once so abundant off the central coast of California that you could just pluck them out of the water, their numbers have been dwindling severely in the last four decades due to pollution, overharvesting and the loss of habitat. Commercial fishing was outlawed in 1998, making abalone farms the only legal purveyors of these slimy creatures. One such farm is Ocean Rose Abalone Farm (☎ 805-995-2495; w www.abalonefarm.com), about 4mi north of Cayucos, where about one million California red abalone are raised from infancy to adulthood in about four years. For a fascinating look at how it's done, join a tour ($3) offered by appointment on Saturday and Sunday between May and September. To get there, turn west toward the ocean off Hwy 1 onto Villa Creek Rd and follow the short dirt road to the farm.

CAMBRIA

About ½mi inland, Cambria (population 5400) is a cutesy village whose lively Main St is lined with mostly tourist-oriented knickknacks stores and art galleries wedged in between B&Bs, inns and restaurants. The crowds can get a bit too much in summer, but from October to May this is a pleasant place to while away an afternoon or spend the night.

Fans of the crazy and curious should make a beeline for **Nit Wit Ridge** (☎ 805-927-2690; 881 Hillcrest Dr), a three-level house built entirely out of recycled materials – abalone shells to beer cans, tiles to toilet seats. This 'palace of junk' is the creation of one Arthur Harold Beal (aka Captain Nit Wit, aka Der Tinkerpaw) and was hand-built by him over a period of 51 years. Beal died in 1992, but his life's work can still be admired during tours, which are offered by appointment from 9am to 4pm daily for $10/8/5 adult/concession/child.

Cambria's coast hugs **Moonstone Beach**, named for the opalescent stones once abundant here. It has low bluffs and a sand beach across from a strip of mid- and high-priced motels. At the beach's northern end, **Leffingwell Landing** offers dramatic views and a picnic area shaded by Monterey cypress trees.

South of Cambria, off Hwy 1, minuscule **Harmony** (population 18) is a quirky slice of Americana. It consists of an old creamery housing artists' workshops and deserves a quick browse.

For information, drop in at the village's **chamber of commerce** (☎ 805-927-3624; 767 Main St).

Places to Stay & Eat

Cambria's choicest lodgings are along Moonstone Beach Dr, but those in the village are more affordable.

Bridge Street Inn (☎ 805-927-7653; 4314 Bridge St; www.bridgestreetinncambria.com; bunk beds $20, rooms $40-70) is a B&B cum hostel with character, charm and comfort by the bucket at prices a pauper can afford. Prices include breakfast, use of the communal kitchen and parking. It's small, so call ahead for reservations.

The Bluebird (☎ 805-927-4634, 800-552-5434, fax 805-927-5215; 1880 Main St; rooms $40-140 Apr-Oct, $48-180 Nov-Mar), with a peaceful and fragrant garden overlooking a creek, has imaginatively appointed rooms, including some with fireplace and private terrace or balcony.

Creekside Inn (☎ 805-927-4021, 800-269-5212; 2618 Main St; w www.moonstone hotels.com; rooms $59-149) has 23 rooms, including some with a balcony facing a creek. Rates include a small continental breakfast.

Cambria Shores Inn (☎ 805-927-8644, 800-433-9179, fax 805-927-4070; w www.cambriashores.com; 6276 Moonstone Beach Dr; rooms $89-160), on the beach, looks like a motel but comes with B&B-type amenities

such as in-room gourmet breakfasts and a free appetizer hour. It's pet-friendly.

Linn's (☎ 805-927-0371; 2277 Main St; dishes $5.50-14) is a casual eatery with high ceilings and art-covered walls. It's famous for pot pies and outlandish desserts, but the menu is extensive enough to satisfy just about any craving.

Robin's (☎ 805-927-5007; 4095 Burton Dr; lunch $5.50-13, dinner $11-17) serves dishes from around the globe, and tofu and tempeh too. Portions are big and lines are long, especially if you've got your eye on a table on the lovely vine-clad patio.

More formal dinner-only places include **Sow's Ear Cafe** (☎ 805-927-4865; 2248 Main St; mains $13-23) and **Brambles Dinner House** (☎ 805-927-4716; 4005 Burton Dr; mains $10-22), both of which serve classic continental food.

SAN SIMEON

San Simeon (population 360) began life in the 1850s as a whaling station. In 1865, George Hearst bought 45,000 acres of land and established a beachside settlement on the western side of Hwy 1, across from today's entrance to Hearst Castle. The Hearst Corporation still owns most of the land here, and the Julia Morgan houses (formerly inhabited by Hearst Castle staff) are now home to the cowboys who run the corporation's 80,000-acre cattle ranch.

Adjacent to the houses, **Hearst Memorial State Beach** (day-use fee $2) has a pleasant sandy stretch with intermittent rock outcroppings and a rickety wooden pier (fishing permitted).

Three miles south of the original San Simeon (just off the Hearst Corporation's property), the town of San Simeon is a mile-long strip of unexciting motels and equally unimpressive restaurants.

The **chamber of commerce** (☎ 805-927-3500, 800-342-5613; 9511 Hearst Dr) can provide information on lodging and other topics.

There are better places to stay in Cambria or points further south which are still close to Hearst Castle, but if you must spend the night, try **Silver Surf Motel** (☎ 805-927-4661, 800-621-3999, fax 805-927-3225; 9390 Castillo Dr; rooms $49-104). It's nothing special but it's decent value for money and has a small indoor pool and spa.

California Seacoast Lodge (☎ 805-927-3878; 9215 Hearst Dr; rooms $89-169) has frilly rooms – think drapes, antiques and overstuffed armchairs – equipped with all mod-cons. Some have ocean views, and breakfast is included.

San Simeon State Park

San Simeon State Park (☎ 805-927-2035) embraces the **San Simeon Natural Preserve**, a popular wintering spot for monarch butterflies, and the **Pānu Cultural Preserve**, the site of archeological finds dating back 6000 years. A 3mi trail meanders through the park, which is fringed by a long sandy beach. Camping is available at the 134-site **San Simeon Creek Campground** (reservations ☎ 800-444-7275; campsites $12) with hot showers and flush toilets, and the undeveloped **Washburn Campground** (campsites $7), with 60 sites, which are allocated on a first-come, first-served basis.

HEARST CASTLE

Imagine driving up the winding road to the imposing castle looming above and arriving there for dinner at the 50ft dining table. Charlie Chaplin is to your right, a reigning queen is on your left and the newest screen heartthrob is batting eyes at you over the roast pheasant. All of this takes place under the intense scrutiny of newspaper magnate William Randolph Hearst – one of the most powerful men in the world – who literally launched the Spanish-American War to sell his newspapers. Well, you never made the list of the world's most desirable dinner guests, but you can still relive the moment at Hearst Castle.

Perched high on a hill dubbed 'The Enchanted Hill' by Hearst, and overlooking vast pastureland and the Pacific Ocean, Hearst Castle (recorded message ☎ 805-927-2020; w www.hearst-castle.org) is a monument to wealth and ambition. The estate sprawls out over 127 acres of lushly landscaped gardens, accentuated by shimmering pools and fountains and statues from ancient Greece and Moorish Spain. It has 165 rooms in four houses, all of them furnished with Italian and Spanish antiques and enhanced by 41 fireplaces and 61 bathrooms. There's a lavish private chapel and numerous entertainment rooms.

Hearst's art collection was so vast that an accurate calculation of its size or value was

never possible. Spanish cathedral ceilings covered with flags from the Palio in Siena, Italy, hover above a French refectory table. The display of wealth borders on the grotesque, and the amalgam of styles and periods is enough to make any architect or historian grimace. But to visit the castle is to 'ooh' and 'aah' at Hearst's casual, if clumsy, attempt at becoming royal. And the subterranean Roman pool, where Errol Flynn and his ilk dallied, is worth the price of admission all by itself.

Information

Hearst Castle, a state historical monument, is open for tours daily except on Thanksgiving, Christmas and New Year's Day. The first tour starts at 8:20am; the last leaves at 3:20pm (later in summer). The castle is inundated with visitors between May and September and on holiday weekends, so reservations are advised. Call ☎ 800-444-4445 (☎ 916-414-8400 from overseas) or go online.

All tours start at the visitor center at the bottom of the hill. Besides the ticket office, you'll find a surprisingly bad snack bar, an espresso bar and two gift shops. There's also a free exhibit that looks at the various roles Hearst played during his lifetime; you don't need tour tickets to see it.

Also at the visitor center is the **National Geographic Theater** (☎ 805-927-6811), with its five-story large-screen theater, which shows a saccharine but nonetheless interesting 40-minute film on Hearst's life, the construction of the castle and daily life up there.

Admission to the theater is included in Tour 1. If you're on another tour but still want to see the movie, you can get discounted tickets for $6/4 adult/child; otherwise admission is $7.50/5.50.

Organized Tours

There are four tours of the estate; all include visits to the estate's stunning Greco-Roman outdoor Neptune Pool and the indoor Roman Pool, lined with gold and Venetian glass. Tour 1 costs $14/7 adult/child six to 17. Tours 2, 3 and 4 cost $10/5 and the evening Tour 5 $20/10. Tours 1 to 4 last 1¼ hours, including the ride up to the castle and back to the visitor center. The evening tour takes 2¼ hours. Tour frequency range from one per hour in winter to up to six per hour at peak times.

The Man & His Castle: William Randolph Hearst

It's certain that absolute power combined with unlimited wealth accounts for some of the most heinous architecture in all of history. Witness the Orwellian hell dreamed up by mobsters in Las Vegas, or the warped grotesqueries visited on Germany by those mental midgets of the Third Reich. Great wealth and taste are mutually exclusive: the filthily moneyed should be drawn and quartered if ever they utter the word: 'blueprints.' But build their piles they will, à la Trump, and the rest of us just have to put up with their monumental droppings.

But occasionally these lurid legacies in concrete and Carborundum are of such a scale and lunacy that they become endearing. Witness Hearst Castle, where a spirited 'little boy' with unlimited 'building blocks' went quietly off his nut. No-one in the kingdom of William Randolph Hearst ever said, 'Uh, Bill...Don't you think a hundred rooms might *almost* be enough?' Nope. Bill's rooms propagated like spastic spores until they reached 165. Their combined impact seems to have been designed by an architectural firm formed by Dolly Parton, Louis XIV and the Three Stooges. But hell, it made Bill happy.

Born into great wealth in San Francisco, Hearst was 10 years old when his mother took him on a grand tour of Europe. There, he developed his lifelong appetites for art and culture. But taste? Perhaps he missed Paris...He then went on to Harvard and journalism. Grasping his father's *Examiner* newspaper in 1887 and a following $20 million fortune, he proved a genius at making enemies. The mere mention of his name made politicians as twitchy as chipmunks in a mustard gas attack. His papers covered stories – true or not – that others wouldn't touch. And if there were no stories, well...headlines such as 'Spaniards Rape American Women in Cuba!' (which didn't happen) helped launch the Spanish–American War. Didn't bother Bill and, boy, did he sell a *lot* of newspapers!

Hearst eventually built a tremendous empire of more than 50 papers across USA and then turned his attention to building his 'private home.' The mere sound of its name – La Cuesta Encantada or, the Enchanted Hill – should have sent the local elephant seal colony swimming for Japan. He hired architect Julia Morgan to turn his fancies into reality. Reality simply frog-marched off a cliff. Morgan should have headed off with the seals.

Continually jerked around by Hearst among various wings and salons, her work soon took on surreal proportions. It had to house, after all, Hearst's lust for art – *and* his girlfriend, Hollywood actress Marion Davies. As Hearst hauled in cathedral ceilings and Roman columns, Morgan did her best to rake his accumulation into something habitable. Bill and Marion wooed Hollywood's elite to weekends where they played tennis and cavorted in grottos amid the chaos. And if ever things got a little banal, why, they all just drove off through Hearst's zoo – tootling the disoriented ostriches and giraffes that must have thought they were in a bad movie.

When Hearst died in 1951 – his reputation as bon vivant extraordinaire secure throughout the realms of the rich – his enormous unfinished project mercifully ended. He was, finally, nothing at all like the embittered 'King Lear' portrayed in *Citizen Kane*, the Orson Welles film supposedly based on his life. By contrast, reports from Hearst's last years reveal a man who seemed, in spite of his bizarre excesses, oddly content. It is unknown if the giraffes shared that opinion.

David Peevers

Tour 1 This 1¾-hour tour is the best for first-timers. In Casa Grande, the main house, you'll visit the huge Assembly sitting room, the refectory (dining room), the Billiard Room and the theater where old home movies of celebrities frolicking at the castle are shown. You'll also see the esplanade, gardens and the Casa del Sol guest cottage.

Tour 2 This tour shows off the upper floors of Casa Grande, including Hearst's Gothic-style private suite and study, the library with 5000 books and ancient Greek vases, the well-equipped and surprisingly modern pantry and kitchen, and the beautiful Doge Suite, modeled after the Doge's Palace in Venice.

Tour 3 Good for those interested in architecture, this tour takes you to the northern wing of Casa Grande, which is the least altered part of the entire estate and was built during Hearst's final years (it's totally different from anything else). You'll also see a video about the construction of Hearst Castle as well as all rooms of Casa del Monte, a 10-room guest cottage.

Tour 4 This tour, available April to October, shows a 'hidden terrace and gardens,' once part of the original plans but covered up in later construction and rediscovered during more recent restoration. The tour also covers the esplanade, a guest cottage, the pool dressing rooms and the wine cellar of Casa Grande.

Tour 5 Offered in spring and fall only, the hugely popular evening tours feature docents in period dress 'acting' as Hearst's guests and staff. Besides touring the most extraordinary rooms of Casa Grande, you'll also see the guest cottage Casa del Mar and the pools and gardens illuminated by hundreds of lights.

PIEDRAS BLANCAS

The coastline north of San Simeon, called Piedras Blancas, is home to California's largest colony of elephant seals, with about 7500 members. From the vista point about 4.5mi north of Hearst Castle, you can observe them wallowing in the sand, swatting away flies, battling each other for turf and chasing their next meal in the ocean. Interpretative panels and docents are around to demystify the behavior of these humongous

mammals. The seals are at their most plentiful between December and February, when you might even be so lucky as to witness a female giving birth. To learn more, drop in at the office of **The Friends of the Elephant Seal** (☎ 805-924-1628; **w** *www.elephantseal.org*) in San Simeon next to the chamber of commerce (see San Simeon earlier in this chapter). See also the boxed text 'Elephant Seals' in the San Francisco Bay chapter.

BIG SUR

Big Sur is an experience rather than one tangible place. Its raw beauty is awe inspiring, its quirky residents endearing. There are no traffic lights, banks or shopping centers, and when the sun goes down, the moon and stars are the only streetlights.

Although there are buses from Monterey to the northern sections of Big Sur, the area is best explored by car, since you'll be itching to stop frequently to take in the rugged beauty and stunning vistas that reveal themselves after every hairpin turn. Note that from June to mid-August, the coast is often shrouded by thick fog.

Although it's only 90mi from San Simeon to Carmel, driving along this narrow two-lane highway is slow going, especially in summer when traffic is dense and passing slower vehicles is difficult and dangerous. Allow at least four hours to cover the distance and be on the lookout for cyclists as well. Traveling after dark is perilous and futile, since you won't be able to see any of the countryside. Keep this in mind, especially if you're in the area during short winter days.

History

The Esselen tribe, known to date back at least 3000 years in the area, occupied settlements along the coast, surviving primarily on acorns, rabbit, deer, bear and sea mammals. They were wiped out by diseases brought by the Spanish before the first US settlers arrived.

Big Sur was named by Spanish settlers living in Carmel's mission who referred to the unexplored wilderness as *el pais grande del sur* (the big country to the south). They named the two coastal rivers *el rio grande del sur* (the big river to the south) and *el rio chiquito del sur* (the little river to the south).

In 1852, John Rogers Cooper (also known as Juan Bautista Rogerio Cooper) filed

BIG SUR

claim to Rancho El Sur, stretching from Cooper Point to the mouth of the Little Sur River. Cooper Point and the headquarters for the ranch are now part of Andrew Molera State Park.

Homesteaders arrived in the early 1900s and supported the canning and lumbering industries. At the turn of the 20th century, Big Sur supported a larger population than it does today. Electricity arrived in the 1950s and TV reception in the 1980s.

In the 1950s and '60s, Big Sur became a favorite retreat for writers and artists, including Henry Miller, who lived here from 1947 to 1964, and Beat Generation members Lawrence Ferlinghetti and Jack Kerouac. Today, Big Sur still attracts its share of New Age mystics and 'artistic' and eccentric types.

Orientation & Information

Visitors often wander into businesses along Hwy 1 and ask, 'How much further to Big Sur?' In fact, there is no *town* of Big Sur as such, though you may see the name on maps. Commercial activity is concentrated along the stretch between Andrew Molera State Park and Pfeiffer Big Sur State Park. Sometimes called 'The Village,' this is where you'll find most of the shops, restaurants and lodging options, including campgrounds; the post office is here as well.

Just south of Pfeiffer is the **Big Sur Ranger Station** (☎ 831-667-2315; open 8am-6pm daily late May–early Sept, 8am-4:30pm rest of year), a good source for information about Los Padres National Forest, the Ventana Wilderness and the state parks. In southern Big Sur, just south of the turnoff to the Nacimiento-Fergusson Rd, is the **Pacific Valley Ranger Station** (☎ 805-927-4211; open 9am-6pm daily May-Sept, Mon-Fri only Oct-Apr).

El Sur Grande, a free newspaper updated annually, is available at nearly every stop and is packed with useful addresses and tips. For a preview check the website **w** www.bigsurcalifornia.org.

The nearest hospital is **Community Hospital** (☎ 831-624-5311) in Monterey, just north of the junction of Hwy 1 and Hwy 68.

Southern Big Sur

For the first 40mi to 45mi of Big Sur – between San Simeon and the Esalen Institute – Hwy 1 is comparatively straight and there is a wider sweep of lowlands between mountain and sea. The landscape is barren and wild compared to Big Sur's river-fed valley further north, and services are few and far between.

Your first taste of Big Sur grandeur comes at **Ragged Point**, a craggy cliff outcropping with fabulous views in both directions of the coastline, about 15mi north of San Simeon. It was originally part of the Hearst empire and is now occupied by a hotel and restaurant called the **Ragged Point Inn & Resort** (☎ 805-927-4502; **w** www.raggedpointinn.com; rooms $89-209; lunch $6-12, dinner $14-23).

Next up is **Gorda** (Spanish for 'Fat'), named for an offshore outcroppings that looks like a fat lady and is now a tourist trap with an overpriced general store and gas station. You can overnight at the **Gorda Springs Resort** (☎ 805-927-3918; studios & cottages $175-325) and fill your belly at **Whale Watchers Café** (☎ 805-927-3918; mains $10-29), but you can probably do better elsewhere.

A few miles north of Gorda is the most scenic stretch of southern Big Sur. In the waters of **Jade Cove** three divers, in 1971, recovered a 9000lb jade boulder that measured 8ft long and brought in $180,000. People still comb the beach today. The best time to find jade, which is black or blue-green and looks dull until you dip it in water, is during low tide or after a big storm.

One of the nicest campgrounds in Big Sur is **Plaskett Creek Campground** (information ☎ 805-434-1996; campsites $16, for hikers & cyclists $5, day-use $5, includes access to Sand Dollar and Pfeiffer beaches), about 2mi

north of Jade Cove. It has 44 spacious first-come, first-served sites shaded by Monterey cypress. There are flush toilets but no showers. A short walk north is the turnoff for the **Sand Dollar Beach picnic area** (day-use $5), from where it's about a five-minute walk down to the area's longest sandy beach.

Next up you'll pass the aforementioned Pacific Valley Ranger Station before coming upon the turnoff to the Nacimiento-Fergusson Rd, which cuts through the forest and connects with Hwy 101 after about 40mi. A worthwhile stop en route is at the Mission San Antonio de Padua (see the section Inland Along Hwy 101 later in this chapter).

The road also gives access to a couple of first-come, first served campgrounds: **Nacimiento** (campsites $8) and, about 2mi further east, the nicer **Ponderosa** (campsites $12), set along a trout stream. Sites have fire pits and tables and there are vault toilets. The Nacimiento Ridge gives views of the ocean and eastern foothills of the Santa Lucia Range.

Back on Hwy 1 are a couple more campgrounds. **Kirk Creek Campground** (walk-ins $5, campsites $16) is a beautiful site on a sunny bluff above the ocean. There are flush toilets but no showers. About 2mi further north is **Limekiln State Park**, whose campground (☎ 831-667-2403, reservations ☎ 800-444-7275; campsites $12, day-use $3) sits right by the entrance tucked under a bridge next to the ocean; it has flush toilets and free hot showers. The park gets

Driving Highway 1

Completed in 1937, after 18 years of construction (mostly with convict labor), Hwy 1 is California's first Scenic Highway, and it certainly deserves the title. The curvy two-lane road isn't meant for quick travel; driving straight from Carmel to San Luis Obispo takes about five hours. Taking in the brilliant coastal scenery here is mandatory: Towering, golden cliffs plummet down to the rock-strewn sea, which can change from peacock blue to the deep purple of a marlin's back in a heartbeat. If you're a shutterbug, load up on film and plan on spending all the daylight hours making the trip. You will, quite literally, find yourself pulling off the road every hundred yards or so for that perfect shot. From December to March, whales migrating north from Baja California make a fantastic roadside attraction.

If you enjoy driving, you will love the banks and swerves of this road. But your patience can be tested: summer brings fog and heavy traffic, and the highway is often closed during winter storms. Just relax and let the road reveal one incredibly beautiful vista after another. Buy gas in Carmel or San Luis Obispo to avoid exorbitant gas prices (sometimes more than double the regular price) and bring a picnic. Beach access is limited since much of the land along Hwy 1 is private and swimming is discouraged because of undertows and rip currents. Trails that do lead to the beach require tennis shoes or sturdy sandals.

its name from the four remaining lime-kilns originally built here in the 1880s to smelt local lime to powder. A ½mi trail through a new redwood grove leads to this historic site. Another short hike leads to a 100ft waterfall.

Continuing north, you'll soon come to the turnoff for a narrow road snaking 2mi up the hillside to the **New Camaldoli Hermitage**. There are spectacular views along the way and benches and picnic tables to enjoy them at leisure. About 30 monks live in this largely self-sufficient community, devoting their lives to prayer and meditation. For information about retreats, call ☎ 831-667-2456.

For more earthly delights, stop in at **Lucia Lodge** (☎ 831-667-2391, fax 831-667-2326; cabins $125-250; lunch $8-28, dinner $17-30), perched about 400ft above the bay 2mi north of the turnoff to the hermitage. It has a restaurant-lounge with an outdoor deck, dreamy views and a menu ranging from sandwiches to fish or steak dinners.

Esalen Institute
Marked only by a lighted sign reading 'Esalen Institute, By Reservation Only,' the Esalen Institute (☎ 831-667-3000; **w** www.esalen.org) is world renowned for its seminars and natural hot springs. Workshops deal with anything that 'promotes human values and potentials,' from African dance to yoga to exploring the inner game of golf. In business for decades, it's sort of the 'old timer' of the New Age, though that term is never used in Esalen-speak.

The Esalen baths are fed by a natural hot spring and sit on a ledge above the center, below the center's main building. Tubs destroyed by El Niño in 1998 were set to be replaced by late 2002 and to be open to the public nightly from 1am to 3:30am (clothing optional). Call ahead.

When space is available, you can also stay at Esalen (and use its new baths) without participating in a seminar. Accommodations are in standard rooms sleeping up to three people ($130 to $150 per person) or in four- to six-bed dorms ($90 to $95 per person). The daily rates include three meals. For room reservations or to book a seminar, call ☎ 831-667-3005. Call or check the website for a free catalog with seminar dates and details.

Julia Pfeiffer Burns State Park
Julia Pfeiffer Burns State Park (☎ 831-667-2315), named for a Big Sur pioneer woman, hugs both sides of Hwy 1 and features redwood, tan oak, madrona and chaparral. At the park entrance (on the east side of Hwy 1) are forested picnic grounds along McWay Creek and an old cabin (on the creek's northern side, just past the picnic area) that housed the Waters, the land's first homesteaders. The Waters built Saddle Rock Ranch here in the 1900s. The Ewoldsen Trail offers good views of the ocean and the Santa Lucia Range.

The park's highlight is California's only coastal waterfall, the 80ft **McWay Falls**, which drops straight into the sea (onto the sand at low tide). To reach the waterfall viewpoint, take the trail heading west from the park entrance and cross beneath Hwy 1. Nearby, two walk-in **campgrounds** (reservations ☎ 800-444-7275; campsites $12) sit on a semiprotected bluff. Camper registration is at Pfeiffer Big Sur campground, about 12mi north (see later in this section).

Partington Cove
From the western side of Hwy 1, a poorly marked steep dirt fire road descends ½mi along Partington Creek to Partington Cove, named for a settler who built the first dock here in the 1880s. Originally, the cove was used for loading tanbark, a cross between an oak and a chestnut whose bark was used in tanning leather; during Prohibition it was an alleged landing for bootleggers. This is a beautiful and often overlooked section of Big Sur with great views, tide pools, swimming in the creek and lovely picnic spots.

The turnoff is inside a large hairpin turn about 2mi north of the Julia Pfeiffer Burns State Park. There are dirt pullouts for parking along the fire road.

Coast Gallery
The Coast Gallery (☎ 831-667-2301; open 9am-5pm daily) consists of several structures made of redwood water tanks. Besides an impressive collection of top-notch crafts by local and national artisans, it also houses an exhibition of watercolors, limited edition prints, books and historic memorabilia by Henry Miller.

There's also several gift shops, a candle studio, and a café serving pastries and light lunches on an ocean-view deck.

Henry Miller Library

About 2mi further north, housed amid gardens and sculptures, the Henry Miller Library (☎ 831-667-2574; w www.henrymiller .org; admission by donation $1; open 11am-6pm Wed-Mon) is Big Sur's most cultured venue. It was the home of Miller's great friend, the painter Emil White, until his death in 1989 and is now run by a nonprofit agency. The library has all of Miller's written works, many of his paintings, translations of his books and a great collection of Big Sur and Beat Generation material. Grabbing a book and hanging out on the deck is encouraged. Official hours are given here (but call ahead). The staff are friendly and extremely well informed. Check the website for poetry, drama, music and other events taking place at the library.

Pfeiffer Big Sur State Park

Pfeiffer Big Sur State Park (☎ 831-667-2315) is the largest state park in Big Sur. Named after Big Sur's first European settlers – Michael and Barbara Pfeiffer, who arrived in 1869 – the park occupies 680 acres of the former Pfeiffer Ranch Resort and contains the original homestead cabin and the graveyard where the Pfeiffers are buried. The rustic administration buildings and Big Sur Lodge (see Places to Stay) were built in the 1930s by the CCC.

A **campground** (reservations ☎ 800-444-7275; campsites $12) is beside the Big Sur River in a flat-bottomed valley shaded by redwood groves; facilities include showers and laundry but no hookups.

Hiking trails loop through the park and head into the adjacent Ventana Wilderness (see the boxed text). Summer crowds are the drawback to this otherwise idyllic scene.

Sycamore Canyon Rd winds 2mi down to **Pfeiffer Beach**, a great spot. The road and the beach were being redeveloped at the time of writing but should have reopened by the time you're reading this.

Andrew Molera State Park

A remote and wild setting, lots of wildlife and great beachcombing are among the assets of the Andrew Molera State Park (☎ 831-667-2315), which once formed part of Juan Bautista Cooper's 9000-acre Rancho El Sur. The first-come, first-served **walk-in campground** (campsites $1), about a third of a mile from the parking lot, has fire pits, vault toilets and drinking water. A gentle ½mi trail leads from the campground past sycamore trees and the **Cooper Cabin**, one of the oldest structures in Big Sur, to a beautiful beach where the Big Sur River runs into the ocean. From here, several trails head south along the bluffs above the beach.

Molera Horseback Tours (☎ 831-625-5486, 800-942-5486; w www.molerahorse backtours.com) offers a variety of guided trail rides from one hour to 2½ hours for $25 to $59 between April and January. Its barn is about ¼mi from the park entrance. Also here is the **Big Sur Cultural & Natural History Center** (☎ 831-455-9514), maintained by the Ventana Wilderness Society; call for its opening hours.

Ventana Wilderness

The 167,000-acre Ventana Wilderness is the backcountry of the Big Sur coast. It lies within the northern part of Los Padres National Forest, which straddles the Santa Lucia Range and runs parallel to the coast for its entire length. Most of the wilderness is covered with oak and chaparral, though canyons cut by the Big Sur and Little Sur rivers support virgin stands of coastal redwoods. Scattered pockets of the endemic Santa Lucia fir grow in rocky outcroppings at elevations above 5000ft.

The Ventana is especially popular with hikers and backpackers. There are 237mi of trails with access to 55 designated backcountry trail camps. One favorite destination is **Sykes Hot Springs**, natural hot mineral pools (ranging from 98°F to 110°F) framed by redwoods, about 10mi from the wilderness boundary via the **Pine Ridge Trail** – the gateway into the wilderness.

The trailhead is at the Big Sur Ranger Station and has parking, fresh water and restrooms. Backcountry and fire permits are available at this ranger station as well as the one in Pacific Valley further south. Note that Ventana has the country's largest concentration of mountain lions (one cat per 10 square miles).

Point Sur Lightstation State Historic Park

About 19mi south of Carmel, Point Sur is an imposing volcanic rock that looks like an island but is actually connected to land by a sandbar. Atop the rock, 361ft above the surf, is the 1899 **Point Sur Lightstation** (☎ 831-625-4419), which remained in operation until 1972. It can only be seen by joining a three-hour tour ($5) offered at 10am Saturday and Sunday year-round. From April to October, tours also run at 10am and 2pm on Wednesday, and in July and August there's an additional tour at 10am on Thursday. Call about the 'moonlight' tour schedule. Tours meet at the farm gate on Hwy 1.

Little Sur River Bridge

Before rising to the lofty Hurricane Point headlands, Hwy 1 passes the low-lying Little Sur River Bridge. Here the Little Sur River makes a gentle sweep – a favorite subject for artists – before it meets the sea, turning the water bright blue with its heavy limestone deposits. During the dry season the river forms a lagoon behind a sandbar. **Pico Blanco**, the white-and-green-striped mountain to the east, stands 3710ft tall and was revered by the Esselen Indians as the sacred birthplace of man and beast.

Bixby Bridge

A much photographed Big Sur landmark, Bixby Bridge spans Bixby Creek and is one of the world's highest single span bridges at 714ft long and 260ft high. Completed in 1932, it was built by prisoners eager to lop time off their sentences.

Before the bridge was built, travelers had to trek 14mi inland on what's called the **Old Coast Rd**, which heads east from Bixby Bridge's northern side and reconnects with Hwy 1 across from Andrew Molera State Park. It's still navigable, but you'll need a sturdy car with high clearance.

Garrapata State Park

Garrapata State Park (☎ 831-624-4909), though often overlooked, is a pleasant spot fronting 2mi of beach and laced with hiking trails running from the ocean into redwood groves. The **Soberanes Canyon Trail** and the **Rocky Ridge Trail** are among the more challenging routes. There's parking along Hwy 1.

Places to Stay

Aside from camping, Big Sur is devoid of budget accommodations. Rooms at the relatively sparse number of cabins, inns and motels are pricey and often booked up weeks, if not months, in advance, especially in summer and on weekends year-round. Make reservations early, hope for cancellations or count on staying outside Big Sur limits. Some places impose a two-night minimum stay. For additional accommodation options, see also the Southern Big Sur section earlier.

Camping There's camping in three of Big Sur's state parks: Andrew Molera State Park, Pfeiffer Big Sur State Park and Julia Pfeiffer Burns State Park. For details about each campground, see the parks' descriptions earlier in this section. There's also undeveloped backcountry camping available in Los Padres National Forest and Ventana Wilderness. For specifics, check with the ranger stations, where you can also get an overnight parking permit ($4) and a free fire permit.

Ventana Campground (☎ 831-667-2712; *campsites Sun-Thur $25, Fri-Sat $35; open Apr-Oct),* just south of Pfeiffer Big Sur State Park and set in a 40-acre redwood grove, has beautiful secluded campsites with a lot of privacy. There's also a tiny general store.

Big Sur Campground & Cabins (☎ 831-667-2322; *campsites $26, tent cabins $50, cabins with bath & kitchen $90-180),* in the 'The Village', has nice sites and small cabins shaded by mature redwoods right along the Big Sur River. The camping store stocks the basics, and there are laundry facilities, hot showers, volleyball and basketball courts and a playground.

Riverside Campground & Cabins (☎ 831-667-2414; *campsites $28, cabins $60-115),* about ½mi further south, is similar. The cheaper cabins don't have private bath.

Inns & Resorts Glen Oaks Motel (☎ 831-667-2105, fax 831-667-1105; **w** *www.glenoaksbigsur.com; rooms $69-104, cottages $130-145),* in 'The Village', has clean, airy and nicely furnished rooms, and cottages set amid trees and flowers. The restaurant serves dinner nightly except Tuesday.

Ripplewood Resort (☎ 831-667-2242; **w** *www.ripplewoodresort.com; cabins $75-125),* next to the Glen Oaks Motel, has cabins with varying amenities. All have kitchens and private bathrooms, some have fireplaces. The cabins along the river are peaceful and surrounded by redwoods, but those on Hwy 1 can be quite noisy. Its café is good for breakfast and lunch and there's a market as well.

Deetjen's Big Sur Inn (☎ 831-667-2377; W www.deetjens.com; rooms $75-195), just south of the Henry Miller Library, is an enchanting conglomeration of rustic rooms, redwoods and wisteria along Castro Creek. Built by a Norwegian immigrant in the early 1930s, each cabin still reflects his personality. None have TV or phones. The inn's cozy restaurant serves breakfast ($4.50 to $11) and gourmet dinners (mains $15 to $29).

Big Sur River Inn (☎ 831-667-2700, 800-548-3610; W www.bigsurriverinn.com; rooms $85-140), in business since 1888, offers cozy country-style lodging right in 'The Village' next to the creek. Facilities include a large heated pool and an all-day restaurant.

Big Sur Lodge (☎ 831-667-3100, 800-424-4787; W www.bigsurlodge.com; cottages $99-229) has pretty cottages, all with deck or balcony. The pricier ones also have kitchens and/or fireplace and sleep up to six people. Rates include admission to the state parks, and there's a restaurant (mains $12.50 to $23) and store.

Ventana Inn & Spa (☎ 831-667-2331, 800-628-6500, fax 831-667-2419; W www.ventanainn.com; rooms $300-975) exudes an aura of serenity and romance, which has not gone unnoticed by a huge stable of Hollywood A-list members, including Anthony Hopkins and Leonardo di Caprio. Rooms come with spa, fireplace and plush robes, and the complex includes a Japanese bathhouse, sauna and two pools.

If that's not posh enough for you, try **Post Ranch Inn** (☎ 831-667-2200; rooms $485-935), across the highway from Ventana, an assemblage of unique guesthouses behind a gated and guarded driveway.

Places to Eat

For additional restaurant options see Places to Stay.

Big Sur Bakery (☎ 831-667-0520; pizzas $9-15, mains $18-24), in a warmly lit, ambience-laden old house in 'The Village', has fresh quiches and bialys and starts making wood-fired pizzas at noon. Dinners are more substantial and mostly meat-based.

Nepenthe (☎ 831-667-2345; mains $11-30), south of Pfeiffer Big Sur State Park, known for its vivid gardens and breathtaking cliff-top location, is especially memorable at sunset. Views are stunning from both the large outdoor terrace and through the panoramic windows in the bar and dining room. Alas, the food's only so-so. For cheaper eats and almost the same views, go downstairs to the self-service **Cafe Kevah** (dishes $8-12; open 9am-4pm daily Mar-Dec).

Cielo (☎ 831-667-2331; lunch $11-17, dinner $25-35), at the Ventana Inn & Spa, has the look of a Zen ski lodge, impeccable service and modern American dishes that are both artistic and tasty.

POINT LOBOS STATE RESERVE

Point Lobos (information ☎ 831-624-4909; admission per vehicle $4, walk-ins free; open 9am-7pm daily during daylight savings time, 9am-5pm rest of year), about 4mi south of Carmel, has a dramatically rocky and convoluted coastline. It takes its name from the Punta de los Lobos Marinos, or the 'Point of the Sea Wolves,' named by the Spanish for the howls of the resident sea lions. Several short walks take in the wild and inspiring scenery. Favorite destinations include **Sea Lion Point** and **Devil's Cauldron**, the latter a whirlpool that gets splashy at high tide. At the end of the main road, **Bird Island** is good for bird-watching and for starting out on long hikes.

The kelp forest in Whaler's Cove is popular with divers, though permits are required ($7; call ☎ 831-624-8413 for details).

CARMEL-BY-THE-SEA

North of Big Sur, Hwy 1 spills out onto the Monterey Peninsula, marked by Carmel in the south and Monterey in the north. Spectacular coastal scenery and a colorful history (as the old Spanish and Mexican capital of California) all come together here.

Carmel (population 4500) began as a planned seaside resort in the 1880s and quickly established a reputation as a bohemian retreat. The artistic flavor survives in the more than 100 galleries that line the town's immaculate streets, but these days 'wealthy' and 'bourgeois' are just as descriptive. Carmel, with its picturesque homes, impressive coastal frontage and upscale shopping, positively glows with smugness.

CENTRAL COAST

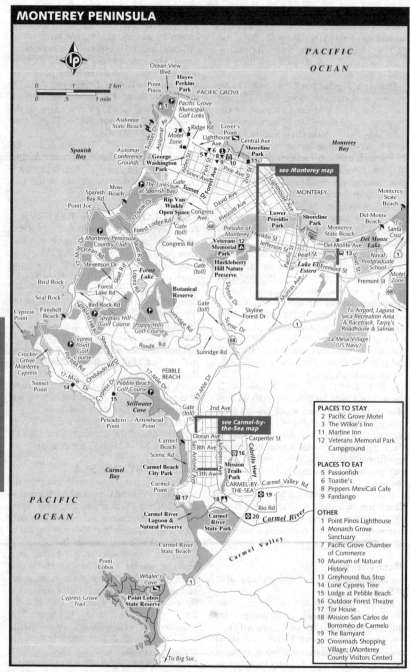

MONTEREY PENINSULA

PACIFIC
OCEAN

0   1   2 km
0   .5   1 mile

Ocean View Blvd
Point Pinos
Hayes Perkins Park
PACIFIC GROVE
Pacific Grove Municipal Golf Links
Asilomar State Beach
Lover's Point
Ridge Rd
Lighthouse Ave
Central Ave
Shoreline Park
Motel Zone
Pine Ave
George Washington Park
Asilomar Conference Grounds
Spanish Bay
Monterey Bay
Sinex Ave
The Links at Spanish Bay
Rip Van Winkle Open Space
Sunset Dr
David Ave
Congress Ave
MONTEREY
Moss Beach
Spanish Bay Rd
Point Joe
Forest Lodge Rd
Gate (toll)
Congress Rd
Prescott Ave
Lower Presidio Park
Shoreline Park
Monterey State Beach
Del Monte Beach
Monterey State Beach
To Santa Cruz
Del Monte Ave
Del Monte Lake
Presidio of Monterey
Veterans Memorial Park
Naval Postgraduate School
Monterey Peninsula Country Club
Ocean Rd
Stevenson Dr
Huckleberry Hill Nature Preserve
Pearl St
Jefferson St
Lake El Estero
Fremont St
Motel Zone
Bird Rock Rd
Forest Lake Rd
Forest Lake
Botanical Reserve
Gate (toll)
Skyline Dr
Munras Ave
Seal Rock
Bird Rock
Cypress Point
Fanshell Beach
Spyglass Hill Golf Course
Poppy Hills Golf Course
Sunridge Rd
Skyline Forest Dr
To Airport, Laguna Seca Recreation Area & Racetrack, Tarpy's Roadhouse & Salinas
Crocker Grove Monterey Cypress
Cypress Point Golf Course
Portola Rd
Ondulado Rd
Ronda Rd
Sunridge Rd
La Mesa Village (US Navy)
Sunset Point
Pebble Beach Golf Course
PEBBLE BEACH
Gate (toll)
2nd Ave
see Carmel-by-the-Sea map
Stillwater Cove
Pescadero Point
Arrowhead Point
Carmel Beach
Scenic Rd
Ocean Ave
8th Ave
Carpenter St
Cabrillo Hwy
Carmel Beach City Park
Mission Trails Park
CARMEL-BY-THE-SEA
Carmel Valley Rd
Carmel Bay
PACIFIC OCEAN
Carmel Point
13th Ave
Carmel River
Rio Rd
Carmel River Lagoon & Natural Preserve
Carmel River State Park
Carmel River
Carmel Valley
Carmel River State Beach
Point Lobos
Whaler's Cove
Cypress Grove Trail
Point Lobos State Reserve
To Big Sur

PLACES TO STAY
2 Pacific Grove Motel
3 The Wilkie's Inn
11 Martine Inn
12 Veterans Memorial Park Campground

PLACES TO EAT
5 Passionfish
6 Toastie's
8 Peppers MexiCali Cafe
9 Fandango

OTHER
1 Point Pinos Lighthouse
4 Monarch Grove Sanctuary
7 Pacific Grove Chamber of Commerce
10 Museum of Natural History
13 Greyhound Bus Stop
14 Lone Cypress Tree
15 Lodge at Pebble Beach
16 Outdoor Forest Theatre
17 Tor House
18 Mission San Carlos de Borroméo de Carmelo
19 The Barnyard
20 Crossroads Shopping Village; (Monterey County Visitors Center)

CENTRAL COAST

The town's manicured appearance is ensured by strict local bylaws, which forbid neon signs, billboards and hot dog stands. A permit is required to wear high heels (to prevent you from suing the city should you slip on the cobbled sidewalks!). Residents pick up their mail from the post office and houses have no street numbers, so addresses always specify the block and side of street. Even public phones, garbage cans and newspaper vending boxes are quaintly shingled.

Orientation & Information

Most of the shops, restaurants and hotels are along Ocean Ave, San Carlos and Dolores Sts. Also on San Carlos, between 5th & 6th St, is the **Carmel Business Association** (☎ 831-624-2522, 800-550-4333, fax 831-624-1329; open 8am-5pm Mon-Fri), which distributes town maps and information, though only about its members.

For information about Carmel and beyond, including Monterey and Big Sur, visit the **Monterey County Visitors Center** (☎ 831-626-1424, 888-221-1010, fax 831-626-1426; 137 Crossroads Blvd; open 10am-5pm daily June-Sept, 10am-4pm Oct-May). It's in the Crossroads Shopping Village, off Hwy 1 at Rio Rd.

Mission San Carlos de Borroméo de Carmelo

The original Monterey mission was founded by Padre Serra in 1769, but poor soil forced the move to the riverside site in Carmel in 1771. Although the missionaries founded 20 other missions in California, this one remained Serra's base. He died here in 1784 and was buried in the mission church beside his compatriot, Padre Juan Crespi.

The mission church was originally built of wood, then replaced by an adobe structure and, in 1793, by the present stone church. In the 19th century, the mission went into decline; it was secularized in 1834 and virtually abandoned in 1836 when the padres moved to Monterey. The ruin was roofed over in 1884, which at least slowed the decay, but restoration didn't really commence until 1931. Today it is one of the most attractive and complete of the California missions, with a superb museum relating the story of Serra and the missions.

CARMEL-BY-THE-SEA

PLACES TO EAT
5 Forge in the Forest
6 Jack London's
8 Village Corner
10 Caffé Napoli
11 Carmel Bakery
12 Caffé Cardinale
13 Patisserie Boissiere
14 The Fabulous Toots Lagoon
15 Tuck Box

PLACES TO STAY
1 Svensgaards Inn
2 Carmel Wayfarer Inn
3 Candle Light Inn
9 Pine Inn

OTHER
4 Post Office
7 Carmel Business Association
16 The Golden Bough Theatre

The mission (☎ 831-624-1271; 3080 Rio Rd; museum & church adult/child under 18 $4/1; open 9:30am-7:30pm Mon-Sat, 10:30am-4:30pm Sun, 9:30am-7:30pm daily June-Aug) is off Hwy 1 in southern Carmel.

Tor House

Poet Robinson Jeffers was one of the creators of the Carmel ethos, and his strikingly rugged home, the Tor House (☎ 831-624-1813; 26304 Ocean View Ave), off Scenic Ave, has become a pilgrimage point. Tours take in the house as well as the gardens and a climb up Hawk Tower, inspired by ancient Irish stone towers. Tours (adult/student $7/4) operate hourly from 10am to 3pm Friday and Saturday; reservations are recommended and no children under 12 are allowed.

Places to Stay

Accommodation is not cheap in Carmel – Motel 6s are definitely not welcome. Instead you'll find a slew of small boutique hotels and cozy B&Bs, many of which impose a two-night minimum stay on weekends and often fill up quickly, particularly in summer.

Carmel Wayfarer Inn (☎ 831-624-2711, 800-624-2711, fax 831-625-1210; cnr Mission St & 4th Ave; rooms $89-259) is a charming country inn dating back to 1919. No room is the same and some have glorious sunset views. Rates include a generous continental breakfast with homemade bread.

Candle Light Inn (☎ 831-624-6451, 800-433-4732, fax 831-624-6732; San Carlos St between 4th & 5th Aves; rooms Nov-May $129-179, June-Oct $185-275) has snug and comfortable rooms with coffeemakers, and is run by a friendly French woman who's a treasure trove of information about the area's restaurants. A continental breakfast is left outside your room in a basket.

Svensgaards Inn (☎ 831-624-1511, 800-433-4732, fax 831-624-5661; cnr San Carlos St & 4th Ave; rooms Nov-May $99-275, June-Oct $150-300) is a charmer wrapped around a lush courtyard with a large heated pool. The nicest rooms come with fireplaces, kitchenette and large whirlpool tubs with TV. A continental breakfast arrives at your door in the morning.

Pine Inn (☎ 831-624-3851, 800-228-3851, fax 831-624-3030; w tallyho-inn.com; Ocean Ave & Lincoln St; rooms $125-250) has a pedigree going back to 1889 and oozes the kind of timeless elegance usually found in European luxury abodes. Rich carpets, shiny wood-paneling, fine antiques and cozy lighting conspire to create an ambience of comfort and style. There's no smoking anywhere (a $250 fine applies if you light up).

Places to Eat

Carmel's restaurant scene is a delight, with plenty of good-value places loaded with atmosphere. Note that most restaurants stop serving dinner at around 9pm.

Caffé Cardinale (☎ 831-626-2095; Ocean Ave between San Carlos & Dolores Sts; snacks $3-8; open 7am-6pm daily) gets rave reviews for its rich coffee (roasted on the premises) but also does dependable baked goods and sandwiches. It's tucked away in an alley off Ocean Ave.

Caffé Napoli (☎ 831-625-4033; Ocean Ave near Lincoln St; mains $10-20) is a hugely popular southern-Italian restaurant serving hand-tossed pizzas, rich pastas and risottos and various fish specials. It's tiny, so reservations are advised.

Carmel Bakery (☎ 831-626-8885; Ocean Ave between Lincoln & Delores Sts; baked dishes $0.50-3; closes at 6pm Sun-Thur, 7pm Fri-Sat) has been the place for baked goods since 1935. A small menu of salads and sandwiches under $7 is also available.

The Fabulous Toots Lagoon (☎ 831-625-1915; Dolores St between Ocean & 7th Aves; mains $10-30) is best known for its finger-lickin' ribs and juicy steaks, although the pizzas are a good bet as well. The bar is a popular gathering spot for locals.

Forge in the Forest (☎ 831-624-2233; cnr 5th Ave & Junípero St; mains $13-31) is one of the best and most fun places in town. You can dine seated on the flowery patio or in the rustic interior anchored by an authentic blacksmith's forge. The food is American/Californian and mid-priced, and there's a daily happy hour with free appetizers.

Jack London's (☎ 831-624-2336; Dolores St between 5th & 6th Aves; dishes $4-19) in a walkway off Dolores St, serves hot food until midnight. A Carmel mainstay since 1973, it pairs upscale pub grub with a selection of local microbrews and killer margaritas. The burgers and baby back ribs are specialties and breakfast is served anytime.

Patisserie Boissiere (☎ 831-624-5008; Mission St between Ocean & 7th Aves; lunch daily $8-13, dinner Wed-Sun $9-18), part of the Carmel Plaza mall, is a charming place whose antique-filled dining room with fireplace feels like the home of a good friend. The food is French, bien sûr, and made with fresh homegrown ingredients.

Tuck Box (☎ 831-624-6365; Dolores St between Ocean & 7th Aves; breakfast & lunch $7-9.50, afternoon tea from $6) is a snug British tea room in a 'Hansel-and-Gretel' house which draws patrons with its homemade scones and pies. Breakfast is served from 7am.

Village Corner (☎ 831-624-3588; cnr Dolores St & 6th Ave; breakfast $5-8.50, lunch $7-16.50, dinner $16-25) is a classic California bistro with a lovely, flower-filled patio anchored by an open-pit fire. Portions are generous and the service is fast and friendly.

Entertainment

Outdoor Forest Theatre (☎ *831-626-1681; Mountain View between Forest & Guadalupe Sts*) was founded in 1910. Musicals, drama and comedies as well as movie screenings take place in a lovely setting surrounded by trees and anchored by two large fire pits.

Golden Bough Theatre (☎ *831-622-0100; Monte Verde between 8th & 9th Aves*) is the home of the Pacific Repertory Theatre, whose menu ranges from Chekhov to Shakespeare.

In July and August, Carmel hosts the well-respected **Carmel Bach Festival** (☎ *831-624-2046;* w *www.bachfestival.org*) at venues around town.

Shopping

Shopping is a favorite pastime for locals and visitors alike, and Carmel has plenty of outlets to satisfy the urge, with a particular abundance of art and craft galleries and shops selling the kind of knickknacks you really don't need but which are nice to have anyway. Carmel galleries are laden with happy dolphin sculptures, oil paintings of local scenery (would you believe paintings of golf courses?) and pictures by artists who discovered impressionism a century too late. More stores cluster in a couple of small malls, including the beautifully designed **Carmel Plaza** (*cnr Ocean Ave & Mission St*). East of the town centre is **The Barnyard** (*Carmel Rancho between Carmel Valley & Rio Rds*) with 40 more specialty shops.

Getting There & Around

Carmel is only 5mi south of Monterey by Hwy 1. **Monterey-Salinas Transit** (*MST;* ☎ *831-899-2555*) bus Nos 4 and 5 go north to Monterey and south to the mission and The Barnyard shopping mall, while No 22 passes through en route to Big Sur. Free unlimited car parking can be found at **Vista Lobos Park** (*cnr 3rd Ave & Torres St*).

17-MILE DRIVE

Carmel and Pacific Grove are linked by the spectacularly scenic 17-Mile Drive, which meanders through Pebble Beach, a resort and residential area that potently symbolizes the peninsula's affluence. Open sunrise to sunset, entry is via five gates and costs $8.50 per car, including a map. Bicycles enter free, but on weekends and holidays cyclists can use only the Pacific Grove gate. Use caution when cycling, as drivers tend to be *very* distracted by the views.

To reach the drive from central Carmel, follow Ocean Ave west, then turn north on N San Antonio Ave. This gets you to the Carmel Gate, where the toll is collected. The road continues on as Carmel Way to the junction with 17-Mile Drive where you turn left.

The road winds through the Del Monte Forest to emerge at Pebble Beach, a playground of choice for the Rolls Royce crowd and home of the famous Pebble Beach Golf Course and the utterly posh Lodge at Pebble Beach. A few miles north, the **Lone Cypress** has inspired far too many local artists and photographers and is also the (copyrighted!) symbol of the Pebble Beach Company, which is trying to claim copyright to all uses of the image, even in paintings.

Beyond here, the drive meanders through **Crocker Grove**, with its Monterey cypress, to the **Cypress Point Lookout** for one of the finest views along the entire drive, even if it's somewhat spoiled by an ugly wire fence. Next up, **Fanshell Beach** and **Seal Rock** attract seals and other bay life, although for animal close-ups it's best to stop a bit further on at **Bird Rock**. Sea lions, harbor seals and many birds make their home in this area, which is easily explored on a 1mi nature walk.

Continuing on leads you past the treacherously rocky **Point Joe**, which in the past was often mistaken for the entrance to Monterey Bay and thus became the site of several shipwrecks. Past the point is **Spanish Bay** where explorer Gaspar de Portolá dropped anchor in 1769. From there it's only a short drive to the northern terminus of the drive at the Pacific Grove Gate.

While most of us normal mortals can only afford to sample the splendid setting on a drive-through, Pebble Beach is a playground of choice for the Rolls-Royce crowd. There are fancy resorts such as The Lodge at Pebble Beach and The Inn at Spanish Bay, elite golf courses (seven of them, including the famous Pebble Beach Golf Course) and the 5000-acre Del Monte Forest.

PACIFIC GROVE

Pacific Grove ('PG' to locals; population 16,000) is a tranquil community that began as a Methodist summer retreat in 1875. To this day, numerous stately Victorian homes line its nicely manicured residential streets. In summer, hordes of tourists descend upon the town, but in winter PG is invaded by swarms of monarch butterflies, which make the local pine groves their temporary home. PG also has a couple of worthwhile museums, a historic lighthouse and one of the peninsula's best surfing beaches, the Asilomar State Beach, which is also a good spot to watch sunsets.

Orientation & Information

Central and Lighthouse Aves are PG's main commercial arteries; Lighthouse continues southeast to Monterey. The **chamber of commerce** (☎ 831-373-3304, 800-656-6650, fax 831-373-3317; **w** www.pacificgrove.org; cnr Central & Forest Aves; open 9:30am-5pm Mon-Fri, 10am-4pm Sat) dispenses visitor information and maps.

Things to See & Do

Fronted by a sculpture of a gray whale, the **Museum of Natural History** (☎ 831-648-3116; 165 Forest Ave; admission free; open 10am-5pm Tues-Sun) has some of that old-fashioned 'dead zoo' flavor, but there are also interesting exhibits about Big Sur, sea otters and the monarch butterflies.

If you're in town during butterfly season (roughly October to March), the best place to see them cluster by the millions is at the **Monarch Grove Sanctuary**, a grove of pines on Ridge Rd off Lighthouse Ave (follow the signs). The **Butterfly Parade**, marking the return of the monarchs to PG, is in October.

At the northwestern end of Lighthouse Ave, at the tip of the Monterey Peninsula, you'll find **Point Pinos Lighthouse** (☎ 831-648-3116; admission free; open 1pm-4pm Thur-Sun), the oldest continuously operating lighthouse on the West Coast. It's been warning ships of this hazardous point with the same lenses and prisms and in the same building since 1855. Inside are exhibits on its history and on local shipwrecks.

Places to Stay & Eat

Most of PG's hotels and B&Bs are of the upscale variety and are northwest of the commercial center along Lighthouse Ave.

Pacific Grove Motel (☎ 831-372-3431, 800-525-3373, fax 831-643-0235; 204 Grove Acre Ave at Lighthouse Ave; rooms $59-149)

has a pool and spa, and its rates include a small continental breakfast.

The Wilkie's Inn (☎ 831-372-5960, 866-372-5960, fax 831-655-1681; **w** www.wilkiesinn.com; 1038 Lighthouse Ave; rooms $70-189) has a motel-look but a good range of amenities, including free continental breakfast and rooms with ocean views and kitchenettes.

Martine Inn (☎ 831-373-3388, 800-852-5588, fax 831-373-3896; **w** www.martineinn.com; 255 Ocean View Blvd; rooms $135-300) exudes charm and comfort by the bucket. Staying here means relaxing in your antique-filled room (some with fireplace), sampling wine and appetizers at cocktail hour, listening to the sound of waves crashing against the rocky shoreline and waking up to a hearty breakfast. The owner is an antique car aficionado; ask to see his classic MG roadsters.

Toastie's (☎ 831-373-7543; 702 Lighthouse Ave; dishes $3.50-8.50), an unpretentious café, has built its reputation on satisfying breakfasts and lunches.

Peppers MexiCali Cafe (☎ 831-373-6892; 170 Forest Ave; dishes $6.50-12.50) serves the gamut of belly-busting Mexican classics as well as some nicely spiced seafood dishes.

Fandango (☎ 831-372-3456; 223 17th St; lunch $8-22, dinner $12-28) takes you on a culinary journey around the Mediterranean in a distinctly California setting.

Pasta Mia (☎ 831-375-7709; 481 Lighthouse Ave; dinner $11-20) is one of the most beloved Italian restaurants on the peninsula, with tasty antipasti, pizza, pasta, steak and fish dishes.

Passionfish (☎ 831-655-3311; 701 Lighthouse Ave; dinner $11-27) keeps regulars happy by pairing fresh fish and choice meats with a United Nations of ingredients, lemongrass sauce to mint pesto. Good wine list too.

MONTEREY

California's Spanish and Mexican history is encountered elsewhere, but nowhere is evidence of the state's Hispanic heritage richer than in Monterey (population 30,000). The city has numerous lovingly restored adobe buildings from the Spanish and Mexican periods, and it's enlightening to spend a day wandering about the town's historic quarter. Monterey also offers a fine Maritime Museum and a world-famous aquarium, not to mention the relative tourist traps of Fisherman's Wharf and Cannery Row.

Monterey Bay is one of the world's richest and most varied marine environments. It boasts dense kelp forests and a diverse range of marine life, including mammals such as sea otters, seals and sea lions, elephant seals, dolphins and whales.

Starting only a few hundred yards offshore from Moss Landing (a few miles north of Monterey), the Monterey Canyon plummets to a depth of over 10,000ft. In summer the upwelling currents carry cold water from this deep submarine canyon, sending a rich supply of nutrients up toward the surface level to feed the bay's diverse marine life. These frigid currents also account for the bay's generally low water temperatures and the fog that often blankets the peninsula in summer.

History

The Ohlone tribe, who had been on the peninsula since around 500 BC, may have spotted Spanish explorer Juan Rodríguez Cabrillo, the first European visitor, who sailed by in 1542. He was followed in 1602 by Sebastián Vizcaíno, who landed near the site of today's downtown Monterey and named it after his patron, the Duke of Monte Rey. A long hiatus followed before the Spanish returned in 1770 to establish Monterey as their first presidio in Alta California. The expedition was led by Gaspar de Portolá and accompanied by mission founder Padre Junípero Serra. A year later, Serra decided to separate church and state by shifting the mission to Carmel, a safe distance from the military presence.

Monterey became the capital of Alta California after Mexico broke from Spain in 1821. Freed from the tight Spanish trading constraints, it also became a bustling international trading port where East Coast Yankees mixed with Russian fur traders and seafarers carrying exotic goods from China.

The stars and stripes were temporarily raised over Monterey in 1842 when Commodore Thomas Jones, hearing a rumor that war had been declared between Mexico and the USA, took the town. A red-faced withdrawal took place a few days later when the rumor turned out to be false. When war really did break out in 1846, Commodore John Sloat's takeover was almost reluctant; he clearly did not want to repeat the mistake.

The American takeover signaled an abrupt change in the town's fortunes, for San Jose soon replaced Monterey as the state capital, and the 1849 gold rush drained much of the remaining population.

The town spent 30 years as a forgotten backwater, its remaining residents eking out an existence from whaling, an industry replaced by tourism in the 1880s. After Southern Pacific Railroad entrepreneurs built the luxurious Hotel del Monte, wealthy San Franciscans discovered Monterey as a convenient getaway. The former hotel is now part of the US Navy's postgraduate school.

Around the same time, fishermen began to capitalize on the teeming marine life in Monterey Bay, and the first sardine canneries soon opened. By the 1930s, Cannery Row had made the port the 'Sardine Capital of the World,' but overfishing and climatic changes caused the industry's sudden collapse in the 1950s. Fortunately, in more recent decades, tourism came to the rescue once again; modern Monterey is an enormously popular and heavily visited city.

Orientation & Information

Monterey's historic downtown is a compact area surrounding Alvarado St, which ends with Portola and Custom House plazas, near Fisherman's Wharf. This area is known as Old Monterey, as distinct from Cannery Row, about a mile northwest. Cannery Row segues straight into Pacific Grove.

For advance planning, you might want to contact the call center operated by the **Monterey County Convention & Visitors Bureau** (☎ 888-221-1010; 9am-5pm Mon-Fri), or check the website at ⓦ www.monterey info.org. There's also a 24-hour hotline with recorded information at ☎ 831-649-1770.

In town, there are several visitor centres, including one on the shore of El Estero Lake east of Old Monterey (☎ 831-649-1770, fax 831-648-5373; cnr Camino El Estero & Franklin St; open 9am-6pm Mon-Sat, 9am-5pm Sun Apr-Oct; 9am-5pm Mon-Sat, 10am-4pm Sun Nov-Mar). It has a free direct-call phone system for checking room availability and prices at dozens of hotels and motels.

A more central branch (☎ 831-649-1770, fax 831-648-5373; 5 Custom House Plaza; open 10am-5pm daily) is in the Stanton Center, also home to the Maritime Museum, near Fisherman's Wharf. A short walk south of

CENTRAL COAST

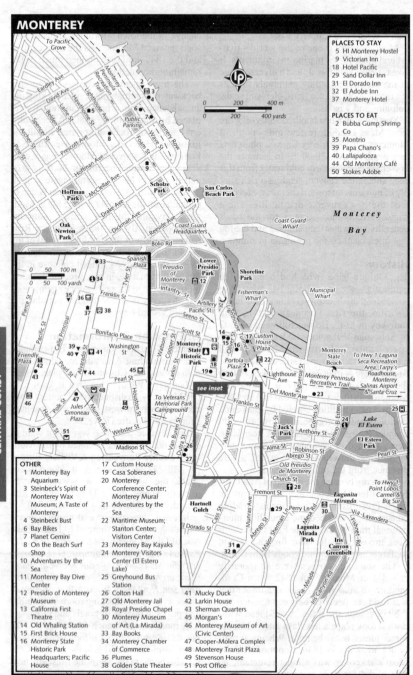

MONTEREY

CENTRAL COAST

here, the **Monterey Chamber of Commerce** (*380 Alvarado St; open 8:30am-5pm Mon-Fri)* dispenses information about its members.

Bay Books (*☎ 831-375-1855; 316 Alvarado St)* has a superb range of books and a coffee bar.

Monterey State Historic Park

Old Monterey is home to an extraordinary assemblage of 19th-century brick and adobe buildings, administered as the Monterey State Historic Park and covered on a 2mi walking tour called **Path of History**. Admission to any of the buildings is free. Tours start at the Maritime Museum, where you can also watch a free and very worthwhile 15-minute introductory film covering the period from 1770 to 1879; it screens more or less continuously from 10am to 4:30pm.

You can join a docent-led 90-minute tour (adult/child $5/2) offered at 10am and 2pm daily and also at 11am Friday to Sunday, although this may change. Alternatively, pick up a free brochure for a self-guided tour from the visitors center inside the Stanton Center or from the **park headquarters** (*☎ 831-649-7118)* across the street in the historic Pacific House. The latter also houses a **museum** (*admission free; open 10am-5pm daily)* highlighting various facets of state history.

There are also free tours of some of the individual houses. Pick up a current schedule at the park headquarters.

Custom House In 1822, newly independent Mexico ended the Spanish trade monopoly but stipulated that any traders bringing goods to Alta California must first unload their cargoes at the Monterey Custom House for duty assessment. The restored 1827 building displays an exotic selection of the goods traders brought in to exchange for Californian cowhides, including rice and spices as well as such 'luxury' items as chandeliers, liquor, machinery and furniture. In 1846, the American flag was raised over the Custom House, and California was formally annexed from Mexico.

Casa Soberanes A beautiful garden fronts Casa Soberanes, built in 1842 during the late Mexican period. Across Pacific St, the large and colorful **Monterey Mural** mosaic, on the modern Monterey Conference Center, tells the history of Monterey.

Larkin House Thomas Larkin arrived from New England in 1832 and made a fortune from the burgeoning regional trade. His fine 1842 house is a combination of New England design and adobe construction, known today as Monterey colonial. Larkin was US consul in Monterey during the US takeover and subsequently played an important role in the transition from Mexican to American rule.

Stevenson House Robert Louis Stevenson came to Monterey in 1879 to meet with his wife-to-be, Fanny Osbourne. This building, then the French Hotel, was reputedly where he stayed while writing *Treasure Island.* The rooms were pretty primitive – they only cost about $2 a month – but he was still a penniless unknown at that time. The 1840 building houses a superb collection of Stevenson memorabilia. The house was closed for renovation at the time of writing but should reopen sometime during 2003.

Cooper-Molera Complex This spacious adobe was built between 1827 and 1900 by John Rogers Cooper (a sea captain from New England and harbormaster of Monterey) and three generations of his family. During those years, it was partitioned and extended, gardens were added, and it was eventually willed to the National Trust.

Other Historic Buildings

Other structures along the Path of History include Monterey's **First Brick House** and the **Old Whaling Station** (both from 1847) – note the front walkway made of whalebone. The **California First Theatre** started out in 1844 as a saloon and lodging house; soldiers staying here are credited with staging California's first theatrical productions. Closed for renovation, performances were scheduled to resume in late 2002.

In 1849, California's state constitution was drawn up in **Colton Hall**, named for Walter Colton, navy chaplain for Commodore Sloat. The upstairs room re-creates the chamber where the document was debated and drafted. The adjacent **Old Monterey Jail** is featured in John Steinbeck's *Tortilla Flat.*

The **Sherman Quarters** on Pacific St was built by Thomas Larkin but takes its name from famed General Sherman of the Civil War, who lived there in 1847. The **Royal Presidio Chapel**, built of stone and adobe in

1795, was the military headquarters of Spanish and Mexican Monterey. The original mission church stood on this site in 1770 before being moved to Carmel. Until the 1820s the presidio's fortified walls embraced pretty much the entire town. As Monterey expanded, the old buildings were all gradually destroyed, leaving the chapel as a sole reminder of the old presidio's presence.

Maritime Museum

Monterey's Maritime Museum (☎ 831-372-2608; Stanton Center, 5 Custom House Plaza; adult/concession $5/2.50; open 10am-5pm daily) presents local naval history from the days of the early explorers to the 20th century. Highlights of the excellent collection include the Fresnel lens from Point Sur Lightstation, a great ship-in-a-bottle collection and interesting displays on Monterey's history, particularly of the rise and rapid fall of the sardine business.

Fisherman's Wharf

Like its larger namesake in San Francisco, the wharf is a tourist trap at heart, but good fun nonetheless. Noisy seals make regular visits to the wharf, and it's also the base for a variety of boat trips, including whale-watching expeditions (see later).

Presidio of Monterey Museum

The Presidio of Monterey Museum (☎ 831-646-3456; Corporal Ewing Rd, Bldg 113; admission free; open 10am-4pm Thur-Sat, 1pm-4pm Sun) is the latest addition to Monterey's museum landscape. Come here to learn about Monterey's history from a military perspective covering the Native American, Mexican and American periods and up to the present. The museum stands on the grounds of the original fort, now home to the Defense Language Institute Foreign Language Center.

Monterey Museum of Art

Monterey's premier art museum has two locations. The branch at the Civic Center (☎ 831-372-5477; 559 Pacific St; adult/student/child under 12 $5/2.50/free; open 11am-5pm Wed-Sat, 1pm-4pm Sun) is particularly strong with regard to California painters and photographers, including Ansel Adams and Edward Weston.

The second site is in a charming villa called La Mirada (☎ 831-372-3689; 720 Via Mirada; adult/student/child under 12 $5/2.50/free; open 11am-5pm Wed-Sat, 1pm-4pm Sun) whose humble adobe origins are well concealed indeed. It displays primarily selections from the museum's Asian collection and is backed by a lovely rose and rhododendron garden. A ticket bought at one branch entitles you to also visit the other.

Cannery Row

John Steinbeck's novel Cannery Row immortalized the sardine-canning business that Monterey lived on for the first half of the 20th century. He describes Cannery Row as 'a poem, a stink, a grating noise, a quality of light, a tone, a habit, a nostalgia, a dream.'

Predictions that overfishing could decimate the business were ignored when the catch reached a peak of 250,000 tons in 1945. Just five years later, figures plummeted to 33,000 tons, and by 1951 most of the sardine canneries had closed, many of them mysteriously catching fire.

Nowadays, Cannery Row is a touristy enclave of restaurants, bars and souvenir shops. A bronze bust of the writer sits at the bottom of Prescott Ave, right next to the restored warehouse containing the Steinbeck's Spirit of Monterey Wax Museum (☎ 831-375-1010; adult/child 7-12 $4.95/2.95; open 9am-9pm daily). This fairly hokey affair seeks to dramatize historic life on Cannery Row with more than a hundred life-sized wax figures, plus animation and sound effects.

Upstairs in the same complex is A Taste of Monterey (☎ 888-646-5446; open 11am-6pm daily), a wine visitor center with a small exhibit, gift shop and – best of all – a tasting room with panoramic views of the bay. Here you can sample the often excellent product grown in the nearby Monterey Wine Country. The fee of $5 for six wines ($10 for reserve wines) is credited toward any wine purchase. The center also hands out free maps of the wine country for self-touring.

Monterey Bay Aquarium

Monterey's most mesmerizing experience is a visit to this amazing aquarium (☎ 831-648-4888; 886 Cannery Row; adult/senior & student/child 3-12 $18/15/8; open 10am-6pm daily, 9:30am-6pm late May–early Sept & holidays), built on the site of what was once the city's largest sardine cannery. You'll encounter countless aquatic denizens, from slow-moving starfish and slimy sea slugs to animated sea lions and sea otters.

All galleries are fascinating, but the top prize goes to the new 'Jellies: Living Art' exhibit, at the aquarium until 2005. It not only presents these pulsing and wafting creatures in all their ethereal beauty and amazing variety, but also shows how they have inspired artists working in all media. There's glass sculpture by Dale Chihuly, paintings by Jackson Pollock, poetry by Jimi Hendrix, lava lamps and lots more. Standing in the infinity mirror room surrounded by what seems like millions of moon jellies is definitely a near-psychedelic moment. Even more jellyfish are on display in the Outer Bay Wing.

Other not-to-be-missed exhibits include the gigantic **kelp forest** and a three-story tank teeming with hundreds of animals – from sharks to sardines, all of which are fed at 11:30am and 4pm daily. Even more fun are the sea otter feeding sessions at 10:30am, 1:30pm and 3:30pm. At other times, these bouncy creatures can often be seen basking in the **Great Tide Pool** outside the aquarium, where they are quite free to roam around as they please. Harbor seals also drop by on occasion.

Small children love **Splash Zone**, an interactive area and home of the penguins. The **touch pools**, where you can get close to sea cucumbers, bat rays and other animals, are also a winner, and not just with the elementary school crowd.

Allow at least three hours for your visit. To avoid long lines in summer, on weekends and holidays, get tickets in advance from your hotel or by calling ☎ 831-648-4937 or ☎ 800-756-3737 ($3 transaction fee). There are several shops, a cafeteria and a restaurant with decent and affordable food.

Activities
The peninsula has some great surfing spots, though not usually for beginners. Strong rip currents and unpredictable rogue waves lie in wait for the unwary, not to mention the presence of those famous sharks. Local surfers vote Asilomar State Beach (in Pacific Grove) and Moss Landing (north of Monterey and Marina) as having the best and most consistent breaks. For surf gear and rentals, head to **On the Beach** (☎ *831-646-9283; 693 Lighthouse Ave*) in the Cannery Row area.

Monterey Bay's rich kelp forests teem with diverse marine life, making this a renowned scuba-diving site. Good spots are off San Carlos Beach near the Coast Guard Wharf in Monterey; Lovers Point in Pacific Grove; and in the Point Lobos State Preserve (see earlier in this chapter).

Monterey Bay Dive Center (☎ *831-656-0454, 800-607-2822; 225 Cannery Row*) offers instruction and equipment rental. Full standard dive outfits go for $69; snorkeling kits cost $39. Private guided tours cost $59/89 for a one/two-tank dive.

Monterey Bay Kayaks (☎ *831-373-5357, 800-649-5357; 693 Del Monte Ave*) rents open and closed kayaks from $25 per day,

Some Critters You 'Otter' Not Miss

Sea otters are one of the major attractions of the Monterey Bay Aquarium, but these charming creatures can be found all around Monterey Bay as far north as Santa Cruz.

Not long ago, the sea otter was on the brink of extinction, ruthlessly hunted down by 18th- and 19th-century fur traders because of its exceptionally dense fur (sea otters can have more than a million hairs per square inch, the thickest fur of any mammal). In 1977, the US Fish & Wildlife Service placed sea otters on the endangered species list. Otters enjoy special protection along the entire length of Big Sur in what is called the California Sea Otter Game Refuge.

Sea otters are one of the few animal species to use tools. They may be seen floating on their backs using a rock to break open shellfish. Their playful nature and laid-back appearance are what make them so popular. Besides the Monterey Bay Aquarium, other good places to see otters are Fisherman's Wharf in Monterey, several of the rocky points along 17-Mile Drive and Point Lobos State Reserve. For more information about these animals, contact the nonprofit **Friends of the Sea Otter** (☎ *831-373-2747, 800-279-3088;* **w** *www.seaotters.org; 125 Ocean View Blvd*) in Pacific Grove, or stop in at its education center and shop at 381 Cannery Row in Monterey.

offers instruction courses every weekend and operates a range of natural history tours for $50 (three hours). Adventures by the Sea is another professional outfitter.

You can spot whales off the coast of Monterey pretty much year-round. The season for blue and humpback whales runs from May to November, while gray whales pass by from mid-December to April. **Whale-watching** boats leave from Fisherman's Wharf, with three-hour trips starting at $25/18 adult/child.

Thanks to stunning scenery and paved bike paths, cycling is a very popular peninsula activity. The paved **Monterey Peninsula Recreational Trail** travels for 18 car-free miles along the waterfront from Lovers Point in Pacific Grove to Seaside, passing by Fisherman's Wharf and Cannery Row in Monterey.

For bike rentals, try the two outlets of **Adventures by the Sea** (☎ 831-372-1807 • 201 Alvarado St • 299 Cannery Row). Rentals cost $6 per hour, $18 for four hours or $24 per day. A 2½-hour guided tour is $45. In-line skates rent for $12 for two hours or $24 for all day.

Bay Bikes (☎ 831-646-9090; 640 Wave St) is another respected rental outfit in the Cannery Row area, with similar rates.

Special Events

The Monterey Peninsula keeps an active schedule of festivals and special events that attract locals and visitors year-round. Highlights include the popular **Monterey Wine Festival** (☎ 800-656-4282; w montereywine.com) in April, and the internationally famed **Monterey Jazz Festival** (☎ 831-373-3366; w www.montereyjazzfestival.org) in September; reserve tickets well in advance for both festivals.

Two Pebble Beach events also fill the area to capacity: the **AT&T Pebble Beach National Pro-Am** (☎ 831-649-1533; w www.attpbgolf.com) golf tournament in late January and the **Concours d'Elegance** (☎ 831-659-0663) classic car exhibit in August.

Places to Stay

Monterey is not noted for bargain accommodations, but if you're economizing there's camping and a great new hostel in town. Those with their own transportation can take advantage of lower prices in Salinas, about a half hour drive east of Monterey.

Prices on the peninsula are seasonal and skyrocket in summer and on weekends year-round. Central reservation agencies include **Monterey Peninsula Reservations** (☎ 888-655-3424; w www.monterey-reservations.com) and **Vacation Centers Reservations** (☎ 800-466-6283; w www.stayinmonterey.com).

Camping & Hostels The centrally located **Veterans Memorial Park Campground** (☎ 831-646-3865; campsites per vehicle $18, walk-ins $5; 3-day maximum stay) has 40 well-kept and mostly sunny sites without electricity on a first-come, first-served basis. Amenities include hot showers, flush toilets and lockers. Coming from Hwy 1, take Hwy 68 to Skyline Forest Dr to Skyline Dr north. From downtown Monterey, follow Jefferson St west into the park.

Laguna Seca Recreation Area (☎ 831-755-4899, reservations ☎ 888-588-2267; Monterey-Salinas Hwy 68; tent/RV sites $18/22) is about 9mi east of town en route to Salinas. It's a nicely maintained area with 175 spaces (102 with hookups), hot showers, flush toilets, picnic tables and fire pits.

HI Monterey Hostel (☎/fax 831-649-0375; w www.montereyhostel.com; 778 Hawthorne St; dorm beds $18-21) is a much-welcome newcomer just four blocks from the Monterey Bay Aquarium and Cannery Row. There's room for 45 and reservations are required from June to September. To get there, take bus No 1 from the Transit Center (see Getting Around later).

Motels & Hotels The cheapest accommodations are along Monterey's motel row, about 2.5mi northeast of Old Monterey on N Fremont St, east of Hwy 1 (take the Fremont St exit). Off-season prices can dip as low as $45, although you're more likely looking at $60 to $90 in the Best Westerns and Travelodge category.

For lodging options closer to central Monterey try **El Dorado Inn** (☎ 831-373-2921, 800-722-1836, fax 831-758-4509; 900 Munras Ave; rooms $45-195), a small motel within walking distance of Old Monterey. Rooms are fairly basic and imbued with a run-down feel, though some have fireplaces. Rates include a small in-room breakfast. Bus No 22 from the Transit Center to Big Sur stops right outside.

El Adobe Inn (☎ 831-372-5409, 800-433-4732, fax 831-375-7236; 936 Munras Ave; rooms $49-199), next door, is similar but has a bit more charm. It's a neat and well-kept property and rates include continental breakfast, free local calls and use of a hot tub.

Sand Dollar Inn (☎ 831-372-7551, 800-982-1986, fax 831-372-0916; ⓦ www.sanddollarinn.com; 755 Abrego St; rooms $69-149) is friendly and has cheerfully decorated rooms. It has amenities such as a heated pool and Jacuzzi, and its rates include a small breakfast.

Monterey Hotel (☎ 831-375-3184, 800-727-0960, fax 831-373-2899; ⓦ www.montereyhotel.com; 406 Alvarado St; rooms $119-329) is an historic place in a beautiful building on lively Alvarado St, right in Old Monterey. Rooms are furnished in old-world style, and rates include a good-sized continental breakfast.

Victorian Inn (☎ 831-373-8000, 800-232-4141, fax 831-373-4815; 487 Foam St; rooms $159-389), near Cannery Row, is a sprawling affair. It doesn't exactly look Victorian, but rooms do emanate the soothing elegance of a comfortable retreat.

Hotel Pacific (☎ 831-373-5700, 800-554-5542, fax 831-373-6921; ⓦ www.hotelpacific.com; 300 Pacific St; rates $189-429), an all-suite property, is one of those places where you feel welcome the moment you set foot in the door. Rooms come with elegant Spanish-style furniture, heavenly feather-beds, a large fireplace, and a kitchenette and dining area. The day starts with a plentiful continental breakfast, while the afternoon brings tea hour with cheese and fruit.

Places to Eat

Old Monterey Café (☎ 831-646-1021; 489 Alvarado St; dishes $5-11; open 7am-2:30pm daily), resolutely old-fashioned, is *the* place for plate-warping breakfasts, plus soups, sandwiches and salads.

Papa Chano's (☎ 831-646-9587; 462 Alvarado St; dishes $2-6), across the street, is a simple Mexican eatery with fresh tacos and big burritos.

Stokes Adobe (☎ 831-373-1110; 500 Hartnell St; small plates $4-8, large plates $12-20) is a highly regarded restaurant in a historic building of the same name. The varied menu focuses on the rich, rustic flavors

of Mediterranean country cooking. Think lavender-infused pork chops or pasta with fennel sausage.

Bubba Gump Shrimp Co (☎ 831-373-1884; 720 Cannery Row; mains $8-18), touristy but fun, is a rollicking theme restaurant based on the movie *Forrest Gump*. Movie stills decorate the lobby, and outside you can quite literally step into Forrest's shoes.

Lallapalooza (☎ 831-645-9036; 474 Alvarado St; mains $8-22) is a hip and sprawling restaurant-cum-martini-bar serving classic and innovative concoctions. The menu features updated versions of American classics.

Montrio (☎ 831-648-8880; 414 Calle Principal; dinner $16-29), in downtown Monterey, is a classy and uncluttered bistro with romantically spot-lit tables and the loftiness of a gallery space. The 'clouds' above the bar are excellent conversation starters. Foodwise it's California eclectic, with a good selection of creative salads and wonderful desserts not intended for waist watchers.

Tarpy's Roadhouse (☎ 831-647-1444; 2999 Monterey-Salinas Hwy No 1; mains $7-37) is in a rustic 1917 homestead about 3.5mi east of town. Locals love it for its cozy ambience and creative and often elaborate interpretations of continental fare. The menu should fit all wallet sizes.

Entertainment

For comprehensive 'what's on' listings, restaurant reviews and other information, pick up free copies of the *Coast Weekly* and *Go!*, available in bookstores, restaurants and at the visitor centers.

Most of the after-dark activity centers on Alvarado St, which is lined with pubs, coffeehouses, cinemas and restaurants.

Mucky Duck (☎ 831-655-3031; 479 Alvarado St) is a lively English-style pub while **Lallapalooza** (see Places to Eat) is famous for its selection of martinis. **Plumes** (☎ 831-373-4526; 400 Alvarado St) is a cool place to hang for a chat and a hot cup of Java. **Morgan's** (☎ 831-373-5601; 498 Washington St), a couple of block east of Alvarado, is an off-beat place with an artsy vibe and occasional live music and poetry readings. **Golden State Theater** (☎ 831-372-4555; 417 Alvarado St) is a fine old cinema in a historic building.

Cannery Row also has its share of nightlife, though most places have that irksome 'touristy' feel. **Planet Gemini** (☎ 831-373-1449; 625 Cannery Row) draws a youthful clientele with its live music and comedy shows (usually Thursday to Saturday). Enter from Hoffman Ave.

Getting There & Away

American/American Eagle, America West and United Express operate flights to Los Angeles, San Francisco and Phoenix out of **Monterey Peninsula Airport** (☎ 831-648-7000; Olmsted Rd), about 4mi southeast of downtown.

Greyhound (☎ 831-373-4735; 1042 Del Monte Ave) operates up to four direct buses daily to Santa Cruz ($10.25, 1¼ hours) and San Francisco ($17.25, three to 3¼ hours). Most buses to Los Angeles ($38.50, seven to 10 hours) require an easy change in Salinas. The bus station is at the Monterey Bay Gas & Minimart.

The nearest Amtrak station is in Salinas, about 17mi east of Monterey. It's a stop for the *Coast Starlight* on its route from Seattle to Los Angeles. Shuttle buses to Monterey run throughout the day and cost $8 each way. Call ☎ 800-872-7245 for information.

Monterey is 120mi south of San Francisco (scenic and slow by Hwy 1, quicker via Hwys 101 and 156). If you need to rent a car, all major companies – Budget, Hertz etc – have offices in Monterey. For locations, call the toll-free numbers in the Getting Around chapter or check the *Yellow Pages*.

Getting Around

Monterey-Salinas Transit (MST; ☎ 831-899-2555; w www.mst.org) bus No 21 travels from the airport to the Monterey Transit Plaza in downtown Monterey. Other reasonably close airports are those in San Francisco and San Jose (see those sections). **Monterey-Salinas Airbus** (reservations ☎ 831-883-2871) provides shuttle service to either airport from the Transit Plaza ($30/55 one way/round-trip, 10 a day).

Monterey-Salinas Transit operates bus services throughout the peninsula, inland to Salinas and south to Point Lobos and Big Sur as far as Nepenthe. Tickets cost from $1.75 to $3.50 and all-day passes are available.

Routes converge at the **Monterey Transit Plaza** (Jules Simoneau Plaza, Alvarado St). From here, bus No 1 makes the trip out to Cannery Row and Pacific Grove. Other useful routes include bus Nos 4 and 5 to Carmel; No 22 to Big Sur via Carmel (May to October only) and Nos 20 and 21 to Salinas (No 21 goes via Laguna Seca and the airport).

From late May to early September, you can save the fare by taking the free **WAVE** (Waterfront Area Visitors Express; ☎ 831-899-2555), a shuttle that loops around Old Monterey, Fisherman's Wharf and Cannery Row daily from 9am to 6:30pm.

AROUND MONTEREY
Mazda Raceway Laguna Seca

Just off Hwy 68, about midway between Salinas and Monterey, the Mazda Raceway Laguna Seca (☎ 831-648-5111, 800-373-0533) attracts racing fans with a year-round schedule of top-rated race car, vintage car and motorcycle events. Details are available on w www.laguna-seca.com. Back in the early 1950s, races used to take place on a road circuit in the Del Monte Forest at Pebble Beach, but the track was very unsafe and the Laguna Seca track replaced it in 1956.

SALINAS

Just 17mi east of Monterey, Salinas (population 120,000) is the birthplace of John Steinbeck and a major agricultural center whose top crop is the lowly iceberg lettuce. From May to September, more than six million heads are harvested each day, a feat that's garnered the area the nickname 'the world's salad bowl.' Easily reached by public transportation or by car via Hwy 68, Salinas makes a strong contrast with the conspicuous affluence of other peninsula cities. Its historic center stretches out along Main St, whose northern end is punctuated by the town's main attraction, the National Steinbeck Center.

Pick up information and maps at the **Salinas Visitors Center** (☎ 831-424-7611, fax 831-424-8639; 119 E Alisal St; open 8:30am-5pm Mon-Fri), four blocks east of Main St.

Seasonal highlights include the **California Rodeo** (☎ 831-775-3100; w www.carodeo.com) in July and the **California International Airshow** (☎ 888-845-7469; w www.ca-airshow.com) in September or October.

National Steinbeck Center

The vast, state-of-the-art National Steinbeck Center (☎ 831-796-3833; w www.steinbeck.org; 1 Main St; adult/concession $8/7; open 10am-5pm daily) is a fitting homage to Salinas' Nobel Prize–winning native son, John Steinbeck (1902–68). Steinbeck's literary explorations were influenced and inspired by the people and daily life of the area; his observations on Cannery Row in Monterey resulted in the eponymous 1945 book.

The interactive exhibit chronicles the writer's life and works in a creative and engaging fashion. Each of seven theme galleries stages scenes from famous books such as *The Grapes of Wrath*, *East of Eden* and *Of Mice and Men*, incorporating quotes and artifacts such as letters and books. There's also a small theater showing film clips. Prized exhibits include Rocinante, the customized camper in which Steinbeck traveled around America while researching *Travels with Charley*. A short biographical film provides an introduction to the man and his volatile career.

Steinbeck was born and spent much of his boyhood in what is now **Steinbeck House** (☎ 831-424-2735; 132 Central Ave), two blocks west of the center. It's now a fancy restaurant, open for lunch daily except Sunday. Steinbeck is buried in the **Garden of Memories Cemetery** family plot.

Places to Stay & Eat

Salinas has plenty of chain motels, making it a less expensive base from which to explore the Monterey Peninsula. Properties include: **Econo Lodge** (☎ 831-422-5111; 180 Sanborn Rd; rooms $48-99); **Days Inn** (☎ 831-759-9900; 1226 De La Torre St; rooms $68-170); **Comfort Inn** (☎ 831-758-8850; 144 Kern St; rooms $79-299); **Super 8 Motel** (☎ 831-422-6486; 1030 Fairview Ave; rooms $50-100); and **Vagabond Inn** (☎ 831-758-4693; 131 Kern St; rooms $80-160).

Laurel Inn (☎ 831-449-2474, 800-354-9831, fax 831-449-2476; w www.laurelinnmotel.com; 801 W Laurel Dr; rooms $60-150) is family-owned and a good choice if chains don't do it for you. Rooms are clean with welcoming decor and there's a large pool, hot tub and sauna for relaxing. It's right off the Hwy 101 Laurel Dr exit.

If hunger strikes, you'll find several options along Main St near the Steinbeck Center, including these two gems:

John Steinbeck

Traipse through the word houses built by many West Coast writers, and you'll encounter the large footprints of John Steinbeck, just leaving the room. Steinbeck is as thoroughly an American writer as Mark Twain. A writer defined by the land in which he lived and by the people he lived among.

A roughneck, Stanford dropout, social critic, humorist, screenwriter and war correspondent, Steinbeck grew up and worked with the desperate people who toiled, often on the edge of starvation, in the fields of his native Salinas. His knowledge of the human condition was largely shaped by his observations of the eternal struggle to hold on to some shred of human dignity in the face of utmost poverty.

The honesty of his feelings about life's inequities is nowhere more powerful than in his greatest novel, *The Grapes of Wrath*, which garnered him a Pulitzer Prize. It's the wrenching story of a family of 1930s dust bowl farmers who reach the end of their road in the farm fields of California and whose trials, humiliation and ultimate defeat are met with stoicism and nobility. This theme – of redemption in the face of disaster – is one that echoes through much of Steinbeck's work.

When awarded the Nobel Prize for Literature in 1962, Steinbeck said in his acceptance speech: 'Literature...grew out of the human need for it, and it has not changed much except to become more needed. The writer is delegated to declare and to celebrate man's proven capacity for greatness of heart and spirit – for gallantry in defeat, for courage, compassion and love.' Reading Steinbeck is still to be put in touch with something profoundly American.

David Peevers

First Awakening (☎ 831-784-1125; 171 S Main St; dishes $4.50-8.50; open 7am-2pm daily), in a beautiful turreted building, does breakfasts that will easily sustain you until the afternoon. At lunch, it's mostly salads and sandwiches.

Hullaballoo (☎ 831-757-3663; 228 S Main St; lunch $7-18, dinner $8-25) has a lively, artistic feel and a seasonally changing menu billed as 'bold American cooking.'

Expect lots of local produce combined creatively with lamb, steak, chicken and fish.

Getting There & Away
MST buses from Monterey (No 20 via Marina or No 21 via Hwy 68; $3.50) stop at the Salinas Transit Center, one block west of the Steinbeck Center. The Amtrak station is two blocks north of the transit center, via N Main St.

ALONG HIGHWAY 101
Traveling inland along Hwy 101 is a good alternative for people wanting to travel quickly between the Monterey Peninsula and San Luis Obispo. The landscape seems monotonous compared to the striking scenery along Hwy 1, but there are a few worthwhile stops, including several California missions as well as the small but interesting Pinnacles National Monument.

Paso Robles
About 30mi north of San Luis Obispo, Paso Robles (population 23,000) is at the heart of an agricultural region where grapes now constitute the biggest crop. Several dozen wineries along Hwy 46 produce a good number of increasingly respectable bottles. Paso Robles' other claim to fame is its hot springs which were recently re-drilled and can once again be enjoyed at the Paso Robles Inn as well as at the **Paso Robles Hot Springs & Spa** (☎ 805-238-4600; 3725 Buena Vista Dr).

The town's historic core centers on Park and 12th Sts, where the restored Carnegie Historic Library Museum and the Clocktower Building serve as reminders of the past. The **chamber of commerce** (☎ 805-238-0506, 800-406-4040, fax 805-238-0527; w www.pasorobleschamber.com; 1225 Park St) has maps and information.

About 25mi east of Hwy 101, on Hwy 46, a monument marks the spot where James Dean died in a car crash on September 30 1955 at the age of 24.

Paso Robles Wine Country The wine country surrounding Paso Robles is worth a day's exploration, as it has not yet attained the notoriety, throngs of people or price levels of Napa or Sonoma. Most wineries are concentrated along Hwy 46 West, off Hwy 101 south of town, although a few more line Hwy 46 East due east of town.

Most vineyards have tasting rooms and free tours. Maps are available from the chamber of commerce and various businesses around town. Good stops include **Eberle Winery** (☎ 805-238-9607; Hwy 46 East; tastings 10am-6pm daily), which has a lovely deck with vineyard views, and offers tours of its wine caves. It's 3.5mi east of Hwy 101. **York Mountain Winery** (☎ 805-238-3925; Hwy 46 West; tastings 10am-5pm daily), 7mi west of Hwy 101, is the oldest winery around here and has a tasting room in an old log cabin.

Places to Stay & Eat Paso Robles' accommodations are concentrated along Spring St, the town's main thoroughfare.

Melody Ranch Motel (☎ 805-238-3911, 800-909-3911; 939 Spring St; rooms $45-70) is the cheapest place in town, but rooms are quite adequate and there's even a small pool.

Adelaide Inn (☎ 805-238-2770, 800-549-7276; 1215 Ysabel Ave; rooms $55-90), in a pleasant setting, has a pool, spa and sauna for relaxing, although the rooms are pretty standard.

Paso Robles Inn (☎ 805-238-2660, 800-676-1713, 805-238-4707; w www.pasorob lesinn.com; 1103 Spring St; rooms $95-245), in the town center, is *the* most fun place in town. It's an historic building sitting above mineral hot springs whose restful qualities you can enjoy in the privacy of your own in-room therapy spa. Many rooms also feature fireplaces. It's all set in a pretty garden, and there's a restaurant on the premises.

Lolo's (☎ 805-239-5777; 305 Spring St; dishes $4.50-9.50) is an inexpensive Mexican eatery with an outdoor patio.

Bistro Laurent (☎ 805-226-8191; 1202 Pine St; mains $15-20) is helmed by a skilled chef who knows his way around a French menu. It's housed in a nice old brick building with plenty of atmosphere.

Getting There & Away CCAT bus No 9 from San Luis Obispo makes the trip to Paso Robles several times daily (90 minutes). Amtrak's *Coast Starlight* also stops in town once daily, as do several Greyhound buses.

Mission San Miguel Arcángel
North of Paso Robles off Hwy 101, Mission San Miguel Arcángel (☎ 805-467-3256; 775 Mission St; admission by donation; open

9:30am-4:30pm daily) is the most accessible and one of the most authentic of the California missions. Established in 1797 as a stopover between Mission San Antonio de Padua and Mission San Luis Obispo de Tolosa, Mission San Miguel was number 16 in the chain of 21 missions. The current structure dates back to 1818 and has not been significantly altered since, as is evident from its rough and water-stained appearance. Murals painted by Chumash Indians, using pigment from local rock, are visible in the main church. It's still run by Franciscan friars.

A self-guided walking tour begins in the gift shop and goes through the mission's interior rooms and garden; allow half an hour. The enormous cactus in front of the mission was planted about the same time the mission was built. Mass is held on Sundays and church holidays.

Rios Caledonia Adobe

A ¼mi south of the mission is the Rios Caledonia Adobe *(☎ 805-467-3357; admission free; open 10am-4pm Wed-Sun)*, which stands on mission property that Governor Pio Pico illegally sold to Petronillo Rios in 1846. Using Chumash labor, Rios built the two-story adobe as a ranch headquarters and hacienda for his family, later turning it into an inn and stagecoach stop on the route between Los Angeles and San Francisco. Original adobe bricks are visible where the whitewash has peeled off. Coming from Hwy 101, take the Stagecoach Rd exit.

Lake Nacimiento

About 17mi northwest of Paso Robles (reached via Lake Nacimiento Rd, clearly marked from Hwy 101), Lake Nacimiento is best visited on the way to or from Mission San Antonio de Padua, unless you are a water-skier, in which case it deserves priority status. With its sprawling inlets, the pine- and oak-fringed reservoir is considered one of the best water-skiing spots in the USA. The lake is crowded with boats from April to October, especially on weekends and holidays. Most lakeshore property is privately owned.

Lake Nacimiento Resort *(☎ 805-238-3256, 800-323-3839; ⓦ www.nacimiento resort.com; day-use fee for 2 people Mar-Oct $10, Nov-Feb $7, additional people $3 each; campsites $25/18, RV sites $35/24, rental trailers from $115, lodges from $195)* pro-vides the only public access; rates include use of a swimming pool, hot tub and other facilities. The restaurant serves good breakfast and lunch and marginal dinners during summer. There are six campgrounds with 260 sites, both for tents and RVs, and various cabins sleeping from four to 10 people. A variety of boats are for rent from $65 to $400 per day; kayaks and canoes rent for $5/18 per hour/day, pedal boats for $10/25.

Mission San Antonio de Padua

The remote location of this mission *(☎ 831-385-4478; admission by donation; open 8am-6pm daily May-Oct, 8am-5pm Nov-Apr)* is a disincentive to many, but it's well worth the trip. Just getting there is interesting because the mission is in the middle of Fort Hunter Ligget, an active army base, and you have to pass a military checkpoint before being allowed to proceed.

The mission was founded in 1771 by Padre Serra and built with Native American labor from Salinas. The church is nicely restored, with decorative flourishes adorning the whitewashed walls – note the wooden pulpit and elaborate canopied altar. A creaky door leads to a garden anchored by a fountain and ringed by tall cypress trees. The mission museum has a good collection of Native American baskets, embroidered garments and furnishings as well as such utilitarian items as an olive press, a loom and other equipment used in the mission's workshops. There's more to explore on the grounds, where you can see the remains of a grist mill, rip saw, corral, reservoir and irrigation system.

A quarter mile before the mission, on a hill, is the Spanish-style **Hacienda Milpitas Ranch House** *(rooms $33, with bath $46-55, 2-bedroom apartment $125)* designed in 1930 by Julia Morgan for William Randolph Hearst. The inn is privately owned and has a restaurant and bar, both popular with the soldiers. The food is neither gourmet nor military grub, but you can get a big steak and all the trimmings for around $10. This is also a great place to spend the night for those on a budget. All rooms are large and equipped with TV and VCR, microwave, coffeemaker and fridge, although the furniture is a bit frayed at the edges.

Getting There & Away From the north, take the Jolon exit (just before King City) off

Hwy 101 and follow Jolon Rd (G14) 20mi south to Mission Rd. From the south, take the Hwy 101 exit marked San Antonio Mission/Lake San Antonio Recreation Area (north of Bradley) and head 22mi northwest on G18. You'll pass a few markets and gas stations on the northern shore of Lake San Antonio (good for swimming) and eventually pass through the military checkpoint. From here, it's a few more miles to the mission.

You can also reach the mission from Hwy 1, about 28mi away via the Nacimiento-Fergusson Rd.

Pinnacles National Monument

Pinnacles National Monument (☎ 831-389-4485; w www.nps.gov/pinn; open 7:30am-8pm daily) gets its name from the spires and crags that rise abruptly up to 1200ft out of the oak- and chaparral-covered hills of the Salinas Valley. The rocks are remains of an ancient volcano that formed along the San Andreas Rift Zone about 23 million years ago. Their arches, spires and crags are the result of millions of years of erosion. The monument is open year-round but spring and fall are the best seasons to visit. Summers are scorching, while winter brings rain.

Orientation & Information The rock formations divide the park into East Pinnacles and West Pinnacles. While there is no road connecting the two sides, you can hike from one end to the other in about an hour.

Information, maps, books and bottled water are available from **Bear Gulch Visitor Center** (eastern side) and **Chaparral Ranger Station** (western side).

The monument is open for day-use only (no overnight camping) and there's a $5 fee per vehicle, valid for seven consecutive days. You'll also receive an illustrated park map. The best time to visit is midweek as parking lots at trailheads fill up quickly on busy weekends.

Activities The Pinnacles' stark beauty is best appreciated on a hike. Due to the park's fairly small size, none are terribly long but nevertheless range from easy to strenuous. Pick up a map at the visitor centers.

Among the park's main attractions are its two talus caves (formed by piles of large boulders), one of which – the **Balconies Cave** – is open for exploration. Scrambling through here is not an exercise recommended for the claustrophobic as it's pitch-black inside, making a flashlight essential (for sale at the visitor centers). The route is not always obvious to the inexperienced, so be prepared to get lost a bit.

The cave is 0.7mi from the Chaparral ranger station. From the eastern side, park at the Chalone Creek trailhead, then head north on the easy Old Pinnacles Trail for about 2.3mi. The other cave, called Bear Gulch Cave, has been closed to visitors since 1997 so as not to disturb a large colony of Townsend's big-eared bats in residence there.

Rock climbing is very popular, although the Pinnacles' volcanic tufa crumbles easily, making it suitable only for experienced climbers. Climbing access signs direct people to the best spots, most of which are on the eastern side. For vital information, check with the rangers or consult the *Climber's Guide to Pinnacles National Monument* by David Rubine.

Other activities include **bird-watching** and **wildflower walks** in spring. **Cycling** is limited to the paved roads.

Places to Stay There's no camping within the park, but the private **Pinnacles Campground** (☎ 831-389-4462; tent/RV per person Sun-Thur $7/9.50, Fri-Sat $14/17), just outside the East Pinnacles entrance, has 78 tent sites and 36 RV hookups. Rates include hot showers. It also has a swimming pool and convenience store.

Off Hwy 101, Soledad has a bank, gas station, market, a few Mexican restaurants and some budget motels.

Getting There & Away For West Pinnacles follow Hwy 146, going east off Hwy 101 at Soledad, for about 12mi. The eastern entrance is a bit harder to reach. Coming from the south, turn east onto route G13 at King City, follow it for about 17mi, then continue north on Hwy 25 for another 13mi to the turnoff for the monument. From the north, take Hwy 25 just south of Gilroy and follow it for about 35mi to the turnoff.

Thanks

Many thanks to the travellers who used the last edition and wrote to us with helpful hints, useful advice and interesting anecdotes:

Jo Abbie, Elizabeth Abbott, Maria Amuchastegui, Morten Andersen-Gott, Lars Anderson, Trygve Anderson, Warren Anderson, Stephen andrew Lee, Linda Appanaitis, Charlie Appleby, Ofra Arbel, Ofra & Youval Arbel, Neil Bage, J Baker, Magdalena Balcerek, Theodore C. Bale, Sarah-Jane Bateman, Mehdi Bazargan, Darren Beckett, Judith Beery, Caroline Bell, Tony Benfield, Stacy Benjamin, Bruce Berger, Bob Bergevin, Ken Berry, Carolyn Bickford, Jo Billingham, Emma H Black, Mike Blencowe, Joseph Blum, Jan Bohuslav, Renee Bremer, David Bridgman, Elizabeth Brightwell, Andrew Britton, Norman Broad, Kevin Broughton, Sheila Bryans, John Bryant, Pam Bryant, Felicity Buddell, Hollywood Bungalows, Nicholas Burton, Heidi Buxton, Heidi & Richard Buxton, Vassili Bykov, Regina Campbell, Camiel Camps, Florence Caplow, Michael Cartwright, Robin Catto, Jacky Chalk, Kam Chan, Brenda J. Chapel, Kevin Chapman, Darrin Charmley, Jennifer E. Chase, Xavier Chavez, Hua Chee Ooi, RA Cherriman, Lovan Chetty, Kate Chmiel, Lars Bruun Christensen, Veronica Cocco, Bethany collings, JE Collins, John Connell, Geoff Cook, Sharon Cooper, Sena Copson, Sena & Ray Copson, Graeme Cornwallis, Kevin Cotter, Scott Crawford, Robert Crisp, Robert Cross, Angel Cuadras, Adele Cushing, Jorgen Dahl, Lucy Dallas, Chris Dalton, Helen Daunt, Robin Daus, C. David Gibbons, Jim Davis, Joshana Davis-Twomey, Vicki Dawkins, Hermelinda De La Torre, Karin de Lauje, Trisha Delbridge, Chris Delodder, Christina Demetriou, Susan Derby, Pam Dickson, Michele DiNunzio, Jean-Noël Doan, Tim Dolta, Scott Donahue, Mike Dowling, Karina Duffy, Joanne Duggan, Monica Ehman, Sue Ellen Shaneyfelt, Nivine Emeran, Lotta Emgard, Jenni Empson-Ridler, Marilee Enge, Johanna Fabre, Colin Falls, Marian Ferrari, MOnica ferrari, Tami Fichter, Amy-lynn Fischer, Jane Fitzpatrick, Grant Fletcher, Andrea Foley, A Ford, Steve Fox, Jerry Franks, Nick Freeman, Eleanor Friedman, Neville Fursdon, Alessandro Gagliardi, Vanessa Gajewska, Claire Gardner, Joanne Garrah, Jennifer Gaylord, Indraneel Ghose, Charlotte Gibson, Rafael Gilliam, Graham Gilpin, Erik Gothberg, Rodrigo Gouvea Rosique, Martin Green, Keith Greenfield, Chantal Grisanti, Patrick Grove, JC Gwilliam, Annika Hacin, Claire Haddon,

Jody Hansen, Prine Hansen, Robert Hanson, David Harcombe, Piers Harding, Piers & Marysia Harding, Shea Hardy, Stephen Harris, Sue Harvey, Camilla Heath, Brian Heeney, Nico Heijnen, Kathleen Helgesen, Oyvind Henriksen, Barbara Hess, Barbara & Art Hess, Ric Higgins, P Hill, P & W R Hill, Andrew Hindmarch, Vincent Hogenboom, Noor Hogeweg, Kai Holderbaum, Muei Hoon Tan, Damien Horigan, Janet Howell, Faridah Iriani Tahir, Jude Isherwood, Mary Jacob, Bailey T James, Michela Janni, Asker Jeukendrup, Pam Johnson, Paul Johnson, Alan Jones, Christopher Jones, Darryl Jones, Margaret Jones, Romy Jouen, Teresa Kamieniak, Lyndis Kang, Michael Keary, Rachel Keary, John Kelleher, Bas Kempen, Karen Kester, Heidi Kestnebaum, Jennifer Keys, Don Kilburg, Alan Kirsner, Michael R. Kluge, Anke Kolbe, Ernst & Annelies Koningsveld, Cherrill Kousal, Winston Kousal, Vera Kramer, Pierre Kruse, Hartmut Kuhne, Frances Kwok, Karen Lally, Nathan Landau, Silviu Landman, JM Latham, Wilbur Lawson, Adrian le Hanne, Elli Levy, Erin Lewis, Hope Liebersohn, Krista Lighthall, Keith Liker, Felicia Lim, JD Lindsay, Brian livingstone, Fiona Llewellyn, Kieron Lo, Kristy Lombardo, Kristy & Anthony Lombardo, Margaret Lord, Wendi Lunn, Christine Lutz, Jack Lynch, Jamie Mackenzie, JL Macomber, Christine Magnor, Andreas Mahn, Evan Malonai, Mary Marcia Pope, Philippe Margaron, Sheryl Maring, Della Markey, P Marquis, Marc Marsh-Desmarais, Don Martine, Marti Matulis, Jade Mawbey, Eve Mayberry, Eve & Frank Mayberry, Frank Mayberry, Sally Maynard, Annette McCormick, Iain McCormick, Jim McGillis, Daryl & Dia McKee, Colin McKinlay, Chris McLaughlin, Darren McLean, Jenny McRae, Kristine Melby, Mercedes Meras, Finn Mikkelsen, Finn & Lene Mikkelsen, Frances Millane, Melina Mingari, John Mitchell, Erik Moderegger, Karin Monnink, Chris Mono, Patrick Mounsey, Nanelle Mulligan, Christian Mussegaard, Claire Nash-Wortham, Claire & Fiona Nash-Wortham, Mickey Nee, Julie Needham, Richard Nelson, Serwind Netzler, Kenneth Newman, Leslie Newman, Tracey Nicholls, Juanita Nicholson, Hemming Nielsen, Ellen Nobels, Nathalie Nollet, Marc Norman, David Nutt, Mike Ocon, Regina O'Connor, Leah Oehlert, Janet Oflynn, Markku Paalanen, Amy Packer, Miles Parker, Brett Paterson, Katerina Pavlou, Nigel Peacock, Stephen Pearce, Rachel J. Pearcey, Grant Pearse, Virginia Persson, DJ Peterson, Dennis Phelan, Leighton & Jane Phillips, Jo Pilkington-Down,

David Pinder, Eliose de Paula Piva, Petr Polednak, Monta Pooley, Lindsay Pulliam, Christpher Race, Linda Rafferty, Maria Ralph, Thomas Rau, Jessica Raymond, Michiel Reneman, Theresa Rieder, Alex ro, Jon Roberts, Kelly Roberts, Alan F. Robilliard, Ruud Roemeling, Andrea Rogge, Ryon Rosovold, Neil J. Rubenking, Raymond Rudd, David Rutter, Sally-Ann Ryder, Hannah Salvidge, S Sanderson, Shornj Sandhu, Lee Savage, Kari Schjolberg Henriksen, Ronald Schlosberg, Link Schrader, Martin Seed, Martin & Mary Seed, Liz Seers, Himanshu Sharma, Alan Sharp, Mick Sharry, Mick & Liz Sharry, Nicole Shaw, Sue Shepard, Kamer Sidhy, Pernilla Siebenfreund, Andreas Silzle, Elaine Simer, Simon Skerrit, Joyce Slaton, David W Smith, L. Smith, Rachael Smith, Rob smith, Claire Snel, Christian Sobotta, Christian & Heike Sobotta, Maibritt Sorensen, Henrik Stender Christensen, Rob Stevens, Jeannette Stewart, Caroline Stout, Valerie Straayer, Valerie & Ilinois State Geological Survey Straayer, Joe Suchman, Jean e Sunderland, Selvi Supramaniam, Joe Szper, Jane Tate, Melanie Thomas, Richard Thompson, Gemma Tinsdale, Hannah Treworgy, Wendy Tucker, Anita Tveter, C B Valdez, Huub van der Linden, Niels van der Werff, Govert van Ginkel, Margo & Fred van Roosmalen, Christa Van Schaardenburg, Erica Van Zon, Krista Vanggaard, Stephanie Vincent, Paul von Wichert, Sally Wade, Barbara Wall, Tobias Wall, Adrian Watson, A Weekes, Norman Weisser, Jodie Whan, Steve White, Gill Whitfield, Stephanie Wickersham, Erika Wienecke, David Wignall, Monique Williamson, Clare Winkel, Adriaan Witjes, David Wlfhart, Allan Wong, Karen Wong, Kenneth Woolley, Bruce Wright, Jim Wright, Richard Yates, Dave Yoshimoto, Donna Zalan, Suki Zoe, Sheila Zompa.

LONELY PLANET

You already know that Lonely Planet produces more than this one guidebook, but you might not be aware of the other products we have on this region. Here is a selection of titles that you may want to check out as well:

Los Angeles condensed
ISBN 1 74059 334 0
US$11.99 • UK£6.99

Las Vegas
ISBN 1 74059 169 0
US$15.99 • UK£9.99

World Food California
ISBN 1 74059 430 4
US$14.99 • UK£9.99

Las Vegas condensed
ISBN 1 74059 453 3
US$12.99 • UK£6.99

USA
ISBN 1 86450 308 4
US$24.99 • UK£14.99

San Francisco
ISBN 1 86450 309 2
US$15.99 • UK£9.99

San Francisco condensed
ISBN 1 74059 380 4
US$11.99 • UK£6.99

Cycling USA - West Coast
ISBN 1 86450 324 6
US$21.99 • UK£13.99

Hiking in the Sierra Nevada
ISBN 1 74059 272 7
US$17.99 • UK£11.99

San Francisco map
ISBN 1 86450 014 X
US$5.95 • UK£3.99

Los Angeles map
ISBN 1 86450 258 4
US$5.99 • UK£3.99

Diving & Snorkeling Southern California & the Channel Islands
ISBN 1 86450 293 2
US$16.99 • UK£10.99

Available wherever books are sold

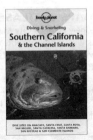

LONELY PLANET

ON THE ROAD

Travel Guides explore cities, regions and countries, and supply information on transport, restaurants and accommodation, covering all budgets. They come with reliable, easy-to-use maps, practical advice, cultural and historical facts and a rundown on attractions both on and off the beaten track. There are over 200 titles in this classic series, covering nearly every country in the world.

 Lonely Planet Upgrades extend the shelf life of existing travel guides by detailing any changes that may affect travel in a region since a book has been published. Upgrades can be downloaded for free from **www.lonelyplanet.com/upgrades**

For travellers with more time than money, **Shoestring** guides offer dependable, first-hand information with hundreds of detailed maps, plus insider tips for stretching money as far as possible. Covering entire continents in most cases, the six-volume shoestring guides are known around the world as 'backpackers bibles'.

For the discerning short-term visitor, **Condensed** guides highlight the best a destination has to offer in a full-colour, pocket-sized format designed for quick access. They include everything from top sights and walking tours to opinionated reviews of where to eat, stay, shop and have fun.

CitySync lets travellers use their Palm™ or Visor™ hand-held computers to guide them through a city with handy tips on transport, history, cultural life, major sights, and shopping and entertainment options. It can also quickly search and sort hundreds of reviews of hotels, restaurants and attractions, and pinpoint their location on scrollable street maps. CitySync can be downloaded from **www.citysync.com**

MAPS & ATLASES

Lonely Planet's **City Maps** feature downtown and metropolitan maps, as well as transit routes and walking tours. The maps come complete with an index of streets, a listing of sights and a plastic coat for extra durability.

Road Atlases are an essential navigation tool for serious travellers. Cross-referenced with the guidebooks, they also feature distance and climate charts and a complete site index.

LONELY PLANET

ESSENTIALS

Read This First books help new travellers to hit the road with confidence. These invaluable predeparture guides give step-by-step advice on preparing for a trip, budgeting, arranging a visa, planning an itinerary and staying safe while still getting off the beaten track.

Healthy Travel pocket guides offer a regional rundown on disease hot spots and practical advice on predeparture health measures, staying well on the road and what to do in emergencies. The guides come with a user-friendly design and helpful diagrams and tables.

Lonely Planet's **Phrasebooks** cover the essential words and phrases travellers need when they're strangers in a strange land. They come in a pocket-sized format with colour tabs for quick reference, extensive vocabulary lists, easy-to-follow pronunciation keys and two-way dictionaries.

Miffed by blurry photos of the Taj Mahal? Tired of the classic 'top of the head cut off' shot? **Travel Photography: A Guide to Taking Better Pictures** will help you turn ordinary holiday snaps into striking images and give you the know-how to capture every scene, from frenetic festivals to peaceful beach sunrises.

Lonely Planet's **Travel Journal** is a lightweight but sturdy travel diary for jotting down all those on-the-road observations and significant travel moments. It comes with a handy time-zone wheel, a world map and useful travel information.

Lonely Planet's eKno is an all-in-one communication service developed especially for travellers. It offers low-cost international calls and free email and voicemail so that you can keep in touch while on the road. Check it out on **www.ekno.lonelyplanet.com**

FOOD & RESTAURANT GUIDES

Lonely Planet's **Out to Eat** guides recommend the brightest and best places to eat and drink in top international cities. These gourmet companions are arranged by neighbourhood, packed with dependable maps, garnished with scene-setting photos and served with quirky features.

For people who live to eat, drink and travel, **World Food** guides explore the culinary culture of each country. Entertaining and adventurous, each guide is packed with detail on staples and specialities, regional cuisine and local markets, as well as sumptuous recipes, comprehensive culinary dictionaries and lavish photos good enough to eat.

LONELY PLANET

OUTDOOR GUIDES

For those who believe the best way to see the world is on foot, Lonely Planet's **Walking Guides** detail everything from family strolls to difficult treks, with 'when to go and how to do it' advice supplemented by reliable maps and essential travel information.

Cycling Guides map a destination's best bike tours, long and short, in day-by-day detail. They contain all the information a cyclist needs, including advice on bike maintenance, places to eat and stay, innovative maps with detailed cues to the rides, and elevation charts.

The **Watching Wildlife** series is perfect for travellers who want authoritative information but don't want to tote a heavy field guide. Packed with advice on where, when and how to view a region's wildlife, each title features photos of over 300 species and contains engaging comments on the local flora and fauna.

With underwater colour photos throughout, **Pisces Books** explore the world's best diving and snorkelling areas. Each book contains listings of diving services and dive resorts, detailed information on depth, visibility and difficulty of dives, and a roundup of the marine life you're likely to see through your mask.

LONELY PLANET

OFF THE ROAD

Journeys, the travel literature series written by renowned travel authors, capture the spirit of a place or illuminate a culture with a journalist's attention to detail and a novelist's flair for words. These are tales to soak up while you're actually on the road or dip into as an at-home armchair indulgence.

The range of lavishly illustrated **Pictorial** books is just the ticket for both travellers and dreamers. Off-beat tales and vivid photographs bring the adventure of travel to your doorstep long before the journey begins and long after it is over.

Lonely Planet **Videos** encourage the same independent, tough-minded approach as the guidebooks. Currently airing throughout the world, this award-winning series features innovative footage and an original soundtrack.

Yes, we know, work is tough, so do a little bit of deskside dreaming with the spiral-bound Lonely Planet **Diary** or a Lonely Planet **Wall Calendar**, filled with great photos from around the world.

TRAVELLERS NETWORK

Lonely Planet Online. Lonely Planet's award-winning Web site has insider information on hundreds of destinations, from Amsterdam to Zimbabwe, complete with interactive maps and relevant links. The site also offers the latest travel news, recent reports from travellers on the road, guidebook upgrades, a travel links site, an online book-buying option and a lively travellers bulletin board. It can be viewed at **www.lonelyplanet.com** or AOL keyword: lp.

Planet Talk is a quarterly print newsletter, full of gossip, advice, anecdotes and author articles. It provides an antidote to the being-at-home blues and lets you plan and dream for the next trip. Contact the nearest Lonely Planet office for your free copy.

Comet, the free Lonely Planet newsletter, comes via email once a month. It's loaded with travel news, advice, dispatches from authors, travel competitions and letters from readers. To subscribe, click on the Comet subscription link on the front page of the Web site.

LONELY PLANET

Guides by Region

L onely Planet is known worldwide for publishing practical, reliable and no-nonsense travel information in our guides and on our Web site. The Lonely Planet list covers just about every accessible part of the world. Currently there are 16 series: Travel guides, Shoestring guides, Condensed guides, Phrasebooks, Read This First, Healthy Travel, Walking guides, Cycling guides, Watching Wildlife guides, Pisces Diving & Snorkeling guides, City Maps, Road Atlases, Out to Eat, World Food, Journeys travel literature and Pictorials.

AFRICA Africa on a shoestring • Botswana • Cairo • Cairo City Map • Cape Town • Cape Town City Map • East Africa • Egypt • Egyptian Arabic phrasebook • Ethiopia, Eritrea & Djibouti • Ethiopian Amharic phrasebook • The Gambia & Senegal • Healthy Travel Africa • Kenya • Malawi • Morocco • Moroccan Arabic phrasebook • Mozambique • Namibia • Read This First: Africa • South Africa, Lesotho & Swaziland • Southern Africa • Southern Africa Road Atlas • Swahili phrasebook • Tanzania, Zanzibar & Pemba • Trekking in East Africa • Tunisia • Watching Wildlife East Africa • Watching Wildlife Southern Africa • West Africa • World Food Morocco • Zambia • Zimbabwe, Botswana & Namibia
Travel Literature: Mali Blues: Traveling to an African Beat • The Rainbird: A Central African Journey • Songs to an African Sunset: A Zimbabwean Story

AUSTRALIA & THE PACIFIC Aboriginal Australia & the Torres Strait Islands •Auckland • Australia • Australian phrasebook • Australia Road Atlas • Cycling Australia • Cycling New Zealand • Fiji • Fijian phrasebook • Healthy Travel Australia, NZ & the Pacific • Islands of Australia's Great Barrier Reef • Melbourne • Melbourne City Map • Micronesia • New Caledonia • New South Wales • New Zealand • Northern Territory • Outback Australia • Out to Eat – Melbourne • Out to Eat – Sydney • Papua New Guinea • Pidgin phrasebook • Queensland • Rarotonga & the Cook Islands • Samoa • Solomon Islands • South Australia • South Pacific • South Pacific phrasebook • Sydney • Sydney City Map • Sydney Condensed • Tahiti & French Polynesia • Tasmania • Tonga • Tramping in New Zealand • Vanuatu • Victoria • Walking in Australia • Watching Wildlife Australia • Western Australia
Travel Literature: Islands in the Clouds: Travels in the Highlands of New Guinea • Kiwi Tracks: A New Zealand Journey • Sean & David's Long Drive

CENTRAL AMERICA & THE CARIBBEAN Bahamas, Turks & Caicos • Baja California • Belize, Guatemala & Yucatán • Bermuda • Central America on a shoestring • Costa Rica • Costa Rica Spanish phrasebook • Cuba • Cycling Cuba • Dominican Republic & Haiti • Eastern Caribbean • Guatemala • Havana • Healthy Travel Central & South America • Jamaica • Mexico • Mexico City • Panama • Puerto Rico • Read This First: Central & South America • Virgin Islands • World Food Caribbean • World Food Mexico • Yucatán
Travel Literature: Green Dreams: Travels in Central America

EUROPE Amsterdam • Amsterdam City Map • Amsterdam Condensed • Andalucía • Athens • Austria • Baltic States phrasebook • Barcelona • Barcelona City Map • Belgium & Luxembourg • Berlin • Berlin City Map • Britain • British phrasebook • Brussels, Bruges & Antwerp • Brussels City Map • Budapest • Budapest City Map • Canary Islands • Catalunya & the Costa Brava • Central Europe • Central Europe phrasebook • Copenhagen • Corfu & the Ionians • Corsica • Crete • Crete Condensed • Croatia • Cycling Britain • Cycling France • Cyprus • Czech & Slovak Republics • Czech phrasebook • Denmark • Dublin • Dublin City Map • Dublin Condensed • Eastern Europe • Eastern Europe phrasebook • Edinburgh • Edinburgh City Map • England • Estonia, Latvia & Lithuania • Europe on a shoestring • Europe phrasebook • Finland • Florence • Florence City Map • France • Frankfurt City Map • Frankfurt Condensed • French phrasebook • Georgia, Armenia & Azerbaijan • Germany • German phrasebook • Greece • Greek Islands • Greek phrasebook • Hungary • Iceland, Greenland & the Faroe Islands • Ireland • Italian phrasebook • Italy • Kraków • Lisbon • The Loire • London • London City Map • London Condensed • Madrid • Madrid City Map • Malta • Mediterranean Europe • Milan, Turin & Genoa • Moscow • Munich • Netherlands • Normandy • Norway • Out to Eat – London • Out to Eat – Paris • Paris • Paris City Map • Paris Condensed • Poland • Polish phrasebook • Portugal • Portuguese phrasebook • Prague • Prague City Map • Provence & the Côte d'Azur • Read This First: Europe • Rhodes & the Dodecanese • Romania & Moldova • Rome • Rome City Map • Rome Condensed • Russia, Ukraine & Belarus • Russian phrasebook • Scandinavian & Baltic Europe • Scandinavian phrasebook • Scotland • Sicily • Slovenia • South-West France • Spain • Spanish phrasebook • Stockholm • St Petersburg • St Petersburg City Map • Sweden • Switzerland • Tuscany • Ukrainian phrasebook • Venice • Vienna • Wales • Walking in Britain • Walking in France • Walking in Ireland • Walking in Italy • Walking in Scotland • Walking in Spain • Walking in Switzerland • Western Europe • World Food France • World Food Greece • World Food Ireland • World Food Italy • World Food Spain **Travel Literature:** After Yugoslavia • Love and War in the Apennines • The Olive Grove: Travels in Greece • On the Shores of the Mediterranean • Round Ireland in Low Gear • A Small Place in Italy

LONELY PLANET

Mail Order

Lonely Planet products are distributed worldwide. They are also available by mail order from Lonely Planet, so if you have difficulty finding a title please write to us. North and South American residents should write to 150 Linden St, Oakland, CA 94607, USA; European and African residents should write to 10a Spring Place, London NW5 3BH, UK; and residents of other countries to Locked Bag 1, Footscray, Victoria 3011, Australia.

INDIAN SUBCONTINENT & THE INDIAN OCEAN Bangladesh • Bengali phrasebook • Bhutan • Delhi • Goa • Healthy Travel Asia & India • Hindi & Urdu phrasebook • India • India & Bangladesh City Map • Indian Himalaya • Karakoram Highway • Kathmandu City Map • Kerala • Madagascar • Maldives • Mauritius, Réunion & Seychelles • Mumbai (Bombay) • Nepal • Nepali phrasebook • North India • Pakistan • Rajasthan • Read This First: Asia & India • South India • Sri Lanka • Sri Lanka phrasebook • Tibet • Tibetan phrasebook • Trekking in the Indian Himalaya • Trekking in the Karakoram & Hindukush • Trekking in the Nepal Himalaya • World Food India **Travel Literature**: The Age of Kali: Indian Travels and Encounters • Hello Goodnight: A Life of Goa • In Rajasthan • Maverick in Madagascar • A Season in Heaven: True Tales from the Road to Kathmandu • Shopping for Buddhas • A Short Walk in the Hindu Kush • Slowly Down the Ganges

MIDDLE EAST & CENTRAL ASIA Bahrain, Kuwait & Qatar • Central Asia • Central Asia phrasebook • Dubai • Farsi (Persian) phrasebook • Hebrew phrasebook • Iran • Israel & the Palestinian Territories • Istanbul • Istanbul City Map • Istanbul to Cairo • Istanbul to Kathmandu • Jerusalem • Jerusalem City Map • Jordan • Lebanon • Middle East • Oman & the United Arab Emirates • Syria • Turkey • Turkish phrasebook • World Food Turkey • Yemen **Travel Literature**: Black on Black: Iran Revisited • Breaking Ranks: Turbulent Travels in the Promised Land • The Gates of Damascus • Kingdom of the Film Stars: Journey into Jordan

NORTH AMERICA Alaska • Boston • Boston City Map • Boston Condensed • British Columbia • California & Nevada • California Condensed • Canada • Chicago • Chicago City Map • Chicago Condensed • Florida • Georgia & the Carolinas • Great Lakes • Hawaii • Hiking in Alaska • Hiking in the USA • Honolulu & Oahu City Map • Las Vegas • Los Angeles • Los Angeles City Map • Louisiana & the Deep South • Miami • Miami City Map • Montreal • New England • New Orleans • New Orleans City Map • New York City • New York City City Map • New York City Condensed • New York, New Jersey & Pennsylvania • Oahu • Out to Eat – San Francisco • Pacific Northwest • Rocky Mountains • San Diego & Tijuana • San Francisco • San Francisco City Map • Seattle • Seattle City Map • Southwest • Texas • Toronto • USA • USA phrasebook • Vancouver • Vancouver City Map • Virginia & the Capital Region • Washington, DC • Washington, DC City Map • World Food New Orleans **Travel Literature**: Caught Inside: A Surfer's Year on the California Coast • Drive Thru America

NORTH-EAST ASIA Beijing • Beijing City Map • Cantonese phrasebook • China • Hiking in Japan • Hong Kong & Macau • Hong Kong City Map • Hong Kong Condensed • Japan • Japanese phrasebook • Korea • Korean phrasebook • Kyoto • Mandarin phrasebook • Mongolia • Mongolian phrasebook • Seoul • Shanghai • South-West China • Taiwan • Tokyo • Tokyo Condensed • World Food Hong Kong • World Food Japan **Travel Literature**: In Xanadu: A Quest • Lost Japan

SOUTH AMERICA Argentina, Uruguay & Paraguay • Bolivia • Brazil • Brazilian phrasebook • Buenos Aires • Buenos Aires City Map • Chile & Easter Island • Colombia • Ecuador & the Galapagos Islands • Healthy Travel Central & South America • Latin American Spanish phrasebook • Peru • Quechua phrasebook • Read This First: Central & South America • Rio de Janeiro • Rio de Janeiro City Map • Santiago de Chile • South America on a shoestring • Trekking in the Patagonian Andes • Venezuela **Travel Literature**: Full Circle: A South American Journey

SOUTH-EAST ASIA Bali & Lombok • Bangkok • Bangkok City Map • Burmese phrasebook • Cambodia • Cycling Vietnam, Laos & Cambodia • East Timor phrasebook • Hanoi • Healthy Travel Asia & India • Hill Tribes phrasebook • Ho Chi Minh City (Saigon) • Indonesia • Indonesian phrasebook • Indonesia's Eastern Islands • Java • Lao phrasebook • Laos • Malay phrasebook • Malaysia, Singapore & Brunei • Myanmar (Burma) • Philippines • Pilipino (Tagalog) phrasebook • Read This First: Asia & India • Singapore • Singapore City Map • South-East Asia on a shoestring • South-East Asia phrasebook • Thailand • Thailand's Islands & Beaches • Thailand, Vietnam, Laos & Cambodia Road Atlas • Thai phrasebook • Vietnam • Vietnamese phrasebook • World Food Indonesia • World Food Thailand • World Food Vietnam

ALSO AVAILABLE: Antarctica • The Arctic • The Blue Man: Tales of Travel, Love and Coffee • Brief Encounters: Stories of Love, Sex & Travel • Buddhist Stupas in Asia: The Shape of Perfection • Chasing Rickshaws • The Last Grain Race • Lonely Planet ... On the Edge: Adventurous Escapades from Around the World • Lonely Planet Unpacked • Lonely Planet Unpacked Again • Not the Only Planet: Science Fiction Travel Stories • Ports of Call: A Journey by Sea • Sacred India • Travel Photography: A Guide to Taking Better Pictures • Travel with Children • Tuvalu: Portrait of an Island Nation

Index

Bold indicates maps.

Boxed Text

Bold indicates maps.

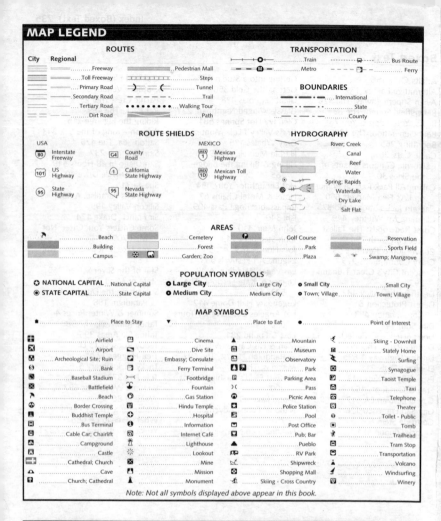

MAP LEGEND

ROUTES

City / Regional

Freeway
Toll Freeway
Primary Road
Secondary Road
Tertiary Road
Dirt Road

Pedestrian Mall
Steps
Tunnel
Trail
Walking Tour
Path

TRANSPORTATION

Train
Metro
Bus Route
Ferry

ROUTE SHIELDS

USA
- 80 Interstate Freeway
- 101 US Highway
- 95 State Highway

- G4 County Road
- 1 California State Highway
- 95 Nevada State Highway

MEXICO
- 1 Mexican Highway
- 1D Mexican Toll Highway

BOUNDARIES

International
State
County

HYDROGRAPHY

River; Creek
Canal
Reef
Water
Spring; Rapids
Waterfalls
Dry Lake
Salt Flat

AREAS

Beach
Building
Campus

Cemetery
Forest
Garden; Zoo

Golf Course
Park
Plaza

Reservation
Sports Field
Swamp; Mangrove

POPULATION SYMBOLS

○ NATIONAL CAPITAL .... National Capital
◉ STATE CAPITAL .... State Capital

● Large City .... Large City
● Medium City .... Medium City

● Small City .... Small City
● Town; Village .... Town; Village

MAP SYMBOLS

■ .... Place to Stay
▼ .... Place to Eat
● .... Point of Interest

Airfield
Airport
Archeological Site; Ruin
Bank
Baseball Stadium
Battlefield
Beach
Border Crossing
Buddhist Temple
Bus Terminal
Cable Car; Chairlift
Campground
Castle
Cathedral; Church
Cave
Church; Cathedral

Cinema
Dive Site
Embassy; Consulate
Ferry Terminal
Footbridge
Fountain
Gas Station
Hindu Temple
Hospital
Information
Internet Café
Lighthouse
Lookout
Mine
Mission
Monument

Mountain
Museum
Observatory
Park
Parking Area
Pass
Picnic Area
Police Station
Pool
Post Office
Pub; Bar
Pueblo
RV Park
Shipwreck
Shopping Mall
Skiing - Cross Country

Skiing - Downhill
Stately Home
Surfing
Synagogue
Taoist Temple
Taxi
Telephone
Theater
Toilet - Public
Tomb
Trailhead
Tram Stop
Transportation
Volcano
Windsurfing
Winery

Note: Not all symbols displayed above appear in this book.

LONELY PLANET OFFICES

Australia
Locked Bag 1, Footscray, Victoria 3011
☎ 03 8379 8000 fax 03 8379 8111
email: talk2us@lonelyplanet.com.au

UK
10a Spring Place, London NW5 3BH
☎ 020 7428 4800 fax 020 7428 4828
email: go@lonelyplanet.co.uk

USA
150 Linden St, Oakland, CA 94607
☎ 510 893 8555 TOLL FREE: 800 275 8555
fax 510 893 8572
email: info@lonelyplanet.com

France
1 rue du Dahomey, 75011 Paris
☎ 01 55 25 33 00 fax 01 55 25 33 01
email: bip@lonelyplanet.fr
www.lonelyplanet.fr

World Wide Web: www.lonelyplanet.com *or* AOL keyword: lp
Lonely Planet Images: www.lonelyplanetimages.com